See the Difference with LearningCurve

MW00668013

LearningCurve
macmillan learning

learningcurveworks.com

LearningCurve is a winning solution for everyone: students come to class better prepared and instructors have more flexibility to go beyond the basic facts and concepts in class. LearningCurve's game-like quizzes are book-specific and link back to the textbook in LaunchPad so that students can brush up on the reading when they get stumped by a question. The reporting features help instructors track overall class trends and spot topics that are giving students trouble so that they can adjust lectures and class activities.

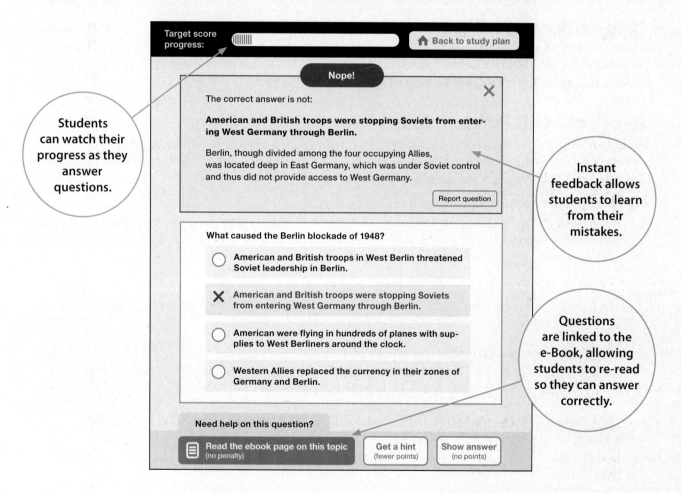

Students can watch their progress as they answer questions.

Instant feedback allows students to learn from their mistakes.

Questions are linked to the e-Book, allowing students to re-read so they can answer correctly.

LearningCurve is easy to assign, easy to customize, and easy to complete. See the difference LearningCurve makes in teaching and learning history.

CONTEMPORARY EUROPE

ATLANTIC OCEAN

North Sea

NORWAY • Bergen • Oslo **SWEDEN** • Stockholm

• Göteborg

Baltic Sea

DENMARK • Aarhus • Copenhagen **RUSSIA**

• Kaliningrad

• Gdańsk

SCOTLAND • Edinburgh

NORTHERN IRELAND • Glasgow

• Belfast

IRELAND ⊛ Dublin

UNITED KINGDOM

• Liverpool

• Cork

• Birmingham

WALES **ENGLAND**

Thames R.

London •

NETHERLANDS

Amsterdam • • Berlin

• Rotterdam

Antwerp • **GERMANY** **POLAND**

Brussels ⊛ Elbe R. Vistula R.

BELGIUM • Frankfurt • Warsaw

Rhine R.

Luxembourg ⊛ • Prague **CZECH REP.** • Kraków

LUXEMBOURG Oder R. • Brno

English Channel **SLOVAKIA** • Miskolc

Seine R. • Vienna ⊛ Bratislava

Paris ⊛ **LIECHTENSTEIN** • Munich Danube R.

FRANCE Zürich • • Vaduz **AUSTRIA** ⊛ Budapest

Loire R. Bern ⊛ • Innsbruck **HUNGARY**

SWITZERLAND • Graz

A L P S **SLOVENIA**

Bay of Biscay Lyons • Ljubljana ⊛ • Zagreb

• Milan Po R. **CROATIA**

Rhône R. **SAN** San • Belgrade

SAN MARINO Marino **BOSNIA AND**

ANDORRA A **HERZEGOVINA** **SERBIA**

PYRENEES Andorra P **MONACO** P Sarajevo ⊛

Oporto • la Vella Marseilles • E Adriatic Sea

Ebro R. • Barcelona N Podgorica ⊛

N • Split

PORTUGAL • Madrid I **MONTENEGRO**

N Rome ⊛ • Tiranë

Lisbon ⊛ **SPAIN** Corsica E **ITALY**

S **ALBANIA**

• Seville • Naples

Balearic Is. Sardinia

Gibraltar Tyrrhenian

(Gr. Br.) Sea Ionian Sea

• Algiers

• Rabat • Tunis • Palermo

Sicily

MOROCCO Valletta ⊛

MALTA

TUNISIA Mediterranean

ALGERIA

⊛ Tripoli

LIBYA

20°W 10°W 0° 10°E

60°N

50°N

40°N

Elevation

Feet	Meters
Over 13,120	Over 4,001
6,561–13,120	2,001–4,000
1,641–6,560	501–2,000
661–1,640	201–500
0–660	0–200
Below sea level	Below sea level

⊛ National capital
• Major city

0   150   300 miles
0 150 300 kilometers

THE CONTEMPORARY WORLD

Greenland
(Den.)

ICELAND

UNITED
KINGDOM

IRELAND

FRANCE

SPAIN

PORTUGAL

Azores
(Port.)

MOROCCO

Canary Is.
(Sp.)

Western Sahara
(Mor.)

MAURITANIA

CAPE
VERDE

SENEGAL   MALI

GAMBIA

GUINEA-BISSAU

GUINEA

BURKINA FASO

SIERRA LEONE

LIBERIA

CÔTE D'IVOIRE

GHANA

CANADA

Alaska
(U.S.)

UNITED STATES

ATLANTIC
OCEAN

Bermuda (U.K.)

Hawaii (U.S.)

MEXICO

BAHAMAS

DOMINICAN
REPUBLIC

HAITI

CUBA

Puerto Rico (U.S.)

JAMAICA   ST. KITTS AND NEVIS

BELIZE   ANTIGUA AND BARBUDA

Guadeloupe (Fr.)   DOMINICA

HONDURAS   Martinique (Fr.)   ST. VINCENT AND THE GRENADINES

GUATEMALA   ST. LUCIA   BARBADOS

EL SALVADOR   NICARAGUA   GRENADA

COSTA RICA   TRINIDAD AND TOBAGO

GUYANA

PANAMA   SURINAME

VENEZUELA   French Guiana (Fr.)

COLOMBIA

PACIFIC OCEAN

Equator

Galápagos Is.
(Ec.)

ECUADOR

BRAZIL

SAMOA

PERU

TONGA

BOLIVIA

Easter I.
(Chile)

PARAGUAY

CHILE

ATLANTIC
OCEAN

URUGUAY

ARGENTINA

0   1,500   3,000 miles

0   1,500   3,000 kilometers

Falkland Is.
(U.K.)

80°N

60°N

40°N

20°N

0°

20°S

40°S

60°S

80°S

160°W   140°W   120°W   100°W   80°W   60°W   40°W   20°W

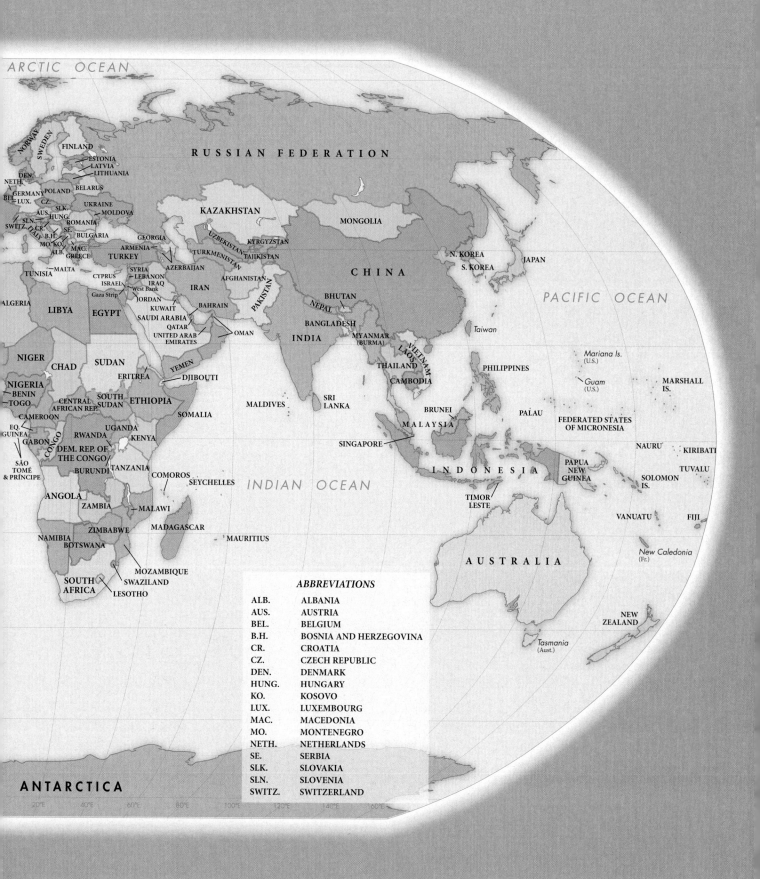

ARCTIC OCEAN

NORWAY
SWEDEN
FINLAND
DEN.
NETH.
GERMANY
BEL.
LUX.
CZ.
AUS.
SWITZ.
SLN.
ITALY
CR.
B.H.
MO.
ALB.
MAC.
GREECE
TUNISIA
MALTA
POLAND
BELARUS
UKRAINE
SLK.
HUNG.
ROMANIA
SE.
BULGARIA
GEORGIA
ARMENIA
TURKEY
AZERBAIJAN
CYPRUS
LEBANON
ISRAEL
SYRIA
IRAQ
Gaza Strip
West Bank
JORDAN
KUWAIT

RUSSIAN FEDERATION

KAZAKHSTAN

UZBEKISTAN
TURKMENISTAN
KYRGYZSTAN
TAJIKISTAN
AFGHANISTAN
IRAN
PAKISTAN

MONGOLIA

N. KOREA
S. KOREA
JAPAN

CHINA

PACIFIC OCEAN

BHUTAN
NEPAL
BANGLADESH
INDIA
MYANMAR
(BURMA)
VIETNAM
LAOS
THAILAND
CAMBODIA

Taiwan

PHILIPPINES

Mariana Is.
(U.S.)

Guam
(U.S.)

MARSHALL
IS.

ALGERIA
LIBYA
EGYPT

NIGER
CHAD
SUDAN

NIGERIA
BENIN
TOGO
CAMEROON
EQ.
GUINEA
GABON
SÃO
TOMÉ
& PRÍNCIPE

CENTRAL
AFRICAN REP.
SOUTH
SUDAN
ETHIOPIA

CONGO
DEM. REP. OF
THE CONGO

SAUDI ARABIA
QATAR
UNITED ARAB
EMIRATES
BAHRAIN
OMAN

YEMEN
ERITREA
DJIBOUTI

SOMALIA

MALDIVES

SRI
LANKA

BRUNEI

MALAYSIA

PALAU

SINGAPORE

FEDERATED STATES
OF MICRONESIA

NAURU
KIRIBATI

UGANDA
RWANDA
KENYA
BURUNDI
TANZANIA

COMOROS
SEYCHELLES

INDIAN OCEAN

INDONESIA

PAPUA
NEW
GUINEA

TUVALU

SOLOMON
IS.

ANGOLA
ZAMBIA
MALAWI
NAMIBIA
ZIMBABWE
BOTSWANA
MADAGASCAR
MAURITIUS

TIMOR
LESTE

VANUATU
FIJI

New Caledonia
(Fr.)

MOZAMBIQUE
SWAZILAND
SOUTH
AFRICA
LESOTHO

AUSTRALIA

NEW
ZEALAND

Tasmania
(Aust.)

ABBREVIATIONS	
ALB.	ALBANIA
AUS.	AUSTRIA
BEL.	BELGIUM
B.H.	BOSNIA AND HERZEGOVINA
CR.	CROATIA
CZ.	CZECH REPUBLIC
DEN.	DENMARK
HUNG.	HUNGARY
KO.	KOSOVO
LUX.	LUXEMBOURG
MAC.	MACEDONIA
MO.	MONTENEGRO
NETH.	NETHERLANDS
SE.	SERBIA
SLK.	SLOVAKIA
SLN.	SLOVENIA
SWITZ.	SWITZERLAND

ANTARCTICA

20°E   40°E   60°E   80°E   100°E   120°E   140°E   160°E

A History of Western Society

TWELFTH EDITION

VOLUME 2
From the Age of Exploration to the Present

John P. McKay
University of Illinois at Urbana-Champaign

Bennett D. Hill
Late of *Georgetown University*

John Buckler
Late of *University of Illinois at Urbana-Champaign*

Clare Haru Crowston
University of Illinois at Urbana-Champaign

Merry E. Wiesner-Hanks
University of Wisconsin–Milwaukee

Joe Perry
Georgia State University

bedford/st.martin's
Macmillan Learning

Boston | New York

FOR BEDFORD/ST. MARTIN'S

Vice President, Editorial, Macmillan Learning Humanities: Edwin Hill
Publisher for History: Michael Rosenberg
Director of Development for History: Jane Knetzger
Acquiring Editor for History: Laura Arcari
Senior Developmental Editor: Leah R. Strauss
Senior Production Editor: Christina M. Horn
Senior Media Producer: Michelle Camisa
Senior Production Supervisor: Jennifer Wetzel
History Marketing Manager: Melissa Famiglietti
Media Editor: Jennifer Jovin
Associate Editor: Tess Fletcher
Editorial Assistant: Melanie McFadyen
Copy Editor: Jennifer Brett Greenstein
Indexer: Leoni Z. McVey

Cartography: Mapping Specialists, Ltd.
Photo Editor: Robin Fadool
Photo Researcher: Bruce Carson
Permissions Editor: Eve Lehmann
Senior Art Director: Anna Palchik
Text Design: Boynton Hue Studio
Cover Design: William Boardman
Volume 2 Cover Art: Black Man with a Mandolin, ca. 1930 (oil on canvas) (see also 287577), André Derain (1880–1954)/Musée de l'Orangerie, Paris, France/Bridgeman Images/© 2016 Artists Rights Society (ARS), New York/ADAGP, Paris
Composition: Jouve
Printing and Binding: RR Donnelley and Sons

Copyright © 2017, 2014, 2011, 2008 by Bedford/St. Martin's

All rights reserved. No part of this book may be reproduced, stored in a retrieval system, or transmitted in any form or by any means, electronic, mechanical, photocopying, recording, or otherwise, except as may be expressly permitted by the applicable copyright statutes or in writing by the Publisher.

Manufactured in the United States of America.

1 0 9 8 7 6
f e d c b a

For information, write: Bedford/St. Martin's, 75 Arlington Street, Boston, MA 02116   (617-399-4000)

ISBN 978-1-319-03101-5 (Combined Edition)
ISBN 978-1-319-03102-2 (Volume 1)
ISBN 978-1-319-03103-9 (Volume 2)
ISBN 978-1-319-04041-3 (Volume A)

ISBN 978-1-319-04042-0 (Volume B)
ISBN 978-1-319-04043-7 (Volume C)
ISBN 978-1-319-04040-6 (Since 1300)

ACKNOWLEDGMENTS

Acknowledgments and copyrights appear on the same page as the text and art selections they cover; these acknowledgments and copyrights constitute an extension of the copyright page.

A History of Western Society grew out of the initial three authors' desire to infuse new life into the study of Western Civilization. The three current authors, Clare Haru Crowston, Merry E. Wiesner-Hanks, and Joe Perry, who first used the book as students or teachers and took over full responsibilities with the eleventh edition, continue to incorporate the latest and best scholarship in the field. All three of us regularly teach introductory history courses and thus bring insights into the text from the classroom, as well as from new secondary works and our own research in archives and libraries.

In this new twelfth edition we aimed to enhance the distinctive attention to daily life that sparks students' interest while also providing a number of innovative tools—both print and digital—designed to help students think historically and master the material. In response to the growing emphasis on historical thinking skills in the teaching of history at all levels, as well as to requests from our colleagues and current adopters, we have significantly expanded the book's primary source program to offer a wide variety of sources, both written and visual, presented in several ways. Every chapter now includes **"Thinking Like a Historian"** (one per chapter), which groups at least five sources around a central question, and **"Evaluating the Evidence"** (three per chapter), which features an individual text or visual source.

The Story of *A History of Western Society*: Bringing the Past to Life for Students

At the point when *A History of Western Society* was first conceptualized, social history was dramatically changing the ways we understood the past, and the original authors decided to create a book that would re-create the lives of ordinary people in appealing human terms, while also giving major economic, political, cultural, and intellectual developments the attention they unquestionably deserve. The current authors remain committed to advancing this vision for today's classroom, with a broader definition of social history that brings the original idea into the twenty-first century.

History as a discipline never stands still, and over the last several decades cultural history has joined social history as a source of dynamism. Because of its emphasis on the ways people made sense of their lives, *A History of Western Society* has always included a large amount of cultural history, ranging from foundational works of philosophy and literature to popular songs and stories. This focus on cultural history has been enhanced in recent editions in a way that highlights the interplay between men's and women's lived experiences and the ways men and women reflect on these experiences to create meaning. The joint social and cultural perspective requires—fortunately, in our opinion—the inclusion of objects as well as texts as important sources for studying history, which has allowed us to incorporate the growing emphasis on material culture in the work of many historians. We know that engaging students' interest in the past is often a challenge, but we also know that the text's hallmark approach—the emphasis on daily life and individual experience in its social and cultural dimensions—connects with students and makes the past vivid and accessible.

"Life" Chapters Connect the Past to the Present

Although social and cultural history can be found in every chapter, they are particularly emphasized in the acclaimed "Life" chapters that spark student interest by making the past palpable and approachable in human terms. The five chapters are Chapter 4: Life in the Hellenistic World, 336–30 B.C.E.; Chapter 10: Life in Villages and Cities of the High Middle Ages, 1000–1300; Chapter 18: Life in the Era of Expansion, 1650–1800; Chapter 22: Life in the Emerging Urban Society, 1840–1914; and Chapter 30: Life in an Age of Globalization, 1990 to the Present. Because we know that a key challenge of teaching history—and Western Civilization in particular—is encouraging students to appreciate the relevance of the past to our lives today, these five "Life" chapters each include a feature called **"The Past Living Now"** that examines an aspect of life today with origins in the period covered in that chapter. Featuring engaging topics such as the development of the modern university (Chapter 10) and the dawn of commercialized sports (Chapter 18), these essays were conceived with student interest in mind.

Primary Sources and Historical Thinking

Because understanding the past requires that students engage directly with sources on their own, this edition features a more expansive primary source program within its covers. **"Thinking Like a Historian"** (one in each chapter) groups at least five sources around a central question, with additional questions to guide students' analysis of the evidence and suggestions for essays that will allow them to put these sources together with what they have learned in class. Topics include "Land Ownership and Social Conflict in the Late Republic" (Chapter 5); "The Rights of Which Men?" (Chapter 19); and "The Conservative Reaction to Immigration and Islamist Terrorism" (Chapter 30). **"Evaluating the Evidence"** (three in each chapter) features an individual source, with headnotes and questions that help students understand the source and connect it to the information in the rest of the chapter. Selected for their interest and carefully integrated into their historical context, these sources provide students with firsthand encounters with people of the past along with the means and tools for building historical skills, including chronological reasoning, explaining causation, evaluating context, and assessing perspective. The suggestions for essays based on the primary sources encourage students to further expand their skills as they use their knowledge to develop historical arguments and write historical analyses.

To give students abundant opportunities to hone their textual and visual analysis skills, as well as a sense of the variety of sources on which historians rely, the primary source program includes a mix of canonical and lesser-known sources; a diversity of perspectives representing ordinary and prominent individuals alike; and a wide variety of source types, from tomb inscriptions, diaries, sermons, letters, poetry, and drama to artifacts, architecture, and propaganda posters. In addition, we have quoted extensively from a wide range of primary sources in the narrative, demonstrating that such quotations are the "stuff" of history. We believe that our extensive use of primary source extracts as an integral part of the narrative as well as in extended form in the primary source boxes will give students ample practice in thinking critically and historically.

Finally, the thoroughly revised companion reader, *Sources for Western Society*, Third Edition, provides a rich selection of documents to complement each chapter of the text and is FREE when packaged with the textbook.

Distinctive Essay Features Punctuate Larger Developments

In addition to the expanded primary source program and **"The Past Living Now,"** we are proud of the two unique boxed essay features in each chapter — **"Individuals in Society"** and **"Living in the Past"** — that personalize larger developments and make them tangible.

To give students a chance to see the past through ordinary people's lives, each chapter includes one of the popular **"Individuals in Society" biographical essays**, which offer brief studies of individuals or groups, informing students about the societies in which they lived. We have found that readers empathize with these human beings as they themselves seek to define their own identities. The spotlighting of individuals, both famous and obscure, perpetuates the book's continued attention to cultural and intellectual developments, highlights human agency, and reflects changing interests within the historical profession as well as the development of "microhistory." Features include essays on Aristophanes, the ancient Athenian playwright who mercilessly satirized the demagogues and thinkers of his day; Anna Jansz of

Rotterdam, an Anabaptist martyr; Hürrem, a concubine who became a powerful figure in the Ottoman Empire during the sixteenth century; Rebecca Protten, a former slave and leader in the Moravian missionary movement; Samuel Crompton, the inventor of the spinning mule during the Industrial Revolution who struggled to control and profit from his invention; and Edward Snowden, a former CIA operative who leaked classified documents about American surveillance programs to the world press and was considered by some a hero and by others a traitor.

To introduce students to the study of material culture, **"Living in the Past"** essays use social and cultural history to show how life in the past was both similar to and different from our lives today. These features are richly illustrated with images and artifacts and include a short essay and questions for analysis. We use these essays to explore the deeper ramifications of aspects of their own lives that students might otherwise take for granted, such as consumer goods, factories, and even currency. Students connect to the people of the past through a diverse range of topics such as "Farming in the Hellenistic World," "Roman Table Manners," "Child's Play," "Coffeehouse Culture," "The Immigrant Experience," "Nineteenth-Century Women's Fashion," and "The Supermarket Revolution."

New Coverage and Updates to the Narrative

This edition is enhanced by the incorporation of a wealth of new scholarship and subject areas that immerse students in the dynamic and ongoing work of history. Chapters 1–6 incorporate the exciting cross-disciplinary scholarship that has emerged over the last several decades on the Paleolithic and Neolithic eras, river valley civilizations, and the ancient Mediterranean. For example, archaeologists working at Göbekli Tepe in present-day Turkey have unearthed rings of massive, multi-ton, elaborately carved limestone pillars built around 9000 B.C.E. by groups of foragers, which has led to a rethinking of the links between culture, religion, and the initial development of agriculture. Similarly, new research on the peoples of Mesopotamia, based on cuneiform writing along with other sources, has led scholars to revise the view that Mesopotamians were fatalistic and to emphasize instead that they generally anticipated being well treated by the gods if they behaved morally. Throughout these chapters, material on cross-cultural connections, the impact of technologies, and changing social relationships has been added. In Chapter 14, we have updated and expanded the coverage of the conquest of the Aztec and Inca Empires and the impact of the conquest on indigenous peoples, including new material on the economic exploitation of indigenous people, religious conversion, and European debates about indigenous people. In Chapter 16, there are several significant revisions. First, there is more coverage of global/colonial issues and of the interaction between intellectual ideas and social change. Second, with regard to the Scientific

Revolution, there is a new section called "Why Europe?" that asks why the Scientific Revolution happened in Europe, as well as an expanded discussion of the relationship between religion and science. Third, a new section called "The Social Life of the Enlightenment" draws attention to recent scholarship linking the ideas of the Enlightenment to the social changes of the eighteenth century; this section includes coverage of the impact of contact with non-Europeans, debates on race, and women's role in the Enlightenment. Chapter 20 pays increased attention to the global context of industrialization, including two new sections: "Why Britain?" explains why the Industrial Revolution originated in Britain and not elsewhere in the world, such as China or India; and "The Global Picture" discusses the global spread of industrialization. A new section on living standards for the working class addresses the impact of industrialization on working people.

Other additions include a streamlined discussion of the role of women in classical Athens (Chapter 3); updated coverage of medicine in the Hellenistic period (Chapter 4); new material on the Vikings of western Europe (Chapter 8); expanded treatment of the growth of Russia's land empire to complement attention to western European acquisition of overseas empires and new material on Peter the Great's campaigns against the Ottomans (Chapter 15); increased coverage of communities and identities of the Atlantic world with material on the way colonial contacts help create national European identities as well as "African" and "Indian" identities (Chapter 17); updated coverage of the history of the family, popular culture, and medicine, including material on the use of colonial plants as medicines (Chapter 18); new material on the Congress of Vienna (Chapter 21) and expanded coverage of political ideologies of liberalism, republicanism, and nationalism (Chapters 21 and 23); new material on women's roles in the European colonies and on women and imperialism (Chapter 24); expanded coverage of the First World War in the Middle East, the collapse of the Ottoman Empire, and the postwar mandate system (Chapter 25); new discussion of Jewish resistance to the Holocaust and extended coverage of anti-Semitism and eugenics in Nazi Germany (Chapter 27); new material on violence and decolonization in the Algerian War of Independence (Chapter 28); and up-to-date coverage of contemporary events in the final chapter, including the refugee crisis, the euro crisis and Greek debt relief, Russian expansionism, issues surrounding terrorism and anti-Muslim sentiment in Europe, and the potential fragmentation of the European Union (Chapter 30).

Helping Students Understand the Narrative

We know firsthand and take seriously the challenges students face in understanding, retaining, and mastering so much material that is often unfamiliar. With the goal of making this the most student-centered edition yet, we continued to enhance the book's pedagogy on many fronts. To focus students' reading, each chapter opens with **a chapter preview with focus questions** keyed to the main chapter headings. These questions are repeated within the chapter and again in the **"Review & Explore" section** at the end of each chapter that provides helpful guidance for reviewing key topics. Each "Review & Explore" section concludes with a **"Suggested Reading and Media Resources"** listing that includes up-to-date readings on the vast amount of new work being done in many fields, as well as recommended documentaries, feature films, television, and Web sites.

To help students understand the bigger picture and prepare for exams, each chapter includes **"Looking Back, Looking Ahead" conclusions** that provide an insightful synthesis of the chapter's main developments, while connecting to events that students will encounter in the chapters to come. In this way students are introduced to history as an ongoing process of interrelated events. These conclusions are followed by **"Make Connections" questions** that prompt students to assess larger developments across chapters, thus allowing them to develop skills in evaluating change and continuity, making comparisons, and analyzing context and causation.

To promote clarity and comprehension, boldface **key terms** in the text are defined in the margins and listed in the chapter review. **Phonetic spellings** are located directly after terms that readers are likely to find hard to pronounce. The **chapter chronologies**, which review major developments discussed in each chapter, mirror the key events of the chapter, and the topic-specific **thematic chronologies** that appear in many chapters provide a more focused timeline of certain developments. Once again, we also provide a **unified timeline** at the end of the text. Comprehensive and easy to locate, this timeline allows students to compare developments over the centuries.

The high-quality art and map program has been thoroughly revised and features hundreds of **contemporaneous illustrations**. To make the past tangible, and as an extension of our attention to cultural history, we include numerous **artifacts** — from swords and fans to playing cards and record players. As in earlier editions, all illustrations have been carefully selected to complement the text, and all include captions that inform students while encouraging them to read the text more deeply. High-quality **full-size maps** illustrate major developments in the narrative, and helpful spot maps are embedded in the narrative to locate areas under discussion. We recognize students' difficulties with geography, and the new edition includes the popular **"Mapping the Past" map activities**. Included in each chapter, these activities give students valuable skills in reading and interpreting maps by asking them to analyze the maps and make connections to the larger processes discussed in the narrative.

In addition, whenever an instructor assigns the **LaunchPad e-Book** (which is free when bundled with the print book), students get full access to **LearningCurve**, an online adaptive learning tool that promotes mastery of the book's content and diagnoses students' trouble spots. With this adaptive quizzing, students accumulate points toward a target score as they go, giving the interaction a game-like feel. Feedback for incorrect responses explains why the answer is incorrect and directs students back to the text to review before they attempt to answer the question again. The end result is a better understanding of the key elements of the text. Instructors who actively assign LearningCurve report their students come to class prepared for discussion and their students enjoy using it. In addition, LearningCurve's reporting feature allows instructors to quickly diagnose which concepts students in their classes are struggling with so they can adjust lectures and activities accordingly. The LaunchPad e-Book with LearningCurve is thus an invaluable asset for instructors who need to support students in all settings, from traditional lectures to hybrid, online, and newer "flipped" classrooms. To learn more about the benefits of LearningCurve and LaunchPad, see the "Versions and Supplements" section on page xv.

Helping Instructors Teach with Digital Resources

As noted, *A History of Western Society* is offered in Macmillan's premier learning platform, **LaunchPad**, an intuitive, interactive e-Book and course space. Free when packaged with the print text or available at a low price when used stand-alone, LaunchPad grants students and teachers access to a wealth of online tools and resources built specifically for our text to enhance reading comprehension and promote in-depth study.

Developed with extensive feedback from history instructors and students, **LaunchPad for *A History of Western Society*** includes the complete narrative of the print book; the companion reader, *Sources for Western Society*; and **LearningCurve**, an adaptive learning tool that is designed to get students to read before they come to class. With **new source-based questions in the test bank and in the LearningCurve**, instructors now have more ways to test students on their understanding of sources and narrative in the book.

This edition also includes **Guided Reading Exercises** that prompt students to be active readers of the chapter narrative and autograded **primary source quizzes** to test comprehension of written and visual sources. These features, plus **additional primary source documents, video sources and tools for making video assignments, map activities, flashcards, and customizable test banks**, make LaunchPad a great asset for any instructor who wants to enliven the history of Western Civilization for students.

These new directions have not changed the central mission of the book, which is to introduce students to the broad sweep of Western Civilization in a fresh yet balanced manner. Every edition has incorporated new research to keep the book up-to-date and respond to the changing needs of readers and instructors, and we have continued to do this in the twelfth edition. As we have made these changes, large and small, we have sought to give students and teachers an integrated perspective so that they can pursue — on their own or in the classroom — the historical questions that they find particularly exciting and significant. To learn more about the benefits of LearningCurve and LaunchPad, see the "Versions and Supplements" section on page xv.

Acknowledgments

It is a pleasure to thank the instructors who read and critiqued the manuscript through its development:

Robert Blackey, California State University, San Bernardino
Kevin Caldwell, Blue Ridge Community College
Amy Colon, SUNY Sullivan
Maia Conrad, Thomas Nelson Community College
Scott Gavorsky, Great Basin College
George Kaloudis, Rivier College
Roy Koepp, University of Nebraska at Kearney
Jesse Lynch, Shasta College
Michael McKeown, Daytona State College
Jennifer Morris, Mount St. Joseph University
Stephen Santelli, Northern Virginia Community College
Calvin Tesler, Lehigh University
Doris Tishkoff, Quinnipiac University

It is also a pleasure to thank the many editors who have assisted us over the years, first at Houghton Mifflin and now at Bedford/St. Martin's. At Bedford/St. Martin's these include senior development editor Leah Strauss, senior production editor Christina Horn, associate editor Tess Fletcher, editorial assistant Melanie McFadyen, director of development Jane Knetzger, and publisher for history Michael Rosenberg. Other key contributors were photo researcher Bruce Carson, text permissions editor Eve Lehmann, text designer Cia Boynton, copy editor Jennifer Brett Greenstein, proofreaders Linda McLatchie and Angela Morrison, indexer Leoni McVey, and cover designer Billy Boardman.

Many of our colleagues at the University of Illinois, the University of Wisconsin–Milwaukee, and Georgia State University continue to provide information and stimulation, often without even knowing it. We thank them for it. We also thank the many students over the years with whom we have used earlier editions of this book. Their reactions and opinions helped shape the revisions to this edition, and we hope it remains worthy of the ultimate praise that they bestowed on it: that it's "not boring like most textbooks." Merry Wiesner-Hanks would, as always, also like to thank her husband, Neil, without whom work on this project would not be possible. Clare Haru Crowston thanks her husband, Ali, and her children, Lili, Reza, and Kian, who are a joyous reminder of the vitality of life that we try to showcase in this book. Joe Perry thanks his colleagues and students at Georgia State for their intellectual stimulation and is grateful to Joyce de Vries for her unstinting support and encouragement.

Each of us has benefited from the criticism of our coauthors, although each of us assumes responsibility for what he or she has written. Merry Wiesner-Hanks intensively reworked John Buckler's Chapters 1–6 and revised Chapters 7–13; Clare Crowston wrote and revised Chapters 14–19 and took responsibility for John McKay's Chapter 20; and Joe Perry took responsibility for John McKay's Chapters 21–24 and wrote and revised Chapters 25–30.

We'd especially like to thank the founding authors, John P. McKay, Bennett D. Hill, and John Buckler, for their enduring contributions and for their faith in each of us to carry on their legacy.

CLARE HARU CROWSTON
MERRY E. WIESNER-HANKS
JOE PERRY

Adopters of *A History of Western Society* and their students have access to abundant print and digital resources and tools, including documents, assessment and presentation materials, the acclaimed Bedford Series in History and Culture volumes, and much more. The LaunchPad course space provides access to the narrative with all assignment and assessment opportunities at the ready. See below for more information, visit **macmillanlearning.com**, or contact your local Bedford/St. Martin's sales representative.

Get the Right Version for Your Class

To accommodate different course lengths and course budgets, *A History of Western Society* is available in several different formats, including a Concise Edition (narrative with select features, maps, and images), a Value Edition (narrative only in two colors with select maps and images), three-hole-punched loose-leaf versions, and low-priced PDF e-Books. And for the best value of all, package a new print book with LaunchPad at no additional charge to get the best each format offers—a print version for easy portability and reading with a LaunchPad interactive e-Book and course space with LearningCurve and loads of additional assignment and assessment options.

- **Combined Edition** (Chapters 1–30): available in paperback, Concise Edition, Value Edition, loose-leaf, e-Book formats, and in LaunchPad
- **Volume 1, From Antiquity to the Enlightenment** (Chapters 1–16): available in paperback, Concise Edition, Value Edition, loose-leaf, e-Book formats, and in LaunchPad
- **Volume 2, From the Age of Exploration to the Present** (Chapters 14–30): available in paperback, Concise Edition, Value Edition, loose-leaf, e-Book formats, and in LaunchPad
- **Volume A, From Antiquity to 1500** (Chapters 1–12): available in paperback, e-Book formats, and in LaunchPad
- **Volume B, From the Later Middle Ages to 1815** (Chapters 11–19): available in paperback, e-Book formats, and in LaunchPad
- **Volume C, From the Revolutionary Era to the Present** (Chapters 19–30): available in paperback, e-Book formats, and in LaunchPad
- **Since 1300** (Chapters 11–30): available in paperback, e-Book formats, and in LaunchPad

As noted below, any of these volumes can be packaged with additional titles for a discount. To get ISBNs for discount packages, visit **macmillanlearning.com** or contact your Bedford/St. Martin's representative.

Assign LaunchPad—an Assessment-Ready Interactive e-Book and Course Space

Available for discount purchase on its own or for packaging with new books at no additional charge, LaunchPad is a breakthrough solution for today's courses. Intuitive and easy to use for students and instructors alike, LaunchPad is ready to use as is and can be edited, customized with your own material, and assigned quickly. LaunchPad for *A History of Western Society* provides Bedford/St. Martin's high-quality content all in one place, including the full interactive e-Book and companion reader, *Sources for Western Society*, plus LearningCurve formative quizzing; guided reading activities designed to help students read actively for key concepts; autograded quizzes for primary sources; and chapter summative quizzes. Through a wealth of formative and summative assessment, including the adaptive learning program of LearningCurve (see the full description ahead), students gain confidence and get into their reading before class. These features, plus additional primary source documents, video tools for making video assignments, map activities, flashcards, and customizable test banks, make LaunchPad an invaluable asset for any instructor.

LaunchPad easily integrates with course management systems, and with fast ways to build assignments, rearrange chapters, and add new pages, sections, or links, it lets teachers build the courses they want to teach and hold students accountable. For more information, visit **launchpadworks.com**, or to arrange a demo, contact us at **history@macmillan.com**.

Assign LearningCurve So Your Students Come to Class Prepared

Students using LaunchPad receive access to LearningCurve for *A History of Western Society*. Assigning LearningCurve in place of reading quizzes is easy for instructors, and the reporting features help instructors track overall class trends and spot topics that are giving students trouble so they can adjust their lectures and class activities. This online learning tool is popular with students because it was designed to help them rehearse content at their own pace in a nonthreatening, game-like environment. The feedback for wrong answers provides instructional coaching and sends students back to the book for review. Students answer as many questions as necessary to reach a target score, with repeated chances to revisit material they haven't mastered. When LearningCurve is assigned, students come to class better prepared.

Take Advantage of Instructor Resources

Bedford/St. Martin's has developed a rich array of teaching resources for this book and for this course. They range from lecture and presentation materials and assessment tools to course management options. Most can be found in LaunchPad or can be downloaded or ordered at macmillanlearning.com.

Bedford Coursepack for Blackboard, Canvas, Brightspace by D2L, or Moodle. We can help you integrate our rich content into your course management system. Registered instructors can download coursepacks that include our popular free resources and book-specific content for *A History of Western Society.*

Instructor's Manual. The *Instructor's Manual* offers both experienced and first-time instructors tools for presenting textbook material in engaging ways. It includes content learning objectives, annotated chapter outlines, and strategies for teaching with the textbook, plus suggestions on how to get the most out of LearningCurve and a survival guide for first-time teaching assistants.

Guide to Changing Editions. Designed to facilitate an instructor's transition from the previous edition of *A History of Western Society* to this new edition, this guide presents an overview of major changes as well as of changes in each chapter.

Online Test Bank. The test bank includes a mix of fresh, carefully crafted multiple-choice, matching, short-answer, and essay questions for each chapter. Many of the multiple-choice questions feature a map, an image, or a primary source excerpt as the prompt. All questions appear in easy-to-use test bank software that allows instructors to add, edit, re-sequence, and print questions and answers. Instructors can also export questions into a variety of course management systems.

The Bedford Lecture Kit: Lecture Outlines, Maps, and Images. Look good and save time with *The Bedford Lecture Kit.* These presentation materials include fully customizable multimedia presentations built around chapter outlines that are embedded with maps, figures, and images from the textbook and are supplemented by more detailed instructor notes on key points and concepts.

Print, Digital, and Custom Options for More Choice and Value

For information on free packages and discounts up to 50%, visit macmillanlearning.com or contact your local Bedford/St. Martin's sales representative.

Sources for Western Society, Third Edition. This primary source collection—available in Volume 1, Volume 2, and Since 1300 versions—provides a revised and expanded selection of sources to accompany *A History of Western Society,* Twelfth Edition. Each chapter features five or six written and visual sources by well-known figures and ordinary individuals alike. With over fifty new selections—including a dozen new visual sources—and enhanced pedagogy throughout, this book gives students the tools to engage critically with canonical and lesser-known sources and prominent and ordinary voices. Each chapter includes a "Sources in Conversation" feature that presents differing views on key topics. This companion reader is an exceptional value for students and offers plenty of assignment options for instructors. Available free when packaged with the print text and included in the LaunchPad e-Book. Also available on its own as a downloadable PDF e-Book.

NEW *Bedford Custom Tutorials for History.* Designed to customize textbooks with resources relevant to individual courses, this collection of brief units, each sixteen pages long and loaded with examples, guides students through basic skills such as using historical evidence effectively, working with primary sources, taking effective notes, avoiding plagiarism and citing sources, and more. Up to two tutorials can be added to a Bedford/St. Martin's history survey title at no additional charge, freeing you to spend your class time focusing on content and interpretation. For more information, visit macmillanlearning.com/historytutorials.

The Bedford Series in History and Culture. More than one hundred titles in this highly praised series combine first-rate scholarship, historical narrative, and important primary documents for undergraduate courses. Each book is brief, inexpensive, and focused on a specific topic or period. Revisions of several bestselling titles, such as *The Prince by Niccolò Machiavelli with Related Documents,* edited by William J. Connell; *The Enlightenment: A Brief History with Documents,* by Margaret C. Jacob; *Candide by Voltaire with Related Documents,* edited by Daniel Gordon; and *The French Revolution and Human Rights: A Brief History with Documents,* by Lynn Hunt, are now available. For a complete list of titles, visit macmillanlearning.com. Package discounts are available.

Rand McNally Atlas of Western Civilization. This collection of over fifty full-color maps highlights social, political, and cross-cultural change and interaction from classical Greece and Rome to the postindustrial Western world. Each map is thoroughly indexed for fast reference. Free when packaged.

Trade Books. Titles published by sister companies Hill and Wang; Farrar, Straus and Giroux; Henry Holt and Company; St. Martin's Press; Picador; and Palgrave Macmillan are available at a 50% discount when packaged with Bedford/St. Martin's textbooks. For more information, visit macmillanlearning.com/tradeup.

A Pocket Guide to Writing in History. This portable and affordable reference tool by Mary Lynn Rampolla provides reading, writing, and research advice useful to students in all history courses. Concise yet comprehensive advice on approaching typical history assignments, developing critical reading skills, writing effective history papers, conducting research, using and documenting sources, and avoiding plagiarism—enhanced with practical tips and examples throughout—has made this slim reference a bestseller. Package discounts are available.

A Student's Guide to History. This complete guide to success in any history course provides the practical help students need to be successful. In addition to introducing students to the nature of the discipline, author Jules Benjamin teaches a wide range of skills from preparing for exams to approaching common writing assignments, and explains the research and documentation process with plentiful examples. Package discounts are available.

The Social Dimension of Western Civilization. Combining current scholarship with classic pieces, this reader's forty-eight secondary sources, compiled by Richard M. Golden, hook students with the fascinating and often surprising details of how everyday Western people worked, ate, played, celebrated, worshipped, married, procreated, fought, persecuted, and died. Package discounts are available.

The West in the Wider World: Sources and Perspectives. Edited by Richard Lim and David Kammerling Smith, the first college reader to focus on the central historical question "How did the West become the West?" offers a wealth of written and visual source materials that reveal the influence of non-European regions on the origins and development of Western Civilization. Package discounts are available.

Brief Contents

Contents

14 European Exploration and Conquest
1450–1650   426

photo: Detail from a Namban Ryobu Japanese painted screen/Museu Nacional de Soares dos Reis, Porto, Portugal/Bridgeman Images

15 Absolutism and Constitutionalism
ca. 1589–1725   464

photo: By Charles Le Brun (1619–1690), 1678/Museum of Fine Arts, Budapest, Hungary/Erich Lessing/Art Resource, NY

16 Toward a New Worldview
1540–1789   504

photo: *An Experiment on a Bird in the Air Pump*, 1768/National Gallery, London/Bridgeman Images

17 The Expansion of Europe
1650–1800   542

18 *Life* in the Era of Expansion
1650–1800   574

photo: *Bristol Docks and Quay*, ca. 1760 (oil on canvas)/© Bristol Museum and Art Gallery, UK/Bridgeman Images

photo: *A Market Day*, 1765, Central European School (oil on canvas)/© Sotheby's/akg-images

xxiv   Contents

19 Revolutions in Politics
1775–1815 610

20 The Revolution in Energy and Industry
ca. 1780–1850 648

photo: *The Taking of the Bastille, 14 July 1789*/French School/Château de Versailles, France/Bridgeman Images

photo: *The Falcon Glassworks*, c. 1840 (oil on canvas)/© Museum of London/HIP/The Image Works

photo: By Gustave Wappers (1803–1874), (oil on canvas)/Musée Royaux des Beaux-Arts
de Belgique, Brussels, Belgium/© Leemage/Bridgeman Images

photo: By Alexander Blaikley (1816–1903)/© Fine Art Photographic Library/Corbis

23 The Age of Nationalism
1850–1914   754

24 The West and the World
1815–1914   792

photo: By Gerolamo Induno (1825–1890) (oil on canvas)/Civico Museo del Risorgimento, Milano, Italy/De Agostini Picture Library/Alfredo Dagli Orti/Bridgeman Images

photo: From *The Spanish and American Illustration*, 1886/Photo © Tarker/Bridgeman Images

photo: *The Menin Road*, 1919/Imperial War Museum, London, UK/Bridgeman Images   photo: Art © Estate of George Grosz/Licensed by VAGA, New York, NY/photo: akg-images

27 Dictatorships and the Second World War

1919–1945   902

28 Cold War Conflict and Consensus

1945–1965   942

photo: De Agostini/Getty Images

photo: © Georgios Makkas/Alamy Stock Photo

29 Challenging the Postwar Order
1960–1991   980

30 *Life* in an Age of Globalization
1990 to the Present   1018

photo: Bernd Kammerer/picture-alliance/dpa/akg-images

photo: *The Standing March* is the collaborative work by the French artist known as JR and the U.S. filmmaker Darren Aronofsky/photo: Eric Feferberg/AFP/Getty Images

Maps, Figures, and Tables

Maps

Figures and Tables

Special Features

INDIVIDUALS IN SOCIETY

LIVING IN THE PAST

MAPPING THE PAST

The notion of "the West" has ancient origins. Greek civilization grew up in the shadow of earlier civilizations to the south and east of Greece, especially Egypt and Mesopotamia. Greeks defined themselves in relation to these more advanced cultures, which they lumped together as "the East." They passed this conceptualization on to the Romans, who in turn transmitted it to the peoples of western and northern Europe. When Europeans established overseas colonies in the late fifteenth century, they believed they were taking Western culture with them, even though many of its elements, such as Christianity, had originated in what Europeans by that point regarded as the East. Throughout history, the meaning of "the West" has shifted, but in every era it has meant more than a geographical location.

The Ancient World

The ancient world provided several cultural elements that the modern world has inherited. First came the traditions of the Hebrews, especially their religion, Judaism, with its belief in one god and in themselves as a chosen people. The Hebrews developed their religious ideas in books that were later brought together in the Hebrew Bible, which Christians term the Old Testament. Second, Greek architectural, philosophical, and scientific ideas have exercised a profound influence on Western thought. Third, Rome provided the Latin language, the instrument of verbal and written communication for more than a thousand years, and concepts of law and government that molded Western ideas of political organization. Finally, Christianity, the spiritual faith and ecclesiastical organization that derived from the life and teachings of a Jewish man, Jesus of Nazareth, also came to condition Western religious, social, and moral values and systems.

The Hebrews

The Hebrews were nomadic pastoralists who may have migrated into the Nile Delta from the east, seeking good land for their herds of sheep and goats. According to the Hebrew Bible, they were enslaved by the Egyptians but were led out of Egypt by a charismatic leader named Moses. The Hebrews settled in the area between the Mediterranean and the Jordan River known as Canaan. They were organized into tribes, each tribe consisting of numerous families who thought of themselves as all related to one another and having a common ancestor.

In Canaan, the nomadic Hebrews encountered a variety of other peoples, whom they both learned from and fought. The Bible reports that the inspired leader Saul established a monarchy over the twelve Hebrew tribes and that the kingdom grew under the leadership of King David. David's successor, Solomon (r. ca. 965–925 B.C.E.), launched a building program including cities, palaces, fortresses, roads, and a temple at Jerusalem, which became the symbol of Hebrew unity. This unity did not last long, however, as at Solomon's death his kingdom broke into two separate states, Israel and Judah.

In their migration, the Hebrews had come in contact with many peoples, such as the Mesopotamians and the Egyptians, who had many gods. The Hebrews came to believe in a single god, Yahweh, who had created all things and who took a strong personal interest in the individual. According to the Bible, Yahweh made a covenant with the Hebrews: if they worshipped Yahweh as their only god, he would consider them his chosen people and protect them from their enemies. This covenant was to prove a constant force in the Hebrews' religion, Judaism, a word taken from the kingdom of Judah.

A Golden Calf   According to the Hebrew Bible, Moses descended from Mount Sinai, where he had received the Ten Commandments, to find the Hebrews worshipping a golden calf, which was against Yahweh's laws. In July 1990 an American archaeological team found this model of a gilded calf inside a pot. The figurine, which dates to about 1550 B.C.E., is strong evidence for the existence in Canaan of religious traditions that involved animals as divine symbols. (www.BibleLandPictures.com/Alamy Stock Photo)

Worship was embodied in a series of rules of behavior, the Ten Commandments, which Yahweh gave to Moses. These required certain kinds of religious observances and forbade the Hebrews to steal, lie, murder, or commit adultery, thus creating a system of ethical absolutes. From the Ten Commandments a complex system of rules of conduct was created and later written down as Hebrew law, beginning with the Torah — the first five books of the Hebrew Bible. Hebrew Scripture, a group of books written over many centuries, also contained history, hymns of praise, prophecy, traditions, advice, and other sorts of writings. Jews today revere these texts, as do many Christians, and Muslims respect them, all of which gives them particular importance.

The Greeks

The people of ancient Greece built on the traditions and ideas of earlier societies to develop a culture that fundamentally shaped Western civilization. Drawing on their day-to-day experiences as well as logic and empirical observation, the Greeks developed ways of understanding and explaining the world around them, which grew into modern philosophy and science. They also created new political forms, including the small independent city-state known as the *polis*. Scholars label the period dating from around 1100 B.C.E. to 323 B.C.E., in which the polis predominated, the Hellenic period. Two poleis were especially powerful: Sparta, which created a military state in which men remained in the army most of their lives, and Athens, which created a democracy in which male citizens had a direct voice.

Athens created a brilliant culture, with magnificent art and architecture whose grace and beauty still speak to people. In their comedies and tragedies, Athenians Aeschylus, Sophocles, and Euripides were the first playwrights to treat eternal problems of the human condition. Athens also experimented with the political system we call democracy. Greek democracy meant the rule of citizens, not "the people" as a whole, and citizenship was generally limited to free adult men whose parents were citizens. Women were citizens for religious and reproductive purposes, but their citizenship did not give them the right to participate in government. Slaves, resident foreigners, and free men who were not children of a citizen were not citizens and had no political voice. Thus ancient Greek democracy did not reflect the modern concept that all people are created equal, but it did permit male citizens to share in determining the diplomatic and military policies of the polis.

Classical Greece of the fifth and fourth centuries B.C.E. also witnessed an incredible flowering of philosophical ideas. Some Greeks began to question their old beliefs and myths, and sought rational rather than supernatural explanations for natural phenomena. They began an intellectual revolution with the idea that nature was predictable, creating what we now call philosophy and science. These ideas also emerged in medicine: Hippocrates, the most prominent physician and teacher of medicine of his time, sought natural explanations for diseases and natural means to treat them.

The Sophists, a group of thinkers in fifth-century-B.C.E. Athens, applied philosophical speculation to politics and language, questioning the beliefs and laws of the polis to understand their origin. They believed that excellence in both politics and language could be taught, and they provided lessons for the young men of Athens who wished to learn how to persuade others in the often-tumultuous Athenian democracy.

Socrates (ca. 470–399 B.C.E.), whose ideas are known only through the works of others, also applied philosophy to politics and to people. Because he posed questions rather than giving answers, it is difficult to say exactly what Socrates thought about many things, although he does seem to have felt that through knowledge people could approach the supreme good and thus find happiness. Most of what we know about Socrates comes from his student Plato (427–347 B.C.E.), who wrote dialogues in which Socrates asks questions and who also founded the Academy, a school dedicated to philosophy. Plato developed the theory that there are two worlds: the impermanent, changing world that we know through our senses, and the eternal, unchanging realm of "forms" that constitute the essence of true reality. According to Plato, true knowledge and the possibility of living a virtuous life come from contemplating ideal forms. Plato's student Aristotle (384–322 B.C.E.) also thought that true knowledge was possible, but he believed that such knowledge came from observation of the world, analysis of natural phenomena, and logical reasoning, not contemplation. He investigated the nature of government, ideas of matter and motion, outer space, ethics, and language and literature, among other subjects. Aristotle's ideas later profoundly shaped both Muslim and Western philosophy and theology.

Echoing the broader culture, Plato and Aristotle viewed philosophy as an exchange between men in which women had no part. The ideal for Athenian citizen women was a secluded life, although how far this ideal was actually a reality is impossible to know. Women in citizen families probably spent most of their time at home, leaving the house only to attend religious festivals and perhaps occasionally plays.

Greek political and intellectual advances took place against a background of constant warfare. The long and bitter struggle between the cities of Athens and Sparta called the Peloponnesian War (431–404 B.C.E.) ended in Athens's defeat. Shortly afterward, Sparta, Athens, and Thebes contested for hegemony in Greece, but no single state was strong enough to dominate the others. Taking advantage of the situation, Philip II (r. 359–336 B.C.E.) of Macedonia, a small kingdom encompassing part of modern Greece and other parts of the Balkans, defeated a combined Theban-Athenian army in 338 B.C.E. Unable to resolve their domestic quarrels, the Greeks lost their freedom to the Macedonian invader.

Philip was assassinated just two years after he had conquered Greece, and his throne was inherited by his son, Alexander. In twelve years, Alexander conquered an

Hellenistic Married Life This small terra-cotta figurine from Myrina, in what is now Turkey, made in the second century B.C.E., shows a newly married couple sitting on a bridal bed. The groom is drawing back the bride's veil, and she is exhibiting the modesty that was a desired quality in young women. Figurines representing every stage of life became popular in the Hellenistic period and were used for religious offerings in temples and sacred places. This one was found in a tomb. (Musée du Louvre, Paris, France/Erich Lessing/Art Resource, NY)

empire stretching from Macedonia across the Middle East into Asia as far as India. He established cities and military colonies in strategic spots as he advanced eastward, but he died at the age of thirty-two while planning his next campaign.

Alexander left behind an empire that quickly broke into smaller kingdoms, but more important, his death ushered in an era, the Hellenistic, in which Greek culture, the Greek language, and Greek thought spread widely, blending with local traditions. The Hellenistic period stretches from Alexander's death in 323 B.C.E. to the Roman conquest in 30 B.C.E. of the kingdom established in Egypt by Alexander's successors. Greek immigrants moved to the cities and colonies established by Alexander and his successors, spreading the Greek language, ideas, and traditions in a process scholars later called Hellenization. Local people who wanted to rise in wealth or status learned Greek. The economic and cultural connections of the Hellenistic world later proved valuable to the Romans, allowing them to trade products and ideas more easily over a broad area.

The mixing of peoples in the Hellenistic era influenced religion, philosophy, and science. The Hellenistic kings built temples to the old Greek gods and promoted rituals and ceremonies that honored them, but new deities, such as Tyche—the goddess and personification of luck, fate, chance, and fortune—also gained prominence. More people turned to mystery religions, which blended Greek and non-Greek elements and offered their adherents secret knowledge, unification with a deity, and sometimes life after death. Others turned to practical philosophies that provided advice on how to live a good life. These included Epicureanism, which advocated moderation to achieve a life of contentment, and Stoicism, which advocated living in accordance with nature. In the scholarly realm, Hellenistic thinkers made advances in mathematics, astronomy, and mechanical design. Additionally, physicians used observation

and dissection to better understand the way the human body works.

Despite the new ideas, the Hellenistic period did not see widespread improvements in the way most people lived and worked. Cities flourished, but many people who lived in rural areas were actually worse off than they had been before, because of higher levels of rents and taxes. Technology was applied to military needs, but not to the production of food or other goods.

The Greek world was largely conquered by the Romans, and the various Hellenistic monarchies became part of the Roman Empire. In cultural terms the lines of conquest were reversed, however, as the Romans were tremendously influenced by Greek art, philosophy, and ideas, all of which have had a lasting impact on the modern world as well.

Rome: From Republic to Empire

The city of Rome, situated near the center of the boot-shaped peninsula of Italy, conquered all of Italy, then the western Mediterranean basin, and then areas in the east that had been part of Alexander's empire, creating an empire that at its largest stretched from England to Egypt and from Portugal to Persia. The Romans spread the Latin language throughout much of their empire, providing a common language for verbal and written communication for more than a thousand years. They also established concepts of law and government that molded Western legal systems, ideas of political organization, and administrative practices.

The city of Rome developed from small villages and was influenced by the Etruscans who lived to the north.

Sometime in the sixth century B.C.E. a group of aristocrats revolted against the ruling king and established a republican form of government in which the main institution of power was the Senate, an assembly of aristocrats, rather than a single monarch. According to tradition, this happened in 509 B.C.E., so scholars customarily divide Roman history into two primary stages: the republic, from 509 to 27 B.C.E., in which Rome was ruled by the Senate; and the empire, from 27 B.C.E. to 476 C.E., in which Roman territories were ruled by an emperor.

In the years following the establishment of the republic, the Romans fought numerous wars with their neighbors on the Italian peninsula. Their superior military institutions, organization, and manpower allowed them to conquer or take into their influence most of Italy by about 265 B.C.E. Once they had conquered an area, the Romans built roads and often shared Roman citizenship. Roman expansion continued. In a series of wars they conquered lands all around the Mediterranean, creating an overseas empire that brought them unheard-of power and wealth. First they defeated the Carthaginians in the Punic Wars, and then they turned east. Declaring the Mediterranean *mare nostrum*, "our sea," the Romans began to create a political and administrative machinery to hold the Mediterranean together under a mutually shared cultural and political system of provinces ruled by governors sent from Rome.

The Romans created several assemblies through which men elected high officials and passed ordinances. The most important of these was the Senate, a political assembly—initially only of hereditary aristocrats called patricians—that advised officials and handled government finances. The common people of Rome, known as plebeians, were initially excluded from holding offices or sitting in the Senate, but a long political and social struggle led to a broadening of the base of political power to include male plebeians. The basis of Roman society for both patricians and plebeians was the family, headed by the paterfamilias, who held authority over his wife, children, and servants. Households often included slaves, who also provided labor for fields and mines.

A lasting achievement of the Romans was their development of law. Roman civil law consisted of statutes, customs, and forms of procedure that regulated the lives of citizens. As the Romans came into more frequent contact with foreigners, Roman officials applied a broader "law of the peoples," to such matters as peace treaties, the treatment of prisoners of war, and the exchange of diplomats. All sides were to be treated the same regardless of their nationality. By the late republic, Roman jurists had widened this still further into the concept of natural law based in part on Stoic ideas they had learned from Greek thinkers. Natural law, according to these thinkers, is made up of rules that govern human behavior that come from applying reason rather than customs or traditions, and so apply to all societies. In reality, Roman officials generally interpreted the law to the advantage of Rome, of course, at least to the extent that the strength of Roman armies allowed them to enforce it. But Roman law came to be seen as one of the most important contributions Rome made to the development of Western civilization.

Law was not the only facet of Hellenistic Greek culture to influence the Romans. The Roman conquest of the Hellenistic East led to the wholesale confiscation of Greek sculpture and paintings to adorn Roman temples and homes. Greek literary and historical classics were translated into Latin; Greek philosophy was studied in the Roman schools; educated people learned Greek as well as Latin as a matter of course. Public baths based on the Greek model—with exercise rooms, swimming pools, and reading rooms—served not only as centers for recreation and exercise but also as centers of Roman public life.

The wars of conquest eventually created serious political problems for the Romans, which surfaced toward the end of the second century B.C.E. Overseas warfare required huge armies for long periods of time. A few army officers gained fabulous wealth, but most soldiers did not and returned home to find their farms in ruins. Those with cash to invest bought up small farms, creating vast estates called *latifundia*. Landless veterans migrated to Rome seeking work. Unable to compete with the tens of thousands of slaves in Rome, they formed a huge unemployed urban population. Rome divided into political factions, each of which named a supreme military commander, who led Roman troops against external enemies but also against each other. Civil war erupted.

Out of the violence and disorder emerged Julius Caesar (100–44 B.C.E.), a victorious general, shrewd politician, and highly popular figure. He took practical steps to end the civil war, such as expanding citizenship and sending large numbers of the urban poor to found colonies and spread Roman culture in Gaul, Spain, and North Africa. Fearful that Caesar's popularity and ambition would turn Rome into a monarchy, a group of aristocratic conspirators assassinated him in 44 B.C.E. Civil war was renewed. In 31 B.C.E. Caesar's grandnephew and adopted son Octavian defeated his rivals and became master of Rome. For his success, the Senate in 27 B.C.E. gave Octavian the name Augustus, meaning "revered one." Although the Senate did not mean this to be a decisive break, that date is generally used to mark the end of the Roman Republic and the start of the Roman Empire.

Augustus rebuilt effective government. Although he claimed that he was restoring the republic, he actually transformed the government into one in which all power was held by a single ruler, gradually taking over many of the offices that traditionally had been held by separate people. Without specifically saying so, Augustus created the office of emperor. The English word *emperor* is derived from the Latin word *imperator*, an origin that reflects the fact that Augustus's command of the army was the main source of his power.

Augustus ended domestic turmoil and secured the provinces. He founded new colonies, mainly in the

Gladiator Mosaic Made in the first half of the fourth century, this mosaic from an estate outside Rome includes the name of each gladiator next to the figure. In the back a gladiator stands in a victory pose, while the fallen gladiator in the front is marked with the symbol Ø, indicating that he has died in combat. Many of the gladiators in this mosaic, such as those at the left, appear less fit and fearsome than the gladiators depicted in movies, more closely reflecting the reality that gladiatorial combat was a job undertaken by a variety of people, including captives, veterans, and poor immigrants to the city. (Galleria Borghese, Rome, Italy/Alinari/Bridgeman Images)

western Mediterranean basin, which promoted the spread of Greco-Roman culture and the Latin language to the West. Magistrates exercised authority in their regions as representatives of Rome. Augustus broke some of the barriers between Italy and the provinces by extending citizenship to many of the provincials who had supported him. Later emperors added more territory, and a system of Roman roads and sea-lanes united the empire, with trade connections extending to India and China. For two hundred years the Mediterranean world experienced what later historians called the *pax Romana*—a period of prosperity, order, and relative peace. The city of Rome grew to a huge size, and the emperor provided grain and bread at low prices to prevent social unrest. Emperors and other wealthy citizens also entertained the city's residents with gladiatorial contests, chariot racing, and other forms of popular entertainment.

In the third century C.E. this prosperity and stability gave way to a period of domestic upheaval and foreign invasion. Rival generals backed by their troops contested the imperial throne in civil wars. Groups the Romans labeled "barbarians," such as the Visigoths, Ostrogoths, Gauls, and others, migrated into and invaded the Roman Empire

from the north and east. Civil war and invasions devastated towns and farms, causing severe economic depression. The emperors Diocletian (r. 284–305 C.E.) and Constantine (r. 306–337 C.E.) tried to halt the general disintegration by reorganizing the empire, expanding the state bureaucracy, building more defensive works, and imposing heavier taxes. For administrative purposes, Diocletian divided the empire into a western half and an eastern half, and Constantine established the new capital city of Constantinople in the East. Their attempts to solve the empire's problems failed, however. The emperors ruling from Constantinople could not provide enough military assistance to repel invaders in the western half of the Roman Empire. In 476 a Germanic chieftain, Odoacer, deposed the Roman emperor in the West and did not take on the title of emperor, calling himself instead the king of Italy. This date thus marks the official end of the Roman Empire in the West, although the Roman Empire in the East, later called the Byzantine Empire, would last for nearly another thousand years.

After the Western Roman Empire's decline, the rich legacy of Greco-Roman culture was absorbed by the medieval world. The Latin language remained the basic medium of communication among educated people in central and western Europe for the next thousand years; for almost two thousand years, Latin literature formed the core of all Western education. Roman roads, buildings, and aqueducts remained in use. Rome left its mark on the legal and political systems of most European countries. Rome had preserved the best of ancient culture for later times.

The Spread of Christianity

The ancient world also left behind a powerful religious legacy, Christianity. Christianity derives from the teachings of a Jewish man, Jesus of Nazareth (ca. 3 B.C.E.–29 C.E.). According to the accounts of his life written down and preserved by his followers, Jesus preached of a heavenly kingdom of eternal happiness in a life after death and of the importance of devotion to God and love of others. His teachings were based on Hebrew Scripture and reflected a conception of God and morality that came from Jewish tradition, but he deviated from traditional Jewish teachings in insisting that he taught in his own name, not simply in the name of Yahweh. He came to establish a spiritual kingdom, he said, not an earthly one, and he urged his followers and listeners to concentrate on the world to come, not on material goods or earthly relationships. Some Jews believed that Jesus was the long-awaited savior who would bring prosperity and happiness, while others thought he was religiously dangerous. The Roman official of Judaea, Pontius Pilate, feared that the popular agitation surrounding Jesus could lead to revolt against Rome. He arrested Jesus, met with him, and sentenced him to death by crucifixion—the usual method for common criminals. Jesus's followers maintained that he rose from the dead three days later.

Those followers might have remained a small Jewish sect but for the preaching of a Hellenized Jew, Paul of Tarsus (ca. 5–67 C.E.). Paul traveled widely and wrote letters of advice, many of which were copied and circulated, transforming Jesus's ideas into more specific moral teachings. Paul urged that Jews and non-Jews be accepted on an equal basis, and the earliest converts included men and women from all social classes. People were attracted to Christian teachings for a variety of reasons: it offered a message of divine forgiveness and eternal life, taught that every individual has a role to play in building the kingdom of God, and fostered a deep sense of community and identity in the often highly mobile Roman world.

Some Roman officials and emperors opposed Christianity and attempted to stamp it out, but most did not, and by the second century Christianity began to establish more permanent institutions, including a hierarchy of officials. It attracted more highly educated individuals, and modified teachings that seemed upsetting to Romans. In 313 the emperor Constantine legalized Christianity, and in 380 the emperor Theodosius made it the official religion of the empire. Carried by settlers, missionaries, and merchants to Gaul, Spain, North Africa, and Britain, Christianity formed a basic element of Western civilization.

Christian writers also played a powerful role in the conservation of Greco-Roman thought. They used Latin as their medium of communication, thereby preserving it. They copied and transmitted classical texts. Writers such as Saint Augustine of Hippo (354–430) used Roman rhetoric and Roman history to defend Christian theology. In so doing, they assimilated classical culture into Christian teaching.

The Middle Ages

Fifteenth-century scholars believed that they were living in a period of rebirth that had recaptured the spirit of ancient Greece and Rome. What separated their time from classical antiquity, in their opinion, was a long period of darkness to which a seventeenth-century professor gave the name "Middle Ages." In this conceptualization, Western history was divided into three periods—ancient, medieval, and modern—an organization that is still in use today. Recent scholars have demonstrated, however, that the thousand-year period between roughly the fifth and fourteenth centuries was not one of stagnation, but one of great changes in every realm of life: social, political, intellectual, economic, and religious. The men and women of the Middle Ages built on the cultural heritage of the Greco-Roman world and on the traditions of barbarian groups to create new ways of doing things.

The Early Middle Ages

The time period that historians mark off as the early Middle Ages, extending from about the fifth to the tenth centuries, saw the emergence of a distinctly Western society and culture. The geographical center of that society shifted northward from the Mediterranean basin to western Europe. Whereas a rich urban life and flourishing trade had characterized the ancient world, the barbarian invasions led to the decline of cities and the destruction of commerce. Early medieval society was rural and local, with the village serving as the characteristic social unit.

Several processes were responsible for the development of European culture. First, Europe became Christian. Missionaries traveled throughout Europe instructing Germanic, Celtic, and Slavic peoples in the basic tenets of the Christian faith. Seeking to gain more converts, the Christian Church incorporated pagan beliefs and holidays, creating new rituals and practices that were meaningful to people, and creating a sense of community through parish churches and the veneration of saints.

Second, as barbarian groups migrated into the Western Roman Empire, they often intermarried with the old Roman aristocracy. The elite class that emerged held the dominant political, social, and economic power in early—and later—medieval Europe. Barbarian customs and tradition, such as ideals of military prowess and bravery in battle, became part of the mental furniture of Europeans.

Third, in the seventh and eighth centuries, Muslim military conquests carried Islam, the religion inspired by the prophet Muhammad (ca. 571–632), from the Arab lands across North Africa, the Mediterranean basin, and Spain into southern France. The Arabs eventually translated many Greek texts. When, beginning in the ninth century, those texts were translated from Arabic into Latin, they came to play a role in the formation of European scientific and philosophical thought.

Monasticism, an ascetic form of Christian life first practiced in Egypt and characterized by isolation from the broader society, simplicity of living, and abstention from sexual activity, flourished and expanded in both the Byzantine East and the Latin West. Medieval people believed that the communities of monks and nuns provided an important service: prayer on behalf of the broader society. In a world lacking career opportunities, monasteries also offered education for the children of the upper classes. Men trained in monastery schools served royal and baronial governments as advisers, secretaries, diplomats, and treasurers; monks in the West also pioneered the clearing of wasteland and forestland.

One of the barbarian groups that settled within the Roman Empire and allied with the Romans was the Franks, and after the Roman Empire collapsed they expanded their holdings, basing some of their government on Roman principles. In the eighth century the dynamic warrior-king of the Franks, Charles the Great, or Charlemagne (r. 768–814), came to control most of central and western continental Europe except Muslim Spain, and western Europe achieved a degree of political unity. Charlemagne supported Christian missionary efforts and encouraged both classical and Christian scholarship. His coronation in 800 by the pope at Rome in a ceremony filled with Latin anthems represented a fusion of classical, Christian, and barbarian elements, as did Carolingian culture more generally. In the ninth century Vikings, Muslims, and Magyars (early Hungarians) raided and migrated into Europe, leading to the collapse of centralized power. Charlemagne's empire was divided, and real authority passed into the hands of local strongmen. Out of this vulnerable society, which was constantly threatened by outside invasions, a new political form involving mutual obligations, later called "feudalism," developed. The power of the local nobles in the feudal structure rested on landed estates worked by peasants in another system of mutual obligation termed "manorialism," in which the majority of peasants were serfs, required to stay on the land where they were born and pay obligations to a lord in labor and products.

The High and Later Middle Ages

By the beginning of the eleventh century, the European world showed distinct signs of recovery, vitality, and creativity. Over the next three centuries, a period called the High Middle Ages, that recovery and creativity manifested itself in every facet of culture—economic, social, political, intellectual, and artistic. A greater degree of peace paved the way for these achievements.

The Viking, Muslim, and Magyar invasions gradually ended. Warring knights supported ecclesiastical pressure against violence, and disorder declined. A warming climate, along with technological improvements such as water mills and horse-drawn plows, increased the available food supply. Most people remained serfs, living in simple houses in small villages, but a slow increase in population led to new areas being cultivated, and some serfs were able to buy their freedom.

Relative security and the increasing food supply allowed for the growth and development of towns in the High Middle Ages. Towns gained legal and political rights, merchant and craft guilds grew more powerful, and towns became centers of production as well as trading centers. In medieval social thinking, three classes existed: the clergy, who prayed; the

Medieval Mother and Child   In this illustration from the margins of a fourteenth-century French book of poetry, a mother carries her infant in a cradle. The baby is tightly swaddled in cloth, a common practice that came from medieval ideas about how children's limbs developed and from concerns about an infant's safety in households with open fires where domestic animals walked freely and parents and older siblings had work to do. (The Pierpont Morgan Library, New York, NY, USA/Art Resource, NY)

nobility, who fought; and the peasantry, who tilled the land. The merchant class, engaging in manufacturing and trade, seeking freedom from the jurisdiction of feudal lords, and pursuing wealth with a fiercely competitive spirit, fit none of the standard categories. Townspeople represented a radical force for change. Trade brought in new ideas as well as merchandise, and towns developed into intellectual and cultural centers.

The growth of towns and cities went hand in hand with a revival of regional and international trade. For example, Italian merchants traveled to the regional fairs of France and Flanders to exchange silk from China and slaves from the Crimea for English woolens, French wines, and Flemish textiles. Merchants adopted new business techniques and a new attitude toward making money. They were eager to invest surplus capital to make more money. These developments added up to what scholars have termed a commercial revolution, a major turning point in the economic and social life of the West. The development of towns and commerce was to lay the foundations for Europe's transformation, centuries later, from a rural agricultural society into an urban industrial society—a change with global implications.

The High Middle Ages also saw the birth of the modern centralized state. The concept of the state had been one of Rome's great legacies to Western civilization, but for almost five hundred years after the disintegration of the Roman Empire in the West, political authority was weak. Charlemagne had far less control of what went on in his kingdom than Roman emperors had, and after the Carolingian Empire broke apart, political authority was completely decentralized, with power spread among many feudal lords. Beginning in the last half of the tenth century, however, feudal rulers started to develop new institutions of law and government that enabled them to assert their power over lesser lords and the general population. Centralized states slowly crystallized, first in France and England, and then in Spain and northern Europe. In Italy and Germany, however, strong independent local authorities predominated.

Medieval rulers required more officials, larger armies, and more money with which to pay for them. They developed financial bureaucracies, of which the most effective were those in England. They also sought to transform a hodgepodge of oral and written customs and rules into a uniform system of laws acceptable and applicable to all their peoples. In France, local laws and procedures were maintained, but the king also established a royal court that published laws and heard appeals. In England, the king's court regularized procedures, and the idea of a common law that applied to the whole country developed. Fiscal and legal measures enacted by King John led to opposition from the high nobles of England, who in 1215 forced him to sign the Magna Carta, agreeing to observe the law. English kings following John recognized this common law, a law that their judges applied throughout the country. Exercise of common law often involved juries of local people to answer questions of fact. The common law and jury systems

of the Middle Ages have become integral features of Anglo-American jurisprudence. In the fourteenth century kings also summoned meetings of the leading classes in their kingdoms, and thus were born representative assemblies, most notably the English Parliament.

In their work of consolidation and centralization, kings increasingly used the knowledge of university-trained officials. Universities first emerged in western Europe in the twelfth century. Medieval universities were educational institutions for men that produced trained officials for the new bureaucratic states. The universities at Bologna in Italy and Montpellier in France, for example, were centers for the study of Roman law. Paris became the leading university for the study of philosophy and theology. Medieval Scholastics (philosophers and theologians) sought to harmonize Greek philosophy, especially the works of Aristotle, with Christian teaching. They wanted to use reason to deepen the understanding of what was believed on faith. At the University of Paris, Thomas Aquinas (1225–1274) wrote an important synthesis of Christian revelation and Aristotelian philosophy in his *Summa Theologica*. Medieval universities developed the basic structures familiar to modern students: colleges, universities, examinations, and degrees. Colleges and universities are another major legacy of the Middle Ages to the modern world.

At the same time that states developed, energetic popes built their power within the Western Christian Church and asserted their superiority over kings and emperors. A papal call to retake the holy city of Jerusalem led to nearly two centuries of warfare between Christians and Muslims. Christian warriors, clergy, and settlers moved out from western and central Europe in all directions, so that through conquest and colonization border regions were gradually incorporated into a more uniform European culture.

Most people in medieval Europe were Christian, and the village or city church was the center of community life, where people attended services, honored the saints, and experienced the sacraments. The village priest blessed the fields before the spring planting and the fall harvesting. In everyday life people engaged in rituals heavy with religious symbolism, and every life transition was marked by a ceremony with religious elements. Guilds of merchants sought the protection of patron saints and held elaborate public celebrations on the saints' feast days. Indeed, the veneration of saints—men and women whose lives contemporaries perceived as outstanding in holiness—and an increasingly sophisticated sacramental system became central features of popular religion. University lectures and meetings of parliaments began with prayers. Kings relied on the services of bishops and abbots in the work of the government. Gothic cathedrals, where people saw beautiful stained-glass windows and listened to complex music, manifested medieval people's deep Christian faith and their pride in their own cities.

The high level of energy and creativity that characterized the twelfth and thirteenth centuries could not be sustained indefinitely. In the fourteenth century every conceivable

Violence in the Late Middle Ages   In this French manuscript illumination from 1465, armored knights kill a priest and official in a castle and a peasant while he plows. In the background, other knights steal cloth from a woman (and the distaff on which she made it) and approach a man at work in a field. Aristocratic violence was a common feature of late medieval life, although nobles would generally not have bothered to put on their armor to harass villagers. (Musée Condé, Chantilly, France/Bridgeman Images)

disaster struck western Europe. The climate turned colder and wetter, leading to poor harvests and widespread famine. People weakened by hunger were more susceptible to disease, and in the middle of the fourteenth century the bubonic plague (or Black Death) swept across the continent, taking a terrible toll on population. England and France became deadlocked in a long and bitter struggle known as the Hundred Years' War (1337–1453). War devastated the countryside, especially in France, leading to widespread discontent and peasant revolts. Workers in cities also revolted against dismal working conditions, and violent crime and ethnic tensions increased. Many urban residents were increasingly dissatisfied with the Christian Church and turned to heretical movements that challenged church power. Schism in the Catholic Church resulted in the simultaneous claim by two popes of jurisdiction. Yet, in spite of the pessimism and crises, important institutions and cultural forms, including representative assemblies and national literatures, emerged.

Early Modern Europe

While war gripped northern Europe, a new culture emerged in southern Europe. The fourteenth century witnessed the beginning of remarkable changes in many aspects of Italian intellectual, artistic, and cultural life. Artists and writers thought they were living in a new golden age, but not until the sixteenth century was this change given the label we use today — the Renaissance, from the French version of a word meaning "rebirth." The term was first used by the artist and art historian Giorgio Vasari (1511–1574) to describe the art of "rare men of genius" such as his contemporary Michelangelo. Through their works, Vasari judged, the glory of the classical past had been reborn after centuries of darkness, or had perhaps even been surpassed. Vasari used the word *Renaissance* to describe painting, sculpture, and architecture, what he termed the "Major Arts." Gradually, however, *Renaissance* was used to refer to many aspects of life at this time, first in Italy and then in the rest of Europe. This new attitude had a slow diffusion out of Italy, with the result that the Renaissance happened at different times in different parts of Europe. Italian art of the fourteenth through the early sixteenth centuries is described as "Renaissance," as is English literature of the late sixteenth century (including Shakespeare).

About a century after Vasari coined the word *Renaissance*, scholars began to view the cultural and political changes of the Renaissance, along with the religious changes of the Reformation and the European voyages of exploration, as ushering in the "modern" world. Since then, some historians have chosen to view the Renaissance as a bridge between the medieval and modern eras, as it corresponded chronologically with the late medieval period and as there was much continuity along with the changes. Others have questioned whether the word *Renaissance* should be used at all to describe an era in which many social groups saw decline rather than advancement. These debates remind us that the labels *medieval*, *Renaissance*, and *modern* are intellectual constructs devised after the fact. They all contain value judgments, as do other chronological designations, such as the "golden age" of Athens and the "Roaring Twenties."

The Renaissance

In the commercial revival of the Middle Ages, ambitious merchants amassed great wealth, especially in the city-states of northern Italy. These city-states were communes in which all citizens shared power, but political instability often led to their transformation into city-states ruled by single individuals. As their riches and power grew, rulers and merchants displayed their wealth in great public buildings as well as magnificent courts—palaces where they lived and conducted business. Political rulers, popes, and powerful families hired writers, artists, musicians, and architects through the system of patronage, which allowed for a great outpouring of culture.

The Renaissance was characterized by self-conscious awareness among fourteenth- and fifteenth-century Italians—particularly scholars and writers known as humanists—that they were living in a new era. Key to this attitude was a serious interest in the Latin classics, a belief in individual potential, and a more secular attitude toward life. All of these are evident in the political theory developed in the Renaissance, particularly that of Machiavelli. Humanists opened schools to train boys and young men for active lives of public service, but had doubts about whether humanist education was appropriate for women. As humanism spread to northern Europe, religious concerns became more pronounced, and Christian humanists set out plans for the reform of church and society. Their ideas reached a much wider audience than did those of early humanists because of the development of the printing press with movable metal type, which revolutionized communication.

Interest in the classical past and in the individual also shaped Renaissance art in terms of style and subject matter.

Painting became more naturalistic, and the individual portrait emerged as a distinct artistic genre. Wealthy merchants, cultured rulers, and powerful popes all hired painters, sculptors, and architects to design and ornament public and private buildings. Art in Italy became more secular and classical, while that in northern Europe retained a more religious tone. Artists began to understand themselves as having a special creative genius, though they continued to produce works on order for patrons, who often determined the content and form.

Social hierarchies in the Renaissance built on those of the Middle Ages, with the addition of new features that evolved into the modern social hierarchies of race, class, and gender. In the fifteenth century black slaves entered Europe in sizable numbers for the first time since the collapse of the Roman Empire, and Europeans fit them into changing understandings of ethnicity and race. The medieval hierarchy of orders based on function in society intermingled with a new hierarchy based on wealth, with new types of elites becoming more powerful. The Renaissance debate about women led many to discuss women's nature and proper role in society, a discussion sharpened by the presence of a number of ruling queens in this era.

Beginning in the fifteenth century rulers utilized aggressive methods to rebuild their governments. First in the regional states of Italy, then in the expanding monarchies of France, England, and Spain, rulers began the work of reducing violence, curbing unruly nobles, and establishing domestic order. They attempted to secure their borders and enhanced methods of raising revenue. The monarchs of western Europe emphasized royal majesty and royal sovereignty and insisted on the respect and loyalty of all subjects, including the nobility. In central Europe the Holy Roman emperors attempted to do the same, but they were not able to overcome the power of local interests to create a unified state.

The Reformation

Calls for reform of the Christian Church began very early in its history. When Christianity became the official religion of the Roman Empire in the fourth century, many believers thought that the church had abandoned its original mission, and they called for a return to a church that was not linked to the state. Throughout the Middle Ages, individuals and groups argued that the church had become too wealthy and powerful, and urged monasteries, convents, bishoprics, and the papacy to give up their property and focus on service to the poor. Some asserted that basic teachings of the church were not truly Christian and that changes were needed in theology as well as in institutional structures and practices. The Christian humanists of the late fifteenth and early sixteenth centuries urged reform, primarily through educational and social change. Throughout the centuries, men and women believed that the early Christian Church represented a golden age akin to the golden age of the classical past celebrated by Renaissance humanists.

Thus sixteenth-century cries for reformation were hardly new. What was new, however, was the breadth with which they were accepted and their ultimate impact. In 1500 there was one Christian Church in western Europe to which all Christians at least nominally belonged. Fifty years later there were many, a situation that continues today. Thus, along with the Renaissance, the Reformation is often seen as a key element in the creation of the "modern" world.

In 1517 Martin Luther (1483–1546), a priest and professor of theology at a small German university, launched an attack on clerical abuses. The Catholic Church in the early sixteenth century had serious problems, and many individuals and groups had long called for reform. This background of discontent helps explain why Martin Luther's ideas found such a ready audience. Luther and other Protestants developed a new understanding of Christian doctrine that emphasized faith, the power of God's grace, and the centrality of the Bible. Protestant ideas were attractive to educated people and urban residents, and they spread rapidly through preaching, hymns, and the printing press. By 1530 many parts of the Holy Roman Empire and Scandinavia had broken with the Catholic Church.

Some reformers developed more radical ideas about infant baptism, ownership of property, and the separation between church and state. Both Protestants and Catholics regarded these as dangerous, and radicals were banished or executed. The German Peasants' War, in which Luther's ideas were linked to calls for social and economic reform, was similarly put down harshly. The Protestant reformers did not break with medieval ideas about the proper gender hierarchy, though they did elevate the status of marriage by denying the value of clerical celibacy and viewed orderly households as the key building blocks of society.

The progress of the Reformation was shaped by the political situation in the Holy Roman Empire. The Habsburg emperor, Charles V, ruled almost half of Europe along with Spain's overseas colonies. Within the empire his authority was limited, however, and local princes, nobles, and cities actually held the most power. This decentralization allowed the Reformation to spread. Charles remained firmly Catholic, and in the 1530s religious wars began in Germany. These were brought to an end with the Peace of Augsburg in 1555, which allowed rulers to choose whether their territory would be Catholic or Lutheran.

Martin Luther and Katharina von Bora   Luther and other Protestants thought that marriage was the ideal state for nearly all people. Luther married a former nun, Katharina von Bora, and his favorite artist Lucas Cranach the Elder painted this double marriage portrait to celebrate the wedding. The couple quickly became a model of the ideal marriage, and more than sixty similar paintings, with slight variations, were produced by Cranach's workshop and hung in churches and wealthy homes. (Galleria degli Uffizi, Florence, Italy/Alinari/Bridgeman)

In England, the political issue of the royal succession triggered that country's break with Rome, and a Protestant Church was established. Protestant ideas also spread into France and eastern Europe. In all these areas, a second generation of reformers built on Lutheran and Zwinglian ideas to develop their own theology and plans for institutional change. The most important of the second-generation reformers was John Calvin, whose ideas would come to shape Christianity over a much wider area than did Luther's. The Roman Catholic Church responded slowly to the Protestant challenge, but by the 1530s the papacy was leading a movement for reform within the church instead of blocking it. Catholic doctrine was reaffirmed at the Council of Trent, and reform measures, such as the opening of seminaries for priests and a ban on holding multiple church offices, were introduced. New religious orders such as the Jesuits and the Ursulines spread Catholic ideas through teaching, and in the case of the Jesuits through missionary work.

Religious differences led to riots, civil wars, and international conflicts in the later sixteenth century. In France and the Netherlands, Calvinist Protestants and Catholics used violence against each other, and religious differences became mixed with political and economic grievances. Long civil wars resulted; one in the Netherlands became an international conflict. War ended in France with the Edict of Nantes in which Protestants were given some civil rights, and in the Netherlands with a division of the country into a Protestant north and a Catholic south. The era of religious wars was also the time of the most extensive witch persecutions in European history, as both Protestants and Catholics tried to rid their cities and states of people they regarded as linked to the Devil.

The Renaissance and the Reformation are often seen as two of the key elements in the creation of the "modern" world. The radical changes brought by the Reformation contained many aspects of continuity, however. Sixteenth-century reformers looked back to the early Christian Church for their inspiration, and many of their reforming ideas had been advocated for centuries. Most Protestant reformers worked with political leaders to make religious changes, just as early church officials had worked with Emperor Constantine and his successors as Christianity became the official religion of the Roman Empire in the fourth century. The spread of Christianity and the spread of Protestantism were accomplished not only by preaching, persuasion, and teaching, but also by force and violence. The Catholic Reformation was carried out by activist popes, a church council, and new religious orders, as earlier reforms of the church had been.

Just as they linked with earlier developments, the events of the Reformation were also closely connected with what is often seen as the third element in the "modern" world, discussed in the first chapter of this book: European Exploration and Conquest. Only a week after Martin Luther stood in front of Emperor Charles V at the Diet of Worms declaring his independence in matters of religion, Ferdinand Magellan, a Portuguese sea captain with Spanish ships, was killed in a group of islands off the coast of Southeast Asia. Charles V had provided the backing for Magellan's voyage, the first to circumnavigate the globe. Magellan viewed the spread of Christianity as one of the purposes of his trip, and later in the sixteenth century institutions created as part of the Catholic Reformation, including the Jesuit order and the Inquisition, would operate in European colonies overseas as well as in Europe itself. The islands where Magellan was killed were later named the Philippines, in honor of Charles's son Philip, who sent an ill-fated expedition, the Spanish Armada, against Protestant England. Philip's opponent Queen Elizabeth was similarly honored when English explorers named a huge chunk of territory in North America "Virginia" as a tribute to their "Virgin Queen." The desire for wealth and power was an important motivation in the European voyages and colonial ventures, but so was religious zeal.

14

European Exploration and Conquest

1450–1650

In 1450 Europeans were relatively marginal players in a centuries-old trading system that linked Africa, Asia, and Europe. The Indian Ocean was the locus of a vibrant cosmopolitan Afroeurasian trade world in which Arab, Persian, Turkish, Indian, African, Chinese, and European merchants and adventurers competed for trade in spices, silks, and other goods. Elites everywhere prized Chinese porcelains and silks, while wealthy members of the Celestial Kingdom, as China called itself, wanted gold, ivory, and rhinoceros horn from Africa, and exotic goods and peacocks from India. African people wanted textiles from India and cowrie shells from the Maldives in the Indian Ocean. Europeans craved Asian silks and spices, but they had few desirable goods to offer their trading partners.

By 1550 the European search for better access to Asian trade goods had led to a new overseas empire in the Indian Ocean and the accidental discovery of the Western Hemisphere. South and North America were soon drawn into a global network of trade centers and political empires, which Europeans came to dominate. The era of globalization had begun, creating new political systems and forms of economic exchange as well as cultural assimilation, conversion, and resistance. Europeans sought to impose their values on the peoples they encountered while struggling to comprehend these peoples' societies. The Age of Discovery (1450–1650), as the time of these encounters is known, laid the foundations for the modern world. ■

CHAPTER PREVIEW

Life in the Age of Discovery
The arrival of the Portuguese in Japan in 1453 inspired a series of artworks depicting the *namban-jin*, or southern barbarians, as they were known. This detail from an early-seventeenth-century painted screen shows Portuguese sailors unloading trade goods from a merchant ship. (Detail from a Namban Byobu Japanese painted screen/ Museu Nacional de Soares dos Reis, Porto, Portugal/Bridgeman Images)

World Contacts Before Columbus

FOCUS QUESTION *What was the Afroeurasian trading world prior to the era of European exploration?*

In the fifteenth century a type of world economy, known as the Afroeurasian trade world, linked the products and people of Asia, Africa, and Europe. Before Christopher Columbus began his voyages to the New World in 1492, the West was not the dominant player in world trade. Nevertheless, wealthy Europeans were eager consumers of luxury goods from the East, which they received through Venetian and Genoese middlemen.

The Trade World of the Indian Ocean

The Indian Ocean was the center of the Afroeurasian trade world, serving as a crossroads for exchange among China, India, the Middle East, Africa, and Europe (Map 14.1). From the seventh through the fourteenth centuries, the volume of this trade steadily increased, declining only during the catastrophic years of the Black Death.

Merchants congregated in a series of cosmopolitan port cities strung around the Indian Ocean. Most of these cities had some form of autonomous self-government. Mutual self-interest largely limited violence and prevented attempts to monopolize trade. The most developed area of this commercial web was the South China Sea. In the fifteenth century the port of Malacca became a great commercial entrepôt (AHN-truh-poh), a trading post to which goods were shipped for storage while awaiting redistribution. To Malacca came Chinese porcelains, silks, and camphor (used in the manufacture of many medications); pepper, cloves, nutmeg, and raw materials such as sandalwood from the Moluccas; sugar from the Philippines; and Indian textiles, copper weapons, incense, dyes, and opium.

The Mongol emperors opened the doors of China to the West, encouraging Europeans like the Venetian trader and explorer Marco Polo to do business there. Marco Polo's tales of his travels from 1271 to 1295 and his encounter with the Great Khan fueled Western fantasies about the exotic Orient. Polo vividly recounted the splendors of the khan's court and the city of Hangzhou, which he described as "the finest and noblest in the world" in which "the number and wealth of the merchants, and the amount of goods that passed through their hands, was so enormous that no man could form a just estimate thereof."[1] After the Mongols fell to the Ming Dynasty in 1368, China entered a period of economic expansion, population growth, and urbanization. By the end of the dynasty in 1644, the Chinese population had tripled to between 150 million and 200 million people. The city of Nanjing had 1 million inhabitants, making it the largest city in the world, while the new capital, Beijing, had more than 600,000 inhabitants, more than any European city. Historians agree that China had the most advanced economy in the world until at least the start of the eighteenth century.

China also took the lead in exploration, sending Admiral Zheng He's fleet along the trade web as far west as Egypt. From 1405 to 1433 each of his seven expeditions involved hundreds of ships and tens of thousands of men. In one voyage alone, Zheng He (JEHNG HUH) sailed more than 12,000 miles, compared to Columbus's 2,400 miles on his first voyage some sixty years later.[2] Although the ships brought back many wonders, such as giraffes and zebras, the purpose of the voyages was primarily diplomatic, to enhance China's prestige and seek tribute-paying alliances. The high expense of the voyages in a period of renewed Mongol encroachment led to the abandonment of the maritime expeditions after the deaths of Zheng He and the emperor. China's turning away from external trade opened new opportunities for European states to expand their role in Asian trade.

Another center of trade in the Indian Ocean was India. The subcontinent had ancient links with its neighbors to the northwest: trade between South Asia and Mesopotamia dates back to the origins of human civilization. The Roman Empire acquired cotton textiles, exotic animals, and other luxury goods from India. Arab merchants who circumnavigated India on their way to trade in the South China Sea established trading posts along the southern coast of India, where the cities of Calicut and Quilon became thriving commercial centers. India was an important contributor of goods to the world trading system. Most of the world's pepper was grown in India, and Indian cotton and silk textiles, mainly from the Gujarat region, were also highly prized.

The Trading States of Africa

By 1450 Africa had a few large empires along with hundreds of smaller states. From 1250 until its defeat by the Ottomans in 1517, the Mamluk Egyptian empire was one of the most powerful on the continent. Its capital, Cairo, was a center of Islamic learning and religious authority as well as a hub for Indian Ocean trade goods. Sharing in Cairo's prosperity was the African highland state of Ethiopia, a Christian kingdom with scattered contacts with European rulers. On the east coast of Africa, Swahili-speaking city-states engaged in the Indian Ocean trade, exchanging ivory, rhinoceros horn, tortoise shells, and slaves for textiles, spices, cowrie shells, porcelain, and other goods. Peopled by confident and urbane merchants, cities like Kilwa, Malindi, Mogadishu, and Mombasa were known for their prosperity and culture.

In the fifteenth century most of the gold that reached Europe came from the western part of the Sudan region in West Africa and from the Akan (AH-kahn) peoples living near present-day Ghana. Transported across the Sahara by Arab and African traders on camels, the gold was sold in the ports of North Africa. Other trading routes led to the Egyptian cities of Alexandria and Cairo, where the Venetians held commercial privileges.

Inland nations that sat astride the north-south caravan routes grew wealthy from this trade. In the mid-thirteenth century the kingdom of Mali emerged as an important player on the overland trade route, gaining prestige from its ruler Mansa Musa's fabulous pilgrimage to Mecca in 1324/25. Mansa Musa reportedly came to the throne after the previous king failed to return from a naval expedition he led to explore the Atlantic Ocean. A document by a contemporary scholar, al-Umari,

Chronology

1271–1295	Marco Polo travels to China
1443	Portuguese establish first African trading post at Arguin
1492	Columbus lands in the Americas
1511	Portuguese capture Malacca from Muslims
1518	Spanish king authorizes slave trade to New World colonies
1519–1522	Magellan's expedition circumnavigates the world
1521	Cortés conquers the Mexica Empire
1533	Pizarro conquers the Inca Empire
1602	Dutch East India Company established

quoted Mansa Musa's description of his predecessor as a man who "did not believe that the ocean was impossible to cross. He wished to reach the other side and was passionately interested in doing so."[3] After only one ship returned from an earlier expedition, the king set out himself at the head of a fleet of two thousand vessels, a voyage from which no one returned. Corroboration of these early expeditions is lacking, but this report underlines the wealth and ambition of Mali in this period.

The Port of Calicut in India The port of Calicut, located on the west coast of India, was a center of the Indian Ocean spice trade during the Middle Ages. Vasco da Gama arrived in Calicut in 1498 and obtained permission to trade there, leading to hostilities between the Portuguese and the Arab traders who had previously dominated the port. (From *Civitates Orbis Terrarum*, ca. 1572/Private Collection/The Stapleton Collection/Bridgeman Images)

CALECHVT CELEBERRI: MVM INDIÆ EMPORIVM.

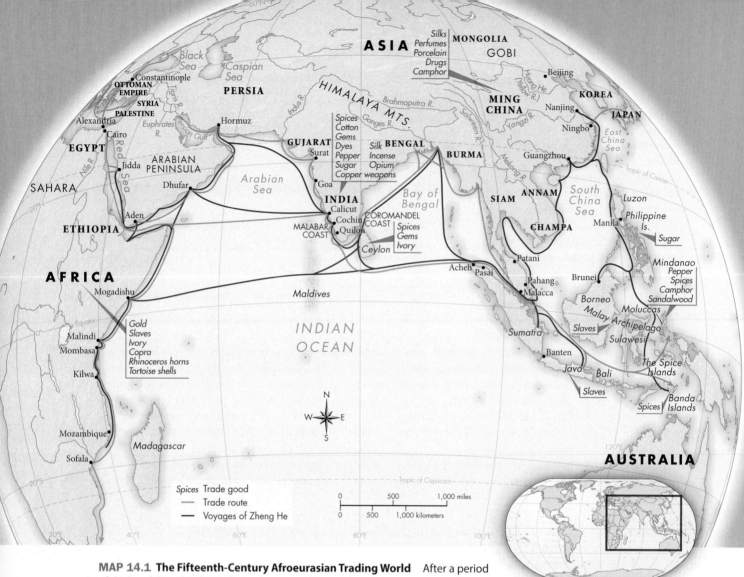

Silks
Perfumes
Porcelain
Drugs
Camphor

Spices
Cotton
Gems
Dyes
Pepper
Sugar
Copper

Silk
Incense
Opium
weapons

Spices
Gems
Ivory

Gold
Slaves
Ivory
Copra
Rhinoceros horns
Tortoise shells

Slaves

Slaves

Slaves

Pepper
Spices
Camphor
Sandalwood

Spices

Sugar

Spices Trade good
—— Trade route
—— Voyages of Zheng He

0   500   1,000 miles
0   500   1,000 kilometers

MAP 14.1 **The Fifteenth-Century Afroeurasian Trading World**   After a period of decline following the Black Death and the Mongol invasions, trade revived in the fifteenth century. Muslim merchants dominated trade, linking ports in East Africa and the Red Sea with those in India and the Malay Archipelago. Chinese admiral Zheng He's voyages (1405–1433) followed the most important Indian Ocean trade routes, in the hope of imposing Ming dominance of trade and tribute.

In later centuries the diversion of gold away from the trans-Sahara routes would weaken the inland states of Africa politically and economically.

Gold was one important object of trade; slaves were another. Slavery was practiced in Africa, as it was virtually everywhere else in the world, long before the arrival of Europeans. Arab and African merchants took West African slaves to the Mediterranean to be sold in European, Egyptian, and Middle Eastern markets and also brought eastern Europeans—a major element of European slavery—to West Africa as slaves. In addition, Indian and Arab merchants traded slaves in the coastal regions of East Africa.

Legends about Africa played an important role in Europeans' imagination of the outside world. They long cherished the belief in a powerful Christian nation in Africa ruled by a mythical king, Prester John, who was believed to be a descendant of one of the three kings who visited Jesus after his birth.

The Ottoman and Persian Empires

The Middle East served as an intermediary for trade between Asia, Africa, and Europe and was also an important supplier of goods for foreign exchange, especially silk and cotton. Two great rival Muslim empires, the Persian Safavids (sah-FAH-vidz) and the Turkish Ottomans, dominated the region. Persian merchants could be found in trading communities as far away as the Indian Ocean. Persia was also a major producer and exporter of silk.

The Persians' Shi'ite Muslim faith clashed with the Ottomans' adherence to Sunnism. Economically, the two competed for control over western trade routes to the East. Under Sultan Mohammed II (r. 1451–1481), the Ottomans captured Europe's largest city, Constantinople, in May 1453. Renamed Istanbul, the city became the capital of the Ottoman Empire. By the mid-sixteenth

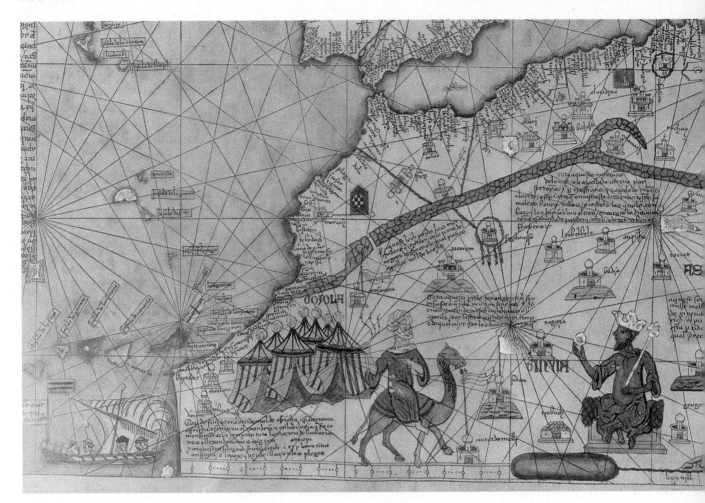

Detail from the *Catalan Atlas*, 1375   This detail from a medieval map depicts Mansa Musa (lower right), who ruled the powerful West African empire of Mali from 1312 to 1337. Musa's golden crown and scepter, and the gold ingot he holds in his hand, testify to the empire's wealth as well as to the European mapmakers' interest in the precious metal mined in the area. (Detail from the *Catalan Atlas*, 1375/Abraham Cresques/Getty Images)

century the Ottomans controlled the sea trade in the eastern Mediterranean, Syria, Palestine, Egypt, and the rest of North Africa, and their power extended into Europe as far west as Vienna.

Ottoman expansion frightened Europeans. The Ottoman armies seemed invincible and the empire's desire for expansion limitless. In France in the sixteenth century, only forty books were published on the American discoveries compared to eighty on Turkey and the Turks.[4] The strength of the Ottomans helps explain some of the missionary fervor Christians brought to new territories. It also raised economic concerns. With trade routes to the East dominated by the Ottomans, Europeans wished to find new trade routes free of Ottoman control.

Genoese and Venetian Middlemen

Compared to the riches and vibrancy of the East, Europe constituted a minor outpost of the world trading sys-

tem. European craftsmen produced few products to rival the fine wares and coveted spices of Asia. In the late Middle Ages, the Italian city-states of Venice and Genoa controlled the European luxury trade with the East.

In 1304 Venice established formal relations with the sultan of Mamluk Egypt, opening operations in Cairo, a gateway to Asian trade. Venetian merchants specialized in goods like spices, silks, and carpets, which they obtained from middlemen in the eastern Mediterranean and Asia Minor. A little went a long way. Venetians purchased no more than five hundred tons of spices a year around 1400, with a profit of about 40 percent. The most important spice was pepper, grown in India and Indonesia, which constituted 60 percent of the spices they purchased in 1400.[5]

The Venetians exchanged Eastern luxury goods for European products they could trade abroad, including Spanish and English wool, German metal goods, Flemish textiles, and silk cloth made in their own manufactures with imported raw materials. Eastern demand for such items, however, was low, leading Venetians to fund their purchases through shipping and trade in firearms and slaves. At least half of what they traded with the East took the form of precious metal, much of it acquired in Egypt and North Africa. When the Portuguese arrived in Asia in the late fifteenth century, they found Venetian coins everywhere.

Venice's ancient rival was Genoa. In the wake of the Crusades, Genoa dominated the northern route to Asia through the Black Sea. Expansion in the thirteenth and fourteenth centuries took the Genoese as far as Persia and the Far East. In 1291 they sponsored an expedition into the Atlantic in search of India. The ships were lost, and their exact destination and motivations remain unknown. This voyage reveals the long roots of Genoese interest in Atlantic exploration.

In the fifteenth century, with Venice claiming victory in the spice trade, the Genoese shifted focus from trade to finance and from the Black Sea to the western Mediterranean. Located on the northwestern coast of Italy, Genoa had always been active in the western Mediterranean, trading with North African ports, southern France, Spain, and even England and Flanders through the Strait of Gibraltar. When Spanish and Portuguese voyages began to explore the western Atlantic, Genoese merchants, navigators, and financiers provided their skills and capital to the Iberian monarchs. The Genoese, for example, ran many of the sugar plantations established on the Atlantic islands colonized by the Portuguese. Genoese merchants would eventually help finance Spanish colonization of the New World.

A major element of Italian trade was slavery. Merchants purchased slaves, many of whom were fellow Christians, in the Balkans. The men were sold to Egypt for the sultan's army or sent to work as agricultural laborers in the Mediterranean. Young girls, who constituted the majority of the trade, were sold in western Mediterranean ports as servants or concubines. After the loss of the Black Sea—and thus the source of slaves—to the Ottomans, the Genoese sought new supplies of slaves in the West, taking the Guanches (indigenous peoples from the Canary Islands), Muslim prisoners, Jewish refugees from Spain, and by the early 1500s both black and Berber Africans. With the growth of Spanish colonies in the New World, Genoese and Venetian merchants would become important players in the Atlantic slave trade.

Italian experience in colonial administration, slaving, and international trade served as a model for the Iberian states as they pushed European expansion to new heights. Mariners, merchants, and financiers from Venice and Genoa—most notably Christopher Columbus—played a crucial role in bringing the fruits of this experience to the Iberian Peninsula and to the New World.

The European Voyages of Discovery

FOCUS QUESTION *How and why did Europeans undertake ambitious voyages of expansion?*

As we have seen, Europe was by no means isolated before the voyages of exploration and its "discovery" of the New World. But because they did not produce many products desired by Eastern elites, Europeans played only a small role in the Indian Ocean trading world. As Europe recovered from the Black Death, new European players entered the scene with novel technology, eager to spread Christianity and to undo Italian and Ottoman domination of trade with the East. A century after the plague, Iberian explorers began the overseas voyages that helped create the modern world, with staggering consequences for their own continent and the rest of the planet.

Causes of European Expansion

European expansion had multiple causes. The first was economic. By the middle of the fifteenth century, Europe was experiencing a revival of population and economic activity after the lows of the Black Death. This revival created demand for luxuries, especially spices, from the East. The fall of Constantinople and subsequent Ottoman control of trade routes created obstacles to fulfilling these demands. Europeans needed to find new sources of precious metal to trade with the Ottomans or trade routes that bypassed the Ottomans.

Why were spices so desirable? Introduced into western Europe by the Crusaders in the twelfth century, pepper, nutmeg, ginger, mace, cinnamon, and cloves added flavor and variety to the monotonous European diet. Not only did spices serve as flavorings for food, but they were also used in anointing oil and as incense for religious rituals, and as perfumes, medicines, and dyes in daily life. Apart from their utility, the expense and exotic origins of spices meant that they were a high-status good, which European elites could use to demonstrate their social status.

Religious fervor and the crusading spirit were another important catalyst for expansion. Just seven

---

■ **conquistador** Spanish for "conqueror"; Spanish soldier-explorers, such as Hernán Cortés and Francisco Pizarro, who sought to conquer the New World for the Spanish crown.

■ **caravel** A small, maneuverable, three-mast sailing ship developed by the Portuguese in the fifteenth century that gave the Portuguese a distinct advantage in exploration and trade.

■ **Ptolemy's *Geography*** A second-century-C.E. work that synthesized the classical knowledge of geography and introduced the concepts of longitude and latitude. Reintroduced to Europeans about 1410 by Arab scholars, its ideas allowed cartographers to create more accurate maps.

months separated Isabella and Ferdinand's conquest of the emirate of Granada, the last remaining Muslim state on the Iberian Peninsula, and Columbus's departure across the Atlantic. Overseas exploration thus transferred the militarist religious fervor of the reconquista (reconquest) to new non-Christian territories. As they conquered indigenous empires, Iberians brought the attitudes and administrative practices developed during the reconquista to the Americas. Conquistadors fully expected to be rewarded with land, titles, and power over conquered peoples, just as the leaders of the reconquista had been.

Like other men of the Renaissance era, explorers sought to win glory for their amazing exploits and demonstrated a genuine interest in learning more about unknown waters. The European discoveries thus constituted one manifestation of Renaissance curiosity about the physical universe. The detailed journals many voyagers kept attest to their wonder and fascination with the new peoples and places they visited.

Individual explorers often manifested all of these desires at once. Christopher Columbus, a devout Christian, aimed to discover new territories where Christianity could be spread while seeking a direct trade route to Asia. The motives of the Portuguese explorer Bartholomew Diaz were, in his own words, "to serve God and His Majesty, to give light to those who were in darkness and to grow rich as all men desire to do." When the Portuguese explorer Vasco da Gama reached the port of Calicut, India, in 1498 and a native asked what he wanted, he replied, "Christians and spices."[6]

The bluntest of the Spanish **conquistadors** (kohn-KEES-tuh-dorz), Hernán Cortés, announced as he prepared to conquer Mexico, "I have come to win gold, not to plow the fields like a peasant."[7] Eagerness for exploration was heightened by a lack of opportunity at home. After the reconquista, young men of the Spanish upper classes found their economic and political opportunities greatly limited. The ambitious turned to the sea to seek their fortunes.

Ordinary sailors were ill paid, and life at sea meant danger, overcrowding, and hunger. For months at a time, 100 to 120 people lived and worked in a space of 1,600 to 2,000 square feet. A lucky sailor would find enough space on deck to unroll his sleeping mat. Horses, cows, pigs, chickens, rats, and lice accompanied sailors on the voyages. As one scholar concluded, "traveling on a ship must have been one of the most uncomfortable and oppressive experiences in the world."[8]

Men chose to join these miserable crews to escape poverty at home, to continue a family trade, or to find better lives as illegal immigrants in the colonies. Many orphans and poor boys were placed on board as apprentices and had little say in the decision. Women also paid a price for the voyages of exploration. Left alone for months or years at a time, and frequently widowed, sailors' wives struggled to feed their families. The widow of a sailor lost on a voyage in 1519 had to wait almost thirty years to collect her husband's salary from the Spanish crown.[9]

The people who stayed at home had a powerful impact on the process. Merchants provided the capital for many early voyages and had a strong say in their course. To gain authorization and financial support for their expeditions, they sought official sponsorship from the Crown. Competition among European monarchs for the prestige and profit of overseas exploration was a crucial factor in encouraging the steady stream of expeditions that began in the late fifteenth century.

The small number of Europeans who could read provided a rapt audience for tales of fantastic places and unknown peoples. Cosmography, natural history, and geography aroused enormous interest among educated people in the fifteenth and sixteenth centuries. One of the most popular books of the time was the fourteenth-century text *The Travels of Sir John Mandeville*, which purported to be a firsthand account of the author's travels in the Middle East, India, and China. Although we now know the stories were fictional, these fantastic tales of cannibals, one-eyed giants, men with the heads of dogs, and other marvels convinced audiences through their vividly and persuasively described details. Christopher Columbus took a copy of Mandeville and the equally popular and more reliable *The Travels of Marco Polo* on his voyage in 1492.

Technology and the Rise of Exploration

The Iberian powers actively sought technological improvements in shipbuilding, weaponry, and navigation in order to undertake successful voyages of exploration and trade. Medieval European seagoing vessels consisted of single-masted sailing ships or narrow, open galleys propelled by oars, which were common in Mediterranean trade. Though adequate for short journeys that hugged the shoreline, such vessels were incapable of long-distance journeys or high-volume trade. To sail to the Indian Ocean or cross the Atlantic, larger and sturdier craft were necessary. In the course of the fifteenth century, the Portuguese developed the **caravel**, a three-mast sailing ship. Its multiple sails and sternpost rudder made the caravel a more maneuverable vessel that required fewer crewmen to operate. It could carry more cargo than a galley, which meant it could sail farther without stopping for supplies and return with a larger cache of profitable goods. When fitted with cannon, it could dominate larger vessels and bombard port cities.[10]

Great strides in cartography and navigational aids were also made during this period. Around 1410 Arab scholars reintroduced Europeans to **Ptolemy's** *Geography*.

Written in the second century C.E. by a Hellenized Egyptian, the work synthesized the geographical knowledge of the classical world. Ptolemy's work provided significant improvements over medieval cartography, clearly depicting the world as round and introducing the idea of latitude and longitude to plot position accurately. It also contained crucial errors. Unaware of the Americas, Ptolemy showed the world as much smaller than it is, so that Asia appeared not very distant from Europe to the west. Both the assets and the flaws of Ptolemy's work shaped the geographical knowledge that explorers like Christopher Columbus brought to their voyages.

Originating in China, the compass was brought to the West in the late Middle Ages; by using the compass to determine their direction and estimating their speed of travel over a set length of time, mariners could determine the course of a ship's voyage, a system of navigation known as "dead reckoning." In the late fifteenth century Portuguese scholars devised a new technique of "celestial reckoning," which involved using the astrolabe, an instrument invented by the ancient Greeks to determine the position of the stars and other celestial bodies. Commissioned by Portuguese king John II, a group of astronomers in the 1480s showed that mariners could determine their latitude at sea by using a specially designed astrolabe to determine the altitude of the polestar or the sun, and consulting tables of these bodies' movements. This was a crucial step forward in maritime navigational techniques.

Much of the new technology that Europeans used on their voyages was borrowed from the East. Gunpowder, the compass, and the sternpost rudder were Chinese inventions. The triangular lateen sail, which allowed caravels to tack against the wind, was a product of the Indian Ocean trade world. Advances in navigational techniques and cartography, including the maritime astrolabe, drew on a rich Iberian tradition of Jewish and Arab mathematics and astronomy. Sometimes assistance to Europeans came from humans rather than instruments. The famed explorer Vasco da Gama employed a local Indian pilot to guide his expedition from the East African coast to India. In exploring new territories, European sailors thus called on techniques and knowledge developed

Ptolemy's *Geography* The recovery of Ptolemy's *Geography* in the early fifteenth century gave Europeans new access to ancient geographical knowledge. This 1486 world map, based on Ptolemy, is a great advance over medieval maps but contains errors with significant consequences for future exploration. It shows a single continent watered by a single ocean, with land covering three-quarters of the world's surface. Africa and Asia are joined with Europe, making the Indian Ocean a landlocked sea and rendering the circumnavigation of Africa impossible. Australia and the Americas are nonexistent, and the continent of Asia is stretched far to the east, greatly shortening the distance from Europe to Asia via the Atlantic. (Bibliothèque Nationale, Paris, France/Giraudon/Bridgeman Images)

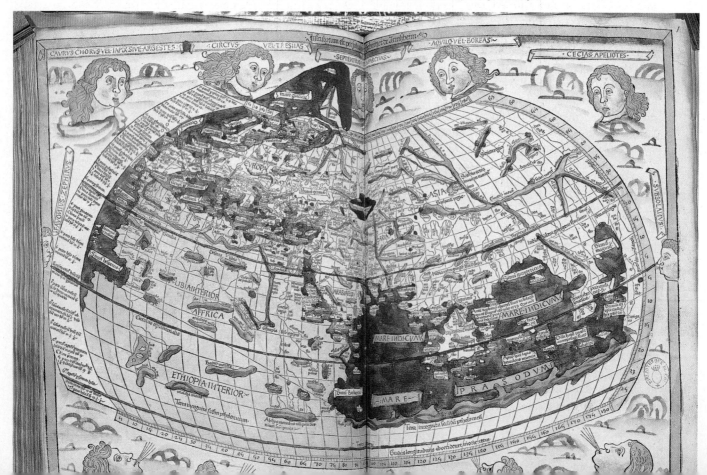

over centuries in China, the Muslim world, and the Indian Ocean.

The Portuguese Overseas Empire

For centuries Portugal was a small, poor nation on the margins of European life whose principal activities were fishing and subsistence farming. It would have been hard for a European to predict Portugal's phenomenal success overseas after 1450. Yet Portugal had a long history of seafaring and navigation. Blocked from access to western Europe by Spain, the Portuguese turned to the Atlantic and North Africa, whose waters they knew better than other Europeans did. Nature favored the Portuguese: winds blowing along their coast offered passage to Africa, its Atlantic islands, and, ultimately, Brazil. Once they had mastered the secret to sailing against the wind to return to Europe (by sailing further west to catch winds from the southwest), they were ideally poised to lead Atlantic exploration.

In the early phases of Portuguese exploration, Prince Henry (1394–1460), a younger son of the king, played a leading role. A nineteenth-century scholar dubbed Henry "the Navigator" because of his support for the study of geography and navigation and for the annual expeditions he sponsored down the western coast of Africa. Although he never personally participated in voyages of exploration, Henry's involvement ensured that Portugal did not abandon the effort despite early disappointments.

The objectives of Portuguese exploration included military glory; the conversion of Muslims; and a quest to find gold, slaves, and an overseas route to the spice markets of India. Portugal's conquest of Ceuta, an Arab city in northern Morocco, in 1415 marked the beginning of European overseas expansion. In the 1420s, under Henry's direction, the Portuguese began to settle the Atlantic islands of Madeira (ca. 1420) and the Azores (1427). In 1443 they founded their first African commercial settlement at Arguin in North Africa. By the time of Henry's death in 1460, his support for exploration was vindicated—from the Portuguese point of view—by thriving sugar plantations on the Atlantic islands, the first arrival of enslaved Africans in Portugal (see page 451), and new access to African gold.

The Portuguese next established fortified trading posts, called factories, on the gold-rich Guinea coast and penetrated into the African continent all the way to Timbuktu (Map 14.2). By 1500 Portugal controlled the flow of African gold to Europe. In contrast to the Spanish conquest of the Americas (see pages 440–444), the Portuguese did not establish large settlements in West Africa or seek to control the political or cultural lives of those with whom they traded. Instead, they sought easier and faster profits by inserting themselves into pre-existing trading systems. For the first century

Brass Astrolabe　Between 1500 and 1635 over nine hundred ships sailed from Portugal to ports on the Indian Ocean, in annual fleets composed of five to ten ships. Portuguese sailors used astrolabes, such as the one shown here, to accurately plot their position. (British Museum, London, UK/Werner Forman/Universal Images Group/Getty Images)

of their relations, African rulers were equal partners with the Portuguese, benefiting from their experienced armies and European vulnerability to tropical diseases.

The Portuguese then pushed farther south down the west coast of Africa. In 1487 Bartholomew Diaz rounded the Cape of Good Hope at the southern tip of Africa, but storms and a threatened mutiny forced him to turn back. A decade later Vasco da Gama succeeded in rounding the Cape while commanding a fleet of four ships in search of a sea route to India. With the help of an Indian guide, da Gama reached the port of Calicut in India. He returned to Lisbon loaded with spices and samples of Indian cloth, having proved the possibility of lucrative trade with the East via the Cape route. Thereafter, a Portuguese convoy set out for passage around the Cape every March.

Lisbon became the entrance port for Asian goods into Europe, but this was not accomplished without a fight. Muslim-controlled port city-states had long controlled the rich trade of the Indian Ocean, and they did not surrender their dominance willingly. From 1500 to 1515 the Portuguese used a combination of bombardment and diplomatic treaties to establish trading forts at Goa, Malacca, Calicut, and Hormuz, thereby laying the foundation for a Portuguese trading empire in the sixteenth and seventeenth centuries. The acquisition of port cities and their trade routes brought riches to Portugal, but, as in Africa, the Portuguese had limited impact on the lives and religious faith of peoples beyond their coastal holdings. Moreover, despite their advances in shipbuilding, weaponry, and navigation, the Portuguese were never able to enforce a total monopoly on trading in the Indian Ocean.

Inspired by the Portuguese, the Spanish had also begun the quest for empire. Theirs was to be a second, entirely different, mode of colonization, leading to the conquest of existing empires, large-scale settlement, and the assimilation of a subjugated indigenous population.

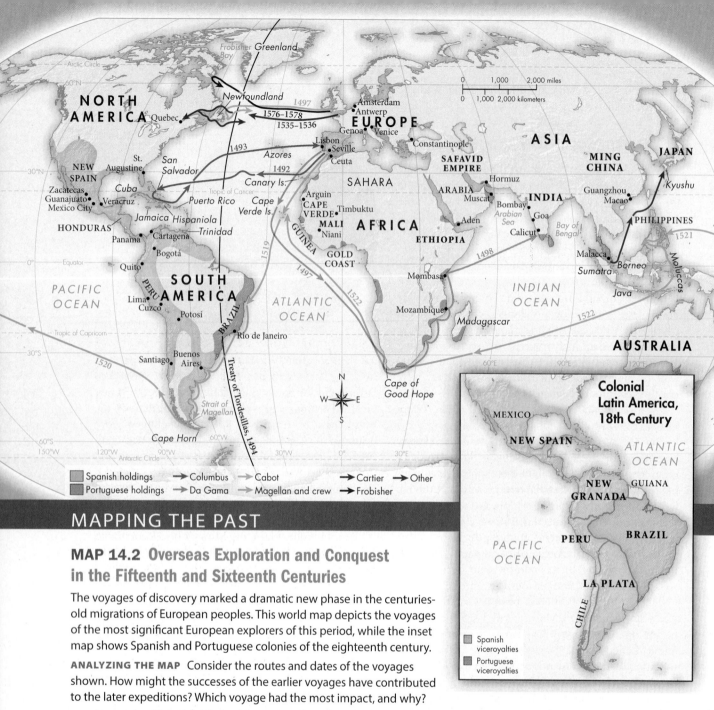

MAP 14.2 Overseas Exploration and Conquest in the Fifteenth and Sixteenth Centuries

The voyages of discovery marked a dramatic new phase in the centuries-old migrations of European peoples. This world map depicts the voyages of the most significant European explorers of this period, while the inset map shows Spanish and Portuguese colonies of the eighteenth century.

ANALYZING THE MAP Consider the routes and dates of the voyages shown. How might the successes of the earlier voyages have contributed to the later expeditions? Which voyage had the most impact, and why?

CONNECTIONS How would you compare Spanish and Portuguese New World holdings in the sixteenth century with those of the eighteenth century? How would you explain the differences and continuities over time?

Spain's Voyages to the Americas

We now know that Christopher Columbus was not the first to explore the Atlantic. Ninth-century Vikings established short-lived settlements in Newfoundland, and it is probable that others made the voyage, either on purpose or accidentally, carried by westward currents off the coast of Africa. In the late fifteenth century the achievements of Portugal's decades of exploration made the moment right for Christopher Columbus's attempt to find a westward route across the Atlantic to Asia.

A native of the port city of Genoa, Christopher Columbus was early on drawn to the life of the sea. He became an experienced seaman and navigator and worked as a mapmaker in Lisbon. He was familiar with *portolans*—written descriptions of the courses along which ships sailed—and the use of the compass for dead reckoning. (He carried an astrolabe on his first voyage, but did not use it for navigation.) As he asserted in his journal: "I have spent twenty-three years at sea and have not left it for any length of time worth mentioning, and I have seen every thing from east to west [meaning he had been to England] and I have been to Guinea [North and West Africa]."[11]

Columbus was also a deeply religious man. He had witnessed the Spanish conquest of Granada and shared fully in the religious and nationalistic fervor surrounding that event. Like the Spanish rulers and most Europeans of his age, Columbus understood Christianity as a missionary religion that should be carried to all places of the earth. He viewed himself as a divine agent: "God made me the messenger of the new heaven and the new earth of which he spoke in the Apocalypse of St. John . . . and he showed me the post where to find it."[12]

Rejected for funding by the Portuguese in 1483 and by Ferdinand and Isabella in 1486, Columbus's project to find a westward passage to the Indies finally won the backing of the Spanish monarchy in 1492. Buoyed by the success of the reconquista and eager to earn profits from trade, the Spanish crown named Columbus viceroy over any territory he might discover and promised him one-tenth of the material rewards of the journey.

Columbus and his small fleet left Spain on August 3, 1492. Inspired by the stories of Mandeville and Marco Polo, Columbus dreamed of reaching the court of the Mongol emperor, the Great Khan (not realizing that the Ming Dynasty had overthrown the Mongols in 1368). Based on Ptolemy's *Geography* and other texts, he expected to pass the islands of Japan and then land on the east coast of China.

After a brief stop in the Canary Islands, he landed in the Bahamas, which he christened San Salvador, on October 12, 1492. In a letter he wrote to Ferdinand and Isabella on his return to Spain, Columbus described the natives as handsome, peaceful, and primitive people whose body painting reminded him of that of the Canary Islands natives. Believing he was somewhere off the east coast of Japan, in what he considered the Indies, he called them "Indians," a name later applied to all inhabitants of the Americas. Columbus concluded that they would make good slaves and could easily be converted to Christianity. (See "Evaluating the Evidence 14.1: Columbus Describes His First Voyage," page 438.)

Scholars have identified the inhabitants of the islands as the Taino people, speakers of the Arawak language, who inhabited Hispaniola (modern-day Haiti and Dominican Republic) and other islands in the Caribbean. From San Salvador, Columbus sailed southwest, landing on Cuba on October 28. Deciding that he must be on the mainland near the coastal city of Quinsay (now Hangzhou), he sent a small embassy inland with

Columbus's First Voyage to the New World, 1492–1493

letters from Ferdinand and Isabella and instructions to locate the grand city. Although they found no large settlement or any evidence of a great kingdom, the sight of Taino people wearing gold ornaments on Hispaniola suggested that gold was available in the region. In January, confident that its source would soon be found, he headed back to Spain to report on his discovery. News of his voyage spread rapidly across Europe.[13]

On his second voyage, Columbus forcibly subjugated the island of Hispaniola and enslaved its indigenous peoples. On this and subsequent voyages, Columbus brought with him settlers for the new Spanish territories, along with agricultural seed and livestock. Columbus himself, however, had limited skills in governing. Revolt soon broke out against him and his brother on Hispaniola. A royal expedition sent to investigate returned the brothers to Spain in chains, and a royal governor assumed control of the colony.

Columbus was very much a man of his times. To the end of his life in 1506, he believed that he had found small islands off the coast of Asia. He never realized the scope of his achievement: he had found a vast continent unknown to Europeans, except for a fleeting Viking presence centuries earlier. He could not know that the scale of his discoveries would revolutionize world power and set in motion a new era of trade, empire, and human migration.

Spain "Discovers" the Pacific

The Florentine navigator Amerigo Vespucci (veh-SPOO-chee) (1454–1512) realized what Columbus had not. Writing about his discoveries on the coast of modern-day Venezuela, Vespucci stated: "Those new regions which we found and explored with the fleet . . . we may rightly call a New World." This letter, titled *Mundus Novus* (The New World), was the first document to describe America as a continent separate from Asia. In recognition of Amerigo's bold claim, the continent was named for him.

To settle competing claims to the Atlantic discoveries, Spain and Portugal turned to Pope Alexander VI. The resulting **Treaty of Tordesillas** (tor-duh-SEE-yuhs) in 1494 gave Spain everything to the west of an imaginary line drawn down the Atlantic, and Portugal everything to the east. This arbitrary division worked in Portugal's favor when in 1500 an expedition led by Pedro Álvares

■ **Treaty of Tordesillas** The 1494 agreement giving Spain everything to the west of an imaginary line drawn down the Atlantic and giving Portugal everything to the east.

Columbus Describes His First Voyage

On his return voyage to Spain in February 1493, Christopher Columbus composed a letter intended for wide circulation and had copies of it sent ahead to Queen Isabella and King Ferdinand. Because the letter sums up Columbus's understanding of his achievements, it is considered the most important document of his first voyage. Remember that his knowledge of Asia rested heavily on Marco Polo's Travels, *published around 1298.*

Since I know that you will be pleased at the great success with which the Lord has crowned my voyage, I write to inform you how in thirty-three days I crossed from the Canary Islands to the Indies, with the fleet which our most illustrious sovereigns gave me. I found very many islands with large populations and took possession of them all for their Highnesses; this I did by proclamation and unfurled the royal standard. No opposition was offered.

I named the first island that I found "San Salvador," in honour of our Lord and Saviour who has granted me this miracle. . . . When I reached Cuba, I followed its north coast westwards, and found it so extensive that I thought this must be the mainland, the province of Cathay. . . .* From there I saw another island eighteen leagues eastwards which I then named "Hispaniola." . . .†

Hispaniola is a wonder. The mountains and hills, the plains and meadow lands are both fertile and beautiful. They are most suitable for planting crops and for raising cattle of all kinds, and there are good sites for building towns and villages. The harbours are incredibly fine and there are many great rivers with broad channels and the majority contain gold.‡ The trees, fruits and plants are very different from those of Cuba. In Hispaniola there are many spices and large mines of gold and other metals. . . .§

The inhabitants of this island, and all the rest that I discovered or heard of, go naked, as their mothers bore them, men and women alike. A few of the women,

however, cover a single place with a leaf of a plant or piece of cotton which they weave for the purpose. They have no iron or steel or arms and are not capable of using them, not because they are not strong and well built but because they are amazingly timid. All the weapons they have are canes cut at seeding time, at the end of which they fix a sharpened stick, but they have not the courage to make use of these, for very often when I have sent two or three men to a village to have conversation with them a great number of them have come out. But as soon as they saw my men all fled immediately, a father not even waiting for his son. And this is not because we have harmed any of them; on the contrary, wherever I have gone and been able to have conversation with them, I have given them some of the various things I had, a cloth and other articles, and received nothing in exchange. But they have still remained incurably timid.

True, when they have been reassured and lost their fear, they are so ingenuous and so liberal with all their possessions that no one who has not seen them would believe it. If one asks for anything they have they never say no. On the contrary, they offer a share to anyone with demonstrations of heartfelt affection, and they are immediately content with any small thing, valuable or valueless, that is given them. I forbade the men to give them bits of broken crockery, fragments of glass or tags of laces, though if they could get them they fancied them the finest jewels in the world. . . .

I hoped to win them to the love and service of their Highnesses and of the whole Spanish nation and to persuade them to collect and give us of the things which they possessed in abundance and which we needed. They have no religion and are not idolaters; but all believe that power and goodness dwell in the sky and they are firmly convinced that I have come from the sky with these ships and people. In this belief they gave me a good reception everywhere, once they had overcome their fear; and this is not because they are stupid — far from it, they are men of great intelligence, for they navigate all those seas, and give a marvellously good account of every thing — but because they have never before seen men clothed or ships like these. . . .

In all these islands the men are seemingly content with one woman, but their chief or king is allowed more than

*Cathay is the old name for China. In the logbook and later in this letter, Columbus accepts the native story that Cuba is an island that can be circumnavigated in something more than twenty-one days, yet he insists here and during the second voyage that it is part of the Asiatic mainland.

†Hispaniola is the second-largest island of the West Indies. Haiti occupies the western third of the island, the Dominican Republic the rest.

‡This did not prove to be true.

§These statements are also inaccurate.

Cabral, en route to India, landed on the coast of Brazil, which Cabral claimed as Portuguese territory.

The search for profits determined the direction of Spanish exploration. Because its profits from Hispaniola and other Caribbean islands were insignificant compared to the enormous riches that the Portuguese

were reaping in Asia, Spain renewed the search for a western passage to Asia. In 1519 Charles V of Spain sent the Portuguese mariner Ferdinand Magellan (1480–1521) to find a sea route to the spices of the Moluccas off the southeast coast of Asia. Magellan sailed southwest across the Atlantic to Brazil, and after

twenty. The women appear to work more than the men and I have not been able to find out if they have private property. As far as I could see whatever a man had was shared among all the rest and this particularly applies to food. . . . In another island, which I am told is larger than Hispaniola, the people have no hair. Here there is a vast quantity of gold, and from here and the other islands I bring Indians as evidence.

In conclusion, to speak only of the results of this very hasty voyage, their Highnesses can see that I will give them as much gold as they require, if they will render me some very slight assistance; also I will give them all the spices and cotton they want. . . . I will also bring them as much aloes as they ask and as many slaves, who will be taken from the idolaters. I believe also that I have found rhubarb and cinnamon and there will be countless other things in addition. . . .

So all Christendom will be delighted that our Redeemer has given victory to our most illustrious King and Queen and their renowned kingdoms, in this great matter. They should hold great celebrations and render solemn thanks to the Holy Trinity with many solemn prayers, for the great triumph which they will have, by the conversion of so many peoples to our holy faith and for the temporal benefits which will follow, for not only Spain, but all Christendom will receive encouragement and profit.

This is a brief account of the facts. Written in the caravel off the Canary Islands.**

15 February 1493

At your orders   THE ADMIRAL

EVALUATE THE EVIDENCE

1. How did Columbus explain the success of his voyage?
2. What was Columbus's view of the Native Americans he met?
3. In what ways does he exaggerate about the Caribbean islands' possessing gold, cotton, and spices?

Source: Approximately 1,109 words from *The Four Voyages of Christopher Columbus*, pp. 115–123, ed. and trans. J. M. Cohen (Penguin Classics, 1969). Reproduced by permission of Penguin Books Ltd.

**Actually, Columbus was off Santa Maria in the Azores.

then headed west into the immense expanse of the Pacific toward the Malay Archipelago. (Some of these islands were conquered later, in the 1560s, and named the "Philippines" for Philip II of Spain.)

Magellan's first impressions of the Pacific were terribly mistaken. Terrible storms, disease, starvation, and violence devastated the expedition. Magellan had set out with a fleet of five ships and around 270 men. Sailors on two of the ships attempted mutiny on the South American coast; one ship was lost, and another ship deserted and returned to Spain before even traversing the straits. The trip across the Pacific took ninety-eight days, and the men survived on rats and sawdust. Magellan himself died in a skirmish in the Malay Archipelago. Only one ship, with eighteen men aboard, returned to Spain from the east by way of the Indian Ocean, the Cape of Good Hope, and the Atlantic in 1522. The voyage—the first to circumnavigate the globe—had taken close to three years.

Despite the losses, this voyage revolutionized Europeans' understanding of the world by demonstrating the vastness of the Pacific. The earth was clearly much larger than Ptolemy's map had shown. Although the voyage made a small profit in spices, it also demonstrated that the westward passage to the Indies was too long and dangerous for commercial purposes. Spain soon abandoned the attempt to oust Portugal from the Eastern spice trade and concentrated on exploiting her New World territories.

Early Exploration by Northern European Powers

Spain's northern European rivals also set sail across the Atlantic during the early days of exploration in search of a northwest passage to the Indies. In 1497 John Cabot, a Genoese merchant living in London, undertook a voyage to Brazil, but landed on Newfoundland instead. The next year he returned and reconnoitered the New England coast. These forays proved futile, and the English established no permanent colonies in the territories they explored. News of the riches of Mexico and Peru later inspired the English to renew their efforts, this time in the extreme north. Between 1576 and 1578 Martin Frobisher made three voyages in and around the Canadian bay that now bears his name. Frobisher hopefully brought a quantity of ore back to England with him, but it proved to be worthless.

Early French exploration of the Atlantic was equally frustrating. Between 1534 and 1541 Frenchman Jacques Cartier made several voyages and explored the St. Lawrence River of Canada, searching for a passage to the wealth of Asia. His exploration of the St. Lawrence was halted at the great rapids west of the present-day island

a long search along the coast he located the treacherous straits that now bear his name (see Map 14.2). The new ocean he sailed into after a rough passage through the straits seemed so calm that Magellan dubbed it the Pacific, from the Latin word for peaceful. His fleet sailed north up the west coast of South America and

of Montreal; he named the rapids "La Chine" in the optimistic belief that China lay just beyond. When this hope proved vain, the French turned to a new source of profit within Canada itself: trade in beavers and other furs. As had the Portuguese in Asia, French traders bartered with local peoples, who maintained control over their trade goods. French fishermen also competed with Spanish and English ships for the teeming schools of cod they found in the Atlantic waters around Newfoundland. Fishing vessels salted the catch on board and brought it back to Europe, where a thriving market for fish was created by the Catholic prohibition on eating meat on Fridays and during Lent.

Conquest and Settlement

FOCUS QUESTION *How did European powers acquire colonies in the Americas, and how were they governed?*

Before Columbus's arrival, the Americas were inhabited by thousands of groups of indigenous peoples with different languages and cultures. These groups ranged from hunter-gatherer tribes organized into tribal confederations to settled agriculturalists to large-scale empires containing bustling cities and towns. The best estimate is that the peoples of the Americas numbered between 35 and 50 million in 1492. Their lives were radically transformed by the arrival of Europeans.

The growing European presence in the New World transformed its land and its peoples forever. While Iberian powers conquered enormous territories in Central and South America, incorporating pre-existing peoples and empires, the northern European powers came later to colonization and established scattered settlements hugging the North American coastline.

Spanish Conquest of the Aztec and Inca Empires

The first two decades after Columbus's arrival in the New World saw Spanish settlement of Hispaniola, Cuba, Puerto Rico, and other Caribbean islands. Based on rumors of a wealthy mainland civilization, the Spanish governor in Cuba sponsored expeditions to the Yucatán coast of the Gulf of Mexico, including one in 1519 under the command of the conquistador Hernán Cortés (1485–1547). Alarmed by Cortés's ambition, the governor decided to withdraw his support, but Cortés quickly set sail before being removed from command. Accompanied by 11 ships, 450 men, 16 horses, and 10

- → Cortés's original route, 1519
- → Cortés's retreat, 1520
- → Cortés's return route, 1520–1521

Invasion of Tenochtitlan, 1519–1521

cannon, Cortés landed on the Mexican coast on April 21, 1519. His camp soon received visits by delegations of unarmed Aztec leaders bearing gifts and news of their great emperor.

The **Aztec Empire**, an alliance between the Mexica people and their conquered allies, had risen rapidly in size and power in the early fifteenth century. At the time of the Spanish arrival, the empire was ruled by Moctezuma II (r. 1502–1520), from his capital at Tenochtitlan (tay-nawch-teet-LAHN), now Mexico City. The Aztecs were a sophisticated civilization with an advanced understanding of mathematics, astronomy, and engineering; and with oral poetry and historical traditions. As in European nations at the time, a hereditary nobility dominated the army, the priesthood, and the state bureaucracy, living from the proceeds of the agricultural labor of the common people.

Within weeks of his arrival, Cortés acquired translators who provided vital information on the empire and its weaknesses (see "Thinking Like a Historian: Who Was Doña Marina?" page 442). To legitimize his authority, Cortés founded the settlement of Veracruz and had himself named its military commander. He then burned his ships to prevent any disloyal or frightened followers from returning to Cuba.

The vulnerability Cortés discovered was local resentment against the Aztec Empire. The Aztec state practiced warfare against neighboring peoples to secure captives for religious sacrifices and laborers for agricultural and building projects. Once conquered, subject tribes paid continual tribute to the empire through their local chiefs. Realizing that he could exploit dissensions within the empire to his own advantage, Cortés forged an alliance with Tlaxcala (tlah-SKAH-lah) and other subject kingdoms. In October a combined Spanish-Tlaxcalan force occupied the city of Cholula, second largest in the empire, and massacred many thousand inhabitants. Strengthened by this display of ruthless power, Cortés made alliances with other native kingdoms. In November 1519, with a few hundred Spanish men and some six thousand indigenous warriors, Cortés marched on Tenochtitlan.

Historians have long debated Moctezuma's response to the arrival of the Spanish. Unlike other native leaders, he refrained from attacking the Spaniards but instead welcomed Cortés and his men into Tenochtitlan. Moctezuma was apparently deeply impressed by Spanish victories and believed the Spanish were invincible. Sources written after the conquest claimed that the emperor believed Cortés was an embodiment of the god Quetzalcoatl, whose return was promised in Aztec myth.

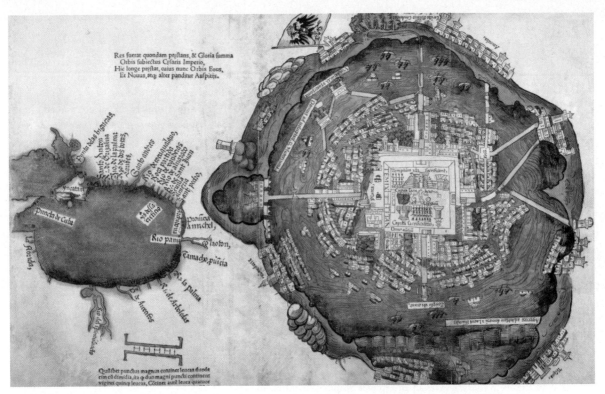

The Mexica Capital of Tenochtitlan This woodcut map was published in 1524 along with Cortés's letters describing the conquest of the Mexica. As it shows, Tenochtitlan occupied an island and was laid out in concentric circles. The administrative and religious buildings were at the heart of the city, which was surrounded by residential quarters. Cortés himself marveled at the city in his letters: "The city is as large as Seville or Cordoba. . . . There are bridges, very large, strong, and well constructed, so that, over many, ten horsemen can ride abreast. . . . The city has many squares where markets are held. . . . There is one square . . . where there are daily more than sixty thousand souls, buying and selling. In the service and manners of its people, their fashion of living was almost the same as in Spain, with just as much harmony and order." (Newberry Library, Chicago, Illinois, USA/Bridgeman Images)

While it is impossible to verify those claims, it is clear that Moctezuma's long hesitation proved disastrous. When Cortés — with incredible boldness — took Moctezuma hostage, the emperor's influence crumbled. During the ensuing attacks and counterattacks, Moctezuma was killed. The Spaniards and their allies escaped from the city, suffering heavy losses. Cortés quickly began gathering forces and making new alliances against the Aztecs. In May 1521 he conducted a second assault on Tenochtitlan, leading an army of approximately one thousand Spanish and seventy-five thousand native warriors.[14]

Spanish victory in late summer 1521 was hard-won and greatly aided by the effects of smallpox, which had devastated the besieged population of the city. After establishing a new capital in the ruins of Tenochtitlan, Cortés and other conquistadors began the systematic conquest of Mexico.

More surprising than the defeat of the Aztecs was the fall of the remote **Inca Empire**. Perched more than 9,800 feet above sea level, the Incas were isolated from North American indigenous cultures and knew nothing of the Aztec Empire or its collapse. Like the Mexica,

the Incas had created a polity that rivaled that of the Europeans in population and complexity. The Incas' strength lay largely in their bureaucratic efficiency. They divided their empire into four major regions containing eighty provinces and twice as many districts. Officials at each level used an extensive network of roads to transmit information and orders back and forth through the empire. While the Aztecs used a system of glyphs for writing, the Incas had devised a complex system of colored and knotted cords, called *khipus*, for administrative bookkeeping. The empire also benefited from the use of llamas as pack animals (by contrast, no beasts of burden existed in Mesoamerica).

By the time of the Spanish invasion, however, the Inca Empire had been weakened by a civil war over succession and an epidemic of disease, possibly smallpox, which may have spread through trade with groups in contact with Europeans. Francisco Pizarro

■ **Aztec Empire** A large and complex Native American civilization in modern Mexico and Central America that possessed advanced mathematical, astronomical, and engineering technology.

■ **Inca Empire** The vast and sophisticated Peruvian empire centered at the capital city of Cuzco that was at its peak from 1438 until 1532.

Who Was Doña Marina?

In April 1519 Doña Marina was among twenty women given to the Spanish as slaves. Fluent in Nahuatl (NAH-wah-tuhl) and Yucatec Maya (spoken by a Spanish priest accompanying Cortés), she acted as an interpreter and diplomatic guide for the Spanish. She had a close relationship with Cortés and bore his son, Don Martín Cortés, in 1522. Although no writings by Doña Marina survive, she figures prominently in both Spanish and indigenous sources on the conquest.

1 Cortés's letter to Charles V, 1522. This letter to Charles V contains one of only two written references to Doña Marina found in Cortés's correspondence with the emperor. He describes her as his "interpreter."

During the three days I remained in that city they fed us worse each day, and the lords and principal persons of the city came only rarely to see and speak with me. And being somewhat disturbed by this, my interpreter, who is an Indian woman from Putunchan, which is the great river of which I spoke to Your Majesty in the first letter, was told by another Indian woman and a native of this city that very close by many of Mutezuma's men were gathered, and that the people of the city had sent away their women and children and all their belongings, and were about to fall on us and kill us all; and that if she wished to escape she should go with her and she would shelter her. All this she told to Gerónimo de Aguilar, an interpreter whom I acquired in Yucatán, of whom I have also written to Your Highness; and he informed me.

2 Díaz's account of the conquest of the Aztecs. Bernal Díaz del Castillo participated in the conquest of the Aztecs alongside Cortés. His historical account of the conquest, written much later in life, provides the lengthiest descriptions of Doña Marina.

Early the next morning many Caciques and chiefs of Tabasco and the neighbouring towns arrived and paid great respect to us all, and they brought a present of gold, . . . and some other things of little value. . . . This present, however, was worth nothing in comparison with the twenty women that were given us, among them one very excellent woman called Doña Marina, for so she was named when she became a Christian.

. . . Cortés allotted one of the women to each of his captains and Doña Marina, as she was good looking and intelligent and without embarrassment, he gave to Alonzo Hernández Puertocarrero. When Puertocarrero went to Spain, Doña Marina lived with Cortés, and bore him a son named Don Martin Cortés.

. . . Her father and mother were chiefs and Caciques of a town called Paynala. . . . Her father died while she was still a little child, and her mother married another Cacique, a young man, and bore him a son. It seems that the father and mother had a great affection for this son and it was agreed between them that he should succeed to their honours when their days were done. So that there should be no impediment to this, they gave the little girl, Doña Marina, to some Indians from Xicalango, and this they did by night so as to escape observation, and they then spread the report that she had died, and as it happened at this time that a child of one of their Indian slaves died they gave out that it was their daughter and the heiress who was dead.

The Indians of Xicalango gave the child to the people of Tabasco and the Tabasco people gave her to Cortés.

. . . As Doña Marina proved herself such an excellent woman and good interpreter throughout the wars in New Spain, Tlaxcala and Mexico (as I shall show later on) Cortés always took her with him, and during that expedition she was married to a gentleman named Juan Jaramillo at the town of Orizaba.

Doña Marina was a person of the greatest importance and was obeyed without question by the Indians throughout New Spain.

ANALYZING THE EVIDENCE

1. How would you compare the attitudes toward Doña Marina displayed in Cortés's letter to the Spanish crown (Source 1) and Díaz's account of the conquest (Source 2)? Why would Cortés downplay his reliance on Doña Marina in correspondence with the Spanish emperor?
2. What skills and experience enabled Doña Marina to act as an intermediary between the Spanish and the Aztecs? Based on the evidence, what role did she play in interactions between the Spanish and the Aztecs?
3. According to Díaz (Source 2), how did Doña Marina feel about her relationship with Cortés and the Spanish? How do you interpret this passage? Is there any evidence in the other sources that supports or undermines the sentiments he attributed to her?
4. Based on the evidence of these sources, what role did indigenous women play in relations between Spanish and Aztec men? How exceptional was Doña Marina?

(Granger, NYC—All rights reserved)

3 **Doña Marina translating for Hernán Cortés during his meeting with Moctezuma.** This image was created by Tlaxcalan artists shortly after the conquest of Mexico and represents one indigenous perspective on the events.

Marina . . . said that God had been very gracious to her in freeing her from the worship of idols and making her a Christian, and letting her bear a son to her lord and master Cortés and in marrying her to such a gentleman as Juan Jaramillo, who was now her husband. That she would rather serve her husband and Cortés than anything else in the world, and would not exchange her place to be Cacica of all the provinces in New Spain.

Doña Marina knew the language of Coatzacoalcos, which is that common to Mexico, and she knew the language of Tabasco, as did also Jerónimo de Aguilar, who spoke the language of Yucatan and Tabasco, which is one and the same. So that these two could understand one another clearly, and Aguilar translated into Castilian for Cortés.

This was the great beginning of our conquests and thus, thanks be to God, things prospered with us. I have made a point of explaining this matter, because without the help of Doña Marina we could not have understood the language of New Spain and Mexico.

4 **The *Florentine Codex*.** In the decades following the conquest, a Franciscan monk, Bernardino de Sahagún, worked with indigenous partners to compile a history of Aztec society. Known today as the *Florentine Codex*, it contains images and text written in both Nahuatl and Spanish. The following excerpt describes the entry of the victorious Spanish into Tenochtitlan.

Next they went to Motecuhzoma's storehouse, in the place called Totocalco, where his personal treasures were kept. The Spaniards grinned like little beasts and patted each other with delight.

When they entered the hall of treasures, it was as if they had arrived in Paradise. They searched everywhere and coveted everything; they were slaves to their own greed. . . .

They seized these treasures as they were their own, as if this plunder were merely a stroke of good luck. And when they had taken all the gold, they heaped up everything else in the middle of the patio.

La Malinche [Doña Marina] called all the nobles together. She climbed up to the palace roof and cried: "Mexicanos, come forward! The Spaniards need your help! Bring them food and pure water. They are tired and hungry; they are almost fainting from exhaustion! Why do you not come forward? Are you angry with them?"

The Mexicas were too frightened to approach. They were crushed by terror and would not risk coming forward. They shied away as if the Spaniards were wild beasts, as if the hour were midnight on the blackest night of the year. Yet they did not abandon the Spaniards to hunger and thirst. They brought them whatever they needed, but shook with fear as they did so. They delivered the supplies to the Spaniards with trembling hands, then turned and hurried away.

PUTTING IT ALL TOGETHER

Using the sources above, along with what you have learned in class and in this chapter, imagine the events and experiences described in these sources from Doña Marina's point of view. Reflect on the various aspects of Doña Marina described in the sources—betrayed daughter, slave, concubine, mother, wife, interpreter, and commander—and write an essay that uses her experience to explore the interaction among Spanish, Aztec, and other indigenous groups during the conquest period.

Sources: (1) Hernán Cortés to Emperor Carlos V, 1522, in *Hernán Cortés: Letters from Mexico,* trans. and ed. Anthony Pagden (New Haven: Yale University Press, 1986), pp. 72–74; (2) Bernal Díaz del Castillo, *The Discovery and Conquest of Mexico, 1517–1521,* trans. A. P. Maudslay (New York: Noonday Press, 1965), pp. 62–63, 64, 66–67; (4) Miguel León-Portilla, ed., *The Broken Spears: The Aztec Account of the Conquest of Mexico,* pp. 68–69. Copyright © 1962, 1990 by Miguel León-Portilla. Expanded and Updated Edition © 1992 by Miguel León-Portilla. Reprinted by permission of Beacon Press, Boston.

(ca. 1475–1541), a conquistador of modest Spanish origins, landed on the northern coast of Peru on May 13, 1532, the very day the Inca leader Atahualpa (ah-tuh-WAHL-puh) won control of the empire after five years of fighting. As Pizarro advanced across the steep Andes toward Cuzco, the capital of the Inca Empire, Atahualpa was also heading there for his coronation.

Like Moctezuma in Mexico, Atahualpa was aware of the Spaniards' movements. He sent envoys to invite the Spanish to meet him in the provincial town of Cajamarca. His plan was to lure the Spanish into a trap, seize their horses and ablest men for his army, and execute the rest. With an army of some forty thousand men stationed nearby, Atahualpa felt he had little to fear. Instead, the Spaniards ambushed and captured him, collected an enormous ransom in gold, and then executed him in 1533 on trumped-up charges. The Spanish then marched on to Cuzco, profiting once again from internal conflicts to form alliances with local peoples. When Cuzco fell in 1533, the Spanish plundered immense riches in gold and silver.

How was it possible for several hundred Spanish conquistadors to defeat powerful empires commanding large armies, vast wealth, and millions of inhabitants? Historians seeking answers to this question have emphasized a combination of factors: the boldness and audacity of conquistadors like Cortés and Pizarro; the military superiority provided by Spanish firepower and horses; divisions within the Aztec and Inca Empires, which produced many native allies for the Spanish; and, of course, the devastating impact of contagious diseases among the indigenous population. Ironically, the well-organized, urban-based Aztec and Inca Empires were more vulnerable to wholesale takeover than more decentralized and fragmented groups like the Maya in the Yucatán peninsula, whose independence was not wholly crushed until the end of the seventeenth century.

Portuguese Brazil

Unlike Mesoamerica or the Andes, the territory of Brazil contained no urban empires, but instead roughly 2.5 million nomadic and settled people divided into small tribes and many different language groups. In 1500 the Portuguese crown named Pedro Álvares Cabral commander of a fleet headed for the spice trade of the Indies. En route the fleet sailed far to the west, accidentally landing on the coast of Brazil, which Cabral claimed for Portugal under the terms of the Treaty of Tordesillas (see page 437). The Portuguese soon undertook a profitable trade with local people in brazilwood, a valued source of red dye.

In the 1520s Portuguese settlers brought sugarcane production to Brazil. They initially used enslaved indigenous laborers on sugar plantations, but the rapid decline in the indigenous population soon led to the use of forcibly transported Africans (see pages 451–452). In Brazil the Portuguese thus created a new form of colonization in the Americas: large plantations worked by enslaved people. This model would spread throughout the Caribbean along with sugar production in the seventeenth century.

Colonial Empires of England and France

For almost a century after the fall of the Aztec capital of Tenochtitlan, the Spanish and Portuguese dominated European overseas trade and colonization. In the early seventeenth century, however, northern European powers profited from Spanish weakness to challenge its monopoly over the seas. They eventually succeeded in creating multisited overseas empires, consisting of settler colonies in North America, plantations with slaves in the Caribbean, and scattered trading posts in West Africa and Asia. Competition among them was encouraged by mercantilist economic doctrine, which dictated that foreign trade was a zero-sum game in which one country's gains necessarily entailed another's loss (see Chapter 15).

Unlike the Iberian powers, whose royal governments financed exploration and directly ruled the colonies, England, France, and the Netherlands conducted the initial phase of colonization via chartered companies endowed with monopolies over settlement and trade in a given area. These corporate bodies were granted extensive powers over faraway colonies, including exclusive rights to conduct trade, wage war, raise taxes, and administer justice.

The first English colony was founded at Roanoke (in what is now North Carolina) in 1585. After a three-year loss of contact with England, the settlers were found to have disappeared; their fate remains a mystery. The colony of Virginia, founded at Jamestown in 1607, initially struggled to grow sufficient food and faced hostility from the Powhatan Confederacy. Eventually it thrived by producing tobacco for a growing European market. Indentured servants obtained free passage to the colony in exchange for several years of work and the promise of greater opportunity for economic and social advancement than in England. In the 1670s English colonists from the Caribbean island of Barbados settled Carolina, where conditions were suitable for large rice plantations. During the late seventeenth century enslaved Africans replaced indentured servants as laborers on tobacco and rice plantations, and a harsh racial divide was imposed.

For the first settlers on the coast of New England, the reasons for seeking a new life in the colonies were more religious than economic. Many of these colonists were radical Protestants escaping Anglican repression. The small and struggling outpost of Plymouth Colony (1620) was followed by Massachusetts Bay Colony (1630), which grew into a prosperous settlement. Religious disputes in Massachusetts led to the dispersion of settlers into the new communities of Providence, Connecticut, Rhode Island, and New Haven. Because New England lacked the conditions for plantation agriculture, slavery was always a minor element of life there.

Whereas the Spanish established wholesale dominance over Mexico and Peru and its indigenous inhabitants, English settlements hugged the Atlantic coastline and excluded indigenous people from their territories rather than incorporating them. In place of the unified rule exerted by the Spanish crown, England's colonization was haphazard and decentralized in nature, leading to greater autonomy and diversity among its colonies. As the English crown grew more interested in colonial expansion, efforts were made to acquire the territory between New England in the north and Virginia in the south. The goal was to unify English holdings and minimize French and Dutch competition on the Atlantic seaboard. The results of these efforts were the mid-Atlantic colonies: the Catholic settlement of Maryland (1632); New York, captured from the Dutch in 1664; and the Quaker colony of Pennsylvania (1681).

Whereas English settlements were largely agricultural, the French established trading factories in present-day Canada, much like those of the Portuguese in Asia and Africa. In 1608 Samuel de Champlain founded the first permanent French settlement at Quebec as a post for trading beaver pelts with local Algonquin and Huron peoples. The settlement of Ville-Marie, later named Montreal, followed in 1642. Louis XIV's capable economic minister, Jean-Baptiste Colbert, established direct royal control over New France (Canada) and tried to enlarge its population by sending colonists. French immigration to New Canada was always minuscule compared with the stream of settlers who came to British North America; nevertheless, the French were energetic and industrious traders and explorers. Following the waterways of the St. Lawrence River, the Great Lakes, and the Mississippi River, they ventured into much of North America in the 1670s and 1680s. In 1673 the Jesuit Jacques Marquette and the merchant Louis Joliet sailed down the Mississippi and claimed possession of the land on both sides of the river as far south as present-day Arkansas. In 1682 Robert de La Salle traveled the Mississippi to the Gulf of Mexico, opening the way for French occupation of Louisiana.

In the first decades of the seventeenth century, English and French naval captains also defied Spain's hold over the Caribbean Sea (see Map 14.2, page 436). The English seized control of Bermuda (1612), Barbados (1627), and a succession of other islands. The French took Cayenne (1604), St. Christophe (1625), Martinique and Guadeloupe (1635), and, finally, Saint-Domingue (1697) on the western half of Spanish-occupied Hispaniola. These islands acquired new importance after 1640, when the Portuguese brought sugar plantations to Brazil. Sugar and slaves quickly followed in the West Indies (see pages 449–452), making the Caribbean plantations the most lucrative of all colonial possessions.

Northern European expansion also occurred in the Old World. In the seventeenth century France and England—along with Denmark and other northern European powers—established fortified trading posts in West Africa as bases for purchasing slaves and in India and the Indian Ocean as bases for purchasing spices and other luxury goods. Thus, by the end of the seventeenth century, a handful of European powers possessed overseas empires that truly spanned the globe.

Colonial Administration

While the earliest exploration and conquest were undertaken by private initiatives (authorized and sponsored by the state), the Spanish and Portuguese governments quickly assumed direct control of overseas territories. In 1503 the Spanish granted the port of Seville a monopoly over all traffic to the New World and established the House of Trade, or *Casa de la Contratación*, to oversee economic matters. In 1523 Spain added to this body the Royal and Supreme Council of the Indies, with authority over all colonial affairs, subject to approval by the king. Spanish territories themselves were divided initially into two **viceroyalties**, or administrative divisions: New Spain, created in 1535, with its capital at Mexico City; and Peru, created in 1542, with its capital at Lima. In the eighteenth century two additional viceroyalties were added: New Granada, with Bogotá as its administrative center; and La Plata, with Buenos Aires as its capital (see Map 14.2, page 436).

Within each territory the viceroy, or imperial governor, exercised broad military and civil authority as the direct representative of Spain. The viceroy presided over the *audiencia* (ow-dee-EHN-see-ah), a board of twelve to fifteen judges that served as his advisory council and the highest judicial body. As in Spain, settlement in the Americas was centered on cities and towns. In each city, the municipal council, or *cabildo*, exercised local authority. Women were denied participation in public life, a familiar pattern from both Spain and precolonial indigenous society.

Portugal adopted similar patterns of rule, with India House in Lisbon functioning much like the Spanish House of Trade and royal representatives overseeing Portuguese possessions in West Africa and Asia. To secure the vast expanse of Brazil, in the 1530s the Portuguese implemented the system of captaincies,

■ **viceroyalties** The name for the four administrative units of Spanish possessions in the Americas: New Spain, Peru, New Granada, and La Plata.

hereditary grants of land given to nobles and loyal officials who bore the costs of settling and administering their territories. Over time, the Crown secured greater power over the captaincies, appointing royal governors to act as administrators. The captaincy of Bahia was the site of the capital, Salvador, home to the governor general and other royal officials.

Throughout the Americas, the Catholic Church played an integral role in Iberian rule. Churches and cathedrals were consecrated, often on precolonial sacred sites, and bishoprics were established. The papacy allowed Portuguese and Spanish officials greater control over the church than was the case at home, allowing them to appoint clerics and collect tithes. This control allowed colonial powers to use the church as an instrument to indoctrinate indigenous people in European ways of life (see page 448).

By the end of the seventeenth century the French crown had followed the Iberian example and imposed direct rule over its North American colonies. The king appointed military governors to rule alongside intendants, royal officials possessed of broad administrative and financial authority within their intendancies. In the mid-eighteenth century reform-minded Spanish king Charles III (r. 1759–1788) adopted the intendant system for the Spanish colonies.

England's colonies followed a distinctive path. Drawing on English traditions of representative government (see Chapter 15), its colonists established their own proudly autonomous assemblies to regulate local affairs. Wealthy merchants and landowners dominated the assemblies, yet common men had more say in politics than was the case in England. Up to the mid-eighteenth century, the Crown found little reason to dispute colonial liberties in the north, but it did acquire greater control over the wealthy plantation colonies of the Caribbean and tobacco-rich Virginia.

The Era of Global Contact

FOCUS QUESTION *How was the era of global contact shaped by new forms of exploitation, commercial exchange, and forced migration?*

The New and Old Worlds were brought into contact and forever changed by the European voyages of discovery and their aftermath. For the first time, a truly global economy emerged in the sixteenth and seventeenth centuries, and it forged new links among far-flung peoples, cultures, and societies. The ancient civilizations of Europe, Africa, the Americas, and Asia confronted each other in new and rapidly evolving ways. Those confrontations led to conquest, forced migration, devastating

population losses, and brutal exploitation. The exchange of goods and people between Europe and the New World brought highly destructive diseases to the Americas, but it also gave both the New and Old Worlds new crops that eventually altered consumption patterns across the globe.

Indigenous Population Loss and Economic Exploitation

From the time of Christopher Columbus in Hispaniola, the Spanish made use of the **encomienda system** to profit from the peoples and territories they subjugated in the Americas. This system was a legacy of the methods used to reward military leaders in the time of the reconquista, when victorious officers received feudal privileges over conquered areas in return for their service. First in the Caribbean and then on the mainland, conquistadors granted their followers the right to employ groups of indigenous people as laborers and to demand tribute payments from them in exchange for providing food, shelter, and instruction in the Christian faith. Commonly, an individual conquistador was assigned a tribal chieftain along with all of the people belonging to his kin group. This system was first used in Hispaniola to work gold fields and then in Mexico for agricultural labor and, when silver was discovered in the 1540s, for silver mining.

A 1512 Spanish law authorizing the use of encomiendas called for indigenous people to be treated fairly, but in practice the system led to terrible abuses, including overwork, beatings, and sexual violence. Spanish missionaries publicized these abuses, leading to debates in Spain about the nature and proper treatment of indigenous people (see pages 457–458). King Charles I responded to such complaints in 1542 with the New Laws, which set limits on the authority of encomienda holders, including their ability to transmit their privileges to heirs.

The New Laws provoked a revolt in Peru and were little enforced throughout Spanish territories. Nonetheless, the Crown gradually gained control over encomiendas in central areas of the empire and required indigenous people to pay tributes in cash, rather than in labor. To respond to a growing shortage of indigenous workers, royal officials established a new government-run system of forced labor, called *repartimiento* in New Spain and *mita* in Peru. Administrators assigned a certain percentage of the inhabitants of native communities to labor for a set period each year in public works, mining, agriculture, and other tasks. Laborers received modest wages in exchange, which they could use to fulfill tribute obligations. In the seventeenth century, as land became a more important source of wealth than labor, elite settlers purchased *haciendas*, enormous tracts of farmland worked by dependent indigenous laborers and slaves.

■ **encomienda system** A system whereby the Spanish crown granted the conquerors the right to forcibly employ groups of Indians in exchange for providing food, shelter, and Christian teaching.

Interpreting the Spread of Disease Among Natives

Thomas Hariot participated in the 1585 expedition to Roanoke, the short-lived English colony. After his return, he wrote A Briefe and True Report of the New Found Land of Virginia, *which describes the natural environment and the indigenous peoples he encountered. Although biased by his Christian faith and European way of life, Hariot strove to present an accurate, detailed, and balanced viewpoint, making his work a precious source on Native American life and early contacts with Europeans. In this passage, he describes the disastrous effects on the Carolina Algonquins of contagious disease, perhaps measles, smallpox, or influenza.*

～

There was no town where we had any subtle device [cunning maneuvers] practiced against us, we leaving it unpunished or not revenged (because we sought by all means possible to win them by gentleness) but that within a few days after our departure from every such town, the people began to die very fast, and many in short space; in some towns about twenty, in some forty, in some sixty, & in one six score, which in truth was very many in respect of their numbers. This happened in no place that we could learn but where we had been, where they used some practice against us, and after such time; The disease also so strange, that they neither knew what it was, nor how to cure it; the like by report of the oldest men in the country never happened before, time out of mind. A thing specially observed by us as also by the natural inhabitants themselves.

Insomuch that when some of the inhabitants which were our friends . . . had observed such effects in four or five towns to follow their wicked practices [of harming the Englishmen], they were persuaded that it was the work of our God through our means, and that we by him might kill and slay whom we would without weapons and not come near them.

And thereupon when it had happened that they had understanding that any of their enemies had abused us in our journeys, hearing that we had wrought no revenge with our weapons, . . . [they] did come and entreat us that we would be a means to our God that [their enemies] as others that had dealt with us might in like sort die; alleging how much it would be for our credit and profit, as also theirs; and hoping furthermore that we would do so much at their requests in respect of the friendship we profess them.

Whose entreaties although we showed that they were ungodly, affirming that our God would not subject himself to any such prayers and requests of me: that indeed all things have been and were to be done according to his good pleasure as he had ordained: and that we to show ourselves his true servants ought rather to make petition for the contrary, that they with them might live together with us, be made partakers of his truth & serve him in righteousness; but notwithstanding in such sort, that we refer that as all other things, to be done according to his divine will & pleasure, and as by his wisdom he had ordained to be best.

EVALUATE THE EVIDENCE

1. According to Hariot, how did the Native Americans allied with the English interpret the epidemics of disease that struck indigenous villages? How do they seem to have viewed their relations with the English?
2. This document sheds light on how one group of indigenous people experienced the suffering and death brought by European diseases. Based on your reading in this chapter, could you imagine differing responses among other groups?

Source: Thomas Hariot, *A Briefe and True Report of the New Found Land of Virginia* (1590; New York: J. Sabin & Sons, 1871), p. 28. Spelling modernized.

Spanish systems for exploiting the labor of indigenous peoples were both a cause of and a response to the disastrous decline in their numbers that began soon after the arrival of Europeans. Some indigenous people died as a direct result of the violence of conquest and the disruption of agriculture and trade caused by warfare. The most important cause of death, however, was infectious disease, a tragic consequence of the Europeans' arrival (see page 449).

Indigenous people's ability to survive infectious disease was reduced by overwork and exhaustion. Moreover, labor obligations diverted local people from tending to their own crops and thus contributed to malnutrition, reduced fertility rates, and starvation. Women were separated from their babies, producing high infant mortality rates. Malnutrition and hunger in turn lowered resistance to disease.

The pattern of devastating disease and population loss established in the Spanish colonies was repeated everywhere Europeans settled. (See "Evaluating the Evidence 14.2: Interpreting the Spread of Disease Among Natives," above.) Overall, population declined by as much as 90 percent or more across the Americas after European contact, but with important regional variations. In general, densely populated urban centers were worse hit than rural areas, and tropical, low-lying regions suffered more than cooler, higher-altitude ones. Some scholars have claimed that losses may have been overreported, since many indigenous people fled their communities — or listed themselves as mixed race (and thus immune from forced labor) — to escape Spanish exploitation. By the mid-seventeenth century the worst losses had occurred and a slight recovery began.

Colonial administrators responded to native population decline by forcibly combining dwindling indigenous communities into new settlements and imposing the rigors of the encomienda and the repartimiento. By the end of the sixteenth century the search for fresh sources of labor had given birth to the new tragedy of the Atlantic slave trade (see page 451).

Life in the Colonies

Many factors helped shape life in European colonies, including geographical location, pre-existing indigenous cultures, patterns of European settlement, and the policies and cultural values of the European nations that claimed them as empire. Throughout the New World, colonial settlements were hedged by immense borderlands where European power was weak and Europeans and non-Europeans interacted on a more equal basis.

Women played a crucial role in the emergence of colonial societies. The first explorers formed unions with native women, through coercion or choice, and relied on them as translators and guides and to form alliances with indigenous powers. As settlement developed, the character of each colony was influenced by the presence or absence of European women. Where women and children accompanied men, as in the British colonies and the Spanish mainland colonies, new settlements took on European languages, religion, and ways of life that have endured, with input from local cultures, to this day. Where European women did not accompany men, as on the west coast of Africa and most European outposts in Asia, local populations largely retained their own cultures, to which male Europeans acclimatized themselves. The scarcity of women in all colonies, at least initially, opened up opportunities for those who did arrive, leading one cynic to comment that even "a whore, if handsome, makes a wife for some rich planter."[15]

It was not just the availability of Englishwomen that prevented Englishmen from forming unions with indigenous women. English cultural attitudes drew strict boundaries between "civilized" and "savage," and even settlements of Christianized native peoples were segregated from the English. This was in strong contrast with the situation in New France, where royal officials initially encouraged French traders to form ties with indigenous people, including marrying local women. Assimilation of the native population was seen as one solution to the low levels of immigration from France.

The vast majority of women who crossed the Atlantic were captive Africans, constituting four-fifths of the female newcomers before 1800.[16] Wherever slavery existed, masters profited from their power to engage in sexual relations with enslaved women. One important difference among European colonies was in the status of children born from such unions. In some colonies, mostly those dominated by the Portuguese, Spanish, or French, substantial populations of free people of color descended from the freed children of such unions. In English colonies, masters were less likely to free children they fathered with female slaves.

The mixing of indigenous peoples with Europeans and Africans created whole new populations and ethnicities and complex forms of identity (see Chapter 17). In Spanish America the word *mestizo* — *métis* in French — described people of mixed Native American and European descent. The blanket terms "mulatto" and "people of color" were used for those of mixed African and European origin. With its immense slave-based plantation agriculture system, large indigenous population, and relatively low Portuguese immigration, Brazil developed a particularly complex racial and ethnic mosaic.

A Mixed-Race Procession The Incas used drinking vessels, known as *keros*, for the ritual consumption of maize beer at feasts. This kero from the early colonial period depicts a multiracial procession: an Inca dignitary is preceded by a Spanish trumpet player and an African drummer. This is believed to be one of the earliest visual representations of an African in the Americas. (British Museum, London, UK/ Werner Forman/Universal Images Group/Getty Images)

Indians Working i Belgian engraver T published many i exploration and settleme World. De Bry never crossed the himself, instead using images and sto by those who did. This image depicts the exploitation of indigenous people in a Spanish sugar mill. (Engraving by Theodor de Bry [1528–1598], ca. 1540/Bibliothèque Nationale, Paris, France/ Snark/Art Resource, NY)

The Columbian Exchange

The travel of people and goods between the Old and New Worlds led to an exchange of animals, plants, and diseases, a complex process known as the **Columbian exchange**. As we have seen, the introduction of new diseases to the Americas had devastating consequences. But other results of the exchange brought benefits not only to the Europeans but also to indigenous peoples.

European immigrants to the Americas wanted a familiar diet, so they searched for climatic zones favorable to familiar crops. Everywhere they settled, the Spanish and Portuguese brought and raised wheat with labor provided by the encomienda system. Grapes and olives brought over from Spain did well in parts of Peru and Chile. Europeans also introduced domestic livestock and horses, which allowed for faster travel and easier transport of heavy loads. In turn, Europeans returned home with many food crops that became central elements of their diet, such as potatoes, maize (corn), and tomatoes. (See "Living in the Past: Foods of the Columbian Exchange," page 450.)

While the exchange of foods was a great benefit to both cultures, the introduction of European pathogens to the New World had a disastrous impact on the native population. In Europe, infectious diseases like smallpox, measles, and influenza—originally passed on from domestic animals living among the population—killed many people each year. Given the size of the population and the frequency of outbreaks, in most of Europe these diseases were experienced in childhood, and survivors carried immunity or resistance. Over

centuries of dealing with these diseases, the European population had had time to adapt. Prior to contact with Europeans, indigenous peoples of the New World suffered from insect-borne diseases and some infectious ones, but their lack of domestic livestock spared them the host of highly infectious diseases known in the Old World. The arrival of Europeans spread these microbes among a completely unprepared population, and they fell victim in vast numbers (see pages 447–448.) The wave of catastrophic epidemic disease that swept the Western Hemisphere after 1492 can be seen as an extension of the swath of devastation wreaked by the Black Death in the fourteenth century, first on Asia and then on Europe. The world after Columbus was thus unified by disease as well as by trade and colonization.

Sugar and Slavery

Two crucial and interrelated elements of the Columbian exchange were the transatlantic trade in sugar and slaves. Throughout the Middle Ages slavery was deeply entrenched in the Mediterranean, but it was not based on race; many slaves were European in origin. How, then, did black African slavery enter the European picture and take root in the Americas? In 1453 the Ottoman capture of Constantinople halted the flow of slaves from the eastern Mediterranean to western Europe. Additionally, the successes of the Iberian

■ **Columbian exchange** The exchange of animals, plants, and diseases between the Old and the New Worlds.

LIVING IN THE PAST
Foods of the Columbian Exchange

Many people are aware of the devastating effects of European diseases on peoples of the New World and of the role of gunpowder and horses in the conquest of native civilizations. They may be less aware of how New World foodstuffs transformed Europeans' daily life.

Prior to Christopher Columbus's voyages, many common elements of today's European diet were unknown in Europe. It's hard to imagine Italian pizza without tomato sauce or Irish stew without potatoes, yet tomatoes and potatoes were both unknown in Europe before 1492. Additional crops originating in the Americas included many varieties of beans, squash, pumpkins, avocados, and peppers.

One of the most important of such crops was maize (corn), first introduced to Europe by Columbus in 1493. Because maize gives a high yield per unit of land, has a short growing season, and thrives in climates too dry for rice and too wet for wheat, it proved an especially important crop for Europeans. By the late seventeenth century the crop had become a staple in Spain, Portugal, southern France, and Italy, and in the eighteenth century it became one of the chief foods of southeastern Europe. Even more valuable was the nutritious white potato, which slowly spread from west to east — to Ireland, England, and France in the seventeenth century, and to Germany, Poland, Hungary, and Russia in the eighteenth, contributing everywhere to a rise in population. Ironically, the white potato reached New England from old England in the early eighteenth century.

Europeans' initial reaction to these crops was often fear or hostility. Adoption of the tomato and the potato was long hampered by the belief that they were unfit for human consumption and potentially poisonous. Both plants belong to the deadly nightshade family, and both contain poison in their leaves and stems. It took time and persuasion for these plants to win over tradition-minded European peasants, who used potatoes mostly as livestock feed. During the eighteenth-century Enlightenment, scientists and doctors played an important role in popularizing the nutritive benefits of the potato.

Columbus himself contributed to misconceptions about New World foods when he mistook the chili pepper for black pepper, one of the spices he had hoped to find in the Indies. The Portuguese quickly began exporting chili peppers from Brazil to Africa, India, and Southeast Asia along the trade routes they dominated. The chili pepper arrived in North America through its place in the diet of enslaved Africans.

Saint Diego of Alcala Feeding the Poor (1645–1646), by Bartolomé Esteban Murillo, the first dated European depiction of the potato in art. (Real Academia de Bellas Artes de San Fernando, Madrid, Spain/Bridgeman Images)

Inca women milking goats, from a collection of illustrations by a Spanish bishop that offers a valuable view of life in Peru in the 1780s. (Palacio Real de Madrid, Spain/Photo © AISA/Bridgeman Images)

European settlers introduced various foods to the native peoples of the New World, including rice, wheat, lettuce, and onions. Perhaps the most significant introduction to the diet of Native Americans came via the meat and milk of the livestock that the early conquistadors brought with them, including cattle, sheep, and goats.

The foods of the Columbian exchange traveled a truly global path. They provided important new sources of nutrition to people all over the world, as well as creating new and beloved culinary traditions. French fries with ketchup, anyone?

QUESTIONS FOR ANALYSIS

1. Why do you think it was so difficult for Europeans to accept new types of food, even when they were high in nutritional quality?
2. What do the painting and illustration shown here suggest about the importance of the Columbian exchange?
3. List the foods you typically eat in a day. How many of them originated in the New World, and how many in the Old World? How does your own life exemplify the outcome of the Columbian exchange?

reconquista drastically diminished the supply of Muslim captives. Cut off from its traditional sources of slaves, Mediterranean Europe turned to sub-Saharan Africa, which had a long history of internal slave trading. (See "Individuals in Society: Juan de Pareja," page 453.)

As Portuguese explorers began their voyages along the western coast of Africa, one of the first commodities they sought was slaves. In 1444 the first ship returned to Lisbon with a cargo of enslaved Africans. While the first slaves were simply seized by small raiding parties, Portuguese merchants soon found that it was easier to trade with local leaders, who were accustomed to dealing in slaves captured through warfare with neighboring powers. In 1483 the Portuguese established an alliance with the kingdom of Kongo. The royal family eventually converted to Christianity, and Portuguese merchants intermarried with Kongolese women, creating a permanent Afro-Portuguese community. From 1490 to 1530 Portuguese traders brought hundreds of enslaved Africans to Lisbon each year (Map 14.3), where they eventually constituted 10 percent of the city's population.

In this stage of European expansion, the history of slavery became intertwined with the history of sugar. Originally sugar was an expensive luxury, but population increases and monetary expansion in the fifteenth century led to increasing demand. Native to the South Pacific, sugar was taken in ancient times to India, where farmers learned to preserve cane juice as granules that could be stored and shipped. From there, sugar crops traveled to China and the Mediterranean, where islands like Crete and Sicily had the warm and wet climate needed for growing sugarcane. When Genoese and other Italians colonized the Canary Islands and the Portuguese settled on the Madeira Islands, sugar plantations came to the Atlantic.

Sugar was a particularly difficult crop to produce for profit. Seed-stems were planted by hand, thousands to the acre. When mature, the cane had to be harvested and processed rapidly to avoid spoiling. Moreover, sugar has a virtually constant growing season, meaning that there was no fallow period when workers could recuperate from the arduous labor. The invention of roller mills to crush the cane more efficiently meant that yields could be significantly augmented, but only if a sufficient labor force was found to supply the mills. Europeans solved the labor problem by forcing first native islanders and then enslaved Africans to provide the backbreaking work.

The transatlantic slave trade began in 1518 when the Spanish emperor Charles V authorized traders to bring enslaved Africans to the Americas. The Portuguese brought the first slaves to Brazil around 1550; by 1600 four thousand were being imported annually. After its founding in 1621, the Dutch West India

MAP 14.3 Seaborne Trading Empires in the Sixteenth and Seventeenth Centuries   By the mid-seventeenth century trade linked all parts of the world except for Australia. Notice that trade in slaves was not confined to the Atlantic but involved almost all parts of the world.

Company, with the full support of the United Provinces, transported thousands of Africans to Brazil and the Caribbean, mostly to work on sugar plantations. In the mid-seventeenth century the English got involved. From 1660 to 1698 the Royal African Company held a monopoly over the slave trade from the English crown.

Before 1700, when slavers decided it was better business to improve conditions, some 20 percent of slaves died on the voyage.[17] The most common cause of death was from dysentery induced by poor-quality food and water, crowding, and lack of sanitation. Men were often kept in irons during the passage, while women and girls were considered fair game for sailors. To increase profits, slave traders packed several hundred captives on each ship. One slaver explained that he removed his boots before entering the slave hold because he had to crawl over the slaves' packed bodies.[18] On sugar plantations, death rates from the brutal pace of labor were

extremely high, leading to a constant stream of new shipments of slaves from Africa.

In total, scholars estimate that European traders embarked over 12 million enslaved Africans across the Atlantic from 1500 to 1875 (of whom roughly 10.7 million disembarked), with the peak of the trade occurring in the eighteenth century.[19] By comparison, only 2 to 2.5 million Europeans migrated to the New World during the same period. Slaves worked in an infinite variety of occupations: as miners, soldiers, sailors, servants, and artisans and in the production of sugar, cotton, rum, indigo, tobacco, wheat, and corn.

Spanish Silver and Its Economic Effects

The sixteenth century has often been called Spain's golden century, but silver mined in the Americas was the true source of Spain's wealth. In 1545, at an altitude

INDIVIDUALS IN SOCIETY

Juan de Pareja

During the long wars of the reconquista, Muslims and Christians captured each other in battle and used the defeated as slaves. As the Muslims were gradually eliminated from Iberia in the fifteenth and sixteenth centuries, the Spanish and Portuguese turned to the west coast of Africa for a new supply of slaves. Most slaves worked as domestic servants, rather than in the fields. Some received specialized training as artisans.

Not all people of African descent were slaves, and some experienced both freedom and slavery in a single lifetime. The life and career of Juan de Pareja (pah-REH-huh) illustrates the complexities of the Iberian slave system and the heights of achievement possible for those who gained freedom.

Pareja was born in Antequera, an agricultural region and the old center of Muslim culture near Seville in southern Spain. Of his parents we know nothing. Because a rare surviving document calls him a "mulatto," one of his parents must have been white and the other must have had some African blood. In 1630 Pareja applied to the mayor of Seville for permission to travel to Madrid to visit his brother and "to perfect his art." The document lists his occupation as "a painter in Seville." Since it mentions no other name, it is reasonable to assume that Pareja arrived in Madrid a free man. Sometime between 1630 and 1648, however, he came into the possession of the artist Diego Velázquez (1599–1660); Pareja became a slave.

How did Velázquez acquire Pareja? By purchase? As a gift? Had Pareja fallen into debt or committed some crime and thereby lost his freedom? We do not know. Velázquez, the greatest Spanish painter of the seventeenth century, had a large studio with many assistants. Pareja was set to grinding powders to make colors and to preparing canvases. He must have demonstrated ability because when Velázquez went to Rome in 1648, he chose Pareja to accompany him.

In 1650, as practice for a portrait of Pope Innocent X, Velázquez painted Pareja. The portrait shows Pareja dressed in fine clothing and gazing self-confidently at the viewer. Displayed in Rome in a public exhibition of Velázquez's work, the painting won acclaim from his contemporaries. That same year, Velázquez signed the document that gave Pareja his freedom, to become effective in 1654. Pareja lived out the rest of his life as an independent painter.

What does the public career of Pareja tell us about the man and his world? Pareja's career suggests that a person of African descent might fall into slavery and yet still acquire professional training and work alongside his master in a position of confidence. Moreover, if lucky enough to be freed, a former slave could exercise a profession and live his own life in Madrid. Pareja's experience was far from typical for a slave in the seventeenth century, but it reminds us of the myriad forms that slavery took in this period.

Velázquez, *Juan de Pareja*, 1650. (Metropolitan Museum of Art, New York, USA/photo © Christie's Images/Bridgeman Images)

QUESTIONS FOR ANALYSIS

1. Since slavery was an established institution in Spain, speculate on Velázquez's possible reasons for giving Pareja his freedom.

2. In what ways does Pareja represent Europe's increasing participation in global commerce and exploration?

Sources: Jonathan Brown, *Velázquez: Painter and Courtier* (New Haven, Conn.: Yale University Press, 1986); *Grove Dictionary of Art* (New York: Macmillan, 2000); Sister Wendy Beckett, *Sister Wendy's American Collection* (New York: Harper Collins Publishers, 2000), p. 15.

of fifteen thousand feet, the Spanish discovered an extraordinary source of silver at Potosí (poh-toh-SEE) (in present-day Bolivia) in territory conquered from the Inca Empire. The frigid place where nothing grew had been unsettled. A half century later 160,000 people lived there, making it about as populous as the city of London. By 1550 Potosí yielded perhaps 60 percent of all the silver mined in the world. From Potosí and the mines at Zacatecas (za-kuh-TAY-kuhhs) and Guanajuato (gwah-nah-HWAH-toh) in Mexico, huge quantities of precious metals poured forth. To protect this treasure from French and English pirates, armed convoys transported it to Spain each year. Between 1503 and 1650, 35 million pounds of silver and over 600,000 pounds of gold entered Seville's port. Spanish predominance, however, proved temporary.

In the sixteenth century Spain experienced a steady population increase, creating a sharp rise in the demand for food and goods. Spanish colonies in the Americas also demanded consumer goods, such as cloth and luxury goods. Since Spain had expelled some of its best farmers

and businessmen—the Muslims and Jews—in the fifteenth century, the Spanish economy was suffering and could not meet the new demands. The excess of demand over supply led to widespread inflation. The result was a rise in production costs and a further decline in Spain's productive capacity.

Did the flood of silver bullion from America cause the inflation? Prices rose most steeply before 1565, but bullion imports reached their peak between 1580 and 1620. Thus silver did not cause the initial inflation. It did, however, greatly exacerbate the situation, and, along with the ensuing rise in population, the influx of silver significantly contributed to the upward spiral of prices. Inflation severely strained government budgets. Several times between 1557 and 1647, Spain's King Philip II and his successors wrote off the state debt, thereby undermining confidence in the government and leaving the economy in shambles. After 1600, when the population declined, prices gradually stabilized.

As Philip II paid his armies and foreign debts with silver bullion, Spanish inflation was transmitted to the rest of Europe. Between 1560 and 1600 much of Europe experienced large price increases. Prices doubled and in some cases quadrupled. Spain suffered most severely, but all European countries were affected. Because money bought less, people who lived on fixed incomes, such as nobles, were badly hurt. Those who owed fixed sums of money, such as the middle class, prospered because in a time of rising prices, debts lessened in value each year. Food costs rose most sharply, and the poor fared worst of all.

In many ways, though, it was not Spain but China that controlled the world trade in silver. The Chinese demanded silver for their products and for the payment of imperial taxes. China was thus the main buyer of world silver, absorbing half the world's production. The silver market drove world trade, with New Spain and Japan being mainstays on the supply side and China dominating the demand side. The world trade in silver is one of the best examples of the new global economy that emerged in this period.

Philip II, ca. 1533 This portrait of Philip II as a young man and crown prince of Spain is by the celebrated artist Titian, court painter to Philip's father, Charles V. After taking the throne, Philip became another great patron of the artist. (Palazzo Pitti, Florence, Italy/Bridgeman Images)

The Birth of the Global Economy

With the Europeans' discovery of the Americas and their exploration of the Pacific, the entire world was linked for the first time in history by seaborne trade. The opening of that trade brought into being three successive commercial empires: the Portuguese, the Spanish, and the Dutch.

The Portuguese were the first worldwide traders. In the sixteenth century they controlled the sea route to India (see Map 14.3). From their fortified bases at Goa on the Arabian Sea and at Malacca on the Malay Peninsula, ships carried goods to the Portuguese settlement at Macao, founded in 1557, in the South China Sea. From Macao Portuguese ships loaded with Chinese silks and porcelains sailed to the Japanese port of Nagasaki and to the Philippine port of Manila, where Chinese goods were exchanged for Spanish silver from New Spain. Throughout Asia the Portuguese traded in slaves—sub-Saharan Africans, Chinese, and Japanese. The Portuguese exported horses from Mesopotamia and copper from Arabia to India; from India they exported hawks and peacocks for the Chinese and Japanese markets. Back to Portugal they

Goods from the Global Economy Spices from Southeast Asia were a driving force behind the new global economy, and among the most treasured European luxury goods. They were used not only for cooking but also as medicines and health tonics. This fresco (below right) shows a fifteenth-century Italian pharmacist measuring out spices for a customer. After the discovery of the Americas, a wave of new items entered European markets, silver foremost among them. The incredibly rich silver mines at Potosí (modern-day Bolivia) were the source of this eight-reale coin (right) struck at the mine during the reign of Charles II. Such coins were the original "pieces of eight" prized by pirates and adventurers. Soon Asian and American goods were mixed together by enterprising tradesmen. This mid-seventeenth-century Chinese teapot (below left) was made of porcelain with the traditional Chinese design prized in the West, but with a silver handle added to suit European tastes. (teapot: Private Collection/Paul Freeman/Bridgeman Images; spice shop: Issogne Castle, Val d'Aosta, Italy, Alfredo Dagli Orti/The Art Archive at Art Resource, NY; coin: Hoberman Collection/SuperStock)

brought Asian spices that had been purchased with textiles produced in India and with gold and ivory from East Africa. They also shipped back sugar from their colony in Brazil, produced by enslaved Africans whom they had transported across the Atlantic.

Coming to empire a few decades later than the Portuguese, the Spanish were determined to claim their place in world trade. The Spanish Empire in the New World was basically a land empire, but across the Pacific the Spaniards built a seaborne empire centered at Manila in the Philippines. The city of Manila served as the transpacific bridge between Spanish America and China. In Manila, Spanish traders used silver from American mines to purchase Chinese silk for European markets. The European demand for silk was so huge that in 1597, for example, 12 million pesos of silver, almost the total value of the transatlantic trade, moved from Acapulco in New Spain to Manila (see Map 14.3).

In the final years of the sixteenth century the Dutch challenged the Spanish and Portuguese Empires. During this period the Protestant Dutch were engaged in a long war of independence from their Spanish Catholic overlords. The joining of the Portuguese crown to Spain in 1580 meant that the Dutch had both strategic and commercial reasons to attack Portugal's commercial empire. In 1599 a Dutch fleet returned to Amsterdam carrying 600,000 pounds of pepper and 250,000 pounds of cloves and nutmeg. Those who had invested in the expedition received a 100 percent profit. The voyage led to the establishment in 1602 of the Dutch East India Company, founded with the stated intention of capturing the Asian spice trade from the Portuguese.

In return for assisting Indonesian princes in local squabbles and disputes with the Portuguese, the Dutch won broad commercial concessions. Through agreements, seizures, and outright military aggression, they gained control of the western access to the Indonesian archipelago in the first half of the seventeenth century. Gradually, they acquired political domination over the archipelago itself. The Dutch were willing to use force more ruthlessly than the Portuguese and had superior organizational efficiency. These factors allowed them to expel the Portuguese from Ceylon and other East Indian islands in 1660 and henceforth control the immensely lucrative production and trade of spices. The company also established the colony of Cape Town on the southern tip of Africa as a provisioning point for its Asian fleets.

Not content with challenging the Portuguese in the Indian Ocean, the Dutch also aspired to a role in the Americas. Founded in 1621, during their war with Spain, the Dutch West India Company aggressively sought to open trade with North and South America and capture Spanish territories there. The company captured or destroyed hundreds of Spanish ships, seized the Spanish silver fleet in 1628, and captured portions of Brazil and the Caribbean. The Dutch also successfully interceded in the transatlantic slave trade, establishing a large number of trading stations on the west coast of Africa. Ironically, the nation that was known throughout Europe as a bastion of tolerance and freedom came to be one of the principal operators of the slave trade starting in the 1640s.

Changing Attitudes and Beliefs

FOCUS QUESTION *How did new encounters shape cultural attitudes and beliefs in Europe and the rest of the world?*

The age of overseas expansion heightened Europeans' contacts with the rest of the world. Religion was one of the most important arenas of cultural contact, as European missionaries aimed to spread Christianity in both the New World and East Asia, with mixed results. While Christianity was embraced in parts of the New World, it was met largely with suspicion in China and Japan. However, the East-West contacts did lead to exchanges of influential cultural and scientific ideas.

These contacts also gave birth to new ideas about the inherent superiority or inferiority of different races, sparking vociferous debate about the status of Africans and indigenous peoples of the Americas. The essays of Michel de Montaigne epitomized a new spirit of skepticism and cultural relativism, while the plays of William Shakespeare reflected the efforts of one great writer to come to terms with the cultural complexity of his day.

Religious Conversion

Converting indigenous people to Christianity was one of the most important justifications for European expansion. Jesuit missionaries were active in Japan and China in the sixteenth and seventeenth centuries, until authorities banned their teachings. The first missionaries to the New World accompanied Columbus on his second voyage and more than 2,500 Franciscans, Dominicans, Jesuits, and other friars crossed the Atlantic in the following century. Later French explorers were also accompanied by missionaries who preached to the Native American tribes with whom the French traded.

Catholic friars were among the first Europeans to seek an understanding of native cultures and languages as part of their effort to render Christianity comprehensible to indigenous people. In Mexico they not only learned the Nahuatl language, but also taught it to non-Nahuatl-speaking groups to create a shared language for Christian teaching. They were also the most

Tenochtitlan Leaders Respond to Spanish Missionaries

For the conquered peoples of the New World, the imposition of Christianity and repression of their pre-existing religions represented yet another form of loss. This document describes the response of the vanquished leaders of Tenochtitlan to Franciscan missionaries seeking to convert them in 1524. The account was written down in the 1560s by or for Bernardino de Sahagún, a Franciscan missionary. Sahagún is well known for his General History of the Things of New Spain *(also known as the* Florentine Codex*), a multivolume account of Mexica history, culture, and society he produced in collaboration with indigenous artists and informants.*

~

You have told us that we do not know the One who gives us life and being, who is Lord of the heavens and of the earth. You also say that those we worship are not gods. This way of speaking is entirely new to us, and very scandalous. We are frightened by this way of speaking because our forebears who engendered and governed us never said anything like this. On the contrary, they left us this our custom of worshiping our gods, in which they believed and which they worshiped all the time that they lived here on earth. They taught us how to honor them. And they taught us all the ceremonies and sacrifices that we make. They told us that through them [our gods] we live and are, and that we were beholden to them, to be theirs and to serve countless centuries before the sun began to shine and before there was daytime. They said that these gods that we worship give us everything we need for our physical existence: maize, beans, chia seeds, etc. We appeal to them for the rain to make the things of the earth grow.

These our gods are the source of great riches and delights, all of which belong to them. They live in very delightful places where there are always flowers, vegetation, and great freshness, a place unknown to mere mortals, called Tlalocan, where there is never hunger, poverty, or illness. It is they who bestow honors, property, titles, and kingdoms, gold and silver, precious feathers, and gemstones.

There has never been a time remembered when they were not worshiped, honored, and esteemed. Perhaps it is a century or two since this began; it is a time beyond counting. . . .

It is best, our lords, to act on this matter very slowly, with great deliberation. We are not satisfied or convinced by what you have told us, nor do we understand or give credit to what has been said of our gods. . . . All of us together feel that it is enough to have lost, enough that the power and royal jurisdiction have been taken from us. As for our gods, we will die before giving up serving and worshiping them.

EVALUATE THE EVIDENCE

1. What reasons do the leaders of Tenochtitlan offer for rejecting the missionaries' teachings? In their view, what elements of their lives will be affected by abandoning the worship of their gods?
2. What insight does this document provide into the mind-set of Mexica people shortly following conquest?

Source: *Coloquios y doctrina Cristiana*, ed. Miguel León-Portilla, in *Colonial Spanish America: A Documentary History*, ed. Kenneth Mills and William B. Taylor (Wilmington, Del.: SR Books, 1998), pp. 21–22. Used by permission of Rowman & Littlefield.

---

vociferous opponents of abuses committed by Spanish settlers (see the next section).

Religion had been a central element of pre-Columbian societies, and many—if not all—indigenous people were receptive to the new religion that accompanied the victorious Iberians. (See "Evaluating the Evidence 14.3: Tenochtitlan Leaders Respond to Spanish Missionaries," above.) It is estimated that missionaries had baptized between 4 and 9 million indigenous people in New Spain by the mid-1530s.[20] In addition to spreading Christianity, missionaries taught indigenous peoples European methods of agriculture and instilled loyalty to colonial masters.

Despite the success of initial conversion efforts, authorities became suspicious about the thoroughness of native peoples' conversion and their lingering belief

in the old gods. They could not prevent the melding together of Catholic teachings with elements of pagan beliefs and practices. For example, a sixteenth-century apparition of the Virgin Mary in Mexico City, known as the Virgin of Guadalupe, which became a central icon of New World Catholicism, seems to have been based on veneration of the Aztec Mother Earth goddess, Tonantzin.

European Debates About Indigenous Peoples

Iberian exploitation of the native population of the Americas began from the moment of Columbus's arrival in 1492. Denunciations of this abuse by Catholic missionaries, however, quickly followed,

Spanish Atrocities in the New World   The illustrations provided by Theodor de Bry to accompany Bartolomé de Las Casas's *Short Account of the Destruction of the Indies* depict atrocities committed by the Spanish in their conquest and settlement of the Americas. De Bry, a converted Protestant, thereby contributed to the "Black Legend" of Spanish colonization. (Engraving by Theodor de Bry, from a work by Bartolomé de Las Casas, 1598/Photo 12/UIG via Getty Images)

inspiring vociferous debates both in Europe and in the colonies about the nature of indigenous peoples and how they should be treated. Bartolomé de Las Casas (1474–1566), a Dominican friar and former encomienda holder, was one of the earliest and most outspoken critics of the brutal treatment inflicted on indigenous peoples. He wrote:

> To these quiet Lambs . . . came the Spaniards like most c(r)uel Tygres, Wolves and Lions, enrag'd with a sharp and tedious hunger; for these forty years past, minding nothing else but the slaughter of these unfortunate wretches, whom with divers kinds of torments neither seen nor heard of before, they have so cruelly and inhumanely butchered, that of three millions of people which Hispaniola itself did contain, there are left remaining alive scarce three hundred persons.[21]

Mounting criticism in Spain led King Charles I to assemble a group of churchmen and lawyers to debate the issue in 1550 in the city of Valladolid. One side, led by Juan Ginés de Sepúlveda, argued that conquest and forcible conversion were both necessary and justi-

fied to save indigenous people from the horrors of human sacrifice, cannibalism, and idolatry. He described them as barbarians who belonged to a category of inferior beings identified by the ancient Greek philosopher Aristotle as naturally destined for slavery. Against these arguments, Las Casas and his supporters depicted indigenous people as rational and innocent children, who deserved protection and tutelage from more advanced civilizations. Both sides claimed victory in the debate, but it had little effect on the situation in the Americas.

Eagerly reading denunciations of Spanish abuses by critics like Las Casas, northern Europeans derived the **"Black Legend"** of Spanish colonialism, the notion that the Spanish were uniquely brutal and cruel in their conquest and settlement of the Americas. However, the legend also helped northern European powers, like France and England, overlook their own record of colonial violence and exploitation.

New Ideas About Race

At the beginning of the transatlantic slave trade, most Europeans would have thought of Africans, if they thought of them at all, as savages in their social customs, religious practices, language, and methods of war. They grouped Africans into the despised categories of pagan heathens and Muslim infidels.

As Europeans turned to Africa for new sources of slaves, they drew on beliefs about Africans' supposed primitiveness and barbarity to defend slavery and even argue, like Sepúlveda with regard to indigenous Americans, that enslavement benefited Africans by bringing them the light of Christianity. In 1444 an observer defended the enslavement of the first Africans by Portuguese explorers as necessary for their salvation "because they lived like beasts, without any of the customs of rational creatures, since they did not even know what were bread and wine, nor garments of cloth, nor life in the shelter of a house; and worse still was their ignorance, which deprived them of knowledge of good, and permitted them only a life of brutish idleness."[22]

Over time, the institution of slavery fostered unprecedented ideas about racial inequality. Africans gradually became seen as utterly distinct from and wholly inferior to Europeans. From rather vague assumptions about Africans' non-Christian religious beliefs and general lack of civilization, Europeans developed increasingly rigid ideas of racial superiority and inferiority to safeguard the growing profits gained from plantation slavery. Black skin became equated with slavery itself as Europeans at home and in the colonies convinced themselves that blacks were destined by God to serve them as slaves in perpetuity.

Support for this belief went back to the Greek philosopher Aristotle's argument that some people are naturally destined for slavery and to biblical associations between darkness and sin. A more explicit justification was found in the story of Noah's curse upon the descendants of his disobedient son Ham to be the "servant[s] of servants." Biblical genealogies listing Ham's sons as those who peopled North Africa and Cush (which includes parts of modern Egypt and Sudan) were read to mean that all inhabitants of those regions bore Noah's curse. From the sixteenth century onward, many defenders of slavery cited this story as justification for their actions.

After 1700 the emergence of new methods of observing and describing nature led to the use of science to define race. Although the term originally referred to a nation or an ethnic group, henceforth "race" would be used to describe supposedly biologically distinct groups of people, whose physical differences produced differences in culture, character, and intelligence. Biblical justifications for inequality thereby gave way to supposedly scientific ones (see pages 525–526).

Michel de Montaigne and Cultural Curiosity

Racism was not the only possible reaction to the new worlds emerging in the sixteenth century. Decades of religious fanaticism, bringing civil anarchy and war, led some Catholics and Protestants to doubt that any one faith contained absolute truth. Added to these doubts was the discovery of peoples in the New World who had radically different ways of life. These shocks helped produce ideas of skepticism and cultural relativism. Skepticism is a school of thought founded on doubt that total certainty or definitive knowledge is ever attainable. The skeptic is cautious and critical and suspends judgment. Cultural relativism suggests that one culture is not necessarily superior to another, just different. Both notions found expression in the work of Frenchman Michel de Montaigne (duh mahn-TAYN) (1533–1592).

Montaigne developed a new literary genre, the essay — from the French *essayer*, meaning "to test or try" — to express his ideas. Published in 1580, Montaigne's *Essays* consisted of short reflections drawing on his extensive reading in ancient texts, his experience as a government official, and his own moral judgment. Intending his works to be accessible to ordinary people, Montaigne wrote in French rather than Latin and in an engaging conversational style. His essays were quickly translated into other European languages and became some of the most widely read texts of the early modern period.

Montaigne's essay "Of Cannibals" reveals the impact of overseas discoveries on one thoughtful European. In contrast to the prevailing views of his day, he rejected the notion that one culture is superior to another. Speaking of native Brazilians, he wrote:

> I find that there is nothing barbarous and savage in this nation [Brazil], . . . except, that everyone gives the title of barbarism to everything that is not according to his usage; as, indeed, we have no other criterion of truth and reason, than the example and pattern of the opinions and customs of the place wherein we live. . . . They are savages in the same way that we say fruits are wild, which nature produces of herself and by her ordinary course; whereas, in truth, we ought rather to call those wild whose natures we have changed by our artifice and diverted from the common order.[23]

In his own time, few would have agreed with Montaigne's challenge to ideas of European superiority or his even more radical questioning of the superiority

■ **"Black Legend"** The notion that the Spanish were particularly ruthless and cruel in their conquest and domination of the Americas, an idea often propagated by Spain's rivals.

of humans over animals. Nevertheless, his popular essays contributed to a basic shift in attitudes. "Wonder," he said, "is the foundation of all philosophy, research is the means of all learning, and ignorance is the end."[24] Montaigne thus inaugurated an era of doubt.

William Shakespeare and His Influence

In addition to the essay as a literary genre, the period fostered remarkable creativity in other branches of literature. England—especially in the latter part of Queen Elizabeth I's reign and in the first years of her successor, James I (r. 1603–1625)—witnessed remarkable literary expression. The undisputed master of the period was the dramatist William Shakespeare, whose genius lay in the originality of his characterizations, the diversity of his plots, his understanding of human psychology, and his unsurpassed gift for language. Born in 1564 to a successful glove manufacturer in Stratford-upon-Avon, Shakespeare grew into a Renaissance man with a deep appreciation of classical culture, individualism, and humanism. Although he wrote sparkling comedies and stirring historical plays, his greatest masterpieces were his later tragedies, including *Hamlet*, *Othello*, and *Macbeth*, which explore an enormous range of human problems and are open to an almost infinite variety of interpretations.

Like Montaigne's essays, Shakespeare's work reveals the impact of the new discoveries and contacts of his day. The title character of *Othello* is described as a "Moor of Venice." In Shakespeare's day, the term "Moor" referred to Muslims of North African origin, including those who had migrated to the Iberian Peninsula. It could also be applied, though, to natives of the Iberian Peninsula who converted to Islam or to non-Muslim Berbers in North Africa. To complicate things even more, references in the play to Othello as "black" in skin color have led many to believe that Shakespeare intended him to be a sub-Saharan African. This confusion in the play aptly reflects the uncertainty in Shakespeare's own time about racial and religious classifications. In contrast to the prevailing view of Moors as inferior, Shakespeare presents Othello as a complex human figure, whose only crime is to have "loved [his wife] not wisely, but too well."

Shakespeare's last play, *The Tempest*, also highlights the issue of race and race relations. The plot involves the stranding on an island of sorcerer Prospero and his daughter Miranda. There Prospero finds and raises Caliban, a native of the island, whom he instructs in his own language and religion. After

Caliban's attempted rape of Miranda, Prospero enslaves him, earning the hatred of his erstwhile pupil. Modern scholars often note the echoes between this play and the realities of imperial conquest and settlement in Shakespeare's day. It is no accident, they argue, that the poet portrayed Caliban as a monstrous dark-skinned island native who was best suited for slavery. Shakespeare himself borrows words from Montaigne's essay "Of Cannibals," suggesting that he may have intended to criticize, rather than endorse, racial intolerance. Shakespeare's work shows us one of the finest minds of the age grasping to come to terms with the racial and religious complexities around him.

NOTES

1. Marco Polo, *The Book of Ser Marco Polo, the Venetian: Concerning the Kingdoms and Marvels of the East*, vol. 2, trans. and ed. Colonel Sir Henry Yule (London: John Murray, 1903), pp. 185–186.
2. Thomas Benjamin, *The Atlantic World: Europeans, Africans, Indians and Their Shared History, 1400–1900* (Cambridge: Cambridge University Press, 2009), p. 56.
3. Quoted in J. Devisse, "Africa in Inter-Continental Relations," in *General History of Africa*, vol. 4, *Africa from the Twelfth to the Sixteenth Century*, ed. D. T. Niane (Berkeley, Calif.: Heinemann Educational Books, 1984), p. 664.
4. Geoffrey Atkinson, *Les nouveaux horizons de la Renaissance française* (Paris: Droz, 1935), pp. 10–12.
5. G. V. Scammell, *The World Encompassed: The First European Maritime Empires, c. 800–1650* (Berkeley: University of California Press, 1981), p. 101.
6. Quoted in C. M. Cipolla, *Guns, Sails, and Empires: Technological Innovation and the Early Phases of European Expansion, 1400–1700* (New York: Minerva Press, 1965), p. 132.
7. Quoted in F. H. Littell, *The Macmillan Atlas: History of Christianity* (New York: Macmillan, 1976), p. 75.
8. Pablo E. Pérez-Mallaína, *Spain's Men of the Sea: Daily Life on the Indies Fleet in the Sixteenth Century* (Baltimore: Johns Hopkins University Press, 1998), p. 133.
9. Ibid., p. 19.
10. John Law, "On the Methods of Long Distance Control: Vessels, Navigation, and the Portuguese Route to India," in *Power, Action and Belief: A New Sociology of Knowledge?* ed. John Law, Sociological Review Monograph 32 (London: Routledge & Kegan Paul, 1986), pp. 234–263.
11. Quoted in F. Maddison, "Tradition and Innovation: Columbus' First Voyage and Portuguese Navigation in the Fifteenth Century," in *Circa 1492: Art in the Age of Exploration*, ed. J. A. Levenson (Washington, D.C.: National Gallery of Art, 1991), p. 69.
12. Quoted in R. L. Kagan, "The Spain of Ferdinand and Isabella," in *Circa 1492: Art in the Age of Exploration*, ed. J. A. Levenson (Washington, D.C.: National Gallery of Art, 1991), p. 60.
13. Peter Hulme, *Colonial Encounters: Europe and the Native Caribbean, 1492–1797* (London: Methuen, 1986), pp. 22–31.
14. Benjamin, *The Atlantic World*, p. 141.
15. Cited in Geoffrey Vaughn Scammell, *The First Imperial Age: European Overseas Expansion, c. 1400–1715* (London: Routledge, 2002), p. 62.
16. Ibid., p. 432.
17. Herbert S. Klein, "Profits and the Causes of Mortality," in *The Atlantic Slave Trade*, ed. David Northrup (Lexington, Mass.: D. C. Heath and Co., 1994), p. 116.

18. Malcolm Cowley and Daniel P. Mannix, "The Middle Passage," in *The Atlantic Slave Trade*, ed. David Northrup (Lexington, Mass.: D. C. Heath and Co., 1994), p. 101.

19. Voyages: The Trans-Atlantic Slave Trade Database, http://www.slavevoyages.org/tast/assessment/estimates.

20. David Carrasco, *The Oxford Encyclopedia of Mesoamerican Cultures* (Oxford: Oxford University Press, 2001), p. 208.

21. Quoted in C. Gibson, ed., *The Black Legend: Anti-Spanish Attitudes in the Old World and the New* (New York: Knopf, 1971), pp. 74–75.

22. Quoted in James H. Sweet, "The Iberian Roots of American Racist Thought," *The William and Mary Quarterly* 54 (1997): 155.

23. C. Cotton, trans., *The Essays of Michel de Montaigne* (New York: A. L. Burt, 1893), pp. 207, 210.

24. Ibid., p. 523.

LOOKING BACK LOOKING AHEAD

In 1517 Martin Luther issued his "Ninety-five Theses," launching the Protestant Reformation; just five years later, Ferdinand Magellan's expedition sailed around the globe, shattering European notions of terrestrial geography. Within a few short years, old medieval certainties about Heaven and earth began to collapse. In the ensuing decades, Europeans struggled to come to terms with religious difference at home and the multitudes of new peoples and places they encountered abroad. While some Europeans were fascinated and inspired by this new diversity, too often the result was violence. Europeans endured decades of civil war between Protestants and Catholics, and indigenous peoples suffered massive population losses as a result of European warfare, disease, and exploitation. Tragically, both Catholic and Protestant religious leaders condoned the African slave trade that brought suffering and death to millions of people.

Even as the voyages of discovery coincided with the fragmentation of European culture, they also played a role in longer-term processes of state centralization and consolidation. The new monarchies of the Renaissance produced stronger and wealthier governments capable of financing the huge expenses of exploration and colonization. Competition to gain overseas colonies became an integral part of European politics. Spain's investment in conquest proved spectacularly profitable and yet, as we will see in Chapter 15, the ultimate result was a weakening of its power. Over time the Netherlands, England, and France also reaped tremendous profits from colonial trade, which helped them build modernized, centralized states. The path from medieval Christendom to modern nation-states led through religious warfare and global encounter.

Make Connections

Think about the larger developments and continuities within and across chapters.

1. Michel de Montaigne argued that people's assessments of what was "barbaric" merely drew on their own habits and customs; based on the earlier sections of this chapter, how widespread was this openness to cultural difference? Was he alone or did others share this view?

2. To what extent did the European voyages of expansion and conquest inaugurate an era of global history? Is it correct to date the beginning of "globalization" from the late fifteenth century? Why or why not?

14 REVIEW & EXPLORE

Identify Key Terms

Identify and explain the significance of each item below.

conquistador (p. 433)

caravel (p. 433)

Ptolemy's *Geography* (p. 433)

Treaty of Tordesillas (p. 437)

Aztec Empire (p. 440)

Inca Empire (p. 441)

viceroyalties (p. 445)

encomienda system (p. 446)

Columbian exchange (p. 449)

"Black Legend" (p. 458)

Review the Main Ideas

Answer the focus questions from each section of the chapter.

◆ What was the Afroeurasian trading world prior to the era of European exploration? (p. 428)

◆ How and why did Europeans undertake ambitious voyages of expansion? (p. 432)

◆ How did European powers acquire colonies in the Americas, and how were they governed? (p. 440)

◆ How was the era of global contact shaped by new forms of exploitation, commercial exchange, and forced migration? (p. 446)

◆ How did new encounters shape cultural attitudes and beliefs in Europe and the rest of the world? (p. 456)

Suggested Reading and Media Resources

BOOKS

◆ Crosby, Alfred W. *The Columbian Exchange: Biological and Cultural Consequences of 1492*, 30th anniversary ed. 2003. An innovative and highly influential account of the environmental impact of the transatlantic movement of animals, plants, and microbes inaugurated by Columbus.

◆ Elliot, J. H. *Empires of the Atlantic World: Britain and Spain in America, 1492–1830*. 2006. A masterful comparative account of the British and Spanish Empires in the Americas.

◆ Fernández-Armesto, Felipe. *Columbus*. 1992. An excellent biography of Christopher Columbus.

◆ Games, Alison. *The Web of Empire: English Cosmopolitans in an Age of Empire, 1560–1660*. 2008. Explores England's successful challenge to Spanish domination of the Americas and the foundations of its empire in the East Indies.

◆ Mann, Charles C. *1491: New Revelations on the Americas Before Columbus*, 2d ed. 2011. A highly readable account of the peoples and societies of the Americas before the arrival of Europeans.

◆ Menard, Russell R. *Sweet Negotiations: Sugar, Slavery, and Plantation Agriculture in Early Barbados*. 2006. Explores the intertwined history of sugar plantations and slavery in seventeenth-century Barbados.

◆ Parker, Charles H. *Global Interactions in the Early Modern Age, 1400–1800*. 2010. An examination of the rise of global connections in the early modern period, which situates the European experience in relation to the world's other empires and peoples.

◆ Pomeranz, Kenneth, and Steven Topik. *The World That Trade Created: Society, Culture, and the World Economy, 1400 to the Present*. 1999. The creation of a world market presented through rich and vivid stories of merchants, miners, slaves, and farmers.

◆ Restall, Matthew. *Seven Myths of Spanish Conquest*. 2003. A re-examination of common misconceptions about why and how the Spanish conquered native civilizations in the New World.

- Rountree, Helen C. *Pocahontas, Powhatan, Opechanca-nough: Three Indian Lives Changed by Jamestown.* 2005. Biographies of three important Native Americans involved in the Jamestown settlement, presenting a rich portrait of the life of the Powhatan people and their encounter with the English.
- Subrahmanyam, Sanjay. *The Portuguese Empire in Asia, 1500–1700: A Political and Economic History,* 2d ed. 2012. A masterful study of the Portuguese overseas empire in Asia that draws on both European and Asian sources.

DOCUMENTARIES

- *America Before Columbus* (National Geographic, 2010). Explores the complex societies and cultures of North America before contact with Europeans and the impact of the Columbian exchange.
- *Conquistadors* (PBS, 2000). Traveling in the footsteps of the Spanish conquistadors, the narrator tells their story while following the paths and rivers they used. Includes discussion of the perspectives and participation of native peoples.
- *1421: The Year China Discovered America?* (PBS, 2004). Investigates the voyages of legendary Chinese admiral Zheng He, exploring the possibility that he and his fleet reached the Americas decades before Columbus.

FEATURE FILMS AND TELEVISION

- *Black Robe* (Bruce Beresford, 1991). A classic film about French Jesuit missionaries among Algonquin and Huron Indians in New France in the seventeenth century.
- *Marco Polo* (Hallmark Channel, 2007). A made-for-television film that follows Italian merchant Marco Polo as he travels to China to establish trade ties with Mongol emperor Kublai Khan.
- *The New World* (Terrence Malick, 2005). Set in 1607 at the founding of the Jamestown settlement, this film retells the story of John Smith and Pocahontas.

WEB SITES

- *The Globalization of Food and Plants.* Hosted by the Yale University Center for the Study of Globalization, this Web site provides information on how various foods and plants—such as spices, coffee, and tomatoes—traveled the world in the Columbian exchange. **yaleglobal.yale.edu/about/food.jsp**
- *Historic Jamestowne.* Showcasing archaeological work at the Jamestown settlement, the first permanent English settlement in America, this site provides details of the latest digs along with biographical information about settlers, historical background, and resources for teachers and students. **www.historicjamestowne.org**
- *Plymouth Colony Archive Project.* A site hosted by the anthropology department at the University of Illinois that contains a collection of searchable primary and secondary sources relating to the Plymouth colony, including court records, laws, seventeenth-century journals and memoirs, wills, maps, and biographies of colonists. **www.histarch.uiuc.edu/Plymouth/index .html**

15

Absolutism and Constitutionalism

ca. 1589–1725

The seventeenth century was a period of crisis and transformation in Europe. Agricultural and manufacturing slumps led to food shortages and shrinking population rates. Religious and dynastic conflicts led to almost constant war, visiting violence and destruction on ordinary people and reshaping European states. With Louis XIV of France taking the lead, armies grew larger than they had been since the time of the Roman Empire, resulting in new government bureaucracies and higher taxes. Yet even with these obstacles, European states succeeded in gathering more power, and by 1680 much of the unrest that originated with the Reformation was resolved.

These crises were not limited to western Europe. Central and eastern Europe experienced even more catastrophic dislocation, with German lands serving as the battleground of the Thirty Years' War and borders constantly vulnerable to attack from the east. In Prussia and in Habsburg Austria absolutist states emerged in the aftermath of this conflict. Russia and the Ottoman Turks also experienced turmoil in the midseventeenth century, but maintained their distinctive styles of absolutist government. The Russian and Ottoman Empires seemed foreign and exotic to western Europeans, who saw them as far removed from their political, religious, and cultural values.

While absolutism emerged as the solution to crisis in many European states, a small minority adopted a different path, placing sovereignty in the hands of privileged groups rather than the Crown. Historians refer to states where executive power was limited by law as "constitutional." The two most important seventeenth-century constitutionalist states were England and the Dutch Republic. Constitutionalism should not be confused with democracy. The elite rulers of England and the Dutch Republic pursued the same policies as absolute monarchs: increased taxation, government authority, and social control. Nonetheless, they served as influential models to onlookers across Europe as forms of government that checked the power of a single ruler. ■

CHAPTER PREVIEW

Life at the French Royal Court
King Louis XIV receives foreign ambassadors to celebrate a peace treaty. The king grandly occupied the center of his court, which in turn served as the pinnacle for the French people and, at the height of his glory, for all of Europe. (By Charles Le Brun [1619–1690], 1678/Museum of Fine Arts, Budapest, Hungary/Erich Lessing/Art Resource, NY)

Seventeenth-Century Crisis and Rebuilding

FOCUS QUESTION *What were the common crises and achievements of seventeenth-century European states?*

Historians often refer to the seventeenth century as an "age of crisis," when Europe was challenged by population losses, economic decline, and social and political unrest. These difficulties were partially due to climate changes that reduced agricultural productivity, but they also resulted from bitter religious divides, war, and increased governmental pressures. Peasants and the urban poor were hit especially hard by the economic problems, and they frequently rose in riot against high food prices.

The atmosphere of crisis encouraged governments to take emergency measures to restore order, measures that they successfully turned into long-term reforms that strengthened the power of the state. These included a spectacular growth in army size as well as increased taxation, the expansion of government bureaucracies, and the acquisition of land or maritime empires. In the long run, European states proved increasingly able to impose their will on the populace.

The Social Order and Peasant Life

Peasants occupied the lower tiers of a society organized in hierarchical levels. At the top, the monarch was celebrated as a semidivine being, chosen by God to embody the state. In Catholic countries, the clergy occupied the second level, due to their sacred role interceding with God and the saints on behalf of their flocks. Next came nobles, whose privileged status derived from their ancient bloodlines and centuries of leadership on the battlefield. Traditional Christian prejudices against commerce and money meant that merchants could never lay claim to the highest honors. However, many prosperous mercantile families had bought their way into the nobility through service to the rising monarchies of the fifteenth and sixteenth centuries and constituted a second tier of nobles. Those lower on the social scale, the peasants and artisans who constituted the vast majority of the population, were expected to defer to their betters with humble obedience. This was the "Great Chain of Being" that linked God to his creation in a series of ranked social groups.

In addition to being rigidly hierarchical, European societies were patriarchal in nature, with men assuming authority over women as a God-given prerogative. The family thus represented a microcosm of the social order. The father ruled his family like a king ruled his domains. Religious and secular law commanded a man's wife, children, servants, and apprentices to defer to his will. Fathers did not possess the power of life and death, like Roman patriarchs, but they were entitled to use physical violence, imprisonment, and other forceful measures to impose their authority. These powers were balanced by expectations that a good father would provide and care for his dependents.

In the seventeenth century most Europeans lived in the countryside. The hub of the rural world was the small peasant village centered on a church and a manor. Life was in many ways circumscribed by the village,

Peasants Working the Land
Working the land was harsh toil for seventeenth-century peasants, but strong family and community bonds gave life meaning and made survival possible. The rich and colorful clothing of the peasants shown here reflects an idealized vision of the peasants' material circumstances.
(*The Month of March*, by the Studio of Pieter de Witte [ca. 1548–1628], [oil on canvas], undated/ © Sotheby's/akg-images)

although we should not underestimate the mobility induced by war, food shortage, and the desire to seek one's fortune or embark on religious pilgrimage.

In western Europe, a small number of peasants in each village owned enough land to feed themselves and had the livestock and plows necessary to work their land. These independent farmers were leaders of the peasant village. They employed the landless poor, rented out livestock and tools, and served as agents for the noble lord. Below them were small landowners and tenant farmers who did not have enough land to be self-sufficient. These families sold their best produce on the market to earn cash for taxes, rent, and food. At the bottom were villagers who worked as dependent laborers and servants. In eastern Europe, the vast majority of peasants toiled as serfs for noble landowners and did not own land in their own right (see page 481).

Rich or poor, east or west, bread was the primary element of the diet. The richest ate a white loaf, leaving brown bread to those who could not afford better. Peasants paid stiff fees to the local miller for grinding grain into flour and sometimes to the lord for the right to bake bread in his oven. Bread was most often accompanied by a soup made of roots, herbs, beans, and perhaps a small piece of salt pork. An important annual festival in many villages was the killing of the family pig. The whole family gathered to help, sharing a rare abundance of meat with neighbors and carefully salting the extra and putting down the lard. In some areas, menstruating women were careful to stay away from the kitchen because of superstitious fears that they would cause the lard to spoil.

Famine and Economic Crisis

European rural society lived on the edge of subsistence. Because of the crude technology and low crop yield, peasants were constantly threatened by scarcity and famine. In the seventeenth century a period of colder and wetter climate throughout Europe, dubbed the "little ice age" by historians, meant a shorter farming season with lower yields. A bad harvest created food shortages; a series of bad harvests could lead to famine. Recurrent famines significantly reduced the population of early modern Europe. Most people did not die of outright starvation but perished through the spread of diseases like smallpox and typhoid, which

Chronology

ca. 1500–1650	Consolidation of serfdom in eastern Europe
1533–1584	Reign of Ivan the Terrible in Russia
1589–1610	Reign of Henry IV in France
1598–1613	Time of Troubles in Russia
1620–1740	Growth of absolutism in Austria and Prussia
1642–1649	English civil war, which ends with execution of Charles I
1643–1715	Reign of Louis XIV in France
1653–1658	Military rule in England under Oliver Cromwell (the Protectorate)
1660	Restoration of English monarchy under Charles II
1665–1683	Jean-Baptiste Colbert applies mercantilism to France
1670	Charles II agrees to re-Catholicize England In secret agreement with Louis XIV
1670–1671	Cossack revolt led by Stenka Razin
ca. 1680–1750	Construction of absolutist palaces
1682	Louis XIV moves court to Versailles
1682–1725	Reign of Peter the Great in Russia
1683–1718	Habsburgs push the Ottoman Turks from Hungary
1685	Edict of Nantes revoked in France
1688–1689	Glorious Revolution in England
1701–1713	War of the Spanish Succession

were facilitated by malnutrition and exhaustion. Outbreaks of bubonic plague continued in Europe until the 1720s.

The Estates of Normandy, a provincial assembly, reported on the dire conditions in northern France during an outbreak of plague:

Of the 450 sick persons whom the inhabitants were unable to relieve, 200 were turned out, and these we saw die one by one as they lay on the roadside. A large number still remain, and to each of them it is only possible to dole out the least scrap of bread. We only give bread to those who would otherwise die. The staple dish here consists of mice, which the inhabitants hunt, so desperate are they from hunger. They devour roots which the animals cannot eat; one can, in fact, not put into words the things one sees. . . . We certify to having ourselves seen herds, not of cattle, but of men and women, wandering about the fields between Rheims and Rhétel, turning up the earth like pigs to find a few roots; and as they can only find rotten ones, and not half enough of them, they become so weak that they have not strength left to seek food.[1]

Industry also suffered. The output of woolen textiles, one of the most important European manufactures, declined sharply in the first half of the seventeenth century. Food prices were high, wages stagnated, and unemployment soared. This economic crisis was not universal: it struck various regions at different times and to different degrees. In the middle decades of the century, for example, Spain, France, Germany, and England all experienced great economic difficulties, but these years were the golden age of the Netherlands.

The urban poor and peasants were the hardest hit. When the price of bread rose beyond their capacity to pay, they frequently expressed their anger by rioting. In towns they invaded bakers' shops to seize bread and resell it at a "just price." In rural areas they attacked convoys taking grain to the cities. Women often led these actions, since their role as mothers gave them some impunity in authorities' eyes. Historians have used the term "moral economy" for this vision of a world in which community needs predominate over competition and profit.

The Thirty Years' War

Harsh economic conditions in the seventeenth century were greatly exacerbated by the decades-long conflict known as the Thirty Years' War (1618–1648). The Holy Roman Empire was a confederation of hundreds of principalities, independent cities, duchies, and other polities loosely united under an elected emperor. The uneasy truce between Catholics and Protestants created by the Peace of Augsburg in 1555 deteriorated as the faiths of various areas shifted. Lutheran princes felt compelled to form the Protestant Union (1608), and Catholics retaliated with the Catholic League (1609). Each alliance was determined that the other should make no religious or territorial advance. Dynastic interests were also involved; the Spanish Habsburgs strongly supported the goals of their Austrian relatives: the unity of the empire and the preservation of Catholicism within it.

The war is traditionally divided into four phases. The first, or Bohemian, phase (1618–1625) was characterized by civil war in Bohemia between the Catholic League and the Protestant Union. In 1620 Catholic forces defeated Protestants at the Battle of the White Mountain. The second, or Danish, phase of the war (1625–1629)—so called because of the leadership of the Protestant king Christian IV of Denmark (r. 1588–1648)—witnessed additional Catholic victories. The Catholic imperial army led by Albert of Wallenstein swept through Silesia, north to the Baltic, and east into Pomerania, scoring smashing victories. Under Charles I, England briefly and unsuccessfully

intervened in this phase of the conflict by entering alliances against France and Spain. Habsburg power peaked in 1629. The emperor issued the Edict of Restitution, whereby all Catholic properties lost to Protestantism since 1552 were restored, and only Catholics and Lutherans were allowed to practice their faiths.

The third, or Swedish, phase of the war (1630–1635) began with the arrival in Germany of the Swedish king Gustavus Adolphus (r. 1594–1632) and his army. The ablest administrator of his day and a devout Lutheran, he intervened to support the empire's Protestants. The French chief minister, Cardinal Richelieu, subsidized the Swedes, hoping to weaken Habsburg power in Europe. Gustavus Adolphus won two important battles but was fatally wounded in combat. The final, or French, phase of the war (1635–1648) was prompted by Richelieu's concern that the Habsburgs would rebound after the death of Gustavus Adolphus. Richelieu declared war on Spain and sent military as well as financial assistance. Finally, in October 1648 peace was achieved.

The 1648 **Peace of Westphalia** that ended the Thirty Years' War marked a turning point in European history. For the most part, conflicts fought over religious faith receded. The treaties recognized the independent authority of more than three hundred German princes (Map 15.1), reconfirming the emperor's severely limited authority. The Augsburg agreement of 1555 became permanent, adding Calvinism to Catholicism and Lutheranism as legally permissible creeds. The north German states remained Protestant, the south German states Catholic.

The Thirty Years' War was the most destructive event for the central European economy and society prior to the world wars of the twentieth century. Perhaps one-third of urban residents and two-fifths of the rural population died, leaving entire areas depopulated. Trade in southern German cities, such as Augsburg, was virtually destroyed. Agricultural areas suffered catastrophically. Many small farmers lost their land, allowing nobles to enlarge their estates and consolidate their control.[2]

Achievements in State-Building

In the context of warfare, economic crisis, and demographic decline, seventeenth-century monarchs took urgent measures to restore order and rebuild their states. Traditionally, historians have distinguished between the absolutist governments of France, Spain, central Europe, and Russia and the constitutionalist governments of England and the Dutch Republic. Whereas absolutist monarchs gathered all power under their personal control, English and Dutch rulers were obliged to respect laws passed by representative institutions. More recently, historians have emphasized commonalities among these powers. Despite their political differences, all these

■ **Peace of Westphalia** The name of a series of treaties that concluded the Thirty Years' War in 1648 and marked the end of large-scale religious violence in Europe.

MAP 15.1 Europe After the Thirty Years' War This map shows the political division of Europe after the Treaty of Westphalia (1648) ended the war. France emerged as the strongest power in Europe at the end of the Thirty Years' War. Based on this map, what challenges did the French state still face in dominating Europe after 1648? How does the map represent Swedish gains and Spanish losses in the Treaty of Westphalia?

states shared common projects of protecting and expanding their frontiers, raising new taxes, consolidating central control, and competing for the new colonies opening up in the New and Old Worlds. In so doing, they followed a broad pattern of state-building and consolidation of power found across Eurasia in this period.

Rulers encountered formidable obstacles in achieving these goals. Without paved roads, telephones, or other modern technology, it took weeks to convey orders from the central government to the provinces and even longer to distant colonies. Rulers also suffered from lack of reliable information about their realms, making it impossible to police and tax the population effectively. Local power structures presented another serious obstacle. Nobles, the church, provincial and national assemblies, town councils, guilds, and other bodies held legal privileges, which could not easily be rescinded. Many kingdoms were composed of groups of people of different ethnicities who spoke a language different from that of the ruling dynasty, which further diminished their willingness to obey.

Nonetheless, over the course of the seventeenth century both absolutist and constitutional governments achieved new levels of power and national unity.

They did so by transforming emergency measures of wartime into permanent structures of government and by subduing privileged groups through the use of force and through economic and social incentives. Increased state authority may be seen in four areas in particular: greater taxation, growth in armed forces, larger and more efficient bureaucracies, and territorial expansion both within Europe and overseas.

Over time, centralized power added up to something close to sovereignty. A state may be termed sovereign when it possesses a monopoly over the instruments of justice and the use of force within clearly defined boundaries. In a sovereign state, no system of courts, such as church tribunals, competes with state courts in the dispensation of justice; and private armies, such as those of feudal lords, present no threat to central authority. While seventeenth-century states did not acquire total sovereignty, they made important strides toward that goal.

Warfare and the Growth of Army Size

The driving force of seventeenth-century state-building was warfare. In medieval times, feudal lords had raised armies only for particular wars or campaigns; now monarchs began to recruit their own forces and maintain permanent standing armies. Instead of serving their own interests, army officers were required to be loyal and obedient to state officials. New techniques for training and deploying soldiers meant a rise in the professional standards of the army.

Along with professionalization came an explosive growth in army size. The French took the lead, with the army growing from roughly 125,000 men in the Thirty Years' War to 340,000 at the end of the seventeenth century.[3] Changes in the style of armies encouraged this growth. Mustering a royal army took longer than simply hiring a mercenary band, giving enemies time to form coalitions. For example, the large coalitions Louis XIV confronted (see pages 478–479) required him to fight on multiple fronts with huge armies. In turn, the relative size and wealth of France among European nations allowed Louis to field enormous armies and thereby to pursue the ambitious foreign policies that caused his alarmed neighbors to form coalitions against him.

Noble values of glory and honor outshone concerns for safety or material benefit. Because they personally led their men in battle, noble officers experienced high death rates on the battlefield. Nobles also fell into debt because they had to purchase their positions in the army and the units they commanded, which meant that they were obliged to assume many of the costs involved in creating and maintaining their units. It was not until the 1760s that the French government assumed the full cost of equipping troops.

The Professionalization of the Swedish Army Swedish king Gustavus Adolphus, surrounded by his generals, gives thanks to God for the safe arrival of his troops in Germany during the Thirty Years' War. A renowned military leader, the king imposed constant training drills and rigorous discipline on his troops, which contributed to their remarkable success in the war. (Military Academy of Karlberg)

Other European powers were quick to follow the French example. The rise of absolutism in central and eastern Europe was thus accompanied by a vast expansion in the size of armies. Great Britain followed a similar, albeit distinctive pattern. Instead of building a land army, the island nation focused on naval forces and eventually built the largest navy in the world.

Popular Political Action

As governments continuously raised taxes to meet the costs of war, neighborhood riots over the cost of bread turned into armed uprisings. Popular revolts were extremely common in England, France, Spain, Portugal, and Italy during the Thirty Years' War. In 1640 Philip IV of Spain faced revolt in Catalonia, the economic center of his realm. At the same time he struggled to put down uprisings in Portugal and in the northern provinces of the Netherlands. In 1647 the city of Palermo, in Spanish-occupied Sicily, exploded in protest over food shortages caused by a series of bad harvests. Fearing public unrest, the city government subsidized the price of bread, attracting even more starving peasants from the countryside. When Madrid ordered an end to subsidies, municipal leaders decided to lighten the loaf rather than raise prices. Not fooled by this change, local women led a bread riot, shouting "Long live the king and down with the taxes and the bad government!" Insurgency spread to the rest of the island and eventually to Naples on the mainland. Apart from affordable food, rebels demanded the suppression of extraordinary taxes and participation in municipal government. Some dreamed of a republic that would abolish noble tax exemptions. Despite initial successes, the revolt lacked unity and strong leadership and could not withstand the forces of the state.

In France urban uprisings became a frequent aspect of the social and political landscape. Beginning in 1630 and continuing intermittently through the early 1700s, major insurrections occurred at Dijon, Bordeaux (bor-DOH), Montpellier, Lyons, and Amiens. All were characterized by deep popular anger and violence directed at outside officials sent to collect taxes. These officials were sometimes seized, beaten, and hacked to death. For example, in 1673 Louis XIV's imposition of new taxes on legal transactions, tobacco, and pewter ware provoked an uprising in Bordeaux.

Municipal and royal authorities often struggled to overcome popular revolt. They feared that stern repressive measures, such as sending in troops to fire on crowds, would create martyrs and further inflame the situation, while full-scale occupation of a city would be very expensive and detract from military efforts elsewhere. The limitations of royal authority gave some leverage to rebels. To quell riots, royal edicts were sometimes suspended, prisoners released, and discussions initiated.

By the beginning of the eighteenth century this leverage had largely disappeared. Municipal governments were better integrated into the national structure, and local authorities had prompt military support from the central government. People who publicly opposed royal policies and taxes received swift and severe punishment.

Absolutism in France and Spain

FOCUS QUESTION *What factors led to the rise of the French absolutist state under Louis XIV, and why did absolutist Spain experience decline in the same period?*

In the Middle Ages jurists held that as a consequence of monarchs' coronation and anointment with sacred oil, they ruled "by the grace of God." Law was given by God; kings "found" the law and acknowledged that they must respect and obey it. Kings in absolutist states amplified these claims, asserting that they were responsible to God alone. They claimed exclusive power to make and enforce laws, denying any other institution or group the authority to check their power. In France the founder of the Bourbon monarchy, Henry IV, established foundations upon which his successors Louis XIII and Louis XIV built a stronger, more centralized French state. Louis XIV is often seen as the epitome of an "absolute" monarch, with his endless wars, increased taxes and economic regulation, and glorious palace at Versailles. In truth, his success relied on collaboration with nobles, and thus his example illustrates both the achievements and the compromises of absolutist rule.

As French power rose in the seventeenth century, the glory of Spain faded. Once the fabulous revenue from American silver declined, Spain's economic stagnation could no longer be disguised, and the country faltered under weak leadership.

The Foundations of French Absolutism

At the beginning of the seventeenth century France's position appeared extremely weak. Struggling to recover from decades of religious civil war, France posed little threat to Spain's predominance in Europe. Yet by the end of the century the countries' positions were reversed.

Henry IV (r. 1589–1610) inaugurated a remarkable recovery by defusing religious tensions and rebuilding France's economy. He issued the Edict of Nantes, allowing

What Was Absolutism?

Historians have long debated the nature of "absolutism" in seventeenth-century Europe. While many historians have emphasized the growth of state power in this period, especially under Louis XIV of France, others have questioned whether such a thing as "absolutism" ever existed. The following documents will allow you to draw your own conclusions about absolutism.

1 **Jacques-Bénigne Bossuet, political treatise, 1709.** In 1670 Louis XIV appointed Bishop Bossuet tutor to his son and heir, known as the dauphin. In *Politics Drawn from the Very Words of Holy Scripture,* Bossuet argued that royal power was divine and absolute, but not without limits.

It appears from all this that the person of the king is sacred, and that to attack him in any way is sacrilege. God has the kings anointed by his prophets with the holy unction in like manner as he has bishops and altars anointed. But even without the external application in thus being anointed, they are by their very office the representatives of the divine majesty deputed by Providence for the execution of his purposes. Accordingly God calls Cyrus his anointed. "Thus saith the Lord to his anointed, to Cyrus, whose right hand I have holden, to subdue nations before him." Kings should be guarded as holy things, and whosoever neglects to protect them is worthy of death. ...There is something religious in the respect accorded to a prince. The service of God and the respect for kings are bound together. St. Peter unites these two duties when he says, "Fear God. Honour the king."...But kings, although their power comes from on high, as has been said, should not regard themselves as masters of that power to use it at their pleasure;...they must employ it with fear and self-restraint, as a thing coming from God and of which God will demand an account.

2 **Letter of the prince of Condé, royal governor of the province of Burgundy, to Controller General Jean-Baptiste Colbert, June 18, 1662.** In this letter, the king's representative in the province of Burgundy reports on his efforts to compel the leaders of the province to pay taxes levied by the royal government. The Estates of Burgundy comprised representatives of the three orders, or estates, of society: the clergy, the nobility, and the commoners.

Since then the Estates have deliberated every day, persuaded that the extreme misery in this province—caused by the great levies it has suffered, the sterility [of the land] in recent years, and the disorders that have recently occurred—would induce the king to give them some relief. That is why they offered only 500,000 for the free gift. Then, after I had protested this in the appropriate manner, they raised it to 600,000, then 800,000, and finally 900,000 livres. Until then I had stood firm at 1.5 million, but when I saw that they were on the verge of deciding not to give any more...I finally came down to the 1.2 million livres contained in my instructions and invited them to deliberate again, declaring that I could not agree to present any other proposition to the king and that I believed that there was no better way to serve their interests than to obey the king blindly. They agreed with good grace and came this morning to offer me a million. They begged me to leave it at that and not to demand more from them for the free gift; and since I told them they would have to do a little better to satisfy the king completely on this occasion, they again exaggerated their poverty and begged me to inform the king of it, but said that, rather than not please him, they preferred to make a new effort, and they would leave it up to me to declare what they had to do. I told them that I believed His Majesty would have the goodness to be satisfied with 1.05 million livres for the free gift, and they agreed.... So Monsieur, there is the deed done.

ANALYZING THE EVIDENCE

1. What elements of royal authority does the portrait of Louis XIV in Source 4 present to viewers? How would you compare this depiction of political power with images from modern-day politicians? How would you explain the differences?
2. What justification do the sources offer for Louis's claim to exercise "absolute" political authority? Based on his own words in Source 3, how do you think Louis would have viewed the constitutional governments of England and the Dutch Republic?
3. Compare and contrast the evidence for Louis's power given in these sources with evidence for limitations on it. What resources would a king have to muster to enlarge his army drastically (Source 5)? What insight do the negotiations over taxation (Source 2) give you into the ways the royal government acquired those resources?

3 Louis XIV, *Memoir for the Instruction of the Dauphin.*

In 1670 Louis XIV finished a memoir he had compiled for the education of his son and heir. Presented in the king's voice — although cowritten with several royal aides — the memoir recounts the early years of Louis's reign and explains his approach to absolute rule.

For however it be held as a maxim that in every thing a Prince should employ the most mild measures and first, and that it is more to his advantage to govern his subjects by persuasive than coercive means, it is nevertheless certain that whenever he meets with impediments or rebellion, the interest of his crown and the welfare of his people demand that he should cause himself to be indispensably obeyed; for it must be acknowledged there is nothing can so securely establish the happiness and tranquility of a country as the perfect combination of all authority in the single person of the Sovereign. The least division in this respect often produces the greatest calamities; and whether it be detached into the hands of individuals or those of corporate bodies, it always is there in a state of fermentation.

... [B]esides the insurrections and the intestine commotions which the ambition of power infallibly produces when it is not repressed, there are still a thousand other evils created by the inactivity of the Sovereign. Those who are nearest his person are the first to observe his weakness, and are also the first who are desirous of profiting by it. Every one of those persons have necessarily others who are subservient to their avaricious views, and to whom they at the same time give the privilege of imitating them. Thus, from the highest to the lowest is a systematic corruption communicated, and it becomes general in all classes.

(*Louis XIV in Royal Costume*, 1701, by Hyacinthe François Rigaud [1659–1743] [oil on canvas])/Musée du Louvre, Paris, France/Bridgeman Images)

4 Hyacinthe Rigaud, portrait of Louis XIV, 1701.

This was one of Louis XIV's favorite portraits of himself. He liked it so much that he had many copies of the portrait made; his successors had their own portraits painted in the same posture with the same clothing and accoutrements.

5 Growth of the French Army.

Time Period	Size of Army
Middle Ages	10,000 men
1635 (Louis XIII and Richelieu enter Thirty Years' War)	125,000 men
1670s (Louis XIV wages Dutch War)	280,000 men
1690s (Louis XIV wages Nine Years' War)	340,000 men

PUTTING IT ALL TOGETHER

Using the sources above, along with what you have learned in class and in this chapter, what was "absolutism"? Write a brief essay explaining what contemporaries thought absolute power entailed and the extent to which Louis XIV achieved such power.

Sources: (1) J. H. Robinson, ed., *Readings in European History*, vol. 2 (Boston: Ginn, 1906), p. 274; (2) William Beik, ed., *Louis XIV and Absolutism: A Brief Study with Documents* (Boston: Bedford/St. Martin's, 2000), pp. 127–128; (3) *Memoirs of Lewis the Fourteenth, Written by Himself, and Addressed to His Son*, vol. 1 (London: Longman, Hurst, Rees and Orme, 1806), pp. 13–14; (5) Based on information from John A. Lynn, *The Wars of Louis XIV, 1667–1714* (London: Routledge, 2013), pp. 5–51.

Huguenots (French Protestants) the right to worship in 150 traditionally Protestant towns throughout France. He built new roads and canals to repair the ravages of years of civil war and raised revenue by selling royal offices instead of charging high taxes. Despite his efforts at peace, Henry was murdered in 1610 by a Catholic zealot.

Cardinal Richelieu (1585–1642) became first minister of the French crown on behalf of Henry's young son, Louis XIII (r. 1610–1643). Richelieu's domestic policies were designed to strengthen royal control. He acted to repress Protestantism, which he viewed as a divisive force in the realm. He also extended the use of intendants, commissioners for each of France's thirty-two districts who were appointed directly by the monarch, to whom they were solely responsible. These officials recruited men for the army, supervised tax collection, presided over the administration of local law, checked up on the local nobility, and regulated economic activities in their districts. As the intendants' power increased under Richelieu, so did the power of the centralized French state.

Richelieu's main foreign policy goal was to destroy the Habsburgs' grip on territories that surrounded France. Consequently, Richelieu supported Habsburg enemies, including Protestants during the Thirty Years' War (see page 468). For the French cardinal, interests of state outweighed religious considerations.

Cardinal Jules Mazarin (1602–1661) succeeded Richelieu as chief minister for the next child-king, the four-year-old Louis XIV, who inherited the throne from his father in 1643. Along with the regent, Queen Mother Anne of Austria, Mazarin continued Richelieu's centralizing policies. His struggle to increase royal revenues to meet the costs of war led to the uprisings of 1648–1653 known as the **Fronde**. In Paris, magistrates of the Parlement of Paris, the nation's most important law court, were outraged by the Crown's autocratic measures. These so-called robe nobles (named for the robes they wore in court) encouraged violent protest by the common people. As rebellion spread outside Paris and to the sword nobles (the traditional warrior nobility), civil order broke down completely, and young Louis XIV had to flee Paris for his safety.

Much of the rebellion died away, however, when Louis XIV was declared king in his own right in 1651, ending the regency of his mother Anne of Austria. (French law prohibited a woman from inheriting the throne, so periods when a queen mother acted as regent for a child-king were always vulnerable moments.) The French people were desperate for peace and stability after the disorders of the Fronde and were willing to accept a strong monarch who could reimpose order. Louis pledged to do just that when he assumed personal rule of his realm at Mazarin's death in 1661.

Louis XIV and Absolutism

In the reign of Louis XIV (r. 1643–1715), the longest in European history, the French monarchy reached the peak of absolutist development. Louis believed in the doctrine of the divine right of kings: God had established kings as his rulers on earth, and they were answerable ultimately to him alone. To symbolize his central role in the divine order, when he was fifteen years old Louis danced at a court ballet dressed as the sun, thereby acquiring the title "Sun King."

In addition to parading his power before the court, Louis worked very hard at the business of governing. He ruled his realm through several councils of state and insisted on taking a personal role in many of their decisions. He selected councilors from the recently ennobled or the upper middle class and offered this explanation: "[T]he public should know, from the rank of those whom I chose to serve me, that I had no intention of sharing power with them."[4] Despite increasing financial problems, Louis never called a meeting of the Estates General, thereby depriving nobles of united expression or action. Nor did Louis have a first minister. In this way he avoided the inordinate power of a Richelieu.

Although personally tolerant, Louis hated division within the realm and insisted that religious unity was essential to his royal dignity and to the security of the state. He thus pursued the policy of Protestant repression launched by Richelieu. In 1685 Louis revoked the Edict of Nantes. The new law ordered the Catholic baptism of Huguenots (French Calvinists), the destruction of Huguenot churches, the closing of schools, and the exile of Huguenot pastors who refused to renounce their faith. Around two hundred thousand Protestants, including some of the king's most highly skilled artisans, fled into exile.

Despite his claims to absolute authority, multiple constraints existed on Louis's power. As a representative of divine power, he was obliged to rule in a manner consistent with virtue and benevolence. (See "Thinking Like a Historian: What Was Absolutism?" page 472.) He had to uphold the laws issued by his royal predecessors. Moreover, he also relied on the collaboration of nobles, who maintained tremendous prestige and authority in their ancestral lands. Without their cooperation, it would have been impossible to extend his power throughout France or wage his many foreign wars. Louis's efforts to elicit noble cooperation can be witnessed in the court life he created at his spectacular palace at Versailles.

Life at Versailles

Through most of the seventeenth century the French court had no fixed home, following the monarch to his

■ **Fronde** A series of violent uprisings during the early reign of Louis XIV triggered by growing royal control and increased taxation.

Letter from Versailles

Born in 1652, the German princess Elisabeth-Charlotte was the daughter of the elector of the Palatinate, one of the many small states of the Holy Roman Empire. In 1671 she married the duke of Orléans, brother of Louis XIV. When Louis's wife died in 1683, Elisabeth-Charlotte became the highest-ranked woman at the French court. Despite the considerable pride she took in her position, her correspondence reveals her unhappiness and boredom with court life and her longing for home, as shown in the letter to her sister excerpted below.

I have nothing new to tell you; I walk and read and write; sometimes the king drives me to the hunt in his calèche. There are hunts every day; Sundays and Wednesdays are my son's days; the king hunts Mondays and Thursdays; Wednesdays and Saturdays Monseigneur [heir to the throne] hunts the wolf; M. le Comte de Toulouse, Mondays and Wednesdays; the Duc du Maine, Tuesdays; and M. le Duc, Fridays. They say if all the hunting kennels were united there would be from 900 to 1000 dogs. Twice a week there is a comedy. But you know, of course, that I go nowhere [due to mourning for her recently deceased husband]; which vexes me, for I must own that the theatre is the greatest amusement I have in the world, and the only pleasure that remains to me. . . .

If the Court of France was what it used to be one might learn here how to behave in society; but — excepting the king and Monsieur [the king's brother, her deceased husband] — no one any longer knows what politeness is.

The young men think only of horrible debauchery. I do not advise any one to send their children here; for instead of learning good things, they will only take lessons in misconduct. You are right in blaming Germans who send their sons to France; how I wish that you and I were men and could go to the wars! — but that's a completely useless wish to have. . . . If I could with propriety return to Germany you would see me there quickly. I love that country; I think it more agreeable than all others, because there is less of luxury that I do not care for, and more of the frankness and integrity which I seek. But, be it said between ourselves, I was placed here against my will, and here I must stay till I die. There is no likelihood that we shall see each other again in this life; and what will become of us after that God only knows.

EVALUATE THE EVIDENCE

1. What are the principal amusements of court life, according to Elisabeth-Charlotte? What comparison does she draw between life in Germany and France?

2. How does the image of Versailles conveyed by Elisabeth-Charlotte contrast with the images of the palace found elsewhere in this chapter? How do you explain this contrast? If courtiers like her found life so dreary at court, why would they stay?

Source: The Correspondence of Madame, Princess Palatine, Marie-Adélaïde de Savoie, and Madame de Maintenon, ed. and trans. Katharine Prescott Wormeley (Boston: Hardy, Pratt, 1902), pp. 50–52.

numerous palaces and country residences. In 1682 Louis moved his court and government to the newly renovated palace at Versailles, a former hunting lodge. The palace quickly became the center of political, social, and cultural life. The king required all great nobles to spend at least part of the year in attendance on him there, so he could keep an eye on their activities. Since he controlled the distribution of state power and wealth, nobles had no choice but to obey and compete with each other for his favor at Versailles.

The glorious palace, with its sumptuous interiors and extensive formal gardens, was a mirror to the world of French glory, soon copied by would-be absolutist monarchs across Europe. (See "Living in the Past: The Absolutist Palace," page 476.) The reality of daily life in the palace was less glamorous. Versailles served as government offices for royal bureaucrats, as living quarters for the royal family and nobles, and as a place of work for hundreds of domestic servants. It

was also open to the public at certain hours of the day. As a result, it was crowded with three thousand to ten thousand people every day. Even high nobles had to put up with cramped living space, and many visitors complained of the noise, smell, and crowds. (See "Evaluating the Evidence 15.1: Letter from Versailles," above.)

Louis further revolutionized court life by establishing an elaborate set of etiquette rituals to mark every moment of his day, from waking up and dressing in the morning to removing his clothing and retiring at night. Courtiers vied for the honor of participating in these ceremonies, with the highest in rank claiming the privilege of handing the king his shirt. Endless squabbles broke out over what type of chair one could sit on at court and the order in which great nobles entered and were seated in the chapel for Mass.

These rituals may seem absurd, but they were far from trivial. The king controlled immense resources

LIVING IN THE PAST
The Absolutist Palace

By 1700 palace building had become a veritable obsession for European rulers. Their dramatic palaces symbolized the age of absolutist power, just as soaring Gothic cathedrals had expressed the idealized spirit of the High Middle Ages. With its classically harmonious, symmetrical, and geometric design, Versailles served as the model for the wave of palace building that began in the last decade of the seventeenth century. Royal palaces like Versailles were intended to overawe the people and proclaim their owners' authority and power.

Located ten miles southwest of Paris, Versailles began as a modest hunting lodge built by Louis XIII in 1623. His son Louis XIV spent decades enlarging and decorating the original structure. Between 1668 and 1670 architect Louis Le Vau (luh VOH) enveloped the old building within a much larger one that still exists today. In 1682 the new palace became the official residence of the Sun King and his court, although construction continued until 1710, when the royal chapel was completed. At any one time, several thousand people occupied the bustling and crowded palace. The awesome splendor of the eighty-yard Hall of Mirrors, replete with floor-to-ceiling mirrors and ceiling murals illustrating the king's triumphs, contrasted with the strong odors from the courtiers who commonly relieved themselves in discreet corners.

In 1693 Charles XI of Sweden, having reduced the power of the aristocracy, ordered the construction of his Royal Palace, which dominates the center of Stockholm to this day. Another such palace was Schönbrunn, an enormous Viennese Versailles begun in 1695 by Emperor Leopold to celebrate Austrian military victories and Habsburg might. Shown at lower right is architect Joseph Bernhard Fischer von Erlach's ambitious plan for Schönbrunn palace. Fischer's plan emphasizes the palace's vast size and its role as a site for military demonstrations. Ultimately, financial constraints resulted in a more modest building.

In central and eastern Europe the favorite noble servants of royalty became extremely rich and powerful, and they, too, built grandiose palaces in the capital cities. These palaces were in part an extension of the monarch, for they surpassed the buildings of less-favored nobles and showed all the high road to fame and fortune. Take, for example, the palaces of Prince Eugene of Savoy, a French nobleman who became Austria's most famous military hero. It was Eugene who led the Austrian army, smashed the Turks, fought Louis XIV to a standstill, and generally guided the triumph of absolutism in Austria. Rewarded with

Prince Eugene's Summer Palace in Vienna. (Erich Lessing/Art Resource, NY)

and privileges; access to him meant favored treatment for government offices, military and religious posts, state pensions, honorary titles, and a host of other benefits. Courtiers sought these rewards for themselves and their family members and followers. A system of patronage—in which a higher-ranked individual protected a lower-ranked one in return for loyalty and services—flowed from the court to the provinces. Through this mechanism Louis gained cooperation from powerful nobles.

Although they could not hold public offices or posts, women played a central role in the patronage system. At court the king's wife, mistresses, and other female relatives recommended individuals for honors,

great wealth by his grateful king, Eugene called on the leading architects of the day, Fischer von Erlach and Johann Lukas von Hildebrandt, to consecrate his glory in stone and fresco. Fischer built Eugene's Winter (or Town) Palace in Vienna, and he and Hildebrandt collaborated on the prince's Summer Palace on the city's outskirts. The prince's summer residence featured two baroque gems, the Lower Belvedere and the Upper Belvedere, completed in 1722 and shown at left. The building's interior is equally stunning, with crouching giants serving as pillars and a magnificent great staircase.

QUESTIONS FOR ANALYSIS

1. Compare these images. What did concrete objects and the manipulation of space accomplish for these rulers that mere words could not?
2. What disadvantages might stem from using architecture as a political tool?
3. Is the use of space and monumental architecture still a political tool in today's world?

Louis XIV leading a tour of the extensive grounds at Versailles. (Château de Versailles, France/Bridgeman Images)

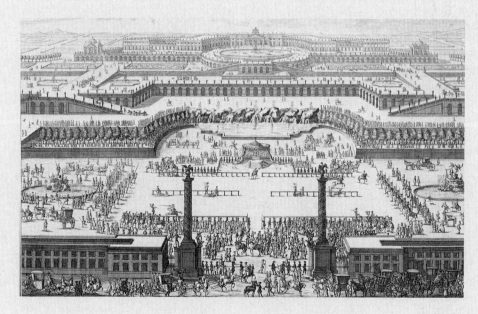

Plans for the Palace at Schönbrunn, ca. 1700. (Private Collection/The Stapleton Collection/Bridgeman Images)

advocated policy decisions, and brokered alliances between factions. Noblewomen played a similar role, bringing their family connections to marriage to form powerful social networks. Onlookers sometimes resented the influence of powerful women at court. The duke of Saint-Simon said of Madame de Maintenon, Louis XIV's mistress and secret second wife, "Many people have been ruined by her, without having been able to discover the author of the ruin, search as they might."

Louis XIV was also an enthusiastic patron of the arts, commissioning many sculptures and paintings for Versailles as well as performances of dance and music. Scholars characterize the art and literature of the age of

Louis XIV as French classicism. By this they mean that the artists and writers of the late seventeenth century imitated the subject matter and style of classical antiquity, that their work resembled that of Renaissance Italy, and that French art possessed the classical qualities of discipline, balance, and restraint. Louis XIV also loved the stage, and in the plays of Molière and Racine his court witnessed the finest achievements in the history of French theater. In this period aristocratic ladies wrote many genres of literature and held salons in their Parisian mansions where they engaged in witty and cultured discussions of poetry, art, theater, and the latest worldly events. Their refined conversational style led Molière and other observers to mock them as "*précieuses*" (PREH-see-ooz; literally "precious"), or affected and pretentious. Despite this mockery, the précieuses represented an important cultural force ruled by elite women.

With Versailles as the center of European politics, French culture grew in international prestige. French became the language of polite society and international diplomacy, gradually replacing Latin as the language of scholarship and learning. Royal courts across Europe spoke French, and the great aristocrats of Russia, Sweden, Germany, and elsewhere were often more fluent in French than in the tongues of their homelands. France inspired a cosmopolitan European culture in the late seventeenth century that looked to Versailles as its center.

The French Economic Policy of Mercantilism

France's ability to build armies and fight wars depended on a strong economy. Fortunately for Louis, his controller general, Jean-Baptiste Colbert (1619–1683), proved to be a financial genius. Colbert's central principle was that the wealth and the economy of France should serve the state. To this end, from 1665 to his death in 1683, Colbert rigorously applied mercantilist policies to France.

Mercantilism is a collection of governmental policies for the regulation of economic activities by and for the state. It derives from the idea that a nation's international power is based on its wealth, specifically its supply of gold and silver. To accumulate wealth, a country always had to sell more goods abroad than it bought. To decrease French purchases of goods from outside the country, Colbert insisted that French industry should produce everything needed by the French people.

To increase exports, Colbert supported old industries and created new ones, focusing especially on tex-

tiles, which were the most important sector of manufacturing, Colbert enacted new production regulations, created guilds to boost quality standards, and encouraged foreign craftsmen to immigrate to France. To encourage the purchase of French goods, he abolished many domestic tariffs and raised tariffs on foreign products. In 1664 Colbert founded the Company of the East Indies with (unfulfilled) hopes of competing with the Dutch for Asian trade.

Colbert also hoped to make Canada—rich in untapped minerals and some of the best agricultural land in the world—part of a vast French empire. He sent four thousand colonists to Quebec, whose capital had been founded in 1608 under Henry IV. Subsequently, the Jesuit Jacques Marquette and the merchant Louis Joliet sailed down the Mississippi River, which they named Colbert in honor of their sponsor (the name soon reverted to the original Native American one). Marquette and Joliet claimed possession of the land on both sides of the river as far south as present-day Arkansas. In 1684 French explorers continued down the Mississippi to its mouth and claimed vast territories for Louis XIV. The area was called, naturally, "Louisiana."

During Colbert's tenure as controller general, Louis was able to pursue his goals without massive tax increases and without creating a stream of new offices. The constant pressure of warfare after Colbert's death, however, undid many of his economic achievements.

Louis XIV's Wars

Louis XIV wrote that "the character of a conqueror is regarded as the noblest and highest of titles." In pursuit of the title of conqueror, he kept France at war for thirty-three of the fifty-four years of his personal rule. François le Tellier, marquis de Louvois, Louis's secretary of state for war, equaled Colbert's achievements in the economic realm. Louvois created a professional army in which the French state, rather than private nobles, employed the soldiers. Uniforms and weapons were standardized, and a rational system of training and promotion was devised. Many historians believe that the new loyalty, professionalism, and growth of the French army represented the peak of Louis's success in reforming government. As in so many other matters, his model was followed across Europe.

Louis's goal was to expand France to what he considered its natural borders. His armies managed to extend French borders to include

.Paris

FRANCHE-
COMTÉ

FRANCE

Territory gained
☐ 1668
☐ 1678
☐ 1713

**The Acquisitions of
Louis XIV, 1668–1713**

important commercial centers in the Spanish Netherlands and Flanders as well as the entire province of Franche-Comté between 1667 and 1678. In 1681 Louis seized the city of Strasbourg, and three years later he sent his armies into the province of Lorraine. At that moment the king seemed invincible. In fact, Louis had reached the limit of his expansion. The wars of the 1680s and 1690s brought no additional territories but placed unbearable strains on French resources. Colbert's successors resorted to desperate measures to finance these wars, including devaluation of the currency and new taxes.

Louis's last war was endured by a French people suffering high taxes, crop failure, and widespread malnutrition and death. In 1700 the childless Spanish king Charles II (r. 1665–1700) died, opening a struggle for control of Spain and its colonies. His will bequeathed the Spanish crown and its empire to Philip of Anjou, Louis XIV's grandson (Louis's wife, Maria-Theresa, was Charles's sister). The will violated a prior treaty by which the European powers had agreed to divide the Spanish possessions between the king of France and the Holy Roman emperor, both brothers-in-law of Charles II. Claiming that he was following both Spanish and French interests, Louis broke with the treaty and accepted the will, thereby triggering the War of the Spanish Succession (1701–1713).

In 1701 the English, Dutch, Austrians, and Prussians formed the Grand Alliance against Louis XIV. War dragged on until 1713. The **Peace of Utrecht**, which ended the war, allowed Louis's grandson Philip to remain king of Spain on the understanding that the French and Spanish crowns would never be united. France surrendered Nova Scotia, Newfoundland, and the Hudson Bay territory to England, which also acquired Gibraltar, Minorca, and control of the African slave trade from Spain (Map 15.2).

The Peace of Utrecht represented the balance-of-power principle in operation, setting limits on the extent to which any one power—in this case, France—could expand. It also marked the end of French expansion. Thirty-five years of war had given France the rights to all of Alsace and some commercial centers in the north. But at what price? In 1714 an exhausted France hovered on the brink of bankruptcy. It is no wonder that when Louis XIV died on September 1, 1715, many subjects felt as much relief as they did sorrow.

The Decline of Absolutist Spain in the Seventeenth Century

At the beginning of the seventeenth century France's position appeared extremely weak. Struggling to recover from decades of religious civil war that had destroyed its infrastructure and economy, France could not dare to compete with Spain's empire or its mighty military. Yet by the end of the century their positions

Charles II, King of Spain, and His Wife Kneeling Before the Eucharist From the royal family to the common peasant, fervent Catholic religious faith permeated seventeenth-century Spanish society, serving as a binding force for the newly unified nation. (Musée Eucharistique du Hieron, Paray le-Monial, France/Gianni Dagli Orti/The Art Archive at Art Resource, NY)

were reversed, and France had surpassed all expectations to attain European dominance.

By the early seventeenth century the seeds of Spanish disaster were sprouting. Between 1610 and 1650 Spanish trade with the colonies in the New World fell 60 percent due to competition from local industries in the colonies and from Dutch and English traders. At the same time, the native Indian and African slaves who toiled in the South American silver mines suffered frightful epidemics of disease. Ultimately, the mines that filled the empire's treasury started to run dry, and the quantity of metal produced steadily declined after 1620.

In Madrid, however, royal expenditures constantly exceeded income. To meet mountainous state debt, the

■ **mercantilism** A system of economic regulations aimed at increasing the power of the state based on the belief that a nation's international power was based on its wealth, specifically its supply of gold and silver.

■ **Peace of Utrecht** A series of treaties, from 1713 to 1715, that ended the War of the Spanish Succession, ended French expansion in Europe, and marked the rise of the British Empire.

North America, 1714

HUDSON'S BAY
COMPANY
QUEBEC *Newfoundland*
NEW
FRANCE   NOVA
SCOTIA
LOUISIANA
THIRTEEN COLONIES
SP.
FLORIDA

Claims
□ British
■ French
■ Spanish

Legend:
■ French Bourbon lands
■ Spanish Bourbon lands
■ Austrian Habsburg lands
□ Prussian lands
□ Great Britain
■ Russian Empire
— Boundary of the Holy Roman Empire

MAP 15.2 Europe After the Peace of Utrecht, 1715

The series of treaties commonly called the Peace of Utrecht ended the War of the Spanish Succession and redrew the map of Europe. A French Bourbon king succeeded to the Spanish throne. France surrendered the Spanish Netherlands (later Belgium), then in French hands, to Austria, and recognized the Hohenzollern rulers of Prussia. Spain ceded Gibraltar to Great Britain, for which it has been a strategic naval station ever since. Spain also granted Britain the *asiento*, the contract for supplying African slaves to the Americas.

ANALYZING THE MAP Identify the areas on the map that changed hands as a result of the Peace of Utrecht. How did these changes affect the balance of power in Europe?

CONNECTIONS How and why did so many European countries possess scattered or noncontiguous territories? What does this suggest about European politics in this period? Does this map suggest potential for future conflict?

Crown repeatedly devalued the coinage and declared bankruptcy, which resulted in the collapse of national credit. Meanwhile, manufacturing and commerce shrank. In contrast to the other countries of western Europe, Spain had a tiny middle class. The elite condemned moneymaking as vulgar and undignified. Thousands entered economically unproductive professions: there were said to be nine thousand monasteries in the province of Castile alone. To make matters worse, the Crown expelled some three hundred thousand *Moriscos*, or former Muslims, in 1609, significantly reducing the pool of skilled workers and merchants. Those working in the textile industry were forced out of business by steep inflation that pushed their production costs to the point where they could not compete in colonial and international markets.[5]

Spanish aristocrats, attempting to maintain an extravagant lifestyle they could no longer afford, increased the rents on their estates. High rents and heavy taxes in turn drove the peasants from the land, leading to a decline in agricultural productivity. In cities wages and production stagnated. Spain also ignored new scientific methods that might have improved agricultural or manufacturing techniques because they came from the heretical nations of Holland and England.

The Spanish crown had no solutions to these dire problems. Philip III (r. 1598–1621), a melancholy and deeply pious man, handed the running of the government over to the duke of Lerma, who used it to advance his personal and familial wealth. Philip IV (r. 1621–1665) left the management of his several kingdoms to Gaspar de Guzmán, Count-Duke of Olivares. Olivares was an able administrator who has often been compared to Richelieu. He did not lack energy and ideas, and he succeeded in devising new sources of revenue. But he clung to the grandiose belief that the solution to Spain's difficulties rested in a return to the imperial tradition of the sixteenth century. Unfortunately, the imperial tradition demanded the revival of war with the Dutch at the expiration of a twelve-year truce in 1622 and a long war with France over Mantua (1628–1659). Spain thus became embroiled in the Thirty Years' War. These conflicts, on top of an empty treasury, brought disaster.

Spain's situation worsened with internal conflicts and fresh military defeats through the remainder of the seventeenth century. In 1640 Spain faced serious revolts in Catalonia and Portugal. In 1643 the French inflicted a crushing defeat on a Spanish army at Rocroi in what is now Belgium. By the Treaty of the Pyrenees of 1659, which ended the French-Spanish conflict, Spain was compelled to surrender extensive territories to France. In 1688 the Spanish crown reluctantly recognized the independence of Portugal, almost a century after the two crowns were joined. The era of Spanish dominance in Europe had ended.

Absolutism in Austria and Prussia

FOCUS QUESTION *What were the social conditions of eastern Europe, and how did the rulers of Austria and Prussia transform their nations into powerful absolutist monarchies?*

The rulers of eastern Europe also labored to build strong absolutist states in the seventeenth century. But they built on social and economic foundations far different from those in western Europe, namely serfdom and the strong nobility who benefited from it. The endless wars of the seventeenth century allowed monarchs to increase their power by building large armies, increasing taxation, and suppressing representative institutions. In exchange for their growing political authority, monarchs allowed nobles to remain as unchallenged masters of their peasants, a deal that appeased both king and nobility, but left serfs at the mercy of the lords. The most successful states were Austria and Prussia, which witnessed the rise of absolutism between 1620 and 1740.

The Return of Serfdom in the East

While economic and social hardship was common across Europe, important differences existed between east and west. In the west the demographic losses of the Black Death allowed peasants to escape from serfdom as they acquired enough land to feed themselves. In eastern Europe seventeenth-century peasants had largely lost their ability to own land independently. Eastern lords dealt with the labor shortages caused by the Black Death by restricting the right of their peasants to move to take advantage of better opportunities elsewhere. In Prussian territories by 1500 the law required that runaway peasants be hunted down and returned to their lords. Moreover, lords steadily took more and more of their peasants' land and arbitrarily imposed heavier labor obligations. By the early 1500s lords in many eastern territories could command their peasants to work for them without pay for as many as six days a week.

The gradual erosion of the peasantry's economic position was bound up with manipulation of the legal system. The local lord was also the local prosecutor, judge, and jailer. There were no independent royal officials to provide justice or uphold the common law. The power of the lord reached far into serfs' everyday lives. Not only was their freedom of movement restricted, but they also required permission to marry or could be forced to marry. Lords could reallocate the lands worked by their serfs at will or sell serfs apart from their families. These conditions applied even on lands owned by the church.

Between 1500 and 1650 the consolidation of serfdom in eastern Europe was accompanied by the growth of commercial agriculture, particularly in Poland and eastern Germany. As economic expansion and population growth resumed after 1500, eastern lords increased the production of their estates by squeezing sizable surpluses out of the impoverished peasants. They then sold these surpluses to foreign merchants, who exported them to the growing cities of wealthier western Europe. The Netherlands and England benefited the most from inexpensive grain from the east.

It was not only the peasants who suffered in eastern Europe. With the approval of kings, landlords systematically undermined the medieval privileges of the towns and the power of the urban classes. Instead of selling products to local merchants, landlords sold directly to foreigners, bypassing local towns. Eastern towns also lost their medieval right of refuge and were compelled to return runaways to their lords. The population of the towns and the urban middle classes declined greatly. This development both reflected and promoted the supremacy of noble landlords in most of eastern Europe in the sixteenth century.

The Austrian Habsburgs

Like all the people of central Europe, the Habsburgs emerged from the Thirty Years' War impoverished and exhausted. Their efforts to destroy Protestantism in the German lands and to turn the weak Holy Roman Empire into a real state had failed. Although the Habsburgs remained the hereditary emperors, real power lay in the hands of a bewildering variety of separate political jurisdictions. Defeat in central Europe encouraged the Habsburgs to turn away from a quest for imperial dominance and to focus inward and eastward in an attempt to unify their diverse holdings. If they could not impose Catholicism in the empire, at least they could do so in their own domains.

Habsburg victory over Bohemia during the Thirty Years' War was an important step in this direction. Ferdinand II (r. 1619–1637) drastically reduced the power of the Bohemian Estates, the largely Protestant representative assembly. He also confiscated the landholdings of Protestant nobles and gave them to loyal Catholic nobles and to the foreign aristocratic mercenaries who led his armies. After 1650 a large portion of the Bohemian nobility was of recent origin and owed its success to the Habsburgs.

With the support of this new nobility, the Habsburgs established direct rule over Bohemia. Under their rule the condition of the enserfed peasantry worsened substantially: three days per week of unpaid labor became the norm. Protestantism was also stamped out. These changes were significant advances in creating absolutist rule in Bohemia.

Ferdinand III (r. 1637–1657) continued to build state power. He centralized the government in the empire's German-speaking provinces, which formed the core Habsburg holdings. For the first time, a permanent standing army was ready to put down any internal opposition. The Habsburg monarchy then turned east toward the plains of Hungary, which had been divided between the Ottomans and the Habsburgs in the early sixteenth century. Between 1683 and 1699 the Habsburgs pushed the Ottomans from most of Hungary and Transylvania. The recovery of all the former kingdom of Hungary was completed in 1718.

The Hungarian nobility, despite its reduced strength, effectively thwarted the full development of Habsburg absolutism. Throughout the seventeenth century Hungarian nobles rose in revolt against attempts to impose absolute rule. They never triumphed decisively, but neither were they crushed the way the nobility in Bohemia had been in 1620. In 1703, with the Habsburgs bogged down in the War of the Spanish Succession, the Hungarians rose in one last patriotic rebellion under Prince Francis Rákóczy. The prince and his forces were eventually defeated, but the Habsburgs agreed to restore many of the traditional privileges of the aristocracy in return for Hungarian acceptance of hereditary Habsburg rule. Thus Hungary, unlike Austria and Bohemia, was never fully integrated into a centralized, absolute Habsburg state.

Despite checks on their ambitions in Hungary, the Habsburgs made significant achievements in state-building elsewhere by forging consensus with the church and the nobility. A sense of common identity and loyalty to the monarchy grew among elites in Habsburg lands, even to a certain extent in Hungary. German became the language of the state, and zealous Catholicism helped fuse a collective identity.

Vienna became the political and cultural center of the empire. By 1700 it was a thriving city with a population of one hundred thousand and its own version of Versailles, the royal palace of Schönbrunn.

Prussia in the Seventeenth Century

In the fifteenth and sixteenth centuries the Hohenzollern family had ruled parts of eastern Germany as the imperial electors of Brandenburg and the dukes of Prussia. The title of "elector" gave its holder the privilege of being one of only seven princes or archbishops entitled to elect the Holy Roman emperor, but the electors had little real power. When he came to power in 1640, the twenty-year-old Frederick William, later known as the "Great Elector," was determined to unify his three provinces and enlarge his holdings. These provinces were Brandenburg; Prussia, inherited in 1618; and scattered territories along the Rhine inherited in 1614 (Map 15.3). Each was inhabited by German-speakers, but each had its own estates. Although the estates had not met regularly during the chaotic Thirty Years' War, taxes could not be levied without their consent. The estates of Brandenburg and Prussia were dominated by the nobility and the landowning classes, known as the **Junkers**.

Frederick William profited from ongoing European war and the threat of invasion from Russia when he argued for the need for a permanent standing army. In 1660 he persuaded Junkers in the estates to accept taxation without consent in order to fund an army. They agreed to do so in exchange for reconfirmation of their own privileges, including authority over the serfs. Having won over the Junkers, the king crushed poten-

■ **Junkers** The nobility of Brandenburg and Prussia, they were reluctant allies of Frederick William in his consolidation of the Prussian state.

MAP 15.3 The Growth of Austria and Brandenburg-Prussia to 1748   Austria expanded to the southwest into Hungary and Transylvania at the expense of the Ottoman Empire. It was unable to hold the rich German province of Silesia, however, which was conquered by Brandenburg-Prussia.

tial opposition to his power from the towns. One by one, Prussian cities were eliminated from the estates and subjected to new taxes on goods and services.

Thereafter, the estates' power declined rapidly, for the Great Elector had both financial independence and superior force. He revealed his strategy toward managing the estates in the written instructions he left his son:

> Always regulate the expenditures according to the revenues, and have officials diligently render receipts every year. When the finances are in a good state again, then you will have enough means, and you will not have to request money from the estates or address them. Then it is also not necessary to hold the many and expensive parliaments, because the more parliaments you hold, the more authority is taken from you, because the estates always try something that is detrimental to the majesty of the ruler.[6]

By following his own advice, Frederick William tripled state revenue during his reign and expanded the army drastically. In 1688 a population of 1 million

supported a peacetime standing army of 30,000. In 1701 the elector's son, Frederick I, received the elevated title of king of Prussia (instead of elector) as a reward for aiding the Holy Roman emperor in the War of the Spanish Succession.

The Consolidation of Prussian Absolutism

Frederick William I, "the Soldiers' King" (r. 1713–1740), completed his grandfather's work, eliminating the last traces of parliamentary estates and local self-government. It was he who truly established Prussian absolutism and transformed Prussia into a military state. Frederick William was intensely attached to military life. He always wore an army uniform, and he lived the highly disciplined life of the professional soldier. Years later he followed the family tradition by leaving his own written instructions to his son: "A formidable army and a war chest large enough to make this army mobile in times of need can create great respect for you in the world, so that you can speak a word like the other powers."[7]

A Prussian Giant Grenadier   Frederick William I wanted tall, handsome soldiers. He dressed them in tight, bright uniforms to distinguish them from the peasant population from which most soldiers came. He also ordered several portraits of his favorites, such as this one, from his court painter, J. C. Merk. Grenadiers (greh-nuh-DEERZ) wore the miter cap instead of an ordinary hat so that they could hurl their heavy grenades unimpeded by a broad brim. (Deutsches Historisches Museum, Berlin, Germany/© DHM/ The Bridgeman Art Library)

Penny-pinching and hard-working, Frederick William achieved results. The king and his ministers built an exceptionally honest and conscientious bureaucracy to administer the country and foster economic development. Twelfth in Europe in population, Prussia had the fourth-largest army by 1740. The Prussian army was the best in Europe, astonishing foreign observers with its precision, skill, and discipline. As one Western traveler put it: "There is no theatre in Berlin whatsoever, diversion is understood to be the handsome troops who parade daily. A special attraction is the great Potsdam Grenadier Regiment . . . when they practice drill, when they fire and when they parade up and down, it is as if they form a single body."[8]

Nevertheless, Prussians paid a heavy and lasting price for the obsessions of their royal drillmaster.

Army expansion was achieved in part through forced conscription, which was declared lifelong in 1713. Desperate draftees fled the country or injured themselves to avoid service. Finally, in 1733 Frederick William I ordered that all Prussian men would undergo military training and serve as reservists in the army, allowing him to preserve both agricultural production and army size. To appease the Junkers, the king enlisted them to lead his growing army. The proud nobility thus commanded the peasantry in the army as well as on the estates.

With all men harnessed to the war machine, Prussian civil society became rigid and highly disciplined. As a Prussian minister later summed up, "To keep quiet is the first civic duty."[9] Thus the policies of Frederick William I, combined with harsh peasant bondage and Junker tyranny, laid the foundations for a highly militaristic country.

The Development of Russia and the Ottoman Empire

FOCUS QUESTION *What were the distinctive features of Russian and Ottoman absolutism?*

Russia occupied a unique position among Eurasian states. With borders straddling eastern Europe and northwestern Asia, its development into a strong imperial state drew on elements from both continents. Like the growth of the Muslim empires in Central and South Asia and the Ming Dynasty in China, the expansion of Russia was a result of the weakening of the great Mongol Empire. After declaring independence from the Mongols, the Russian tsars conquered a vast empire, extending through North Asia all the way to the Pacific Ocean. State-building and territorial expansion culminated during the reign of Peter the Great, who forcibly introduced elements of Western culture and society.

While Europeans debated, and continued to debate, whether or not Russia was a Western society, there was no question in their minds that the Ottomans were outsiders. Even absolutist rulers disdained Ottoman sultans as cruel and tyrannical despots. Despite stereotypes, however, the Ottoman Empire was in many ways more tolerant than its Western counterparts, providing protection and security to other religions while steadfastly maintaining the Muslim faith. The Ottoman state combined the Byzantine heritage of the territory it had conquered with Persian and Arab traditions. Flexibility and openness to other ideas and practices were sources of strength for the empire.

Mongol Rule in Russia and the Rise of Moscow

In the thirteenth century the Mongols had conquered Kievan Rus, the medieval Slavic state centered first at Novgorod and then at Kiev, a city on the Dnieper River; this state included most of present-day Ukraine, Belarus, and part of northwest Russia. For two hundred years, the Mongols forced the Slavic princes to submit to their rule and to render tribute and slaves. The princes of the Grand Duchy of Moscow, a principality within Kievan Rus, became particularly adept at serving the Mongols. They loyally put down uprisings and collected the khan's taxes. Eventually the Muscovite princes were able to destroy the other princes who were their rivals for power. Ivan III (r. 1462–1505), known as Ivan the Great, successfully expanded the principality of Moscow eastward toward the Baltic Sea and westward to the Ural Mountains and the Siberian frontier.

By 1480 Ivan III was strong enough to refuse to pay tribute to the Mongols and declare the autonomy of Moscow. To legitimize their new position, Ivan and his successors borrowed elements of Mongol rule. They forced weaker Slavic principalities to render tribute previously paid to Mongols and borrowed Mongol institutions such as the tax system, postal routes, and census. Loyalty from the highest-ranking nobles, or **boyars**, helped the Muscovite princes consolidate their power.

Another source of legitimacy for Moscow was its claim to the political and religious legacy of the Byzantine Empire. After the fall of Constantinople to the Turks in 1453, the princes of Moscow saw themselves as the heirs of both the Byzantine caesars (or emperors) and the empire's Orthodox Christianity. The title "tsar," first taken by Ivan IV in 1547, is in fact a contraction of *caesar*. The tsars considered themselves rightful and holy rulers, an idea promoted by Orthodox churchmen who spoke of "holy Russia" as the "Third Rome." The marriage of Ivan III to the daughter of the last Byzantine emperor further enhanced Moscow's assertion of imperial authority.

Building the Russian Empire

Developments in Russia took a chaotic turn with the reign of Ivan IV (r. 1533–1584), the famous "Ivan the Terrible," who rose to the throne at age three. His mother died, possibly poisoned, when he was eight, leaving Ivan to suffer insults and neglect from the boyars at court. At age sixteen Ivan pushed aside his advisers, and in an awe-inspiring ceremony, with gold coins pouring down on his head, he majestically crowned himself tsar.

After the sudden death of his wife, however, Ivan began a campaign of persecution against those he suspected of opposing him. He executed members of leading boyar families, along with their families, friends, servants, and peasants. To replace them, Ivan created a new service nobility, whose loyalty was guaranteed by their dependence on the state for land and titles.

As landlords demanded more from the serfs who survived the persecutions, growing numbers of peasants fled toward wild, recently conquered territories to the east and south. There they joined free groups and warrior bands known as **Cossacks**. Ivan responded by tying peasants ever more firmly to the land and to noble landholders. Simultaneously, he ordered that urban dwellers be bound to their towns and jobs so that he could tax them more heavily. The urban classes had no security in their property, and even the wealthiest merchants were dependent agents of the tsar. These restrictions checked the growth of the Russian middle classes and stood in sharp contrast to economic and social developments in western Europe.

Ivan combined domestic oppression with external aggression. His reign was successful in defeating the remnants of Mongol power, adding vast new territories to the realm, and laying the foundations for the huge, multiethnic Russian empire. In the 1550s, strengthened by an alliance with Cossack bands, Ivan conquered the Muslim khanates of Kazan and Astrakhan and brought the fertile steppe region around the Volga River under Russian control. In the 1580s Cossacks fighting for the Russian state crossed the Ural Mountains and began the long conquest of Siberia. Because of the size of the new territories and their distance from Moscow, the Russian state did not initially seek to impose the Orthodox religion and maintained local elites in positions of honor and leadership, buying their loyalty with grants of land. In relying on cooperation from local elites and ruthlessly exploiting the common people, the Russians followed the pattern of the Spanish and other early modern European imperial states.

Following Ivan's death, Russia entered a chaotic period known as the "Time of Troubles" (1598–1613).

- Moscow, ca. 1300
- Gains by 1505
- Gains by 1584
- Gains by 1725
- ✳ Major battle

SWEDEN
FINLAND
St. Petersburg
Novgorod
POLAND-LITHUANIA
Moscow
Kiev
Cossacks
Poltava 1709
Cossacks
URAL MTS.
CAUCASUS MTS.

The Expansion of Russia to 1725

■ **boyars** The highest-ranking members of the Russian nobility.

■ **Cossacks** Free groups and outlaw armies originally comprising runaway peasants living on the borders of Russian territory from the fourteenth century onward. By the end of the sixteenth century they had formed an alliance with the Russian state.

Russian Peasant An eighteenth-century French artist visiting Russia recorded his impressions of the daily life of the Russian people in this etching of a fish merchant pulling his wares through a snowy village on a sleigh. Two caviar vendors behind him make a sale to a young mother standing at her doorstep with her baby in her arms. (Pierson: Les Amis de Paris–Saint Pétersbourgh)

While Ivan's relatives struggled for power, Cossacks and peasants rebelled against nobles and officials. This social explosion from below brought the nobles together. They crushed the Cossack rebellion and brought Ivan's sixteen-year-old grandnephew, Michael Romanov, to the throne (r. 1613–1645). The Romanov dynasty would endure as one of the most successful European absolutist dynasties until the Russian Revolution of 1917.

Like their Western counterparts, the Romanov tsars made several important achievements in state-building during the second half of the seventeenth century. After a long war, Russia gained land in Ukraine from Poland in 1667 and completed the conquest of Siberia by the end of the century. Territorial expansion was accompa-

nied by growth of the bureaucracy and the army. The tsars employed foreign experts to reform the Russian army, and enlisted Cossack warriors to fight Siberian campaigns. The great profits from Siberia's natural resources, especially furs, funded the Romanovs' bid for Great Power status. Russian imperialist expansion to the east paralleled the Western powers' exploration and conquest of the Atlantic world in the same period.

The growth of state power did nothing to improve the lot of the common people. In 1649 a new law code extended serfdom to all peasants in the realm, giving lords unrestricted rights over their serfs and establishing penalties for harboring runaways. The new code also removed the privileges that non-Russian elites had enjoyed within the empire and required conversion to

Peter the Great This compelling portrait by Grigory Musikiysky captures the strength and determination of the warrior-tsar in 1723, after more than three decades of personal rule. In his hand Peter holds the scepter, symbol of royal sovereignty, and across his breastplate is draped an ermine fur, a mark of honor. In the background are the battleships of Russia's new Baltic fleet and the famous St. Peter and St. Paul Fortress that Peter built in St. Petersburg. (Hermitage/St. Petersburg, Russia/Bridgeman Art Library)

Peter the Great and Foreign Experts

John Deane, an eminent shipbuilder, was one of the many foreign artisans and experts brought to Russia by Peter the Great after the latter's foreign tour of 1697. Several months after his arrival in Russia, Deane sent a glowing account of the tsar's technical prowess to his patron in England, the marquess of Carmarthen, admiral of the English fleet.

~

At my arrival in Moscow, I fell very ill of the Bloody-Flux, which made me be in Moscow when his Majesty came home: About the latter end of October I was somewhat recovered, his Majesty then carried me down to Voronize* with him. Voronize is about 400 English Miles South-East from Moscow. There the Czar immediately set up a ship of 60 guns, where he is both Foreman and Master-Builder; and not to flatter him, I'll assure your Lordship it will be the best ship among them, and 'tis all from his own Draught; How he fram'd her together and how he made the Mould, and in so short a time as he did is really wonderful: But he is able at this day to put his own notions into practice, and laugh at his Dutch and Italian builders for their ignorance. There are several pieces of workmanship, as in the keel, stem, and post, which are all purely his own invention, and sound good work, and would be approved of by all the shipwrights of England if they saw it. . . .

After some time [I] fell sick again; and at Christmas, when his Majesty came to Moscow, he brought me

*Site of the naval shipyard.

back again for recovery of my health, where I am at present. . . . The whole place is inhabited by the Dutch; I believe there may be 400 families. Last Sunday and Monday the strangers were invited to the consecration of General La Fort's house, which is the noblest building in Russia, and finely furnisht. There were all the envoys, and as near as I could guess 200 gentlemen, English, French, and Dutch, and about as many ladies; each day were dancing and musick. All the envoys, and all the lords (but three in Moscow) are going to Voronize to see the fleet, I suppose. His majesty went last Sunday to Voronize with Prince Alexander and I am to go down (being something recovered) with the Vice-Admiral about six days hence.

EVALUATE THE EVIDENCE

1. According to Deane, what evidence did Peter give of his skills in shipbuilding? Based on this document, how would you characterize the relationship between Peter the Great and his foreign experts?
2. What other evidence does Deane provide of the impact of foreigners on life in Russia?

Source: John Deane, *A Letter from Moscow to the Marquess of Carmarthen, Relating to the Czar of Muscovy's Forwardness in His Great Navy, & c. Since His Return Home*, London, 1699.

Russian Orthodoxy. Henceforth, Moscow maintained strict control of trade and administration throughout the empire.

The peace imposed by harsh Russian rule was disrupted in 1670 by a rebellion led by the Cossack Stenka Razin, who attracted a great army of urban poor and peasants. He and his followers killed landlords and government officials and proclaimed freedom from oppression, but their rebellion was defeated in 1671. The ease with which Moscow crushed the rebellion testifies to the success of the Russian state in unifying and consolidating its empire.

The Reforms of Peter the Great

Heir to Romanov efforts at state-building, Peter the Great (r. 1682–1725) embarked on a tremendous campaign to accelerate and complete these processes. A giant for his time at six feet seven inches, and possessing enormous energy and willpower, Peter built on the service obligations of Ivan the Terrible and his suc-

cessors and continued their tradition of territorial expansion. In particular, he was determined to gain access to the sea for his virtually landlocked state.

Peter realized a first step toward this goal by conquering the Ottoman fort of Azov in 1696 and quickly built Russia's first navy base. In 1697 the tsar led a group of 250 Russian officials and young nobles on an eighteen-month tour of western European capitals. Peter was fascinated by foreign technology and he hoped to forge an anti-Ottoman alliance to strengthen his claims on the Black Sea. Traveling unofficially to avoid lengthy diplomatic ceremonies, Peter met with foreign kings, master shipbuilders, gunners, and other specialists. He failed to secure a military alliance, but he did learn his lessons from the growing power of the Dutch and the English. He also engaged more than a hundred foreign experts to return with him to Russia to help build the navy and improve Russian infrastructure. (See "Evaluating the Evidence 15.2: Peter the Great and Foreign Experts," above.)

Having failed to gain support for an anti-Ottoman alliance and suffering a reversal of fortune at Azov, Peter switched tactics and entered into a secret agreement with Denmark and Poland to wage a sudden war of aggression against Sweden with the goal of securing access to the Baltic Sea. Peter and his allies believed that their combined forces could win easy victories because Sweden was in the hands of a new and inexperienced king.

Eighteen-year-old Charles XII of Sweden (1697–1718) surprised Peter. He defeated Denmark quickly in 1700, then turned on Russia. In a blinding snowstorm, his well-trained professional army attacked and routed unsuspecting Russians besieging the Swedish fortress of Narva on the Baltic coast. It was, for the Russians, a grim beginning to the long and brutal Great Northern War, which lasted from 1700 to 1721.

Peter responded to this defeat with new measures to increase state power, strengthen his military forces, and gain victory. He required all nobles to serve in the army or in the civil administration—for life. Since a more modern army and government required skilled experts, Peter created new schools and universities and required every young nobleman to spend five years in education away from home. Peter established an interlocking military-civilian bureaucracy with fourteen ranks, and he decreed that all had to start at the bottom and work toward the top. The system allowed some people of non-noble origins to rise to high positions, a rarity in Europe at the time. These measures gradually combined to make the army and government more powerful and efficient.

Peter also greatly increased the service requirements of commoners. In the wake of the Narva disaster, he established a regular standing army of more than two hundred thousand peasant-soldiers, drafted for life and commanded by noble officers. He added an additional hundred thousand men in special regiments of Cossacks and foreign mercenaries. To fund the army, taxes on peasants increased threefold during Peter's reign. Serfs were also arbitrarily assigned to work in the growing number of factories and mines that supplied the military. Under Peter, Russia's techniques for governing its territories—including the policing of borders and individual identity documents—were far ahead of those of most other imperial powers.

Peter the Great Cutting a Boyar's Beard As part of his westernization program, Peter the Great obliged Russian men to shave their long beards, a shock to traditional Orthodox notions of masculinity. Like many of his reforms, these were aimed primarily at the noble boyars; many peasants continued to wear beards in the countryside. (Universal History Archive/Getty Images)

In 1709 Peter's new war machine was able to crush the small army of Sweden in Ukraine at Poltava, one of the most significant battles in Russian history. Russia's victory against Sweden was conclusive in 1721, and Estonia and present-day Latvia came under Russian rule for the first time. The cost was high: warfare consumed 80 to 85 percent of all revenues. But Russia became the dominant power in the Baltic and very much a great European power.

After his victory at Poltava, Peter channeled enormous resources into building a new Western-style capital on the Baltic to rival the great cities of Europe. Originally a desolate and swampy Swedish outpost, the magnificent city of St. Petersburg was designed to reflect modern urban planning, with wide, straight avenues, buildings set in a uniform line, and large parks. Each summer, twenty-five thousand to forty thousand peasants were sent to provide construction labor in St. Petersburg without pay.

There were other important consequences of Peter's reign. For Peter, modernization meant westernization, and he encouraged the spread of Western culture along with technology and urban planning. Peter required nobles to shave their heavy beards and wear Western clothing, previously banned in Russia. He also ordered them to attend parties where young men and women would mix together and freely choose their own spouses. From these efforts a new elite class of Western-oriented Russians began to emerge.

Peter's reforms were unpopular with many Russians. For nobles, one of Peter's most detested reforms was the imposition of unigeniture—inheritance of land by one son alone—cutting daughters and other sons from family property. For peasants, the reign of the tsar saw a significant increase in the bonds of serfdom, and the gulf between the enserfed peasantry and the educated nobility increased. Despite the unpopularity of Peter's reforms, his modernizing and westernizing of Russia paved the way for it to move somewhat closer to the European mainstream in its thought and institutions during the Enlightenment, especially under Catherine the Great.

The Ottoman Empire

Most Christian Europeans perceived the Ottomans as the antithesis of their own values and traditions and viewed the empire as driven by an insatiable lust for warfare and conquest. In their view the fall of Constantinople was a historic catastrophe and the taking of the Balkans a form of despotic imprisonment. To Ottoman eyes, the world looked very different. The siege of Constantinople liberated a glorious city from its long decline under the Byzantines. Rather than being a despoiled captive, the Balkans were a haven for refugees fleeing the growing intolerance of Western Christian powers. The Ottoman Empire provided a safe haven for Jews, Muslims, and even some Christians from the Inquisition and religious war.

The Ottomans came out of Central Asia as conquering warriors, settled in Anatolia (present-day Turkey), and, at their peak in the mid-sixteenth century, ruled one of the most powerful empires in the world (see Chapter 14). Their possessions stretched from western Persia across North Africa and into the heart of central Europe (Map 15.4).

The Ottoman Empire was built on a unique model of state and society. Agricultural land was the personal hereditary property of the **sultan**, and peasants paid taxes to use the land. There was therefore an almost complete absence of private landed property and no hereditary nobility. The Ottomans also employed a distinctive form of government administration. The top ranks of the bureaucracy were staffed by the sultan's slave corps. Because Muslim law prohibited enslaving other Muslims, the sultan's agents purchased slaves along the borders of the empire. Within the realm, the sultan levied a "tax" of one thousand to three thousand male children on the conquered Christian populations in the Balkans every year. These young slaves were raised in Turkey as Muslims and were trained to fight and to administer. Unlike enslaved Africans in European colonies, who faced a dire fate, the most talented Ottoman slaves rose to the top of the bureaucracy, where they might acquire wealth and power. The less fortunate formed the core of the sultan's army, the **janissary corps**. These highly organized and efficient troops gave the Ottomans a formidable advantage in war with western Europeans. By 1683 service in the janissary corps had become so prestigious that the sultan ceased recruitment by force, and it became a volunteer army open to Christians and Muslims.

The Ottomans divided their subjects into religious communities, and each *millet*, or "nation," enjoyed autonomous self-government under its religious leaders. The Ottoman Empire recognized Orthodox Christians, Jews, Armenian Christians, and Muslims as distinct millets, but despite its tolerance, the empire was an explicitly Islamic state. The **millet system** created a powerful bond between the Ottoman ruling class and religious leaders, who supported the sultan's rule in return for extensive authority over their own

■ **sultan** The ruler of the Ottoman Empire; he owned all the agricultural land of the empire and was served by an army and bureaucracy composed of highly trained slaves.

■ **janissary corps** The core of the sultan's army, composed of slave conscripts from non-Muslim parts of the empire; after 1683 it became a volunteer force.

■ **millet system** A system used by the Ottomans whereby subjects were divided into religious communities, with each millet (nation) enjoying autonomous self-government under its religious leaders.

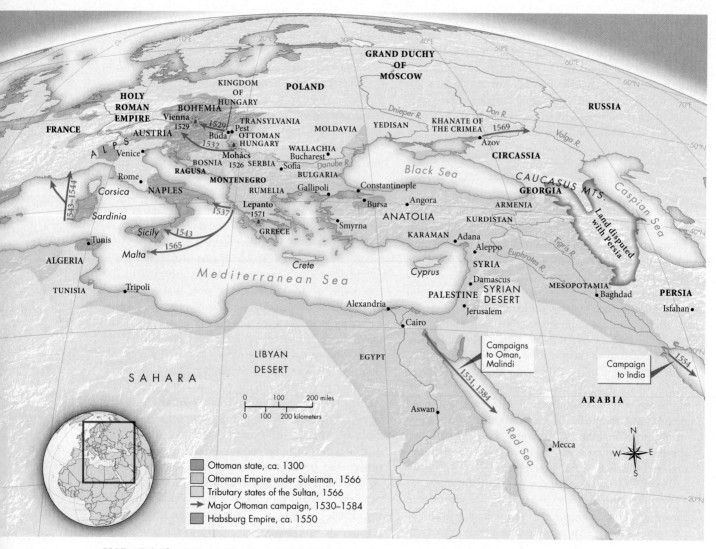

MAP 15.4 The Ottoman Empire at Its Height, 1566 The Ottomans, like their great rivals the Habsburgs, rose to rule a vast dynastic empire encompassing many different peoples and ethnic groups. The army and the bureaucracy served to unite the disparate territories into a single state under an absolutist ruler.

communities. Each millet collected taxes for the state, regulated group behavior, and maintained law courts, schools, houses of worship, and hospitals for its people.

Istanbul (known outside the empire by its original name, Constantinople) was the capital of the empire. The "old palace" was for the sultan's female family members, who lived in isolation under the care of eunuchs, men who were castrated to prevent sexual relations with women. The newer Topkapi palace was where officials worked and young slaves trained for future administrative or military careers. Sultans married women of the highest social standing, while keeping many concubines of low rank. To prevent the elite families into which they married from acquiring influence over the government, sultans procreated only with their concubines and not with official wives. They also adopted a policy of allowing each concubine to

produce only one male heir. At a young age, each son went to govern a province of the empire accompanied by his mother. These practices were intended to stabilize power and prevent a recurrence of the civil wars of the late fourteenth and early fifteenth centuries.

Sultan Suleiman undid these policies when he boldly married his concubine, a former slave of Polish origin named Hürrem, and had several children with her. (See "Individuals in Society: Hürrem," at right.) Starting with Suleiman, imperial wives began to take on more power. Marriages were arranged between sultans' daughters and high-ranking servants, creating powerful new members of the imperial household. Over time, the sultan's exclusive authority waned in favor of a more bureaucratic administration.

Like European states, the Ottoman Empire suffered significant crises in the late sixteenth and early

In Muslim culture, *harem* means a sacred place or a sanctuary. The term was applied to the part of the household occupied by women and children and forbidden to men outside the family. The most famous harem member in Ottoman history was Hürrem, wife of Suleiman the Magnificent.

Like many of the sultan's concubines, Hürrem (1505?–1558) was of foreign birth. Tradition holds that she was born Aleksandra Lisowska in the kingdom of Poland (present-day Ukraine). Captured during a Tartar raid and enslaved, she entered the imperial harem between 1517 and 1520, when she was about fifteen years old. Reports from Venetian visitors claimed that she was not outstandingly beautiful, but was possessed of wonderful grace, charm, and good humor, earning her the Turkish nickname Hürrem, or "joyful one." Soon after her arrival, Hürrem became the imperial favorite.

Suleiman's love for Hürrem led him to set aside all precedents for the role of a concubine, including the rule that concubines must cease having children once they gave birth to a male heir. By 1531 Hürrem had given Suleiman one daughter and five sons. In 1533 or 1534 Suleiman entered formal marriage with his consort—an unprecedented and scandalous honor for a concubine. Suleiman reportedly lavished attention on his wife and defied convention by allowing her to remain in the palace throughout her life instead of accompanying her son to a provincial governorship.

Contemporaries were shocked by Hürrem's influence over the sultan and resentful of the apparent role she played in politics and diplomacy. The Venetian ambassador Bassano wrote that "the Janissaries and the entire court hate her and her children likewise, but because the Sultan loves her, no one dares to speak."* Court rumors circulated that Hürrem used witchcraft to control the sultan and ordered the sultan's execution of his first-born son by another mother.

The correspondence between Suleiman and Hürrem, unavailable until the nineteenth century, along with Suleiman's own diaries, confirms her status as the sultan's most trusted confidant and adviser. During his frequent absences, the pair exchanged passionate love letters. Hürrem included political information and warned of potential uprisings. She also intervened in affairs between the empire and her former home, apparently helping Poland attain its privileged diplomatic status. She brought a feminine touch to diplomatic relations, sending personally embroidered articles to foreign leaders.

Hürrem used her enormous pension to contribute a mosque, two schools, a hospital, a fountain, and two public baths to Istanbul. In Jerusalem, Mecca, and Istanbul, she provided soup kitchens and hospices for pilgrims and the poor. She died in 1558, eight years before her husband. Her son Selim II (r. 1566–1574) inherited the throne.

This portrait emphasizes the beauty and sensual allure of Hürrem, who journeyed from slave to harem favorite to wife of the sultan and mother of his successor. (Pictures from History/akg-images)

Relying on Western observers' reports, historians traditionally depicted Hürrem as a manipulative and power-hungry social climber. They portrayed her career as the beginning of a "sultanate of women" in which strong imperial leadership gave way to court intrigue and debauchery. More recent historians have emphasized the intelligence and courage Hürrem demonstrated in navigating the ruthlessly competitive world of the harem.

Hürrem's journey from Ukrainian maiden to concubine to sultan's wife captured enormous public attention. She is the subject of numerous paintings, plays, and novels, as well as an opera, a ballet, and a symphony by the composer Haydn. Interest in and suspicion of Hürrem continues. In 2003 a Turkish miniseries once more depicted her as a scheming intriguer.

QUESTIONS FOR ANALYSIS

1. What types of power did Hürrem exercise during her lifetime? How did her gender enable her to attain certain kinds of power and also constrain her ability to exercise it?
2. What can an exceptional woman like Hürrem reveal about the broader political and social world in which she lived?

*Quoted in Galina Yermolenko, "Roxolana: The Greatest Empresse of the East," *The Muslim World* 95 (2005): 235.

Source: Leslie P. Pierce, *The Imperial Harem: Women and Sovereignty in the Ottoman Empire* (New York: Oxford University Press, 1993).

seventeenth centuries. Raised in the harem rather than taking on provincial governorships, the sultans who followed Suleiman were inexperienced and faced numerous political revolts. Ottoman finances suffered from the loss of international trade to the Portuguese and the Dutch, and the empire—like Spain—suffered from rising prices and a shrinking population. While the Bourbon monarchy was modernizing and enlarging the French army, the Ottomans failed to adopt new military technologies and training methods. As a result, its military strength, long feared throughout Europe, declined, leading ultimately to the ceding of Hungary and Transylvania to the Austrian Habsburgs in 1699 (see page 482). The Ottoman state adapted to these challenges with some measure of success, but did not recover the glory it held under Suleiman.

Constitutional Rule in England and the Dutch Republic

FOCUS QUESTION *Why and how did the constitutional state triumph in the Dutch Republic and England?*

While France, Prussia, Russia, and Austria developed absolutist states, England and the Netherlands evolved toward **constitutionalism**, which is the limitation of government by law. Constitutionalism also implies a balance between the authority and power of the government, on the one hand, and the rights and liberties of the subjects, on the other. By definition, all constitutionalist governments have a constitution, be it written or unwritten. A nation's constitution may be embodied in one basic document and occasionally revised by amendment, like the Constitution of the United States. Or it may be only partly formalized and include parliamentary statutes, judicial decisions, and a body of traditional procedures and practices, like the English and Dutch constitutions.

Despite their common commitment to constitutional government, England and the Dutch Republic represented significantly different alternatives to absolute rule. After decades of civil war and an experiment with **republicanism**, the English opted for a

■ **constitutionalism** A form of government in which power is limited by law and balanced between the authority and power of the government, on the one hand, and the rights and liberties of the subjects or citizens on the other hand; could include constitutional monarchies or republics.

■ **republicanism** A form of government in which there is no monarch and power rests in the hands of the people as exercised through elected representatives.

■ **Puritans** Members of a sixteenth- and seventeenth-century reform movement within the Church of England that advocated purifying it of Roman Catholic elements, like bishops, elaborate ceremonials, and wedding rings.

constitutional monarchy in 1688. This settlement, which has endured to this day, retained a monarch as the titular head of government but vested sovereignty in an elected parliament. Upon gaining independence from Spain in 1648, the Dutch rejected monarchical rule, adopting a republican form of government in which elected estates held supreme power. Neither was democratic by any standard, but to frustrated inhabitants of absolutist states they were shining examples of the restraint of arbitrary power and the rule of law.

Religious Divides and Civil War

In 1588 Queen Elizabeth I of England (r. 1558–1603) exercised very great personal power; by 1689 the English monarchy was severely circumscribed. A rare female monarch, Elizabeth was able to maintain control over her realm in part by refusing to marry and submit to a husband. She was immensely popular with her people, but left no immediate heir to continue her legacy.

In 1603 Elizabeth's Scottish cousin James Stuart succeeded her as James I (r. 1603–1625). Like Louis XIV, James believed that a monarch has a divine right to his authority and is responsible only to God. James went so far as to lecture the House of Commons: "There are no privileges and immunities which can stand against a divinely appointed King." Such a view ran directly counter to the long-standing English tradition that a person's property could not be taken away without due process of law. James I and his son Charles I (r. 1625–1649) considered such constraints intolerable and a threat to their divine-right prerogative. Consequently, bitter squabbles erupted between the Crown and the House of Commons. The expenses of England's intervention in the Thirty Years' War, through hostilities with Spain (1625–1630) and France (1627–1629), only exacerbated tensions. Charles I's response was to refuse to summon Parliament from 1629 onward.

Religious issues also embittered relations between the king and the House of Commons. In the early seventeenth century many English people felt dissatisfied with the Church of England established by Henry VIII (r. 1509–1547). Calvinist **Puritans** wanted to take the Reformation further by "purifying" the Anglican Church of Roman Catholic elements—elaborate vestments and ceremonials, bishops, and even the giving and wearing of wedding rings.

James I responded to such ideas by declaring, "No bishop, no king." For James, bishops were among the chief supporters of the throne. His son and successor, Charles I, further antagonized religious sentiments by marrying a French princess and supporting the heavy-handed policies of the archbishop of Canter-

Van Dyck, *Charles I at the Hunt*, ca. 1635   Anthony Van Dyck was the greatest of Rubens's many students. In 1633 he became court painter to Charles I. This portrait of Charles just dismounted from a horse emphasizes the aristocratic bearing, elegance, and innate authority of the king. Van Dyck's success led to innumerable commissions by members of the court and aristocratic society. He had a profound influence on portraiture in England and beyond; some scholars believe that this portrait influenced Rigaud's 1701 portrayal of Louis XIV (see page 473). (Musée du Louvre, Paris, France/Bridgeman Images)

bury William Laud (1573–1645). Laud provoked outrage by imposing two new elements on church organization in Scotland: a new prayer book, modeled on the Anglican *Book of Common Prayer*, and bishoprics.

Charles avoided addressing grievances against him by refusing to call Parliament into session from 1629 to 1640. Instead, he financed his government through extraordinary stopgap levies considered illegal by most English people. However, when Scottish Calvinists revolted against his religious policies, Charles was forced to summon Parliament to obtain funds for an army to put down the revolt. Accordingly, this Parliament, called the "Long Parliament" because it sat from 1640 to 1660, enacted legislation that limited the power of the monarch, and made government without Parliament impossible.

In 1641 the Parliament passed the Triennial Act, which compelled the king to summon Parliament every three years. The Commons impeached Archbishop Laud and then threatened to abolish bishops.

King Charles, fearful of a Scottish invasion—the original reason for summoning Parliament—reluctantly accepted these measures.

The next act in the conflict was precipitated by the outbreak of rebellion in Ireland, where English governors and landlords had long exploited the people. In 1641 the Catholic gentry of Ireland led an uprising in response to a feared invasion by anti-Catholic forces of the British Long Parliament.

Without an army, Charles I could neither come to terms with the Scots nor respond to the Irish rebellion. After a failed attempt to arrest parliamentary leaders, Charles left London for the north of England, where he began to raise an army. In response, Parliament formed its own army, the New Model Army, composed of the militia of the city of London and country squires with business connections. During the spring of 1642 both sides prepared for war. In July a linen weaver became the first casualty of the civil war during a skirmish between royal and parliamentary forces in Manchester.

The English Civil War, 1642–1649

The English civil war (1642–1649) pitted the power of the king against that of the Parliament. After three years of fighting, Parliament's New Model Army defeated the king's armies at the Battles of Naseby and Langport in the summer of 1645. Charles, though, refused to concede defeat. Both sides jockeyed for position, waiting for a decisive event. This arrived in the form of the army under the leadership of Oliver Cromwell, a member of the House of Commons and a devout Puritan. In 1647 Cromwell's forces captured the king and dismissed anti-Cromwell members of the Parliament. In 1649 the remaining representatives, known as the "Rump Parliament," put Charles on trial for high treason. Charles was found guilty and beheaded on January 30, 1649, an act that sent shock waves around Europe.

The Puritan Protectorate

With the execution of Charles, kingship was abolished. The question remained of how the country would be governed. One answer was provided by philosopher Thomas Hobbes (1588–1679). Hobbes held a pessimistic view of human nature and believed that, left to themselves, humans would compete violently for power and wealth. The only solution, as he outlined in his 1651 treatise *Leviathan*, was a social contract in which all members of society placed themselves under the absolute rule of the sovereign, who would maintain peace and order. Hobbes imagined society as a human body in which the monarch served as head and individual subjects together made up the body. Just as the body cannot sever its own head, so Hobbes believed that society could not, having accepted the contract, rise up against its king.

Hobbes's longing for a benevolent absolute monarch was not widely shared in England. Instead, Oliver Cromwell and his supporters enshrined a commonwealth, or republican government, known as the **Protectorate**. Theoretically, legislative power rested in the surviving members of Parliament, and executive power was lodged in a council of state. In fact, the army controlled the government, and Oliver Cromwell controlled the army, ruling what was essentially a military dictatorship.

The army prepared a constitution, the Instrument of Government (1653), that invested executive power in a lord protector (Cromwell) and a council of state. It provided for triennial parliaments and gave Parliament the sole power to raise taxes. But after repeated disputes, Cromwell dismissed Parliament in 1655, and the instrument was never formally endorsed. Cromwell continued the standing army and proclaimed quasi-martial law. He divided England into twelve military districts,

The Family of Henry Chorley, Haberdasher of Preston, ca. 1680   This painting celebrates the Puritan family values of order, discipline, and self-restraint. The wife is surrounded by her young children, emphasizing her motherly duties, while her husband is flanked by their grown sons. Nevertheless, the woman's expression suggests she is a strong-minded partner to her husband, not meekly subservient. The couple probably worked side by side in the family business of selling men's clothing and accessories. (Oil on canvas/Harris Museum and Art Gallery, Preston, Lancashire, UK/Bridgeman Images)

Puritan Occupations
These twelve engravings depict typical Puritan occupations and show that the Puritans came primarily from the artisan and lower middle classes. The governing classes and peasants made up a much smaller percentage of the Puritans and generally adhered to the traditions of the Church of England. (Private Collection/© Look and Learn/Peter Jackson Collection/Bridgeman Images)

each governed by a major general. Reflecting Puritan ideas of morality, Cromwell's state forbade sports, closed the theaters, and rigorously censored the press.

On the issue of religion, Cromwell favored some degree of toleration, and the Instrument of Government gave all Christians except Roman Catholics the right to practice their faith. Cromwell had long associated Catholicism in Ireland with sedition and heresy, and led an army there to reconquer the country in August 1649. One month later, his forces crushed a rebellion at Drogheda and massacred the garrison. After Cromwell's departure for England, atrocities worsened. The English banned Catholicism in Ireland, executed priests, and confiscated land from Catholics for English and Scottish settlers. These brutal acts left a legacy of Irish hatred for England.

Cromwell adopted mercantilist policies similar to those of absolutist France. He enforced a Navigation Act (1651) requiring that English goods be transported on English ships. The act was a great boost to the development of an English merchant marine and brought about a short but successful war with the commercially threatened Dutch. While mercantilist legislation ultimately benefited English commerce, for ordinary people the turmoil of foreign war only added to the harsh conditions of life induced by years of civil war. Cromwell also welcomed the immigration of Jews because of their skills in business, and they began to return to England after four centuries of absence.

The Protectorate collapsed when Cromwell died in 1658 and his ineffectual son succeeded him. Fed up with military rule, the English longed for a return to civilian government and, with it, common law and social stability. By 1660 they were ready to restore the monarchy.

The Restoration of the English Monarchy

The Restoration of 1660 brought to the throne Charles II (r. 1660–1685), eldest son of Charles I, who had been living on the continent. Both houses of Parliament were also restored, together with the established

■ **Protectorate** The English military dictatorship (1653–1658) established by Oliver Cromwell following the execution of Charles I.

Anglican Church. The Restoration failed to resolve two serious problems, however. What was to be the attitude of the state toward Puritans, Catholics, and dissenters from the established church? And what was to be the relationship between the king and Parliament?

To answer the first question, Parliament enacted the **Test Act** of 1673 against those outside the Church of England, denying them the right to vote, hold public office, preach, teach, attend the universities, or even assemble for meetings. But these restrictions could not be enforced. When the Quaker William Penn held a meeting of his Friends and was arrested, the jury refused to convict him.

In politics, Charles II's initial determination to work well with Parliament did not last long. Finding that Parliament did not grant him an adequate income, in 1670 Charles entered into a secret agreement with his cousin Louis XIV. The French king would give Charles £200,000 annually, and in return Charles would relax the laws against Catholics, gradually re-Catholicize England, and convert to Catholicism himself. When the details of this treaty leaked out, a great wave of anti-Catholic sentiment swept England.

When Charles died and his Catholic brother James became king, the worst English anti-Catholic fears were realized. In violation of the Test Act, James II (r. 1685–1688) appointed Roman Catholics to positions in the army, the universities, and local government. When these actions were challenged in the courts, the judges, whom James had appointed, decided in favor of the king. James and his supporters opened new Catholic churches and schools and issued tracts promoting Catholicism. Attempting to broaden his base of support with Protestant dissenters and nonconformists, James granted religious freedom to all.

James's opponents, a powerful coalition of eminent persons in Parliament and the Church of England, bitterly resisted James's ambitions. They offered the English throne to James's heir, his Protestant daughter Mary, and her Dutch husband, Prince William of Orange. In December 1688 James II, his queen, and their infant son fled to France and became pensioners of Louis XIV. Early in 1689 William and Mary were crowned king and queen of England.

Constitutional Monarchy

The English call the events of 1688 and 1689 the "Glorious Revolution" because they believe it replaced one king with another with barely any bloodshed. In truth, William's arrival sparked revolutionary riots and violence across the British Isles and in North American cities such as Boston and New York. Uprisings by supporters of James, known as Jacobites, occurred in 1689 in Scotland. In Ireland, the two sides waged outright war from 1689 to 1691. William's victory at the Battle of the Boyne (1690) and the subsequent Treaty of Limerick (1691) sealed his accession to power.

In England, the revolution represented the final destruction of the idea of divine-right monarchy. The men who brought about the revolution framed their intentions in the Bill of Rights, which was formulated in direct response to Stuart absolutism. Law was to be made in Parliament; once made, it could not be suspended by the Crown. Parliament had to be called at least once every three years. The independence of the judiciary was established, and there was to be no standing army in peacetime. Protestants could possess arms, but the Catholic minority could not. A Catholic could not inherit the throne. Additional legislation granted freedom of worship to Protestant dissenters, but not to Catholics. William and Mary accepted these principles when they took the throne, and the House of Parliament passed the Bill of Rights in December 1689.

The Glorious Revolution and the concept of representative government found its best defense in political philosopher John Locke's *Two Treatises of Government* (1690). Locke (1632–1704) maintained that a government that oversteps its proper function—protecting the natural rights of life, liberty, and property—becomes a tyranny. (See "Evaluating the Evidence 15.3: John Locke, *Two Treatises of Government*," at right.) By "natural" rights Locke meant rights basic to all men because all have the ability to reason. Under a tyrannical government, the people have the natural right to rebellion. On the basis of this link, he justified limiting the vote to property owners. Locke's idea that there are natural or universal rights equally valid for all peoples and societies was especially popular in colonial America. American colonists also appreciated his arguments that Native Americans had no property rights since they did not cultivate the land and, by extension, no political rights because they possessed no property.

Although the events of 1688 and 1689 brought England closer to Locke's ideal, they did not constitute a democratic revolution. The revolution placed sovereignty in Parliament, and Parliament represented the upper classes. The age of aristocratic government lasted at least until 1832 and in many ways until 1928, when women received full voting rights.

■ **Test Act** Legislation, passed by the English Parliament in 1673, to secure the position of the Anglican Church by stripping Puritans, Catholics, and other dissenters of the right to vote, preach, assemble, hold public office, and teach at or attend the universities.

■ **stadholder** The executive officer in each of the United Provinces of the Netherlands, a position often held by the princes of Orange.

John Locke, *Two Treatises of Government*

In 1688 opponents of King James II invited his daughter Mary and her husband, the Dutch prince William of Orange, to take the throne of England. James fled for the safety of France. One of the most outspoken proponents of the "Glorious Revolution" that brought William and Mary to the throne was philosopher John Locke. In this passage, Locke argues that sovereign power resides in the people, who may reject a monarch who does not obey the law.

~

But government into whosoever hands it is put, being as I have before shown, entrusted with this condition, and for this end, that men might have and secure their properties, the prince or senate, however it may have power to make laws for the regulation of property between the subjects one amongst another, yet can never have a power to take to themselves the whole, or any part of the subjects' property, without their own consent. For this would be in effect to leave them no property at all. . . .

'Tis true, governments cannot be supported without great charge, and 'tis fit every one who enjoys his share of the protection, should pay, out of this estate, his proportion for the maintenance of it. But still it must be with his own consent, i.e., the consent of the majority, giving it either by themselves, or their representatives chosen by them; for if any one shall claim a power to lay and levy taxes on the people, by his own authority, and without such consent of the people, he thereby invades the fundamental law of property, and subverts the end of government. For what

property have I in that which another may be right to take when he pleases to himself. . . .

The constitution of the legislative is the first and fundamental act of society, whereby provision is made for the continuation of their union, under the direction of persons, and bonds of laws, made by persons authorized thereunto, by the consent and appointment of the people, without which no one man, or number of men, amongst them, can have authority of making laws that shall be binding to the rest. When any one, or more, shall take upon them to make laws, whom the people have not appointed so to do, they make laws without authority, which the people are not therefore bound to obey; by which means they come again to be out of subjection, and may constitute to themselves a new legislative, as they think best, being in full liberty to resist the force of those, who, without authority, would impose any thing upon them.

EVALUATE THE EVIDENCE

1. For what reason do people form a government, according to Locke? What would be the justification for disobeying laws and rejecting the authority of government?
2. In what ways does this document legitimize the events of the Glorious Revolution?

Source: John Locke, *Two Treatises of Government*. Reprinted in *England's Glorious Revolution, 1688–1689*, ed. Steven C. A. Pincus (Boston: Bedford/St. Martin's, 2006), pp. 161–162, 164.

The Dutch Republic in the Seventeenth Century

In the late sixteenth century the seven northern provinces of the Netherlands fought for and won their independence from Spain. The independence of the Republic of the United Provinces of the Netherlands was recognized in 1648 in the treaty that ended the Thirty Years' War. In this period, often called the "golden age" of the Netherlands, Dutch ideas and attitudes played a profound role in shaping a new and modern worldview. At the same time, the United Provinces developed its own distinctive model of a constitutional state.

Rejecting the rule of a monarch, the Dutch established a republic, a state in which power rested in the hands of the people and was exercised through elected representatives. Other examples of republics in early modern Europe included the Swiss Confederation

and several autonomous city-states of Italy and the Holy Roman Empire. Among the Dutch, an oligarchy of wealthy businessmen called regents handled domestic affairs in each province's Estates (assemblies). The provincial Estates held virtually all the power. A federal assembly, or States General, handled foreign affairs and war, but it did not possess sovereign authority. All issues had to be referred back to the local Estates for approval, and each of the seven provinces could veto any proposed legislation. Holland, the province with the largest navy and the most wealth, usually dominated the republic and the States General.

In each province, the Estates appointed an executive officer, known as the **stadholder**, who carried out ceremonial functions and was responsible for military defense. Although in theory the stadholder was freely chosen by the Estates and was answerable to them, in

Jan Steen, *The Merry Family*, 1668   In this painting from the Dutch golden age, a happy family enjoys a boisterous song while seated around the dining table. Despite its carefree appearance, the painting was intended to teach a moral lesson. The children are shown drinking wine and smoking, bad habits they have learned from their parents. The inscription hanging over the mantelpiece (upper right) spells out the message clearly: "As the Old Sing, so Pipe the Young." (Oil on canvas/Rijksmuseum, Amsterdam, The Netherlands/Album/Art Resource, NY)

practice the strong and influential House of Orange usually held the office of stadholder in several of the seven provinces of the republic. This meant that tensions always lingered between supporters of the House of Orange and those of the staunchly republican Estates, who suspected that the princes of Orange harbored monarchical ambitions. When one of them, William III, took the English throne in 1688 with his wife, Mary, the republic simply continued without stadholders for several decades.

The political success of the Dutch rested on their phenomenal commercial prosperity. The Dutch originally came to dominate European shipping by putting profits from their original industry—herring fishing—into shipbuilding. They boasted the lowest shipping rates and largest merchant marine in Europe, allowing them to undersell foreign competitors (see Chapter 14). In the seventeenth century global trade and commerce brought the Dutch the highest standard of living in Europe, perhaps in the world. Salaries were high, and all classes of society ate well. A scholar has described the Netherlands as "an island of plenty in a sea of want." Consequently, the Netherlands experienced very few of the food riots that characterized the rest of Europe.[10]

The moral and ethical bases of Dutch commercial wealth were thrift, frugality, and religious toleration. Although there is scattered evidence of anti-Semitism, Jews enjoyed a level of acceptance and assimilation in business and general culture unique in early modern Europe. In the Dutch Republic, toleration paid off: it attracted a great deal of foreign capital and investment. After Louis XIV revoked the Edict of Nantes, many Huguenots fled France for the Dutch Republic. They brought with them a high level of artisanal skill and business experience as well as a loathing for state repression that would inspire the political views of the Enlightenment (see page 518).

Baroque Art and Music

Throughout European history, the cultural tastes of one age have often seemed unsatisfactory to the next. So it was with the baroque. The term *baroque* may have come from the Portuguese word for an "odd-shaped, imperfect pearl" and was commonly used by late-eighteenth-century art critics as an expression of scorn for what they considered an overblown, unbalanced style. Specialists now agree that the baroque style marked one of the high points in the history of European culture.

Rome and the revitalized Catholic Church of the late sixteenth century spurred the early development of the baroque. The papacy and the Jesuits encouraged the growth of an intensely emotional, exuberant art. These patrons wanted artists to go beyond the Renaissance focus on pleasing a small, wealthy cul-

tural elite. They wanted artists to appeal to the senses and thereby touch the souls and kindle the faith of ordinary churchgoers while proclaiming the power and confidence of the reformed Catholic Church. In addition to this underlying religious emotionalism, the baroque drew its sense of drama, motion, and ceaseless striving from the Catholic Reformation. The interior of the famous Jesuit Church of Jesus in Rome—the Gesù—combined all these characteristics in its lavish, wildly active decorations and frescoes.

Taking definite shape in Italy after 1600, the baroque style in the visual arts developed with exceptional vigor in Catholic countries—in Spain and Latin America, Austria, southern Germany, and Poland. Yet baroque art was more than just "Catholic art" in the seventeenth century and the first half of the eighteenth. True, neither Protestant England nor the Netherlands

Satire on Tulipmania   This painting mocks the speculative boom in tulips that hit the Dutch Republic in the 1630s. The left side of the image depicts a group of monkeys dressed as wealthy investors engaged in buying and selling tulips. On the right side, investors experience the pain of the crash, as one monkey urinates on a worthless tulip and another is brought to trial for debt. (By Jan Brueghel the Younger [1601–1678], [oil on panel]/Private Collection/Johnny Van Haeften Ltd., London/Bridgeman Images)

Rubens, *Garden of Love*, 1633–1634   This painting is an outstanding example of the lavishness and richness of baroque art. Born and raised in northern Europe, Peter Paul Rubens trained as a painter in Italy. Upon his return to the Spanish Netherlands, he became a renowned and amazingly prolific artist, patronized by rulers across Europe. Rubens was a devout Catholic, and his work conveys the emotional fervor of the Catholic Reformation. (Oil on canvas/Prado, Madrid, Spain/Giraudon/Bridgeman Images)

ever came fully under the spell of the baroque, but neither did Catholic France. And Protestants accounted for some of the finest examples of baroque style, especially in music. The baroque style spread partly because its tension and bombast spoke to an agitated age that was experiencing great violence and controversy in politics and religion.

In painting, the baroque reached maturity early with Peter Paul Rubens (1577–1640), the most outstanding and most representative of baroque painters. Studying in his native Flanders and in Italy, where he was influenced by masters of the High Renaissance such as Michelangelo, Rubens developed his own rich, sensuous, colorful style, which was characterized by animated figures, melodramatic contrasts, and monumental size. Rubens excelled in glorifying monarchs such as Queen Mother Marie de' Medici of France. He was also a devout Catholic; nearly half of his pictures treat Christian subjects. Yet one of Rubens's trademarks was the fleshy, sensual nudes who populate his canvases as Roman goddesses, water nymphs, and remarkably voluptuous saints and angels.

In music, the baroque style reached its culmination almost a century later in the dynamic, soaring lines of the endlessly inventive Johann Sebastian Bach (1685–1750). Organist and choirmaster of several Lutheran churches across Germany, Bach was equally at home writing secular concertos and sublime religious cantatas. Bach's organ music combined the baroque spirit of invention, tension, and emotion in an unforgettable striving toward the infinite. Unlike Rubens, Bach was not fully appreciated in his lifetime, but since the early nineteenth century his reputation has grown steadily.

NOTES

1. Quoted in Cecile Hugon, *Social France in the XVII Century* (London: McMilland, 1911), p. 189.
2. H. Kamen, "The Economic and Social Consequences of the Thirty Years' War," *Past and Present* 39 (1968): 44–61.
3. John A. Lynn, "Recalculating French Army Growth," in *The Military Revolution Debate: Readings on the Military Transformation of Early Modern Europe*, ed. Clifford J. Rogers (Boulder, Colo.: Westview Press, 1995), p. 125.
4. Quoted in John A. Lynn, *Giant of the Grand Siècle: The French Army, 1610–1715* (Cambridge: Cambridge University Press, 1997), p. 74.
5. J. H. Elliott, *Imperial Spain, 1469–1716* (New York: Mentor Books, 1963), pp. 306–308.
6. German History Documents, http://germanhistorydocs.ghi-dc .org/docpage.cfm?docpage_id=3733.
7. H. Rosenberg, *Bureaucracy, Aristocracy, and Autocracy: The Prussian Experience, 1660–1815* (Boston: Beacon Press, 1966), p. 43.
8. Cited in Giles MacDonogh, *Frederick the Great: A Life in Deed and Letters* (New York: St. Martin's, 2001), p. 23.
9. Rosenberg, *Bureaucracy, Aristocracy, and Autocracy*, p. 40.
10. S. Schama, *The Embarrassment of Riches: An Interpretation of Dutch Culture in the Golden Age* (New York: Alfred A. Knopf, 1987), pp. 165–170; quotation is on p. 167.

LOOKING BACK LOOKING AHEAD

The seventeenth century represented a difficult passage between two centuries of dynamism and growth. On one side lay the sixteenth century of religious enthusiasm and strife, overseas expansion, rising population, and vigorous commerce. On the other side stretched the eighteenth-century era of renewed population growth, economic development, and cultural flourishing. The first half of the seventeenth century was marked by the spread of religious and dynastic warfare across Europe, resulting in the death and dislocation of many millions. This catastrophe was compounded by recurrent episodes of crop failure, famine, and epidemic disease, all of which contributed to a stagnant economy and population loss. In the middle decades of the seventeenth century, the very survival of the European monarchies established in the Renaissance appeared in doubt.

With the re-establishment of order in the second half of the century, maintaining political and social stability was of paramount importance to European rulers and elites. In western and eastern Europe, a host of monarchs proclaimed their God-given and "absolute" authority to rule in the name of peace, unity, and good order. Rulers' ability to impose such claims in reality depended a great deal on compromise with local elites, who acquiesced to state power in exchange for privileges and payoffs. In this way, absolutism and constitutionalism did not always differ as much as they claimed. Both systems relied on political compromises forged from decades of strife.

The eighteenth century was to see this status quo thrown into question by new Enlightenment aspirations for human society, which themselves derived from the inquisitive and self-confident spirit of the Scientific Revolution. By the end of the century, demands for real popular sovereignty would challenge the foundations of the political order so painfully achieved in the seventeenth century.

Make Connections

Think about the larger developments and continuities within and across chapters.

1. This chapter has argued that, despite their political differences, rulers in absolutist and constitutionalist nations faced similar obstacles in the mid-seventeenth century and achieved many of the same goals. What evidence for this argument do you find in the chapter? Do you think that absolutist and constitutionalist rulers were, on the whole, more similar or more different?

2. Proponents of absolutism in western Europe believed that their form of monarchical rule was fundamentally different from and superior to what they saw as the "despotism" of Russia and the Ottoman Empire. What was the basis of this belief, and how accurate do you think it was?

15 REVIEW & EXPLORE

Identify Key Terms

Identify and explain the significance of each item below.

Peace of Westphalia (p. 468)

Fronde (p. 474)

mercantilism (p. 478)

Peace of Utrecht (p. 479)

Junkers (p. 482)

boyars (p. 485)

Cossacks (p. 485)

sultan (p. 489)

janissary corps (p. 489)

millet system (p. 489)

constitutionalism (p. 492)

republicanism (p. 492)

Puritans (p. 492)

Protectorate (p. 494)

Test Act (p. 496)

stadholder (p. 497)

Review the Main Ideas

Answer the focus questions from each section of the chapter.

◆ What were the common crises and achievements of seventeenth-century European states? (p. 466)

◆ What factors led to the rise of the French absolutist state under Louis XIV, and why did absolutist Spain experience decline in the same period? (p. 471)

◆ What were the social conditions of eastern Europe, and how did the rulers of Austria and Prussia transform their nations into powerful absolutist monarchies? (p. 481)

◆ What were the distinctive features of Russian and Ottoman absolutism? (p. 484)

◆ Why and how did the constitutional state triumph in the Dutch Republic and England? (p. 492)

Suggested Reading and Media Resources

BOOKS

- Beik, William. *A Social and Cultural History of Early Modern France.* 2009. An overview of early modern French history, by one of the leading authorities on the period.
- Benedict, Philip, and Myron P. Gutmann, eds. *Early Modern Europe: From Crisis to Stability.* 2005. A helpful introduction to the many facets of the crises of the seventeenth century.
- Elliott, John H. *Imperial Spain, 1469–1716,* 2d ed. 2002. An authoritative account of Spain's rise to imperial greatness and its slow decline.
- Gaunt, Peter, ed. *The English Civil War: The Essential Readings.* 2000. A collection showcasing leading historians' interpretations of the civil war.
- Goldgard, Anne. *Tulipmania: Money, Honor, and Knowledge in the Dutch Golden Age.* 2007. A fresh look at the speculative fever for tulip bulbs in the early-seventeenth-century Dutch Republic.
- Hagen, William W. *Ordinary Prussians: Brandenburg Junkers and Villagers, 1500–1840.* 2002. Provides a fascinating encounter with the people of a Prussian estate.
- Hughes, Lindsey, ed. *Peter the Great and the West: New Perspectives.* 2001. Essays by leading scholars on the reign of Peter the Great and his opening of Russia to the West.
- Ingrao, Charles W. *The Habsburg Monarchy, 1618–1815,* 2d ed. 2000. An excellent synthesis of the political and social development of the Habsburg empire in the early modern period.
- Kettering, Sharon. *Patronage in Sixteenth- and Seventeenth-Century France.* 2002. A collection of essays on courtly patronage, emphasizing the role of women in noble patronage networks.
- Pincus, Steven. *1688: The First Modern Revolution.* 2009. Revisionary account of the Glorious Revolution, emphasizing its toll in bloodshed and destruction of property and its global repercussions.
- Roman, Rolf, ed. *Baroque: Architecture, Sculpture, Painting.* 2007. A beautifully illustrated presentation of multiple facets of the baroque across Europe.
- Romaniello, Matthew P. *The Elusive Empire: Kazan and the Creation of Russia, 1552–1671.* 2012. A study of the conquest of Kazan by Ivan the Terrible in 1552 and the Russian empire built in its aftermath.
- Wilson, Peter H. *The Thirty Years War: Europe's Tragedy.* 2009. An overview of the origins and outcomes of the Thirty Years' War, focusing on political and economic issues in addition to religious conflicts.

DOCUMENTARIES

- *The Art of Baroque Dance* (Dancetime Publications, 2006). An introduction to baroque dance incorporating images of the architecture and art of the period alongside dance performances and information on major elements of the style.
- *Rubens: Passion, Faith, Sensuality and the Art of the Baroque* (Kultur Studio, 2011). A documentary introducing viewers to the work of Peter Paul Rubens, one of the greatest artists of the baroque style.

FEATURE FILMS AND TELEVISION

- *Alastriste* (Agustín Díaz Yanes, 2006). Set in the declining years of Spain's imperial glory, this film follows the violent adventures of an army captain who takes the son of a fallen comrade under his care.
- *Charles II: The Power and the Passion* (BBC, 2003). An award-winning television miniseries about the son of executed English king Charles I and the Restoration that brought him to the throne in 1660.
- *Cromwell* (Ken Hughes, 1970). The English civil war from its origin to Oliver Cromwell's victory, with battle scenes as well as personal stories of Cromwell and other central figures.
- *Girl with a Pearl Earring* (Peter Webber, 2003). The life and career of painter Johannes Vermeer told through the eyes of a fictional servant girl who becomes his assistant and model.
- *Molière* (Laurent Tirard, 2007). A film about the French playwright Molière, a favorite of King Louis XIV, which fancifully incorporates characters and plotlines from some of the writer's most celebrated plays.

WEB SITES

- *The Jesuit Relations.* This site contains the entire English translation of *The Jesuit Relations and Allied Documents,* the reports submitted by Jesuit missionaries in New France to authorities in the home country. **puffin.creighton.edu/jesuit/relations/**
- *Tour of Restoration London.* A Web site offering information on the places, food, and people of Restoration London, inspired by the novel *Invitation to a Funeral* by Molly Brown (1999). **www.okima.com/**
- *Versailles Palace.* The official Web site of the palace of Versailles, built by Louis XIV and inhabited by French royalty until the revolution of 1789. **en.chateauversailles.fr/homepage**

16

Toward a New Worldview

1540–1789

The intellectual developments of the sixteenth and seventeenth centuries created the modern worldview that the West continues to hold—and debate—to this day. In this period, fundamentally new ways of understanding the natural world emerged. Those leading the changes saw themselves as philosophers and referred to their field of study as "natural philosophy." Whereas medieval scholars looked to authoritative texts like the Bible or the classics, early modern natural philosophers performed experiments and relied on increasingly complex mathematical calculations. The resulting conception of the universe and its laws remained in force until Albert Einstein's discoveries at the beginning of the twentieth century. Along with new discoveries in botany, zoology, chemistry, and other domains, these developments constituted a fundamental shift in the basic framework for understanding the natural world and the methods for examining it known collectively as the "Scientific Revolution."

In the eighteenth century philosophers extended the use of reason from the study of nature to human society. They sought to bring the light of reason to bear on the darkness of prejudice, outmoded traditions, and ignorance. Self-proclaimed members of an "Enlightenment" movement, they wished to bring the same progress to human affairs as their predecessors had brought to the understanding of the natural world. While the Scientific Revolution ushered in modern science, the Enlightenment created concepts of human rights, equality, progress, universalism, and tolerance that still guide Western societies today. At the same time, some people used their new understanding of nature and reason to proclaim their own superiority, thus rationalizing attitudes now regarded as racist and sexist. Transformations in science and philosophy were enabled and encouraged by European overseas expansion, which challenged traditional ways of thinking by introducing an enormous variety of new peoples, plants, and animals. ◼

CHAPTER PREVIEW

The Scientific Revolution

What revolutionary discoveries were made in the sixteenth and seventeenth centuries, and why did they occur in Europe?

Important Changes in Scientific Thinking and Practice

What intellectual and social changes occurred as a result of the Scientific Revolution?

The Rise and Spread of Enlightenment Thought

How did the Enlightenment emerge, and what were major currents of Enlightenment thought?

The Social Life of the Enlightenment

How did Enlightenment thinkers address issues of racial and social difference, and how did new institutions and social practices diffuse Enlightenment thought?

Enlightened Absolutism

What impact did new ways of thinking have on political developments and monarchical absolutism?

Life During the Scientific Revolution
This 1768 painting by Joseph Wright captures the popularization of science and experimentation during the Enlightenment. Here, a scientist demonstrates the creation of a vacuum by withdrawing air from a flask, with the suffocating cockatoo serving as shocking proof of the experiment. (*An Experiment on a Bird in the Air Pump*, 1768/National Gallery, London/Bridgeman Images)

The Scientific Revolution

FOCUS QUESTION *What revolutionary discoveries were made in the sixteenth and seventeenth centuries, and why did they occur in Europe?*

Until the middle of the sixteenth century, Europeans relied on an understanding of motion and matter drawn from the ancient Greek philosopher Aristotle and adapted to Christian theology. The rise of the university, along with the intellectual vitality of the Renaissance and technological advancements, inspired European scholars to seek better explanations. From the sun-centered universe proposed by the Polish astronomer Nicolaus Copernicus to the great synthesis of physics and astronomy accomplished by the English scientist Isaac Newton, a revolutionary new understanding of the universe had emerged by the end of the seventeenth century. Collectively known as the "Scientific Revolution," the work of these scientists constituted highly significant milestones in the creation of modern science.

Hailed today as pioneers of a modern worldview, the major figures of the Scientific Revolution were for the most part devout Christians who saw their work as heralding the glory of creation and who combined older traditions of magic, astrology, and alchemy with their pathbreaking experimentation. Their discoveries took place in a broader context of international trade, imperial expansion, and cultural exchange. Alongside developments in modern science and natural philosophy, the growth of natural history in this period is now recognized by historians as a major achievement of the Scientific Revolution.

Why Europe?

In 1500 scientific activity flourished in many parts of the world. With the expansion of Islam into the lands of the Byzantine Empire in the seventh and eighth centuries, Muslim scholars inherited ancient Greek learning, which itself was built on centuries of borrowing from older civilizations in Egypt, Babylonia, and India. The interaction of peoples and cultures across the vast Muslim world, facilitated by religious tolerance and the common scholarly language of Arabic, was highly favorable to advances in learning.

In a great period of cultural and intellectual flourishing from 1000 to 1500, Muslim scholars thrived in cultural centers such as Baghdad and Córdoba, the capital of Islamic Spain. They established the world's first universities in Constantinople, Fez (Morocco), and Cairo. In this fertile atmosphere, scholars surpassed the texts they had inherited in areas such as mathematics, physics, astronomy, and medicine. Arab and Persian mathematicians, for example, invented algebra, the concept of the algorithm, and decimal point notation, while Arab astronomers improved on measurements recorded in ancient works.

China was also a vital center of scientific activity, which reached a peak in the mid-fourteenth century. Among its many achievements, papermaking, gunpowder, and the use of the compass in navigation were the most influential for the West. In Mesoamerica, civilizations such as the Maya and the Aztecs devised complex calendar systems based on astronomical observations and developed mathematics and writing.

Given the multiple world sites of learning and scholarship, it was by no means inevitable that Europe would take the lead in scientific thought or that "modern science" as we know it would emerge. In world history, periods of advancement produced by intense cultural interaction, such as those that occurred after the spread of Islam, are often followed by stagnation and decline during times of conflict and loss of authority. This is what happened in western Europe after the fall of the Western Roman Empire in the fifth century and in the Maya civilization after the collapse of its cultural and political centers around 900. The Muslim world successfully resisted a similar threat after the Mongol invasions.

The re-establishment of stronger monarchies and the growth of trade in the High Middle Ages contributed to a renewal of learning in western Europe. As Europeans began to encroach on Islamic lands in Iberia, Sicily, and the eastern Mediterranean, they became aware of the rich heritage of ancient Greek learning in these regions and the ways scholars had improved upon received knowledge. In the twelfth century many Greek texts—including works of Aristotle, Ptolemy, Galen, and Euclid previously unknown in the West—were translated into Latin, along with the commentaries of Arab scholars. A number of European cities created universities in which Aristotle's works dominated the curriculum.

As Europe recovered from the ravages of the Black Death in the late fourteenth and fifteenth centuries, the intellectual and cultural movement known as the Renaissance provided a crucial foundation for the Scientific Revolution (see Chapter 12). Scholars called humanists, working in the bustling mercantile city-states of Italy, emphasized the value of acquiring knowledge for the practical purposes of life. The quest to restore the glories of the ancient past led to the rediscovery of other classical texts such as Ptolemy's *Geography*, which was translated into Latin around 1410. An encyclopedic treatise on botany by Theophrastus was rediscovered in the 1450s moldering on the shelves of the Vatican library. The fall of Constantinople to the Ottomans in 1453 resulted in a great influx of little-known Greek works, as Christian scholars fled to Italy with their precious texts.

In this period, western European universities established new professorships of mathematics, astronomy, and natural philosophy. The prestige of the new fields was low, especially mathematics, which was reserved for practical problems such as accounting, surveying, and computing planetary tables, but not used as a tool to understand the functioning of the physical world itself. Nevertheless, these professorships eventually enabled the union of mathematics with natural philosophy that was to be a hallmark of the Scientific Revolution.

European overseas expansion in the fifteenth and sixteenth centuries provided another catalyst for new thought about the natural world. In particular, the navigational problems of long oceanic voyages in the age of expansion stimulated scientific research and invention. To help solve these problems, inventors developed many new scientific instruments, such as the telescope, barometer, thermometer, pendulum clock, microscope, and air pump. Better instruments, which permitted more accurate observations, often led to important new knowledge. Another crucial technology in this period was printing, which provided a faster and less expensive way to circulate knowledge.

Political and social conflicts were widespread in Eurasia in the sixteenth and early seventeenth centuries, but they had different results. The three large empires of the Muslim world—the Ottomans, Safavid Persians, and Mughals—that arose in the wake of the Mongol Empire sought to restore order and assert legitimacy in part by imposing Islamic orthodoxy. Their failure to adopt the printing press can be seen as part of a wider reaction against earlier traditions of innovation. Similarly, in China, under the Qing Dynasty, political newcomers legitimized their authority through stricter adherence to traditional ways. In contrast, western Europe remained politically fragmented into smaller competitive nations, divisions that were augmented by the religious fracturing of the Protestant Reformation. These conditions made it impossible for authorities to impose one orthodox set of ideas and thus allowed individuals to question dominant patterns of thinking.

Scientific Thought to 1500

The term *science* as we use it today came into use only in the nineteenth century. For medieval scholars, philosophy was the path to true knowledge about the world, and its proofs consisted of the authority of the

Chronology

ca. 1540–1700	Scientific Revolution
ca. 1690–1789	Enlightenment
ca. 1700–1800	Growth of book publishing
1720–1780	Rococo style in art and decoration
1740–1748	War of the Austrian Succession
1740–1780	Reign of the empress Maria Theresa of Austria
1740–1786	Reign of Frederick the Great of Prussia
ca. 1740–1789	Salons led by Parisian elites
1751–1772	Philosophes publish *Encyclopedia: The Rational Dictionary of the Sciences, the Arts, and the Crafts*
1756–1763	Seven Years' War
1762–1796	Reign of Catherine the Great of Russia
1780–1790	Reign of Joseph II of Austria
1791	Establishment of the Pale of Settlement

ancients (as interpreted by Christian theologians) and their techniques of logical argumentation. Questions about the physical nature of the universe and how it functioned belonged to a minor branch of philosophy, called **natural philosophy**. Natural philosophy was based primarily on the ideas of Aristotle, the great Greek philosopher of the fourth century B.C.E. Medieval theologians such as Thomas Aquinas brought Aristotelian philosophy into harmony with Christian doctrines. According to the Christianized view of Aristotle, a motionless earth stood at the center of the universe and was encompassed by ten separate concentric crystal spheres in which were embedded the moon, the sun, planets, and stars. Beyond the spheres was Heaven, with the throne of God and the souls of the saved. Angels kept the spheres moving in perfect circles.

Aristotle's views also dominated thinking about physics and motion on earth. Aristotle had distinguished between the world of the celestial spheres and that of the earth—the sublunar world. The spheres consisted of a perfect, incorruptible "quintessence," or fifth essence. The sublunar world, however, was made up of four imperfect, changeable elements: air, fire, water, and earth. Aristotle and his followers also believed that a uniform force moved an object at a constant speed and that the object would stop as soon as that force was removed.

Aristotle's cosmology made intellectual sense, but it could not account for the observed motions of the stars

■ **natural philosophy** An early modern term for the study of the nature of the universe, its purpose, and how it functioned; it encompassed what we would call "science" today.

The Aristotelian Universe as Imagined in the Sixteenth Century A round earth is at the center, surrounded by spheres of water, air, and fire. Beyond this small nucleus, the moon, the sun, and the five planets were embedded in their own rotating crystal spheres, with the stars sharing the surface of one enormous sphere. Beyond, the heavens were composed of unchanging ether. (From *Cosmographia*, by Peter Apian, 1630/Universal History Archive/UIG/ Bridgeman Images)

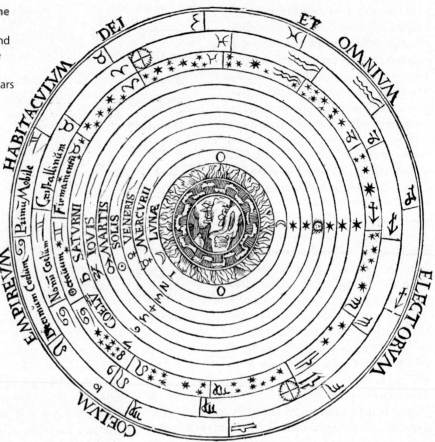

and planets and, in particular, provided no explanation for the apparent backward motion of the planets (which we now know occurs as planets closer to the sun periodically overtake the earth on their faster orbits). The great second-century scholar Ptolemy, a Hellenized Egyptian, offered a theory for this phenomenon. According to Ptolemy, the planets moved in small circles, called epicycles, each of which moved in turn along a larger circle, or deferent. Ptolemaic astronomy was less elegant than Aristotle's neat nested circles and required complex calculations, but it provided a surprisingly accurate model for predicting planetary motion.

The work of Ptolemy also provided the basic foundation of knowledge about the earth. Rediscovered around 1410, his *Geography* presented crucial advances on medieval cartography by representing a round earth divided into 360 degrees with the major latitude marks. Ptolemy's work reintroduced the idea of using coordinates of latitude and longitude to plot points on the earth's surface, a major advantage for long-distance navigation. However, Ptolemy's map reflected the limits of ancient knowledge, showing only the continents of Europe, Africa, and Asia, with land covering three-quarters of the world. Lacking awareness of the Pacific Ocean and the Americas, Ptolemy vastly underestimated the distance west from Europe to Asia.

These two frameworks reveal the strengths and limitations of European knowledge on the eve of the Scientific Revolution. Overcoming the authority of the ancients to develop a new understanding of the natural world, derived from precise techniques of observation and experimentation, was a monumental achievement. Europeans were not the first to use experimental methods—of which there was a long tradition in the Muslim world and elsewhere—but they were the first to separate scientific knowledge decisively from philosophical and religious beliefs and to accord mathematics a fundamental role in understanding the natural world.

The Copernican Hypothesis

The first great departure from the medieval system was the work of the Polish cleric Nicolaus Copernicus (1473–1543). Copernicus studied astronomy, medicine, and church law at the famed universities of Bologna, Padua, and Ferrara before taking up a church position in East Prussia. Copernicus came to believe that Ptolemy's cumbersome rules detracted from the majesty of a perfect creator. He preferred an idea espoused by some ancient Greek and Arab scholars: that the sun, rather than the earth, was at the center of the universe. Without questioning the Aristotelian belief in crystal spheres or the idea that circular motion was divine, Copernicus theorized that the stars and planets, including the earth, revolved around a fixed sun. Copernicus worked on his hypothesis from 1506 to 1530, but, fearing the ridicule of other scholars, he did not publish his *On the Revolutions of the Heavenly Spheres* until 1543, the year of his death.

The **Copernican hypothesis** had enormous scientific and religious implications, many of which the conservative Copernicus did not anticipate. First, it put the stars at rest, their apparent nightly movement simply a result of the earth's rotation. Thus it destroyed the main reason for believing in crystal spheres capable of moving the stars around the earth. Second, Copernicus's theory suggested a universe of staggering size. If in the course of a year the earth moved around the sun and yet the stars appeared to remain in the same place, then the universe was unthinkably large. Third, by using mathematics, instead of philosophy, to justify his theories, Copernicus challenged the traditional hierarchy of the disciplines. Finally, by characterizing the earth as just another planet, Copernicus destroyed the basic idea of Aristotelian physics—that the earthly sphere was quite different from the heavenly one. Where then were Heaven and the throne of God?

Religious leaders varied in their response to Copernicus's theories. A few Protestant scholars became avid Copernicans, while others accepted some elements of his criticism of Ptolemy, but firmly rejected the notion that the earth moved, a doctrine that contradicted the literal reading of some passages of the Bible. Among Catholics, Copernicus's ideas drew little attention prior to 1600. Because the Catholic Church had never held to literal interpretations of the Bible, it did not officially declare the Copernican hypothesis false until 1616.

Other events were almost as influential in creating doubts about traditional astronomy. In 1572 a new star appeared and shone very brightly for almost two years. The new star, which was actually a distant exploding star, made an enormous impression on people. It seemed to contradict the idea that the heavenly spheres were unchanging and therefore perfect. In 1577 a new comet suddenly moved through the sky, cutting a straight path across the supposedly impenetrable crystal spheres. It was time, as a sixteenth-century scientific writer put it, for "the radical renovation of astronomy."[1]

Brahe, Kepler, and Galileo: Proving Copernicus Right

One astronomer who agreed with the Copernican hypothesis was the Danish astronomer Tycho Brahe (TEE-koh BRAH-hee) (1546–1601). Brahe established himself as Europe's leading astronomer with his detailed observations of the new star that appeared in 1572. Impressed by his work, the king of Denmark

Hevelius and His Wife Portable sextants were used to chart a ship's position at sea by measuring the altitude of celestial bodies above the horizon. Astronomers used much larger sextants to measure the angular distances between two bodies. Here, Johannes Hevelius makes use of the great brass sextant at the Danzig observatory, with the help of his wife, Elisabetha. Six feet in radius, this instrument was closely modeled on the one used by Tycho Brahe. (Engraving from *Machina Coelestis*, 1673, by Johannes Hevelius/SSPL/Getty Images)

provided funds for Brahe to build the most sophisticated observatory of his day.

Upon the king's death, Brahe acquired a new patron in the Holy Roman emperor Rudolph II and built a new observatory in Prague. For twenty years Brahe observed the stars and planets with the naked eye in order to create new and improved tables of planetary motions, dubbed the *Rudolphine Tables* in honor of his patron. His limited understanding of mathematics and his sudden death in 1601, however, prevented him from making much sense out of his mass of data. Part Ptolemaic, part Copernican, he believed that all the

■ **Copernican hypothesis** The idea that the sun, not the earth, was the center of the universe.

planets except the earth revolved around the sun and that the entire group of sun and planets revolved in turn around the earth-moon system.

Brahe's assistant, Johannes Kepler (1571–1630), carefully re-examined his predecessor's notations and came to believe that they could not be explained by Ptolemy's astronomy. Abandoning the notion of epicycles and deferents—which even Copernicus had retained in part—Kepler developed three revolutionary laws of planetary motion. First, largely through observations of the planet Mars, he demonstrated that the orbits of the planets around the sun are elliptical rather than circular. Second, he demonstrated that the planets do not move at a uniform speed in their orbits. When a planet is close to the sun it moves more rapidly, and it slows as it moves farther away from the sun. Finally, Kepler's third law stated that the time a planet takes to make its complete orbit is precisely related to its distance from the sun.

Kepler's contribution was monumental. Whereas Copernicus had used mathematics to describe planetary movement, Kepler proved mathematically the precise relations of a sun-centered (solar) system. He thus united for the first time the theoretical cosmology of natural philosophy with mathematics. His work demolished the old system of Aristotle and Ptolemy, and with his third law he came close to formulating the idea of universal gravitation (see the next section). In 1627 he also completed Brahe's *Rudolphine Tables*, which were used by astronomers for many years.

While Kepler was unraveling planetary motion, a young Florentine named Galileo Galilei (1564–1642) was challenging Aristotelian ideas about motion on earth. Like Kepler and so many early scientists, Galileo was a poor nobleman first marked for a religious career. Instead, his fascination with mathematics led to a professorship in which he examined motion and mechanics in a new way. Galileo focused on deficiencies in Aristotle's theories of motion. He measured the movement of a rolling ball across a surface, repeating the action again and again to verify his results. In his famous acceleration experiment, he showed that a uniform force—in this case, gravity—produced a uniform acceleration. Through another experiment, he formulated the **law of inertia**. He found that rest was not the natural state of objects. Rather, an object continues in motion forever unless stopped by some external force. His discoveries proved Aristotelian physics wrong.

On hearing details about the invention of the telescope in Holland, Galileo made one for himself and

trained it on the heavens. He quickly discovered the first four moons of Jupiter, which clearly suggested that Jupiter could not possibly be embedded in an impenetrable crystal sphere as Aristotle and Ptolemy maintained. This discovery provided new evidence for the Copernican theory, in which Galileo already believed. Galileo then pointed his telescope at the moon. He wrote in 1610 in *The Sidereal Messenger*: "By the aid of a telescope anyone may behold [the Milky Way] in a manner which so distinctly appeals to the senses that all the disputes which have tormented philosophers through so many ages are exploded by the irrefutable evidence of our eyes, and we are freed from wordy disputes upon the subject."[2] (See "Evaluating the Evidence 16.1: Galileo Galilei, *The Sidereal Messenger*," at right.)

Reading these famous lines, one feels a crucial corner in Western civilization being turned. No longer should one rely on established authority. A new method of learning and investigating was being developed, one that proved useful in any field of inquiry. A historian investigating documents of the past, for example, is not so different from a Galileo studying stars and rolling balls.

Newton's Synthesis

By about 1640 the work of Brahe, Kepler, and Galileo had been largely accepted by the scientific community despite opposition from religious leaders. The old Aristotelian astronomy and physics were in ruins, and several fundamental breakthroughs had been made. But the new findings failed to explain what forces controlled the movement of the planets and objects on earth. That challenge was taken up by English scientist Isaac Newton (1642–1727), a genius who spectacularly united the experimental and theoretical-mathematical sides of modern science.

Newton was born into the lower English gentry, and he enrolled at Cambridge University in 1661. He arrived at some of his most basic ideas about physics in 1666 at age twenty-four, but was unable to prove them mathematically. In 1684, after years of studying optics, Newton returned to physics for eighteen intensive months. The result was his towering accomplishment, a single explanatory system that could integrate the astronomy of Copernicus, as corrected by Kepler's laws, with the physics of Galileo and his predecessors. Newton did this through a set of mathematical laws that explain motion and mechanics. These laws were published in 1687 in Newton's *Mathematical Principles of Natural Philosophy* (also known as the *Principia*). Because of their complexity, it took scientists and engineers two hundred years to work out all their implications.

The key feature of the Newtonian synthesis was the **law of universal gravitation**. According to this law,

■ **law of inertia** A law formulated by Galileo that states that motion, not rest, is the natural state of an object, and that an object continues in motion forever unless stopped by some external force.

■ **law of universal gravitation** Newton's law that all objects are attracted to one another and that the force of attraction is proportional to the objects' quantity of matter and inversely proportional to the square of the distance between them.

Galileo Galilei, *The Sidereal Messenger*

In this passage from The Sidereal Messenger *(1610), Galileo Galilei recounts his experiments to build a telescope and his observations of the moon. By discovering the irregularity of the moon's surface, Galileo disproved a central tenet of medieval cosmography: that the heavens were composed of perfect, unblemished spheres essentially different from the base matter of earth.*

About ten months ago a report reached my ears that a Dutchman had constructed a telescope, by the aid of which visible objects, although at a great distance from the eye of the observer, were seen distinctly as if near. . . . A few days after, I received confirmation of the report in a letter written from Paris . . . , which finally determined me to give myself up first to inquire into the principle of the telescope, and then to consider the means by which I might compass [achieve] the invention of a similar instrument, which a little while after I succeeded in doing, through deep study of the theory of refraction; and I prepared a tube, at first of lead, in the ends of which I fitted two glass lenses, both plane on one side, but on the other side one spherically convex, and the other concave. . . . At length, by sparing neither labour nor expense, I succeeded in constructing for myself an instrument so superior that objects seen through it appear magnified nearly a thousand times, and more than thirty times nearer than if viewed by the natural powers of sight alone. . . .

Let me speak first of the surface of the moon, which is turned towards us. For the sake of being understood more easily, I distinguish two parts in it, which I call respectively the brighter and the darker. The brighter part seems to surround and pervade the whole hemisphere, but the darker part, like a sort of cloud, discolours the moon's surface and makes it appear covered with spots. Now these spots . . . are plain to every one, and every age has seen them, wherefore I shall call them *great* or *ancient* spots, to distinguish them from other spots, smaller in size, but so thickly scattered that they sprinkle the whole surface of the moon, but especially the brighter portion of it. These spots have never been observed by any one before me, and from my observations of them, often repeated, I have been led to that opinion which I have expressed, namely, that I feel sure that the surface of the moon is not perfectly smooth, free from inequalities and exactly spherical, as a large school of philosophers considers with regard to the moon and the other heavenly bodies, but that, on the contrary, it is full of inequalities, uneven, full of hollows and protuberances, just like the surface of the earth itself, which is varied everywhere by lofty mountains and deep valleys.

EVALUATE THE EVIDENCE

1. What did the telescope permit Galileo to see on the moon that was not visible to the naked eye, and how did he interpret his observations?
2. Why were Galileo's observations so important to the destruction of the Ptolemaic universe?

Source: Galileo Galilei, *The Sidereal Messenger* (London: Rivingtons, 1880), pp. 10–11, 14–15.

every body in the universe attracts every other body in the universe in a precise mathematical relationship, whereby the force of attraction is proportional to the quantity of matter of the objects and inversely proportional to the square of the distance between them. The whole universe—from Kepler's elliptical orbits to Galileo's rolling balls—was unified in one majestic system. Newton's synthesis of mathematics with physics and astronomy prevailed until the twentieth century and established him as one of the most important figures in the history of science. Yet, near the end of his life, this acclaimed figure declared: "I do not know what I may appear to the world; but to myself I seem to have been only like a boy, playing on the seashore, and diverting myself, in now and then finding a smoother pebble or a prettier shell than ordinary, whilst the great ocean of truth lay all undiscovered before me."[3]

Natural History and Empire

At the same time that they made advances in astronomy and physics, Europeans embarked on the pursuit of knowledge about unknown geographical regions and the useful and valuable resources they contained. Because they were the first to acquire a large overseas empire, the Spanish pioneered these efforts. Following the conquest of the Aztec and Inca Empires (see Chapter 14), they sought to learn about and profit from their New World holdings. The Spanish crown sponsored many scientific expeditions to gather information and specimens, out of which emerged new discoveries that reshaped the fields of botany, zoology, cartography, and metallurgy, among others. These accomplishments have attracted less attention from historians in part because the strict policy of secrecy imposed on scientific discoveries by the Spanish crown limits the number of available documents about them.

Plants were a particular source of interest because they offered tremendous profits in the form of spices, medicines, dyes, and cash crops. King Philip II of Spain sent his personal physician, Francisco Hernández, to New Spain for seven years in the 1560s. Hernández filled fifteen volumes with illustrations of three thousand plants previously unknown in Europe. He extensively interviewed local healers about the plants' medicinal properties, thereby benefiting from centuries of Mesoamerican botanical knowledge. In the seventeenth century, for example, the Spanish obtained a monopoly on the world's supply of cinchona bark, which comes from a tree native to the high altitudes of the Andes and was the first effective treatment for malaria.

Other countries followed the Spanish example as their global empires expanded, relying on both official expeditions and the private initiative of merchants, missionaries, and settlers. (See "Evaluating the Evidence 16.2: 'An Account of a Particular Species of Cocoon,'" page 514.) Royal botanical gardens served as living laboratories for cultivating valuable foreign plants. Over time, the stream of new information about plant and animal species overwhelmed existing intellectual frameworks. Carl Linnaeus (1707–1778) of Sweden sent his students on exploratory voyages around the world and, based on their observations and the specimens they collected, devised a formal system of naming and classifying living organisms still used today (with substantial revisions).

New encyclopedias of natural history popularized this knowledge with realistic drawings and descriptions emphasizing the usefulness of animals and plants. Audiences at home eagerly read the accounts of naturalists, who braved the heat, insects, and diseases of tropical jungles to bring home exotic animal, vegetable, and mineral specimens (along with indigenous human subjects). They heard much less about the many local guides, translators, and practitioners of medicine and science who made these expeditions possible and who contributed rich knowledge about the natural world.

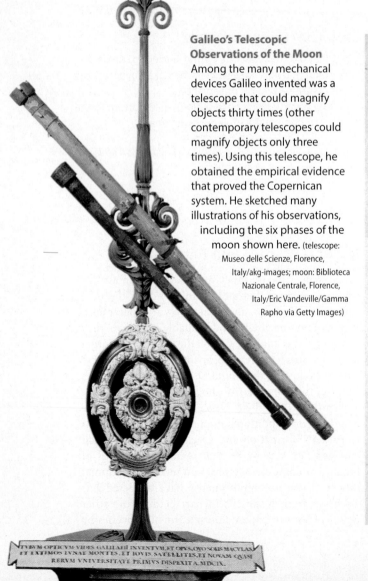

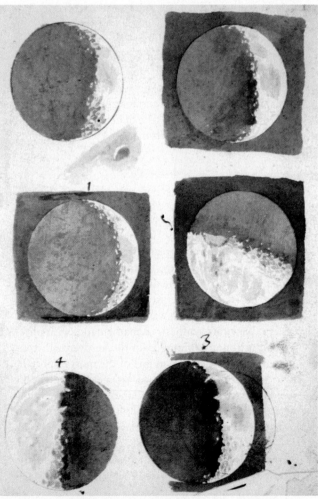

Galileo's Telescopic Observations of the Moon Among the many mechanical devices Galileo invented was a telescope that could magnify objects thirty times (other contemporary telescopes could magnify objects only three times). Using this telescope, he obtained the empirical evidence that proved the Copernican system. He sketched many illustrations of his observations, including the six phases of the moon shown here. (telescope: Museo delle Scienze, Florence, Italy/akg-images; moon: Biblioteca Nazionale Centrale, Florence, Italy/Eric Vandeville/Gamma Rapho via Getty Images)

Magic and Alchemy

Recent historical research on the Scientific Revolution has focused on the contribution of ideas and practices that no longer belong to the realm of science, such as astrology and alchemy. For most of human history, interest in astronomy was inspired by the belief that the movement of heavenly bodies influenced events on earth. Many of the most celebrated astronomers also worked as astrologers. Used as a diagnostic tool in medicine, astrology formed a regular part of the curriculum of medical schools.

Centuries-old practices of magic and alchemy also remained important traditions for natural philosophers. Early modern practitioners of magic strove to understand and control hidden connections they perceived among different elements of the natural world, such as that between a magnet and iron. The idea that objects possessed hidden or "occult" qualities that allowed them to affect other objects was a particularly important legacy of the magical tradition. Belief in occult qualities—or numerology or cosmic harmony—was not antithetical to belief in God. On the contrary, adherents believed that only a divine creator could infuse the universe with such meaningful mystery.

Johannes Kepler exemplifies the interaction among these different strands of interest in the natural world. His duties as court mathematician included casting horoscopes for the royal family, and he guided his own life by astrological principles. He also wrote at length on cosmic harmonies and explained elliptical motion through ideas about the beautiful music created by the combined motion of the planets. Kepler's fictional account of travel to the moon, written partly to illustrate the idea of a non-earth-centered universe, caused controversy and may have contributed to the arrest and trial of his mother as a witch in 1620. Kepler also suffered because of his unorthodox brand of Lutheranism, which led to his condemnation by both Lutherans and Catholics.

Another example of the interweaving of ideas and beliefs is Sir Isaac Newton, who was both intensely religious and fascinated by alchemy, whose practitioners believed (among other things) that base metals could be turned into gold. Critics complained that his idea of universal gravitation was merely a restatement of old magical ideas about the innate sympathies between bodies; Newton himself believed that the attraction of gravity resulted from God's actions in the universe.

Important Changes in Scientific Thinking and Practice

FOCUS QUESTION *What intellectual and social changes occurred as a result of the Scientific Revolution?*

The Scientific Revolution was not accomplished by a handful of brilliant individuals working alone. Advancements occurred in many fields—medicine, chemistry, and botany, among others—as scholars developed new methods to seek answers to long-standing problems. They did so in collaboration with skilled craftsmen who invented new instruments and helped conduct experiments. These results circulated in an intellectual community from which women were usually excluded.

Metamorphoses of the Caterpillar and Moth Maria Sibylla Merian (1647–1717), the stepdaughter of a Dutch painter, became a celebrated scientific illustrator in her own right. Her finely observed pictures of insects in the South American colony of Suriname introduced many new species. For Merian, science was intimately tied with art: she not only painted but also bred caterpillars and performed experiments on them. Her two-year stay in Suriname, accompanied by a teenage daughter, was a daring feat for a seventeenth-century woman. (From *Metamorphosis Insectorum Surinamensium*, 1705/akg-images)

"An Account of a Particular Species of Cocoon"

To disseminate its members' work, the Royal Society of England published the results of its meetings in the Philosophical Transactions of the Royal Society. *The passage below is excerpted from a presentation made to the society in the mid-eighteenth century by the Reverend Samuel Pullein, a graduate of Trinity College in Dublin. A relative of the governor of Jamaica, Pullein became fascinated by the idea of introducing silkworm cultivation to the American colonies. His presentation exemplifies the contribution of many minor enthusiasts to the progress of science in this period and the importance of colonialism to the new knowledge.*

Having lately seen the aurelia of a particular species of caterpillar, I judged, from its texture and consistence, that there might be procured from it a silk not inferior to that of the common silk-worm in its quality, and in its quantity much superior. I have made some experiments on this new species of silk-pod, which strengthen this opinion.

This pod is about three inches and a quarter in length, and above one inch in diameter; its outward form not so regular an oval as that of the common silk-worm; its consistence somewhat like that of a dried bladder, when not fully blown; its colour of a reddish brown; its whole weight 21 grains.

Upon cutting open this outer integument, there appeared in the inside a pod completely oval, as that of the silk-worm. It was covered with some floss-silk, by which it was connected to the outer coat, being of the same colour. Its length was two inches; its diameter nearly one inch; and its weight nine grains.

The pod could not be easily unwinded, because it was perforated by the moth: but, upon putting it in hot water, I reeled off so much as sufficed to form a judgment of the strength and staple of its silk.

The single thread winded off the pod in the same manner as that of the common silk-worm; seeming in all respects as fine, and as tough. I doubled this thread so often as to contain twenty in thickness; and the compound thread was as smooth, as elastic, and as glossy, as that of the common silk-worm. I tried what weight it would bear; and it bore fifteen ounces and a half, and broke with somewhat less than sixteen, upon several trials. . . .

The caterpillar which produces this pod is a native of America. It was found in Pennsylvania: the pod was fixed to the small branch of a tree, which seemed to be either of the crab or hawthorn species. . . .

I do not conceive that it will be at all difficult to find out the caterpillar, or the tree it feeds on; or to reel such a quantity of the silk as shall, when woven into ribband, more fully demonstrate whether it be of that value which I judge it. For by comparing it with the *cocoon* of the wild Chinese silk-worm, from which an excellent species of silk is made, I have no doubt of its being the same species; and would be glad if, by this memorial, I could induce the people of America to make trial of it.

EVALUATE THE EVIDENCE

1. What is Pullein's aim in presenting his research to the Royal Society? How does he try to establish the credibility of his claims about the silkworm?
2. In what ways does this document belong to the "Scientific Revolution" as discussed in this chapter? What does Pullein's presentation tell us about the nature of "science" presented to the Royal Society in the mid-eighteenth century?

Source: "An Account of a Particular Species of Cocoon, or Silk-Pod, from America," Reverend Samuel Pullein, M.A., *Philosophical Transactions of the Royal Society* 15 (1759): 54–57.

The Methods of Science: Bacon and Descartes

One of the keys to the achievement of a new worldview in the seventeenth century was the development of better ways of obtaining knowledge. Two important thinkers, Francis Bacon (1561–1626) and René Descartes (day-KAHRT) (1596–1650), were influential in describing and advocating for improved scientific methods based, respectively, on experimentation and mathematical reasoning.

The English politician and writer Francis Bacon was the greatest early propagandist for the experimental method. Rejecting the Aristotelian and medieval method of using speculative reasoning to build general theories, Bacon argued that new knowledge had to be pursued through empirical research. The researcher who wants to learn more about leaves or rocks, for example, should not speculate about the subject but rather collect a multitude of specimens and then compare and analyze them to derive general principles. Bacon formalized the empirical method, which had already been used by Brahe and Galileo, into the general theory of inductive reasoning known as **empiricism**. Bacon's work, and his prestige as lord chancellor under James I, led to the widespread adoption of what was called "experimental philosophy" in England after his death. In 1660 followers of Bacon created the Royal Society (still in existence), which met weekly to conduct experiments and discuss the latest findings of scholars across Europe.

On the continent, more speculative methods retained support. In 1619, as a twenty-three-year-old soldier serving in the Thirty Years' War, the French philosopher René Descartes experienced a life-changing intellectual vision. Descartes saw that there was a perfect correspondence between geometry and algebra and that geometrical spatial figures could be expressed as algebraic equations and vice versa. A major step forward in the history of mathematics, Descartes's discovery of analytic geometry provided scientists with an important new tool.

Descartes used mathematics to elaborate a highly influential vision of the workings of the cosmos. Accepting Galileo's claim that all elements of the universe are composed of the same matter, Descartes began to investigate the basic nature of matter. Drawing on ancient Greek atomist philosophies, Descartes developed the idea that matter was made up of identical "corpuscles" (tiny particles) that collided together in an endless series of motions, akin to the workings of a machine. All occurrences in nature could be analyzed as matter in motion and, according to Descartes, the total "quantity of motion" in the universe was constant. Descartes's mechanistic view of the universe depended on the idea that a vacuum was impossible, which meant that every action had an equal reaction, continuing in an eternal chain reaction.

Although Descartes's hypothesis about the vacuum was proved wrong, his notion of a mechanistic universe intelligible through the physics of motion proved inspirational. Decades later, Newton rejected Descartes's idea of a full universe and several of his other ideas, but retained the notion of a mechanistic universe as a key element of his own system.

Descartes's greatest achievement was to develop his initial vision into a whole philosophy of knowledge and science. The Aristotelian cosmos was appealing in part because it corresponded with the evidence of the human senses. When experiments proved that sensory impressions could be wrong, Descartes decided it was necessary to doubt them and everything that could reasonably be doubted, and to then, as in geometry, use deductive reasoning from self-evident truths, which he called "first principles," to ascertain scientific laws. Descartes's reasoning ultimately reduced all sub-stances to "matter" and "mind" — that is, to the physical and the spiritual. The devout Descartes believed that God had endowed man with reason for a purpose and that rational speculation could provide a path to the truths of creation. His view of the world as consisting of two fundamental entities is known as **Cartesian dualism**. Descartes's thought was highly influential in France and the Netherlands, but less so in England, where experimental philosophy won the day.

Both Bacon's inductive experimentalism and Descartes's deductive mathematical reasoning had flaws. Bacon's inability to appreciate the importance of mathematics and his obsession with practical results

Major Contributors to the Scientific Revolution

Nicolaus Copernicus (1473–1543)	*On the Revolutions of the Heavenly Spheres* (1543); theorized that the sun, rather than the earth, was the center of the galaxy
Paracelsus (1493–1541)	Swiss physician and alchemist who pioneered the use of chemicals and drugs to address illness
Andreas Vesalius (1514–1564)	*On the Structure of the Human Body* (1543)
Tycho Brahe (1546–1601)	Built observatory and compiled data for the *Rudolphine Tables*, a new table of planetary data
Francis Bacon (1561–1626)	Advocated experimental method, formalizing theory of inductive reasoning known as empiricism
Galileo Galilei (1564–1642)	Used telescopic observation to provide evidence for Copernican hypothesis; experimented to formulate laws of physics, such as inertia
Johannes Kepler (1571–1630)	Used Brahe's data to mathematically prove the Copernican hypothesis; his new laws of planetary motion united for the first time natural philosophy and mathematics; completed the *Rudolphine Tables* in 1627
William Harvey (1578–1657)	Discovery of circulation of blood (1628)
René Descartes (1596–1650)	Used deductive reasoning to formulate the theory of Cartesian dualism
Robert Boyle (1627–1691)	Boyle's law (1662) governing the pressure of gases
Isaac Newton (1642–1727)	*Principia Mathematica* (1687); set forth the law of universal gravitation, synthesizing previous findings of motion and matter

■ **empiricism** A theory of inductive reasoning that calls for acquiring evidence through observation and experimentation rather than deductive reason and speculation.

■ **Cartesian dualism** Descartes's view that all of reality could ultimately be reduced to mind and matter.

clearly showed the limitations of antitheoretical empiricism. Likewise, some of Descartes's positions demonstrated the inadequacy of rigid, dogmatic rationalism. For example, he believed that it was possible to deduce the whole science of medicine from first principles. Although insufficient on their own, Bacon's and Descartes's extreme approaches are combined in the modern scientific method, which began to crystallize in the late seventeenth century.

Medicine, the Body, and Chemistry

The Scientific Revolution, which began with the study of the cosmos, soon transformed the understanding of the microcosm of the human body. For many centuries the ancient Greek physician Galen's explanation of the body carried the same authority as Aristotle's account of the universe. According to Galen, the body contained four humors: blood, phlegm, black bile, and yellow bile. Illness was believed to result from an imbalance of humors, which is why doctors frequently prescribed bloodletting to expel excess blood.

Swiss physician and alchemist Paracelsus (1493–1541) was an early proponent of the experimental method in medicine and pioneered the use of chemicals and drugs to address what he saw as chemical, rather than humoral, imbalances. Another experimentalist, Flemish physician Andreas Vesalius (1516–1564), studied anatomy by dissecting human bodies, often those of executed criminals. In 1543, the same year Copernicus published *On the Revolutions*, Vesalius issued his masterpiece, *On the Structure of the Human Body*. Its two hundred precise drawings revolutionized the understanding of human anatomy, disproving Galen, just as Copernicus and his successors had disproved Aristotle and Ptolemy. The experimental approach also led English royal physician William Harvey (1578–1657) to discover the circulation of blood through the veins and arteries in 1628. Harvey was the first to explain that the heart worked like a pump and to explain the function of its muscles and valves.

Robert Boyle (1627–1691) was a key figure in the victory of experimental methods in England and helped create the Royal Society in 1660. Boyle's scientific work led to the development of modern chemistry. Following Paracelsus's lead, he undertook experiments to discover the basic elements of nature, which he believed was composed of infinitely small atoms. Boyle was the first to create a vacuum, thus disproving Descartes's belief that a vacuum could not exist in nature, and he discovered Boyle's law (1662), which states that the pressure of a gas varies inversely with volume.

Science and Religion

It is sometimes assumed that the relationship between science and religion is fundamentally hostile and that the pursuit of knowledge based on reason and proof is incompatible with faith. Yet during the Scientific Revolution most practitioners were devoutly religious and saw their work as contributing to the celebration of God's glory rather than undermining it. However, the concept of heliocentrism, which displaced the earth from the center of the universe, threatened the understanding of the place of mankind in creation as stated in Genesis. All religions derived from the

ANDREÆ VESALII.

AN. ÆT. XXVIII.   M.D.XLII.

Frontispiece to *De Humani Corporis Fabrica* (*On the Structure of the Human Body*) The frontispiece to Vesalius's pioneering work, published in 1543, shows him dissecting a corpse. This was a revolutionary new hands-on approach for physicians, who usually worked from a theoretical, rather than a practical, understanding of the body. Based on direct observation, Vesalius replaced ancient ideas drawn from Greek philosophy with a much more accurate account of the structure and function of the body. (© SSPL/Science Museum/The Image Works)

Old Testament—Catholic, Protestant, Jewish, and Muslim—thus faced difficulties accepting the Copernican system. The leaders of the Catholic Church were initially less hostile than Protestant and Jewish religious leaders, but in the first decades of the sixteenth century the Catholic attitude changed. In 1616 the Holy Office placed the works of Copernicus and his supporters, including Kepler, on a list of books Catholics were forbidden to read.

Out of caution, Galileo Galilei silenced his views on heliocentrism for several years, until 1623 saw the ascension of Pope Urban VIII, a man sympathetic to the new science. However, Galileo's 1632 *Dialogue on the Two Chief Systems of the World* went too far. Published in Italian and widely read, it openly lampooned the Aristotelian view and defended Copernicus. In 1633 Galileo was tried for heresy by the papal Inquisition. Imprisoned and threatened with torture, the aging Galileo recanted, "renouncing and cursing" his Copernican errors.

Thereafter, the Catholic Church became more hostile to science, a change that helped account for the decline of science in Italy (but not in Catholic France) after 1640. At the same time, some Protestant countries, including the Netherlands, Denmark, and England, became quite "pro-science." This was especially true in countries without a strong religious authority capable of imposing religious orthodoxy on scientific questions.

Science and Society

The rise of modern science had many consequences. First, it created a new social group—the international scientific community. Members of this community were linked together by common interests and values as well as by scholarly journals and associations. The personal success of scientists and scholars depended on making new discoveries, and science became competitive. Second, as governments intervened to support and sometimes direct research, the new scientific community became closely tied to the state and its agendas. National academies of science were created under state sponsorship in London in 1660, Paris in 1666, Berlin in 1700, and later across Europe.

It was long believed that the Scientific Revolution had little relationship to practical concerns and the life of the masses until the late-eighteenth-century Industrial Revolution (see Chapter 20). More recently, historians have emphasized the importance of skilled craftsmen in the rise of science, particularly in the development of the experimental method. Many artisans developed a strong interest in emerging scientific ideas, and, in turn, the practice of science in the seventeenth century often relied on artisans' expertise in making instruments and conducting precise experiments.

Some things did not change in the Scientific Revolution. For example, scholars willing to challenge received ideas about the natural universe did not question the seemingly natural inequalities between the sexes. Instead, the emergence of professional science may have worsened them in some ways. When Renaissance courts served as centers of learning, talented noblewomen could find niches in study and research. But the rise of a scientific community raised new barriers for women because the universities and academies that furnished professional credentials refused them entry.

There were, however, a number of noteworthy exceptions. In Italy, universities and academies did offer posts to women. Across Europe, women worked as makers of wax anatomical models and as botanical and zoological illustrators, like Maria Sibylla Merian. They were also very much involved in informal scientific communities, attending salons (see page 528), participating in scientific experiments, and writing learned treatises. Some female intellectuals became full-fledged members of the philosophical dialogue. In England, Margaret Cavendish, Anne Conway, and Mary Astell all contributed to debates about Descartes's mind-body dualism, among other issues. Descartes himself conducted an intellectual correspondence with the princess Elizabeth of Bohemia, of whom he stated: "I attach more weight to her judgment than to those messieurs the Doctors, who take for a rule of truth the opinions of Aristotle rather than the evidence of reason."[4]

The Rise and Spread of Enlightenment Thought

FOCUS QUESTION *How did the Enlightenment emerge, and what were major currents of Enlightenment thought?*

The political, intellectual, and religious developments of the early modern period that gave rise to the Scientific Revolution further contributed to a series of debates about key issues in eighteenth-century Europe and the wider world that came to be known as the **Enlightenment**. The conflicts of the Reformation that led to the devastating violence of the Thirty Years' War brought old religious certainties into question; the strong states that emerged to quell the disorder soon inspired questions about political sovereignty and its limits. Increased movement of peoples, goods, and ideas within and among the continents of Asia, Africa, Europe, and America offered examples of surprisingly different ways of life and values. Finally, the tremendous achievements of the Scientific Revolution inspired intellectuals to believe that answers to all the

■ **Enlightenment** The influential intellectual and cultural movement of the late seventeenth and eighteenth centuries that introduced a new worldview based on the use of reason, the scientific method, and progress.

questions being asked could be found through observation and the use of reason.

Intellectual turmoil in the late seventeenth century thus gave rise to the new worldview of the eighteenth-century Enlightenment. This worldview, which has played a large role in shaping the modern mind, grew out of a rich mix of diverse and often conflicting ideas that were debated in international networks. Despite the diversity, three central concepts stand at the core of Enlightenment thinking. The first and foremost idea was that the methods of natural science could and should be used to examine and understand all aspects of life. This was what intellectuals meant by *reason*, a favorite word of Enlightenment thinkers. Nothing was to be accepted on faith; everything was to be submitted to **rationalism**, a secular, critical way of thinking. A second important Enlightenment concept was that the scientific method was capable of discovering the laws of human society as well as those of nature. These tenets led to the third key idea, that of progress. Enlightenment thinkers believed that, armed with the proper method of discovering the laws of human existence, human beings could create better societies and better people.

The Early Enlightenment

Loosely united by certain key ideas, the European Enlightenment (ca. 1690–1789) was a broad intellectual and cultural movement that gained strength gradually and did not reach its maturity until about 1750. Its origins in the late seventeenth century lie in a combination of developments, including political opposition to absolutist rule; religious conflicts between Protestants and Catholics and within Protestantism; European contacts with other cultures; and the attempt to apply principles and practices from the Scientific Revolution to human society. The generation that came of age between the publication of Newton's *Principia* in 1687 and the death of Louis XIV in 1715 thus tied the knot between the Scientific Revolution and a new outlook on life. Whereas medieval and Reformation thinkers had been concerned primarily with abstract concepts of sin and salvation, and Renaissance humanists had drawn their inspiration from the classical past, Enlightenment thinkers believed that their era had gone far beyond antiquity and that intellectual progress was within their reach.

A key crucible for Enlightenment thought was the Dutch Republic, with its proud commitment to religious tolerance and republican rule. When Louis XIV demanded that all Protestants convert to Catholicism, around two hundred thousand French Protestants, or Huguenots, fled the country, many destined for the Dutch Republic. From this haven of tolerance, Huguenots and their supporters began to publish tracts denouncing religious intolerance and suggesting that only a despotic monarch, not a legitimate ruler, would deny religious freedom. Their challenge to authority thus combined religious and political issues.

These dual concerns drove the career of one important early Enlightenment writer, Pierre Bayle (1647–1706), a Huguenot who took refuge in the Dutch Republic. Bayle critically examined the religious beliefs and persecutions of the past in his *Historical and Critical Dictionary* (1697). Demonstrating that human beliefs had been extremely varied and very often mistaken, he concluded that nothing can ever be known beyond all doubt, a view known as skepticism. His influential *Dictionary* was found in more private libraries of eighteenth-century France than any other book.

The Dutch Jewish philosopher Baruch Spinoza (1632–1677) was another key figure in the transition from the Scientific Revolution to the Enlightenment. Deeply inspired by advances in science—in particular by debates about Descartes's thought—Spinoza sought to apply natural philosophy to thinking about human society. He borrowed Descartes's emphasis on rationalism and his methods of deductive reasoning, but rejected the French thinker's mind-body dualism. Instead, Spinoza came to espouse monism, the idea that mind and body were united in one substance and that God and nature were merely two names for the same thing. He envisioned a deterministic universe in which good and evil were merely relative values and human actions were shaped by outside circumstances, not free will. Spinoza was excommunicated by the relatively large Jewish community of Amsterdam for his controversial religious ideas, but he was heralded by his Enlightenment successors as a model of personal virtue and courageous intellectual autonomy.

The German philosopher and mathematician Gottfried Wilhelm von Leibniz (1646–1716), who had developed calculus independently of Isaac Newton, refuted both Cartesian dualism and Spinoza's monism. Instead, he adopted the idea of an infinite number of substances, or "monads," from which all matter is composed. His *Theodicy* (1710) declared that ours must be "the best of all possible worlds" because it was created by an omnipotent and benevolent God. Leibniz's optimism was later ridiculed by the French philosopher Voltaire in *Candide or Optimism* (1759).

Out of this period of intellectual turmoil came John Locke's *Essay Concerning Human Understanding*

■ **rationalism** A secular, critical way of thinking in which nothing was to be accepted on faith, and everything was to be submitted to reason.

■ **sensationalism** The idea that all human ideas and thoughts are produced as a result of sensory impressions.

■ **philosophes** A group of French intellectuals who proclaimed that they were bringing the light of knowledge to their fellow humans in the Age of Enlightenment.

(1690). In this work Locke (1632–1704), a physician and member of the Royal Society, brilliantly set forth a new theory about how human beings learn and form their ideas. Whereas Descartes based his deductive logic on the conviction that certain first principles, or innate ideas, are imbued in humans by God, Locke insisted that all ideas are derived from experience. The human mind at birth is like a blank tablet, or tabula rasa, on which understanding and beliefs are inscribed by experience. Human development is therefore determined by external forces, like education and social institutions, not innate characteristics. Locke's essay contributed to the theory of **sensationalism**, the idea that all human ideas and thoughts are produced as a result of sensory impressions.

Along with Newton's *Principia*, the *Essay Concerning Human Understanding* was one of the great intellectual inspirations of the Enlightenment. Locke's equally important contribution to political theory, *Two Treatises of Government* (1690), insisted on the sovereignty of the Parliament against the authority of the Crown (see Chapter 15).

The Influence of the Philosophes

Divergences among the early thinkers of the Enlightenment show that, while they shared many of the same premises and questions, the answers they found differed widely. The spread of this spirit of inquiry owed a great deal to the work of the **philosophes** (fee-luh-ZAWFZ), a group of intellectuals in France who proudly proclaimed that they, at long last, were bringing the light of reason to their ignorant fellow humans.

Philosophe is the French word for "philosopher," and in the mid-eighteenth century France became a hub of Enlightenment thought. There were at least three reasons for this. First, French was the international language of the educated classes, and France was the wealthiest and most populous country in Europe. Second, the rising unpopularity of King Louis XV and his mistresses generated growing discontent and calls for reform among the educated elite. Third, the French philosophes made it their goal to reach a larger audience of elites, many of whom were joined together in a concept inherited from the Renaissance known as the Republic of Letters—an imaginary transnational realm of the critical thinkers and writers.

To appeal to the public and get around the censors, the philosophes wrote novels and plays, histories and philosophies, and dictionaries and encyclopedias, all filled with satire and double meanings to spread their message. One of the greatest philosophes, the baron de Montesquieu (mahn-tuhs-KYOO) (1689–1755), pioneered this approach in *The Persian Letters*, an extremely influential social satire published in 1721 and considered the first major work of the French Enlightenment.

Major Figures of the Enlightenment

Baruch Spinoza (1632–1677)	Early Enlightenment thinker excommunicated from the Jewish religion for his concept of a deterministic universe
John Locke (1632–1704)	*Essay Concerning Human Understanding* (1690)
Gottfried Wilhelm von Leibniz (1646–1716)	German philosopher and mathematician known for his optimistic view of the universe
Pierre Bayle (1647–1706)	*Historical and Critical Dictionary* (1697)
Montesquieu (1689–1755)	*The Persian Letters* (1721); *The Spirit of Laws* (1748)
Voltaire (1694–1778)	Renowned French philosophe and author of more than seventy works
David Hume (1711–1776)	Central figure of the Scottish Enlightenment; *Of Natural Characters* (1748)
Jean-Jacques Rousseau (1712–1778)	*The Social Contract* (1762)
Denis Diderot (1713–1784) and Jean le Rond d'Alembert (1717–1783)	Editors of *Encyclopedia: The Rational Dictionary of the Sciences, the Arts, and the Crafts* (1751–1772)
Adam Smith (1723–1790)	*The Theory of Moral Sentiments* (1759); *An Inquiry into the Nature and Causes of the Wealth of Nations* (1776)
Immanuel Kant (1724–1804)	*What Is Enlightenment?* (1784); *On the Different Races of Man* (1775)
Moses Mendelssohn (1729–1786)	Major philosopher of the Haskalah, or Jewish Enlightenment
Cesare Beccaria (1738–1794)	*On Crimes and Punishments* (1764)

It consisted of amusing letters supposedly written by two Persian travelers who as outsiders saw European customs in unique ways, thereby allowing Montesquieu a vantage point for criticizing existing practices and beliefs.

Disturbed by the growth in absolutism under Louis XIV and inspired by the example of the physical sciences, he set out to apply the critical method to the problem of government in *The Spirit of Laws* (1748). Arguing that forms of government were shaped by history and geography, Montesquieu identified three main types: monarchies, republics, and despotisms. A great admirer of the English parliamentary system, Montesquieu argued for a separation of powers, with

Philosophes' Dinner Party This engraving depicts one of the famous dinners hosted by Voltaire at Ferney, the estate on the French-Swiss border where he spent the last twenty years of his life. A visit to the great philosophe (pictured in the center with arm raised) became a cherished pilgrimage for Enlightenment writers. (Engraving by Jean Huber [1721–1786]/Album/Art Resource, NY)

political power divided among different classes and legal estates holding unequal rights and privileges. Montesquieu was no democrat; he was apprehensive about the uneducated poor and he did not question the sovereignty of the French monarchy. But he was concerned that absolutism in France was drifting into tyranny and believed that strengthening the influence of intermediary powers was the best way to prevent it. Decades later, his theory of separation of powers had a great impact on the constitutions of the young United States in 1789 and of France in 1791.

The most famous philosophe was François Marie Arouet, known by the pen name Voltaire (vohl-TAIR) (1694–1778). In his long career, Voltaire wrote more than seventy witty volumes, hobnobbed with royalty, and died a millionaire through shrewd speculations. His early career, however, was turbulent, and he was twice arrested for insulting noblemen. To avoid a prison term, Voltaire moved to England for three years and there he came to share Montesquieu's enthusiasm for English liberties and institutions.

Returning to France, Voltaire met Gabrielle-Emilie Le Tonnelier de Breteuil, marquise du Châtelet (SHAH-tuh-lay) (1706–1749), a gifted noblewoman. Madame du Châtelet invited Voltaire to live in her country house at Cirey in Lorraine and became his long-time companion, under the eyes of her tolerant husband. Passionate about science, she studied physics and mathematics and published scientific articles and translations, including the first translation of Newton's *Principia* into French, still in use today. Excluded from the Royal Academy of Sciences because she was a woman, Madame du Châtelet had

no doubt that women's limited role in science was due to their unequal education. Discussing what she would do if she were a ruler, she wrote, "I would reform an abuse which cuts off, so to speak, half the human race. I would make women participate in all the rights of humankind, and above all in those of the intellect."[5]

While living at Cirey, Voltaire wrote works praising England and popularizing English science. Yet, like almost all of the philosophes, Voltaire was a reformer, not a revolutionary, in politics. He pessimistically concluded that the best one could hope for in the way of government was a good monarch, since human beings "are very rarely worthy to govern themselves." Nor did Voltaire believe in social and economic equality. The only realizable equality, Voltaire thought, was that "by which the citizen only depends on the laws which protect the freedom of the feeble against the ambitions of the strong."[6]

Voltaire's philosophical and religious positions were much more radical. Voltaire believed in God, but he rejected Catholicism in favor of **deism**, belief in a distant noninterventionist deity. Drawing on mechanistic philosophy, he envisioned a universe in which God acted like a great clockmaker who built an orderly system and then stepped aside to let it run. Above all, Voltaire and most of the philosophes hated all forms of religious intolerance, which they believed led to fanaticism and cruelty. (See "Thinking Like a Historian: The Enlightenment Debate on Religious Tolerance," page 522.)

The strength of the philosophes lay in their dedication and organization. Their greatest achievement was a group effort—the seventeen-volume *Encyclopedia: The Rational Dictionary of the Sciences, the Arts, and the Crafts*, edited by Denis Diderot (DEE-duh-roh)

■ **deism** Belief in a distant, noninterventionist deity; common among Enlightenment thinkers.

(1713–1784) and Jean le Rond d'Alembert (dah-luhm-BEHR) (1717–1783). The two men set out in 1751 to find coauthors who would examine the rapidly expanding whole of human knowledge and teach people how to think critically and objectively about all matters. As Diderot said, he wanted the *Encyclopedia* to "change the general way of thinking."[7]

Completed in 1765 despite opposition from the French state and the Catholic Church, the *Encyclopedia* contained seventy-two thousand articles by leading scientists, writers, skilled workers, and progressive priests. Science and the industrial arts were exalted, religion and immortality questioned. Intolerance, legal injustice, and out-of-date social institutions were openly criticized. The *Encyclopedia* also included many articles describing non-European cultures and societies, including acknowledgment of Muslim scholars' contribution to the development of Western science. Summing up the new worldview of the Enlightenment, the *Encyclopedia* was widely read, especially in less expensive reprint editions, and it was extremely influential.

After about 1770 a number of thinkers and writers began to attack the philosophes' faith in reason and progress. The most famous of these was Jean-Jacques Rousseau (1712–1778). The son of a poor Swiss watchmaker, Rousseau made his way into the Parisian Enlightenment through his brilliant intellect. Rousseau was both one of the most influential voices of the Enlightenment and, in his ultimate rejection of rationalism and civilized sociability, a harbinger of reaction against Enlightenment ideals.

Like other Enlightenment thinkers, Rousseau was passionately committed to individual freedom. Unlike them, however, he attacked rationalism and civilization as destroying, rather than liberating, the individual. Warm, spontaneous feeling, Rousseau believed, had to complement and correct cold intellect. Moreover, he asserted, the basic goodness of the individual and the unspoiled child had to be protected from the cruel refinements of civilization. Rousseau's ideals greatly influenced the early Romantic movement, which rebelled against the culture of the Enlightenment in the late eighteenth century.

Rousseau's contribution to political theory in *The Social Contract* (1762) was based on two fundamental concepts: the general will and popular sovereignty. According to Rousseau, the general will is sacred and absolute, reflecting the common interests of all the people, who have displaced the monarch as the holder of sovereign power. The general will is not necessarily the will of the majority, however. At times the general will may be the authentic, long-term needs of the people as correctly interpreted by a farsighted minority. Little noticed before the French Revolution, Rousseau's concept of the general will appealed greatly to democrats and nationalists after 1789.

Enlightenment Movements Across Europe

The Enlightenment was a movement of international dimensions, with thinkers traversing borders in a constant exchange of visits, letters, and printed materials. Voltaire alone wrote almost eighteen thousand letters to correspondents in France and across Europe. The Republic of Letters, as this international group of scholars and writers was called, was a truly cosmopolitan set of networks stretching from western Europe to its colonies in the Americas, to Russia and eastern Europe, and along the routes of trade and empire to Africa and Asia.

Within this broad international conversation, scholars have identified numerous regional and national particularities. Outside of France, many strains of Enlightenment — Protestant, Catholic, and Jewish — sought to reconcile reason with faith, rather than emphasizing the errors of religious fanaticism and intolerance. Some scholars point to a distinctive "Catholic Enlightenment" that aimed to renew and reform the church from within, looking to divine grace rather than human will as the source of progress.

The Scottish Enlightenment, which was centered in Edinburgh, was marked by an emphasis on common sense and scientific reasoning. After the Act of Union with England in 1707, Scotland was freed from political crisis to experience a vigorous period of intellectual growth. Advances in philosophy were also stimulated by the creation of the first public educational system in Europe.

A central figure in Edinburgh was David Hume (1711–1776), whose emphasis on civic morality and religious skepticism had a powerful impact at home and abroad. Hume strove to apply Newton's experimental methods to what he called the "science of man." Building on Locke's writings on learning, Hume argued that the human mind is really nothing but a bundle of impressions. These impressions originate only in sensory experiences and our habits of mentally joining these experiences together. Therefore, reason cannot tell us anything about questions that cannot be verified by sensory experience (in the form of controlled experiments or mathematics), such as the origin of the universe or the existence of God. Hume further argued, in opposition to Descartes, that reason alone could not supply moral principles and that they derived instead from emotions and desires, such as feelings of approval or shame. Hume's rationalistic inquiry thus ended up undermining the Enlightenment's faith in the power of reason by emphasizing the superiority of the senses and the passions over reason in driving human thought and behavior.

Hume's emphasis on human experience, rather than abstract principle, had a formative influence on another major figure of the Scottish Enlightenment,

The Enlightenment Debate on Religious Tolerance

Enlightenment philosophers questioned many aspects of European society, including political authority, social inequality, and imperialism. A major focus of their criticism was the dominance of the established church and the persecution of minority faiths. While many philosophers defended religious tolerance, they differed widely in their approaches to the issue.

1 Moses Mendelssohn, "Reply to Lavater," 1769.
In 1769 Johann Caspar Lavater, a Swiss clergyman, called on Moses Mendelssohn to either refute proofs of Christianity publicly or submit to baptism. Mendelssohn's reply is both a call for toleration and an affirmation of his religious faith.

It is, of course, the natural obligation of every mortal to diffuse knowledge and virtue among his fellow men, and to do his best to extirpate their prejudices and errors. One might think, in this regard, that it was the duty of every man publicly to oppose the religious opinions that he considers mistaken. But not all prejudices are equally harmful, and hence the prejudices we may think we perceive among our fellow men must not all be treated in the same way. Some are directly contrary to the happiness of the human race.... These must be attacked outright by every friend of humanity.... Of this kind are all people's errors and prejudices that disturb their own or their fellows' peace and contentment and kill every seed of the true and the good in man before it can germinate. On the one hand, fanaticism, misanthropy, and the spirit of persecution, and on the other, frivolity, luxury, and libertinism.

Sometimes, however, the opinions of my fellow men, which in my belief are errors, belong to the higher theoretical principles which are too remote from practical life to do any direct harm; but, precisely because of their generality, they form the basis on which the nation that upholds them has built its moral and social system, and thus happen to be of great importance to this part of the human race. To oppose such doctrines in public, because we consider them prejudices, is to dig up the ground to see whether it is solid and secure, without providing any other support for the building that stands on it. Anyone who cares more for the good of humanity than for his own fame will be slow to voice his opinion about such prejudices, and will take care not to attack them outright without extreme caution.

2 Voltaire, *Treatise on Toleration*, 1763.
Voltaire, the prominent French philosophe, began his *Treatise on Toleration* by recounting the infamous trial of Jean Calas. Although all the evidence pointed toward suicide, the judges concluded that Calas had killed his son in order to prevent him from converting to Catholicism, and Calas was brutally executed in 1762. For Voltaire, the Calas affair was a battle between fanaticism and reason, extremism and moderation.

Some fanatic in the crowd cried out that Jean Calas had hanged his son Marc Antoine. The cry was soon repeated on all sides; some adding that the deceased was to have abjured Protestantism on the following day, and that the family and young Lavaisse had strangled him out of hatred of the Catholic religion. In a moment all doubt had disappeared. The whole town was persuaded that it is a point of religion with the Protestants for a father and mother to kill their children when they wish to change their faith.

... There was not, and could not be, any evidence against the family; but a deluded religion took the place of proof.... [The judges] were confounded when the old man, expiring on the wheel, prayed God to witness his innocence, and begged him to pardon his judges.

The daughters were taken from the mother and put in a convent. The mother, almost sprinkled with the blood of her husband, her eldest son dead, the younger banished, deprived of her daughters and all her property, was alone in the world, without bread, without hope, dying of the intolerable misery. Certain persons, having carefully examined the circumstances of this horrible adventure, were so impressed that they urged the widow, who had retired into solitude, to go and demand justice at the feet of the throne.... She reached Paris almost at the point of death. She was astonished at her reception, at the help and the tears that were given to her.

At Paris reason dominates fanaticism, however powerful it be; in the provinces fanaticism almost always overcomes reason.

ANALYZING THE EVIDENCE

1. Based on these sources, what attitudes did eighteenth-century Europeans manifest toward religions other than their own? Were such attitudes always negative?
2. What justifications did Enlightenment philosophers use to argue in favor of religious tolerance? Were arguments in favor of religious tolerance necessarily antireligious?
3. Why did Judaism figure so prominently in debates about religious tolerance in eighteenth-century Europe? In what ways do you think Mendelssohn's experience as a Jew (Source 1) shaped his views on religious tolerance?

3 **Bernard Picart, "Jewish Meal During the Feast of the Tabernacles," from *Ceremonies and Customs of All the Peoples of the World*, 1724.** Eighteenth-century travel literature provided eager audiences with images and descriptions of religious practices from around the world. This image emphasizes the prosperity and warm family relations of a Jewish family enjoying a holiday meal, echoing the tolerant mind-set of the author.

(Meal of the Jews During the Festival of the Tents, engraving by Bernard Picart, from *Religious Ceremonies and Customs*, 1724/Jewish Chronicle/Heritage Images/Getty Images)

4 **Gotthold Ephraim Lessing, *Nathan the Wise*, 1779.** In this excerpt from *Nathan the Wise*, a play by German writer Gotthold Ephraim Lessing, the sultan Saladin asks a Jewish merchant named Nathan to tell him which is the true religion: Islam, Christianity, or Judaism. Nathan responds with a parable about a man who promised to leave the same opal ring, a guarantor of divine favor, to each of his three beloved sons. He then had two exact replicas of the ring made so that each son would believe he had inherited the precious relic.

NATHAN: Scarce was the father dead.
When each one with his ring appears
Claiming each the headship of the house.
Inspections, quarrelling, and complaints ensue;
But all in vain, the veritable ring
Was not distinguishable —
(*After a pause, during which he expects the Sultan's answer*)
Almost as indistinguishable as to us,
Is now — the true religion.

SALADIN: What? Is that meant as answer to my question?

NATHAN: 'Tis meant but to excuse myself, because
I lack the boldness to discriminate between the rings,
Which the father by express intent had made
So that they might not be distinguished.

SALADIN: The rings! Don't play with me.
I thought the faiths which I have named

Were easily distinguishable,
Even to their raiment, even to meat and drink.

NATHAN: But yet not as regards their proofs:
For do not all rest upon history, written or traditional?
And history can also be accepted
Only on faith and trust. Is it not so?
Now, whose faith and confidence do we least misdoubt?
That of our relatives? Of those whose flesh and blood we are,
Of those who from our childhood
Have lavished on us proofs of love,
Who ne'er deceived us, unless 'twere wholesome for us so?
How can I place less faith in my forefathers
Than you in yours? or the reverse?
Can I desire of you to load your ancestors with lies,
So that you contradict not mine? Or the reverse?
And to the Christian the same applies.
Is that not so?

PUTTING IT ALL TOGETHER

Using the sources above, along with what you have learned in class and in this chapter, compare and contrast the views on religious toleration presented in the sources. On what would the authors of these works have agreed? How did their arguments in favor of toleration differ? What explanation can you offer for the differences you note?

Sources: (1) Ritchie Robertson, ed., *The German-Jewish Dialogue: An Anthology of Literary Texts, 1749–1993* (New York: Oxford University Press, 1999), pp. 41–42; (2) Voltaire, *A Treatise on Toleration and Other Essays*, trans. Joseph McCabe (Amherst, N.Y.: Prometheus Books, 1994), pp. 147–149, 152–153; (4) Crane Brinton, ed., *The Portable Age of Reason Reader* (New York: Viking Press, 1956), pp. 383–389.

Adam Smith (1723–1790). Smith argued that social interaction produced feelings of mutual sympathy that led people to behave in ethical ways, despite inherent tendencies toward self-interest. By observing others and witnessing their feelings, individuals imaginatively experienced such feelings and learned to act in ways that would elicit positive sentiments and avoid negative ones. Smith believed that the thriving commercial life of the eighteenth century was likely to produce civic virtue through the values of competition, fair play, and individual autonomy. In *An Inquiry into the Nature and Causes of the Wealth of Nations* (1776), Smith attacked the laws and regulations created by mercantilist governments that, he argued, prevented commerce from reaching its full capacity (see Chapter 17).

Inspired by philosophers of moral sentiments, like Hume and Smith, as well as by physiological studies of the role of the nervous system in human perception, the celebration of sensibility became an important element of eighteenth-century culture. *Sensibility* referred to an acute sensitivity of the nerves and brains to outside stimuli, which produced strong emotional and physical reactions. Novels, plays, and other literary genres depicted moral and aesthetic sensibility as a particular characteristic of women and the upper classes. The proper relationship between reason and the emotions (or between *Sense and Sensibility* as Jane Austen put it in the title of her 1811 novel) became a key question.

After 1760 Enlightenment ideas were hotly debated in the German-speaking states, often in dialogue with Christian theology. Immanuel Kant (1724–1804), a professor in East Prussia, was the greatest German philosopher of his day. Kant posed the question of the age when he published a pamphlet in 1784 titled *What Is Enlightenment?* He answered, "*Sapere Aude* [dare to know]! 'Have the courage to use your own understanding' is therefore the motto of enlightenment." He argued that if intellectuals were granted the freedom to exercise their reason publicly in print, enlightenment would almost surely follow. Kant was no revolutionary; he also insisted that in their private lives, individuals must obey all laws, no matter how unreasonable, and should be punished for "impertinent" criticism. Like other Enlightenment figures in central and east-central Europe, Kant thus tried to reconcile absolute monarchical authority and religious faith with a critical public sphere.

Northern Europeans often regarded the Italian states as culturally backward, yet important developments in Enlightenment thought took place in the Italian peninsula. After achieving independence from Habsburg rule (1734), the kingdom of Naples entered a period of intellectual flourishing as reformers struggled to lift the heavy weight of church and noble power. In northern Italy a central figure was Cesare Beccaria (1738–1794), a nobleman educated at Jesuit schools and the University of Pavia. His *On Crimes and Punishments* (1764) was a passionate plea for reform of the penal system that decried the use of torture, arbitrary imprisonment, and capital punishment, and advocated the prevention of crime over the reliance on punishment. The text was quickly translated into French and English and made an impact throughout Europe and its colonies.

The Social Life of the Enlightenment

FOCUS QUESTION *How did Enlightenment thinkers address issues of racial and social difference, and how did new institutions and social practices diffuse Enlightenment thought?*

The Scientific Revolution and the political and religious conflicts of the late seventeenth century were not the only developments that influenced European thinkers. Europeans' increased interactions with non-European peoples and cultures also helped produce the Enlightenment spirit.

Global Contacts

In the wake of the great discoveries of the fifteenth and sixteenth centuries, the rapidly growing travel literature taught Europeans that the peoples of China, India, Africa, and the Americas had very different beliefs and customs. Europeans shaved their faces and let their hair grow. Ottomans shaved their heads and let their beards grow. In Europe a man bowed before a woman to show respect. In Siam a man turned his back on a woman when he met her because it was disrespectful to look directly at her. Countless similar examples discussed in travel accounts helped change the perspective of educated Europeans. They began to look at truth and morality in relative, rather than absolute, terms. If anything was possible, who could say what was right or wrong?

The powerful and advanced nations of Asia were obvious sources of comparison with the West. Seventeenth-century Jesuit missionaries served as a conduit for transmission of knowledge to the West about Chinese history and culture. The philosopher and mathematician Leibniz corresponded with Jesuits stationed in China, coming to believe that Chinese ethics and political philosophy were superior but that Europeans had equaled China in science and technology; some scholars believe his concept of monads was influenced by Confucian teaching on the inherent harmony between the cosmic order and human society.[8]

During the eighteenth-century Enlightenment, opinion on China was divided. Voltaire and some other philosophes revered China—without ever visiting or seriously studying it—as an ancient culture replete with wisdom and learning, ruled by benevolent absolutist monarchs. They enthusiastically embraced Confucianism as a natural religion in which universal moral truths were uncovered by reason. By contrast, Montesquieu and Diderot criticized China as a despotic land ruled by fear.

Attitudes toward Islam and the Muslim world were similarly mixed. As the Ottoman military threat receded at the end of the seventeenth century, some Enlightenment thinkers assessed Islam favorably. Some deists praised Islam as superior to Christianity and Judaism in its rationality, compassion, and tolerance. Others, including Spinoza, saw Islamic culture as superstitious and favorable to despotism. In most cases, writing about Islam and Muslim cultures served primarily as a means to reflect on Western values and practices. Thus Montesquieu's *Persian Letters* used the Persian harem as a symbol of despotic rule that he feared his own country was adopting. Voltaire's play about the life of the Prophet portrayed Muhammad as the epitome of the religious fanaticism the philosophes opposed.

One writer with considerable personal experience in a Muslim country was Lady Mary Wortley Montagu, wife of the English ambassador to the Ottoman Empire. Her letters challenged prevailing ideas by depicting Turkish people as sympathetic and civilized. Montagu also disputed the notion that women were oppressed in Ottoman society.

Apart from debates about Asian and Muslim lands, the "discovery" of the New World and subsequent explorations in the Pacific Ocean also destabilized existing norms and values in Europe. One popular idea, among Rousseau and others, was that indigenous peoples of the Americas were living examples of "natural man," who embodied the essential goodness of humanity uncorrupted by decadent society. Other popular candidates for utopian natural men were the Pacific Island societies explored by Captain James Cook and others from the 1770s on.

Enlightenment Debates About Race

As scientists developed taxonomies of plant and animal species in response to discoveries in the Americas, they also began to classify humans into hierarchically ordered "races" and to speculate on the origins of such races. In *The System of Nature* (1735), Swedish botanist

Carl von Linné argued that nature was organized into a God-given hierarchy. The comte de Buffon (komt duh buh-FOHN) argued that humans originated with one species that then developed into distinct races due largely to climatic conditions.

Enlightenment thinkers such as David Hume and Immanuel Kant helped popularize these ideas. In *Of Natural Characters* (1748), Hume wrote:

> I am apt to suspect the negroes and in general all other species of men (for there are four or five different kinds) to be naturally inferior to the whites. There never was a civilized nation of any other complexion than white, nor even any individual eminent amongst them, no arts, no sciences. . . . Such a uniform and constant difference could not happen, in so many countries and ages if nature had not made an original distinction between these breeds of men.[9]

Kant taught and wrote as much about "anthropology" and "geography" as he did about standard philosophical themes such as logic, metaphysics, and moral philosophy. He elaborated his views about race in *On the Different Races of Man* (1775), claiming that there were four human races, each of which had derived from an original race. According to Kant, the closest descendants of the original race were the white inhabitants of northern Germany. (Scientists now know the human race originated in Africa.)

Using the word *race* to designate biologically distinct groups of humans, akin to distinct animal species, was new. Previously, Europeans had grouped other peoples into "nations" based on their historical, political, and cultural affiliations, rather than on supposedly innate physical differences. Unsurprisingly, when European thinkers drew up a hierarchical classification of human species, their own "race" was placed at the top. Europeans had long believed they were culturally superior to "barbaric" peoples in Africa and, since 1492, the New World. Now emerging ideas about racial difference taught them they were biologically superior as well. In turn, scientific racism helped legitimate and justify the tremendous growth of slavery that occurred during the eighteenth century. If one "race" of humans was fundamentally different and inferior, its members could be seen as particularly fit for enslavement and liable to benefit from tutelage by the superior race.

Racist ideas did not go unchallenged. The abbé Raynal's *History of the Two Indies* (1770) fiercely attacked slavery and the abuses of European colonization. *Encyclopedia* editor Denis Diderot adopted Montesquieu's technique of criticizing European

***Encyclopedia* Image of the Cotton Industry**   This romanticized image of slavery in the West Indies cotton industry was published in Diderot and d'Alembert's *Encyclopedia*. It shows enslaved men, at right, gathering and picking over cotton bolls, while the woman at left mills the bolls to remove their seeds. The *Encyclopedia* presented mixed views on slavery; one article described it as "indispensable" to economic development, while others argued passionately for the natural right to freedom of all mankind. (Universal History Archive/UIG via Getty Images)

attitudes through the voice of outsiders in his dialogue between Tahitian villagers and their European visitors. (See "Evaluating the Evidence 16.3: Denis Diderot, 'Supplement to Bougainville's Voyage,'" at right.) Scottish philosopher James Beattie (1735–1803) responded directly to claims of white superiority by pointing out that Europeans had started out as savage as nonwhites supposedly were and that many non-European peoples in the Americas, Asia, and Africa had achieved high levels of civilization. Former slaves, like Olaudah Equiano (see Chapter 17) and Ottobah Cugoana, published eloquent memoirs testifying to the horrors of slavery and the innate equality of all humans. These challenges to racism, however, were in the minority. Many other Enlightenment voices supporting racial inequality—Thomas Jefferson among them—may be found.

Women and the Enlightenment

Dating back to the Renaissance *querelle des dames*, the debate over women's proper role in society and the nature of gender differences continued to fascinate Enlightenment thinkers. Some philosophes championed greater rights and expanded education for women, claiming that the position and treatment of women were the best indicators of a society's level of civilization and decency.[10] In *Persian Letters*, Montesquieu used the oppression of women in the harem, described in letters from the wives of Usbek—one of the Persian voyagers—as a potent symbol of the political tyranny he identified with the Persian Empire. At the end of the book, the rebellion of the harem against the cruel eunuchs Usbek left in charge serves to make Montesquieu's point that despotism must ultimately fail.

Denis Diderot, "Supplement to Bougainville's Voyage"

Denis Diderot was born in a provincial town in eastern France and educated in Paris. Rejecting careers in the church and the law, he devoted himself to literature and philosophy. In 1749, sixty years before Charles Darwin's birth, Diderot was jailed by Parisian authorities for publishing an essay questioning God's role in creation and suggesting the autonomous evolution of species. Following these difficult beginnings, Diderot's editorial work and writing on the Encyclopedia were the crowning intellectual achievements of his life and, according to some, of the Enlightenment itself.

Like other philosophes, Diderot employed numerous genres to disseminate Enlightenment thought, ranging from scholarly articles in the Encyclopedia to philosophical treatises, novels, plays, book reviews, and erotic stories. His "Supplement to Bougainville's Voyage" (1772) was a fictional account of a European voyage to Tahiti inspired by the writings of traveler Louis-Antoine de Bougainville. In this passage, Diderot expresses his own loathing of colonial conquest and exploitation through the voice of an elderly Tahitian man. The character's praise for his own culture allows Diderot to express his Enlightenment idealization of "natural man," free from the vices of civilized societies.

He was the father of a large family. When the Europeans arrived he looked upon them with scorn, showing neither astonishment, nor fear, nor curiosity. On their approach he turned his back and retired into his hut. Yet his silence and anxiety revealed his thoughts only too well; he was inwardly lamenting the eclipse of his countrymen's happiness. When Bougainville was leaving the island, as the natives swarmed on the shore, clutching his clothes, clasping his companions in their arms and weeping, the old man made his way forward and proclaimed solemnly, "Weep, wretched natives of Tahiti, weep. But let it be for the coming and not the leaving of these ambitious, wicked men. One day you will know them better. One day they will come back, bearing in one hand the piece of wood you see in that man's belt, and, in the other, the sword hanging by the side of that one, to enslave you, slaughter you, or make you captive to their follies and vices. One day you will be subject to them, as corrupt, vile and miserable as they are. . . ."

Then turning to Bougainville, he continued, "And you, leader of the ruffians who obey you, pull your ship away swiftly from these shores. We are innocent, we are content, and you can only spoil that happiness. We follow the pure instincts of nature, and you have tried to erase its impression from our hearts. Here, everything belongs to everyone, and you have preached I can't tell what distinction between 'yours' and 'mine.' . . . If a Tahitian should one day land on your shores and engrave on one of your stones or on the bark of one of your trees, *This land belongs to the people of Tahiti*, what would you think

then? You are stronger than we are, and what does that mean? When one of the miserable trinkets with which your ship is filled was taken away, what an uproar you made, what revenge you exacted! At that moment, in the depths of your heart, you were plotting the theft of an entire country! You are not a slave, you would rather die than be one, and yet you wish to make slaves of us. Do you suppose, then, that a Tahitian cannot defend his own liberty and die for it as well? This inhabitant of Tahiti, whom you wish to ensnare like an animal, is your brother. You are both children of Nature. What right do you have over him that he does not have over you? You came; did we attack you? Have we plundered your ship? Did we seize you and expose you to the arrows of our enemies? Did we harness you to work with our animals in the fields? We respected our own image in you.

"Leave us our ways; they are wiser and more decent than yours. We have no wish to exchange what you call our ignorance for your useless knowledge. Everything that we need and is good for us we already possess. Do we merit contempt because we have not learnt how to acquire superfluous needs? When we are hungry, we have enough to eat. When we are cold, we have enough to wear. You have entered our huts; what do you suppose we lack? Pursue as far as you wish what you call the comforts of life, but let sensible beings stop when they have no more to gain from their labours than imaginary benefits. If you persuade us to go beyond the strict bounds of necessity, when will we finish our work? When will we enjoy ourselves? We have kept our annual and daily labours within the smallest possible limits, because in our eyes nothing is better than rest. Go back to your own country to agitate and torment yourselves as much as you like. But leave us in peace. Do not fill our heads with your factitious needs and illusory virtues. . . ."

EVALUATE THE EVIDENCE

1. On what grounds does the speaker argue for the Tahitians' basic equality with the Europeans?
2. What is the good life according to the speaker, and how does it contrast with the European way of life? Which do you think is the better path?
3. In what ways could Diderot's thoughts here be seen as representative of Enlightenment ideas? Are there ways in which they are not?
4. How realistic do you think this account is? How might defenders of expansion respond?

Source: Edited excerpts from pp. 41–43 in Denis Diderot, *Political Writings*, translated and edited by John Hope Mason and Robert Wokler. Copyright © 1992 by Cambridge University Press. Reprinted by permission of Cambridge University Press.

In the 1780s the marquis de Condorcet, a celebrated mathematician and contributor to the *Encyclopedia*, went so far as to urge that women should share equal rights with men. This was an extremely rare position. Most philosophes accepted that women were inferior to men intellectually as well as physically. They sought moderate reform at best, particularly in the arena of female education, and had no desire to upend men's traditional dominance over women.

From the first years of the Enlightenment, women writers made crucial contributions both to debates about women's rights and to the broader Enlightenment discussion. In 1694 Mary Astell published *A Serious Proposal to the Ladies*, which encouraged women to aspire to the life of the mind and proposed the creation of a women's college. Astell also harshly criticized the institution of marriage. Echoing arguments made against the absolute authority of kings during the Glorious Revolution (see Chapter 15), she argued that husbands should not exercise absolute control over their wives in marriage. Yet Astell, like most female authors of the period, was careful to acknowledge women's God-given duties to be good wives and mothers.

The explosion of printed literature over the eighteenth century (see the next section) brought significant numbers of women writers into print, but they remained a small proportion of published authors. In the second half of the eighteenth century, women produced some 15 percent of published novels, the genre in which they enjoyed the greatest success. They represented a much tinier proportion of nonfiction authors.[11]

If they remained marginal in the world of publishing, women played a much more active role in the informal dimensions of the Enlightenment: conversation, letter writing, travel, and patronage. A key element of their informal participation was as salon hostesses, or *salonnières* (sah-lahn-ee-EHRZ). **Salons** were weekly meetings held in wealthy households, which brought together writers, aristocrats, financiers, and noteworthy foreigners for meals and witty discussions of the latest trends in literature, science, and philosophy. One prominent salonnière was Madame du Deffand, whose weekly Parisian salon included such guests as Montesquieu, d'Alembert, and Benjamin Franklin, then serving as the first U.S. ambassador to France. Invitations to salons were highly coveted; introductions to the rich and powerful could make the career of an ambitious writer, and, in turn, the social elite found amusement and cultural prestige in their ties to up-and-coming artists and men of letters.

Elite women also exercised great influence on artistic taste. Soft pastels, ornate interiors, sentimental portraits, and starry-eyed lovers protected by hovering cupids were all hallmarks of the style they favored. This style, known as **rococo** (ruh-KOH-koh), was popular throughout Europe in the period from 1720 to 1780. It was particularly associated with the mistress of Louis XV, Madame de Pompadour, who used her position to commission paintings, furniture, and other luxury objects in the rococo style.

Women's prominent role as society hostesses and patrons of the arts and letters outraged some Enlightenment thinkers. According to Jean-Jacques Rousseau, women and men were radically different by nature and should play diametrically opposed roles in life. Destined by nature to assume the active role in sexual relations, men were naturally suited for the rough-and-tumble of politics and public life. Women's role was to attract male sexual desire in order to marry and create families and then to care for their homes and children in private. For Rousseau, wealthy Parisian women's love for attending social gatherings and pulling the strings of power was unnatural and had a corrupting effect on both politics and society. Some women eagerly accepted Rousseau's idealized view of their domestic role, but others—such as the English writer Mary Wollstonecraft—vigorously rejected his notion of women's limitations.

Rousseau's emphasis on the natural laws governing women echoed a wider shift in ideas about gender during this period, as doctors, scientists, and philosophers increasingly agreed that women's essential characteristics were determined by their sexual organs and reproductive functions. This turn to nature, rather than tradition or scripture, as a means to understand human society had parallels in contemporary views on racial difference. Just as writers like Rousseau used women's "natural" passivity to argue for their subordinate role in society, so Kant and others used ideas about non-Europeans' "natural" inferiority to defend slavery and colonial domination. The new powers of science and reason were thus marshaled to imbue traditional stereotypes with the force of natural law. Scholars continue to debate the apparent paradox between Enlightenment thinkers' ideals of equality, progress, and reason and their acceptance of racial and gender inequality.

Urban Culture and Life in the Public Sphere

Enlightenment ideas did not float on thin air. A series of new institutions and practices encouraged the spread of enlightened ideas. From about 1700 to 1789, the production and consumption of books grew significantly and the types of books people read changed dramatically. For example, the proportion of religious and devotional books published in Paris declined after

Madame de Pompadour, Mistress to French King Louis XV   Madame de Pompadour used the wealth at her command to patronize many highly skilled artists and craftsmen. She helped popularize the ornate, lightly colored, and highly decorative rococo style, epitomized by the sumptuous trimmings of her dress. (By François Boucher [1703–1770], [oil on canvas]/© Scottish National Gallery, Edinburgh/Bridgeman Images)

1750; history and law held constant; the arts and sciences surged.

Reading more books on many more subjects, the educated public approached reading in a new way. The old style of reading in Europe had been centered on a core of sacred texts read aloud by the father to his assembled family. Now reading involved a broader field of books that constantly changed. Reading became individual and silent, and texts could be questioned.

For those who could not afford to purchase books, lending libraries offered access to the new ideas of the Enlightenment. Coffeehouses, which first appeared in the late seventeenth century, became meccas of philosophical discussion. (See "Living in the Past: Coffeehouse Culture," page 530.) In addition to these institutions, book clubs, debating societies, Masonic lodges (groups of Freemasons, a secret society that accepted craftsmen and shopkeepers as well as middle-class men and nobles), salons, and newspapers all played roles in the creation of a new **public sphere** that celebrated open debate informed by critical reason. The public sphere was an idealized space where members of society came together as individuals to discuss issues relevant to the society, economics, and politics of the day.

What of the common people? Did they participate in the Enlightenment? Enlightenment philosophes did not direct their message to peasants or urban laborers. They believed that the masses had no time or talent for philosophical speculation and that elevating them would be a long and potentially dangerous process. Deluded by superstitions and driven by violent passions, the people, they thought, were like children in need of firm parental guidance. D'Alembert characteristically made a sharp distinction between "the truly enlightened public" and "the blind and noisy multitude."[12]

■ **salon** Regular social gathering held by talented and rich Parisians in their homes, where philosophes and their followers met to discuss literature, science, and philosophy.

■ **rococo** A popular style in Europe in the eighteenth century, known for its soft pastels, ornate interiors, sentimental portraits, and starry-eyed lovers protected by hovering cupids.

■ **public sphere** An idealized intellectual space that emerged in Europe during the Enlightenment, where the public came together to discuss important issues relating to society, economics, and politics.

LIVING IN THE PAST
Coffeehouse Culture

Customers in today's coffee shops may be surprised to learn that they are participating in a centuries-old institution that has contributed a great deal to the idea of "modernity." Tradition has it that an Ethiopian goatherd first discovered coffee when he noticed that his goats became frisky and danced after consuming the berries. Botanists agree that coffee probably originated in Ethiopia and then spread to Yemen and across the Arabian peninsula by around 1000 C.E. In 1457 the first public coffeehouse opened in Istanbul, and from there coffeehouses became a popular institution throughout the Muslim world.

European travelers in Istanbul were astonished at its inhabitants' passion for coffee, which one described as "blacke as soote, and tasting not much unlike it."* However, Italian merchants introduced coffee to Europe around 1600, and the first European coffee shop opened in Venice in 1645, soon followed by shops in Oxford, England, in 1650, London in 1652, and Paris in 1672. By the 1730s coffee shops had be-

come so popular in London that one observer noted, "There are some people of moderate Fortunes, that lead their Lives mostly in Coffee-Houses, they eat, drink and sleep (in the Day-time) in them."†

Coffeehouses helped spread the ideas and values of the Scientific Revolution and the Enlightenment. They provided a new public space where urban Europeans could learn about and debate the issues of the day. Within a few years, each political party, philosophical sect, scientific society, and literary circle had its own coffeehouse, which served as a central gathering point for its members and an informal recruiting site for new ones. Coffeehouses self-consciously distinguished themselves from the rowdy atmosphere of the tavern; whereas alcohol dulled the senses, coffee sharpened the mind for discussion.

European coffeehouses also played a key role in the development of modern business, as their proprietors began to provide specialized commercial news to attract customers.

Seventeenth-century English coffeehouse. (Granger, NYC — All rights reserved)

*Quoted in Markman Ellis, *The Coffee House: A Cultural History* (London: Phoenix, 2004), p. 8.
†Quoted ibid, p. 198.

Lloyd's of London, the famous insurance company, got its start in the shipping lists published by coffeehouse owner Edward Lloyd in the 1690s. The streets around London's stock exchange were crowded with coffeehouses where merchants and traders congregated to strike deals and hear the latest news.

Coffeehouses succeeded in Europe because they met a need common to politics, business, and intellectual life: the spread and sharing of information. In the late seventeenth century newspapers were rare and expensive, there were few banks to guarantee credit, and politics was limited to a tiny elite. To break through these constraints, people needed reliable information. The coffeehouse was an ideal place to acquire it, along with a new kind of stimulant that provided the energy and attention to fuel a lively discussion.

QUESTIONS FOR ANALYSIS

1. What do the images shown here suggest about the customers of seventeenth- and eighteenth-century coffeehouses? Who frequented these establishments? Who was excluded?
2. What limitations on the exchange of information existed in early modern Europe? Why were coffeehouses so useful as sites for exchanging information?
3. What social role do coffeehouses play where you live? Do you see any continuities with the seventeenth- and eighteenth-century coffeehouse?

Eighteenth-century Viennese coffeehouse. (Private Collection/Erich Lessing/Art Resource, NY)

Despite these prejudices, the ideas of the philosophes did find an audience among some members of the common people. At a time of rising literacy, book prices were dropping and many philosophical ideas were popularized in cheap pamphlets and through public reading. Although they were barred from salons and academies, ordinary people were not immune to the new ideas in circulation.

Enlightened Absolutism

FOCUS QUESTION *What impact did new ways of thinking have on political developments and monarchical absolutism?*

How did the Enlightenment influence political developments? To this important question there is no easy answer. Most Enlightenment thinkers outside of England and the Netherlands, especially in central and eastern Europe, believed that political change could best come from above—from the ruler—rather than from below. Royal absolutism was a fact of life, and the monarchs of Europe's leading states clearly had no intention of giving up their great power. Therefore, the philosophes and their sympathizers realistically concluded that a benevolent absolutism offered the best opportunities for improving society.

Many government officials were interested in philosophical ideas. They were among the best-educated members of society, and their daily involvement in complex affairs of state made them naturally attracted to ideas for improving human society. Encouraged and instructed by these officials, some absolutist rulers tried to reform their governments in accordance with Enlightenment ideals—what historians have called the **enlightened absolutism** of the later eighteenth century. In both Catholic and Protestant lands, rulers typically fused Enlightenment principles with religion, drawing support for their innovations from reform-minded religious thinkers. The most influential of the new-style monarchs were in Prussia, Russia, and Austria, and their example illustrates both the achievements and

Prussia, 1740
Prussian gains, 1742
Austria, 1740
— Boundary of the Holy Roman Empire

Königsberg

Berlin

POLAND

SILESIA

Prague

Vienna

AUSTRIA

HUNGARY

The War of the Austrian Succession, 1740–1748

the great limitations of enlightened absolutism. France experienced its own brand of enlightened absolutism in the contentious decades prior to the French Revolution (see Chapter 19).

Frederick the Great of Prussia

Frederick II (r. 1740–1786), commonly known as Frederick the Great, built masterfully on the work of his father, Frederick William I (see Chapter 15). Although in his youth he embraced culture and literature rather than the militarism championed by his father, by the time he came to the throne Frederick was determined to use the splendid army he had inherited.

Therefore, when the young empress Maria Theresa of Austria inherited the Habsburg dominions upon the death of her father, Charles VI, Frederick pounced. He invaded her rich province of Silesia (sigh-LEE-zhuh), defying solemn Prussian promises to respect the Pragmatic Sanction, a diplomatic agreement that had guaranteed Maria Theresa's succession. In 1742, as other greedy powers vied for her lands in the European War of the Austrian Succession (1740–1748), Maria Theresa was forced to cede almost all of Silesia to Prussia. In one stroke Prussia had doubled its population to 6 million people. Now Prussia unquestionably stood as a European Great Power.

Though successful in 1742, Frederick had to fight against great odds to save Prussia from total destruction after the ongoing competition between Britain and France for colonial empire brought another great conflict in 1756. Maria Theresa, seeking to regain Silesia, formed an alliance with the leaders of France and Russia. The aim of the alliance during the resulting Seven Years' War (1756–1763) was to conquer Prussia and divide up its territory. Despite invasions from all sides, Frederick fought on with stoic courage. In the end he was miraculously saved: Peter III came to the Russian throne in 1762 and called off the attack against Frederick, whom he greatly admired.

The terrible struggle of the Seven Years' War tempered Frederick's interest in territorial expansion and brought him to consider how more humane policies for his subjects might also strengthen the state. Thus Frederick went beyond a superficial commitment to

■ **enlightened absolutism** Term coined by historians to describe the rule of eighteenth-century monarchs who, without renouncing their own absolute authority, adopted Enlightenment ideals of rationalism, progress, and tolerance.

Enlightenment culture for himself and his circle. He tolerantly allowed his subjects to believe as they wished in religious and philosophical matters. He promoted the advancement of knowledge, improving his country's schools and permitting scholars to publish their findings. Moreover, Frederick tried to improve the lives of his subjects more directly. As he wrote to his friend Voltaire, "I must enlighten my people, cultivate their manners and morals, and make them as happy as human beings can be, or as happy as the means at my disposal permit."

The legal system and the bureaucracy were Frederick's primary tools. Prussia's laws were simplified, torture was abolished, and judges decided cases quickly and impartially. Prussian officials became famous for their hard work and honesty. After the Seven Years' War ended in 1763, Frederick's government energetically promoted the reconstruction of agriculture and industry. Frederick himself set a good example. He worked hard and lived modestly, claiming that he was "only the first servant of the state." Thus Frederick justified monarchy in terms of practical results and said nothing of the divine right of kings.

Frederick's dedication to high-minded government went only so far, however. While he condemned serfdom in the abstract, he accepted it in practice and did not free the serfs on his own estates. He accepted and extended the privileges of the nobility, who remained the backbone of the army and the entire Prussian state.

In reforming Prussia's bureaucracy, Frederick drew on the principles of **cameralism**, the German science of public administration that emerged in the decades following the Thirty Years' War. Influential throughout the German lands, cameralism held that monarchy was the best of all forms of government, that all elements of society should be placed at the service of the state, and that, in turn, the state should make use of its resources and authority to improve society. Predating the Enlightenment, cameralist interest in the public good was usually inspired by the needs of war. Cameralism shared with the Enlightenment an emphasis on rationality, progress, and utilitarianism.

Catherine the Great of Russia

Catherine the Great of Russia (r. 1762–1796) was one of the most remarkable rulers of her age, and the French philosophes adored her. Catherine was a German princess from Anhalt-Zerbst, an insignificant principality sandwiched between Prussia and Saxony. Her father commanded a regiment of the Prussian army, but her mother was related to the Romanovs of Russia, and that proved to be Catherine's opening to power.

Catherine's Romanov connection made her a suitable bride at the age of fifteen for the heir to the Russian throne. It was a mismatch from the beginning, but her *Memoirs* made her ambitions clear: "I did not care about Peter, but I did care about the crown." When her husband, Peter III, came to power during the Seven Years' War, his decision to withdraw Russian troops from the coalition against Prussia alienated the army. Catherine profited from his unpopularity to form a conspiracy to depose her husband. In 1762 Catherine's lover Gregory Orlov and his three brothers, all army officers, murdered Peter, and the German princess became empress of Russia.

Catherine had drunk deeply at the Enlightenment well. Never questioning that absolute monarchy was the best form of government, she set out to rule in an enlightened manner. She had three main goals. First, she worked hard to continue Peter the Great's effort to bring the culture of western Europe to Russia (see Chapter 15). To do so, she imported Western architects, musicians, and intellectuals. She bought masterpieces of Western art and patronized the philosophes. An enthusiastic letter writer, she corresponded extensively with Voltaire and praised him as the "champion of the human race." When the French government banned the *Encyclopedia*, she offered to publish it in St. Petersburg, and she sent money to Diderot when he needed it. With these actions, Catherine won good press in the West for herself and for her country. Moreover, this intellectual ruler, who wrote plays and loved good talk, set the tone for the entire Russian nobility. Peter the Great westernized Russian armies, but it was Catherine who westernized the imagination of the Russian nobility.

Catherine's second goal was domestic reform, and she began her reign with sincere and ambitious projects. In 1767 she appointed a legislative commission to prepare a new law code. This project was never completed, but Catherine did restrict the practice of torture and allowed limited religious toleration. She also tried to improve education and strengthen local government. The philosophes applauded these measures and hoped more would follow.

Such was not the case. In 1773 a common Cossack soldier named Emelian Pugachev sparked a gigantic uprising of serfs, very much as Stenka Razin had done a century earlier (see Chapter 15). Proclaiming himself the true tsar, Pugachev issued orders abolishing serfdom, taxes, and army service. Thousands joined his cause, slaughtering landlords and officials over a vast area of southwestern Russia. Pugachev's untrained forces eventually proved no match for Catherine's

■ **cameralism** View that monarchy was the best form of government, that all elements of society should serve the monarch, and that, in turn, the state should use its resources and authority to increase the public good.

Catherine the Great and Denis Diderot   Self-proclaimed adherent of Enlightenment ideals, Russian empress Catherine the Great enthusiastically corresponded with philosophes like Voltaire and Denis Diderot. When Diderot put his library on sale to raise much-needed funds, Catherine sent him the money but allowed him to keep his books. Historians have long debated the "enlightened despotism" represented by Catherine and other absolutist rulers. (Catherine: Based on a work by Alexander Roslin [1718–1793], [oil on canvas]/Museum of Art, Serpukhov, Russia/Bridgeman Images; Diderot: By Louis Michel van Loo [1707–1771]/Musée du Louvre, Paris, France/Fine Art Images/Heritage Images/Getty Images)

noble-led army. Betrayed by his own company, Pugachev was captured and savagely executed.

Pugachev's rebellion put an end to any intentions Catherine had about reforming the system. The peasants were clearly dangerous, and her empire rested on the support of the nobility. After 1775 Catherine gave the nobles absolute control of their serfs, and she extended serfdom into new areas, such as Ukraine. In 1785 she freed nobles forever from taxes and state service. Under Catherine the Russian nobility attained its most exalted position, and serfdom entered its most oppressive phase.

Catherine's third goal was territorial expansion, and in this respect she was extremely successful. Her armies subjugated the last descendants of the Mongols and the Crimean Tartars, and began the conquest of the Caucasus (KAW-kuh-suhs). Her greatest coup by far was the partition of Poland (Map 16.1). When, between 1768 and 1772, Catherine's armies scored unprecedented victories against the Ottomans and thereby

threatened to disturb the balance of power between Russia and Austria in eastern Europe, Frederick of Prussia obligingly came forward with a deal. He proposed that Turkey be let off easily and that Prussia, Austria, and Russia each compensate itself by taking a gigantic slice of the weakly ruled Polish territory. Catherine jumped at the chance. The first partition of Poland took place in 1772. Subsequent partitions in 1793 and 1795 gave away the rest of Polish territory, and the ancient republic of Poland vanished from the map.

The Austrian Habsburgs

Another female monarch, Maria Theresa (r. 1740–1780) of Austria, set out to reform her nation, although traditional power politics was a more important motivation for her than were Enlightenment teachings. A devoutly Catholic mother and wife who inherited power from her father, Charles VI, Maria Theresa was a remarkable but old-fashioned absolutist. Her more radical son,

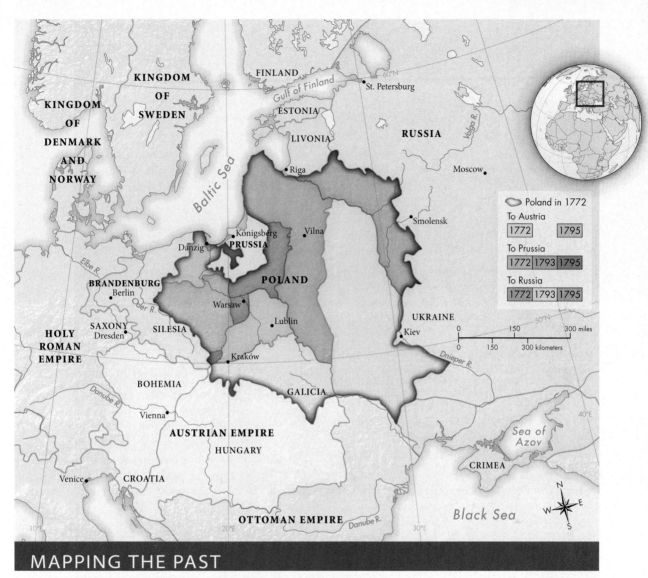

MAPPING THE PAST

MAP 16.1 The Partition of Poland, 1772–1795

In 1772 war between Russia and Austria threatened over Russian gains from the Ottoman Empire. To satisfy desires for expansion without fighting, Prussia's Frederick the Great proposed that parts of Poland be divided among Austria, Prussia, and Russia. In 1793 and 1795 the three powers partitioned the remainder, and the republic of Poland ceased to exist.

ANALYZING THE MAP Of the three powers that divided the kingdom of Poland, which gained the most territory? How did the partition affect the geographical boundaries of each state, and what was the significance? What border with the former Poland remained unchanged? Why do you think this was the case?

CONNECTIONS What does it say about European politics at the time that a country could simply cease to exist on the map? Could that happen today?

Joseph II (r. 1780–1790), drew on Enlightenment ideals, earning the title of "revolutionary emperor."

Emerging from the long War of the Austrian Succession in 1748 with the serious loss of Silesia, Maria Theresa was determined to introduce reforms that would make the state stronger and more efficient. First, she initiated church reform, with measures aimed at limiting the papacy's influence, eliminating many religious holidays, and reducing the number of monasteries. Second, a whole series of administrative renovations strengthened the central bureaucracy, smoothed out some provincial differences, and revamped the tax system, taxing even the lands of nobles, previously exempt from taxation. Third, the

Maria Theresa   The empress and her husband pose with twelve of their sixteen children at Schönbrunn palace in this family portrait by court painter Martin Meytens (1695–1770). Joseph, the heir to the throne, stands at the center of the star on the floor. Wealthy women often had very large families, in part because they, unlike poor women, seldom nursed their babies. (Château de Versailles, France/Bridgeman Images)

government sought to improve the lot of the agricultural population, cautiously reducing the power of lords over their hereditary serfs and their partially free peasant tenants.

Coregent with his mother from 1765 onward and a strong supporter of change from above, Joseph II moved forward rapidly when he came to the throne in 1780. Most notably, Joseph abolished serfdom in 1781, and in 1789 he decreed that peasants could pay land-lords in cash rather than through labor on their land. This measure was violently rejected not only by the nobility but also by the peasants it was intended to help, because they lacked the necessary cash. When a disillusioned Joseph died prematurely at forty-nine, the entire Habsburg empire was in turmoil. His brother Leopold II (r. 1790–1792) canceled Joseph's radical edicts in order to re-establish order. Peasants once again were required to do forced labor for their lords.

I n 1743 a small, humpbacked Jewish boy with a stammer left his poor parents in Dessau in central Germany and walked eighty miles to Berlin, the capital of Frederick the Great's Prussia. According to one story, when the boy reached the Rosenthaler (ROH-zuhn-taw-lehr) Gate, the only one through which Jews could pass, he told the inquiring watchman that his name was Moses and that he had come to Berlin "to learn." The watchman laughed and waved him through. "Go Moses, the sea has opened before you."*

In Berlin the young Mendelssohn studied Jewish law and eked out a living copying Hebrew manuscripts in a beautiful hand. But he was soon fascinated by an intellectual world that had been closed to him in the Dessau ghetto. There, like most Jews throughout central Europe, he had spoken Yiddish — a mixture of German, Polish, and Hebrew. Now, working mainly on his own, he mastered German; learned Latin, Greek, French, and English; and studied mathematics and Enlightenment philosophy. Word of his exceptional abilities spread in Berlin's Jewish community (the dwelling of 1,500 of the city's 100,000 inhabitants). He began tutoring the children of a wealthy Jewish silk merchant, and he soon became the merchant's clerk and later his partner. But his great passion remained the life of the mind and the spirit, which he avidly pursued in his off-hours.

Gentle and unassuming in his personal life, Mendelssohn was a bold thinker. Reading eagerly in Western philosophy since antiquity, he was, as a pious Jew, soon convinced that Enlightenment teachings need not be opposed to Jewish thought and religion. He concluded that reason could complement and strengthen religion, although each would retain its integrity as a separate sphere.† Developing his idea in his first great work, *On the Immortality of the Soul* (1767), Mendelssohn used the neutral setting of a philosophical dialogue between Socrates and his followers in ancient Greece to argue that the human soul lived forever. In refusing to bring religion and critical thinking into conflict, he was strongly influenced by contemporary German philosophers who argued similarly on behalf of Christianity. He reflected the way the German Enlightenment generally supported established religion, in contrast to the French Enlightenment, which attacked it.

Mendelssohn's treatise on the human soul captivated the educated German public, which marveled that a Jew could have written a philosophical masterpiece. In the excitement, a Christian zealot named Johann Casper Lavater challenged Mendelssohn in a pamphlet to demonstrate how the Christian

Lavater (right) attempts to convert Mendelssohn, in a painting by Moritz Oppenheim of an imaginary encounter. (By Moritz Daniel Oppenheim [1800–1882], [oil on canvas]/akg-images)

faith was not "reasonable" or to accept Christianity. Replying politely but passionately, the Jewish philosopher affirmed that his studies had only strengthened him in his faith, although he did not seek to convert anyone not born into Judaism. Rather, he urged toleration in religious matters and spoke up courageously against Jewish oppression.

Orthodox Jew and German philosophe, Moses Mendelssohn serenely combined two very different worlds. He built a bridge from the ghetto to the dominant culture over which many Jews would pass, including his novelist daughter Dorothea and his famous grandson, the composer Felix Mendelssohn.

QUESTIONS FOR ANALYSIS

1. How did Mendelssohn seek to influence Jewish religious thought in his time?
2. How do Mendelssohn's ideas compare with those of the French Enlightenment?

*H. Kupferberg, *The Mendelssohns: Three Generations of Genius* (New York: Charles Scribner's Sons, 1972), p. 3.
†David Sorkin, *Moses Mendelssohn and the Religious Enlightenment* (Berkeley: University of California Press, 1996), pp. 8ff.

Despite differences in their policies, Joseph II and the other absolutists of the later eighteenth century combined old-fashioned state-building with the culture and critical thinking of the Enlightenment. In doing so, they succeeded in expanding the role of the state in the life of society. They perfected bureaucratic machines that were to prove surprisingly adaptive and enduring. Their failure to implement policies we would recognize as humane and enlightened—such as abolishing serfdom—may reveal inherent limitations in Enlightenment thinking about equality and social justice, rather than deficiencies in their execution of Enlightenment programs. The fact that leading philosophes supported rather than criticized eastern rulers' policies exposes the blind spots of the era.

The Pale of Settlement, 1791

Jewish Life and the Limits of Enlightened Absolutism

Perhaps the best example of the limitations of enlightened absolutism are the debates surrounding the emancipation of the Jews. Europe's small Jewish populations lived under highly discriminatory laws. For the most part, Jews were confined to tiny, overcrowded ghettos, were excluded by law from most professions, and could be ordered out of a kingdom at a moment's notice. Still, a very few did manage to succeed and to obtain the right of permanent settlement, usually by performing some special service for the state. Many rulers relied on Jewish bankers for loans to raise armies and run their kingdoms. Jewish merchants prospered in international trade because they could rely on contacts with colleagues in Jewish communities scattered across Europe.

In the eighteenth century an Enlightenment movement known as the **Haskalah** emerged from within the European Jewish community, led by the Prussian philosopher Moses Mendelssohn (1729–1786). (See "Individuals in Society: Moses Mendelssohn and the Jewish Enlightenment," page 537.) Christian and Jewish Enlightenment philosophers, including Mendelssohn, began to advocate for freedom and civil rights for European Jews. In an era of reason and progress, they argued, restrictions on religious grounds could not stand. The Haskalah accompanied a period of controversial social change within Jewish communities, in

which rabbinic controls loosened and heightened interaction with Christians took place.

Arguments for tolerance won some ground. The British Parliament passed a law allowing naturalization of Jews in 1753, but later repealed the law due to public outrage. The most progressive reforms took place under Austrian emperor Joseph II. Among his liberal edicts of the 1780s were measures intended to integrate Jews more fully into society, including eligibility for military service, admission to higher education and artisanal trades, and removal of requirements for special clothing or emblems. Welcomed by many Jews, these reforms raised fears among traditionalists of assimilation into the general population.

Many monarchs rejected all ideas of emancipation. Although he permitted freedom of religion to his Christian subjects, Frederick the Great of Prussia firmly opposed any general emancipation for the Jews, as he did for the serfs. Catherine the Great, who acquired most of Poland's large Jewish population when she annexed part of that country in the late eighteenth century, similarly refused. In 1791 she established the Pale of Settlement, a territory including parts of modern-day Poland, Latvia, Lithuania, Ukraine, and Belarus, in which most Jews were required to live. Jewish habitation was restricted to the Pale until the Russian Revolution in 1917.

The first European state to remove all restrictions on the Jews was France under the French Revolution. Over the next hundred years, Jews gradually won full legal and civil rights throughout the rest of western Europe. Emancipation in eastern Europe took even longer and aroused more conflict and violence.

NOTES

1. Quoted in H. Butterfield, *The Origins of Modern Science* (New York: Macmillan, 1951), p. 47.
2. Ibid., p. 120.
3. Quoted in John Freely, *Aladdin's Lamp: How Greek Science Came to Europe Through the Islamic World* (New York: Knopf, 2009), p. 225.
4. Jacqueline Broad, *Women Philosophers of the Seventeenth Century* (Cambridge: Cambridge University Press, 2003), p. 17.
5. L. Schiebinger, *The Mind Has No Sex? Women in the Origins of Modern Science* (Cambridge, Mass.: Harvard University Press, 1989), p. 64.
6. Quoted in G. L. Mosse et al., eds., *Europe in Review* (Chicago: Rand McNally, 1964), p. 156.
7. Quoted in P. Gay, "The Unity of the Enlightenment," *History* 3 (1960): 25.
8. D. E. Mungello, *The Great Encounter of China and the West, 1500–1800*, 2d ed. (Lanham, Md.: Rowman & Littlefield, 2005), p. 98.

■ **Haskalah** The Jewish Enlightenment of the second half of the eighteenth century, led by the Prussian philosopher Moses Mendelssohn.

9. Quoted in Emmanuel Chukwudi Eze, ed., *Race and the Enlightenment: A Reader* (Oxford: Blackwell, 1997), p. 33.
10. See E. Fox-Genovese, "Women in the Enlightenment," in *Becoming Visible: Women in European History*, 2d ed., ed. R. Bridenthal, C. Koonz, and S. Stuard (Boston: Houghton Mifflin, 1987), esp. pp. 252–259, 263–265.

11. Aurora Wolfgang, *Gender and Voice in the French Novel, 1730–1782* (Aldershot, U.K.: Ashgate, 2004), p. 8.
12. Jean Le Rond d'Alembert, *Eloges lus dans les séances publiques de l'Académie française* (Paris, 1779), p. ix, quoted in Mona Ozouf, "'Public Opinion' at the End of the Old Regime," *The Journal of Modern History* 60, Supplement: Rethinking French Politics in 1788 (September 1988): S9.

LOOKING BACK LOOKING AHEAD

Hailed as the origin of modern thought, the Scientific Revolution must also be seen as a product of its past. Medieval universities gave rise to important new scholarship, and the ambition and wealth of Renaissance patrons nurtured intellectual curiosity. Religious faith also influenced the Scientific Revolution, inspiring thinkers to understand the glory of God's creation, while bringing censure and personal tragedy to others. Natural philosophers following Copernicus pioneered new methods of observing and explaining nature while drawing on centuries-old traditions of mysticism, astrology, alchemy, and magic.

The Enlightenment ideas of the eighteenth century were a similar blend of past and present; they could serve as much to bolster absolutist monarchical regimes as to inspire revolutionaries to fight for individual rights and liberties. Although the Enlightenment fostered critical thinking about everything from science to religion, the majority of Europeans, including many prominent thinkers, remained devout Christians.

The achievements of the Scientific Revolution and the Enlightenment are undeniable. Key Western values of rationalism, human rights, and open-mindedness were born from these movements. With their new notions of progress and social improvement, Europeans would embark on important revolutions in industry and politics in the centuries that followed. Nonetheless, others have seen a darker side. For these critics, the mastery over nature permitted by the Scientific Revolution now threatens to overwhelm the earth's fragile equilibrium, and the Enlightenment belief in the universal application of reason can lead to arrogance and intolerance of other people's spiritual, cultural, and political values. Such vivid debates about the legacy of these intellectual and scientific developments testify to their continuing importance in today's world.

Make Connections

Think about the larger developments and continuities within and across chapters.

1. How did the era of European exploration and discovery (Chapter 14) affect the ideas of scientists and philosophers discussed in this chapter? In what ways did contact with new peoples and places stimulate new forms of thought among Europeans?

2. What was the relationship between the Scientific Revolution and the Enlightenment? How did new ways of understanding the natural world influence thinking about human society?

3. Compare the policies and actions of seventeenth-century absolutist rulers (Chapter 15) with their "enlightened" descendants described in this chapter. How accurate is the term *enlightened absolutism*?

16   REVIEW & EXPLORE

Identify Key Terms

Identify and explain the significance of each item below.

natural philosophy (p. 507)

Copernican hypothesis (p. 509)

law of inertia (p. 510)

law of universal gravitation (p. 510)

empiricism (p. 514)

Cartesian dualism (p. 515)

Enlightenment (p. 517)

rationalism (p. 518)

sensationalism (p. 519)

philosophes (p. 519)

deism (p. 520)

salon (p. 528)

rococo (p. 528)

public sphere (p. 529)

enlightened absolutism (p. 532)

cameralism (p. 533)

Haskalah (p. 538)

Review the Main Ideas

Answer the focus questions from each section of the chapter.

◆ What revolutionary discoveries were made in the sixteenth and seventeenth centuries, and why did they occur in Europe? (p. 506)

◆ What intellectual and social changes occurred as a result of the Scientific Revolution? (p. 513)

◆ How did the Enlightenment emerge, and what were major currents of Enlightenment thought? (p. 517)

◆ How did Enlightenment thinkers address issues of racial and social difference, and how did new institutions and social practices diffuse Enlightenment thought? (p. 524)

◆ What impact did new ways of thinking have on political developments and monarchical absolutism? (p. 532)

Suggested Reading and Media Resources

BOOKS

◆ Cañizares-Esguerra, Jorge. *Nature, Empire, and Nation: Explorations of the History of Science in the Iberian World*. 2006. Explores the role of Spain and Spanish America in the development of science in the early modern period.

◆ Curran, Andrew S. *The Anatomy of Blackness: Science and Slavery in an Age of Enlightenment*. 2013. Examines how Enlightenment thinkers transformed traditional thinking about people of African descent into ideas about biological racial difference.

◆ Dear, Peter. *Revolutionizing the Sciences: European Knowledge and Its Ambitions, 1500–1700*, 2d ed. 2009. An accessible and well-illustrated introduction to the Scientific Revolution.

◆ Delbourgo, James, and Nicholas Dew, eds. *Science and Empire in the Atlantic World*. 2008. A collection of essays examining the relationship between the Scientific Revolution and the imperial expansion of European powers across the Atlantic.

◆ Ellis, Markman. *The Coffee House: A Cultural History*. 2004. An engaging study of the rise of the coffeehouse and its impact on European cultural and social life.

◆ Massie, Robert K. *Catherine the Great: Portrait of a Woman*. 2012. Recounts the life story of Catherine, from obscure German princess to enlightened ruler of Russia.

- McMahon, Darrin M. *Happiness: A History.* 2006. Discusses how worldly pleasure became valued as a duty of individuals and societies in the Enlightenment.
- Messbarger, Rebecca. *The Lady Anatomist: The Life and Work of Anna Morandi Manzolini.* 2010. The life of an Italian woman artist and scientist who showed the opportunities and constraints for eighteenth-century women.
- Robertson, John. *The Case for the Enlightenment: Scotland and Naples, 1680–1760.* 2005. A comparative study of Enlightenment movements in Scotland and Naples, emphasizing commonalities between these two small kingdoms on the edges of Europe.
- Shapin, Steven. *The Scientific Revolution.* 1996. A concise and well-informed general introduction to the Scientific Revolution.
- Sorkin, David. *Moses Mendelssohn and the Religious Enlightenment.* 1996. A brilliant study of the Jewish philosopher and of the role of religion in the Enlightenment.

DOCUMENTARIES

- *Galileo's Battle for the Heavens* (PBS, 2002). Recounts the story of Galileo's struggle with the Catholic Church over his astronomical discoveries, featuring re-enactments of key episodes in his life.
- *Newton's Dark Secrets* (PBS, 2005). Explores Isaac Newton's fundamental scientific discoveries alongside his religious faith and practice of alchemy.

FEATURE FILMS AND TELEVISION

- *Catherine the Great* (A&E, 1995). A made-for-television movie starring Catherine Zeta-Jones as the German princess who becomes Catherine the Great.
- *Dangerous Liaisons* (Stephen Frears, 1988). Based on a 1782 novel, the story of two aristocrats who cynically manipulate others, until one of them falls in love with a chaste widow chosen as his victim.
- *Longitude* (A&E, 2000). A television miniseries that follows the parallel stories of an eighteenth-century clockmaker striving to find a means to measure longitude at sea and a modern-day veteran who restores the earlier man's clocks.
- *Ridicule* (Patrice Leconte, 1996). When a provincial nobleman travels to the French court in the 1780s to present a project to drain a malarial swamp in his district, his naïve Enlightenment ideals incur the ridicule of decadent courtiers.

WEB SITES

- *The Encyclopedia of Diderot & d'Alembert Collaborative Translation Project.* A collaborative project to translate the *Encyclopedia* edited by Denis Diderot and Jean le Rond d'Alembert into English, with searchable entries submitted by students and scholars and vetted by experts. **quod.lib.umich.edu/d/did/**
- *The Hermitage Museum.* The Web site of the Russian Hermitage Museum founded by Catherine the Great in the Winter Palace in St. Petersburg, with virtual tours of the museum's rich collections. **http://www.hermitagemuseum.org/wps/portal/hermitage**
- *Mapping the Republic of Letters.* A site hosted by Stanford University showcasing projects using mapping software to create spatial visualizations based on correspondence and travel of members of the eighteenth-century Republic of Letters. **republicofletters.stanford.edu/**

17

The Expansion of Europe

1650–1800

Absolutism and aristocracy, a combination of raw power and elegant refinement, were a world apart from the common people. For most people in the eighteenth century, life remained a struggle with poverty and uncertainty, with the landlord and the tax collector. In 1700 peasants on the land and artisans in their shops lived little better than had their ancestors in the Middle Ages, primarily because European societies still could not produce very much as measured by modern standards. Despite the hard work of ordinary men, women, and children, there was seldom enough good food, warm clothing, and decent housing. The idea of progress, of substantial improvement in the lives of great numbers of people, was still the dream of only a small elite in fashionable salons.

Yet the economic basis of European life was beginning to change. In the course of the eighteenth century, the European economy emerged from the long crisis of the seventeenth century, responded to challenges, and began to expand once again. Population resumed its growth, while colonial empires extended and developed. Some areas were more fortunate than others. The rising Atlantic powers—the Dutch Republic, France, and above all England—and their colonies led the way. The expansion of agriculture, industry, trade, and population marked the beginning of a surge comparable to that of the eleventh- and twelfth-century springtime of European civilization. But this time, broadly based expansion was not cut short by plague and famine. This time the response to new challenges led toward one of the most influential developments in human history, the Industrial Revolution, considered in Chapter 20. ■

CHAPTER PREVIEW

The Port of Bristol
Starting in the late seventeenth century the English port of Bristol prospered through colonial trade with the West Indies and North America. In the eighteenth century it became a major hub of the slave trade, shipping finished goods to Africa to purchase captives, who were in turn transported to the Americas in exchange for sugar, rum, and tobacco for English markets. (*Bristol Docks and Quay*, ca. 1760 [oil on canvas]/© Bristol Museum and Art Gallery, UK/Bridgeman Images)

Working the Land

FOCUS QUESTION *What important developments led to increased agricultural production, and how did these changes affect peasants?*

At the end of the seventeenth century the economy of Europe was agrarian. With the exception of the Dutch Republic and England, at least 80 percent of the people of western Europe drew their livelihoods from agriculture. In eastern Europe the percentage was considerably higher. Men and women were tied to the land, plowing fields and sowing seed, reaping harvests and storing grain. Yet even in a rich agricultural region such as the Po Valley in northern Italy, every bushel of wheat seed sown yielded on average only five or six bushels of grain at harvest. By modern standards, output was distressingly low.

In most regions of Europe, climatic conditions produced poor or disastrous harvests every eight or nine years. In famine years the number of deaths soared far above normal. A third of a village's population might disappear in a year or two. But new developments in agricultural technology and methods gradually brought an end to the ravages of hunger in western Europe.

The Legacy of the Open-Field System

Why, in the late seventeenth century, did many areas of Europe produce barely enough food to survive? The answer lies in patterns of farming inherited from the Middle Ages, which sustained fairly large numbers of people, but did not produce material abundance. From the Middle Ages up to the seventeenth century, much of Europe was farmed through the open-field system. The land to be cultivated was divided into several large fields, which were in turn cut up into long, narrow strips. The fields were open, and the strips were not enclosed into small plots by fences or hedges. The whole peasant village followed the same pattern of plowing, sowing, and harvesting in accordance with long-standing traditions.

The ever-present problem was soil exhaustion. Wheat planted year after year in a field will deplete nitrogen in the soil. Since the supply of manure for fertilizer was limited, the only way for the land to recover was to lie fallow for a period of time. Clover and other annual grasses that sprang up in unplanted fields restored nutrients to the soil and also provided food for livestock. In the early Middle Ages a year of fallow was alternated with a year of cropping; then three-year rotations were introduced. On each strip of land, a year of wheat or rye was followed by a year of oats or beans and only then by a year of fallow. Peasants staggered the rotation of crops,

so some wheat, legumes, and pastureland were always available. The three-year system was an important achievement because cash crops could be grown two years out of three, rather than only one year in two.

Traditional village rights reinforced communal patterns of farming. In addition to rotating field crops in a uniform way, villages maintained open meadows for hay and natural pasture. After the harvest villagers also pastured their animals on the wheat or rye stubble. In many places such pasturing followed a brief period, also established by tradition, for the gleaning of grain. In this process, poor women would go through the fields picking up the few single grains that had fallen to the ground in the course of the harvest. Many villages were surrounded by woodlands, also held in common, which provided essential firewood, building materials, and nutritional roots and berries.

The state and landlords continued to levy heavy taxes and high rents, thereby stripping peasants of much of their meager earnings. The level of exploitation varied. Generally speaking, the peasants of eastern Europe were worst off. As we saw in Chapter 15, they were serfs bound to their lords in hereditary service. In much of eastern Europe, working several days per week on the lord's land was not uncommon. Well into the nineteenth century, individual Russian serfs and serf families were regularly bought and sold.

Social conditions were better in western Europe, where peasants were generally free from serfdom. In France, western Germany, England, and the Low Countries (modern-day Belgium and the Netherlands), peasants could own land and could pass it on to their children. In years with normal harvests, most people had enough food to fill their bellies. Yet life in the village was hard, and poverty was the reality for most people.

New Methods of Agriculture

The seventeenth century saw important gains in productivity in some regions that would slowly extend to the rest of Europe. By 1700 less than half of the population of Britain and the Dutch Republic worked in agriculture, producing enough to feed the remainder of the population. Many elements combined in this production growth, but the key was new ways of rotating crops that allowed farmers to forgo the unproductive fallow period altogether and maintain their land in continuous cultivation. The secret to eliminating the fallow lay in deliberately alternating grain with crops that restored nutrients to the soil, such as peas and beans, root crops like turnips and potatoes, and clover and other grasses.

Clover was one of the most important crops, because it restores nitrogen directly to the soil through its roots. Other crops produced additional benefits. Potatoes and many types of beans came to Europe as part of the sixteenth-century Columbian exchange between the New and the Old Worlds (see Chapter 14). Originally perceived by Europeans as fit only for animal feed, potatoes eventually made their way to the human table, where they provided a nutritious supplement to the peasant's meager diet. With more fodder, hay, and root vegetables for the winter months, peasants and larger farmers could build up their herds of cattle and sheep. More animals meant more manure to fertilize and restore the soil. More animals also meant more meat and dairy products as well as more power to pull plows in the fields and bring carts to market.

Over time, crop rotation spread to other parts of Europe, and farmers developed increasingly specialized patterns of crop rotation to suit different kinds of soils. For example, in the late eighteenth century farmers in French Flanders near Lille alternated a number of grain, root, and hay crops in a given field on a ten-year schedule. Ongoing experimentation, fueled by developments in the Scientific Revolution (see Chapter 16), led to more methodical farming.

Advocates of the new crop rotations, who included an emerging group of experimental scientists, some government officials, and a few big landowners, believed that new methods were scarcely possible within the traditional framework of open fields and common rights. A farmer who wanted to experiment with new methods would have to get all the landholders in the village to agree to the plan. Advocates of improvement argued that innovating agriculturalists needed to enclose and consolidate their scattered holdings into compact, fenced-in fields in order to farm more effectively. In doing so, the innovators also needed to enclose the village's natural pastureland, or common, into individual shares. According to proponents of this movement, known as **enclosure**, the upheaval of village life was the necessary price of technical progress.

That price seemed too high to many rural people who had small, inadequate holdings or very little land at all. Traditional rights were precious to these poor peasants, who used commonly held pastureland to graze livestock, and marshlands or forest outside the village as a source for foraged goods that could make the difference between survival and famine in harsh times. Thus, when the small landholders and the village poor could effectively oppose the enclosure of the open fields and the common lands, they did so. In many countries they found allies among the larger, predominantly noble landowners who were also wary

Chronology

1600–1850	Growth in agriculture, pioneered by the Dutch Republic and England
1651–1663	British Navigation Acts
1652–1674	Anglo-Dutch wars
1700–1790	Height of Atlantic slave trade; expansion of rural industry in Europe
1701–1763	British and French mercantilist wars of empire
1720–1722	Last outbreak of bubonic plague in Europe
1720–1789	Growth of European population
1756–1763	Seven Years' War
1760–1815	Height of parliamentary enclosure in England
1763	Treaty of Paris; France cedes its possessions in India and North America
1770	James Cook claims the east coast of Australia for England
1776	Adam Smith publishes *An Inquiry into the Nature and Causes of the Wealth of Nations*
1805	British takeover of India complete
1807	British slave trade abolished

of enclosure because it required large investments in purchasing and fencing land and thus posed risks for them as well.

The old system of unenclosed open fields and the new system of continuous rotation coexisted in Europe for a long time. Open fields could still be found in much of France and Germany as late as the nineteenth century because peasants there had successfully opposed eighteenth-century efforts to introduce the new techniques. Through the end of the eighteenth century, the new system of enclosure was extensively adopted only in the Low Countries and England.

The Leadership of the Low Countries and England

The seventeenth-century Dutch Republic, already the most advanced country in Europe in many areas of human endeavor (see Chapter 15), pioneered advancements in agriculture. By the middle of the seventeenth century intensive farming was well established, and the innovations of enclosed fields, continuous rotation, heavy manuring, and a wide variety of crops were all present. Agriculture was highly specialized and commercialized, especially in the province of Holland.

■ **enclosure** The movement to fence in fields in order to farm more effectively, at the expense of poor peasants who relied on common fields for farming and pasture.

One reason for early Dutch leadership in farming was that the area was one of the most densely populated in Europe. In order to feed themselves and provide employment, the Dutch were forced at an early date to seek maximum yields from their land and to increase the cultivated area through the steady draining of marshes and swamps. The pressure of population was connected with the second cause: the growth of towns and cities. Stimulated by commerce and overseas trade, Amsterdam grew from thirty thousand to two hundred thousand inhabitants in its golden seventeenth century. The growing urban population provided Dutch peasants with markets for all they could produce and allowed each region to specialize in what it did best. Thus the Dutch could develop their potential, and the Low Countries became, as one historian wrote, "the Mecca of foreign agricultural experts who came . . . to see Flemish agriculture with their own eyes, to write about it and to propagate its methods in their home lands."[1]

The English were among their best students. In the mid-seventeenth century English farmers borrowed the system of continuous crop rotation from the Dutch. They also drew on Dutch expertise in drainage and water control. Large parts of seventeenth-century Holland had once been sea and sea marsh, and the efforts of centuries had made the Dutch the world's leaders in drainage. In the first half of the seventeenth century, Dutch experts made a great contribution to draining the extensive marshes, or fens, of wet and rainy England. The most famous of these Dutch engineers, Cornelius Vermuyden, directed one large

drainage project in Yorkshire and another in Cambridgeshire. In the Cambridge fens, Vermuyden and his Dutch workers eventually reclaimed forty thousand acres, which were then farmed intensively in the Dutch manner. Swampy wilderness was converted into thousands of acres of some of the best land in England.

Based on the seventeenth-century achievements, English agriculture continued to progress during the eighteenth century, growing enough food to satisfy a rapidly growing population. Jethro Tull (1674–1741), part crank and part genius, was an important English innovator. A true son of the early Enlightenment, Tull adopted a critical attitude toward accepted ideas about farming and tried to develop better methods through empirical research. He was especially enthusiastic about using horses, rather than slower-moving oxen, for plowing. He also advocated sowing seed with drilling equipment rather than scattering it by hand. Drilling distributed seed in an even manner and at the proper depth. There were also improvements in livestock, inspired in part by the earlier successes of English country gentlemen in breeding ever-faster horses for the races and fox hunts that were their passions. Selective breeding of ordinary livestock was a marked improvement over the haphazard breeding of the past.

One of the most important—and bitterly contested—aspects of English agricultural development was the enclosure of open fields and commons. More than half the farmland in England was enclosed through private initiatives prior to 1700; Parliament completed this work in the eighteenth century. From the 1760s to

The Seed Drill   The seed drill had a metal plow in front (depicted behind the horse's back feet) to dig channels in the earth and a container behind it that distributed seed evenly into the channels. The drill allowed farmers to plant seeds at consistent depths and in straight lines, a much more efficient system than the old method of simply scattering seed across the field. (Prisma/UIG via Getty Images)

Arthur Young on the Benefits of Enclosure

In the 1760s Arthur Young farmed his family property in Essex, England, devoting himself to experiments in the latest techniques of agriculture and animal husbandry. He traveled through the British Isles and France meeting with farmers and collecting information on their crop yields and methods of cultivation. His published observations — and his optimistic views on progress in agriculture — were widely read and acclaimed in his day. In the passage below, Young expounds on the benefits of enclosing open fields.

Respecting open field lands, the quantity of labour in them is not comparable to that of enclosures; for, not to speak of the great numbers of men that in enclosed countries are constantly employed in winter in hedging and ditching, what comparison can there be between the open field system of one half or a third of the lands being in fallow, receiving only three ploughings; and the same portion now tilled four, five, or six times by Midsummer, then sown with turnips, those hand-hoed twice, and then drawn by hand, and carted to stalls for beasts; or else hurdled out in portions for fatting sheep! What a scarcity of employment in one case, what a variety in the other! And consider the vast tracts of land in the kingdom (no less than the whole upon which turnips are cultivated) that have undergone this change since the last century. I should also remind the reader of other systems of management; beans and peas hand-hoed for a fallow — the culture of potatoes — of carrots, of coleseed, &c. — the hoeing of white corn — with the minuter improvements in every part of the culture of all crops — every article of which is an increase of labour. Then he should remember the vast tracts of country uncultivated in the last century, which have been enclosed and converted into new farms, a much greater tract in 80 years than these writers dream of: all this is the effect of enclosures, and consequently they also have yielded a great increase of employment. . . .

The fact is this; in the central counties of the kingdom, particularly Northamptonshire, Leicestershire, and parts of Warwick, Huntingdon and Buckinghamshires, there have been within 30 years large tracts of the open field arable under that vile course, 1 fallow, 2 wheat, 3 spring corn, enclosed and laid down to grass, being much more suited to the wetness of the soil than corn; and yields in beef, mutton, hides and wool, beyond comparison a greater neat produce than when under corn. . . . Thus the land yields a greater neat produce in food for mankind — the landlord doubles his income, which enables him to employ so many more manufacturers and artisans — the farmer increases his income, by means of which he also does the same — the hides and wool are a creation of so much employment for other manufacturers.

EVALUATE THE EVIDENCE

1. What are the various improvements in agriculture described by Young in this passage? How do they relate to one another?
2. Why does Young think that enclosures produce more employment opportunities than open fields do? Based on your reading in the chapter, did everyone perceive the benefits produced by enclosure in the same way as Young?

Source: Arthur Young, Political Arithmetic: Containing Observations on the Present State of Great Britain; and the Principles of Her Policy in the Encouragement of Agriculture (London: W. Nicoll, 1774), pp. 72–73, 148.

1815 a series of acts of Parliament enclosed most of the remaining common land. Arthur Young, another agricultural experimentalist, celebrated large-scale enclosure as a necessary means to achieve progress. (See "Evaluating the Evidence 17.1: Arthur Young on the Benefits of Enclosure," above.) Many of his contemporaries, as well as the historians that followed him, echoed that conviction. More recent research, however, has shown that regions that maintained open-field farming were still able to adopt crop rotation and other innovations, suggesting that enclosures were not a prerequisite for increased production.

Many critics of Arthur Young's day emphasized the social upheaval caused by enclosure. By eliminating common rights and greatly reducing the access of poor men and women to the land, the eighteenth-century enclosure movement marked the completion of two major historical developments in England — the rise of capitalist market-oriented estate agriculture and the emergence of a landless rural proletariat. By the early nineteenth century a tiny minority of wealthy English and Scottish landowners held most of the land and pursued profits aggressively, leasing their holdings through agents at competitive prices to middle-size farmers, who relied on landless laborers for their workforce. These landless laborers worked very long hours, usually following a dawn-to-dusk schedule six days a week all year long. Not only was the small landholder deprived of his land, but improvements in technology meant that fewer laborers were needed to work the large farms, and unemployment spread throughout the countryside. As one observer commented:

> It is no uncommon thing for four or five wealthy graziers to engross a large inclosed lordship, which was before in the hands of twenty or thirty farmers, and as many smaller tenants or proprietors. All these are thereby thrown out of their livings, and many other families, who were chiefly employed and supported by them, such as blacksmiths, carpenters, wheelwrights and other artificers and tradesmen, besides their own labourers and servants.[2]

In no other European country had this **proletarianization**—this transformation of large numbers of small peasant farmers into landless rural wage earners—gone so far. England's village poor found the cost of change heavy and unjust.

The Beginning of the Population Explosion

FOCUS QUESTION *Why did the European population rise dramatically in the eighteenth century?*

Another factor that affected the existing order of life and drove economic changes in the eighteenth century was the beginning of the population explosion. Explosive growth continued in Europe until the twentieth century, by which time it was affecting non-Western areas of the globe. In this section we examine the background and causes of the population growth; the following section considers how the challenge of more mouths to feed and more hands to employ affected the European economy.

Long-Standing Obstacles to Population Growth

Until 1700 the total population of Europe grew slowly much of the time, and it followed an irregular cyclical pattern (Figure 17.1). This cyclical pattern had a great influence on many aspects of social and economic life. The terrible ravages of the Black Death of 1348–1350 caused a sharp drop in population and food prices after 1350 and also created a labor shortage throughout Europe. Some economic historians calculate that for common people in western Europe who managed to steer clear of warfare and of power struggles within the ruling class, the later Middle Ages was an era of exceptional well-being.

By the mid-sixteenth century much of Europe had returned to its pre-plague population levels. In this buoyant period, farmers brought new land into cultivation and urban settlements grew significantly. But this well-being eroded in the course of the sixteenth century. Population growth outstripped the growth of production after about 1500. There was less food, housing, fuel, and other resources per person, and prices rose more rapidly than wages, a development intensified by the inflow of precious metals from the Americas (see Chapter 14). The century-long period of general, if uneven, inflation that followed, known as the European price revolution, substantially lowered living standards. Population figures stagnated or declined across much of Europe, and widespread poverty was an undeniable reality.

During the seventeenth century births and deaths, fertility and mortality, returned to a crude but effective balance. The population grew modestly in normal years at a rate of perhaps 0.5 to 1 percent, or enough to double the population in 70 to 140 years. This is, of course, a generalization encompassing many different patterns. In areas such as Russia and colonial New England, where there was a great deal of frontier to be settled, the annual rate of natural increase, not counting immigration, might well have exceeded 1 percent. In a country such as France, where the land had long been densely settled, the rate of increase might have been less than 0.5 percent.

Although population growth of even 1 percent per year seems fairly modest, it will produce a very large increase over a long period: in three hundred years it will result in sixteen times as many people. Yet such significant increases did not occur in agrarian Europe. In certain abnormal years and tragic periods—the Black Death was only the most extreme example—many more people died than were born, and total population fell sharply, even catastrophically. A number of years of modest growth would then be necessary to make up for those who had died in an abnormal year. Such savage increases in deaths occurred periodically in the seventeenth century on a local and regional scale, and these demographic crises combined to check the growth of population until after 1700.

The grim reapers of demographic crisis were famine, epidemic disease, and war. Episodes of famine were inevitable in all eras of premodern Europe, given low crop yields and unpredictable climatic conditions. In the seventeenth century much of Europe experienced unusually cold and wet weather, which produced even more severe harvest failures and food shortages than usual. Contagious diseases, like typhus, smallpox, syphilis, and the ever-recurring bubonic plague, also continued to ravage Europe's population on a periodic basis. War was another scourge, and its indirect effects were even more harmful than the

■ **proletarianization** The transformation of large numbers of small peasant farmers into landless rural wage earners.

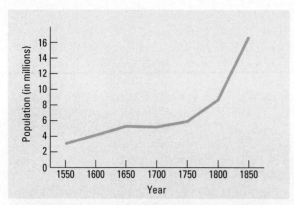

FIGURE 17.1 The Growth of Population in England, 1550–1850 England is a good example of both the uneven increase of European population before 1700 and the third great surge of growth that began in the eighteenth century. (Source: Data from E. A. Wrigley et al., *English Population History from Family Reconstitution, 1580–1837* [Cambridge: Cambridge University Press, 1997], p. 614.)

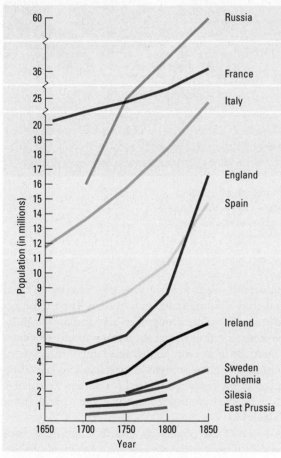

FIGURE 17.2 The Increase of Population in Europe, 1650–1850 Population grew across Europe in the eighteenth century, though the most dramatic increases occurred after 1750. Russia experienced the largest increase and emerged as Europe's most populous state, as natural increase was complemented by growth from territorial expansion. (Source: Data from Massimo Livi Bacci, *The Population of Europe* [Wiley-Blackwell, 2000], p. 8.)

purposeful killing during military campaigns. Soldiers and camp followers passed all manner of contagious diseases throughout the countryside. Armies requisitioned scarce food supplies and disrupted the agricultural cycle while battles destroyed precious crops, livestock, and farmlands. The Thirty Years' War (1618–1648) witnessed all possible combinations of distress (see Chapter 15). The number of inhabitants in the German states alone declined by more than two-thirds in some large areas and by at least one-third almost everywhere else.

The New Pattern of the Eighteenth Century

In the eighteenth century the traditional demographic pattern of Europe was transformed. Growth took place unevenly, with Russia growing very quickly after 1700 and France much more slowly. Nonetheless, the explosion of population was a major phenomenon in all European countries. Europeans grew in numbers steadily from 1720 to 1789, with especially dramatic increases after about 1750 (Figure 17.2). Between 1700 and 1835 the population of Europe doubled in size.

What caused this population growth? In some areas, especially England, women had more babies than before because new opportunities for employment in rural industry (see page 553) allowed them to marry at an earlier age. But the basic cause of European population increase as a whole was a decline in mortality—fewer deaths.

One of the primary reasons behind this decline was the still-unexplained disappearance of the bubonic plague. Following the Black Death in the fourteenth century, plague had remained part of the European experience, striking again and again with savage force, particularly in towns. In 1720 a ship from Syria and the Levant brought the disease to Marseilles. As a contemporary account described it, "The Porters employ'd in unloading the Vessel, were immediately seiz'd with violent Pains in the Head . . . soon after they broke out in Blotches and Buboes, and died in three Days."[3] Plague quickly spread within and beyond Marseilles, killing up to one hundred thousand. By 1722 the epidemic had passed, and that was the last time plague fell on western and central Europe. Exactly why plague disappeared is unknown. Stricter measures of quarantine in Mediterranean ports and along the Austrian border with the Ottoman Empire helped by carefully isolating human carriers of plague. Chance and plain good luck were probably just as important.

Advances in medical knowledge did not contribute much to reducing the death rate in the eighteenth century. The most important advance in preventive medicine in this period was inoculation against smallpox, a disease that killed approximately four hundred

The Plague at Marseilles   The bishop of Marseilles blesses victims of the plague that overwhelmed Marseilles in 1720. Some one hundred thousand people died in the outbreak, which was the last great episode of plague in western Europe. (By Nicolas-André Monsiau [1754–1837], [oil on canvas]/Photo: Christian Jean/Musée du Louvre, Paris, France/© RMN–Grand Palais/Art Resource, NY)

thousand people each year in Europe. Widely practiced in the Ottoman Empire, inoculation was popularized in England in the 1720s by the wife of the former English ambassador, but did not spread to the rest of the continent for decades. Improvements in the water supply and sewage, which were frequently promoted by strong absolutist monarchies, did contribute to somewhat better public health and helped reduce such diseases as typhoid and typhus in urban areas of western Europe. Improvements in water supply and the drainage of swamps also reduced Europe's large insect population. Flies and mosquitoes played a major role in spreading diseases, especially those striking children and young adults. Thus early public health measures contributed to the decline in mortality that began with the disappearance of plague and continued into the early nineteenth century.

Human beings also became more successful in their efforts to safeguard the supply of food. The

eighteenth century was a time of considerable canal and road building in western Europe. These advances in transportation, which were also among the more positive aspects of strong absolutist states, lessened the impact of local crop failure and famine. Emergency supplies could be brought in, and localized starvation became less frequent. Wars became less destructive than in the seventeenth century and spread fewer epidemics.

None of the population growth would have been possible if not for the advances in agricultural production in the seventeenth and eighteenth centuries, which increased the food supply and contributed nutritious new foods, particularly the potato from South America. In short, population grew in the eighteenth century primarily because years of higher-than-average death rates were less catastrophic. Famines, epidemics, and wars continued to occur and to affect population growth, but their severity moderated.

Population growth intensified the imbalance between the number of people and the economic opportunities available to them. Deprived of land by the enclosure movement, the rural poor were forced to look for new ways to make a living.

The Growth of Rural Industry

FOCUS QUESTION *How and why did rural industry intensify in the eighteenth century?*

The growth of population increased the number of rural workers with little or no land, and this in turn contributed to the development of industry in rural areas. The poor in the countryside increasingly needed to supplement their agricultural earnings with other types of work, and urban capitalists were eager to employ them, often at lower wages than urban workers received. **Cottage industry**, which consisted of manufacturing with hand tools in peasant cottages and work sheds, grew markedly in the eighteenth century and became a crucial feature of the European economy.

To be sure, peasant communities had always made clothing, processed food, and constructed housing for their own use. But medieval peasants did not produce manufactured goods on a large scale for sale in a market. By the eighteenth century, however, the pressures of rural poverty led many poor villagers to seek additional work, and far-reaching changes for daily rural life were set in motion.

The Putting-Out System

Cottage industry was often organized through the **putting-out system**. The two main participants in the putting-out system were the merchant capitalist and the rural worker. In this system, the merchant loaned, or "put out," raw materials to cottage workers, who processed the raw materials in their own homes and returned the finished products to the merchant. There were endless variations on this basic relationship. Sometimes rural workers bought their own raw materials and produced goods that they sold to the merchant. Sometimes whole families were involved in domestic industry; at other times the tasks were closely associated with one gender or age group. Sometimes several workers toiled together to perform a complicated process in a workshop outside the home. The relative importance of earnings from the land and from industry varied greatly for handicraft workers, although industrial wages usually became more important for a given family with time.

As industries grew in scale and complexity, production was often broken into many stages. For example, a merchant would provide raw wool to one group of workers for spinning into thread. He would then pass the thread to another group of workers to be bleached, to another for dyeing, and to another for weaving into cloth. The merchant paid outworkers by the piece and proceeded to sell the finished product to regional, national, or international markets.

The putting-out system grew because it had competitive advantages. Underemployed labor was abundant, and poor peasants and landless laborers would work for low wages. Since production in the countryside was unregulated, workers and merchants could change procedures and experiment as they saw fit. Because workers did not need to meet rigid guild standards, cottage industry became capable of producing many kinds of goods. Textiles; all manner of knives, forks, and housewares; buttons and gloves; and clocks could be produced quite satisfactorily in the countryside. Although luxury goods for the rich, such as exquisite tapestries and fine porcelain, demanded special training, close supervision, and centralized workshops, the limited skills of rural industry were sufficient for everyday articles.

Rural manufacturing did not spread across Europe at an even rate. It developed most successfully in England, particularly for the spinning and weaving of woolen cloth. By 1500 half of England's textiles were being produced in the countryside. By 1700 English industry was generally more rural than urban and heavily reliant on the putting-out system. Most continental countries, with the exception of Flanders and the Dutch Republic, developed rural industry more slowly. The latter part of the eighteenth century witnessed a remarkable expansion of rural industry in certain densely populated regions of continental Europe (Map 17.1).

The Lives of Rural Textile Workers

Until the nineteenth century the industry that employed the most people in Europe was textiles. The making of linen, woolen, and eventually cotton cloth was the typical activity of cottage workers engaged in the putting-out system. A look inside the cottage of the English weaver illustrates a way of life as well as an economic system. The rural worker lived in a small cottage with tiny windows and little space. The cottage was often a single room that served as workshop,

---

■ **cottage industry** A stage of industrial development in which rural workers used hand tools in their homes to manufacture goods on a large scale for sale in a market.

■ **putting-out system** The eighteenth-century system of rural industry in which a merchant loaned raw materials to cottage workers, who processed them and returned the finished products to the merchant.

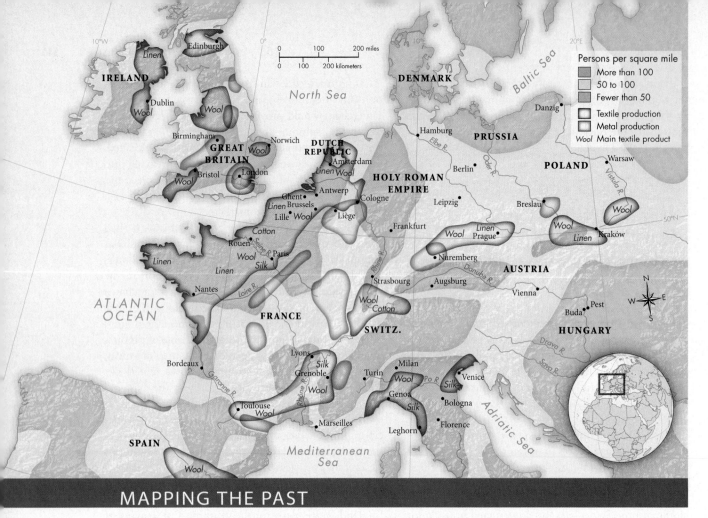

MAPPING THE PAST

MAP 17.1 Industry and Population in Eighteenth-Century Europe

The growth of cottage manufacturing in rural areas helped country people increase their income and contributed to population growth. The putting-out system began in England, and much of the work was in the textile industry. Cottage industry was also strong in the Low Countries — modern-day Belgium and the Netherlands.

ANALYZING THE MAP What does this map suggest about the relationship between population density and the growth of textile production? What geographical characteristics seem to have played a role in encouraging this industry?

CONNECTIONS How would you account for the distribution of each type of cloth across Europe? Did metal production draw on different demographic and geographical conditions? Why do you think this was the case?

---

kitchen, and bedroom. There were only a few pieces of furniture, of which the weaver's loom was by far the largest and most important. That loom changed somewhat in the early eighteenth century when John Kay's invention of the flying shuttle enabled the weaver to throw the shuttle back and forth between the threads with one hand. Aside from that improvement, however, the loom was as it had been for much of history and as it would remain until the arrival of mechanized looms in the first decades of the nineteenth century.

Handloom weaving was a family enterprise. All members of the family helped in the work, so that "every person from seven to eighty (who retained their sight and who could move their hands) could earn their bread," as one eighteenth-century English observer put it.[4] Operating the loom was usually considered a man's job,

reserved for the male head of the family. Women and children worked at auxiliary tasks; they prepared the warp (vertical) threads and mounted them on the loom, wound threads on bobbins for the weft (horizontal) threads, and sometimes operated the warp frame while the father passed the shuttle.

The work of four or five spinners was needed to keep one weaver steadily employed. Since the weaver's family usually could not produce enough thread, merchants hired the wives and daughters of agricultural workers, who took on spinning work in their spare time. In England, many widows and single women also became "spinsters," so many in fact that the word became a synonym for an unmarried woman. In parts of Germany, spinning employed whole families and was not reserved for women.

Relations between workers and employers were often marked by sharp conflict. (See "Thinking Like a Historian: Rural Industry: Progress or Exploitation?" page 554.) There were constant disputes over the weights of materials and the quality of finished work. Merchants accused workers of stealing raw materials, and weavers complained that merchants delivered underweight bales. Suspicion abounded.

Conditions were particularly hard for female workers. While men could earn decent wages through long hours of arduous labor, women's wages were usually much lower because they were not considered the family's primary wage earner. In England's Yorkshire wool industry, a male wool comber earned a good wage of 12 shillings or more a week, while a female spinner could hope for only 3½ shillings.[5] A single or widowed spinner faced a desperate struggle with poverty. Any period of illness or unemployment could spell disaster for her and any children she might have. In 1788 one English writer condemned the low wages of spinners in Norwich: "The suffering of thousands of wretched individuals, willing to work, but starving from their ill requited labour; of whole families of honest industrious children offering their little hands to the wheel, and asking bread of the helpless mother, unable through this well regulated manufacture to give it to them."[6]

From the merchant capitalist's point of view, the problem was not low wages but maintaining control over the labor force. Cottage workers were scattered across the countryside and their work depended on the agricultural calendar. In spring and late summer planting and hay-making occupied all hands in the rural village, leading to shortages in the supply of thread. Merchants bitterly resented their lack of control over rural labor because their own livelihood depended on their ability to meet orders on time. They accused workers—especially female spinners—of laziness, drunkenness, and immorality. If workers failed to produce enough thread, they reasoned, it must be because their wages were too high and they had little incentive to work.

Merchants thus insisted on maintaining the lowest possible wages to force the "idle" poor into productive labor. They also lobbied for, and obtained, new police powers over workers. Imprisonment and public whipping became common punishments for pilfering small amounts of yarn or cloth. For poor workers, their right to hold on to the bits and pieces left over in the production process was akin to the traditional peasant right of gleaning in common lands. With progress came the loss of traditional safeguards for the poor.

The Industrious Revolution

One scholar has used the term **industrious revolution** to summarize the social and economic changes taking place in northwestern Europe in the late seventeenth and early eighteenth centuries.[7] This occurred as households reduced leisure time, stepped up the pace of work, and, most important, redirected the labor of women and children away from the production of goods for household consumption and toward wage work. In the countryside the spread of cottage industry can be seen as one manifestation of the industrious revolution, while in the cities there was a rise in female employment outside the home (see page 557). By working harder and increasing the number of wageworkers, rural and urban households could purchase more goods, even in a time of stagnant or falling wages.

The effect of these changes is still debated. While some scholars lament the encroachment of longer work hours and stricter discipline on traditional family life, others insist that poor families made decisions based on their own self-interests. With more finished goods becoming available at lower prices, households sought cash income to participate in an emerging consumer economy.

The role of women and girls in this new economy is particularly controversial. When women entered the labor market, they almost always worked at menial, tedious jobs for very low wages. Yet when women earned their own wages, they also seem to have exercised more independence in marriage choices and household decision making. Most of their scant earnings went for household necessities, items of food and clothing they could no longer produce now that they worked full-time, but sometimes a few shillings were left for a ribbon or a new pair of stockings. Women's use of their surplus income thus helped spur the rapid growth of the textile industries in which they labored so hard.

These new sources and patterns of labor established important foundations for the Industrial Revolution of the late eighteenth and nineteenth centuries (see Chapter 20). They created households in which all members worked for wages rather than in a family business and in which consumption relied on market-produced rather than homemade goods. It was not until the mid-nineteenth century, with rising industrial wages, that a new model emerged in which the male "breadwinner" was expected to earn enough to support the whole family and women and children were relegated back to the domestic sphere. With women estimated to compose more than 40 percent of the global workforce, today's world is experiencing a second industrious revolution in a similar climate of stagnant wages and increased demand for consumer goods.[8]

■ **industrious revolution** The shift that occurred as families in northwestern Europe focused on earning wages instead of producing goods for household consumption; this reduced their economic self-sufficiency but increased their ability to purchase consumer goods.

Rural Industry: Progress or Exploitation?

Eighteenth-century commentators noted the effects of the growth of rural industry on families and daily life. Some were greatly impressed by the rise in living standards made possible by the putting-out system, while others criticized the rising economic inequality between merchants and workers and the power the former acquired over the latter.

1 Daniel Defoe's observations of English industry. Novelist and economic writer Daniel Defoe claimed that the labor of women and children in spinning and weaving brought in as much income as or more income than the man's agricultural work, allowing the family to eat well and be warmly clothed.

◇ *Being a compleat prospect of the trade of this nation, as well the home trade as the foreign,* 1728.

[A] poor labouring man that goes abroad to his Day Work, and Husbandry, Hedging, Ditching, Threshing, Carting, &c. and brings home his Week's Wages, suppose at eight Pence to twelve Pence a Day, or in some Counties less; if he has a Wife and three or four Children to feed, and who get little or nothing for themselves, must fare hard, and live poorly; 'tis easy to suppose it must be so.

But if this Man's Wife and Children can at the same Time get Employment, if at next Door, or at the next Village there lives a Clothier, or a Bay Maker, or a stuff or Drugget Weaver;* the Manufacturer sends the poor Woman combed Wool, or carded Wool every Week to spin, and she gets eight Pence or nine Pence a day at home; the Weaver sends for her two little Children, and they work by the Loom, winding, filling quills, &c. and the two bigger Girls spin at home with their Mother, and these earn three Pence or four Pence a Day each: So that put it together, the Family at Home gets as much as the Father gets Abroad, and generally more.

This alters the Case extremely, the Family feels it, they all feed better, are cloth'd warmer, and do not so easily nor so often fall into Misery and Distress; the Father gets them Food, and the Mother gets them Clothes; and as they grow, they do not run away to be Footmen and Soldiers, Thieves and Beggars or sell themselves to the Plantations to avoid the Gaol and the Gallows, but have a Trade at their Hands, and every one can get their Bread.

*Bay, stuff, and drugget were types of coarse woolen cloth typical of the inexpensive products of rural weaving.

2 Anonymous, "The Clothier's Delight." Couched in the voice of the ruthless cloth merchant, this song from around 1700 expresses the bitterness and resentment textile workers felt against the low wages paid by employers. One can imagine a group of weavers gathered at the local tavern singing their protest on a rare break from work.

◇ Of all sorts of callings that in England be
There is none that liveth so gallant as we;
Our trading maintains us as brave as a knight,
We live at our pleasure and take our delight;
We heapeth up richest treasure great store
Which we get by griping and grinding the poor.
　　And this is a way for to fill up our purse
　　Although we do get it with many a curse.

Throughout the whole kingdom, in country and
　　　town,
There is no danger of our trade going down,
So long as the Comber can work with his comb,
And also the Weaver weave with his lomb;
The Tucker and Spinner that spins all the year,
We will make them to earn their wages full dear.
　　And this is a way, etc.

3 Late-eighteenth-century diary. This diary entry from 1788 illustrates the dangers of bringing textile manufacture into the family home.

◇ Fire at Isaac Hardy's, which burnt 6 lbs. of cotton, 5 pairs of stockings and set the cradle on fire, with a child in which was much burnt. It happened through the wife improvidently holding the candle under the cotton as it was drying.

ANALYZING THE EVIDENCE

1. What impression of cottage industry does the painting of the Irish linen industry in Source 4 present? How does this contrast with the impressions from the written sources?
2. Do you think the personal accounts of a diary (Source 3) or a memoir (Source 5) are more reliable sources on rural industry than a social commentator's opinion (Source 1) or a song (Source 2)? Why or why not?
3. Who was involved in the work of rural textile manufacture, and what tasks did these workers perform? How does this division of labor resemble or differ from the household in which you grew up?

4 **The linen industry in Ireland.**
Many steps went into making textiles.
Here the women are beating away the
woody part of the flax plant so that
the man can comb out the soft
part. The combed fibers will
then be spun into thread and
woven into cloth by this
family enterprise.
(From *The Linen Manufactory of Ireland*,
1791, by William Hincks [1752–1797]/
Private Collection/The Stapleton
Collection/Bridgeman Images)

5 **Samuel Crompton's memories of childhood labor.** In his memoir, Samuel Crompton
recalled his childhood labor in the cotton industry of the mid-eighteenth century. When
he grew up, he invented the spinning mule, which greatly improved the efficiency of the
process (see Chapter 20).

I recollect that soon after I was able to walk I was employed in the cotton manufacture. My
mother used to bat the cotton wool on a wire riddle. It was then put into a deep brown mug with a
strong ley of soap suds. My mother then tucked up my petticoats about my waist, and put me into
the tub to tread upon the cotton at the bottom. When a second riddleful was batted I was lifted out,
it was placed in the mug, and I again trod it down. This process was continued untill the mug became
so full that I could no longer safely stand in it, when a chair was placed beside it, and I held on by
the back. When the mug was quite full the soapsuds were poured off, and each separate dollop [i.e.,
lump] of wool well squeezed to free it from moisture. They were then placed on the bread-rack under
the beams of the kitchen-loft to dry. My mother and my grand-mother carded the cotton wool by
hand, taking one of the dollops at a time, on the simple hand cards. When carded they were put aside
in separate parcels ready for spinning.

PUTTING IT ALL TOGETHER

Using the sources above, along with what you have learned in class and in this chapter, write
an essay assessing the impact of the putting-out industry on rural families and their way of life.
Make sure to consider the experiences of all members of the household.

Sources: (1) Daniel Defoe, *A Plan of the English Commerce: Being a compleat prospect of the trade of this nation, as well the home trade as the foreign*
(London, 1728), pp. 90–91; (2) Paul Mantoux and Marjorie Vernon, eds., *The Industrial Revolution in the Eighteenth Century: An Outline of the Beginnings
of the Modern Factory System in England* (1928; Abingdon, U.K.: Taylor and Francis, 2006), pp. 75–76; (3, 5) Ivy Pinchbeck, *Women Workers and the
Industrial Revolution, 1750–1850* (1930; Abingdon, U.K.: Frank Cass, 1977), p. 114.

The Debate over Urban Guilds

FOCUS QUESTION *What were guilds, and why did they become controversial in the eighteenth century?*

One consequence of the growth of rural industry was an undermining of the traditional **guild system** that protected urban artisans. Guilds continued to dominate production in towns and cities, providing their masters with economic privileges as well as a proud social identity, but they increasingly struggled against competition from rural workers. Meanwhile, those excluded from guild membership—women, day laborers, Jews, and foreigners—worked on the margins of the urban economy.

In the second half of the eighteenth century, critics like Adam Smith attacked the guilds as outmoded institutions that obstructed technical progress and innovation. Until recently, most historians repeated that view. An ongoing reassessment of guilds now emphasizes their ability to adapt to changing economic circumstances.

Urban Guilds

Originating around 1200 during the economic boom of the Middle Ages, the guild system reached its peak in most of Europe in the seventeenth and eighteenth centuries. During this period, urban guilds increased dramatically in cities and towns across Europe. In Louis XIV's France, for example, finance minister Jean-Baptiste Colbert revived the urban guilds and used them to encourage high-quality production and to collect taxes (see Chapter 15). The number of guilds in the city of Paris grew from 60 in 1672 to 129 in 1691.

Guild Procession in Seventeenth-Century Brussels   Guilds played an important role in the civic life of the early modern city. They collected taxes from their members, imposed quality standards and order on the trades, and represented the interests of commerce and industry to the government. In return, they claimed exclusive monopolies over their trades and the right to govern their own affairs. Guilds marched in processions, like the one shown here, at important city events, proudly displaying their corporate insignia. (*The Senior Guilds*, 1616, by Denis van Alsloot [fl. 1599–1628]/Victoria and Albert Museum, London, UK/V & A Images, London/Art Resource, NY)

Guild masters occupied the summit of the world of work. Each guild possessed a detailed set of privileges, including exclusive rights to produce and sell certain goods, access to restricted markets in raw materials, and the rights to train apprentices, hire workers, and open shops. Any individual who violated these monopolies could be prosecuted. Guilds also served social and religious functions, providing a locus of sociability and group identity to the middling classes of European cities.

To ensure there was enough work to go around, guilds restricted their membership to men who were Christians, had several years of work experience, paid membership fees, and successfully completed a masterpiece. Masters' sons enjoyed automatic access to their fathers' guilds, while outsiders — including Jews and Protestants in Catholic countries — were barred from entering. Most urban men and women worked in non-guild trades as domestic servants, manual laborers, and vendors of food, used clothing, and other goods.

The guilds' ability to enforce their barriers varied a great deal across Europe. In England, national regulations superseded guild rules, sapping their importance. In France, the Crown developed an ambiguous attitude toward guilds, relying on them for taxes and enforcement of quality standards, yet allowing non-guild production to flourish in the countryside in the 1760s, and even in some urban neighborhoods. The German guilds were perhaps the most powerful in Europe, and the most conservative. Journeymen in German cities, with their masters' support, violently protested the encroachment of non-guild workers.

While most were hostile to women, a small number of guilds did accept women. Most involved needlework and textile production, occupations that were considered appropriate for women. In 1675 seamstresses gained a new all-female guild in Paris, and soon seamstresses joined tailors' guilds in parts of France, England, and the Dutch Republic. By the mid-eighteenth century male masters began to hire more female workers, often in defiance of their own guild statutes.

Adam Smith and Economic Liberalism

At the same time that cottage industry began to infringe on the livelihoods of urban artisans, new Enlightenment ideals called into question the very existence of the guild system. Eighteenth-century critics derided guilds as outmoded and exclusionary institutions that obstructed technical innovation and progress. One of the best-known critics of government regulation of trade and industry was Adam Smith (1723–1790), a leading figure

of the Scottish Enlightenment (see Chapter 16). Smith developed the general idea of freedom of enterprise and established the basis for modern economics in his groundbreaking work *Inquiry into the Nature and Causes of the Wealth of Nations* (1776). Smith criticized guilds for their stifling restrictions, a critique he extended to all state monopolies and privileged companies. Far preferable, in his view, was free competition, which would protect consumers from price gouging and give all citizens an equal right to do what they did best. Smith advocated a more highly developed "division of labor," which entailed separating craft production into individual tasks to increase workers' speed and efficiency. (See "Evaluating the Evidence 17.2: Adam Smith on the Division of Labor," page 558.)

In keeping with his fear of political oppression and with the "system of natural liberty" that he championed, Smith argued that government should limit itself to "only three duties": it should provide a defense against foreign invasion, maintain civil order with courts and police protection, and sponsor certain indispensable public works and institutions that could never adequately profit private investors. He believed that the pursuit of self-interest in a competitive market would be sufficient to improve the living conditions of citizens, a view that quickly emerged as the classic argument for **economic liberalism**.

However, Smith did not advocate unbridled capitalism. Unlike many disgruntled merchant capitalists, he applauded the modest rise in real wages of British workers in the eighteenth century, stating: "No society can surely be flourishing and happy, of which the far greater part of the members are poor and miserable." Smith also acknowledged that employers were "always and everywhere in a sort of tacit, but constant and uniform combination, not to raise the wages of labor above their actual rate" and sometimes entered "into particular combinations to sink the wages even below this rate." While he celebrated the rise in productivity allowed by the division of labor, he also acknowledged its demoralizing effects on workers and called for government intervention to raise workers' living standards.[9]

Many educated people in France, including government officials, shared Smith's ideas. In 1774, the reform-minded economics minister Anne-Robert-Jacques Turgot issued a law in the name of Louis XV, ordering the grain trade to be freed from state regulation. Two years later, another edict abolished all French guilds. The law stated:

▪ **guild system** The organization of artisanal production into trade-based associations, or guilds, each of which received a monopoly over its trade and the right to train apprentices and hire workers.

▪ **economic liberalism** A belief in free trade and competition based on Adam Smith's argument that the invisible hand of free competition would benefit all individuals, rich and poor.

Adam Smith on the Division of Labor

In An Inquiry into the Nature and Causes of the Wealth of Nations *(1776), Scottish philosopher Adam Smith argued that commercial society — his term for the early capitalism of his age — was finally freeing the individual from the constraints of tradition, superstition, and cumbersome regulations. The passage below contains Smith's famous description of the division of labor, which permits a small number of men to do the work of many more. Although Smith lauded the gains in efficiency, skilled artisans bitterly resented the loss of control and specialized knowledge imposed by dividing production into isolated, repetitive steps.*

To take an example, therefore, from a very trifling manufacture; but one in which the division of labor has been very often taken notice of, the trade of the pin-maker; a workman not educated to this business . . . nor acquainted with the use of the machinery employed in it . . . could scarce, perhaps, with his utmost industry, make one pin in a day, and certainly could not make twenty. But in the way in which this business is now carried on, not only the whole work is a peculiar trade, but it is divided into a number of branches, of which the greater part are likewise peculiar trades. One man draws out the wire, another straightens it, a third cuts it, a fourth points it, a fifth grinds it at the top for receiving the head; to make the head requires two or three distinct operations; to put it on, is a peculiar business, to whiten the pins is another; it is even a trade by itself to put them into the paper; and the important business of making a pin is, in this manner, divided into about eighteen distinct operations, which, in some manufactories, are all performed by distinct hands, though in others the same man will sometimes perform two or three of them. I have seen a small manufactory of this kind where ten men only were employed, and where some of them consequently performed two or three distinct operations. But though they were very poor, and therefore but indifferently accommodated with the necessary machinery, they could, when they exerted themselves, make among them about twelve pounds of pins in a day. There are in a pound upward of four thousand pins of a middling size. Those ten persons, therefore, could make among them upward of forty-eight thousand pins in a day. Each person, therefore, making a tenth part of forty-eight thousand pins, might be considered as making four thousand eight hundred pins in a day. But if they had all wrought separately and independently, and without any of them having been educated to this peculiar business, they certainly could not each of them have made twenty, perhaps not one pin in a day; that is, certainly not the two hundred and fortieth, perhaps not the four thousand eight hundredth part of what they are at present capable of performing, in consequence of a proper division and combination of their different operations.

EVALUATE THE EVIDENCE

1. Into what steps — what Smith calls "peculiar trades" — is pin making divided? How do these steps make it possible for ten men to do the work of hundreds?
2. Why would skilled craftsmen oppose the division of labor described by Smith? What disadvantages did it create for them? For their guilds?

Source: Adam Smith, *The Wealth of Nations*, part 1 (New York: P. F. Collier & Son, 1902), pp. 44–45.

We wish to abolish these arbitrary institutions, which do not allow the poor man to earn his living; which reject a sex whose weakness has given it more needs and fewer resources . . . ; which destroy emulation and industry and nullify the talents of those whose circumstances have excluded them from membership of a guild; which deprive the state and the arts of all the knowledge brought to them by foreigners; which retard the progress of these arts . . . ; [and which] burden industry with an oppressive tax, which bears heavily on the people.[10]

Vociferous popular protest against these measures led to Turgot's disgrace shortly afterward and the cancellation of his reforms, but the legislators of the French Revolution (see Chapter 19) returned to a liberal economic agenda in 1789. The National Assembly definitively abolished guilds in 1791. Other European countries followed suit more slowly, with guilds surviving in central Europe and Italy into the second half of the nineteenth century. By the middle of the nineteenth century economic liberalism was championed by most European governments and elites.

Some artisans welcomed the deregulation espoused by Smith and Turgot, but many continued to uphold the ideals of the guilds. In the late eighteenth and early nineteenth centuries, skilled artisans across Europe espoused the values of high-quality hand craftsmanship and limited competition in contrast to the proletarianization and loss of skills they endured in mechanized production. Recent scholarship has challenged wholly negative views of the guilds, emphasizing the flexibility and adaptability of the guild system and the role it played in fostering confidence in quality standards.

The Atlantic World and Global Trade

FOCUS QUESTION *How did colonial markets boost Europe's economic and social development, and what conflicts and adversity did world trade entail?*

In addition to agricultural improvement, population pressure, and growing cottage industry, the expansion of Europe in the eighteenth century was characterized by the increase of world trade. Adam Smith himself declared that "the discovery of America and that of a passage to the East Indies by the Cape of Good Hope, are the two greatest and most important events recorded in the history of mankind."[11] In the eighteenth century Spain and Portugal revitalized their empires and began drawing more wealth from renewed colonial development. Yet once again the countries of northwestern Europe—the Dutch Republic, France, and above all Great Britain—benefited most.

The Atlantic economy that these countries developed from 1650 to 1790 would prove crucial in the building of a global economy. Great Britain, which was formed in 1707 by the union of England and Scotland into a single kingdom, gradually became the leading maritime power. Thus the British played the critical role in building a fairly unified Atlantic economy that provided remarkable opportunities for them and their colonists. They also competed ruthlessly with France and the Netherlands for trade and territory in the Americas and Asia.

Mercantilism and Colonial Competition

Britain's commercial leadership in the eighteenth century had its origins in the mercantilism of the seventeenth century (see Chapter 15). Eventually eliciting criticism from Enlightenment thinker Adam Smith and other proponents of free trade in the late eighteenth century, European mercantilism was a system of economic regulations aimed at increasing the power of the state. As practiced by a leading figure such as Colbert under Louis XIV, mercantilism aimed particularly at creating a favorable balance of foreign trade in order to increase a country's stock of gold. A

country's gold holdings served as an all-important treasure chest that could be opened periodically to pay for war in a violent age.

In England, the desire to increase both military power and private wealth resulted in the mercantile system of the **Navigation Acts**. Oliver Cromwell established the first of these laws in 1651, and the restored monarchy of Charles II extended them in 1660 and 1663. The acts required that most goods imported from Europe into England and Scotland (Great Britain after 1707) be carried on British-owned ships with British crews or on ships of the country producing the articles. Moreover, these laws gave British merchants and shipowners a virtual monopoly on trade with British colonies. The colonists were required to ship their products on British (or American) ships and to buy almost all European goods from Britain. It was believed that these economic regulations would eliminate foreign competition, thereby helping British merchants and workers as well as colonial plantation owners and farmers. It was hoped, too, that the emerging British Empire would develop a shipping industry with a large number of experienced seamen who could serve during wartime in the Royal Navy.

The Navigation Acts were a form of economic warfare. Their initial target was the Dutch, who were far ahead of the English in shipping and foreign trade in the mid-seventeenth century (see Chapter 15). In conjunction with three Anglo-Dutch wars between 1652 and 1674, the Navigation Acts seriously damaged Dutch shipping and commerce. The British seized the thriving Dutch colony of New Amsterdam in 1664 and renamed it New York. By the late seventeenth century the Dutch Republic was falling behind England in shipping, trade, and colonies.

Thereafter France stood clearly as England's most serious rival in the competition for overseas empire. Rich in natural resources, with a population three or four times that of England, and allied with Spain, continental Europe's leading military power was already building a powerful fleet and a worldwide system of rigidly monopolized colonial trade. Thus from 1701 to 1763 Britain and France were locked in a series of wars to decide, in part, which nation would become the leading maritime power and claim the profits of Europe's overseas expansion (Map 17.2).

The first round was the War of the Spanish Succession (see Chapter 15), which started in 1701 when Louis XIV accepted the Spanish crown willed to his grandson. Besides upsetting the continental balance of power, a union of France and Spain threatened to encircle and destroy the British colonies in North America (see Map 17.2). Defeated by a great coalition of states after twelve years of fighting, Louis XIV

■ **Navigation Acts** A series of English laws that controlled the import of goods to Britain and British colonies.

Colonel James Tod of the East India Company Traveling by Elephant through Rajasthan, India
By the end of the eighteenth century agents of the British East India Company exercised growing military and political authority in India, in addition to monopolizing Britain's lucrative economic trade with the subcontinent.
(Victoria and Albert Museum, London, UK/Bridgeman Images)

was forced in the Peace of Utrecht (YOO-trehkt) in 1713 to cede his North American holdings in Newfoundland, Nova Scotia, and the Hudson Bay territory to Britain. Spain was compelled to give Britain control of its West African slave trade—the so-called *asiento* (ah-SYEHN-toh)—and to let Britain send one ship of merchandise into the Spanish colonies annually.

Conflict continued among the European powers over both domestic and colonial affairs. The War of the Austrian Succession (1740–1748), which started when Frederick the Great of Prussia seized Silesia from Austria's Maria Theresa (see Chapter 16), gradually became a world war that included Anglo-French conflicts in India and North America. The war ended with no change in the territorial situation in North America. This inconclusive standoff helped set the stage for the Seven Years' War (1756–1763; see Chapter 19). In central Europe, France aided Austria's Maria Theresa in her quest to win back Silesia from the Prussians, who had formed an alliance with England. In North America, French and British settlers engaged in territorial skirmishes that eventually resulted in all-out war

that drew in Native American allies on both sides of the conflict (see Map 19.1, page 614). By 1763 Prussia had held off the Austrians, and British victory on all colonial fronts was ratified in the **Treaty of Paris**. British naval power, built in large part on the rapid growth of the British shipping industry after the passage of the Navigation Acts, had triumphed decisively: Britain had realized its goal of monopolizing a vast trading and colonial empire.

The Atlantic Economy

As the volume of transatlantic trade increased, the regions bordering the ocean were increasingly drawn into an integrated economic system. Commercial exchange in the Atlantic has often been referred to as the "triangle trade," designating a three-way transport of goods: European commodities, like guns and textiles, to Africa; enslaved Africans to the colonies; and colonial goods, such as cotton, tobacco, and sugar, back to Europe (see Map 17.2).

Over the course of the eighteenth century, the economies of European nations bordering the Atlantic

■ **Treaty of Paris** The treaty that ended the Seven Years' War in Europe and the colonies in 1763, and ratified British victory on all colonial fronts.

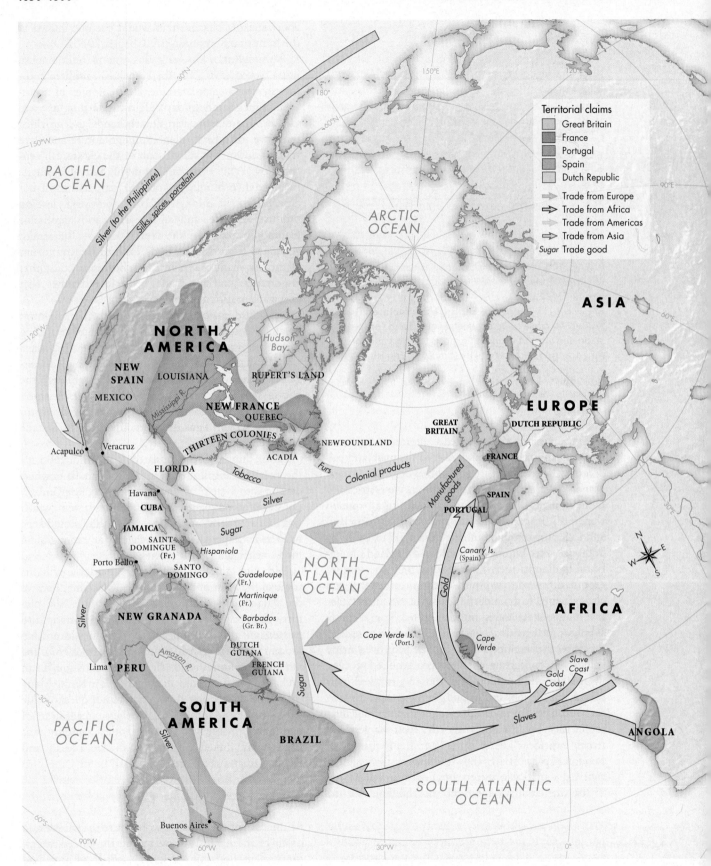

MAP 17.2 The Atlantic Economy in 1701 The growth of trade encouraged both economic development and military conflict in the Atlantic basin. Four continents were linked together by the exchange of goods and people.

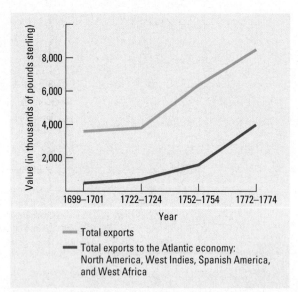

FIGURE 17.3 Exports of English Manufactured Goods, 1700–1774 While trade between England and Europe stagnated after 1700, English exports to Africa and the Americas boomed and greatly stimulated English economic development.
(Source: Data from R. Davis, "English Foreign Trade, 1700–1774," *Economic History Review*, 2d ser., 15 [1962]: 302–303.)

Ocean, especially England, relied more and more on colonial exports. In England, sales to the mainland colonies of North America and the West Indian sugar islands—with an important assist from West Africa and Latin America—soared from £500,000 to £4 million (Figure 17.3). Exports to England's colonies in Ireland and India also rose substantially from 1700 to 1800. By 1800 sales to European countries—England's traditional trading partners—represented only one-third of exports, down from two-thirds a century earlier. England also benefited from importing colonial products. Colonial monopolies allowed the English to obtain a steady supply of such goods at beneficial prices and to re-export them to other nations at high profits. Moreover, many colonial goods, like sugar and tobacco, required processing before consumption and thus contributed new manufacturing jobs in England. In the eighteenth century, stimulated by trade and empire building, England's capital city, London, grew into the West's largest and richest city. (See "Living in the Past: The Remaking of London," page 564.) Thus the mercantilist system achieved remarkable success for England, and by the 1770s the country stood on the threshold of the

epoch-making changes that would become known as the Industrial Revolution (see Chapter 20).

Although they lost many possessions to the English in the Seven Years' War, the French still profited enormously from colonial trade. The colonies of Saint-Domingue (modern-day Haiti), Martinique, and Guadeloupe remained in French hands and provided immense fortunes in plantation agriculture and slave trading during the second half of the eighteenth century. By 1789 the population of Saint-Domingue included five hundred thousand slaves whose labor had allowed the colony to become the world's leading producer of coffee and sugar and the most profitable plantation colony in the New World.[12] The wealth generated from colonial trade fostered the confidence of the merchant classes in Paris, Bordeaux, and other large cities, and merchants soon joined other elite groups clamoring for political reforms.

The third major player in the Atlantic economy, Spain, also saw its colonial fortunes improve during the eighteenth century. Not only did it gain Louisiana from France in 1763, but its influence expanded westward all the way to northern California through the efforts of Spanish missionaries and ranchers. Its mercantilist goals were boosted by a recovery in silver production, which had dropped significantly in the seventeenth century.

Silver mining also stimulated food production for the mining camps, and wealthy Spanish landowners developed a system of **debt peonage** to keep indigenous workers on their estates. Under this system, which was similar to serfdom, a planter or rancher would keep workers in perpetual debt bondage by advancing them food, shelter, and a little money.

Although the "triangle trade" model highlights some of the most important flows of commerce across the Atlantic, it significantly oversimplifies the picture. For example, a brisk intercolonial trade also existed, with the Caribbean slave colonies importing food in the form of fish, flour, and livestock from the northern colonies and rice from the south, in exchange for sugar and slaves (see Map 17.2). Many colonial traders violated imperial monopolies to trade with the most profitable partners, regardless of nationality. Moreover, the Atlantic economy was inextricably linked to trade with the Indian and Pacific Oceans (see pages 569–571).

The Atlantic Slave Trade

At the core of the Atlantic world were the misery and profit of the **Atlantic slave trade**. The forced migration of millions of Africans—cruel, unjust, and tragic—was a key element in the Atlantic system and western European economic expansion throughout the eighteenth century. The brutal practice intensified

■ **debt peonage** A form of serfdom that allowed a planter or rancher to keep his workers or slaves in perpetual debt bondage by periodically advancing food, shelter, and a little money.

■ **Atlantic slave trade** The forced migration of Africans across the Atlantic for slave labor on plantations and in other industries; the trade reached its peak in the eighteenth century and ultimately involved more than 12 million Africans.

dramatically after 1700 and especially after 1750 with the growth of trade and demand for slave-produced goods like sugar and cotton. According to the most authoritative source, European traders purchased and shipped 6.5 million enslaved Africans across the Atlantic between 1701 and 1800—more than half of the estimated total of 12.5 million Africans transported between 1450 and 1900, of whom 15 percent died in procurement and transit.[13] By the peak decade of the 1780s, shipments averaged about eighty thousand individuals per year in an attempt to satisfy the constantly rising demand for labor power—and also for slave owners' profits—in the Americas.

The rise of plantation agriculture was responsible for the tremendous growth of the slave trade. Among all European colonies, the plantations of Portuguese Brazil received by far the largest number of enslaved Africans over the entire period of the slave trade—45 percent of the total. Another 45 percent were divided among the many Caribbean colonies. The colonies of mainland North America took only 3 percent of slaves arriving from Africa, a little under four hundred thousand, relying mostly on natural growth of the enslaved population.

Eighteenth-century intensification of the slave trade resulted in fundamental changes in its organization. After 1700, as Britain became the undisputed leader in shipping slaves across the Atlantic, European governments and ship captains cut back on fighting among themselves and concentrated on commerce. They generally adopted the shore method of trading, which was less expensive than maintaining fortified trading posts. Under this system, European ships sent boats ashore to trade with African dealers or invited dealers to bring traders and slaves out to their ships. This method allowed ships to move easily along the coast from market to market and to depart more quickly for the Americas.

Some African merchants and rulers who controlled exports profited from the greater demand for slaves. With their newfound wealth, some Africans gained access to European and colonial goods, including firearms. But generally such economic returns did not spread very far, and the negative consequences of the expanding slave trade predominated. Wars among African states to obtain salable captives increased, and leaders used slave profits to purchase more arms than textiles and consumer goods. While the populations of Europe and Asia grew substantially in the eighteenth century, the population of Africa

Plantation Zones, ca. 1700

stagnated or possibly declined. As one contemporary critic observed:

> I do not know if coffee and sugar are essential to the happiness of Europe, but I know that these two products have accounted for the unhappiness of two great regions of the world: America has been depopulated so as to have land on which to plant them; Africa has been depopulated so as to have the people to cultivate them.[14]

Most Europeans did not personally witness the horrors of the slave trade between Africa and the Americas, and until the early part of the eighteenth century they considered the African slave trade a legitimate business. But as details of the plight of enslaved people became known, a campaign to abolish slavery developed in Britain. (See "Evaluating the Evidence 17.3: Olaudah Equiano's Economic Arguments for Ending Slavery," page 567.) In the late 1780s the abolition campaign grew into a mass movement of public opinion, the first in British history. British women were prominent in this movement, denouncing the immorality of human bondage and stressing the cruel and sadistic treatment of enslaved women and families. These attacks put the defenders of slavery on the defensive. In 1807 Parliament abolished the British slave trade, although slavery continued in British colonies and the Americas for decades.

Identities and Communities of the Atlantic World

As contacts between the Atlantic coasts of the Americas, Africa, and Europe became more frequent, and as European settlements grew into well-established colonies, new identities and communities emerged. The term *Creole* referred to people of Spanish ancestry born in the Americas. Wealthy Creoles and their counterparts throughout the Atlantic colonies prided themselves on following European ways of life. In addition to their lavish plantation estates, they maintained townhouses in colonial cities built on the European model, with theaters, central squares, churches, and coffeehouses. They purchased luxury goods made in Europe, and their children were often sent to be educated in the home country.

Over time, however, the colonial elite came to feel that their circumstances gave them different interests and characteristics from those of their home population.

LIVING IN THE PAST
The Remaking of London

The imperial capital of London dominated Britain and astonished the visitor. Equal in population to Paris with 400,000 inhabitants in 1650, London grew to 900,000 by 1800, while second-place Paris had 600,000. And as London grew, its citizens created a new urban landscape and style of living.

In 1666 the Great Fire of London destroyed about 80 percent of the old, predominantly wooden central city. Reconstruction proceeded quickly, with brick structures made mandatory to prevent fires. As London rebuilt and kept growing, noble landowners sought to increase their incomes by setting up residential developments on their estates west of the city. A landowner would lay out a square with streets and building lots and lease the lots to speculative builders who put up fine houses for sale or rent. Soho Square, first laid out in the 1670s and shown at top right as it appeared in 1731, was fairly typical. The spacious square with its gated park is surrounded by three-story row houses on deep, narrow lots. Set in the country but close to the city, a square like Soho was a kind of elegant village with restrictive building codes that catered to aristocrats, officials, and successful professionals who were served by the artisans and shopkeepers living in side streets. The elegant new area, known as the West End, contrasted sharply with the shoddy rentals and makeshift shacks of laborers and sailors in the mushrooming East End, which artists rarely painted. Residential segregation by income level increased substantially in eighteenth-century London and became a key feature of the modern city.

As the suburban villages grew and gradually merged, the West End increasingly attracted the well-to-do from all over England. Rural landowners and provincial notables came for the social season from October to May. The picture at bottom right of Bloomsbury Square in 1787 and the original country mansion of the enterprising noble developer provides a glimpse into this wellborn culture.

London Before the Great Fire. (Hulton Archive/Getty Images)

As one observer explained, "A turn of mind peculiar to the planter, occasioned by a physical difference of constitution, climate, customs, and education, tends . . . to repress the remains of his former attachment to his native soil."[15] Colonial elites became "Americanized" by adopting native foods, like chocolate and potatoes, and sought relief from tropical disease in native remedies. Creole traders and planters, along with their counterparts in English colonies, increasingly resented the regulations and taxes imposed by colonial bureaucrats. Such resentment would eventually lead to revolution against colonial powers (see Chapter 19).

Not all Europeans in the colonies were wealthy; indeed, many arrived as indentured servants and had to labor for several years before acquiring freedom. Numerous poor or middling whites worked as clerks, shopkeepers, craftsmen, and, in North America, farmers and laborers. With the exception of British North America, white Europeans made up a minority of the population; they were outnumbered in Spanish America by indigenous peoples and in the Caribbean by the growing numbers of enslaved people of African descent. Since European migrants were disproportionately male, much of the population of the Atlantic world descended from unions—forced or through choice—of European men and indigenous or African women (see the painting on page 569). Colonial attempts to identify and control racial

Soho Square, 1731. (From *Stow's Survey of London*, by Sutton Nicholls [fl. 1700–1740]/Private Collection/The Stapleton Collection/Bridgeman Images)

Bloomsbury Square, 1787. (By Edward Dayes [1763–1804]/Private Collection/© Look and Learn/ Peter Jackson Collection/Bridgeman Images)

QUESTIONS FOR ANALYSIS

1. Examining the picture shown at left, how would you characterize London before the Great Fire?
2. Compare the paintings of Soho and Bloomsbury Squares. How are they complementary? Why did the artist choose to include a milkmaid and her cows in the illustration of Bloomsbury Square?

categories greatly influenced developing Enlightenment thought on racial difference (see Chapter 16).

Mixed-race populations sometimes rose to the colonial elite. The Spanish conquistadors often consolidated their power through marriage to the daughters of local rulers, and their descendants were among the most powerful inhabitants of Spanish America. In the Spanish and French Caribbean, as in Brazil, many masters acknowledged and freed their mixed-race children, leading to sizable populations of free people of color. Advantaged by their fathers, some became wealthy land and slave owners in their own right. In the second half of the eighteenth century, the prosperity of some free people of color brought a backlash from the white population of Saint-Domingue in the form of new race laws prohibiting nonwhites from marrying whites and forcing them to adopt distinctive attire.

British colonies followed a distinctive pattern. There, whole families, rather than individual men, migrated, resulting in a rapid increase in the white population. This development was favored by British colonial law, which forbade marriage between English men and women and Africans or Native Americans. In the British colonies of the Caribbean and the southern mainland, masters tended to leave their mixed-race progeny in slavery rather than freeing them, maintaining a stark discrepancy between free whites and enslaved people of color.[16] The identities inspired by the Atlantic world were equally complex. In some ways, the colonial encounter helped create new and more fixed forms of identity. Inhabitants of distinct regions of European nations came to see themselves as "Spanish" or "English" when they crossed the Atlantic; similarly, their colonial governments imposed the identity of "Indian" and "African" on peoples with vastly different linguistic, cultural, and political origins. The result was the creation of new Creole communities that melded cultural and social elements of various groups of origin with the new European cultures.

The status of mixed-race people, known as mestizos in Spanish America and métis in New France, was ambiguous. Spanish administrators applied purity of blood (*limpieza de sangre*) laws — originally used to exclude Jews and Muslims during the reconquista — to indigenous and African peoples. Some mixed-race people sought to enter Creole society and obtain its many official and unofficial privileges by passing as white. Over time, where they existed in any number, mestizos and free people of color established their own communities and social hierarchies based on wealth, family connections, occupation, and skin color.

Converting indigenous people to Christianity was a key ambition for all European powers in the New World. Galvanized by the Protestant Reformation and the perceived need to protect and spread Catholicism, Catholic powers actively sponsored missionary efforts. Jesuits, Franciscans, Dominicans, and other religious orders established missions throughout Spanish, Portuguese, and French colonies (see Chapter 14). In Central and South America, large-scale conversion forged enduring Catholic cultures in Portuguese and Spanish colonies. Conversion efforts in North America were less effective because indigenous settlements were more scattered and native people were less integrated into colonial communities. On the whole, Protestants were less active as missionaries in this period, although some dissenters, like Moravians, Quakers, and Methodists, did seek converts among indigenous and enslaved people. (See "Individuals in Society: Rebecca Protten," page 568.)

The practice of slavery reveals important limitations on efforts to spread Christianity. Slave owners often refused to baptize their slaves, fearing that enslaved people would use their Christian status to claim additional rights. In some areas, particularly among the mostly African-born slaves of the Caribbean, elements of African religious belief and practice endured, often incorporated with Christian traditions.

Restricted from owning land and holding many occupations in Europe, Jews were eager participants in the new Atlantic economy and established a network

The Atlantic Slave Trade This engraving from 1814 shows traders leading a group of slaves to the West African coast, where they will board ships to cross the Atlantic. Many slaves died en route or arrived greatly weakened and ill. The newspaper advertisement of the sale of a ship's cargo of slaves in Charleston, South Carolina, promises "fine healthy negroes," testifying to the dangers of the crossing and to the frequency of epidemic diseases like smallpox. (engraving: Bibliothèque de l'Arsenal, Paris / Archives Charmet / Bridgeman Images; advertisement: Granger, NYC — All rights reserved)

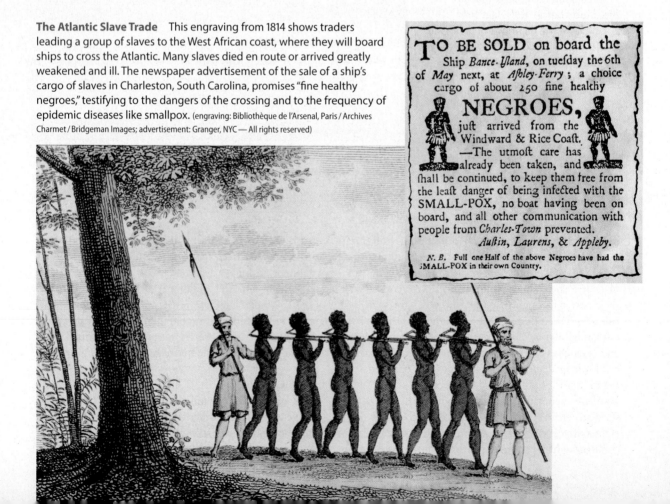

TO BE SOLD on board the Ship *Bance-Island*, on tuesday the 6th of *May* next, at *Ashley-Ferry*; a choice cargo of about 250 fine healthy NEGROES, just arrived from the Windward & Rice Coast. —The utmost care has already been taken, and shall be continued, to keep them free from the least danger of being infected with the SMALL-POX, no boat having been on board, and all other communication with people from *Charles-Town* prevented. *Austin, Laurens, & Appleby.*

N. B. Full one Half of the above Negroes have had the SMALL-POX in their own Country.

Olaudah Equiano's Economic Arguments for Ending Slavery

According to his autobiography, first published in 1789, Olaudah Equiano was born in Benin (modern Nigeria) of Ibo ethnicity and was abducted and transported across the Atlantic as a child. Equiano served a British Royal Navy officer, who educated the boy, but then sold him to a Quaker merchant. Equiano eventually bought his freedom from his master and returned to England, where he worked as a hairdresser and merchant seaman. Having won fame by publishing his life story, Equiano campaigned ardently to end slavery, as documented in the excerpt below.

~

Tortures, murder, and every other imaginable barbarity and iniquity, are practised upon the poor slaves with impunity. I hope the great slave trade will be abolished. I pray it may be an event at hand. The great body of manufacturers, uniting in the cause, will considerably facilitate and expedite it; and, as I have already stated, it is most substantially their interest and advantage, and as such the nation's at large (except those persons concerned in the manufacturing [of] neck-yokes, collars, chains, hand-cuffs, leg-bolts, drags, thumbscrews, iron muzzles, and coffins; cats, scourges, and other instruments of torture used in the slave trade). In a short time one sentiment alone will prevail, from motives of interest as well as justice and humanity. Europe contains one hundred and twenty million of inhabitants. Query — How many millions doth Africa contain? Supposing the

Africans, collectively and individually, to expend 5£ a head in raiment and furniture yearly when civilized, &c. an immensity beyond the reach of imagination!

This I conceive to be a theory founded upon facts, and therefore an infallible one. If the blacks were permitted to remain in their own country, they would double themselves every fifteen years. In proportion to such increase will be the demand for manufactures. Cotton and indigo grow spontaneously in most parts of Africa; a consideration this of no small consequence to the manufacturing towns of Great Britain. It opens a most immense, glorious, and happy prospect — the clothing, &c. of a continent ten thousand miles in circumference, and immensely rich in productions of every denomination in return for manufactures.

EVALUATE THE EVIDENCE

1. Why does Equiano believe England will profit more by trading with free Africans than by enslaving them? Who do you think the audience for this document was, and how might the audience have affected the message?
2. What broader economic and cultural developments in eighteenth-century England does Equiano's plea reflect?

Source: Olaudah Equiano, *The Interesting Narrative of the Life of Olaudah Equiano*, ed. Robert J. Allison, 2d ed. (Boston: Bedford/St. Martin's, 2007), p. 213.

of mercantile communities along its trade routes. As in the Old World, Jews in European colonies faced discrimination; for example, restrictions existed on the number of slaves they could own in Barbados in the early eighteenth century.[18] Jews were considered to be white Europeans and thus ineligible to be slaves, but they did not enjoy equal status with Christians. The status of Jews adds one more element to the complexity of Atlantic identities.

The Atlantic Enlightenment

Enlightenment ideas thrived in the colonies, although with as much diversity and disagreement as in Europe (see Chapter 16). The colonies of British North America were deeply influenced by the Scottish Enlightenment, with its emphasis on pragmatic approaches to the problems of life. Following the Scottish model, leaders in the colonies adopted a moderate, "common-sense" version of the Enlightenment that emphasized self-improvement and ethical conduct. In most cases,

this version of the Enlightenment was perfectly compatible with religion and was chiefly spread through the growing colleges and universities of the colonies, which remained church-based institutions.

Some thinkers went even further in their admiration for Enlightenment ideas. Benjamin Franklin's writings and political career provide an outstanding example of the combination of the pragmatism and economic interests of the Scottish Enlightenment with the constitutional theories of John Locke, Jean-Jacques Rousseau, and the baron de Montesquieu. Franklin was privately a lifelong deist, meaning that he believed in God but not in organized religion. Nonetheless, he continued to attend church and respect religious proprieties, a cautious pattern followed by fellow deist Thomas Jefferson and other leading thinkers of the American Enlightenment.

Northern Enlightenment thinkers often depicted Spain and its American colonies as the epitome of the superstition and barbarity they contested. The Catholic Church strictly controlled the publication of books on

INDIVIDUALS IN SOCIETY

Rebecca Protten

In the mid-1720s a young English-speaking girl who came to be known as Rebecca traveled by ship from Antigua to the small Danish sugar colony of St. Thomas, today part of the U.S. Virgin Islands. Eighty-five percent of St. Thomas's four thousand inhabitants were of African descent, almost all enslaved. Sugar plantations demanded backbreaking work, and slave owners used extremely brutal methods to maintain control, including amputations and beheadings for runaways.

Surviving documents refer to Rebecca as a "mulatto," indicating a mixed European and African ancestry. A wealthy Dutch-speaking planter named van Beverhout purchased the girl for his household staff, sparing her a position in the grueling and deadly sugar fields. Rebecca won the family's favor, and they taught her to read, write, and speak Dutch. They also shared with her their Protestant faith and took the unusual step of freeing her.

As a free woman, she continued to work as a servant for the van Beverhouts and to study the Bible and spread its message of spiritual freedom. In 1736 she met some missionaries for the Moravian Church, a German-Protestant sect that emphasized emotion and communal worship and devoted its mission work to the enslaved peoples of the Caribbean. The missionaries were struck by Rebecca's piety and her potential to assist their work. As one wrote: "She researches diligently in the Scriptures, loves the Savior, and does much good for other Negro women because she does not simply walk alone with her good ways but instructs them in the Scriptures as well." A letter Rebecca sent to Moravian women in Germany declared: "Oh how good is the Lord. My heart melts when I think of it. His name is wonderful. Oh! Help me to praise him, who has pulled me out of the darkness. I will take up his cross with all my heart and follow the example of his poor life."*

Rebecca soon took charge of the Moravians' female missionary work. Every Sunday and every evening after work, she would walk for miles to lead meetings with enslaved and free black women. The meetings consisted of reading and writing lessons, prayers, hymns, a sermon, and individual discussions in which she encouraged her new sisters in their spiritual growth.

In 1738 Rebecca married a German Moravian missionary, Matthaus Freundlich, a rare but not illegal case of mixed marriage. The same year, her husband bought a plantation, with slaves, to serve as the headquarters of their mission work. The Moravians—and presumably Rebecca herself—wished to spread Christian faith among slaves and improve their treatment, but did not oppose the institution of slavery itself.

Authorities nonetheless feared that baptized and literate slaves would agitate for freedom, and they imprisoned

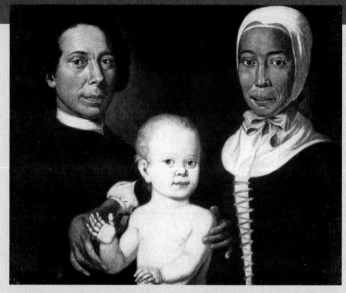

A portrait of Rebecca Protten with her second husband and their daughter, Anna-Maria. (Courtesy of Jon F. Sensbach. Used by permission of the Moravian Archives [Unity Archives, Herrnhut, Germany], GS-393)

Rebecca and Matthaus and tried to shut down the mission. Only the unexpected arrival on St. Thomas of German aristocrat and Moravian leader Count Zinzendorf saved the couple. Exhausted by their ordeal, they left for Germany in 1741 accompanied by their small daughter, but both father and daughter died soon after their arrival.

In Marienborn, a German center of the Moravian faith, Rebecca encountered other black Moravians, who lived in equality alongside their European brethren. In 1746 she married another missionary, Christian Jacob Protten, son of a Danish sailor and, on his mother's side, grandson of a West African king. She and another female missionary from St. Thomas were ordained as deaconesses, probably making them the first women of color to be ordained in the Western Christian Church.

In 1763 Rebecca and her husband set out for her husband's birthplace, the Danish slave fort at Christiansborg (in what is now Accra, Ghana) to establish a school for mixed-race children. Her husband died in 1769, leaving Rebecca a widow once more. After declining the offer of passage back to the West Indies in 1776, she died in obscurity near Christiansborg in 1780.

QUESTIONS FOR ANALYSIS

1. Why did Moravian missionaries assign such an important leadership role to Rebecca? What particular attributes did she offer?
2. Why did Moravians, including Rebecca, accept the institution of slavery instead of fighting to end it?
3. What does Rebecca's story teach us about the Atlantic world of the mid-eighteenth century?

*Quotations from Jon F. Sensbach, *Rebecca's Revival: Creating Black Christianity in the Atlantic World* (Cambridge, Mass.: Harvard University Press, 2006), pp. 61, 63.

the Iberian Peninsula and in Spanish America. None-theless, the Bourbon dynasty that took power in Spain in the early eighteenth century followed its own course of enlightened absolutism, just like its counterparts in the rest of Europe (see Chapter 16). Under King Carlos III (r. 1759–1788) and his son Carlos IV (r. 1788–1808), Spanish administrators attempted to strengthen colonial rule by posting a standing army in the colonies and increasing royal monopolies and taxes to pay for it. They also ordered officials to gather more accurate information about the colonies as a basis for improving the government. Enlightened administrators debated the status of indigenous peoples and whether it would be better for these peoples (and for the prosperity of Spanish America) if they maintained their distinct legal status or were integrated into Spanish society.

Educated Creoles were well aware of the new currents of thought, and the universities, newspapers, and salons of Spanish America produced their own reform ideas. The establishment of a mining school in Mexico City in 1792, the first in the Spanish colonies, illuminates the practical achievements of reformers. As in other European colonies, one effect of Enlightenment thought was to encourage Creoles to criticize the policies of the mother country and aspire toward greater autonomy.

Trade and Empire in Asia and the Pacific

As the Atlantic economy took shape, Europeans continued to vie for dominance in the Asian trade. Between 1500 and 1600 the Portuguese had become major players in the Indian Ocean trading world, eliminating Venice as Europe's chief supplier of spices and other Asian luxury goods. The Portuguese dominated but did not fundamentally alter the age-old pattern of Indian Ocean trade, which involved merchants from many areas as more or less autonomous players. This situation changed radically with the intervention of the Dutch and then the English (see Chapter 14).

Formed in 1602, the Dutch East India Company had taken control of the Portuguese spice trade in the Indian Ocean, with the port of Batavia (Jakarta) in Java as its center of operations. Within a few decades they had expelled the Portuguese from Ceylon and other East Indian islands. Unlike the Portuguese, the Dutch transformed the Indian Ocean trading world. Whereas East Indian states and peoples maintained independence under the Portuguese, who treated them as autonomous business partners, the Dutch established outright control and reduced them to dependents.

After these successes, the Dutch hold in Asia faltered in the eighteenth century due to the company's failure to diversify to meet changing consumption patterns. Spices continued to compose much of its shipping, despite their declining importance in the European

Castas Painting   In the second half of the eighteenth century, fascination with the emerging mixed-race population of Spanish America gave rise to the genre of *castas* paintings, sets of sixteen families, each depicting a specific racial mixture. Here the painter has identified the mother as "Indian" and the father as a *chino*, a term referring to the offspring of a union between an Indian and an African. (*A Half-Breed and His Lobo Indian Wife and Their Child*, Mexican [oil on canvas]/Museo de America, Madrid, Spain/Index/Bridgeman Images)

diet, probably due to changing fashions in food and luxury consumption. Fierce competition from its main rival, the English East India Company (established 1600), also severely undercut Dutch trade.

Britain initially struggled for a foothold in Asia. With the Dutch monopolizing the Indian Ocean, the British turned to India, the source of lucrative trade in silks, textiles, and pepper. Throughout the seventeenth century the English East India Company relied on trade concessions from the powerful Mughal emperor, who granted only piecemeal access to the subcontinent. Finally, in 1716 the Mughals conceded empire-wide trading privileges. As Mughal power waned, British East India Company agents increasingly intervened in local affairs and made alliances or waged war against Indian princes.

Britain's great rival for influence in India was France. During the War of the Austrian Succession, British and

India, 1805

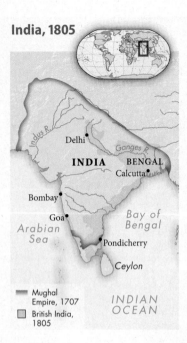

French forces in India supported opposing rulers in local power struggles. In 1757 East India Company forces under Robert Clive conquered the rich northeastern province of Bengal at the Battle of Plassey. French-English rivalry was finally resolved by the Treaty of Paris, which granted all of France's possessions in India to the British with the exception of Pondicherry, an Indian Ocean port city. With the elimination of their rival, British ascendancy in India accelerated. In 1765 the Mughal shah granted the East India Company *diwani*, the right to civil administration and tax collection, in Bengal and neighboring provinces. By the early nineteenth century the company had overcome vigorous Indian resistance to gain economic and political dominance of much of the subcontinent; direct administration by the British government replaced East India Company rule after a large-scale rebellion in 1857.

The late eighteenth century also witnessed the beginning of British settlement of the continent of Australia. The continent was first sighted by Europeans in the early seventeenth century, and thereafter parts of the coast were charted by European ships. Captain James Cook claimed the east coast of Australia for England in 1770, naming it New South Wales. The first colony was established there in the late 1780s, relying on the labor of convicted prisoners forcibly transported from Britain. Settlement of the western portion of the continent followed in the 1790s. The first colonies struggled for survival and, after an initial period of friendly relations, soon aroused the hostility and resistance of aboriginal peoples. Cook himself was killed by islanders in Hawaii in 1779, having charted much of the Pacific Ocean for the first time.

The rising economic and political power of Europeans in this period drew on the connections they established between the Asian and Atlantic trade worlds. An outstanding example is the trade in cowrie shells. These seashells, originating in the Maldive Islands in the Indian Ocean, were used as a form of currency in West Africa. European traders obtained them in Asia, packing them alongside porcelains, spices, and silks for the journey home. The cowries were then brought from European ports to the West African coast to be traded for slaves. Indian textiles were also prized in Africa and played a similar role in exchange. Thus the trade of the

The British in India, ca. 1785 This Indian miniature shows the wife (center) of a British officer attended by many Indian servants. A British merchant (left) awaits her attention. The picture reflects the luxurious lifestyle of British elites in India, many of whom returned home with colossal fortunes. (The British Library, London, UK/Werner Forman Archive/Art Resource, NY)

Atlantic was inseparable from Asian commerce, and Europeans were increasingly found dominating commerce in both worlds.

NOTES

1. B. H. Slicher van Bath, *The Agrarian History of Western Europe, A.D. 500–1850* (New York: St. Martin's Press, 1963), p. 240.

2. Quoted in Paul Mantoux, *The Industrial Revolution in the Eighteenth Century: An Outline of the Beginnings of the Modern Factory System* (1961; Abingdon, U.K.: Routledge, 2005), p. 175.

3. Thomas Salmon, *Modern History: Or the Present State of All Nations* (London, 1730), p. 406.

4. Quoted in I. Pinchbeck, *Women Workers and the Industrial Revolution, 1750–1850* (1930; Abingdon, U.K.: Frank Cass, 1977), p. 113.

5. Richard J. Soderlund, "'Intended as a Terror to the Idle and Profligate': Embezzlement and the Origins of Policing in the Yorkshire Worsted Industry, c. 1750–1777," *Journal of Social History* 31 (Spring 1998): 658.

6. Quoted in Maxine Berg, *The Age of Manufactures, 1700–1820: Industry, Innovation, and Work in Britain* (London: Routledge, 1994), p. 124.

7. Jan de Vries, *The Industrious Revolution: Consumer Behavior and the Household Economy, 1650 to the Present* (Cambridge: Cambridge University Press, 2008).

8. Jan de Vries, "The Industrial Revolution and the Industrious Revolution," *The Journal of Economic History* 54, no. 2 (June 1994): 249–270; discusses the industrious revolution of the second half of the twentieth century.

9. R. Heilbroner, *The Essential Adam Smith* (New York: W. W. Norton, 1986), p. 196.

10. S. Pollard and C. Holmes, eds., *Documents of European Economic History*, vol. 1, *The Process of Industrialization, 1750–1870* (New York: St. Martin's Press, 1968), p. 53.

11. Ibid., p. 281.

12. Laurent Dubois and John D. Garrigus, *Slave Revolution in the Caribbean, 1789–1904* (New York: Palgrave, 2006), p. 8.

13. Figures obtained from Voyages: The Trans-Atlantic Slave Trade Database, http://www.slavevoyages.org/assessment/estimates (accessed January 17, 2016).

14. Quoted in Thomas Benjamin, *The Atlantic World: Europeans, Africans, Indians and Their Shared History, 1400–1900* (Cambridge: Cambridge University Press, 2009), p. 211.

15. Pierre Marie François Paget, *Travels Round the World in the Years 1767, 1768, 1769, 1770, 1771*, vol. 1 (London, 1793), p. 262.

16. Orlando Patterson, *Slavery and Social Death* (Cambridge, Mass.: Harvard University Press, 1982), p. 255.

17. Tamar Herzog, "Identities and Processes of Identification in the Atlantic World," in *The Oxford Handbook of the Atlantic World, 1450–1850*, ed. Nicholas Canny and Philip Morgan (Oxford: Oxford University Press, 2011), pp. 480–491.

18. Erik R. Seeman, "Jews in the Early Modern Atlantic: Crossing Boundaries, Keeping Faith," in *The Atlantic in Global History, 1500–2000*, ed. Jorge Cañizares-Esguerra and Erik R. Seeman (Upper Saddle River, N.J.: Pearson Prentice Hall, 2007), p. 43.

LOOKING BACK LOOKING AHEAD

By the turn of the eighteenth century, western Europe had begun to shake off the effects of a century of famine, disease, warfare, economic depression, and demographic stagnation. The eighteenth century witnessed a breakthrough in agricultural production that, along with improved infrastructure and the retreat of epidemic disease, contributed to a substantial increase in population. One crucial catalyst for agricultural innovation was the Scientific Revolution, which provided new tools of empirical observation and experimentation. The Enlightenment as well, with its emphasis on progress and public welfare, convinced government officials, scientists, and informed landowners to seek better solutions to old problems. By the end of the century, industry and trade had also attracted enlightened commentators who advocated free markets and less government control. Modern ideas of political economy thus constitute one more legacy of the Enlightenment, but — like the Enlightenment itself — they drew criticism from nineteenth- and twentieth-century thinkers.

As the era of European exploration and conquest gave way to colonial empire building, the eighteenth century witnessed increased consolidation of global markets and bitter competition among Europeans for the spoils of empire. From its slow inception in the mid-fifteenth century, the African slave trade reached brutal heights in the second half of the eighteenth century. The eighteenth-century Atlantic world thus tied the shores of Europe, the Americas, and Africa in a web of commercial and human exchange that also had strong ties with the Pacific and the Indian Oceans.

The new dynamics of the eighteenth century prepared the way for world-shaking changes. Population growth and rural industry began to undermine long-standing traditions of daily life in western Europe. The transformed families of the industrious revolution developed not only new habits of work, but also a new sense of confidence in their abilities. By the 1770s England was approaching an economic transformation fully as significant as the great political upheaval destined to develop shortly in neighboring France. In the same period, the first wave of resistance to European domination rose up in the colonies. The great revolutions of the late eighteenth century would change the world forever.

Make Connections

Think about the larger developments and continuities within and across chapters.

1. How did agriculture, industry, and population affect each other in the eighteenth century? How and why did developments in one area affect the other areas?

2. Compare the economic and social situation of western Europe in the mid-eighteenth century with that of the seventeenth century (Chapter 15). What were the achievements of the eighteenth century, and what factors allowed for such progress to be made?

3. The eighteenth century was the period of the European Enlightenment, which celebrated tolerance and human liberty (Chapter 16). Paradoxically, it was also the era of a tremendous increase in slavery, which brought suffering and death to millions. How can you explain this paradox?

17 REVIEW & EXPLORE

Identify Key Terms

Identify and explain the significance of each item below.

enclosure (p. 545)

proletarianization (p. 548)

cottage industry (p. 551)

putting-out system (p. 551)

industrious revolution (p. 553)

guild system (p. 556)

economic liberalism (p. 557)

Navigation Acts (p. 559)

Treaty of Paris (p. 560)

debt peonage (p. 562)

Atlantic slave trade (p. 562)

Review the Main Ideas

Answer the focus questions from each section of the chapter.

◆ What important developments led to increased agricultural production, and how did these changes affect peasants? (p. 544)

◆ Why did the European population rise dramatically in the eighteenth century? (p. 548)

◆ How and why did rural industry intensify in the eighteenth century? (p. 551)

◆ What were guilds, and why did they become controversial in the eighteenth century? (p. 556)

◆ How did colonial markets boost Europe's economic and social development, and what conflicts and adversity did world trade entail? (p. 559)

Suggested Reading and Media Resources

BOOKS

* Allen, Robert, et al., eds. *Living Standards in the Past: New Perspectives on Well-Being in Asia and Europe.* 2004. Offers rich comparative perspectives on population growth and living standards among common people.

* Anderson, Virginia DeJohn. *Creatures of Empire: How Domestic Animals Transformed Early America.* 2004. Explores the importance of domestic animals in the colonization of North America and the conflicting attitudes of English settlers and Native Americans toward animals.

* Bell, Dean Phillip. *Jews in the Early Modern World.* 2008. A broad examination of Jewish life and relations with non-Jews in the early modern period.

* Carpenter, Roger M. *The Renewed, the Destroyed, and the Remade: The Three Thought Worlds of the Iroquois and the Huron, 1609–1650.* 2004. Explores the culture and beliefs of two Native American peoples in the period of European colonization.

* Farr, James R. *Artisans in Europe, 1300–1914.* 2000. An overview of guilds and artisanal labor in early modern Europe.

* Gullickson, Gary L. *Spinners and Weavers of Auffay: Rural Industry and the Sexual Division of Labor in a French Village, 1750–1850.* 1986. Examines women's labor in cottage industry in northern France.

* Klein, Herbert S. *The Atlantic Slave Trade.* 1999. An excellent short synthesis on slavery in the Atlantic world.

* Morgan, Jennifer Lyle. *Laboring Women: Reproduction and Gender in New World Slavery.* 2004. Focuses on the role of women's labor in the evolution of slavery in Britain's North American colonies.

* Ormrod, David. *The Rise of Commercial Empires: England and the Netherlands in the Age of Mercantilism, 1650–1770.* 2003. Examines the battle for commercial and maritime supremacy in the North Sea.

* Rediker, Marcus. *The Slave Ship: A Human History.* 2007. The horrors of the transatlantic slave trade from the perspective of the captains, sailors, and captives of the ships that crossed the ocean.

* Walsh, Lorena S. *Motives of Honor, Pleasure and Profit: Plantation Management in the Colonial Chesapeake, 1607–1763.* 2010. A study of the economic and social rationales at work in the management of tobacco plantations and their enslaved labor force.

DOCUMENTARIES

* *Blackbeard: Terror at Sea* (National Geographic, 2006). A documentary recounting the exploits of the most famous eighteenth-century pirate.

* *Tales from the Green Valley* (BBC, 2005). A television series exploring life on a British farm in the seventeenth century.

FEATURE FILMS AND TELEVISION

* *Amazing Grace* (Michael Apted, 2006). An idealistic Briton's struggle to end his country's involvement in the slave trade alongside allies Olaudah Equiano and a repentant former slave-ship captain.

* *The Last of the Mohicans* (Michael Mann, 1992). Set among the battles of the Seven Years' War (known as the French and Indian War in the colonies), a man raised as a Mohican saves the daughter of an English officer.

* *Rob Roy* (Michael Caton-Jones, 1995). A Scottish Highlander's effort to better his village by borrowing money to raise and sell cattle is challenged by the treachery of a noble lord and greedy bankers.

* *Word and Utopia* (Manoel de Oliveira, 2000). A Portuguese missionary struggles to improve the treatment of indigenous people in seventeenth-century Brazil.

WEB SITES

* *The Bubble Project.* A Web site presenting historical and modern resources on the South Sea Bubble of 1720, one of the first major international financial crises. **myweb.dal.ca/dmcneil/bubble/bubble.html**

* *Common-place: The Interactive Journal of Early American Life.* Aimed at a diverse audience of scholars, teachers, students, and history buffs, with articles, blogs, and other resources on early America. **www.common-place.org**

* *Olaudah Equiano, or, Gustavus Vassa, the African.* A Web site featuring material on the movement to abolish slavery and the career of Olaudah Equiano, a former slave who published an autobiography in which he discussed his experience in bondage. **www.brycchancarey.com/equiano**

* *The Trans-Atlantic Slave Trade Database.* Presents the results of decades of research into the voyages of the transatlantic slave trade, interpretive articles, and an interactive database including ships, ports of arrival and departure, captains, and information on individuals taken in slavery. **www.slavevoyages.org**

18

Life in the Era of Expansion

1650–1800

The discussion of agriculture and industry in the last chapter showed the common people at work, straining to make ends meet within the larger context of population growth, gradual economic expansion, and ferocious competition at home and overseas. This chapter shows us how that world of work was embedded in a rich complex of family organization, community practices, everyday experiences, and collective attitudes. As with the economy, traditional habits and practices of daily life changed considerably over the eighteenth century. Change was particularly dramatic in the growing cities of northwestern Europe, where traditional social controls were undermined by the anonymity and increased social interaction of the urban setting.

Historians have studied many aspects of popular life, including marriage patterns and family size, childhood and education, nutrition, health care, and religious worship. Uncovering the life of the common people is a formidable challenge because they left few written records and regional variations abounded. Yet imaginative research has resulted in major findings and much greater knowledge. It is now possible to follow the common people into their homes, workshops, churches, and taverns and to ask, "What were the everyday experiences and attitudes of ordinary people, and how did they change over the eighteenth century?" ■

CHAPTER PREVIEW

Marriage and the Family

What changes occurred in marriage and the family in the course of the eighteenth century?

Children and Education

What was life like for children, and how did attitudes toward childhood evolve?

Popular Culture and Consumerism

How did increasing literacy and new patterns of consumption affect people's lives?

Religious Authority and Beliefs

What were the patterns of popular religion, and how did they interact with the worldview of the educated public and their Enlightenment ideals?

Medical Practice

How did the practice of medicine evolve in the eighteenth century?

Market Day
Open-air markets provided city dwellers with fresh produce, meat, and dairy products. They were also a lively site for meeting friends, catching up on the latest news, and enjoying the passing spectacle of urban life. In European cities, this tradition has continued to the present day. (*A Market Day*, 1765, Central European School [oil on canvas]/© Sotheby's/akg-images)

Marriage and the Family

FOCUS QUESTION *What changes occurred in marriage and the family in the course of the eighteenth century?*

The basic unit of social organization is the family. Within the structure of the family, human beings love, mate, and reproduce. The family bears primary responsibility to teach the child, imparting values and customs that condition an individual's behavior for a lifetime. The family is also an institution woven into the web of history. It evolves and changes, assuming different forms in different times and places. The eighteenth century was an important moment of change in family life, as patterns of marriage shifted and individuals adapted and conformed to the new and changing realities of the family unit.

Late Marriage and Nuclear Families

Because census data before the modern period are rare, historians have turned to parish registers of births, deaths, and marriages to uncover details of European family life before the nineteenth century. These registers reveal that the three-generation extended family was a rarity in western and central Europe. When young European couples married, they normally established their own households and lived apart from their parents, much like the nuclear families (a family group consisting of parents and their children with no other relatives) common in the United States today. If a three-generation household came into existence, it was usually because a widowed parent moved into the home of a married child.

Most people did not marry young in the seventeenth and eighteenth centuries. The average person married surprisingly late, many years after reaching adulthood and many more after beginning to work. Studies of western Europe in the seventeenth and eighteenth centuries show that both men and women married for the first time at an average age of twenty-five to twenty-seven. Furthermore, 10 to 20 percent of men and women in western Europe never married at all. Matters were different in eastern Europe, where the multigeneration household was the norm, marriage occurred around age twenty, and permanent celibacy was much less common.

Why did young people in western Europe delay marriage? The main reason was that couples normally did not marry until they could start an independent household and support themselves and their future children. Peasants often needed to wait until their father's death to inherit land and marry. In the towns, men and women worked to accumulate enough savings to start a small business and establish their own home. As one father stated in an advice book written for his son: "Money is the sinew of love, as well as war; you can do nothing happily in wedlock without it; the other [virtue and beauty] are court-cards, but they are not of the trump-suit and are foiled by every sneaking misadventure."[1]

Laws and tradition also discouraged early marriage. In some areas couples needed permission from the local lord or landowner in order to marry. Poor couples had particular difficulty securing the approval of local officials, who believed that freedom to marry for the lower classes would result in more landless paupers, more abandoned children, and more money for welfare. Village elders often agreed.

The custom of late marriage combined with the nuclear-family household distinguished western European society from other areas of the world. Historians have argued that this late-marriage pattern was responsible for at least part of the economic advantage western Europeans acquired relative to other world regions. Late marriage joined a mature man and a mature woman—two adults who had already accumulated social and economic capital and could transmit self-reliance and skills to the next generation. The relative closeness in age between husband and wife favored a greater degree of gender equality than existed in areas where older men married much younger women.

Work Away from Home

Many young people worked within their families until they could start their own households. Boys plowed and wove; girls spun and tended the cows. Many others left home to work elsewhere. Around age fifteen, an apprentice from a rural village would typically move to a city or town to learn a trade, earning little and working hard. If he was lucky and had connections, he might eventually be admitted to a guild and establish his economic independence. Many poor families could not afford apprenticeships for their sons. Without craft skills, these youths drifted from one tough job to another: hired hand for a small farmer, wage laborer on a new road, carrier of water or domestic servant in a nearby town.

Many adolescent girls also left their families to work. The range of opportunities open to them was more limited, however. Apprenticeship was sometimes available with mistresses in traditionally female occupations like seamstress, linen draper, or midwife. With the growth in production of finished goods for the emerging consumer economy during the eighteenth century (see Chapter 17), demand rose for skilled female labor and, with it, a wider range of jobs became available for women. Nevertheless, women still continued to earn much lower wages for their work than men.

Service in another family's household was by far the most common job for girls, and even middle-class families often sent their daughters into service. The legions of young servant girls worked hard but had little independence. Constantly under the eye of her mistress, the servant girl had many tasks—cleaning, shopping, cooking, and child care. Often the work was endless, for there were few laws to limit exploitation. Court records are full of servant girls' complaints of physical mistreatment by their mistresses. There were many like the fifteen-year-old English girl in the early eighteenth century who told the judge that her mistress had not only called her "very opprobrious names, as Bitch, Whore and the like," but also "beat her without provocation and beyond measure."[2]

Chronology

1684	Jean-Baptiste de la Salle founds Brothers of the Christian Schools
1717	Elementary school attendance mandatory in Prussia
1750–1790	John Wesley preaches revival in England
1750–1850	Illegitimacy explosion
1757	Madame du Coudray publishes *Manual on the Art of Childbirth*
1762	Jean-Jacques Rousseau advocates more attentive child care in *Emile*
1763	Louis XV orders Jesuits out of France
1774	Elementary school attendance mandatory in Austria
1776	Thomas Paine publishes *Common Sense*
1796	Edward Jenner performs first smallpox vaccination

Young Serving Girl Increased migration to urban areas in the eighteenth century contributed to a loosening of traditional morals and soaring illegitimacy rates. Young women who worked as servants or shopgirls could not be supervised as closely as those who lived at home. The themes of seduction, fallen virtue, and familial conflict were popular in eighteenth-century art. (*The Beautiful Kitchen Maid*, by François Boucher [1703–1770], [oil on canvas]/Musée Cognacq-Jay, Paris, France/Bridgeman Images)

Male apprentices told similar tales of abuse and they shared the legal status of "servants" with housemaids, but they were far less vulnerable to the sexual exploitation that threatened young girls. In theory, domestic service offered a girl protection and security in a new family. But in practice, she was often the easy prey of a lecherous master or his sons or friends. If the girl became pregnant, she could be fired and thrown out in disgrace. Many families could not or would not accept such a girl back into the home. Forced to make their own way, these girls had no choice but to turn to a harsh life of prostitution (see page 580) and petty thievery. "What are we?" exclaimed a bitter Parisian prostitute. "Most of us are unfortunate women, without origins, without education, servants and maids for the most part."[3] Adult women who remained in service, at least in large towns and cities, could gain more autonomy and distressed their employers by changing jobs frequently.

Premarital Sex and Community Controls

Ten years between puberty and marriage was a long time for sexually mature young people to wait. Many unmarried couples satisfied their sexual desires with fondling and petting. Others went further and engaged in premarital intercourse. Those who did so risked pregnancy and the stigma of illegitimate birth. Birth control was not unknown in Europe before the nineteenth century, but it was primitive and unreliable. Condoms, made from sheep intestines, became available in the mid-seventeenth century, replacing uncomfortable earlier versions made from cloth. They were expensive and mainly used by aristocratic libertines and prostitutes. The most common method of contraception was coitus interruptus—withdrawal by the male before ejaculation. The French, who were early leaders in contraception, were using this method extensively by the end of the eighteenth century.

Despite the lack of reliable contraception, premarital sex did not result in a large proportion of illegitimate births in most parts of Europe until 1750. English parish registers seldom listed more than one illegitimate child out of every twenty children baptized. Some French parishes in the seventeenth century had extraordinarily low rates of illegitimacy, with less than 1 percent of babies born out of wedlock. Illegitimate babies were apparently a rarity, at least as far as the official records are concerned.

Where collective control over sexual behavior among youths failed, community pressure to marry often prevailed. A comparison of marriage and birth dates of seven representative parishes in seventeenth-century England shows that around 20 percent of children must have been conceived before the couple was married, but only 2 percent were born out of wedlock.[4] Figures for the French village of Auffay in Normandy in the eighteenth century were remarkably similar. No doubt many of these French and English couples were already engaged, or at least in a committed relationship, before they entered into intimate relations, and pregnancy simply set the marriage date once and for all.

The combination of low rates of illegitimate birth with large numbers of pregnant brides reflects the powerful **community controls** of the traditional village, particularly the open-field village, with its pattern of cooperation and common action. An unwed mother with an illegitimate child was inevitably viewed as a grave threat to the economic, social, and moral stability of the community. Irate parents, anxious village elders, indignant priests, and stern landlords all combined to pressure young people who wavered about marriage in the face of unexpected pregnancies. In the countryside these controls meant that premarital sex was not entered into lightly and that it was generally limited to those contemplating marriage.

The concerns of the village and the family weighed heavily on couples' lives after marriage as well. Whereas uninvolved individuals today try to stay out of the domestic disputes of their neighbors, the people in peasant communities gave such affairs loud and unfavorable publicity either at the time or during the carnival season (see page 588). Relying on degrading public rituals, known as **charivari**, the young men of the village would typically gang up on their victim and force him or her to sit astride a donkey facing backward and holding up the donkey's tail. They would parade the overly brutal spouse-beater or the adulterous couple around the village, loudly proclaiming the offenders' misdeeds. The donkey ride and other colorful humiliations ranging from rotten vegetables splattered on the doorstep to obscene and insulting midnight serenades were common punishments throughout much of Europe. They epitomized the community's effort to police personal behavior and maintain moral standards.

New Patterns of Marriage and Illegitimacy

In the second half of the eighteenth century, long-standing patterns of marriage and illegitimacy shifted dramatically. One important change was an increased

■ **community controls** A pattern of cooperation and common action in a traditional village that sought to uphold the economic, social, and moral stability of the closely knit community.

■ **charivari** Degrading public rituals used by village communities to police personal behavior and maintain moral standards.

■ **illegitimacy explosion** The sharp increase in out-of-wedlock births that occurred in Europe between 1750 and 1850, caused by low wages and the breakdown of community controls.

The Village Wedding The spirited merrymaking of a peasant wedding was a popular theme of European artists in the eighteenth century. Given the harsh conditions of life, a wedding provided a treasured moment of feasting, dancing, and revelry. With the future of the village at stake, the celebration of marriage was a public event. (Private Collection/Bridgeman Images)

ability for young people to make decisions about marriage for themselves, rather than following the interests of their families. This change occurred because social and economic transformations made it harder for families and communities to supervise their behavior. More youths in the countryside worked for their own wages, rather than on a family farm, and their economic autonomy translated into increased freedom of action. Moreover, many youths joined the flood of migrants to the cities, either with their families or in search of work on their own. Urban life provided young people with more social contacts and less social control.

A less positive outcome of loosening social control was an **illegitimacy explosion**, concentrated in England, France, Germany, and Scandinavia. In Frankfurt, Germany, for example, births out of wedlock rose steadily from about 2 percent of all births in the early eighteenth century to a peak of about 25 percent around 1850. In Bordeaux, France, 36 percent of all babies were being born out of wedlock by 1840. Small towns and villages experienced less startling climbs, but between 1750 and

1850 increases from an initial range of 1 to 3 percent to a range of 10 to 20 percent were commonplace. Given the meager economic opportunities open to single mothers, their circumstances were desperate.

Why did the number of illegitimate births skyrocket? One reason was a rise in sexual activity among young people. The loosened social controls that gave young people more choice in marriage also provided them with more opportunities to yield to sexual desire. As in previous generations, many of the young couples who engaged in sexual activity intended to marry. In one medium-size French city in 1787–1788, the great majority of unwed mothers stated that sexual intimacy had followed promises of marriage. Their sisters in rural Normandy frequently reported that they had been "seduced in anticipation of marriage."[5]

The problem for young women who became pregnant was that fewer men followed through on their promises. The second half of the eighteenth century witnessed sharply rising prices for food, homes, and other necessities of life. Many soldiers, day laborers, and male servants were no doubt sincere in their

579

proposals, but their lives were insecure, and they hesitated to take on the burden of a wife and child.

The romantic yet practical dreams and aspirations of young people were thus frustrated by low wages, inequality, and changing economic and social conditions. Old patterns of marriage and family were breaking down. Only in the late nineteenth century would more stable patterns reappear.

Sex on the Margins of Society

Not all sex acts took place between men and women hopeful of marriage. Prostitution offered both single and married men an outlet for sexual desire. After a long period of relative tolerance, prostitutes encountered increasingly harsh and repressive laws in the sixteenth and early seventeenth centuries as officials across Europe closed licensed brothels and declared prostitution illegal.

Despite this repression, prostitution continued to flourish in the eighteenth century. Most prostitutes were working women who turned to the sex trade when confronted with paltry wages and unemployment. Such women did not become social pariahs, but retained ties with the communities of laboring poor to which they belonged. If caught by the police, however, they were liable to imprisonment or banishment. Venereal disease was also a constant threat. Prostitutes were subjected to humiliating police examinations for disease, although medical treatments were at best rudimentary. Farther up the social scale were courtesans whose wealthy protectors provided apartments, servants, fashionable clothing, and cash allowances. After a brilliant but brief career, an aging courtesan faced with the loss of her wealthy client could descend once more to streetwalking.

Relations between individuals of the same sex attracted even more condemnation than did prostitution, since they defied the Bible's limitation of sex to the purposes of procreation. Male same-sex relations, described as "sodomy" or "buggery," were prohibited by law in most European states, under pain of death. Such laws, however, were enforced unevenly, most strictly in Spain and far less so in the Scandinavian countries and Russia.[6]

Protected by their status, nobles and royals sometimes openly indulged their same-sex desires, which were accepted as long as they married and produced legitimate heirs. It was common knowledge that King James I, sponsor of the first translation of the Bible into English, had male lovers, but these relationships were tolerated because they did not prevent him from having seven children with his wife, Anne of Denmark. The duchess of Orléans, sister-in-law of French king Louis XIV, complained in her letters about her husband's male lovers, one of whom was appointed tutor to the couple's son. She also repeated rumors about the homosexual inclinations of King William of England, hero of the Glorious Revolution (see Chapter 15).

In the late seventeenth century homosexual subcultures began to emerge in Paris, Amsterdam, and London, with their own slang, meeting places, and styles of dress. Unlike the relations described above, which involved men who took both wives and male lovers, these groups included men exclusively oriented toward other men. In London, they called themselves "mollies," a term originally applied to prostitutes, and some began to wear women's clothing and adopt effeminate behavior. A new self-identity began to form among homosexual men: a belief that their same-sex desire made them fundamentally different from other men. As a character in one late-eighteenth-century fiction declared, he was in "a category of men different from the other, a class Nature has created in order to diminish or minimize propagation."[7]

Same-sex relations existed among women as well, but they attracted less anxiety and condemnation than those among men. Some women were prosecuted for "unnatural" relations; others attempted to escape the narrow confines imposed on them by dressing as men. Cross-dressing women occasionally snuck into the armed forces, such as Ulrika Elenora Stålhammar, who served as a man in the Swedish army for thirteen years and married a woman. After confessing her transgressions, she was sentenced to a lenient one-month imprisonment.[8] The beginnings of a distinctive lesbian subculture appeared in London and other large cities at the end of the eighteenth century.

Across the early modern period, traditional tolerance for sexual activities outside of heterosexual marriage—be they sex with prostitutes or same-sex relations among male courtiers—faded. This process accelerated in the eighteenth century as Enlightenment critics attacked court immorality and preached virtue and morality for middle-class men, who were expected to prove their worthiness to claim the reins of political power.

Children and Education

FOCUS QUESTION *What was life like for children, and how did attitudes toward childhood evolve?*

On the whole, western European women married late, but then began bearing children rapidly. If a woman married before she was thirty, and if both she and her husband lived to fifty, she would most likely give birth to six or more children. Infant mortality varied across Europe, but was very high by modern standards, and many women died in childbirth due to limited medical knowledge and technology.

For those children who did survive, Enlightenment ideals that emerged in the latter half of the century stressed the importance of parental nurturing. The new worldview also led to an increase in elementary schools throughout Europe. Despite the efforts of enlightened absolutists and religious institutions, however, formal education reached only a minority of ordinary children.

Child Care and Nursing

Newborns entered a dangerous world. They were vulnerable to infectious diseases, and many babies died of dehydration brought about by bad bouts of ordinary diarrhea. Of those who survived infancy, many more died in childhood. Even in a rich family, little could be done for an ailing child. Childbirth was also dangerous. Women who bore six children faced a cumulative risk of dying in childbirth of 5 to 10 percent, a thousand times as great as the risk in Europe today.[9] They died from blood loss and shock during delivery and from infections caused by unsanitary conditions. The joy of pregnancy was thus shadowed by fear of loss of the mother or her child.

In the countryside, women of the lower classes generally breast-fed their infants for two years or more. Although not a foolproof means of birth control, breast-feeding decreases the likelihood of pregnancy by delaying the resumption of ovulation. By nursing their babies, women limited their fertility and spaced their children two or three years apart. Nursing also saved lives: breast-fed infants received precious immunity-producing substances and were more likely to survive than those who were fed other food.

Areas where babies were not breast-fed — typically in northern France, Scandinavia, and central and eastern Europe — experienced the highest infant mortality rates. In these areas, many people believed that breast-feeding was bad for a woman's health or appearance. Across Europe, women of the aristocracy and upper middle class seldom nursed their own children because they found breast-feeding undignified and it interfered with their social responsibilities. The alternatives to breast-feeding consisted of feeding babies cow's or goat's milk or paying lactating women to provide their milk.

Wealthy women hired live-in wet nurses to suckle their babies (which usually meant sending the nurse's own infant away to be nursed by someone else). Working women in the cities also relied on wet nurses because they needed to earn a living. Unable to afford live-in wet nurses, they often turned to the cheaper services of women in the countryside. Rural **wet-nursing** was a widespread business in the eighteenth century, conducted within the framework of the putting-out system. The traffic was in babies rather than in yarn or cloth, and two or three years often passed before the wet-nurse worker in the countryside finished her task.

Wet-nursing was particularly common in northern France. Toward the end of the century, roughly twenty thousand babies were born in Paris each year. Almost half were placed with rural wet nurses through a government-supervised distribution network; 20 to 25 percent were placed in the homes of Parisian nurses personally selected by their parents; and another 20 to 25 percent were abandoned to foundling hospitals, which would send them to wet nurses in the countryside. The remainder (perhaps 10 percent) were nursed at home by their mothers or live-in nurses.[10]

Reliance on wet nurses raised levels of infant mortality because of the dangers of travel, the lack of supervision of conditions in wet nurses' homes, and the need to share milk between a wet nurse's own baby and the one or more babies she was hired to feed. A study of mortality rates in mid-eighteenth-century France shows that 25 percent of babies died before their first birthday, and another 30 percent before age ten.[11] In England, where more mothers nursed, only some 30 percent of children did not reach their tenth birthday.

Within each country and across Europe, tremendous regional variation existed. Mortality rates were higher in overcrowded and dirty cities; in low-lying, marshy regions; and during summer months when rural women were busy in agricultural work and had less time to tend to infants. The corollary of high infant mortality was high fertility. Women who did not breast-feed their babies or whose children died in infancy became pregnant more quickly and bore more children. Thus, on balance, the number of children who survived to adulthood tended to be the same across Europe, with higher births balancing the greater loss of life in areas that relied on wet-nursing.

In the second half of the eighteenth century, critics mounted a harsh attack against wet-nursing. Enlightenment thinkers proclaimed that wet-nursing was robbing European society of reaching its full potential. They were convinced, incorrectly, that the population was declining (in fact it was rising, but they lacked accurate population data) and blamed this decline on women's failure to nurture their children properly. Some also railed against practices of contraception and masturbation, which they believed were robbing their nations of potential children. Despite these complaints, many women continued to rely on wet nurses for convenience or from necessity.

Foundlings and Infanticide

The young woman who could not provide for an unwanted child had few choices, especially if she had no prospect of marriage. Abortions were illegal,

---

■ **wet-nursing** A widespread and flourishing business in the eighteenth century in which women were paid to breast-feed other women's babies.

dangerous, and apparently rare. In desperation, some women, particularly in the countryside, hid unwanted pregnancies, delivered in secret, and smothered their newborn infants. The punishment for infanticide was death. Yet across Europe, convictions for infanticide dropped in the second half of the eighteenth century, testimony, perhaps, to growing social awareness of the crushing pressures caused by unwanted pregnancies.

Another sign of this awareness was the spread of homes for abandoned children in cities across Europe. Homes for abandoned children first took hold in Italy, Spain, and Portugal in the sixteenth century, spreading to France in 1670 and the rest of Europe thereafter. In eighteenth-century England the government acted on a petition calling for a foundling hospital "to prevent the frequent murders of poor, miserable infants at birth" and "to suppress the inhuman custom of exposing newborn children to perish in the streets."

By the end of the eighteenth century, European foundling hospitals were admitting annually about one hundred thousand abandoned children, nearly all of them infants. One-third of all babies born in Paris in the 1770s were immediately abandoned to foundling homes. There appears to have been no differentiation by sex in the numbers of children sent to foundling hospitals. Many of the children were the offspring of single women, the result of the illegitimacy explosion of the second half of the eighteenth century. But fully one-third of all the foundlings were abandoned by married couples too poor to feed another child.[12]

At their best, foundling homes were a good example of Christian charity and social concern in an age of great poverty and inequality. They provided the rudiments of an education and sought to place the children in apprenticeship or domestic service once they reached an appropriate age. Philosopher Jean-Jacques Rousseau defended his decision to place his five illegitimate children in a foundling home—despite their mother's opposition—on the grounds of "poverty and misfortune." He also claimed that the hospital would shield them from the stigma of illegitimacy and provide a home that was "better, or at least more secure, than what [he] would have been able to provide."[13]

Yet the foundling home was no panacea. Even in the best of these homes, 50 percent of the babies normally died within a year. In the worst, fully 90 percent did not survive, falling victim to infectious disease, malnutrition, and neglect.[14] None of Rousseau's children are known to have survived.

Attitudes Toward Children

What were the typical circumstances of children's lives? Some scholars have claimed that high mortality rates prevented parents from forming emotional attachments to young children. With a reasonable expectation that a child might die, some scholars believe, parents maintained an attitude of indifference, if not downright negligence. Most historians now believe, however, that seventeenth- and eighteenth-century parents did love their children, suffered anxiously when they fell ill, and experienced extreme anguish when they died.

Parents were well aware of the dangers of infancy and childhood. The great eighteenth-century English historian Edward Gibbon (1737–1794) wrote, with some exaggeration, that "the death of a new born child before that of its parents may seem unnatural but it is a strictly probable event, since of any given number the greater part are extinguished before the ninth year, before they possess the faculties of the mind and the body." Gibbon's father named all his boys Edward after himself, hoping that at least one of them would survive to carry his name. His prudence was not misplaced. Edward the future historian and eldest survived. Five brothers and sisters who followed him all died in infancy.

Emotional prudence could lead to emotional distance. The French essayist Michel de Montaigne, who lost five of his six daughters in infancy, wrote, "I cannot abide that passion for caressing new-born children, which have neither mental activities nor recognisable bodily shape by which to make themselves loveable and I have never willingly suffered them to be fed in my presence."[15] In contrast to this harsh picture, however, historians have drawn ample evidence from diaries, letters, and family portraits that parents of all social classes did cherish their children. This was equally true of mothers and fathers and of attitudes toward sons and daughters. The English poet Ben Jonson wrote movingly in "On My First Son" of the death of his six-year-old son Benjamin, which occurred during a London plague outbreak in 1603:

> Farewell, thou child of my right hand, and joy;
> My sin was too much hope of thee, loved boy.
> Seven years thou wert lent to me, and I thee pay,
> Exacted by thy fate, on the just day.

In a society characterized by much violence and brutality, discipline of children was often severe. The axiom "Spare the rod and spoil the child" seems to have been coined in the mid-seventeenth century. Susannah Wesley (1669–1742), mother of John Wesley, the founder of Methodism (see page 598), agreed. According to her, the first task of a parent toward her children was "to conquer the will, and bring them to an obedient temper." She reported that her babies were "taught to fear the rod, and to cry softly; by which means they escaped the abundance of correction they might otherwise have had, and that most odious noise of the crying of children was rarely heard in the house."[16] They were

Parisian Boyhood

The life of Jacques-Louis Ménétra, a Parisian glazier, exempli-fied many of the social patterns of his day. He lost his mother in infancy, was educated at a parish school, married late, and had four children, two of whom died. Ménétra distinguished himself from other workingmen, however, by writing an auto-biography describing his tumultuous childhood, his travels around France as a journeyman, and his settled life as a guild master. Ménétra's father was often violent, but he fiercely defended his son against rumored child abductions in Paris (in reality the police had overstepped orders to arrest children loitering in the streets).

I was born on 13 July 1738 a native of this great city. My father belonged to the class usually called artisans. His profession was that of glazier. Hence it is with him that I begin my family tree and I shall say nothing about my ancestors. My father married and set himself up at the same time and wed a virtuous girl who gave him four children, three daughters and one boy, myself, all of whose little pranks I'm going to write about.

My father became a widower when I was two years old. I had been put out to nurse. My grandmother who always loved me a great deal and even idolized me, knowing that the nurse I was with had her milk gone bad, came to get me and after curing me put me back out to nurse [where] I ended up with a pretty good woman who taught me early on the profession of begging. My [grand]mother and my godfather when they came to see me . . . found me in a church begging charity. They took me home and from then until the age of eleven I lived with my good grandmother. My father wanted me back, afraid that he would have to pay my board. He put me to work in his trade even though several people tried to talk him out of it [but] he wouldn't listen to them. . . .

When I felt a little better, I went back to my usual ways which is to say that my father was always angry with me. One night when I was lighting the way in a staircase where he was installing a casement and not mounting it the way he wanted with an angry kick [he] knocked out all my teeth. When I got back home my (step)mother took me to a dentist by the name of Ricie who put back the teeth that weren't broken and I went three weeks eating nothing but bouillon and soup.

In those days it was rumored that they were taking young boys and bleeding them and that they were lost forever and that their blood was used to bathe a princess suffering from a disease that could only be cured with human blood. There was plenty of talk about that in Paris. My father came to get me at school as many other fathers did along with seven big coopers armed with crowbars. The rumor was so strong that the windows of the police station were broken and several poor guys were assaulted and one was even burned in the place de Grève because he looked like a police informer. Children weren't allowed to go outside; three poor wretches were hanged in the place de Grève to settle the matter and restore calm in Paris.

EVALUATE THE EVIDENCE

1. What hardships did the young Ménétra face in his childhood? What attitude did he display toward his childhood experiences?
2. What characteristic elements of eighteenth-century family life does Ménétra's childhood reflect? Does his story provide evidence for or against the thesis that parents deeply loved their children?

Source: Jacques-Louis Ménétra, *Journal of My Life*, ed. Daniel Roche, trans. Arthur Goldhammer, pp. 18, 21–22. Copyright © 1986 Columbia University Press. Reprinted with permission of the publisher.

beaten for lying, stealing, disobeying, and quarreling, and forbidden from playing with other neighbor chil-dren. Susannah's methods of disciplining her children were probably extreme even in her own day, but they do reflect a broad consensus that children were born with an innately sinful will that parents must overcome. (See "Evaluating the Evidence 18.1: Parisian Boyhood," above.)

The Enlightenment produced an enthusiastic new discourse about childhood and child rearing. Starting around 1760 critics called for greater tenderness toward children and proposed imaginative new teach-ing methods. In addition to supporting foundling homes and urging women to nurse their babies, these new voices ridiculed the practice of swaddling babies and using whaleboned corsets to mold children's bones. Rejecting the custom of dressing children in miniature versions of adult clothing, critics called for comfortable clothing to allow freedom of movement. Rather than emphasizing original sin, these enlight-ened voices celebrated the child as an innocent prod-uct of nature. Since they viewed nature as inherently positive, Enlightenment educators advocated safe-guarding and developing children's innate qualities rather than thwarting and suppressing them. Accord-ingly, they believed the best hopes for a new society, untrammeled by the prejudices of the past, lay in a radical reform of child-rearing techniques.

The First Step of Childhood This tender snapshot of a baby's first steps toward an adoring mother exemplifies new attitudes toward children and raising them ushered in by the Enlightenment. Authors like Jean-Jacques Rousseau encouraged elite mothers like the one pictured here to take a more personal interest in raising their children, instead of leaving them in the hands of indifferent wet nurses and nannies. Many women responded eagerly to this call, and the period saw a more sentimentalized view of childhood and family life. (By François Gerard [1770–1837]/Fogg Art Museum, Harvard Art Museums, Cambridge, Massachusetts, USA/Erich Lessing/Art Resource, NY)

One of the century's most influential works on child rearing was Jean-Jacques Rousseau's *Emile, or On Education* (1762), inspired in part, Rousseau claimed, by remorse for the abandonment of his own children. In *Emile*, Rousseau argued that boys' education should include plenty of fresh air and exercise and that boys should be taught practical craft skills in addition to book learning. Reacting to what he perceived as the vanity and frivolity of upper-class Parisian women, Rousseau insisted that girls' education focus on their future domestic responsibilities. For Rousseau, women's "nature" destined them solely for a life of marriage and child rearing. The sentimental ideas of Rousseau and other reformers were enthusiastically adopted by elite women, some of whom began to nurse their own children.

The Spread of Elementary Schools

The availability of education outside the home gradually increased over the early modern period. The wealthy led the way in the sixteenth century with special colleges, often run by Jesuits in Catholic areas. Schools charged specifically with educating children of the common people began to appear in the second half of the seventeenth century. They taught six- to twelve-year-old children basic literacy, religion, and perhaps some arithmetic for the boys and needlework for the girls. The number of such schools expanded in the eighteenth century, although they were never sufficient to educate the majority of the population.

Religion played an important role in the spread of education. From the middle of the seventeenth century, Presbyterian Scotland was convinced that the path to salvation lay in careful study of the Scriptures, and it established an effective network of parish schools for rich and poor alike. The Church of England and the dissenting congregations—Puritans, Presbyterians, Quakers, and so on—established "charity schools" to instruct poor children. The first proponents of universal education, in Prussia, were inspired by the Protestant idea that every believer should be able to read the Bible and by the new idea of raising a population capable of effectively serving the state. As early as 1717 Prussia made attendance at elementary schools compulsory for boys and girls in areas where schools existed.[17] More Protestant German states, such as Saxony and Württemberg (VUHR-tuhm-burg), followed suit in the eighteenth century.

Catholic states pursued their own programs of popular education. In the 1660s France began setting up charity schools to teach poor children their catechism and prayers as well as reading and writing. These were run by parish priests or by new educational teaching orders. One of the most famous orders was Jean-Baptiste de la Salle's Brothers of the Christian Schools. Founded in 1684, the schools had thirty-five thousand students across France by the 1780s. Enthusiasm for popular education was even greater in the Habsburg empire. Inspired by the expansion of schools in rival Protestant German states, Maria Theresa issued her own compulsory education edict in 1774, imposing five hours of school, five days a week, for all children aged six to twelve.[18] Across Europe some elementary education was becoming a reality, and schools became increasingly significant in the life of the child.

Popular Culture and Consumerism

FOCUS QUESTION *How did increasing literacy and new patterns of consumption affect people's lives?*

Because of the new efforts in education, basic literacy expanded among the popular classes, whose reading habits centered primarily on religious material, but who also began to incorporate more practical and entertaining literature. In addition to reading, people of all classes enjoyed a range of leisure activities including storytelling, fairs, festivals, and sports.

One of the most important developments in European society in the eighteenth century was the emergence of a fledgling consumer culture. Much of the expansion took place among the upper and upper-middle classes, but a boom in cheap reproductions of luxury items also opened doors for people of modest means. From food to ribbons and from coal stoves to umbrellas, the material worlds of city dwellers grew richer and more diverse. This "consumer revolution," as it has been called, created new expectations for comfort, hygiene, and self-expression, thus dramatically changing European daily life in the eighteenth century.

Popular Literature

The surge in childhood education in the eighteenth century led to a remarkable growth in literacy between 1600 and 1800. Whereas in 1600 only one male in six was barely literate in France and Scotland, and one in four in England, by 1800 almost nine out of ten Scottish males, two out of three French males (Map 18.1), and more than half of English males were literate. In all three countries, most of the gains occurred in the eighteenth century. Women were also increasingly literate, although they lagged behind men.

The growth in literacy promoted growth in reading, and historians have carefully examined what the common people read. While the Bible remained the overwhelming favorite, especially in Protestant countries, short pamphlets known as chapbooks were the staple of popular literature. Printed on the cheapest paper, many chapbooks featured Bible stories, prayers, and the lives of saints and exemplary Christians. This pious literature gave believers moral teachings and a faith that helped them endure their daily struggles.

Entertaining, often humorous stories formed a second element of popular literature. Fairy tales, medieval romances, true crime stories, and fantastic adventures were some of the delights that filled the peddler's pack as he approached a village. These tales presented a world of danger and magic, of supernatural powers, fairy godmothers, and evil trolls, that provided a temporary flight from harsh everyday reality. They also contained nuggets of ancient folk wisdom, counseling prudence in a world full of danger and injustice, where wolves dress like grandmothers and eat Little Red Riding Hoods.

Finally, some popular literature was highly practical, dealing with rural crafts, household repairs, useful plants, and similar matters. Much lore was stored in almanacs, where calendars listing secular, religious, and astrological events were mixed with agricultural schedules, arcane facts, and jokes. The almanac was highly appreciated even by many in the comfortable

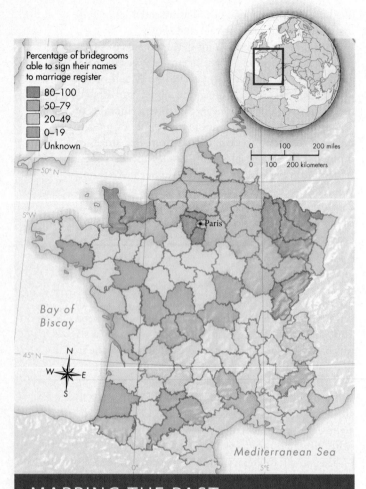

Percentage of bridegrooms
able to sign their names
to marriage register

■ 80–100
■ 50–79
□ 20–49
■ 0–19
■ Unknown

MAPPING THE PAST

MAP 18.1 Literacy in France, ca. 1789

Literacy rates increased but still varied widely between and within states in eighteenth-century Europe.

ANALYZING THE MAP What trends in French literacy rates does this map reveal? Which regions seem to be ahead? How would you explain the regional variations?

CONNECTIONS Note the highly variable nature of literacy rates across the country. Why might the rate of literacy be higher closer to the capital city of Paris? Why would some areas have low rates?

classes. In this way, elites shared some elements of a common culture with the masses.

While it is safe to say that the vast majority of ordinary people—particularly peasants in isolated villages—did not read the great works of the Enlightenment, they were not immune from the new ideas. Urban working people were exposed to Enlightenment thought through the news and gossip that spread across city streets, workshops, markets, and taverns.

■ **blood sports** Events such as bullbaiting and cockfighting that involved inflicting violence and bloodshed on animals and that were popular with the eighteenth-century European masses.

They also had access to cheap pamphlets that helped translate Enlightenment critiques into ordinary language. Servants, who usually came from rural areas and traveled home periodically, were well situated to transmit ideas from educated employers to the village.

Certainly some ordinary people did assimilate Enlightenment ideals. Thomas Paine, author of some of the most influential texts of the American Revolution, was an English corset-maker's son who left school at age twelve and carried on his father's trade before emigrating to the colonies. His 1776 pamphlet *Common Sense* attacked the weight of custom and the evils of government against the natural society of men. This text, which sold 120,000 copies in its first months of publication, is vivid proof of working people's reception of Enlightenment ideas. Paine's stirring mastery of such ideas was perhaps unique, but his access to them was certainly not.

Leisure and Recreation

Despite the spread of literacy, the culture of the village remained largely oral rather than written. In the cold, dark winter months, peasant families gathered around the fireplace to sing, tell stories, do craftwork, and keep warm. In some parts of Europe, women would gather together in someone's cottage to chat, sew, spin, and laugh. Sometimes a few young men would be invited so that the daughters (and mothers) could size up potential suitors in a supervised atmosphere. A favorite recreation of men was drinking and talking with buddies in public places, and it was a sorry village that had no tavern. In addition to old favorites such as beer and wine, the common people turned with gusto to cheap and potent hard liquor, which fell in price because of improved techniques for distilling grain in the eighteenth century.

Towns and cities offered a wider range of amusements, including pleasure gardens, theaters, and lending libraries. Urban fairs featured prepared foods, acrobats, and conjuring acts. Leisure activities were another form of consumption marked by growing commercialization. For example, commercial, profit-making spectator sports emerged in this period, including horse races, boxing matches, and bullfights. (See "The Past Living Now: The Commercialization of Sports," at right.) Modern sports heroes, such as brain-bashing heavyweight champions and haughty bullfighting matadors, made their appearance on the historical scene.

Blood sports, such as bullbaiting and cockfighting, also remained popular with the masses. In bullbaiting, the bull, usually staked on a chain in the courtyard of an inn, was attacked by ferocious dogs for the amusement of the innkeeper's clients. Eventually the maimed and tortured animal was slaughtered by a butcher and sold as meat. In cockfighting, two roosters, carefully

Ask people to name their most cherished memory of school and, as likely as not, you will hear about a victory at football or volleyball or another encounter with organized sports.

Today's world of college and professional sports owes a great deal to the entrepreneurs of seventeenth- and eighteenth-century Europe who produced the first commercialized spectator sports, in which trained athletes, usually male, engaged in organized competitions for the entertainment of ticket-buying fans. These spectacles were part of the array of new leisure-time activities introduced in this era. When they were not strolling in pleasure gardens, debating philosophy in coffeehouses, or perusing fashions in fancy boutiques, crowds of men and women gathered to watch boxing matches and horse races, as well as rowing, walking, and running competitions.

Kings and aristocrats had raced their horses privately for centuries, but first began breeding them for this purpose in the seventeenth and eighteenth centuries, producing the thoroughbred strains still prized today. The first large-scale race meets began in the mid-seventeenth century at Newmarket, still home to today's British racing industry. Originally treated as lowly domestic servants, jockeys gained recognition as independent professionals in the early nineteenth century. Aristocrats also deployed their footmen in pedestrian races, which then grew in popularity and attracted semiprofessional competitors. These races sometimes featured female competitors, including a toddler who in 1749 beat the odds by walking half a mile of a London street in under thirty minutes.*

Professional boxing had less exalted origins in the popular blood sports of the day. In 1719 a London prizefighter named James Figg became the first boxing entrepreneur, opening an "amphitheater" where he staged animal fights and contests among human boxers and swordsmen. With the growing popularity of the sport, the first rules of boxing appeared in the 1740s, calling for fights to include gloves, referees, and judges, and outlawing hitting a man when he was down.

The football and soccer games so central to school spirit in our day arose from the ball games played by peasants across medieval Europe, sometimes taking the form of all-out competitions between rival villages. Elite boarding schools transformed these riotous events into organized and regulated games, because their masters believed that team sports strengthened the body and disciplined the mind. The Rugby School thus produced the first written rules of rugby in 1845. The games of soccer and football developed from these

origins in the nineteenth century, and the first professional leagues began in the 1890s.

Along with commercialization of sports came gambling, cheating, and disorderly crowds, problems that continue to confront professional athletics. A spirit of competition and thirst for victory may be seen as constant elements of the human character; however, historical events profoundly shape the way individuals manifest these qualities. In turn, the way we play and watch sports reveals a great deal about the societies in which we live.

In this early-eighteenth-century painting, two men spar in a boxing match staged in London for the entertainment of the gathered crowd. (Gemaeldegalerie Alte Meiser, Museumslandschaft Hessen Kassel, Germany/bpk, Berlin/Art Resource, NY)

QUESTIONS FOR ANALYSIS

1. In what ways did the commercial sporting events of the eighteenth century reflect the overall "consumer revolution" of this period? How do the professional sports of today's world reflect our own patterns of consumption?

2. What continuities do you see in the social and commercial function of sports between the eighteenth century and today? Conversely, what are the various ways you or those around you "consume" or participate in sports that an eighteenth-century individual might never have dreamed of?

*Allen Guttmann, *Sports: The First Five Millennia* (Amherst: University of Massachusetts Press, 2007), p. 72.

trained by their owners and armed with razor-sharp steel spurs, slashed and clawed each other in a small ring until the victor won—and the loser died. An added attraction of cockfighting was that the screaming spectators could bet on the lightning-fast combat.

Popular recreation merged with religious celebration in a variety of festivals and processions throughout the year. The most striking display of these religiously inspired events was **carnival**, a time of reveling and excess in Catholic Europe, especially in Mediterranean countries. Carnival preceded Lent—the forty days of fasting and penitence before Easter—and for a few exceptional days in February or March, a wild release of drinking, masquerading, and dancing reigned. Moreover, a combination of plays, processions, and raucous spectacles turned the established order upside down. Peasants dressed as nobles and men as women, and rich masters waited on their servants at the table. This annual holiday gave people a much-appreciated chance to release their pent-up frustrations and aggressions before life returned to the usual pattern of hierarchy and hard work.

The rowdy pastimes of the populace attracted criticism from clerical and lay elites in the second half of the eighteenth century. In 1772 the Spanish crown banned dragons and giants from the Corpus Christi parade, and the vibrant carnival of Venice was outlawed under Napoleon's rule in 1797. In the same period English newspapers publicly denounced boxing, gambling, blood sports, and other uncouth activities; one described bullbaiting in 1791 as "a disgrace to a civilized people."[19] However, historians have tended to overstate claims for a "culture war" between elites and the populace in the eighteenth century. Certainly, many wealthy and educated Europeans continued to enjoy the folktales of the chapbooks and they shared the love of gambling, theater, and sport. Moreover, both peasants and patricians—even most enlightened thinkers—shared a deep religiosity. In turn, as we have seen, common people were by no means cut off from the new currents of thought. Thus cultural elements continued to be shared across social divides.

New Foods and Appetites

At the beginning of the eighteenth century, ordinary men and women depended on grain as fully as they had in the past. Bread was quite literally the staff of life. Peasants in the Beauvais region of France ate two pounds of bread a day, washing it down with water, wine, or beer. Their dark bread was made from roughly ground wheat and rye—the standard flour of the

common people. Even peasants normally needed to buy some grain for food, and, in full accord with landless laborers and urban workers, they believed in the moral economy and the **just price**. That is, they believed that prices should be "fair," protecting both consumers and producers, and that just prices should be imposed by government decree if necessary. When prices rose above this level, they often took action in the form of bread riots (see Chapter 15).

The rural poor also ate a quantity of vegetables. Peas and beans were probably the most common. Grown as field crops in much of Europe since the Middle Ages, they were eaten fresh in late spring and summer. Dried, they became the basic ingredients in the soups and stews of the long winter months. In most regions other vegetables appeared on the tables of the poor in season, primarily cabbages, carrots, and wild greens. Fruit was mostly limited to the summer months. Too precious to drink, milk was used to make cheese and butter, which peasants sold in the market to earn cash for taxes and land rents.

The common people of Europe ate less meat in 1700 than in 1500 because their general standard of living had declined and meat was more expensive. Moreover, harsh laws in most European countries reserved the right to hunt and eat game, such as rabbits, deer, and partridges, to nobles and large landowners. Few laws were more bitterly resented—or more frequently broken—by ordinary people than those governing hunting.

The diet of small traders and artisans—the people of the towns and cities—was less monotonous than that of the peasantry. Bustling markets provided a substantial variety of meats, vegetables, and fruits, although bread and beans still formed the bulk of such families' diets. Not surprisingly, the diet of the rich was quite different from that of the poor. The upper classes were rapacious carnivores, and a truly elegant dinner consisted of an abundance of rich meat and fish dishes laced with piquant sauces and complemented with sweets, cheeses, and wine in great quantities. During such dinners, it was common to spend five or more hours at table, eating and drinking and enjoying the witty banter of polite society.

Patterns of food consumption changed markedly as the century progressed. Because of a growth of market gardening, a greater variety of vegetables appeared in towns and cities. This was particularly the case in the Low Countries and England, which pioneered new methods of farming. Introduced into Europe from the Americas—along with corn, squash, tomatoes, and many other useful plants—the humble potato provided an excellent new food source. Containing a good supply of carbohydrates, calories, and vitamins A and C, the potato offset the lack of vitamins in the poor person's winter and early-spring diet, and it provided a much higher caloric yield than grain for a given piece

■ **carnival** The few days of revelry in Catholic countries that preceded Lent and that included drinking, masquerading, dancing, and rowdy spectacles that upset the established order.

■ **just price** The idea that prices should be fair, protecting both consumers and producers, and that they should be imposed by government decree if necessary.

Chocolate Drinking These Spanish tiles from 1710 illustrate the new practice of preparing and drinking hot chocolate. Originating in the New World, chocolate was one of the many new foods imported to Europe in the wake of the voyages of discovery. The first Spanish chocolate mills opened in the mid-seventeenth century, and consumption of chocolate rapidly increased. The inclusion of these tiles in the decoration of a nobleman's house testifies to public interest in the new drink. (Detail of ceiling tile, from Teia, Spain/Museu de Ceramica, Barcelona, Spain/Album/Art Resource, NY)

of land. After initial resistance, the potato became an important dietary supplement in much of Europe by the end of the century.

The most remarkable dietary change in the eighteenth century was in the consumption of commodities imported from abroad. Originally expensive and rare luxury items, goods like tea, sugar, coffee, chocolate, and tobacco became staples for people of all social classes. With the exception of tea—which originated in China—most of the new consumables were produced in European colonies in the Americas. In many cases, the labor of enslaved peoples enabled the expansion in production and drop in prices that allowed such items to spread to the masses.

Why were colonial products so popular? Part of the motivation for consuming these products was a desire to emulate the luxurious lifestyles of the elite. Having seen pictures of or read about the fine lady's habit of "tea-time" or the gentleman's appreciation for a pipe, common Europeans sought to experience these pleasures for themselves. Moreover, the quickened pace of work in the eighteenth century created new needs for stimulants among working people. (See "Evaluating the Evidence 18.2: A Day in the Life of Paris," page 590.) Whereas the gentry took tea as a leisurely and genteel ritual, the lower classes drank tea or coffee at work to fight

monotony and fatigue. With the widespread adoption of these products (which turned out to be mildly to extremely addictive), working people in Europe became increasingly dependent on faraway colonial economies and enslaved labor. Their understanding of daily necessities and how to procure those necessities shifted definitively, linking them to global trade networks they could not comprehend or control.

Toward a Consumer Society

Along with foodstuffs, all manner of other goods increased in variety and number in the eighteenth century. This proliferation led to a growth in consumption and new attitudes toward consumer goods so wide-ranging that some historians have referred to an eighteenth-century **consumer revolution**.[20] The result of this revolution was the birth of a new type of society in which people derived their self-identity as much from their consuming practices as from their working lives and place in the production process. As people gained the opportunity to pick and choose among a wide variety of consumer goods, new notions of individuality and self-expression developed. A shopgirl

■ **consumer revolution** The wide-ranging growth in consumption and new attitudes toward consumer goods that emerged in the cities of northwestern Europe in the second half of the eighteenth century.

A Day in the Life of Paris

Louis-Sébastien Mercier (1740–1814) was the best chronicler of everyday life in eighteenth-century Paris. His masterpiece was the Tableau de Paris *(1781–1788), a multivolume work composed of 1,049 chapters that covered subjects ranging from convents to cafés, bankruptcy to booksellers, the latest fashions to royal laws. As this excerpt demonstrates, he aimed to convey the infinite diversity of people, places, and things he saw around him, and in so doing he left future generations a precious record of the changing dynamics of Parisian society in the second half of the eighteenth century.*

Mercier's family belonged to the respectable artisan classes. This middling position ideally situated Mercier to observe the extremes of wealth and poverty around him. Although these volumes contain many wonderful glimpses of daily life, they should not be taken for an objective account. Mercier brought his own moral and political sensibilities, influenced by Jean-Jacques Rousseau, to the task of description.

Chapter 39: How the Day Goes

It is curious to see how, amid what seems perpetual life and movement, certain hours keep their own characteristics, whether of bustle or of leisure. Every round of the clock-hand sets another scene in motion, each different from the last, though all about equal in length. Seven o'clock in the morning sees all the gardeners, mounted on their nags and with their baskets empty, heading back out of town again. No carriages are about, and not a presentable soul, except a few neat clerks hurrying to their offices. Nine o'clock sets all the barbers in motion, covered from head to foot with flour — hence their soubriquet of "whitings"* — wig in one hand, tongs in the other. Waiters from the lemonade-shops are busy with trays of coffee and rolls, breakfast for those who live in furnished rooms. . . . An hour later the Law comes into action; a black cloud of legal practitioners and hangers-on descend upon the Châtelet,† and the other courts; a procession of wigs and gowns and briefbags, with plaintiffs and defendants at their heels. Midday is the stockbrokers' hour, and the idlers'; the former hurry off to the Exchange, the latter to the Palais-Royal.‡ The Saint-Honoré§ quarter, where all the financiers live, is at its busiest now, its streets are crowded with the customers and clients of the great.

At two o'clock those who have invitations to dine set out, dressed in their best, powdered, adjusted, and walking on tiptoe not to soil their stockings. All the cabs are engaged, not one is to be found on the rank; there is a good deal of competition for these vehicles, and you may see two would-be passengers jumping into a cab together from different sides, and furiously disputing which was first. . . .

Three o'clock and the streets are not so full; everyone is at dinner; there is a momentary calm, soon to be broken, for at five fifteen the din is as though the gates of hell were opened, the streets are impassable with traffic going all ways at once, towards the playhouses or the public gardens. Cafés are at their busiest.

Towards seven the din dies down, everywhere and all at once. You can hear the cab-horses' hoofs pawing the stones as they wait — in vain. It is as though the whole town were gagged and bound, suddenly, by an invisible hand. This is the most dangerous time of the whole day for thieves and such, especially towards autumn when the days begin to draw in; for the watch is not yet about, and violence takes its opportunity.

Night falls; and, while scene-shifters set to work at the playhouses, swarms of other workmen, carpenters, masons and the like, make their way towards the poorer quarters. They leave white footprints from the plaster on their shoes, a trail that any eye can follow. They are off home, and to bed, at the hour which finds elegant ladies sitting down to their dressing-tables to prepare for the business of the night.

*Small fish typically rolled in flour and fried.
†The main criminal court of Paris.
‡A garden surrounded by arcades with shops and cafés.
§A fashionable quarter for the wealthy.

could stand out from her peers by her choice of a striped jacket, a colored parasol, or simply a new ribbon for her hair. The full emergence of a consumer society did not take place until much later, but its roots lie in the eighteenth century.

Increased demand for consumer goods was not merely an innate response to increased supply. Eighteenth-century merchants cleverly pioneered new techniques to incite demand: they initiated marketing campaigns, opened fancy boutiques with large windows, and advertised the patronage of royal princes and princesses. By diversifying their product lines and greatly accelerating the turnover of styles, they seized the reins of fashion from the courtiers who had earlier controlled it. Instead of setting new styles, duchesses and marquises now bowed to the dictates of fashion merchants. (See "Individuals in Society: Rose Bertin, 'Minister of Fashion,'" page 593.) Fashion also extended beyond court circles to touch many more items and social groups.

At nine this begins; they all set off for the play. Houses tremble as the coaches rattle by, but soon the noise ceases; all the fine ladies are making their evening visits, short ones, before supper. Now the prostitutes begin their night parade, breasts uncovered, heads tossing, colour high on their cheeks, and eyes as bold as their hands. These creatures, careless of the light from shop-windows and street lamps, follow and accost you, trailing through the mud in their silk stockings and low shoes, with words and gestures well matched for obscenity. . . .

By eleven, renewed silence. People are at supper, private people, that is; for the cafés begin at this hour to turn out their patrons, and to send the various idlers and workless and poets back to their garrets for the night. A few prostitutes still linger, but they have to use more circumspection, for the watch is about, patrolling the streets, and this is the hour when they "gather 'em in"; that is the traditional expression.

A quarter after midnight, a few carriages make their way home, taking the non–card players back to bed. These lend the town a sort of transitory life; the tradesman wakes out of his first sleep at the sound of them, and turns to his wife, by no means unwilling. More than one young Parisian must owe his existence to this sudden passing rattle of wheels. . . .

At one in the morning six thousand peasants arrive, bringing the town's provision of vegetables and fruits and flowers, and make straight for the Halles.** . . . As for the market itself, it never sleeps. . . . Perpetual noise, perpetual motion, the curtain never rings down on the enormous stage; first come the fishmongers, and after these the egg-dealers, and after these the retail buyers; for the Halles keep all the other markets of Paris going; they are the warehouses whence these draw their supplies. The food of the whole city is shifted and sorted in high-piled baskets; you may see eggs, pyramids of eggs, moved here and

there, up steps and down, in and out of the throngs, miraculous; not one is ever broken. . . .

This impenetrable din contrasts oddly with the sleeping streets, for at that hour none but thieves and poets are awake.

Twice a week, at six, those distributors of the staff of life, the bakers of Gonesse,†† bring in an enormous quantity of loaves to the town, and may take none back through the barriers. And at this same hour workmen take up their tools, and trudge off to their day's labour. Coffee with milk is, unbelievably, the favoured drink among these stalwarts nowadays. . . .

So coffee-drinking has become a habit, and one so deep-rooted that the working classes will start the day on nothing else. It is not costly, and has more flavour to it, and more nourishment too, than anything else they can afford to drink; so they consume immense quantities, and say that if a man can only have coffee for breakfast it will keep him going till nightfall.

EVALUATE THE EVIDENCE

1. What different social groups does Mercier describe? Does he approve or disapprove of Parisian society as he describes it?

2. How do the social classes described by Mercier differ in their use of time, and why? Do you think the same distinctions exist today?

3. What evidence of the consumer revolution can you find in Mercier's account? How do the goods used by eighteenth-century Parisians compare to the ones you use in your life today?

Source: Excerpt from *Panorama of Paris: Selections from "Le Tableau de Paris,"* by Louis-Sébastien Mercier, based on the translation by Helen Simpson, edited with a new preface and translations by Jeremy D. Popkin. Copyright © 1999 The Pennsylvania State University. Reprinted by permission of Penn State Press.

**The city's central wholesale food market.

††A suburb of Paris, famous for the excellent bread baked there.

Clothing was one of the chief indicators of the growth of consumerism. Shrewd entrepreneurs made fashionable clothing seem more desirable, while legions of women entering the textile and needle trades made it ever cheaper. As a result, eighteenth-century western Europe witnessed a dramatic rise in the consumption of clothing, particularly in large cities. One historian has documented an enormous growth in the size and value of Parisians' wardrobes from 1700 to 1789, as well as a new level of diversity in garments and accessories,

colors, and fabrics.[21] Colonial economies again played an important role in lowering the cost of materials, such as cotton cloth and vegetable dyes, largely due to the unpaid toil of enslaved Africans. Cheaper copies of elite styles made it possible for working people to aspire to follow fashion for the first time.

Elite onlookers were sometimes shocked by the sight of lower-class people in stylish outfits. In 1784 Mrs. Fanny Cradock described encountering her milkman during an evening stroll "dressed in a fashionable suit, with an embroidered waistcoat, silk knee-breeches and lace cuffs."[22] The spread of fashion challenged the traditional social order of Europe by blurring the boundaries between social groups and making it harder to distinguish between noble and commoner on the bustling city streets.

Mrs. Cradock's milkman notwithstanding, women took the lead in the spread of fashion. Parisian women significantly out-consumed men, acquiring larger and more expensive wardrobes than those of their husbands, brothers, and fathers. This was true across the social spectrum; in ribbons, shoes, gloves, and lace, European working women reaped in the consumer

First Hot-Air Balloon Flight, 1783   This engraving depicts the world's first free hot-air balloon flight as seen from the Parisian residence of Benjamin Franklin, who was then serving as American ambassador to France. The balloon, invented by the Montgolfier brothers, traveled over five miles in a twenty-minute flight to great public acclaim. (Bibliothèque Nationale, Paris, France/Bridgeman Images)

revolution what they had sown in the industrious revolution (see Chapter 17). There were also new gender distinctions in dress. Previously, noblemen had vied with noblewomen in the magnificence of their apparel; by the end of the eighteenth century men had renounced brilliant colors and voluptuous fabrics to don early versions of the plain dark suit that remains standard male formal wear in the West. This was one more aspect of the increasingly rigid boundaries drawn between appropriate male and female behavior.

Changes in outward appearances were reflected in inner spaces, as new attitudes about privacy, individualism, and intimate life also emerged. Historians have used notaries' probate inventories to peer into ordinary people's homes. In 1700 the cramped home of a modest family consisted of a few rooms, each of which had multiple functions. The same room was used for sleeping, receiving friends, and working. In the eighteenth century rents rose sharply, making it impossible to gain more space, but families began attributing specific functions to specific rooms. They also began to erect inner barriers within the home to provide small niches in which individuals could seek privacy. (See "Thinking Like a Historian: A New Subjectivity," page 594.)

New levels of comfort and convenience accompanied this trend toward more individualized ways of life. In 1700 a meal might be served in a common dish, with each person dipping his or her spoon into the pot. By the end of the eighteenth century even humble households contained a much greater variety of cutlery and dishes, making it possible for each person to eat from his or her own plate. More books and prints, which also proliferated at lower prices, decorated the shelves and walls. Improvements in glassmaking provided more transparent glass, which allowed daylight to penetrate into gloomy rooms. Cold and smoky hearths were increasingly replaced by more efficient and cleaner coal stoves, which also eliminated the backache of cooking over an open fire. Rooms were warmer, better lit, more comfortable, and more personalized, and the spread of street lighting made it safer to travel in cities at night.

Standards of bodily and public hygiene also improved. Public bathhouses, popular across Europe in the Middle Ages, had gradually closed in the early modern period due to concerns over sexual promiscuity and infectious disease. Many Europeans came to fear that immersing the body in hot water would allow harmful elements to enter the skin. Carefully watched by his physician, Louis XIII of France took his first bath at age seven, while James I of England refused to wash more than his hands. Personal cleanliness consisted of wearing fresh linen and using perfume to mask odors, both expensive practices that

One day in 1779, as the French royal family rode in a carriage through the streets of Paris, Queen Marie Antoinette noticed her fashion merchant, Rose Bertin, observing the royal procession. "Ah! there is mademoiselle Bertin," the queen exclaimed, waving her hand. Bertin responded with a curtsy. The king then stood and greeted Bertin, followed by the royal family and their entourage.* The incident shocked the public, for no common merchant had ever received such homage from royalty.

Bertin had come a long way from her humble beginnings. Born in 1747 to a poor family in northern France, she moved to Paris in the 1760s to work as a shop assistant. Bertin eventually opened her own boutique on the fashionable rue Saint Honoré. In 1775 Bertin received the highest honor of her profession when she was selected by Marie Antoinette as one of her official purveyors.

Based on the queen's patronage, and riding the wave of the new consumer revolution, Bertin became one of the most successful entrepreneurs in Europe. Bertin established not only a large clientele, but also a reputation for pride and arrogance. She refused to work for non-noble customers, claiming that the orders of the queen and the court required all her attention. She astounded courtiers by referring to her "work" with the queen, as though the two were collaborators rather than absolute monarch and lowly subject. Bertin's close relationship with Marie Antoinette and the fortune the queen spent on her wardrobe hurt the royal family's image. One journalist derided Bertin as a "minister of fashion," whose influence outstripped that of all the others in royal government.

In January 1787 rumors spread through Paris that Bertin had filed for bankruptcy with debts of 2 to 3 million livres (a garment worker's annual salary was around 200 livres). Despite her notoriously high prices and rich clients, this news did not shock Parisians, because the nobility's reluctance to pay its debts was equally well known. Bertin somehow held on to her business. Some said she had spread the bankruptcy rumors herself to shame the court into paying her bills.

Bertin remained loyal to the Crown during the tumult of the French Revolution (see Chapter 19) and sent dresses to the queen even after the arrest of the royal family. Fearing for her life, she left France for Germany in 1792 and continued to ply her profession in exile. She returned to France in 1800 and died in 1813, one year before the restoration of the Bourbon monarchy might have renewed her acclaim.†

Rose Bertin scandalized public opinion with her self-aggrandizement and ambition, yet history was on her side. She

In this 1746 painting by François Boucher, a leisured lady has just been coiffed by her hairdresser. Wearing the cape she donned to protect her clothing from the hair powder, she receives a fashion merchant, who displays an array of ribbons and other finery. (*The Milliner*/DEA Picture Library/Getty Images)

was the first celebrity fashion stylist and one of the first self-made career women to rise from obscurity to fame and fortune based on her talent, taste, and hard work. Her legacy remains in the exalted status of today's top fashion designers and in the dreams of small-town girls to make it in the big city.

QUESTIONS FOR ANALYSIS

1. Why was the relationship between Queen Marie Antoinette and Rose Bertin so troubling to the public? Why would relations between a queen and a fashion merchant have political implications?
2. Why would someone who sold fashionable clothing and accessories rise to such a prominent position in business and society? What makes fashion so important in the social world?

*Mémoires secrets pour servir à l'histoire de la république des lettres en France, vol. 13, 299, 5 mars 1779 (London: John Adamson, 1785).
†On Rose Bertin, see Clare Haru Crowston, "The Queen and Her 'Minister of Fashion': Gender, Credit and Politics in Pre-Revolutionary France," *Gender and History* 14, no. 1 (April 2002): 92–116.

A New Subjectivity

Traditional European society was organized into groups that shared common values: families, parishes, guilds, and social ranks. Most people's time was spent working and socializing alongside people of the same milieu. The eighteenth century introduced a new, more private and individualized sense of self. Artisans and merchants created a host of material goods that allowed men and women to pursue this new subjectivity in comfort and style.

1 **Jean-Jacques Rousseau, *The Confessions*, 1782.** Swiss philosopher Jean-Jacques Rousseau felt driven to understand and express his inner feelings. His autobiography, *The Confessions*, had an enormous impact on European culture, stirring generations of Europeans to strive for greater self-knowledge.

~I have resolved on an enterprise which has no precedent, and which, once complete, will have no imitator. My purpose is to display to my kind a portrait in every way true to nature, and the man I shall portray will be myself.

Simply myself. I know my own heart and understand my fellow man. But I am made unlike any one I have ever met; I will even venture to say that I am like no one in the whole world. I may be no better, but at least I am different. Whether Nature did well or ill in breaking the mould in which she formed me, is a question which can only be resolved after the reading of my book. . . .

I have displayed myself as I was, as vile and despicable when my behavior was such, as good, generous, and noble when I was so. I have bared my secret soul as Thou thyself hast seen it, Eternal Being! So let the numberless legion of my fellow men gather round me, and hear my confessions.

3 **The dressing gown.** Dressing gowns became popular in the eighteenth century as a warm and comfortable garment for reading, writing, and relaxing in the privacy of the home, before putting on formal wear to go out to dinner or the theater.

(*Young Man at the Clavichord*, 1767, French School (oil on canvas)/Musée du Louvre, Paris, France/Bridgeman Images)

2 **Pierre Choderlos de Laclos, *Les Liaisons Dangereuses*, 1782.** Like other elite young women of her day, the fictional heroine of this novel found privacy in a small room, or cabinet, of her own where she could read, write, and reflect. It contained a locked desk where she hid her love letters.

~You see, my good friend, [that] I am keeping my word to you, and that bonnets and pompons do not take up all my time; there is some left for you. . . . Mama has consulted me about everything; she treats me much less like a schoolgirl than she used to. I have my own chambermaid; I have a bedroom and a cabinet to myself, and I am writing to you on a very pretty Secretary, to which I have been given the key, and in which I can hide whatever I wish.

ANALYZING THE EVIDENCE

1. What did Rousseau think was new and important about the autobiography he was writing (Source 1)?
2. What do the material objects displayed in Sources 3, 4, and 5 tell us about the new subjectivity? Why would historians turn to material objects to understand shifts in the understanding of the self? Do you see advantages or limitations to this approach?
3. Think about how different groups of people might have experienced subjectivity in distinctive ways. Why might a private room and a locked desk be particularly important for a young woman (Source 2)? What challenges would the poor face in following the path traced by Rousseau (Source 1)?

4 **The bedroom.** Architects helped create private spaces where the new subjectivity could develop. As Louis-Sébastien Mercier declared, "Wise and ingenious divisions economize the property, multiply it and give it new and precious comforts." This alcove bedchamber provided a cozy nook for receiving intimate friends and engaging in private self-reflection.

(Musée de la Ville de Paris, Musée Carnavalet, Paris, France/Bridgeman Images)

5 **Dressing table.** This dressing table could double as a writing desk when its cleverly constructed drawers were folded away. Probate inventories show a strong rise in the number of mirrors, writing desks, and toilette items owned by men and women over the course of the eighteenth century.
(George III Rudd's table, ca. 1770 [mahogany and marquetry], English/Private Collection/Photo © Christie's Images/Bridgeman Images)

PUTTING IT ALL TOGETHER

Using the sources above, along with what you have learned in class and in this chapter, write an essay that explores the connection in the eighteenth century between social relationships, the changing material circumstances of life, and developing ideas of the individual and the self.

Sources: (1) Jean-Jacques Rousseau, *The Confessions* (London: Penguin, 1953), p. 17; (2) Dena Goodman, *Becoming a Woman in the Age of Letters* (Ithaca: Cornell University Press, 2009), p. 243.

The Consumer Revolution   From the mid-eighteenth century on, the cities of western Europe witnessed a new proliferation of consumer goods. Items once limited to the wealthy few — such as fans, watches, snuffboxes, umbrellas, ornamental containers, and teapots — were now reproduced in cheaper versions for middling and ordinary people. (jar: Etui, Bilson enamel/Victoria and Albert Museum, London, UK/ Bridgeman Images; fan: Musée Condé, Chantilly, France/Scala/White Images/Art Resource, NY)

bespoke wealth and social status. From the mid-eighteenth century on, enlightened doctors revised their views and began to urge more frequent bathing. Spa towns, like Bath, England, became popular sites for the wealthy to see each other and be seen. Officials also took measures to improve the cleaning of city streets in which trash, human soil, and animal carcasses were often left to rot.

The scope of the new consumer economy should not be exaggerated. These developments were concentrated in large cities in northwestern Europe and North America. Even in these centers the elite benefited the most from new modes of life. This was not yet the society of mass consumption that emerged toward the end of the nineteenth century with the full expansion of the Industrial Revolution. The eighteenth century did, however, lay the foundations for one of the most distinctive features of modern Western life: societies based on the consumption of goods and services obtained through the market in which individuals form their identities and self-worth through the goods they consume.

Religious Authority and Beliefs

FOCUS QUESTION *What were the patterns of popular religion, and how did they interact with the worldview of the educated public and their Enlightenment ideals?*

Though the critical spirit of the Enlightenment made great inroads in the eighteenth century, the majority of ordinary men and women, especially those in rural areas, retained strong religious faith. The church promised salvation, and it gave comfort in the face of sorrow and death. Religion also remained strong because it was embedded in local traditions and everyday social experience.

Yet the popular religion of village Europe was also enmeshed in a larger world of church hierarchies and state power. These powerful outside forces sought to regulate religious life at the local level. Their efforts created tensions that helped set the scene for vigorous religious revivals in Protestant Germany and England as well as in Catholic France.

Church Hierarchy

In the eighteenth century religious faith not only endured, but grew more fervent in many parts of Europe. The local parish church remained the focal point of religious devotion and community cohesion. Congregants gossiped and swapped stories after services, and neighbors came together in church for baptisms, marriages, funerals, and special events. Priests and parsons kept the community records of births, deaths, and marriages; distributed charity; looked after orphans; and provided primary education to the common people. Thus the parish church was woven into the very fabric of community life.

While the parish church remained central to the community, it was also subject to greater control from the state. In Protestant areas, princes and monarchs headed the official church, and they regulated their "territorial churches" strictly, selecting personnel and imposing detailed rules. Clergy of the official church dominated education, and followers of other faiths suffered religious and civil discrimination. By the eighteenth century the radical ideas of the Reformation had resulted in another version of church bureaucracy.

Catholic monarchs in this period also took greater control of religious matters in their kingdoms, weakening papal authority. In both Spain and Portugal, the Catholic Church was closely associated with the state, a legacy of the long internal reconquista and sixteenth-century imperial conquests overseas. In the eighteenth century the Spanish crown took firm control of ecclesiastical appointments. Papal proclamations could not even be read in Spanish churches without prior approval from the government. In Portugal, religious enthusiasm led to a burst of new churches and monasteries in the early eighteenth century.

France went even further in establishing a national Catholic Church, known as the Gallican Church. Louis XIV's expulsion of Protestants in 1685 was accompanied by an insistence on the king's prerogative to choose and control bishops and issue laws regarding church affairs. Catholicism gained new ground in the Holy Roman Empire with the conversion of a number of Protestant princes and successful missionary work by Catholic orders among the populace. While it could not eradicate Protestantism altogether, the Habsburg monarchy successfully consolidated Catholicism as a pillar of its political control.

The Jesuit order played a key role in fostering the Catholic faith, providing extraordinary teachers, missionaries, and agents of the papacy. In many Catholic countries they exercised tremendous political influence, holding high government positions and educating the nobility in their colleges. By playing politics so effectively, however, the Jesuits elicited a broad coalition of enemies. Bitter controversies led Louis XV to order the Jesuits out of France in 1763 and to confiscate their property. France and Spain then pressured Rome to dissolve the Jesuits completely. In 1773 a reluctant pope caved in, although the order was revived after the French Revolution.

The Jesuit order was not the only Christian group to come under attack in the middle of the eighteenth century. The dominance of the larger Catholic Church and established Protestant churches was also challenged, both by enlightened reformers from above and by the faithful from below. Influenced by Enlightenment ideals, some Catholic rulers believed that the clergy in monasteries and convents should make a more practical contribution to social and religious life. Austria, a leader in controlling the church (see Chapter 16) and promoting primary education, showed how far the process could go. Maria Theresa began by sharply restricting entry into what she termed "unproductive" orders. In his Edict on Idle Institutions, her successor, Joseph II, abolished contemplative orders, henceforth permitting only orders that were engaged in teaching, nursing, or other practical work. The state expropriated the dissolved monasteries and convents and used their wealth to create more parishes throughout Austria. This edict had a disproportionate effect on women because most of their orders were cloistered from the outside world and thus were not seen as "useful." Joseph II also issued edicts of religious tolerance, including for Jews, making Austria one of the first European states to lift centuries-old restrictions on its Jewish population.

Protestant Revival

Official efforts to reform state churches in the eighteenth century were confronted by a wave of religious enthusiasm from below. By the late seventeenth century the vast transformations of the Protestant Reformation were complete and had been widely adopted in most Protestant churches. Medieval practices of idolatry, saint worship, and pageantry were abolished; stained-glass windows were smashed and murals whitewashed. Yet many official Protestant churches had settled into a smug complacency. This, along with the growth of state power and bureaucracy in local parishes, threatened to eclipse one of the Reformation's main goals—to bring all believers closer to God.

In the Reformation heartland, one concerned German minister wrote that the Lutheran Church "had become paralyzed in forms of dead doctrinal conformity" and badly needed a return to its original inspiration.[23] His

Advice to Methodists

John Wesley (1703–1791) was the fifteenth child of an Anglican rector and a strict mother. As a small child, he was rescued from certain death in a house fire; in later years, he saw this moment as a sign of providential grace. Along with his brother Charles, John Wesley is recognized as the founder of Methodism, an evangelical movement that began within the Church of England and was influenced by German Pietism. In the passage below, Wesley offers his advice to followers of the new religious movement he had inspired, who had been dubbed "Methodists" for their scrupulous and methodical approach to religious worship.

By *Methodists* I mean, a People who profess to pursue (in whatsoever Measure they have attained) Holiness of Heart and Life, inward and outward Conformity in all Things to the revealed Will of God: Who place Religion in an uniform Resemblance of the great Object of it; in a steady Imitation of Him they worship, in all his inimitable Perfections; more particularly, in Justice, Mercy, and Truth, or universal Love filling the Heart, and governing the Life. . . .

Your *Name* is new (at least, as used in a religious Sense), not heard of, till a few Years ago, either in our own, or any other Nation. Your *Principles* are new, in this respect, That there is no other Set of People among us (and, possibly, not in the Christian World) who hold them all, in the same Degree and Connection; who so strenuously and continually insist on the absolute Necessity of universal Holiness both in Heart and Life; of a peaceful, joyous Love of God; of a supernatural Evidence of Things not seen; of an inward Witness that we are the Children of God, and of the Inspiration of the Holy Ghost, in order to any good Thought, or Word, or Work. And perhaps there is no other Set of People (at least not visibly united together), who lay *so much*, and yet *no more* Stress than you do, on Rectitude of *Opinions*, on outward *Modes of Worship*, and the Use of those *Ordinances* which you acknowledge to be of God. . . .

Your *Strictness* of Life, taking the whole of it together, may likewise be accounted new. I mean, your making it a Rule, to abstain from fashionable *Diversions*, from *reading* Plays, Romances, or Books of Humour, from *singing* innocent Songs, or *talking* in a merry, gay, diverting Manner; your *Plainness* of Dress; your *Manner of Dealing* in Trade; your Exactness in observing the *Lord's Day*; your Scrupulosity as to Things that have *not paid Custom*; your total Abstinence from *spirituous Liquors* (unless in Cases of Extreme Necessity); your Rule, "not to mention the Fault of an absent Person, in Particular, of *Ministers*, or of *those in Authority*," may justly be termed new.

EVALUATE THE EVIDENCE

1. What elements of the Methodist faith does Wesley identify as "new" in this document? To what or whom is he comparing Methodists?
2. To what changes under way in English society does this document appear to be responding? What social practices do Methodists oppose, according to Wesley?

Source: John Wesley, *Advice to the People Call'd Methodists* (Bristol: Felix Farley, 1745), pp. 3, 5–6.

---

voice was one of many that prepared and then guided a Protestant revival that succeeded because it answered the intense but increasingly unsatisfied needs of common people.

The Protestant revival began in Germany in the late seventeenth century. It was known as **Pietism** (PIGH-uh-tih-zum), and three aspects helped explain its powerful appeal. First, Pietism called for a warm, emotional religion that everyone could experience. Enthusiasm—in prayer, in worship, in preaching, in life itself—was the key concept. "Just as a drunkard becomes full of wine, so must the congregation become filled with spirit," declared one exuberant writer.[24]

Second, Pietism reasserted the earlier radical stress on the priesthood of all believers, thereby reducing the gulf between official clergy and Lutheran laity. Bible reading and study were enthusiastically extended to all classes, and this provided a powerful spur for popular literacy as well as individual religious development. Pietists were largely responsible for the educational reforms implemented by Prussia in the early eighteenth century (see page 585). Third and finally, Pietists believed in the practical power of Christian rebirth in everyday affairs. Reborn Christians were expected to lead good, moral lives and to come from all social classes.

Pietism soon spread through the German-speaking lands and to Scandinavia. It also had a major impact on John Wesley (1703–1791), who served as the catalyst for popular religious revival in England. (See "Evaluating the Evidence 18.3: Advice to Methodists," above.) Wesley came from a long line of ministers, and when he went to Oxford University to prepare for the clergy, he mapped a fanatically earnest "scheme of religion." After becoming a teaching fellow at Oxford, Wesley organized a Holy Club for similarly minded

Hogarth's Satirical View of the Church William Hogarth (1697–1764) was one of the foremost satirical artists of his day. This image mocks a London Methodist meeting, where the congregation swoons in enthusiasm over the preacher's sermon. The woman in the foreground giving birth to rabbits is an allusion to a hoax perpetrated in 1726 by a servant named Mary Tofts; the gullibility of those who believed Tofts is likened to that of the Methodist congregation. (From *Hogarth Restored: The Whole Works of the Celebrated William Hogarth*, 1812/Private Collection/The Stapleton Collection/Bridgeman Images)

students, who were soon known contemptuously as **Methodists** because they were so methodical in their devotion. Yet like the young Martin Luther, Wesley remained intensely troubled about his own salvation even after his ordination as an Anglican priest in 1728.

Wesley's anxieties related to grave problems of the faith in England. The government shamelessly used the Church of England to provide favorites with high-paying jobs. Both church and state officials failed to respond to the spiritual needs of the people, and services and sermons had settled into an uninspiring routine. The separation of religion from local customs and social life was symbolized by church doors that were customarily locked on weekdays. Moreover, Enlightenment skepticism was making inroads among the educated classes, and deism—a belief in God but not in organized religion—was becoming popular. Some bishops and church leaders seemed to believe that

doctrines such as the virgin birth were little more than elegant superstitions.

Wesley's inner search in the 1730s was deeply affected by his encounter with Moravian Pietists, whom he first met on a ship as he traveled across the Atlantic to take up a position in Savannah, Georgia. The small Moravian community in Georgia impressed him as a productive, peaceful, and pious world, reflecting the values of the first apostles. (For more on the Moravian Church, see "Individuals in Society: Rebecca Protten," in Chapter 17 on page 568.) After returning to London, following a disastrous failed engagement and

■ **Pietism** A Protestant revival movement in early-eighteenth-century Germany and Scandinavia that emphasized a warm and emotional religion, the priesthood of all believers, and the power of Christian rebirth in everyday affairs.

■ **Methodists** Members of a Protestant revival movement started by John Wesley, so called because they were so methodical in their devotion.

the disappointment of his hopes to convert Native Americans, he sought spiritual counseling from a Pietist minister from Germany. Their conversations prepared Wesley for a mystical, emotional "conversion" in 1738. He described this critical turning point in his *Journal*:

> In the evening I went to a [Christian] society in Aldersgate Street where one was reading Luther's preface to the Epistle to the Romans. About a quarter before nine, while he was describing the change which God works in the heart through faith in Christ, I felt my heart strangely warmed. I felt I did trust in Christ, Christ alone for salvation; and an assurance was given me that he had taken away my sins, even mine, and saved me from the law of sin and death.[25]

Wesley's emotional experience resolved his intellectual doubts about the possibility of his own salvation. Moreover, he was convinced that any person, no matter how poor or uneducated, might have a similarly heartfelt conversion and gain the same blessed assurance. He took the good news to the people, traveling some 225,000 miles by horseback and preaching more than forty thousand sermons between 1750 and 1790. Since existing churches were often overcrowded and the church-state establishment was hostile, Wesley preached in open fields. People came in large numbers. Of critical importance was Wesley's rejection of Calvinist predestination—the doctrine of salvation granted to only a select few. Instead, he preached that all men and women who earnestly sought salvation might be saved. It was a message of hope and joy, of free will and universal salvation.

Wesley's ministry used lay preachers to reach new converts, formed Methodist cells, and eventually resulted in a new denomination. And just as Wesley had been inspired by the Pietist revival in Germany, so evangelicals in the Church of England and the old dissenting groups now followed Wesley's example of preaching to all people, giving impetus to an even broader awakening among the lower classes. Thus in Protestant countries religion continued to be a vital force in the lives of the people.

Catholic Piety

Religion also flourished in Catholic Europe around 1700, but there were important differences from Protestant practice. First, the visual contrast was striking; baroque art still lavished rich and emotionally exhilarating figures and images on Catholic churches, whereas most Protestant churches had removed their art during the Reformation. Moreover, people in Catholic Europe on the whole participated more

actively in formal worship than did Protestants. More than 95 percent of the population probably attended church for Easter communion, the climax of the religious year.

The tremendous popular strength of religion in Catholic countries can in part be explained by the church's integral role in community life and popular culture. Thus, although Catholics reluctantly confessed their sins to priests, they enthusiastically came together in religious festivals to celebrate the passage of the liturgical year. In addition to the great processional days—such as Palm Sunday, the joyful re-enactment of Jesus's triumphal entry into Jerusalem—each parish had its own saints' days, processions, and pilgrimages. Led by its priest, a congregation might march around the village or across the countryside to a local shrine. Millions of Catholic men and women also joined religious associations, known as confraternities, where they participated in prayer and religious services and collected funds for poor relief and members' funerals. The Reformation had largely eliminated such activities in Protestant areas.

Catholicism had its own version of the Pietist revivals that shook Protestant Europe. **Jansenism** has been described by one historian as the "illegitimate offspring of the Protestant Reformation and the Catholic Counter-Reformation."[26] It originated with Cornelius Jansen (1585–1638), bishop of Ypres in the Spanish Netherlands, who called for a return to the austere early Christianity of Saint Augustine. In contrast to the worldly Jesuits, Jansen emphasized the heavy weight of original sin and accepted the doctrine of predestination. Although outlawed by papal and royal edicts as Calvinist heresy, Jansenism attracted Catholic followers eager for religious renewal, particularly among the French. Many members of France's urban elite, especially judicial nobles and some parish priests, became known for their Jansenist piety and spiritual devotion. Such stern religious values encouraged the judiciary's increasing opposition to the French monarchy in the second half of the eighteenth century.

Among the urban poor, a different strain of Jansenism took hold. Prayer meetings brought men and women together in ecstatic worship, and some participants fell into convulsions and spoke in tongues. The police of Paris posted spies to report on such gatherings and conducted mass raids and arrests.

Marginal Beliefs and Practices

In the countryside, many peasants continued to hold religious beliefs that were marginal to the Christian faith altogether, often of obscure or even pagan origin. On the Feast of Saint Anthony, for example, priests were expected to bless salt and bread for farm animals to protect them from disease. Catholics believed that

■ **Jansenism** A sect of Catholicism originating with Cornelius Jansen that emphasized the heavy weight of original sin and accepted the doctrine of predestination; it was outlawed as heresy by the pope.

saints' relics could bring fortune or attract lovers, and there were healing springs for many ailments. In 1796 the Lutheran villagers of Beutelsbach in southern Germany incurred the ire of local officials when they buried a live bull at a crossroads to ward off an epidemic of hoof-and-mouth disease.[27] The ordinary person combined strong Christian faith with a wealth of time-honored superstitions.

Inspired initially by the fervor of the Reformation era, then by the critical rationalism of the Enlightenment, religious and secular authorities sought increasingly to "purify" popular spirituality. Thus one parish priest in France lashed out at his parishioners, claiming that they were "more superstitious than devout . . . and sometimes appear as baptized idolators."[28] French priests particularly denounced the "various remnants of paganism" found in popular bonfire ceremonies during Lent, in which young men, "yelling and screaming like madmen," tried to jump over the bonfires in order to help the crops grow and to protect themselves from illness. One priest saw rational Christians regressing into pagan animals — "the triumph of Hell and the shame of Christianity."[29]

The severity of the attack on popular belief varied widely by country and region. Where authorities pursued purification vigorously, as in Austria under Joseph II, pious peasants saw only an incomprehensible attack on age-old faith and drew back in anger. It was in this era of rationalism and disdain for superstition that the persecution of witches slowly came to an end across Europe. Common people in the countryside continued to fear the Devil and his helpers, but the elite increasingly dismissed such fears and refused to prosecute suspected witches. The last witch was executed in England in 1682, the same year France prohibited witchcraft trials. By the late eighteenth century the witchcraft hunts had ended across Europe.

Medical Practice

FOCUS QUESTION *How did the practice of medicine evolve in the eighteenth century?*

Although significant breakthroughs in medical science would not come until the middle and late nineteenth century, the Enlightenment's inherent optimism and its focus on improving human life through understanding of the laws of nature produced a great deal of research and experimentation in the eighteenth century. Medical practitioners greatly increased in number, although their techniques did not differ much from those of previous generations. Care of the sick in this era was the domain of several competing groups: traditional healers, apothecaries (pharmacists), physicians, surgeons, and midwives. From the Middle Ages through the seventeenth century,

both men and women were medical practitioners. However, since women were generally denied admission to medical colleges and lacked the diplomas necessary to practice, the range of medical activities open to them was restricted. In the eighteenth century women's traditional roles as midwives and healers eroded even further.

Faith Healing and General Practice

In the course of the eighteenth century, traditional healers remained active, drawing on centuries of folk knowledge about the curative properties of roots, herbs, and other plants. Faith healing also remained popular, especially in the countryside. Faith healers and their patients believed that evil spirits caused illness by lodging in people and that the proper treatment was to exorcise, or drive out, the offending devil. Religious and secular officials did their best to stamp out such practices, but with little success.

In the larger towns and cities, apothecaries sold a vast number of herbs, drugs, and patent medicines for every conceivable "temperament and distemper." By the eighteenth century many of these medicines were derived from imported plants. The Asian spices prized since medieval times often had medicinal uses; from the sixteenth century onward, the Portuguese and then the Dutch dominated the Indian Ocean trade in these spices (see Chapter 14). As Europeans expanded to the New World, they brought a keen interest in potentially effective and highly profitable medicinal plants. Botanists accompanied European administrators and explorers to the Americas, where they profited from the healing traditions of indigenous peoples and, in the plantation societies of the Caribbean, enslaved Africans. They returned to Europe with a host of medicinal plants such as ipecacuanha, sarsaparilla, opium, and cinchona, the first effective treatment for fever. Over the course of the seventeenth century, imports of medicinal plants boomed. By the late eighteenth century, England was importing annually £100,000 worth of drugs, compared to only £1,000 or £2,000 in 1600.[30]

Like all varieties of medical practitioners, apothecaries advertised their wares, their high-class customers, and their miraculous cures in newspapers and commercial circulars. Medicine, like food and fashionable clothing, thus joined the era's new and loosely regulated commercial culture.

Physicians, who were invariably men, were apprenticed in their teens to practicing physicians for several years of on-the-job training. This training was then rounded out with hospital work or some university courses. Seen as gentlemen who did not labor with their hands, many physicians diagnosed and treated patients by correspondence or through oral dialogue, without conducting a physical examination. Because their

Most women in eighteenth-century Europe gave birth to at least five or six children over their lifetimes. They were assisted in the arduous, often dangerous process of childbirth by friends, relatives, and, in many cases, professional midwives. Birth took place at home, sometimes with the aid of a birthing chair, such as the folding chair from Sicily shown here.

The training and competency of midwives were often rudimentary, especially in the countryside. Enlightenment interest in education and public health helped inspire a movement across Europe to raise standards. One of its pioneers was Madame Angelique Marguerite Le Boursier du Coudray. Du Coudray herself had undergone a rigorous three-year apprenticeship and was a member of the Parisian surgeons' guild. She set off on a mission to teach rural midwives in the French province of Auvergne.

Du Coudray saw that her unlettered pupils learned through the senses, not through books. Thus she made, possibly for the first time in history, a life-size obstetrical model — a "machine" — out of fabric and stuffing for use in her classes. She reported, "I had . . . the students maneuver in front of me on a machine . . . which represented the pelvis of a woman, the womb, its opening, its ligaments, the conduit called the vagina, the bladder, and *rectum intestine*. I added [an artificial] child of natural size, whose joints were flexible enough to be able to be put in different positions."* Now du Coudray could demonstrate the problems of childbirth, and each student could practice on the model in the "lab session."

As her reputation grew, du Coudray sought to reach a national audience. In 1757 she published her *Manual on the Art of Childbirth*. The *Manual* incorporated her hands-on teaching method and served as a reference for students and graduates. In 1759 the government authorized du Coudray to carry her instruction "throughout the realm" and promised financial support.

Her classes brought women from surrounding villages to meet mornings and afternoons six days a week, with ample time to practice on the mannequin. After two to three months of instruction, Madame du Coudray and her entourage moved on. Teaching thousands of midwives, Madame du Coudray and her model may well have contributed to the decline in infant mortality and to the increase in population occurring in France in the eighteenth century — an increase she and her royal supporters fervently desired. Certainly she spread better knowledge about childbirth from the educated elite to the common people.

Eighteenth-century birthing chair from Sicily. (SSPL/Getty Images)

Life-size model showing twin fetuses. (Obstetrical Museum, Palazzo Poggi, University of Bologna, Italy/© Hal Beral/VWPics/age-fotostock)

*Quotes are from Nina Gelbart, *The King's Midwife: A History and Mystery of Madame du Coudray* (Berkeley: University of California Press, 1998), pp. 60–61.

Childbirth was traditionally a woman's world that brought female relatives, friends, and the midwife to the laboring woman's bedside, as shown in this Dutch painting from the late seventeenth century. (*The Newborn Baby*, 1675, by Matthys Naiveu [1647–1726], [oil on canvas]/Image copyright © The Metropolitan Museum of Art, New York, New York, USA/Image source: Art Resource, NY)

QUESTIONS FOR ANALYSIS

1. How do you account for du Coudray's remarkable success? What does her story suggest about women's lives in this period, both within their families and in the economic realm? What kind of opportunities were available to women?
2. What is painted on the Italian birthing chair where a woman's head would rest during labor? What might this suggest about childbirth in this period?
3. How might the Dutch painting of childbirth shown here differ if painted by a Western artist today?

"Incorrect method of delivery" from du Coudray's *Manual*. (Bibliothèque de la Faculté de Médecine, Paris, France/Archive Charmet/ Bridgeman Images)

training was expensive, physicians came mainly from prosperous families and they usually concentrated on urban patients from similar social backgrounds. Nevertheless, even poor people spent hard-won resources to seek treatment for their loved ones.

Physicians in the eighteenth century were increasingly willing to experiment with new methods, but time-honored practices lay heavily on them. They laid great stress on purging, and bloodletting was still considered a medical cure-all. It was the way "bad blood," the cause of illness, was removed and the balance of humors necessary for good health was restored.

Improvements in Surgery

Long considered to be craftsmen comparable to butchers and barbers, surgeons began studying anatomy seriously and improved their art in the eighteenth century. With endless opportunities to practice, army surgeons on gory battlefields led the way. They learned that a soldier with an extensive wound, such as a shattered leg or arm, could perhaps be saved if the surgeon could obtain a flat surface above the wound that could be cauterized with fire. Thus, if a soldier had a broken limb and the bone stuck out, the surgeon amputated so that the remaining stump could be cauterized and the likelihood of death reduced.

The eighteenth-century surgeon (and patient) labored in the face of incredible difficulties. Almost all operations were performed without painkillers, for the anesthesia of the day was hard to control and too dangerous for general use. Many patients died from the agony and shock of such operations. Surgery was also performed in utterly unsanitary conditions, for there was no knowledge of bacteriology and the nature of infection. The simplest wound treated by a surgeon could fester and lead to death.

Midwifery

Midwives continued to deliver the overwhelming majority of babies throughout the eighteenth century. Trained initially by another woman practitioner — and regulated by a guild in many cities — the midwife primarily assisted in labor and delivering babies. She also treated female problems, such as irregular menstrual cycles, breast-feeding difficulties, infertility, and venereal disease, and ministered to small children.

The midwife orchestrated labor and birth in a woman's world, where friends and relatives assisted the pregnant woman in the familiar surroundings of her own home. The male surgeon (and the husband) rarely entered this female world, because most births, then as now, were normal and spontaneous. After the invention of forceps became publicized in 1734, surgeon-physicians used their monopoly over this and other instruments to seek lucrative new business. Attacking midwives as ignorant and dangerous, they sought to undermine faith in midwives and persuaded growing numbers of wealthy women of the superiority of their services. As one male expert proclaimed:

> A midwife is usually a creature of the lowest class of human beings, and of course utterly destitute of education, who from indigence, and that she is incapable of everything else, has been compelled to follow, as the last and sole resources a profession which people fondly imagine no very difficult one, never dreaming that the least glimpse of previous instruction is required for that purpose. . . . Midwives are universally ignorant. For where or how should she come by any thing deserving the name of knowledge.[31]

Research suggests that women practitioners successfully defended much but not all of their practice in the eighteenth century. One enterprising French midwife, Madame du Coudray, wrote a widely used textbook, *Manual on the Art of Childbirth* (1757), in order to address complaints about incompetent midwives. She then secured royal financing for her campaign to teach birthing techniques. Du Coudray traveled all over France using a life-size model of the female torso and fetus to help teach illiterate women. (See "Living in the Past: Improvements in Childbirth," page 602.) Despite criticism, it appears that midwives generally lost no more babies than did male doctors, who were still summoned to treat non-elite women only when life-threatening situations required surgery.

Women also continued to perform almost all nursing. Female religious orders ran many hospitals, and at-home nursing was almost exclusively the province of women. Thus, although they were excluded from the growing ranks of formally trained and authorized practitioners, women continued to perform the bulk of informal medical care. Nursing as a secular profession did not emerge until the nineteenth century.

The Conquest of Smallpox

Experimentation and the intensified search for solutions to human problems led to some real advances in medicine after 1750. The eighteenth century's greatest medical triumph was the eradication of smallpox. With the progressive decline of bubonic plague, smallpox became the most terrible of the infectious diseases, and it is estimated that 60 million Europeans died of it in the eighteenth century.

The first step in the conquest of this killer in Europe came in the early eighteenth century. An English aristocrat whose beauty had been marred by the pox, Lady Mary Wortley Montagu, learned about the long-

The Wonderful Effects of the New Inoculation!   The talented caricaturist James Gillray satirized widespread anxieties about the smallpox vaccination in this lively image. The discoveries of Edward Jenner a few years prior to Gillray's caricature had led to the adoption of a safer vaccine derived from cowpox. The artist mocks this breakthrough by showing cows bursting from the boils supposedly brought on by the vaccine. (Private Collection/Bridgeman Images)

established practice of smallpox inoculation in the Muslim lands of western Asia while her husband was serving as British ambassador to the Ottoman Empire. She had her own son successfully inoculated with the pus from a smallpox victim and was instrumental in spreading the practice in England after her return in 1722. But inoculation was risky and was widely condemned because about one person in fifty died from it. In addition, people who had been inoculated were infectious and often spread the disease.

While the practice of inoculation with the smallpox virus was refined over the century, the crucial breakthrough was made by Edward Jenner (1749–1823), a talented country doctor. His starting point was the countryside belief that dairymaids who had contracted cowpox did not get smallpox. Cowpox produces sores that resemble those of smallpox, but the disease is mild and is not contagious.

For eighteen years Jenner practiced a kind of Baconian science, carefully collecting data. Finally, in 1796 he performed his first vaccination on a young boy using matter taken from a milkmaid with cowpox.

After performing more successful vaccinations, Jenner published his findings in 1798. The new method of treatment spread rapidly, and smallpox soon declined to the point of disappearance in Europe and then throughout the world.

NOTES

1. Archibald Campbell, Marquis of Argyll, *Instructions to a Son, Containing Rules of Conduct in Publick and Private Life* (Glasgow: E. Foulis, 1743), p. 33.
2. Quoted in J. M. Beattie, "The Criminality of Women in Eighteenth-Century England," *Journal of Social History* 8 (Summer 1975): 86.
3. Quoted in R. Cobb, *The Police and the People: French Popular Protest, 1789–1820* (Oxford: Clarendon Press, 1970), p. 238.
4. Peter Laslett, *Family Life and Illicit Love: Essays in Historical Sociology* (Cambridge: Cambridge University Press, 1977).
5. G. Gullickson, *Spinners and Weavers of Auffay: Rural Industry and the Sexual Division of Labor in a French Village, 1750–1850* (Cambridge: Cambridge University Press, 1986), p. 186.
6. Louis Crompton, *Homosexuality and Civilization* (Cambridge, Mass.: Belknap Press, 2003), p. 321.
7. D. S. Neff, "Bitches, Mollies, and Tommies: Byron, Masculinity and the History of Sexualities," *Journal of the History of Sexuality* 11, no. 3 (July 2002): 404.

8. George E. Haggerty, ed., *Encyclopedia of Gay Histories and Cultures* (New York: Garland Publishing, 2000), pp. 1311–1312.

9. Pier Paolo Viazzo, "Mortality, Fertility, and Family," in *Family Life in Early Modern Times, 1500–1789*, ed. David I. Kertzer and Marzio Barbagli (New Haven, Conn.: Yale University Press, 2001), p. 180.

10. George Sussman, *Selling Mother's Milk: The Wet-Nursing Business in France, 1715–1914* (Urbana: University of Illinois Press, 1982), p. 22.

11. Yves Blayo, "La Mortalité en France de 1740 à 1820," *Population*, special issue 30 (1975): 135.

12. Viazzo, "Mortality, Fertility, and Family," pp. 176–178.

13. Quoted in Matthew Gerber, *Bastards: Politics, Family, and Law in Early Modern France* (Oxford: Oxford University Press, 2012), p. 125.

14. Alysa Levene, "The Estimation of Mortality at the London Foundling Hospital, 1741–99," *Population Studies* 59, no. 1 (2005): 87–97.

15. Quoted in Robert Woods, "Did Montaigne Love His Children? Demography and the Hypothesis of Parental Indifference," *Journal of Interdisciplinary History* 33, no. 3 (2003): 421.

16. Quoted in Gay Ochiltree and Don Edgar, *The Changing Face of Childhood* (Melbourne: Institute of Family Studies, 1981), p. 11.

17. James Van Horn Melton, *Absolutism and the Eighteenth-Century Origins of Compulsory Schooling in Prussia and Austria* (Cambridge: Cambridge University Press, 2003), p. 46.

18. James Van Horn Melton, "The Theresian School Reform of 1774," in *Early Modern Europe*, ed. James B. Collins and Karen L. Taylor (Oxford: Blackwell, 2006).

19. Jeremy Black, *The English Press in the Eighteenth Century* (Philadelphia: University of Pennsylvania Press, 1987), p. 262.

20. Neil McKendrik, John Brewer, and J. H. Plumb, *The Birth of a Consumer Society: The Commercialization of Eighteenth-Century England* (Bloomington: Indiana University Press, 1982).

21. Daniel Roche, *The Culture of Clothing: Dress and Fashion in the Ancien Regime*, trans. Jean Birrell (Cambridge: Cambridge University Press, 1996).

22. Quoted in Cissie Fairchilds, "The Production and Marketing of Populuxe Goods in Eighteenth-Century Paris," in *Consumption and the World of Goods*, ed. John Brewer and Roy Porter (London: Routledge, 1993), p. 228.

23. Quoted in K. Pinson, *Pietism as a Factor in the Rise of German Nationalism* (New York: Columbia University Press, 1934), p. 13.

24. Ibid., pp. 43–44.

25. Quoted in S. Andrews, *Methodism and Society* (London: Longmans, Green, 1970), p. 327.

26. Dale Van Kley, "The Rejuvenation and Rejection of Jansenism in History and Historiography," *French Historical Studies* 29 (Fall 2006): 649–684.

27. David Sabean, *The Power in the Blood: Popular Culture and Village Discourse in Early Modern Germany* (Cambridge: Cambridge University Press, 1984), p. 174.

28. Quoted in I. Woloch, *Eighteenth-Century Europe: Tradition and Progress, 1715–1789* (New York: W. W. Norton, 1982), p. 292.

29. Quoted in T. Tackett, *Priest and Parish in Eighteenth-Century France* (Princeton, N.J.: Princeton University Press, 1977), p. 214.

30. Patrick Wallis, "Exotic Drugs and English Medicine: England's Drug Trade, c. 1550–c. 1800," *Social History of Medicine* 2, no. 1 (2012): 26.

31. Louis Lapeyre, *An Enquiry into the Merits of These Two Important Questions: I. Whether Women with Child Ought to Prefer the Assistance of Their Own Sex to That of Men-Midwives? II. Whether the Assistance of Men-Midwives Is Contrary to Decency?* (London: S. Bladon, 1772), p. 29.

LOOKING BACK LOOKING AHEAD

The fundamental patterns of life in early modern Europe remained very much the same up to the eighteenth century. The vast majority of people lived in the countryside and followed age-old rhythms of seasonal labor in the fields and farmyard. Community ties were close in small villages, where the struggle to prevail over harsh conditions called on all hands to work together and to pray together. The daily life of a peasant in 1700 would have been familiar to his ancestors in the fifteenth century. Indeed, the three orders of society enshrined in the medieval social hierarchy — clergy, nobility, peasantry — were binding legal categories in France up to 1789.

And yet, the economic changes inaugurated in the late seventeenth century — intensive agriculture, cottage industry, the industrious revolution, and colonial expansion — contributed to the profound social and cultural transformation of daily life in eighteenth-century Europe. Men and women of the laboring classes, especially in the cities, experienced change in many facets of their daily lives: in loosened community controls over sex and marriage, rising literacy rates, new goods and new forms of self-expression, and a wave of religious piety that challenged traditional orthodoxies. Lay and secular elites attacked some forms of popular life, but considerable overlap continued between popular and elite culture.

Economic, social, and cultural change would culminate in the late eighteenth century with the outbreak of revolution in the Americas and Europe. Initially led by the elite, political upheavals relied on the enthusiastic participation of the poor and their desire for greater inclusion in the life of the nation. Such movements also encountered resistance from the common people when revolutionaries trampled on their religious faith. For many observers, contemporaries and historians alike, the transformations of the eighteenth century constituted a fulcrum between the old world of hierarchy and tradition and the modern world with its claims to equality and freedom.

Make Connections

Think about the larger developments and continuities within and across chapters.

1. How did the expansion of agriculture and trade (Chapter 17) contribute to changes in daily life in the eighteenth century?

2. What were the main areas of improvement in the lives of the common people in the eighteenth century, and what aspects of life remained unchanged or even deteriorated?

3. How did Enlightenment thought (Chapter 16) affect education, child care, medicine, and religion in the eighteenth century?

18 REVIEW & EXPLORE

Identify Key Terms

Identify and explain the significance of each item below.

community controls (p. 578)   just price (p. 588)

charivari (p. 578)   consumer revolution (p. 589)

illegitimacy explosion (p. 579)   Pietism (p. 598)

wet-nursing (p. 581)   Methodists (p. 599)

blood sports (p. 586)   Jansenism (p. 600)

carnival (p. 588)

Review the Main Ideas

Answer the focus questions from each section of the chapter.

◆ What changes occurred in marriage and the family in the course of the eighteenth century? (p. 576)

◆ What was life like for children, and how did attitudes toward childhood evolve? (p. 580)

◆ How did increasing literacy and new patterns of consumption affect people's lives? (p. 585)

◆ What were the patterns of popular religion, and how did they interact with the worldview of the educated public and their Enlightenment ideals? (p. 596)

◆ How did the practice of medicine evolve in the eighteenth century? (p. 601)

Suggested Reading and Media Resources

BOOKS

- Bergin, Joseph. *Church, Society, and Religious Change in France, 1580–1730.* 2009. A study of changing religious views in France from the wars of religion to the Enlightenment and the interaction of church and society.

- Bongie, Laurence L. *From Rogue to Everyman: A Foundling's Journey to the Bastille.* 2005. The story of an eighteenth-century orphan and, through his eyes, the Parisian underworld of gamblers, prostitutes, and police spies.

- Burke, Peter. *Popular Culture in Early Modern Europe,* 3d ed. 2009. An updated version of a classic introduction to everyday life, mentalities, and leisure pursuits.

- Crawford, Katherine. *European Sexualities, 1400–1800.* 2007. A broad survey of cultural and social aspects of sex and sexuality in early modern Europe.

- Gawthrop, Richard. *Pietism and the Making of Eighteenth-Century Prussia.* 2006. An examination of the importance of Pietist morality and institutions in the making of the Prussian state.

- Gelbart, Nina. *The King's Midwife: A History and Mystery of Madame du Coudray.* 2002. A vivid and accessible biography of the most famous midwife of eighteenth-century France.

- Gerber, Matthew. *Bastards: Politics, Family, and Law in Early Modern France.* 2012. A study of legal disputes over the rights of illegitimate children in France that illuminates the gradual destigmatization of illegitimacy in the eighteenth century.

- Goodman, Dena. *Becoming a Woman in the Age of Letters.* 2009. An exploration of women as writers in the eighteenth century, delving into their use of writing as a form of self-expression and the material culture of desks, pens, and rooms that enabled them to write.

- Kertzer, David I., and Marzio Barbagli, eds. *Family Life in Early Modern Times, 1500–1789.* 2001. A rich collection of essays on the history of the family, women, and children in early modern Europe.

- Kushner, Nina. *Erotic Exchanges: The World of Elite Prostitution in Eighteenth-Century Paris.* 2013. A study of the lives and careers of courtesans in the French capital.

- Trentman, Frank, ed. *The Oxford Handbook of the History of Consumption.* 2012. A series of essays presenting the most recent research on the history of consumption, including global perspectives.

DOCUMENTARIES

- *A History of Private Life* (BBC Radio 4, 2009). A radio documentary series, available on CD, that examines four hundred years of domestic life, drawn from letters and diaries.

- *At Home with the Georgians* (BBC, 2011). A documentary examining the new domestic ideals of the eighteenth century, with re-enactments of daily life in British homes in all ranks of society.

FEATURE FILMS AND TELEVISION

- *Barry Lyndon* (Stanley Kubrick, 1975). The adventures of an eighteenth-century Irish rogue who marries a rich widow.

- *Becoming Jane* (Julian Jarrold, 2007). The early life of famous novelist Jane Austen; mixes fact with fiction to make her the protagonist of a romance in the spirit of her own novels.

- *City of Vice* (Channel 4, 2008). A British crime series focusing on Henry Fielding, the eighteenth-century writer and magistrate who founded the first police force of London, the Bow Street Runners.

- *The Fortunes and Misfortunes of Moll Flanders* (PBS, 1996). A lively Masterpiece Theater adaptation of Daniel Defoe's famous novel recounting an orphaned girl's struggle to survive in eighteenth-century London.

WEB SITES

- *Colonial Williamsburg.* The Web site for Colonial Williamsburg offers many resources for exploring everyday life in the eighteenth century, including an online tour of the historic site, descriptions of the eighteenth-century people and trades, as well as short videos illustrating many aspects of daily life. **http://www.history.org/**

- *London Lives.* A collection of almost 250,000 searchable digitized primary sources about ordinary people in eighteenth-century London, including criminal trials, hospital records, and other documents. **www.londonlives.org/static/Project.jsp**

19
Revolutions in Politics

1775–1815

A great wave of revolution rocked both sides of the Atlantic Ocean in the last decades of the eighteenth century. As trade goods, individuals, and ideas circulated in ever-greater numbers across the Atlantic Ocean, debates and events in one locale soon influenced those in another. As changing social realities challenged the old order of life and Enlightenment ideals of freedom and equality flourished, reformers in many places demanded fundamental changes in politics and government. At the same time, wars fought for dominance of the Atlantic economy left European states weakened by crushing debts, making them vulnerable to calls for reform.

The revolutionary era began in North America in 1775, and the United States of America won freedom from Britain in 1783. Then in 1789, France, the most populous country in western Europe and a center of culture and intellectual life, became the leading revolutionary nation. It established first a constitutional monarchy, then a radical republic, and finally a new empire under Napoleon that would last until 1815. During this period of constant domestic turmoil, French armies brought revolution to much of Europe. Inspired both by the ideals of the Revolution on the continent and by their own experiences and desires, the slaves of Saint-Domingue rose up in 1791. Their rebellion would eventually lead to the creation of the new independent nation of Haiti in 1804. In Europe and its colonies abroad, the age of modern politics was born. ■

CHAPTER PREVIEW

The Taking of the Bastille, July 14, 1789
The French Revolution began on July 14, 1789, when a group of angry Parisians attacked a royal prison on the east side of the city, known as the Bastille. Although only seven prisoners were being held at the time, the prison had become a symbol of despotic rule. (*The Taking of the Bastille, 14 July 1789*/French School/Château de Versailles, France/Bridgeman Images)

Background to Revolution

FOCUS QUESTION *What were the factors leading to the revolutions of the late eighteenth century?*

The origins of the late-eighteenth-century revolutions in British North America, France, and Haiti were complex. No one cause lay behind them, nor was revolution inevitable or certain of success. However, a set of shared factors helped set the stage for revolt. Among them were fundamental social and economic changes and political crises that eroded state authority. Another significant cause of revolutionary fervor was the impact of political ideas derived from the Enlightenment. Even though most Enlightenment writers were cautious about political reform, their confidence in reason and progress helped inspire a new generation to fight for greater freedom from repressive governments. Perhaps most important, financial crises generated by the expenses of imperial warfare brought European states to their knees and allowed abstract discussions of reform to become pressing realities.

Social Change

Eighteenth-century European society was legally divided into groups with special privileges, such as the nobility and the clergy, and groups with special burdens, such as the peasantry. Nobles were the largest landowners, possessing one-quarter of the agricultural land of France, while constituting less than 2 percent of the population. They enjoyed exemption from direct taxation as well as exclusive rights to hunt game, bear swords, and use gold thread in their clothing. In most countries, various middle-class groups—professionals, merchants, and guild masters—enjoyed privileges that allowed them to monopolize all sorts of economic activity. Poor peasants and urban laborers, who constituted the vast majority of the population, bore the brunt of taxation and were excluded from the world of privilege.

Traditional prerogatives persisted in societies undergoing dramatic and destabilizing change. Europe's population rose rapidly after 1750, and its cities and towns swelled in size. Inflation kept pace with population growth, making it ever more difficult to find affordable food and living space. One way the poor kept up, and even managed to participate in the new consumer revolution (see Chapter 18), was by working harder and for longer hours. More women and children entered the paid labor force, challenging the traditional hierarchies and customs of village life.

Economic growth created new inequalities between rich and poor. While the poor struggled with rising prices, investors grew rich from the spread of rural manufacture and overseas trade, including the trade in enslaved Africans and in the products of slave labor. Old distinctions between landed aristocracy and city merchants began to fade as enterprising nobles put money into trade and rising middle-class bureaucrats and merchants purchased landed estates and noble titles. Marriages between proud nobles and wealthy, educated commoners (called the *bourgeoisie* [boor-ZHWAH-zee] in France) served both groups' interests, and a mixed-caste elite began to take shape. In the context of these changes, ancient privileges seemed to pose an intolerable burden to many observers.

Another social change involved the racial regimes established in European colonies to legitimize and protect slavery. By the late eighteenth century European law accepted that only Africans and people of African descent were subject to slavery. Even free people of color—a term for nonslaves of African or mixed African-European descent—were subject to special laws restricting the property they could own, whom they could marry, and what clothes they could wear. Racial privilege conferred a new dimension of entitlement on European settlers in the colonies, and they used extremely brutal methods to enforce it. The contradiction between slavery and the Enlightenment ideals of liberty and equality was all too evident to the enslaved and the free people of color.

Growing Demands for Liberty and Equality

In addition to destabilizing social changes, the ideals of liberty and equality helped fuel revolutions in the Atlantic world. What did these concepts mean to eighteenth-century politicians and other people, and why were they so radical and revolutionary in their day?

The call for liberty was first of all a call for individual human rights. Before the revolutionary period, even the most enlightened monarchs believed they needed to regulate what people wrote and believed. Opposing this long-standing practice, supporters of the cause of individual liberty (who became known as "liberals" in the early nineteenth century) demanded freedom to worship according to the dictates of their consciences, an end to censorship, and freedom from arbitrary laws and from judges who simply obeyed orders from the government. The Declaration of the Rights of Man and of the Citizen, issued at the beginning of the French Revolution, proclaimed that "liberty consists in being able to do anything that does not harm another person." In the context of the monarchical and absolutist forms of government then dominating Europe, this was a truly radical idea.

The call for liberty was also a call for a new kind of government. Reformers believed that the people had sovereignty—that is, that the people alone had the authority to make laws limiting an individual's freedom of action. In practice, this system of government meant choosing legislators who represented the people and were accountable to them. Monarchs might retain their thrones, but their rule should be constrained by the will of the people.

Equality was a more ambiguous idea. Eighteenth-century liberals argued that, in theory, all citizens should have identical rights and liberties and that the nobility had no right to special privileges based on birth. However, they accepted a number of distinctions. First, most eighteenth-century liberals were men of their times, and they generally believed that equality between men and women was neither practical nor desirable. Women played an important political role in the revolutionary movements at several points, but the men who wrote constitutions for the new republics limited formal political rights—the right to vote, to run for office, and to participate in government—to men. Second, few questioned the superiority of people of European descent over those of indigenous or African origin. Even those who believed that the slave trade was unjust and should be abolished usually felt that emancipation was so dangerous that it needed to be an extremely gradual process.

Third, liberals never believed that everyone should be equal economically. Although Thomas Jefferson wrote in an early draft of the American Declaration of Independence that everyone was equal in "the pursuit of property," liberals certainly did not expect equal success in that pursuit. (Jefferson later changed "property" to the more noble-sounding "happiness.") Great differences in fortune between rich and poor were perfectly acceptable. The essential point was that every free white male should have a legally equal chance at economic gain. However limited they appear to modern eyes, these demands for liberty and equality were revolutionary, given that a privileged elite had long existed with little opposition.

The two most important Enlightenment references for late-eighteenth-century liberals were John Locke and the baron de Montesquieu (see Chapter 16). Locke maintained that England's long political tradition rested on "the rights of Englishmen" and on representative government through Parliament. He argued that if a government oversteps its proper function of protecting the natural rights of life, liberty, and private property, it becomes a tyranny. Montesquieu was also inspired by English constitutional history and the

Chronology

1775–1783	American Revolution
1786–1789	Height of French monarchy's financial crisis
1789	Ratification of U.S. Constitution; storming of the Bastille; feudalism abolished in France
1789–1799	French Revolution
1790	Burke publishes *Reflections on the Revolution in France*
1791	Slave insurrection in Saint-Domingue
1792	Wollstonecraft publishes *A Vindication of the Rights of Woman*
1793	Execution of Louis XVI
1793–1794	Robespierre's Reign of Terror
1794	Robespierre deposed and executed; France abolishes slavery in all territories
1794–1799	Thermidorian reaction
1799–1815	Napoleonic era
1804	Haitian republic declares independence
1812	Napoleon invades Russia
1814–1815	Napoleon defeated and exiled

Glorious Revolution of 1688–1689, which placed sovereignty in Parliament (see Chapter 15). He, too, believed that powerful "intermediary groups"—such as the judicial nobility of which he was a proud member—offered the best defense of liberty against despotism.

The belief that representative institutions could defend their liberty and interests appealed powerfully to the educated middle classes. Yet liberal ideas about individual rights and political freedom also appealed to members of the hereditary nobility, at least in western Europe and as formulated by Montesquieu. Representative government did not mean democracy, which liberal thinkers tended to equate with mob rule. Rather, they envisioned voting for representatives as being restricted to men who owned property—those with "a stake in society." The blurring of practical distinctions between landed aristocrats and wealthy commoners meant that there was no clear-cut opposition between nobles and non-nobles on political issues.

Revolutions thus began with aspirations for equality and liberty among the social elite. Soon, however, dissenting voices emerged as some revolutionaries became frustrated with the limitations of liberal notions of equality and liberty and clamored for a fuller realization of these concepts. Depending on location, their demands included universal male suffrage, political rights for women and free people of color, the emancipation

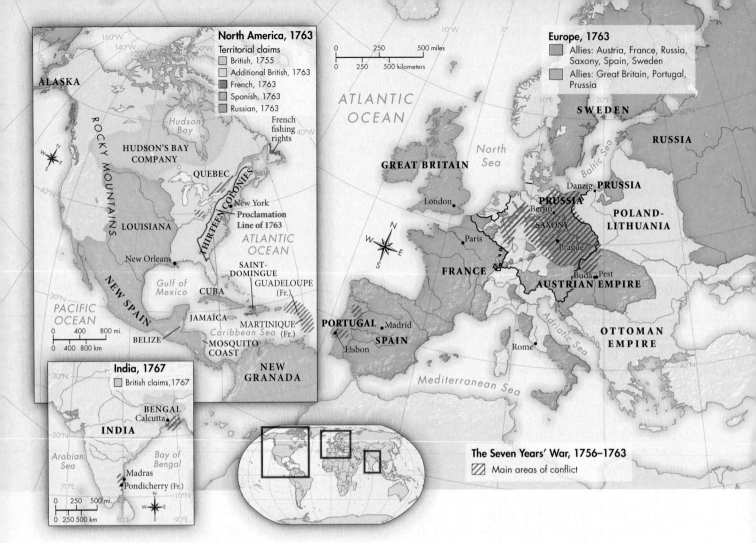

MAP 19.1 The Seven Years' War in Europe, North America, and India, 1755–1763 As a result of the war, France lost its vast territories in North America and India. In an effort to avoid costly conflicts with Native Americans living in the newly conquered territory, the British government in 1763 prohibited colonists from settling west of the Appalachian Mountains. One of the few remaining French colonies in the Americas, Saint-Domingue (on the island of Hispaniola) was the most profitable plantation colony in the New World.

of slaves, and government regulations to reduce economic inequality. The age of revolution was thus marked by bitter conflicts over how far reform should go and to whom it should apply.

The Seven Years' War

The roots of revolutionary ideas could be found in Enlightenment texts, but it was by no means inevitable that their ideas would result in revolution. Many members of the educated elite were satisfied with the status quo or too intimidated to challenge it. Instead, events — political, economic, and military — created crises that opened the door for the development of radical thought and action. One of the most important was the global conflict known as the Seven Years' War (1756–1763).

The war's battlefields stretched from central Europe to India to North America (where the conflict was

known as the French and Indian War), pitting a new alliance of England and Prussia against the French, Austrians, and, later, Spanish. Its origins were in conflicts left unresolved at the end of the War of the Austrian Succession in 1748 (see Chapter 16), during which Prussia seized the Austrian territory of Silesia. In central Europe, Austria's Maria Theresa vowed to win back Silesia and to crush Prussia, thereby re-establishing the Habsburgs' traditional leadership in German affairs. By the end of the Seven Years' War, Maria Theresa had almost succeeded, but Prussia survived with its boundaries intact.

Unresolved tensions also lingered in North America, particularly regarding the border between the French and British colonies. The encroachment of English settlers into territory claimed by the French in the Ohio Valley resulted in skirmishes that soon became war. Although the inhabitants of New France were greatly outnumbered — Canada counted 55,000 inhabitants, compared to 1.2 million in the thirteen English colonies—French forces achieved major victories until 1758. Both sides relied on the participation of Native American tribes with whom they had long-standing trading contacts and actively sought new indigenous allies during the conflict. The tide of the conflict turned when the British diverted resources from the war in Europe, using superior sea power to destroy France's fleet and choke its commerce around the world. In 1759 the British laid siege to Quebec for four long months, finally defeating the French in a battle that sealed the nation's fate in North America.

British victory on all colonial fronts was ratified in the 1763 Treaty of Paris. Canada and all French territory east of the Mississippi River passed to Britain, and France ceded Louisiana to Spain as compensation for Spain's loss of Florida to Britain. France also gave up most of its holdings in India, opening the way to British dominance on the subcontinent (Map 19.1).

By 1763 Britain had realized its goal of monopolizing a vast trading and colonial empire, but at a tremendous cost in war debt. France emerged from the conflict humiliated and broke, but with its profitable Caribbean colonies intact. In the aftermath of war, both British and French governments had to raise taxes to repay loans, raising a storm of protest and demands for fundamental reform. Since the Caribbean colony of Saint-Domingue remained French, political turmoil in the mother country would directly affect its population. The seeds of revolutionary conflict in the Atlantic world were thus sown.

Commemorative Teapot   Manufacturers were quick to bring products to the market celebrating weighty political events, like this British teapot heralding "Stamp Act Repeal'd." By purchasing such items, ordinary people could champion political causes of the day and bring public affairs into their private lives. (Made by the Cockhill Pit Factory, 1766/ © Peabody Essex Museum, Salem, Massachusetts, USA/Bridgeman Images)

The American Revolutionary Era, 1775–1789

FOCUS QUESTION *Why and how did American colonists forge a new, independent nation?*

Increased taxes and government control were a crucial factor behind colonial protests in the New World, where the era of liberal political revolution began. After revolting against their home country, the thirteen mainland colonies of British North America succeeded in establishing a new unified government. Participants in the revolution believed they were demanding only the traditional rights of English men and women. But those traditional rights were liberal rights, and in the American context they had strong democratic and popular overtones. Thus the American Revolution was fought in the name of ideals that were still quite radical for their time. In founding a government based on liberal principles, the Americans set an example that would have a forceful impact on France and its colonies. Yet the revolution did not resolve the question of social and political equality, which eluded the enslaved, women, free blacks, and indigenous people.

The Origins of the Revolution

The high cost of the Seven Years' War doubled the British national debt. Anticipating further expenses to defend the half a billion acres in new territory granted by the Treaty of Paris, the government in London imposed bold new administrative measures. Breaking with a tradition of loose colonial oversight, the British announced that they would maintain a large army in North America and tax the colonies directly. In 1765 Parliament passed the Stamp Act, which levied taxes on a long list of commercial and legal documents, diplomas, newspapers, almanacs, and playing cards. A stamp glued to each article indicated that the tax had been paid.

These measures seemed perfectly reasonable to the British, for a much heavier stamp tax already existed in Britain, and proceeds from the tax were to fund the defense of the colonies. Nonetheless, the colonists vigorously protested the Stamp Act by rioting and by boycotting British goods. Thus Parliament reluctantly repealed it.

Another area of contention was settlement of the new territory acquired by the Treaty of Paris. At the end of the Seven Years' War, land-squeezed settlers quickly moved west across the Appalachian Mountains into the Ohio Valley, sparking conflict with the Ottawa and other tribes already present in the region as well as remaining French settlers. To prevent costly wars in distant territory, the British government in 1763 issued a royal proclamation prohibiting colonists to settle west of the Appalachian Mountains. The so-called Proclamation Line did little to stem land speculation and the flow of migrants, but it did exacerbate suspicion and tensions between Britain and its colony. These disputes raised important political questions. To what extent could the British government reassert its power while limiting the authority of elected colonial bodies? Who had the right to make laws for Americans? The British government replied that Americans were represented in Parliament, albeit indirectly (like most British people), and that Parliament ruled throughout the empire. Many Americans felt otherwise. In the words of John Adams, a major proponent of colonial independence, "A Parliament of Great Britain can have no more rights to tax the colonies than a Parliament of Paris." Thus British colonial administration and parliamentary supremacy came to appear as unacceptable threats to existing American liberties.

Americans' resistance to these threats was fed by the great degree of independence they had long enjoyed. In British North America, unlike in England and Europe, no powerful established church existed, and religious freedom was taken for granted. Colonial assemblies made the important laws, which were seldom overturned by the British government. Also, the right to vote was much more widespread than in England. In many parts of colonial Massachusetts, for example, as many as 95 percent of adult males could vote.

Moreover, greater political equality was matched by greater social and economic equality, at least for the free white population. No hereditary nobility exercised privileges over peasants and other social groups. Instead, independent farmers dominated colonial society. This was particularly true in the northern colonies, where the revolution originated.

In 1773 disputes over taxes and representation flared up again. Under the Tea Act of that year, the British government permitted the financially hard-pressed East India Company to ship tea from China directly to its agents in the colonies, rather than through London middlemen, who sold to independent merchants in the colonies. Thus the company secured a profitable monopoly on the tea trade, and colonial merchants were excluded. The price on tea was actually lowered for colonists, but the act generated a great deal of opposition because of its impact on local merchants.

In protest, Boston men disguised as Native Americans staged a rowdy protest (later called the "Tea Party") by boarding East India Company ships and throwing tea from them into the harbor. In response, the so-called Coercive Acts of 1774 closed the port of Boston, curtailed local elections, and expanded the royal governor's power. County conventions in Massachusetts urged that the acts be "rejected as the attempts of a wicked administration to enslave America." Other colonial assemblies joined in the denunciations. In September 1774 the First Continental Congress—consisting of colonial delegates who sought at first to peacefully resolve conflicts with Britain—met in Philadelphia. The more radical members of this assembly argued successfully against concessions to the English crown. The British Parliament also rejected compromise, and in April 1775 fighting between colonial and British troops began at Lexington and Concord.

Independence from Britain

As fighting spread, the colonists moved slowly toward open calls for independence. The uncompromising attitude of the British government and its use of German mercenaries did much to dissolve loyalties to the home country and to unite the separate colonies. *Common Sense* (1775), a brilliant attack by the recently arrived English radical Thomas Paine (1737–1809), also mobilized public opinion in favor of independence. A runaway bestseller with sales of 120,000 copies in a few months, Paine's tract ridiculed the idea of a small island ruling a great continent. In his call for freedom and republican government, Paine expressed Americans' growing sense of separateness and moral superiority.

On July 4, 1776, the Second Continental Congress adopted the Declaration of Independence. Written by Thomas Jefferson and others, this document boldly listed the tyrannical acts committed by George III (r. 1760–1820) and confidently proclaimed the natural rights of mankind and the sovereignty of the American states. The Declaration of Independence in effect universalized the traditional rights of English people and made them the rights of all mankind. It stated that "all Men are created equal, that they are endowed by their Creator with certain unalienable Rights, that among these are Life, Liberty, and the Pursuit of Happiness." No other American political document has ever caused such excitement, either at home or abroad.

After the Declaration of Independence, the conflict often took the form of a civil war pitting patriots against Loyalists, those who maintained an allegiance to the Crown. The Loyalists, who numbered up to 20 percent of the total white population, tended to be wealthy and politically moderate. They were small in number in New England and Virginia, but more common in the Deep South and on the western frontier. British commanders also recruited Loyalists from enslaved people by promising freedom to any slave who left his master to fight for the mother country.

Many wealthy patriots—such as John Hancock and George Washington—willingly allied themselves with farmers and artisans in a broad coalition. This coalition harassed the Loyalists and confiscated their property to help pay for the war, causing 60,000 to 80,000 of them to flee, mostly to Canada. The broad social base of the revolutionaries tended to make the revolution democratic. State governments extended the right to vote to many more men, including free African American men in many cases, but not to women.

On the international scene, the French wanted revenge against the British for the humiliating defeats of the Seven Years' War. Thus they sympathized with the rebels and supplied guns and gunpowder from the beginning of the conflict. By 1777 French volunteers were arriving in Virginia, and a dashing young nobleman, the marquis de Lafayette (1757–1834), quickly became one of the most trusted generals of George Washington, who was commanding American troops. In 1778 the French government offered a formal alliance to the American ambassador in Paris, Benjamin Franklin, and in 1779 and 1780 the Spanish and Dutch declared war on Britain. Catherine the Great of Russia helped organize the League of Armed Neutrality to protect neutral shipping rights and succeeded in hampering Britain's naval power.

Thus by 1780 Britain was engaged in a war against most of Europe as well as the thirteen colonies. In these circumstances, and in the face of severe reverses in India, in the West Indies, and at Yorktown in Virginia, a new British government decided to cut its losses and end the war. American officials in Paris were receptive to negotiating a deal with England alone, for they feared that France wanted a treaty that would bottle up the new nation east of the Appalachian Mountains and give British holdings west of the Appalachians to France's ally, Spain. Thus the American negotiators deserted their French allies and accepted the extraordinarily favorable terms Britain offered.

Under the Treaty of Paris of 1783, Britain recognized the independence of the thirteen colonies and ceded all its territory between the Allegheny Mountains and the Mississippi River to the Americans. Out of the bitter rivalries of the Old World, the Americans snatched dominion over a vast territory.

Framing the Constitution

The liberal program of the American Revolution was consolidated by the federal Constitution, the Bill of Rights, and the creation of a national republic. Assembling in Philadelphia in the summer of 1787, the delegates to the Constitutional Convention were determined to end the period of economic depression, social uncertainty, and leadership under a weak central government that had followed independence. The delegates thus decided to grant the federal, or central, government important powers: regulation of domestic and foreign trade, the right to tax, and the means to enforce its laws.

Strong rule would be placed squarely in the context of representative self-government. Senators and congressmen would be the lawmaking delegates of the

The American Revolution

1765	Britain passes the Stamp Act
1773	Britain passes the Tea Act
1774	Britain passes the Coercive Acts in response to the Tea Party in the colonies; the First Continental Congress refuses concessions to the English crown
April 1775	Fighting begins between colonial and British troops
July 4, 1776	Second Continental Congress adopts the Declaration of Independence
1777–1780	The French, Spanish, and Dutch side with the colonists against Britain
1783	Treaty of Paris recognizes the independence of the American colonies
1787	U.S. Constitution is signed
1791	The first ten amendments to the Constitution (the Bill of Rights) are ratified

voters, and the president of the republic would be an elected official. The central government would operate in Montesquieu's framework of checks and balances, under which authority was distributed across three different branches — the executive, legislative, and judicial branches — that would prevent one interest from gaining too much power. The power of the federal government would in turn be checked by that of the individual states.

When the results of the Constitutional Convention were presented to the states for ratification, a great public debate began. The opponents of the proposed Constitution — the Antifederalists — charged that the framers of the new document had taken too much power from the individual states and made the federal government too strong. Moreover, many Antifederalists feared for the individual freedoms for which they had fought. To overcome these objections, the Federalists promised to spell out these basic freedoms as soon as the new Constitution was adopted. The result was the first ten amendments to the Constitution, which the first Congress passed shortly after it met in New York in March 1789. These amendments, ratified in 1791, formed an effective Bill of Rights to safeguard the individual. Most of them — trial by jury, due process of law, the right to assemble, freedom from unreasonable search — had their origins in English law and the English Bill of Rights of 1689. Other rights — the freedoms of speech, the press, and religion — reflected natural-law theory and the strong value colonists had placed on independence from the start.

Abigail Adams, "Remember the Ladies"

Abigail Adams wrote many letters to her husband, John Adams, during the long years of separation imposed by his political career. In March 1776 he was serving in the Continental Congress in Philadelphia as Abigail and their children experienced the British siege of Boston and a smallpox epidemic. This letter, written from the family farm in Braintree, Massachusetts, combines news from home with pressing questions about the military and political situation, and a call to "Remember the Ladies" when drafting a new constitution.

March 31, 1776

I wish you would ever write me a Letter half as long as I write you; and tell me if you may where your Fleet are gone? What sort of Defence Virginia can make against our common Enemy? Whether it is so situated as to make an able Defence? . . .

Do not you want to see Boston; I am fearful of the smallpox, or I should have been in before this time. I got Mr. Crane to go to our House and see what state it was in. I find it has been occupied by one of the Doctors of a Regiment, very dirty, but no other damage has been done to it. The few things which were left in it are all gone. . . .

I feel very differently at the approach of spring to what I did a month ago. We knew not then whether we could plant or sow with safety, whether when we had toiled we could reap the fruits of our own industry, whether we could rest in our own Cottages, or whether we should not be driven from the sea coasts to seek shelter in the wilderness, but now we feel as if we might sit under our own vine and eat the good of the land. . . .

I long to hear that you have declared an independency— and by the way in the new Code of Laws which I suppose it will be necessary for you to make I desire you would Remember the Ladies, and be more generous and favorable to them than your ancestors. Do not put such unlimited power in the hands of the Husbands. Remember all men would be tyrants if they could. If particular care and attention is not paid to the Ladies we are determined to foment a Rebellion, and will not hold ourselves bound by any Laws in which we have no voice, or Representation.

That your Sex are Naturally Tyrannical is a Truth so thoroughly established as to admit of no dispute, but such of you as wish to be happy willingly give up the harsh title of Master for the more tender and endearing one of Friend. Why then, not put it out of the power of the vicious and the Lawless to use us with cruelty and indignity with impunity. Men of Sense in all Ages abhor those customs which treat us only as the vassals of your Sex. Regard us then as beings placed by providence under your protection and in imitation of the Supreme Being make use of that power only for our happiness.

EVALUATE THE EVIDENCE

1. What does Adams's letter suggest about her relationship with her husband and the role of women in the family in this period?
2. What does Adams's letter tell us about what it was like to live through the American Revolution and how a woman might perceive the new liberties demanded by colonists?

Source: Letter from Abigail Adams to John Adams, 31 March–5 April 1776 (electronic edition), *Adams Family Papers: An Electronic Archive*, Massachusetts Historical Society, http://www.masshist.org/digitaladams/. Used by permission.

Limitations of Liberty and Equality

The American Constitution and the Bill of Rights exemplified the strengths and the limits of what came to be called classical liberalism. Liberty meant individual freedoms and political safeguards. Liberty also meant representative government, but it did not mean democracy, with its principle of one person, one vote. Equality meant equality before the law, not equality of political participation or wealth. It did not mean equal rights for slaves, indigenous peoples, or women.

A vigorous abolitionist movement during the 1780s led to the passage of emancipation laws in all northern states, but slavery remained prevalent in the South, and discord between pro- and antislavery delegates roiled the Constitutional Convention of 1787. The result was a compromise stipulating that an enslaved person would count as three-fifths of a person in tallying population numbers for taxation and proportional representation in the House of Representatives. This solution levied higher taxes on the South, but also guaranteed slaveholding states greater representation in Congress, which they used to oppose emancipation. Congress did ban slavery in federal territory in 1789, then the export of slaves from any state, and finally, in 1808, the import of slaves to any state.

The new republic also failed to protect the Native American tribes whose lands fell within or alongside the territory ceded by Britain at the Treaty of Paris. The 1787 Constitution promised protection to Native Americans and guaranteed that their land would not be taken without consent. Nonetheless, the federal government forced tribes to concede their land for meager returns; state governments and the rapidly expanding population paid even less heed to the Constitution and often simply seized Native American land for new settlements.

Although lacking the voting rights enjoyed by so many of their husbands and fathers in the relatively democratic colonial assemblies, women played a vital role in the American Revolution. As household provisioners, women were essential participants in boycotts of British goods, like tea, which squeezed profits from British merchants and fostered the revolutionary spirit. After the outbreak of war, women raised funds for the Continental Army and took care of homesteads, workshops, and other businesses when their men went off to fight. Yet despite Abigail Adams's plea to her husband, John Adams, that the framers of the Declaration of Independence should "remember the ladies," women did not receive the right to vote in the new Constitution, an omission confirmed by a clause added in 1844. (See "Evaluating the Evidence 19.1: Abigail Adams, 'Remember the Ladies,'" at left.)

Revolution in France, 1789–1791

FOCUS QUESTION *How did the events of 1789 result in a constitutional monarchy in France, and what were the consequences?*

No country felt the consequences of the American Revolution more deeply than France. Hundreds of French officers served in America and were inspired by the experience. The most famous of these, the young and impressionable marquis de Lafayette, left home as a great aristocrat determined to fight France's traditional foe, England. He returned with a love of liberty and firm republican convictions. French intellectuals engaged in passionate analysis of the federal Constitution as well as the constitutions of the various states of the new United States. The American Revolution undeniably fueled dissatisfaction with the old monarchical order in France. Yet the French Revolution did not mirror the American example. It was more radical and more complex, more influential and more controversial, more loved and more hated. For Europeans and most of the rest of the world, it was the great revolution of the eighteenth century, the revolution that opened the modern era in politics.

Breakdown of the Old Order

As did the American Revolution, the French Revolution had its immediate origins in the government's financial difficulties. The efforts of the ministers of King Louis XV (r. 1715–1774) to raise taxes to meet the expenses of the War of the Austrian Succession and the

Seven Years' War were thwarted by the high courts, known as the parlements. The noble judges of the parlements resented the Crown's threat to their exemption from taxation and decried the government's actions as a form of royal despotism.

When renewed efforts to reform the tax system similarly failed in 1776, the government was forced to finance its enormous expenditures during the American war with borrowed money. As a result, the national debt soared. In 1786 the finance minister informed the timid king Louis XVI that the nation was on the verge of bankruptcy. Fully 50 percent of France's annual budget went to interest payments on the ever-increasing debt. Another 25 percent went to maintain the military, while 6 percent was absorbed by the royal family and the court at Versailles. Less than 20 percent of the national budget served the productive functions of the state, such as transportation and general administration.

Unlike England, which had a far larger national debt relative to its population, France had no central bank and no paper currency. Therefore, when a depressed economy and a lack of public confidence made it increasingly difficult for the government to obtain new loans, the government could not respond simply by printing more money. It had no alternative but to try increasing taxes. Because France's tax system was unfair and out-of-date, increased revenues were possible only through fundamental reforms. Such reforms, which would affect all groups in France's complex and fragmented society, were guaranteed to create social and political unrest.

Financial crisis struck a monarchy that had lost much of its mantle of royal authority. Louis XV scandalized the country with a series of mistresses of low social origins. To make things worse, he refused to take communion because his adultery placed him in a state of sin. The king was being stripped of the sacred aura of God's anointed on earth (a process called desacralization) and was being reinvented in the popular imagination as a degenerate. Maneuverings among political factions at court further distracted the king and prevented decisive action from his government.

Despite the progressive desacralization of the monarchy, Louis XV would probably have prevailed had he lived longer, but he died in 1774. The new king, Louis XVI (r. 1774–1792), was a shy twenty-year-old with good intentions. Taking the throne, he is reported to have said, "What I should like most is to be loved."[1] The eager-to-please monarch Louis waffled on political reform and the economy, and proved unable to quell the rising storm of opposition.

The Formation of the National Assembly

Spurred by a depressed economy and falling tax receipts, Louis XVI's minister of finance revived old proposals to impose a general tax on all landed property as

The Awakening of the Third Estate
This cartoon from July 1789 represents the third estate as a common man throwing off his chains and rising up against his oppression, as the first estate (the clergy) and the second estate (the nobility) look on in fear. (*The Awakening of the Third Estate, July 1789*/French School/colored engraving/Musée de la Ville de Paris, Musée Carnavalet, Paris, France/Bridgeman Images)

well as to form provincial assemblies to help administer the tax, and he convinced the king to call an assembly of notables in 1787 to gain support for the idea. The assembled notables, mainly aristocrats and high-ranking clergy, declared that such sweeping tax changes required the approval of the **Estates General**, the representative body of all three estates, which had not met since 1614.

Facing imminent bankruptcy, the king tried to reassert his authority. He dismissed the notables and established new taxes by decree. The judges of the Parlement of Paris promptly declared the royal initiative null and void. When the king tried to exile the judges, a tremendous wave of protest swept the country. Frightened investors refused to advance more loans to the state. Finally in July 1788, a beaten Louis XVI bowed to public opinion and called for the Estates General. Absolute monarchy was collapsing.

As its name indicates, the Estates General was a legislative body with representatives from the three orders, or **estates**, of society: the clergy, nobility, and everyone else. Following centuries-old tradition, each estate met separately to elect delegates, first at a local and then at a regional level. Results of the elections reveal the mindset of each estate on the eve of the Revolution. The local assemblies of the clergy, representing the first estate, elected mostly parish priests rather than church leaders, demonstrating their dissatisfaction with the church hierarchy. The nobility, or second estate, voted in a

majority of conservatives, primarily from the provinces, where nobles were less wealthy, more devout, and more numerous. Nonetheless, fully one-third of noble representatives were liberals committed to major changes. Commoners of the third estate, who constituted over 95 percent of the population, elected primarily lawyers and government officials to represent them, with few delegates representing business and the poor.

The petitions for change drafted by the assemblies showed a surprising degree of consensus about the key issues confronting the realm. In all three estates, voices spoke in favor of replacing absolutism with a constitutional monarchy in which laws and taxes would require the consent of the Estates General in regular meetings. There was also the strong feeling that individual liberties would have to be guaranteed by law and that economic regulations should be loosened.

On May 5, 1789, the twelve hundred delegates of the three estates gathered in Versailles for the opening session of the Estates General. Despite widespread hopes for serious reform, the Estates General quickly deadlocked over the issue of voting procedures. Controversy had begun during the electoral process itself, when the government confirmed that, following precedent, each estate should meet and vote separately. During the lead-up to the Estates General, critics had demanded a single assembly dominated by the third estate. In his famous pamphlet *What Is the Third Estate?* the abbé Emmanuel Joseph Sieyès (himself a member of the first estate) argued that the nobility was a tiny, overprivileged minority and that the third estate constituted the true strength of the French nation. (See "Evaluating the Evidence 19.2: Abbé Sieyès, *What Is the Third Estate?*" page 622.) The government granted the third estate as many delegates as the clergy and the nobility combined, but then nullified the reform by

■ **Estates General** A legislative body in prerevolutionary France made up of representatives of each of the three classes, or estates. It was called into session in 1789 for the first time since 1614.

■ **estates** The three legal categories, or orders, of France's inhabitants: the clergy, the nobility, and everyone else.

■ **National Assembly** The first French revolutionary legislature, made up primarily of representatives of the third estate and a few from the nobility and clergy, in session from 1789 to 1791.

The Tennis Court Oath, June 20, 1789 Painted two years after the event shown, this dramatic painting by Jacques-Louis David depicts a crucial turning point in the early days of the Revolution. On June 20 delegates of the third estate arrived at their meeting hall in the Versailles palace to find the doors closed and guarded. Fearing the king was about to dissolve their meeting by force, the deputies reassembled at a nearby indoor tennis court and swore a solemn oath not to disperse until they had been recognized as the National Assembly. (Musée de la Ville de Paris, Musée Carnavalet, Paris/Bridgeman Images)

granting one vote per estate instead of one vote per person. This meant that the two privileged estates could always outvote the third.

In angry response, in June 1789 delegates of the third estate refused to meet until the king ordered the clergy and nobility to sit with them in a single body. On June 17 the third estate, which had been joined by a few parish priests, voted to call itself the **National Assembly**. On June 20, excluded from their hall because of "repairs," the delegates moved to a large indoor tennis court where they swore the famous Tennis Court Oath, pledging not to disband until they had been recognized as a national assembly and had written a new constitution.

The king's response was disastrously ambivalent. On June 23 he made a conciliatory speech urging reforms, and four days later he ordered the three estates to meet together. At the same time, Louis apparently followed the advice of relatives and court nobles who urged him to dissolve the Assembly by force. The king

called an army of eighteen thousand troops toward the capital to bring the delegates under control, and on July 11 he dismissed his finance minister and other more liberal ministers. It appeared that the monarchy was prepared to use violence to restore its control.

Popular Uprising and the Rights of Man

While delegates at Versailles were pressing for political rights, economic hardship gripped the common people. Conditions were already tough, due to the government's disastrous financial situation. A poor grain harvest in 1788 caused the price of bread to soar, and inflation spread quickly through the economy. As a result, demand for manufactured goods collapsed, and many artisans and small traders lost work. In Paris perhaps 150,000 of the city's 600,000 people were unemployed by July 1789.

Against this background of poverty and political crisis, the people of Paris entered decisively onto the

Abbé Sieyès, *What Is the Third Estate?*

In the flood of pamphlets that appeared after Louis XVI's call for a meeting of the Estates General, the most influential was written in 1789 by a Catholic priest named Emmanuel Joseph Sieyès. In "What Is the Third Estate?" the abbé Sieyès vigorously condemned the system of privilege that lay at the heart of French society. The term privilege *combined the Latin words for "private" and "law." In Old Regime France, no one set of laws applied to all; over time, the monarchy had issued a series of particular laws, or privileges, that enshrined special rights and entitlements for select individuals and groups. Noble privileges were among the weightiest.*

Sieyès rejected this entire system of legal and social inequality. Deriding the nobility as a foreign parasite, he argued that the common people of the third estate, who did most of the work and paid most of the taxes, constituted the true nation. His pamphlet galvanized public opinion and played an important role in convincing representatives of the third estate to proclaim themselves a "National Assembly" in June 1789. Sieyès later helped bring Napoleon Bonaparte to power, abandoning the radicalism of 1789 for an authoritarian regime.

1. What is the Third Estate? Everything.
2. What has it been until now in the political order? Nothing.
3. What does it want? To become something.

. . . What is a Nation? A body of associates living under a *common* law and represented by the same *legislature.*

Is it not more than certain that the noble order has privileges, exemptions, and even rights that are distinct from the rights of the great body of citizens? Because of this, it [the noble order] does not belong to the common order, it is not covered by the law common to the rest. Thus its civil rights already make it a people apart inside the great Nation. It is truly *imperium in imperio* [a law unto itself].

As for its *political* rights, the nobility also exercises them separately. It has its own representatives who have no mandate from the people. Its deputies sit separately, and even when they assemble in the same room with the deputies of the ordinary citizens, the nobility's representation still remains essentially distinct and separate: it is foreign to the Nation by its very principle, for its mission

does not emanate from the people, and by its purpose, since it consists in defending, not the general interest, but the private interests of the nobility.

The Third Estate therefore contains everything that pertains to the Nation and nobody outside of the Third Estate can claim to be part of the Nation. What is the Third Estate? EVERYTHING. . . .

By Third Estate is meant the collectivity of citizens who belong to the common order. Anybody who holds a legal privilege of any kind leaves that common order, stands as an exception to the common law, and in consequence does not belong to the Third Estate. . . . It is certain that the moment a citizen acquires privileges contrary to common law, he no longer belongs to the common order. His new interest is opposed to the general interest; he has no right to vote in the name of the people. . . .

In vain can anyone's eyes be closed to the revolution that time and the force of things have brought to pass; it is none the less real. Once upon a time the Third Estate was in bondage and the noble order was everything that mattered. Today the Third is everything and nobility but a word. Yet under the cover of this word a new and intolerable aristocracy has slipped in, and the people has every reason to no longer want aristocrats. . . .

What is the will of a Nation? It is the result of individual wills, just as the Nation is the aggregate of the individuals who compose it. It is impossible to conceive of a legitimate association that does not have for its goal the common security, the common liberty, in short, the public good. No doubt each individual also has his own personal aims. He says to himself, "protected by the common security, I will be able to peacefully pursue my own personal projects, I will seek my happiness where I will, assured of encountering only those legal obstacles that society will prescribe for the common interest, in which I have a part, and with which my own personal interest is so usefully allied." . . .

Advantages which differentiate citizens from one another lie outside the purview of citizenship. Inequalities of wealth or ability are like the inequalities of age, sex, size, etc. In no way do they detract from the *equality* of citizenship. These individual advantages no doubt benefit from the protection of the law; but it is not the legislator's

---

revolutionary stage. They believed that, to survive, they should have steady work and enough bread at fair prices. They also feared that the dismissal of the king's liberal finance minister would put them at the mercy of aristocratic landowners and grain speculators. At the beginning of July, knowledge spread of the massing of troops near Paris. On July 14, 1789, several hundred people

stormed the Bastille (ba-STEEL), a royal prison, to obtain weapons for the city's defense. Faced with popular violence, Louis soon announced the reinstatement of his finance minister and the withdrawal of troops from Paris. The National Assembly was now free to continue its work.

Just as the laboring poor of Paris had decisively intervened in the revolution, the struggling French

task to create them, to give privileges to some and refuse them to others. The law grants nothing; it protects what already exists until such time that what exists begins to harm the common interest. These are the only limits on individual freedom. I imagine the law as being at the center of a large globe; we the citizens without exception, stand equidistant from it on the surface and occupy equal places; all are equally dependent on the law, all present it with their liberty and their property to be protected; and this is what I call the *common rights* of citizens, by which they are all alike. All these individuals communicate with each other, enter into contracts, negotiate, always under the common guarantee of the law. If in this general activity somebody wishes to get control over the person of his neighbor or usurp his property, the common law goes into action to repress this criminal attempt and puts everyone back in their place at the same distance from the law. . . .

It is impossible to say what place the two privileged orders [the clergy and the nobility] ought to occupy in the social order: this is the equivalent of asking what place one wishes to assign to a malignant tumor that torments and undermines the strength of the body of a sick person. It must be *neutralized*. We must re-establish the health and working of all organs so thoroughly that they are no longer susceptible to these fatal schemes that are capable of sapping the most essential principles of vitality.

EVALUATE THE EVIDENCE

1. What criticism of noble privileges does Sieyès offer? Why does he believe nobles are "foreign" to the nation?
2. How does Sieyès define the nation, and why does he believe that the third estate constitutes the nation?
3. What relationship between citizens and the law does Sieyès envision? What limitations on the law does he propose?

Source: Excerpt from pp. 65–70 in *The French Revolution and Human Rights: A Brief Documentary History*, edited, translated, and with an introduction by Lynn Hunt. Copyright © 1996 by Bedford Books of St. Martin's Press. Used by permission of the publisher.

peasantry also took matters into their own hands. Peasants bore the brunt of state taxation, church tithes, and noble privileges. Since most did not own enough land to be self-sufficient, they were hard-hit by the rising price of bread. In the summer of 1789, throughout France peasants began to rise in insurrection against their lords, ransacking manor houses and burning

feudal documents that recorded their obligations. In some areas peasants reoccupied common lands enclosed by landowners and seized forests. Fear of marauders and vagabonds hired by vengeful landlords—called the **Great Fear** by contemporaries—seized the rural poor and fanned the flames of rebellion.

Faced with chaos, the National Assembly responded to the swell of popular uprising with a surprise maneuver on the night of August 4, 1789. By a decree of the Assembly, all the old noble privileges—peasant serfdom where it still existed, exclusive hunting rights, fees for having legal cases judged in the lord's court, the right to make peasants work on the roads, and a host of other dues—were abolished along with the tithes paid to the church. From this point on, French peasants would seek mainly to protect and consolidate this victory.

The Great Fear, 1789

On August 27, 1789, the Assembly further issued the Declaration of the Rights of Man and of the Citizen. This clarion call of the liberal revolutionary ideal guaranteed equality before the law, representative government for a sovereign people, and individual freedom. This revolutionary credo, only two pages long, was disseminated throughout France and the rest of Europe and around the world.

The National Assembly's declaration had little practical effect for the poor and hungry people of France. The economic crisis worsened after the fall of the Bastille, as aristocrats fled the country and the luxury market collapsed. Foreign markets also shrank, and unemployment among the urban working classes grew. In addition, women—the traditional managers of food and resources in poor homes—could no longer look to the church, which had been stripped of its tithes, for aid.

On October 5 some seven thousand women marched the twelve miles from Paris to Versailles to demand action. This great crowd, "armed with scythes, sticks and pikes," invaded the National Assembly. Interrupting a delegate's speech, an old woman defiantly shouted into the debate, "Who's that talking down there? Make the chatterbox shut up. That's not the point: the point is that we want bread."[2] Hers was the genuine voice of the people, essential to any understanding of the French Revolution. The women invaded the royal apartments, killed some of the royal bodyguards, and searched for the queen, Marie

■ **Great Fear** The fear of noble reprisals against peasant uprisings that seized the French countryside and led to further revolt.

The Figure of Liberty In this painting, the figure of Liberty bears a copy of the Declaration of the Rights of Man and of the Citizen in one hand and a pike to defend them in the other. The painting, by female artist and ardent revolutionary Nanine Vallain, hung in the Jacobin Club until its fall from power. (By Nanine Vallain [1767–1815]/De Agostini/Getty Images)

National Assembly abolished the nobility, and in July the king swore to uphold the as-yet-unwritten constitution, effectively enshrining a constitutional monarchy. The king remained the head of state, but all lawmaking power now resided in the National Assembly, elected by French males who possessed a set amount of property, comprising roughly half the male population. The constitution passed in September 1791 was the first in French history. It legalized divorce and broadened women's rights to inherit property and to obtain financial support for illegitimate children from fathers, but excluded women from political office and voting.

This decision was attacked by a small number of men and women who believed that the rights of man should be extended to all French citizens. Politically active women wrote pamphlets, formed clubs, and petitioned the assembly on behalf of women's right to participate in the life of the nation. Olympe de Gouges (1748–1793), a self-taught writer and woman of the people, protested the evils of slavery as well as the injustices done to women. In September 1791 she published her *Declaration of the Rights of Woman*. This pamphlet echoed its famous predecessor, the Declaration of the Rights of Man and of the Citizen, proclaiming, "Woman is born free and remains equal to man in rights." De Gouges's position found little sympathy among leaders of the Revolution, however. (See "Thinking Like a Historian: The Rights of Which Men?" page 626.)

In addition to ruling on women's rights, the National Assembly replaced the complicated patchwork of historic provinces with eighty-three departments of approximately equal size, a move toward more rational and systematic methods of administration. In the name of economic liberty, the deputies prohibited guilds and workers' associations, and abolished internal customs fees. Thus the National Assembly applied the spirit of the Enlightenment in a thorough reform of France's laws and institutions.

The National Assembly also imposed a radical reorganization on religious life. The Assembly granted religious freedom to the small minority of French Protestants and Jews. In November 1789 it nationalized the property of the Catholic Church and abolished monasteries. The government used all former church property as collateral to guarantee a new paper currency, the assignats (A-sihg-nat), and then sold the property in an attempt to put the state's finances on a solid footing.

Imbued with the rationalism and skepticism of the eighteenth-century Enlightenment, many delegates distrusted popular piety and "superstitious religion." Thus in July 1790, with the Civil Constitution of the Clergy, they established a national church with priests chosen by voters. The National Assembly then forced the Catholic clergy to take an oath of loyalty to the new government. The pope formally condemned this

Antoinette, who was widely despised for her frivolous and supposedly immoral behavior. It seems likely that only the intervention of Lafayette and the National Guard saved the royal family. But the only way to calm the disorder was for the king to live closer to his people in Paris, as the crowd demanded.

Liberal elites brought the Revolution into being and continued to lead politics. Yet the people of France were now roused and would henceforth play a crucial role in the unfolding of events.

A Constitutional Monarchy and Its Challenges

The day after the women's march on Versailles, the National Assembly followed the king to Paris, and the next two years, until September 1791, saw the consolidation of the liberal revolution. In June 1790 the

The Women of Paris March to Versailles On October 5, 1789, thousands of poor Parisian women marched to Versailles to protest the price of bread. For the common people, the king was the baker of last resort, responsible for feeding his people during times of scarcity. The image of a set of scales one woman holds aloft (along with a loaf of bread stuck on the tip of her pike) symbolizes the crowd's desire for justice and for bread to be sold at the same price per pound as it always had been. The women forced the royal family to return with them to live in Paris, rather than remain isolated from their subjects at court. (*The Women's March on Versailles in October 1789*, 18th-century French print/DEA/Gianni Dagli Orti/Getty Images)

measure, and only half the priests of France swore the oath. Many sincere Christians, especially those in the countryside, were appalled by these changes in the religious order.

World War and Republican France, 1791–1799

FOCUS QUESTION *Why and how did the French Revolution take a radical turn entailing terror at home and war with European powers?*

When Louis XVI accepted the National Assembly's constitution in September 1791, a young provincial lawyer and delegate named Maximilien Robespierre (1758–1794) concluded that "the Revolution is over." Robespierre was right in the sense that the most constructive and lasting reforms were in place. Yet he was wrong in suggesting that turmoil had ended, for a much more radical stage lay ahead, one that would bring war with foreign powers, the declaration of terror at home, and a transformation in France's government.

The International Response

The outbreak of revolution in France produced great excitement and a sharp division of opinion in Europe and the United States. On the one hand, liberals and radicals saw a mighty triumph of liberty over despotism. On the other hand, conservative leaders such as British statesman Edmund Burke (1729–1797) were intensely troubled. In 1790 Burke published *Reflections on the Revolution in France*, in which he defended inherited privileges. He glorified Britain's unrepresentative Parliament and predicted that reform like that occurring in France would lead only to chaos and tyranny.

One passionate rebuttal came from a young writer in London, Mary Wollstonecraft (1759–1797). Incensed by Burke's book, Wollstonecraft (WOOL-stuhn-kraft) wrote a blistering attack, *A Vindication of the Rights of Man* (1790). Two years later, she published her masterpiece, *A Vindication of the Rights of Woman* (1792). Like de Gouges in France, Wollstonecraft demanded equal rights for women. She also advocated coeducation out of the belief that it would make women better wives and mothers, good citizens, and economically independent. Considered very radical for the time, the book became a founding text of the feminist movement.

The kings and nobles of continental Europe, who had at first welcomed the Revolution in France as weakening a competing power, now feared its impact. In June 1791 the royal family was arrested after a failed attempt to escape France. To supporters of the Revolution, the attempted flight was proof that the king was treacherously seeking foreign support for an invasion of France. To the monarchs of Austria and Prussia, the arrest of a crowned monarch was unacceptable. Two

The Rights of Which Men?

In August 1789 the legislators of the French Revolution adopted the Declaration of the Rights of Man and of the Citizen, enshrining full legal equality under the law for French citizens. Who exactly could become a citizen and what rights they might enjoy quickly became contentious issues.

1 **Robespierre on the distinction between active and passive citizenship.** In a November 1789 letter, Maximilien Robespierre denounced the decision to limit political participation to those with a certain amount of wealth. In 1792 a new law installed universal suffrage, but wealth restrictions returned under the Directory in 1795.

No doubt you know that a specific sum of money is being demanded of citizens for them to exercise the rights of citizens; that they must pay a tax equivalent to three days' work in order to participate in the primary assemblies; ten days' to be a member of the secondary assemblies which are called departments; finally 54 livres tax and possession of landed property to be eligible for the national assembly. These provisions are the work of the aristocratic party in the Assembly which has not even permitted the others to defend the rights of the people and has constantly shouted them down; so that the most important of all our deliberations was taken without discussion, carried off in tumult. . . .

[I]t seems to me that a representation founded on the bases I have just indicated could easily raise up an aristocracy of riches on the ruins of the feudal aristocracy; and I do not see that the people which should be the aim of every political institution will gain much from this kind of arrangement. Moreover I fail to see how representatives who derive their power from their constituents, that is to say from all the citizens without distinction of wealth, have the right to despoil the major part of these constituents of the power which they have confided to them.

2 **Petition of the French Jews.** After granting civil rights to Protestants in December 1789, the National Assembly began to consider the smaller but more controversial population of French Jews. Eager to become citizens in their own right, the Jews of Paris, Alsace, and Lorraine presented a joint petition to the National Assembly in January 1790.

A great question is pending before the supreme tribunal of France. *Will the Jews be citizens or not?* . . .

In general, civil rights are entirely independent from religious principles. And all men of whatever religion, whatever sect they belong to, whatever creed they practice, provided that their creed, their sect, their religion does not offend the principles of a pure and severe morality, all these men, we say, equally able to serve the fatherland, defend its interests, contribute to its splendor, should all equally have the title and the rights of citizen. . . .

Reflect, then, on the condition of the Jews. Excluded from all the professions, ineligible for all the positions, deprived even of the capacity to acquire property, not daring and not being able to sell openly the merchandise of their commerce, to what extremity are you reducing them? You do not want them to die, and yet you refuse them the means to live: you refuse them the means, and you crush them with taxes. You leave them therefore really no other resource than usury [lending money with interest]. . . .

Everything is changing; the lot of the Jews must change at the same time; and the people will not be more surprised by this particular change than by all those which they see around them everyday.

ANALYZING THE EVIDENCE

1. Both the active-passive citizenship distinction discussed by Robespierre in Source 1 and the petition by the Jews of France in Source 2 raise the issue of the relationship between economic status and citizenship rights. What is this relationship in each case, and how do the relationships differ from each other?
2. Compare the arguments made by the free men of color in Source 3 and Etta Palm d'Aelders on behalf of women in Source 5. Why did the free men of color insist on the strong contributions they had already made while d'Aelders emphasized women's weakness and humiliation? What do these rhetorical strategies tell you about contemporary ideas about masculinity and femininity?
3. In Source 4, what arguments does the Colonial Committee advance in favor of legal autonomy of the colonies? Why would autonomy favor the position of colonial landowners?

3 **Free men of color address the National Assembly.** In the first years of the Revolution, debate raged over the question of political equality in Saint-Domingue. In October 1789 a group of free men of color appeared before the National Assembly to present an appeal for political rights for themselves (but not for the enslaved).

~ [C]itizens of all classes have been called to the great work of public regeneration; all have contributed to writing complaints and nominating deputies to defend their rights and set forth their interests.

The call of liberty has echoed in the other hemisphere.

It should certainly have erased even the memory of these outrageous distinctions between citizens of the same land; instead, it has brought forth even more appalling ones. . . . In this strange system, the citizens of color find themselves represented by the white colonists' deputies, although they have still never been included in their partial assemblies and they have not entrusted any power to these deputies. Their opposition interests, which sadly are only too obvious, make such representation absurd and contradictory. . . . The citizens of color are clearly as qualified as the whites to demand this representation.

Like them they are all citizens, free and French; the edict of March 1685 accords them all such rights and guarantees them all such privileges. . . . Like them they are property owners and farmers; like them they contribute to the relief of the state by paying the levies and bearing all expenses that they and the whites share. Like them they have already shed their blood and are prepared to spill it again for the defense of the fatherland. Like them, finally, though with less encouragement and means, they have proven their patriotism again and again.

4 **The Colonial Committee defends colonists' autonomy.** In March 1790 the Colonial Committee—dominated by slaveholding plantation owners—recommended that colonial assemblies be given the right to make their own laws. This meant that any laws passed in France on the abolition of slavery or the enfranchisement of people of color would not affect the colonies. A member of the committee summarized its views.

~ It would be a mistake as dangerous as it is unforgivable to envisage the colonies as provinces, and to want to subject them to the same regime. . . . [A] land so different from ours in every way, inhabited by different classes of people, distinguished from each other by characteristics unfamiliar to us, and for whom our social distinctions offer no analogy . . . needs laws which might be called indigenous. . . . [I]t belongs only to the inhabitants of our colonies, convened in the colonies themselves, to gather to elect the body of representatives to work in virtue of its powers and without leaving its territory, to create the constitution, that is to say the form of the internal regime and local administration which is most suited to assure colonials of the advantages of civil society.

5 **Etta Palm d'Aelders on the rights of women.** During the Revolution, Dutch-born Etta Palm d'Aelders became one of the most outspoken advocates for women's rights. In her *Address of French Citizenesses to the National Assembly* in 1791, she addresses the National Assembly in opposition to a proposed law reserving for husbands the capacity to seek legal redress for adultery.

~ It is a question of your duty, your honor, your interest, to destroy down to their roots these gothic laws which abandon the weakest but [also] the most worthy half of humanity to a humiliating existence, to an eternal slavery.

You have restored to man the dignity of his being in recognizing his rights; you will no longer allow woman to groan beneath an arbitrary authority; that would be to overturn the fundamental principles on which rests the stately edifice you are raising by your untiring labors for the happiness of Frenchmen. It is too late to equivocate. Philosophy has drawn truth from the darkness; the time has come; justice, sister of liberty, calls all individuals to the equality of rights, without discrimination of sex; the laws of a free people must be equal for all beings, like the air and the sun. . . .

[T]he powers of husband and wife must be equal and separate. The law cannot establish any difference between these two authorities; they must give equal protection and maintain a perpetual balance between the two married people. . . .

You will complete your work by giving girls a moral education equal to that of their brothers; for education is for the soul what watering is for plants; it makes it fertile, causes it to bloom, fortifies it, and carries the germ productive of virtue and talents to a perfect maturity.

PUTTING IT ALL TOGETHER

Using the sources above, along with what you have learned in class and in this chapter, write a short essay exploring how different groups drew on the events, language, and principles of the French Revolution to make their claims. Keep in mind both differences and similarities in their rhetorical strategies as well as any additional sources of legitimation they employed.

Sources: (1) John Hardman, *The French Revolution Sourcebook* (London: Arnold, 2002), pp. 120–121; (2) Excerpt from pp. 93, 95–97 in *The French Revolution and Human Rights: A Brief Documentary History*, edited, translated, and with an introduction by Lynn Hunt; (3) Laurent Dubois and John D. Garrigus, *Slave Revolution in the Caribbean, 1789–1804: A Brief History with Documents* (Boston: Bedford/St. Martin's, 2006), pp. 68–69; (4) Frédéric Régent, "Slavery and the Colonies," in Peter McPhee, *A Companion to the French Revolution* (Chichester: Wiley Blackwell, 2015), p. 401; (5) Darline Gay Levy, Harriet Branson Applewhite, and Mary Durham Johnson, eds., *Women in Revolutionary Paris, 1789–1795* (Champaign-Urbana: University of Illinois Press, 1981), pp. 75–77.

The French Revolution

National Assembly (1789–1791)

May 5, 1789	Estates General meets at Versailles
June 17, 1789	Third estate declares itself the National Assembly
June 20, 1789	Tennis Court Oath
July 14, 1789	Storming of the Bastille
July–August 1789	Great Fear
August 4, 1789	Abolishment of feudal privileges
August 27, 1789	Declaration of the Rights of Man and of the Citizen
October 5, 1789	Women march on Versailles; royal family returns to Paris
November 1789	National Assembly confiscates church land
July 1790	Civil Constitution of the Clergy establishes a national church; Louis XVI agrees to constitutional monarchy
June 1791	Royal family arrested while fleeing France
August 1791	Declaration of Pillnitz

Legislative Assembly (1791–1792)

April 1792	France declares war on Austria
August 1792	Mob attacks the palace, and Legislative Assembly takes Louis XVI prisoner

National Convention (1792–1795)

September 1792	September Massacres; National Convention abolishes monarchy and declares France a republic
January 1793	Louis XVI executed
February 1793	France declares war on Britain, the Dutch Republic, and Spain; revolts take place in some provinces
March 1793	Struggle between Girondists and the Mountain
April 1793	Creation of the Committee of Public Safety
June 1793	Arrest of Girondist leaders
September 1793	Price controls instituted
October 1793	National Convention bans women's political societies
1793–1794	Reign of Terror
Spring 1794	French armies victorious on all fronts
July 1794	Robespierre executed; Thermidorian reaction begins

The Directory (1795–1799)

1795	Economic controls abolished; suppression of the sans-culottes begins
1799	Napoleon seizes power

months later they issued the Declaration of Pillnitz, proclaiming their willingness to intervene in France to restore Louis XVI's rule if necessary. But the crowned heads of Europe misjudged the situation. The new French representative body, called the Legislative Assembly, that convened in October 1791 had new delegates and a different character. Although the delegates were still prosperous, well-educated middle-class men, they were younger and less cautious than their predecessors. Since the National Assembly had declared sitting deputies ineligible for re-election, none of them had previously served as national representatives. Many of them belonged to the political **Jacobin Club**. Such clubs had proliferated in Parisian neighborhoods since the beginning of the Revolution, drawing men and women to debate the political issues of the day.

Jacobins and other deputies reacted with patriotic fury to the Declaration of Pillnitz. They said that if the kings of Europe were attempting to incite war against France, then "we will incite a war of people against kings. . . . Ten million Frenchmen, kindled by the fire of liberty, armed with the sword, with reason, with eloquence would be able to change the face of the world and make the tyrants tremble on their thrones."[3] In April 1792 France declared war on Francis II of Austria, the Habsburg monarch.

France's crusade against tyranny went poorly at first. Prussia joined Austria against the French, who broke and fled at their first military encounter with this First Coalition of foreign powers united against the Revolution. On behalf of the crowns of Austria and Prussia, the duke of Brunswick, commander of the coalition armies, issued a declaration threatening to destroy Paris if harm came to the royal family. The Legislative Assembly declared the country in danger, and volunteers rallied to the capital. The Brunswick manifesto heightened suspicion of treason on the part of the French king and queen. On August 10, 1792, a revolutionary crowd attacked the royal palace at the Tuileries (TWEE-luh-reez), while the royal family fled to the Legislative Assembly. Rather than offering refuge, the Assembly suspended the king from all his functions, imprisoned him, and called for a constitutional assembly to be elected by universal male suffrage.

The Second Revolution and the New Republic

The fall of the monarchy marked a radicalization of the Revolution, a phase that historians often call the **second revolution**. Louis's imprisonment was followed by the September Massacres. Fearing invasion by the Prussians and riled up by rumors that counter-revolutionaries would aid the invaders, angry crowds stormed the prisons and killed jailed priests and aristocrats. In late September 1792 the new, popularly elected National Convention, which replaced the Legislative Assembly, proclaimed France a republic, a nation in which the people, instead of a monarch, held sovereign power.

As with the Legislative Assembly, many members of the new National Convention belonged to the Jacobin Club of Paris. But the Jacobins themselves were increasingly divided into two bitterly opposed groups—the **Girondists** (juh-RAHN-dihsts) and **the Mountain**, led by Robespierre and another young lawyer, Georges Jacques Danton.

This division emerged clearly after the National Convention overwhelmingly convicted Louis XVI of treason. The Girondists accepted his guilt but did not wish to put the king to death. By a narrow majority, the Mountain carried the day, and Louis was executed on January 21, 1793, by guillotine, which the French had recently perfected. Marie Antoinette suffered the same fate later that year. But both the Girondists and the Mountain were determined to continue the "war against tyranny." The Prussians had been stopped at the Battle of Valmy on September 20, 1792, one day before the republic was proclaimed. French armies then invaded Savoy and captured Nice, moved into the German Rhineland, and by November 1792 were occupying the entire Austrian Netherlands (modern Belgium).

Everywhere they went, French armies of occupation chased princes, abolished feudalism, and found support among some peasants and middle-class people. But French armies also lived off the land, requisitioning food and supplies and plundering local treasures. The liberators therefore looked increasingly like foreign invaders. Meanwhile, international tensions mounted. In February 1793 the National Convention, at war with Austria and Prussia, declared war on Britain, the Dutch Republic, and Spain

as well. Republican France was now at war with almost all of Europe.

Groups within France added to the turmoil. Peasants in western France revolted against being drafted into the army, with the Vendée region of Brittany emerging as the epicenter of revolt. Devout Catholics, royalists, and foreign agents encouraged their rebellion, and the counter-revolutionaries recruited veritable armies to fight for their cause.

In March 1793 the National Convention was locked in a life-and-death political struggle between members of the Mountain and the more moderate Girondists. With the middle-class delegates so bitterly divided, the people of Paris once again emerged as the decisive political factor. The laboring poor and the petty traders were often known as the **sans-culottes** because their men wore trousers instead of the knee breeches of the aristocracy and the solid middle class. (See "Evaluating the Evidence 19.3: Contrasting Visions of the Sans-Culottes," page 630.) They demanded radical political action to defend the Revolution. The Mountain, sensing an opportunity to outmaneuver the Girondists, joined with sans-culottes activists to engineer a popular uprising. On June 2, 1793, armed sans-culottes invaded the Convention and forced its deputies to arrest twenty-nine Girondist deputies for treason. All power passed to the Mountain.

Areas of Insurrection, 1793

The Convention also formed the Committee of Public Safety in April 1793 to deal with threats from within and outside France. The committee, led by Robespierre, held dictatorial power, allowing it to use whatever force necessary to defend the Revolution. Moderates in leading provincial cities revolted against the committee's power and demanded a decentralized government. Counter-revolutionary forces in the

■ **Jacobin Club** A political club in revolutionary France whose members were well-educated radical republicans.

■ **second revolution** From 1792 to 1795, the second phase of the French Revolution, during which the fall of the French monarchy introduced a rapid radicalization of politics.

■ **Girondists** A moderate group that fought for control of the French National Convention in 1793.

■ **the Mountain** Led by Robespierre, the French National Convention's radical faction, which seized legislative power in 1793.

■ **sans-culottes** The laboring poor of Paris, so called because the men wore trousers instead of the knee breeches of the aristocracy and middle class; the word came to refer to the militant radicals of the city.

Contrasting Visions of the Sans-Culottes

These two images offer profoundly different representations of a sans-culotte woman. The image on the left was created by a French artist, while the image on the right is English. The French words above the image on the right read in part, "Heads! Blood! Death! . . . I am the Goddess of Liberty! . . . Long Live the Guillotine!"

(Musée de la Ville de Paris, Musée Carnavalet, Paris, France/Bridgeman Images)

A PARIS BELLE.

(© Courtesy of the Warden and Scholars of New College, Oxford, UK/Bridgeman Images)

EVALUATE THE EVIDENCE

1. How would you describe the woman on the left? What qualities does the artist seem to ascribe to her, and how do you think these qualities relate to the sans-culottes and the Revolution? How would you characterize the facial expression and attire of the woman on the right? How does the inclusion of the text contribute to your impressions of her?
2. What does the contrast between these two images suggest about differences between French and English perceptions of the sans-culottes and of the French Revolution? Why do you think the artists have chosen to depict women?

Vendée won significant victories, and the republic's armies were driven back on all fronts. By July 1793 only the areas around Paris and on the eastern frontier were firmly held by the central government. Defeat seemed imminent.

Total War and the Terror

A year later, in July 1794, the central government had reasserted control over the provinces, and the Austrian Netherlands and the Rhineland were once again in French hands. This remarkable change of fortune was due to the revolutionary government's success in harnessing the explosive forces of a planned economy, revolutionary terror, and modern nationalism in a total war effort.

Robespierre and the Committee of Public Safety advanced on several fronts in 1793 and 1794, seeking to impose republican unity across the nation. First, they collaborated with the sans-culottes, who continued pressing the common people's case for fair prices and a moral economic order. Thus in September 1793 Robespierre and his coworkers established a planned economy with egalitarian social overtones. Rather than let supply and demand determine prices, the government set maximum prices for key products. Though the state was too weak to enforce all its price regulations, it did fix the price of bread in Paris at levels the poor could afford.

The people were also put to work, producing arms, munitions, uniforms, boots, saddles, and other necessary supplies, for the war effort. The government told craftsmen what to produce, nationalized many small workshops, and requisitioned raw materials and grain. These reforms amounted to an emergency form of socialism, which thoroughly frightened Europe's propertied classes and greatly influenced the subsequent development of socialist ideology.

Second, while radical economic measures furnished the poor with bread and the armies with supplies, the **Reign of Terror** (1793–1794) enforced compliance with republican beliefs and practices. The Constitution of 1793, which had been completed in June 1793 and approved by a national referendum, was indefinitely suspended in favor of a "revolutionary government." Special courts responsible only to Robespierre's Committee of Public Safety tried "enemies of the nation" for political crimes. Some forty thousand French men and women were executed or died in prison and around three hundred thousand were arrested, making Robespierre's Reign of Terror one of the most controversial phases of the Revolution. Presented as a necessary measure to save the republic, the Terror was a weapon directed against all suspected of opposing the revolutionary government. As Robespierre himself put it, "Terror is nothing more than prompt, severe inflexible justice."[4] For many Europeans of the time, however, the Reign of Terror represented a frightening perversion of the ideals of 1789.

In their efforts to impose unity, the Jacobins also took actions to suppress women's participation in political debate, which they perceived as disorderly and a distraction from women's proper place in the home. On October 30, 1793, the National Convention declared that "the clubs and popular societies of women, under whatever denomination are prohibited." Among those convicted of sedition was writer Olympe de Gouges, who was sent to the guillotine in November 1793.

The third element of the Committee's program was to bring about a cultural revolution that would transform former royal subjects into republican citizens. The government sponsored revolutionary art and songs as well as a new series of secular festivals to celebrate republican virtue and patriotism. It also attempted to rationalize French daily life by adopting the decimal system for weights and measures and a new calendar based on ten-day weeks. (See "Living in the Past: A Revolution of Culture and Daily Life," page 632.) Another important element of this cultural revolution was the campaign of de-Christianization, which aimed to eliminate Catholic symbols and beliefs. Fearful of the hostility aroused in rural France, however, Robespierre called for a halt to de-Christianization measures in mid-1794.

The final element in the program of the Committee of Public Safety was its appeal to a new sense of national identity and patriotism. With a common language and a common tradition newly reinforced by the revolutionary ideals of popular sovereignty and democracy, many French people developed an intense emotional commitment to the defense of the nation, and they saw the war against foreign opponents as a life-and-death struggle between good and evil. This was the birth of modern nationalism, which would have a profound effect on subsequent European history.

The all-out mobilization of French resources under the Terror combined with the fervor of nationalism to create an awesome fighting machine. A decree of August 1793 imposed the draft on all unmarried young men, and by January 1794 French armed forces outnumbered those of their enemies almost four to one.[5] Well trained, well equipped, and constantly indoctrinated, the enormous armies of the republic were led by young, impetuous generals. These generals often had risen from the ranks, and they personified the opportunities the Revolution offered gifted sons of the people. By spring 1794 French armies were victorious on all fronts and domestic revolt was largely suppressed. The republic was saved.

The Thermidorian Reaction and the Directory

The success of French armies led the Committee of Public Safety to relax the emergency economic controls, but the Committee extended the political Reign of Terror. In March 1794 the revolutionary tribunal sentenced many of its critics to death. Two weeks later Robespierre sent long-standing collaborators who he believed had turned against him, including Danton, to the guillotine. In June 1794 a new law removed defendants' right of legal counsel and criminalized criticism of the Revolution. A group of radicals and moderates in the Convention, knowing that they might be next, organized a conspiracy. They howled down Robespierre when he tried to speak to the National Convention on July 27, 1794—a date known as 9 Thermidor according to France's newly adopted republican calendar. The next day it was Robespierre's turn to be guillotined.

As Robespierre's closest supporters followed their leader to the guillotine, the respectable middle-class lawyers and professionals who had led the liberal

■ **Reign of Terror** The period from 1793 to 1794 during which Robespierre's Committee of Public Safety tried and executed thousands suspected of treason and a new revolutionary culture was imposed.

The French Revolution brought sweeping political and social change to France, removing one of the oldest monarchies in Europe in favor of broad-based representative government and eliminating age-old distinctions between nobles and commoners. Revolutionaries feared, however, that these measures were not enough to transform the nation. They therefore undertook a parallel revolution of culture intended to purify and regenerate the French people and turn former royal subjects into patriotic citizens capable of realizing the dream of liberty, equality, and fraternity.

To bring about cultural revolution, officials of the new republic targeted the most fundamental elements of daily life: the experience of space and time. Prior to the Revolution, regions of France had their own systems of measurement, meaning that the length of an inch or the weight of a pound differed substantially across the realm. Disgusted with the inefficiency of this state of affairs and determined to impose national unity, the government adopted the decimal-based metric system first proposed in 1670. The length of the meter was scientifically set at one ten-millionth of the distance from the pole to the equator. Henceforth all French citizens would inhabit spaces that were measured and divided in the same way.

The government attempted a similar rationalization of the calendar. Instead of twelve months of varying lengths, each of the twelve months on the new revolutionary calendar was made up of three ten-day weeks, with a

five- or six-day interval at the end of each year. To mark the total rebirth of time, the new calendar began at Year 1 on the day of the foundation of the French republic (September 22, 1792). A series of festivals with patriotic themes replaced the traditional Catholic feast days. One of the most important was the festival of the Cult of the Supreme Being (a form of deism promoted by Robespierre as the state religion). There was even a short-lived attempt to put the clock on a decimal system.

Cultural revolution also took on more concrete forms. Every citizen was required to wear a tricolor cockade on his or her hat to symbolize loyalty to the republic. Enterprising merchants sold a plethora of everyday goods with revolutionary themes. One could eat from revolutionary plates, drink from revolutionary mugs, waft revolutionary fans, and even decorate the home with revolutionary wallpaper. Living the French Revolution meant entering a whole new world of sense and experience.

Plate showing a festival of the Cult of the Supreme Being.
(Musée de la Ville de Paris, Musée Carnavalet, Paris, France/Erich Lessing/Art Resource, NY)

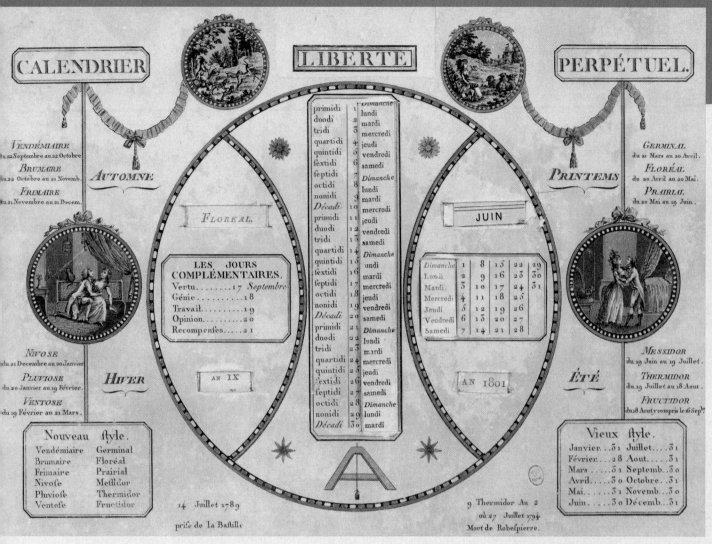

Revolutionary calendar. (Musée de la Ville de Paris, Musée Carnavalet, Paris, France/Bridgeman Images)

QUESTIONS FOR ANALYSIS

1. How easy do you think it would have been to follow the new revolutionary calendar? Why did revolutionaries believe it was necessary to create a new calendar?
2. How would you describe the festival of the Cult of the Supreme Being as it is shown on the plate? What values of the Revolution does it seem to emphasize?
3. Why were ordinary objects, like plates and playing cards, decorated with symbols of the Revolution? What does this tell you about the ways everyday life was drawn into the experience of revolution?

Revolutionary playing card.
(Musée de la Ville de Paris, Musée Carnavalet, Paris, France/Bridgeman Images)

633

The Guillotine Prior to the French Revolution, methods of execution included hanging and being broken at the wheel. Only nobles enjoyed the privilege of a relatively swift and painless death by decapitation, delivered by an executioner's ax. The guillotine, a model of which is shown here, was devised by a French revolutionary doctor named Guillotin as a humane and egalitarian form of execution. Ironically, due to the mass executions under the Terror, it is now seen instead as a symbol of revolutionary cruelty. (Musée de la Ville de Paris, Musée Carnavalet, Paris/Bridgeman Images)

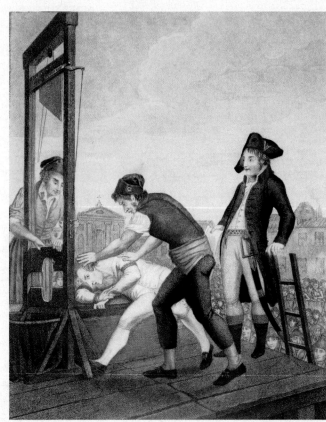

The Execution of Robespierre After overseeing the Terror, during which thousands of men and women accused of being enemies of the Revolution faced speedy trial and execution, it was Maximilien Robespierre's turn to face the guillotine on 9 Thermidor Year II (July 28, 1794). (Musée de la Ville de Paris, Musée Carnavalet, Paris, France/Bridgeman Images)

Revolution of 1789 reasserted their authority. This period of **Thermidorian reaction**, as it was called, hearkened back to the ideals of the early Revolution; the new leaders of government proclaimed an end to the revolutionary expediency of the Terror and the return of representative government, the rule of law, and liberal economic policies. In 1795 the National Convention abolished many economic controls, let prices rise sharply, and severely restricted the local political organizations through which the sans-culottes exerted their strength.

In the same year, members of the National Convention wrote a new constitution to guarantee their economic position and political supremacy. As in previous elections, the mass of the population could vote only for electors who would in turn elect the legislators, but the new constitution greatly reduced the number of men eligible to become electors by instating a substantial property requirement. It also inaugurated a bicameral legislative system for the first time in the Revolution, with a Council of 500 serving as the lower house that initiated legislation and a Council of Elders (composed of about 250 members aged forty years or older) acting as the upper house that approved new laws. To prevent a new Robespierre from monopolizing power, the new Assembly granted executive power to a five-man body, called the Directory.

The Directory continued to support French military expansion abroad. War was no longer so much a crusade as a response to economic problems. Large, victorious French armies reduced unemployment at home. However, the French people quickly grew weary of the corruption and ineffectiveness that characterized the Directory. The trauma of years of military and political violence had alienated the public, and the Directory's heavy-handed and opportunistic policies did not reverse the situation. This general dissatisfaction revealed itself clearly in the national elections of 1797, which returned a large number of conservative and even monarchist deputies who favored peace at almost any price. Two years later Napoleon Bonaparte ended the Directory in a coup d'état (koo day-TAH) and substituted a strong dictatorship for a weak one.

■ **Thermidorian reaction** A reaction to the violence of the Reign of Terror in 1794, resulting in the execution of Robespierre and the loosening of economic controls.

The Napoleonic Era, 1799–1815

FOCUS QUESTION *How did Napoleon Bonaparte assume control of France and much of Europe, and what factors led to his downfall?*

For almost fifteen years, from 1799 to 1814, France was in the hands of a keen-minded military dictator of exceptional ability. One of history's most fascinating leaders, Napoleon Bonaparte (1769–1821) realized that he needed to put an end to civil strife in France in order to create unity and consolidate his rule. And he did. But Napoleon saw himself as a man of destiny, and the glory of war and the dream of universal empire proved irresistible. For years he spiraled from victory to victory, but in the end he was destroyed by a mighty coalition united in fear of his restless ambition.

Napoleon's Rule of France

Born in Corsica into an impoverished noble family in 1769, Napoleon left home and became a lieutenant in the French artillery in 1785. Converted to the revolutionary cause and rising rapidly in the republican army, Napoleon was placed in command of French forces in Italy and won brilliant victories there in 1796 and 1797. His next campaign, in Egypt, was a failure, but Napoleon returned to France before the fiasco was generally known, and his reputation remained intact.

French aggression in Egypt and elsewhere provoked the British to organize a new alliance in 1798, the Second Coalition, that also included Austria and Russia.

Napoleon soon learned that some prominent members of the legislature were plotting against the Directory. The plotters' dissatisfaction stemmed not so much from the Directory's ruling dictatorially as from the fact that it was a weak dictatorship. Ten years of upheaval and uncertainty had made firm rule much more appealing than liberty and popular politics to these disillusioned revolutionaries. The abbé Sieyès personified this evolution in thinking. In 1789 he had written that the nobility was grossly overprivileged and that the entire people should rule the French nation. Now Sieyès's motto was "Confidence from below, authority from above."

The flamboyant thirty-year-old Napoleon, nationally revered for his heroism, was an ideal figure of authority. On November 9, 1799, Napoleon and his conspirators ousted the Directors, and the following day soldiers disbanded the legislature at bayonet point. Napoleon was named first consul of the republic, and a new constitution consolidating his position was overwhelmingly approved by a nationwide vote in December 1799. Republican appearances were maintained, but Napoleon became the real ruler of France.

Napoleon's domestic policy centered on using his popularity and charisma to maintain order and end civil strife. He did so by appeasing powerful groups in France by according them favors in return for loyal

Napoleon Bonaparte Visits Plague Victims in Jaffa, Syria This image of Napoleon Bonaparte visiting plague victims during a campaign in Jaffa in 1799 emphasizes the general's courage and compassion, evoking the biblical scene of Jesus touching and healing lepers. Bonaparte commissioned this painting to defend himself against accusations that he had failed in his duty toward the sick. (By Jan-Antoine Gros [1771–1835]/Art Media/Print Collector/Getty Images)

The Napoleonic Era

November 1799	Napoleon overthrows the Directory
December 1799	Napoleon's new constitution approved
1800	Foundation of the Bank of France
1801	France defeats Austria and acquires Italian and German territories in the Treaty of Lunéville; Napoleon signs papal Concordat
1802	Treaty of Amiens
March 1804	Napoleonic Code
December 1804	Napoleon crowned emperor
October 1805	Britain defeats the French fleet at the Battle of Trafalgar
December 1805	Napoleon defeats Austria and Russia at the Battle of Austerlitz
1807	Napoleon redraws map of Europe in the treaties of Tilsit
1808	Spanish revolt against French occupation
1810	Height of the Grand Empire
June 1812	Napoleon invades Russia
Fall–Winter 1812	Napoleon makes a disastrous retreat from Russia
March 1814	Russia, Prussia, Austria, and Britain sign the Treaty of Chaumont, pledging alliance to defeat Napoleon
April 1814	Napoleon abdicates and is exiled to Elba; Louis XVIII restored to constitutional monarchy
February–June 1815	Napoleon escapes from Elba but is defeated at the Battle of Waterloo; Louis XVIII restored to throne for second time

service. Napoleon's bargain with the solid middle class was codified in the famous Civil Code of March 1804, also known as the **Napoleonic Code**, which reasserted two of the fundamental principles of the Revolution of 1789: equality of all male citizens before the law, and security of wealth and private property. Napoleon and the leading bankers of Paris established the privately owned Bank of France in 1800, which served the interests of both the state and the financial oligarchy. Napoleon won over peasants by defending the gains in land and status they had won during the Revolution.

At the same time, Napoleon consolidated his rule by recruiting disillusioned revolutionaries to form a network of ministers, prefects, and centrally appointed mayors. Nor were members of the old nobility slighted. In 1800 and again in 1802 Napoleon granted amnesty to one hundred thousand émigrés on the condition that they return to France and take a loyalty oath. Members of this returning elite soon ably occupied

many high posts in the expanding centralized state. Napoleon also created a new imperial nobility in order to reward his most talented generals and officials.

Napoleon applied his diplomatic skills to healing the Catholic Church in France so that it could serve as a bulwark of social stability. After arduous negotiations, Napoleon and Pope Pius VII (pontificate 1800–1823) signed the Concordat (kuhn-KOHR-dat) of 1801. The pope obtained the right for French Catholics to practice their religion freely, but Napoleon gained political power: his government now nominated bishops, paid the clergy, and exerted great influence over the church.

The domestic reforms of Napoleon's early years were his greatest achievement. Much of his legal and administrative reorganization has survived in France to this day, but order and unity had a price: authoritarian rule. Women lost many of the gains they had made in the 1790s. Under the Napoleonic Code, women were dependents of either their fathers or their husbands, and they could not make contracts or have bank accounts in their own names. Napoleon and his advisers aimed at re-establishing a family monarchy, where the power of the husband and father was as absolute over the wife and the children as that of Napoleon was over his subjects. He also curtailed free speech and freedom of the press and manipulated voting in the occasional elections. After 1810 political suspects were held in state prisons, as they had been during the Terror.

Napoleon's Expansion in Europe

Napoleon was above all a great military man. After coming to power in 1799, he sent peace feelers to Austria and Great Britain, the two remaining members of the Second Coalition that had been formed against France in 1798. When they rejected his overtures, Napoleon's armies decisively defeated the Austrians. In the Treaty of Lunéville (1801), Austria accepted the loss of almost all its Italian possessions, and German territory on the west bank of the Rhine was incorporated into France. The British agreed to the Treaty of Amiens in 1802, allowing France to control the former Dutch Republic (known as the Batavian Republic since 1795), the Austrian Netherlands, the west bank of the Rhine, and most of the Italian peninsula. The Treaty of Amiens was a diplomatic triumph for Napoleon, and peace with honor and profit increased his popularity at home.

In 1802 Napoleon was secure but driven to expand his power. Aggressively redrawing the map of German-speaking lands so as to weaken Austria and encourage the secondary states of southwestern Germany to side with France, Napoleon tried to restrict British trade with all of Europe. He then plotted to attack Great Britain, but his Mediterranean fleet was destroyed by Lord Nelson at the Battle of Trafalgar on October 21, 1805. Invasion of England was henceforth impossible. Renewed fighting had its advantages, however, for the first consul used the wartime atmosphere to have himself proclaimed emperor in late 1804.

Austria, Russia, and Sweden joined with Britain to form the Third Coalition against France shortly before the Battle of Trafalgar. Actions such as Napoleon's assumption of the Italian crown had convinced both Alexander I of Russia and Francis II of Austria that Napoleon was a threat to the European balance of power. Yet they were no match for Napoleon, who scored a brilliant victory over them at the Battle of Austerlitz in December 1805. Alexander I decided to pull back, and Austria accepted large territorial losses in return for peace as the Third Coalition collapsed.

Napoleon then reorganized the German states to his liking. In 1806 he abolished many of the tiny German states as well as the ancient Holy Roman Empire and established by decree the German Confederation of the Rhine, a union of fifteen German states minus Austria, Prussia, and Saxony. Naming himself "protector" of the confederation, Napoleon firmly controlled western Germany.

Napoleon's intervention in German affairs alarmed the Prussians, who mobilized their armies after more than a decade of peace with France. Napoleon attacked and won two more brilliant victories in October 1806 at Jena and Auerstädt, where the Prussians were outnumbered two to one. The war with Prussia, now joined by Russia, continued into the following spring. After Napoleon's larger armies won another victory, Alexander I of Russia was ready to negotiate the peace. In the subsequent treaties of Tilsit in 1807, Prussia lost half of its population, while Russia accepted Napoleon's reorganization of western and central Europe and promised to enforce Napoleon's economic blockade against British goods.

German Confederation of the Rhine, 1806

The Grand Empire and Its End

Increasingly, Napoleon saw himself as the emperor of Europe, not just of France. The so-called **Grand Empire** he built had three parts. The core, or first part, was an ever-expanding France, which by 1810 included today's Belgium and the Netherlands, parts of northern Italy, and German territories on the east bank of the Rhine. The second part consisted of a number of dependent satellite kingdoms, on the thrones of which Napoleon placed members of his large family. The third part comprised the independent but allied states of Austria, Prussia, and Russia. After 1806 Napoleon expected both satellites and allies to support his **Continental System**, a blockade in which no ship coming from Britain or her colonies could dock at a port controlled by the French. It was intended to halt all trade between Britain and continental Europe, thereby destroying the British economy and its military force.

The impact of the Grand Empire on the peoples of Europe was considerable. In the areas incorporated into France and in the satellites (Map 19.2), Napoleon abolished feudal dues and serfdom to the benefit of the peasants and middle class. Yet Napoleon had to put the prosperity and special interests of France first in order to safeguard his power base. Levying heavy taxes in money and men for his armies, he came to be regarded more as a conquering tyrant than as an enlightened liberator. Thus French rule sparked patriotic upheavals and encouraged the growth of reactive nationalism, for individuals in different lands learned to identify emotionally with their own embattled national families as the French had done earlier.

The first great revolt occurred in Spain. In 1808 Napoleon deposed Spanish king Ferdinand VII and placed his own brother Joseph on the throne. However, a coalition of Catholics, monarchists, and patriots rebelled against Napoleon's attempts to make Spain a French satellite. French armies occupied Madrid, but the foes of Napoleon fled to the hills and waged uncompromising

■ **Napoleonic Code** French civil code promulgated in 1804 that reasserted the 1789 principles of the equality of all male citizens before the law and the absolute security of wealth and private property, as well as restricting rights accorded to women by previous revolutionary laws.

■ **Grand Empire** The empire over which Napoleon and his allies ruled, encompassing virtually all of Europe except Great Britain and Russia.

■ **Continental System** A blockade imposed by Napoleon to halt all trade between continental Europe and Britain, thereby weakening the British economy and military.

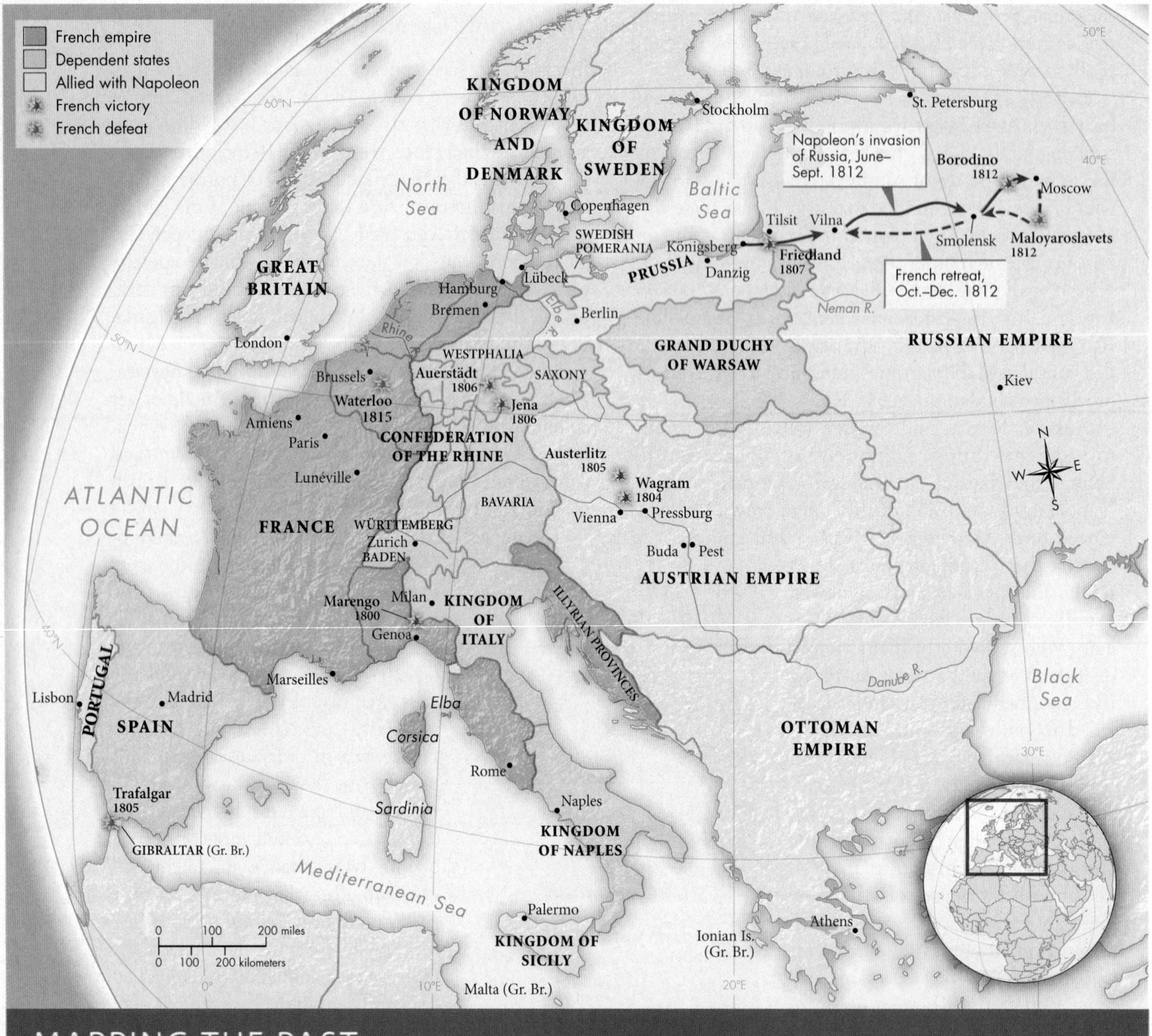

MAPPING THE PAST

MAP 19.2 Napoleonic Europe in 1812

At the height of the Grand Empire in 1810, Napoleon had conquered or allied with every major European power except Britain. But in 1812, angered by Russian repudiation of his ban on trade with Britain, Napoleon invaded Russia with disastrous results. Compare this map with Map 15.2 (page 480), which shows the division of Europe in 1715.

ANALYZING THE MAP How had the balance of power shifted in Europe from 1715 to 1812? What changed, and what remained the same? What was the impact of Napoleon's wars on Germany and the Italian peninsula?

CONNECTIONS Why did Napoleon succeed in achieving vast territorial gains where Louis XIV did not?

guerrilla warfare. Spain was a clear warning: resistance to French imperialism was growing.

Yet Napoleon pushed on. In 1810, when the Grand Empire was at its height, Britain still remained at war with France, helping the guerrillas in Spain and Portugal. The Continental System was a failure. Instead of harming Britain, the system provoked the British to set up a counter-blockade, which created hard times in France. Perhaps looking for a scapegoat, Napoleon turned on Alexander I of Russia, who in 1811 openly repudiated Napoleon's war of prohibitions against British goods.

Napoleon's invasion of Russia began in June 1812 with a force that eventually numbered 600,000, probably the largest force yet assembled in a single army. Only

Francisco Goya, *The Third of May 1808* Spanish master Francisco Goya created a passionate and moving indictment of the brutality of war in this painting from 1814, which depicts the close-range execution of Spanish rebels by Napoleon's forces in May 1808. Goya's painting evoked the bitterness and despair of many Europeans who suffered through Napoleon's invasions. (Prado, Madrid, Spain/Bridgeman Images)

one-third of this army was French, however; nationals of all the satellites and allies were drafted into the operation. Originally planning to winter in the Russian city of Smolensk, Napoleon recklessly pressed on toward Moscow. The great Battle of Borodino that followed was a draw. Alexander ordered the evacuation of Moscow, which the Russians then burned in part, and he refused to negotiate. Finally, after five weeks in the scorched and abandoned city, Napoleon ordered a retreat, one of the greatest military disasters in history. The Russian army, the Russian winter, and starvation cut Napoleon's army to pieces. When the frozen remnants staggered into Poland and Prussia in December, 370,000 men had died and another 200,000 had been taken prisoner.[6]

Leaving his troops to their fate, Napoleon raced to Paris to raise yet another army. Possibly he might still have saved his throne if he had been willing to accept a France reduced to its historical size—the proposal offered by Austria's foreign minister, Prince Klemens von Metternich. But Napoleon refused. Austria and Prussia deserted Napoleon and joined Russia and Great Britain in the Treaty of Chaumont in March 1814, by

which the four powers formed the Quadruple Alliance to defeat the French emperor.

All across Europe patriots called for a "war of liberation" against Napoleon's oppression. Less than a month later, on April 4, 1814, a defeated Napoleon abdicated his throne. After this unconditional abdication, the victorious allies granted Napoleon the island of Elba off the coast of Italy as his own tiny state. Napoleon was allowed to keep his imperial title, and France was required to pay him a yearly income of 2 million francs.

The allies also agreed to the restoration of the Bourbon dynasty under Louis XVIII (r. 1814–1824) and promised to treat France with leniency in a peace settlement. The new monarch sought support among the people by issuing the Constitutional Charter, which accepted many of France's revolutionary changes and guaranteed civil liberties.

Yet Louis XVIII lacked the magnetism of Napoleon. Hearing of political unrest in France and diplomatic tensions in Vienna, Napoleon staged a daring escape from Elba in February 1815 and marched on Paris with a small band of followers. French officers and soldiers who had fought so long for their emperor responded to the call. Louis XVIII fled, and once more Napoleon took command. But Napoleon's gamble was a desperate long shot, for the allies were united against him. At the end of a frantic period known as the Hundred Days, they crushed his forces at Waterloo on June 18, 1815, and imprisoned him on the rocky island of St. Helena, off the western coast of Africa. Louis XVIII returned to the throne, and the allies dealt more harshly with the French. As for Napoleon, he took revenge by writing his memoirs, nurturing the myth that he had been Europe's revolutionary liberator, a romantic hero whose lofty work had been undone by oppressive reactionaries.

The Haitian Revolution, 1791–1804

FOCUS QUESTION *How did slave revolt on colonial Saint-Domingue lead to the creation of the independent nation of Haiti in 1804?*

The events that led to the creation of the independent nation of Haiti constitute the third, and perhaps most extraordinary, chapter of the revolutionary era in the late eighteenth century. Prior to 1789 Saint-Domingue, the French colony that was to become Haiti, reaped huge profits through a ruthless system of slave-based plantation agriculture. News of revolution in France lit a powder keg of contradictory aspirations among white planters, free people of color, and slaves. While revolutionary authorities debated how far to extend the rights of man on Saint-Domingue, first free people of color and then enslaved people took matters into their own hands, rising up to claim their freedom. They succeeded, despite invasion by the British and Spanish and Napoleon Bonaparte's bid to reimpose French control. In 1804 Haiti became the only nation in history to claim its freedom through slave revolt.

Revolutionary Aspirations in Saint-Domingue

On the eve of the French Revolution, Saint-Domingue—the most profitable of all Caribbean colonies—was even more rife with social tensions than France itself. The colony, which occupied the western third of the island of Hispaniola, was inhabited by a variety of social groups who resented and mistrusted one another. The European population included French colonial officials, wealthy plantation owners and merchants, and poor artisans and clerks. Individuals of French or European descent born in the colonies were called "Creoles," and over time they had developed their own interests, at times distinct from those of metropolitan France. Vastly

outnumbering the white population were the colony's five hundred thousand enslaved people alongside a sizable population of some forty thousand free people of African and mixed African and European descent. Members of this last group referred to themselves as free people of color.

Legal and economic conditions on Saint-Domingue vastly favored the white population. Most of the island's enslaved population performed grueling toil in the island's sugar plantations. The highly outnumbered planters used extremely brutal methods, such as beating, maiming, and executing slaves, to maintain their control. The 1685 Code Noir (Black Code) that set the parameters of slavery was intended to provide minimal standards of humane treatment, but its tenets were rarely enforced. Masters calculated that they could earn more by working slaves ruthlessly and purchasing new ones when they died, than by providing the food, rest, and medical care needed to allow the enslaved population to reproduce naturally. This meant a constant inflow of newly enslaved people from Africa was necessary to work the plantations.

Despite their brutality, slaveholders on Saint-Domingue freed a surprising number of their slaves, mostly their own mixed-race children, thereby producing one of the largest populations of free people of color in any slaveholding colony. The Code Noir had originally granted free people of color the same legal status as whites: they could own property, live where they wished, and pursue any education or career they desired. From the 1760s on, however, the rising prosperity and visibility of this group provoked resentment from the white population. In response, colonial administrators began rescinding the rights of free people of color, and by the time of the French Revolution myriad aspects of their lives were subject to discriminatory laws.

The political and intellectual turmoil of the 1780s, with its growing rhetoric of liberty, equality, and fraternity, raised new challenges and possibilities for each of Saint-Domingue's social groups. For enslaved people, who constituted approximately 90 percent of the population, news of abolitionist movements in France led to hopes that the mother country might grant them freedom. Free people of color looked to reforms in Paris as a means of gaining political enfranchisement and reasserting equal status with whites. The Creole elite, not surprisingly, saw matters very differently. Infuriated by talk of abolition and determined to protect their way of life, they looked to revolutionary ideals of representative government for the chance to gain control of their own affairs, as had the American colonists before them.

The National Assembly frustrated the hopes of all these groups. Cowed by colonial representatives who claimed that support for free people of color would result in slave insurrection and independence, the Assembly refused to extend French constitutional safeguards to the colonies. After dealing this blow to the

Saint-Domingue Slave Life   Although the brutal conditions of plantation slavery left little time or energy for leisure, slaves on Saint-Domingue took advantage of their day of rest on Sunday to engage in social and religious activities. The law officially prohibited slaves of different masters from mingling together, but such gatherings were often tolerated if they remained peaceful. This image depicts a fight between two slaves, precisely the type of unrest and violence feared by authorities. (By Agostino Brunias [1728–1796]/Yale Center for British Art, Paul Mellon Collection, USA/Bridgeman Images)

aspirations of slaves and free people of color, the Assembly also reaffirmed French monopolies over colonial trade, thereby angering Creole planters as well. Like the American settlers before them, the colonists chafed under the rule of the mother country.

In July 1790 Vincent Ogé (aw-ZHAY) (ca. 1750–1791), a free man of color, returned to Saint-Domingue from Paris determined to win rights for his people. He raised an army of several hundred and sent letters to the new Provincial Assembly of Saint-Domingue demanding political rights for all free citizens. But Ogé's demands were refused, so he and his followers turned to armed insurrection. After initial victories, his army was defeated, and Ogé was tortured and executed by colonial officials. Revolutionary leaders in Paris were more sympathetic to Ogé's cause. In May 1791, responding to what it perceived as partly justified grievances, the National Assembly granted political rights to free people of color born to two free parents who possessed sufficient property. When news of this legislation arrived in Saint-Domingue, the white elite was furious, and the colonial governor refused to enact it. Violence now erupted between groups of whites and free people of color in parts of the colony.

The Outbreak of Revolt

Just as the sans-culottes helped push forward more radical reforms in France, the second stage of revolution in Saint-Domingue also resulted from decisive action from below. In August 1791 slaves, who had witnessed the confrontation between whites and free people of color for over a year, took events into their own hands. Groups of slaves held a series of nighttime meetings to plan a mass insurrection. In doing so, they drew on their own considerable military experience; the majority of slaves had been born in Africa, and many had served in the civil wars of the kingdom of Kongo and other conflicts before being taken into slavery.[7] They also drew on a long tradition of slave resistance prior to 1791, which had ranged from work slowdowns, to running away, to taking part in African-derived religious rituals and dances known as *vodou* (or voodoo). According to some sources, the August 1791 pact to take up arms was sealed by such a voodoo ritual.[8]

Revolts began on a few plantations on the night of August 22. Within a few days the uprising had swept much of the northern plain, creating a slave army

Slave Revolt on Saint-Domingue This illustration, from the proslavery perspective, emphasizes the violence and destructiveness of the slave rebellion in Saint-Domingue. Many white settlers fled to the United States and other Caribbean islands with as much of their property, including slaves, as they could take with them. (The Library Company of Philadelphia)

estimated at around 2,000 individuals. By August 27 it was described by one observer as "10,000 strong, divided into 3 armies, of whom 700 or 800 are on horseback, and tolerably well-armed."[9] During the next month enslaved combatants attacked and destroyed hundreds of sugar and coffee plantations.

On April 4, 1792, as war loomed with the European states, the National Assembly issued a decree extending full citizenship rights to free people of color, including the right to vote. As in France, voting rights and the ability to hold public office applied to men only. The Assembly hoped this measure would win the loyalty of free people of color and their aid in defeating the slave rebellion.

Warfare in Europe soon spread to Saint-Domingue (Map 19.3). Since the beginning of the slave insurrection, the Spanish colony of Santo Domingo, on the eastern side of the island of Hispaniola, had supported rebel slaves. In early 1793 the Spanish began to bring slave leaders and their soldiers into the Spanish army. Toussaint L'Ouverture (TOO-sahn LOO-vair-toor) (1743–1803), a freed slave who had joined the revolt, was named a Spanish officer. In September the British navy blockaded the colony, and invading British troops captured French territory on the island. For the Spanish and British, revolutionary chaos provided a tempting opportunity to capture a profitable colony.

Desperate for forces to oppose France's enemies, commissioners sent by the newly elected National Convention promised to emancipate all those who fought for France. By October 1793 they had abolished slavery throughout the colony. On February 4, 1794, the Convention ratified the abolition of slavery and extended it to all French territories, including the Caribbean colonies of Martinique and Guadeloupe. In some ways this act merely acknowledged the achievements already won by the slave insurrection itself.

The tide of battle began to turn when Toussaint L'Ouverture switched sides, bringing his military and political skills, along with four thousand well-trained soldiers, to support the French war effort. By 1796 the French had regained control of the colony, and L'Ouverture had emerged as a key military leader. (See "Individuals in Society: Toussaint L'Ouverture," page 644.) In May 1796 he was named commander of the western province of Saint-Domingue (see Map 19.3). The increasingly conservative nature of the French government during the Thermidorian reaction, however, threatened to undo the gains made by former slaves and free people of color.

The War of Haitian Independence

With Toussaint L'Ouverture acting increasingly as an independent ruler of the western province of Saint-Domingue, another general, André Rigaud (1761–1811), set up his own government in the southern peninsula.

Tensions mounted between L'Ouverture and Rigaud. While L'Ouverture was a freed slave of African descent, Rigaud belonged to the free colored elite. This elite resented the growing power of former slaves like L'Ouverture, who in turn accused them of adopting the racism of white settlers. Civil war broke out between the two sides in 1799, when L'Ouverture's forces, led by his lieutenant, Jean Jacques Dessalines (1758–1806), invaded the south. Victory over Rigaud in 1800 gave L'Ouverture control of the entire colony.

This victory was soon challenged by Napoleon, who had his own plans for re-establishing slavery and using the profits as a basis for expanding French power. Napoleon ordered his brother-in-law, General Charles-Victor-Emmanuel Leclerc (1772–1802), to lead an expedition to the island to crush the new regime. In 1802 Leclerc landed in Saint-Domingue and ordered the arrest of Toussaint L'Ouverture. The rebel leader, along with his family, was deported to France, where he died in 1803.

It was left to L'Ouverture's lieutenant, Jean Jacques Dessalines, to unite the resistance, and he led it to a crushing victory over French forces. On January 1, 1804,

The Haitian Revolution

May 1791	French National Assembly enfranchises free men of color born of two free parents
August 1791	Slave insurrections in Saint-Domingue
April 1792	French National Assembly grants full citizenship rights to free people of color, including the right to vote for men
September 1793	British troops invade Saint-Domingue
February 1794	Abolition of slavery in all French territories
1796	France regains control of Saint-Domingue under Toussaint L'Ouverture
1803	Death of Toussaint L'Ouverture in France
January 1804	Declaration of Haitian independence
May 1805	First Haitian constitution

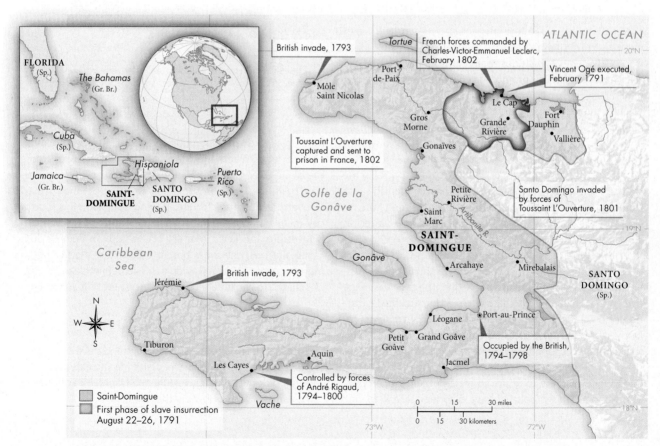

MAP 19.3 The War of Haitian Independence, 1791–1804   Neighbored by the Spanish colony of Santo Domingo, Saint-Domingue was the most profitable European colony in the Caribbean. In 1770 the French transferred the capital from Le Cap to Port-au-Prince. Slave revolts erupted in the north near Le Cap in 1791. Port-au-Prince became the capital of the newly independent Haiti in 1804.

INDIVIDUALS IN SOCIETY

Toussaint L'Ouverture

Little is known of the early life of Saint-Domingue's brilliant military and political leader Toussaint L'Ouverture. He was born in 1743 on a plantation outside Le Cap owned by the Count de Bréda. According to tradition, L'Ouverture was the eldest son of a captured African prince from modern-day Benin. Toussaint Bréda, as he was then called, occupied a privileged position among slaves. Instead of performing backbreaking labor in the fields, he served his master as a coachman and livestock keeper. He also learned to read and write French and some Latin, but he was always more comfortable with the Creole dialect.

During the 1770s the plantation manager emancipated L'Ouverture, who subsequently leased his own small coffee plantation and slaves. He married Suzanne Simone, who already had one son, and the couple had another son during their marriage. In 1791 he joined the slave uprisings that swept Saint-Domingue, and he took on the *nom de guerre* (war name) "L'Ouverture," meaning "the opening." L'Ouverture rose to prominence among rebel slaves allied with Spain and by early 1794 controlled his own army. A devout Catholic who led a frugal and ascetic life, L'Ouverture impressed others with his enormous physical energy, intellectual acumen, and air of mystery. In 1794 he defected to the French side and led his troops to a series of victories against the Spanish. In 1795 the National Convention promoted L'Ouverture to brigadier general.

Over the next three years L'Ouverture successively eliminated rivals for authority on the island. First he freed himself of the French commissioners sent to govern the colony. With a firm grip on power in the northern province, L'Ouverture defeated General André Rigaud in 1800 to gain control in the south. His army then marched on the capital of Spanish Santo Domingo on the eastern half of the island, meeting little resistance. The entire island of Hispaniola was now under his command.

With control of Saint-Domingue in his hands, L'Ouverture was confronted with the challenge of building a post-emancipation society, the first of its kind. The task was made even more difficult by the chaos wreaked by war, the destruction of plantations, and bitter social and racial tensions. For L'Ouverture the most pressing concern was to re-establish the plantation economy. Without revenue to pay his army, the gains of the rebellion could be lost. He therefore encouraged white planters to return to reclaim their property. He also adopted harsh policies toward former slaves, forcing

Equestrian portrait of Toussaint L'Ouverture. (© Photos 12/ Alamy Stock Photo)

them back to their plantations and restricting their ability to acquire land. When they resisted, he sent troops across the island to enforce submission. L'Ouverture's 1801 constitution reaffirmed his draconian labor policies and named L'Ouverture governor for life, leaving Saint-Domingue as a colony in name alone. In June 1802 French forces arrested L'Ouverture and jailed him at Fort de Joux in France's Jura Mountains near the Swiss border. L'Ouverture died of pneumonia on April 7, 1803. It was left to his lieutenant, Jean Jacques Dessalines, to win independence for the new Haitian nation.

QUESTIONS FOR ANALYSIS

1. Toussaint L'Ouverture was both slave and slave owner. How did each experience shape his life and actions?
2. What did Toussaint L'Ouverture and Napoleon Bonaparte have in common? How did they differ?

Dessalines formally declared the independence of Saint-Domingue and the creation of the new sovereign nation of Haiti, the name used by the pre-Columbian inhabitants of the island. The Haitian constitution was ratified in 1805.

Haiti, the second independent state in the Americas and the first in Latin America, was born from the first successful large-scale slave revolt in history. This event spread shock and fear through slaveholding societies in the Caribbean and the United States, bringing to life their worst nightmares of the utter reversal of their power and privilege. Fearing the spread of rebellion to the United States, President Thomas Jefferson refused to recognize Haiti as an independent nation. The liberal proponents of American revolution thus chose to protect slavery at the expense of revolutionary ideals of universal human rights. The French government imposed crushing indemnity charges on Haiti to recompense the loss of French property, dealing a harsh blow to the fledgling nation's economy.

Yet Haitian independence had fundamental repercussions for world history, helping spread the idea that liberty, equality, and fraternity must apply to all people. The next phase of Atlantic revolution soon opened in the Spanish American colonies.

NOTES

1. Quoted in G. Wright, *France in Modern Times*, 4th ed. (New York: W. W. Norton, 1987), p. 34.
2. G. Pernoud and S. Flaisser, eds., *The French Revolution* (Greenwich, Conn.: Fawcett, 1960), p. 61.
3. Quoted in L. Gershoy, *The Era of the French Revolution, 1789–1799* (New York: Van Nostrand, 1957), p. 150.
4. Quoted in Wim Klooster, *Revolutions in the Atlantic World: A Comprehensive History* (New York: New York University Press, 2009), p. 74.
5. T. Blanning, *The French Revolutionary Wars, 1787–1802* (London: Arnold, 1996), pp. 116–128.
6. D. Sutherland, *France, 1789–1815: Revolution and Counterrevolution* (New York: Oxford University Press, 1986), p. 420.
7. John K. Thornton, "'I Am the Subject of the King of Congo': African Political Ideology and the Haitian Revolution," *Journal of World History* 4, no. 2 (Fall 1993): 181–214.
8. Laurent Dubois, *Avengers of the New World: The Story of the Haitian Revolution* (Cambridge, Mass.: Belknap Press, 2004), pp. 43–45, 99–100.
9. Quoted ibid., p. 97.

LOOKING BACK LOOKING AHEAD

A great revolutionary wave swept both sides of the Atlantic Ocean in the late eighteenth century. The revolutions in British North America, France, and Haiti were individual and unique, but they had common origins and consequences for Western and, indeed, world history. Despite the French monarchy's ongoing claims to the absolutist rule imposed by Louis XIV, the eighteenth century had inaugurated monumental changes, as population grew, urbanization spread, and literacy increased. Enlightenment ideals, especially those of John Locke and the baron de Montesquieu, influenced all orders of society, and reformers increasingly championed limiting monarchical authority in the name of popular sovereignty.

The Atlantic world was the essential context for this age of revolutions. The movement of peoples, commodities, and ideas across the Atlantic Ocean in the eighteenth century created a world of common debates, conflicts, and aspirations. Moreover, the high stakes of colonial empire heightened competition among European states, leading to a series of wars that generated crushing costs for overburdened treasuries. For both the British in their North American colonies and the French at home, the desperate need for new taxes weakened government authority and opened the door to revolution. In turn, the ideals of the French Revolution inspired slaves and free people of color in Saint-Domingue, thus opening the promise of liberty, equality, and fraternity to people of all races.

The chain reaction did not end with the birth of an independent Haiti in 1804. On the European continent throughout the nineteenth and early twentieth centuries, periodic convulsions occurred as successive generations struggled over political rights first proclaimed by the generation of 1789. Meanwhile, as dramatic political events unfolded, a parallel economic revolution was gathering steam. This was the Industrial Revolution, originating around 1780 and accelerating through the end of the eighteenth century (see Chapter 20). After 1815 the twin forces of industrialization and democratization would combine to transform Europe and the world.

Make Connections

Think about the larger developments and continuities within and across chapters.

1. What were major differences and similarities among the American, French, and Haitian Revolutions?

2. How did the increased circulation of goods, people, and ideas across the Atlantic in the eighteenth century (Chapter 17) contribute to the outbreak of revolution on both sides of the ocean?

3. To what extent would you characterize the revolutions discussed in this chapter as Enlightenment movements (Chapter 16)?

19 REVIEW & EXPLORE

Identify Key Terms

Identify and explain the significance of each item below.

Estates General (p. 620)	the Mountain (p. 629)
estates (p. 620)	sans-culottes (p. 629)
National Assembly (p. 621)	Reign of Terror (p. 631)
Great Fear (p. 623)	Thermidorian reaction (p. 634)
Jacobin Club (p. 628)	Napoleonic Code (p. 636)
second revolution (p. 629)	Grand Empire (p. 637)
Girondists (p. 629)	Continental System (p.637)

Review the Main Ideas

Answer the focus questions from each section of the chapter.

◆ What were the factors leading to the revolutions of the late eighteenth century? (p. 612)

◆ Why and how did American colonists forge a new, independent nation? (p. 615)

◆ How did the events of 1789 result in a constitutional monarchy in France, and what were the consequences? (p. 619)

◆ Why and how did the French Revolution take a radical turn entailing terror at home and war with European powers? (p. 625)

◆ How did Napoleon Bonaparte assume control of France and much of Europe, and what factors led to his downfall? (p. 635)

◆ How did slave revolt on colonial Saint-Domingue lead to the creation of the independent nation of Haiti in 1804? (p. 640)

Suggested Reading and Media Resources

BOOKS

- Armitage, David, and Sanjay Subrahmanyam, eds. *The Age of Revolutions in Global Context, c. 1760–1840.* 2009. Presents the international causes and consequences of the age of revolutions.

- Auslander, Leora. *Cultural Revolutions: Everyday Life and Politics in Britain, North America, and France.* 2009. An innovative interpretation of the revolutions in England, America, and France as cultural revolutions that politicized daily life.

- Bell, David A. *The First Total War: Napoleon's War and the Birth of Warfare as We Know It.* 2007. Argues that the French Revolution created a new form of "total" war that prefigured the world wars of the twentieth century.

- Calloway, Colin G. *The Scratch of a Pen: 1763 and the Transformation of North America.* 2006. A study of the dramatic impact of the Seven Years' War on the British and French colonies of North America.

- Desan, Suzanne. *The Family on Trial in Revolutionary France.* 2004. Studies the effects of revolutionary law on the family, including the legalization of divorce.

- Dubois, Laurent. *Avengers of the New World: The Story of the Haitian Revolution.* 2004. An excellent and highly readable account of the revolution that transformed the French colony of Saint-Domingue into the independent state of Haiti.

- Gould, Eliga H., and Peter S. Onuf, eds. *Empire and Nation: The American Revolution in the Atlantic World.* 2005. A collection of essays placing the American Revolution in its wider Atlantic context, including studies of its impact on daily life in the new republic and the remaining British Empire.

- Klooster, Wim. *Revolutions in the Atlantic World: A Comparative History.* 2009. An accessible and engaging comparison of the revolutions in North America, France, Haiti, and Spanish America.

- McPhee, Peter, ed. *A Companion to the French Revolution.* 2013. A wide-ranging collection of essays on the French Revolution, written by outstanding experts in the field.

- Schechter, Ronald. *Obstinate Hebrews: Representations of Jews in France, 1715–1815.* 2003. An illuminating study of Jews and attitudes toward them in France, from the Enlightenment to emancipation.

- Sepinwall, Alyssa, ed. *Haitian History: New Perspectives.* 2013. A collection of essays showcasing the most important new scholarship on the Haitian Revolution.

- Wood, Gordon S. *The American Revolution: A History.* 2003. A concise introduction to the American Revolution by a Pulitzer Prize–winning historian.

DOCUMENTARIES

- *Égalité for All: Toussaint Louverture and the Haitian Revolution* (PBS, 2009). Uses music, interviews, voodoo rituals, and dramatic re-enactments to explore the Haitian Revolution and its fascinating leader, Toussaint L'Ouverture.

- *Liberty! The American Revolution* (PBS, 1997). A dramatic documentary about the American Revolution, consisting of six hour-long episodes that cover events from 1763 to 1788.

- *The War That Made America* (PBS, 2006). A miniseries about the French and Indian War that focuses on alliances between Native Americans and the French and British, including George Washington's role in the conflict as a young officer.

FEATURE FILMS AND TELEVISION

- *Colonel Chabert* (Yves Angelo, 1994). A Napoleonic cavalryman severely wounded in battle and left for dead recovers and returns home to find that his wife has remarried an ambitious politician.

- *Farewell, My Queen* (Benoît Jacquot, 2012). A fictional view of the final days of the French monarchy, from the perspective of a female servant whose job is to read to Queen Marie Antoinette.

- *John Adams* (HBO, 2008). An award-winning miniseries on the life of one of the Founding Fathers of the United States.

- *Master and Commander: The Far Side of the World* (Peter Weir, 2003). A British navy captain pursues a French vessel along the coast of South America during the Napoleonic Wars.

WEB SITES

- *French Revolution Digital Archive.* A Web site hosted by Stanford University that includes fourteen thousand digital images from the French Revolution. **http://frda.stanford.edu/**

- *Haiti Digital Library.* A guide to online primary sources, articles, and Web sites related to Haitian history, from the revolution to modern times; sponsored by the Haiti Laboratory at Duke University. **sites.duke.edu/haitilab/english/**

- *Liberty, Equality, Fraternity: Exploring the French Revolution.* Features a large image and document collection from the era of the French Revolution, as well as songs, maps, and thematic essays written by expert scholars in the field. **chnm.gmu.edu/revolution/**

- *The Papers of George Washington.* A site with online versions of many documents pertaining to and written by George Washington, accompanied by articles on themes related to Washington's life and views. **gwpapers.virginia.edu/**

20

The Revolution in Energy and Industry

ca. 1780–1850

While revolutions in France and across the Atlantic were opening a new political era, another revolution was beginning to transform economic and social life. The Industrial Revolution took off around 1780 in Great Britain and soon began to influence continental Europe and the United States. Non-European nations began to industrialize after 1860.

Industrialization profoundly modified much of human experience. It changed patterns of work, transformed the social class structure and the way people thought about class, and eventually altered the international balance of political power. Quite possibly only the development of agriculture during Neolithic times had a comparable impact and significance.

What was revolutionary about the Industrial Revolution was not its pace or that it represented a sharp break with the previous period. On the contrary, the Industrial Revolution built on earlier developments, and the rate of progress was slow. What was remarkable about the Industrial Revolution was that it inaugurated a period of sustained economic and demographic growth that has continued to the present day. Although it took time, the Industrial Revolution eventually helped ordinary people in the West gain a higher standard of living as the widespread poverty of preindustrial Europe gradually receded.

Such fundamental transitions did not occur overnight. National wealth rose much more quickly than improvements in the European standard of living until about 1850. This was because, even in Britain, only a few key industries experienced a technological revolution. Many more industries continued to use old methods. In addition, wage increases were modest until the mid-nineteenth century, and the gradual withdrawal of children and married women from paid work meant that the household as a whole earned the same or less. ■

CHAPTER PREVIEW

Life in the Industrial Revolution
Daily life for industrial workers was harsh, especially for the many child laborers who worked in the new factories and in other industries, like the glassworks pictured here. Long hours of work, strict discipline, and low wages were the lot of most industrial workers, whose living standards did not improve until the 1840s. (*The Falcon Glassworks*, c. 1840, [oil on canvas]/© Museum of London/HIP/The Image Works)

The Industrial Revolution in Britain

FOCUS QUESTION *Why did the Industrial Revolution begin in Britain, and how did it develop between 1780 and 1850?*

The Industrial Revolution began in Great Britain, the nation created in 1707 by the formal union of Scotland, Wales, and England. The transformation in industry was something new in history, and it was unplanned. With no models to copy and no idea of what to expect, Britain pioneered not only in industrial technology but also in social relations and urban living. Just as France was a trailblazer in political change, Britain was the leader in economic development, and it must therefore command special attention.

Why Britain?

Perhaps the most important debate in economic history focuses on why the Industrial Revolution originated in western Europe, and Britain in particular, rather than in other parts of the world, such as Asia. Historians continue to debate this issue, but the best answer seems to be that Britain possessed a unique set of possibilities and constraints—abundant coal, high wages, a relatively peaceful and centralized government, well-developed financial systems, innovative culture, highly skilled craftsmen, and a strong position in empire and global trade—that spurred its people to adopt a capital-intensive, machine-powered system of production. The long-term economic advantages of this system were not immediately apparent, and its adoption by the British was more a matter of circumstance than a planned strategy.

Thus a number of factors came together over the long term to give rise to the Industrial Revolution in Britain. The Scientific Revolution and the Enlightenment fostered a new world-view that embraced progress and the role of research and experimentation in understanding and mastering the natural world. Britain's intellectual culture emphasized the public sharing of knowledge, including that of scientists and technicians from other countries. The British Royal Society of Arts, for example, sponsored prizes for innovations in machinery and agriculture and played a pivotal part in the circulation of "useful knowledge."

In the economic realm, the seventeenth-century expansion of rural industry produced a surplus of English woolen cloth. Exported throughout Europe, English cloth brought commercial profits and high wages to the detriment of traditional producers in Flanders and Italy. By the eighteenth century the expanding Atlantic economy and trade with India and China were also serving Britain well. The mercantilist colonial empire Britain aggressively built, augmented by a strong position in Latin America and in the transatlantic slave trade, provided raw materials like cotton and a growing market for British manufactured goods (see Chapter 17). Strong demand for British manufacturing meant that British workers earned high wages compared to the rest of Europe.

Agriculture also played an important role in bringing about the Industrial Revolution in Britain. English farmers were second only to the Dutch in productivity in 1700, and they were continually adopting new methods of farming. The result, especially before 1760, was a period of bountiful crops and low food prices. Because of increasing efficiency, landowners were able to produce more food with a smaller workforce. By the mid-eighteenth century, on the eve of the Industrial Revolution, less than half of Britain's population worked in agriculture. The enclosure movement had deprived many small landowners of their land, leaving the landless poor to work as hired agricultural laborers or in cottage industry. These groups created a large pool of potential laborers for the new factories.

Abundant food and high wages in turn meant that the ordinary English family no longer had to spend almost everything it earned just to buy bread. Thus the family could spend more on manufactured goods—a razor for the man or a shawl for the woman. They could also pay to send their children to school. Britain's populace enjoyed high levels of literacy and numeracy (knowledge of mathematics) compared to the rest of Europe. Moreover, in the eighteenth century the members of the average British family were redirecting their labor away from unpaid work for household consumption and toward work for wages that they could spend on goods, a trend reflecting the increasing commercialization of the entire European economy.

Britain also benefited from rich natural resources and a well-developed infrastructure. In an age when it was much cheaper to ship goods by water than by land, no part of England was more than fifty miles from navigable water. Beginning in the 1770s a

Cottage Industry and Transportation in Eighteenth-Century Great Britain

Industrial areas
- ■ Coal deposit
- ○ Metal goods
- ■ Woolen cloth
- — Canals, 1800
- — Navigable rivers

SCOTLAND

Newcastle

North Sea

Manchester — Sheffield

Birmingham — *Iron*

WALES

ENGLAND

Iron

London

Bath   *Iron*

Exeter

English Channel

canal-building boom enhanced this advantage. Rivers and canals provided easy movement of England's and Wales's enormous deposits of iron and coal, resources that would be critical raw materials in Europe's early industrial age. The abundance of coal combined with high wages in manufacturing placed Britain in a unique position among European nations: its manufacturers had extremely strong incentives to develop technologies to draw on the power of coal to increase workmen's productivity. In parts of the world with lower wages, such as India and China, the costs of mechanization at first outweighed potential gains in productivity.

A final factor favoring British industrialization was the heavy hand of the British state and its policies, especially in the formative decades of industrial change. Despite its rhetoric in favor of "liberty," Britain's parliamentary system taxed its population aggressively. The British state collected twice as much per capita as the supposedly "absolutist" French monarchy and spent the money on a navy to protect imperial commerce and on an army that could be used to quell uprisings by disgruntled workers. Starting with the Navigation Acts under Oliver Cromwell (see Chapter 15), the British state also adopted aggressive tariffs, or duties, on imported goods to protect its industries.

All these factors combined to initiate the **Industrial Revolution**, a term first coined by awed contemporaries in the 1820s to describe the burst of major inventions and technical changes under way. This technical revolution went hand in hand with an impressive quickening in the annual rate of industrial growth in Britain. Whereas industry had grown at only 0.7 percent between 1700 and 1760 (before the Industrial Revolution), it grew at the much higher rate of 3 percent between 1801 and 1831 (when industrial transformation was in full swing).[1]

Technological Innovations and Early Factories

The pressure to produce more goods for a growing market and to reduce the labor costs of manufacturing was directly related to the first decisive breakthrough of the Industrial Revolution: the creation of the world's first machine-powered factories in the British cotton textile industry. Technological innovations in the manufacture of cotton cloth led to a new system of production and social relationships. This was not the first time in European history that large numbers of people were systematically put to work in a single locale; the military arsenals of late medieval Venice are one example of a much older form of "factory." The crucial innovation in Britain was the introduction of machine power into the factory and the organization of labor around the functioning of highly productive machines.

The putting-out system that developed in the seventeenth-century textile industry involved a merchant who loaned, or "put out," raw materials to cottage workers who processed the raw materials in their own homes and returned the finished products to the merchant. There was always a serious imbalance in

Chronology

ca. 1765	Hargreaves invents spinning jenny; Arkwright creates water frame
1769	Watt patents modern steam engine
ca. 1780–1850	Industrial Revolution; population boom in Britain
1799	Combination Acts passed in England
1802–1833	Series of Factory Acts passed by British government to limit the workday of child laborers and set minimum hygiene and safety requirements
1805	Egypt begins process of modernization
1810	Strike of Manchester cotton spinners
ca. 1815	Western European countries seek to adopt British industrial methods
1824	Combination Acts repealed
1829	Stephenson's *Rocket*, an early locomotive
1830s	Industrial banks in Belgium
1834	*Zollverein* erected among most German states
1842	Mines Act passed in Britain
1844	Engels, *The Condition of the Working Class in England*
1850s	Japan begins to adopt Western technologies; industrial gap widens between the West and the rest of the world
1851	Great Exhibition held at Crystal Palace in London
1860s	Germany and the United States begin to rapidly industrialize

> ■ **Industrial Revolution** A term first coined in 1799 to describe the burst of major inventions and economic expansion that began in Britain in the late eighteenth century.

Woman Working a Spinning Jenny
The loose cotton strands on the slanted bobbins shown in this illustration of Hargreaves's spinning jenny passed up to the sliding carriage and then on to the spindles (inset) in back for fine spinning. The worker, almost always a woman, regulated the sliding carriage with one hand, and with the other she turned the crank on the wheel to supply power. By 1783 one woman could spin by hand a hundred threads at a time. (spinning jenny: © Mary Evans Picture Library/The Image Works; spindle: Picture Research Consultants & Archives)

textile production based on cottage industry: the work of four or five spinners was needed to keep one weaver steadily employed. Cloth weavers constantly had to find more thread and more spinners. During the eighteenth century the putting-out system grew across Europe, but most extensively in Britain. There, pressured by growing demand, the system's limitations began to outweigh its advantages around 1760.

Many a tinkering worker knew that a better spinning wheel promised rich rewards. It proved hard to spin the traditional raw materials—wool and flax—with improved machines, but cotton was different. Cotton textiles had first been imported into Britain from India by the East India Company as a rare and delicate luxury for the upper classes. In the eighteenth century a lively market for cotton cloth emerged in

West Africa, where the English and other Europeans traded it in exchange for slaves. By 1760 a tiny domestic cotton industry had emerged in northern England, but it could not compete with cloth produced in India and other parts of Asia. At this time, Indian cotton textiles dominated the world market, due to their workers' mastery over design and dyeing techniques, easy access to raw materials, and relatively low wages. International competition thus drove English entrepreneurs to invent new technologies to bring down labor costs.

After many experiments over a generation, a gifted carpenter and jack-of-all-trades, James Hargreaves, invented his cotton-spinning jenny about 1765. At almost the same moment, a barber-turned-manufacturer named Richard Arkwright invented (or possibly pirated) another kind of spinning machine, the water frame. These breakthroughs produced an explosion in the infant cotton textile industry in the 1780s, when it was increasing the value of its output at an unprecedented rate of about 13 percent each year. By 1790 the new machines were producing ten times as much cotton yarn as had been made in 1770.

Hargreaves's **spinning jenny** was simple, inexpensive, and powered by hand. In early models from six to twenty-four spindles were mounted on a sliding carriage, and each spindle spun a fine, slender thread.

The machines were usually worked by women, who moved the carriage back and forth with one hand and turned a wheel to supply power with the other. Now it was the male weaver who could not keep up with the vastly more efficient female spinner.

Arkwright's spinning frame employed a different principle, using a series of rollers to stretch the yarn. It quickly acquired a capacity of several hundred spindles and demanded much more power than a single operator could provide. A solution was found in waterpower. The **water frame** required large specialized mills located beside rivers in factories that employed as many as one thousand workers. The water frame did not completely replace cottage industry, however, for it could spin only a coarse, strong thread, which was then put out for respinning on hand-operated cottage jennies. Around 1780 a hybrid machine—called a mule—invented by Samuel Crompton proved capable of spinning very fine and strong thread in large quantities. (See "Individuals in Society: Samuel Crompton," page 654.) Gradually, all cotton spinning was concentrated in large-scale water-powered factories.

These revolutionary developments in the textile industry allowed British manufacturers to compete successfully in international markets in both fine and coarse cotton thread. At first, the machines were too expensive to build and did not provide enough savings in labor to be adopted in continental Europe or elsewhere. Where wages were low and investment capital was scarce, there was little point in adopting mechanized production until significant increases in the machines' productivity, and a drop in the cost of manufacturing them, occurred in the first decades of the nineteenth century.[2]

Families using cotton in cottage industry were freed from their constant search for adequate yarn from scattered part-time spinners, since all the thread needed could be spun in the cottage on the jenny or obtained from a nearby factory. The income of weavers, now hard-pressed to keep up with the spinners, rose markedly until about 1792. They were among the highest-earning workers in England. As a result, large numbers of agricultural laborers became handloom weavers, while mechanics and capitalists sought to invent a power loom to save on labor costs. This Edmund Cartwright achieved in 1785. But the power looms of the factories worked poorly at first and did not replace handlooms until the 1820s.

Working conditions in the early cotton factories were so poor that adult weavers and spinners were reluctant to work in them. Factory owners often turned to young orphans and children instead. By placing them in "apprenticeship" with factory owners, parish officers charged with caring for such children saved money. At the same time, the factory owners gained workers over whom they exercised almost the authority

of slave owners. Apprenticed as young as five or six years of age, boy and girl workers were forced by law to labor for their masters for as many as fourteen years. Housed, fed, and locked up nightly in factory dormitories, the young workers labored thirteen or fourteen hours a day for little or no pay. Harsh physical punishment maintained brutal discipline. To be sure, poor children typically worked long hours in many types of demanding jobs, but this wholesale coercion of orphans as factory apprentices constituted exploitation on a truly unprecedented scale.

The creation of the world's first machine-powered factories in the British cotton textile industry in the 1770s and 1780s, which grew out of the putting-out system of cottage production, was a major historical development. Both symbolically and substantially, the big new cotton mills marked the beginning of the Industrial Revolution in Britain. By 1831 the largely mechanized cotton textile industry accounted for fully 22 percent of the country's entire industrial production.

The Steam Engine Breakthrough

Human beings have long used their toolmaking abilities to construct machines that convert one form of energy into another for their own benefit. In the medieval period, Europeans began to adopt water mills to grind their grain and windmills to pump water and drain swamps. More efficient use of water and wind in the sixteenth and seventeenth centuries enabled them to accomplish more. Nevertheless, even into the eighteenth century Europe, like other areas of the world, continued to rely mainly on wood for energy, and human beings and animals continued to perform most work. This dependence meant that Europe and the rest of the world remained poor in energy and power.

By the eighteenth century wood was in ever-shorter supply in Britain. Processed wood (charcoal) was the fuel that was mixed with iron ore in the blast furnace to produce pig iron, crude iron molded into ingots called "pigs" that could be processed into steel, cast iron, or wrought iron. The iron industry's appetite for wood was enormous, and by 1740 the British iron industry was stagnating. Vast forests enabled Russia in the eighteenth century to become the world's leading producer of iron, much of which was exported to Britain. As wood became ever more scarce, the British looked to coal (combustible rock composed of fossilized organic matter) as an alternative. They had first

■ **spinning jenny** A simple, inexpensive, hand-powered spinning machine created by James Hargreaves in 1765.

■ **water frame** A spinning machine created by Richard Arkwright that had a capacity of several hundred spindles and used waterpower; it therefore required a larger and more specialized mill—a factory.

INDIVIDUALS IN SOCIETY

Samuel Crompton

Samuel Crompton's life story illustrates the remarkable ingenuity and determination of the first generation of inventors of the Industrial Revolution as well as the struggles they faced in controlling and profiting from their inventions. Crompton was born in 1753 in Bolton-in-the Moors, a Lancashire village active in the domestic production of cotton thread and cloth. Crompton descended from small landowners and weavers, but his grandfather had lost the family land and his father died shortly after his birth.

Crompton's mother was a pious and energetic woman who supported the family by tenant farming and spinning and weaving cotton. Crompton spent years spinning in childhood until he was old enough to begin weaving. His mother ensured that he was well educated at the local school, and as a teenager he attended night classes, studying algebra, mathematics, and trigonometry.

This was the period when John Kay's invention of the flying shuttle doubled the speed of handloom weaving, leading to a drastic increase in the demand for thread (see Chapter 17). Crompton's family acquired one of the new spinning jennies — invented by James Hargreaves — and he saw for himself how they advanced production. He was also acquainted with Richard Arkwright, inventor of the water frame, who then operated a barbershop in Bolton.

In 1774 Crompton began work on the spinning machine that would consume what little free time, and spare money, he possessed over the next five years. Solitary by nature, and fearful of competition and the violence of machine breakers, Crompton worked alone and in secret. He earned a little extra money playing violin in the Bolton theater orchestra, and he possessed a set of tools left over from his father's own mechanical experiments.

The result of all this effort was the spinning mule, so called because it combined the rollers of Arkwright's water frame with the moving carriage of Hargreaves's spinning jenny. With the mule, spinners could produce very fine and strong thread in large quantities, something no previous machine had permitted. The mule effectively ended England's reliance on India for the finest muslin cloth.

In 1780, possessed of a spectacular technological breakthrough and a beloved bride, Crompton seemed poised for a prosperous and happy life. Demand surged for the products of his machine, and manufacturers were desperate to learn its secrets. Too poor and naïve to purchase a patent for his invention, Crompton shared it with manufacturers through a subscription agreement. Unfortunately, he received little of the promised money in return.

Once exposed to the public, the spinning mule quickly spread across Great Britain. Crompton continued to make high-quality yarn, but had to compete with all the other

Samuel Crompton, inventor of the spinning mule. (Engraving by Thomas Barlow [1824–1889], based on a painting by Charles Allingham/SSPL/Getty Images)

Replica of the spinning mule, a hybrid machine that combined features from Hargreaves's spinning jenny and Arkwright's water frame. (SSPL/Getty Images)

workshops using his machine. Moreover, he could not keep skilled workers, since they were constantly lured away by his competitors' higher wages.

As others earned great wealth with the mule, Crompton grew frustrated by his relative poverty. In 1811 he toured Great Britain to document his invention's impact. He estimated that 4,600,000 mules were then in operation that directly employed 70,000 people. Crompton's supporters took these figures to Parliament, which granted him a modest reward of £5,000. However, this boost did little to improve his fortunes, and his subsequent business ventures failed. In 1824 local benefactors took up a small subscription to provide for his needs, but he died in poverty in 1827 at the age of seventy-four.

QUESTIONS FOR ANALYSIS

1. What factors in Crompton's life enabled him to succeed as an inventor?
2. Why did Crompton fail to profit from his inventions?
3. What does the contrast between Richard Arkwright's fantastic success and Crompton's relative failure tell us about innovation and commercial enterprise in the Industrial Revolution?

Source: Gilbert James France, *The Life and Times of Samuel Crompton, Inventor of the Spinning Machine Called the Mule* (London: Simpkin Marshall, 1859).

James Nasmyth's Mighty Steam Hammer   Nasmyth's invention was the forerunner of the modern pile driver, and its successful introduction in 1832 epitomized the rapid development of steam-power technology in Britain. In this painting by the inventor himself, workers manipulate a massive iron shaft being hammered into shape at Nasmyth's foundry near Manchester. (Ann Ronan Pictures/Print Collector/Getty Images)

used coal in the late Middle Ages as a source of heat. By 1640 most homes in London were heated with coal, and it was also used in industry to provide heat for making beer, glass, soap, and other products. The breakthrough came when industrialists began to use coal to produce mechanical energy and to power machinery.

To produce more coal, mines had to be dug deeper and deeper and, as a result, were constantly filling with water. Mechanical pumps, usually powered by animals walking in circles at the surface, had to be installed. Animal power was expensive and bothersome. In an attempt to overcome these disadvantages, Thomas Savery in 1698 and Thomas Newcomen in 1705 invented the first primitive **steam engines**. Both engines burned coal to produce steam, which was then used to operate a pump. Although both models were extremely inefficient, by the early 1770s many of the Savery engines and hundreds of the Newcomen engines were operating successfully in English and Scottish mines.

In 1763 a gifted young Scot named James Watt (1736–1819) was drawn to a critical study of the steam engine. Watt was employed at the time by the University of Glasgow as a skilled craftsman making scientific instruments. Scotland's Enlightenment emphasis on practicality and social progress had caused its universities to become pioneers in technical education. In 1763 Watt was called on to repair a Newcomen engine being used in a physics course. After a series of observations, Watt saw that the Newcomen engine's waste of energy could be reduced by adding a separate condenser. This splendid invention, patented in 1769, greatly increased the efficiency of the steam engine.

To invent something is one thing; to make it a practical success is quite another. Watt needed skilled

■ **steam engines** A breakthrough invention by Thomas Savery in 1698 and Thomas Newcomen in 1705 that burned coal to produce steam, which was then used to operate a pump; the early models were superseded by James Watt's more efficient steam engine, patented in 1769.

workers, precision parts, and capital, and the relatively advanced nature of the British economy proved essential. A partnership in 1775 with Matthew Boulton, a wealthy English industrialist, provided Watt with adequate capital and exceptional skills in salesmanship. Among Britain's highly skilled locksmiths, tinsmiths, and millwrights, Watt found mechanics who could install, regulate, and repair his sophisticated engines. From ingenious manufacturers such as the cannon-maker John Wilkinson, Watt was gradually able to purchase precision parts. This support allowed him to create an effective vacuum in the condenser and regulate a complex engine. In more than twenty years of constant effort, Watt made many further improvements. By the late 1780s the firm of Boulton and Watt had made the steam engine a practical and commercial success in Britain.

The coal-burning steam engine of Watt and his followers was the Industrial Revolution's most fundamental advance in technology. For the first time in history, humanity had, at least for a few generations, almost unlimited power at its disposal. For the first time, inventors and engineers could devise and implement all kinds of power equipment to aid people in their work. The steam-power plant began to replace waterpower in cotton-spinning factories during the 1780s, contributing greatly to that industry's phenomenal rise. Steam also took the place of waterpower in flour mills, in the malt mills used in breweries, in the flint mills supplying the pottery industry, and in the mills exported by Britain to the West Indies to crush sugarcane.

The British iron industry was radically transformed. Originally, the smoke and fumes resulting from coal burning meant that coal could not be substituted for charcoal in smelting iron. Starting around 1710, ironmakers began to use coke—a smokeless and hot-burning fuel produced by heating coal to rid it of water and other impurities—to smelt pig iron. After 1770 the adoption of steam-driven bellows in blast furnaces allowed for great increases in the quantity of pig iron produced by British ironmakers. In the 1780s Henry Cort developed the puddling furnace, which allowed pig iron to be refined in turn with coke.

Strong, skilled ironworkers—the puddlers—"cooked" molten pig iron in a great vat, raking off globs of refined iron for further processing. Cort also developed steam-powered rolling mills, which were capable of turning out finished iron in every shape and form. The economic consequence of these technical innovations was a great boom in the British iron industry. In 1740 annual British iron production was only 17,000 tons. With the spread of coke smelting and the impact of Cort's inventions, production had reached 260,000 tons by 1806. In 1844 Britain produced 3 million tons of iron. Once expensive, iron became the cheap, basic, indispensable building block of the British economy.

Steam-Powered Transportation

The coal industry had long used plank roads and rails to move coal wagons within mines and at the surface. Rails reduced friction and allowed a horse or a human being to pull a much heavier load. Thus, once a rail capable of supporting a heavy locomotive was developed in 1816, all sorts of experiments with steam engines on rails went forward.

The first steam locomotive was built by Richard Trevithick after much experimentation. George Stephenson acquired glory for his locomotive named *Rocket*, which sped down the track of the just-completed Liverpool and Manchester Railway at a maximum speed of 35 miles per hour, without a load, in 1829. (See "Living in the Past: The Steam Age," page 658.) The line from Liverpool to Manchester was a financial as well as a technical success, and many private companies quickly began to build more rail lines. Within twenty years they had completed the main trunk lines of Great Britain (Map 20.1). Other countries were quick to follow, with the first steam-powered trains operating in the United States in the 1830s and in Brazil, Chile, Argentina, and the British colonies of Canada, Australia, and India in the 1850s.

The arrival of the railroad had many significant consequences. It dramatically reduced the cost and uncertainty of shipping freight over land. Previously, markets had tended to be small and local; as the barrier of high transportation costs was lowered, markets became larger and even nationwide. Larger markets encouraged larger factories with more sophisticated machinery in a growing number of industries. Such factories could make goods more cheaply and gradually subjected most cottage workers and many urban artisans to severe competitive pressures. In all countries, the construction of railroads created a strong demand for unskilled labor and contributed to the growth of a class of urban workers.

The steam engine also transformed water travel. French engineers completed the first steamships in the 1770s, and the first commercial steamships came into use in North America several decades later. The *Clermont* began to travel the waters of the Hudson River in New York State in 1807, shortly followed by ships belonging

■ *Rocket* The name given to George Stephenson's effective locomotive that was first tested in 1829 on the Liverpool and Manchester Railway at 35 miles per hour.

■ **Crystal Palace** The location of the Great Exhibition in 1851 in London; an architectural masterpiece made entirely of glass and iron.

■ **iron law of wages** Theory proposed by English economist David Ricardo suggesting that the pressure of population growth prevents wages from rising above the subsistence level.

to brewer John Molson on the St. Lawrence River. The steamship brought the advantages of the railroad—speed, reliability, efficiency—to water travel.

Industry and Population

In 1851 London hosted an industrial fair called the Great Exhibition in the newly built **Crystal Palace**. More than 6 million visitors from all over Europe marveled at the gigantic new exhibition hall set in the middle of a large, centrally located park. The building was made entirely of glass and iron, both of which were now cheap and abundant. Sponsored by the British royal family, the exhibition celebrated the new era of industrial technology and the kingdom's role as world economic leader.

Britain's claim to be the "workshop of the world" was no idle boast, for it produced two-thirds of the world's coal and more than half of all iron and cotton cloth. More generally, in 1860 Britain produced a remarkable 20 percent of the entire world's output of industrial goods, whereas it had produced only about 2 percent of the total in 1750.[3] As the British economy significantly increased its production of manufactured goods, the gross national product (GNP) rose roughly fourfold at constant prices between 1780 and 1851. At the same time, the population of Britain boomed, growing from about 9 million in 1780 to almost 21 million in 1851. Thus growing numbers consumed much of the increase in total production.

Rapid population growth in Britain was key to industrial development. More people meant a more mobile labor force, with many young workers in need of employment and ready to go where the jobs were. Sustaining the dramatic increase in population, in turn, was only possible through advances in production in agriculture and industry. Based on the lessons of history, many contemporaries feared that the rapid growth in population would inevitably lead to disaster. In his *Essay on the Principle of Population* (1798), Thomas Malthus (1766–1834) examined the dynamics of human populations. He argued:

> There are few states in which there is not a constant effort in the population to increase beyond the means of subsistence. This constant effort as constantly tends to subject the lower classes of society to distress, and to prevent any great permanent melioration of these conditions.[4]

Given the limited resources available, Malthus concluded that the only hope of warding off such "positive checks" to population growth as famine and disease was "prudential restraint." That is, young men and

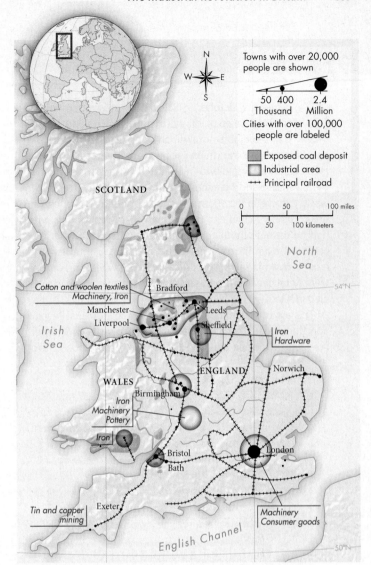

MAP 20.1 The Industrial Revolution in Great Britain, ca. 1850 Industry concentrated in the rapidly growing cities of the north and the center of England, where rich coal and iron deposits were close to one another.

women had to limit the growth of population by marrying late in life. But Malthus was not optimistic about this possibility. The powerful attraction of the sexes, he feared, would cause most people to marry early and have many children.

Economist David Ricardo (1772–1823) spelled out the pessimistic implications of Malthus's thought. Ricardo's depressing **iron law of wages** posited that over an extended period of time, because of the pressure of population growth, wages would always sink to subsistence level. That is, wages would be just high enough to keep workers from starving.

Malthus, Ricardo, and their followers were proved wrong in the long run, largely because industrialization improved productivity beyond what they could imagine.

On Tuesday, October 6, 1829, a huge crowd gathered at the small town of Rainhill in northern England. Pedestrians and horse-drawn carriages jostled for space as a band played and the Union Jack waved. The occasion was a race over a newly laid two-mile stretch of track sponsored by the Liverpool and Manchester Railway Company. The victor was the *Rocket*, a locomotive designed by George Stephenson, the company's chief engineer, a man of modest origins who had no formal schooling. Pulling heavy wagons, *Rocket* first achieved over 13 miles per hour and then astounded the crowds by whizzing by at 24 miles per hour when the wagons were detached. It was probably the fastest a vehicle had traveled in history.*

The last and culminating invention of the Industrial Revolution, the railroad dramatically revealed the power and increased the speed of the new age. Until the coming of the railroad, travel was largely measured by the distance that a human or a horse could cover before becoming exhausted. Steam power created a revolution in human transportation, allowing a constant, rapid rate of travel with no limits on its duration. Time and space suddenly and drastically contracted, as faraway places could be reached in one-third the time or less. As the poet Heinrich Heine proclaimed in 1843, "What changes must now occur, in our way of looking at things, in our notions! . . . I feel as if the mountains and forests of all countries were advancing on Paris. Even now, I can smell the German linden trees; the North Sea's breakers are rolling against my door."†

Racing down the track at speeds that reached 50 miles per hour by 1850 was an overwhelming experience. Some great painters, notably Joseph M. W. Turner (1775–1851) and Claude Monet (1840–1926), succeeded in expressing this sense of power and awe. Contemporary novelists also recorded their impres-

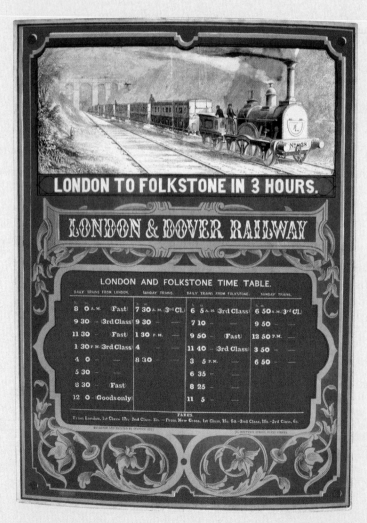

LONDON TO FOLKSTONE IN 3 HOURS.

LONDON & DOVER RAILWAY

A colorful timetable poster lists the trains from London to Folkstone, the English Channel's gateway port to the European continent, and proudly proclaims a speedy journey. Tunneling through hills and spanning rivers with bridges, railroad construction presented innumerable challenges and required enormous amounts of capital and labor. (Private Collection/Bridgeman Images)

*Christopher McGowan, *Rail, Steam, and Speed: The "Rocket" and the Birth of Steam Locomotion* (New York: Columbia University Press, 2004), p. 21.

†Quoted in Wolfgang Schivelbusch, *The Railway Journey: The Industrialization of Time and Space in the Nineteenth Century* (Berkeley: University of California Press, 1986), p. 37.

Turner's *Rain, Steam, and Speed.* This 1844 painting captures the rush of an oncoming train as it swoops across the Maidenhead railway bridge on a rainy day. (National Gallery, London, UK/Bridgeman Images)

sions of early train travel, as in this striking passage by Charles Dickens: "Through the hollow, on the height, by the heath, by the orchard, by the park, by the garden, over the canal, across the river, where the sheep are feeding, where the mill is going, where the barge is floating, where the dead are lying, where the factory is smoking, where the stream is running, where the village clusters . . . away with a strike and a roar and a rattle, and no trace to leave behind but dust and vapour."‡ After surviving a terrible railroad crash, Dickens himself developed an intense fear of train travel. The increase in speed also led doctors to worry about the effects of the constant noise and vibration on passengers and crew.

Despite these concerns, the railroad quickly became a central institution of society. So did the massive new train stations, the cathedrals of the industrial age. Leading railway engineers such as Isambard Kingdom Brunel and Thomas Brassey, whose tunnels pierced mountains and whose bridges spanned valleys, became public idols — the astronauts of their day.

QUESTIONS FOR ANALYSIS

1. Why was the train so revolutionary? What evidence is provided here for contemporaries' perceptions of train travel?
2. Why is the train less important in today's culture?

‡Charles Dickens, *Dombey and Son* (Ware, U.K.: Wordsworth Editions, 1999), p. 262.

An advertisement announcing the *Rocket* as winner of the 1829 Liverpool and Manchester Railway race for the fastest locomotive. (Granger, NYC — All rights reserved)

Interior View of the Crystal Palace   Built for the Great Exhibition of 1851, the Crystal Palace was a spectacular achievement in engineering, prefabricated from three hundred thousand sheets of glass. With almost fifteen thousand exhibitors, the event constituted the first international industrial exhibition, showcasing manufactured products from Britain, its empire, and the rest of the world. Later, the building was disassembled and moved to another site in London, where it stood until destroyed by fire in 1936. (Engraved by William Simpson [1832–1899] from an original by J. McNevin, color lithograph/London Metropolitan Archives, City of London, UK/Bridgeman Images)

However, until the 1820s, or even the 1840s, contemporary observers might reasonably have concluded that the economy and the total population were racing neck and neck, with the outcome very much in doubt. There was another problem as well. Perhaps workers, farmers, and ordinary people did not get their rightful share of the new wealth. Perhaps only the rich got richer, while the poor got poorer or made no progress. We will turn to this great issue after situating the process of industrialization in its European and global context.

Industrialization in Europe and the World

FOCUS QUESTION *How did countries in Europe and around the world respond to the challenge of industrialization?*

As new technologies and a new organization of labor began to revolutionize production in Britain, other countries took notice and began to emulate its example. With the end of the Napoleonic Wars, the nations of the European continent quickly adopted British inventions and achieved their own pattern of technological innovation and economic growth. By the last decades of the nineteenth century, western European countries as well as the United States and Japan had industrialized their economies to a considerable, albeit variable, degree.

Industrialization in other parts of the world proceeded more gradually, with uneven jerks and national and regional variations. Scholars are still struggling to explain these variations as well as the dramatic gap that emerged for the first time in history between Western and non-Western levels of economic production. These questions are especially important because they may offer valuable lessons for poor countries that today are seeking to improve their material condition through industrialization and economic development. The latest findings on the nineteenth-century experience are encouraging. They suggest that there were alternative paths to the industrial world and that there was and is no need to follow a rigid, predetermined British model.

National and International Variations

Comparative data on industrial production in different countries over time help give us an overview of what happened. One set of data, the work of a Swiss scholar, compares the level of industrialization on a per capita basis in several countries from 1750 to 1913. These data are far from perfect, but they reflect basic trends and are presented in Table 20.1 for closer study.

Table 20.1 presents a comparison of how much industrial product was produced, on average, for each person in a given country in a given year. All the numbers are expressed in terms of a single index number of 100, which equals the per capita level of industrial goods in Great Britain in 1900. Every number in the table is thus a percentage of the 1900 level in Britain and is directly comparable with other numbers. The countries are listed in roughly the order that they began to use large-scale, power-driven technology.

What does this overview tell us? First, one sees in the first column that in 1750 all countries were fairly close together, including non-Western nations such as China and India. Both China and India had been extremely important players in early modern world trade; both were sophisticated, technologically advanced, and economically powerful up to 1800 (see Chapter 14). However, the column headed 1800 shows that Britain had opened up a noticeable lead over all countries by 1800, and that gap progressively widened as the Industrial Revolution accelerated through 1830 and reached full maturity by 1860.

Second, the table shows that Western countries began to emulate the British model successfully over the course of the nineteenth century, with significant variations in the timing and in the extent of industrialization. Belgium, achieving independence from the Netherlands in 1831 and rich in iron and coal, led in adopting Britain's new technology, and it experienced a great surge between 1830 and 1860. France developed factory production more gradually and did not experience "revolutionary" growth in overall industrial output.

Slow but steady growth in France was overshadowed by the spectacular rise of the German lands and the United States after 1860 in what has been termed the "second industrial revolution." In general, eastern and southern Europe began the process of modern industrialization later than northwestern and central Europe. Nevertheless, these regions made real progress in the late nineteenth century, as growth after 1880 in Austria-Hungary, Italy, and Russia suggests. This meant that all European states as well as the United States managed to raise per capita industrial levels in the nineteenth century.

These increases stood in stark contrast to the decreases that occurred at the same time in many non-Western countries, most notably in China and India, as Table 20.1 shows. European countries industrialized to a greater or lesser extent even as most of the non-Western world stagnated. Japan, which is not included in this table, stands out as an exceptional area of non-Western industrial

growth in the second half of the nineteenth century. After the forced opening of the country to the West in the 1850s, Japanese entrepreneurs began to adopt Western technology and manufacturing methods, resulting in a production boom by the late nineteenth century. Different rates of wealth- and power-creating industrial development, which heightened disparities within Europe, also greatly magnified existing inequalities between Europe and the rest of the world.

Industrialization in Continental Europe

Throughout Europe the eighteenth century was an era of agricultural improvement, population increase, expanding foreign trade, and growing cottage industry. Thus, when the pace of British industry began to accelerate in the 1780s, continental businesses began to emulate the new methods. British industry enjoyed clear superiority, but the European continent was close behind. During the period of the revolutionary and Napoleonic wars, from 1793 to 1815, however, western Europe experienced tremendous political and social upheaval that temporarily halted economic development. With the return of peace in 1815, western European countries again began to play catch-up.

They faced significant challenges. In the newly mechanized industries, British goods were being produced very economically, and these goods had come to dominate world markets. In addition, British technology had become so advanced that few engineers or skilled technicians outside England understood it. Moreover, the technology of steam power had grown much more expensive. It involved large investments in the iron and coal industries and, after 1830, in railroads. Continental business people had difficulty amassing the large sums

TABLE 20.1 Per Capita Levels of Industrialization, 1750–1913

	1750	1800	1830	1860	1880	1900	1913
Great Britain	10	16	25	64	87	100	115
Belgium	9	10	14	28	43	56	88
United States	4	9	14	21	38	69	126
France	9	9	12	20	28	39	59
Germany	8	8	9	15	25	52	85
Austria-Hungary	7	7	8	11	15	23	32
Italy	8	8	8	10	12	17	26
Russia	6	6	7	8	10	15	20
China	8	6	6	4	4	3	3
India	7	6	6	3	2	1	2

Note: All entries are based on an index value of 100, equal to the per capita level of industrialization in Great Britain in 1900. Data for Great Britain includes Ireland, England, Wales, and Scotland.

Source: P. Bairoch, "International Industrialization Levels from 1750 to 1980," *Journal of European Economic History* 11 (Spring 1982): 294, U.S. Journals at Cambridge University Press.

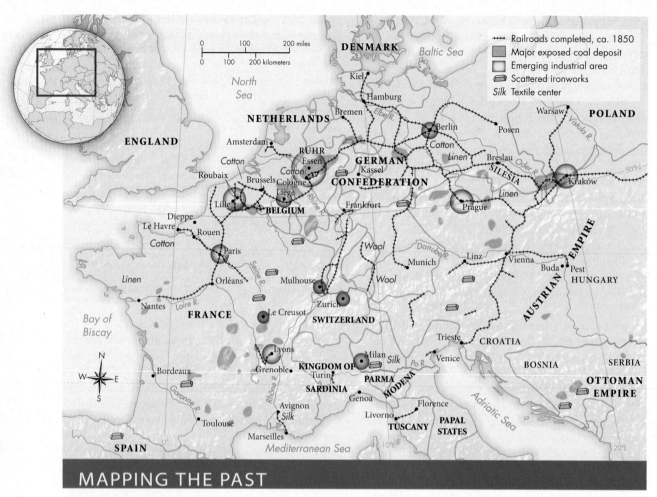

MAPPING THE PAST

MAP 20.2 Continental Industrialization, ca. 1850

Although continental countries were beginning to make progress by 1850, they still lagged far behind Great Britain. For example, continental railroad building was still in an early stage, whereas the British rail system was essentially complete (see Map 20.1). Coal played a critical role in nineteenth-century industrialization both as a power source for steam engines and as a raw material for making iron and steel.

ANALYZING THE MAP Locate the major exposed (that is, known) coal deposits in 1850. Which countries and areas appear rich in coal resources, and which appear poor? Is there a difference between northern and southern Europe?

CONNECTIONS What is the relationship between known coal deposits and emerging industrial areas in continental Europe? In Great Britain (see Map 20.1)?

of money the new methods demanded, and laborers bitterly resisted the move to working in factories. All these factors slowed the spread of machine-powered industry (Map 20.2).

Nevertheless, western European nations possessed a number of advantages that helped them respond to these challenges. First, most had rich traditions of putting-out enterprise, merchant capitalists, and skilled urban artisans. These assets gave their firms the ability to adapt and survive in the face of new market conditions. Second, continental capitalists did not need to develop their own advanced technology. Instead, they

could simply "borrow" the new methods developed in Great Britain. European countries also had a third asset that many non-Western areas lacked in the nineteenth century: they had strong, independent governments that did not fall under foreign political control. These governments would use the power of the state to promote industry and catch up with Britain.

Most continental businesses adopted factory technology slowly, and handicraft methods lived on. Indeed, continental industrialization usually brought substantial but uneven expansion of handicraft industry in both rural and urban areas for a time. Artisan production of luxury items grew in France as the rising income of the international middle class created increased foreign demand for silk scarves, embroidered needlework, perfumes, and fine wines. Focusing on artisanal luxury production made sense for French entrepreneurs given their long history of dominance in that sector. Rather than being a "backward" refusal to modernize, it represented a sound strategic choice that allowed the French to capitalize on their know-how and international reputation for high-quality goods.

Agents of Industrialization

Western European success in adopting British methods took place despite the best efforts of the British to prevent it. The British realized the great value of their technical discoveries and tried to keep their secrets to themselves. Until 1825 it was illegal for artisans and skilled mechanics to leave Britain; until 1843 the export of textile machinery and other equipment was forbidden. Many talented, ambitious workers, however, slipped out of the country illegally and introduced the new methods abroad.

One such man was William Cockerill, a Lancashire carpenter. He and his sons began building cotton-spinning equipment in French-occupied Belgium in 1799. In 1817 the most famous son, John Cockerill, built a large industrial enterprise in Liège in southern Belgium, which produced machinery, steam engines, and then railway locomotives. He also established modern ironworks and coal mines. Cockerill's plants in the Liège area became a center for the gathering and transmitting of industrial information across Europe. Many skilled British workers came to work for Cockerill, and some went on to found their own companies throughout Europe.

Thus British technicians and skilled workers were a powerful force in the spread of early industrialization. A second agent of industrialization consisted of talented entrepreneurs such as Fritz Harkort (1793–1880), a pioneer in the German machinery industry. Serving in England as a Prussian army officer during the Napoleonic Wars, Harkort was impressed with what he saw. Harkort set up shop building steam engines in the Ruhr Valley, on the western border with France. In spite of problems obtaining skilled workers and machinery, Harkort succeeded in building and selling engines. However, his ambitious efforts also resulted in large financial losses for himself and his partners. His career illustrates both the great efforts of a few important business leaders to duplicate the British achievement and the difficulty of the task.

National governments played an even more important role in supporting industrialization in continental Europe than in Britain. **Tariff protection** was one such support and it proved to be important. The French, for

example, responded to a flood of cheap British goods in 1815 after the Napoleonic Wars by laying high taxes on imported goods. Customs agreements emerged among some German states starting in 1818, and in 1834 a number of states signed a treaty creating a customs union, or *Zollverein*. The treaty allowed goods to move between member states without tariffs, while erecting a single uniform tariff against other nations.

After 1815 continental governments also bore the cost of building roads, canals, and railroads to improve transportation. Belgium led the way in the 1830s and 1840s. Built rapidly as a unified network, Belgium's state-owned railroads stimulated the development of heavy industry and made the country an early industrial leader. In France, the state shouldered all the expense of acquiring and laying roadbed, including bridges and tunnels. In short, governments helped pay for railroads, the all-important leading sector in continental industrialization.

Finally, banks also played a larger and more creative role on the continent than in Britain. Previously, almost all banks in Europe had been private. Because of the possibility of unlimited financial loss, the partners of private banks tended to be conservative and were content to deal with a few rich clients and a few big merchants. They generally avoided industrial investment as being too risky.

In the 1830s two important Belgian banks pioneered in a new direction. They received permission from the growth-oriented government to establish themselves as corporations enjoying limited liability. That is, if the bank went bankrupt, stockholders could now lose only their original investments in the bank's common stock, and they could not be forced by the courts to pay for any additional losses out of other property they owned. Limited liability helped these Belgian banks attract investors. They mobilized impressive resources for investment in big companies, became industrial banks, and successfully promoted industrial development.

Similar corporate banks became important in France and the German lands in the 1850s and 1860s. Usually working in collaboration with governments, corporate banks established and developed many railroads and many companies working in heavy industry, which were also increasingly organized as limited liability corporations.

The combined efforts of governments, skilled workers, entrepreneurs, and industrial banks meshed successfully after 1850 and the financial crash of 1873. In Belgium, France, and the German states, key indicators of modern industrial development — such as railway mileage, iron and coal production, and steam

■ **tariff protection** A government's way of supporting and aiding its own economy by laying high taxes on imported goods from other countries, as when the French responded to cheaper British goods flooding their country by imposing high tariffs on some imported products.

The Circle of the Rue Royale, Paris, 1868   The Circle of the Rue Royale was an exclusive club of aristocrats, bankers, railway owners, and other members of Parisian high society. This group portrait projects the wealth and elegance of the club's members, who are gathered on the balcony of a hotel. (*The Circle of the Rue Royale, Paris, 1868*, by James Jacques Joseph Tissot [1836–1902], [oil on canvas]/Fine Art Images/Heritage Images/Getty Images)

engine capacity—increased at average annual rates of 5 to 10 percent. As a result, rail networks were completed in western and much of central Europe, and the leading continental countries mastered the industrial technologies that had first been developed by the British. In the early 1870s Britain was still Europe's most industrial nation, but a select handful of nations had closed the gap.

The Global Picture

The Industrial Revolution did not have a transformative impact beyond Europe prior to the 1860s, with the exception of the United States and Japan, both early adopters of British practices. In many countries, national governments and pioneering entrepreneurs did make efforts to adopt the technologies and methods of production that had proved so successful in Britain, but they fell short of transitioning to an industrial economy. For example, in Russia the imperial government brought steamships to the Volga River and a railroad to the capital, St. Petersburg, in the first decades of the nineteenth century. By midcentury ambitious entrepreneurs had established steam-powered cotton factories using imported

British machines. However, these advances did not lead to overall industrialization of the country, most of whose people remained mired in rural servitude. Instead, Russia confirmed its role as provider of raw materials, especially timber and grain, to the hungry West.

Egypt, a territory of the Ottoman Empire, similarly began an ambitious program of modernization after a reform-minded viceroy took power in 1805. This program included the use of imported British technology and experts in textile manufacture and other industries. These industries, however, could not compete with lower-priced European imports. Like Russia, Egypt fell back on agricultural exports to European markets, like sugar and cotton.

Such examples of faltering efforts at industrialization could be found in many other regions of the Middle East, Asia, and Latin America. Where European governments maintained direct or indirect political control, they acted to monopolize colonial markets as both sources of raw materials and consumers for their own products, rather than encouraging the spread of industrialization. Such regions could not respond to low-cost imports by raising tariffs, as the United States and western European nations had done, because they were controlled by imperial powers that did not allow them to do so. In India, millions of poor textile workers lost their livelihood because they could not compete with industrially produced British cottons. The British charged stiff import duties on Indian cottons entering the kingdom, but prohibited the Indians from doing the same to British imports. As a British trade encyclopedia boasted in 1844:

> The British manufacturer brings the cotton of India from a distance of 12,000 miles, commits it to his spinning jennies and power-looms, carries back their products to the East, making them again to travel 12,000 miles; and in spite of the loss of time, and of the enormous expense incurred by this voyage of 24,000 miles, the cotton manufactured by his machinery becomes less costly than the cotton of India spun and woven by the hand near the field that produced it.[5]

Latin American economies were disrupted by the early-nineteenth-century wars of independence. As these countries' economies recovered in the mid-nineteenth century, they increasingly adopted steam power for sugar and coffee processing and for transportation. Like elsewhere, this technology first supported increased agricultural production for export and only later drove domestic industrial production. As in India, the arrival of cheap British cottons destroyed the pre-existing textile industry that had employed many people.

The rise of industrialization in Britain, western Europe, and the United States thus caused other regions of the world to become increasingly economically dependent. Instead of industrializing, many territories underwent a process of deindustrialization due to imperialism and economic competition. In turn, relative economic weakness made them vulnerable to the new wave of imperialism undertaken by industrialized nations in the second half of the nineteenth century (see Chapter 24).

As for China, it did not adopt mechanized production until the end of the nineteenth century, but continued as a market-based, commercial society with a massive rural sector and industrial production based on traditional methods. Some regions of China experienced slow economic growth, while others were stagnant. In the 1860s and 1870s, when Japan was successfully adopting industrial methods, the Chinese government showed similar interest in Western technology and science. However, China faced widespread uprisings in the mid-nineteenth century, which drained attention and resources to the military. With China poised to surpass the United States in economic production by 2020, scholars now wonder whether the ascension of Europe and the West from 1800 was merely a brief interruption in a much longer pattern of Asian dominance.

New Patterns of Working and Living

FOCUS QUESTION *How did work evolve during the Industrial Revolution, and how did daily life change for working people?*

Having first emerged in the British countryside in the late eighteenth century, factories and industrial labor began migrating to cities by the early nineteenth century. As factories moved from rural to urban areas, their workforce evolved as well, from pauper children to families to men and women uprooted from their traditional rural communities. Many women, especially young single women and poor women, continued to work, but married women began to limit their participation in the workforce when possible. For some people, the Industrial Revolution brought improvements, but living and working conditions for the poor stagnated or even deteriorated until around 1850, especially in overcrowded industrial cities.

Work in Early Factories

The first factories of the Industrial Revolution were cotton mills, which began functioning in the 1770s along fast-running rivers and streams and were often located in sparsely populated areas. Cottage workers, accustomed to the putting-out system, were reluctant to work in the new factories even when they received relatively good wages. In a factory, workers had to keep up with the machine and follow its relentless tempo. Moreover, they had to show up every day, on time, and work long, monotonous hours under the constant supervision of demanding overseers, and they were punished systematically if they broke the work rules. For example, if a worker was late to work, or accidentally spoiled material, the employer deducted fines from the weekly pay. Employers frequently beat children and adolescents for their infractions.

Cottage workers were not used to that way of life. All members of the family worked hard and long, but in spurts, setting their own pace. They could interrupt their work when they wished. Women and children could break up their long hours of spinning with other tasks. On Saturday afternoon the head of the family delivered the week's work to the merchant manufacturer and got paid. Saturday night was a time of relaxation and drinking, especially for the men.

Also, early factories resembled English poorhouses, where destitute people went to live at public expense. Some poorhouses were industrial prisons, where the inmates had to work in order to receive food and lodging. The similarity between large brick factories and large stone poorhouses increased the cottage workers' fear of factories and their hatred of factory discipline. It was cottage workers' reluctance to work in factories that prompted early cotton mill owners to turn to pauper children. Mill owners contracted with local officials to employ large numbers of such children, who had no say in the matter. Attitudes began to change in the last decade of the eighteenth century, as middle-class reformers publicized the brutal toil imposed on society's most vulnerable members.

Working Families and Children

By the 1790s the early pattern had begun to change. The use of pauper apprentices was in decline, and in 1802 it was forbidden by Parliament. Many more textile factories were being built, mainly in urban areas, where they could use steam power rather than water-power and attract a workforce more easily than in the countryside. People came from near and far to work in the cities, as factory workers and as porters, builders, and domestic servants. Collectively, these wage laborers came to be known as the "working class," a term first used in the late 1830s.

In some cases, workers accommodated to the system by carrying over familiar working traditions. Some came to the mills and the mines in the family units in which they had labored on farms and in the putting-out system. The mill or mine owner bargained with the head of the family and paid him or her for the efforts of the whole family. In the cotton mills, children worked for their mothers or fathers, collecting scraps and "piecing" broken threads together. In the mines, children sorted coal and worked the ventilation equipment. Their mothers hauled coal in the tunnels below the surface, while their fathers hewed with pick and shovel at the face of the seam.

Ties of kinship were particularly important for newcomers, who often traveled great distances to find work. Many urban workers in Great Britain were from Ireland. They were forced out of rural Ireland by population growth and deteriorating economic conditions from 1817 on, and their numbers increased dramatically in the desperate years of the potato famine, from 1845 to 1851 (see Chapter 21). As early as 1824 most of the workers in the Glasgow cotton mills were Irish; in 1851 one-sixth of the population of Liverpool was Irish. Like many other immigrant groups held together by ethnic and religious ties, however, the Irish worked together, formed their own neighborhoods, and preserved their cultural traditions.

In the early decades of the nineteenth century, however, technical changes made it less and less likely that workers could continue to labor in family groups. As control and discipline passed into the hands of impersonal managers and overseers, adult workers began to protest against inhuman conditions on behalf of their children. Some enlightened employers and social reformers in Parliament argued that more humane standards were necessary, and they used widely circulated parliamentary reports to influence public opinion. For example, Robert Owen (1771–1858), a successful manufacturer in Scotland, testified in 1816 before an investigating committee on the basis of his experience. He argued that employing children under ten years of age as factory workers was "injurious to the children, and not beneficial to the proprietors."[6] Workers also provided graphic testimony at such hearings as reformers pressed Parliament to pass corrective laws. These efforts resulted in a series of British **Factory Acts** from 1802 to 1833 that progressively limited the workday of child laborers and set minimum hygiene and safety requirements. (See "Evaluating the Evidence 20.1: Debate over Child Labor Laws," page 667.) The Factory Act of 1833 installed a system of full-time professional inspectors to enforce the provisions of previous acts. Children between ages nine and thirteen could work a maximum of eight hours per day, not including two hours for education. Teenagers aged fourteen to eighteen could work up to twelve hours, while those under nine were banned from employment. The Factory Acts constituted significant progress in preventing the exploitation of children. One unintended drawback of restrictions on child labor, however, was that they broke the pattern of whole families working together in the factory because efficiency required standardized shifts for all workers. After 1833 the number of children employed in industry declined rapidly.

The New Sexual Division of Labor

With the restriction of child labor and the collapse of the family work pattern in the 1830s came a new sexual division of labor. By 1850 the man was emerging as the family's primary wage earner, while the married woman found only limited job opportunities. Generally denied good jobs at high wages in the growing urban economy, wives were expected to concentrate on their duties at home.

This new pattern of **separate spheres** had several aspects. First, all studies agree that married women from the working classes were much less likely to work full-time for wages outside the house after the first child arrived, although they often earned small amounts doing putting-out handicrafts at home and taking in boarders. Second, when married women did

■ **Factory Acts** English laws passed from 1802 to 1833 that limited the workday of child laborers and set minimum hygiene and safety requirements.

■ **separate spheres** A gender division of labor with the wife at home as mother and homemaker and the husband as wage earner.

Debate over Child Labor Laws

The Cotton Mills and Factories Act of 1819 was one of a series of acts intended to prevent the exploitation of child laborers in Britain, largely by restricting their working hours. Debate in the House of Commons over the legislation pitted those arguing for humanitarian considerations against defenders of economic freedom. A passionate proponent of the bill was Sir Robert Peel, himself a factory owner and father of a future British prime minister.

19 February 1818

   Sir Robert Peel. . . . About fifteen years ago he had brought in a Bill for the Regulation of Apprentices in Cotton Manufactories. At that time they were the description of persons most employed in those manufactories. He himself had a thousand of them. . . . Since that time, however, the business had been much extended. Manufactories were established in large towns, and the proprietors availed themselves of all the poor population of those towns. In Manchester alone 20,000 persons were employed in the cotton manufactories, and in the whole of England about three times that number. . . . It was notorious that children of a very tender age were dragged from their beds some hours before day light, and confined in the factories not less than fifteen hours; and it was also notoriously the opinion of the faculty, that no children of eight or nine years of age could bear that degree of hardship with impunity to their health and constitution. It had been urged by the humane, that there might be two sets of young labourers for one set of adults. He was afraid this would produce more harm than good. The better way would be to shorten the time of working for adults as well as for children; and to prevent the introduction of the latter at a very early age. . . . The children . . . were prevented from growing to their full size. In consequence, Manchester, which used to furnish numerous

recruits for the army, was now wholly unproductive in that respect. . . .

   Lord Lascelles. . . . The individuals who were the objects of the hon. gentleman's proposition were free labourers. This excited his jealousy; for, were the principle of interference with free labourers once admitted, it was difficult to say how far it might not be carried. . . .

   Mr. Philips strongly objected to the adoption of any measure of this description, and denied that the employment of children in the cotton factories operated, as had been described, to stint their growth, impair their comfort, or scatter disease amongst them. . . . Small factories were often ill ventilated, and from that circumstance the health of a person might suffer more in six hours in one of these factories, than in fifteen hours in a factory which was well ventilated and properly constructed in other respects. But how could this evil be cured by any bill? The small factories generally went to ruin, and that was the cure for the evil. From the returns made to the House, out of 31,117, the number of persons employed in these returns, 1717, or 5½ per cent, were of the age of 10 and under, 13,203 from 10 to 18, and 16,197 of the age of 18 and upwards. Out of 27,827 persons, there were 1,830 only who could not read.

EVALUATE THE EVIDENCE

1. What arguments for and against labor regulation do the two sides offer? What rhetorical strategies do they use to strengthen their arguments?
2. In what ways do these arguments reflect the changes in working and living patterns described in the text?

Source: Commons Sitting of 19 February 1818, series 1, vol. 37, Cotton Factories Bill, cc559-66, http://hansard.millbanksystems.com/commons/1818/feb/19/cotton-factories-bill.

work for wages outside the house, they usually came from the poorest families, where the husbands were poorly paid, sick, unemployed, or missing. Third, these poor married or widowed women were joined by legions of young unmarried women, who worked full-time but only in certain jobs, of which textile factory work, laundering, and domestic service were particularly important. Fourth, all women were generally confined to low-paying, dead-end jobs. Evolving gradually, but largely in place by 1850, the new sexual division of labor constituted a major development in the history of women and of the family.

   Several factors combined to create this new sexual division of labor. First, the new and unfamiliar discipline of

the clock and the machine was especially hard on married women of the laboring classes. Relentless factory discipline conflicted with child care in a way that labor on the farm or in the cottage had not. A woman operating earsplitting spinning machinery could mind a child of seven or eight working beside her (until such work was outlawed), but she could no longer pace herself through pregnancy or breast-feed her baby on the job. Thus a working-class woman had strong incentives to stay home, if she could afford it. Caring for babies was a less important factor in areas of continental Europe, such as northern France and Scandinavia, where women relied on paid wet nurses instead of breast-feeding their babies (see Chapter 18).

Women Workers on Break   This painting from mid-nineteenth-century northern England shows women textile workers as they relax and socialize on their lunch break. Most of the workers are young and probably unmarried. (*The Dinner Break, Wigan*, 1874, by Eyre Crowe [1824–1910], [oil on canvas]/Manchester Art Gallery, UK/Bridgeman Images)

Second, running a household in conditions of primitive urban poverty was an extremely demanding job in its own right. There were no supermarkets or public transportation. Shopping, washing clothes, and feeding the family constituted a never-ending challenge. Taking on a brutal job outside the house—a "second shift"—had limited appeal for the average married woman from the working class. Thus many women might well have accepted the emerging division of labor as the best available strategy for family survival in the industrializing society.[7]

Third, to a large degree the young, generally unmarried women who did work for wages outside the home were segregated from men and confined to certain "women's jobs" because the new sexual division of labor replicated long-standing patterns of gender segregation and inequality. In the preindustrial economy, a small sector of the labor market had always been defined as "women's work," especially tasks involving needlework, spinning, food preparation, child care, and nursing. This traditional sexual

division of labor took on new overtones, however, in response to the factory system. Previously, at least in theory, young people worked under a watchful parental eye. The growth of factories and mines brought unheard-of opportunities for girls and boys to mix on the job, free of familial supervision. Such opportunities led to more unplanned pregnancies and fueled the illegitimacy explosion that had begun in the late eighteenth century and that gathered force until at least 1850. Thus segregation of jobs by gender was partly an effort by older people to control the sexuality of working-class youths.

Investigations into the British coal industry before 1842 provide a graphic example of this concern. (See "Evaluating the Evidence 20.2: The Testimony of Young Mine Workers," page 670.) The middle-class men leading the inquiry professed horror at the sight of girls and women working without shirts, which was a common practice because of the heat, and they quickly assumed the prevalence of licentious sex with the male miners, who also wore very little clothing. In fact, many girls and married women worked for related males in a family unit that provided considerable

■ **Mines Act of 1842** English law prohibiting underground work for all women and girls as well as for boys under ten.

protection and restraint. Yet many witnesses from the working class also believed that the mines were inappropriate and dangerous places for women and girls. Some miners stressed particularly the danger of sexual aggression for girls working past puberty. As one explained, "I consider it a scandal for girls to work in the pits. Till they are 12 or 14 they may work very well but after that it's an abomination. . . . The work of the pit does not hurt them, it is the effect on their morals that I complain of."[8] The **Mines Act of 1842** prohibited underground work for all women and girls as well as for boys under ten.

Some women who had to support themselves protested against being excluded from coal mining, which paid higher wages than most other jobs open to working-class women. But provided they were part of families that could manage economically, the girls and the women who had worked underground were generally pleased with the law. In explaining her satisfaction in 1844, one mother of four provided real insight into why many married working women accepted the emerging sexual division of labor:

> While working in the pit I was worth to my [miner] husband seven shillings a week, out of which we had to pay 2½ shillings to a woman for looking after the younger children. I used to take them to her house at 4 o'clock in the morning, out of their own beds, to put them into hers. Then there was one shilling a week for washing; besides, there was mending to pay for, and other things. The house was not guided. The other children broke things; they did not go to school when they were sent; they would be playing about, and get ill-used by other children, and their clothes torn. Then when I came home in the evening, everything was to do after the day's labor, and I was so tired I had no heart for it; no fire lit, nothing cooked, no water fetched, the house dirty, and nothing comfortable for my husband. It is all far better now, and I wouldn't go down again.[9]

A final factor encouraging working-class women to withdraw from paid labor was the domestic ideals emanating from middle-class women, who had largely

Child Labor in Coal Mines   Public sentiment against child labor in coal mines was provoked by the publication of dramatic images of the harsh working conditions children endured. The Mines Act of 1842 prohibited the employment underground of women and girls, and boys under the age of ten. (*Child Labour in an English Coal Mine*, 1844, colored lithograph/akg-images)

The Testimony of Young Mine Workers

The use of child labor in British industrialization quickly attracted the attention of humanitarians and social reformers. This interest led to investigations by parliamentary commissions, which resulted in laws limiting the hours and the ages of children working in large factories. Designed to build a case for remedial legislation, parliamentary inquiries gave large numbers of workers a rare chance to speak directly to contemporaries and to historians.

The moving passages that follow are taken from testimony gathered in 1841 and 1842 by the Ashley Mines Commission. Interviewing employers and many male and female workers, the commissioners focused on the physical condition of the youth and on the sexual behavior of workers far underground. The subsequent Mines Act of 1842 sought to reduce immoral behavior and sexual bullying by prohibiting underground work for all women and girls (and for boys younger than ten).

Mr. Payne, coal master

That children are employed generally at nine years old in the coal pits and sometimes at eight. In fact, the smaller the vein of coal is in height, the younger and smaller are the children required; the work occupies from six to seven hours per day in the pits; they are not ill-used or worked beyond their strength; a good deal of depravity exists but they are certainly not worse in morals than in other branches of the Sheffield trade, but upon the whole superior; the morals of this district are materially improving; Mr. Bruce, the clergyman, has been zealous and active in endeavoring to ameliorate their moral and religious education.

Ann Eggley, hurrier, 18 years old

I'm sure I don't know how to spell my name. We go at four in the morning, and sometimes at half-past four. We begin to work as soon as we get down. We get out after four, sometimes at five, in the evening. We work the whole time except an hour for dinner, and sometimes we haven't time to eat. I hurry [move coal wagons underground] by myself, and have done so for long. I know the corves [small coal wagons] are very heavy, they are the biggest corves anywhere about. The work is far too hard for me; the sweat runs off me all over sometimes. I am very tired at night. Sometimes when we get home at night we have not power to wash us, and then we go to bed. Sometimes we fall asleep in the chair. Father said last night it was both a shame and a disgrace for girls to work as we do, but there was naught else for us to do. I began to hurry when I was seven and I have been hurrying ever since. I have been 11 years in the pits. The girls are always tired.

I was poorly twice this winter; it was with headache. I hurry for Robert Wiggins; he is not akin to me. . . . We don't always get enough to eat and drink, but we get a good supper. I have known my father go at two in the morning to work . . . and he didn't come out till four. I am quite sure that we work constantly 12 hours except on Saturdays. We wear trousers and our shifts in the pit and great big shoes clinkered and nailed. The girls never work naked to the waist in our pit. The men don't insult us in the pit. The conduct of the girls in the pit is good enough sometimes and sometimes bad enough. I never went to a day-school. I went a little to a Sunday-school, but I soon gave it over.

I thought it too bad to be confined both Sundays and week-days. I walk about and get the fresh air on Sundays. I have not learnt to read. I don't know my letters. I never learnt naught. I never go to church or chapel; there is no church or chapel at Gawber, there is none nearer than a mile. . . . I have never heard that a good man came into the world who was God's son to save sinners. I never heard of Christ at all. Nobody has ever told me about him, nor have my father and mother ever taught me to pray. I know no prayer; I never pray.

Patience Kershaw, aged 17

My father has been dead about a year; my mother is living and has ten children, five lads and five lasses; the oldest is about thirty, the youngest is four; three lasses go to mill; all the lads are colliers, two getters and three hurriers; one lives at home and does nothing; mother does nought but look after home.

All my sisters have been hurriers, but three went to the mill. Alice went because her legs swelled from hurrying in cold water when she was hot. I never went to day-school; I go to Sunday-school, but I cannot read or write; I go to pit at five o'clock in the morning and come out at five in the evening; I get my breakfast of porridge and milk first; I take my dinner with me, a cake, and eat it as I go; I do not stop or rest any time for the purpose; I get nothing else until I get home, and then have potatoes and meat, not every day meat. I hurry in the clothes I have now got on, trousers and ragged jacket; the bald place upon my head is made by thrusting the corves; my legs have never swelled, but sisters' did when they went to mill; I hurry the corves a mile and more under ground and back; they weigh 300 cwt.;* I hurry 11 a day; I wear a belt and chain at the workings to get the corves out; the putters [miners] that I work for are *naked* except their caps; they pull off all their clothes; I see them at work when I go up; sometimes they beat me, if I am not quick enough, with their

*An old English unit of weight equaling 112 pounds.

hands; they strike me upon my back; the boys take liberties with me, sometimes, they pull me about; I am the only girl in the pit; there are about 20 boys and 15 men; all the men are naked; I would rather work in mill than in coal-pit.

Isabel Wilson, 38 years old, coal putter

When women have children thick [fast] they are compelled to take them down early. I have been married 19 years and have had 10 bairns [children]; seven are in life. When on Sir John's work was a carrier of coals, which caused me to miscarry five times from the strains, and was gal [very] ill after each. Putting is no so oppressive; last child was born on Saturday morning, and I was at work on the Friday night.

Once met with an accident; a coal brake my cheek-bone, which kept me idle some weeks. I have wrought below 30 years, and so has the guid man; he is getting touched in the breath now.

None of the children read, as the work is no regular. I did read once, but no able to attend to it now; when I go below lassie 10 years of age keeps house and makes the broth or stir-about.

EVALUATE THE EVIDENCE

1. How does Payne's testimony compare with that of Ann Eggley and Patience Kershaw?
2. Describe the work of Eggley, Kershaw, and Wilson. What strikes you most about the testimonies of these workers?
3. The witnesses were responding to questions from middle-class commissioners. What did the commissioners seem interested in? Why?

Source: *Voices of the Industrial Revolution: Selected Readings from the Liberal Economists and Their Critics*, pp. 87–90, edited by J. Bowditch and C. Ramsland (Ann Arbor: The University of Michigan Press, 1961). Reprinted by permission of the publisher.

embraced the "separate spheres" ideology. Middle-class reformers published tracts and formed societies to urge poor women to devote more care and attention to their homes and families.

Living Standards for the Working Class

Despite the best efforts of hard-working men and women, living conditions for the industrialized poor were often abysmal. Although the evidence is complex and sometimes contradictory, most historians of the Industrial Revolution now agree that overall living standards for the working class did not rise substantially until the 1840s at the earliest. British wages were always high compared to those in the rest of Europe, but the stresses of war with France from 1792 to 1815 led to a decline in the average British worker's real wages and standard of living. These difficult war years, with high unemployment and inflation, lent a grim color to the new industrial system. Factory wages began to rise after 1815, but these gains were modest and were offset by a decline in the labor of children and married women, meaning that many households had less total income than before. Moreover, many people still worked outside the factories as cottage workers or rural laborers, and in those sectors wages declined. Thus the increase in the productivity of industry did not lead to an increase in the purchasing power of the British working classes. Only after 1830, and especially after 1840, did real wages rise substantially, so that the average worker earned roughly 30 percent more in real terms in 1850 than in 1770.[10]

Up to that point, the demands of labor in the new industries probably outweighed their benefits as far as working people were concerned. Many landless poor people in the late eighteenth century were self-employed cottage workers living in close-knit rural communities; with industrialization they worked longer and harder at jobs that were often more grueling and more dangerous. In England nonagricultural workers labored about 250 days per year in 1760 as compared to 300 days per year in 1830, while the normal workday remained an exhausting eleven hours throughout the entire period. In 1760 nonagricultural workers still observed many religious and public holidays by not working, and many workers took Monday off. These days of leisure and relaxation declined rapidly after 1760, and by 1830 nonagricultural workers had joined landless agricultural laborers in toiling six rather than five days a week.[11]

As the factories moved to urban areas, workers followed them in large numbers, leading to an explosion in the size of cities, especially in the north of England.

Life in the new industrial cities, such as Manchester and Glasgow, was grim. Migrants to the booming cities found expensive, hastily constructed, overcrowded apartments and inadequate sanitary systems. Infant mortality, disease, malnutrition, and accidents took such a high toll in human life that life expectancy was only around twenty-five to twenty-seven years, some fifteen years less than the national average.[12] Perhaps the most shocking evidence of the impact of the Industrial Revolution on living standards is the finding that child mortality levels rose after 1825, especially in industrial areas.

Another way to consider the workers' standard of living is to look at the goods they purchased. Such evidence is somewhat contradictory, but generally suggestive of stagnant or declining living standards until the middle of the nineteenth century. One important area of improvement was in the consumption of cotton goods, which became much cheaper and could be enjoyed by all classes. Now millions of poor people could afford to wear cotton slips and underpants as well as cotton dresses and shirts. However, in other areas, food in particular, the modest growth in factory wages was not enough to compensate for rising prices.

From the 1840s onward, matters improved considerably as wages made substantial gains and the prices of many goods dropped. A greater variety of foods became available, including the first canned goods. Some of the most important advances were in medicine. Smallpox vaccination became routine and surgeons began to use anesthesia in the late 1840s. By 1850 trains had revolutionized transportation for the masses, while the telegraph made instant communication possible for the first time in human history. In addition, gaslights greatly expanded the possibilities of nighttime activity. Gas lighting is one of the most important examples of a direct relationship between the scientific advances of the eighteenth century—in this case, chemistry—and the development of new technologies of the Industrial Revolution.

More difficult to measure than real wages or life expectancy was the impact of the Industrial Revolution on community and social values. As young men and women migrated away from their villages to seek employment in urban factories, many close-knit rural communities were destroyed. Village social and cultural traditions disappeared without new generations to carry them on. Although many young people formed new friendships and appreciated the freedoms of urban life, they also suffered from the loneliness of life in the anonymous city. The loss of skills and work autonomy, along with the loss of community, must be included in the assessment of the Industrial Revolution's effect on the living conditions of workers.

Relations Between Capital and Labor

FOCUS QUESTION *How did the changes brought about by the Industrial Revolution lead to new social classes, and how did people respond to the new structure?*

In Great Britain, industrial development led to the creation of new social groups and intensified long-standing conflicts between capital and labor. A new class of factory owners and industrial capitalists arose. These men and women and their families strengthened the wealth and size of the middle class, which had previously been made up mainly of merchants and professional people. The demands of modern industry regularly brought the interests of the middle-class industrialists into conflict with those of the people who worked for them—the working class. (See "Thinking Like a Historian: Making the Industrialized Worker," page 674.) As observers took notice of these changes, they raised new questions about how industrialization affected social relationships. Meanwhile, enslaved labor in European colonies contributed to the industrialization process in multiple ways.

The New Class of Factory Owners

Early industrialists operated in a highly competitive economic system. As the careers of James Watt and Fritz Harkort illustrate, there were countless production problems, and success and large profits were by no means certain. Manufacturers therefore waged a constant battle to cut their production costs and stay afloat. Much of the profit had to go back into the business for new and better machinery.

Most early industrialists drew upon their families and friends for labor and capital, but they came from a variety of backgrounds. Many, such as Harkort, were from well-established families with rich networks of contacts and support. Others, such as Watt and Cockerill, were of modest means, especially in the early days. Artisans and skilled workers of exceptional ability had unparalleled opportunities. Members of ethnic and religious groups who had been discriminated against jumped at the new chances and often helped each other. Scots, Quakers, and other Protestant dissenters were tremendously important in Britain; Protestants and Jews dominated banking in Catholic France. Many of the industrialists were newly rich, and, not surprisingly, they were very proud and self-satisfied.

As factories and firms grew larger, opportunities declined, at least in well-developed industries. It became

Luddite Rioters Named after a mythic leader, "General Ludd," the Luddite riots began in 1811 in Nottinghamshire and quickly spread to manufacturing districts throughout England. Their target was the mechanized looms that led to lower wages and unemployment among hand-weavers. Machine breaking was quickly declared a capital crime, and a number of Luddites were executed. (*Luddite Rioters*, 19th century English engraving/Private Collection/Bridgeman Images)

considerably harder for a gifted but poor young mechanic to start a small enterprise and end up as a wealthy manufacturer. Formal education became more important for young men as a means of success and advancement, but studies at the advanced level were expensive. In Britain by 1830 and in France and Germany by 1860, leading industrialists were more likely to have inherited their well-established enterprises, and they were financially much more secure than their struggling parents had been. They also had a greater sense of class-consciousness; they were fully aware that ongoing industrial development had widened the gap between themselves and their workers.

Just like working-class women, the wives and daughters of successful businessmen found fewer opportunities for active participation in Europe's increasingly complex business world. Rather than contributing as vital partners in a family-owned enterprise, as so many middle-class women had done, these women were increasingly valued for their ladylike gentility. By 1850 some influential women writers and most businessmen assumed that middle-class wives and daughters should avoid work in offices and factories. Rather, a middle-class lady was expected to concentrate on her proper role as wife and mother, preferably in an elegant residential area far removed from ruthless commerce and the volatile working class. (See "Evaluating the Evidence 20.3: Advice for Middle-Class Women," page 676.)

Responses to Industrialization

From the beginning, the British Industrial Revolution had its critics. Among the first were the Romantic poets. William Blake (1757–1827) called the early factories "satanic mills" and protested against the hard life of the London poor. William Wordsworth (1770–1850) lamented the destruction of the rural way of life and the pollution of the land and water. Some handicraft workers—notably the **Luddites**, who attacked factories in northern England in 1811 and later—smashed the new machines, which they believed were putting them out of work. Doctors and reformers wrote of problems in the factories and new towns, while Malthus and Ricardo concluded that workers would earn only enough to stay alive.

This pessimistic view was accepted and reinforced by Friedrich Engels (1820–1895), the future revolutionary and colleague of Karl Marx (see Chapter 21). After studying conditions in northern England, this young son of a wealthy Prussian cotton manufacturer published in 1844 *The Condition of the Working Class in England*, a blistering indictment of the capitalist classes. "At the bar of world opinion," he wrote, "I charge the English middle classes with mass murder, wholesale robbery, and all the other crimes in the calendar." The new poverty of industrial workers was worse than the old poverty of cottage workers and agricultural laborers, according to Engels. The culprit was industrial capitalism, with its relentless competition and constant technical change. Engels's extremely influential charge of capitalist exploitation and increasing worker poverty was embellished by Marx and later socialists (see Chapter 21).

Analysis of industrial capitalism, often combined with reflections on the French Revolution, led to the development of a new overarching interpretation—a

■ **Luddites** Group of handicraft workers who attacked factories in northern England in 1811 and later, smashing the new machines that they believed were putting them out of work.

THINKING LIKE A HISTORIAN

Making the Industrialized Worker

Looking back from the vantage point of the 1820s and 1830s, contemporary observers saw in early industrialization a process that was as much about social transformation as it was about technological transformation—a process in which changes in work conditions were closely tied to changes in workers' family lives, values, and mental habits.

1 **Peter Gaskell, *The Manufacturing Population of England: Its Moral, Social, and Physical Conditions, and the Changes Which Have Arisen from the Use of Steam Machinery*, 1833.** In this excerpt, Peter Gaskell sketches the moral, social, and physical conditions of English workers *before* industrialization took hold, linking these characteristics to preindustrial work conditions.

Prior to the year 1760, manufactures were in a great measure confined to the demands of the home market. At this period, and down to 1800 . . . the majority of the artisans engaged in them had laboured in their own houses, and in the bosoms of their families. . . .

These were, undoubtedly, the golden times of manufactures, considered in reference to the character of the labourers. By all the processes being carried on under a man's own roof, he retained his individual respectability; he was kept apart from associations that might injure his moral worth, whilst he generally earned wages which were sufficient not only to live comfortably upon, but which enabled him to rent a few acres of land; thus joining in his own person two classes, that are now daily becoming more and more distinct. . . .

Thus, removed from many of those causes which universally operate to the deterioration of the moral character of the labouring man, when brought into large towns . . . the small farmer, spinner, or hand-loom weaver presents as orderly and respectable an appearance as could be wished. It is true that the amount of labour gone through was but small; that the quantity of cloth or yarn produced was but limited—for he worked by the rule of his strength and convenience. They were, however, sufficient to clothe and feed himself and family decently, and according to their station; to lay

by a penny for an evil day, and to enjoy those amusements and bodily recreations then in being. He was a respectable member of society; a good father, a good husband, and a good son.

2 **Richard Guest, *A Compendious History of the Cotton-Manufacture*, 1823.** Like Peter Gaskell, Richard Guest, one of the earliest historians of the English textile industry, believed that industrialization had "introduced great changes into the manners and habits of the people." Unlike Gaskell, however, Guest was convinced that these changes had been for the better. Where Gaskell saw moral decline, Guest saw moral awakening.

The progress of the Cotton Manufacture introduced great changes into the manners and habits of the people. The operative workmen being thrown together in great numbers had their faculties sharpened and improved by constant communication. Conversation wandered over a variety of topics not before essayed; the questions of Peace and War, which interested them importantly, inasmuch as they might produce a rise or fall of wages, became highly interesting, and this brought them into the vast field of politics and discussions on the character of their Government, and the men who composed it. They took a greater interest in the defeats and victories of their country's arms, and from being only a few degrees above their cattle in the scale of intellect, they became Political Citizens. . . .

The facility with which the Weavers changed their masters, the constant effort to find out and obtain the largest remuneration for their labour, the excitement to ingenuity which the higher wages for fine manufactures and skillful workman-

ANALYZING THE EVIDENCE

1. How does Richard Guest's characterization of preindustrial workers and conditions in Source 2 compare to Peter Gaskell's in Source 1? Why did Gaskell think industrialization would harm workers' morals while Guest saw it as a force for moral improvement?
2. Early-nineteenth-century artists produced many images of the new factories. How would you describe the textile mill shown in Source 4?
3. According to the German doctor in Source 3, what challenges confronted working-class women in their daily lives? To what extent does he seem to blame the women themselves for their situation? How might observations like these have affected the new sexual division of labor discussed in the text?
4. In what ways were Robert Owen's innovations (Source 5) a response to the negative impacts of industrialization highlighted by the German doctor (Source 3)?

ship produced, and a conviction that they depended mainly on their own exertions, produced in them that invaluable feeling, a spirit of freedom and independence, and that guarantee for good conduct and improvement of manners, a consciousness of the value of character and of their own weight and importance.

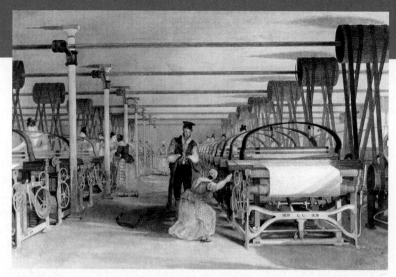

3 **Living conditions of the working class, 1845.** As middle-class reformers began to investigate working-class living conditions, they were shocked at what they found. This excerpt comes from an 1845 interview of doctors in a German industrial city.

～QUESTION: What is your usual experience regarding the cleanliness of these classes?

DR. BLUEMNER: Bad! Mother has to go out to work, and can therefore pay little attention to the domestic economy, and even if she makes an effort, she lacks time and means. A typical woman of this kind has four children, of whom she is still suckling one, she has to look after the whole household, to take food to her husband at work, perhaps a quarter of a mile away on a building site; she therefore has no time for cleaning and then it is such a small hole inhabited by so many people. The children are left to themselves, crawl about the floor or in the streets, and are always dirty; they lack the necessary clothing to change more often, and there is no time or money to wash these frequently. There are, of course, gradations; if the mother is healthy, active and clean, and if the poverty is not too great, then things are better.

4 **Power loom weaving, 1834.** This engraving shows adult women operating power looms under the supervision of a male foreman, and it accurately reflects both the decline of family employment and the emergence of a gender-based division of labor in many British factories. The jungle of belts and shafts connecting the noisy looms to the giant steam engine on the ground floor created a constant din. (The LIFE Picture Collection/Time Life Pictures/Getty Images)

5 **Robert Owen, *A New View of Society*, 1831.** Manufacturer and social reformer Robert Owen was also interested in the lessons of the early years of industrialization. He wished not to defend or decry industrialization, but to apply those lessons to the design and operation of his textile factory at New Lanark, Scotland.

～The system of receiving apprentices from public charities was abolished; permanent settlers with large families were encouraged, and comfortable houses built for their accommodation. The practice of employing children in the mills, of six, seven, and eight years of age, was discontinued, and their parents advised to allow them to acquire health and education until they were ten years old.... The children were taught reading, writing, and arithmetic during five years, that is, from five to ten, in the village school, without expense to their parents....

[A]ttention was given to the domestic arrangements of the community. Their houses were rendered more comfortable, their streets were improved, the best provisions were purchased, and sold to them at low rates.... They were taught to be rational, and they acted rationally. Thus both parties experienced the incalculable advantages of the system which had been adopted. Those employed became industrious, temperate, healthy, faithful to their employers, and kind to each other; while the proprietors were deriving services ... far beyond those which could be obtained by any other means than those of mutual confidence and kindness.

PUTTING IT ALL TOGETHER

Using the sources above, along with what you have learned in class and in this chapter, create a comparison of industrial and preindustrial conditions, written from the perspective of a nineteenth-century observer. Your observer can come from any social background: he or she could be a scholar like Peter Gaskell or Richard Guest, a factory owner like Robert Owen, or an actual factory worker. As you write, be sure to consider the influence of your observer's background on his or her characterization of the changes brought by industrialization. What differences would your observer highlight? Why?

Sources: (1) Peter Gaskell, *The Manufacturing Population of England: Its Moral, Social, and Physical Conditions, and the Changes Which Have Arisen from the Use of Steam Machinery* (London: Baldwin and Cradock, 1833), pp. 15–16, 18; (2) E. Royston Pike, *Human Documents of the Industrial Revolution in Britain* (London: George Allen & Unwin, 1970), pp. 26–28; (3) Laura L. Frader, ed., *The Industrial Revolution: A History in Documents* (Oxford: Oxford University Press, 2006), pp. 85–86; (5) Pike, *Human Documents of the Industrial Revolution in Britain*, pp. 37–42.

Advice for Middle-Class Women

The adoption of steam-powered machines generated tremendous profits during the Industrial Revolution. Factory owners and managers enjoyed new wealth, and skilled male workers eventually began to hope for wages high enough to keep their wives and children at home. These social changes encouraged the nineteenth-century "separate spheres" ideology, which emphasized the importance of women's role as caretakers of the domestic realm. Sarah Stickney Ellis's The Women of England: Their Social Duties and Domestic Habits, *excerpted below, was one of a flood of publications offering middle-class women advice on shopping, housekeeping, and supervising servants.*

"What shall I do to gratify myself—to be admired—or to vary the tenor of my existence?" are not the questions which a woman of right feelings asks awaking to the avocations of the day. Much more congenial to the highest attributes of woman's character, are inquiries such as these: "How shall I endeavor through this day to turn the time, the health, and the means permitted me to enjoy, to the best account? Is any one sick, I must visit their chamber without delay, and try to give their apartment an air of comfort, by arranging such things as the wearied nurse may not have thought of. Is any one about to set off on a journey, I must see that the early meal is spread, to prepare it with my own hands, in order that the servant, who was working late last night, may profit by unbroken rest. Did I fail in what was kind or considerate to any of the family yesterday; I will meet her this morning with a cordial welcome, and show, in the most delicate way I can, that I am anxious to atone for the past. Was any one exhausted by the last day's exertion, I will be an hour before them this morning, and let them see that their labor is so much in advance. Or, if nothing extraordinary occurs to claim my attention, I will meet the family with a consciousness that, being the least engaged of any member of it, I am consequently the most at liberty to devote myself to the general good of the whole, by cultivating cheerful conversation, adapting myself to the prevailing tone of feeling, and leading those who are least happy, to think and speak of what will make them more so."

EVALUATE THE EVIDENCE

1. What daily tasks and duties does Sarah Stickney Ellis prescribe for the mother of the family?
2. How does this document exemplify the changes in the sexual division of labor and ideals of domesticity described in the text?

Source: Sarah Stickney Ellis, *The Women of England: Their Social Duties and Domestic Habits*, in *The Past Speaks*, 2d ed., ed. Walter Arnstein (Lexington, Mass.: D. C. Heath, 1993), 2:173.

new paradigm—regarding social relationships. Briefly, this paradigm argued that individuals were members of separate classes based on their relationship to the means of production, that is, the machines and factories that dominated the new economy. As owners of expensive industrial machinery and as dependent laborers in their factories, the two main groups of society had separate and conflicting interests. Accordingly, the comfortable, well-educated "public" of the eighteenth century came increasingly to be defined as the middle class ("middle" because they were beneath the small group of aristocracy at the top of society who claimed to be above industrial activity), and the "people" gradually began to perceive themselves as composing a modern working class. And if the new class interpretation was more of a simplification than a fundamental truth for some critics, it appealed to many because it seemed to explain what was happening. Therefore, conflicting classes existed, in part, because many individuals came to believe they existed and developed an awareness that they belonged to a particular social class—what Karl Marx called **class-consciousness**.

Meanwhile, other observers believed that conditions were improving for the working people. In his 1835 study of the cotton industry, Andrew Ure (yoo-RAY) wrote that conditions in most factories were not harsh and were even quite good. Edwin Chadwick, a government official well acquainted with the problems of the working population, concluded that the "whole mass of the laboring community" was increasingly able "to buy more of the necessities and minor luxuries of life."[13] Nevertheless, those who thought—correctly—that conditions were getting worse for working people were probably in the majority.

The Early British Labor Movement

Not everyone worked in large factories and coal mines during the Industrial Revolution. In 1850 more British people still worked on farms than in any other single occupation, although rural communities were suffering from outward migration. The second-largest occupation was domestic service, with more than 1 million household servants, 90 percent of whom were women.

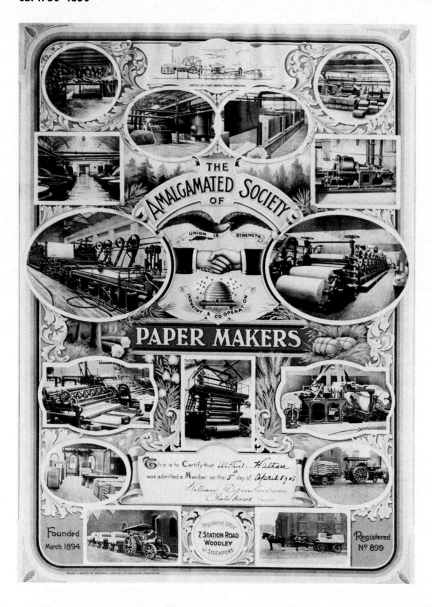

Union Membership Certificate
This handsome membership certificate belonged to Arthur Watton, a properly trained and certified papermaker of Kings Norton in Birmingham, England. Members of such unions proudly framed their certificates and displayed them in their homes, showing that they were skilled workers. (Courtesy, Sylvia Waddell)

Thus many old, familiar jobs outside industry lived on and provided alternatives to industrial labor.

Within industry itself, the pattern of artisans working with hand tools in small shops remained unchanged in many trades, even as others were revolutionized by technological change. For example, the British iron industry was completely dominated by large-scale capitalist firms by 1850. Many large ironworks had more than one thousand people on their payrolls. Yet the firms that fashioned iron into small metal goods, such as tools, tableware, and toys, employed on average fewer than ten wage workers who used handicraft skills. The survival of small workshops gave many workers an alternative to factory employment.

Working-class solidarity and class-consciousness developed both in small workshops and in large factories. In the northern factory districts, anticapitalist sentiments were frequent by the 1820s. Commenting in 1825 on a strike in the woolen center of Bradford

and the support it had gathered from other regions, one newspaper claimed with pride that "it is all the workers of England against a few masters of Bradford."[14] Even in trades that did not undergo mechanization, unemployment and stagnant wages contributed to class awareness.

Such sentiments ran contrary to the liberal tenets of economic freedom championed by eighteenth-century thinkers like Adam Smith. Liberal economic principles were embraced by statesmen and middle-class business owners in the late eighteenth century and continued to gather strength in the early nineteenth century. In 1799 Parliament passed the **Combination Acts**, which

■ **class-consciousness** Awareness of belonging to a distinct social and economic class whose interests might conflict with those of other classes.

■ **Combination Acts** British laws passed in 1799 that outlawed unions and strikes, favoring capitalist business people over skilled artisans. Bitterly resented and widely disregarded by many craft guilds, the acts were repealed by Parliament in 1824.

outlawed unions and strikes. In 1813 and 1814 Parliament repealed an old law regulating the wages of artisans and the conditions of apprenticeship. As a result of these and other measures, certain skilled artisan workers, such as bootmakers and high-quality tailors, found aggressive capitalists ignoring traditional work rules and trying to flood their trades with unorganized women workers and children to beat down wages.

The capitalist attack on artisan guilds and work rules was bitterly resented by many craftworkers, who subsequently played an important part in Great Britain and in other countries in gradually building a modern labor movement. The Combination Acts were widely disregarded by workers. Printers, papermakers, carpenters, tailors, and other such craftsmen continued to take collective action, and societies of skilled factory workers also organized unions in defiance of the law. Unions sought to control the number of skilled workers, to limit apprenticeship to members' own children, and to bargain with owners over wages.

They were not afraid to strike; there was, for example, a general strike of adult cotton spinners in Manchester in 1810. In the face of widespread union activity, Parliament repealed the Combination Acts in 1824, and unions were tolerated, though not fully accepted, after 1825.

The next stage in the development of the British trade-union movement was the attempt to create a single large national union. This effort was led not so much by working people as by social reformers such as Robert Owen. Owen, a self-made cotton manufacturer (see page 675), had pioneered in industrial relations by combining firm discipline with concern for the health, safety, and hours of his workers. After 1815 he experimented with cooperative and socialist communities, including one at New Harmony, Indiana. Then in 1834 Owen was involved in the organization of one of the largest and most visionary of the early national unions, the Grand National Consolidated Trades Union.

When Owen's and other ambitious schemes collapsed, the British labor movement moved once again after 1851 in the direction of craft unions. The most famous of these was the Amalgamated Society of Engineers, which represented skilled machinists. These unions won real benefits for members by fairly conservative means and thus became an accepted part of the industrial scene.

British workers also engaged in direct political activity in defense of their interests. After the collapse of Owen's national trade union, many working people went into the Chartist movement, which sought political democracy. The key Chartist demand—that all men be given the right to vote—became the great hope of millions of common people. Workers were also active in campaigns to limit the workday in factories to ten hours and to permit duty-free importation of wheat into Great Britain to secure cheap bread. Thus working people developed a sense of their own identity and played an active role in shaping the new industrial system. They were neither helpless victims nor passive beneficiaries.

The Impact of Slavery

Another mass labor force of the Industrial Revolution was composed of the millions of enslaved men, women, and children who toiled in European colonies in the Caribbean and in North and South America. Historians have long debated the extent to which revenue from slavery contributed to Britain's achievements in the Industrial Revolution.

Most now agree that profits from colonial plantations and slave trading were a small portion of British national income in the eighteenth century and were probably more often invested in land than in industry. Nevertheless, the impact of slavery on Britain's economy was much broader than its direct profits alone. In the mid-eighteenth century the need for items to exchange for colonial cotton, sugar, tobacco, and slaves stimulated demand for British manufactured goods in the Caribbean, North America, and West Africa. Britain's dominance in the slave trade also led to the development of finance and credit institutions that helped early industrialists obtain capital for their businesses. Investments in canals, roads, and railroads made possible by profits from colonial trade provided the necessary infrastructure to move raw materials and products of the factory system.

The British Parliament abolished the slave trade in 1807 and freed all slaves in British territories in 1833, but by 1850 most of the cotton processed by British mills was supplied by the labor of enslaved people in the southern United States. Thus the Industrial Revolution was deeply entangled with the Atlantic world and the misery of slavery.

NOTES

1. N. F. R. Crafts, *British Economic Growth During the Industrial Revolution* (Oxford: Oxford University Press, 1985), p. 32.
2. Robert C. Allen, *The British Industrial Revolution in Global Perspective* (Cambridge: Cambridge University Press, 2009), pp. 1–2.
3. P. Bairoch, "International Industrialization Levels from 1750 to 1980," *Journal of European Economic History* 11 (Spring 1982): 269–333.
4. Quoted in J. Bowditch and C. Ramsland, eds., *Voices of the Industrial Revolution* (Ann Arbor: University of Michigan Press, 1961), p. 55, from the fourth edition of Thomas Malthus, *Essay on the Principle of Population* (1807).
5. Quoted in Emma Griffin, *A Short History of the British Industrial Revolution* (Basingstoke, U.K.: Palgrave Macmillan, 2010), p. 126.
6. Quoted in E. R. Pike, *"Hard Times": Human Documents of the Industrial Revolution* (New York: Praeger, 1966), p. 109.
7. See especially J. Brenner and M. Rama, "Rethinking Women's Oppression," *New Left Review* 144 (March–April 1984): 33–71, and sources cited there.
8. J. Humphries, ". . . 'The Most Free from Objection' . . . The Sexual Division of Labor and Women's Work in Nineteenth-Century England," *Journal of Economic History* 47 (December 1987): 941; Pike, *"Hard Times,"* p. 266.
9. Quoted in Pike, *"Hard Times,"* p. 208.
10. Joel Mokyr, *The Enlightened Economy: An Economic History of Britain, 1700–1850* (New Haven, Conn.: Yale University Press, 2009), pp. 460–461.
11. Hans-Joachim Voth, *Time and Work in England, 1750–1830* (Oxford: Oxford University Press, 2000), pp. 118–133, 268–270.
12. Mokyr, *The Enlightened Economy*, p. 455.
13. Quoted in W. A. Hayek, ed., *Capitalism and the Historians* (Chicago: University of Chicago Press, 1954), p. 126.
14. Quoted in D. Geary, ed., *Labour and Socialist Movements in Europe Before 1914* (Oxford: Berg, 1989), p. 29.

LOOKING BACK LOOKING AHEAD

The Industrial Revolution was a long process of economic innovation and growth occurring first in Britain around 1780 and spreading to the European continent after 1815. The development of machines powered first by water and then by steam allowed for a tremendous growth in productivity, which enabled Britain to assume the lead in the world's production of industrial goods. Industrialization fundamentally changed the social landscape of European countries, creating a new elite of wealthy manufacturers and a vast working class of urban wage laborers whose living conditions remained grim until the mid-nineteenth century.

One popular idea in the 1830s, first developed by a French economist, was that Britain's late-eighteenth-century "industrial revolution" paralleled the political events in France during the French Revolution. One revolution was economic, while the other was political; one was ongoing and successful, while the other had failed and come to a definite end in 1815, when Europe's conservative monarchs defeated Napoleon and restored the French kings of the Old Regime.

In fact, in 1815 the French Revolution, like the Industrial Revolution, was an unfinished revolution. Just as Britain was in the midst of its economic transformation and the states of northwestern Europe had only begun industrialization, so too after 1815 were the political conflicts and ideologies of revolutionary France still very much alive. The French Revolution had opened the era of modern political life not just in France but across Europe. It had brought into existence many of the political ideologies that would interact with the social and economic forces of industrialization to refashion Europe and create a new urban society. Moreover, in 1815 the unfinished French Revolution carried the very real possibility of renewed political upheaval. This possibility, which conservatives feared and radicals longed for, would become dramatic reality in 1848, when political revolutions swept across Europe like a whirlwind.

Make Connections

Think about the larger developments and continuities within and across chapters.

1. Why did Great Britain take the lead in industrialization, and when did other countries begin to adopt the new techniques and organization of production?

2. How did the achievements in agriculture and rural industry of the late seventeenth and eighteenth centuries (Chapter 17) pave the way for the Industrial Revolution of the late eighteenth century?

3. How would you compare the legacy of the political revolutions of the late eighteenth century (Chapter 19) with that of the Industrial Revolution? Which seems to you to have created the most important changes, and why?

20 REVIEW & EXPLORE

Identify Key Terms

Identify and explain the significance of each item below.

Industrial Revolution (p. 651)

spinning jenny (p. 652)

water frame (p. 653)

steam engines (p. 655)

Rocket (p. 656)

Crystal Palace (p. 657)

iron law of wages (p. 657)

tariff protection (p. 663)

Factory Acts (p. 666)

separate spheres (p. 666)

Mines Act of 1842 (p. 669)

Luddites (p. 673)

class-consciousness (p. 676)

Combination Acts (p. 677)

Review the Main Ideas

Answer the focus questions from each section of the chapter.

◆ Why did the Industrial Revolution begin in Britain, and how did it develop between 1780 and 1850? (p. 650)

◆ How did countries in Europe and around the world respond to the challenge of industrialization? (p. 660)

◆ How did work evolve during the Industrial Revolution, and how did daily life change for working people? (p. 665)

◆ How did the changes brought about by the Industrial Revolution lead to new social classes, and how did people respond to the new structure? (p. 672)

Suggested Reading and Media Resources

BOOKS

- Allen, Robert C. *The British Industrial Revolution in Global Perspective.* 2009. Explains the origins of the Industrial Revolution and why it took place in Britain and not elsewhere.

- Davidoff, Leonore, and Catherine Hall. *Family Fortunes: Men and Women of the English Middle Class, 1750–1850,* rev. ed. 2003. Examines both economic activities and cultural beliefs with great skill.

- Griffin, Emma. *A Short History of the British Industrial Revolution.* 2010. An accessible and lively introduction to the subject.

- Horn, Jeff, Leonard N. Rosenband, and Merritt Roe Smith. *Reconceptualizing the Industrial Revolution.* 2010. A collection of essays by leading scholars that re-examines the most contentious debates in the field.

- Humphries, Jane. *Childhood and Child Labour in the British Industrial Revolution.* 2010. A moving account of the experience of children during the Industrial Revolution, based on numerous autobiographies.

- James, Harold. *Family Capitalism.* 2006. A study of the entrepreneurial dynasties of the British Industrial Revolution.

- Mokyr, Joel. *The Enlightened Economy: An Economic History of Britain, 1700–1850.* 2009. A masterful explanation of industrialization and economic growth in Britain that emphasizes the impact of Enlightenment openness and curiosity.

- Morris, Charles R. *The Dawn of Innovation: The First American Industrial Revolution.* 2012. Tells the story of the individuals, inventions, and trade networks that transformed the United States from a rural economy to a global industrial power.

- Prados de la Escosura, Leandro, ed. *Exceptionalism and Industrialisation: Britain and Its European Rivals, 1688–1815.* 2004. Compares the path toward economic development in Britain and the rest of Europe.

- Rosenthal, Jean-Laurent, and R. Bin Wong. *Before and Beyond Divergence: The Politics of Economic Change in China and Europe.* 2011. A study of the similarities and differences between Europe and China that led to the origins and growth of industrialization in Europe.

- Stearns, Peter N. *The Industrial Revolution in World History,* 4th ed. 2012. A useful brief survey.

DOCUMENTARIES

- *The Children Who Built Victorian Britain* (BBC, 2011). An account of the role of child labor in the Industrial Revolution, based on written testimonies from children of that era.

- *Great Victorian Railway Journeys: How Modern Britain Was Built by Victorian Steam Power* (BBC, 2012). A popular British television series re-creates five journeys by train from the Victorian era, showing the impact of rail travel on English culture and society.

- *Mill Times* (PBS, 2006). A combination of documentary video and animated re-enactments that tells the story of the mechanization of the cotton industry in Britain and the United States.

FEATURE FILMS AND TELEVISION

- *Germinal* (Claude Berri, 1993). In a European coal-mining town during the Industrial Revolution, exploited workers go on strike and encounter brutal repression from the authorities.

- *Hard Times* (Granada TV, 1977). A four-hour miniseries adaptation of Charles Dickens's famous novel about the bitter life of mill workers in England during the Industrial Revolution.

- *Oliver Twist* (Roman Polanski, 2005). A film based on a novel by Charles Dickens depicting the harsh conditions of life for orphans and poor children in nineteenth-century London.

WEB SITES

- *Images of the Industrial Revolution in Britain.* A collection of annotated images from the eighteenth and nineteenth centuries covering various aspects of the Industrial Revolution. **http://www.netnicholls.com/neh2001/index.html**

- *Spinning the Web.* A Web site offering comprehensive information on the people, places, industrial processes, and products involved in the mechanization of the British cotton industry. **www.spinningtheweb.org.uk/industry**

- *Women Working, 1800–1930.* A digital collection of the Harvard University Library, with sources and links related to women's labor in the nineteenth and early twentieth centuries. **ocp.hul.harvard.edu/ww**

21

Ideologies and Upheavals

1815–1850

The momentous economic and political transformation of modern times that began in the late eighteenth century with the "unfinished" revolutions—the Industrial Revolution in England and the political revolution in France—would play out with unpredictable consequences in the first half of the nineteenth century. Attempts to halt the spread of the progressive forces associated with the French Revolution led first to a reassertion of conservative political control in continental Europe. Following the leadership of Austrian foreign minister Klemens von Metternich, the aristocratic leaders of the Great Powers sought to stamp out the spread of liberal and democratic reforms.

The political and cultural innovations made possible by the unfinished revolutions, however, proved difficult to contain. In politics, powerful new ideologies—liberalism, nationalism, and socialism—emerged to oppose Metternich's revitalized conservatism. In literature, art, and music, Romanticism—an intellectual and artistic movement that challenged the certainties of the Enlightenment and fed the growth of popular nationalism—captured the intensity of the era. A successful revolution in Greece, liberal reform in Great Britain, and popular unrest in France gave voice to ordinary people's desire for political and social change. All these movements helped launch the great wave of revolutions that swept across Europe in 1848, and the dramatic results would have a lasting impact on the shape of Western civilization. ∎

CHAPTER PREVIEW

Life in the Revolutionary Era
Between 1830 and 1848 crowds stormed public areas to force political change in many parts of Europe. In this dramatic scene from the revolutions of 1830, rioters in Brussels demand Belgian national independence from the Netherlands. At the top right, a patriot clutches the Belgian tricolor flag while another brandishes a list of revolutionary demands; at the center, a youth has died in the fight for the nation, inspiring fellow citizens to join the cause. (By Gustave Wappers [1803–1874], [oil on canvas]/Musée Royaux des Beaux-Arts de Belgique, Brussels, Belgium/© Leemage/ Bridgeman Images)

The Aftermath of the Napoleonic Wars

FOCUS QUESTION *How was peace restored and maintained after 1815?*

The eventual eruption of revolutionary political forces in 1848 was by no means predictable as the Napoleonic era ended. Quite the contrary. After finally defeating Napoleon, the conservative, aristocratic monarchies of Russia, Prussia, Austria, and Great Britain—known as the Quadruple Alliance—reaffirmed their determination to hold France in line. Even before Napoleon's final defeat, the allies had agreed to meet to fashion a general peace accord in 1814 at the Congress of Vienna, where they faced a great challenge: how could they construct a lasting settlement that would not sow the seeds of another war? By carefully managing the balance of power, redrawing the boundaries of formerly French-held territories, and embracing conservative restoration, they brokered an agreement that contributed to fifty years of peace in Europe (Map 21.1).

The European Balance of Power

Elite representatives of the Quadruple Alliance (plus a representative of the restored Bourbon monarch of France)—including Tsar Alexander I of Russia, King Friedrich Wilhelm III of Prussia, Emperor Franz II of Austria, and their foreign ministers—met to fashion

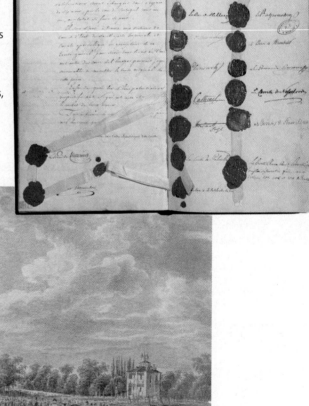

Congress of Vienna The Congress of Vienna was renowned for its intense diplomatic deal making, resulting in the Treaty of Vienna, the last page of which was signed and sealed in 1815 by the representatives of the various European states attending the conference (inset). The congress won additional notoriety for its ostentatious parades, parties, and dance balls. The painting here portrays a mounted group of European royalty, led by the Prussian emperor and the Russian tsar, in a flamboyant parade designed to celebrate Napoleon's defeat the year before. Onlookers toast the victorious monarchs. The display of flags, weapons, and heraldic emblems symbolizes the unity of Europe's Great Powers, while the long tables in the background suggest the extent of the festivities. Such images were widely distributed to engender popular support for the conservative program. (treaty: Archives du Ministère des Affaires Étrangères, Paris, France/Archives Charmet/Bridgeman Images; painting: *The Celebration of the Prater in the Presence of the Reigning Monarchs, 1815*/Collection of the Palaces Artstetten and Luberegg/akg-image)

the peace at the **Congress of Vienna** from September 1814 to June 1815. A host of delegates from the smaller European states also attended the conference and offered minor assistance.

Such a face-to-face meeting of kings and emperors was very rare at the time. Professional ambassadors and court representatives had typically conducted state-to-state negotiations; now national leaders engaged in what we would today call "summit diplomacy." Participants at the congress enjoyed any number of festivities associated with aristocratic court culture, including formal receptions, military parades and reviews, sumptuous dinner parties, fancy ballroom dances, fireworks displays, and operatic and theatrical productions. Participation in Vienna's vibrant salon culture offered further opportunities to socialize, discuss current issues, and make informal deals that could be confirmed at the conference table. All the while, newspapers, pamphlets, periodicals, and satiric cartoons kept readers across Europe up-to-date on social events as well as the latest political developments and agreements. The conference thus marked an important transitional moment in Western history. The salon society and public sphere of the seventeenth-century Enlightenment (see Chapter 16) gradually shifted toward nineteenth-century cultures of publicity and public opinion informed by more modern mass-media campaigns.[1]

The allied powers were concerned first and foremost with the defeated enemy, France. Self-interest and traditional ideas about the balance of power motivated allied moderation toward the former foe. To Klemens von Metternich (MEH-tuhr-nihk) and Robert Castlereagh (KA-suhl-ray), the foreign ministers of Austria and Great Britain, the balance of power meant an international equilibrium of political and military forces that would discourage aggression by any combination of states or, worse, the domination of Europe by any single state. Their French negotiating partner, the skillful and cynical diplomat Charles Talleyrand, concurred.

The allies offered France lenient terms after Napoleon's abdication. They agreed to restore the Bourbon king to the French throne. The first Treaty of Paris, signed before the conference (and before Napoleon escaped from Elba and attacked the Bourbon regime), gave

Chronology

1790s–1840s	Romantic movement in literature and the arts
1809–1848	Metternich serves as Austrian foreign minister
1810	Germaine de Staël publishes *On Germany*
1814–1815	Congress of Vienna
1815	Revision of Corn Laws in Great Britain; Holy Alliance formed
June 18, 1815	Napoleon defeated at the Battle of Waterloo
1819	Karlsbad Decrees issued by German Confederation
1820	Congress of Troppau proclaims the principle of intervention to maintain autocratic regimes
1821	Austria crushes a liberal revolution in Naples and restores the Sicilian autocracy
1823	French armies restore the Spanish crown
1830	Greece wins independence from Ottomans
	France invades Algeria
	Charles X repudiates the Constitutional Charter; insurrection and collapse of the government follow
	Louis Philippe succeeds to the throne and maintains a narrowly liberal regime
1832	Reform Bill in Britain
1839	Socialist Louis Blanc publishes *The Organization of Work*
1840	Anarchist Pierre-Joseph Proudhon publishes *What Is Property?*
1845–1851	Great Famine in Ireland
1847	Ten Hours Act in Britain
1848	Revolutions in France, Austria, and Prussia; Marx and Engels publish *The Communist Manifesto*

France the boundaries it had possessed in 1792, which were larger than those of 1789. In addition, France did not have to pay war reparations. Thus the victorious powers avoided provoking a spirit of victimization and desire for revenge in the defeated country.

The Quadruple Alliance combined leniency with strong defensive measures designed to raise barriers against the possibility of renewed French aggression. Belgium and Holland—incorporated into the French empire under Napoleon—were united under an enlarged and independent "Kingdom of the Netherlands" capable of opposing French expansion to the north. The German-speaking lands on France's eastern border, also

■ **Congress of Vienna** A meeting of the Quadruple Alliance (Russia, Prussia, Austria, and Great Britain), restoration France, and smaller European states to fashion a general peace settlement that began after the defeat of Napoleon's France in 1814.

MAPPING THE PAST

MAP 21.1 Europe in 1815

In 1815 Europe contained many different states, but after the defeat of Napoleon international politics was dominated by the five Great Powers: Russia, Prussia, Austria, Great Britain, and France. (The number rises to six if one includes the Ottoman Empire.) At the Conference of Vienna, the Great Powers redrew the map of Europe.

ANALYZING THE MAP Trace the political boundaries of each Great Power. What are their geographical strengths and weaknesses? Compare these boundaries to those established at the height of Napoleonic power (see Map 19.2, page 638). What are the most important changes?

CONNECTIONS How did Prussia's and Austria's territorial gains contribute to the balance of power established at the Congress of Vienna? What other factors enabled the Great Powers to achieve such a long-lasting peace?

taken by Napoleon (see Chapter 19), were returned to Prussia. As a famous German anthem put it, the expanded Prussia would now stand as the "watch on the Rhine" against French attack. In addition, the allies reorganized the German-speaking territories of central Europe. A new German Confederation, a loose association of German-speaking states based on Napoleon's reorganization of the territory dominated by Prussia and Austria, replaced the roughly three hundred principalities, free cities, and dynastic states of the Holy Roman Empire with just thirty-eight German states (see Map 21.1).

Austria, Britain, Prussia, and Russia furthermore used the balance of power to settle their own potentially dangerous disputes. The victors generally agreed that each of them should receive compensation in the form of territory for their victory over the French. Great Britain had already won colonies and strategic outposts during the long wars. Austria gave up territories in Belgium and southern Germany but expanded greatly elsewhere, taking the rich provinces of Venetia and Lombardy in northern Italy as well as former Polish possessions and new lands on the eastern coast of the Adriatic.

Russian and Prussian claims for territorial expansion were more contentious. When Russia had pushed Napoleon out of central Europe, its armies had expanded its control over Polish territories. Tsar Alexander I wished to make Russian rule permanent. But when France, Austria, and Great Britain all argued for limits on Russian gains, the tsar ceded territories back to Prussia and accepted a smaller Polish kingdom. Prussian claims on the state of Saxony, a wealthy kingdom in the German Confederation, were particularly contentious. The Saxon king had supported Napoleon to the bitter end; now Wilhelm III wanted to incorporate Saxony into Prussia. Under pressure, he agreed to partition the state, leaving an independent Saxony in place, a change that posed no real threat to its Great Power neighbors but soothed their fears of Prussian expansionism. These territorial changes and compromises fell very much within the framework of balance-of-power ideology.

Unfortunately for France, in February 1815 Napoleon suddenly escaped from his "comic kingdom" on the island of Elba and re-ignited his wars of expansion for a brief time (see Chapter 19). Yet the second Treaty of Paris, concluded in November 1815 after Napoleon's final defeat at Waterloo, was still relatively moderate toward France. The elderly Louis XVIII was restored to his throne for a second time. France lost only a little territory, had to pay an indemnity of 700 million francs, and was required to support a large army of occupation for five years. The rest of the settlement concluded at the Congress of Vienna was left intact. The members of the Quadruple Alliance, however, did agree to meet periodically to discuss their common interests and to consider ap-

propriate measures for the maintenance of peace in Europe. This agreement marked the beginning of the European "Congress System," which lasted long into the nineteenth century and settled many international crises peacefully, through international conferences or "congresses" and balance-of-power diplomacy.

Metternich and Conservatism

The political ideals of conservatism, often associated with Austrian foreign minister Prince Klemens von Metternich (1773–1859), dominated Great Power discussions at the Congress of Vienna. Metternich's determined defense of the monarchical status quo made him a villain in the eyes of most progressive, liberal thinkers of the nineteenth century. Yet rather than denounce his politics, we can try to understand the general conservatism he represented. Born into the landed nobility of the Rhineland, Metternich was an internationally oriented aristocrat who made a brilliant diplomatic career. Austrian foreign minister from 1809 to 1848, the cosmopolitan and conservative Metternich had a pessimistic view of human nature, which he believed was ever prone to error, excess, and self-serving behavior. The disruptive events of the French Revolution and the Napoleonic Wars confirmed these views, and Metternich's conservatism would emerge as a powerful new political ideological force in response to the revolutionary age.

Metternich firmly believed that liberalism, as embodied in revolutionary America and France, bore the responsibility for the untold bloodshed and suffering caused by twenty-five years of war. Like Edmund Burke (see Chapter 19) and other conservatives, Metternich blamed liberal middle-class revolutionaries for stirring up the lower classes. Authoritarian, aristocratic government, he concluded, was necessary to protect society from the baser elements of human behavior, which were easily released in a democratic system. Organized religion was another pillar of strong government. Metternich despised the anticlericalism of the Enlightenment and the French Revolution and maintained that Christian morality was a vital bulwark against radical change.

Metternich defended his elite class and its rights and privileges with a clear conscience. The church and nobility were among Europe's most ancient and valuable institutions, and conservatives regarded tradition as the basic foundation of human society.

The threat of liberalism appeared doubly dangerous to Metternich because it generally went with aspirations for national independence. Liberals believed that each people, each national group, had a right to establish its own independent government and fulfill its own destiny. Though Metternich and other conservatives might accept some form of constitutional monarchy, the idea of national self-determination under

Prince Klemens von Metternich This portrait by Sir Thomas Lawrence reveals much about Metternich, the foreign minister of the Austrian Empire. Handsome, refined, and intelligent, this grand aristocrat passionately defended his class and its interests. (Royal Collection Trust © Her Majesty Queen Elizabeth II, 2015/Bridgeman Images)

liberal constitutional government was repellent because it threatened to revolutionize central Europe and destroy the Austrian Empire.

After centuries of war, royal intermarriage, and territorial expansion, the vast Austrian Empire of the Habsburgs included many regions and peoples within its borders (Map 21.2). The numerous kingdoms, duchies, and principalities under Habsburg rule included the lands of the Austrian crown, the Kingdom of Hungary, the Kingdom of Bohemia, and the Kingdom of Lombardy-Venetia, to name just the largest. Noble houses in these territories maintained some control, but ultimate authority rested with the Habsburg emperor. The peoples of the Austrian Empire spoke at least eleven different languages and observed vastly different customs; an astonishing variety of different ethnic groups mingled in the same provinces and the

■ **Holy Alliance** An alliance formed by the conservative rulers of Austria, Prussia, and Russia in September 1815 that became a symbol of the repression of liberal and revolutionary movements all over Europe.

■ **Karlsbad Decrees** Issued in 1819, these repressive regulations were designed to uphold Metternich's conservatism, requiring the German states to root out subversive ideas and squelch any liberal organizations.

same villages. They included about 8 million Germans, about one-fourth of the population. Some 5.5 million Magyars (Hungarians), 5 million Italians, 4 million Czechs, and 2 million Poles lived alongside each other in the imperial state, as did smaller groups of Slovenes, Croats, Serbs, Romanians, Jews, and Armenians.[2] The various Slavic groups, together with the Italians and the Romanians, lived in widely scattered regions, yet they outnumbered the politically dominant Germans and Hungarians (see Map 21.2).

The multiethnic empire Metternich served had strengths and weaknesses. A large population and vast territories gave the empire economic and military clout, but its potentially dissatisfied ethnicities and nationalities undermined political unity. In these circumstances, Metternich and the Habsburg dynasty virtually had to oppose liberalism and nationalism—if Austria was to remain intact and powerful, it could hardly accommodate ideologies that demanded national independence.

On the Austrian Empire's borders, the Russian Empire and, to a lesser extent, the Ottoman Empire supported and echoed Metternich's efforts to hold back liberalism and nationalism. Bitter enemies, the far-flung Russian and Ottoman Empires were both absolutist states with powerful armies and long traditions of expansion and conquest. Because of those conquests, both were also multinational empires with many peoples, languages, and religions, but in each case most of the ruling elite came from the dominant ethnic group—the Orthodox Christian Russians of central and northern Russia and the Muslim Ottoman Turks of Anatolia (much of modern Turkey). After 1815 both of these multinational absolutist states worked to preserve their respective traditional conservative orders. Only after 1840 did each in turn experience a profound crisis and embark on a program of fundamental reform and modernization, as we shall see in Chapter 23.

Repressing the Revolutionary Spirit

Conservative political ideologies had important practical consequences. Under Metternich's leadership, Austria, Prussia, and Russia embarked on a decades-long crusade against the liberties and civil rights associated with the French and American Revolutions. The first step was the formation in September 1815 of the **Holy Alliance** by Austria, Prussia, and Russia. First proposed by Russia's Alexander I, the alliance worked to repress reformist and revolutionary movements and stifle desires for national independence across Europe.

The conservative restoration first brought its collective power to bear on southern Europe. In 1820 revolutionaries successfully forced the kings of Spain and the southern Italian Kingdom of the Two Sicilies to establish constitutional monarchies, with press free-

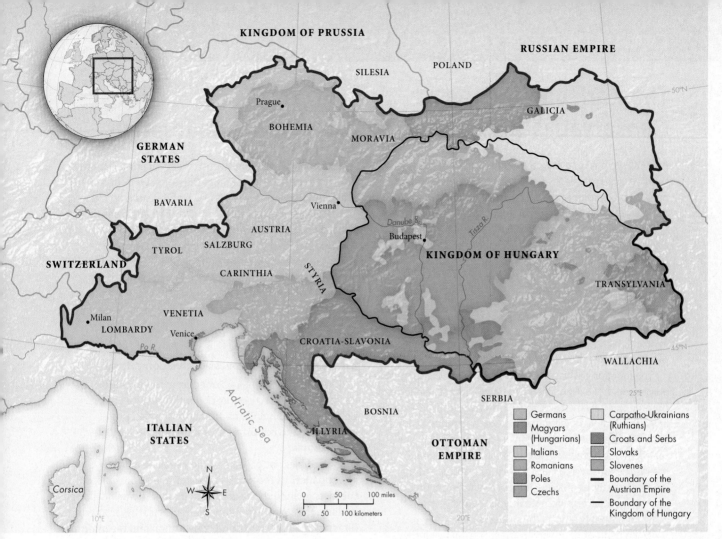

50°N

45°N

25°E

20°E

10°E

15°E

KINGDOM OF PRUSSIA

RUSSIAN EMPIRE

POLAND

SILESIA

GALICIA

Prague

BOHEMIA

MORAVIA

GERMAN
STATES

BAVARIA

Vienna

Danube R.

Tisza R.

AUSTRIA

Budapest

KINGDOM OF HUNGARY

SALZBURG

TYROL

SWITZERLAND

CARINTHIA

STYRIA

TRANSYLVANIA

Milan

VENETIA

LOMBARDY

Venice

CROATIA-SLAVONIA

WALLACHIA

Po R.

Adriatic Sea

ITALIAN
STATES

ILLYRIA

BOSNIA

SERBIA

OTTOMAN
EMPIRE

Corsica

N
W E
S

0   50   100 miles

0   50   100 kilometers

Germans

Magyars
(Hungarians)

Italians

Romanians

Poles

Czechs

Carpatho-Ukrainians
(Ruthians)

Croats and Serbs

Slovaks

Slovenes

Boundary of the
Austrian Empire

Boundary of the
Kingdom of Hungary

MAP 21.2 Peoples of the Habsburg Monarchy, 1815 The old dynastic state ruled by the Habsburg monarchy was a patchwork of nationalities and ethnic groups, in which territorial borders barely reflected the diversity of where different peoples actually lived. Note especially the widely scattered pockets of Germans and Hungarians. How do you think this ethnic diversity might have led to the rise of national independence movements in the Austrian Empire?

doms, universal male suffrage, and other liberal reforms. Metternich was horrified; revolution was rising once again. Calling a conference at Troppau in Austria, he and Alexander I proclaimed the principle of active intervention to maintain all autocratic regimes whenever they were threatened. Austrian forces then marched into Naples in 1821 and restored the autocratic power of Ferdinand I in the Two Sicilies. A French invasion of Spain in 1823 likewise returned power to the king there.

The conservative policies of Metternich and the Holy Alliance limited reform not only in Austria and the Italian peninsula but also in the entire German Confederation. The states in the German Confederation retained independence, and though ambassadors from each met in a Confederation Diet, or assembly, it had little real political power. When liberal reformers and university students began to protest for the national unification of the German states, the Austrian and Prussian leadership used the diet to issue and en-

force the infamous **Karlsbad Decrees** in 1819. These decrees required the German states to outlaw liberal political organizations, police their universities and newspapers, and establish a permanent committee with spies and informers to clamp down on liberal or radical reformers. (See "Evaluating the Evidence 21.1: The Karlsbad Decrees: Conservative Reaction in the German Confederation," page 690.)

The forces of reaction squelched reform in Russia as well. In St. Petersburg in December 1825, a group of about three thousand army officers inspired by liberal ideals staged a protest against the new tsar, Nicholas I. Troops loyal to Nicholas I surrounded and assaulted the group with gunfire, cavalry, and cannon, leaving some sixty men dead; the surviving leaders were publicly hanged, and the rest sent to exile in Siberia. Through censorship, military might, secret police, imprisonment, and execution, conservative regimes in central Europe used the powers of the state to repress liberal reform wherever possible.

The Karlsbad Decrees: Conservative Reaction in the German Confederation

In 1819 a member of a radical student fraternity at the German University of Jena assassinated the conservative author and diplomat August von Kotzebue. Metternich used the murder as an excuse to promulgate the repressive Karlsbad Decrees, excerpted below, which clamped down on liberal nationalists in the universities and the press throughout the German Confederation.

Law on Universities

1. A special representative of the ruler of each state shall be appointed for each university, with appropriate instructions and extended powers, and shall reside in the place where the university is situated. . . .

The function of this agent shall be to see to the strictest enforcement of existing laws and disciplinary regulations; to observe carefully the spirit which is shown by the instructors in the university in their public lectures and regular courses, and, without directly interfering in scientific matters or in the methods of teaching, to give a salutary direction to the instruction, having in view the future attitude of the students. Lastly, he shall devote unceasing attention to everything that may promote morality, good order, and outward propriety among the students. . . .

2. The confederated governments mutually pledge themselves to remove from the universities or other public educational institutions all teachers who, by obvious deviation from their duty, or by exceeding the limits of their functions, or by the abuse of their legitimate influence over the youthful minds, or by propagating harmful doctrines hostile to public order or subversive of existing governmental institutions, shall have unmistakably proved their unfitness for the important office intrusted to them. . . .

[Articles 3 and 4 ordered the universities to enforce laws against secret student societies.]

Press Law

1. So long as this decree shall remain in force no publication which appears in the form of daily issues, or as a serial not exceeding twenty sheets of printed matter, shall go to press in any state of the union without the previous knowledge and approval of the state officials. . . .

6. The Diet shall have the right, moreover, to suppress on its own authority, without being petitioned, such writings included in Article 1, in whatever German state they may appear, as, in the opinion of a commission appointed by it, are inimical to the honor of the union, the safety of individual states, or the maintenance of peace and quiet in Germany. There shall be no appeal from such decisions. . . .

Establishment of an Investigative Committee

1. Within a fortnight, reckoned from the passage of this decree, there shall convene, under the auspices of the Confederation . . . an extraordinary commission of investigation to consist of seven members, including the chairman.

2. The object of the commission shall be a joint investigation, as thorough and extensive as possible, of the facts relating to the origin and manifold ramifications of the revolutionary plots and demagogical associations directed against the existing constitution and the internal peace both of the union and of the individual states.

EVALUATE THE EVIDENCE

1. How do these regulations express the spirit of reactionary politics after the Napoleonic Wars? Why were university professors and students singled out as special targets?
2. The Karlsbad Decrees were periodically renewed until finally overturned during the revolutions of 1848. Do you think they were effective in checking the growth of liberal politics?

Source: James Harvey Robinson, *Readings in European History*, vol. 2 (Boston: Ginn and Company, 1906), pp. 547–550.

Limits to Conservative Power and Revolution in South America

Metternich liked to call himself "the chief Minister of Police in Europe," and the members of the Holy Alliance continually battled liberal political change.[3] Metternich's system proved quite effective in central Europe, at least until 1848, but the monarchists failed to stop dynastic change in France in 1830 or prevent Belgium from winning independence from the Netherlands in 1831.

The most dramatic challenge to conservative power occurred not in Europe, but overseas in South America. In the 1820s South American elites rose up and broke away from the Spanish crown and established a number of new republics based at first on liberal Enlightenment ideals. The leaders of the revolutions were primarily wealthy Creoles, direct descendants of Spanish parents born in the Americas. The well-established and powerful Creoles—only about 5 percent of the population—resented the political and economic control of an even smaller elite minority of *peninsulares*, people born in Spain who lived in and ruled the colonies. The vast majority of the population, composed of "mestizos" and "mulattos" (people of ethnically mixed heritage), enslaved and freed Africans, and native indigenous peoples, languished at the bottom of the social pyramid.

By the late 1700s the Creoles had begun to question Spanish policy and even the necessity of further colonial rule. The spark for revolt came during the Napoleonic Wars, when the French occupation of Spain in 1808 weakened the power of the autocratic Spanish crown and the Napoleonic rhetoric of rights inspired revolutionaries. Yet the Creoles hesitated, worried that open revolt might upend the social pyramid or even lead to a slave revolution as in Haiti (see Chapter 19).

The South American revolutions thus began from below, with spontaneous uprisings by subordinated peoples of color. Creole leaders quickly took control of a struggle that would prove to be more prolonged and violent than the American Revolution, with outcomes less clear. In the north, the competent general Simón Bolívar—the Latin American equivalent of George Washington—defeated Spanish forces and established a short-lived "Gran Colombia," which lasted from 1819 to 1830. Bolívar, the "people's liberator," dreamed of establishing a federation of South American states, modeled on the United States. To the south, José de San Martín, a liberal-minded military commander, successfully threw off Spanish control by 1825.

Dreams of South American federation and unity proved difficult to realize. By 1830 the large northern state established by Bolívar had fractured, and by 1840 the borders of the new nations looked much like the map of Latin America today. Most of the new states initially received liberal constitutions, but these were difficult to implement in lands where the vast majority of people had no experience with constitutional rule and women and the great underclass of non-Creoles were not allowed to vote. Experiments with liberal constitutions soon gave way to a new political system controlled by *caudillos* (cow-DEE-yohs), or strong men, sometimes labeled warlords. Often former Creoles, the caudillos ruled limited territories on the basis of military strength, family patronage, and populist politics. The South American revolutions had failed to establish lasting constitutional republics, but they did demonstrate the revolutionary potential of liberal ideals and the limits on conservative control.

The Spread of Radical Ideas

FOCUS QUESTION *What new ideologies emerged to challenge conservatism?*

In the years following the peace settlement of 1815, intellectuals and social observers sought to harness the radical ideas of the revolutionary age to new political movements. Many rejected conservatism, with its stress on tradition, a hereditary monarchy, a privileged landowning aristocracy, and an official state church. Often inspired by liberties championed during the French Revolution, radical thinkers developed and refined alternative ideologies—or political philosophies—and tried to convince people to follow them. In so doing, they helped articulate the basic political ideals that continue to shape Western society today.

Liberalism and the Middle Class

The principal ideas of **liberalism**—liberty and equality—were by no means defeated in 1815. First realized successfully in the American Revolution and then achieved in part in the French Revolution, liberalism demanded representative government as opposed to autocratic monarchy, and equality before the law for all as opposed to separate classes with separate legal rights. Liberty also meant specific individual freedoms: freedom of the press, freedom of speech, freedom of assembly, freedom of worship, and freedom from arbitrary arrest. Such ideas are still the guiding beliefs in modern democratic states, but in Europe in 1815 only France with Louis XVIII's Constitutional Charter and Great Britain with its Parliament had realized any of the liberal program. Even in those countries, liberalism had only begun to succeed.

Although conservatives still saw liberalism as a profound threat, it had gained a group of powerful adherents: the new upper classes made wealthy through growing industrialization and global commerce. This group promoted the liberal economic doctrine of **laissez faire** (lay-say FEHR), which called for free trade (including relaxation of import/export duties), unrestricted private enterprise, and no government interference in the economy.

As we saw in Chapter 17, Adam Smith posited the idea of economic liberalism and free-market capitalism in 1776 in opposition to mercantilism and its attempt

■ **liberalism** The principal ideas of this movement were equality and liberty; liberals demanded representative government and equality before the law as well as individual freedoms such as freedom of the press, freedom of speech, freedom of assembly, freedom of worship, and freedom from arbitrary arrest.

■ **laissez faire** A doctrine of economic liberalism that calls for unrestricted private enterprise and no government interference in the economy.

to regulate trade. Smith argued that freely competitive private enterprise would give all citizens a fair and equal opportunity to do what they did best and would result in greater income for everyone, not just the rich. (Smith's form of liberalism is often called "classical liberalism" in the United States, in order to distinguish it sharply from modern American liberalism, which generally favors more government programs to meet social needs and regulate the economy.)

In the first half of the nineteenth century, liberal political ideals became closely associated with narrow class interests. Starting in the 1820s in Britain, business elites enthusiastically embraced laissez-faire policies because they proved immensely profitable, and used liberal ideas to defend their right to do as they wished in their factories. Labor unions were outlawed because, these elites argued, unions restricted free competition and the individual's "right to work." Early-nineteenth-century liberals favored representative government, but they generally wanted property qualifications attached to the right to vote. In practice, this meant limiting the vote to very small numbers of the well-to-do. Workers, peasants, and women, as well as middle-class shopkeepers, clerks, and artisans, did not own the necessary property and thus could not vote.

As liberalism became increasingly identified with upper-class business interests, some opponents of conservatism felt that liberalism did not go nearly far enough. Inspired by memories of the French Revolution and the example of Jacksonian democracy in the young American republic, this group embraced republicanism: an expanded liberal ideology that endorsed universal democratic voting rights, at least for males, and radical equality for all. Republicans were more willing than most liberals to endorse violent upheaval to achieve goals. In addition, republicans might advocate government action to create jobs, redistribute income, and level social differences. As the results of the revolutions of 1830 and 1848 suggest, liberals and radical republicans could join forces against conservatives only up to a point. (See "Thinking Like a Historian: The Republican Spirit in 1848," page 694.)

The Growing Appeal of Nationalism

Nationalism — destined to have an enormous influence in the modern world — was another radical idea that gained popularity in the years after 1815. The nascent power of nationalism was revealed in the success of the French armies in the revolutionary and Napoleonic wars, when soldiers inspired by patriotic loyalty to the French nation achieved victory after victory (see Chapter 19). Early nationalists found inspiration in the vision of a people united by a common language, a common history and culture, and a common territory. In German-speaking central Europe,

defeat by Napoleon's armies had made the vision of a national people united in defense of their "fatherland" particularly attractive.

In the early nineteenth century such national unity was more a dream than a reality as far as most ethnic groups or nationalities were concerned. Local dialects abounded, even in relatively cohesive countries like France, where peasants from nearby villages often failed to understand each other. Moreover, a variety of ethnic groups shared the territory of most states, not just the Austrian, Russian, and Ottoman Empires discussed earlier. Over the course of the nineteenth century, nationalism nonetheless gathered force as a political philosophy. Advancing literacy rates, the establishment of a mass press, the growth of large state bureaucracies, compulsory education, and conscription armies all created a common culture that encouraged ordinary people to take pride in their national heritage.

In multiethnic states, however, nationalism could promote disintegration. Recognizing the power of the "national idea," European nationalists — generally educated, middle-class liberals and intellectuals — sought to turn the cultural unity that they desired into political reality. They believed that every nation, like every citizen, had the right to exist in freedom and to develop its unique character and spirit, and they hoped to make the territory of each people coincide with well-defined borders in an independent nation-state.

This political goal made nationalism explosive, particularly in central and eastern Europe, where different peoples overlapped and intermingled. As discussed, the Austrian, Russian, and Ottoman central states refused to allow national minorities independence. This suppression fomented widespread discontent among nationalists who wanted freedom from oppressive imperial rule. In the many different principalities of the Italian peninsula and the German Confederation, to the contrary, nationalists yearned for national unification across what they saw as divisive and obsolete state borders. Whether they sought independence or unification, before 1850 nationalist movements were fresh, idealistic, and progressive, if not revolutionary.

In recent years historians have tried to understand why the nationalist vision, which typically fit poorly with existing conditions and promised much upheaval, was so successful in the long run. Of fundamental importance in the rise of nationalism was the development of a complex industrial and urban society, which required more sophisticated forms of communication between individuals and groups.[4] The need for improved communication promoted the use of a standardized national language in many areas, creating at least a superficial cultural unity as a standard tongue spread through mass education and the emergence of the popular press. When a minority population was large and concentrated, the nationalist campaign for a standardized language often led the minority group to push for a separate nation-state.

Scholars generally argue that nations are recent creations, the product of a new, self-conscious nationalist ideology. Thus nation-states emerged in the nineteenth century as "imagined communities" that sought to bind millions of strangers together around the abstract concept of an all-embracing national identity. This meant bringing citizens together with emotionally charged symbols and ceremonies, such as independence holidays and patriotic parades. On these occasions the imagined nation of equals might celebrate its most hallowed traditions, which were often recent inventions.[5]

Between 1815 and 1850 most people who believed in nationalism also believed in either liberalism or radical republicanism. They typically shared a deep belief in the creativity and nobility of the people. Liberals and especially republicans, for example, saw the people as the ultimate source of all government. Yet nationally minded liberals and republicans agreed that the benefits of self-government would be possible only if individuals were bonded together by common traditions that transcended local interests and even class differences. Thus in the early nineteenth century the liberty of the individual and the love of a free nation overlapped greatly.

Despite some confidence that a world system based on independent nation-states would promote global harmony, early nationalists eagerly emphasized the differences between peoples and developed a strong sense of "us" versus "them." To this "us-them" outlook, nationalists could all too easily add two highly volatile ingredients: a sense of national mission and a sense of national superiority. As Europe entered an age of increased global interaction, these powerful ideas would lead to aggression and conflict, as powerful nation-states backed by patriotic citizens competed with each other on the international stage.

The Foundations of Modern Socialism

More radical than liberalism or nationalism was **socialism**. Early socialist thinkers were a diverse group with wide-ranging ideas. Yet they shared a sense that the political revolution in France, the growth of industrialization in Britain, and the rise of laissez faire had created a profound spiritual and moral crisis. Modern capitalism, they believed, fomented a selfish individualism that encouraged inequality and split the community into isolated fragments. Society urgently required fundamental change to re-establish cooperation and a new sense of community.

Early socialists felt an intense desire to help the poor, and they preached that the rich and the poor should be more nearly equal economically. To this end, they believed that private property should be strictly regulated by the government, or abolished outright and replaced by state or community ownership. Economic planning, greater social equality, and state regulation of property were the key ideas of early socialism — and have remained central to all socialism since.

One influential group of early socialist advocates became known as the "utopian socialists" because their grand schemes for social improvement ultimately proved unworkable. The Frenchmen Count Henri de Saint-Simon (awn-REE duh san-see-MOHN) (1760–1825) and Charles Fourier (sharl FAWR-ee-ay) (1772–1837), as well as the British industrialist Robert Owen, all founded movements intended to establish model communities that would usher in a new age of happiness and equality.

Saint-Simon's "positivism" optimistically proclaimed the tremendous possibilities of industrial development: "The golden age of the human species . . . is before us!"[6] The key to progress was proper social organization that required the "parasites" — the court, the aristocracy, lawyers, and churchmen — to give way, once and for all, to the "doers" — the leading scientists, engineers, and industrialists. The doers would carefully plan the economy and guide it forward by undertaking vast public works projects and establishing investment banks. Saint-Simon also stressed in highly moralistic terms that every social institution ought to have as its main goal improved conditions for the poor.

After 1830 the utopian critique of capitalism became sharper. Charles Fourier called for the construction of mathematically precise, self-sufficient communities called "phalanxes," each made up of 1,620 people. In the phalanx, all property was owned by the community and used for the common good. Fourier was an early proponent of the total emancipation of women. According to Fourier, under capitalism young single women were shamelessly "sold" to their future husbands for dowries and other financial considerations. Therefore, he called for the abolition of marriage and for sexual freedom and free unions based only on love. The great British utopian Robert Owen, an early promoter of labor unions, likewise envisaged a society organized into socialistic industrial-agricultural communities. Saint-Simon, Fourier, and Owen all had followers who tried to put their ideas into practice. Though these attempts had mostly collapsed by the 1850s, utopian socialist ideas remained an inspiration for future reformers and revolutionaries.

■ **nationalism** The idea that each people had its own genius and specific identity that manifested itself especially in a common language and history, and often led to the desire for an independent political state.

■ **socialism** A backlash against the emergence of individualism and the fragmentation of industrial society, and a move toward cooperation and a sense of community; the key ideas were economic planning, greater social equality, and state regulation of property.

The Republican Spirit in 1848

Political leaders, prominent intellectuals, and ordinary citizens were all inspired by powerful reformist ideologies in the revolutions of 1848: liberalism and especially republicanism. Though the revolutions were crushed, the political ideals articulated by the revolutionaries lived on. How do the various ideas and policies embodied in the "republican spirit" continue to influence politics today?

1 **Decrees of the provisional republican government in Paris, February 1848.** After a revolutionary mob overturned the bourgeois monarchy of Louis Philippe, the provisional republican government issued the following decrees.

The Overthrow of the Orléanist Monarchy

In the name of the French people:

A reactionary and oligarchical government has just been overthrown by the heroism of the people of Paris. That government has fled, leaving behind it a trail of blood that forbids it ever to retrace its steps.

The blood of the people has flowed as in July [1830]; but this time this noble people shall not be deceived. It has won a national and popular government in accord with the rights, the progress, and the will of this great and generous nation.

A provisional government, the result of pressing necessity and ratified by the voice of the people and of the deputies of the departments, in the session of February 24, is for the moment invested with the task of assuring and organizing the national victory....

The provisional government wishes to establish a republic,—subject, however, to ratification by the people, who shall be immediately consulted.

The unity of the nation (formed henceforth of all the classes of citizens who compose it); the government of the nation by itself; liberty, equality, and fraternity, for fundamental principles, and "the people" for our emblem and watchword: these constitute the democratic government which France owes to itself, and which our efforts shall secure for it....

Decrees Relating to the Workingmen

The provisional government of the French republic pledges itself to guarantee the means of subsistence of the workingman by labor.

It pledges itself to guarantee labor to all citizens.

It recognizes that workingmen ought to enter into associations among themselves in order to enjoy the advantage of their labor....

The provisional government of the French republic decrees that all articles pledged at the pawn shops since the first of February, consisting of linen, garments, or clothes, etc., upon which the loan does not exceed ten francs, shall be given back to those who pledged them....

The provisional government of the republic decrees the immediate establishment of national workshops.

2 ***Demands of the German People*** **(political pamphlet from Mannheim, Germany), 1848.** In small towns and communities across German-speaking lands, citizens inspired by republicanism met and confronted autocratic governments with lists of demands in pamphlets and petitions.

A German parliament, freely elected by the people. Every German man of 21 years of age and above should have the right to vote in a parliamentary election....

Unconditional freedom of the press.

Complete freedom of religion, conscience and teaching.

Administration of justice before a jury.

General granting of citizen's rights for German citizens.

A just system of taxation based on income.

Prosperity, training, and teaching for all.

Protection and security of jobs.

Balancing out of disparities between capital and labor.

Popular and just State administration.

Responsibility of Ministers and civil servants.

Removal of all prejudices.

ANALYZING THE EVIDENCE

1. Why would republican ideologies appeal to ordinary people in 1848? What groups might oppose or be indifferent to republicanism? Why did reformists present liberal-republican ideals in visual formats, as in Source 3?
2. Review the section on liberalism and republicanism in this chapter (pages 691–692). Which aspects of the evidence presented in Sources 1–4 appear more liberal, and which appear more republican? Does a close reading of the sources reveal conflicts between liberal and republican ideals?
3. In Source 4, how does Carl Schurz explain the benefits of radical republicanism but also its potential problems?

(Musée de la Ville Paris, Musée Carnavalet, Paris, France/Bridgeman Images)

3 **Frederic Sorrieu, *Universal Democratic and Social Republic: The Pact*, 1848.** The subtitle of this French lithograph, which celebrates the revolutionary breakthroughs of 1848, reads "People, Forge a Holy Alliance and Hold Hands." An embodiment of the republican ethos, it portrays the peoples of Europe holding their respective national flags. A heavenly host blesses the gathering, and the shattered symbols of Europe's monarchies litter the foreground.

4 **Carl Schurz, *The Reminiscences of Carl Schurz*, 1913.** Politician and journalist Carl Schurz explains how the threat of autocratic "reaction" (or political repression) led to radical republicanism.

[T]he visible development of the reaction had the effect of producing among many of those who stood earnestly for national unity and constitutional government a state of mind more open to radical tendencies. The rapid progress of these developments was clearly perceptible in my own surroundings. Our democratic club was composed in almost equal parts of students and citizens, among whom there were many of excellent character, of some fortune and good standing, and of moderate views, while a few others had worked themselves into a state of mind resembling that of the terrorists in the French Revolution. . . .

At first the establishment of a constitutional monarchy with universal suffrage and well-secured civil rights would have been quite satisfactory to us. But the reaction, the threatened rise of which we were observing, gradually made many of us believe that there was no safety for popular liberty except in a republic. . . .

The idealism which saw in the republican citizen the highest embodiment of human dignity we had imbibed from the study of classic antiquity; and the history of the French Revolution satisfied us that a republic could be created in Germany and could maintain its existence in the European system of states. In that history we found striking examples of the possibility of accomplishing the seemingly impossible, if only the whole energy existing in a great nation were awakened and directed with unflinching boldness.

Most of us, indeed, recoiled from the wild excesses which had stained with streams of innocent blood the national uprising in France during the Reign of Terror; but we hoped to stir up the national energies without such terrorism. At any rate, the history of the French Revolution furnished to us models in plenty that mightily excited our imagination. How dangerously seductive such a play of the imagination is we were, of course, then unaware.

PUTTING IT ALL TOGETHER

Using the sources above, along with what you have learned in class and in this chapter, write a short essay that evaluates the appeal of republicanism in 1848. What is the role of "the people" or "the citizen" in the republican spirit of 1848? How does that differ from the conservative viewpoint?

Sources: (1) James Harvey Robinson, *Readings in European History*, vol. 2 (Boston: Ginn and Company, 1906), pp. 559–561; (2) *Questions on German History: Ideas, Forces, Decisions from 1800 to the Present* (Bonn: German Bundestag, Press and Information Centre, Publications Section, 1984), p. 119 (punctuation has been updated); (4) Carl Schurz, *The Reminiscences of Carl Schurz*, vol. 1 (Garden City, N.Y.: Doubleday, Page & Co., 1913), pp. 136–137 (punctuation has been updated).

Some socialist thinkers embraced the even more radical ideas of anarchism. In his 1840 pamphlet *What Is Property?* Pierre-Joseph Proudhon (1809–1865), a self-educated printer, famously argued "property is theft!" Property, he claimed, was profit that was stolen from the worker, the source of all wealth. Distrustful of all authority and political systems, Proudhon believed that states should be abolished and that society should be organized in loose associations of working people.

Other early socialists, like Louis Blanc (1811–1882), a sharp-eyed, intelligent journalist, focused on more practical reforms. In his *Organization of Work* (1839), he urged workers to agitate for universal voting rights and take control of the state peacefully. Blanc believed that the government should set up publicly funded workshops and factories to guarantee full employment. The right to work had to become as sacred as any other right.

As industrialization advanced in European cities, working people began to embrace the socialist message. This happened first in France, where workers cherished the memory of the radical phase of the French Revolution and became violently opposed to laissez-faire laws that denied their right to organize in guilds and unions. Developing a sense of class in the process of their protests, workers favored collective action and government intervention in economic life. Thus the aspirations of workers and radical theorists reinforced each other, and a genuine socialist movement emerged in Paris in the 1830s and 1840s.

The Birth of Marxist Socialism

In the 1840s France was the center of socialism, but in the following decades the German intellectual Karl Marx (1818–1883) would weave the diffuse strands of socialist thought into a distinctly modern ideology. Marxist socialism—or **Marxism**—would have a lasting impact on political thought and practice.

The son of a Jewish lawyer who had converted to Lutheranism, the young Marx was a brilliant student. After earning a Ph.D. in philosophy at Humboldt University in Berlin in 1841, he turned to journalism, and his critical articles about the laboring poor caught the attention of the Prussian police. Forced to flee Prussia in 1843, Marx traveled around Europe, promoting socialism and avoiding the authorities. He lived a modest, middle-class life with his wife, Jenny, and their children, often relying on his friend and colleague Friedrich Engels (see Chapter 20) for financial support. After the revolutions of 1848, Marx settled in London, where he spent the rest of his life as an advocate of working-class revolution. *Capital*, his magnum opus, appeared in 1867.

Karl Marx and His Family   Active in the revolutions of 1848, Marx fled Germany and eventually settled in London, where he wrote *Capital*, the weighty exposition of his socialist theories. Despite his advocacy of radical revolution, Marx and his wife, Jenny, pictured here with two of their daughters, lived a respectable though modest middle-class life. Standing on the left is Friedrich Engels, an accomplished writer and political theorist who was Marx's long-time friend, financial supporter, and intellectual collaborator. (© Mary Evans Picture Library/Marx Memorial Library/The Image Works)

Marx was a dedicated scholar, and his work united sociology, economics, philosophy, and history in an impressive synthesis. From Scottish and English political economists like Adam Smith and David Ricardo, Marx learned to apply social-scientific analysis to economic problems, though he pushed these liberal ideas in radical directions. Deeply influenced by the utopian socialists, Marx championed ideals of social equality and community. He criticized his socialist predecessors, however, for their fanciful utopian schemes, claiming that his version of "scientific" socialism was rooted in historic law, and therefore realistic. Following German philosophies of idealism associated with

Georg Hegel (1770–1831), Marx came to believe that history had patterns and purpose and moved forward in stages toward an ultimate goal.

Bringing these ideas together, Marx argued that class struggle over economic wealth was the great engine of human history. In his view, one class had always exploited the other, and with the advent of modern industry, society was split more clearly than ever before: between the upper class—the **bourgeoisie** (boor-ZHWAH-zee)—and the working class—the **proletariat**. The bourgeoisie, a tiny minority, owned the means of production and grew rich by exploiting the labor of workers. Over time, Marx argued, the proletariat would grow ever larger and ever poorer, and their increasing alienation would lead them to develop a sense of revolutionary class-consciousness. Then, just as the bourgeoisie had triumphed over the feudal aristocracy in the French Revolution, the proletariat would overthrow the bourgeoisie in a violent revolutionary cataclysm. The result would be the end of class struggle and the arrival of communism, a system of radical equality.

Fascinated by the rapid expansion of modern capitalism, Marx based his revolutionary program on an insightful yet critical analysis of economic history. Under feudalism, he wrote, labor had been organized according to long-term contracts of rights and privileges. Under capitalism, to the contrary, labor was a commodity like any other, bought and sold for wages in the free market. The goods workers produced were always worth more than what those workers were paid, and the difference—"surplus value," in Marx's terms—was pocketed by the bourgeoisie in the form of profit.

According to Marx, capitalism was immensely productive but highly exploitative. In a never-ending search for profit, the bourgeoisie would squeeze workers dry and then expand across the globe, until all parts of the world were trapped in capitalist relations of production. Contemporary ideals, such as free trade, private property, and even marriage and Christian morality, were myths that masked and legitimized class exploitation. To many people, Marx's argument that the contradictions inherent in this unequal system would eventually be overcome in a working-class revolution appeared to be the irrefutable capstone of a brilliant interpretation of historical trends.

When Marx and Engels published *The Communist Manifesto* on the eve of the revolutions of 1848, their opening claim that "a spectre is haunting Europe—the spectre of Communism" was highly exaggerated. The Communist movement was in its infancy. Scattered groups of socialists, anarchists, and labor leaders were hardly united around Marxist ideas. But by the time Marx died in 1883, Marxist socialism had profoundly

reshaped left-wing radicalism in ways that would inspire revolutionaries around the world for the next one hundred years.

The Romantic Movement

FOCUS QUESTION *What were the characteristics of the Romantic movement?*

The early nineteenth century brought changes to literature and the other arts as well as political ideas. Followers of the new Romantic movement, or Romanticism, revolted against the emphasis on rationality, order, and restraint that characterized the Enlightenment and the controlled style of classicism. Forerunners appeared from about 1750 on, but the movement crystallized fully in the 1790s, primarily in England and Germany. Romanticism gained strength and swept across Europe until the 1840s, when it gradually gave way to Realism.

The Tenets of Romanticism

Like other cultural movements, **Romanticism** was characterized by intellectual diversity. Nonetheless, common parameters stand out. Artists inspired by Romanticism repudiated the emphasis on reason associated with well-known Enlightenment philosophes like Voltaire or Montesquieu (see Chapter 16). Romantics championed instead emotional exuberance, unrestrained imagination, and spontaneity in both art and personal life. Preoccupied with emotional excess, Romantic works explored the awesome power of love and desire and of hatred, guilt, and despair.

Where Enlightenment thinkers applied the scientific method to social issues and cast rosy predictions for future progress, Romantics valued intuition and nostalgia for the past. Where Enlightenment thinkers embraced secularization, Romantics sought the inspiration of religious ecstasy. Where Enlightenment thinkers valued public life and civic affairs, Romantics delved into the supernatural and turned inward, to the

---

■ **Marxism** An influential political program based on the socialist ideas of German radical Karl Marx, which called for a working-class revolution to overthrow capitalist society and establish a Communist state.

■ **bourgeoisie** The middle-class minority who owned the means of production and, according to Marx, exploited the working-class proletariat.

■ **proletariat** The industrial working class who, according to Marx, were unfairly exploited by the profit-seeking bourgeoisie.

■ **Romanticism** An artistic movement at its height from about 1790 to the 1840s that was in part a revolt against classicism and the Enlightenment, characterized by a belief in emotional exuberance, unrestrained imagination, and spontaneity in both art and personal life.

English Romantic Poets

These poems by Percy Bysshe Shelley and John Keats stand as sublime examples of literary Romanticism.

~

OZYMANDIAS

Percy Bysshe Shelley, 1818

I met a traveller from an antique land
Who said: "Two vast and trunkless legs of stone
Stand in the desert. Near them, on the sand,
Half sunk, a shattered visage lies, whose frown,
And wrinkled lip, and sneer of cold command,
Tell that its sculptor well those passions read
Which yet survive, stamped on these lifeless things,
The hand that mocked them and the heart that fed.
And on the pedestal these words appear—
'My name is Ozymandias, king of kings:
Look on my works, ye Mighty, and despair!'
Nothing beside remains. Round the decay
Of that colossal wreck, boundless and bare,
The lone and level sands stretch far away."

BRIGHT STAR

John Keats, 1819

Bright star, would I were stedfast as thou art—
    Not in lone splendour hung aloft the night
And watching, with eternal lids apart,
    Like nature's patient, sleepless Eremite,

The moving waters at their priestlike task
    Of pure ablution round earth's human shores,
Or gazing on the new soft-fallen mask
    Of snow upon the mountains and the moors—
No—yet still stedfast, still unchangeable,
    Pillow'd upon my fair love's ripening breast,
To feel for ever its soft fall and swell,
    Awake for ever in a sweet unrest,
Still, still to hear her tender-taken breath,
And so live ever—or else swoon to death.

EVALUATE THE EVIDENCE

1. How do these poems express some of the basic tenets of Romanticism? How, for example, do they explore notions of decline and death?

2. Are the powerful emotions described in and evoked by these poems incompatible with Enlightenment rationalism?

Source: George Edward Woodberry, ed., *The Complete Poetical Works of Percy Bysshe Shelley* (Boston: Houghton, Mifflin, and Company, 1892), p. 201; H. Buxton Forman, ed., *The Complete Works of John Keats*, vol. 3 (Glasgow: Gowars and Gray, 1901), p. 224.

---

hidden recesses of the self. As the Austrian composer Franz Schubert exclaimed in 1824:

> Oh imagination, thou supreme jewel of mankind, thou inexhaustible source from which artists and scholars drink! Oh, rest with us—despite the fact that thou art recognized only by a few—so as to preserve us from that so-called Enlightenment, that ugly skeleton without flesh or blood![7]

Nowhere was the break with Enlightenment classicism more apparent than in Romanticism's general conception of nature. Classicists were not particularly interested in nature. The Romantics, in contrast, were enchanted by stormy seas, untouched forests, and icy arctic wastelands. Nature could be awesome and tempestuous, a source of beauty or spiritual inspiration. Most Romantics saw the growth of modern industry as an ugly, brutal attack on their beloved nature and on venerable traditions. They sought escape—in the unspoiled Lake District of northern England, in exotic North Africa, in an imaginary and idealized Middle Ages.

The study of history became a Romantic obsession. History held the key to a universe now perceived to be organic and dynamic, not mechanical and static, as Enlightenment thinkers had believed. Historical novels like Sir Walter Scott's *Ivanhoe* (1820), a passionate romance set in twelfth-century England, found eager readers among the literate middle classes. Professional historians influenced by Romanticism, such as Jules Michelet, went beyond the standard accounts of great men or famous battles. Michelet's many books on the history of France consciously promoted the growth of national aspirations; by fanning the embers of memory, Michelet encouraged the French people to search the past for their special national destiny.

Romanticism was a lifestyle as well as an intellectual movement. Many early-nineteenth-century Romantics lived lives of tremendous emotional intensity. Obsessive love affairs, duels to the death, madness, strange illnesses, and suicide were not uncommon. Romantic artists typically led bohemian lives, wearing their hair long and uncombed in preference to donning powdered wigs, and rejecting the manners and morals of refined society. Great individualists, the Romantics believed that the full development of one's unique human potential was the supreme purpose in life.

Romantic Literature

Romanticism found its distinctive voice in poetry, as the Enlightenment had in prose. Though Romantic poetry had important forerunners in the German "Storm and Stress" movement of the 1770s and 1780s, its first great poets were English: William Blake, William Wordsworth, Samuel Taylor Coleridge, and Sir Walter Scott were all active by 1800, followed shortly by Lord Byron, Percy Bysshe Shelley, and John Keats. (See "Evaluating the Evidence 21.2: English Romantic Poets," at left.)

A towering leader of English Romanticism, William Wordsworth was deeply influenced by Rousseau and the spirit of the early French Revolution. Wordsworth settled in the rural Lake District of England with his sister, Dorothy, and Samuel Taylor Coleridge (1772–1834). In 1798 Wordsworth and Coleridge published their *Lyrical Ballads*, which abandoned flowery classical conventions for the language of ordinary speech and endowed simple subjects with the loftiest majesty. Wordsworth believed that all natural things were sacred, and his poetry often expressed a mystical appreciation of nature:

> To every natural form, rock, fruit or flower
> Even the loose stones that cover the high-way
> I gave a moral life, I saw them feel,
> Or link'd them to some feeling: the great mass
> Lay bedded in a quickening soul, and all
> That I beheld, respired with inward meaning.[8]

Here Wordsworth expressed his love of nature in commonplace forms that a variety of readers could appreciate. The short stanza well illustrates his famous conception of poetry as the "spontaneous overflow of powerful feeling [which] takes its origin from emotion recollected in tranquility."[9]

In France under Napoleon, classicism remained strong and at first inhibited the growth of Romanticism. An early French champion of the new movement, Germaine de Staël (duh STAHL) (1766–1817) urged the French to throw away their worn-out classical models. Her study *On Germany* (1810) extolled the spontaneity and enthusiasm of German writers and thinkers, and it had a powerful impact on the post-1815 generation in France. (See "Individuals in Society: Germaine de Staël," page 700.) Between 1820 and 1850 the Romantic impulse broke through in the poetry and prose of Alphonse de Lamartine, Victor Hugo, and George Sand (pseudonym of the woman

Casper David Friedrich, *Two Men Contemplating the Moon,* **1820** Friedrich's reverence for the mysterious powers of nature radiates from this masterpiece of Romantic art. The painting shows two relatively small, anonymous figures mesmerized by the sublime beauty of the full moon. Viewers of the painting, positioned by the artist to look over the shoulders of the men, are likewise compelled to experience nature's wonder. In a subtle expression of the connection between Romanticism and political reform, Friedrich has clothed the men in old-fashioned, traditional German dress, which radical students had adopted as a form of protest against the repressive conservatism of the post-Napoleonic era. (Galerie Neue Meister Dresden, Germany/© Staatliche Kunstsammlungen Dresden/Bridgeman Images)

INDIVIDUALS IN SOCIETY

Germaine de Staël

Rich, intellectual, passionate, and assertive, Germaine Necker de Staël (1766–1817) astonished contemporaries and still fascinates historians. She was strongly influenced by her parents, poor Swiss Protestants who soared to the top of prerevolutionary Parisian society. Her brilliant but rigid mother filled Germaine's head with knowledge, and each week the precocious child listened, wide-eyed and attentive, to illustrious writers and philosophers debating ideas at her mother's salon. At age twelve, she suffered a physical and mental breakdown. Only then was she allowed to have a playmate to romp about with on the family estate. Her adoring father was Jacques Necker, a banker who made an enormous fortune and became France's reform-minded minister of finance before the Revolution. Worshipping her father in adolescence, Germaine also came to love politics.

Accepting at nineteen an arranged marriage with Baron de Staël-Holstein, a womanizing Swedish diplomat bewitched by her dowry, Germaine began her life's work. She opened her own intellectual salon and began to write and publish. Her wit and exuberance attracted foreigners and liberal French aristocrats, one of whom became the first of many lovers as her marriage soured and she searched unsuccessfully for the happiness of her parents' union. Fleeing Paris in 1792 and returning after the Thermidorian reaction (see Chapter 19), she subsequently angered Napoleon by criticizing his dictatorial rule. In 1803 he permanently banished her from Paris.

Germaine de Staël. (Portrait by Marie Eleomore Godefroid [1778–1849], copy of a painting by François Gerard/Château de Versailles, France/ Bridgeman Images)

Retiring again to her isolated estate in Switzerland and skillfully managing her inherited wealth, Staël fought insomnia with opium and boredom with parties that attracted luminaries from all over Europe. Always seeking stimulation for her restless mind, she traveled widely in Italy and Germany and drew upon these experiences in her novel *Corinne* (1807) and her study *On Germany* (1810). Both works summed up her Romantic faith and enjoyed enormous success.

Staël urged creative individuals to abandon traditional rules and classical models. She encouraged them to embrace experimentation, emotion, and enthusiasm. Enthusiasm, which she had in abundance, was the key, the royal road to creativity, personal fulfillment, and human improvement. Thrilling to music, for example, she felt that only an enthusiastic person could really appreciate this gift of God, this wordless message that "unifies our dual nature and blends senses and spirit in a common rapture."*

Yet a profound sadness runs through her writing. This sadness, so characteristic of the Romantic temperament, grew in part out of disappointments in love and prolonged exile. But it also grew out of the insoluble predicament of being an enormously gifted woman in an age of intense male sexism. Little wonder that uneasy male competitors and literary critics took delight in ridiculing and defaming her as a neurotic and masculine woman, a mediocre and unnatural talent who had foolishly dared to enter the male world of serious thought and action. Even her supporters could not accept her for what she was. Poet Lord Byron recognized her genius and called her "the most eminent woman author of this, or perhaps of any century" but quickly added that "she should have been born a man."†

Buffeted and saddened by this scorn and condescension, Staël advocated equal rights for women throughout her life. Only with equal rights and duties—in education and careers, in love and marital relations—could a woman ever hope to realize her intellectual and emotional potential. Practicing what she preached as best she could, Germaine de Staël was a trailblazer in the struggle for women's rights.

QUESTIONS FOR ANALYSIS

1. In what ways did Germaine de Staël's life and thought reflect basic elements of the Romantic movement?
2. Why did male critics often attack Staël? What do these criticisms tell us about gender relations in the early nineteenth century?

*Quoted in G. R. Besser, *Germaine de Staël Revisited* (New York: Twayne Publishers, 1994), p. 106. Enhanced by a feminist perspective, this fine study is highly recommended.
†Quoted ibid., p. 139.

writer Amandine-Aurore-Lucile Dudevant). Of these, Victor Hugo (1802–1885) became the most well known.

Son of a Napoleonic general, Hugo achieved an amazing range of rhythm, language, and image in his lyric poetry. His powerful novels exemplified the Romantic fascination with fantastic characters, exotic historical settings, and extreme emotions. The hero of Hugo's famous *The Hunchback of Notre Dame* (1831) is the great cathedral's deformed bell-ringer, a "human gargoyle" overlooking the teeming life of fifteenth-century Paris. Renouncing his early conservatism, Hugo equated freedom in literature with liberty in politics and society. His political evolution was thus exactly the opposite of Wordsworth's, in whom youthful radicalism gave way to middle-aged caution. As the contrast between the two artists suggests, Romanticism was compatible with many political beliefs.

In central and eastern Europe, literary Romanticism and early nationalism often reinforced one another. Well-educated Romantics championed their own people's histories, cultures, and unique greatness. Like modern anthropologists, they studied peasant life and transcribed the folk songs, tales, and proverbs that the cosmopolitan Enlightenment had disdained. The brothers Jacob and Wilhelm Grimm were particularly successful at rescuing German fairy tales from oblivion. (See "Evaluating the Evidence 21.3: Jacob and Wilhelm Grimm, *Children's Stories and Household Tales*," page 702.) In the Slavic lands, Romantics played a decisive role in converting spoken peasant languages into modern written languages. In the vast Austrian, Russian, and Ottoman Empires, with their many ethnic minorities, the combination of Romanticism and nationalism was particularly potent. Ethnic groups dreaming of independence could find revolutionary inspiration in Romantic visions of a historic national destiny.

Romanticism in Art and Music

Romantic concerns with nature, history, and the imagination extended well beyond literature, into the realms of art and music. France's Eugène Delacroix (oo-ZHEHN deh-luh-KWAH) (1798–1863), one of Romanticism's greatest artists, painted dramatic, colorful scenes that stirred the emotions. Delacroix was

Delacroix, *Massacre at Chios*, 1824 This moving masterpiece by Romantic artist Eugène Delacroix portrays an Ottoman massacre of ethnic Greeks on the island of Chios during the struggle for national independence in Greece. The Greek revolt won the enthusiastic support of European liberals, nationalists, and Romantics, and this massive oil painting (ca. 13 feet by 11 feet) portrays the Ottomans as cruel and violent oppressors holding back the course of history. (Musée du Louvre, Paris, France/Bridgeman Images)

Jacob and Wilhelm Grimm, *Children's Stories and Household Tales*

Familiar fairy tales such as "Snow White" and "Little Red Riding Hood" are the legacy of the Brothers Grimm — Jacob (1785–1863) and Wilhelm (1768–1859) — university-trained linguists who traveled through rural Germany recording folktales in the first decades of the nineteenth century. Determined to preserve what Wilhelm called "a world of magic" in a time of rapid change, their work uncovered a popular oral culture that worked mythic, pagan, and Christian themes into folktales and legends about the trials and joys of everyday life. In 1812 the brothers published the first volume of Children's Stories and Household Tales, *which marked the start of a collaborative, scholarly study of German myth and history. The Grimms brought together the Romantic idealization of simple rural virtues and the growing appreciation of national character and difference. Collecting German folktales at the height of the Napoleonic Wars and the French occupation of German territories helped popularize a specifically national tradition, which set the Germans apart from the French and offered at least passive resistance to the foreign invaders. In the passages below, Wilhelm eloquently describes the importance of uncovering lost tales and emphasizes the unique "riches of German poetry" found in folktales.*

~

From *Children's Stories and Household Tales*, Volume 1, 1812

When a storm of some other calamity from the heavens destroys an entire crop, it is reassuring to find that a small spot on a path lined by hedges or bushes has been spared and that a few stalks, at least, remain standing. If the sun favors them with light, they continue to grow, alone and unobserved, and no scythe comes along to cut them down prematurely for vast storage bins. But near the end of the summer, once they have ripened and become full, poor devout hands seek them out; ear upon ear, carefully bound and esteemed more highly than entire sheaves, they are brought home, and for the entire winter they provide nourishment, perhaps the only seed for the future. That is how it all seems to us when we review the riches of German poetry from earlier times and discover that nothing of it has been kept alive. Even the memory of it is lost — folk songs and these innocent household tales are all that remain. . . .

We know them and we love them just because we happen to have heard them in a certain way, and we like them without reflecting on why. . . . [O]ne quickly discovers that the custom [of telling these tales] persists only in places where there is a warm openness to poetry or where there are imaginations not yet deformed by the perversities of modern life. . . .

We have tried to collect these tales in as pure a form as possible. In many, the narrative flow is interrupted by rhymes and lines of verse, which sometimes clearly alliterate but are never sung during the telling of a tale. Precisely these are the oldest and best tales. No details have been added or embellished or changed, for we would have been reluctant to expand stories already so rich by adding analogies and allusions. They cannot be invented. A collection of this kind has never existed in Germany.

From *Children's Stories and Household Tales*, Volume 2, 1815

The true value of these tales must really be set quite high: they put our ancient heroic poetry in a new light that could not have been produced in any other way. Briar Rose [or Sleeping Beauty], who is put to sleep after being pricked by a spindle, is really Brunhilde, put to sleep after being pricked by a thorn. . . . Snow White sleeps peacefully with the same glowing red colors of life on her cheeks as Snaefrid, the most beautiful woman of all, at whose coffin sits Harald the Fair-Haired [Brunhilde, Snaefrid, and Harald are characters from ancient Germanic myths]. . . . These folktales have kept intact German myths that were thought to be lost, and we are firmly convinced that if a search were conducted in all the hallowed regions

fascinated with remote and exotic subjects, whether lion hunts in Morocco or dreams of languishing, sensuous women in a sultan's harem. The famous German painter Casper David Friedrich (1774–1840) preferred somber landscapes of ruined churches or remote arctic shipwrecks, which captured the divine presence in natural forces.

In England the Romantic painters Joseph M. W. Turner (1775–1851) and John Constable (1776–1837) were fascinated by nature, but their interpretations of it contrasted sharply, aptly symbolizing the tremendous emotional range of the Romantic movement. Turner depicted nature's power and terror; wild storms and sinking ships were favorite subjects. Constable painted gentle Wordsworthian landscapes in which human beings lived peacefully with their environment, the comforting countryside of unspoiled rural England.

of our fatherland, long neglected treasures would transform themselves into fabulous treasures and help to found the study of the origins of our poetry. It works the same way with the many dialects of our language. In them a large part of the words and peculiarities that we had long held to be defunct live on undetected.

The aim of our collection was not just to serve the cause of the history of poetry. It was also our intention that the poetry living in it be effective, bringing pleasure when it could, and that it therefore become a manual of manners. . . .

We have published variant forms, along with relevant notes, in the appendix. Those who feel indifferent to such things will find it easier to skip over them than we would have found to omit them. They belong to the book, since it is a contribution to the history of German folk poetry. These different versions seem more noteworthy to us than they do to those who see in them nothing more than variants or corrupt forms of a once extant archetypal form. For us, they are more likely to be attempts to capture, through numerous approaches, an inexhaustibly rich ideal type.

EVALUATE THE EVIDENCE

1. How does the view of German history promoted by the Grimms bring together Romanticism and nationalism? How do the folktales lend authenticity to ideas about the historical roots of the German nation?
2. In the selections above, Wilhelm claims that the stories were collected in "as pure a form as possible" without added details or embellishments, and he later underscores the importance of including "variant forms" of each story. Why does he make these appeals to the scientific method? Would it matter if the Grimm brothers had embellished the tales?

Source: Maria Tatar, ed., *The Annotated Brothers Grimm*, bicentennial ed. (New York: Norton, 2012), pp. 435–436; 440; 443–445.

Musicians and composers likewise explored the Romantic sensibility. Abandoning well-defined musical structures, the great Romantic composers used a wide range of forms to create profound musical landscapes that evoked powerful emotions. They transformed the small classical orchestra, tripling its size by adding wind instruments, percussion, and more brass and strings. The crashing chords evoking the surge of the masses in Chopin's "Revolutionary

Etude" and the bottomless despair of the funeral march in Beethoven's Third Symphony — such were the modern orchestra's musical paintings that plumbed the depths of human feeling.

This range and intensity gave music and musicians much greater prestige and publicity than in the past. Music no longer simply complemented a church service or helped a nobleman digest his dinner. It became a sublime end in itself, most perfectly realizing the endless yearning of the soul. The unbelievable one-in-a-million performer — the great virtuoso who could transport the listener to ecstasy and hysteria — became a cultural hero. People swooned, for example, for Franz Liszt (1811–1886), the greatest pianist of his age, as they scream for rock stars today.

The first great Romantic composer is also the most famous today. Ludwig van Beethoven (1770–1827) used contrasting themes and tones to produce dramatic conflict and inspiring resolutions. As one contemporary admirer wrote, "Beethoven's music sets in motion the lever of fear, of awe, of horror, of suffering, and awakens just that infinite longing which is the essence of Romanticism."[10] Beethoven's range and output were tremendous. At the peak of his fame, he began to lose his hearing. He considered suicide but eventually overcame despair: "I will take fate by the throat; it will not bend me completely to its will."[11] Beethoven continued to pour out immortal music, although his last years were silent, spent in total deafness.

Reforms and Revolutions Before 1848

FOCUS QUESTION *How and where was conservatism challenged after 1815?*

While the Romantics enacted a revolution in the arts, liberal, national, and socialist forces battered against the conservative restoration of 1815. Political change could result from gradual and peaceful reform or from violent insurrection, but everywhere it took the determination of ordinary people standing up to the prerogatives of the powerful. Between 1815 and 1848 three important countries — Greece, Great Britain, and France — experienced variations on this basic theme.

National Liberation in Greece

Though conservative statesmen had maintained the autocratic status quo despite revolts in Spain and the Two Sicilies, a national revolution succeeded in Greece in the 1820s. Since the fifteenth century the Greeks had lived under the domination of the Ottoman Turks. In spite of centuries of foreign rule, the Greeks had survived as a people, united by their language and the Greek Orthodox religion. In the early nineteenth century the general growth of national aspirations inspired a desire for independence. This rising national movement led to the formation of secret societies and then to open revolt in 1821, led by Alexander Ypsilanti (ihp-suh-LAN-tee), a Greek patriot and a general in the Russian army.

Greek Independence, 1830

At first, the Great Powers, particularly Metternich, opposed the revolution and refused to back Ypsilanti, primarily because they sought a stable Ottoman Empire as a bulwark against Russian interests in southeast Europe. Yet the Greek cause had powerful defenders. Educated Europeans and Americans cherished the culture of classical Greece; Russians admired the piety of their Orthodox brethren. Writers and artists, moved by the Romantic impulse, responded enthusiastically to the Greek national struggle. The famous English Romantic poet Lord Byron even joined the Greek revolutionaries to fight (as he wrote in a famous poem) "that Greece might yet be free."

The Greeks, though often quarreling among themselves, battled the Ottomans while hoping for the support of European governments. In 1827 Britain, France, and Russia yielded to popular demands at home and directed Ottoman leaders to accept an armistice. When they refused, the navies of these three powers trapped the Ottoman fleet at Navarino. Russia then declared another of its periodic wars of expansion against the Ottomans. This led to the establishment of a Russian protectorate over much of present-day Romania, which had also been under Ottoman rule. Great Britain, France, and Russia finally declared Greece independent in 1830 and installed a German prince as king of the new country in 1832. Despite this imposed regime, which left the Greek people restive, they had won their independence in a heroic war of liberation against a foreign empire.

Liberal Reform in Great Britain

Pressure from below also reshaped politics in Great Britain, but through a process of gradual reform rather than revolution. Eighteenth-century Britain had been remarkably stable. The landowning aristocracy dominated

society, but that class was neither closed nor rigidly defined. Successful business and professional people could buy land and become gentlefolk, while the common people enjoyed limited civil rights. Yet the constitutional monarchy was hardly democratic. With only about 8 percent of the population allowed to vote, the British Parliament, easily manipulated by the king, remained in the hands of the upper classes. Government policies supported the aristocracy and the new industrial capitalists at the expense of the laboring classes.

By the 1780s there was growing interest in some kind of political reform, and organized union activity began to emerge in force during the Napoleonic Wars (see Chapter 19). Yet the radical aspects of the French Revolution threw the British aristocracy into a panic for a generation, making it extremely hostile to any attempts to change the status quo.

In 1815 open conflict between the ruling class and laborers emerged when the aristocracy rammed far-reaching changes in the **Corn Laws** through Parliament. Britain had been unable to import cheap grain from eastern Europe during the war years, leading to high prices and large profits for the landed aristocracy. With the war over, grain (which the British generically called "corn") could be imported again, allowing the price of wheat and bread to go down and benefiting almost everyone—except aristocratic landlords. The new Corn Laws placed high tariffs (or fees) on imported grain. Its cost rose to improbable levels, ensuring artificially high bread prices for working people and handsome revenues for aristocrats. Seldom has a class legislated more selfishly for its own narrow economic advantage or done more to promote a class-based view of political action.

The change in the Corn Laws, coming as it did at a time of widespread unemployment and postwar economic distress, triggered protests and demonstrations by urban laborers, who enjoyed the support of radical intellectuals. In 1817 the Tory government, controlled completely by the landed aristocracy, responded by temporarily suspending the traditional rights of peaceable assembly and habeas corpus, which gives a person under arrest the right to a trial. Two years later, Parliament passed the infamous Six Acts, which, among other things, placed controls on a heavily taxed press and practically eliminated all mass meetings. These acts followed an enormous but orderly protest, at Saint Peter's Fields in Manchester, which was savagely broken up by armed cavalry. Nicknamed the **Battle of Peterloo**, in scornful reference to the British victory at Waterloo, this incident demonstrated the government's determination to repress dissenters.

Strengthened by ongoing industrial development, emerging manufacturing and commercial groups insisted on a place for their new wealth alongside the landed wealth of the aristocracy in the framework of

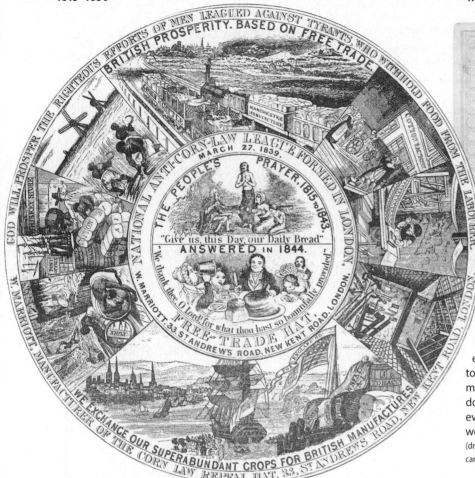

Anti–Corn Law League   This line drawing, printed on silk fabric, graced the interior crown of a top hat sold as the "Corn Law Repeal Hat." The Anti–Corn Law League, a forerunner of today's political pressure groups, successfully used a number of propaganda techniques to mobilize a broad urban coalition dedicated to free trade and the end of tariffs on imported grain. For example, each league supporter was encouraged to join the national organization and receive a membership card like the one pictured here. How do the various texts and scenes on the hat lining evoke arguments against the Corn Laws? Why would these arguments win popular support? (drawing: Universal History Archive/UIG/Bridgeman Images; card: © Museum of London, UK/Bridgeman Images)

political power and social prestige. They called for many kinds of liberal reform: changes in town government, organization of a new police force, more rights for Catholics and dissenters, and reform of the Poor Laws to provide aid to some low-paid workers. In the 1820s a less frightened Tory government moved in the direction of better urban administration, greater economic liberalism, civil equality for Catholics, and limited imports of foreign grain. These actions encouraged the middle classes to press on for reform of Parliament so they could have a larger say in government.

The Whig Party, though led like the Tories by elite aristocrats, had by tradition been more responsive to middle-class commercial and manufacturing interests. In 1830 a Whig ministry introduced "an act to amend the representation of the people of England and Wales." After a series of setbacks, the Whigs' **Reform Bill of 1832** was propelled into law by a mighty surge of popular support. Significantly, the bill moved British politics in a democratic direction and allowed the House of Commons to emerge as the all-important legislative body, at the expense of the aristocrat-dominated House of Lords. The new industrial areas of the country gained representation in the Commons, and many old "rotten boroughs"—electoral districts that had very few voters and that the landed aristocracy had bought and

sold—were eliminated. The number of voters increased by about 50 percent, to include about 12 percent of adult men in Britain and Ireland. Comfortable middle-class groups in the urban population, as well as some substantial farmers who leased their land, received the vote. Thus the conflicts building in Great Britain were successfully—though only temporarily—resolved. Continued peaceful reform within the system appeared difficult but not impossible.

The "People's Charter" of 1838 and the Chartist movement it inspired pressed British elites for yet more radical reform (see Chapter 20). Inspired by the economic distress of the working class in the 1830s and 1840s, the Chartists demanded universal male (but not female) suffrage. They saw complete political democracy and rule by the common people—the great majority of

■ **Corn Laws**   British laws governing the import and export of grain, which were revised in 1815 to prohibit the importation of foreign grain unless the price at home rose to improbable levels, thus benefiting the aristocracy but making food prices high for working people.

■ **Battle of Peterloo**   The army's violent suppression of a protest that took place at Saint Peter's Fields in Manchester in reaction to the revision of the Corn Laws.

■ **Reform Bill of 1832**   A major British political reform that increased the number of male voters by about 50 percent and gave political representation to new industrial areas.

the population—as the means to a good and just society. Hundreds of thousands of people signed gigantic petitions calling on Parliament to grant all men the right to vote, first in 1839, again in 1842, and yet again in 1848. Parliament rejected all three petitions. In the short run, the working poor failed with their Chartist demands, but they learned a valuable lesson in mass politics.

While calling for universal male suffrage, many working-class people joined with middle-class manufacturers in the Anti–Corn Law League, founded in Manchester in 1839. Mass participation made possible a popular crusade led by fighting liberals, who argued that lower food prices and more jobs in industry depended on repeal of the Corn Laws. Much of the working class agreed. When Ireland's potato crop failed in 1845 and famine prices for food seemed likely in England, Tory prime minister Robert Peel joined with the Whigs and a minority of his own party to repeal the Corn Laws in 1846 and allow free imports of grain. England escaped famine. Thereafter the liberal doctrine of free trade became almost sacred dogma in Great Britain.

The following year, the Tories passed a bill designed to help the working classes, but in a different way. The Ten Hours Act of 1847 limited the workday for women and young people in factories to ten hours. In competition with the middle class for the support of the working class, Tory legislators continued to support legislation regulating factory conditions. This competition between a still-powerful aristocracy and a strong middle class was a crucial factor in Great Britain's peaceful political evolution. The working classes could make temporary alliances with either competitor to better their own conditions.

Ireland and the Great Famine

The people of Ireland did not benefit from the political competition in England. In the mid-nineteenth century, Ireland was an agricultural nation, and the great majority of the rural population (outside of the northern counties of Ulster, which were partly Presbyterian) were Irish Catholics. They typically rented their land from a tiny minority of Church of England Protestant landowners, who often resided in England. Using a middleman system, these absentee landlords leased land for short periods only, set rents at will, and easily evicted their tenants. In short, landlords used their power to grab as much profit as possible.

Trapped in an exploitative tenant system driven by a pernicious combination of religion and class, Irish peasants lived in abominable conditions. Wretched one-room mud cabins dotted the Irish countryside; the typical tenant farmer could afford neither shoes nor stockings. Hundreds of shocking accounts described hopeless poverty. The novelist Sir Walter Scott wrote:

> The poverty of the Irish peasantry is on the extreme verge of human misery; their cottages would scarce serve for pig styes even in Scotland; and their rags seem the very refuse of a sheep, and are spread over their bodies with such an ingenious variety of wretchedness that you would think nothing but some sort of perverted taste could have assembled so many shreds together.[12]

A compassionate French traveler agreed, writing that Ireland was "pure misery, naked and hungry. . . . I saw

Devoués à la mort.

Fabrique de balles Patriotiques.

Secours au courage malheureux.

the American Indian in his forests and the black slave in his chains, and I believed that I was seeing the most extreme form of human misery; but that was before I knew the lot of poor Ireland."[13]

Despite the terrible conditions, population growth sped upward, part of Europe's general growth trend begun in the early eighteenth century (see Chapter 17). Between 1780 and 1840 the Irish population doubled from 4 million to 8 million. Extensive cultivation of the humble potato was largely responsible for this rapid growth. A single acre of land planted with the nutritious potato could feed a family of six for a year, and the hardy tuber thrived on Ireland's boggy wastelands. About one-half of the Irish population subsisted on potatoes and little else. Needing only a big potato patch to survive, the rural poor married early. To be sure, a young couple faced a life of extreme poverty. They would literally live on potatoes, supplemented perhaps with a bit of grain or milk. Yet the decision to marry and have large families made sense. A couple could manage rural poverty better than someone living alone, and children meant extra hands in the fields.

As population and potato dependency grew, however, conditions became more precarious. From 1820 onward, deficiencies and diseases in the potato crop occurred with disturbing frequency. Then in 1845 and 1846, and again in 1848 and 1851, the potato crop failed in Ireland. Blight attacked the young plants, and leaves and tubers rotted. Unmitigated disaster—the **Great Famine**—followed, as already impoverished peasants experienced widespread sickness and starvation.

The British government, committed to rigid free-trade ideology, reacted slowly. Relief efforts were tragically inadequate. Moreover, the government continued to collect taxes, landlords demanded their rents, and tenants who could not pay were evicted and their homes destroyed. Famine or no, Ireland remained the conquered jewel of foreign landowners.

The Great Famine shattered the pattern of Irish population growth. Fully 1 million emigrants fled the famine between 1845 and 1851, mostly to the United States and Canada, and up to 1.5 million people died. The elderly and the very young were hardest hit. Alone among the countries of Europe, Ireland experienced a declining population in the second half of the nineteenth century, as it became a land of continuous out-migration, early death, late marriage, and widespread celibacy.

The Great Famine intensified anti-British feeling and promoted Irish nationalism, for the bitter memory of starvation, exile, and British inaction burned deeply into the popular consciousness. Patriots of the later nineteenth and early twentieth centuries could call on powerful collective emotions in their campaigns for land reform, home rule, and, eventually, Irish independence.

The Revolution of 1830 in France

Like Greece and the British Isles, France experienced dramatic political change in the first half of the nineteenth century, and the French experience especially illustrates the disruptive potential of popular liberal politics. The Constitutional Charter granted by Louis XVIII in the Bourbon restoration of 1814 was a limited

L'Amazóne de 1830.

Scenes from the Revolution of 1830 in Paris   Titled "Game of the Heroes of the Memorable Days of July," these hand-colored playing cards portray incidents from the uprising in Paris in July 1830. The captions at the bottom read, from left, "Duty unto Death"; "Making the Bullets of Patriotism"; "Aid to the Ill-Fated Brave One"; and "The Amazon of 1830." These fanciful yet moving scenes idealize the revolutionary zeal of the ordinary men and women who fought government troops and helped overthrow the rule of King Charles X. In reality, though, their efforts replaced the king but not the system. (Musée de la Ville de Paris, Musée Carnavalet, Paris, France/Bridgeman Images)

■ **Great Famine** The result of four years of potato crop failure in the late 1840s in Ireland, a country that had grown dependent on potatoes as a dietary staple.

liberal constitution (see Chapter 19). The charter protected economic and social gains made by sections of the middle class and the peasantry in the French Revolution, permitted some intellectual and artistic freedom, and created a parliament with upper and lower houses. Immediately after Napoleon's abortive Hundred Days, the moderate, worldly king refused to bow to the wishes of die-hard aristocrats who wanted to sweep away all the revolutionary changes. Instead, Louis appointed as his ministers moderate royalists, who sought and obtained the support of a majority of the representatives elected to the lower Chamber of Deputies between 1816 and Louis's death in 1824.

Louis XVIII's charter was liberal but hardly democratic. Only about 100,000 of the wealthiest males out of a total population of 30 million had the right to vote for the deputies who, with the king and his ministers, made the laws of the nation. Nonetheless, the "notable people" who did vote came from very different backgrounds. There were wealthy businessmen, war profiteers, successful professionals, ex-revolutionaries, large landowners from the old aristocracy and the middle class, Bourbons, and Bonapartists. The old aristocracy, with its pre-1789 mentality, was a minority within the voting population.

Louis's conservative successor, Charles X (r. 1824–1830), a true reactionary, wanted to re-establish the old order in France. Increasingly blocked by the opposition of the deputies, Charles's government turned in 1830 to military adventure in an effort to rally French nationalism and gain popular support. A long-standing economic and diplomatic dispute with Muslim Algeria, a vassal state of the Ottoman Empire, provided the opportunity.

In June 1830 a French force of thirty-seven thousand crossed the Mediterranean, landed to the west of Algiers, and took the capital city in three short weeks. Victory seemed complete, but in 1831 Algerians in the interior revolted and waged a fearsome war that lasted until 1847, when French armies finally subdued the country. The conquest of Algeria marked the rebirth of French imperial expansion, and the colonial government encouraged French, Spanish, and Italian immigrants to move to Algeria and settle on large tracts of land expropriated from the region's Muslim inhabitants.

Emboldened by the initial good news from Algeria, Charles repudiated the Constitutional Charter in an attempted coup in July 1830. He censored the press and issued decrees stripping much of the wealthy middle class of its voting rights. The immediate reaction, encouraged by liberal lawyers, journalists, and middle-class businessmen, was an insurrection in the capital. Printers, other artisans, and small traders fired up by popular republicanism rioted in the streets of Paris, and three days of vicious street fighting brought down the government. Charles fled. Then the upper middle class, which had fomented the revolt, abandoned the more radical workers and skillfully seated Charles's cousin, Louis Philippe, duke of Orléans, on the vacant throne.

Events in Paris reverberated across Europe. In the Netherlands, Belgian Catholics revolted against the Dutch king and established the independent kingdom of Belgium. In Switzerland, regional liberal assemblies forced cantonal governments to amend their constitutions, leading to two decades of political conflict. And in partitioned Poland, an armed nationalist rebellion against the tsarist government was crushed by the Russian Imperial Army.

Despite the abdication of Charles X, in France the political situation remained fundamentally unchanged. The new king, Louis Philippe (r. 1830–1848), accepted the Constitutional Charter of 1814 and adopted the red, white, and blue flag of the French Revolution. Beyond these symbolic actions, however, popular demands for more thorough reform went unanswered. The upper middle class had effected a change in dynasty that maintained the status quo and the narrowly liberal institutions of 1815. Republicans, democrats, social reformers, and the poor of Paris were bitterly disappointed. They had made a revolution, but it seemed for naught.

The Revolutions of 1848

FOCUS QUESTION *What were the main causes and results of the revolutions of 1848?*

In the late 1840s Europe entered a period of tense economic and political crisis. Bad harvests across the continent caused widespread distress. Uneven industrial development failed to provide jobs or raise incomes, and boosted the popularity of radical ideologies. As a result, limited revolts broke out across Europe: a rebellion in the northern part of Austria in 1846, a civil war in Switzerland in 1847, and an uprising in Naples, Italy, in January 1848.

Full-scale revolution broke out in France in February 1848, and its shock waves rippled across the continent. Only the most developed countries—Great Britain, Belgium, and the Netherlands—and the least developed—the Ottoman and Russian Empires—escaped untouched. Elsewhere governments toppled, as monarchs and ministers bowed or fled. National independence, liberal democratic constitutions, and social reform: the lofty aspirations of a generation seemed at hand. Yet in the end, the revolutions failed.

A Democratic Republic in France

By the late 1840s revolution in Europe was almost universally expected, but it took events in Paris—once again—to turn expectations into realities. For eighteen years Louis Philippe's reign, labeled the "bourgeois monarchy" because it served the selfish interests of France's wealthy elites, had been characterized by stubborn inaction and complacency. Corrupt politicians refused to approve social legislation or consider electoral reform. Frustrated desires for change, high-level financial scandals, and a general sense of stagnation dovetailed with a severe depression that began with crop failures in 1846 to 1847. The government did little to prevent the agrarian crisis from dragging down the entire economy.

The government's failures united a diverse group of opponents against the king. Bourgeois merchants, opposition deputies, and liberal intellectuals shared a sense of outrage with middle-class shopkeepers, skilled artisans, and unskilled working people. Widespread discontent eventually touched off a popular revolt in Paris. On the night of February 22, 1848, workers joined by some students began tearing up cobblestones and building barricades. Armed with guns and dug in behind their makeshift fortresses, the workers and students demanded a new government. On February 24 the National Guard broke ranks and joined the revolutionaries. Louis Philippe refused to call in the army and abdicated in favor of his grandson. But the common people in arms would tolerate no more monarchy. This refusal led to the proclamation of a provisional republic, headed by a ten-man executive committee and certified by cries of approval from the revolutionary crowd.

The revolutionaries immediately set about drafting a democratic, republican constitution for France's Second Republic. Building such a republic meant giving the right to vote to every adult male, and this was quickly done. Bold decrees issued by the provisional republican government expressed sympathy for revolutionary freedoms by calling for liberty, fraternity, and equality (see page 694). The revolutionary government guaranteed workplace reforms, freed all slaves in French colonies, and abolished the death penalty. Yet there were profound differences within the revolutionary coalition. On the one hand, the moderate liberal republicans of the middle class viewed universal male suffrage as the ultimate concession to dangerous popular forces, and they strongly opposed any further radical social measures. On the other hand, radical republicans, influenced by a generation of utopian socialists and appalled by the poverty and misery of the urban poor, were committed to some kind of socialism. Hard-pressed urban artisans, who hated the unrestrained competition of cutthroat capitalism, advocated a combination of strong craft unions and worker-owned businesses.

The Revolutions of 1848

1848

January	Uprising in Naples, Italy
February	Revolution in Paris; proclamation of provisional republic
March	Revolt in Austrian Empire; Hungarian autonomy movement; uprisings in German cities; insurrections in Lombardy-Venetia
May	Frankfurt parliament convenes to write a constitution for a united Germany
June	Republican army defeats "June Days" workers' uprising in Paris; Austrian army crushes working-class revolt in Prague
August	Austrian army represses insurrection in northern Italian states
September–November	Counter-revolutionary forces push back reformers in Prussia and the German states
December	Franz Joseph crowned Austrian emperor; Louis Napoleon elected president in France

1849

March	Frankfurt parliament completes draft constitution, elects Friedrich Wilhelm of Prussia emperor of a Lesser Germany, which he rejects
June	Russian troops subdue Hungarian autonomy movement; Prussian troops dissolve the remnants of the Frankfurt parliament

Worsening depression and rising unemployment brought these conflicting goals to the fore in 1848. Louis Blanc (see page 696), who along with a worker named Albert represented the republican socialists in the provisional government, pressed for recognition of a socialist right to work. Blanc urged the creation of the permanent government-sponsored cooperative workshops he had advocated in *The Organization of Work*. Such workshops would be an alternative to capitalist employment and a decisive step toward a new, noncompetitive social order.

The moderate republicans, willing to provide only temporary relief, wanted no such thing. The resulting compromise set up national workshops—soon to become little more than a vast program of pick-and-shovel public works—and established a special commission under Blanc to "study the question." This satisfied no one. The national workshops were, however, better than nothing. An army of desperate poor from the French provinces and even from foreign countries streamed into Paris to sign up for the workshops. As the economic crisis worsened, the number enrolled in the workshops soared from 10,000 in March to 120,000 by June, and another 80,000 tried unsuccessfully to join.

LIVING IN THE PAST
Revolutionary Experiences in 1848

The striking similarities between the different national revolutions in 1848 suggest that Europeans lived through common experiences that shaped a generation, and this was indeed true. The first such experience was raising the barricades, fighting in the streets, and overthrowing rulers or forcing major concessions. The result of this astonishing triumph was a tremendous surge in political participation and civic activity throughout most of Europe. This unprecedented mass politics took many forms. Politics in the streets—demonstrations, protests, open-air meetings—played an ongoing role as large crowds pressured kings and legislatures. Newspaper publishing exploded as censorship ended and interest in public affairs soared. In Paris, where many new papers like *Le Salut Public* (The Public Safety) appeared, daily newspaper production increased eightfold in three months. In the Austrian Empire, urban workers and artisans listened to newspapers read aloud in taverns and followed developments. Intense political activity led to a multitude of political clubs and associations based on occupation. Women also formed organizations for the welfare of children and families, although few women as yet pushed for equal rights.

Newly politicized and increasingly divided into competing groups, the peoples of Europe then shared the onslaught of reaction and the trauma of defeat and civil war. In Prague and in Paris, almost simultaneously, army commanders found a deadly way to respond to urban uprisings. First they used cannon and field artillery to bombard and destroy the fighters behind their makeshift fortifications. Only then did obedient infantrymen attack and take the barricades in hand-to-hand combat, as Prussian soldiers did later in Frankfurt. Fleeing insurgents were hunted down and often shot. Thus the remembered experiences of 1848 included a tragic finale of grief and mourning. This is captured in the painting *Memory of the Civil War* by Ernest Meissonier, an artillery captain in the French National Guard who viewed at close range the carnage of the June Days in Paris. Though the revolutions of 1848 ended in bloody defeat, hard-won lessons in civic organizing and mass politics would remain important tools for political activists in the second half of the nineteenth century.

Ernest Meissonier, *Memory of the Civil War*.
(Musée du Louvre, Paris, France/Bridgeman Images)

While the Paris workshops grew, the French people went to the election polls in late April. The result was a bitter loss for the republicans. Voting in most cases for the first time, the people of France elected to the new 900-person Constituent Assembly 500 monarchists and conservatives, only about 270 moderate republicans, and just 80 radicals or socialists.

One of the moderate republicans was the author of *Democracy in America*, Alexis de Tocqueville (1805–1859), who had predicted the overthrow of Louis Philippe's government. He explained the election results by observing that the socialist movement in Paris aroused the fierce hostility of France's peasants as well as the middle and upper classes. The French

Street fighting in Frankfurt, 1848. (Granger, NYC — All rights reserved)

QUESTIONS FOR ANALYSIS

1. What do these three images reveal about the role of violence in the rise of mass politics in 1848?
2. The 1848 revolutions increased political activity, yet they were crushed. How does the scene of fighting in Frankfurt help explain this outcome?
3. Take a close look at Meissonier's *Memory of the Civil War*. Does the painting promote a political message? How do societies transmit and revise their historical memories?

Front page of *Le Salut Public*. (akg-images)

peasants owned land, and according to Tocqueville, "private property had become with all those who owned it a sort of bond of fraternity."[14] Tocqueville saw that a majority of the members of the new Constituent Assembly was firmly committed to centrist moderation and strongly opposed to the socialists and their artisan allies, a view he shared.

This clash of ideologies — of liberal moderation and radical socialism — became a clash of classes and arms after the elections. The new government's executive committee dropped Blanc and thereafter included no representative of the Parisian working class. Fearing that their socialist hopes were about to be dashed, artisans and unskilled workers invaded the Constituent

Assembly on May 15 and tried to proclaim a new revolutionary state. The government used the middle-class National Guard to squelch this uprising. As the workshops continued to fill and grow more radical, the fearful but powerful propertied classes in the Assembly took the offensive. On June 22 the government dissolved the workshops in Paris, giving the workers the choice of joining the army or going to workshops in the provinces.

A spontaneous and violent uprising followed. Frustrated in their thwarted attempt to create a socialist society, masses of desperate people were now losing even their life-sustaining relief. Barricades sprang up again in the narrow streets of Paris, and a terrible class war began. Working people fought with the courage of utter desperation, but this time the government had the army and the support of peasant France. After three terrible "June Days" of street fighting and the death or injury of more than ten thousand people, the republican army under General Louis Cavaignac stood triumphant in a sea of working-class blood and hatred. (See "Living in the Past: Revolutionary Experiences in 1848," page 710.)

The revolution in France thus ended in spectacular failure. The February coalition of the middle and working classes had in four short months become locked in mortal combat. In place of a generous democratic republic, the Constituent Assembly completed a constitution featuring a strong executive. This allowed Louis Napoleon, nephew of Napoleon Bonaparte, to win a landslide victory in the election of December 1848. The appeal of his great name as well as the desire of the propertied classes for order at any cost had led to what would become a semi-authoritarian regime.

Revolution and Reaction in the Austrian Empire

Throughout central Europe, the first news of the upheaval in France evoked feverish excitement and then popular revolution, lending credence to Metternich's famous quip "When France sneezes, all Europe catches cold." Across the Austrian Empire and the German Confederation, liberals demanded written constitutions, representative government, and greater civil liberties from authoritarian regimes (Map 21.3). When governments hesitated, popular revolts broke out. Urban workers and students served as the shock troops, but they were allied with middle-class liberals and peasants. In the face of this united front, monarchs made quick concessions. The revolutionary coalition, having secured great and easy victories, then broke down as it had in France. The traditional forces—the monarchy, the aristocracy, the regular army—recovered their nerve, reasserted their authority, and revoked many, though not all, of the reforms. Reaction was everywhere victorious.

The revolution in the Austrian Empire began in Hungary in March 1848, when nationalistic Hungarians demanded national autonomy, full civil liberties, and universal suffrage. Anti-imperial insurrection broke out in the northern Italian territories of Lombardy-Venetia the same month, and Austrian forces retreated after five days of street fighting. As the monarchy in Vienna hesitated, radicalized Viennese students and workers took to the streets of the imperial capital and raised barricades in defiance of the government. Meanwhile, peasant disturbances broke out across the empire. The Habsburg emperor Ferdinand I (r. 1835–1848) capitulated and promised reforms and a liberal constitution. When Metternich refused to compromise, the aging conservative was forced to resign and fled to London. The old absolutist order seemed to be collapsing with unbelievable rapidity.

Yet the revolutionary coalition lacked stability. When the monarchy abolished serfdom, with its degrading forced labor and feudal services, the newly free peasants lost interest in the political and social questions agitating the cities. Meanwhile, the coalition of urban revolutionaries broke down along class lines over the issue of socialist workshops and universal voting rights for men.

Conflicting national aspirations further weakened and ultimately destroyed the revolutionary coalition. In March the Hungarian revolutionary leaders pushed through an extremely liberal, almost democratic, constitution for the Kingdom of Hungary. But the Hungarian revolutionaries also sought to transform the mosaic of provinces and peoples in their territories into a unified, centralized Hungarian nation. The minority groups that formed half of the population—the Croats, Serbs, and Romanians—rejected such unification (see Map 21.2). Each group felt entitled to political autonomy and cultural independence. In a similar way, Czech nationalists based in Prague and other parts of Bohemia came into conflict with German nationalists living in the same region. Thus desires for national autonomy within the Austrian Empire enabled the monarchy to play off one ethnic group against the other.

Finally, conservative aristocratic forces rallied under the leadership of the archduchess Sophia, a Bavarian princess married to the Habsburg emperor's brother. Deeply ashamed of the emperor's collapse before a "mess of students," she insisted that Ferdinand I, who had no heir, abdicate in favor of her son, Franz Joseph.[15] Powerful nobles organized around Sophia in a secret conspiracy to reverse and crush the revolution.

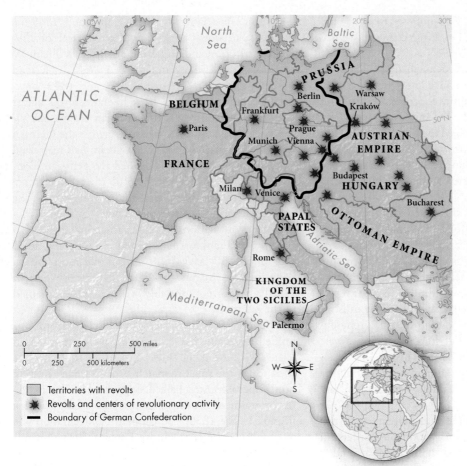

MAP 21.3 The Revolutions of 1848
In February and March 1848 revolutions broke out in the European heartlands: France, the Austrian Empire, and the German Confederation. In contrast, relative stability reigned in Great Britain, Belgium, the Netherlands, and the Russian and Ottoman Empires. Why did some regions descend into revolution, and not others? Can a study of geography help explain the difference?

The first conservative breakthrough came when the army bombarded Prague and savagely crushed a working-class revolt there on June 17, 1848. By August the Austrians had crushed the Italian insurrection. At the end of October, the well-equipped, predominantly peasant troops of the regular Austrian army bombarded the student and working-class radicals dug in behind barricades in Vienna with heavy artillery. They retook the city at the cost of more than four thousand casualties. The determination of the Austrian aristocracy and the loyalty of its army sealed the triumph of reaction and the defeat of revolution.

When Franz Joseph (r. 1848–1916) was crowned emperor of Austria immediately after his eighteenth birthday in December 1848, only the Hungarians had yet to be brought under control. Another determined conservative, Nicholas I of Russia (r. 1825–1855), obligingly lent his iron hand. On June 6, 1849, 130,000 Russian troops poured into Hungary and subdued the country after bitter fighting. For a number of years, the Habsburgs ruled the Kingdom of Hungary as a conquered territory.

Prussia, the German Confederation, and the Frankfurt National Parliament

After Austria, Prussia was the largest and most influential kingdom in the German Confederation. Since the Napoleonic Wars, liberal German reformers had sought to transform absolutist Prussia into a constitutional monarchy, hoping it would then lead the thirty-eight states of the German Confederation into a unified nation-state. The agitation that followed the fall of Louis Philippe, on top of several years of crop failure and economic crises, encouraged liberals to press their demands. In March 1848 excited crowds in urban centers across the German Confederation called for liberal reforms and a national parliament, and many regional rulers quickly gave in to their demands.

When artisans and factory workers rioted in Berlin, the capital of Prussia, and joined temporarily with the middle-class liberals in the struggle against the monarchy, the autocratic yet compassionate Prussian king, Friedrich Wilhelm IV (r. 1840–1861), vacillated and then caved in. On March 21 he promised to grant Prussia a liberal constitution and to merge Prussia into a new national German state.

But urban workers wanted much more—and the Prussian aristocracy wanted much less—than the moderate constitutional liberalism conceded by the king. The workers issued a series of democratic and vaguely socialist demands that troubled their middle-class allies. An elected Prussian Constituent Assembly met in Berlin to write a constitution for the Prussian state, and a conservative clique gathered around the king to urge counter-revolution.

At the same time, elections were held across the German Confederation for a national parliament, which convened to write a federal constitution that would lead to national unification. When they met in Frankfurt that May, the state officials, lawyers, professors, and businessmen elected to parliament represented the interests of the social elite. Their calls for constitutional monarchy, free speech, religious tolerance, and abolition of aristocratic privilege were typical of moderate national liberalism. The deputies essentially ignored calls for more radical action from industrial workers, peasants, republicans, and socialists.

In October 1848 the Frankfurt parliament turned to the question of national unification and borders. At first, the deputies proposed unification around a **Greater Germany** that would include the German-speaking lands of the Austrian Empire in a national state—but not non-German territories in Italy and central Europe. This proposal foundered on Austrian determination to maintain its empire, and some parliamentarians advocated a Lesser Germany that would unify Prussia and other German states without Austria. Even as the deputies debated Germany's future in the autumn of 1848, the forces of counter-revolution pushed back reformists and revolutionaries in Prussia and the other German states.

Despite Austrian intransigence, in March 1849 the national parliament finally completed its draft of a liberal constitution and requested Friedrich Wilhelm IV of Prussia to serve as emperor of a "lesser" German national state (minus Austria). By early 1849, however, reaction had rolled back liberal reforms across the German Confederation. Prussian troops had already crushed popular movements across the German Confederation, and Friedrich Wilhelm had reasserted his royal authority and disbanded the Prussian Constituent Assembly. He contemptuously refused to accept the "crown from the gutter" offered by the parliament in Frankfurt. Bogged down by their preoccupation with nationalist issues, the reluctant revolutionaries in Frankfurt had waited too long and acted too timidly. By May 1849 all but the most radical deputies had resigned from the parliament, and in June Prussian troops forcibly dissolved what remained of the assembly.

Friedrich Wilhelm in fact wanted to be emperor of a unified Germany, but only on his own authoritarian terms. With the liberal threat successfully squelched, he tried to get the small monarchies of Germany to elect him emperor. Austria balked. Supported by Russia, the Austrians forced Prussia to renounce all schemes of unification in late 1850. The German Confederation was re-established in 1851, and a decade of reaction followed. In an echo of the Karlsbad Decrees, state security forces monitored universities, civic organizations, and the press throughout the confederation. Former revolutionaries fled into exile, and German liberals gave up demands for national unification. In the various German states, reactionary monarchs, aided by ever-growing state bureaucracies, granted their subjects conservative constitutions and weak parliaments that maintained aristocratic control. Attempts to unite the Germans—first in a liberal national state and then in a conservative Prussian empire—had failed completely.

■ Greater Germany A liberal plan for German national unification that included the German-speaking parts of the Austrian Empire, put forth at the national parliament in 1848 but rejected by Austrian rulers.

NOTES

1. See B. E. Vick, *The Congress of Vienna: Power and Politics after Napoleon* (Cambridge, Mass.: Harvard University Press, 2014), pp. 11–14.
2. A. Sked, *The Decline and Fall of the Habsburg Empire, 1815–1918* (London: Longman, 1989), pp. 1–2.
3. Quoted in D. Blackbourn, *The Long Nineteenth Century: A History of Germany, 1780–1918* (New York: Oxford University Press, 1998), p. 122.
4. E. Gellner, *Nations and Nationalism* (Oxford: Basil Blackwell, 1983), especially pp. 19–39.
5. This paragraph draws on the influential views of B. Anderson, *Imagined Communities: Reflections on the Origins and Spread of Nationalism*, rev. ed. (London: Verso, 1991), and E. J. Hobsbawm and T. Ranger, eds., *The Invention of Tradition* (Cambridge: Cambridge University Press, 1983).
6. Quoted in F. E. Manuel and F. P. Manuel, *Utopian Thought in the Western World* (Cambridge, Mass.: Harvard University Press, 1979), p. 589.
7. Quoted in H. G. Schenk, *The Mind of the European Romantics* (New York: Oxford University Press, 1979), p. 5.
8. Quoted ibid., p. 169.
9. Quoted in O. Frey, *Emotions Recollected in Tranquility—Wordsworth's Concept of Poetry in "I Wandered Lonely as a Cloud"* (Munich: GRIN Verlag, 2008), p. 5.
10. Quoted in A. Comini, *The Changing Image of Beethoven: A Study in Mythmaking* (Santa Fe, N.M.: Sunstone Press, 2008), p. 79.
11. Quoted in F. B. Artz, *From the Renaissance to Romanticism: Trends in Style in Art, Literature, and Music, 1300–1830* (Chicago: University of Chicago Press, 1962), pp. 276, 278.
12. Quoted in G. O'Brien, *The Economic History of Ireland from the Union to the Famine* (London: Longmans, Green, 1921), p. 21.
13. Quoted ibid., pp. 23–24.
14. A. de Tocqueville, *Recollections* (New York: Columbia University Press, 1949), p. 94.
15. W. L. Langer, *Political and Social Upheaval, 1832–1852* (New York: Harper & Row, 1969), p. 361.

LOOKING BACK LOOKING AHEAD

Viewed from a broad historical perspective, Europe's economic and social foundations in 1750 remained agricultural and rural. Although Enlightenment thought was beginning to question the status quo, authoritarian absolutism dominated political life. One hundred years later, the unfinished effects of the Industrial and French Revolutions had brought fundamental changes to the social fabric of daily life and politics across Europe. The liberal ideals of representative government and legal equality realized briefly in revolutionary France inspired intellectuals and social reformers, who adopted ideologies of liberalism, nationalism, Romanticism, and socialism to challenge the conservative order. The uneven spread of industrial technologies and factory organization into developed areas across Europe spurred the growth of an urban working class, but did little to raise the living standards of most workers, peasants, and artisans. Living on the edge of subsistence, the laboring poor in rural and urban areas alike remained subject to economic misfortune, mass unemployment, and food shortages, and they turned repeatedly to protest, riots, and violent insurrection in pursuit of economic and political rights.

In 1848 the poor joined middle- and upper-class reformers in a great wave of revolution that forced conservative monarchs across the continent to grant liberal and national concessions — at least for a moment. Divisions in the revolutionary coalition and the power of the autocratic state forced back the wave of reform, and the revolutions ended in failure. Conservative monarchies revived, nationalist movements collapsed, and hopes for German unification withered. Yet protest on the barricades and debate in liberal parliaments had given a generation a wealth of experience with new forms of participatory politics, and the ideologies associated with the French Revolution would continue to invigorate reformers and revolutionaries after 1850. Nationalism, with its commitment to the imagined community of a great national family and the nation-state, would become a dominant political force, particularly as European empires extended their reach after 1875. At the same time, as agriculture and rural life gradually declined in economic importance, the consolidation of industrialization would raise living standards, sustain a growing urban society, and reshape family and class relationships. Diverse, complicated, and fascinating, pockets of this new urban society already existed in 1850. By 1900 it dominated northwestern Europe and was making steady inroads to the east and south.

Make Connections

Think about the larger developments and continuities within and across chapters.

1. Why did the ideas of the Romantic movement so easily support reformist and radical political ideas, including liberalism, republicanism, and nationalism? What does this reveal about the general connections between art and politics?

2. How did the spread of radical ideas and the movements for reform and revolution explored in this chapter draw on the "unfinished" political and industrial revolutions (Chapters 19 and 20) of the late eighteenth century?

3. The years between 1815 and 1850 witnessed the invention of a number of new political ideologies and the application of these ideologies in a variety of struggles for political power. What impact would these ideologies and struggles have later in the nineteenth and twentieth centuries? Do they still have an impact today?

21 REVIEW & EXPLORE

Identify Key Terms

Identify and explain the significance of each item below.

Congress of Vienna (p. 685)

Holy Alliance (p. 688)

Karlsbad Decrees (p. 689)

liberalism (p. 691)

laissez faire (p. 691)

nationalism (p. 692)

socialism (p. 693)

Marxism (p. 696)

bourgeoisie (p. 697)

proletariat (p. 697)

Romanticism (p. 697)

Corn Laws (p. 704)

Battle of Peterloo (p. 704)

Reform Bill of 1832 (p. 705)

Great Famine (p. 707)

Greater Germany (p. 714)

Review the Main Ideas

Answer the focus questions from each section of the chapter.

◆ How was peace restored and maintained after 1815? (p. 684)

◆ What new ideologies emerged to challenge conservatism? (p. 691)

◆ What were the characteristics of the Romantic movement? (p. 697)

◆ How and where was conservatism challenged after 1815? (p. 703)

◆ What were the main causes and results of the revolutions of 1848? (p. 708)

Suggested Reading and Media Resources

BOOKS

- Brewer, David. *The Greek War of Independence: The Struggle for Freedom and from Ottoman Oppression.* 2001. A compelling narrative history that places nation building at the center of the Greek Revolution.

- Evans, Richard J. W. *Austria, Hungary, and the Habsburgs: Central Europe c. 1683–1867.* 2008. A collection of essays by a prominent historian of Germany and central Europe that places special emphasis on nationalism, ethnic diversity, and the revolutions of 1848.

- Ferber, Michael. *Romanticism: A Very Brief Introduction.* 2010. An accessible overview of the ideas and people associated with European Romanticism.

- Green, Abigail. *Fatherlands: State-Building and Nationhood in Nineteenth-Century Germany.* 2001. A brilliant discussion of the struggle to shape a sense of national identity in three smaller German states.

- Hobsbawm, Eric. *The Age of Revolution, 1789–1848.* 1996. An engaging survey of the transformative effects of the Industrial and French Revolutions.

- Kelly, John. *The Graves Are Walking: The Great Famine and the Saga of the Irish People.* 2012. A well-received, moving history of the Irish potato famine and its social and political causes and consequences.

- Kolakowski, Leszek. *Main Currents of Marxism: The Founders, the Golden Age, the Breakdown.* 1978. In over one thousand pages, this famous masterpiece offers a critical view of the history of Marxist thought.

- Merriman, John. *Police Stories: Building the French State, 1815–1851.* 2006. An outstanding and innovative study of the way the professionalization of the police force contributed to the construction of the central state in France.

- Pilbeam, Pamela. *French Socialists Before Marx: Workers, Women, and the Social Question.* 2000. Shows the significant role of women in utopian socialism.

- Rapport, Mike. *1848: Year of Revolution.* 2008. A stimulating, well-written account that examines all of Europe.

- Sked, Alan. *Metternich and Austria: An Evaluation.* 2008. Explores Metternich's role in domestic and foreign affairs in the first half of the nineteenth century.

- Sperber, Jonathan. *Karl Marx: A Nineteenth-Century Life.* 2013. An evenhanded cradle-to-grave biography of the famous revolutionary theorist.

- Vick, Brian E. *The Congress of Vienna: Power and Politics After Napoleon.* 2014. An original analysis of political culture at the Congress of Vienna and the celebratory spectacles that accompanied Napoleon's defeat and the return of European peace.

DOCUMENTARIES

- *English Poetry Anthology: The Romantic Poets* (Kultur Video, 2006). Documents the Romantic poetry movement in England, featuring Wordsworth, Byron, and Keats.

- *Landmarks of Western Art: Romanticism* (Kultur Video, 2003). Documents the Romantic movement in painting, highlighting artists such as Turner, Constable, Goya, and Géricault.

- *The Rise*, from *Heaven on Earth: The Rise and Fall of Socialism* (PBS, 2005). The first part of a three-part series, this documentary follows the rise of the socialist movement.

FEATURE FILMS

- *Bright Star* (Jane Campion, 2009). A romantic drama about the British Romantic poet John Keats and Fanny Brawne, whose relationship was cut short by Keats's early death.

- *Frankenstein* (James Whale, 1931). Based on the classic Romantic novel by Mary Shelley, the film tells the story of an obsessed scientist who creates a living being in a bizarre science experiment.

- *Les Misérables* (Bille August, 1998). Adapted from Victor Hugo's epic novel, the film portrays ex-convict Jean Valjean's pursuit of redemption. Set in early-nineteenth-century France, the film is also a commentary on the social unrest in France and depicts the student uprising in Paris in 1832.

WEB SITES

- *Following the Famine.* Information about the Irish famine and the passage that many took to North America to escape the famine. **irishfamine.ca/**

- *Fordham University Internet Modern History Sourcebook.* An expansive collection of primary sources from all periods, including topics from this chapter such as Metternich and conservatism, liberalism, Romanticism, and the 1848 revolts. **www.fordham.edu/Halsall/mod/modsbook.asp**

- *Heilbrunn Timeline of Art History: Romanticism.* The Metropolitan Museum of Art's overview of the Romantic movement within art, along with a slide show of eighteen pieces of artwork from the period. **www.metmuseum.org/toah/hd/roma/hd_roma.htm**

- *Marxists Internet Archive.* This archive offers a vast amount of material and sources related to Karl Marx, communism, and Communist revolutions. **marxists.org/index.htm**

22

Life in the Emerging Urban Society

1840–1914

When Londoners gathered in 1860 at the Grand Fete in the Crystal Palace (see painting on right), they enjoyed the pleasures of an established urban society that would have been unthinkable just sixty years earlier. Across the nineteenth century, as industrialization expanded exponentially, Europeans left their farms and country villages to find work in the ever-growing towns and cities. By 1900, in much of developed western Europe, more than half the population lived in urban conglomerations, a trend of rural-to-urban migration that would spread and continue across the twentieth century.

Despite the happy faces in the London crowd pictured here, the emerging urban society brought costs as well as benefits. On the whole, living standards rose in the nineteenth century, but wages and living conditions varied greatly, and many city dwellers were still poor. Advances in public health and urban planning brought some relief to the squalid working-class slums, yet vast differences in income, education, and occupation still divided people into socially stratified groups. As a result, rather than discuss "the working class" or "the middle class," it is more accurate to speak of "working classes" and "middle classes" and consider the blurred boundaries between the two. Major changes in family life and gender roles accompanied this diversified class system. Dramatic breakthroughs in chemistry, medicine, and electrical engineering further transformed urban society after 1880, and a new generation of artists, writers, and professional social scientists struggled to explain and portray the vast changes wrought by urbanization. ■

CHAPTER PREVIEW

Taming the City
How did urban life change in the nineteenth century?

Rich and Poor and Those in Between
What did the emergence of urban industrial society mean for rich and poor and those in between?

Changing Family Lifestyles
How did urbanization affect family life and gender roles?

Science and Thought
How and why did intellectual life change in this period?

Life in the Nineteenth-Century City
The excitement and variety of urban life sparkle in this depiction of a public entertainment gala in 1860, sponsored by London's Royal Dramatic College and held in the city's fabulous Crystal Palace. (By Alexander Blaikley [1816–1903]/© Fine Art Photographic Library/Corbis)

Taming the City

FOCUS QUESTION *How did urban life change in the nineteenth century?*

Since the Middle Ages, European cities had been centers of government, culture, and large-scale commerce. They had also been congested, dirty, and unhealthy. Beginning in the early nineteenth century, the Industrial Revolution took these unfortunate realities of urban life to unprecedented levels. While historians may debate whether the overall social impact of industrialization was generally positive or negative, there is little doubt that rapid urban growth worsened long-standing overcrowding, pollution, and unhealthy living conditions. Taming the city posed a frightening challenge for society. Only the full-scale efforts of government

leaders, city planners, reformers, scientists, and civic-minded citizens would ameliorate the ferocious savagery of the industrial metropolis.

Industry and the Growth of Cities

The main causes of the poor quality of urban life—dense overcrowding, pervasive poverty, and lack of medical knowledge—had existed for centuries. Because the typical city had always been a "walking city," with no public transportation, great masses of people needed to live in close proximity to shops, markets, and workplaces. Packed together almost as tightly as possible, people in cities suffered and died from the spread of infectious disease in far greater numbers than their rural counterparts. In the larger towns, more people died each year than were born, on average, and

MAPPING THE PAST

MAP 22.1 European Cities of 100,000 or More, 1800–1900

There were more large cities in Great Britain in 1900 than in all of Europe in 1800.

ANALYZING THE MAP Compare the spatial distribution of cities in 1800 with the distribution in 1900. Where in 1900 are large cities concentrated in clusters? What does their distribution tell us about the scale and location of industrialization in nineteenth-century Europe?

CONNECTIONS In 1800, what common characteristics were shared by many large European cities? (For example, how many big cities were capitals or leading ports?) Were any common characteristics shared by the large cities in 1900? What does this suggest about the reasons behind this dramatic growth?

urban populations maintained their numbers only because newcomers continually arrived from rural areas.

The Industrial Revolution exacerbated these deplorable conditions. The steam engine freed industrialists from dependence on the energy of fast-flowing streams and rivers so that by 1800 there was every incentive to build new factories in urban areas, which had many advantages. Cities had better transportation facilities than the countryside and thus better supplies of coal and raw materials. Cities had many hands wanting work, for they drew people like a magnet, and as a result concentrated demand for manufactured goods. And it was a great advantage for a producer to have other factories nearby to supply the business's needs and buy its products. Therefore, as industry grew, already overcrowded and unhealthy cities expanded rapidly.

Great Britain, the first country in the world to go through the early stages of the Industrial Revolution (see Chapter 20), was forced to face the acute challenges of a changing urban environment early on. In the 1820s and 1830s the populations of a number of British cities increased by 40 to 70 percent each decade. The number of people living in cities of 20,000 or more in England and Wales jumped from 1.5 million in 1801 to 6.3 million in 1851 and reached 15.6 million in 1891. Such cities accounted for 17 percent of the total English population in 1801, 35 percent as early as 1851, and fully 54 percent in 1891. Other countries duplicated the English pattern as they industrialized (Map 22.1). (See "Evaluating the Evidence 22.1: First Impressions of the World's Biggest City," page 722.)

Except on the outskirts, early-nineteenth-century cities in Britain used every scrap of available land to the fullest extent. Parks and open areas were almost nonexistent. Developers erected buildings on the smallest possible lots in order to pack the maximum number of people into a given space. Narrow houses were built attached to one another in long rows. These row houses had neither front nor back yards, and only a narrow alley in back separated one row from the next. Other buildings were built around courtyards completely enclosed on all four sides. Many people lived in tiny apartments or small, overcrowded cellars or attics. "Six, eight, and even ten occupying one room is anything but uncommon," wrote a Scottish doctor for a government investigation in 1842.

These highly concentrated urban populations lived in extremely unsanitary and unhealthy conditions. Open drains and sewers flowed alongside or down the

Chronology

ca. 1840s–1890s	Realism dominant in Western arts and literature
1848	Cholera epidemic and first public health law in Britain
ca. 1850–1870	Modernization of Paris
1850–1914	Condition of working classes improves
1854	Pasteur begins studying fermentation and in 1863 develops pasteurization
1854–1870	Development of germ theory
1859	Darwin publishes *On the Origin of Species by the Means of Natural Selection*
1865	Completion of London sewer system
1869	Mendeleev creates periodic table
1880–1913	Second Industrial Revolution; birthrate steadily declines in Europe
1890	Max Weber publishes *The Protestant Ethic and the Spirit of Capitalism*
1890s	Electric streetcars introduced in Europe

middle of unpaved streets. Toilet facilities were primitive and inadequate. In parts of Manchester, as many as two hundred people shared a single outhouse. Such privies filled up rapidly, and since they were infrequently emptied, sewage often overflowed and seeped into cellar dwellings. Moreover, some courtyards in poorer neighborhoods became dunghills, collecting excrement that was sometimes sold as fertilizer and sometimes simply continued to accumulate. As one historian put it, by the 1840s the better-off classes had come to the "shocking realization that millions of English men, women, and children were living in shit."[1]

The environmental costs of rapid urbanization and industrialization were enormous as well. Black soot from coal-fired factories and train engines fouled city air, and by 1850 the River Thames was little better than an open sewer.

Who or what bore responsibility for these awful conditions? The crucial factors included the tremendous pressure of more people and the total absence of public transportation. People simply had to jam themselves together to get to shops and factories on foot. In addition, government in Great Britain, both local and national, only slowly established sanitary facilities and adequate building codes. Scientific understanding of the causes and consequences of urban crowding advanced slowly, and some elites rigidly opposed government action. Certainly, Great Britain had no monopoly on overcrowded and unhealthy urban conditions. Many continental cities were every bit as bad.

First Impressions of the World's Biggest City

In this anonymous, tongue-in-cheek passage, first published as a humorous sketch around 1870, a country man describes his first impressions of urban life. At that time London, with over 4 million inhabitants, was the largest city in the world.

A man's first residence in London is a revolution in his life and feelings. He loses at once no small part of his individuality. He was a man before, now he is a "party." No longer known as Mr. Brown, but as (say) No. XXI., he feels as one of many cogs in one of the many wheels of an incessantly wearing, tearing, grinding, system of machinery. His country notions must be modified, and all his life-long ways and takings-for-granted prove crude and questionable. He is hourly reminded "This is not the way in London; that this won't work here," or, "people always expect," and "you'll soon find the difference." . . .

Competition in London is very rife. The cheap five-shilling hatter was soon surprised by a four-and-nine-penny shop opposite. Few London men could live but by a degree of energy which the country dealer little knows. The wear and tear of nerve-power and the discharge of brain-power in London are enormous. The London man lives fast. . . .

Many other things contribute to make our new Londoner feel smaller in his own eyes. The living stream flows by him in the streets; he never saw so many utter strangers to him and to each other before; their very pace and destination are different; there is a walk and business determination distinctly London. In other towns men saunter they know not whither, but nearly every passer-by in London has his point, and is making so resolutely towards it that it seems not more his way than his destination as he is carried on with the current; and of street currents there are two, to the City and from the City, so distinct and persistent, that our friend can't get out of one without being jostled by the other. . . .

Self-dependence is another habit peculiarly of London growth. Men soon discover they have no longer the friend, the relative or the neighbour of their own small town to fall back upon. . . .

No doubt there are warm friendships and intimacies in London as well as in the country, but few and far between. People associate more at arm's length, and give their hand more readily than their heart, and hug themselves within their own domestic circles. You know too little of people to be deeply interested either in them or their fortunes, so you expect nothing and are surprised at nothing. An acquaintance may depart London life, and even this life, or be sold up and disappear, without the same surprise or making the same gap as in a village circle.

EVALUATE THE EVIDENCE

1. Why does the author assert, "The London man lives fast"?
2. Does this account of modern city life support or contradict the arguments of the new sociologists, discussed later in the chapter?
3. Is this a realistic portrait of city life? How does the author use humor to engage the reader?

Source: Henry Mayhew et al., "Life in London," in *London Characters and the Humorous Side of London Life* (London: Chatto and Windus, 1881), pp. 277–281.

Most responsible of all was the sad legacy of rural housing conditions in preindustrial society combined with an appalling ignorance of germs and basic hygiene. When ordinary people moved to the city, housing was far down on their list of priorities, and they generally took dirt for granted. One English miner told an investigator, "I do not think it usual for the lasses [in the coal mines] to wash their bodies; my sisters never wash themselves." As for the men, "their legs and bodies are as black as your hat."[2]

The Advent of the Public Health Movement

Around the middle of the nineteenth century, people's fatalistic acceptance of their overcrowded, unsanitary surroundings began to give way to a growing interest in reform and improvement. Edwin Chadwick, one of the commissioners charged with the administration of relief to paupers under Britain's revised Poor Law of 1834, emerged as a powerful voice for reform. Chadwick found inspiration in the ideas of radical philosopher Jeremy Bentham (1748–1832), whose approach to social issues, called **utilitarianism**, had taught that public problems ought to be dealt with on a rational, scientific basis to advance the "greatest good for the greatest number." Applying these principles, Chadwick soon became convinced that disease and death actually caused poverty, because a sick worker was an unemployed worker and orphaned children were poor children. Most important, Chadwick believed that government could help prevent disease by cleaning up the urban environment.

Chadwick collected detailed reports from local Poor Law officials on the "sanitary conditions of the laboring population" and published his hard-hitting findings in 1842. This mass of widely publicized evidence proved that disease was related to filthy environmental conditions, which were in turn caused largely by lack of drainage, sewers, and garbage collection.

Chadwick correctly believed that the stinking excrement of communal outhouses could be dependably carried off by water through sewers at less than one-twentieth the cost of removing it by hand. The inexpensive iron pipes and tile drains of the industrial age would provide running water and sewerage for all sections of town, not just the wealthy ones. In 1848, with the cause strengthened by a cholera epidemic that raged across Britain, Chadwick's report became the basis of Great Britain's first public health law, which created a national health board and gave cities broad authority to build modern sanitation systems. (See "The Past Living Now: Modern Sewage Systems," page 724.)

The public health movement won dedicated supporters in the United States, France, and Germany from the late 1840s on. Governments accepted at least limited responsibility for the health of all citizens, and their programs broke decisively with the age-old fatalism of urban populations. By the 1860s and 1870s European cities were making real progress toward adequate water supplies and sewer systems. Though factories and coal stoves continued to pump black smoke into the air, and pollution remained a serious problem, city dwellers started to reap the reward of better health, and death rates began to decline (Figure 22.1).

The Bacterial Revolution

Although improved sanitation in cities promoted a better quality of life and some improvements in health care, effective control of communicable disease required a great leap forward in medical knowledge and biological theory. Early reformers, including Chadwick, were seriously handicapped by their adherence to the prevailing miasmatic theory of disease—the belief that people contracted disease when they inhaled the bad odors of decay and putrefying excrement. In the 1840s and 1850s keen observation by doctors and public health officials pinpointed the role of bad drinking water in the transmission of disease and suggested that contagion was spread through physical contact with filth, not by its odors, thus weakening the miasmatic idea.

The breakthrough in understanding how bad drinking water and filth actually made people sick arrived when the French chemist Louis Pasteur developed the **germ theory** of disease. Pasteur (pas-TUHR) (1822–1895), who began studying fermentation for brewers in 1854, used a microscope to develop a simple test that brewers could use to monitor the fermentation process and avoid spoilage. He found that fermentation depended on the growth of living organisms and that the activity of these organisms

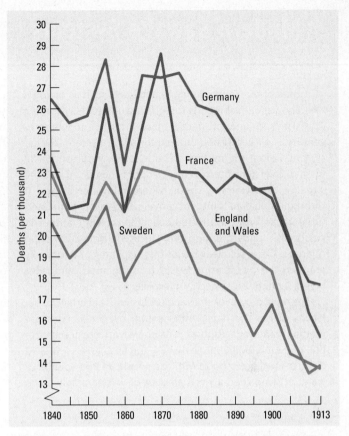

FIGURE 22.1 The Decline of Death Rates in England and Wales, Germany, France, and Sweden, 1840–1913 A rising standard of living, improvements in public health, and better medical knowledge all contributed to the dramatic decline of death rates in the nineteenth century.

could be suppressed by heating the beverage—a process that came to be called pasteurization, which he first implemented in the early 1860s. The breathtaking implication of this discovery was that specific diseases were caused by specific living organisms—germs—and that those organisms could be controlled.

By 1870 the work of Pasteur and others had demonstrated the general connection between germs and disease. When, in the middle of the 1870s, German country doctor Robert Koch (kawkh) and his coworkers developed pure cultures of harmful bacteria and described their life cycles, the dam broke. Over the next twenty years, researchers—mainly Germans—identified the organisms responsible for disease after disease. These discoveries led to the development of a number of effective vaccines, though some infections resisted treatment until scientists developed antibiotics in the middle of the next century.

■ **utilitarianism** The idea of Jeremy Bentham that social policies should promote the "greatest good for the greatest number."

■ **germ theory** The idea that disease was caused by the spread of living organisms that could be controlled.

Some of our most mundane activities, such as taking a shower or flushing the toilet, bring us into daily contact with an unappreciated marvel of late-nineteenth-century engineering and urban reform: the modern sewage system. Before the mid-nineteenth century, human waste was typically deposited in chamber pots and tossed into the street with a warning shout, where rainwater carried it through open canals into local rivers. In densely populated urban areas, waste was often collected through latrines in cesspools, underground pits located beneath living quarters. Cesspool cleaners, or "nightsoilmen," periodically emptied the pits, carting waste to designated dumpsites where it might be turned into fertilizer.

The rapid growth of cities and explosive rise in urban populations across the nineteenth century overwhelmed these methods of sewage disposal. In an ironic twist, the popularization of a sanitation improvement—the flush toilet—spelled disaster for the cesspool. With each flush, a large volume of water accompanied a small amount of waste, rapidly filling cesspools with liquid. Cesspool pits then leaked, spilling untreated sewage into waterways. The results—unbearably odorous—were also deadly. Water polluted with the bacteria that cause cholera and typhoid seeped into drinking supplies, causing mass epidemics across Europe.

London, the largest city in the world at the time, was a perfect example. As the population more than tripled from about 1.3 million in 1825 to 4.2 million in 1875, the sewage problem became catastrophic. Cesspools overflowed, and flush toilets installed in new buildings drained directly into the River Thames, the main source of drinking water for London residents. Over twenty thousand died in the cholera epidemics of 1832 and 1849, and another eleven thousand perished of the same disease in 1854. Though urban reformers initially blamed the epidemics on foul smells (or "miasmas") rather than bacteria, they did correctly identify putrid water as the cause and called on urban authorities to take action. The famous "Great Stink" of the summer of 1858, when appalling fumes from the fetid river threatened to

"What Torrents of Filth Come from That Walbrook Sewer!!" This 1832 cartoon by satirist George Cruikshank shows the director of the Southwark Water Works, a main source of London's drinking water, enthroned on an intake valve in the midst of a heavily polluted River Thames. Wearing a chamber pot for a hat and holding a trident with an impaled dog, cat, and rat, he raises a glass of foul liquid to cries of "Give Us Clean Water!" and "It Makes Me Sick!" (SSPL/Getty Images)

shut down the city, underscored the urgent need for change.

In response, between 1858 and 1865 the London Metropolitan Board of Works, led by engineer Joseph Bazalgette, built a massive network of new sewers that one Sunday paper called "the most extensive and wonderful work of modern times."* Bazalgette and his construction crews enclosed open canals in underground channels that combined flows of rainwater and human waste. London's massive interception sewers now emptied sewage into irrigation fields and treatment plants rather than directly into the Thames.

Inspired by London's example, urban engineers across Europe and North America built their own sewers and treatment plants, which limited the dumping of raw waste into local rivers, lakes, or seas. Sewage systems have improved since then, but the basic nineteenth-century designs—and often the drainage systems themselves—remain a vital if unacknowledged aspect of everyday life in the twenty-first century.

QUESTIONS FOR ANALYSIS

1. Why would contemporaries view Bazalgette's sewer system as a "wonderful work of modern times"?
2. How did progressive ideas about public health and urban reform drive the construction of late-nineteenth-century sewage systems? What other public works projects or public health initiatives promoted today have roots in nineteenth-century visions of social progress?

*Quoted in Stephen Halliday, *Water: A Turbulent History* (Gloucestershire, U.K.: Sutton, 2004), p. 15.

Acceptance of germ theory brought about dramatic improvements in the deadly environment of hospitals and operating rooms (see Chapter 18). In 1865, when Pasteur showed that the air was full of bacteria, English surgeon Joseph Lister (1827–1912) immediately grasped the connection between aerial bacteria and the problem of wound infection. He reasoned that a chemical disinfectant applied to a wound dressing would "destroy the life of the floating particles" (or germs). Lister's antiseptic principle worked wonders. In the 1880s German surgeons developed the more sophisticated practice of sterilizing not only the wound but also everything—hands, instruments, clothing—that entered the operating room.

The achievements of the bacterial revolution coupled with the public health movement saved millions of lives, particularly after about 1880. Mortality rates began to decline dramatically in European countries (see Figure 22.1) as the awful death sentences of the past—diphtheria, typhoid, typhus, cholera, yellow fever—became vanishing diseases. City dwellers especially benefited from these developments. By 1910 a great silent revolution had occurred: the death rates for people of all ages in urban areas were generally no greater than those for people in rural areas, and sometimes they were lower.

Improvements in Urban Planning

In addition to public health improvements, more effective urban planning was an important key to unlocking a better quality of urban life in the nineteenth century. France took the lead in this area during the rule of Napoleon III (r. 1848–1870), who used government action to promote the welfare of his subjects. Napoleon III believed that rebuilding much of Paris would provide employment, improve living conditions, limit the outbreak of cholera epidemics—and testify to the power and glory of his empire. He hired Baron Georges Haussmann (HOWS-muhn) (1809–1884), an aggressive, impatient Alsatian, to modernize the city. An authoritarian manager and capable city planner, Haussmann bulldozed both buildings and opposition. In twenty years Paris was completely transformed (Map 22.2).

The Paris of 1850 was a labyrinth of narrow, dark streets, the results of desperate overcrowding and a lack of effective planning. More than one-third of the city's 1 million inhabitants lived in a central district not twice the size of New York's Central Park. Residents faced terrible conditions and extremely high death rates. The entire metropolis had few open spaces and only two public parks.

For two decades Haussmann and his fellow planners proceeded on many interrelated fronts. With a bold energy that often shocked their contemporaries,

MAP 22.2 The Modernization of Paris, ca. 1850–1870 The addition of broad boulevards, large parks, and grand train stations transformed Paris. The cutting of the new north-south axis — known as the Boulevard Saint-Michel — was one of Haussmann's most controversial projects. His plan razed much of Paris's medieval core and filled the Île de la Cité with massive government buildings. Note the addition of new streets and light rail systems (the basis of the current Parisian subway system, the "metro") that encircle the city core, emblematic of the public transportation revolution that enhanced living conditions in nineteenth-century European cities.

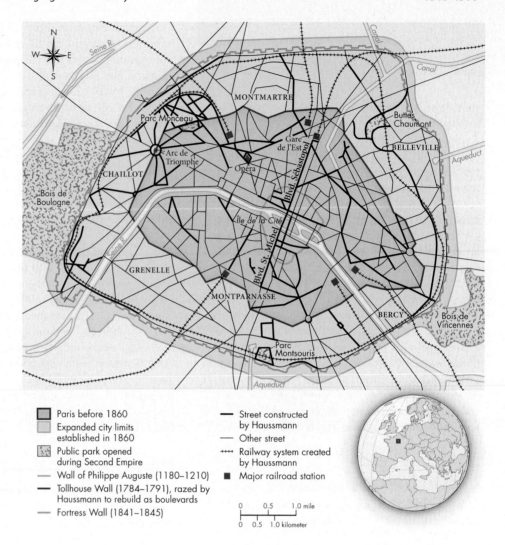

Paris before 1860

Expanded city limits established in 1860

Public park opened during Second Empire

Wall of Philippe Auguste (1180–1210)

Tollhouse Wall (1784–1791), razed by Haussmann to rebuild as boulevards

Fortress Wall (1841–1845)

Street constructed by Haussmann

Other street

Railway system created by Haussmann

Major railroad station

0   0.5   1.0 mile
0   0.5   1.0 kilometer

they razed old buildings in order to cut broad, straight, tree-lined boulevards through the center of the city as well as in new quarters rising on the outskirts (see Map 22.2). These boulevards, designed in part to prevent the easy construction and defense of barricades by revolutionary crowds, permitted traffic to flow freely and afforded impressive vistas. Their creation demolished some of the worst slums. New streets stimulated the construction of better housing, especially for the middle classes. Planners created small neighborhood parks and open spaces throughout the city and developed two very large parks suitable for all kinds of holiday activities — one on the affluent west side and one on the poor east side of the city. The city improved its sewers, and a system of aqueducts more than doubled the city's supply of clean, fresh water.

Rebuilding Paris provided a new model for urban planning and stimulated urban reform throughout Europe, particularly after 1870. In city after city, public authorities mounted a coordinated attack on many of the interrelated problems of the urban environment. As in Paris, improvements in public health through better water supply and waste disposal often went hand in hand with new boulevard construction. Urban planners in cities such as Vienna and Cologne followed the Parisian example of tearing down old walled fortifications and replacing them with broad, circular boulevards on which they erected office buildings, town halls, theaters, opera houses, and museums. These ring roads and the new boulevards that radiated outward from the city center eased movement and encouraged urban expansion (see Map 22.2). Zoning expropriation laws, which allowed a majority of the owners of land in a given quarter of the city to impose major street or sanitation improvements on a reluctant minority, were an important mechanism of the urban reform movement.

Public Transportation

The development of mass public transportation often accompanied urban planning, further enhancing living conditions. In the 1870s many European cities authorized private companies to operate horse-drawn streetcars, which had been developed in the United States, to carry riders along the growing number of

Urban Poverty Nineteenth-century London was notorious for its urban squalor, captured in this 1895 photo of Kensington High Street. For the families that lived in these ramshackle apartments, this small, unsanitary courtyard served as a cramped recreation, market, and working space. (*Market Court, Kensington High Street, London, c. 1895/English Heritage/Heritage Images/Getty Images*)

major thoroughfares. Then in the 1890s the real revolution occurred: European countries adopted another American transit innovation, a streetcar that ran on the newly harnessed power of electricity.

Electric streetcars were cheaper, faster, more dependable, cleaner, and more comfortable than their horse-drawn counterparts. Workers, shoppers, and schoolchildren hopped on board during the workweek. On weekends and holidays, streetcars carried urban dwellers on happy outings to parks and the countryside, to racetracks and music halls. In 1886 the horse-drawn streetcars of Austria-Hungary, France, Germany, and Great Britain carried about 900 million riders per year. By 1910 electric streetcar systems in those four countries were carrying 6.7 billion riders.[3]

Mass transit helped greatly in the struggle for decent housing. The new boulevards and horse-drawn streetcars facilitated a middle-class move to better and more spacious housing in the 1860s and 1870s; after 1890 electric streetcars meant people of even modest means could access new, improved housing. Though still densely populated, cities expanded and became less congested. In England in 1901, only 9 percent of the urban population was overcrowded in terms of the official definition of more than two persons per room. On the continent, many city governments in the early twentieth century built electric streetcar and light rail systems to provide transporta-

tion to the growing number of workers who lived in the new public and private housing developments built beyond the city limits. Suburban commuting was born.

Rich and Poor and Those in Between

FOCUS QUESTION *What did the emergence of urban industrial society mean for rich and poor and those in between?*

As the quality of urban life improved across Europe, the class structure became more complex and diverse. Urban society featured many distinct social groups, all of which existed in a state of constant flux and competition. The gap between rich and poor remained enormous and quite traditional, but there were numerous gradations between the extremes.

The Distribution of Income

By 1850 at the latest, real wages — that is, wages received by workers adjusted for changes in the prices they paid — were rising for the mass of the population, and they continued to do so until 1914. The real wages of British workers, for example, almost doubled between 1850 and 1906. Similar increases occurred in continental countries as industrial development quickened after 1850. Ordinary people took a major step forward in the centuries-old battle against poverty, reinforcing efforts to improve many aspects of human existence.

Greater economic rewards for the average person did not, however, eliminate hardship and poverty. Nor did they make the wealth and income of the rich and the poor significantly more equal, as contemporary critics argued and economic historians have clearly demonstrated. The aristocracy—with imposing wealth, unrivaled social prestige, and substantial political influence—retained its position at the very top of the social ladder, followed closely by a new rich elite, composed mainly of the most successful business families from banking, industry, and large-scale commerce. In fact, the prominent families of the commercial elite tended to marry into the old aristocracy, to form a new upper class of at most 5 percent of the population. Much of the aristocracy welcomed this development. Having experienced a sharp decline in its relative income in the course of industrialization, the landed aristocracy had met big business coming up the staircase and was often delighted to trade titles, country homes, and snobbish elegance for good, hard cash. Some of the best bargains were made through marriages to American heiresses. Correspondingly, wealthy aristocrats tended increasingly to exploit their agricultural and mineral resources as if they were business people.

Income inequality reflected social status. In almost every advanced country around 1900, the richest 5 percent of all households in the population received about a third of all national income, and the richest 20 percent of households received from 50 to 60 percent of it. As a result, the lower 80 percent received only 40 to 50 percent of all income—far less per household than the two richest classes. Moreover, the bottom 30 percent of all households received 10 percent or less of all income.

To understand the full significance of these statistics, one must realize that the middle classes were much smaller than they are today. In the nineteenth century they accounted for less than 20 percent of the population (that is, only about one in five families earned enough to be labeled "middle class"). Moreover, in the nineteenth century (and for centuries before as well) income taxes on the wealthy were light or nonexistent. Thus the gap between rich and poor remained enormous at the beginning of the twentieth century. Indeed, it was probably almost as great as it had been in the late eighteenth century, in the age of agriculture and aristocracy.

The great gap between rich and poor endured, in part, because industrial and urban development made society more diverse and classes less unified; though the satirical drawing of "Apartment Living in Paris" at right pokes fun at social difference, the effects were serious.

Society had not split into two sharply defined opposing classes, as Karl Marx had predicted (see Chapter 21). Instead, the economic specialization that enabled society to produce goods more effectively had created a remarkable variety of new social groups. There developed an almost unlimited range of jobs, skills, and earnings; one group or subclass blended into another in a complex, confusing hierarchy. Between the tiny elite of the very rich and the sizable mass of the dreadfully poor lived a range of subclasses, each filled with individuals struggling to rise or at least to hold their own in the social order. In this atmosphere of competition and hierarchy, neither the "middle class" nor the "working class" actually acted as a single unified force. Rather, the social and occupational hierarchy developed enormous variations, though the age-old pattern of great economic inequality remained firmly intact.

The People and Occupations of the Middle Classes

By the beginning of the twentieth century, the diversity and range within the urban middle class were striking. Indeed, it makes sense to replace the idea of a single "middle class" with a group of "middle classes" whose members engaged in occupations requiring mental, rather than physical, skill.

Below the wealthy top tier, the much larger, much less wealthy, and increasingly diversified middle class included moderately successful industrialists and merchants as well as professionals in law, business, and medicine. As industry and technology expanded in the nineteenth century, a growing demand developed for experts with specialized knowledge, and advanced education soared in importance among the middle classes. Engineering, for example, emerged from the world of skilled labor as a full-fledged profession with considerable prestige. Architects, chemists, accountants, and surveyors, to name only a few, first achieved professional standing in this period. They established criteria for advanced training and certification and banded together in organizations to promote and defend their interests. As governments grew and provided more services, and very large corporations (such as railroads or arms manufacturers) controlled ever-larger numbers of human and physical resources, middle-class professionals also found jobs as managers in large public and private institutions. Government officials and private executives had specialized knowledge and the capacity to earn a good living.

Industrialization expanded and diversified the lower middle class as well. The number of independent, property-owning shopkeepers and small business people grew, and so did the number of white-collar employees—a mixed group of traveling salesmen, bookkeepers, store managers, and clerks who staffed the offices and branch stores of large corporations.

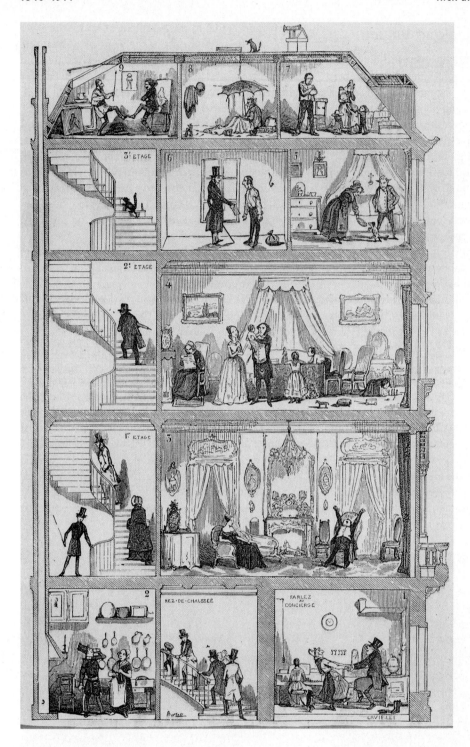

Apartment Living in Paris   This satirical cartoon shows a cutaway view of a typical layout for a city apartment in Europe around 1850. Take a close look at the inhabitants of each floor, at their possessions and behaviors. Can an analysis of household goods help define the social class of the various residents? How is social status coded in living space? (By Charles Albert Arnoux [1820–1883]/from *Tableau de Paris*, 1852/akg-images)

White-collar employees owned little property and often earned no more than better-paid skilled or semiskilled workers. Yet white-collar workers were fiercely committed to the middle class ideal of upward social mobility. The suit, the tie, the soft, clean hands that accompanied low-level retail and managerial work became important status symbols that set this group above those who earned a living through manual labor.

Relatively well educated but without complex technical skills, many white-collar occupational groups strove to achieve professional standing and higher social status. Elementary school teachers largely succeeded in this effort. Miserably paid part-time workers in the early nineteenth century, teachers rode the wave of mass education to respectable middle-class status and income. Nurses also rose from the lower ranks of unskilled labor to precarious middle-class standing. Dentistry was taken out of the hands of working-class barbers and placed in the hands of highly trained (and middle-class) professionals.

Middle-Class Culture and Values

Despite growing occupational diversity and conflicting interests, lifestyle preferences loosely united the European middle classes. Food, housing, clothes, and behavior all expressed middle-class values and testified to the superior social standing of this group over the working classes.

Unlike the working classes, the middle classes had the money to eat well, and spent a substantial portion of their household budget on food and entertainment. They consumed meat in abundance: a well-off family might spend 10 percent of its annual income on meat and fully 25 percent on food and drink. The dinner party—a favored social occasion—boosted spending. A wealthy middle-class family might give a lavish party for eight to twelve almost every week, and such parties were especially common on holidays.

The middle-class wife could cope with this endless procession of meals, courses, and dishes because she had servants as well as money at her disposal. Indeed, the employment of at least one full-time maid to cook and clean was the clearest sign that a family had crossed the cultural divide separating the working classes from what some contemporary observers called the "servant-keeping classes." The greater a family's income, the greater the number of servants it employed. Servants absorbed about another 25 percent of income at all levels of the middle class.

Well fed and well served, the middle classes were also well housed by 1900. Many prosperous families rented, rather than owned, their homes, complete with tiny rooms for servants in the basement or under the eaves of the top floor. And, just as the aristocracy had long divided the year between palatial country estates and lavish townhouses during "the season," so the upper middle class purchased country places or built beach houses for weekend and summer use.

The middle classes paid great attention to outward appearances, especially their clothes. The factory, the sewing machine, and the department store had all helped reduce the cost and expand the variety of clothing. Middle-class women were particularly attentive to the dictates of fashion, though men also wore the now-appropriate business suit. (See "Living in the Past: Nineteenth-Century Women's Fashion," page 732.) Ownership of private coaches and carriages, expensive items in the city, further testified to rising social status.

Rich Europeans could devote more time to "culture" and leisure pursuits than less wealthy or well-established families could. The keystones of culture and leisure were books, music, and travel. The long Realist novel, the heroic operas of composers Wagner and Verdi, the diligent striving of the dutiful daughter at the piano, and the packaged tour to a foreign country were all sources of middle-class pleasure.

In addition to their material tastes, the middle classes generally agreed upon a strict code of behavior, manners, and morality. They stressed hard work, self-discipline, and personal achievement. Middle-class social reformers denounced drunkenness and gambling as vices and celebrated sexual purity and fidelity as virtues, especially for women. Men and women who fell into vice, crime, or

A Corner of the Table (1904)
With photographic precision, the French artist Paul-Émile Chabas (1869–1937) captures the elegance and intimacy of a sumptuous dinner party. Throughout Europe, members of the upper middle class and aristocracy enjoyed dinners like this with eight or nine separate courses, beginning with appetizers and ending with coffee and liqueurs. (Musée des Beaux-Arts, Tourcoing, France/Bridgeman Images)

Rat Catching Although antivivisectionist reform groups successfully pressured city and state authorities to ban many forms of cruelty to animals, the sport of "ratting" continued to attract working- and middle-class crowds well into the nineteenth century. In this 1852 painting, an all-male crowd at the Blue Anchor Tavern on the outskirts of London lays bets on the trained Manchester terrier Tiny as he tries to kill two hundred rats in a single hour. Because they saw rats as verminous pests that brought filth and disease into Europe's rapidly growing cities, the authorities tolerated rat killing for sport, a pastime that was a throwback to the inhumane bullbaiting and cockfighting popular in the early modern era (see Chapter 18). (© Museum of London, UK/Bridgeman Images)

poverty were held responsible for their own circumstances. A stern sense of Christian morals, preached tirelessly by religious leaders, educators, and politicians, reaffirmed these values. The middle-class individual was supposed to know right from wrong and act accordingly.

The People and Occupations of the Working Classes

At the beginning of the twentieth century, about four out of five people belonged to the working classes — that is, people whose livelihoods depended primarily on physical labor and who did not employ domestic servants. Many of them were still small landowning peasants and hired farm hands, and this was especially the case in eastern Europe. In western and central Europe, however, the typical worker had left the land. By 1900 less than 8 percent of the people in Great Britain worked in agriculture, and in rapidly industrializing Germany only 25 percent were employed in agriculture and forestry. Even in less industrialized France, under 50 percent of the population worked the land.

The urban working classes were even less unified and homogeneous than the middle classes. First, economic development and increased specialization expanded the traditional range of working-class skills, earnings, and experiences. Meanwhile, the old sharp distinction between highly skilled artisans and unskilled manual workers gradually broke down. To be sure, highly skilled printers and masons as well as unskilled dockworkers and common laborers continued to exist. But between these extremes there appeared ever more semiskilled

groups, including trained factory workers. Skilled, semiskilled, and unskilled workers developed divergent lifestyles and cultural values. These differences contributed to a keen sense of social status and hierarchy within the working classes, creating great diversity and undermining the class unity predicted by Marx.

Highly skilled workers — about 15 percent of the working classes — became known as the **labor aristocracy**. They earned only about two-thirds of the income of the bottom ranks of the servant-keeping classes, but that was fully double the earnings of unskilled workers. The most "aristocratic" of these highly skilled workers were construction bosses and factory foremen, who had risen from the ranks and were fiercely proud of their achievement. The labor aristocracy also included members of the traditional highly skilled handicraft trades that had not been mechanized or placed in factories, like cabinetmakers, jewelers, and printers.

While the labor aristocracy enjoyed its exalted position, maintaining that status was by no means certain. Gradually, as factory production eliminated more and more crafts, lower-paid, semiskilled factory workers replaced many skilled artisans. Traditional woodcarvers and watchmakers virtually disappeared, for example, as the making of furniture and timepieces now took place in factories. At the same time, industrialization opened new opportunities for new kinds of highly skilled workers, such as shipbuilders and railway

■ **labor aristocracy** The highly skilled workers, such as factory foremen and construction bosses, who made up about 15 percent of the working classes from about 1850 to 1914.

In the last third of the nineteenth century, fashionable clothing, especially for middle-class women, became the first modern consumer industry, as shoppers snapped up the constantly changing ready-to-wear goods sold by large department stores. Before the twentieth century, when society fragmented into many different groups expressing themselves in many clothing styles, clothing patterns focused mainly on perceived differences in class and gender. Most changes in women's fashion originated in Paris in the nineteenth century. The crinoline dresses from 1869 shown on this page were worn exclusively by aristocratic and wealthy middle-class women, initially in France, and then across the Western world. These expensive dresses, flawlessly tailored by skilled seamstresses, abounded in elaborate embroidery, rich velvety materials, and fancy accessories. The circular spread of the gowns was created by the crinoline, a slip with a metal hoop that held the skirt out on all sides. Underneath their dress, women wore a corset, the century's most characteristic women's undergarment, which was laced up tightly in back and which pressed unmercifully inward from the breasts to the hips.

By 1875, as shown in this painting of a middle-class interior (opposite, top left), the corset still bound a woman's frame, but the crinoline hoop had been replaced by the bustle, a cotton fan with steel reinforcement that pushed the dress out in back to exaggerate gender differences. Worn initially by the wealthy elite, the bustle became the standard for middle-class women when cheaper ready-to-wear versions became available throughout Europe in department stores or mail-order catalogues. Emulating the elite in style, conventional middle-class women shopped carefully, scouting for sales. They used fashion to distinguish themselves from working-class women, who wore simple cotton clothes, just as the wealthy had tried to use clothing to differentiate themselves from the middle class earlier in the century.

By century's end alternative styles of dress had emerged. The young middle-class Englishwoman in this 1893 photo (opposite, top right) has chosen a woman's tailored suit, the only major English innovation in nineteenth-century women's fashion. This alternative dress combined the tie, suit jacket, vest, and straw hat of male attire with typical feminine elements, such as the skirt and gloves. This practical, socially accepted dress appealed to the growing number of

Crinoline dresses, Paris, 1869.
(Private Collection/Bridgeman Images)

Summer dress with bustle, England, 1875. (Roy Miles Fine Paintings/Bridgeman Images)

Alternative dress, England, 1893. (Manchester Art Gallery, UK/Bridgeman Images)

women in paid employment in the 1890s. By the early part of the twentieth century, the corset had given way entirely to the more flexible brassiere and the mainstream embrace of loose-fitting garments, as illustrated by this 1910 French advertisement (bottom right).

QUESTIONS FOR ANALYSIS

1. What does the image from 1869 tell you about the life of these women (their work, leisure activities, and so on)? What implications, if any, do you think the later styles shown here had for women's lives? For class distinctions?

2. What does the impractical, restrictive clothing in these images reveal about society's view of women during this period? What is the significance of the emergence of loose-fitting or other alternative styles of dress?

3. Historian Diana Crane has argued that women's departure from a dominant style can be seen as a symbolic, nonverbal assertion of independence and equality with men. Do you agree? Did the greater freedom of movement in clothing in the twentieth century reflect the emerging emancipation of Western women? Or was the coquettish femininity of loose, flowing dresses only a repackaging of the dominant culture's sharply defined gender boundaries?

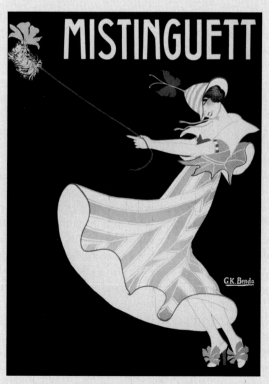

Loose-fitting dress, France, 1910. (Poster by G. K. [Georges Kogelmann] Benda/© Corbis)

locomotive engineers. Thus the labor elite remained in a state of flux, as individuals and whole crafts moved up and down the social scale.

To maintain their precarious standing, the upper working class adopted distinctive values and straitlaced, almost puritanical behavior. Like the middle classes, the labor aristocracy believed firmly in middle-class morality and economic improvement. Families in the upper working class saved money regularly, worried about their children's education, and valued good housing. Wives seldom sought employment outside the home. Despite these similarities, skilled workers viewed themselves not as aspirants to the middle class but as the pacesetters and natural model for the rest of the working classes. Well aware of the degradation not so far below them, they practiced self-discipline and stern morality and generally frowned on heavy drinking and sexual permissiveness. As one German skilled worker somberly warned, "The path to the brothel leads through the tavern" and from there to drastic decline or total ruin.[4]

Below the labor aristocracy stood the enormously complex world of hard work, composed of both semiskilled and unskilled workers. Established construction workers—carpenters, bricklayers, pipe fitters—stood near the top of the semiskilled hierarchy, often flirting with (or sliding back from) the labor elite. A large number of the semiskilled were factory workers, who earned highly variable but relatively good wages. These workers included substantial numbers of unmarried women, who began to play an increasingly important role in the industrial labor force.

Below the semiskilled workers, a larger group of unskilled workers included day laborers such as longshoremen, wagon-driving teamsters, and "helpers" of all kinds. Many of these people had real skills and performed valuable services, but they were unorganized and divided, united only by the common fate of meager earnings and poor living conditions. The same lack of unity characterized street vendors and market people—these self-employed members of the lower working classes competed savagely with each other and with established shopkeepers of the lower middle class.

One of the largest components of the unskilled group was domestic servants, whose numbers grew steadily in the nineteenth century. In Great Britain, for example, one out of every seven employed persons in 1911 was a domestic servant. The great majority were women; indeed, one out of every three girls in Britain between the ages of fifteen and twenty worked as a domestic servant. Throughout Europe, many female domestics in the cities were recent migrants from rural areas. As in earlier times, domestic service meant hard work at low pay with limited personal independence and the danger of sexual exploitation. For the full-time general maid in a lower-middle-class family, an unending routine of baby-sitting, shopping, cooking, and cleaning defined a lengthy working day. In the wealthiest households, the serving girl was at the bottom of a rigid hierarchy of status-conscious butlers and housekeepers.

Nonetheless, domestic service had real attractions for young women from rural areas who had few specialized skills. Marriage prospects were better, or at least more varied, in the city than back home. And though wages were low, they were higher and more regular than in hard agricultural work—which was being replaced by mechanization, at any rate. Finally, as one London observer noted, young girls and other migrants from the countryside were drawn to the city by "the contagion of numbers, the sense of something going on, the theaters and the music halls, the brightly lighted streets and busy crowds—all, in short, that makes the difference between the Mile End fair on a Saturday night, and a dark and muddy country lane, with no glimmer of gas and with nothing to do."[5]

Many young domestics made the successful transition to working-class wife and mother. Yet with an unskilled or unemployed husband, a growing family, and limited household income, many working-class wives had to join the broad ranks of working women in the **sweated industries**. These industries expanded rapidly after 1850 and resembled the old putting-out and cottage industries of earlier times (see Chapter 17). The women normally worked at home and were paid by the piece, not by the hour. They and their young children who helped them earned pitiful wages and lacked any job security. Women decorated dishes or embroidered linens, took in laundry for washing and ironing, or made clothing, especially after the advent of the sewing machine. An army of poor women, usually working at home, accounted for many of the inexpensive ready-made clothes displayed on department store racks and in tiny shops.

Working-Class Leisure and Religion

Notwithstanding hard physical labor and lack of wealth, the urban working classes sought fun and recreation, and they found both. Across Europe, drinking remained unquestionably the favorite leisure-time activity of working people. For many middle-class moralists, as well as moralizing historians since, love of drink was the curse of the modern age—a sign of social dislocation and popular suffering. Certainly, drinking was deadly serious business. One English slum dweller recalled that "drunkenness was by far the commonest cause of dispute and misery in working class homes. On account of it one saw many a decent family drift down through poverty into total want."[6]

Generally, however, heavy problem drinking declined in the late nineteenth century as it became less socially acceptable. This decline reflected in part the moral leadership of the labor aristocracy. At the same time, drinking became more publicly acceptable. Cafés and pubs became increasingly bright, friendly places. Working-class politi-

■ **sweated industries** Poorly paid handicraft production, often carried out by married women paid by the piece and working at home.

Moulin Rouge   A group of barmaids perform the French cancan in 1895 at the Moulin Rouge, a famous Parisian cabaret/nightclub, while a live orchestra plays in the balcony above. The cancan was a fast and provocative dance that involved rapid dips and turns, and high kicks that revealed the performers' legs and frilly underwear. The new industrial society made leisure time available to more and more people of all classes, and mixed-couple entertainment including dance balls, theater performance, and dining out became increasingly popular. (Photo © Dazy René/Bridgeman Images)

cal activities, both moderate and radical, were also concentrated in taverns and pubs. Moreover, social drinking in public places by married couples and sweethearts became an accepted and widespread practice for the first time. This greater participation by women undoubtedly helped civilize the world of drink and hard liquor.

The two other leisure-time passions of working-class culture were sports and music halls. "Cruel sports," such as bullbaiting and cockfighting, still popular in the middle of the century, had greatly declined throughout Europe by the 1880s. Commercialized spectator sports filled their place; horse racing and soccer were the most popular. Working people gambled on sports events, and for many a working person a desire to decipher racing forms provided a powerful incentive toward literacy. Music halls and vaudeville theaters, the working-class counterparts of middle-class opera and classical theater, were enormously popular throughout Europe. In 1900 London had more than fifty such halls and theaters. Music hall audiences included men and women, which may account for the fact that drunkenness, premarital sex, marital difficulties, and mothers-in-law were all favorite themes of broad jokes and bittersweet songs.

In more serious moments, religion continued to provide working people with solace and meaning. The eighteenth-century vitality of popular religion in Catholic

countries and the Protestant rejuvenation exemplified by German Pietism and English Methodism (see Chapter 18) carried over into the nineteenth century. Indeed, many historians see the early nineteenth century as an age of religious revival. Yet historians recognize that by the last few decades of the nineteenth century, a considerable decline in both church attendance and church donations had occurred in most European countries. And it seems clear that this decline was greater for the urban working classes than for their rural counterparts or for the middle classes.

Why did working-class church attendance decline? On one hand, the construction of churches failed to keep up with the rapid growth of urban population, especially in new working-class neighborhoods. On the other, throughout the nineteenth century workers saw Catholic and Protestant churches as conservative institutions that defended status quo politics, hierarchical social order, and middle-class morality. Socialist political parties, in particular, attacked organized religion as a pillar of bourgeois society; and as the working classes became more politically conscious, they tended to see established churches as allied with their political opponents. In addition, religion underwent a process historians call "feminization": in the working and middle classes alike, women were more pious and attended service more regularly than men. Urban workingmen in particular developed vaguely antichurch attitudes, even though they might remain neutral or positive toward religion itself.

The pattern was different in the United States, where most nineteenth-century churches also preached social conservatism. But because church and state had always been separate and because a host of denominations and even different religions competed for members, working people identified churches much less with the political and social status quo. Instead, individual churches in the United States were often closely identified with an ethnic group rather than a social class, and churches thrived, in part, as a means of asserting ethnic identity. This same process occurred in Europe if the church or synagogue had never been linked to the state and served as a focus for ethnic cohesion. Irish Catholic churches in Protestant Britain, Catholic churches in partitioned Polish lands, and Jewish synagogues in Russia were outstanding examples.

Changing Family Lifestyles

FOCUS QUESTION *How did urbanization affect family life and gender roles?*

By the 1850s the family had stabilized considerably after the disruption of the late eighteenth and early nineteenth centuries. With the consolidation caused by industrialization and urbanization, the growing middle classes created a distinctive middle-class lifestyle, which set them off from peasants, workers, and the aristocracy. New ideas about courtship and marriage, family and gender roles, and homemaking and child rearing expressed middle-class norms and values in ways that would have a profound impact on family life in the century to come. Changes in family life affected both men and women and all social classes, but to varying degrees. Leading a middle-class lifestyle was prohibitively expensive for workers and peasants, and middle-class family values at first had little relevance for their lives. Yet as the nineteenth century drew to a close, the middle-class lifestyle increasingly became the norm for all classes.

Middle-Class Marriage and Courtship Rituals

Rather than marry for convenience, or for economic or social reasons—as was still common among workers, peasants, and aristocrats—by the 1850s the middle-class couple was supposed to follow an idealized model: they met, courted, fell deeply in love, and joined for

life because of a shared emotional bond. Of course, economic considerations in marriage by no means disappeared. But an entire culture of romantic love—popularized in advice manuals, popular fiction, and art, and practiced in courtship rituals, weddings, and married life—now surrounded the middle-class couple with a tender emotional charge. The growing popularity among all classes toward the end of the nineteenth century of what historians call **companionate marriage** underscores the impact of historical change on human emotions and behaviors.

Strict rules for courtship and engagement enshrined in the concept of falling in love ensured that middle-class individuals would make an appropriate match. Parents, chaperones, and the general public closely guarded the boundary between courtship and sex, between the proper and the improper. Young couples were seldom alone before they became engaged, and individuals rarely paired off with someone from an inappropriate class background. Premarital sex was taboo for women, though men might experiment, a double standard that revealed the value the middle classes placed on sexual morality and especially women's virginity before marriage.

Engagement also followed a complicated set of rules and rituals. Secret engagements led to public announcements, and then the couple could appear together, though only escorted by chaperones in potentially delicate situations. Couples might walk arm in arm, but custom placed strict limits on physical intimacy. A couple might find ways to experiment with sexual behaviors, but only in secret—secrecy that confirmed the special feelings of "true love" between the couple.

Marriage had its own set of rules. Usually a middle-class man could marry only if he could support a wife, children, and a servant, which meant he had to be well established in his career and fairly prosperous. As a result, some middle-class men never married, because they could not afford it. These customs created special difficulties for young middle-class women, who could rarely pursue an independent career or acquire a home without a husband. The system encouraged mixed-age marriages. A new husband was typically much older than his young wife, who usually had no career and entered marriage directly out of her parents' home or perhaps a girl's finishing school. She would have had little experience with the realities of adult life.

Love meant something different to men and women. Trained to fall passionately in love with "Mr. Right," young women equated marriage with emotional intensity. Men, on the other hand, were supposed to "find a wife": they took a more active but dispassionate role in courtship. Since women generally were quite young, the man was encouraged to see himself as the protector of a young and fragile creature. In short, the typical middle-class marriage was more similar to a child-parent relationship than a partnership of

■ **companionate marriage** Marriage based on romantic love and middle-class family values that became increasingly dominant in the second half of the nineteenth century.

equals, a situation finely portrayed in Henrik Ibsen's famous play *A Doll's House* (1879). The inequality of marriage was codified in European legal systems that, with rare exceptions, placed property ownership in the hands of the husband.

Middle- and Working-Class Sexuality

A double standard in sexual relations paralleled the gender inequalities built into middle-class standards of love and marriage. Middle-class moralists of all stripes cast men as aggressively sexual creatures, while women—the "angel in the house"—were supposed to be pure and chaste and act as a brake on male desire. Contemporary science legitimized this double standard. According to late-nineteenth-century physicians, men, easily aroused by the sight of a wrist or ankle, fell prey to their raging biological drives, while respectable women were supposedly uninterested in sex by nature.

Middle-class moralists assumed that men would enter marriage with some sexual experience, though this was unthinkable for a middle-class woman. When middle-class men did seek premarital sex, middle-class women were off limits. Instead, bourgeois men took advantage of their class status and sought lower-class women, domestic servants, or prostitutes. If a young middle-class woman had experimented with or even was suspected of having had premarital sex, her chances for an acceptable marriage fell dramatically. (See "Evaluating the Evidence 22.2: Stephan Zweig on Middle-Class Youth and Sexuality," page 738.)

The sexual standards of the working classes stood in marked contrast to these norms in the early nineteenth century, but that changed over time. Premarital sex for both men and women was common and more acceptable among workers. In the first half of the nineteenth century, among the lower classes, about one-third of the births in many large European cities occurred outside of wedlock. The second half of the century saw the reversal of this high rate of illegitimacy: in western, northern, and central Europe, more babies were born to married mothers. Young, unmarried workers were probably engaging in just as much sexual activity as their parents and grandparents who had created the illegitimacy explosion of 1750 to 1850 (see Chapter 18). But in the later part of the nineteenth century, pregnancy for a young single woman, which a couple might see as the natural consequence of a serious relationship, led increasingly to marriage and the establishment of a two-parent household. Indeed, one in three working-class women was pregnant when she married. This important development reflected the spread of middle-class ideals of family respectability among the working classes, as well as their gradual economic improvement. Romantic love held working-class families together, and marriage was less of an economic challenge. The urban working-class couple of the late nineteenth cen-

tury thus became more stable, and that stability strengthened the family as an institution.

Prostitution

In the late nineteenth century prostitution was legal in much of Europe. In Italy, France, Great Britain, and much of Germany, the state licensed brothels and registered individual prostitutes. In Paris, 155,000 women were registered as prostitutes between 1871 and 1903, and 750,000 others were suspected of prostitution in the same years. In Berlin, in 1909 alone, the authorities registered over 40,000 prostitutes. The totals are probably low, since most women in the sex trade tried to avoid government registration.

In streets, dance halls, and pubs across Europe, young working-class women used prostitution as a source of second income or as a way to weather a period of unemployment. Their clients were generally lower-class men, soldiers, and sailors, though middle- and upper-class men looking to "sow wild oats" also paid for sexual encounters. Streetwalking offered women some measure of financial independence, but the work was dangerous. Violence and rape, police harassment, and venereal disease were commonplace hazards.

Prostitutes clearly violated middle-class ideals of feminine respectability, but among the working classes prostitution was tolerated as more-or-less acceptable work of a temporary nature. Like domestic service, prostitution was a stage of life, not permanent employment. After working as prostitutes in their youth, many women went on to marry (or live with) men of their own class and establish homes and families.

As middle-class family values became increasingly prominent after the 1860s, prostitution generated great concern among social reformers. The prostitute—immoral, lascivious, and unhealthy in middle-class eyes—served as the dark mirror image of the respectable middle-class woman. Authorities blamed prostitutes for spreading crime and disease, particularly syphilis. Before the discovery of penicillin, syphilis was indeed a terrifying and widespread affliction. Its painful symptoms led to physical and mental decline and often death; medical treatment was embarrassing and for the most part ineffective.

As general concerns with public health gained recognition, state and city authorities across Europe subjected prostitutes—in their eyes the vector of contagious disease—to increased surveillance. The British Contagious Diseases Acts, in force between 1864 and 1886, exemplified the trend. Under these acts, special plainclothes policemen required women identified as "common prostitutes" to undergo biweekly medical exams. If they showed signs of venereal disease, they were interned in a "lock hospital" and forced to undergo treatment; when the outward signs of disease went away, they were released.

Stephan Zweig on Middle-Class Youth and Sexuality

Growing up in Vienna in a prosperous Jewish family, Stephan Zweig (1881–1942) became an influential voice calling for humanitarian values and international culture in early-twentieth-century Europe. Passionately opposed to the First World War, Zweig wrote poetry, plays, and novels. But he was most famous for his biographies: shrewd psychological portraits of historical figures such as Magellan and Marie Antoinette. After Hitler came to power in 1933, Zweig lived in exile until his death in 1942. Zweig's last work was The World of Yesterday *(1943), one of the truly fascinating autobiographies of the twentieth century. In the following passage, Zweig recalls the romantic experiences and sexual separation of middle-class youth before the First World War.*

During the eight years of our higher schooling [beyond grade school], something had occurred which was of great importance to each one of us: we ten-year-olds had grown into virile young men of sixteen, seventeen, and eighteen, and Nature began to assert its rights. . . . It did not take us long to discover that those authorities in whom we had previously confided — school, family, and public morals — manifested an astonishing insincerity in this matter of sex. But what is more, they also demanded secrecy and reserve from us in this connection. . . .

This "social morality," which on the one hand privately presupposed the existence of sexuality and its natural course, but on the other would not recognize it openly at any price, was doubly deceitful. While it winked one eye at a young man and even encouraged him with the other "to sow his wild oats," as the kindly language of the home put it, in the case of a woman it studiously shut both eyes and acted as if it were blind. That a man could experience desires, and was permitted to experience them, was silently admitted by custom. But to admit frankly that a woman could be subject to similar desires, or that creation for its eternal purposes also required a female polarity, would have transgressed the conception of the "sanctity of womanhood." In the pre-Freudian era, therefore, the axiom was agreed upon that a female person could have no physical desires as long as they had not been awakened by man, and that, obviously, was officially permitted only in marriage. But even in those moral times, in Vienna in particular, the air was full of dangerous erotic infection, and a girl of good family had to live in a completely sterilized atmosphere, from the day of her birth until the day when she left the altar on her husband's arm. In order to protect young girls, they were not left alone for a single moment. . . . Every book which they read was inspected, and above all else,

young girls were constantly kept busy to divert their attention from any possible dangerous thoughts. They had to practise the piano, learn singing and drawing, foreign languages, and the history of literature and art. They were educated and overeducated. But while the aim was to make them as educated and as socially correct as possible, at the same time society anxiously took great pains that they should remain innocent of all natural things to a degree unthinkable today. A young girl of good family was not allowed to have any idea of how the male body was formed, or to know how children came into the world, for the angel was to enter into matrimony not only physically untouched, but completely "pure" spiritually as well. "Good breeding," for a young girl of that time, was identical with ignorance of life; and this ignorance ofttimes lasted for the rest of their lives. . . .

What possibilities actually existed for a young man of the middle-class world? In all the others, in the so-called lower classes, the problem was no problem at all. . . . In most of our Alpine villages the number of natural children greatly exceeded the legitimate ones. Among the proletariat, the worker, before he could get married, lived with another worker in free love. . . . It was only in our middle-class society that such a remedy as an early marriage was scorned. . . . And so there was an artificial interval of six, eight, or ten years between actual manhood and manhood as society accepted it; and in this interval the young man had to take care of his own "affairs" or adventures.

Those days did not give him too many opportunities. Only a very few particularly rich young men could afford the luxury of keeping a mistress, that is, taking an apartment and paying her expenses. And only a very few fortunate young men achieved the literary ideal of love of the times — the only one which it was permitted to describe in novels — an affair with a married woman. The others helped themselves for the most part with shopgirls and waitresses, and this offered little inner satisfaction. . . . But, generally speaking, prostitution was still the foundation of the erotic life outside of marriage; in a certain sense it constituted a dark underground vault over which rose the gorgeous structure of middle-class society with its faultless, radiant façade.

The present generation has hardly any idea of the gigantic extent of prostitution in Europe before the [First] World War. Whereas today it is as rare to meet a prostitute on the streets of a big city as it is to meet a wagon in the road, then the sidewalks were so sprinkled with women for sale that it was more difficult to avoid than to find them. To this was added the countless number of "closed houses," the night clubs, the cabarets, the dance parlours with their dancers and singers, and the bars with their "comeon" girls. At that time female wares were offered for sale at every hour and at every price. . . . And this was the same city, the same society, the same morality, that was indignant when young girls rode bicycles, and declared it a disgrace to the dignity of science when Freud in his calm, clear, and penetrating manner established truths that they did not wish to be true. The same world that so pathetically defended the purity of womanhood allowed this cruel sale of women, organized it, and even profited thereby.

We should not permit ourselves to be misled by sentimental novels or stories of that epoch. It was a bad time for youth. The young girls were hermetically locked up under the control of the family, hindered in their free bodily as well as intellectual development. The young men were forced to secrecy and reticence by a morality which fundamentally no one believed or obeyed. Unhampered, honest relationships — in other words, all that could have made youth happy and joyous according to the laws of Nature — were permitted only to the very few.

EVALUATE THE EVIDENCE

1. According to Zweig, how did the sex lives of young middle-class women and young middle-class men differ? What accounted for these differences?
2. What were the differences between the sex lives of the middle class and those of the "so-called lower classes"? What was Zweig's opinion of these differences?
3. Zweig ends with a value judgment: "It was a bad time for youth." Do you agree or disagree? Why?

Source: Excerpts from pp. 67, 76–78, 81–83, 88 in *The World of Yesterday* by Stephan Zweig, translated by Helmut Ripperger. Translation copyright 1943, renewed © 1971 by the Viking Press, Inc. Used by permission of Viking Books, an imprint of Penguin Publishing Group, a division of Penguin Random House LLC.

The Contagious Diseases Acts were controversial from the start. A determined middle-class feminist campaign against the policy, led by feminist Josephine Butler and the Ladies National Association, loudly proclaimed that the acts physically abused poor women, violated their constitutional rights, and legitimized male vice. Under pressure, Parliament repealed the laws in 1886. Yet heavy-handed government regulation had devastated the informality of working-class prostitution. Now branded as "registered girls," prostitutes experienced new forms of public humiliation, and the trade was increasingly controlled by male pimps rather than by the women themselves. Prostitution had never been safe, but it had been accepted, at least among the working classes. Prostitutes were now stigmatized as social and sexual outsiders.

Separate Spheres and the Importance of Homemaking

After 1850 the work of wives became increasingly distinct and separate from that of their husbands in all classes. The preindustrial pattern among both peasants and cottage workers, in which husbands and wives both worked and shared basic household duties, became less common. In wealthier homes, this change was particularly dramatic. The good middle-class family man earned the wages to support the household; the public world of work, education, and politics was male space. Respectable middle-class women did not work outside the home and rarely even traveled alone in public. Working-class women, including servants and prostitutes, were more visible in public places, but if a middle-class woman went out without a male escort, she might be accused of low morals or character. Thus many historians have stressed that the societal ideal in nineteenth-century Europe became a strict division of labor by gender within rigidly constructed **separate spheres**: the "private sphere," where the woman acted as wife, mother, and homemaker, and the "public sphere," where the husband acted as wage earner and family provider.

For the middle classes, the private single-family home, a symbol of middle-class status and a sanctuary from the callous outside world of competitive capitalism, was central to the notion of separate spheres. At the heart of the middle-class home stood the woman: notions of femininity, motherhood, and family life came together in the ideal of domestic space. Middle-class floor plans grew to include separate sleeping rooms for parents and each family member — unheard of among the lower classes — as well as a special drawing room (or parlor), used to entertain guests. Plump

■ **separate spheres** The nineteenth-century gendered division of labor and lifestyles that cast men as breadwinners and women as homemakers.

Christmas and the Sentimental Pleasures of the Middle-Class Home Victorian Christmas celebrated the family values and lifestyles of the middle classes at their most expressive. This clichéd portrait of a wealthy middle-class family holiday—with holly adorning the walls, mistletoe hanging above the fireplace, children singing carols with their parents, and contented grandparents sitting by a warm fire—captures the intimacy and love that increasingly bound together middle-class and working-class families alike during the nineteenth century. Titled *Home Sweet Home* and released for commercial reproduction and sale around 1900, prints of this image of domestic bliss no doubt adorned the walls of many middle-class parlors like the one shown in the painting. (Private Collection/Photo © Christie's Images/Bridgeman Images)

sofas, bric-a-brac, and souvenirs graced domestic interiors; curtains of heavy red velvet and colorful silks draped doors and windows. Such ostentatious displays were far too expensive for the working classes, who made up 80 percent of the population.

Middle-class women were spared the masculine burdens of the outside working world, and lower-class servants ensured that they had free time to turn the private sphere into a domestic refuge of love and privacy. Numerous middle-class housekeeping manuals made the wife's responsibilities quite clear, as this Swedish handbook from 1889 suggests: "A man who spends most of his day away from the family, who has to work outside the home, counts on finding a restful and refreshing atmosphere when he returns home, and sometimes even a little merriment or a surprise. . . . It is his wife's duty to ensure that he is not disappointed in his expectation. She must do her utmost to make his

stay at home as pleasant as possible; she can thus continue to keep her influence over him and retain his affection undiminished."[7]

By 1900 working-class families had adopted many middle-class values, but they did not have the means to fully realize the ideal of separate spheres. Women were the primary homemakers, and, as in the upper classes, men did little or no domestic labor. But many working-class women also made a monetary contribution to family income by taking in a boarder, doing piecework at home in the sweated industries (see page 734), or getting an outside job. While middle-class family life centered on an ample daily meal, working-class women struggled to put sufficient food on the table. Working women worked to create a homelike environment that at least resembled that of the middle class—cleaning house, collecting trinkets, and decorating domestic interiors—but working men often preferred to spend time in the local pub with workmates, rather than come home. Indeed, alcoholism and domestic violence afflicted many working-class families, even as they worked to build a relationship based on romantic love.

Feminist historians have often criticized the middle-class ideal of separate spheres because it restricted women's educational and employment opportunities, and the women's rights movement that emerged in the late nineteenth century certainly challenged the limitations of the model. In recent years, however, some scholars have been rethinking gender roles within the long-term development of consumer behavior and household economies. In the era of industrialization, these scholars suggest, the "breadwinner-homemaker" household that developed from about 1850 onward was rational consumer behavior that improved the lives of all family members, especially in the working classes.[8]

According to this view, when husbands specialized in earning an adequate cash income—the "family wage" that labor unions demanded—and wives specialized in managing the home, the working-class wife could produce desirable benefits that could not be bought in a market, such as improved health, better eating habits, and better behavior. For example, higher wages from the breadwinner could buy more raw food, but only the homemaker's careful selection, processing, and cooking would allow the family to benefit from increased spending on food. Running an urban household was a complicated, demanding, and valuable task. Twice-a-day food shopping, careful economizing, and fighting the growing crusade against dirt—not to mention child rearing—constituted a full-time occupation. Working yet another job for wages outside the home had limited appeal for most married women unless the earnings were essential for family survival. The homemaker's managerial skills, however, enabled the working-class couple to maximize their personal well-being.

The woman's guidance of the household went hand in hand with the increased pride in the home and family and the emotional importance attached to them in working- and middle-class families alike. According to one historian, by 1900 the English song "Home, Sweet Home" had become "almost a second national anthem."[9] Domesticity and family ties were now central to the lives of millions of people of all classes.

Child Rearing

Another striking sign of deepening emotional ties within the family was a growing emphasis on the love and concern that mothers gave their infants. Early emotional bonding and a willingness to make real sacrifices for the welfare of the infant became increasingly important among the comfortable classes by the end of the eighteenth century, though the ordinary mother of modest means adopted new attitudes only as the nine-

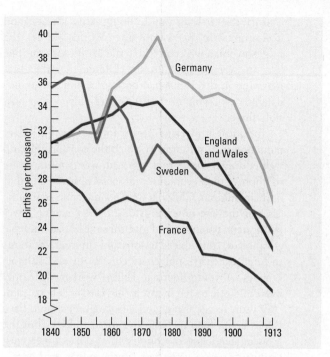

FIGURE 22.2 The Decline of Birthrates in England and Wales, France, Germany, and Sweden, 1840–1913 Women had fewer babies for a variety of reasons, including the fact that their children were increasingly less likely to die before reaching adulthood. How do these numbers compare with those in Figure 22.1?

teenth century progressed. The baby became more important, and women became better mothers.

The surge of maternal feeling was shaped by and reflected in a wave of specialized books on child rearing and infant hygiene, such as French family reformer Gustav Droz's phenomenally successful book *Papa, Mama, and Baby*, which went through 121 editions between 1866 and 1884. Droz urged fathers to become affectionate toward their children and pitied those "who do not know how to roll around on the carpet, play at being a horse and a great wolf, and undress their baby."[10] Following expert advice, mothers increasingly breast-fed their infants, rather than paying wet nurses to do so. Breast-feeding involved sacrifice—a temporary loss of freedom, if nothing else. Yet when there was no good alternative to mother's milk, it saved lives. Another sign, from France, of increased parental affection is that fewer illegitimate babies were abandoned as foundlings after about 1850. Moreover, the practice of swaddling disappeared completely. Instead, ordinary mothers allowed their babies freedom of movement and delighted in their spontaneity.

The loving care lavished on infants was matched by greater concern for older children and adolescents. They, too, were bound in the strong emotional ties of a more intimate and protective family. For one thing, European women began to limit the number of children they bore in order to care adequately for those they had (Figure 22.2). By the end of the nineteenth century, the birthrate was declining across Europe, and it continued to do so until after World War II. The Englishwoman who married in the 1860s, for example, had an average of about six children; her daughter marrying in the 1890s had only four; and her granddaughter marrying in the 1920s had only two or possibly three.

The most important reason for this revolutionary reduction in family size, in which the comfortable and well-educated classes took the lead, was parents' desire to improve their economic and social position and that of their children. Children were no longer an economic asset in the late nineteenth century. By having fewer youngsters, parents could give those they had valuable advantages, from music lessons and summer vacations to long, expensive university educations and suitable dowries. A young German skilled worker with only one child spoke for many in his class when he said, "We want to get ahead, and our daughter should have things better than my wife and sisters did."[11] Thus the growing tendency of couples in the late nineteenth century to use a variety of contraceptive methods— the rhythm method, the withdrawal method, and mechanical devices, including after the 1840s condoms and diaphragms made of vulcanized rubber— reflected increased concern for children.

In middle-class households, parents expended considerable effort to ensure that they raised their children according to prevailing family values. Indeed, many parents, especially in the middle classes, probably became too concerned about their children, unwittingly subjecting them to an emotional pressure cooker of almost unbearable intensity. Professional family experts, including teachers, doctors, and reformers like Droz, produced a vast popular literature on child rearing that encouraged parents to focus on developing their children's self-control, self-fulfillment, and sense of Christian morality. Family specialists recommended against corporal punishment— still common in worker and peasant households— but even though they typically escaped beatings, the children of the wealthy grew up under constant observation and discipline, a style of parenting designed to teach the self-control necessary for adult success. Parents carefully monitored their children's sexual behavior, and masturbation— according to one expert "the most shameful and terrible of all vices"— was of particular concern.[12] (See "Evaluating the Evidence 22.2: Stephan Zweig on Middle-Class Youth and Sexuality," page 738.)

Attempts to repress the child's sexuality generated unhealthy tension, often made worse by the rigid division of gender roles within the family. While family experts lauded parental love, and especially love between mother and child, they believed that relations between father and child were troubled by a lack of emotional bonding. At work all day, the father came home a stranger to his offspring; his world of business was far removed from the maternal world of spontaneous affection. Moreover, the father set demanding rules, often expecting the child to succeed where he himself had failed and making his approval conditional on achievement. This kind of distance was especially the case in the wealthiest families, in which domestic servants, nannies, and tutors did much of the work of child rearing. Wealthy parents saw their children only over dinner, or on special occasions like birthdays or holidays.

The children of the working classes probably had more avenues of escape from such tensions than did those of the middle classes. Unlike their middle-class counterparts, who remained economically dependent on their families until a long education was finished or a proper marriage secured, working-class boys and girls went to work when they reached adolescence. Earning wages on their own, they could bargain with their parents by the time they were sixteen or seventeen for greater independence within the household. If they were unsuccessful in these negotiations, they could and did leave home to live cheaply as paying lodgers in other working-class homes. Not until the twentieth century would middle-class youths be equally free to break away from the family when emotional ties became oppressive.

The Feminist Movement

The ideal of separate spheres and the rigid gender division of labor meant that middle-class women faced great obstacles when they needed— or wanted— to move into the man's world of paid employment outside the home. Married women were subordinated to their husbands by law and lacked many basic legal rights. In England, a wife had no legal identity and hence no right to own property in her own name. Even the wages she might earn belonged to her husband. In France, the Napoleonic Code (see Chapter 19) enshrined the principle of female subordination and gave the wife few legal rights regarding property, divorce, and custody of the children.

Facing discrimination in education and employment and suffering from a lack of legal rights, some women rebelled and began the long-continuing fight for equality of the sexes and the rights of women. Their struggle proceeded on two main paths. First, following in the steps of women such as Mary Wollstonecraft (see Chapter 19), organizations founded by middle-class feminists campaigned for equal legal rights for women as well as access to higher education, professional employment, and the vote. Middle-class feminists argued that unmarried women and middle-class widows with inadequate incomes simply had to have more opportunities to support themselves. Second, feminists argued

■ **suffrage movement** A militant movement for women's right to vote led by middle-class British women around 1900.

First-Wave Feminists in Action   In May 1914 suffragette leader Emily Pankhurst was arrested by a police superintendent when she tried to present a petition to the king at Buckingham Palace. The British suffragettes often engaged in provocative public acts of civic disobedience in their campaign for women's right to vote. How do you account for the reaction of the male onlookers? (© Museum of London, UK/Bridgeman Images)

that paid (as opposed to unpaid) work could relieve the monotony that some women found in their sheltered middle-class existence and add greater meaning to their lives. In the late nineteenth century women's organizations scored some significant victories, such as the 1882 law giving English married women full property rights. More women gradually found professional and white-collar employment, especially after 1880, in fields such as teaching, nursing, and social work.

Progress toward women's rights was slow and hard-won. In Britain, the women's **suffrage movement** mounted a militant struggle for the right to vote, particularly in the decade before World War I. Inspired by the slogan "Deeds Not Words," women "suffragettes" marched in public demonstrations, heckled members of Parliament, and slashed paintings in London's National Gallery. Jailed for political activities, they went

on highly publicized hunger strikes. Yet conservatives dismissed what they called "the shrieking sisterhood," and British women received the vote only in 1919.

In Germany before 1900, women were not admitted as fully registered students at a single university. Determined pioneers had to fight with tremendous fortitude to break through sexist barriers to advanced education and subsequent professional employment. (See "Individuals in Society: Franziska Tiburtius," page 744.) By 1913 the Federation of German Women's Association, an umbrella organization for regional feminist groups, had some 470,000 members. Their protests had a direct impact on the revised German Civil Code of 1906, which granted women substantial gains in family law and property rights.

Women inspired by utopian and especially Marxist socialism (see Chapter 21) blazed an alternative path. Often scorning the reform programs of middle-class feminists, socialist women leaders argued that the liberation of working-class women would come only with the liberation of the entire working class through revolution. In the meantime, they championed the cause of working women and won some practical improvements, especially in Germany, where the socialist movement was most effectively organized. In a general way, these different approaches to women's issues reflected the diversity of classes in urban society.

Science and Thought

FOCUS QUESTION   *How and why did intellectual life change in this period?*

Major changes in Western science and thought accompanied the emergence of urban society. Two aspects of these complex intellectual developments stand out as especially significant. First, scientific knowledge in many areas expanded rapidly. Breakthroughs in chemistry, physics, and electricity profoundly influenced the Western worldview and spurred the creation of new products and whole industries. The natural and social sciences were also established as highly respected fields of study. Second, between about the 1840s and the 1890s Western arts and literature underwent a shift from soaring Romanticism to tough-minded Realism.

The Triumph of Science in Industry

The quickening pace of scientific advancements in the last third of the nineteenth century resulted in many practical benefits. The intellectual achievements of the Scientific Revolution (see Chapter 16) had resulted in few such benefits, and theoretical knowledge had also played a relatively small role in the Industrial Revolution

Franziska Tiburtius

Why did a small number of women in the late nineteenth century brave great odds and embark on professional careers? And how did a few of them manage to reach their objectives? The career and personal reflections of Franziska Tiburtius (tigh-bur-TEE-uhs), a pioneer in German medicine, suggest that talent, determination, and economic necessity were critical ingredients to both the attempt and the success.*

Like many women of her time who studied and pursued professional careers, Franziska Tiburtius (1843–1927) was born into a property-owning family of modest means. The youngest of nine children growing up on a small estate in northeastern Germany, the sensitive child wilted under a harsh governess but flowered with a caring teacher and became an excellent student. Graduating at sixteen and needing to support herself, Tiburtius had few opportunities. A young woman from a "proper" background could work as a governess or teacher without losing her respectability and spoiling her matrimonial prospects, but that was about it. She tried both avenues. Working for six years as a governess in a noble family and no doubt learning that poverty was often one's fate in this genteel profession, she then turned to teaching. Called home from her studies in Britain in 1871 to care for her brother, who had contracted typhus as a field doctor in the Franco-Prussian War, she found her calling. She decided to become a medical doctor.

Supported by her family, Tiburtius's decision was truly audacious. In all Europe, only the University of Zurich accepted female students. Moreover, if it became known that she had studied medicine and failed, she would probably never get a job as a teacher. No parent would entrust a daughter to an emancipated radical who had carved up dead bodies. Although the male students at the university sometimes harassed the female ones with crude pranks, Tiburtius thrived. The revolution of the microscope and the discovery of microorganisms thrilled Tiburtius and she was fascinated by her studies. She became close friends with a fellow female student from Germany, Emilie Lehmus, with whom she would form a lifelong partnership in medicine.

Graduating at age thirty-three in 1876, Tiburtius went to stay with her doctor brother in Berlin. Though well qualified to practice, she was blocked by pervasive discrimination. Not permitted to take the state medical exams, she could practice only as an unregulated (and unprofessional) "natural healer." But after persistent fighting with the bureaucrats, she was able to display her diploma and practice as "Franziska Tiburtius, M.D., University of Zurich."

Soon Tiburtius and Lehmus realized their dream and opened a clinic. Subsidized by a wealthy industrialist, they focused on

Franziska Tiburtius, pioneering woman physician in Berlin.
(1915 photograph/akg-images)

treating women factory workers. The clinic filled a great need and was soon treating many patients. A room with beds for extremely sick women was later expanded into a second clinic.

Tiburtius and Lehmus became famous. For fifteen years, they were the only women doctors in all of Berlin and inspired a new generation of women. Though they added the wealthy to their thriving practice, they always concentrated on the poor, providing them with subsidized and up-to-date treatment. Talented, determined, and working with her partner, Tiburtius experienced fully the joys of personal achievement and useful service. Above all, Tiburtius overcame the tremendous barriers raised up against women seeking higher education and professional careers, providing an inspiring model for those who dared to follow.

QUESTIONS FOR ANALYSIS

1. Analyze Franziska Tiburtius's life. What lessons do you draw from it? How do you account for her bold action and success?
2. In what ways was Tiburtius's career related to improvements in health in urban society and to the expansion of the professions?

*This portrait draws on Conradine Lück, *Frauen: Neun Lebensschicksale* (Reutlingen: Ensslin & Laiblin, n.d.), pp. 153–185.

in England (see Chapter 20). But breakthroughs in in-dustrial technology in the late eighteenth century enormously stimulated basic scientific inquiry as re-searchers sought to explain theoretically how such things as steam engines and blast furnaces actually worked. The result was an explosive growth of funda-mental scientific discoveries from the 1830s onward. In contrast to earlier periods, these theoretical discov-eries were increasingly transformed into material im-provements for the general population.

A perfect example of the translation of better scien-tific knowledge into practical human benefits was the work of Louis Pasteur and his followers in biology and the medical sciences (see page 723). Another was the development of the branch of physics known as **thermodynamics**. Building on Isaac Newton's laws of mechanics and on studies of steam engines, thermody-namics investigated the relationship between heat and mechanical energy. The law of conservation of energy held that different forms of energy—such as heat, elec-tricity, and magnetism—could be converted but nei-ther created nor destroyed. By midcentury, physicists had formulated the fundamental laws of thermodynam-ics, which were then applied to mechanical engineering, chemical processes, and many other fields.

Chemistry and electricity were two other fields characterized by extremely rapid scientific progress. And in both fields, "science was put in the service of industry," as the influential economist Alfred Marshall (1842–1924) argued at the time. Chemists devised ways of measuring the atomic weight of different elements, and in 1869 the Russian chemist Dmitri Mendeleev (mehn-duh-LAY-uhf) (1834–1907) codi-fied the rules of chemistry in the periodic law and the periodic table. Chemistry was subdivided into many specialized branches, including organic chemistry—the study of the compounds of carbon. Applying the-oretical insights gleaned from this new field, researchers in large German chemical companies dis-covered ways of transforming the dirty, useless coal tar that accumulated in coke ovens into beautiful, expen-sive synthetic dyes for the world of fashion. German production of synthetic dyes soared, and by 1900 German chemical companies controlled 90 percent of world production.

Electricity, a scientific curiosity in 1800, was totally transformed by a century of tremendous technological advancement. It became a commercial form of energy, first used in communications (the telegraph, which spurred quick international communication with the laying of underwater cables), then in electrochemistry (refining aluminum, for example), and finally in cen-tral power generation (for lighting, transportation, and industrial motors). And by 1890 the internal combus-tion engine fueled by petroleum was an emerging competitor to steam and electricity alike.

The successful application of scientific research in the fast-growing electrical and organic chemical indus-tries between 1880 and 1913 provided a model for other industries. Systematic "R&D"—research and development—was born in the late nineteenth cen-tury. Above all, the burst of industrial creativity and technological innovation, often called the **Second Industrial Revolution**, promoted the strong economic growth in the last third of the nineteenth century that drove the urban reforms and the rising standard of liv-ing considered in this chapter. (See "Thinking Like a Historian: The Promise of Electricity," page 746.)

The triumph of science and technology had three other significant consequences. First, though ordinary citizens continued to lack detailed scientific knowl-edge, everyday experience and innumerable articles in newspapers and magazines impressed the importance of science on the popular mind. Second, as science became more prominent in popular thinking, the philosophical implications of science formulated in the Enlightenment spread to broad sections of the population. Natural processes appeared to be deter-mined by rigid laws, leaving little room for either di-vine intervention or human will. Yet scientific and technical advances had also fed the Enlightenment's optimistic faith in human progress, which now ap-peared endless and automatic to growing numbers of people. Third, the methods of science acquired unri-valed prestige after 1850. For many, the union of care-ful experiment and abstract theory was the only reliable route to truth and objective reality. The "un-scientific" intuitions of poets and the revelations of saints seemed hopelessly inferior.

Darwin and Natural Selection

Scientific research also progressed rapidly outside of the world of industry and technology, sometimes putting forth direct challenges to traditional beliefs. In geology, for example, Charles Lyell (1797–1875) effectively dis-credited the long-standing view that the earth's surface had been formed by short-lived cataclysms, such as bib-lical floods and earthquakes. Instead, according to Lyell's principle of uniformitarianism, the same geo-logical processes that are at work today slowly formed the earth's surface over an immensely long time. The vast timescale required for the processes that Lyell de-scribed to have these effects undermined traditional beliefs about the age of the earth based on religious teachings. Similarly, the evolutionary view of biological development, first proposed by the Greek Anaximander

---

■ **thermodynamics** A branch of physics built on Newton's laws of mechanics that investigated the relationship between heat and mechanical energy.

■ **Second Industrial Revolution** The burst of industrial creativity and technological innovation that promoted strong economic growth in the last third of the nineteenth century.

The Promise of Electricity

The commercialization and widespread use of electricity around 1900 made possible a broad spectrum of new technologies in the late nineteenth century, including telephones and telegraphs; radio; electric lights in public and private space; electric railroads, trams, and subways; electrochemistry and electrometallurgy; power plants, generators, and batteries; and electric motors and machines. How did the arrival of electricity change people's lives?

1 **The Palace of Electricity, 1900 Universal Exhibition, Paris.** The ever-popular world fairs and expositions organized around the turn of the century typically included brightly lit pavilions dedicated to the wonders of electricity. At the top of the Palace of Electricity in Paris, the "Electric Fairy" held up a torch powered by 50,000 volts.

(From *Le Bon Marché* shop catalogue, 1900/Private Collection/Archives Charmet/Bridgeman Images)

(Russian Master State History Museum, Moscow, Russia/Fine Art Images/Getty Images)

2 **"Luks' — The Least Expensive and Brightest Lighting for All Occasions," ca. 1900.** This Russian poster advertising lighting systems from the Luks' (Deluxe) lighting company in Riga promotes "kerosene and incandescent lights and bulbs" and so marks a transitional period, when lighting companies encouraged consumers to switch from gas to electricity. The poster portrays a princess of light, holding an electric bulb that illuminates first the Russian Empire and then the rest of the globe. The small scene at the bottom shows the historic Tauride Palace in St. Petersburg and suggests the revolutionary effect of electric light in public spaces.

ANALYZING THE EVIDENCE

1. How did the commercialization of electricity reflect and/or contribute to the late-nineteenth-century faith in progress, rationalism, and reform?
2. What sort of research and development model did it take to electrify Europe? What sort of business model? How were the two connected?
3. Even in 1900, it was hard to predict that electricity would be more popular than gas or coal as a source for energy use at home or in the workplace. In Sources 1, 2, and 3, how do electricity's boosters strive to popularize the residential and commercial use of electricity?

3 "Electrical Progress in Great Britain During 1909."

An American journal for electricians offered glowing approval of the electrification of Great Britain. Along with the United States, Britain was a world leader in electrification around 1900; other European nations were not far behind.

〰The most noticeable and at the same time the most hopeful, feature of the year 1909 in the United Kingdom, has been the great progress made in bringing electricity within the compass of the "small man." This movement, which means so much for the future of all electrical industry, has occupied the close attention of a large proportion of the electricity works managers and engineers and of most manufacturing and importing businesses....

[T]he forward movement [of the filament lamp] is now in full swing. The wire lamp is everywhere working wonders in reducing the cost of electric lighting on existing installations and that fact together with the very strong support that is being given by other influences, is making it easier to get electrical applications adopted in many places where it seemed impossible before....

[The London power companies] are now jointly using the daily press in an advertising campaign so conducted as to command the attention of all who read, educating them as to the rightful claims of electricity. One of the companies has opened a model "Electric Home" in its area, fitted throughout with electric lighting, heating, and small power. The house is occupied by a tenant who is under special arrangement to admit the public between certain hours every day, to demonstrate to them the manifold domestic applications of electricity and their convenience and cleanliness. Neither coal nor gas is used for any purpose whatsoever in the house.... This popularizing work is still very necessary indeed, for really the public does not know yet much that it ought to know....

[The report then describes a number of technological advances, including newly built electric-generating plants, electric-powered steel mills, and the use of electric motors in a variety of industrial applications.]

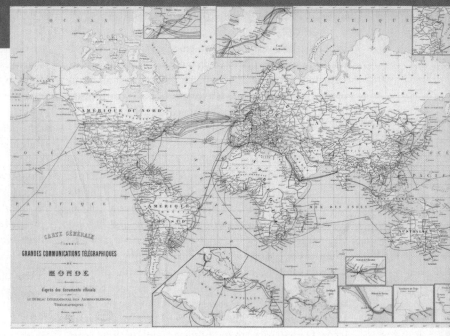

4 "General Map of Large-Scale World Telegraph Communications, 1901/03."

After some equipment failures, British and U.S. engineers successfully completed the first transatlantic telegraph cable, fired by electric current, in 1858. By 1900 telegraph cables circled the globe.
(Boston Public Library, Boston, Massachusetts, USA/Bridgeman Images)

5 Electric trams and lines in Piazza del Duomo, Milan, Italy, ca. 1900.

Electric streetcar and subway systems made quick travel through urban spaces accessible and inexpensive. In Milan, the tracks and streetcars, and the installation of electric streetlights, strike a modern contrast to the Gothic cathedral and Neoclassical triumphal arch that frame the central square.

(DEA Picture Library/Getty Images)

PUTTING IT ALL TOGETHER

Using the sources above, along with what you have learned in class, in Chapter 22, and in the sections on the Industrial Revolution in Chapter 17, write a short essay that describes the effects of electrification on European society. Was electricity a fundamental driving force in the history of Western society?

Sources: (3) Albert H. Bridge, "Electrical Progress in Great Britain in 1909," *Electrical Review and Western Electrician*, January 1, 1910, 17–19.

in the sixth century B.C.E., re-emerged in a more modern form in the work of French naturalist Jean-Baptiste Lamarck (1744–1829). Lamarck asserted that all forms of life had arisen through a long process of continuous adjustment to the environment, a dramatic challenge to the belief in divine creation of species.

Lamarck's work was flawed—he believed that the characteristics parents acquired in the course of their lives could be inherited by their children—and was not accepted, but it helped prepare the way for Charles Darwin (1809–1882), the most influential of all nineteenth-century evolutionary thinkers. As the official naturalist on a five-year scientific cruise to Latin America and the South Pacific beginning in 1831, Darwin carefully collected specimens of the different animal species he encountered on the voyage. Back in England, convinced by fossil evidence and by his friend Lyell that the earth and life on it were immensely ancient, Darwin came to doubt the general belief in a special divine creation of each species of animal. Instead, he concluded, all life had gradually evolved from a common ancestral origin in an unending "struggle for survival." After long hesitation, Darwin published his research, which immediately attracted wide attention.

Darwin's great originality lay in suggesting precisely how biological evolution might have occurred. His theory of **evolution** is summarized in the title of his work *On the Origin of Species by the Means of Natural Selection* (1859). Decisively influenced by the gloomy assertions of Thomas Malthus (MAL-thuhs) that populations naturally grow faster than their food supplies (see Chapter 20), Darwin argued that chance differences among the individual members of a given species help some survive while others die. Thus the variations that prove useful in the struggle for survival are selected naturally, and they gradually spread to the entire species through reproduction.

Darwin's controversial theory had a powerful and many-sided influence on European thought and the European middle classes. Because his ideas seemed to suggest that evolution moved along without God's intervention, and that humans were simply one species among many others, some conservatives accused Darwin of anti-Christian beliefs and mocked him for suggesting that humans descended from apes. Others hailed Darwin as the great scientist par excellence, the "Newton of biology," who had revealed once again the powers of objective science.

Some thinkers went a step further and applied Darwin's theory of biological evolution to human affairs. English philosopher Herbert Spencer (1820–1903) saw the human race as driven forward to ever-greater specialization and progress by a brutal economic struggle that determined the "survival of the fittest." The poor were the ill-fated weak; the prosperous were the chosen strong. Spencer's **Social Darwinism** gained adherents among nationalists, who viewed global competition between countries as a grand struggle for survival, as well as among imperialists, who used Social Darwinist ideas to justify the "natural" rule of the supposedly more civilized West over their colonial subjects and territories.

The Modern University and the Social Sciences

By the 1880s major universities across Europe had been modernized and professionalized. Education now emphasized controlled research projects in newly established clinics and laboratories; advanced students conducted independent research in seminar settings. An increasingly diversified professoriate established many of the academic departments still found in today's universities, from anthropology to zoology. In a striking development, faculty devoted to the newly instituted human or social sciences took their place alongside the hard sciences. Using critical methods often borrowed from natural science, social scientists studied massive sets of numerical data that governments had begun to collect on everything from birthrates to crime and from population to prostitution. Like Karl Marx, they were fascinated by the rise of capitalism and modernity; unlike Marx, they preferred to understand rather than revolutionize society.

Sociology, the critical analysis of contemporary or historical social groups, emerged as a leading social science. Perhaps the most prominent and influential late-nineteenth-century sociologist was the German Max Weber (1864–1920). In his most famous book, *The Protestant Ethic and the Spirit of Capitalism* (1890), Weber argued that the rise of capitalism was directly linked to Protestantism in northern Europe. Pointing to the early and successful modernization of countries like the Netherlands and England, he concluded that Protestantism gave religious approval to hard work, saving, and investing—the foundations for capitalist development—because worldly success was a sign of God's approval. This famous argument seriously challenged the basic ideas of Marxism: ideas, for Weber, were just as important as economics or class struggle in the rise of capitalism. Yet like Marx, Weber held a critical view of the rationalization of the human spirit, trapped in what he called the "iron cage" of capitalist relations. Modern industrial society, according to Weber, had turned people into "specialists without spirit, hedonists without heart." An ambitious scholar, Weber

---

■ **evolution** The idea, applied by thinkers in many fields, that stresses gradual change and continuous adjustment.

■ **Social Darwinism** A body of thought drawn from the ideas of Charles Darwin that applied the theory of biological evolution to human affairs and saw the human race as driven by an unending economic struggle that would determine the survival of the fittest.

■ **Realism** A literary movement that, in contrast to Romanticism, stressed the depiction of life as it actually was.

wrote extensively on capitalist rationalization, modern bureaucracy, industrialization and agriculture, and the forms of political leadership.

In France, the prolific sociologist Émile Durkheim (1858–1917) earned an international reputation for his wide-ranging work. His study of the psychic and social basis of religion, *The Elementary Forms of Religious Life* (1912), remains a classic of social-scientific thought. In his pioneering work of quantitative sociology, *Suicide* (1897), Durkheim concluded that ever-higher suicide rates were caused by widespread feelings of "anomie," or rootlessness. Because modern society had stripped life of all sense of tradition, purpose, and belonging, Durkheim believed, anomie was inescapable; only an entirely new moral order might offer some relief.

Other sociologists contributed to the critique of modern society. The German Ferdinand Tönnies (1855–1936) argued that with industrialization Western civilization had undergone a fundamental transformation from "community" to "society." Rationalized self-interest had replaced traditional values, leading to intensified alienation and a cold bureaucratic age. In *The Crowd* (1895), French sociologist Gustav Le Bon (1841–1931) wrote that the alienated masses were prone to gathering in mass crowds, in which individuals lost control over their emotions and actions.

According to the deeply conservative Le Bon, a strong, charismatic leader could easily manipulate the crowd's collective psyche and turn the servile mass into a violent and dangerous revolutionary mob.

The new sociologists cast a bleak light on urban industrial society. While they acknowledged some benefits of rationalization and modernization, they bemoaned the accompanying loss of community and tradition. In some ways, their diagnosis of the modern individual as an isolated atom suffering from anomie and desperately seeking human connection was chillingly prescient: the powerful Communist and Fascist movements that swept through Europe after World War I seemed to win popular support precisely by offering ordinary people a renewed sense of social belonging.

Realism in Art and Literature

In art and literature, the key themes of **Realism** emerged in the 1840s and continued to dominate Western culture until the 1890s. Realist artists and writers believed that artistic works should depict life exactly as it was. Forsaking the personal, emotional viewpoint of the Romantics for strict, supposedly factual objectivity, the Realists observed and recorded the world around them—often to expose the sordid reality of modern life.

Realism in the Arts   Realist depictions of gritty everyday life challenged the Romantic emphasis on nature and the emotions, as well as the Neoclassical focus on famous men and grand events. French painter Honoré Daumier's *The Third-Class Carriage*, completed in 1864, is a famous example of Realism in the arts that portrays the effects of industrialization in the mid-nineteenth century. In muted colors, Daumier's painting captures the grinding poverty and weariness of the poor but also lends a sense of dignity to their humble lives. (Metropolitan Museum of Art, New York, USA/Bridgeman Images)

Émile Zola and Realism in Literature

"There should no longer be any school, no more formulas, no standards of any sort; there is only life itself, an immense field where each may study and create as he likes," wrote Émile Zola in 1867. The great Realist author applied these precepts in the opening lines of his 1885 masterpiece novel, Germinal, *which championed the rights of French coal miners in the late nineteenth century.*

Over the open plain, beneath a starless sky as dark and thick as ink, a man walked alone along the highway from Marchiennes to Montsou, a straight paved road ten kilometres in length, intersecting the beetroot-fields. He could not even see the black soil before him, and only felt the immense flat horizon by the gusts of March wind, squalls as strong as on the sea, and frozen from sweeping leagues of marsh and naked earth. No tree could be seen against the sky, and the road unrolled as straight as a pier in the midst of the blinding spray of darkness.

The man had set out from Marchiennes about two o'clock. He walked with long strides, shivering beneath his worn cotton jacket and corduroy breeches. A small parcel tied in a check handkerchief troubled him much, and he pressed it against his side, sometimes with one elbow, sometimes with the other, so that he could slip to the bottom of his pockets both the benumbed hands that bled beneath the lashes of the wind. A single idea occupied his head—the empty head of a workman without work and without lodging—the hope that the cold would be less keen after sunrise. For an hour he went on thus, when on the left, two kilometres from Montsou, he saw red flames, three fires burning in the open air and apparently suspended. At first he hesitated, half afraid. Then he could not resist the painful need to warm his hands for a moment. . . .

Suddenly, at a bend in the road, the fires reappeared close to him, though he could not understand how they burnt so high in the dead sky, like smoky moons. But on the level soil another sight had struck him. It was a heavy mass, a low pile of buildings from which rose the silhouette of a factory chimney; occasional gleams appeared from dirty windows, five or six melancholy lanterns were hung outside to frames of blackened wood, which vaguely outlined the profiles of gigantic stages; and from this fantastic apparition, drowned in night and smoke, a single voice arose, the thick, long breathing of a steam escapement that could not be seen.

Then the man recognized a [mine] pit. His despair returned. What was the good? There would be no work. Instead of turning towards the buildings he decided at last to ascend the pit bank, on which burnt in iron baskets the three coal fires which gave light and warmth for work. The labourers in the cutting must have been working late; they were still throwing out the useless rubbish. . . . He could distinguish living shadows tipping over the trains or tubs near each fire.

EVALUATE THE EVIDENCE

1. Zola claimed to represent "only life itself," but the vivid description in his prose often creates heavily dramatized effects, as in this selection. Why does Zola use such deeply poetic imagery?

2. How do the style and subject matter of Realism compare and contrast with those of Romanticism?

Source: Émile Zola, *Germinal*, trans. Havelock Ellis (London: Everyman's Library, 1894).

Emphatically rejecting the Romantic search for the exotic and the sublime, Realism (or "Naturalism," as it was often called) energetically pursued the typical and the commonplace. Beginning with a dissection of the middle classes, from which most of them sprang, many Realists eventually focused on the working classes, especially the urban working classes, which had been neglected in imaginative literature before this time. The Realists put a microscope to many unexplored and taboo subjects, including sex, labor strikes, violence, and alcoholism, and hastened to report that slums and factories teemed with savage behavior. Shocked middle-class critics denounced Realism as ugly sensationalism wrapped provocatively in pseudoscientific declarations and crude language—even as the movement attracted a growing middle-class audience, fascinated by the sensationalist view "from below."

The Realist movement began in France, where Romanticism had never been completely dominant. Artists like Gustave Courbet, Jean-François Millet, and Honoré Daumier painted scenes of laboring workers and peasants in somber colors and simple compositions, exemplified in Daumier's 1864 painting *The Third-Class Carriage* (see page 749). Daumier's art championed the simple virtues of the working class and lampooned the greed and ill will of the rich bourgeoisie; a caricature of King Louis Philippe earned him six months in prison.

Literary Realism also began in France, where Honoré de Balzac, Gustave Flaubert, and Émile Zola became internationally famous novelists. Balzac (1799–1850) spent thirty years writing a vastly ambitious panorama of postrevolutionary French life. Known collectively as *The Human Comedy*, this series of nearly one hundred stories, novels, and essays vividly portrays more than two thousand characters from virtually all sectors of French society. Balzac pictured urban society as grasping, amoral, and brutal. In his novel *Father Goriot* (1835), the hero, a poor student from the provinces, eventually surrenders his idealistic integrity to feverish ambition and society's pervasive greed.

Madame Bovary (1857), the masterpiece of Flaubert (floh-BEHR) (1821–1880), is far narrower in scope than Balzac's work but is still famous for its depth of psychological insight and critique of middle-class values. Unsuccessfully prosecuted as an outrage against public morality and religion, Flaubert's carefully crafted novel tells the ordinary, even banal, story of a frustrated middle-class housewife who has an adulterous love affair and is betrayed by her lover. Without moralizing, Flaubert portrays the provincial middle class as petty, smug, and hypocritical.

Émile Zola (1840–1902) was most famous for his seamy, animalistic view of working-class life. But he also wrote gripping, carefully researched stories featuring the stock exchange, the big department store, and the army, as well as urban slums and bloody battles between police and sturdy coal strikers. Like many later Realists, Zola sympathized with socialism, a view evident in his overpowering novel *Germinal* (1885). (See "Evaluating the Evidence 22.3: Émile Zola and Realism in Literature," at left.)

Realism quickly spread beyond France. In England, Mary Ann Evans (1819–1880), who wrote under the pen name George Eliot, brilliantly achieved a more deeply felt, less sensational kind of Realism in her great novel *Middlemarch: A Study of Provincial Life* (1871–1872). The novels of Thomas Hardy (1840–1928), such as *Tess of the D'Urbervilles* (1891) and *The Return of the Native* (1878), depict ordinary men and women frustrated and crushed by social prejudice, sexual puritanism, and bad luck. The greatest Russian Realist, Count

Leo Tolstoy (1828–1910), combined Realism in description and character development with an atypical moralizing, especially in his later work. In *War and Peace* (1864–1869), a monumental novel set against the background of Napoleon's invasion of Russia in 1812, Tolstoy developed his fatalistic theory of human history, which regards free will as an illusion and the achievements of even the greatest leaders as only the channeling of historical necessity. Yet Tolstoy's central message is one that most of the people discussed in this chapter would have readily accepted: human love, trust, and everyday family ties are life's enduring values.

NOTES

1. S. Marcus, "Reading the Illegible," in *The Victorian City: Images and Realities*, ed. H. J. Dyos and Michael Wolff, vol. 1 (London: Routledge & Kegan Paul, 1973), p. 266.
2. Quoted in E. Chadwick, *Report on the Sanitary Condition of the Labouring Population of Great Britain*, ed. M. W. Flinn (Edinburgh: University of Edinburgh Press, 1965; original publication, 1842), pp. 315–316.
3. J. McKay, *Tramways and Trolleys: The Rise of Urban Mass Transport in Europe* (Princeton, N.J.: Princeton University Press, 1976), p. 81.
4. Quoted in R. P. Neuman, "The Sexual Question and Social Democracy in Imperial Germany," *Journal of Social History* 7 (Winter 1974): 276.
5. Quoted in J. A. Banks, "The Contagion of Numbers," in *The Victorian City: Images and Realities*, ed. H. J. Dyos and Michael Wolff, vol. 1 (London: Routledge & Kegan Paul, 1973), p. 112.
6. Quoted in R. Roberts, *The Classic Slum: Salford Life in the First Quarter of the Century* (Manchester, U.K.: University of Manchester Press, 1971), p. 95.
7. J. Frykman and O. Löfgren, *Culture Builders: A Historical Anthropology of Middle-Class Life* (New Brunswick, N.J.: Rutgers University Press, 1987), p. 134.
8. See the pioneering work of J. de Vries, *The Industrious Revolution: Consumer Behavior and the Household Economy* (Cambridge: Cambridge University Press, 2008), especially pp. 186–237.
9. Roberts, *The Classic Slum*, p. 35.
10. Quoted in T. Zeldin, *France, 1848–1945*, vol. 1 (Oxford: Clarendon Press, 1973), p. 328.
11. Quoted in Neuman, "The Sexual Question," p. 281.
12. Frykman and Löfgren, *Culture Builders*, p. 114.

LOOKING BACK LOOKING AHEAD

When the peoples of northwestern Europe looked out at the economic and social landscape in the early twentieth century, they had good reason to feel that the promise of the Industrial Revolution was being realized. The dark days of urban squalor and brutal working hours had given way after 1850 to a gradual rise in the standard of living for all classes. Scientific discoveries were combining with the applied technology of public health and industrial production to save lives and drive continued economic growth.

Moreover, social and economic advances seemed to be matched by progress in the political sphere. The years following the dramatic failure of the revolutions of 1848 saw the creation of unified nation-states in Italy and Germany, and after 1870, as we shall see in the following chapters, nationalism and the nation-state reigned in Europe. Although the rise of nationalism created tensions among the European countries, these tensions would not explode until 1914 and the outbreak of the First World War. Instead, the most aggressive and destructive aspects of European nationalism found their initial outlet in the final and most powerful surge of Western overseas expansion. Thus Europe, transformed by industrialization and nationalism, rushed after 1875 to seize territory and build new or greatly expanded authoritarian empires in Asia and Africa.

Make Connections

Think about the larger developments and continuities within and across chapters.

1. What were the most important changes in everyday life from the eighteenth century (Chapter 18) to the nineteenth century? What main causes or agents drove these changes?

2. Did the life of ordinary people improve, stay the same, or even deteriorate over the nineteenth century when compared to the previous century? What role did developments in science, medicine, and urban planning play in this process?

3. How did the emergence of a society divided into working and middle classes affect the workplace, homemaking, and family values and gender roles?

22 REVIEW & EXPLORE

Identify Key Terms

Identify and explain the significance of each item below.

utilitarianism (p. 722)	suffrage movement (p. 743)
germ theory (p. 723)	thermodynamics (p. 745)
labor aristocracy (p. 731)	Second Industrial Revolution (p. 745)
sweated industries (p. 734)	evolution (p. 748)
companionate marriage (p. 736)	Social Darwinism (p. 748)
separate spheres (p. 739)	Realism (p. 749)

Review the Main Ideas

Answer the focus questions from each section of the chapter.

- How did urban life change in the nineteenth century? (p. 720)
- What did the emergence of urban industrial society mean for rich and poor and those in between? (p. 727)
- How did urbanization affect family life and gender roles? (p. 736)
- How and why did intellectual life change in this period? (p. 743)

Suggested Reading and Media Resources

BOOKS

- Barnes, David S. *The Great Stink of Paris and the Nineteenth-Century Struggle Against Filth and Germs.* 2006. An outstanding introduction to sanitary developments and attitudes toward public health.
- Cioc, Mark. *The Rhine: An Eco-Biography, 1815–2000.* 2002. An environmental history focused on the Rhine River, Europe's most important commercial waterway.
- Coontz, Stephanie. *Marriage, a History: From Obedience to Intimacy, or How Love Conquered Marriage.* 2005. A lively investigation of the historical background to current practice.
- Davidoff, Leonore, and Catherine Hall. *Family Fortunes: Men and Women of the English Middle Class, 1780–1850.* 1991. A groundbreaking classic that places gender at the center of the construction of middle-class values, lifestyles, and livelihoods.
- De Vries, Jan. *The Industrious Revolution: Consumer Behavior and the Household Economy, 1850 to the Present.* 2008. A major interpretative analysis focusing on married couples and their strategies.
- Kelly, Alfred. *The German Worker: Working-Class Autobiographies from the Age of Industrialization.* 1987. A superb collection of firsthand, primary-source accounts of working-class life, with an excellent introduction on German workers in general.
- Koven, Seth. *Slumming: Sexual and Social Politics in Victorian London.* 2006. A provocative, in-depth account of middle-class encounters with the London working class in the late nineteenth century.
- Maynes, Mary Jo. *Taking the Hard Road: Life Course in French and German Workers' Biographies in the Era of Industrialization.* 1995. Includes fascinating stories that provide insight into how workers saw themselves.
- Perrot, Michelle, ed. *A History of Private Life.* 1990. A fascinating multivolume and multiauthor work that puts private life and family at the center of historical investigation.
- Walkowitz, Judith. *Prostitution and Victorian Society: Women, Class, and the State.* 1980. This important work changed the way historians think about sexuality and prostitution in the second half of the nineteenth century.
- Weiner, Jonathan. *The Beak of the Finch: The Story of Evolution in Our Time.* 1994. A prize-winning, highly readable account of Darwin and evolution.

DOCUMENTARIES

- *Charles Darwin and the Tree of Life* (BBC, 2009). Marking the bicentennial of Darwin's birth, the BBC produced this television documentary about Charles Darwin and his important theory of evolution.
- *George Eliot: A Scandalous Life* (BBC, 2002). A documentary about the life of Mary Ann Evans, who wrote under the pen name George Eliot.
- *Great Russian Writers: Leo Tolstoy* (Kultur Video, 2006). A short documentary about the life and work of Leo Tolstoy.

FEATURE FILMS

- *Anna Karenina* (Joe Wright, 2012). Based on Leo Tolstoy's famous novel, the film focuses on Anna Karenina's affair with Count Vronsky.
- *Germinal* (Claude Berri, 1993). Nineteenth-century coal miners in northern France go on strike in response to repression by the authorities in this film based on Émile Zola's classic Realist novel.
- *Madame Bovary* (Tim Fywell, 2000). A frustrated middle-class housewife named Emma Bovary has an adulterous love affair in this film adaptation of Gustave Flaubert's novel.
- *The Story of Louis Pasteur* (William Dieterle, 1936). A dramatized biography of Louis Pasteur, the French chemist who developed the germ theory.

WEB SITES

- *Cholera and the Thames.* A captivating Web site where one can learn about the problem of cholera in London in the nineteenth century. Includes essays, games, educational resources, and a gallery of images related to the topic. **www.choleraandthethames.co.uk/**
- *Haussmann.* An overview of the life of Georges Haussmann and his transformation of Paris from 1858 to 1870. **gallery.sjsu.edu/paris/architecture/Haussmann.html**
- *History of Contraception: Nineteenth Century.* A discussion of contraception, abortion, and other issues surrounding sexuality in the nineteenth century. **www.glowm.com/?p=glowm.cml/section_view&articleid=375#21001**
- *The Literature Network: Realism.* An extended essay about Realism in literature. The site also has biographies and links to works by several Realist authors, including Balzac, Eliot, Flaubert, Hardy, Tolstoy, and Zola. **www.online-literature.com/periods/realism.php**

23

The Age of Nationalism

1850–1914

In the years that followed the revolutions of 1848, Western society progressively developed, for better or worse, an effective organizing principle capable of coping with the many-sided challenges of the unfinished industrial and political revolutions and the emerging urban society. That principle was nationalism—mass identification with the nation-state. Just as industrialization and urbanization had brought vast changes to class relations, family lifestyles, and science and culture, the triumph of nationalism remade territorial boundaries and forged new relations between the nation-state and its citizens.

The rise of nationalism and the nation-state, enormously significant historical developments, was by no means completely predictable. Nationalism had been a powerful force since at least 1789, but the goal of creating independent nation-states, inhabited by people sharing a common ethnicity, language, history, and territory, had repeatedly failed, most spectacularly in the revolutions of 1848. By 1914, however, most Europeans lived in nation-states, and the ideology of nationalism had become an almost universal faith in the Western world. The governments of the new nation-states took various forms, from conservative authoritarianism to parliamentary monarchy to liberal republicanism. Whatever the political system, in most cases the nation-state became increasingly responsive to the needs of its people, opening the political franchise and offering citizens at least rudimentary social and economic benefits. At the same time, the nation-state demanded more from its citizens, most obviously in the form of rising income taxes and universal military service. Nationalism, which before 1848 appealed primarily to liberals seeking political reform or national independence, became an ever more conservative ideology. At its worst, populists and fanatics eagerly manipulated and sometimes abused the growing patriotism of ordinary people to justify exclusionary policies against Jews and other ethnic minorities, and to promote expansionary projects in overseas colonies. ▪

CHAPTER PREVIEW

Life in the Age of Nationalism
Conscripts in an Italian village cheer a speech by a local dignitary as a soldier bids farewell to his family before joining the army in the field. This portrait pays homage to the Italian peasant, willing to fight for his newborn country. This idealized scene depicts the changing relationship between state and citizen, as nationalism came to predominate at all levels of society. (By Gerolamo Induno [1825–1890], [oil on canvas]/Civico Museo del Risorgimento, Milano, Italy/De Agostini Picture Library/Alfredo Dagli Orti/Bridgeman Images)

Napoleon III in France

FOCUS QUESTION *How did Napoleon III seek to reconcile popular and conservative forces in an authoritarian nation-state?*

Early nationalism was generally liberal and idealistic and could be democratic and radical (see Chapter 21). Yet nationalism also flourished in authoritarian states, which imposed social and economic changes from above. Napoleon Bonaparte's France had already combined national feeling with authoritarian rule. Napoleon's nephew, Louis Napoleon, revived and extended this combination.

France's Second Republic

Although Louis Napoleon Bonaparte had played no part in French politics before 1848, universal male suffrage and widespread popular support gave him three times as many votes as the four other presidential candidates combined in the French presidential election of December 1848. This outcome occurred for several reasons. First, he had the great name of his uncle, whom romantics had transformed into a demigod after 1820. Second, as Karl Marx stressed at the time, middle-class and peasant property owners feared the socialist challenge of urban workers and the chaos of the revolution of 1848, and they wanted a tough ruler to protect their property and provide stability. Third, Louis Napoleon enunciated a positive program for France in pamphlets widely circulated before the election.

Above all, Louis Napoleon promoted a vision of national unity and social progress. He believed that the government should represent the people and help them economically. But how could these tasks be accomplished? Corrupt parliaments and political parties were not the answer, according to Louis Napoleon. French politicians represented special-interest groups, particularly middle-class ones. The answer was a strong, even authoritarian, national leader, like the first Napoleon, whose efforts to provide jobs and stimulate the economy would serve all people, rich and poor. This leader would be linked to each citizen by direct democracy, his sovereignty uncorrupted by politicians and legislative bodies. To the many common people who voted for him, Louis Napoleon appeared to be a strong leader and a forward-looking champion of popular interests.

Elected to a four-year term by an overwhelming majority, Louis Napoleon was required by the constitution to share power with the National Assembly, which was overwhelmingly conservative. With some misgivings, he signed conservative-sponsored bills that

Paris in the Second Empire The flash and glitter of unprecedented prosperity in the Second Empire come alive in this vibrant contemporary painting. Writers and intellectuals chat with elegant women and trade witticisms with financiers and government officials at the Café Tortoni, a favorite rendezvous for fashionable society. Horse-drawn omnibuses with open top decks mingle with cabs and private carriages on the broad new boulevard. (Musée de la Ville de Paris, Musée Carnavalet, Paris, France/Bridgeman Images)

increased greatly the role of the Catholic Church in primary and secondary education and deprived many poor people of the right to vote. He took these steps in hopes that the Assembly would vote funds to pay his personal debts and change the constitution so he could run for a second term.

But in 1851, after the Assembly failed to cooperate with that last aim, Louis Napoleon began to conspire with key army officers. On December 2, 1851, he illegally dismissed the legislature and seized power in a coup d'état. There was some armed resistance in Paris and widespread insurrection in the countryside in southern France, but the army crushed these popular protests. Restoring universal male suffrage and claiming to stand above political bickering, Louis Napoleon called on the French people, as the first Napoleon had done, to legalize his actions. They did: 92 percent voted to make him president for ten years. A year later, in a plebiscite, 97 percent voted to make him hereditary emperor.

Chronology

1839–1876	Western-style Tanzimat reforms in Ottoman Empire
1852–1870	Reign of Napoleon III in France
1859–1870	Unification of Italy
1861	Freeing of Russian serfs
1861–1865	U.S. Civil War
1866	Austro-Prussian War
1870–1871	Franco-Prussian War; unification of Germany
1870–1878	Kulturkampf, Bismarck's attack on Catholic Church
1873	Stock market crash spurs renewed anti-Semitism, beginning in central and eastern Europe
1880s	Educational reforms in France create a secular public school system
1880s–1890s	Widespread return to protectionism among European states
1883	First social security laws to help workers in Germany
1890–1900	Witte initiates second surge of Russian industrialization
1905	Revolution in Russia
1906–1914	Social reform in Great Britain
1908	Young Turks seize power in Ottoman Empire

Napoleon III's Second Empire

Louis Napoleon—now proclaimed Emperor Napoleon III—experienced both success and failure between 1852 and 1870, when he fell from power. In the 1850s his policies led to economic growth. His government promoted the new investment banks and massive railroad construction that were at the heart of the Industrial Revolution on the continent (see Chapter 20). It fostered general economic expansion through an ambitious program of public works, which included rebuilding Paris to improve the urban environment (see Chapter 22). The profits of business owners soared, rising wages of workers outpaced inflation, and unemployment declined greatly.

Initially, Louis Napoleon's hope that economic progress would reduce social and political tensions was at least partially realized. Until the mid-1860s he enjoyed support from France's most dissatisfied group, the urban workers. Government regulation of pawnshops and support for credit unions and better working-class housing were evidence of helpful reform in the 1850s. In the 1860s Louis Napoleon granted workers the right to form unions and the right to strike—important economic rights denied by earlier governments.

At first, political power remained in the hands of the emperor. He alone chose his ministers, who had great freedom of action. At the same time, Louis Napoleon restricted but did not abolish the newly reformed Assembly. Members were elected by universal male suffrage every six years, and Louis Napoleon and his government took these elections very seriously. They tried to entice notable people, even those who had opposed the regime, to stand as government candidates in order to expand the base of support. Moreover, the government used its officials and appointed mayors to spread the word that election of the government's candidates—and defeat of the opposition—would provide roads, tax rebates, and a thousand other local benefits.

In 1857 and again in 1863, Louis Napoleon's system worked brilliantly and produced overwhelming electoral victories for government-backed candidates. In the 1860s, however, this electoral system gradually disintegrated. A sincere nationalist, Napoleon had wanted to reorganize Europe on the principle of nationality and gain influence and territory for France and himself in the process. Instead, problems in Italy and the rising power of Prussia led to increasing criticism at home from his Catholic and nationalist supporters. With increasing effectiveness, the middle-class liberals who had always wanted a less authoritarian regime denounced his rule.

Napoleon was always sensitive to the public mood. Public opinion, he once said, always wins the last victory, and he responded to critics with progressive liberalization. He gave the Assembly greater powers and opposition candidates greater freedom, which they used to good advantage. In 1869 the opposition, consisting of republicans, monarchists, and liberals, polled almost 45 percent of the vote.

The next year, a sick and weary Louis Napoleon again granted France a new constitution, which combined a basically parliamentary regime with a hereditary emperor as chief of state. In a final plebiscite on the eve of the disastrous war with Prussia (see page 763), 7.5 million Frenchmen approved the new constitution—only 1.5 million opposed it. Napoleon III's successful attempt to reconcile a strong central state with universal male suffrage showed that nationalism was compatible with authoritarian government, even as France moved in an increasingly democratic direction.

Nation Building in Italy, Germany, and the United States

FOCUS QUESTION *How did conflict and war lead to the construction of strong nation-states in Italy, Germany, and the United States?*

Louis Napoleon's triumph in 1848 and his authoritarian rule in the 1850s provided the old ruling classes of Europe with a new model in politics. Would the expanding urban middle classes and even portions of the working classes rally to a strong, conservative national state that promised economic growth, social benefits, and national unity, as in France? This was one of the great political questions in the 1850s and 1860s. In Europe, the national unification of Italy and Germany offered a resounding answer. In the United States, nation building marked by sectional differences over slavery offered another.

Italy to 1850

Before 1850 Italy had never been united. The Italian peninsula was divided in the Middle Ages into competing city-states. A battleground for the Great Powers after 1494, Italy was reorganized in 1815 at the Congress of Vienna into a hodgepodge of different states. Austrian foreign minister Prince Klemens von Metternich captured the essence of the situation when

he dismissed Italy as only "a geographical expression" (Map 23.1).

Between 1815 and 1848 the goal of a unified Italian nation captured the imaginations of many Italians. There were three basic approaches. First, the radical and idealistic patriot Giuseppe Mazzini called for a centralized democratic republic based on universal male suffrage and the will of the people. (See "Evaluating the Evidence 23.1: The Struggle for the Italian Nation," page 760.) Second, Vincenzo Gioberti, a Catholic priest, sought a federation of existing states under the presidency of a progressive pope. The third approach centered on Victor Emmanuel II, the autocratic king of Sardinia-Piedmont. Many Italians sought a federation under this prominent king, much as Germans looked to Prussia for national leadership. It helped that Piedmont was one of the most industrialized, modern territories in the Italian peninsula.

The third alternative was strengthened by the failures of 1848, when Austria smashed Mazzini's republicanism. Victor Emmanuel II, crowned in 1849, retained the liberal constitution granted by his father under duress the previous year. This constitution combined a strong monarchy with a fair degree of civil liberties and parliamentary government, though deputies were elected by a limited franchise based on income. To some of the Italian middle classes, the Kingdom of Sardinia-Piedmont appeared to be a liberal, progressive state ideally suited to drive Austria out of northern Italy and lead a united Italy. By contrast, Mazzini's brand of democratic republicanism seemed quixotic and too radical.

As for the papacy, the initial cautious support for unification under Pope Pius IX (pontificate 1846–1878) had given way to hostility after he was temporarily driven from Rome during the upheavals of 1848. For a long generation, the papacy opposed not only national unification but also most modern trends. In 1864 in the *Syllabus of Errors*, Pius IX denounced rationalism, socialism, separation of church and state, and religious liberty. The Catholic Church would be a bulwark against liberalism and progressive reform for the next two decades.

Cavour and Garibaldi in Italy

The struggle for Italian unification under Emmanuel II was supported by a brilliant statesman, Count Camillo Benso di Cavour (kuh-VOOR), who served as prime minister of the Sardinia-Piedmont from 1852 until his death in 1861. A nobleman who made a substantial fortune in business before entering politics, Cavour had limited and realistic national goals. Until 1859 he sought unity only with the states of northern and perhaps central Italy, which would nonetheless greatly expand the existing kingdom.

In the 1850s Cavour worked to consolidate Sardinia-Piedmont as a liberal constitutional state capable of leading northern Italy. His program of building highways and railroads, expanding civil liberties, and opposing clerical privilege increased support for his efforts throughout northern Italy. Yet Cavour realized that Sardinia-Piedmont could not drive Austria out of the north without the help of a powerful ally. Accordingly, he established a secret alliance with Napoleon III against Austria in July 1858.

Cavour then goaded Austria into attacking Piedmont in 1859, and Louis Napoleon came to Italy's defense. After defeating the Austrians at the Battles of Magenta and Solferino, however, Napoleon did a sudden about-face. Worried by criticism from French Catholics for supporting the pope's declared enemy, he abandoned Cavour and made a compromise peace with the Austrians in July 1859. The Kingdom of Sardinia-Piedmont received only Lombardy, the area around Milan, from Austria. The rest of Italy remained essentially unchanged.

Yet the skillful maneuvers of Cavour's allies in the moderate nationalist movement salvaged his plans for Italian unification. While the war against Austria raged in the north, pro-unification nationalists in Tuscany and elsewhere in central Italy encouraged popular revolts that easily toppled their ruling princes. Using and controlling this popular enthusiasm, middle-class nationalist leaders in central Italy called for fusion with Sardinia-Piedmont. This was not at all what the Great Powers wanted, but the nationalists held firm. In early 1860, Cavour regained Napoleon III's support by ceding Savoy and Nice to France. The people of central Italy then voted overwhelmingly to join a greatly enlarged kingdom under Victor Emmanuel. Cavour had achieved his original goal, a united northern Italian state (see Map 23.1).

For superpatriots such as Giuseppe Garibaldi (1807–1882), however, the job of unification was only half done. The son of a poor sailor, Garibaldi personified the romantic, revolutionary nationalism and republicanism of Mazzini and 1848. Leading a corps of volunteers against Austria in 1859, Garibaldi emerged in 1860 as an independent force in Italian politics.

MAP 23.1 The Unification of Italy, 1859–1870
The leadership of Sardinia-Piedmont, nationalist fervor, and Garibaldi's attack on the Kingdom of the Two Sicilies were decisive factors in the unification of Italy.

The Struggle for the Italian Nation

The leading prophet of Italian nationalism and unification before 1848, Giuseppe Mazzini founded a secret society called Young Italy to fight for the unification of the Italian states in a democratic republic. This selection, from the chapter "Duties Towards Your Country" in Mazzini's best-known work, The Duties of Man *(1858), was addressed to Italian workingmen.*

~

Your first Duties . . . are to Humanity. . . . But what can each of you, with his isolated powers, do for the moral improvement, for the progress of Humanity? . . .

God gave you the means of multiplying your forces and your powers of action indefinitely when he gave you a Country, when, like a wise overseer of labor, who distributes the different parts of the work according to the capacity of the workmen, he divided Humanity into distinct groups upon the face of our globe, and thus planted the seeds of nations. Evil governments have disfigured the design of God, which you may see clearly marked out, as far, at least, as regards Europe, by the courses of the great rivers, by the lines of the lofty mountains, and by other geographical conditions; they have disfigured it by conquest, by greed, by jealousy of the just sovereignty of others; disfigured it so much that today there is perhaps no nation except England and France whose confines correspond to this design.

[These evil governments] did not, and they do not, recognize any country except their own families and dynasties, the egoism of caste. But the divine design will infallibly be fulfilled. Natural divisions, the innate spontaneous tendencies of the peoples will replace the arbitrary divisions sanctioned by evil governments. The map of Europe will be remade. The Countries of the People will rise, defined by the voice of the free, upon the ruins of the Countries of Kings and privileged castes. Between these Countries there will be harmony and brotherhood. And then the work of Humanity for the general amelioration, for the discovery and application of the real law of life, carried on in association and distributed according to local capacities, will be accomplished by peaceful and progressive development.

Then each of you, strong in the affections and in the aid of many millions of men speaking the same language, endowed with the same tendencies, and educated by the same historic tradition, may hope by your personal effort to benefit the whole of Humanity.

Without Country you have neither name, voice, nor rights, no admission as brothers into the fellowship of the Peoples. You are the bastards of Humanity. Soldiers without a banner, . . . you will find neither faith nor protection. . . . Do not beguile yourselves with the hope of emancipation from unjust social conditions if you do not first conquer a Country for yourselves; where there is no Country there is no common agreement to which you can appeal; the egoism of self-interest rules alone, and he who has the upper hand keeps it, since there is no common safeguard for the interests of all.

EVALUATE THE EVIDENCE

1. What, according to Mazzini, are the sources of national belonging? What role does religion play in his account? Would you label Mazzini a liberal nationalist?
2. How do Mazzini's ideas on nationhood compare to those of Ernest Renan (see page 780)?

Source: G. Mazzini, *The Duties of Man and Other Essays* (London: J. M. Dent and Sons, 1907), pp. 51–54.

Partly to use him and partly to get rid of him, Cavour secretly supported Garibaldi's bold plan to "liberate" the Kingdom of the Two Sicilies. Landing in Sicily in May 1860, Garibaldi's guerrilla band of a thousand **Red Shirts** captured the imagination of the peasantry, who rose in bloody rebellion against their landlords. Outwitting the twenty-thousand-man royal army, the guerrilla leader won battles, gained volunteers, and took Palermo. Then Garibaldi and his men crossed to the mainland, marched triumphantly toward Naples, and prepared to attack Rome and the pope. The wily Cavour quickly sent Sardinian forces to occupy most of the Papal States (but not Rome) and to intercept Garibaldi.

Cavour realized that an attack on Rome would bring war with France, and he feared Garibaldi's radicalism and popular appeal. He immediately organized a plebiscite in the conquered territories. Despite the urging of some radical supporters, the patriotic Garibaldi did not oppose Cavour, and the people of the south voted to join the kingdom of Sardinia. When Garibaldi and Victor Emmanuel II rode together through Naples to cheering crowds in October 1860, they symbolically sealed the union of north and south, of monarch and nation-state.

Cavour had successfully controlled Garibaldi and turned popular nationalism in a conservative direction. The new kingdom of Italy, which expanded to

Garibaldi and Victor Emmanuel II   The historic 1860 meeting in Naples between the leader of Italy's revolutionary nationalists and the king of Sardinia sealed the unification of northern and southern Italy. With the sleeve of his red shirt showing, Garibaldi offers his hand — and his conquests — to the uniformed king and his moderate monarchical government. The idealized patriotism evident in this painting, completed in 1866, testifies to the growing appeal of popular nationalism. (Detail, fresco, 1886, by Pietro Aldi [1852–1888]/Palazzo Pubblico, Siena, Italy/Bridgeman Images)

include Venice in 1866 and Rome in 1870, was a parliamentary monarchy under Victor Emmanuel II, neither radical nor fully democratic. Only a half million out of 22 million Italians had the right to vote, and the propertied classes and the common people remained divided. A great and growing social and cultural gap also separated the progressive, industrializing north from the stagnant, agrarian south. The new Italy was united on paper, but profound divisions remained.

Growing Austro-Prussian Rivalry

In the aftermath of 1848 the German states were locked in a political stalemate. After Austria and Russia blocked Prussian king Friedrich Wilhelm IV's attempt in 1850 to unify Germany, tension grew between Austria and Prussia as they struggled to dominate the German Confederation (see Chapter 21).

Economic differences exacerbated this rivalry. Austria had not been included in the German Customs Union, or *Zollverein* (TZOLE-fur-ayne), when it was founded

in 1834 to stimulate trade and increase state revenues. By the end of 1853 Austria was the only state in the German Confederation outside the union. As middle-class and business groups profited from participation in the Zollverein, Prussia's leading role within the customs union gave it a valuable advantage in its struggle against Austria.

Prussia had emerged from the upheavals of 1848 with a weak parliament, which was in the hands of the wealthy liberal middle class by 1859. Longing for national unification, these middle-class representatives wanted to establish once and for all that the parliament, not the king, held ultimate political power, including control of the army. At the same time, the national uprising in Italy in 1859 made a profound impression on Prussia's tough-minded Wilhelm I (r. 1861–1888). Convinced that great political change and war — perhaps with Austria, perhaps with France —

■ **Red Shirts** The guerrilla army of Giuseppe Garibaldi, who invaded Sicily in 1860 in an attempt to liberate it, winning the hearts of the Sicilian peasantry.

were quite possible, Wilhelm I and his top military advisers pushed to raise taxes and increase the defense budget in order to double the size of the army. The Prussian parliament rejected the military budget in 1862, and the liberals triumphed completely in new elections. Wilhelm I then appointed Count Otto von Bismarck as Prussian prime minister and encouraged him to defy the parliament. This was a momentous choice.

Bismarck and the Austro-Prussian War

The most important figure in German history between Martin Luther and Adolf Hitler, Otto von Bismarck (1815–1898) has been the object of enormous interest and debate. A great hero to some and a great villain to others, Bismarck was above all a master of practical politics who first honed his political skills as a high-ranking diplomat for the Prussian government. Born into the Prussian landowning aristocracy and devoted to his sovereign, Bismarck had a strong personality and an unbounded desire for power. Yet in his drive to secure power for himself and for Prussia, Bismarck remained extraordinarily flexible and pragmatic. Keeping his options open, Bismarck moved with determination and cunning toward his goal.

When he took office as prime minister in 1862, in the midst of the constitutional crisis caused by the deadlock on the military budget, Bismarck made a strong but unfavorable impression. Declaring that Wilhelm's government would rule without parliamentary consent, he lashed out at the liberal middle-class opposition: "The great questions of the day will not be decided by speeches and resolutions—that was the blunder of 1848 and 1849—but by blood and iron."

Denounced by liberals for his view that "might makes right," Bismarck had the Prussian bureaucracy go right on collecting taxes, even though the parliament refused to approve the budget. Bismarck also reorganized the army. And for four years, from 1862 to 1866, voters continued to express their opposition by sending large liberal majorities to the parliament.

Opposition at home spurred Bismarck to search for success abroad. The extremely complicated question of Schleswig-Holstein—two provinces that belonged to Denmark but were members of the German Confederation (Map 23.2)—provided a welcome opportunity. In 1864, when the Danish king tried, as he had in 1848, to bring these two provinces into a more centralized Danish state against the will of the German Confederation, Prussia enlisted Austria in a short and successful war against Denmark.

Bismarck, however, was convinced that Prussia had to control completely the northern, predominantly Protestant part of the confederation, which meant expelling Austria from German affairs. After the victory over Denmark, Bismarck's clever maneuvering left Prussia in a position to force Austria out by war. Recognizing that such a war would have to be localized to avoid provoking a larger European alliance against Prussia, Bismarck skillfully neutralized Russia and France.

The Austro-Prussian War of 1866 that followed lasted only seven weeks. Using railroads to quickly mobilize troops, who were armed with new and more efficient breech-loading rifles, the Prussian army defeated Austria decisively at the Battle of Sadowa (SAH-dawvah) in Bohemia on July 3. Anticipating Prussia's future needs, Bismarck offered Austria generous peace terms. Austria paid no reparations and lost no territory to Prussia, although Venetia was ceded to Italy. But the existing German Confederation was dissolved, and Austria agreed to withdraw from German affairs. Prussia conquered and annexed several small states north of the Main River and completely dominated the remaining principalities in the newly formed North German Confederation. The mainly Catholic states of the south remained independent but allied with Prussia. Bismarck's fundamental goal of Prussian expansion was partially realized (see Map 23.2).

Taming the German Parliament

Bismarck had long been convinced that the old order he so ardently defended would have to make peace, on its own terms, with the liberal middle class and nationalists. Impressed with Napoleon III's example in France, he realized that nationalists were not necessarily hostile to conservative, authoritarian government. Moreover, the events of 1848 convinced Bismarck that the German middle class could be led to prefer national unity under conservative leadership rather than a long, uncertain battle for a truly liberal state. Thus during the Austrian war, he increasingly identified Prussia's fate with the "national development of Germany."

To consolidate Prussian control, Bismarck fashioned a federal constitution for the new North German Confederation. Each state retained its own local government, but the king of Prussia became president of the confederation, and the chancellor—Bismarck—was responsible only to the president. The federal bureaucracy—under Wilhelm I and Bismarck—controlled the army and foreign affairs. A weak federal legislature, with members of the lower house elected by universal male suffrage, gave some voice to popular opinion. With this radical innovation, Bismarck opened the door to the possibility of going over the head of the middle class directly to the people, as Napoleon III had done in France. All the while, however, ultimate power rested in the hands of the Prussian king and army.

Map labels (as shown on the map):

SWEDEN
DENMARK
SCHLESWIG
Schleswig-Holstein 1864
Kiel
North Sea
Baltic Sea
Königsberg
EAST PRUSSIA
Danzig
POMERANIA
WEST PRUSSIA
Lübeck
HOLSTEIN
Hamburg
MECKLENBURG
Bremen
OLDENBURG
HANOVER
BRANDENBURG
Elbe R.
Berlin
Warta R.
Vistula R.
Warsaw
Hanover
P R U S S I A
POSEN
RUSSIAN EMPIRE
Amsterdam
NETHERLANDS
WESTPHALIA
Essen
Ruhr R.
Leipzig
Mulde R.
Oder R.
POLAND
Antwerp
Cologne
Bonn
Dresden
BELGIUM
RHINE PROVINCE
Weimar
SAXONY
SILESIA
Kraków
Frankfurt
Moselle R.
Rhine R.
Main R.
Sadowa 1866
Prague
Sedan 1870
Luxembourg
Karlsruhe
Neckar R.
BOHEMIA
Vltava R.
Olmütz
MORAVIA
Verdun
Nuremberg
Morava R.
LORRAINE
Nancy
Strasbourg
WÜRTTEMBERG
Stuttgart
BAVARIA
Inn R.
Munich
Danube R.
Vienna
A U S T R I A N   E M P I R E
Pest
Buda
ALSACE
BADEN
FRANCE
SWITZERLAND
Innsbruck
ITALY

Legend:
✳ Major battle
— German Confederation boundary, 1815–1866
▬ Bismarck's German Empire, 1871
▢ Prussia before 1866
▢ Conquered by Prussia in Austro-Prussian War, 1866
▢ Joined with Prussia to form North German Confederation, 1867
▢ South German states joining with Prussia to form German Empire, 1871
▢ Won by Prussia in Franco-Prussian War, 1871

0   50   100 miles
0   50   100 kilometers

MAPPING THE PAST

MAP 23.2 The Unification of Germany, 1864–1871

This map shows how Prussia expanded and a new German Empire was created through the Austro-Prussian War of 1866 and the Franco-Prussian War of 1870–1871.

ANALYZING THE MAP What losses did Austria experience in 1866? What territories did France lose as a result of the Franco-Prussian War?

CONNECTIONS How was central Europe remade and the power of Prussia-Germany greatly increased as a result of the Austro-Prussian War and the Franco-Prussian War?

In Prussia itself, Bismarck held out an olive branch to the parliamentary opposition. Marshaling all his diplomatic skill, Bismarck asked the parliament to pass a special indemnity bill to approve, after the fact, all the government's spending between 1862 and 1866. With German unity in sight, most of the liberals eagerly cooperated. The constitutional struggle in Prussia ended, and the German middle class came to accept the monarchical authority that Bismarck represented.

The Franco-Prussian War

The final act in the drama of German unification followed quickly. Bismarck calculated that a patriotic war with France would drive the south German states into his arms. Taking advantage of a diplomatic issue—whether a distant relative of Prussia's Wilhelm I might become king of Spain—Bismarck pressed France. By 1870 the French leaders of the Second Empire, goaded by Bismarck and alarmed by their powerful new neighbor, declared war to teach Prussia a lesson.

As soon as war began, Bismarck enlisted support of the south German states. While other governments maintained their neutrality — Bismarck's generosity to Austria in 1866 paid big dividends — combined German forces under Prussian leadership decisively defeated the main French army at Sedan on September 1, 1870. Louis Napoleon himself was captured and humiliated. Three days later, French patriots in Paris proclaimed yet another French republic and vowed to continue fighting. But after five months, in January 1871, a besieged and starving Paris surrendered, and France accepted Bismarck's harsh peace terms.

By this time, the south German states had agreed to join a new German Empire. With Bismarck by his side, Wilhelm I was proclaimed emperor of Germany in the Hall of Mirrors in the palace of Versailles. As in the 1866 constitution, the king of Prussia and his min-

isters had ultimate power in the new German Empire, and the lower house of the legislature was elected by universal male suffrage.

Bismarck imposed a severe penalty on France: payment of a colossal indemnity of 5 billion francs and loss of the rich eastern province of Alsace and part of Lorraine to Germany. French men and women of all classes viewed these territorial losses as a terrible crime (see Map 23.2). They could never forget and never forgive, poisoning relations between France and Germany after 1871.

The Franco-Prussian War, which many Europeans saw as a test of nations in a pitiless Darwinian struggle for existence, released an enormous surge of patriotic feeling in the German Empire. Bismarck's genius, the invincible Prussian army, the solidarity of king and people in a unified nation — such themes grew immensely popular with many German citizens during and after the war. The weakest of the Great Powers

Proclaiming the German Empire, January 1871   This commemorative painting by Anton von Werner testifies to the nationalistic intoxication in Germany after the victory over France at Sedan. Wilhelm I of Prussia stands on a platform surrounded by princes and generals in the famous Hall of Mirrors in the palace of Versailles, while officers from all the units around a besieged Paris cheer and salute him with uplifted swords as emperor of a unified Germany. Bismarck, in white (center), stands between king and army. (By Anton Alexander von Werner [1843–1915]/Schloss Friedrichsruhe, Germany/Bridgeman Images)

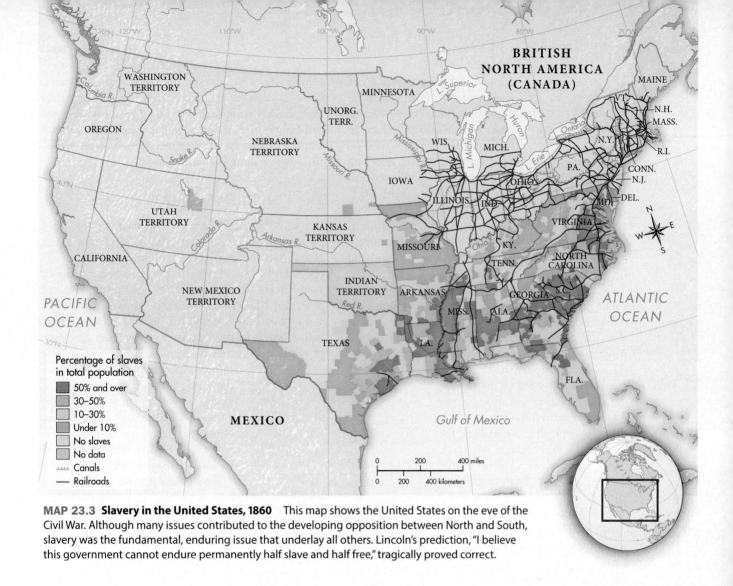

MAP 23.3 Slavery in the United States, 1860 This map shows the United States on the eve of the Civil War. Although many issues contributed to the developing opposition between North and South, slavery was the fundamental, enduring issue that underlay all others. Lincoln's prediction, "I believe this government cannot endure permanently half slave and half free," tragically proved correct.

Percentage of slaves in total population
- 50% and over
- 30–50%
- 10–30%
- Under 10%
- No slaves
- No data
- Canals
- Railroads

in 1862, Prussia with united Germany had become the most powerful state in Europe in less than a decade, and most Germans were enormously proud. Semi-authoritarian nationalism and a new conservatism, based on an alliance of the landed nobles and middle classes, had triumphed in Germany.

Slavery and Nation Building in the United States

The United States also experienced a process of bloody nation building. Nominally united, the country was divided by the slavery question, and economic development in the young republic carried free and slaveholding states in very different directions. Northerners extended family farms westward and began building English-model factories in the northeast. By 1850 an industrializing, urbanizing North was also building canals and railroads and attracting most of the European immigrants arriving in the nation.

In sharp contrast, industry and cities developed more slowly in the South, and European immigrants largely avoided the region. Even though three-quarters of all Southern white families were small farmers and owned no slaves, plantation owners holding twenty or more slaves dominated the economy and society. These profit-minded slave owners used gangs of enslaved Africans to establish a vast plantation economy across the Deep South, where cotton was king (Map 23.3). By 1850 the region produced 5 million bales a year, supplying textile mills in Europe and New England.

The rise of the cotton empire greatly expanded slave-based agriculture in the South, spurred exports, and played a key role in igniting rapid U.S. economic growth. The large profits flowing from cotton led influential Southerners to defend slavery. In doing so, Southern whites developed a strong cultural identity and came to see themselves as a closely knit "we" distinct from the Northern "they." Because Northern whites viewed their free-labor system as more just, and economically and morally superior to slavery, North-South antagonisms intensified.

Tensions reached a climax after 1848 when the United States won the Mexican-American War

U.S. Secession, 1860–1861

(1846–1848) and gained a vast area stretching from west Texas to the Pacific Ocean. Debate over the extension of slavery in this new territory hardened attitudes on both sides. Abraham Lincoln's election as president in 1860 gave Southern secessionists the chance they had been waiting for. Determined to win independence, eleven states left the Union and formed the Confederate States of America.

The resulting Civil War (1861–1865), the bloodiest conflict in American history, ended with the South decisively defeated and the Union preserved. In the aftermath of the war, certain dominant characteristics of American life and national culture took shape. Powerful business corporations emerged, steadfastly supported by the Republican Party during and after the war. The **Homestead Act** of 1862, which gave western land to settlers, and the Thirteenth Amendment of 1865, which ended slavery, reinforced the concept of free labor taking its chances in a market economy. Finally, the success of Lincoln and the North in holding the Union together seemed to confirm that the "manifest destiny" of the United States was indeed to straddle a continent as a great world power. Thus a new American nationalism, grounded in economic and territorial expansion, grew out of a civil war.

competition with other Great Powers. For both states, however, relentless power politics led to serious trouble. Their leaders recognized that they had to "modernize" and embrace the economic, military, and social-political reforms that might enable a country to compete effectively with leading European nations.

The "Great Reforms" in Russia

In the 1850s Russia was a poor agrarian society with a rapidly growing population. Almost 90 percent of the people lived off the land, and industrialization developed slowly. (See "Living in the Past: Peasant Life in Post-Reform Russia," page 768.) Bound to the lord from birth, the peasant serf was little more than a slave, and by the 1840s serfdom had become a central moral and political issue for the government. The slow pace of modernization encouraged the growth of protest movements, from radical Marxists clamoring for socialist revolution to middle-class intellectuals who sought a liberal constitutional state. Then a humiliating Russian defeat in the Crimean War underscored the need for modernizing reforms.

The **Crimean War** (1853–1856) grew out of the breakdown of the European balance of power established at the Congress of Vienna (see Chapter 21), general Great Power competition over the Middle East, and Russian desires to expand into the European territories of the Ottoman Empire. A Russian-French dispute over the protection of Christian shrines in Jerusalem sparked the conflict. Famous for incompetent leadership on all sides, the war revealed the awesome power of modern weaponry, particularly artillery, in ways that anticipated the U.S. Civil War. Massive naval engagements, doomed cavalry charges, and staggering casualties—Russia alone lost about 450,000 soldiers—captured the imagination of home-front audiences, who followed events in the national press. By 1856 France and Great Britain, aided by the Ottoman Empire and Sardinia, had joined forces in an effort to limit Russian territorial expansion. This alliance decisively defeated Russia.

The war convinced Russia's leaders that they had fallen behind the industrializing nations of western Europe. At the very least, Russia needed railroads, better armaments, and military reform to remain a Great Power. Moreover, the disastrous war raised the specter of massive peasant rebellion, making reform of serfdom imperative. Military disaster forced liberal-leaning Tsar Alexander II (r. 1855–1881) and his

The Crimean War, 1853–1856

The Modernization of Russia and the Ottoman Empire

FOCUS QUESTION *What steps did Russia and the Ottoman Turks take toward modernization, and how successful were they?*

The Russian and the Ottoman Empires experienced profound political crises in the mid-nineteenth century. These crises differed from those occurring in Italy and Germany, for both empires were vast multinational states built on long traditions of military conquest and absolutist rule by elites from the dominant Russians and Ottoman Turks. In the early nineteenth century the governing elites in both empires strongly opposed representative government and national independence for ethnic minorities, concentrating on absolutist rule and

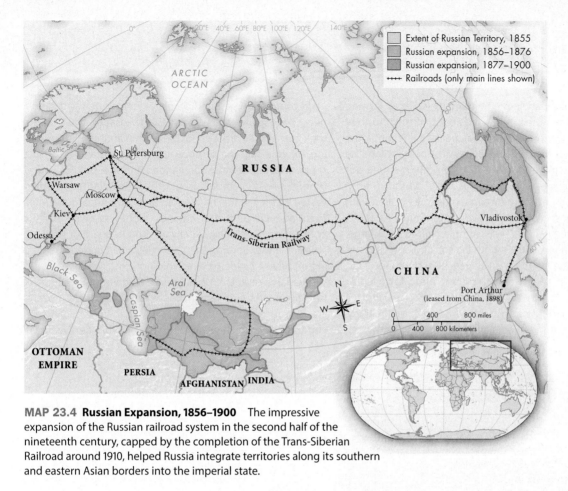

MAP 23.4 **Russian Expansion, 1856–1900**　The impressive expansion of the Russian railroad system in the second half of the nineteenth century, capped by the completion of the Trans-Siberian Railroad around 1910, helped Russia integrate territories along its southern and eastern Asian borders into the imperial state.

ministers along the path of rapid social change and modernization.

In a bold move, Alexander II abolished serfdom in 1861. About 22 million emancipated peasants received citizenship rights and the chance to purchase, on average, about half of the land they cultivated. Yet they had to pay fairly high prices, and because the land was to be owned collectively, each peasant village was jointly responsible for the payments of all the families in the village. Collective ownership made it difficult for individual peasants to improve agricultural methods or leave their villages. Thus old patterns of behavior predominated, limiting the effects of reform.

Most of Alexander II's later reforms were also halfway measures. In 1864 the government established a new institution of local government, the zemstvo. Members of this local assembly were elected by a three-class system of townspeople, peasant villagers, and noble landowners. A zemstvo executive council dealt with local problems. Russian liberals hoped that this reform would lead to an elected national parliament, but it did not. The zemstvos remained subordinate to the traditional bureaucracy and the local nobility. In addition, changes to the legal system established independent courts and equality before

the law. The government relaxed but did not remove censorship, and somewhat liberalized policies toward Russian Jews.

Russian efforts to promote economic modernization proved more successful. Transportation and industry, both vital to the military, were transformed in two industrial surges. The first came after 1860, when the government encouraged and subsidized private railway companies. The railroads linked important cities in the western territories of the empire and enabled Russia to export grain and thus earn money to finance further development. The jewel in the crown of the Russian rail system was the 5,700-mile-long Trans-Siberian Railway. Passing through seven time zones from Moscow to Vladivostok, this crucial rail line brought millions of immigrant peasants from western Russia into the lightly populated areas to the east. The grain they grew was moved west along the line, to help feed the growing cities in Russia's heartland (Map 23.4). Industrial

■ **Homestead Act**　An American law enacted during the Civil War that gave western land to settlers, reinforcing the concept of free labor in a market economy.

■ **Crimean War**　A conflict fought between 1853 and 1856 over Russian desires to expand into Ottoman territory. Russia was defeated by France, Britain, and the Ottomans, underscoring the need for reform in the Russian Empire.

LIVING IN THE PAST
Peasant Life in Post-Reform Russia

The cautious emancipation of 1861, which freed Russian peasants from their noble lords but tied them to their villages, preserved traditional peasant life until the massive industrial surge of the 1890s. Most peasant families continued to live in one- or two-story log cabins strung out along the village's wide dirt road. A cabin typically had a single living room, a storage room (sometimes shared with animals), and a shallow cellar. Simple furniture—a table, benches, storage shelves—was complemented by a large, flat brick oven that was used both for cooking and as a surface for sleeping. On Sundays villagers attended a long Orthodox service in their wooden church, often followed in summer by socializing with family and friends, drinking tea and mild homemade ale, telling stories, and playing the traditional stringed instrument, the balalaika.

In contrast to western Europe, where women had almost never done heavy field work, Russian peasant women always took part in the hard work of plowing, planting, and harvesting. Infertile soil, sparse population, simple hand tools, and short growing seasons demanded intense physical effort from all family members to get the crops planted and harvested before the first hard freeze and the long, brutal winter. Since peasant land, after emancipation, was owned by the entire village, with each family allotted its share of the long strips of land according to its size, fields had no fences marking off private property, which did not exist.

Russian peasants typically needed additional nonagricultural income to supplement the wages they made growing crops. Thus both men and women engaged in many crafts and trades, of which weaving, pottery, embroidery, hauling,

In this photograph (ca. 1875), members of a Russian family gather outside a typical peasant cabin to enjoy a Sunday break from their labors. The man at the rear is playing a song on a balalaika (pictured below), a three-stringed Russian folk instrument similar to a guitar. (family: Granger, NYC—All rights reserved; balalaika: © Akihara Fujikura/The ImageWorks)

Russian agriculture depended on the contribution of women and girls, as this photograph attests. (Granger, NYC — All rights reserved)

logging, and carpentry were particularly important. Wood-workers, like this peasant barrel maker with his birch-bark shoes and homemade leggings, used an abundant raw material to fashion elaborate dolls and attractive wooden tableware as well as workaday items. Peasants also went to towns and cities for temporary work, and many settled there permanently as industrial workers in the 1890s.

QUESTIONS FOR ANALYSIS

1. How did the abolition of serfdom affect peasant life in Russia?
2. What role did peasant women play in Russian agriculture? Why?
3. How did Russian peasants interact with their environment? In what ways did their environment influence peasants' lives?

This 1895 photo of a barrel maker and the image of the antique wooden nesting dolls highlight the importance of woodworking as a source of secondary income for Russian peasants. (barrel maker: akg-images; nesting dolls: Sergiev Posad Toy Museum, Sergiev Posad, Russia/Visual Connection Archive)

suburbs grew up around Moscow and St. Petersburg, and a class of modern factory workers began to take shape. Industrial development and the growing proletariat class helped spread Marxist thought and spurred the transformation of the Russian revolutionary movement after 1890.

Strengthened by industrial development, Russia began to expand by seizing lands on the borders of the empire. Russia took control of territory in far eastern Siberia, on the border with China, and in Central Asia, north of Afghanistan. The imperial state also encroached upon the Islamic lands of the Caucasus, along the northeast border of the Ottoman Empire. Russian peasants, always hungry for land, used the new rail systems to move to and settle in the newly colonized areas, at times displacing local residents (see Map 23.4). The rapid expansion of the Russian Empire to the south and east excited ardent Russian nationalists and superpatriots, who became some of the government's most enthusiastic supporters. Alexander II consolidated imperial control by suppressing nationalist movements among Poles, Ukrainians, and Baltic peoples in the western lands of the Russian Empire. By 1900 the Russian Empire commanded a vast and diverse array of peoples and places.

Alexander II's political reforms outraged reactionaries but never went far enough for liberals and radicals. In 1881 a member of the "People's Will," a small anarchist group, assassinated the tsar, and the era of reform came to an abrupt end. The new tsar, Alexander III (r. 1881–1894), was a determined reactionary. Nevertheless, from 1890 to 1900 economic modernization and industrialization surged ahead for the second time, led by Sergei Witte (suhr-GAY VIH-tuh), finance minister from 1892 to 1903. The tough, competent Witte believed that industrial backwardness threatened Russia's greatness. Under his leadership, the government doubled the network of state-owned railways to thirty-five thousand miles. Witte established high protective tariffs to support Russian industry, and he put the country on the gold standard to strengthen Russian finances.

Witte's greatest innovation was to use Westerners to catch up with the West. He encouraged foreigners to build factories in Russia, believing that "the inflow of foreign capital is . . . the only way by which our industry will be able to supply our country quickly with abundant and cheap products."[1] His efforts to entice western Europeans to locate their factories in Russia were especially successful in southern Russia. There, in eastern Ukraine, foreign entrepreneurs and engineers built an enormous and very modern steel and coal industry. In 1900 peasants still constituted the great majority of the population, but Russia was catching up with the more industrialized West.

The Russian Revolution of 1905

Catching up partly meant further territorial expansion, for this was the age of Western imperialism. By 1903 Russia had established a sphere of influence in Chinese Manchuria and was eyeing northern Korea, which put Russia in conflict with the goals of an equally imperialistic Japan. Tsar Nicholas II (r. 1894–1917), who replaced his father in 1894, ignored their diplomatic protests. In response, the Japanese launched a surprise attack on Port Arthur, a Russian naval base in northern China, in February 1904. The resulting Russo-Japanese war lasted less than a year. After Japan scored repeated victories, which included annihilating a Russian fleet, the humiliated Russians surrendered in September 1905.

Once again, military disaster abroad brought political upheaval at home. The business and professional classes had long wanted a liberal, representative government. Urban factory workers were organized in a radical and still-illegal labor movement. Peasants had gained little from the era of reforms and suffered from poverty and overpopulation. At the same time, the empire's minorities and subject nationalities, such as the Poles, the Ukrainians, and the Latvians, continued to call for self-rule. With the army pinned down in Manchuria, all these currents of discontent converged in the revolution of 1905.

On a Sunday in January 1905, a massive crowd of workers and their families converged peacefully on the Winter Palace in St. Petersburg to present a petition to Nicholas II. Suddenly troops opened fire, killing and wounding hundreds. The **Bloody Sunday** massacre produced a wave of general indignation that turned many Russians against the tsar. (See "Evaluating the Evidence 23.2: Eyewitness Accounts of Bloody Sunday," at right.)

By the summer of 1905 strikes and political rallies, peasant uprisings, revolts among minority nationalities, and mutinies by troops were sweeping the country. The revolutionary surge culminated in October 1905 in a paralyzing general strike that forced the government to capitulate. The tsar then issued the October Manifesto, which granted full civil rights and promised a popularly elected **Duma** (or parliament) with real legislative power. The manifesto split the opposition. Frightened middle-class leaders embraced it, which helped the government repress the popular uprising and survive as a constitutional monarchy.

On the eve of the opening of the first Duma in May 1906, the government issued the new constitution,

■ **Bloody Sunday** A massacre of peaceful protesters at the Winter Palace in St. Petersburg in 1905, triggering a revolution that overturned absolute tsarist rule and made Russia into a conservative constitutional monarchy.

■ **Duma** The Russian parliament that opened in 1906, elected indirectly by universal male suffrage but controlled after 1907 by the tsar and the conservative classes.

Eyewitness Accounts of Bloody Sunday

Newspaper reporters for the Times *(London) and* Le Matin *(Paris) expressed shock at the rapid outbreak of deadly violence on Bloody Sunday (January 22, 1905), one of the events that sparked the Russian Revolution of 1905. The Cossacks referred to in the* Times *account were soldiers recruited from Russia's southern steppes. Father Gapon, also mentioned in that report, was an Orthodox priest who led the march.*

From the *Times* (London)

Event has succeeded event with such bewildering rapidity that the public is staggered and shocked beyond measure. The first trouble began at 11 o'clock, when the military tried to turn back some thousands of strikers at one of the bridges . . . where the constant flow of workmen pressing forward refused to be denied access to the common rendezvous in the Palace Square. The Cossacks at first used their knouts [whips], then the flat of their sabers, and finally they fired. The strikers in the front ranks fell on their knees and implored the Cossacks to let them pass, protesting that they had no hostile intentions. They refused, however, to be intimidated by blank cartridges, and orders were given to load with ball.

The passions of the mob broke loose like a bursting dam. The people, seeing the dead and dying carried away in all directions, the snow on the streets and pavements soaked with blood, cried aloud for vengeance. Meanwhile the situation at the Palace was becoming momentarily worse. The troops were reported to be unable to control the vast masses which were constantly surging forward. Re-enforcements were sent, and at 2 o'clock here also the order was given to fire. Men, women, and children fell at each volley, and were carried away in ambulances, sledges, and carts. The indignation and fury of every class were aroused. Students, merchants, all classes of the population alike were inflamed. At the moment of writing, firing is going on in every quarter of the city.

Father Gapon, marching at the head of a large body of workmen, carrying a cross and other religious emblems, was wounded in the arm and shoulder. The two forces of workmen are now separated. Those on the other side of the river are arming with swords, knives, and smiths' and carpenters' tools, and are busy erecting barricades. The troops are apparently reckless, firing right and left, with or without reason. The rioters continue to appeal to them, saying, "You are Russians! Why play the part of blood-thirsty butchers?" . . .

A night of terror is in prospect.

From *Le Matin* (Paris)

The soldiers of the Preobrazhensky regiment, without any summons to disperse, shoot down the unfortunate people as if they were playing at bloodshed. Several hundred fall; more than a hundred and fifty are killed. They are almost all children, women, and young people. It is terrible. Blood flows on all sides. At 5 o'clock the crowd is driven back, cut down and repelled on all sides. The people, terror-stricken, fly in every direction. Scared women and children slip, fall, rise to their feet, only to fall again farther on. At this moment a sharp word of command is heard and the victims fall en masse. There had been no disturbances to speak of. The whole crowd is unarmed and has not uttered a single threat.

EVALUATE THE EVIDENCE

1. Can you begin to reconstruct the events of Bloody Sunday from these reports? Who seems to be responsible for the violence?
2. Did popular protest help ordinary people win rights from the Russian state?

Source: James Harvey Robinson and Charles Beard, eds., *Readings in Modern European History*, vol. 2 (Boston: Ginn and Company, 1909), pp. 373–374.

---

the Fundamental Laws. The tsar retained great powers. The Duma, elected indirectly by universal male suffrage with a largely appointive upper house, could debate and pass laws, but the tsar had an absolute veto. As in Bismarck's Germany, the tsar appointed his ministers, who did not need to command a majority in the Duma.

The predominantly middle-class liberals, the largest group in the newly elected Duma, saw the Fundamental Laws as a step backward. Cooperation with Nicholas II's ministers soon broke down, and after months of deadlock the tsar dismissed the Duma. Thereupon he and his advisers, including the talented Pyotr Stolypin, who

served as prime minister, unilaterally rewrote the electoral law. These revisions greatly increased the electoral weight of the conservative propertied classes. When new elections were held, the tsar could count on a legislative majority loyal to the monarchy. His government then pushed through important agrarian reforms designed to break down collective village ownership of land and encourage the more enterprising peasants— Stolypin's "wager on the strong and sober," meant to encourage economic growth. The government reformed the education and banking systems, but these acts were accompanied by harsh repression of dissidents and radicals. About three thousand suspected revolutionaries were executed by the state, and the hangman's noose became known as "Stolypin's necktie." In 1914, on the eve of the First World War, Russia was partially modernized, a conservative constitutional monarchy with a peasant-based but industrializing economy and significant pockets of discontent.

Reform and Readjustment in the Ottoman Empire

By the early nineteenth century the economic and political changes reshaping Europe were also at play in the Ottoman Empire, which stretched around the northeastern, eastern, and southern shores of the Mediterranean Sea. The borderlands of this vast empire experienced constant flux and conflict. Russia had occupied Ottoman provinces on the Danube River in the last decades of the eighteenth century and grabbed more during the Napoleonic Wars. In 1816 the Ottomans were forced to grant Serbia local autonomy. In 1830 the Greeks won independence, and French armies began their long and bloody takeover of Ottoman Algeria. Yet the Ottomans achieved important victories during the same decades. Egyptian forces under the leadership of Muhammad Ali, the Ottoman governor in Egypt, restored order in the Islamic holy lands and conquered significant portions of Sudan, south of Egypt.

Muhammad Ali, a ruthless and intelligent soldier-politician, ruled Egypt in the name of the Ottoman sultan from 1805 to 1848. His modernizing reforms of agriculture, industry, and the military (see Chapter 24) helped turn Egypt into the most powerful state in the eastern Mediterranean. In time, his growing strength directly challenged the Ottoman sultan and Istanbul's ruling elite. From 1831 to 1840 Egyptian troops under the leadership of Muhammad Ali's son Ibrahim occupied and governed the Ottoman province of Syria and Palestine, and threatened to depose the Ottoman sultan Mahmud II (r. 1808–1839).

This conflict forced the Ottomans to seek European support. Mahmud II's dynasty survived, but only because the European powers, led by Britain, allied with the Ottomans to discipline Muhammad Ali. The European powers preferred a weak and dependent Ottoman Empire to a strong, economically independent state under a dynamic leader such as Muhammad Ali.

Faced with growing European military and economic competition, liberal Ottoman statesmen in 1839 launched an era of radical reforms known as the **Tanzimat**, or "Reorganization." The Tanzimat reforms, borrowed from western European models, were designed

to modernize the empire. The high point of reform came when the new liberal-minded sultan, Abdul Mejid (r. 1839–1861), issued the Imperial Rescript of 1856, just after the Crimean War. Articles in the decree called for equality before the law regardless of religious faith, a modernized administration and army, and private ownership of land. As part of the reform policy, and under economic pressure from the European powers that had paid for the empire's war against Russia in Crimea, Ottoman leaders adopted free-trade policies. New commercial laws removed tariffs on foreign imports and permitted foreign merchants to operate freely throughout the empire.

The turn to nineteenth-century liberal capitalism had mixed effects. On one hand, with the growth of Western-style banking and insurance systems, elite Christian and Jewish businessmen in the empire prospered. Yet the bulk of the profits went to foreign investors rather than Ottoman subjects. More important, the elimination of traditional state-controlled monopolies sharply cut imperial revenues. In 1851 Sultan Mejid was forced to borrow 55 million francs from British and French bankers to cover state deficits. Other loans followed, and intractable indebtedness led to the bankruptcy of the Ottoman state two decades later.

Intended to bring revolutionary modernization, the Tanzimat permitted partial recovery but fell short of its goals. The Ottoman initiatives did not curtail the appetite of Western imperialists, who secured a stranglehold on the imperial economy via issuing loans. The reforms also failed to halt the growth of nationalism among some Christian subjects in the Balkans, which resulted in crises and increased pressure from neighboring Austria and Russia, eager to gain access to the Balkans and the eastern Mediterranean.

Finally, equality before the law for all citizens, regardless of religious affiliation, actually increased religious disputes, which were often encouraged and manipulated by the European powers eager to seize any pretext for intervention. This development embittered relations between religious conservatives and social liberals, a struggle that ultimately distracted the government from its reform mission. Religious conservatives in both the Muslim and Greek Orthodox communities detested the religious reforms, which they viewed as an impious departure from tradition. These conservatives became dependable supporters of Sultan Abdülhamid II (ahb-dool-hah-MEED) (r. 1876–1909), who in 1876 halted the reform movement and turned away from European liberalism in his long and repressive reign.

Abdülhamid II's government failed to halt foreign efforts to fragment and ultimately take control over key Ottoman territories. Defeat in the Russo-Turkish War (1877–1878) meant the loss to Russia of Ottoman districts in the Caucasus; formal declarations of independence for Romania, Montenegro, and Serbia,

■ **Tanzimat** A set of reforms designed to remake the Ottoman Empire on a western European model.

■ **Young Turks** Fervent patriots who seized power in a 1908 coup in the Ottoman Empire, forcing the conservative sultan to implement reforms.

Pasha Hilim Receiving Archduke Maximilian of Austria   As this painting suggests, Ottoman leaders became well versed in European languages and culture. They also mastered the game of power politics, playing one European state against another to secure the Ottoman Empire's survival. (By Peter Johann Nepomuk Geiger [1805–1880]/Miramare Palace, Trieste, Italy/Alfredo Dagli Orti/The Art Archive at Art Resource, NY)

all former Ottoman territories in the Balkans; and the establishment of an autonomous Bulgaria, still nominally under the Ottoman sultan's control. By the 1890s the government's failures had encouraged a powerful resurgence of the modernizing impulse under the banner of the Committee of Union and Progress (CUP), an umbrella organization that united multiethnic reformist groups from across the empire. These fervent patriots, unofficially called the **Young Turks**, seized power in a 1908 coup and forced the sultan to implement new reforms. Although they failed to stop the rising tide of anti-Ottoman nationalism in the Balkans, the Young Turks helped prepare the way for the rise of modern secular Turkey after the defeat and collapse of the Ottoman Empire in World War I.

The Responsive National State, 1871–1914

FOCUS QUESTION *What general domestic political trends emerged after 1871?*

The decades after 1870 brought rapid change to the structures and ideas of European politics. Despite some major differences between countries, European domestic politics had a new common framework, the nation-state. The common themes within that framework were the emergence of mass politics and growing popular loyalty toward the nation. Traditional elites hardly disappeared, but they were forced into new arrangements in order to exercise power, and a group of new, pragmatic politicians took leading roles. The major states of western Europe adopted constitutions of some sort, and universal male suffrage was granted in Britain, France, and Germany and elsewhere, at least in voting for the lower houses of parliament. New political parties representing a broad spectrum of interests and groups from workers and liberals to Catholics and conservatives engaged in hard-fought election campaigns to provide benefits to their constituencies.

Powerful bureaucracies emerged to govern growing populations and manage modern economies, and the growth of the state spurred a growth in the social responsibilities of government. The new responsive national state offered its citizens free education and some welfare and public health benefits, and for good reason many ordinary people felt increasing loyalty to their governments and their nations.

Building popular support for strong nation-states had a less positive side. Conservative and moderate leaders both found that workers who voted socialist—whose potential revolutionary power they feared—would rally around the flag in a diplomatic crisis or cheer when colonial interests seized a distant territory of doubtful value. Therefore, after 1871 governing elites frequently used antiliberal militarist and imperialist policies in attempts to unite national populations and overcome or mask intractable domestic conflicts. In the end, the manipulation of foreign policy to manage domestic issues inflamed the international tensions that erupted in the cataclysms of World War I and the Russian Revolution.

The German Empire

The history of Germany after 1871 exemplified many of these general political developments. Like the United States, the new German Empire adopted a federal system: a union of Prussia and twenty-four smaller states, each with separate legislatures. Much of the everyday business of government was conducted by the individual states, but there was a strong national government with a chancellor—until 1890, Bismarck—and a popularly elected national parliament called the **Reichstag** (RIKES-tahg). Although Bismarck repeatedly ignored the wishes of the parliamentary majority, he nonetheless preferred to win the support of the Reichstag to lend legitimacy to his policy goals. This situation gave the political parties opportunities to influence national policy. Until 1878 Bismarck relied mainly on the National

Liberals, who had rallied to him after 1866. They supported legislation useful for economic growth and unification of the country.

Less wisely, the National Liberals backed Bismarck's attack on the Catholic Church, the so-called **Kulturkampf** (kool-TOOR-kahmpf), or "culture struggle." Like Bismarck, the middle-class National Liberals were alarmed by Pius IX's declaration of papal infallibility in 1870. That dogma seemed to ask German Catholics to put loyalty to their church, a foreign power, above their loyalty to their newly unified nation. Kulturkampf initiatives aimed at making the Catholic Church subject to government control. However, only in Protestant Prussia did the Kulturkampf have even limited success, because elsewhere Catholics generally voted for the Center Party, which blocked passage of laws hostile to the church.

In 1878 Bismarck abandoned his attack on the church and instead courted the Catholic Center Party, whose supporters included many Catholic small farmers in western and southern Germany. By revoking free-trade policy and enacting high tariffs on cheap grain from the United States, Canada, and Russia, he won over both the Catholic Center and the conservative Protestant Junkers, nobles with large landholdings in East Prussia.

Other governments followed Bismarck's lead, and the 1880s and 1890s saw a widespread return to protectionism in Europe. France, in particular, established very high tariffs to protect agriculture and industry. By raising tariffs, European governments offered an effective response to a major domestic economic problem—foreign competition—in a way that won greater popular loyalty. At the same time, the rise of protectionism exemplified the dangers of self-centered nationalism: new tariffs led to international name-calling and nasty trade wars.

After the failure of the Kulturkampf, Bismarck's government tried to stop the growth of the **German Social Democratic Party (SPD)**, Germany's Marxist, working-class political party, which was established in the 1870s. Both conservative elites and middle-class liberals genuinely feared the SPD's revolutionary language and allegiance to a Marxist movement that transcended the nation-state. In 1878 Bismarck pushed through the Reichstag the Anti-Socialist Laws, which banned Social Democratic associations, meetings, and publications. The Social Democratic Party was driven underground, but it maintained substantial influence, and Bismarck decided to try another tack.

In an attempt to win working-class support, Bismarck urged the Reichstag to enact a variety of state-supported social welfare measures. Big business and some conservatives accused him of creating "state socialism," but Bismarck ably pressed his program in many lively speeches, as the following excerpt suggests:

■ **Reichstag** The popularly elected lower house of government of the new German Empire after 1871.

■ **Kulturkampf** Bismarck's attack on the Catholic Church within Germany from 1870 to 1878, resulting from Pius IX's declaration of papal infallibility.

■ **German Social Democratic Party (SPD)** A German working-class political party founded in the 1870s, the SPD championed Marxism but in practice turned away from Marxist revolution and worked instead in the German parliament for social and workplace reforms.

Give the working-man the right to work as long as he is healthy; assure him care when he is sick; assure him maintenance when he is old. If you do that, and do not fear the [financial] sacrifice, or cry out at State Socialism as soon as the words "provision for old age" are uttered, — if the state would show a little more Christian solicitude for the working-man, then I believe the gentlemen of the Wyden [Social Democratic] program will sound their bird-call in vain, and that the thronging toward them will cease as soon as working-men see that the Government and legislative bodies are earnestly concerned with their welfare.[2]

Bismarck and his supporters carried the day, and his essentially conservative nation-state pioneered in providing social welfare programs. In 1883 he pushed through the Reichstag the first of several social security laws to help wage earners by providing national sickness insurance. An 1884 law created accident insurance; one from 1889 established old-age pensions and retirement benefits. Henceforth sick, injured, and retired workers could look forward to some regular benefits from the state. This national social security system, paid for through compulsory contributions by wage earners and employers as well as grants from the state, was the first of its kind anywhere. Bismarck's social security system did not wean workers from voting socialist, but it did give them a small stake in the system and protect them from some of the uncertainties of the competitive industrial economy. This enormously significant development was a product of political competition, as well as government efforts to win popular support by defusing the SPD's radical appeal.

Increasingly, the key issue in German domestic politics was socialism and, specifically, the rapid growth of the SPD. In 1890 the new emperor, the young, idealistic, and unstable Wilhelm II (r. 1888–1918), opposed Bismarck's attempt to renew the Anti-Socialist Laws. Eager to rule in his own right and to earn the support of the workers, Wilhelm II forced Bismarck to resign. Afterward, German foreign policy changed profoundly and mostly for the worse, but the government did pass new laws to aid workers and legalize socialist political activity.

Yet Wilhelm II was no more successful than Bismarck in getting workers to renounce socialism. Indeed, Social Democrats won more and more seats in the Reichstag, becoming Germany's largest single party in 1912. Though this electoral victory shocked aristocrats and their wealthy, conservative allies, who held exaggerated fears of an impending socialist upheaval, the revolutionary socialists had actually become less radical in Germany. In the years before World War I, the SPD broadened its base by adopting a more patri-

otic tone, allowing for greater military spending and imperialist expansion. German socialists abandoned revolutionary aims to concentrate instead on gradual social and political reform (see pages 785–788).

Republican France

Although Napoleon III's reign made some progress in reducing antagonisms between classes, the Franco-Prussian War undid these efforts. In 1871 France seemed hopelessly divided once again. The patriotic republicans who proclaimed the Third Republic in Paris after the military disaster at Sedan refused to admit defeat by the Germans. They defended Paris with great heroism for weeks, living off rats and zoo animals until they were starved into submission by German armies in January 1871.

When the next national elections sent a large majority of conservatives and monarchists to the National Assembly and France's new leaders decided they had no choice but to surrender Alsace (al-SAS) and Lorraine to Germany, the traumatized Parisians exploded in patriotic frustration and proclaimed the Paris Commune in March 1871. Avowedly radical, the leaders of the Commune wanted to establish a revolutionary government in Paris and rule without interference from the conservative French countryside. Their program included workplace reforms, the separation of church and state, press censorship, and radical feminism. The National Assembly, led by aging politician Adolphe Thiers (TEE-ehr), ordered the French army into Paris and brutally crushed the Commune. Twenty thousand people died in the fighting. As in June 1848, it was Paris against the provinces, French against French.

Out of this tragedy, France slowly formed a new national unity, achieving considerable stability before 1914. How do we account for this? Luck played a part. Until 1875 the monarchists in the ostensibly republican National Assembly had a majority but could not agree on who should be king. The compromise Bourbon candidate refused to rule except under the white flag of his absolutist ancestors—a completely unacceptable condition for many supporters of a constitutional monarchy. In the meantime, Thiers's destruction of the radical Commune and his other firm measures showed the fearful provinces and the middle classes that the Third Republic could be politically moderate and socially conservative. France therefore reluctantly retained republican government. As President Thiers cautiously said, this was "the government which divides us least."

Another stabilizing factor was the skill and determination of moderate republican leaders in the early years. The most famous was Léon Gambetta (gam-BEH-tuh), the son of an Italian grocer, a warm, easygoing, unsuccessful lawyer turned professional politician. By 1879 the great majority of members of both the upper and the lower houses of the National Assembly were republicans, and the Third Republic had firm foundations after almost a decade.

The moderate republicans sought to preserve their creation by winning the allegiance of the next generation. The Assembly legalized trade unions, and France worked to expand its colonial empire. More important, a series of laws between 1879 and 1886 greatly expanded the state system of public, tax-supported schools and established free compulsory elementary education for both girls and boys. In the past, most elementary and much secondary education had occurred in Catholic schools, which had long been hostile to republics and much of secular life. Free compulsory elementary education became secular republican education. Not only in France, but throughout the Western world, the expansion of public education served as a critical nation-building tool in the late nineteenth century.

Although the educational reforms of the 1880s disturbed French Catholics, many of them rallied to the republic in the 1890s. The limited acceptance of the modern world by the more liberal Pope Leo XIII (pontificate 1878–1903) eased conflicts between church and state. Unfortunately, the **Dreyfus affair** renewed church-state tensions.

In 1894 Alfred Dreyfus, a Jewish captain in the French army, was falsely accused and convicted of treason. His family never doubted his innocence and fought to reopen the case, enlisting the support of prominent republicans and intellectuals, including novelist Émile Zola. In 1898 and 1899 the case split France apart. On one side was the army, which had manufactured evidence against Dreyfus, joined by anti-Semites, conservative nationalists, and most of the Catholic establishment. On the other side stood liberals and most of the more radical republicans.

Dreyfus was eventually declared innocent, but the battle revived republican animosity toward the Catholic Church. Between 1901 and 1905 the government severed all ties between the state and the church. The government stopped paying priests' and bishops' salaries and placed committees of lay Catholics in control of all churches. Suddenly on their own financially, Catholic schools soon lost a third of their students, greatly increasing the state school system's reach and thus its power of indoctrination. Thus deep religious and political divisions, as well as a growing socialist

movement (see page 788), challenged the apparent stability of the Third Republic.

Great Britain and Ireland

Historians often cast late-nineteenth-century Britain as a shining example of peaceful and successful political evolution, where an effective two-party Parliament skillfully guided the country from classical liberalism to full-fledged democracy with hardly a misstep. This "Whig view" of Great Britain is not so much wrong as it is incomplete. After the right to vote was granted to males of the wealthy middle class in 1832, opinion leaders and politicians wrestled for some time with further expansion of the franchise. In 1867 the Second Reform Bill of Benjamin Disraeli and the Conservative Party extended the vote to all middle-class males and the best-paid workers in order to broaden their own base of support beyond the landowning class. After 1867 English political parties and electoral campaigns became more modern, and the "lower orders" appeared to vote as responsibly as their "betters." Hence the Third Reform Bill of 1884 gave the vote to almost every adult male.

While the House of Commons drifted toward democracy, the House of Lords was content to slumber nobly. Between 1901 and 1910, however, the Lords tried to reassert itself. Acting as supreme court of the land, it ruled against labor unions in two important decisions. And after the Liberal Party came to power in 1906, the Lords vetoed several measures passed by the Commons, including the so-called **People's Budget**, designed to increase spending on social welfare services. When the king threatened to create enough new peers to pass the bill, the Lords finally capitulated, as they had with the Reform Bill of 1832 (see Chapter 21). Aristocratic conservatism yielded to popular democracy.

Extensive social welfare measures, previously slow to come to Great Britain, were passed in a spectacular rush between 1906 and 1914. During those years the Liberal Party, inspired by the fiery Welshman David Lloyd George (1863–1945), enacted the People's Budget and substantially raised taxes on the rich. This income helped the government pay for national health insurance, unemployment benefits, old-age pensions, and a host of other social measures. The state tried to integrate the urban masses socially as well as politically, though the refusal to grant women the right to vote encouraged a determined and increasingly militant suffrage movement (see Chapter 22).

This record of accomplishment was only part of the story, however. On the eve of World War I, the unanswered question of Ireland brought Great Britain to the brink of civil war. The terrible Irish famine of the 1840s and early 1850s had fueled an Irish

---

■ **Dreyfus affair** A divisive case in which Alfred Dreyfus, a Jewish captain in the French army, was falsely accused and convicted of treason. The Catholic Church sided with the anti-Semites against Dreyfus; after Dreyfus was declared innocent, the French government severed all ties between the state and the church.

■ **People's Budget** A bill proposed after the Liberal Party came to power in Britain in 1906, it was designed to increase spending on social welfare services, but was initially vetoed in the House of Lords.

Irish Home Rule In December 1867 members of the "Fenians," an underground group dedicated to Irish independence from British rule, detonated a bomb outside Clerkenwell Prison in London. Their attempt to liberate Irish Republican activists failed. Though the bomb blew a hole in the prison walls, damaged nearby buildings, and killed twelve innocent bystanders, no Fenians were freed. The British labeled the event the "Clerkenwell Outrage," and its violence evokes revealing parallels with the radical terrorist attacks of today. (From *Illustrierte Zeitung*, Leipzig, Germany, 4 January 1868/akg-images)

revolutionary movement. The Irish Republican Brotherhood, established in 1858 and known as the "Fenians," engaged in violent campaigns against British rule. The British responded with repression and arrests (see image above). Seeking a way out of the conflict, the English slowly granted concessions, such as rights for Irish peasants and the abolition of the privileges of the Anglican Church. Liberal prime minister William Gladstone (1809–1898), who twenty years earlier had proclaimed, "My mission is to pacify Ireland," introduced bills to give Ireland self-government, or home rule, in 1886 and in 1893. They failed to pass, but in 1913 Irish nationalists finally gained such a bill for Ireland.

Thus Ireland, the Emerald Isle, was on the brink of achieving self-government. Yet to the same extent that the Catholic majority in the southern counties wanted home rule, the Protestants of the northern counties of Ulster came to oppose it. Motivated by the accumulated fears and hostilities of generations,

the Ulster Protestants refused to submerge themselves in a majority-Catholic Ireland, just as Irish Catholics had refused to submit to a Protestant Britain.

The Ulsterites vowed to resist home rule. By December 1913 they had raised one hundred thousand armed volunteers, and much of English public opinion supported their cause. In response, in 1914 the Liberals in the House of Lords introduced a compromise home-rule bill that did not apply to the northern counties. This bill, which openly betrayed promises made to Irish nationalists, was rejected in the Commons, and in September the original home-rule bill passed but with its implementation delayed. The Irish question had been overtaken by the earth-shattering world war that began in August 1914, and final resolution was suspended for the duration of the hostilities.

Irish developments illustrated once again the power of national feeling and national movements in the nineteenth century. Moreover, they demonstrated that central governments could not elicit greater loyalty unless they could capture and control that elemental current of national feeling. Though Great Britain had much going for it—power, parliamentary rule, prosperity—none of these availed in the face of the conflicting nationalisms created by Irish Catholics and Protestants. Similarly, progressive Sweden was powerless to stop a Norwegian national movement, which culminated in Norway's leaving Sweden and becoming fully independent in 1905. In this light, one can also understand the difficulties faced by the Ottoman Empire in the Balkans in the late nineteenth century. It was only a matter of time before the Serbs, Bulgarians, and Romanians would break away.

The Austro-Hungarian Empire

The dilemma of conflicting nationalisms in Ireland or the Ottoman Empire helps one appreciate how desperate the situation in the Austro-Hungarian Empire had become by the early twentieth century. In 1848 Magyar nationalism had driven Hungarian patriots to declare an independent Hungarian republic, which Russian and Austrian armies savagely crushed in the summer of 1849 (see Chapter 21). Throughout the 1850s Hungary was ruled as a conquered territory, and Emperor Franz Joseph and his bureaucracy tried hard to centralize the state and Germanize the language and culture of the different ethnic groups there.

Then, in the wake of its defeat by Prussia in 1866 and the loss of northern Italy, a weakened Austria agreed to a compromise and in 1867 established the so-called dual monarchy. The Austrian Empire was divided in two, and the Magyars gained virtual independence for Hungary. Henceforth each half of the empire dealt with its own ethnic minorities. The two states still shared the same monarch and common ministries for finance, defense, and foreign affairs.

In Austria, ethnic Germans were only one-third of the population, and many Germans saw their traditional dominance threatened by Czechs, Poles, and other Slavs. The language used in government and elementary education at the local level became a particularly emotional issue in the Austrian parliament. From 1900 to 1914 the legislature was so divided that ministries generally could not obtain a majority and ruled instead by decree. Efforts by both conservatives and socialists to defuse national antagonisms by stressing economic issues that cut across ethnic lines were largely unsuccessful.

In Hungary, the Magyar nobility in 1867 restored the constitution of 1848 and used it to dominate both the Magyar peasantry and the minority populations until 1914. Only the wealthiest one-fourth of adult males had the right to vote, making the parliament the creature of the Magyar elite. Laws promoting the use of the Magyar language in schools and government were bitterly resented, especially by Croatians and Romanians. While Magyar extremists campaigned loudly for total separation from Austria, the radical leaders of their subject nationalities dreamed of independence from Hungary. Unlike most major countries, which harnessed nationalism to strengthen the state after 1871, the Austro-Hungarian Empire was progressively weakened by it.

The Nation and the People

FOCUS QUESTION *How did popular nationalism evolve in the last decades of the nineteenth century?*

In the first two-thirds of the nineteenth century, nationalism convulsed the autocratic states of Europe. Liberal constitutionalists and radical republicans championed the national idea as a way to challenge authoritarian monarchs, liberate minority groups from imperial rule, and unify diverse territories into a single state. Yet in the decades after 1870—corresponding to the rise of the responsive national state—nationalist ideology evolved in a different direction. Nationalism began to appeal more to those on the right wing of the political spectrum than the left. In these same years the "us-them" outlook associated with nationalism gained force, bolstered by modern scientific racism. Some fanatics and demagogic political leaders sought to build extreme nationalist movements by whipping up racist animosity toward imaginary enemies, especially Jews. The growth of modern anti-Semitism after 1880 epitomized the most negative aspects of European nationalism before the First World War.

Making National Citizens

Responding to national unification, an Italian statesman famously remarked, "We have made Italy. Now we must make Italians." His comment captured the dilemma faced by political leaders in the last third of the nineteenth century. As the nation-state extended voting rights and welfare benefits to more and more people, the question of national loyalty became more and more pressing. Politicians and nationalist ideologues made forceful attempts to ensure the people's conformity to their laws, but how could they ensure that national governments would win their citizens' heartfelt allegiance?

The issue was pressing. The recent unification of Italy and Germany, for example, had brought together a patchwork of previously independent states with different customs, loyalties, and in some cases languages. In Italy, only about 2 percent of the population spoke the language that would become official Italian. In Germany, regional and religious differences and strong traditions of local political autonomy undermined collective feeling. In Great Britain, deep class differences still dampened national unity, and across the territories of central and eastern Europe, overlapping ethnic groups with distinct languages and cultures challenged the logic of nation building. Even in France, where national boundaries had been fairly stable for several centuries, only about 50 percent of the people spoke proper French. The 60 percent of the population that still lived in rural areas often felt stronger allegiance to their village or region than to the distant nation headquartered in Paris.

Yet by the 1890s most ordinary people had accepted, if not embraced, the notion of national belonging. There were various reasons for nationalism's growing popularity. For one, modern nation-states imposed centralized institutions across their entire territories, which reached even the lowliest citizen. Universal military conscription, introduced in most of Europe after the Franco-Prussian War (Britain was an exception), yanked peasants off their land and workers out of their factories and exposed young male conscripts to patriotic values. Free compulsory education leveled out language differences and taught children about glorious national traditions. In Italy and Germany, the introduction of a common currency, standard weights and measurements, and a national post office eroded regional differences. Boasting images of grand historical events or prominent leaders, even postage stamps and banknotes could impart a sense of national solidarity.

Improved transportation and communication networks broke down regional differences and reinforced the national idea as well. The extension of railroad service into hinterlands and the improvement of local roads shattered rural isolation, boosted the growth of national markets for commercial agriculture, and helped turn "peasants into Frenchmen."[3] Literacy rates and compulsory schooling advanced rapidly in the late nineteenth century, and more and more people read about national history or the latest political events in growing numbers of newspapers, magazines, and books.

A diverse group of intellectuals, politicians, and ideologues of all stripes eagerly promoted national pride. At Humboldt University in Berlin, for example, the prominent history professor Heinrich von Treitschke championed German superiority, especially over archrival Great Britain. Scholars like Treitschke uncovered the deep roots of national identity in ancient folk traditions; in shared language, customs, race, and religion; and in historic attachments to national territory. Such accounts, often based on flimsy historical evidence, were popularized in the classroom and the press. Few nationalist thinkers sympathized with French philosopher Ernest Renan, who suggested that national identity was based more on a people's current desire for a "common life" and an invented, heroic past than on actual, true-to-life historical experiences.

A variety of new symbols and rituals brought nationalism into the lives of ordinary people. Each nation had its own unique capital city, flag, military uniform, and national anthem. New symbols, such as Britain's doughty John Bull, France's republican Marianne, America's stern Uncle Sam, and Germany's solid Michel, supposedly embodied shared national characteristics. All citizens could participate in newly invented national holidays, such as Bastille Day in France, first held in 1880 to commemorate the French Revolution, or Sedan Day in Germany, created to celebrate Germany's victory over France in 1871. Royal weddings, coronations, jubilees, and funerals brought citizens into the streets to celebrate the nation's leaders—Queen Victoria's 1887 Golden Jubilee set a high standard. Public squares and parks received prominent commemorative statues and monuments, such as the grand memorial to Victor Emmanuel II in central Rome, or the ostentatious Monument to the Battle of Nations built in Leipzig to honor German victory in the Napoleonic Wars. Surrounded by these inescapable elements of everyday nationalism, most ordinary people grew to see themselves as members of their national communities.[4] (See "Thinking Like a Historian: How to Build a Nation," page 780.)

Nationalism and Racism

Where nationalism in the first two-thirds of the nineteenth century had often been a force for liberal reform and peaceful brotherhood, expressed in its most optimistic form by thinkers like Giuseppe Mazzini (see "Evaluating the Evidence 23.1: The Struggle for the Italian Nation," page 760), it now took on more populist and exclusionary tones. The ideal of national belonging had from the start created an "us-them" outlook (see Chapter 21). After the 1870s the growing popularity of supposedly scientific understandings of racial difference added additional layers of meaning to this dichotomy. Though we now understand that there is no genetic evidence that divides humanity into distinct races, most people in the late nineteenth century believed that race was a product of heredity. Many felt pride in their own national racial characteristics—French, English, German, Jewish, Slavic, and many others—that were supposedly passed down from

How to Build a Nation

Nationalism permeated many aspects of everyday life and became a powerful political ideology in the late nineteenth century. Yet Europeans were divided by opposing regional and religious loyalties, social and class divisions, and ethnic differences, so developing a sense of national belonging among ordinary people posed a problem. How did leaders encourage citizens to embrace national identities?

1 **Ernest Renan, "What Is a Nation?" 1882.** In a famous lecture, French philosopher Ernest Renan argued that national identity depended on an imagined past that had less to do with historical reality than with contemporary aspirations for collective belonging.

A nation is a soul, a spiritual principle. Two things, which in truth are but one, constitute this soul or spiritual principle. One lies in the past, one in the present. One is the possession in common of a rich legacy of memories; the other is present-day consent, the desire to live together, the will to perpetuate the value of the heritage that one has received in an undivided form. . . .

More valuable by far than common customs posts and frontiers conforming to strategic ideas is the fact of sharing, in the past, a glorious heritage and regrets, and of having, in the future, [a shared] programme to put into effect, or the fact of having suffered, enjoyed, and hoped together. These are the kinds of things that can be understood in spite of differences of race and language. I spoke just now of "having suffered together" and, indeed, suffering in common unifies more than joy does. Where national memories are concerned, griefs are of more value than triumphs, for they impose duties, and require a common effort.

A nation is therefore a large-scale solidarity, constituted by the feeling of the sacrifices that one has made in the past and of those that one is prepared to make in the future. It presupposes a past; it is summarized, however, in the present by a tangible fact, namely, consent, the clearly expressed desire to continue a common life. A nation's existence is, if you will pardon the metaphor, a daily plebiscite, just as an individual's existence is a perpetual affirmation of life.

2 **National banknotes and stamps.** Patriotic images turned up in everyday places. An Italian banknote (1881), for example, featured Leonardo da Vinci and King Victor Emmanuel II, while a Belgian stamp (1905) portrayed King Leopold II.

(De Agostini/Alfredo Dagli Orti/Getty Images)

(© CSP_Boris15/age-fotostock)

ANALYZING THE EVIDENCE

1. In Source 1, why does Ernest Renan conclude that "[a] nation's existence is . . . a daily plebiscite"?
2. Consider Sources 2–5. What symbols or ideas are used to promote a sense of national belonging? Why, for example, would an Italian banknote feature an image of the sixteenth-century artist/philosopher Leonardo da Vinci? Why do these sources repeatedly evoke blood, battles, and national leaders?
3. Are nationalists good historians? Do the sources above accurately represent the "true-to-life" historic experiences of specific national peoples?

3 **"The Watch on the Rhine," lyrics 1840, music 1854.** German soldiers sang this triumphal patriotic anthem about the Rhine River, which defines the borderlands between France and Germany, as they marched to fight in the Franco-Prussian War (1870–1871) and World War I (1914–1918).

A voice resounds like thunder-peal,
'Mid dashing waves and clang of steel:
The Rhine, the Rhine, the German Rhine!
Who guards to-day my stream divine?
    [*Chorus*] Dear Fatherland, no danger thine;
    Firm stand thy sons to watch the Rhine!

They stand, a hundred thousand strong,
Quick to avenge their country's wrong;
With filial love their bosoms swell,
They'll guard the sacred landmark well!
    Chorus

The dead of an heroic race
From heaven look down and meet this gaze;
He swears with dauntless heart, "O Rhine,
Be German as this breast of mine!"
    Chorus

While flows one drop of German blood,
Or sword remains to guard thy flood,
While rifle rests in patriot hand,
No foe shall tread thy sacred strand!
    Chorus

Our oath resounds, the river flows,
In golden light our banner glows;
Our hearts will guard thy stream divine:
The Rhine, the Rhine, the German Rhine!
    Chorus

(© Ivan Vdovin/JAI/Corbis)

4 **Monument to the Battle of Nations, Leipzig, Germany, 1913.** This colossal monument commemorates the victory of the Prussians and their allies over Napoleon in 1813. A large statue of the archangel Michael underneath an inscription reading "Gott Mit Uns" (God with Us) guards the entrance, while Teutonic knights with drawn swords stand watch around the memorial's crest. The visitors climbing the stairs at the bottom left of the photo give some idea of the monument's size.

5 **The National Monument to King Victor Emmanuel II, Rome, Italy, 1911.** Nicknamed the "wedding cake" by local wits, this memorial/museum features an equestrian statue of the king above a frieze representing the Italian people, and an imposing Roman-style colonnade crowned by two horse-drawn chariots.

(© Peter Phipp/Travelshots/Bridgeman Images)

PUTTING IT ALL TOGETHER

Using the sources above, along with what you have learned about nationalism in class and in Chapters 21 and 23, write a short essay that applies Ernest Renan's ideas about national identity to the spread of nationalism in the late nineteenth century. Can you explain why nationalism might subsume or erode existing regional, religious, or class differences?

Sources: (1) Ernest Renan, "What Is a Nation?" trans. Martin Thom, in *Nation and Narration*, ed. Homi K. Bhabha (New York: Routledge, 2003), pp. 19–20; (3) Eva March Tappan, ed., *The World's Story: A History of the World in Story, Song and Art*, vol. 7, *Germany, the Netherlands, and Switzerland* (Boston: Houghton Mifflin, 1914), pp. 249–250.

generation to generation. Unfortunately, pride in one's own heritage easily led to denigration of someone else's.

Modern attempts to use race to categorize distinct groups of people had their roots in Enlightenment thought (see Chapter 16). Now a new group of intellectuals, including race theorists such as Count Arthur de Gobineau and Houston Stewart Chamberlain, claimed that their ideas about racial difference were scientific, based on hard biological "facts" about bloodlines and heredity. In his early book *On the Inequality of the Human Races* (1854), Gobineau divided humanity into the white, black, and yellow races based on geographical location and championed the white "Aryan race" for its supposedly superior qualities. Social Darwinist ideas about the "survival of the fittest," when applied to the "contest" between nations and races, drew on such ideas to further popularize stereotypes about inferior and superior races.

The close links between nationalism and scientific racism helped justify imperial expansion, as we shall see in the next chapter. Nationalist racism also fostered domestic persecution and exclusion, as witnessed by Bismarck's Kulturkampf and the Dreyfus affair. According to race theorists, the nation was supposed to be racially pure, and ethnic minorities were viewed as outsiders and targets for reform, repression, and relocation. Thus the ethnic Russian leaders of the Russian Empire targeted minority Poles and Czechs for "Russification," a process by which they might learn the Russian language and assimilate into Russian society. Germans likewise viewed the large number of ethnic Poles living in East Prussia as a "national threat" that required "Germanization" before they could be seen as equals to the supposedly superior Germans. For many nationalists, driven by ugly currents of race hatred, Jews were the ultimate outsiders, the stereotypical "inferior race" that posed the greatest challenge to national purity.

Jewish Emancipation and Modern Anti-Semitism

Changing political principles and the triumph of the nation-state had revolutionized Jewish life in western and central Europe. The decisive turning point came in 1848, when Jews formed part of the revolutionary vanguard in Vienna and Berlin and the Frankfurt Assembly endorsed full rights for German Jews. In 1871 the constitution of the new German Empire consolidated the process of Jewish emancipation in that nation. It abolished all restrictions on Jewish marriage, choice of occupation, place of residence, and property ownership. However, even with this change, exclusion from government employment and discrimination in social relations remained.

The trend toward legal emancipation presented Jews with challenges and opportunities. Traditional Jewish occupations, such as court financial agent, village moneylender, and peddler, were undermined by free-market reforms, but careers in business, the professions, and the arts opened. European Jews excelled in wholesale and retail trade, banking and finance, consumer industries, journalism, medicine, and law, as well as the fine arts. By 1871 a majority of Jewish people in western and central Europe had improved their economic situation enough to enter the middle classes. Middle-class Jews came to identify strongly with their respective nation-states and, with good reason, saw themselves as patriotic citizens.

Vicious anti-Semitism reappeared with force in central and eastern Europe after the stock market crash of 1873. Drawing on long traditions of religious intolerance, segregation into ghettos, and periodic anti-Jewish riots and expulsions (or pogroms), late-nineteenth-century anti-Semitism now drew on the exclusionary aspects of modern popular nationalism and the pseudoscience of race. Fanatic anti-Semites whipped up resentment against Jewish achievement and Jewish "financial control" and claimed that the Jewish race or "blood" (beyond the Jewish religion) posed a biological threat to Christian peoples. Such ideas were popularized by the repeated publication of the notorious forgery "The Protocols of the Elders of Zion," a falsified account of a secret meeting supposedly held at the First Zionist Congress in Basel in 1897. The "Protocols," actually written by the Russian secret police, suggested that Jewish elders planned to dominate the globe. Such anti-Semitic beliefs were particularly popular among conservatives, extreme nationalists, and people who felt threatened by Jewish competition, such as small shopkeepers, officeworkers, and professionals.

Anti-Semites created nationalist political parties that attacked and insulted Jews to win popular support. Anti-Semitism helped Karl Lueger and his Christian Socialist Party, for example, win striking electoral victories in Vienna in the 1890s. Lueger, mayor of Vienna from 1897 to 1910, combined fierce anti-Semitic rhetoric with municipal ownership of basic services, and he appealed especially to the German-speaking lower middle class—and an unsuccessful young artist named Adolf Hitler.

Before 1914 anti-Semitism was most oppressive in eastern Europe, where Jews suffered from social prejudice and rampant poverty. In the western borderlands of the Russian Empire, where 4 million of Europe's 7 million Jewish people lived in 1880 with few legal rights, officials used anti-Semitism to channel popular discontent away from the government and onto the Jewish minority. Russian Jews were regularly denounced as foreign exploiters who corrupted national

■ **Zionism** A movement dedicated to building a Jewish national homeland in Palestine, started by Theodor Herzl.

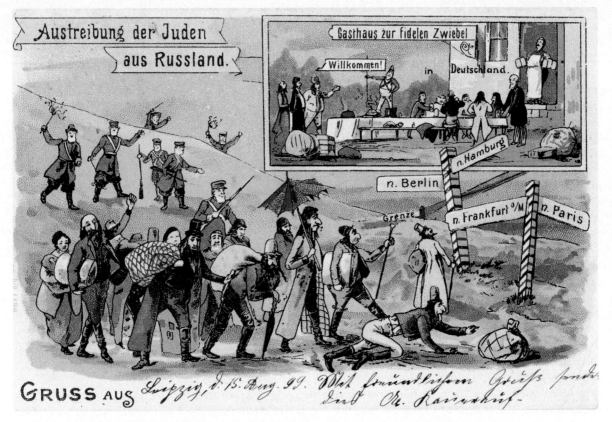

"The Expulsion of the Jews from Russia" So reads this postcard, correctly suggesting that Russian government officials often encouraged the popular anti-Semitism that helped drive many Jews out of Russia in the late nineteenth century. The road signs indicate that these poor Jews are crossing into Germany, where they will find a grudging welcome and a meager meal at the Jolly Onion Inn. Other Jews from eastern Europe settled in France and Britain, thereby creating small but significant Jewish populations in both of these countries for the first time since they had expelled most of their Jews in the Middle Ages. (Alliance Israélite Universelle, Paris, France/Archives Charmet/Bridgeman Images)

traditions, and in 1881 to 1882 a wave of violent pogroms commenced in southern Russia. The police and the army stood aside for days while peasants looted and destroyed Jewish property, and official harassment continued in the following decades.

The growth of radical anti-Semitism spurred the emergence of **Zionism**, a Jewish political movement whose adherents believed that Christian Europeans would never overcome their anti-Semitic hatred. To escape the burdens of anti-Semitism, leading Zionists such as Theodor Herzl advocated the creation of a Jewish state in Palestine—a homeland where European Jews could settle and live free of social oppression. (See "Individuals in Society: Theodor Herzl," page 784.) Zionism was particularly popular among Jews living in Russia. Many embraced self-emancipation and the vision of a Zionist settlement in Palestine, or emigrated to western or central Europe and the United States. About 2.75 million Jews left central and eastern Europe between 1881 and 1914.

Marxism and the Socialist Movement

FOCUS QUESTION *Why did the socialist movement grow, and how revolutionary was it?*

Nationalism served, for better or worse, as a new unifying principle. But what about socialism? Socialist parties, generally Marxist groups dedicated to international proletarian revolution, grew rapidly in these years. Did this mean that national states had failed to gain the support of workers?

The Socialist International

The growth of socialist parties after 1871 was phenomenal. (See "Evaluating the Evidence 23.3: Adelheid Popp, the Making of a Socialist," page 786.) Neither Bismarck's Anti-Socialist Laws nor his extensive social

Theodor Herzl

In September 1897, only days after his vision and energy had called into being the First Zionist Congress in Basel, Switzerland, Theodor Herzl (1860–1904) assessed the results in his diary: "If I were to sum up the Congress in a word — which I shall take care not to publish — it would be this: At Basel I founded the Jewish state. If I said this out loud today I would be greeted by universal laughter. In five years perhaps, and certainly in fifty years, everyone will perceive it."* Herzl's buoyant optimism, which so often carried him forward, was prophetic. Leading the Zionist movement until his death in 1904, at age forty-four, Herzl guided the first historic steps toward modern Jewish political nationhood and the creation of Israel in 1948.

Theodor Herzl was born in Budapest, Hungary, into an upper-middle-class, German-speaking Jewish family. When he was eighteen, his family moved to Vienna, where he studied law. As a university student, he soaked up the liberal beliefs of most well-to-do Viennese Jews, which included the assimilation of German culture. Wrestling with his nonreligious Jewishness and his strong pro-German feeling, Herzl embraced German nationalism and joined a German dueling fraternity. There he discovered that full acceptance required openly anti-Semitic attitudes and a repudiation of all things Jewish. Herzl resigned.

After receiving his law degree, Herzl embarked on a literary career. In 1889 he married into a wealthy Viennese Jewish family, but he and his socialite wife were mismatched and never happy together. Herzl achieved considerable success as both a journalist and a playwright. His witty comedies focused on the bourgeoisie, including Jewish millionaires trying to live like aristocrats. Accepting many German stereotypes, Herzl sometimes depicted eastern Jews as uneducated and grasping. But he believed that the Jewish shortcomings he perceived were the results of age-old persecution and would disappear through education and assimilation. Herzl also took a growing pride in Jewish steadfastness in the face of victimization and suffering.

The emergence of modern anti-Semitism (see page 782) shocked Herzl, as it did many acculturated Jewish Germans. Moving to Paris in 1891 as the correspondent for Vienna's leading liberal newspaper, Herzl studied contemporary politics and pondered recent historical developments. He came to a bold conclusion, published in 1896 as *The Jewish State: An Attempt at a Modern Solution to the Jewish Question.* According to Herzl, Jewish assimilation had failed, and attempts to combat European anti-Semitism would never succeed. Only by building an independent Jewish state could the Jewish people flourish.

Herzl developed his Zionism before the anti-Jewish agitation accompanying the Dreyfus affair, which only served to

Theodor Herzl in Palestine, 1898. (David Wolffsohn/Imagno/Getty Images)

strengthen his faith in his analysis. Generally rebuffed by skeptical Jewish elites in western and central Europe, Herzl turned for support to youthful idealists and the poor Jewish masses. He became an inspiring man of action, rallying the delegates to the annual Zionist congresses, directing the growth of the worldwide Zionist organization, and working himself to death. Herzl also understood that national consciousness required powerful emotions and symbols, such as a Jewish flag. Flags build nations, he said, because people "live and die for a flag."

Putting the Zionist vision before non-Jews and world public opinion, Herzl believed in international diplomacy and political agreements. He traveled constantly to negotiate with European rulers and top officials, seeking their support in securing territory for a Jewish state, usually suggesting that it take form in Palestine, a territory in the Ottoman Empire. Aptly described by an admiring contemporary as "the first Jewish statesman since the destruction of Jerusalem," Herzl proved most successful in Britain. His work paved the way for the 1917 Balfour Declaration, which solemnly pledged British support for a "Jewish homeland" in Palestine.

QUESTIONS FOR ANALYSIS

1. Describe Herzl's background and early beliefs. Do you see a link between Herzl's early German nationalism and his later Zionism?
2. Why did Herzl believe an independent Jewish state with its own national flag was necessary?
3. How did Herzl work as a leader to turn his Zionist vision into a reality?

*Quotes are from Theodor Herzl, *The Diaries of Theodor Herzl*, trans. and ed. with an introduction by Marvin Lowenthal (New York: Grosset & Dunlap, 1962), pp. 224, 22, xxi.

"Greetings from the May Day Festival"   Workers participated enthusiastically in the annual one-day strike on May 1 in Stuttgart, Germany, to honor international socialist solidarity, as this postcard suggests. Speeches, picnics, and parades were the order of the day, and workers celebrated their respectability and independent culture. Picture postcards like this one and the one on page 783 developed with railroads, mass travel, and high-speed printing. (Published by August Henning, Nürnberg, Germany, 1899/akg-images)

security system checked the growth of the German Social Democratic Party, which espoused radical Marxism even though it sought reform through legal parliamentary politics. By 1912 the SPD had millions of followers—mostly people from the working classes—and was the largest party in the Reichstag. Socialist parties grew in other countries as well, though nowhere else with such success. In 1883 Russian exiles in Switzerland founded the Russian Social Democratic Party, and various socialist groups were unified in 1905 in the French Section of the Workers International. Belgium and Austria-Hungary also had strong socialist parties.

As the name of the French party suggests, Marxist socialist parties strove to join together in an international organization, and in 1864 Marx himself helped found the socialist International Working Men's Association, also known as the First International. In the following years, Marx battled successfully to control the organization and used its annual international meetings as a means of spreading his doctrines of socialist revolution. He enthusiastically endorsed the radical patriotism of the Paris Commune and its terrible struggle against the French state as a giant step toward socialist revolution. Marx's fervent embrace of working-class violence frightened many of his early

supporters, especially the more moderate British labor leaders. Internal tensions led to the collapse of the First International in 1876.

Yet international proletarian solidarity remained an important objective for Marxists. In 1889, as the individual parties in different countries grew stronger, socialist leaders came together to form the Second International, which lasted until 1914. Though only a federation of national socialist parties, the Second International had a great psychological impact. It had a permanent executive, and every three years delegates from the different parties met to interpret Marxist doctrines and plan coordinated action. May 1 (May Day) was declared an annual international one-day strike, a day of marches and demonstrations. Prosperous elites and conservative middle-class citizens feared the growing power of socialism and the Second International, but many workers joined the cause.

Labor Unions and Marxist Revisionism

Was socialism really radical and revolutionary in these years? On the whole, it was not. As socialist parties grew and attracted large numbers of members, they

Adelheid Popp, the Making of a Socialist

Nationalism and socialism appeared locked in bitter compe-
tition in Europe before 1914, but they actually complemented
each other in many ways. Both faiths were secular as opposed
to religious, and both fostered political awareness. A working
person who became interested in politics and developed
nationalist beliefs might well convert to socialism at a
later date.

This was the case for Adelheid Popp (1869–1939), a self-
taught working woman who became an influential socialist
leader. Born into a desperately poor working-class family in
Vienna, in what she remembered as a "hard and gloomy
childhood," she was forced by her parents to quit school at
age ten to begin full-time work. She struggled with low-
paying piecework for years before she landed a solid factory
job, as she recounts in the following selection from her widely
read autobiography. Always an avid reader, Popp became
the editor of a major socialist newspaper for German work-
ing women. She then told her life story so that all working
women might share her truth: "Socialism could change and
strengthen others, as it did me."

[Finally] I found work again; I took everything that was
offered me in order to show my willingness to work, and
I passed through much. But at last things became better.
[At age fifteen] I was recommended to a great factory
which stood in the best repute. Three hundred girls and
about fifty men were employed. I was put in a big room
where sixty women and girls were at work.

Against the windows stood twelve tables, and at
each sat four girls. We had to sort the goods which had
been manufactured, others had to count them, and a third
set had to brand on them the mark of the firm. We worked
from 7 A.M. to 7 P.M. We had an hour's rest at noon, half-
an-hour in the afternoon. . . . I had never yet been paid
so much. . . .

I seemed to myself to be almost rich. . . . [Yet] from the
women of this factory one can judge how sad and full of
deprivation is the lot of a factory worker. In none of the
neighbouring factories were the wages so high; we were
envied everywhere. Parents considered themselves
fortunate if they could get their daughters of fourteen
in there on leaving school. . . . And even here, in this
paradise, all were badly nourished. Those who stayed at
the factory for the dinner hour would buy themselves
for a few pennies a sausage or the leavings of a cheese
shop. . . . In spite of all the diligence and economy, every
one was poor, and trembled at the thought of losing her
work. All humbled themselves, and suffered the worst

injustice from the foremen, not to risk losing this good
work, not to be without food. . . .

I did not only read novels and tales; I had begun . . . to
read the classics and other good books. I also began to
take an interest in public events. . . . I was not democratically inclined. I was full of enthusiasm then for emperors,
and kings and highly placed personages played no small
part in my fancies. . . . I bought myself a strict Catholic
paper, that criticised very adversely the workers' movement, which was attracting notice. Its aim was to educate
in a patriotic and religious direction. . . . I took the
warmest interest in the events that occurred in the royal
families, and I took the death of the Crown Prince of
Austria so much to heart that I wept a whole day. . . .
Political events [also] held me in suspense. The possibility
of a war with Russia roused my patriotic enthusiasm. I saw
my brother already returning from the battlefield covered
with glory. . . .

When a particularly strong anti-Semitic feeling
was noticeable in political life, I sympathised with it
for a time. A broad sheet, "How Israel Attained Power
and Sovereignty over all the Nations of the Earth,"
fascinated me. . . .

About this time an Anarchist group was active. Some
mysterious murders which had taken place were ascribed
to the Anarchists, and the police made use of them to
oppress the rising workmen's movement. . . . I followed
the trial of the Anarchists with passionate sympathy. I read
all the speeches, and because, as always happens, Social
Democrats, whom the authorities really wanted to attack,
were among the accused, I learned their views. I became
full of enthusiasm. Every single Social Democrat . . .
seemed to me a hero. . . . There was unrest among the
workers . . . and demonstrations of protest followed.
When these were repeated the military entered the
"threatened" streets. . . . In the evenings I rushed in the
greatest excitement from the factory to the scene of the
disturbance. The military did not frighten me; I only left
the place when it was "cleared."

Later on my mother and I lived with one of my brothers
who had married. Friends came to him, among them
some intelligent workmen. One of these workmen was
particularly intelligent, and . . . could talk on many
subjects. He was the first Social Democrat I knew. He
brought me many books, and explained to me the
difference between Anarchism and Socialism. I heard
from him, also for the first time, what a republic was,
and in spite of my former enthusiasm for royal dynasties,
I also declared myself in favour of a republican form of

government. I saw everything so near and so clearly, that I actually counted the weeks which must still elapse before the revolution of state and society would take place. From this workman I received the first Social Democratic party organ. . . . I first learned from it to understand and judge of my own lot. I learned to see that all I had suffered was the result not of a divine ordinance, but of an unjust organization of society. . . .

In the factory I became another woman. . . . I told my [female] comrades all that I had read of the workers' movement. Formerly I had often told stories when they had begged me for them. But instead of narrating . . . the fate of some queen, I now held forth on oppression and exploitation. I told of accumulated wealth in the hands of a few, and introduced as a contrast the shoemakers who had no shoes and the tailors who had no clothes. On breaks I read aloud the articles in the Social Democratic paper and explained what Socialism was as far as I understood it. . . . [While I was reading] it often happened that one of the clerks passing by shook his head and said to another clerk: "The girl speaks like a man."

EVALUATE THE EVIDENCE

1. How did Popp describe and interpret work in the factory?
2. According to her autobiography, what accounts for Popp's nationalist sentiments early on? How and why did she become a Social Democrat?
3. Was Popp likely to lead other working women to socialism by reading them articles from socialist newspapers? Why or why not?

Source: Slightly adapted from A. Popp, *The Autobiography of a Working Woman*, trans. E. C. Harvey (Chicago: F. G. Browne, 1913), pp. 29, 34–35, 39, 66–69, 71, 74, 82–90.

looked less and less toward revolution, and more and more toward gradual change and steady improvement for the working class. The mainstream of European socialism became militantly moderate. Socialists still liked to alarm mainstream politicians with revolutionary rhetoric. But they increasingly worked within the system, often joining labor unions to win practical workplace reforms.

Workers themselves grew less inclined to follow radical programs for several reasons. As they gained the right to vote and to participate politically in the nation-state, workers focused their attention more on elections than on revolutions. As workers won real, tangible benefits, this furthered the process. And workers were not immune to patriotic education and indoctrination during military service. Many responded positively to drum-beating parades and aggressive foreign policy as they loyally voted for socialists. Nor were workers by any means a unified group with shared social and political interests—as we saw in Chapter 22.

Perhaps most important of all, workers' standard of living rose gradually but substantially after 1850. The quality of life in urban areas improved dramatically as well. For all these reasons, workers became more moderate: they demanded gains, but they were less likely to take to the barricades in pursuit of them.

The growth of labor unions reinforced the trend toward moderation. In the early stages of industrialization, unions were generally prohibited by law. A famous law of the French Revolution had declared all guilds and unions illegal in the name of "liberty" in 1791. In Great Britain, attempts by workers to unite were made criminal conspiracies in 1799. Other countries had similar laws that hampered union development. Unions were considered subversive bodies to be hounded and crushed.

From this sad position workers struggled to escape. Great Britain led the way in 1824 and 1825 when it granted unions the right to exist—though generally not the right to strike. After the collapse of Robert Owen's attempt to form one big national union in the 1830s (see Chapter 20), new and more practical kinds of unions appeared. Limited primarily to highly skilled workers such as machinists and carpenters, these "new model unions" concentrated on winning better wages and hours through collective bargaining and compromise. This approach helped pave the way to the full acceptance of unions in Britain in the 1870s, and after 1890 unions for unskilled workers developed.

Developments in Germany, the most industrialized and unionized continental country by 1914, were particularly instructive. German unions did not receive basic rights until 1869, and until the Anti-Socialist Laws were repealed in 1890, they were frequently harassed by the government as socialist fronts. As a result, in 1895 Germany had only about 270,000 union members in a male industrial workforce of nearly 8 million. Then, with almost all legal harassment eliminated, union membership skyrocketed, reaching roughly 3 million in 1912.

This great expansion both reflected and influenced the changing character of German unions. Increasingly, union activists focused on bread-and-butter issues—wages, hours, working conditions—rather than on fomenting socialist revolution. Genuine collective bargaining, long opposed by socialist intellectuals as a sellout, was officially recognized as desirable by the German Trade Union Congress in 1899. When employers proved unwilling to bargain, a series of strikes forced them to change their minds. In 1913 alone, over ten thousand collective bargaining agreements benefiting 1.25 million workers were signed.

The German trade unions and their leaders were in fact, if not in name, thoroughgoing revisionists. **Revisionism** was an effort by various socialists to update Marx's doctrines to reflect the realities of the time. Thus the socialist Eduard Bernstein (1850–1932) argued in 1899 in his *Evolutionary Socialism* that many of Marx's predictions had been proved false.

> Social conditions have not developed to such an acute opposition of things and classes as is depicted in the Communist Manifesto. . . . The number of members of the possessing classes to-day is not smaller but larger. . . .
>
> In all advanced countries we see the privileges of the capitalist bourgeoisie yielding step by step to democratic organizations. Under the influence of this, and driven by the movement of the working classes which is daily becoming stronger, a social reaction has set in against the exploiting tendencies of capital.[5]

Socialists, according to thinkers like Bernstein, should reform their doctrines and tactics to meet these changed conditions. They should combine with other progressive forces to win continued evolutionary gains for workers through legislation, unions, and further economic development. These views were denounced as heresy by the SPD and later by the Second International. Yet the revisionist, gradualist approach contin-

ued to gain the tacit acceptance of many German socialists, particularly in the trade unions.

Moderation found followers elsewhere. In France, the great socialist leader Jean Jaurès (1859–1914) formally repudiated revisionism in order to establish a unified socialist party, but he remained at heart a gradualist and optimistic secular humanist. Questions of revolution or revisionism also divided Russian Marxists.

By the early twentieth century socialist parties had clear-cut national characteristics. Russians and socialists in the Austro-Hungarian Empire tended to be the most radical. The German party talked revolution and practiced reformism, greatly influenced by its enormous trade-union movement. The French party talked revolution and tried to practice it, unrestrained by a trade-union movement that was both very weak and very radical. In Britain, the socialist but non-Marxist Labour Party, reflecting the well-established union movement, was formally committed to gradual reform. In Spain and Italy, Marxist socialism was very weak. There anarchism, seeking to smash the state rather than the bourgeoisie, dominated radical thought and action.

In short, socialist policies and doctrines varied from country to country. Socialism itself was to a large extent "nationalized" behind the façade of international unity. This helps explain why when war came in 1914, almost all socialist leaders and most workers supported their national governments and turned away from international solidarity.

NOTES

1. Quoted by J. McKay in *Pioneers for Profit: Foreign Entrepreneurship and Russian Industrialization, 1885–1913* (Chicago: University of Chicago Press, 1970), p. 11.
2. W. Dawson, *Bismarck and State Socialism* (London: Swan Sonnenschein & Co., 1890), pp. 63–64.
3. E. Weber, *Peasants into Frenchmen: The Modernization of Rural France, 1870–1914* (Stanford: Stanford University Press, 1976).
4. See E. Hobsbawm, "Mass Producing Traditions: Europe, 1870–1914," in *The Invention of Tradition*, ed. E. Hobsbawm and T. Ranger (New York: Cambridge University Press, 1992), pp. 263–307.
5. E. Bernstein, *Evolutionary Socialism: A Criticism and Affirmation*, trans. E. Harvey (New York: B. W. Huebsch, 1909), pp. x–xvi, quoted in J. H. Hexter et al., *The Traditions of the Western World* (Chicago: Rand McNally, 1967), pp. 797–798.

■ **revisionism** An effort by moderate socialists to update Marxist doctrines to reflect the realities of the late nineteenth century.

LOOKING BACK LOOKING AHEAD

In 1900 the triumph of the national state in Europe seemed almost complete. In the aging Austro-Hungarian, Russian, and Ottoman Empires, ethnic minorities continued to fight for national independence, and class, region, religion, and ethnicity still generated social and political differences across Europe. Nonetheless, the politically unified nation-state, resting solidly upon ongoing industrialization and the emerging urban society, governed with the consent and even the devotion of many of its citizens. Ordinary people developed a sense of patriotic allegiance to the nation and saw themselves as members of a national group—for instance, Swedes, Germans, Italians, or Americans. This newfound sense of national identity often eroded or leveled out other social differences.

Responsive and capable of tackling many practical problems, the European nation-state of 1900 was in part the realization of ideologues and patriots like Mazzini and the middle-class liberals active in the unsuccessful revolutions of 1848. Yet whereas early nationalists had envisioned a Europe of free peoples and international peace, the nationalists of 1900 had been nurtured in an atmosphere of competition between European states and the wars of unification in the 1850s and 1860s. This new generation of nationalists reveled in the strength of their unity, and the nation-state became the foundation stone of a new system of global power.

Thus after 1870, even as the responsive nation-state improved city life and brought social benefits to ordinary people, Europe's leading countries extended their imperial control around the globe. In Asia and Africa, the European powers seized territory, fought brutal colonial wars, and built authoritarian empires. Moreover, in Europe itself the universal faith in nationalism, which usually reduced social tensions within states, promoted a bitter, almost Darwinian, competition between states. Thus European nationalism threatened the very progress and unity it had helped to build. In 1914 the power of unified nation-states would turn on itself, unleashing the First World War and doling out self-inflicted wounds of enormous proportions to all of Europe's peoples.

Make Connections

Think about the larger developments and continuities within and across chapters.

1. By 1900 most countries in Europe and North America had established modern nation-states, but the road to nation building varied dramatically from place to place. Which countries were most successful in building viable nation-states? What accounts for the variation?

2. How and why did the relationship between the state and its citizens change in the last decades of the nineteenth century?

3. Liberalism, socialism, and nationalism first emerged as coherent ideologies in the decades around 1800 (Chapter 21). How had they changed by 1900?

23 REVIEW & EXPLORE

Identify Key Terms

Identify and explain the significance of each item below.

Red Shirts (p. 760)   Reichstag (p. 774)

Homestead Act (p. 766)   Kulturkampf (p. 774)

Crimean War (p. 766)   German Social Democratic Party (SPD) (p. 774)

Bloody Sunday (p. 770)   Dreyfus affair (p. 776)

Duma (p. 770)   People's Budget (p. 776)

Tanzimat (p. 772)   Zionism (p. 783)

Young Turks (p. 773)   revisionism (p. 788)

Review the Main Ideas

Answer the focus questions from each section of the chapter.

◆ How did Napoleon III seek to reconcile popular and conservative forces in an authoritarian nation-state? (p. 756)

◆ How did conflict and war lead to the construction of strong nation-states in Italy, Germany, and the United States? (p. 758)

◆ What steps did Russia and the Ottoman Turks take toward modernization, and how successful were they? (p. 766)

◆ What general domestic political trends emerged after 1871? (p. 773)

◆ How did popular nationalism evolve in the last decades of the nineteenth century? (p. 778)

◆ Why did the socialist movement grow, and how revolutionary was it? (p. 783)

Suggested Reading and Media Resources

BOOKS

◆ Anderson, Benedict. *Imagined Communities: Reflections on the Origin and Spread of Nationalism.* 1991. Famous for its argument about the social construction of nationalism.

◆ Calhoun, Craig. *Nationalism.* 1997. A clear and concise overview of recent theories of nationalism and national identity.

◆ Clyman, Toby W., and Judith Vowles, eds. *Russia Through Women's Eyes: Autobiographies from Tsarist Russia.* 1999. An eye-opening collection detailing women's experiences in Russia.

◆ Findley, Carter Vaughn. *The Turks in World History.* 2005. An exciting reconsideration of the Turks in long-term perspective.

◆ Fink, Carole. *Defending the Rights of Others: The Great Powers, the Jews, and International Minority Protection, 1878–1938.* 2004. Skilled consideration of the cruelty and tragedy of ethnic conflict and minority oppression.

◆ Geary, Dick, ed. *Labour and Socialist Movements in Europe Before 1914.* 1989. An excellent collection that examines labor movements in several different countries.

◆ Hennock, E. P. *The Origin of the Welfare State in England and Germany, 1850–1914.* 2007. Compares Germany's statist approach with England's response to demands from below.

- Hobsbawm, Eric, and Terrence Ranger, eds. *The Invention of Tradition*. 1992. An influential collection of articles on the invented nature of modern nationalism.
- Lazarski, Christopher. *Power Tends to Corrupt: Lord Acton's Study of Liberty*. 2012. A compelling intellectual history that explores the political thought of a seminal British theorist of liberty and its development in Western history.
- Merriman, John. *Massacre: The Life and Death of the Paris Commune*. 2014. An engaging narrative account of a key revolutionary moment.
- Mosse, George. *Nationalism and Sexuality: Respectability and Abnormal Sexuality in Modern Europe*. 1985. A pathbreaking and still-relevant work that calls attention to the links between nationalism, racism, and sexuality.
- Ridley, Jasper. *Garibaldi*. 2001. A thorough study of the world-renowned revolutionary nationalist.
- Tombs, Robert. *France, 1814–1914*. 1996. An impressive survey with a useful bibliography.

DOCUMENTARIES

- *In Search of History: The Infamous Dreyfus Affair* (History Channel, 1998). Examines the false accusations against Alfred Dreyfus in France, also known as the Dreyfus affair.
- *The Internationale* (Peter Miller, 2000). Tells the story of a song written in 1871 after the suppression of the Paris Commune, and how that song went on to inspire many other groups and movements.

FEATURE FILMS AND TELEVISION

- *Fall of Eagles* (BBC, 1974). A thirteen-part television drama about the fall from power of the Habsburgs, Romanovs, and Hohenzollerns in the nineteenth century.
- *La Commune (Paris 1871)* (Peter Watkins, 2000). A unique drama about the Paris Commune that features hundreds of nonprofessional actors in the roles of the revolutionaries.
- *The Leopard* (Luchino Visconti, 1963). An epic tale about the aristocracy of Sicily struggling in the midst of major social upheaval during Garibaldi's invasion in 1860.
- *The Wandering Jew* (Otto Kreisler, 1920). An early pro-Zionist film that tells the story of Theodor Herzl's life.

WEB SITES

- *Discover the Ottomans.* An extensive Web site on the history of the Ottoman Empire, which offers pages on the timeline of the empire, the history of military campaigns, rulers of the empire, and the art and culture of the Ottomans. **www.theottomans.org/english/index.asp**
- *Fordham University Internet Modern History Sourcebook.* "The 19th Century and Western Hegemony," a section of this Web site, includes documents on nineteenth-century Britain, France, Italy (with texts by Cavour, Garibaldi, and Victor Emmanuel), Russia, other western and eastern European countries, and the United States. **www.fordham.edu/Halsall/mod/modsbook.asp**
- *Lorraine Beitler Collection of the Dreyfus Affair.* Information about the Dreyfus affair, including essays and examples of sources that are part of the Lorraine Beitler Collection at the University of Pennsylvania. **sceti.library.upenn.edu/dreyfus/**
- *Napoleon.org.* The history of the rule of Napoleon III through texts, images, and timelines. **www.napoleon.org/en/History/index.asp**

24

The West and the World

1815–1914

While industrialization and nationalism were transforming urban and rural life throughout Europe, western Europeans were reshaping the world. At the peak of its power and pride, the West entered the third and most dynamic phase of the aggressive expansion that had begun with the Crusades and continued with the rise of seaborne colonial empires. At the same time, millions of Europeans picked up stakes and emigrated abroad, primarily to North and South America but also to Australia, North and South Africa, and Asiatic Russia. An ever-growing stream of people, products, and ideas flowed into and out of Europe in the nineteenth century. Hardly any corner of the globe was left untouched.

The most spectacular manifestations of Western expansion came in the late nineteenth century when the leading European nations established or enlarged their far-flung colonial empires. This political annexation of territory in the 1880s—the "New Imperialism," as it is often called by historians—was the capstone of Europe's underlying economic and technological transformation. More directly, Europe's New Imperialism rested on a formidable combination of superior military might and strong authoritarian rule, and it posed a brutal challenge to African and Asian peoples. Different societies met this Western challenge in different ways. By 1914 non-Western elites in many lands were rallying their peoples and leading an anti-imperialist struggle for dignity and genuine independence that would eventually triumph after 1945. ■

CHAPTER PREVIEW

Life on the Imperial Frontier
Colonialism entangled the lives of Europeans, natives, and immigrants, as seen in this 1886 painting of the city of Durban in the British colony of South Africa, the site of a minor gold rush. Here European settlers view an exhibit of gold nuggets found in local mines, as a South Asian migrant laborer and an African Zulu, both dressed in their traditional clothing, pass by. (From *The Spanish and American Illustration*, 1886/Photo © Tarker/Bridgeman Images)

Industrialization and the World Economy

FOCUS QUESTION *What were some of the global consequences of European industrialization between 1815 and 1914?*

The Industrial Revolution created, first in Great Britain and then in continental Europe and North America, a tremendously dynamic economic system. In the course of the nineteenth century, that system expanded across the face of the earth. Some of this extension into non-Western areas was peaceful and beneficial, for the West had many products and techniques the rest of the world desired. If peaceful methods failed, however, Europeans used their superior military power to force non-Western nations to open their doors to Western economic interests. In general, Europeans fashioned the global economic system so that the largest share of the ever-increasing gains from trade, technology, and migration flowed to the West and its propertied classes.

The Rise of Global Inequality

The Industrial Revolution in Europe marked a momentous turning point in human history. Those regions of the world that industrialized in the nineteenth century (mainly Europe and North America) increased their wealth and power enormously in comparison to those that did not. A gap between the core industrializing regions and the soon-to-be colonized or semi-colonized regions outside the European–North American core (mainly in Africa, Asia, the Middle East, and Latin America) emerged and widened throughout the

nineteenth century. Moreover, this pattern of uneven global development became institutionalized, or built into the structure of the world economy. Thus a "lopsided world" evolved, a world with a rich north and a poor south (albeit with regional variations).

In recent years economic historians have charted the long-term evolution of this gap, and Figure 24.1 summarizes the findings of one important study. Three main points stand out. First, in 1750 the average standard of living was no higher in Europe as a whole than in the rest of the world. Second, it was industrialization that opened the gaps in average wealth and well-being among countries and regions. Third, income per person stagnated in the colonized world before 1913, in striking contrast to the industrializing regions. Only after 1945, in the era of decolonization and political independence, did former colonies make real economic progress, beginning in their turn the critical process of industrialization.

The rise of these enormous income disparities, which indicate similar and striking disparities in food and clothing, health and education, and life expectancy and general material well-being, has generated a great deal of debate. One school of interpretation stresses that the West used science, technology, capitalist organization, and even its rational worldview to create massive wealth, and then used that wealth and power to its advantage. Another school argues that the West used its political and economic power to steal much of the world's riches, continuing in the nineteenth and twentieth centuries the rapacious colonialism born of the era of expansion. Because these issues are complex and there are few simple answers, it is helpful to consider them in the context of world trade in the nineteenth century.

FIGURE 24.1   The Growth of Average Income per Person in Industrialized Countries, Nonindustrialized Countries, and Great Britain, 1750–1970   Growth is given in 1960 U.S. dollars and prices.

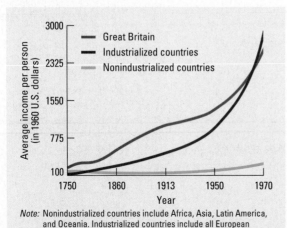

Note: Nonindustrialized countries include Africa, Asia, Latin America, and Oceania. Industrialized countries include all European countries, Canada, the United States, and Japan.

The World Market

Commerce between nations has always stimulated economic development. In the nineteenth century Europe directed an enormous increase in international commerce. Great Britain took the lead in cultivating export markets for its booming industrial output, as British manufacturers looked first to Europe and then around the world, seeking consumers for its growing numbers of mass-produced goods.

Take the case of cotton textiles. By 1820 Britain was exporting 50 percent of its production. Europe bought 50 percent of these cotton textile exports, while India bought only 6 percent and had its own well-established textile industry. Then as European nations and the United States erected protective tariff barriers to promote domestic industry, British cotton textile manufacturers aggressively sought other foreign markets in non-Western areas. By 1850 India was buying 25 percent and Europe only 16 percent of a much larger volume of production. As a British colony, India could not raise tariffs to protect its ancient, indigenous cotton textile industry, which collapsed, leaving thousands of Indian weavers unemployed.

In addition to its dominance in the export market, Britain was also the world's largest importer of goods. From the repeal of the Corn Laws in 1846 (see Chapter 21) to the outbreak of World War I in 1914, Britain remained the world's emporium, the globe's largest trader of agricultural products, raw materials, and manufactured goods. Under free-trade policies, open access to Britain's market stimulated the development of mines and plantations in many non-Western areas.

Improved transportation systems fostered international trade. Wherever railroads were built, they drastically reduced transportation costs, opened new economic opportunities, and called forth new skills and attitudes. European investors funded much of the railroad construction undertaken in Latin America, Asia, and Africa, which connected seaports with resource-rich inland cities and regions, as opposed to linking and developing cities and regions within a given country. Thus railroads dovetailed effectively with Western economic interests, facilitating the inflow and sale of Western manufactured goods and the export and the development of local raw materials.

The power of steam revolutionized transportation by sea as well as by land. Steam power began to supplant sails on the oceans of the world in the late 1860s. Passenger and freight rates tumbled as ship design became more sophisticated, and the intercontinental shipment of low-priced raw materials became feasible. The time needed to cross the Atlantic dropped from three weeks in 1870 to about ten days in 1900, and the opening of the Suez and Panama Canals (in 1869 and 1914, respectively) shortened transport time to other areas of the globe considerably. In addition, improved port facilities made loading and unloading cargo less expensive, faster, and more dependable.

The revolution in land and sea transportation encouraged European entrepreneurs to open up and exploit vast new territories around the world. Improved transportation enabled Asia, Africa, and Latin America to ship not only familiar agricultural products—spices, tea, sugar, coffee—but also new raw materials for industry, such as jute, rubber, cotton, and coconut

Chronology

1805–1848	Muhammad Ali modernizes Egypt
1839–1842	First Opium War; Treaty of Nanking
1853	Perry "opens" Japan for trade
1856–1860	Second Opium War
1857–1858	Britain crushes Great Rebellion in India
1863–1879	Reign of Ismail in Egypt
1867	Meiji Restoration in Japan
1869	Suez Canal opens
1880–1900	Most of Africa falls under European rule
1884–1885	Berlin Conference
1885	Russian expansion reaches borders of Afghanistan
1898	United States takes over Philippines; hundred days of reform in China; Battle of Omdurman
1899	Kipling writes "The White Man's Burden"
1899–1902	South African War
1902	Conrad publishes *Heart of Darkness*; Hobson publishes *Imperialism*
1912	Western-style republic replaces China's Qing Dynasty
1914	Panama Canal opens

oil. The export of raw materials supplied by these "primary producers" to Western manufacturers boosted economic growth in core countries but did little to establish independent industry in the nonindustrialized periphery.

New communications systems were used to direct the flow of goods across global networks. Transoceanic telegraph cables, firmly in place by the 1880s, enabled rapid communications among the financial centers of the world. While a British tramp freighter steamed from Calcutta to New York, a broker in London could arrange by telegram for it to carry American cargo to Australia. The same communications network conveyed world commodity prices instantaneously.

As their economies grew, Europeans began to make massive foreign investments beginning about 1840. By the outbreak of World War I in 1914, Europeans had invested more than $40 billion abroad. Great Britain, France, and Germany were the principal investing countries (Map 24.1). The great gap between rich and poor within Europe meant that the wealthy and moderately well-to-do could and did send great sums abroad in search of interest and dividends.

Most of the capital exported did not go to European colonies or protectorates in Asia and Africa. About

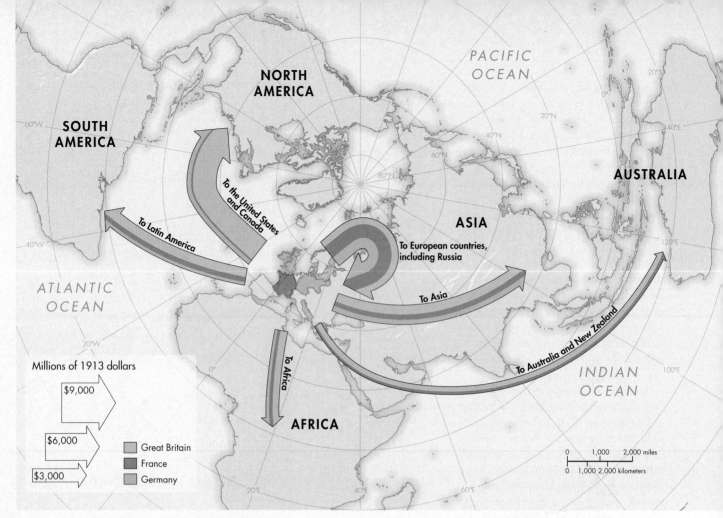

MAP 24.1 European Investment to 1914 Foreign investment grew rapidly after 1850, and Britain, France, and Germany were the major investing nations. As this map suggests, most European investment was not directed to the African and Asian areas seized in the New Imperialism after 1880.

three-quarters of total European investment went to other European countries, or to settler colonies—so-called **neo-Europes**, a term coined by historian Alfred Crosby to describe regions where the climate and topography resembled the European homeland, including the United States, Canada, Australia, New Zealand, Latin America, and parts of Siberia. In these relatively advanced regions, which had already attracted significant settler populations of ethnic Europeans, Europe found its most profitable opportunities for investment in construction of railroads, ports, and utilities. By lending money to construct foreign railroads, Europeans enabled white settlers to buy European rails and locomotives and develop sources of cheap food and raw materials.

Much of this investment was peaceful and mutually beneficial for lenders and borrowers. The extension of Western economic power and the construction of neo-Europes, however, were disastrous for indigenous peoples. Native Americans and Australian Aborigines especially were decimated by the diseases, liquor, and weapons of an aggressively expanding Western society.

The Opening of China

Europe's development of robust offshoots in sparsely populated North America, Australia, and much of Latin America absorbed huge quantities of goods, investments, and migrants. Yet Europe's economic and cultural penetration of old, densely populated civilizations was also profoundly significant. Interaction with such civilizations increased the Europeans' trade and profit, and they were prepared to use force, if necessary, to attain their desires. This was what happened in China, a striking example of the pattern of European intrusion into non-Western lands.

For centuries China had sent more goods and inventions to Europe than it had received, and such was still the case in the early nineteenth century. Trade with Europe was carefully regulated by the Chinese imperial government, ruled by the Qing (ching), or Manchu, Dynasty in the nineteenth century. Qing officials required all foreign merchants to live in the southern port of Guangzhou (Canton) and to buy and sell only to licensed Chinese merchants. Practices considered harmful to Chinese interests were strictly forbidden.

Commissioner Lin Zexu Overseeing the Destruction of Opium at Guangzhou, 1839
A formidable Chinese bureaucrat known for his competence and high moral standards, Lin Zexu
was sent to Guangzhou (Canton) as imperial commissioner in late 1838 to halt the illegal importa-
tion of opium by the British. He made a huge impact on the opium trade within a matter of months.
As a result, British troops invaded China, and the ultimate British victory in the Opium Wars forced
China to grant European merchants one-sided trade agreements. (Pictures from History/Bridgeman Images)

For years the little community of foreign merchants
in Guangzhou had to accept this Chinese system. By
the 1820s, however, the dominant group of these merchants, the British, were flexing their muscles. Moreover, in opium—that "destructive and ensnaring vice"
denounced by Chinese decrees—the British found a
means to break China's self-imposed isolation. British
merchants smuggled opium grown legally in British-
occupied India into China, where its use and sale were
illegal. Huge profits and growing addiction led to a
rapid increase in sales. By 1836 the British merchants
in Guangzhou aggressively demanded the creation of
an independent British colony in China and "safe and
unrestricted liberty" in their Chinese trade. Spurred on
by economic motives, they pressured the British government to take decisive action and enlisted the support of British manufacturers with visions of vast
Chinese markets to be opened to their goods as well.

At the same time, the Qing government decided that
the opium trade had to be stamped out. It was ruining
the people and stripping the empire of its silver, which
went to British merchants to pay for the drug. The government began to vigorously prosecute Chinese drug
dealers. In 1839 it sent special envoy Lin Zexu to
Guangzhou to deal with the crisis. Lin Zexu punished

Chinese who purchased opium and seized the opium
supplies of the British merchants, who then withdrew
to the barren island of Hong Kong. He sent a famous
letter justifying his policy to Queen Victoria in London.

The wealthy, well-connected British merchants
appealed to their allies in London for support, and the
British government responded. It also wanted free,
unregulated trade with China, as well as the establishment of diplomatic relations on the European model,
complete with ambassadors, embassies, and published
treaties. Using troops from India and taking advantage
of its control of the seas, Britain occupied several coastal
cities and in the first of two **Opium Wars** forced China
to give in to British demands. In the Treaty of Nanking
in 1842, the imperial government was required to cede
the island of Hong Kong to Britain forever, pay an
indemnity of $100 million, and open up four large cit-
ies to unlimited foreign trade with low tariffs.

■ **neo-Europes** Settler colonies with established populations of
Europeans, such as North America, Australia, New Zealand, and Latin
America, where Europe found outlets for population growth and its most
profitable investment opportunities in the nineteenth century.

■ **Opium Wars** Two mid-nineteenth-century conflicts between China
and Great Britain over the British trade in opium, which were designed to
"open" China to European free trade. In defeat, China gave European
traders and missionaries increased protection and concessions.

With Britain's new power over Chinese commerce, the opium trade flourished, and Hong Kong developed rapidly as an Anglo-Chinese enclave. But disputes over trade between China and the Western powers continued. Finally, the second Opium War (1856–1860) culminated in the occupation of Beijing by seventeen thousand British and French troops, who intentionally burned down the emperor's summer palace. Another round of one-sided treaties gave European merchants and missionaries greater privileges and protection and forced the Chinese to accept trade and investment on unfavorable terms in several more cities. Thus did Europeans use opium addiction and military aggression to blow a hole in the wall of Chinese seclusion and open the country to foreign trade and foreign ideas.

Japan and the United States

China's neighbor Japan had its own highly distinctive civilization and even less use for Westerners. European traders and missionaries first arrived in Japan, an archipelago nation slightly smaller than California, in the sixteenth century. By 1640 Japanese leaders had reacted quite negatively to their presence. The government decided to expel all foreigners and seal off the country from all European influences in order to preserve traditional Japanese culture and society. When American and British whaling ships began to appear off Japanese coasts almost two hundred years later, the policy of exclusion was still in effect. An order of 1825 commanded Japanese officials to "drive away foreign vessels without second thought."[1]

Japan's unbending isolation seemed hostile and barbaric to the West, particularly to the United States. It complicated the practical problems of ensuring the safety of shipwrecked American sailors and the provisioning of whaling ships and China traders sailing in the eastern Pacific. It also thwarted American business leaders' hope of trade and profit. Moreover, Americans shared the self-confidence and dynamism of expanding Western society, and they felt destined to play a great role in the Pacific. To Americans it seemed the duty of the United States to force the Japanese to open their ports and behave as a "civilized" nation.

After several unsuccessful American attempts to establish commercial relations with Japan, Commodore Matthew Perry steamed into Edo (now Tokyo) Bay in 1853. Relying on **gunboat diplomacy** by threatening to attack, Perry demanded diplomatic negotiations with the emperor. Japan entered a grave crisis. Some Japanese military leaders urged resistance, but senior officials realized how defenseless their cities

were against naval bombardment. Shocked and humiliated, they reluctantly signed a treaty with the United States that opened two ports and permitted trade. Over the next five years, more treaties spelled out the rights and privileges of the Western nations and their merchants in Japan. Japan was "opened." What the British had done in China with two wars, the Americans had achieved in Japan with the threat of one.

Western Penetration of Egypt

Egypt's experience illustrates not only the explosive power of the expanding European economy and society but also their seductive appeal. European involvement in Egypt also led to a new model of formal political control, which European powers applied widely in Africa and Asia after 1882.

Of great importance in African and Middle Eastern history, the ancient land of the pharaohs had since 525 B.C.E. been ruled by a succession of foreigners, most recently by the Ottoman sultans. In 1798 French armies under young General Napoleon Bonaparte invaded the Egyptian part of the Ottoman Empire and occupied the territory for three years. Into the power vacuum left by the French withdrawal stepped an extraordinary Albanian-born, Turkish-speaking general, Muhammad Ali (1769–1849).

First appointed governor of Egypt in 1805 by the Ottoman sultan, Muhammad Ali set out to build his own state on the strength of a large, powerful army organized along European lines. He drafted for the first time the illiterate peasant masses of Egypt, and he hired French and Italian army officers to train both these raw recruits and their Turkish officers in modern military methods. He reformed the government bureaucracy, cultivated new lands, and improved communication networks. By the end of his reign in 1848, Muhammad Ali had established a strong and virtually independent Egyptian state, to be ruled by his family on a hereditary basis within the Ottoman Empire (see Chapter 23).

Muhammad Ali's modernization program attracted large numbers of Europeans to the banks of the Nile. The port city of Alexandria had more than fifty thousand Europeans by 1864. Europeans served not only as army officers but also as engineers, doctors, government officials, and police officers. Others turned to trade, finance, and shipping.

To pay for his ambitious plans, Muhammad Ali encouraged the development of commercial agriculture. This move had profound implications. Egyptian peasants were poor but largely self-sufficient, growing food for their own consumption on state-owned lands allotted to them by tradition. Faced with the possibility of export agriculture, high-ranking officials and members of Muhammad Ali's family began carving large

■ **gunboat diplomacy** The use or threat of military force to coerce a government into economic or political agreements.

■ **global mass migration** The mass movement of people from Europe in the nineteenth century; one reason that the West's impact on the world was so powerful and many-sided.

private landholdings out of the state domain. These new landlords made the peasants their tenants and forced them to grow cash crops such as cotton and rice geared to European markets. Egyptian landowners "modernized" agriculture, but to the detriment of peasant living standards.

These trends continued under Muhammad Ali's grandson Ismail (ihs-MAH-eel), who in 1863 began his sixteen-year rule as Egypt's khedive (kuh-DEEV), or prince. Educated at France's leading military academy, Ismail was a westernizing autocrat. The large irrigation networks he promoted boosted cotton production and exports to Europe, and with his support a French company completed the Suez Canal in 1869. The Arabic of the Egyptian masses replaced the Turkish spoken by Ottoman rulers as the official language. Young Egyptians educated in Europe spread new skills, and Cairo acquired modern boulevards and Western hotels. As Ismail proudly declared, "My country is no longer in Africa, we now form part of Europe."[2]

Yet Ismail was too impatient and reckless. His projects were enormously expensive, and by 1876 Egypt owed foreign bondholders a colossal debt that it could not pay. France and Great Britain intervened and forced Ismail to appoint French and British commissioners to oversee Egyptian finances and ensure payment of the Egyptian debt in full. This momentous decision marked a sharp break with the past. Throughout most of the nineteenth century, Europeans had used military might and political force primarily to make sure that non-Western lands would accept European trade and investment. Now Europeans were going to effectively rule Egypt.

Foreign financial control evoked a violent nationalistic reaction among Egyptian religious leaders, young intellectuals, and army officers. In 1879, under the leadership of Colonel Ahmed Arabi, they formed the Egyptian Nationalist Party. Continuing diplomatic pressure on the government, which forced Ismail to abdicate in favor of his ineffectual son, Tewfiq (r. 1879–1892), resulted in bloody anti-European riots in Alexandria in 1882. A number of Europeans were killed, and Tewfiq and his court had to flee to British ships for safety. When the British fleet bombarded Alexandria, more riots swept the country, and Colonel Arabi led a revolt. But a British expeditionary force put down the rebellion and occupied all of Egypt that year.

The British said their occupation was temporary, but British armies remained in Egypt until 1956. Before the First World War (1914–1918), they maintained the façade of Egypt as an autonomous province of the

The Suez Canal, 1869

Mediterranean Sea

Alexandria

Cairo

Bitter Lakes

Suez Canal

SINAI

EGYPT

Nile R.

Gulf of Suez

OTTOMAN EMPIRE

Red Sea

Ottoman Empire, but the khedive was a mere puppet. British rule did result in tax reforms and somewhat better conditions for peasants, while foreign bondholders received their interest and Egyptian nationalists nursed their injured pride.

The British takeover in Egypt provided a new model for European expansion in densely populated lands. Such expansion was based on military force, political domination, and a self-justifying ideology of beneficial reform. This model predominated until 1914. Thus did Europe's Industrial Revolution lead to tremendous political as well as economic expansion throughout the world after 1880.

Global Migration Around 1900

FOCUS QUESTION *How was massive migration an integral part of Western expansion?*

A poignant human drama accompanied economic expansion: millions of people pulled up stakes and left their ancestral lands in the course of history's greatest migration. To millions of ordinary people for whom the opening of China and the interest on the Egyptian debt had not the slightest significance, this great movement was the central experience in the saga of Western expansion. It was, in part, because of this **global mass migration** that the West's impact on the world in the nineteenth century was so powerful and many-sided.

A note on vocabulary may be in order here: *migration* refers to general human movement; *emigrants* (or *emigration*) refers to people leaving one country for another; *immigrants* (or *immigration*) refers to people entering one country from another. When people migrate, they emigrate from and immigrate to.

The Pressure of Population

In the early eighteenth century European population growth entered its third and decisive stage, which continued unabated until the early twentieth century. Birthrates eventually declined in the nineteenth century, but so did death rates, mainly because of the rising standard of living and the revolution in public health (see Chapter 22). During the hundred years before 1900 the population of Europe (including Asiatic Russia) more than doubled, from approximately 188 million to roughly 432 million.

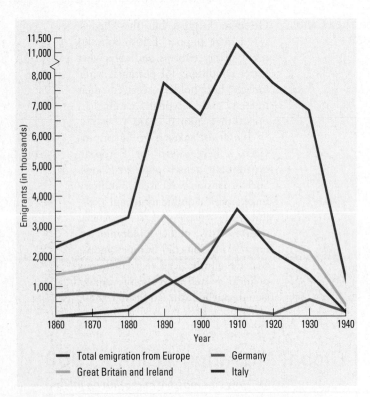

FIGURE 24.2 Emigration from Europe by Decade, 1860–1940
Emigration from Europe followed regional economic trends, as the comparison in this chart suggests. Overall, emigration from Europe grew quickly until the outbreak of World War I in 1914, after which it declined rapidly.

These figures actually understate Europe's population explosion, for between 1815 and 1932 more than 60 million Europeans left the subcontinent. These emigrants went primarily to the rapidly growing neo-Europes—North and South America, Australia, New Zealand, and Siberia. Since the population of native Africans, Asians, and Americans grew more slowly than that of Europeans, the number of Europeans and people of predominantly European origin jumped from about 24 percent of the world's total in 1800 to about 38 percent on the eve of World War I.

The growth of the European population provided further impetus for Western expansion, and it drove more and more people to emigrate. As in the eighteenth century, the rapid increase in numbers in Europe proper led to land hunger and relative overpopulation in area after area. In most countries, emigration increased twenty years after a rapid growth in population, as children grew up, saw little available land and few opportunities, and departed. This pattern was especially prevalent when rapid population increase predated extensive industrial development, which offered the best long-term hope of creating jobs and reducing poverty. Thus millions of country folk in industrialized parts of Europe moved to cities in search of work, while those in more slowly industrializing regions went abroad.

Before looking more closely at the people who emigrated, consider these three facts. First, the number of men and women who left Europe increased rapidly at the end of the nineteenth century and leading up to World War I. As Figure 24.2 shows, more than 11 million left in the first decade of the twentieth century, over five times the number departing in the 1850s. Thus large-scale emigration was a defining characteristic of European society at the turn of the century.

Second, different countries had very different patterns of migration. People left Britain and Ireland in large numbers from the 1840s on. This outflow reflected not only rural poverty but also the movement of skilled industrial technicians and the preferences shown to British migrants in the overseas British Empire. Ultimately, about one-third of all European emigrants between 1840 and 1920 came from the British Isles. German emigration was quite different. It grew irregularly after about 1830, reaching a first peak in the early 1850s and another peak in the early 1880s. Thereafter it declined rapidly, for at that point Germany's rapid industrialization provided adequate jobs at home. This pattern contrasted sharply with that of Italy. More and more Italians left the country right up to 1914, forced out by relatively slow industrial growth and poor living standards in Italian villages. In short, migration patterns mirrored social and economic conditions in the various European countries and provinces.

Third, although the United States did absorb the largest overall number of European emigrants, fewer than half of all these emigrants went to the United States. Asiatic Russia, Canada, Argentina, Brazil, Australia, and New Zealand also attracted large numbers, as Figure 24.3 shows. Moreover, immigrants accounted for a larger proportion of the total population in Argentina, Brazil, and Canada than in the United States. The common American assumption that European emigration meant immigration to the United States is quite inaccurate.

European Emigration

What kind of people left Europe, and what were their reasons for doing so? The European emigrant was generally an energetic small farmer or skilled artisan trying hard to stay ahead of poverty, not a desperately impoverished landless peasant or urban proletarian. Small peasant landowners and village craftsmen typically left Europe because of the lack of available land and the growing availability of inexpensive factory-made goods, which threatened their traditional livelihoods. (See "Living in the Past: The Immigrant Experience," page 802.)

Determined to maintain or improve their status, immigrants brought great benefits to the countries that received them, in large part because the vast majority were young, typically unmarried, and ready to work

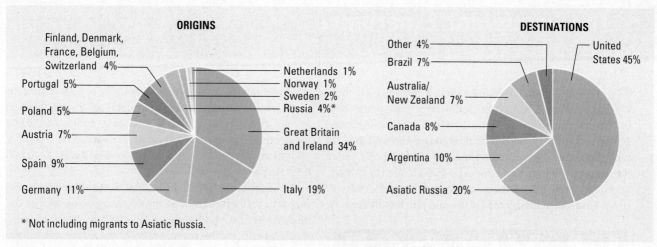

FIGURE 24.3 Origins and Destinations of European Emigrants, 1851–1960 European emigrants came from many countries; almost half of them went to the United States.

hard in the new land, at least for a time. Many Europeans moved but remained within Europe, settling temporarily or permanently in another European country. Jews from central Europe and peasants from Ireland moved to Great Britain; Russians and Poles sought work in Germany; and Spaniards, Portuguese, and Italians went to France. A substantial number of Europeans were actually migrants as opposed to immigrants who settled in new lands—that is, they returned home after some time abroad. One in two immigrants to Argentina and probably one in three to the United States eventually returned to their native lands.

The likelihood of repatriation varied greatly by nationality. People who emigrated from the Balkans, for instance, were much more likely to return to their countries than people from Ireland or eastern European Jews. For those who returned, the possibility of buying land in the old country was of central importance. In Ireland (as well as in England and Scotland), large, often-absentee landowners owned most land; little was up for sale. In Russia, most Jews faced discrimination and were forced to live in the Pale of Settlement (see Chapter 16), and non-Jews owned most property. Therefore, when Irish farmers and Russian Jewish artisans emigrated in search of opportunity, or, for Jews, to escape pogroms (see Chapter 23), it was basically a once-and-for-all departure.

The mass movement of Italians illustrates many of the characteristics of European emigration. As late as the 1880s, three of every four Italians worked in agriculture. With the influx of cheap North American wheat, many small landowning peasants whose standard of living was falling began to leave their country. Numerous Italians went to the United States, but before 1900 even greater numbers went to Argentina and Brazil.

Many Italians had no intention of permanently settling abroad. Some called themselves "swallows." After harvesting their own wheat and flax in Italy, they "flew"

to Argentina to harvest wheat between December and April. Returning to Italy for the spring planting, they repeated this exhausting process. This was a very hard life, but a frugal worker could save $250 to $300 in the course of a season, at a time when an Italian agricultural worker earned less than $1 a day in Italy.

Ties of family and friendship played a crucial role in the emigration process. Many people from a given province or village settled together in rural enclaves or tightly knit urban neighborhoods thousands of miles away. Very often a prominent individual—a businessman, a religious leader, an ambitious family member— would blaze the way, and others would follow, forming a "migration chain."

Many landless young European men and women were spurred to leave by a spirit of revolt and independence. In Sweden and in Norway, in Jewish Russia and in Italy, these young people felt frustrated by the power of the small minority in the privileged classes, which often controlled both church and government and resisted demands for liberal reform and greater opportunity. Many a young Norwegian seconded the passionate cry of Norway's national poet, Martinius Bjørnson (BYURN-sawn): "Forth will I! Forth! I will be crushed and consumed if I stay."[3] Many young Jews wholeheartedly agreed with a spokesman of Kiev's Jewish community in 1882, who summed up his congregation's growing defiance in the face of brutal persecution: "Our human dignity is being trampled upon, our wives and daughters are being dishonored, we are looted and pillaged; either we get decent human rights or else let us go wherever our eyes may lead us."[4]

Thus for many, emigration was a radical way to gain basic human rights. Emigration rates slowed in countries where the people won basic political and social reforms, such as the right to vote, equality before the law, and social security.

LIVING IN THE PAST
The Immigrant Experience

Between 1800 and 1930, 60 million Europeans left their homelands in search of better lives. Just under half moved to the United States; between 1890 and 1925 over 20 million men, women, and children passed through the Ellis Island Immigration Station in New York City harbor. During these years, southern and eastern Europeans, such as Italians, Poles, and Russian Jews, far outnumbered the northern Europeans who had predominated in the mid-nineteenth-century wave of migration to the United States. Today over 40 percent of Americans are descendants of people who went through immigration control on Ellis Island. These figures give some idea of the immense number of people involved in this great migration, but statistics hardly capture what it was like to pull up stakes and move to America.

Transporting migrants across the North Atlantic was big business. Well-established steamship companies such as Cunard, White Star, and Hamburg-America advertised inexpensive fares and good accommodations. The reality was usually different. For the vast majority who could afford only third-class passage in the steerage compartment (so called because it was located near the ship's rudder), the eight- to fourteen-day journey overseas from Naples, Hamburg, or Liverpool was cramped, cold, and unsanitary. Yet poor job prospects and religious or political persecution at home—and the lure of America's booming economy—led many to take the journey.

Once they arrived at Ellis Island, steerage passengers were subjected to a four- to five-hour examination in the Great Hall. Physicians checked their health. Customs officers inspected legal documents. Bureaucrats administered intelligence tests and evaluated the migrants' financial and moral status. The exams worried and sometimes insulted the new arrivals. As one Polish-Jewish immigrant remembered, "They asked us questions. 'How much is two and one? How much is two and two?' But the next young girl, also from our city, went and they asked her, 'How do you wash stairs, from the top or from the bottom?' She says, 'I don't come to America to wash stairs.'"

Migrants with obvious illnesses were required to stay in the island's hospital as long as several weeks to see if they improved. Sick passengers whom officials judged either a threat to public health or a likely drain on public finances were sent home. Suspected anarchists and, later, Bolsheviks were also deported.

Italian poster advertising sailings to the United States, Brazil, Venezuela, Argentina, and Central America, 1906. (National Archives, RG85: 51411/53)

Asian Emigration

Not all emigration was from Europe. A substantial number of Chinese, Japanese, Indians, and Filipinos—to name only four key groups—also responded to rural hardship with temporary or permanent emigration. At least 3 million Asians moved abroad before 1920. Most went as indentured laborers to work under incredibly difficult conditions on the plantations or in the gold mines of Latin America, southern Asia, Africa, California, Hawaii, and Australia. This marked the rise of a new global trend: white estate owners very often used Asian immigrants to replace or supplement black workers after the suppression of the slave trade.

Conditions for steerage passengers were cramped, as shown in this 1902 photo. Passengers were allowed to bring only their most cherished possessions, such as the teddy bear from Switzerland and the Hebrew prayer book from Poland, both of which made the crossing to the United States with their owners in 1921. (steerage: Granger, NYC — All rights reserved; prayer book and teddy bear: Metaform Inc./ Karen Yamauchi of artifacts in the National Park Service Collection, Statue of Liberty National Monument, Ellis Island Immigration Museum. Book: gift of Jean C. Osaja. Bear: gift of Gertrude Schneider Smith)

By today's standards, it was remarkably easy for those seeking to establish permanent residency to enter the United States — only about 2 percent of all migrants were denied entry. After they cleared processing, the new arrivals were ferried to New York City, where they either stayed or departed for other industrialized cities of the Northeast and Midwest. The migrants typically took unskilled jobs for low wages, but by keeping labor costs down, they fueled the rapid industrialization of late-nineteenth-century America. They furthermore transformed the United States from a land of predominantly British and northern European settlers into the multiethnic melting pot of myth and fame.

QUESTIONS FOR ANALYSIS

1. Why did so many Europeans make the difficult and sometimes-dangerous transatlantic trip to the United States?
2. What were the main concerns of U.S. immigration officials as they evaluated the new arrivals? Did U.S. officials treat immigrants fairly?

In the 1840s, for example, the Spanish government actively recruited Chinese laborers to meet the strong demand for field hands in Cuba. Between 1853 and 1873, when such immigration was stopped, more than 130,000 Chinese laborers went to Cuba. The majority spent their lives as virtual slaves. The great landlords of Peru also brought in more than 100,000 workers from China in the nineteenth century, and there were similar movements of Asians elsewhere.

Emigration from Asia would undoubtedly have grown to much greater proportions if planters and mine owners in search of cheap labor had been able to hire as many Asian workers as they wished. But they could not.

Vaccinating Migrants Bound for Hawaii, 1904   First Chinese, then Japanese, and finally Koreans and Filipinos went across the Pacific in large numbers to labor in Hawaii on American-owned sugar plantations in the late nineteenth century. The native Hawaiians had been decimated by disease, creating a severe labor shortage for Hawaii's plantation economy. U.S. plantation owners filled the shortage with East Asian immigrant workers. (© Corbis)

Many Asians fled the plantations and gold mines as soon as possible, seeking greater opportunities in trade and towns. There they came into conflict with local populations, whether in Malaya, southern Africa, or areas settled by Europeans. When that took place in neo-Europes, European settlers demanded a halt to Asian immigration. By the 1880s the American and Australian governments had instituted exclusionary acts—discriminatory laws designed to keep Asians from entering the country.

In fact, the explosion of mass mobility in the late nineteenth century, combined with the growing appeal of nationalism and scientific racism (see Chapter 23), encouraged a variety of attempts to control immigration flows and seal off national borders. National governments established strict rules for granting citizenship and asylum to foreigners. Passports and customs posts monitored

movement across increasingly tight national boundaries. Such attempts were often inspired by **nativism**, beliefs that led to policies giving preferential treatment to established inhabitants above immigrants. Thus French nativists tried to limit the influx of Italian migrant workers, German nativists stopped Poles from crossing eastern borders, and American nativists (in the 1920s) restricted immigration from southern and eastern Europe and banned it outright from much of Asia. (See "Evaluating the Evidence 24.1: Nativism in the United States," at right.)

A crucial factor in migration patterns before 1914 was, therefore, immigration policies that offered preferred status to "acceptable" racial and ethnic groups in the open lands of possible permanent settlement. This, too, was part of Western dominance in the increasingly lopsided world. Largely successful in monopolizing the best overseas opportunities, Europeans and people of European ancestry reaped the main benefits from the mass migration. By 1913 people in Australia, Canada, and the United States had joined the British in having the highest average incomes in the world, while incomes in Asia and Africa lagged far behind.

Western Imperialism, 1880–1914

FOCUS QUESTION *How did Western imperialism change after 1880?*

The expansion of Western society reached its apex between about 1880 and 1914. In those years, the leading European nations not only continued to send massive streams of migrants, money, and manufactured goods around the world, but also rushed to create or enlarge vast empires. This political empire building, under direct European rule, contrasted sharply with the economic penetration of non-Western territories between 1816 and 1880, which had left a China or a Japan "opened" but politically independent. By contrast, the empires of the late nineteenth century recalled the old European colonial empires of the sixteenth to eighteenth centuries. Because this renewed imperial push came after a long pause in European expansionism, contemporaries termed it the **New Imperialism**.

Characterized by a frantic rush to plant the flag over as many people and as much territory as possible, the New Imperialism had momentous consequences. By the early twentieth century almost 84 percent of the globe was dominated by European nations, and Britain alone controlled one-quarter of the earth's territory and one-third of its population. The New Imperialism created tensions among competing European states and led to wars and threats of war with non-European powers.

- **nativism** Policies and beliefs, often influenced by nationalism, scientific racism, and mass migration, that give preferential treatment to established inhabitants over immigrants.

- **New Imperialism** The late-nineteenth-century drive by European countries to create vast political empires abroad.

- **Afrikaners** Descendants of the Dutch settlers in the Cape Colony in southern Africa.

Nativism in the United States

In this 1896 Senate speech, the dynamic and well-respected Republican senator Henry Cabot Lodge expressed nativist anxieties about "race mixing" in the United States and called for rigid immigration restrictions. Most Europeans who immigrated to the United States in the late nineteenth century were Roman Catholics from Italy and central Europe and Jews and Slavs from Poland and Russia — "races" that nativists considered superior to Asians and Africans but far below the Anglo-Saxon Protestants from northern Europe, who constituted the majority of U.S. immigrants until the 1870s.

Restricting Immigration

This bill is intended to amend the existing law so as to restrict still further immigration to the United States. Paupers, diseased persons, convicts, and contract laborers are now excluded. By this bill it is proposed to make a new class of excluded immigrants, and to add to those which have just been named the totally ignorant. . . .

[We propose] to exclude all immigrants who could neither read nor write, and this is the plan which was adopted by the committee. . . . In their report the committee have shown by statistics, which have been collected and tabulated with great care, the emigrants who would be affected by this illiteracy test. . . . It is found . . . that the illiteracy test will bear most heavily upon the Italians, Russians, Poles, Hungarians, Greeks, and Asiatics, and very lightly, or not at all, upon English-speaking emigrants, or Germans, Scandinavians, and French. In other words, the races most affected by the illiteracy test are those whose emigration to this country has begun within the last twenty years and swelled rapidly to enormous proportions, races with which the English-speaking people have never hitherto assimilated, and who are most alien to the great body of the people of the United States. . . .

Immigration and the Economy

There is no one thing which does so much to bring about a reduction of wages and to injure the American wage earner as the unlimited introduction of cheap foreign labor through unrestricted immigration. Statistics show that the change in the race character of our immigration has been accompanied by a corresponding decline in its quality. . . .

Immigration and Citizenship

When we speak of a race, . . . we mean the moral and intellectual characters, which in their association make the soul of a race, and which represent the product of all its past, the inheritance of all its ancestors. . . .

[I]t is on the moral qualities of the English-speaking race that our history, our victories, and all our future rest. There is only one way in which you can lower those qualities or weaken those characteristics, and that is by breeding them out. If a lower race mixes with a higher in sufficient numbers, history teaches us that the lower race will prevail. . . . The lowering of a great race means not only its own decline, but that of civilization. . . .

Mr. President, more precious even than forms of government are the mental and moral qualities which make what we call our race. While those stand unimpaired all is safe. When those decline all is imperiled. . . . The time has certainly come, if not to stop, at least to check, to sift, and to restrict those immigrants. . . . The gates which admit men to the United States and to citizenship in the great republic should no longer be left unguarded.

EVALUATE THE EVIDENCE

1. How does Lodge's understanding of race drive his enthusiasm for immigration restrictions?
2. Why would nativist arguments win popular support in the late nineteenth century?

Source: Henry Cabot Lodge, *Speeches and Addresses, 1884–1909* (Boston: Houghton Mifflin Company, 1909), pp. 245, 247, 249–250, 262, 264–266.

Aimed primarily at Africa and Asia, the New Imperialism put millions of non-Western peoples directly under European rule.

The European Presence in Africa Before 1880

Prior to 1880, European nations controlled only about 10 percent of Africa. The French had begun conquering Algeria in 1830, and by 1880 substantial numbers of French, Italian, and Spanish colonists had settled among the overwhelming Arab majority there. Yet the overall effect on Africa was minor.

At the southern tip of the continent, Britain had taken possession of the Dutch settlements in and around Cape Town during the wars with Napoleon I. This takeover of the Cape Colony had led disgruntled Dutch cattle ranchers and farmers in 1835 to make their so-called Great Trek into the interior, where they fought the Zulu and Xhosa (KO-sah) peoples for land. After 1853 the Boers, or **Afrikaners** (a-frih-KAH-nuhrz), as the descendants of the Dutch in the Cape

European Imperialism at Its Worst   This 1908 English cartoon, "Leopold, King of the Congo, in his national dress," focuses on the barbaric practice of cutting off the hands and feet of Africans who refused to gather as much rubber as Leopold's company demanded. In 1908 an international human rights campaign forced the Belgian king to cede his personal fief to the Belgian state. (Granger, NYC — All rights reserved)

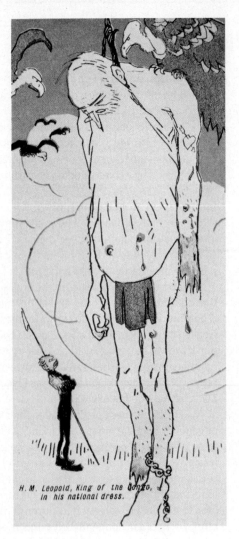

H. M. Leopold, King of the Congo, in his national dress.

The Scramble for Africa After 1880

Between 1880 and 1900 Britain, France, Belgium, Germany, and Italy scrambled for African possessions as if their national livelihoods depended on it (Map 24.2). By 1900 nearly the whole continent had been carved up and placed under European rule: only Ethiopia, which fought off Italian invaders, and Liberia, which had been settled by freed slaves from the United States, remained independent. In all other African territories, European powers tightened their control and established colonial governments in the years before 1914.

In the complex story of the European seizure of Africa, certain events and individuals stand out. Of enormous importance was the British occupation of Egypt in 1882, which established the new model of formal political control (see page 799). King Leopold II of Belgium (r. 1865–1909), an energetic, strong-willed monarch of a tiny country with a lust for distant territory, also played a crucial role. As early as 1861, he had laid out his vision of expansion: "The sea bathes our coast, the world lies before us. Steam and electricity have annihilated distance, and all the nonappropriated lands on the surface of the globe can become the field of our operations and of our success."[5]

By 1876 Leopold's expansionism focused on central Africa. He formed a financial syndicate under his personal control to send Henry M. Stanley, a sensation-seeking journalist and part-time explorer, to the Congo basin. Stanley established trading stations, signed unfair treaties with African chiefs, and planted the Belgian flag. Leopold's actions alarmed the French, who quickly sent out an expedition under Pierre de Brazza. In 1880 de Brazza signed a treaty of protection with the chief of the large Teke tribe and began to establish a French protectorate on the north bank of the Congo River.

Leopold's intrusion into the Congo area called attention to the possibilities of African colonization, and by 1882 Europe had caught "African fever." A gold-rush mentality led to a determined race for territory, and rampant greed threatened the balance of power in Europe. To lay down some basic rules for this new and dangerous global competition, Jules Ferry of France and Otto von Bismarck of Germany arranged an international conference on Africa in Berlin in 1884 and 1885. The **Berlin Conference**, attended by over ten Western powers including the United States, established the principle that European claims to African territory had to rest on "effective occupation" (a strong presence on the ground) to be recognized by other states. This meant that Europeans would push relentlessly into interior regions from all sides and that no single European power would be able to claim the entire continent. The conference recognized Leopold's

Colony were beginning to call themselves, proclaimed their independence and defended it against British armies. By 1880 Afrikaner and British settlers, who detested each other and lived in separate areas, had wrested control of much of South Africa from the Zulu, Xhosa, and other African peoples.

In addition to the French in the north and the British and Afrikaners in the south, European trading posts and forts dating back to the Age of Discovery and the slave trade dotted the coast of West Africa, and the Portuguese maintained a loose hold on their old possessions in Angola and Mozambique. Elsewhere, over the great mass of the continent, Europeans did not rule.

After 1880 the situation changed drastically. In a spectacular manifestation of the New Imperialism, European countries jockeyed for territory in Africa, breaking sharply with previous patterns of colonization and diplomacy.

■ **Berlin Conference** A meeting of European leaders held in 1884 and 1885 in order to lay down some basic rules for imperialist competition in sub-Saharan Africa.

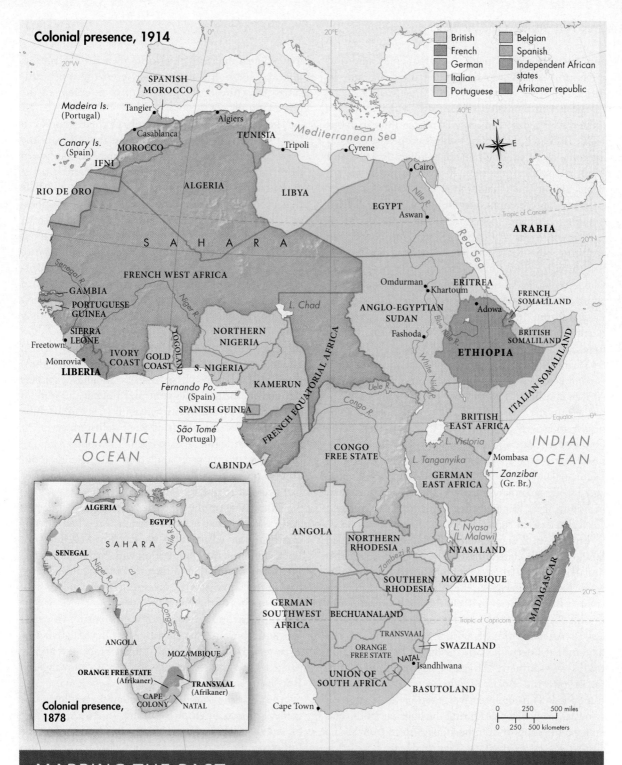

Colonial presence, 1914

British
French
German
Italian
Portuguese
Belgian
Spanish
Independent African states
Afrikaner republic

SPANISH MOROCCO
Madeira Is. (Portugal)
Tangier
Algiers
Casablanca
TUNISIA
Tripoli
Cyrene
Mediterranean Sea
Cairo
Canary Is. (Spain)
MOROCCO
IFNI
RIO DE ORO
ALGERIA
LIBYA
EGYPT
Aswan
ARABIA
Tropic of Cancer
S A H A R A
Senegal R.
FRENCH WEST AFRICA
Niger R.
GAMBIA
PORTUGUESE GUINEA
SIERRA LEONE
Freetown
IVORY COAST
GOLD COAST
TOGOLAND
Monrovia
LIBERIA
L. Chad
NORTHERN NIGERIA
S. NIGERIA
KAMERUN
Fernando Po. (Spain)
SPANISH GUINEA
São Tomé (Portugal)
FRENCH EQUATORIAL AFRICA
CABINDA
Omdurman
Khartoum
ANGLO-EGYPTIAN SUDAN
Fashoda
Blue Nile R.
Adowa
ETHIOPIA
White Nile R.
Uele R.
Congo R.
CONGO FREE STATE
ERITREA
FRENCH SOMALILAND
BRITISH SOMALILAND
ITALIAN SOMALILAND
BRITISH EAST AFRICA
Equator
L. Victoria
L. Tanganyika
Mombasa
Zanzibar (Gr. Br.)
GERMAN EAST AFRICA
Red Sea
Nile R.
ATLANTIC OCEAN
INDIAN OCEAN
ANGOLA
NORTHERN RHODESIA
L. Nyasa (L. Malawi)
NYASALAND
Zambezi R.
SOUTHERN RHODESIA
MOZAMBIQUE
MADAGASCAR
20°S
GERMAN SOUTHWEST AFRICA
BECHUANALAND
TRANSVAAL
ORANGE FREE STATE
SWAZILAND
NATAL
Isandhlwana
Tropic of Capricorn
UNION OF SOUTH AFRICA
BASUTOLAND
Cape Town

0   250   500 miles
0   250 500 kilometers

20°W   0°   20°E   40°E   20°N   0°

Colonial presence, 1878
ALGERIA
EGYPT
SAHARA
SENEGAL
Niger R.
Nile R.
ANGOLA
MOZAMBIQUE
Congo R.
ORANGE FREE STATE (Afrikaner)
TRANSVAAL (Afrikaner)
CAPE COLONY
NATAL

MAPPING THE PAST

MAP 24.2 The Partition of Africa

The European powers carved up Africa after 1880 and built vast political empires. European states also seized territory in Asia in the nineteenth century, although some Asian states and peoples managed to maintain their political independence (see Map 24.3, page 811). Compare the patterns of European imperialism in Africa and Asia, using this map and Map 24.3.

ANALYZING THE MAP What European countries were leading imperialist states in both Africa and Asia, and what lands did they hold? What countries in Africa and Asia maintained their independence? What did the United States and Japan have in common in Africa and Asia?

CONNECTIONS The late nineteenth century was the high point of European imperialism. What were the motives behind the rush for land and empire in Africa and Asia?

personal rule over a neutral Congo Free State and agreed to work to stop slavery and the slave trade in Africa.

The Berlin Conference coincided with Germany's sudden emergence as an imperial power. Prior to about 1880, Bismarck, like many other European leaders at the time, had seen little value in colonies. In 1884 and 1885, as political agitation for expansion increased, Bismarck did an abrupt about-face, and Germany established protectorates over a number of small African kingdoms and tribes in Togo, the Cameroons region, southwest Africa, and, later, East Africa. In acquiring colonies, Bismarck cooperated against the British with France's Jules Ferry, an ardent republican who also embraced imperialism. With Bismarck's tacit approval, the French pressed southward from Algeria, eastward from their old forts on the Senegal coast, and northward from their protectorate on the Congo River to take control of parts of West and Central Africa.

Meanwhile, the British began to enlarge their own African colonies, beginning at the southern tip of the African continent. Led by Cecil Rhodes (1853–1902), prime minister of Britain's Cape Colony, British colonists leapfrogged over the two Afrikaner states—the Orange Free State and the Transvaal (see Map 24.2)—in the early 1890s and established protectorates over Bechuanaland (bech-WAH-nuh-land; now Botswana) and Rhodesia (now Zimbabwe and Zambia), named in honor of its founder. (See "Individuals in Society: Cecil Rhodes," at right.)

English-speaking capitalists like Rhodes developed fabulously rich gold mines in the Transvaal, and this unilateral territorial and economic expansion heightened tensions between the British and Afrikaner (Dutch Boer) settlers. In 1899 the conflict erupted in the bloody South African War, or Boer War (1899–1902). After a series of defeats at the hands of the determined Boers, the British shipped some 180,000 troops to southern Africa. Overwhelming British forces put the Boers on the defensive, and they responded with an intensive guerrilla war that took two years to put down. During the fighting, both sides enlisted the support of indigenous African troops. The British forces resorted to "scorched earth" policies, burning crops and villages in Boer regions, and, most notoriously, placed Boers and native Africans in rudimentary concentration camps in an attempt to halt the guerrilla campaign. News of these tactics provoked liberal outrage at home in Britain.

The war ended with a British victory in 1902, and in 1910 the Afrikaner territories were united with the old Cape Colony and the eastern province of Natal in a new Union of South Africa, established as a largely "self-governing" colony but still under British control. Gradually, however, the defeated Afrikaners used their numerical superiority over the British settlers to take political power, as even the most educated nonwhites lost the right to vote, except in the Cape Colony.

The British also fought to enlarge their colonies in West Africa, impatiently pushing northward from the Cape Colony, westward from Zanzibar, and southward from Egypt. In 1885 British troops stationed in the Sudanese city of Khartoum, an outpost on the Nile that protected imperial interests in Egypt, were massacred by fiercely independent Muslim Sudanese. A decade later the British sought to establish permanent rule in the disputed territory. Under the command of General Sir Herbert Kitchener (who would serve Britain as secretary of state for war during World War I), a well-armed force moved cautiously and more successfully up the Nile River, building a railroad to supply arms and reinforcements as it went. Finally, in 1898 these British troops confronted the poorly armed Sudanese army at the Battle of Omdurman (ahm-duhr-MAHN) (see Map 24.2). Sudanese soldiers charged the British lines time and time again, only to be cut down by the recently invented Maxim machine gun. In the solemn words of one English observer, "It was not a battle but an execution. The bodies were . . . spread evenly over acres and acres." In the end, about 10,000 Sudanese soldiers lay dead, while 28 Britons had been killed and 145 wounded.[6]

Continuing up the Nile after the battle, Kitchener's armies found that a small French force had already occupied the village of Fashoda (fuh-SHOH-duh). Locked in imperial competition with Britain ever since the British occupation of Egypt, France had tried to be first to reach one of Africa's last unclaimed areas—the upper reaches of the Nile. The result was a serious diplomatic crisis and the threat of war between two major European powers. Wracked by the Dreyfus affair (see Chapter 23) and unwilling to fight, France eventually backed down and withdrew its forces, allowing the British to take over.

The British conquest of Sudan exemplifies the general process of empire building in Africa. The fate of the Muslim-Sudanese force at Omdurman was inflicted on native peoples who openly resisted European control: they were blown away by vastly superior military force. The violent German suppression of armed rebellions in the colonies of German East Africa and German Southwest Africa, where revolt led to full-scale warfare and the deaths of some one hundred thousand Herero and Nama Africans, confirmed the rule. But as the Fashoda incident showed, however much the European powers squabbled for territory around the world, they had the sense to stop short of actually fighting each other. Imperial ambitions were not worth a great European war.

Cecil Rhodes

Cecil Rhodes epitomized the dynamism and the ruthlessness of the New Imperialism. He built a corporate monopoly, claimed vast tracts in Africa, and established the famous Rhodes scholarships to develop colonial (and American) leaders who would love and strengthen the British Empire. But to Africans, he left a bitter legacy.

Rhodes came from a large middle-class family and at seventeen went to southern Africa to seek his fortune. He soon turned to diamonds, newly discovered at Kimberley, picked good business partners, and was wealthy by 1876. But Rhodes, often called a dreamer, wanted more. He entered Oxford University, where he studied while returning periodically to Africa. His musings crystallized in a Social Darwinist belief in progress through racial competition and territorial expansion. "I contend," he wrote, "that we [English] are the finest race in the world and the more of the world we inhabit the better it is for the human race."*

Rhodes's belief in British expansion never wavered. In 1880 he formed the De Beers Mining Company, and by 1888 his firm had monopolized southern Africa's diamond production and earned fabulous profits. Rhodes also entered the Cape Colony's legislature and became the colony's all-powerful prime minister from 1890 to 1896.

His main objective was to annex the Afrikaner republics and impose British rule on as much land as possible beyond their northern borders. Working through a state-approved private company financed in part by De Beers, Rhodes's agents forced and cajoled African kings to accept British "protection," and then put down rebellions with machine guns. Britain thus obtained a great swath of empire on the cheap.

But Rhodes, like many high achievers obsessed with power and personal aggrandizement, went too far. He backed, and then declined to call back, the 1896 Jameson Raid, a failed British invasion of the Afrikaner Transvaal, which was designed to topple the Dutch-speaking republic. Repudiated by top British leaders who had encouraged his plan, Rhodes had to resign as prime minister. In declining health, he continued to agitate against the Afrikaner republics. He died at age forty-nine as the South African War (1899–1902) ended.

In accounting for Rhodes's remarkable but flawed achievements, both sympathetic and critical biographers stress his imposing physical size, enormous energy, and charismatic personality. His ideas were commonplace, but he believed in them passionately, and he could persuade and inspire others

Cecil Rhodes, after crushing the last African revolt in Rhodesia in 1896. (© Baldwin H. Ward. Ward & Kathryn C. Ward/Corbis)

to follow his lead. Rhodes the idealist was nonetheless a born negotiator, a crafty deal maker who believed that everyone could be had for a price. According to his most insightful biographer, Rhodes's homosexuality—discreet, partially repressed, but undeniable—was also "a major component of his magnetism and his success."† Never comfortable with women, he loved male companionship. He drew together a "band of brothers," both gay and straight, who shared in his pursuit of power.

Rhodes cared nothing for the rights of Africans and blacks. Both a visionary and an opportunist, he looked forward to an eventual reconciliation of Afrikaners and British in a united white front. Therefore, as prime minister of the Cape Colony, he broke with the colony's liberal tradition and supported Afrikaner demands to reduce drastically the number of black voters and limit black freedoms. This helped lay the foundation for the Union of South Africa's brutal policy of racial segregation known as apartheid after 1948.

QUESTIONS FOR ANALYSIS

1. In what ways did Rhodes's career epitomize the New Imperialism in Africa?
2. How did Rhodes relate to Afrikaners and to black Africans? How do you account for the differences and the similarities?

*Robert I. Rotberg, *The Founder: Cecil Rhodes and the Pursuit of Power* (New York: Oxford University Press, 1988), p. 150.
†Ibid., p. 408.

Imperialism in Asia

Although their sudden division of Africa was more spectacular, Europeans also exerted political control over much of Asia. Here the Dutch were a major player. In 1815 the Dutch ruled little more than the island of Java in the East Indies. Thereafter they gradually brought almost all of the three-thousand-mile Malay Archipelago under their political authority, though— in good imperialist fashion—they had to share some of the spoils with Britain and Germany. In the critical decade of the 1880s, the French under the leadership of Ferry took Indochina. India, Japan, and China also experienced a profound imperialist impact (Map 24.3).

Two other great imperialist powers, Russia and the United States, also acquired territories in Asia. Russia moved steadily forward on two fronts throughout the nineteenth century. Russians conquered Muslim areas to the south in the Caucasus and in Central Asia, reaching the border of Afghanistan in 1885. Russia also proceeded to nibble greedily on China's outlying provinces, especially in the 1890s.

The great conquest by the United States was the Philippines, taken from Spain in 1898 through the Spanish-American War. When it quickly became clear that the United States had no intention of granting the independence it had promised, Philippine patriots rose in revolt and were suppressed only after long, bitter fighting. Some Americans protested the taking of the Philippines, but to no avail. Thus another great Western power joined the imperialist ranks in Asia.

Causes of the New Imperialism

Many factors contributed to the late-nineteenth-century rush for empire, which was in turn one aspect of Western society's overall expansion in the age of industry and nationalism. It is little wonder that controversies have raged over interpretation of the New Imperialism, especially since authors of every persuasion have often exaggerated particular aspects in an attempt to prove their own theories. Yet despite complexity and controversy, basic causes are clearly identifiable.

Economic motives played an important role in the extension of political empires, especially in the British Empire. By the late 1870s France, Germany, and the United States were industrializing rapidly behind rising tariff barriers. Great Britain was losing its early economic lead and facing increasingly tough competition in foreign markets. In this changing economic climate, the seizure of Asian and African territory by continental powers in the 1880s raised alarms in Britain. Fearing that France and Germany would seal off their empires with high tariffs, resulting in the permanent loss of future economic opportunities, the British followed suit and began their own push to expand empire.

Actually, the overall economic gains of the New Imperialism proved quite limited before 1914. The new colonies were simply too poor to buy much, and they offered few immediately profitable investments. Nonetheless, even the poorest, most barren desert was jealously prized, and no territory was ever abandoned.

Tools for Empire Building Western technological advances aided Western political ambitions in Africa and Asia. The Maxim machine gun shown at far right was highly mobile and could lay down a continuous barrage that would decimate charging enemies, as in the slaughter of Muslim soldiers at the Battle of Omdurman in the Sudan. Quinine (near right) was also very important to empire building. First taken around 1850 in order to prevent the contraction of deadly malaria, quinine enabled European soldiers and officials to move safely into the African interior and overwhelm indigenous peoples. (quinine: Science Museum, London, UK/Wellcome Images; gun: © Lordprice Collection/Alamy Stock Photo)

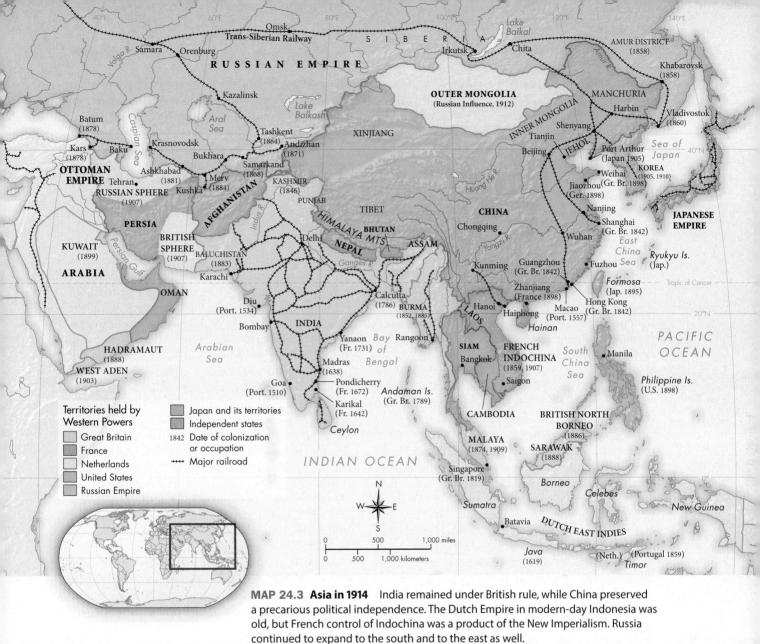

MAP 24.3 Asia in 1914 India remained under British rule, while China preserved a precarious political independence. The Dutch Empire in modern-day Indonesia was old, but French control of Indochina was a product of the New Imperialism. Russia continued to expand to the south and to the east as well.

This was because colonies became important for political and diplomatic reasons. Each leading country saw colonies as crucial to national security and military power. For instance, safeguarding the Suez Canal played a key role in the British occupation of Egypt, and protecting Egypt in turn led to the bloody conquest of Sudan. Far-flung possessions guaranteed ever-growing navies the safe havens and the dependable coaling stations they needed in time of crisis or war.

Along with economic motives, many people were convinced that colonies were essential to great nations. "There has never been a great power without great colonies," wrote one French publicist. The influential nationalist historian of Germany, Heinrich von Treitschke, spoke for many when he wrote: "Every virile people has established colonial power. . . . All great nations in the fullness of their strength have

desired to set their mark upon barbarian lands and those who fail to participate in this great rivalry will play a pitiable role in time to come."[7]

Treitschke's harsh statement reflects not only the increasing aggressiveness of European nationalism after Bismarck's wars of German unification, but also Social Darwinian theories of brutal competition among races (see Chapter 23). As one prominent English economist argued, the "strongest nation has always been conquering the weaker . . . and the strongest tend to be best." Thus European nations, which saw themselves as racially distinct parts of the dominant white race, had to seize colonies to show they were strong and powerful. Moreover, since victory of the fittest in the struggle for survival was nature's inescapable law, the conquest of "inferior" peoples was just. "The path of progress is strewn with the wreck . . . of inferior races," wrote one professor in 1900. "Yet these dead peoples are, in very truth, the stepping stones on which mankind has risen to the higher intellectual and deeper emotional life of today."[8] Social Darwinism and pseudoscientific racial doctrines fostered imperialist expansion.

So did the industrial world's unprecedented technological and military superiority. Three aspects were particularly important. First, the rapidly firing Maxim machine gun, so lethal at Omdurman, was an ultimate weapon in many another unequal battle. Second, newly discovered quinine proved no less effective in controlling malaria, which had previously decimated whites in the tropics whenever they left breezy coastal enclaves and dared to venture into mosquito-infested interiors. Third, the combination of the steamship and the international telegraph permitted Western powers to quickly concentrate their firepower in a given area when it was needed. Never before—and never again after 1914—would the technological gap between the West and non-Western regions of the world be so great.

Social tensions and domestic political conflicts also contributed mightily to overseas expansion. In Germany and Russia, and in other countries to a lesser extent, conservative political leaders manipulated colonial issues to divert popular attention from the class struggle at home and to create a false sense of national unity. Thus imperial propagandists relentlessly stressed that colonies benefited workers as well as capitalists, providing jobs and cheap raw materials that raised workers' standard of living. Government leaders and their allies in the tabloid press successfully encouraged the masses to savor foreign triumphs and to glory in the supposed increase in national prestige. In short, conservative leaders defined imperialism as a national necessity, which they used to justify the status quo and their hold on power.

Finally, certain special-interest groups in each country were powerful agents of expansion. White settlers in the colonial areas demanded more land and greater state protection. Missionaries and humanitarians wanted to spread religion and stop the slave trade within Africa. Shipping companies wanted lucrative subsidies to protect rapidly growing global trade. Military men and colonial officials foresaw rapid advancement and highly paid positions in growing empires. The actions of such groups pushed the course of empire forward.

A "Civilizing Mission"

Western society did not rest the case for empire solely on naked conquest and a Darwinian racial struggle or

■ **white man's burden** The idea that Europeans could and should civilize more primitive nonwhite peoples and that imperialism would eventually provide nonwhites with modern achievements and higher standards of living.

■ **Orientalism** A term coined by literary scholar Edward Said to describe the way Westerners misunderstood and described colonial subjects and cultures.

on power politics and the need for naval bases on every ocean. Imperialists developed additional arguments for imperialism to satisfy their consciences and answer their critics.

A favorite idea was that Westerners could and should civilize more primitive nonwhite peoples. According to this view, Westerners shouldered the responsibility for governing and converting the supposed savages under their charge and strove to remake them on superior European models. Africans and Asians would eventually receive the benefits of industrialization and urbanization, Western education, Christianity, advanced medicine, and finally higher standards of living. In time, they might be ready for self-government and Western democracy. Thus the French repeatedly spoke of their imperial endeavors as a sacred "civilizing mission." Other imperialists agreed; as one German missionary put it, a combination of prayer and hard work under German direction would lead "the work-shy native to work of his own free will" and thus lead him to "an existence fit for human beings."[9] Another argument was that imperial government protected natives from tribal warfare as well as from cruder forms of exploitation by white settlers and business people. In 1899 Rudyard Kipling (1865–1936), who wrote masterfully of Anglo-Indian life and was perhaps the most influential British writer of the 1890s, summarized such ideas in his poem "The White Man's Burden." (See "Evaluating the Evidence 24.2: The White Man's Burden," at right.)

Many Americans accepted the ideology of the **white man's burden**. It was an important factor in the decision to rule, rather than liberate, the Philippines after the Spanish-American War. Like their European counterparts, these Americans believed that their civilization had reached unprecedented heights and that they had unique benefits to bestow on supposedly less advanced peoples.

Though the colonial administrators and military generals in charge of imperial endeavors were men, European women played a central role in the "civilizing mission." Proponents of imperial expansion actively encouraged women to "serve" in the colonies, and many answered the call. Some women worked as colonial missionaries, teachers, and nurses; others accompanied their husbands overseas. Europeans who embraced the "white man's burden" believed that the presence of white women in the colonies might help stop the spread of what they called "race mixing": the tendency of European men to establish cross-race marriages or relationships with indigenous women. If they stayed in the colonies long enough to establish a semipermanent household, European women might oversee native servants. Colonial encounters thus established complicated social hierarchies that entangled race, class, and gender. (See

The White Man's Burden

When it was first published in an American illustrated magazine aimed at the middle class in 1899, Rudyard Kipling's well-known poem was read as encouragement for U.S. occupation of the Philippines in the aftermath of the Spanish-American War. It has since been understood as a forceful if somewhat anxious justification for Western imperialism in general.

Take up the White Man's Burden —
　Send forth the best ye breed —
Go, bind your sons to exile
　To serve your captive's need;
To wait, in heavy harness,
　On fluttered folk and wild —
Your new-caught sullen peoples,
　Half devil and half child.

Take up the White Man's burden —
　In patience to abide,
To veil the threat of terror
　And check the show of pride;
By open speech and simple,
　An hundred times made plain,
To seek another's profit
　And work another's gain.

Take up the White Man's burden —
　The savage wars of peace —
Fill full the mouth of Famine,
　And bid the sickness cease;
And when your goal is nearest
　(The end for others sought)
Watch sloth and heathen folly
　Bring all your hope to nought.

Take up the White Man's burden —
　No iron rule of kings,
But toil of serf and sweeper —
　The tale of common things.
The ports ye shall not enter,
　The roads ye shall not tread,
Go, make them with your living
　And mark them with your dead.

Take up the White Man's burden,
　And reap his old reward —
The blame of those ye better
　The hate of those ye guard —
The cry of those ye humor
　(Ah, slowly!) toward the light: —
"Why brought ye us from bondage,
　Our loved Egyptian night?"

Take up the White Man's burden —
　Ye dare not stoop to less —
Nor call too loud on Freedom
　To cloak your weariness.
By all ye will or whisper,
　By all ye leave or do,
The silent sullen peoples
　Shall weigh your God and you.

Take up the White Man's burden!
　Have done with childish days —
The lightly-proffered laurel,
　The easy ungrudged praise:
Comes now, to search your manhood
　Through all the thankless years,
Cold, edged with dear-bought
　wisdom,
　The judgment of your peers.

EVALUATE THE EVIDENCE

1. What, exactly, is the "white man's burden"? What, according to Kipling, are the costs and rewards of undertaking the "civilizing mission"?
2. Kipling's famous poem is over one hundred years old. Are its assertions for the legitimacy of "westernization" outdated, or do they still have resonance in today's global world?

Source: Reprinted in "The White Man's Versus the Brown Man's Burden," *The Literary Digest*, vol. 18, no. 8 (New York: Funk and Wagnalls, 1899), p. 219.

"Thinking Like a Historian: Women and Empire," page 814.)

Peace and stability under European control also facilitated the spread of Christianity. Catholic and Protestant missionaries — both men and women — competed with Islam south of the Sahara, seeking converts and building schools to spread the Gospel. Many Africans' first real contact with whites was in mission schools. Some peoples, such as the Ibo in Nigeria, became highly Christianized.

Such occasional successes in sub-Saharan Africa contrasted with the general failure of missionary efforts in India, China, and the Islamic world. There Christians often preached in vain to peoples with ancient, complex religious beliefs. Yet the number of Christian believers around the world did increase substantially in the nineteenth century, and missionary groups kept trying.

Orientalism

Even though many Westerners shared a sense of superiority over non-Western peoples, they were often fascinated by foreign cultures and societies. In the late 1970s the influential literary scholar Edward Said (sigh-EED) (1935–2003) coined the term **Orientalism** to describe this fascination and the stereotypical and often racist Western understandings of non-Westerners that dominated nineteenth-century Western thought. Said originally used "Orientalism" to refer to the way Europeans viewed "the Orient," or Arab societies in North Africa and the Middle East. The term caught on, however, and is often used more broadly to refer to Western views of non-Western peoples across the globe.

Said believed that it was almost impossible for people in the West to look at or understand non-Westerners without falling into some sort of Orientalist stereotype.

Women and Empire

Though men played dominant roles in colonial territories, European women also worked as educators, missionaries, nurses, and housewives. What was life like for European women in the colonies?

1 *The Complete Indian Housekeeper & Cook,* **1898.** This book on household management described the domestic duties of the elite British woman (the "memsahib") in colonial India. It was shot through with notions of racial difference and superiority.

〜 This book, it is hoped, will meet the very generally felt want for a practical guide to young housekeepers in India. A large proportion of English ladies in this country come to it newly married, to begin a new life, and take up new responsibilities under absolutely new conditions....

The first duty of a mistress is, of course, to be able to give intelligible orders to her servants; therefore it is necessary she should learn to speak Hindustani....

The second duty is obviously to insist on her orders being carried out. And here we come to the burning question, "how is this to be done?"...The secret lies in making rules, and keeping to them. The Indian servant is a child in everything save age, and should be treated as a child; that is to say, kindly, but with the greatest firmness....[F]irst faults should never go unpunished. By overlooking a first offence, we lose the only opportunity we have of preventing it becoming a habit....

In their own experience the authors have found a system of rewards and punishments perfectly easy of attainment. One of them has for years adopted the plan of engaging her servants at so much a month — the lowest rate at which such service is obtainable — and so much extra as buksheesh [a tip or bribe], conditional on good service....Of course common sense is required to adjust the balance of rewards and punishments, for here again Indian servants are like children, in that they have an acute sense of justice....

We do not wish to advocate an unholy haughtiness; but an Indian household can no more be governed peacefully, without dignity and prestige, than an Indian empire.

2 **Elspeth Huxley,** *The Flame Trees of Thika,* **1959.** In her memoir, Elspeth Huxley described her childhood in British Kenya on the eve of the First World War.

〜 Juma [the family's male Kenyan servant] had a patronizing air that [my mother] resented, and she doubted if he was showing enough respect. Those were the days when to lack respect was a more serious crime than to neglect a child, bewitch a man or steal a cow, and was generally punishable by beating. Indeed respect was the only protection available to Europeans who lived singly, or in scattered families, among thousands of Africans accustomed to constant warfare and armed with spears and poisoned arrows, but had themselves no barricades, and went about unarmed. This respect preserved them [the Europeans] like an invisible coat of mail, or a form of magic, and seldom failed; but it had to be very carefully guarded.

3 **Arguments for "race mixing" in Germany's African colonies.** When Germans first claimed African colonies in the mid-1880s, settlers often married or had close relations with African women.

〜

Max Buchner, *colonial bureaucrat*
As for free social intercourse with the daughters of the country [African colonial subjects], it is to be seen as more helpful than harmful to health. The eternal feminine, also under dark skin, is an excellent charm against low spirits, to which one is so vulnerable in the solitude of Africa.

Carl Büttner, *prominent missionary*
Frau Kleinschmidt [the Nama-African wife of a German missionary is] *highly respected* by whites and natives....[H]er household could be a *model* for all the whites living in Damaraland [central Namibia]....In short, this entire family [with seven children], descended from a mixed marriage, has had an *important* role in the development of this land and one can only wish that there be more like it.

ANALYZING THE EVIDENCE

1. What does the evidence presented in Sources 1–2 and 5–6 reveal about the relationships between European women and colonial subjects? What are the main points of contact and concern?
2. Why is respect a key element in the relationship between colonizers and colonized (Sources 1 and 2)? Why would it be particularly important to women like Elspeth Huxley?
3. In Sources 3 and 4, what are the main arguments for and against "race mixing" in the German colonies? How do they draw on stereotypes about Europeans and Africans?

4 **Arguments against "race mixing" in Germany's African colonies.** After about 1900, colonial authorities tried to halt "race mixing" by condemning and outlawing interracial marriage and encouraging German women to move to colonial Africa.

Paul Rohrbach, *colonial bureaucrat*

[German men are ruined by] keeping a filthy house with the lazy, ignorant, indolent, in a word barbaric and in almost every respect base colored wenches. [German men] for years and years have had no other contact with women besides this intercourse that is down-dragging, demoralizing, and nothing but coarse sensuality.

Editorial, *Hamburg News,* **1912**

The tolerance of mixed marriages would deeply degrade the prestige of the white race in Central Africa and would severely endanger the white women. Mixed marriages would then be permissible for white women as well, with native men. The white woman would thereby lose the only thing that offers her an unconditional protection from attacks in the colonies today, the respect of the colored.

Editorial, *Usambara Post,* **1912**

The European woman alone can solve the problem [of race mixing]. Only she can accomplish something positive, all so-called disciplinary measures belong to the realm of prohibitive and negative decrees, in which no real value resides: nature cannot be driven out with a pitchfork

(Mansell /The LIFE Picture Collection/Getty Images)

5 **Photograph of a British tea party in India, 1896.** Class, race, and gender come together in this revealing photograph of an elite group of British colonists enjoying their tea, accompanied by Indian servants. The British "memsahib" at the center of the picture rests her feet on a tiger-skin rug and holds a tiger cub in her lap.

6 **Timetable for the Christian Missionary Society Girl's School, Ibadan, Nigeria, 1908.** Nigerian schoolchildren learned Western domestic tasks at European missionary schools.

5:00 A.M.	Prepare food, fetch water from river for baths, house, and kitchen
6:15–7:00	Quiet time and prayers
7:00	Domestic Work*
8:00	School
12:00 P.M.	Dinner
1:30	School
3:30	Recreation
4:00	Domestic Work*
6:00	Supper
7:15	Home Lessons
8:15	Prayers

Total time devoted to course work (including domestic subjects): 6 hours
Total time devoted to domestic chores: 4 hours, 15 minutes
*Note: "Domestic Work" tasks varied day by day and could include housework, laundry, ironing, preparing food, gardening, and cleaning.

PUTTING IT ALL TOGETHER

European women played a major role in the colonies during the era of New Imperialism. Using the sources above, along with what you have learned in class and in this chapter, write a short essay that describes their experience. How did women's ideas about race and gender help define the relationship between European colonizers and their colonial subjects?

Sources: (1) F. A. Steel and G. Gardiner, *The Complete Indian Housekeeper & Cook* (London: Heinemann, 1898), pp. 1–4, 9; (2) Quoted in Margaret Strobel, *European Women and the Second British Empire* (Bloomington: Indiana University Press, 1991), p. 23; (3, 4) All quotes from Lora Wildenthal, *German Woman for Empire, 1884–1945* (Durham: Duke University Press, 2001), pp. 81, 86–87, 103, 120–121; (6) "Timetable" in LaRay Denzer, "Domestic Science Training in Colonial Yorubaland, Nigeria," in *African Encounters with Domesticity,* ed. Karen Tranberg Hansen (New Brunswick: Rutgers University Press, 1992), p. 119.

A Missionary School
A Swahili schoolboy leads his classmates in a reading lesson in Dar es Salaam in German East Africa in 1903; portraits of Emperor Wilhelm II and his wife look down on the classroom, a reminder of imperial control. Europeans argued that they were spreading the benefits of a superior civilization with schools like this one, which is unusually well built and furnished because of its strategic location in the capital city. Schoolrooms were typically segregated by sex, and lessons for young men and women adhered to Western notions of gender difference. (ullstein bild/ Granger, NYC — All rights reserved)

Politicians, scholarly experts, writers and artists, and ordinary people readily adopted "us versus them" views of foreign peoples. The West, they believed, was modern, while the non-West was primitive. The West was white, the non-West colored; the West was rational, the non-West emotional; the West was Christian, the non-West pagan or Islamic. As part of this view of the non-West as radically "other," Westerners imagined the Orient as a place of mystery and romance, populated with exotic, dark-skinned peoples, where Westerners might have remarkable experiences of foreign societies and cultures.

Such views swept through North American and European scholarship, arts, and literature in the late nineteenth century. The emergence of ethnography and anthropology as academic disciplines in the 1880s was part of the process. Inspired by a new culture of collecting, scholars and adventurers went into the field, where they studied supposedly primitive cultures and traded for, bought, or stole artifacts from non-Western peoples. The results of their work were reported in scientific studies, articles, and books, and intriguing objects filled the display cases of new public museums of ethnography and natural history. In a slew of novels published around 1900, authors portrayed romance and high adventure in the colonies and so contributed to the Orientalist worldview. Artists followed suit, and dramatic paintings of ferocious Arab warriors, Eastern slave markets, and the sultan's harem adorned museum walls and wealthy middle-class parlors. Scholars, authors, and artists were not necessarily racists or imperialists, but they found it difficult to escape Orientalist stereotypes. In the end they helped spread the notions of Western superiority and justified colonial expansion.

Critics of Imperialism

The expansion of empire aroused sharp, even bitter, critics. The forceful attack made by radical English economist J. A. Hobson (1858–1940) in *Imperialism* (1902), a work that influenced Lenin and others, was exemplary. Deeply angered by British tactics during the unpopular South African (Boer) War, Hobson contended that the rush to acquire colonies was due to the economic needs of unregulated capitalism, particularly the need of the rich to find outlets for their surplus capital. Yet, Hobson argued, imperial possessions did not pay off economically for the entire country. Only unscrupulous special-interest groups profited from them, at the expense of both European taxpayers and the natives. Moreover, Hobson argued that the quest for empire diverted popular attention away from domestic reform and the need to reduce the great gap between rich and poor.

Like Hobson, Marxist critics offered a thorough analysis and critique of Western imperialism. Rosa Luxemburg, a radical member of the German Social Democratic Party, argued that capitalism needed to

Orientalism in Western Society Stereotyped Western impressions of Arabs and the Islamic world became increasingly popular in the West in the nineteenth century. This wave of Orientalism found expression in high art, as in the renowned painting *Women of Algiers in Their Apartment* (1834), by the French painter Eugène Delacroix (left). Delacroix portrays three women and their African servant at rest in a harem, the segregated, women-only living quarters for the wives of elite Muslim men (Islamic law allows a man to have several wives). Orientalist ideas also made their way into the fabric of everyday life, when ordinary people visited museum exhibits, read newspaper articles, or purchased popular colonial products like cigarettes, coffee, and chocolate. (Musée du Louvre, Paris, France/Bridgeman Images)

expand into noncapitalist Asia and Africa to maintain high profits. The Russian Marxist and future revolutionary leader Vladimir Lenin concluded that imperialism represented the "highest stage" of advanced monopoly capitalism and predicted that its onset signaled the coming decay and collapse of capitalist society. These and similar arguments were not very persuasive, however. Most people then (and now) were sold on the idea that imperialism was profitable for the homeland and beneficial to the colonized, and the masses developed a broad and genuine enthusiasm for empire.

Hobson and many other critics struck home, however, with their moral condemnation of whites' imperiously ruling nonwhites. They rebelled against crude Social Darwinian thought. "O Evolution, what crimes are committed in thy name!" cried one foe. Another sardonically coined a new beatitude: "Blessed are the strong, for they shall prey on the weak."[10] Kipling and his kind were lampooned as racist bullies whose rule rested on brutality, racial contempt, and the Maxim gun. (See "Evaluating the Evidence 24.3: The Brown Man's Burden," page 818.) Similarly, in 1902 in the novel *Heart of Darkness*—a demolishing critique of the Belgian exploitation of the Congo—Polish-born novelist Joseph Conrad (1857–1924) castigated the "pure selfishness" of Europeans in supposedly civilizing Africa. The main character, once a liberal scholar, turns into a savage brute.

Critics charged Europeans with applying a degrading double standard and failing to live up to their own noble ideals. At home, Europeans had won or were winning

Travel Guide This "Official Guide" (right) to an exhibition on Cairo held in Berlin offered an exotic look at foreign lands. Note the veiled women in the center and the pyramid and desert mosque in the background. (Private Collection/Archives Charmet/ Bridgeman Images)

representative government, individual liberties, and a certain equality of opportunity. In their empires, Europeans imposed military dictatorships. Colonial administrators forced Africans and Asians to work involuntarily, almost like slaves, and subjected them to shameless discrimination. Only by renouncing imperialism, its critics insisted, and giving captive peoples the freedoms Western society had struggled for since the French Revolution would Europeans be worthy of their traditions. These critics provided colonial peoples with a Western ideology of liberation.

The Brown Man's Burden

As soon as it was published, Kipling's "The White Man's Burden" drew mockery from anti-imperialist intellectuals and politicians. In 1899 British publisher and Parliament member Henry Labouchère, known for his inflammatory views on any number of contemporary issues, wrote one of the most famous satires of Kipling's poem.

Pile on the brown man's burden
    To gratify your greed;
Go clear away the "niggers"
    Who progress would impede;
Be very stern, for truly
    'Tis useless to be mild
With new-caught, sullen peoples,
    Half devil and half child.

Pile on the brown man's burden;
    And if ye rouse his hate,
Meet his old-fashioned reasons
    With Maxims up to date.
With shells and dumdum bullets
    A hundred times made plain
The brown man's loss must ever
    Imply the white man's gain.

Pile on the brown man's burden,
    Compel him to be free;
Let all your manifestoes
    Reek with philanthropy.
And if with heathen folly
    He dares your will dispute,
Then in the name of freedom
    Don't hesitate to shoot.

Pile on the brown man's burden,
    And if his cry be sore,

That surely need not irk you —
    Ye've driven slaves before.
Seize on his ports and pastures,
    The fields his people tread;
Go make from them your living,
    And mark them with his dead.

Pile on the brown man's burden,
    Nor do not deem it hard
If you should earn the rancor
    Of these ye yearn to guard,
The screaming of your eagle
    Will drown the victim's sob —
Go on through fire and slaughter,
    There's dollars in the job.

Pile on the brown man's burden,
    And through the world proclaim
That ye are freedom's agent —
    There's no more paying game!
And should your own past history
    Straight in your teeth be thrown,
Retort that independence
    Is good for whites alone.

Pile on the brown man's burden,
    With equity have done;
Weak, antiquated scruples
    Their squeamish course have run,

And though 'tis freedom's banner
    You're waving in the van,
Reserve for home consumption
    The sacred "rights of man"!

And if by chance ye falter,
    Or lag along the course,
If, as the blood flows freely,
    Ye feel some slight remorse,
Hie ye to Rudyard Kipling,
    Imperialism's prop,
And bid him, for your comfort,
    Turn on his jingo stop.

EVALUATE THE EVIDENCE

1. What means does Labouchère use to mock Kipling's poem?
2. What, according to Labouchère, drives the imperial project? Does Kipling or Labouchère make the better case for the causes and effects of Western imperialism? Why?

Source: Reprinted in "The White Man's Versus the Brown Man's Burden," *The Literary Digest*, vol. 18, no. 8 (New York: Funk and Wagnalls, 1899), p. 219.

Responding to Western Imperialism

FOCUS QUESTION *What was the general pattern of non-Western responses to Western expansion?*

To Africans and Asians, Western expansion represented a profoundly disruptive assault. Everywhere it threatened existing ruling classes, local economies, and long-standing ways of life. Christian missionaries and European secular ideologies challenged established beliefs and values. Non-Western peoples experienced imperialism as an invasion, one made all the more painful by the power and arrogance of the European intruders.

The Pattern of Response

Generally, the initial response of African and Asian rulers to aggressive Western expansion was to try to drive the unwelcome foreigners away. This was the case in China, Japan, and Sudan, as we have seen. Violent antiforeign reactions exploded elsewhere again and again, as in the lengthy U.S.-Indian wars, but the superior military technology of the industrialized West almost invariably prevailed. Beaten in battle, many Africans and Asians concentrated on preserving their cultural traditions at all costs. Others found themselves forced to reconsider their initial hostility. Some (such as Ismail of Egypt) concluded that the West was indeed superior in some ways and that it was therefore necessary to copy some European achievements, especially if they wished to escape full-blown Western political rule.

Thus it is possible to think of responses to the Western impact as a spectrum, with "traditionalists" at one end, "westernizers" or "modernizers" at the other, and many shades of opinion in between. Both before and after European domination, the struggle among these groups was often intense. With time, however, the modernizers tended to gain the upper hand.

When the power of both the traditionalists and the modernizers was thoroughly shattered by superior force, some Asians and Africans accepted imperial rule. Political participation in non-Western lands was historically limited to small elites, and ordinary people often did what their rulers told them to do. In these circumstances Europeans, clothed in power and convinced of their righteousness, tried to govern smoothly and effectively. At times they received considerable support from both traditionalists (local chiefs, landowners, religious leaders) and modernizers (Western-educated professional classes and civil servants).

Nevertheless, imperial rule was in many ways an imposing edifice built on sand. Support for European rule among subjugated peoples was shallow and weak. Colonized lands were primarily peasant societies, and much of the burden of colonization fell on small farmers who tenaciously fought for some measure of autonomy. When colonists demanded extra taxes or crops, peasants played dumb and hid the extent of their harvest; when colonists asked for increased labor, peasants dragged their feet. These "weapons of the weak" stopped short of open defiance but nonetheless presented a real challenge to Western rule.[11] Moreover, native people followed with greater or lesser enthusiasm the few determined personalities who came to openly oppose the Europeans. Such leaders always arose, both when Europeans ruled directly and when they manipulated native governments, for at least two basic reasons.

First, the nonconformists—the eventual anti-imperialist leaders—developed a burning desire for human dignity, economic emancipation, and political independence, all incompatible with foreign rule. Second, and somewhat ironically, potential leaders found in the Western world the ideologies underlying and justifying their protest. They discovered liberalism, with its credos of civil liberties and political self-determination. They echoed the demands of anti-imperialists in Europe and America that the West live up to its own ideals. Above all, they found themselves attracted to nationalism, which asserted that every people had the right to control its own destiny. After 1917 anti-imperialist revolt would find another European-made weapon in Lenin's version of Marxist socialism. Thus the anti-imperialist search for dignity drew strength from Western thought and culture, as is particularly apparent in the development of three major Asian countries—India, Japan, and China.

Empire in India

India was the jewel of the British Empire, and no colonial area experienced a more profound British impact. Unlike Japan and China, which maintained a real if precarious independence, and unlike African territories, which Europeans annexed only at the end of the nineteenth century, India was ruled more or less absolutely by Britain for a very long time.

Arriving in India on the heels of the Portuguese in the seventeenth century, the British East India Company had conquered the last independent native state by 1848. The last "traditional" response to European rule—an attempt by the existing ruling classes to drive the invaders out by military force—was broken in India in 1857 and 1858. Those were the years of the **Great Rebellion** (which the British called a "mutiny"), an insurrection by Muslim and Hindu mercenaries in the British army that spread throughout northern and central India before it was finally crushed, primarily by loyal indigenous troops from southern India. Britain then established direct control until Indian independence was gained in 1947.

India was ruled by the British Parliament in London and administered by a tiny, all-white civil service in India. In 1900 this elite consisted of fewer than 3,500 top officials, who controlled a population of 300 million. The white elite, backed by white officers and indigenous troops, was competent and generally well disposed toward the welfare of the Indian peasant masses. Yet it practiced strict job discrimination and social segregation, and most of its members quite frankly considered what they saw as the jumble of Indian peoples and castes to be racially inferior. As Lord Kitchener, one of the most distinguished top military commanders in India, stated:

The Great Rebellion, 1857–1858

> It is this consciousness of the inherent superiority of the European which has won for us India. However well educated and clever a native may be, and however brave he may prove himself, I believe that no rank we can bestow on him would cause him to be considered an equal of the British officer.[12]

British women played an important part in the imperial enterprise, especially after the opening of the Suez

■ **Great Rebellion** The 1857 and 1858 insurrection by Muslim and Hindu mercenaries in the British army that spread throughout northern and central India before finally being crushed.

Canal in 1869 made it much easier for civil servants and businessmen to bring their wives and children with them to India. These British families tended to live in their own separate communities, where they occupied large houses with well-shaded porches, handsome lawns, and a multitude of servants. It was the wife's responsibility to manage this complex household. Many officials' wives learned to relish their duties, and they directed their households and servants with the same self-confident authoritarianism that characterized their husbands' political rule.

A small minority of British women — many of them feminists, social reformers, or missionaries, both married and single — sought to go further and shoulder what one historian has called the "white women's burden" in India.[13] These women tried especially to improve the lives of Indian women, both Hindu and Muslim, promoting education and legislation to move them closer to the better conditions they believed Western women had attained. Their greatest success was educating some elite Hindu women who took up the cause of reform.

Inspired by the "civilizing mission" — as well as strong feelings of racial and cultural superiority — British imperialists worked energetically to westernize Indian society. Realizing that they needed well-educated Indians to serve as skilled subordinates in both the government and the army, the British established a modern system of secondary education, with all instruction in English. Thus some Indians gained excellent opportunities for economic and social advancement. High-caste Hindus, particularly quick to respond, emerged as skillful intermediaries between the British rulers and the Indian people, and soon they formed a new elite profoundly influenced by Western thought and culture.

This new Indian elite joined British officials and businessmen to promote modern economic development, a second result of British rule. Examples included constructing irrigation projects for agriculture, building the world's third-largest railroad network for good communications, and forming large tea and jute plantations geared to the world economy. Unfortunately, the lot of the Indian masses improved little, for the profits from the increase in production went to indigenous and British elites.

Finally, with a well-educated, English-speaking Indian bureaucracy and steps toward economic development, the British created a unified, powerful state. They placed under the same system of law and administration the different Hindu and Muslim peoples and the vanquished kingdoms of the entire subcontinent — groups that had fought each other for centuries and had been repeatedly conquered by Muslim and Mongol invaders. It was as if Europe, with its many states and varieties of Christianity, had been conquered and united in a single great empire.

Despite these achievements, the decisive reaction to European rule was the rise of nationalism among the Indian elite. No matter how anglicized and necessary a member of the indigenous educated classes became, he or she could never become the white ruler's equal. The top jobs, the best clubs, the modern hotels, and even certain railroad compartments were off limits to darker-skinned Indians. The peasant masses might accept such inequality as the latest version of age-old oppression, but the well-educated, English-speaking elite eventually could not. For them, racial discrimination meant injured pride and bitter injustice. It flagrantly contradicted the cherished Western concepts of human rights and equality that they had learned about in Western schools. Moreover, it was based on dictatorship, no matter how benign.

By 1885, when educated Indians came together to found the predominantly Hindu Indian National Congress, demands were increasing for the equality and self-government that Britain had already granted white-settler colonies, such as Canada and Australia. By 1907, emboldened in part by Japan's success (see the next section), a radical faction in the Indian National Congress called for Indian independence. Although there were sharp divisions between Hindus and Muslims on what shape the Indian future should take, among other issues, Indians were finding an answer to the foreign challenge. The common heritage of British rule and Western ideals, along with the reform and revitalization of the Hindu religion, had created a genuine movement for national independence.

The Example of Japan

When Commodore Matthew Perry arrived in Tokyo in 1853 with his crude but effective gunboat diplomacy, Japan was a complex feudal society. At the top stood a figurehead emperor, but real power was in the hands of a hereditary military governor, the shogun. With the help of a warrior nobility known as samurai, the shogun governed a country of hard-working, productive peasants and city dwellers. The intensely proud samurai were humiliated by the sudden American intrusion and the unequal treaties with Western countries that followed.

When foreign diplomats and merchants began to settle in Yokohama, radical samurai reacted with a wave of antiforeign terrorism and antigovernment assassinations that lasted from 1858 to 1863. In response, an allied fleet of American, British, Dutch, and French warships demolished key forts, further weakening the power and prestige of the shogun's government. Then in 1867 a coalition led by patriotic samurai seized control of the government with hardly any bloodshed and restored the political power of the emperor in the **Meiji Restoration**, a great turning point in Japanese history.

The battle cry of the Meiji (MAY-jee) reformers was "Enrich the state and strengthen the armed forces," and the immediate goal of the new government was to meet the foreign threat. Yet how were these tasks to be accomplished? In a remarkable about-face, the leaders of Meiji Japan dropped their antiforeign attacks.

The Russo-Japanese War, 1904–1905 This 1904 Japanese print portrays the surprise Japanese naval attack on the Russian fleet at Port Arthur as a glorious victory. Though the opening battle was in fact inconclusive, with few losses on either side, the Japanese won the war. Defeat by a supposedly "primitive" Asian nation encouraged reform movements in the Russian Empire and became a factor in the outbreak of the Russian Revolution of 1905 (see Chapter 23). (Universal History Archive/Getty Images)

Convinced that Western civilization was indeed superior in its military and industrial aspects, they initiated a series of measures to reform Japan along modern lines. In the broadest sense, the Meiji leaders tried to harness Western industrialization and political reform to protect their country and catch up with Europe.

In 1871 the new leaders abolished the old feudal structure of aristocratic, decentralized government and formed a strong unified state. Following the example of the French Revolution, they dismantled the four-class legal system and declared social equality. They decreed freedom of movement in a country where traveling abroad had been a serious crime. They created a free, competitive, government-stimulated economy. Japan began to build railroads and modern factories. The new generation adopted many principles of a free, liberal society, and, as in Europe, the resulting freedom resulted in a tremendously creative release of human energy.

Yet the overriding concern of Japan's political leadership was always to maintain a powerful state and a strong military. State leaders created a powerful modern navy and completely reorganized the army along European lines, forming a professional officer corps and requiring three years of military service of all males. This army of draftees effectively put down disturbances in the countryside, and in 1877 it crushed a major rebellion by feudal elements protesting the loss of their privileges. In addition, Japan skillfully adapted the West's science and technology, particularly in industry, medicine, and education, and many Japanese studied abroad. The government paid large salaries to

attract foreign experts, who were replaced by trained Japanese as soon as possible.

By 1890, when the new state was firmly established, the wholesale borrowing of the early restoration had given way to a more selective emphasis on those things foreign that were in keeping with Japanese tradition. Following the model of the German Empire, Japan established an authoritarian constitution and rejected democracy. The power of the emperor and his ministers was vast, that of the legislature limited.

Japan also successfully copied the imperialism of Western society. Expansion proved that Japan was strong and cemented the nation together in a great mission. Having "opened" Korea with its own gunboat diplomacy in 1876, Japan decisively defeated China in a war over Korea in 1894 and 1895 and took Formosa (modern-day Taiwan). In the next years, Japan competed aggressively with European powers for influence and territory in China, particularly in Manchuria, where Japanese and Russian imperialism collided. In 1904 Japan launched the Russo-Japanese War (1904–1905) by attacking Russia without a formal declaration of war. After a series of bloody battles, victorious Japan took over Russia's former protectorate in Port Arthur and emerged with a valuable foothold in China (see Map 24.3). By 1910, with the annexation of Korea, Japan had become a major imperialist power.

Japan became the first non-Western country to use an ancient love of country to transform itself and

■ Meiji Restoration The restoration of the Japanese emperor to power in 1867, leading to the subsequent modernization of Japan.

Demonizing the Boxer Rebellion   The Sunday supplement to *Le Petit Parisien*, a popular French newspaper, ran a series of gruesome front-page pictures of ferocious Boxers burning buildings, murdering priests, and slaughtering Chinese Christians. In this 1910 illustration, Boxer rebels invade a church in Mukden, Manchuria, and massacre the Christian worshippers. Whipping up European outrage about Chinese atrocities was a prelude to harsh reprisals by the Western powers. (From *Le Petit Journal*/Mary Evans Picture Library)

thereby meet the many-sided challenge of Western expansion. Moreover, Japan demonstrated convincingly that a modern Asian nation could defeat and humble a great Western power. Japan's achievement fascinated many Chinese and Vietnamese nationalists and provided patriots throughout Asia and Africa with an inspiring example of national recovery and liberation.

Toward Revolution in China

In 1860 the two-hundred-year-old Qing Dynasty in China appeared on the verge of collapse. Efforts to repel foreigners had failed, and rebellion and chaos wracked the country. Yet the government drew on its

■ **hundred days of reform**   A series of Western-style reforms launched in 1898 by the Chinese government in an attempt to meet the foreign challenge.

traditional strengths and made a surprising comeback that lasted more than thirty years.

Two factors were crucial in this reversal. First, the traditional ruling groups temporarily produced new and effective leadership. Loyal scholar-statesmen and generals quelled disturbances such as the great Tai Ping rebellion. The remarkable empress dowager Tzu Hsi (tsoo shee) governed in the name of her young son, combining shrewd insight with vigorous action to revitalize the bureaucracy.

Second, destructive foreign aggression lessened, for the Europeans had obtained their primary goal of establishing commercial and diplomatic relations. Indeed, some Europeans contributed to the dynasty's recovery. A talented Irishman effectively reorganized China's customs office, increasing government tax receipts, and a sympathetic American diplomat represented China in foreign lands, helping to strengthen the Chinese government. Such efforts dovetailed with the dynasty's efforts to adopt some aspects of Western government and technology while maintaining traditional Chinese values and beliefs.

The parallel movement toward domestic reform and limited cooperation with the West collapsed under the blows of Japanese imperialism. Defeat in the Sino-Japanese War (1894–1895) and the subsequent harsh peace treaty revealed China's helplessness in the face of aggression, triggering a rush by foreign powers for concessions and protectorates. At the high point of this rush in 1898, it appeared that the European powers might actually divide China among themselves, as they had recently divided Africa. Probably only the jealousy each nation felt toward its imperialist competitors saved China from partition. In any event, the tempo of foreign encroachment greatly accelerated after 1894.

China's precarious position after the war with Japan led to a renewed drive for fundamental reforms. Like the leaders of the Meiji Restoration, some modernizers saw salvation in Western institutions. In 1898 they convinced the young emperor to launch a desperate **hundred days of reform** in an attempt to meet the foreign challenge. More radical reformers, such as the revolutionary Sun Yatsen (1866–1925), who came from the peasantry and was educated in Hawaii by Christian missionaries, sought to overthrow the dynasty altogether and establish a republic.

The efforts at radical reform by the young emperor and his allies threatened the Qing establishment and the empress dowager Tzu Hsi, who had dominated the court for a quarter of a century. In a palace coup, she and her supporters imprisoned the emperor, rejected the reform movement, and put reactionary officials in charge. Hope for reform from above was crushed.

A violent antiforeign reaction swept the country, encouraged by the Qing court and led by a secret society that foreigners called the Boxers. The conservative, patriotic Boxers blamed China's ills on foreigners, charging foreign missionaries with undermining Chinese reverence for their ancestors and thereby threatening the Chinese family and the society as a whole. In the agony of defeat and unwanted reforms, the Boxers and other secret societies struck out at their enemies. In northeastern China, more than two hundred foreign missionaries and several thousand Chinese Christians were killed, prompting threats and demands from Western governments. The empress dowager answered by declaring war on the foreign powers, hoping that the Boxers might relieve the foreign pressure on the government.

The imperialist response was swift and harsh. After the Boxers besieged the embassy quarter in Beijing, foreign governments (including Japan, Britain, France, Germany, and the United States) organized an international force of twenty thousand soldiers to rescue their diplomats and punish China. These troops defeated the Boxers and occupied and plundered Beijing. In 1901 China was forced to accept a long list of penalties, including a heavy financial indemnity payable over forty years.

The years after this heavy defeat were ever more troubled. Anarchy and foreign influence spread as the power and prestige of the Qing Dynasty declined still further. Antiforeign, antigovernment revolutionary groups agitated and plotted. Finally, in 1912 a spontaneous uprising toppled the Qing Dynasty. After thousands of years of emperors, a loose coalition of revolutionaries proclaimed a Western-style republic and called for an elected parliament. The transformation of China under the impact of expanding Western society entered a new phase, and the end was not in sight.

NOTES

1. Quoted in J. W. Hall, *Japan: From Prehistory to Modern Times* (New York: Delacorte Press, 1970), p. 250.
2. Quoted in Earl of Cromer, *Modern Egypt* (London, 1911), p. 48.
3. Quoted in T. Blegen, *Norwegian Migration to America*, vol. 2 (Northfield, Minn.: Norwegian-American Historical Association, 1940), p. 468.
4. Quoted in I. Howe, *World of Our Fathers* (New York: Harcourt Brace Jovanovich, 1975), p. 290.
5. Quoted in W. L. Langer, *European Alliances and Alignments, 1871–1890* (New York: Vintage Books, 1931), p. 290.
6. Quoted in J. Ellis, *The Social History of the Machine Gun* (New York: Pantheon Books, 1975), pp. 86, 101. The numbers given for British casualties at the Battle of Omdurman vary; the total casualties quoted here come from an original British army report. See Lieutenant General H. M. L. Rundle, M.G., Chief of Staff, "Herewith Returns of Killed and Wounded of the Expeditionary Force at the Battle of Khartum, on September 2, 1898," Khartum, September 9, 1898, at North East Medals, http://www.britishmedals.us/kevin/other/lgomdurman.html.
7. Quoted in G. H. Nadel and P. Curtis, eds., *Imperialism and Colonialism* (New York: Macmillan, 1964), p. 94.
8. Quoted in W. L. Langer, *The Diplomacy of Imperialism*, 2d ed. (New York: Alfred A. Knopf, 1951), pp. 86, 88.
9. Quoted in S. Conrad, *Globalisation and the Nation in Imperial Germany* (New York: Cambridge University Press, 2010), p. 78.
10. Quoted in Langer, *The Diplomacy of Imperialism*, p. 88.
11. J. C. Scott, *Weapons of the Weak: Everyday Forms of Peasant Resistance* (New Haven: Yale University Press, 1985), p. xvi.
12. Quoted in K. M. Panikkar, *Asia and Western Dominance: A Survey of the Vasco da Gama Epoch of Asian History* (London: George Allen & Unwin, 1959), p. 116.
13. A. Burton, "The White Women's Burden: British Feminists and 'The Indian Women,' 1865–1915," in *Western Women and Imperialism: Complicity and Resistance*, ed. N. Chauduri and M. Strobel (Bloomington: Indiana University Press, 1992), pp. 137–157.

LOOKING BACK LOOKING AHEAD

In the early twentieth century educated Europeans had good reason to believe that they were living in an age of progress. The ongoing triumphs of industry and science and the steady improvements in the standard of living beginning about 1850 were undeniable, and it was generally assumed that these favorable trends would continue. There had also been progress in the political realm. The bitter class conflicts that culminated in the bloody civil strife of 1848 had given way in most European countries to stable nation-states with elected legislative bodies that reflected the general population, responded to real problems, and enjoyed popular support. Moreover, there had been no general European war since Napoleon's defeat in 1815. Only the brief, limited wars connected with German and Italian unification at midcentury had broken the peace in the European heartland.

In the global arena, peace was much more elusive. In the name of imperialism, Europeans (and North Americans) used war and the threat of war to open markets and punish foreign governments around the world. Although criticized by some intellectuals and leftists such as J. A. Hobson, these foreign campaigns resonated with European citizens and stimulated popular nationalism. Like fans in a sports bar, the peoples of Europe followed their colonial teams and cheered them on to victories that were almost certain. Thus imperialism and nationalism reinforced and strengthened each other in Europe, especially after 1875.

This was a dangerous development. Easy imperialist victories over weak states and poorly armed non-Western peoples encouraged excessive pride and led Europeans to underestimate the fragility of their accomplishments as well as the murderous power of their weaponry. Imperialism also made nationalism more aggressive and militaristic. At the same time that European imperialism was dividing the world, the leading European states were also dividing themselves into two opposing military alliances. Thus when the two armed camps stumbled into war in 1914, there would be a superabundance of nationalistic fervor, patriotic sacrifice, and cataclysmic destruction.

Make Connections

Think about the larger developments and continuities within and across chapters.

1. How did the expansion of European empires transform everyday life around the world?

2. Historians often use the term *New Imperialism* to describe the globalization of empire that began in the last decades of the nineteenth century. Was the New Imperialism really that different from earlier waves of European expansion (Chapters 14 and 17)?

3. How did events and trends in European colonies connect to or reflect events and trends in the European homeland?

24 REVIEW & EXPLORE

Identify Key Terms

Identify and explain the significance of each item below.

neo-Europes (p. 796)	Berlin Conference (p. 806)
Opium Wars (p. 797)	white man's burden (p. 812)
gunboat diplomacy (p. 798)	Orientalism (p. 813)
global mass migration (p. 799)	Great Rebellion (p. 819)
nativism (p. 804)	Meiji Restoration (p. 820)
New Imperialism (p. 804)	hundred days of reform (p. 822)
Afrikaners (p. 805)	

Review the Main Ideas

Answer the focus questions from each section of the chapter.

♦ What were some of the global consequences of European industrialization between 1815 and 1914? (p. 794)

♦ How was massive migration an integral part of Western expansion? (p. 799)

♦ How did Western imperialism change after 1880? (p. 804)

♦ What was the general pattern of non-Western responses to Western expansion? (p. 818)

Suggested Reading and Media Resources

BOOKS

- Bagchi, Amiya Kumar. *Perilous Passage: Mankind and the Global Ascendancy of Capital.* 2005. A spirited radical critique of the "rise of the West."
- Bayley, C. A. *The Birth of the Modern World, 1780–1914.* 2004. A broad survey that puts European imperialism and nationalism in a global context.
- Conklin, Alice. *A Mission to Civilize: The French Republican Ideal and West Africa, 1895–1930.* 1997. An outstanding examination of French imperialism.
- Conrad, Sebastian. *Globalisation and the Nation in Imperial Germany.* 2010. Places German nationalism and imperialism in the context of the wave of globalization that took place in the late nineteenth century.
- Cook, Scott B. *Colonial Encounters in the Age of High Imperialism.* 1996. A stimulating overview with a very readable account of the explorer Stanley and central Africa.
- Crews, Robert. *For Prophet and Tsar: Islam and Empire in Russia and Central Asia.* 2006. Considers neglected aspects of Russian imperialism.
- Davis, Mike. *Late Victorian Holocausts: El Niño Famines and the Making of the Third World.* 2002. A passionate condemnation of the links among imperialist policy, environmental catastrophe, and mass starvation in European colonies around 1900.
- Goodlad, Graham. *British Foreign and Imperial Policy, 1865–1919.* 2000. Examines Britain's leading role in European imperialism.
- Hochschild, Adam. *King Leopold's Ghost: A Story of Greed, Terror, and Heroism in Colonial Africa, 1895–1930.* 1997. A chilling account of Belgian imperialism in the Congo.
- Maier, Charles S. *Among Empires: American Ascendancy and Its Predecessors.* 2006. Explores imperial power in history and how well America measures up.
- Midgley, Clare, ed. *Gender and Imperialism.* 1998. Examines the complex questions related to European women and imperialism.
- Pomeranz, Kenneth. *The Great Divergence: China, Europe, and the Making of the Modern Economy.* 2001. This influential book explores the rise of European global influence after 1800.
- Walthall, Anne. *Japan: A Cultural, Social, and Political History.* 2006. A concise, up-to-date overview covering a broad range of developments in East Asia.

DOCUMENTARIES

- *Berlin 1885: The Scramble for Africa* (Joël Calmettes, 2010). A re-enactment of and documentary about the Berlin Conference, where European powers divided up the African continent into colonies.
- *Congo: White King, Red Rubber, Black Death* (Peter Bate, 2003). Covers King Leopold II's horrific exploitation of the Congo.
- *Queen Victoria's Empire* (Paul Bryers, 2001). A PBS four-part series about Queen Victoria and her empire, which included one-fifth of the world's population.

FEATURE FILMS AND TELEVISION

- *The Four Feathers* (Shekhar Kapur, 2002). A British officer resigns his post just before his regiment goes to the Sudan to fight the "rebels." Seen as a coward because of the resignation, the officer goes undercover to regain his honor.
- *Opium War* (Jin Xie, 1997). Depicts the dramatic conflicts between the British and Chinese surrounding the opium trade in the nineteenth century.
- *Rhodes* (BBC, 1996). An eight-part television drama about the British imperialist Cecil Rhodes, known for his success in the diamond industry and his passionate pursuit of British rule in southern Africa.
- *Zulu* (Cy Endfield, 1964). A war film portraying British soldiers and Zulu warriors fighting at the Battle of Rorke's Drift.

WEB SITES

- *BBC's Slavery and the "Scramble for Africa."* Explores the role abolition played in British interests in the colonization of Africa in the nineteenth century. **www.bbc.co.uk/history/british/abolition/scramble_for_africa_article_01.shtml**
- *Muhammad Ali Pasha in Egyptian History.* An introduction to the period of Muhammad Ali in Egypt. **www.egyptianagriculture.com/muhammad_ali.html**
- *The United States and the Opening to Japan, 1853.* The U.S. Office of the Historian's Web site presents an overview of Commodore Matthew Perry's arrival in Japan, as well as other material on U.S. imperial expansion in the nineteenth century. **https://history.state.gov/milestones/1830-1860/opening-to-japan**

25

War and Revolution

1914–1919

In the summer of 1914 the nations of Europe went willingly to war. They believed they had no other choice. Both peoples and governments confidently expected a short war leading to a decisive victory and thought that European society would be able to go on as before. These expectations were totally mistaken. The First World War was long, indecisive, and tremendously destructive. To the shell-shocked generation of survivors, it was known simply as the Great War because of its unprecedented scope and intensity.

From today's perspective, it is clear that the First World War was closely connected to the ideals and developments of the previous century. Industrialization, which promised a rising standard of living, now produced horrendous weapons that killed and maimed millions. Imperialism, which promised to civilize those the Europeans considered savages, now led to intractable international conflicts. Nationalism, which promised to bring compatriots together in a harmonious nation-state, now encouraged hateful prejudice and chauvinism. The extraordinary violence of world war shook confidence in such nineteenth-century certainties to their core.

The war would have an enormous impact on the century that followed. The need to provide extensive supplies and countless soldiers for the war effort created mass suffering, encouraged the rise of the bureaucratic state, and brought women in increasing numbers into the workplace. Millions were killed or wounded at the front, and millions more grieved these losses. Grand states collapsed: the Russian, Austro-Hungarian, and Ottoman Empires passed into history. The trauma of war contributed to the rise of extremist politics—in the Russian Revolution of 1917 the Bolsheviks established a radical Communist regime, and totalitarian Fascist movements gained popularity across Europe in the postwar decades. Explaining the war's causes and consequences remains one of the great challenges for historians of modern Europe. ■

CHAPTER PREVIEW

Life in World War I
This painting by British artist Paul Nash portrays a supply road on the western front. Nash's somber palette, tiny figures, and Cubist-influenced landscape capture the devastation and anonymous violence of total war. (*The Menin Road*, 1919/Imperial War Museum, London, UK/Bridgeman Images)

The Road to War

FOCUS QUESTION *What caused the outbreak of the First World War?*

Historians have long debated why Europeans so readily pursued a war that was long and costly and failed to resolve the problems faced by the combatant nations. There was no single most important cause. Growing competition over colonies and world markets, a belligerent arms race, and a series of diplomatic crises sharpened international tensions. On the home front, new forms of populist nationalism strengthened people's unquestioning belief in "my country right or wrong" while ongoing domestic conflicts encouraged governments to pursue aggressive foreign policies in attempts to bolster national unity. All helped pave the road to war.

Growing International Conflict

The First World War began, in part, because European statesmen failed to resolve the diplomatic problems created by Germany's rise to Great Power status. The Franco-Prussian War and the unification of Germany opened a new era in international relations. By the war's end in 1871, France was defeated, and Bismarck had made Prussia-Germany the most powerful nation in Europe (see Chapter 23). After 1871 Bismarck declared that Germany was a "satisfied" power. Within Europe, he stated, Germany had no territorial ambitions and wanted only peace.

But how was peace to be preserved? Bismarck's first concern was to keep France—bitter over its defeat and the loss of Alsace and Lorraine—diplomatically isolated and without allies. His second concern was the threat to peace posed by the enormous multinational

MAP 25.1 European Alliances at the Outbreak of World War I, 1914   At the start of World War I, Europe was divided into two hostile alliances: the Triple Entente of Britain, France, and Russia, and the Triple Alliance of Germany, Austria-Hungary, and Italy. Italy never fought with the Triple Alliance but instead joined the Entente in 1915.

empires of Austria-Hungary and Russia, particularly in southeastern Europe, where the waning strength of the Ottoman Empire had created a threatening power vacuum in the disputed border territories of the Balkans.

Bismarck's accomplishments in foreign policy were effective, but only temporary. From 1871 to the late 1880s, he maintained German leadership in international affairs, and he signed a series of defensive alliances with Austria-Hungary and Russia designed to isolate France. Yet in 1890 the new emperor Wilhelm II incautiously dismissed Bismarck, in part because he disagreed with the chancellor's friendly policy toward Russia. Under Wilhelm II, Bismarck's carefully planned alliance system began to unravel. Germany refused to renew a nonaggression pact with Russia, the centerpiece of Bismarck's system, in spite of Russian willingness to do so. This fateful move prompted long-isolated republican France to court absolutist Russia, offering loans, arms, and diplomatic support. In early 1894 France and Russia became military allies. As a result, continental Europe was divided into two rival blocs. The **Triple Alliance** of Austria, Germany, and Italy faced an increasingly hostile Dual Alliance of Russia and France, and the German general staff began secret preparations for a war on two fronts (Map 25.1).

As rivalries deepened on the continent, Great Britain's foreign policy became increasingly crucial. After 1891 Britain was the only uncommitted Great Power. Many Germans and some Britons felt that the advanced, racially related Germanic and Anglo-Saxon peoples were natural allies. However, the good relations that had prevailed between Prussia and Great Britain since the mid-eighteenth century gave way to a bitter Anglo-German rivalry.

There were several reasons for this ill-fated development. Commercial rivalry in world markets between Germany and Great Britain increased sharply in the 1890s, as Germany became a great industrial power. Germany's ambitious pursuit of colonies further threatened British interests. Above all, Germany's decision in 1900 to expand significantly its battle fleet posed a challenge to Britain's long-standing naval supremacy. In response to German expansion, British leaders prudently shored up their exposed global position with alliances and agreements. Britain improved its often-strained relations with the United States, concluded an alliance with Japan in 1902, and allied with France in the Anglo-French Entente of 1904, which settled all outstanding colonial disputes between Britain and France.

Alarmed by Britain's closer ties to France, Germany's leaders decided to test the strength of their alliance. In 1905 Wilhelm II declared that Morocco—where France had colonial interests—was an independent, sovereign state and demanded that Germany receive the same trading rights as France. Wilhelm II insisted on an international conference in hopes that his saber rattling would settle the Moroccan question to Germany's benefit. But his crude bullying only brought

Chronology

1914–1918	World War I
June 28, 1914	Serbian nationalist assassinates Archduke Franz Ferdinand
August 1914	War begins
September 1914	Battle of the Marne; German victories on the eastern front
October 1914	Ottoman Empire joins the Central Powers
1915	Italy joins the Triple Entente; German submarine sinks the *Lusitania*; Germany halts unrestricted submarine warfare; Battle of Gallipoli
1915–1918	Armenian genocide; German armies occupy large parts of east-central Europe
1916	Battles of Verdun and the Somme
1916–1918	Antiwar movement spreads throughout Europe; Arab rebellion against Ottoman Empire
1917	Germany resumes unrestricted submarine warfare
March 1917	February Revolution in Russia
April 1917	United States enters the war
October–November 1917	Battle of Caporetto
November 1917	Bolshevik Revolution in Russia; Balfour Declaration on Jewish homeland in Palestine
1918	Treaty of Brest-Litovsk; revolution in Germany
1918–1920	Civil war in Russia
1919	Treaty of Versailles; Allies invade Turkey
1923	Treaty of Lausanne recognizes Turkish independence

■ **Triple Alliance** The alliance of Austria, Germany, and Italy. Italy left the alliance when war broke out in 1914 on the grounds that Austria had launched a war of aggression.

France and Britain closer together, and Germany left the conference empty-handed.

The result of the First Moroccan Crisis in 1905 was something of a diplomatic revolution. Britain, France, Russia, and even the United States began to see Germany as a potential threat. At the same time, German leaders began to see sinister plots to encircle Germany and block its development as a world power. In 1907 Russia, battered by its disastrous war with Japan and the revolution of 1905, agreed to settle its quarrels with Great Britain in Persia and Central Asia and signed the Anglo-Russian Agreement. This agreement laid the foundation of the **Triple Entente** (ahn-TAHNT), an alliance between Britain, Russia, and France.

Germany's decision to expand its navy with a large, enormously expensive fleet of big-gun battleships, known as "dreadnoughts" because of their great size and power, heightened international tensions. German patriots saw a large navy as the legitimate right of a great world power and as a source of national pride. But British leaders saw the German buildup as a military challenge that forced them to spend the "People's Budget" (see Chapter 23) on battleships rather than social welfare. In 1909 the London *Daily Mail* hysterically informed its readers that "Germany is deliberately preparing to destroy the British Empire."[1] By then Britain had sided psychologically, if not officially, with France and Russia.

The leading nations of Europe were divided into two hostile camps, both ill-prepared to deal with the worsening situation in the Balkans. Britain, France, and Russia—the Triple Entente—were in direct opposition to the German-led Triple Alliance (see Map 25.1). This unfortunate treaty system only confirmed the failure of all European leaders to incorporate Bismarck's mighty empire permanently and peacefully into the international system. By 1914 many believed that war was inevitable.

The Mood of 1914

Diplomatic rivalries and international crises played key roles in the rush to war, but a complete understanding of the war's origins requires an account of the "mood of 1914"—the attitudes and convictions of Europeans around 1914.[2] Widespread militarism (the popular approval of military institutions and their values) and nationalism encouraged leaders and citizens alike to see international relations as an arena for the testing of national power, with war if necessary.

Germany was especially famous for its powerful and aggressive army, but military institutions played a prominent role in affairs of state and in the lives of ordinary people across Europe. In a period marked by diplomatic tensions, politicians relied on generals and military experts to help shape public policy. All the Great Powers built up their armed forces and designed mobilization plans to rush men and weapons to the field of battle. Universal conscription in Germany, France, Italy, Austria-Hungary, and Russia—only Britain still relied on a volunteer army—exposed hundreds of thousands of young men each year to military culture and discipline.

The continent had not experienced a major conflict since the Franco-Prussian War (1870–1871), so Europeans vastly underestimated the destructive potential of modern weapons. Encouraged by the patriotic national press, many believed that war was glorious, manly, and heroic. If they expected another conflict, they thought it would be over quickly. Leading politicians and intellectuals likewise portrayed war as a test of strength that would lead to national unity and renewal. Such ideas permeated European society. As one German volunteer wrote in his diary as he left for the front in 1914, "I believe that this war is a challenge for our time and for each individual, a test by fire, that we may ripen into manhood, become men able to cope with the coming stupendous years and events."[3]

Support for military values was closely linked to a growing sense of popular nationalism, the notion that one's country was superior to all others (see Chapters 21 and 23). Since the 1850s the spread of the idea that members of an ethnic group should live together in a homogeneous, united nation-state had provoked all kinds of international conflicts over borders and citizenship rights. Nationalism drove the spiraling arms race and the struggle over colonies. Broad popular commitment to national interests above all else weakened groups that thought in terms of international communities and consequences. Expressions of antiwar sentiment by socialists, pacifists, and women's groups were seen as a betrayal of country in time of need. Inspired by nationalist beliefs, much of the population was ready for war.

Leading statesmen had practical reasons for promoting militarism and nationalism. Political leaders had long used foreign adventurism and diplomatic posturing to distract the people from domestic conflicts. In Great Britain, leaders faced civil war in Northern Ireland and a vocal and increasingly radical women's movement. In Russia, defeat in the Russo-Japanese War (1904–1905) and the revolution of 1905 had greatly weakened support for the tsarist regime. In Germany, the victory of the Marxist Social Democratic Party in the parliamentary elections of 1912 led government authorities to worry that the country was falling apart. The French likewise faced difficult labor and budget problems.

Determined to hold onto power and frightened by rising popular movements, ruling classes across Europe were willing to gamble on diplomatic brinksmanship and even war to postpone dealing with intractable

■ **Triple Entente** The alliance of Great Britain, France, and Russia prior to and during the First World War.

social and political conflicts. Victory promised to pre-serve the privileged positions of elites and rally the masses behind the national cause. The patriotic nationalism bolstered by the outbreak of war did bring unity in the short run, but the wealthy governing classes underestimated the risk of war to themselves. They had forgotten that great wars and great social revolutions very often go hand in hand.

The Outbreak of War

On June 28, 1914, Archduke Franz Ferdinand, heir to the Austro-Hungarian throne, was assassinated by Serbian revolutionaries during a state visit to the Bosnian capital of Sarajevo (sar-uh-YAY-voh). After a series of failed attempts to bomb the archduke's motorcade, Gavrilo Princip, a fanatical member of the radical group the Black Hand, shot the archduke and his wife, Sophie, in their automobile. After his capture, Princip remained defiant, asserting at his trial, "I am a Yugoslav nationalist, aiming for the unification of all Yugoslavs,

and I do not care what form of state, but it must be free from Austria."[4]

Princip's deed, in the crisis-ridden borderlands between the weakened Ottoman and Austro-Hungarian Empires, led Europe into world war. In the early years of the twentieth century, war in the Balkans—"the powder keg of Europe"—seemed inevitable. The reason was simple: between 1900 and 1914 the Western powers had successfully forced the Ottoman rulers to give up their European territories. Serbs, Bulgarians, Albanians, and others now sought to establish independent nation-states, and the ethnic nationalism inspired by these changing state boundaries was destroying the Ottoman Empire and threatening Austria-Hungary (Map 25.2). The only questions were what kinds of wars would result and where they would lead.

By the early twentieth century nationalism in southeastern Europe was on the rise. Independent Serbia was eager to build a state that would include all ethnic Serbs and was thus openly hostile to Austria-Hungary and the Ottoman Empire, since both states

MAP 25.2 The Balkans, 1878–1914   After the Congress of Berlin in 1878, the Ottoman Empire suffered large territorial losses but remained a power in the Balkans. By 1914 Ottoman control had given way to ethnic population groups that flowed across political boundaries, and growing Serbian national aspirations threatened Austria-Hungary.

included substantial Serbian minorities within their borders. To block Serbian expansion, Austria in 1908 annexed the territories of Bosnia and Herzegovina (hehrt-suh-goh-VEE-nuh). The southern part of the Austro-Hungarian Empire now included an even larger Serbian population. Serbians expressed rage but could do nothing without support from Russia, their traditional ally.

The tensions in the Balkans soon erupted into regional warfare. In the First Balkan War (1912), Serbia joined Greece and Bulgaria to attack the Ottoman Empire and then quarreled with Bulgaria over the spoils of victory. In the Second Balkan War (1913), Bulgaria attacked its former allies. Austria intervened and forced Serbia to give up Albania. After centuries, nationalism had finally destroyed the Ottoman Empire in Europe. Encouraged by their success against the Ottomans, Balkan nationalists increased their demands for freedom from Austria-Hungary, dismaying the leaders of that multinational empire.

Within this complex context, the assassination of Archduke Franz Ferdinand instigated a five-week period of intense diplomatic activity that culminated in world war. The leaders of Austria-Hungary concluded that Serbia was implicated in the assassination and deserved severe punishment. On July 23 Austria-Hungary gave Serbia an unconditional ultimatum that

would violate Serbian sovereignty. When Serbia replied moderately but evasively, Austria mobilized its armies and declared war on Serbia on July 28. In this way, multinational Austria-Hungary, desperate to save its empire, deliberately chose war to stem the rising tide of hostile nationalism within its borders.

From the beginning of the crisis, Germany encouraged Austria-Hungary to confront Serbia and thus bore responsibility for turning a little war into a world war. Emperor Wilhelm II and his chancellor Theobald von Bethmann-Hollweg realized that war between Austria and Russia was likely, for a resurgent Russia would not stand by and watch the Austrians crush the Serbs, who were Russia's traditional allies. Yet Bethmann-Hollweg hoped that, although Russia (and its ally France) would go to war, Great Britain would remain neutral, unwilling to fight in the distant Balkans. With that hope, the German chancellor sent a telegram to Austria-Hungary, which promised that Germany would "faithfully stand by" its ally in case of war. This "blank check" of unconditional support encouraged the prowar faction in Vienna to take a hard line against the Serbs at a time when moderation might still have limited the crisis.

The diplomatic situation quickly spiraled out of control as military plans and timetables began to dictate policy. Vast Russia required much more time to

German Militarism   The German emperor Wilhelm II reviews his troops with the Italian king Victor Emmanuel in front of the royal palace in Potsdam in 1902. Aggressive militarism and popular nationalism helped pave the road to war. (© Scherl/SZ Photo/The Image Works)

mobilize its armies than did Germany and Austria-Hungary. And since the complicated mobilization plans of the Russian general staff assumed a two-front war with both Austria and Germany, Russia could not mobilize against one without mobilizing against the other. Therefore, on July 29 Tsar Nicholas II ordered full mobilization, which in effect declared war on both Austria-Hungary and Germany. The German general staff had also long thought in terms of a two-front war. Their misguided **Schlieffen Plan** called for a quick victory over France after a lightning attack through neutral Belgium — the quickest way to reach Paris — before turning on Russia. On August 3 German armies invaded Belgium. Great Britain, infuriated by the German violation of Belgian neutrality, declared war on Germany the following day.

The speed of the so called July Crisis created shock, panic, and excitement, and a bellicose public helped propel Europe into war. In the final days of July and the first few days of August, massive crowds thronged the streets of Paris, London, St. Petersburg, Berlin, and Vienna. Shouting prowar slogans, the enthusiastic crowds pushed politicians and military leaders toward the increasingly inevitable confrontation. Events proceeded rapidly, and those who opposed the war could do little to prevent its arrival. In a little over a month, a limited Austrian-Serbian war had become a European-wide conflict, and the First World War had begun.

The Schlieffen Plan

← Planned German offensive

▢ Neutral nations

NETHERLANDS

GERMANY

Brussels

BELGIUM

Rhine R.

LUX.

Paris   Reims

• Metz

Seine R.   Marne R.

FRANCE

0   100   200 mi.
0   100   200 km.

SWITZ.

Waging Total War

FOCUS QUESTION *How did the First World War differ from previous wars?*

When the Germans invaded Belgium in August 1914, they and many others thought that the war would be short and relatively painless. Many sincerely believed that "the boys will be home by Christmas." They were wrong. On the western front in France and the eastern front in Russia, and on the borders of the Ottoman Empire, the belligerent armies bogged down in a new and extremely costly kind of war, later labeled **total war** by German general Erich Ludendorff. Total war meant new roles for soldiers and civilians alike. At the front, total war meant lengthy, deadly battles fought with all the destructive weapons a highly industrialized

society could produce. At home, national economies were geared toward the war effort. Governments revoked civil liberties, and many civilians lost lives or livelihoods as occupying armies moved through their towns and cities. The struggle expanded outside Europe, and the Middle East, Africa, East Asia, and the United States were all brought into the maelstrom of total war.

Stalemate and Slaughter on the Western Front

In the face of the German invasion, the Belgian army heroically defended its homeland and fell back in good order to join a rapidly landed British army corps near the Franco-Belgian border. At the same time, Russian armies attacked eastern Germany, forcing the Germans to transfer much-needed troops to the east. Instead of quickly capturing Paris as per the Schlieffen Plan, by the end of August dead-tired German soldiers were advancing slowly along an enormous front in the scorching summer heat. Afraid that armed Belgian partisans (called *francs-tireurs*) were attacking German troops behind the lines, the German occupiers dealt harshly with local resistance. German soldiers executed civilians suspected of joining the partisans and, in an out-of-control tragedy, burned the medieval core of the Belgian city of Louvain. Entente propaganda made the most of the German "Rape of Belgium" and the atrocities committed by German troops.

On September 6 the French attacked a gap in the German line at the Battle of the Marne. For three days, France threw everything into the attack. At one point, the French government desperately requisitioned all the taxis of Paris to rush reserves to the front. Finally, the Germans fell back. France had been miraculously saved (Map 25.3).

With the armies stalled, both sides began to dig trenches to protect themselves from machine-gun fire. By November 1914 an unbroken line of four hundred miles of defensive positions extended from the Belgian coast through northern France and on to the Swiss

---

■ **Schlieffen Plan** Failed German plan calling for a lightning attack through neutral Belgium and a quick defeat of France before turning on Russia.

■ **total war** A war in which distinctions between the soldiers on the battlefield and civilians at home are blurred, and where the government plans and controls economic and social life in order to supply the armies at the front with supplies and weapons.

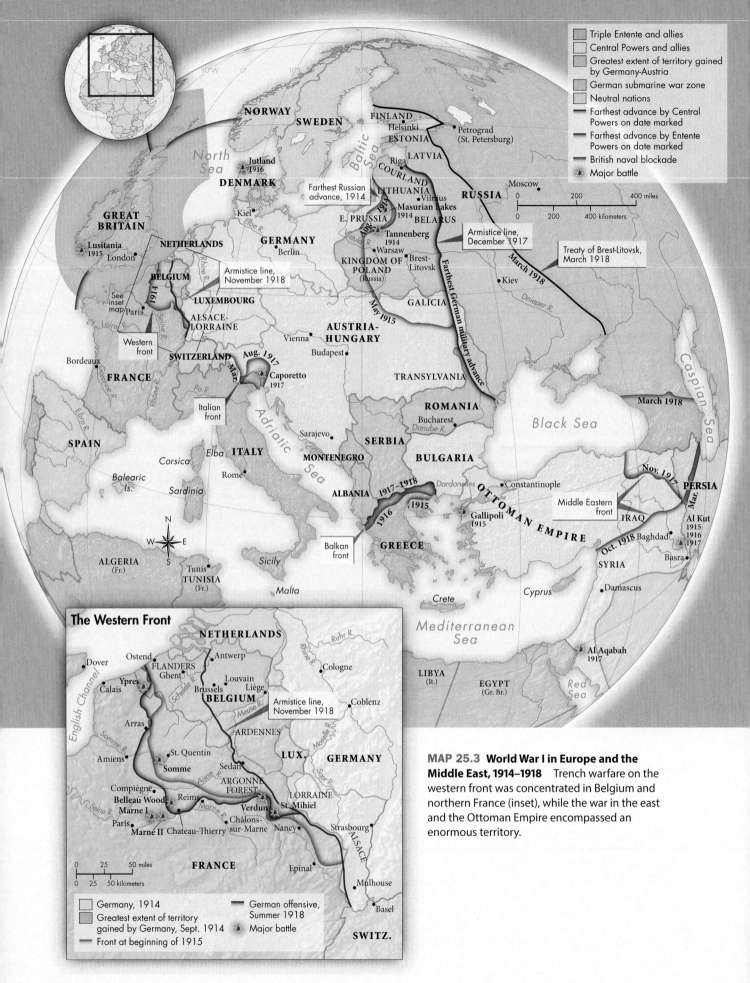

Triple Entente and allies
Central Powers and allies
Greatest extent of territory gained by Germany-Austria
German submarine war zone
Neutral nations
Farthest advance by Central Powers on date marked
Farthest advance by Entente Powers on date marked
British naval blockade
Major battle

NORWAY
SWEDEN
FINLAND
Helsinki
Petrograd (St. Petersburg)
North Sea
Jutland 1916
ESTONIA
DENMARK
Riga
LATVIA
COURLAND
Moscow
Farthest Russian advance, 1914
LITHUANIA
Vilnius
RUSSIA
Armistice line, December 1917
Kiel
E. PRUSSIA
Masurian Lakes 1914
BELARUS
Treaty of Brest-Litovsk, March 1918
GREAT BRITAIN
Lusitania 1915
London
NETHERLANDS
GERMANY
Berlin
Tannenberg 1914
Warsaw
KINGDOM OF POLAND (Russia)
Brest-Litovsk
March 1918
Kiev
BELGIUM
Armistice line, November 1918
LUXEMBOURG
ALSACE-LORRAINE
GALICIA
Dnieper R.
Western front
SWITZERLAND
Aug. 1917
AUSTRIA-HUNGARY
Vienna
Budapest
Farthest German military advance
Bordeaux
FRANCE
Caporetto 1917
TRANSYLVANIA
March 1918
Caspian Sea
Paris
Italian front
Po R.
Adriatic Sea
ROMANIA
Bucharest
Danube R.
Black Sea
SPAIN
Corsica
Elba
ITALY
Rome
Sarajevo
SERBIA
MONTENEGRO
BULGARIA
Nov. 1917
PERSIA
Balearic Is.
Sardinia
1917-1918
ALBANIA
1916
1915
Dardanelles
Constantinople
OTTOMAN EMPIRE
Middle Eastern front
IRAQ
Al Kut 1915 1916 1917
Baghdad
ALGERIA (Fr.)
Tunis
TUNISIA (Fr.)
Sicily
Malta
Balkan front
GREECE
Gallipoli 1915
Oct. 1918
SYRIA
Basra
Crete
Cyprus
Damascus
Mediterranean Sea
LIBYA (It.)
EGYPT (Gr. Br.)
Red Sea
Al Aqabah 1917

The Western Front

English Channel
Dover
Ostend
FLANDERS
Ghent
NETHERLANDS
Antwerp
Ruhr R.
Rhine R.
Calais
Ypres
Brussels
Louvain
Liège
Cologne
BELGIUM
Scheldt R.
Meuse R.
Armistice line, November 1918
Arras
ARDENNES
Coblenz
Amiens
Somme R.
St. Quentin
LUX.
GERMANY
Somme
Sedan
Aisne R.
Moselle R.
Saar R.
Compiègne
Belleau Wood
Reims
ARGONNE FOREST
Verdun
St. Mihiel
LORRAINE
Marne I
Chateau-Thierry
Marne R.
Châlons-sur-Marne
Nancy
Strasbourg
Paris
Marne II
Seine R.
FRANCE
Epinal
ALSACE
Mulhouse
Basel
SWITZ.

Germany, 1914
Greatest extent of territory gained by Germany, Sept. 1914
Front at beginning of 1915
German offensive, Summer 1918
Major battle

MAP 25.3 World War I in Europe and the Middle East, 1914–1918 Trench warfare on the western front was concentrated in Belgium and northern France (inset), while the war in the east and the Ottoman Empire encompassed an enormous territory.

frontier. Armies on both sides dug in behind rows of trenches, mines, and barbed wire, and slaughter on the western front began in earnest. The cost in lives of **trench warfare** was staggering, the gains in territory minuscule. For ordinary soldiers, conditions in the trenches were atrocious. (See "Living in the Past: Life and Death on the Western Front," page 836.) Recently invented weapons, the products of an industrial age, made battle impersonal, traumatic, and extremely deadly. The machine gun, hand grenades, poison gas, flamethrowers, long-range artillery, the airplane, and the tank were all used to murderous effect. All favored the defense, increased casualty rates, and revolutionized the practice of war.

The leading generals of the combatant nations, who had learned military tactics and strategy in the nineteenth century, struggled to understand trench warfare.

For four years they repeated the same mistakes, mounting massive offensives designed to achieve decisive breakthroughs. Brutal frontal assaults against highly fortified trenches might overrun the enemy's frontline, but attacking soldiers rarely captured any substantial territory. The French and British offensives of 1915 never gained more than three miles of territory. In 1916 the unsuccessful German campaign against Verdun left over 700,000 soldiers killed or wounded, and ended with the combatants in their original positions. The results in 1917 were little better. In hard-fought battles on all fronts, millions of young men were wounded or died for no real gain.

The Battle of the Somme, a great British offensive undertaken in the summer of 1916 in northern France, exemplified the horrors of trench warfare. The battle began with a weeklong heavy artillery bombardment

"Greetings from the trenches." This German postcard (left) shows three soldiers writing letters to their loved ones at home; the card was probably produced on a small, frontline printing press, for quick use by soldiers in the field. The post was typically the only connection between soldiers and their relatives, and over 28 billion pieces of mail passed between home and front on all sides during the war. Patriotic, mass-produced postcards, such as the British example also pictured here (right), often played on the connections between absent loved ones and national duty. (British card: Imperial War Museum, London, UK/ The Art Archive at Art Resource, NY; German card: © Sammlung Sauer/dpa/Corbis)

Ein Gruss aus dem Schützengraben.

■ **trench warfare** A type of fighting used in World War I behind rows of trenches, mines, and barbed wire; the cost in lives was staggering and the gains in territory minimal.

Hardship and tedium alternated with spasms of indescribable violence on the western front. Enlisted men rotated in and out of position, at best spending two weeks at base, two weeks in reserve positions, and two weeks in the trenches on the frontlines. They had little leave time to visit loved ones at home, though they exchanged literally billions of letters and postcards with friends and family. At the front, mud and vermin, bad food, damp and cold, and wretched living quarters were the norm. Soldiers spent most of their time repairing rough trenches and dugouts and standing watch for an enemy they rarely saw.

During periods of combat, modern weapons like mustard gas, the machine gun, and long-range artillery resulted in horrific destruction. Units were often decimated in poorly planned frontal assaults, and comrades could rarely retrieve the wounded and dead from no-man's land between the lines. Bodies, mangled by high explosives, were ground into the mud and disappeared, or became part of the earthworks themselves. A British soldier described the appalling effects: "The last I saw of him was two arms straining madly at the ground, blood pouring from his mouth while legs and body sank into a shellhole filled with water."*

The statistics tell a no less staggering story. More than 8 million combatants on all sides died during the war, and

Soldiers and draft animals alike wore gas masks as protection from enemy artillery that fired newly developed shells containing deadly poisonous gas. (Universal History Archive/ UIG via Getty Images)

British soldiers going "over the top." (© Pictorial Press Ltd./Alamy Stock Photo)

CAMPAGNE 1914
La prise d'un drapeau.

This French postcard celebrates victory over the Germans in the 1914 campaign and idealizes the bloody reality of trench warfare. (akg-images)

some 21 million were wounded. One historian estimates that fully half of all dead soldiers went either missing or unidentified; the tidy rows of crosses in military cemeteries mask a horrible reality. For these dead, Woodrow Wilson's words rang true: World War I was indeed "the war to end all wars." Things were less clear for the survivors. The maimed veteran — traumatized by "shell shock" or missing limbs or facial features — became an inescapable element of postwar life and culture.

QUESTIONS FOR ANALYSIS

1. How did highly industrialized warfare affect the everyday experience of enlisted men in the First World War?
2. What were the effects of modern weaponry, and how did these weapons change the way soldiers were buried?
3. How do the images shown here differ in their depiction of war? What might the postcard artist and the photographers have intended in showing these views of World War I?

*Quoted in Denis Winter, *Death's Men: Soldiers of the Great War* (London: Penguin, 1979), p. 180.

on the German lines, intended to cut the barbed wire fortifications, decimate the enemy trenches, and prevent the Germans from making an effective defense. For seven days and nights, the British artillery fired nonstop on the German lines, delivering about 1.5 million shells. On July 1 the British went "over the top," climbing out of the trenches and moving into no-man's land toward the German lines, dug into a series of ridges about half a mile away.

During the bombardment, the Germans had fled to their dugouts — underground shelters dug deep into the trenches — where they suffered from lack of water, food, and sleep. But they survived. As the British soldiers neared the German lines and the shelling stopped, the Germans emerged from their bunkers, set up their machine guns, and mowed down the approaching troops. In many places, the wire had not been cut by the bombardment, so the attackers, held in place by the wire, made easy targets. About 20,000 British men were killed and 40,000 more were wounded on just the first day, a crushing loss that shook troop morale and public opinion at home. The battle lasted until November, and in the end the British did push the Germans back — a whole seven miles. Some 420,000 British, 200,000 French, and 600,000 Germans were killed or wounded fighting over an insignificant scrap of land.

As the war ground on, exhausted soldiers found it difficult to comprehend or describe the bloody reality of their experiences at the front. As one French soldier wrote:

> I went over the top, I ran, I shouted, I hit, I can't remember where or who. I crossed the wire, jumped over holes, crawled through shell craters still stinking of explosives, men were falling, shot in two as they ran; shouts and gasps were half muffled by the sweeping surge of gunfire. But it was like a nightmare mist all around me. . . . Now my part in it is over for a few minutes. . . . Something is red over there; something is burning. Something is red at my feet: blood.[5]

The anonymous, almost unreal qualities of high-tech warfare made their way into the art and literature of the time. In each combatant nation, artists and

0   2.5   5 mi.
0   2.5   5 km.

Bapaume

Nov. 19
Sept. 15
July 15
July 14
Albert   July 1
Somme R.
Peronne

As of July 1, 1916
◻ British- and French-held territory
◻ German-held territory
◔ Woods
— Road
⋯ Front lines July–Nov. 1916

The Battle of the Somme, 1916

Poetry in the Trenches

The trauma of the First World War generated an outburst of cultural creation, and each nation had its favored group of artists and writers. Among the most famous were Britain's "trench poets," including John McCrae, Wilfred Owen, and Siegfried Sassoon. All three served in France. McCrae, a medical officer, died of an infection contracted in a field hospital close to the front. Owen was killed in action one week before the end of the war. Sassoon survived, but was always haunted by the death of his close friend Owen and his horrific memories of the fighting.

John McCrae, "In Flanders Fields"

In Flanders fields the poppies blow
     Between the crosses, row on row
    That mark our place; and in the sky
    The larks, still bravely singing, fly
Scarce heard amid the guns below.

We are the Dead. Short days ago
We lived, felt dawn, saw sunset glow,
    Loved and were loved, and now we lie
          In Flanders fields.

Take up our quarrel with the foe:
To you from failing hands we throw
    The torch; be yours to hold it high.
    If ye break faith with us who die
We shall not sleep, though poppies grow
          In Flanders fields.

Wilfred Owen, "Dulce et Decorum Est"

Bent double, like old beggars under sacks,
Knock-kneed, coughing like hags, we cursed through
    sludge,
Till on the haunting flares we turned our backs
And towards our distant rest began to trudge.
Men marched asleep. Many had lost their boots,
But limped on, blood-shod. All went lame; all blind;
Drunk with fatigue; deaf even to the hoots
Of gas-shells dropping softly behind.

Gas! GAS! Quick, boys! — An ecstasy of fumbling
Fitting the clumsy helmets just in time,
But someone still was yelling out and stumbling
And flound'ring like a man in fire or lime.—
Dim through the misty panes and thick green light,
As under a green sea, I saw him drowning.

In all my dreams before my helpless sight
He plunges at me, guttering, choking, drowning.

If in some smothering dreams, you too could pace
Behind the wagon that we flung him in,

And watch the white eyes writhing in his face,
His hanging face, like a devil's sick of sin,
If you could hear, at every jolt, the blood
Come gargling from the froth-corrupted lungs
Bitter as the cud
Of vile, incurable sores on innocent tongues,—
My friend, you would not tell with such high zest
To children ardent for some desperate glory,
The old Lie: *Dulce et decorum est*
*Pro patria mori.**

Siegfried Sassoon, "Attack"

At dawn the ridge emerges massed and dun
In the wild purple of the glowering sun,
Smouldering through spouts of drifting smoke that
    shroud
The menacing scarred slope; and, one by one,
Tanks creep and topple forward to the wire.
The barrage roars and lifts. Then, clumsily bowed
With bombs and guns and shovels and battle-gear,
Men jostle and climb to meet the bristling fire.
Lines of grey, muttering faces, masked with fear,
They leave their trenches, going over the top,
While time ticks blank and busy on their wrists,
And hope, with furtive eyes and grappling fists,
Flounders in the mud. O Jesu, make it stop!

EVALUATE THE EVIDENCE

1. Each of these poems was written during the war. How does each author bridge the traditional language and rhythm of poetry and the brutality of modern warfare?
2. What messages do the poems have for the reader at home?
3. What do these poems reveal about the effects of World War I on the fine arts and literature?

Sources: John McCrae, *In Flanders Fields and Other Poems* (New York: G. P. Putnam's Sons/Knickerbocker Press, 1919), p. 15; Wilfred Owen, *Poems by Wilfred Owen* (New York: Viking Press, 1921), p. 15; Siegfried Sassoon, *Counter-Attack and Other Poems* (New York: E. P. Dutton, 1918), p. 18.

*It is sweet and fitting / To die for one's country.

writers sought to portray the nightmarish quality of total war. Works by artists like Paul Nash, whose painting *The Menin Road* opens this chapter, or the poems of the famous British "trench poets," may do more to capture the experience of the war than contemporary photos or the dry accounts of historians. (See "Evaluating the Evidence 25.1: Poetry in the Trenches," at left.)

The Widening War

On the eastern front, the slaughter did not immediately degenerate into trench warfare, and the fighting was dominated by Germany. Repulsing the initial Russian attacks, the Germans won major victories at the Battles of Tannenberg and the Masurian Lakes in August and September 1914. Russia put real pressure on the relatively weak Austro-Hungarian army, but by 1915 the eastern front had stabilized in Germany's favor. A staggering 2.5 million Russian soldiers had been killed, wounded, or captured. German armies occupied huge swaths of the Russian Empire in central Europe, including ethnic Polish, Belorussian, and Baltic territories. Yet Russia continued to fight, marking another failure of the Schlieffen Plan.

To govern these occupied territories, the Germans installed a vast military bureaucracy, with some 15,000 army administrators and professional specialists. Anti-Slavic prejudice dominated the mind-set of the occupiers, who viewed the local Slavs as savages and ethnic "mongrels." German military administrators used prisoners of war and refugees as forced labor. They stole animals and crops from local farmers to supply the occupying army or send home to Germany. About one-third of the civilian population died or became refugees under this brutal occupation. In the long run, the German state hoped to turn these territories into German possessions, a chilling forerunner of Nazi policies in World War II.[6]

The changing tides of victory and hopes for territorial gains brought neutral countries into the war (see Map 25.3). Italy, a member of the Triple Alliance since 1882, had declared its neutrality in 1914 on the grounds that Austria had launched a war of aggression. Then in May 1915 Italy switched sides to join the Triple Entente in return for promises of Austrian territory. The war along the Italian-Austrian front was bitter and deadly and cost some 600,000 Italian lives.

In October 1914 the Ottoman Empire joined Austria and Germany, by then known as the Central Powers. The following September Bulgaria followed the Ottoman Empire's lead in order to settle old scores with Serbia. The Balkans, with the exception of Greece, were occupied by the Central Powers.

The entry of the Ottomans carried the war into the Middle East. Heavy fighting between the Ottomans and the Russians in the Caucasus enveloped the Armenians, who lived on both sides of the border and had experienced brutal repression by the Ottomans in 1909. When in 1915 some Armenians welcomed Russian armies as liberators, the Ottoman government, with German support, ordered a mass deportation of its Armenian citizens from their homeland. In this early example of modern ethnic cleansing, often labeled genocide, about 1 million Armenians died from murder, starvation, and disease.

In 1915, at the Battle of Gallipoli, British forces tried and failed to take the Dardanelles and Constantinople from the Ottoman Turks. The invasion force was pinned down on the beaches, and the ten-month-long battle cost the Ottomans 300,000 and the British 265,000 men killed, wounded, or missing.

The British were more successful at inciting the Arabs to revolt against their Ottoman rulers. They bargained with the foremost Arab leader, Hussein ibn-Ali (1856–1931), the chief magistrate (*sharif*) of Mecca, the holiest city in the Muslim world, and ruler for the Ottoman sultan of much of the Ottoman Empire's territory along the Red Sea, an area known as the Hejaz (see map in "Thinking Like a Historian," Source 4, page 859). In a famous exchange of diplomatic notes with Sir Henry McMahon, the British high commissioner in Cairo, Hussein managed in 1915 to win vague British commitments for an independent Arab kingdom. In 1916 Hussein rebelled against the Turks, proclaiming himself king of the Arabs. Hussein was aided by the British liaison officer T. E. Lawrence, who in 1917 helped lead Arab soldiers in a successful guerrilla war against the Turks on the Arabian peninsula.

The British enjoyed similar victories in the Ottoman province of Mesopotamia (today's Iraq). British troops quickly occupied the southern Iraqi city of Basra in 1914, securing their access to the region's oil fields. After a series of setbacks at the hands of Ottoman troops, the British captured Baghdad in 1917. In September 1918 British armies and their Arab allies rolled into Syria, a large and diverse Ottoman territory that included the holy lands of Palestine and the present-day

The Battle of Gallipoli

Suvla Bay

Anzac Cove

Aegean Sea

To Constantinople (Istanbul) and the Black Sea, distance approx. 85 miles

Turkish mine fields

GALLIPOLI PENINSULA

Cape Helles

Dardanelles

British forces landing site, Helles, April 25, 1915

British forces landing site, Suvla Bay, August 6, 1915

Maximum ground gained by Allies

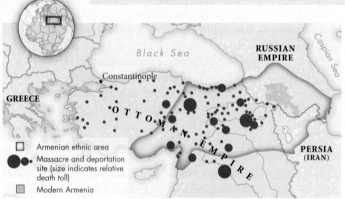

The Armenian Genocide, 1915–1918

Deportation of Ottoman Armenians   In 1915, when some Armenians welcomed Russian armies as liberators after years of persecution, the Ottoman government ordered a mass deportation of its Armenian citizens from their homeland in the empire's eastern provinces. This photo, taken from a hotel window in Kharpert by a German businessman in 1915, shows Turkish guards marching Armenian men off to prison, where they were tortured to death. About 1 million Armenians died from murder, starvation, and disease during World War I. (Photo courtesy of the Armenian Library & Museum of America)

countries of Syria, Lebanon, Jordan, and Israel. This offensive culminated in the triumphal entry of Hussein's son Faisal into Damascus. Arab patriots in Syria and Iraq now expected a large, unified Arab nation-state to rise from the dust of the Ottoman collapse — though they would later be disappointed by the Western powers (see page 856).

The war spread to East Asia and colonial Africa as well. Japan declared war on Germany in 1914, seized Germany's Pacific and East Asian colonies, and used the opportunity to expand its influence in China. In Africa, instead of rebelling as the Germans hoped, colonial subjects of the British and French generally supported the Allied powers and helped local British and French commanders take over German colonies.

The European world war spilled out of European borders and brought non-European peoples into the conflict. More than a million Africans and Asians served in the various armies of the warring powers; more than double that number served as porters to carry equipment and build defenses. The French, facing a shortage of young men, made especially heavy use of colonial troops from North Africa. Soldiers from India played a key role in Britain's campaigns against the Ottomans, though under the command of native British officers. And large numbers of soldiers came from the British Commonwealth, a voluntary association of former British colonies. Canadians, Australians, and New Zealanders fought with the British; those from Australia and New Zealand (the ANZAC Army Corps) fought with particular distinction in the failed Allied assault on Gallipoli.

After three years of refusing to play a fighting role, the United States was finally drawn into the expanding conflict. American intervention grew out of the war at sea and general sympathy for the Triple Entente. At the beginning of the war, Britain and France established a naval blockade to strangle the Central Powers. No neutral cargo ship was permitted to sail to Germany. In early 1915 Germany retaliated with attacks on supply ships from a murderously effective new weapon, the submarine.

In May 1915 a German submarine sank the British passenger liner *Lusitania*, claiming more than 1,000 lives, among them 139 U.S. citizens. President Woodrow Wilson protested vigorously, using the tragedy to incite American public opinion against the Germans. To avoid almost-certain war with the United States, Germany halted its submarine warfare for almost two years.

Early in 1917 the German military command—hoping that improved submarines could starve Britain into submission before the United States could come to its rescue—resumed unrestricted submarine warfare. This was a reckless gamble, and the United States declared war on Germany in April of that year. Eventually the United States tipped the balance in favor of the British, French, and their allies.

The Home Front

FOCUS QUESTION *In what ways did the war transform life on the home front?*

The war's impact on civilians was no less massive than it was on the men crouched in the trenches. Total war encouraged the growth of state bureaucracies, transformed the lives of ordinary women and men, and by the end inspired mass antiwar protest movements.

Mobilizing for Total War

In August 1914 many people greeted the outbreak of hostilities enthusiastically. In every country, ordinary folk believed that their nation was right to defend itself from foreign aggression. With the exception of those on the extreme left, even socialists supported the war. Yet by mid-October generals and politicians had begun to realize that victory would require more than patriotism. Heavy casualties and the stalemate meant each combatant country experienced a desperate need for men and weapons. To keep the war machine moving, national leaders aggressively intervened in society and the economy.

By the late nineteenth century the responsive national state had already shown an eagerness to manage the welfare of its citizens (see Chapter 23). Now, confronted by the crisis of total war, the state intruded even further into people's daily lives. New government ministries mobilized soldiers and armaments, estab-

lished rationing programs, and provided care for war widows and wounded veterans. Censorship offices controlled news about the course of the war. Government planning boards temporarily abandoned free-market capitalism and set mandatory production goals and limits on wages and prices. Government management of highly productive industrial economies worked: it yielded an effective and immensely destructive war effort on all sides.

Germany went furthest in developing a planned economy to wage total war. As soon as war began, the Jewish industrialist Walter Rathenau convinced the government to set up the War Raw Materials Board to ration and distribute raw materials. Under Rathenau's direction, every useful material from foreign oil to barnyard manure was inventoried and rationed. Moreover, the board launched successful attempts to produce substitutes, such as synthetic rubber and nitrates, for scarce war supplies. Food was rationed in accordance with physical need. Germany failed to tax the war profits of private firms heavily enough, however. This failure contributed to massive deficit financing, inflation, the growth of a black market, and the eventual re-emergence of class conflict.

Following the terrible Battles of Verdun and the Somme in 1916, German military leaders forced the Reichstag to accept the Auxiliary Service Law, which required all males between seventeen and sixty to work only at jobs considered critical to the war effort. Women also worked in war factories, mines, and steel mills, where they labored, like men, at heavy and dangerous jobs. While war production increased, people lived on little more than one thousand calories a day.

After 1917 Germany's leaders ruled by decree. Generals Paul von Hindenburg and Erich Ludendorff—heroes of the Battle of Tannenberg—drove Chancellor Bethmann-Hollweg from office. With the support of the newly formed ultraconservative Fatherland Party, the generals established a military dictatorship. Hindenburg called for the ultimate mobilization for total war. Germany could win, he said, only "if all the treasures of our soil that agriculture and industry can produce are used exclusively for the conduct of War. . . . All other considerations must come second."[7] Thus in Germany total war led to the establishment of history's first "totalitarian" society, a model for future National Socialists, or Nazis.

Only Germany was directly ruled by a military government, yet leaders in all the belligerent nations took power from parliaments, suspended civil liberties, and ignored democratic procedures. After 1915 the British Ministry of Munitions organized private industry to produce for the war, allocated labor, set wage and price rates, and settled labor disputes. In France, a weakened parliament met without public oversight, and the courts jailed pacifists who dared criticize the state.

Vera Brittain

Although the Great War upended millions of lives, it struck Europe's young people with the greatest force. For Vera Brittain (1893–1970), as for so many in her generation, the war became life's defining experience, which she captured forever in her famous autobiography, *Testament of Youth* (1933).

Brittain grew up in a wealthy business family in northern England, bristling at small-town conventions and discrimination against women. Very close to her brother Edward, two years her junior, Brittain read voraciously and dreamed of being a successful writer. Finishing boarding school and overcoming her father's objections, she prepared for Oxford's rigorous entry exams and won a scholarship to its women's college. Brittain fell in love with Roland Leighton, an equally brilliant student from a literary family and her brother's best friend. All three, along with two other close friends, Victor Richardson and Geoffrey Thurlow, confidently prepared to enter Oxford in late 1914.

When war suddenly loomed in July 1914, Brittain shared with millions of Europeans a surge of patriotic support for her government, a prowar enthusiasm she later downplayed in her published writings. She wrote in her diary that her "great fear" was that England would declare its neutrality and commit the "grossest treachery" toward France.* She supported Leighton's decision to enlist, agreeing with his glamorous view of war as "very ennobling and very beautiful." Later, exchanging anxious letters with Leighton in France in 1915, Brittain began to see the conflict in personal, human terms. She wondered if any victory or defeat could be worth her fiancé's life.

Struggling to quell her doubts, Brittain redoubled her commitment to England's cause and volunteered as an army nurse. For the next three years, she served with distinction in military hospitals in London, Malta, and northern France, repeatedly torn between the vision of noble sacrifice and the reality of human tragedy. Having lost sexual inhibitions while caring for mangled male bodies, she longed to consummate her love with Leighton. Awaiting his return on leave on Christmas Day in 1915, she was greeted instead with a telegram: he had been killed two days before.

Leighton's death was the first of several devastating blows that eventually overwhelmed Brittain's idealistic patriotism.

Vera Brittain was marked forever by her wartime experiences. (Vera Brittain fonds, William Ready Division of Archives and Research Collections, McMaster University Library)

In 1917 Thurlow and then Richardson died from gruesome wounds. In early 1918, as the last great German offensive covered the floors of her war-zone hospital with maimed and dying German prisoners, the bone-weary Brittain felt a common humanity and saw only more victims. A few weeks later her brother Edward — her last hope — died in action. When the war ended, she was, she said, a "complete automaton," with her "deepest emotions paralyzed if not dead."

Returning to Oxford and finishing her studies, Brittain gradually recovered. She formed a deep, restorative friendship with another talented woman writer, Winifred Holtby; published novels and articles; and became a leader in the feminist campaign for gender equality. She also married and had children. But her wartime memories were always with her. Finally, Brittain succeeded in coming to grips with them in *Testament of Youth*, her powerful antiwar autobiography. The unflinching narrative spoke to the experiences of an entire generation and became a runaway bestseller. Above all, Brittain captured the contradictory character of the war, in which millions of young people found excitement, courage, and common purpose but succeeded only in destroying their lives with their superhuman efforts and futile sacrifices. Increasingly committed to pacifism, Brittain opposed England's entry into World War II.

QUESTIONS FOR ANALYSIS

1. What were Brittain's initial feelings toward the war? How and why did they change as the conflict continued?
2. Why did Brittain volunteer as a nurse, as many women did? How might wartime nursing have influenced women of her generation?
3. In portraying the contradictory character of World War I for Europe's youth, was Brittain describing the character of all modern warfare?

*Quotes from the excellent study P. Berry and M. Bostridge, *Vera Brittain: A Life* (London: Virago Press, 2001), p. 59; additional quotations are from pp. 80 and 136.

Once the United States entered the war, new federal agencies such as the War Labor Board and the War Industries Board regulated industry, labor relations, and agricultural production, while the Espionage and Sedition Acts weakened civil liberties. The war may have been deadly for citizen armies, but it was certainly good for the growth of the bureaucratic nation-state.

The Social Impact

The social changes wrought by total war were no less profound than the economic impact, though again there were important national variations. National conscription sent millions of men to the front, exposing many to foreign lands for the first time in their lives. The insatiable needs of the military created a tremendous demand for workers, making jobs readily available. This situation   seldom, if ever, seen before 1914, when unemployment and poverty had been facts of urban life—brought momentous changes.

The need for workers meant greater power and prestige for labor unions. Unions cooperated with war governments on workplace rules, wages, and production schedules in return for real participation in important decisions. The entry of labor leaders and unions into policymaking councils paralleled the entry of socialist leaders into war governments. Both reflected a new government openness to the needs of those at the bottom of society.

The role of women changed dramatically. The production of vast amounts of arms and ammunition required huge numbers of laborers, and women moved into skilled industrial jobs long considered men's work. Women became highly visible in public—as munitions workers, bank tellers, and mail carriers, and even as police officers, firefighters, and farm laborers. Women also served as auxiliaries and nurses at the front. (See "Individuals in Society: Vera Brittain," at left.)

The war expanded the range of women's activities and helped change attitudes about proper gender roles, but the long-term results were mixed. Women gained experience in jobs previously reserved for men, but at war's end millions of demobilized soldiers demanded their jobs back, and governments forced women out of the workplace. Thus women's employment gains were mostly temporary, except in nursing and social work, already considered "women's work." The great dislocations

Women Workers Building a Truck in a London Workshop, 1917   Millions of men on all sides were drafted to fight in the war, creating a serious labor shortage on the home front. When women began to fill jobs formerly reserved for men, they challenged middle-class gender roles. (© Hulton-Deutsch Collection/Corbis)

of war loosened sexual morality, and some women bobbed their hair, shortened their skirts, and smoked in public. Yet supposedly "loose" women were often criticized for betraying their soldier-husbands away at the front. As a result of women's many-sided war effort, the United States, Britain, Germany, Poland, and other countries granted women the right to vote immediately after the war. Yet women's rights movements faded in the 1920s and 1930s, in large part because feminist leaders found it difficult to regain momentum after the crisis of war.

To some extent, the war promoted greater social equality, blurring class distinctions and lessening the gap between rich and poor. This blurring was most apparent in Great Britain, where the bottom third of the population generally lived better than they ever had, for the poorest gained most from the severe shortage of labor. Elsewhere, greater equality was reflected in full employment, distribution of scarce rations according to physical needs, and a sharing of hardships. In general, despite some war profiteering, European society became more uniform and egalitarian.

Death itself had no respect for traditional social distinctions. It savagely decimated the young aristocratic officers who led the charge, and it fell heavily on the mass of drafted peasants and unskilled workers who followed, leading commentators to speak of a "lost generation." Yet death often spared highly skilled workers and foremen. Their lives were too valuable to squander at the front, for they were needed to train the newly recruited women and older unskilled men laboring valiantly in war plants at home.

Growing Political Tensions

During the first two years of war, many soldiers and civilians supported their governments. Patriotic nationalism and belief in a just cause united peoples behind their national leaders. Each government used rigorous censorship and crude propaganda to bolster popular support. (See "Evaluating the Evidence 25.2: Wartime Propaganda Posters," at right.) German propaganda pictured black soldiers from France's African empire abusing German women, while the French and British ceaselessly recounted and exaggerated German atrocities in Belgium and elsewhere. Patriotic posters and slogans, slanted news, and biased editorials inflamed national hatreds, helped control public opinion, and encouraged soldiers to keep fighting.

Political and social tensions re-emerged, however, and by the spring of 1916 ordinary people were beginning to crack under the strain of total war. Strikes and protest marches over war-related burdens and shortages flared up on every home front. On May 1, 1916, several thousand demonstrators in Berlin heard the radical socialist leader Karl Liebknecht (1871–1919)

attack the costs of the war effort. Liebknecht was arrested and imprisoned, but his daring action electrified Europe's far left. In France, Georges Clemenceau (zhorzh kleh-muhn-SOH) (1841–1929) established a virtual dictatorship, arrested strikers, and jailed without trial journalists and politicians who dared to suggest a compromise peace with Germany.

In April 1916 Irish republican nationalists took advantage of the tense wartime conditions to step up their rebellion against British rule. During the great Easter Rising, armed republican militias took over parts of Dublin and proclaimed an independent Irish Republic. After a week of bitter fighting, British troops crushed the rebels and executed their leaders. Though the republicans were defeated, the punitive aftermath fueled anti-British sentiment in Ireland. The Rising set the stage for the success of the nationalist Sinn Fein Party and a full-scale civil war for Irish independence in the early 1920s.

On all sides, soldiers' morale began to decline. Numerous French units mutinied and refused to fight after the disastrous French offensive of May 1917. Only tough military justice, including executions for mutiny leaders, and a tacit agreement with the troops that there would be no more grand offensives, enabled the new general-in-chief, Henri-Philippe Pétain (pay-TAN), to restore order. Facing defeat, wretched conditions at the front, and growing hopelessness, Russian soldiers deserted in droves, providing fuel for the Russian Revolution of 1917. After the murderous Battle of Caporetto in northern Italy, which lasted from October to November in 1917, the Italian army collapsed in despair. In the massive battles of 1916 and 1917, the British armies had been "bled dry." Only the promised arrival of fresh troops from the United States stiffened the resolve of the Allies.

The strains were even worse for the Central Powers. In October 1916 a young socialist assassinated the chief minister of Austria-Hungary. The following month, when the aging emperor Franz Joseph died, a symbol of unity disappeared. In spite of absolute censorship, political dissatisfaction and conflicts among nationalities grew. Both Czech and Balkan leaders demanded independent states for their peoples. By April 1917 the Austro-Hungarian people and army were exhausted. Another winter of war would bring revolution and disintegration.

Germans likewise suffered immensely. The British naval blockade greatly limited food imports, and the scarcity of basic necessities had horrific results: some 750,000 German civilians starved to death. For the rest, heavy rationing of everyday goods such as matches, bread, cooking oil, and meat undermined morale. A growing minority of moderate socialists in the Reichstag gave voice to popular discontent when they called for a compromise "peace without annexations or reparations."

Such a peace was unthinkable for the Fatherland Party. Yet Germany's rulers faced growing unrest.

Wartime Propaganda Posters

This famous French propaganda poster from 1918 (left) proclaims "They shall not pass" and expresses the French determination to hold back the German invaders at any cost. The American recruitment poster from 1917 (right) encourages "fighting men" to "join the Navy."

(Private Collection/© Galerie Bilderwelt/Bridgeman Images)

(Private Collection/© Galerie Bilderwelt/Bridgeman Images)

EVALUATE THE EVIDENCE

1. Describe the soldier and sailor pictured on these posters. How do the posters present the war?
2. The French poster was created after France had been at war for four years, while the naval recruitment poster came out before American troops were actively engaged overseas. How might the country of origin and the date of publication have affected the messages conveyed in the posters?

When the bread ration was further reduced in April 1917, more than 200,000 workers and women struck and demonstrated for a week in Berlin, returning to work only under the threat of prison and military discipline. That same month, radicals left the Social Democratic Party to form the Independent Social Democratic Party; in 1918 they would found the German Communist Party. Thus Germany, like its ally Austria-Hungary (and its enemy France), was beginning to crack in 1917. Yet it was Russia that collapsed first and saved the Central Powers—for a time.

The Russian Revolution

FOCUS QUESTION *Why did world war lead to revolution in Russia, and what was its outcome?*

Growing out of the crisis of the First World War, the Russian Revolution of 1917 was one of modern history's most momentous events. For some, the revolution was Marx's socialist vision come true; for others, it was the triumph of a despised Communist dictatorship. To all, it presented a radically new prototype of state and society.

The Fall of Imperial Russia

Like their allies and enemies, many Russians had embraced war with patriotic enthusiasm in 1914. At the Winter Palace, throngs of people knelt and sang "God Save the Tsar!" while Tsar Nicholas II (r. 1894–1917) repeated the oath Alexander I had sworn in 1812 during Napoleon's invasion of Russia (see Chapter 19), vowing never to make peace as long as the enemy stood on Russian soil. Russia's lower house of parliament, the Duma, voted to support the war. Conservatives anticipated expansion in the Balkans, while liberals and most socialists believed that alliance with Britain and France would bring democratic reforms. For a moment, Russia was united.

Enthusiasm for the war soon waned as better-equipped German armies inflicted terrible losses. By 1915 substantial numbers of Russian soldiers were being sent to the front without rifles; they were told to find their arms among the dead. Russia's battered peasant army nonetheless continued to fight, and Russia moved toward full mobilization on the home front. The government set up special committees to coordinate defense, industry, transportation, and agriculture. These efforts improved the military situation, but overall Russia mobilized less effectively than the other combatants.

One problem was weak leadership. Under the constitution resulting from the revolution of 1905 (see Chapter 23), the tsar had retained complete control over the bureaucracy and the army. A kindly but narrow-minded aristocrat, Nicholas II distrusted the publicly elected Duma and resisted popular involvement in government, relying instead on the old bureaucracy. Excluded from power, the Duma, the educated middle classes, and the masses became increasingly critical of the tsar's leadership. In September 1915 parties ranging from conservative to moderate socialist formed the Progressive bloc, which called for a completely new government responsible to the Duma instead of the tsar. In answer, Nicholas temporarily adjourned the Duma. The tsar then announced that he was traveling to the front in order to lead and rally Russia's armies, leaving the government in the hands of his wife, the strong-willed and autocratic Tsarina Alexandra.

His departure was a fatal turning point. In his absence, Tsarina Alexandra arbitrarily dismissed loyal political advisers. She turned to her court favorite, the disreputable and unpopular Rasputin, an uneducated Siberian preacher whose influence with the tsarina rested on his purported ability to heal Alexis—Alexandra's only son and heir to the throne—from his hemophilia. In a desperate attempt to right the situation, three members of the high aristocracy murdered Rasputin in December 1916. The ensuing scandal further undermined support for the tsarist government.

Imperial Russia had entered a terminal crisis. Tens of thousands of soldiers deserted, swelling the number of the disaffected at home. By early 1917 the cities were wracked by food shortages, heating fuel was in short supply, and the economy was breaking down. In March violent street demonstrations broke out in Petrograd (now named St. Petersburg), spread to the factories, and then engulfed the city. From the front, the tsar ordered the army to open fire on the protesters, but the soldiers refused to shoot and joined the revolutionary crowd instead. The Duma declared a provisional government on March 12, 1917. Three days later, Nicholas abdicated.

The Provisional Government

The **February Revolution**, then, was the result of an unplanned uprising of hungry, angry people in the capital, but it was eagerly accepted throughout the country. (The name of the revolution matches the traditional Russian calendar, which used a different dating system.) The patriotic upper and middle classes embraced the prospect of a more determined war effort, while workers anticipated better wages and more food. After generations of autocracy, the provisional government established equality before the law, granting freedoms of religion, speech, and assembly, as well as the right of unions to organize and strike.

Yet the provisional government made a crucial mistake: though the Russian people were sick of fighting, the new leaders failed to take Russia out of the war. A government formed in May 1917 included the fiery agrarian socialist Alexander Kerensky, who became prime minister in July. For the patriotic Kerensky, as for other moderate socialists, the continuation of war was still a national duty. Turning his back on needed reforms, Kerensky refused to confiscate large landholdings and give them to peasants, fearing that such drastic action would complete the disintegration of Russia's peasant army. Human suffering and war-weariness grew, testing the limited strength of the provisional government.

From its first day, the provisional government had to share power with a formidable rival — the **Petrograd Soviet** (or council) of Workers' and Soldiers' Deputies. Modeled on the revolutionary soviets of 1905, the Petrograd Soviet comprised two to three thousand workers, soldiers, and socialist intellectuals. Seeing itself as a true grassroots product of revolutionary democracy, the Soviet acted as a parallel government. It issued its own radical orders, weakening the authority of the provisional government.

The most famous edict of the Petrograd Soviet was Army Order No. 1, issued in May 1917, which stripped officers of their authority and placed power in the hands of elected committees of common soldiers. Designed to protect the revolution from resistance by the aristocratic officer corps, the order led to a collapse of army discipline.

In July 1917 the provisional government mounted a poorly considered summer offensive against the Germans. The campaign was a miserable failure, and desertions mounted as peasant soldiers returned home to help their families get a share of the land, which peasants were seizing in a grassroots agrarian revolt. By the summer of 1917 Russia was descending into anarchy. It was an unparalleled opportunity for the most radical and talented of Russia's many revolutionary leaders, Vladimir Ilyich Lenin (1870–1924).

Lenin and the Bolshevik Revolution

Born into the middle class, Lenin became an enemy of imperial Russia when his older brother was executed for plotting to kill archconservative Tsar Alexander III in 1887. As a law student, Lenin eagerly studied Marxist socialism, which began to win converts among radical intellectuals during Russia's industrialization in the 1890s. A pragmatic and flexible thinker, Lenin updated Marx's revolutionary philosophy to address existing conditions in Russia.

Key Events of the Russian Revolution

August 1914	Russia enters World War I
1916–1917	Tsarist government in crisis
March 1917	February Revolution; establishment of provisional government; tsar abdicates
April 1917	Lenin returns from exile
July 1917	Bolshevik attempt to seize power fails
October 1917	Bolsheviks gain a majority in the Petrograd Soviet
November 6–7, 1917	Bolsheviks seize power; Lenin named head of new Communist government
1918–1920	Civil war
March 1918	Treaty of Brest-Litovsk; Trotsky becomes head of the Red Army
1920	Civil war ends; Lenin and Bolshevik-Communists take control of Russia

Three interrelated concepts were central for Lenin. First, he stressed that only violent revolution could destroy capitalism. He tirelessly denounced all "revisionist" theories of a peaceful evolution to socialism (see Chapter 23) as a betrayal of Marx's message of violent class conflict. Second, Lenin argued that under certain conditions a Communist revolution was possible even in a predominantly agrarian country like Russia. Peasants, who were numerous, poor, and exploited, could take the place of Marx's traditional working class in the coming revolutionary conflict.

Third, Lenin believed that the possibility of revolution was determined more by human leadership than by historical laws. He called for a highly disciplined workers' party strictly controlled by a small, dedicated elite of intellectuals and professional revolutionaries. This elite would not stop until revolution brought it to power. Lenin's version of Marxism had a major impact on events in Russia and ultimately changed the way future revolutionaries engaged in radical revolt around the world.

Other Russian Marxists challenged Lenin's ideas. At meetings of the Russian Social Democratic Labor Party in London in 1903, matters came to a head. Lenin demanded a small, disciplined, elitist party dedicated to Communist revolution, while his opponents wanted a more democratic, reformist party with

■ **February Revolution** Unplanned uprisings accompanied by violent street demonstrations begun in March 1917 (old calendar February) in Petrograd, Russia, that led to the abdication of the tsar and the establishment of a provisional government.

■ **Petrograd Soviet** A huge, fluctuating mass meeting of two to three thousand workers, soldiers, and socialist intellectuals modeled on the revolutionary soviets of 1905.

The Radicalization of the Russian Army   Russian soldiers inspired by the Bolshevik cause carry banners with Marxist slogans calling for revolution and democracy, around July 1917. One reads "All Power to the Proletariat," a telling response to the provisional government's failure to pull Russia out of the war. Sick of defeat and wretched conditions at the front, the tsar's troops welcomed Lenin's promises of "Peace, Land, and Bread" and were enthusiastic participants in the Russian Revolution. (Hulton Archive/Getty Images)

mass membership (like the German SPD). The Russian Marxists split into two rival factions. Lenin called his camp the **Bolsheviks**, or "majority group"; his opponents were Mensheviks, or "minority group." The Bolsheviks had only a tenuous majority of a single vote, but Lenin kept the name for propaganda reasons and they became the revolutionary party he wanted: tough, disciplined, and led from above.

Unlike other socialists, Lenin had not rallied around the national flag in 1914. Observing events from neutral Switzerland, where he lived in exile to avoid persecution by the tsar's police, Lenin viewed the war as a product of imperialist rivalries and an opportunity for socialist revolution. After the February Revolution of 1917, the German government provided Lenin with safe passage across Germany and back into Russia. The Germans hoped Lenin would undermine the sagging war effort of the provisional government. They were not disappointed.

Arriving triumphantly at Petrograd's Finland Station on April 3, Lenin attacked at once. He rejected all cooperation with what he called the "bourgeois" provisional government. His slogans were radical in the extreme: "All power to the soviets"; "All land to the peasants"; "Stop the war now." Lenin was a superb tactician. His promises of "Peace, Land, and Bread" spoke to the expectations of suffering soldiers, peasants, and workers and earned the Bolsheviks substantial popular support. The moment for revolution was at hand.

Yet Lenin and the Bolsheviks almost lost the struggle for Russia. A premature attempt to seize power in July collapsed, and Lenin went into hiding. However, this temporary setback made little difference in the long run. The army's commander in chief, General Lavr Kornilov, led a feeble coup against the provisional Kerensky government in September. In the face of this rightist counter-revolutionary threat, the Bolsheviks were rearmed. Kornilov's forces disintegrated, but Kerensky lost all credit with the army, the only force that might have saved democratic government in Russia.

Trotsky and the Seizure of Power

Throughout the summer, the Bolsheviks greatly increased their popular support. Party membership soared from 50,000 to 240,000, and in October the Bolshe-

■ **Bolsheviks** Lenin's radical, revolutionary arm of the Russian party of Marxist socialism, which successfully installed a dictatorial socialist regime in Russia.

viks gained a fragile majority in the Petrograd Soviet. Now Lenin's supporter Leon Trotsky (1879–1940), a spellbinding revolutionary orator and radical Marxist, brilliantly executed the Bolshevik seizure of power.

Painting a vivid but untruthful picture of German and counter-revolutionary plots, Trotsky convinced the Petrograd Soviet to form a special military-revolutionary committee in October and make him its leader. Thus military power in the capital passed into Bolshevik hands.

On the night of November 6, militants from Trotsky's committee joined with trusted Bolshevik soldiers to seize government buildings in Petrograd and arrest members of the provisional government. Then they went on to the Congress of Soviets, where a Bolshevik majority—roughly 390 of 650 excited delegates—declared that all power had passed to the soviets and named Lenin head of the new government. John Reed, a sympathetic American journalist, described the enthusiasm that greeted Lenin at the congress:

> Now Lenin, gripping the edge of the reading stand . . . stood there waiting, apparently oblivious to the long-rolling ovation, which lasted several minutes. When it finished, he said simply, "We shall now proceed to construct the Socialist order!" Again that overwhelming human roar.[8]

The Bolsheviks came to power for three key reasons. First, by late 1917 democracy had given way to anarchy: power was there for those who would take it. Second, in Lenin and Trotsky the Bolsheviks had an utterly determined and superior leadership, which both the tsarist and the provisional governments lacked. Third, as Reed's comment suggests, Bolshevik policies appealed to ordinary Russians. Exhausted by war and weary of tsarist autocracy, they were eager for radical changes. (See "Evaluating the Evidence 25.3: Peace, Land, and Bread for the Russian People," page 850.) With time, many Russians would become bitterly disappointed with the Bolshevik regime, but for the moment they had good reason to hope for peace, better living conditions, and a more equitable society.

Dictatorship and Civil War

The Bolsheviks' truly monumental accomplishment was not taking power, but keeping it. Over the next four years, they conquered the chaos they had helped create and began to build a Communist society. How was this done?

Lenin had the genius to profit from developments over which the Bolsheviks had little control. Since summer, a peasant revolt had swept across Russia, as impoverished peasants had seized for themselves the

Lenin Rallies the Masses Bolshevik leader Vladimir Lenin, known for his fiery speeches, addresses a crowd in Moscow's Red Square in October 1917. (Sovfoto/UIG via Getty Images)

Peace, Land, and Bread for the Russian People

Lenin wrote this dramatic manifesto in the name of the Congress of Soviets in Petrograd, the day after Trotsky seized power in the city. The Bolsheviks boldly promised the Russian people a number of progressive reforms, including an immediate armistice, land reform, democracy in the army, and ample food for all. They also issued a call to arms. The final paragraphs warn of counter-revolutionary resistance and capture the looming descent into all-out civil war.

~

To Workers, Soldiers, and Peasants!

The . . . All-Russia Congress of Soviets of Workers and Soldiers' Deputies has opened. The vast majority of the Soviets are represented at the Congress. A number of delegates from the Peasants' Soviets are also present. . . . Backed by the will of the vast majority of the workers, soldiers, and peasants, backed by the victorious uprising of the workers and the garrison which has taken place in Petrograd, the Congress takes power into its own hands.

The Provisional Government has been overthrown. The majority of the members of the Provisional Government have already been arrested.

The Soviet government will propose an immediate democratic peace to all the nations and an immediate armistice on all fronts. It will secure the transfer of the land of the landed proprietors, the crown and the monasteries to the peasant committees without compensation; it will protect the rights of the soldiers by introducing complete democracy in the army; it will establish workers' control over production; it will ensure the convocation of the Constituent Assembly at the time appointed; it will see to it that bread is supplied to the cities and prime necessities to the villages; it will guarantee all the nations inhabiting Russia the genuine right to self-determination.

The Congress decrees: all power in the localities shall pass to the Soviets of Workers', Soldiers' and Peasants' Deputies, which must guarantee genuine revolutionary order.

The Congress calls upon the soldiers in the trenches to be vigilant and firm. The Congress of Soviets is convinced that the revolutionary army will be able to defend the revolution against all attacks of imperialism until such time as the new government succeeds in concluding a democratic peace, which it will propose directly to all peoples. The new government will do everything to fully supply the revolutionary army by means of a determined policy of requisitions and taxation of the propertied classes, and also will improve the condition of the soldiers' families.

The Kornilov men — Kerensky, Kaledin and others — are attempting to bring troops against Petrograd. Several detachments, whom Kerensky had moved by deceiving them, have come over to the side of the insurgent people.

Soldiers, actively resist Kerensky the Kornilovite! Be on your guard!

Railwaymen, hold up all troop trains dispatched by Kerensky against Petrograd!

Soldiers, workers in factory and office, the fate of the revolution and the fate of the democratic peace is in your hands!

Long live the revolution!

> November 7, 1917
> The All-Russia Congress of Soviets
> Of Workers' and Soldiers' Deputies
> The Delegates from the Peasants' Soviets

EVALUATE THE EVIDENCE

1. How does Lenin's manifesto embody Bolshevik political goals? Why might it appeal to ordinary Russians in the crisis of war and revolution?
2. What historical conditions made it difficult for the Bolsheviks to fulfill the ambitious promises made at the 1917 congress?

Source: Marxists Internet Archive Library, http://www.marxists.org/archive/lenin/works/1917/oct-25-26/25b.htm.

estates of the landlords and the church. Thus when Lenin mandated land reform, he merely approved what peasants were already doing. Similarly, urban workers had established their own local soviets or committees and demanded direct control of individual factories. This, too, Lenin ratified with a decree in November 1917.

The Bolsheviks proclaimed their regime a "provisional workers' and peasants' government," promising that a freely elected Constituent Assembly would draw up a new constitution. But free elections in November produced a stunning setback: the Bolsheviks won only 23 percent of the elected delegates. The Socialist Revolutionary Party—the peasants' party—had a clear plurality with about 40 percent of the vote. After the Constituent Assembly met for one day, however, Bolshevik soldiers acting under Lenin's orders disbanded it. By January 1918 Lenin had moved to establish a one-party state.

Lenin acknowledged that Russia had effectively lost the war with Germany and that the only realistic goal was peace at any price. That price was very high. Germany demanded that the Soviet government give up all its western territories, areas inhabited primarily by Poles, Finns, Lithuanians, and other non-Russians—people who had been conquered by the tsars over three centuries and put into the "prisonhouse of nationalities," as Lenin had earlier called the Russian Empire.

At first, Lenin's fellow Bolsheviks refused to accept such great territorial losses. But when German armies resumed their unopposed march into Russia in February 1918, Lenin had his way in a very close vote. A third of old Russia's population was sliced away by the **Treaty of Brest-Litovsk**, signed with Germany in March 1918. With peace, Lenin escaped the disaster of continued war and could pursue his goal of absolute power for the Bolsheviks—now also called Communists—within Russia.

The peace treaty and the abolition of the Constituent Assembly inspired armed opposition to the Bolshevik regime. People who had supported self-rule in November saw that once again they were getting dictatorship. The officers of the old army organized the so-called White opposition to the Bolsheviks in southern Russia, Ukraine, Siberia, and the area west of Petrograd. The Whites came from many social groups and were united only by their hatred of communism and the Bolsheviks—the Reds.

By the summer of 1918 Russia was in a full-fledged civil war. Eighteen self-proclaimed regional governments—several of which represented minority nationalities—challenged Lenin's government in Moscow. By the end of the year White armies were on the attack. In October 1919 they closed in on central Russia from three sides, and it appeared they might triumph. They did not.

Lenin and the Red Army beat back the counter-revolutionary White armies for several reasons. Most important, the Bolsheviks had quickly developed a better army. Once again, Trotsky's leadership was decisive. At first, the Bolsheviks had preached democracy in the military and had even elected officers in 1917. But beginning in March 1918, Trotsky became war commissar of the newly formed Red Army. He reestablished strict discipline and the draft. Soldiers deserting or disobeying an order were summarily shot. Moreover, Trotsky made effective use of former tsarist army officers, who were actively recruited and given unprecedented powers over their troops. Trotsky's disciplined and effective fighting force repeatedly defeated the Whites in the field.

Ironically, foreign military intervention helped the Bolsheviks. For a variety of reasons, but primarily to stop the spread of communism, the Western Allies (including the United States, Britain, France, and Japan)

sent troops to support the White armies. Yet their efforts were limited and halfhearted. By 1919, with the Great War over, Westerners were sick of war, and few politicians wanted to get involved in a new military crusade. Allied intervention failed to offer effective aid, though it did permit the Bolsheviks to appeal to the patriotic nationalism of ethnic Russians, in particular former tsarist army officers who objected to foreign involvement in Russian affairs.

Other conditions favored a Bolshevik victory as well. Strategically, the Reds controlled central Russia and the crucial cities of Moscow and Petrograd. The Whites attacked from the fringes and lacked coordination. Moreover, the poorly defined political program of the Whites was a mishmash of liberal republicanism and monarchism incapable of uniting the Bolsheviks' enemies. And while the Bolsheviks promised ethnic minorities in Russian-controlled territories substantial autonomy, the nationalist Whites sought to preserve the tsarist empire.

The Bolsheviks mobilized the home front for the war by establishing a system of centralized controls called **War Communism**. The leadership nationalized banks and industries and outlawed private enterprise. Bolshevik commissars introduced rationing, seized grain from peasants to feed the cities, and maintained strict workplace discipline. Although normal economic activity broke down, these measures maintained labor discipline and kept the Red Army supplied with men and material.

Revolutionary terror also contributed to the Communist victory. Lenin and the Bolsheviks set up a fearsome secret police known as the Cheka, dedicated to suppressing counter-revolutionaries. During the civil war, the Cheka imprisoned and executed without trial tens of thousands of supposed "class enemies." Victims included clergymen, aristocrats, the wealthy Russian bourgeoisie, deserters from the Red Army, and political opponents of all kinds. The tsar and his family were callously executed in July 1918. The "Red Terror" of 1918 to 1920 helped establish the secret police as a central tool of the emerging Communist government.

By the spring of 1920 the White armies were almost completely defeated, and the Bolsheviks had retaken much of the territory ceded to Germany under the Treaty of Brest-Litovsk. The Red Army reconquered Belarus and Ukraine, both of which had briefly gained independence. Building on this success, the Bolsheviks

---

■ **Treaty of Brest-Litovsk** Peace treaty signed in March 1918 between the Central Powers and Russia that ended Russian participation in World War I and ceded Russian territories containing a third of the Russian Empire's population to the Central Powers.

■ **War Communism** The application of centralized state control during the Russian civil war, in which the Bolsheviks seized grain from peasants, introduced rationing, nationalized all banks and industry, and required everyone to work.

"The Deceiving Brothers Have Fallen Upon Us!" This pro-Bolshevik propaganda poster from the Russian civil war is loaded with symbolism. It draws on the Greek myth of Hercules battling the Hydra to depict the enemies of the revolution as a many-headed snake. Ugly caricatures of Germany, France, Tsar Nicholas, Britain, and the church bleed from the blows of a powerful Russian worker, who embodies the revolutionary working class. At the bottom of the page, a lengthy poem calls on the Russian people to stand together to defeat the "deceiving brothers," and in the background a booming industrial landscape represents the economic development that will follow Bolshevik victory. (The New York Public Library/Art Resource, NY)

moved westward into Polish territory, but they were halted on the outskirts of Warsaw in August 1920 by troops under the leadership of the Polish field marshal and chief of state Jozef Pilsudski. This defeat halted Bolshevik attempts to spread communism farther into Europe, though in 1921 the Red Army overran the independent national governments of the Caucasus. The Russian civil war was over, and the Bolsheviks had won an impressive victory.

The Peace Settlement

FOCUS QUESTION *In what ways was the Allied peace settlement flawed?*

Even as civil war raged in Russia and chaos engulfed much of central and eastern Europe, the war in the west came to an end in November 1918. Early in 1919 the victorious Western Allies came together in Paris, where they worked out terms for peace with Germany and created the peacekeeping League of Nations. Expectations were high; optimism was almost unlimited. Nevertheless, the peace settlement of 1919 turned out to be a disappointment for peoples and politicians alike. Rather than lasting peace, the immediate postwar years brought economic crisis and violent political conflict.

The End of the War

In early 1918 the German leadership decided that the time was ripe for a last-ditch, all-out attack on France. The defeat of Russia had released men and materials for the western front. The looming arrival of the first U.S. troops and the growth of dissent at home quickened German leaders' resolve. In the great Spring Offensive of 1918, Ludendorff launched an extensive attack on the French lines. German armies came within thirty-five miles of Paris, but Ludendorff's exhausted, overextended forces never broke through. They were stopped in July at the second Battle of the Marne, where 140,000 American soldiers saw action. The late but massive American intervention tipped the scales in favor of Allied victory.

By September British, French, and American armies were advancing steadily on all fronts. Hindenburg and Ludendorff realized that Germany had lost the war. Not wanting to shoulder the blame, they insisted that moderate politicians should take responsibility for the defeat. On October 4 the German emperor formed a new, more liberal civilian government to sue for peace.

As negotiations over an armistice dragged on, frustrated Germans rose up in revolt. On November 3 sailors in Kiel mutinied, and throughout northern Germany soldiers and workers established revolutionary councils modeled on the Russian soviets. The same day, Austria-Hungary surrendered to the Allies and began breaking apart. Revolution erupted in Germany, and masses of workers demonstrated for peace in Berlin. With army discipline collapsing, Wilhelm II abdicated and fled to Holland. Socialist leaders in Berlin proclaimed a German republic on November 9 and agreed to tough Allied terms of surrender. The armistice went into effect on November 11, 1918. The war was over.

Revolution in Austria-Hungary and Germany

Military defeat brought turmoil and revolution to Austria-Hungary and Germany, as it had to Russia. Having started the war to preserve an imperial state, the Austro-Hungarian Empire perished in the attempt. The independent states of Austria, Hungary, and Czechoslovakia, and a larger Romania, Italy, and Poland, were carved out of its territories (Map 25.4). For four months in 1919, until conservative nationalists seized power,

Hungary became a Marxist republic along Bolshevik lines. A greatly expanded Serbian monarchy gained control of the western Balkans and took the name Yugoslavia.

In late 1918 Germany likewise experienced a dramatic revolution that resembled the Russian Revolution of March 1917. In both cases, a genuine popular uprising welled up from below, toppled an authoritarian monarchy, and created a liberal provisional republic. In both countries, liberals and moderate socialist politicians struggled with more radical workers' and soldiers' councils (or soviets) for political dominance. In Germany, however, moderates from the Social Democratic Party and their liberal allies held on to power and established the Weimar Republic — a democratic government that would lead Germany for the next fifteen years. Their success was a deep disappointment for Russia's Bolsheviks, who had hoped that a more radical revolution in Germany would help spread communism across the European continent.

There were several reasons for the German outcome. The great majority of the Marxist politicians in the Social Democratic Party were moderates, not revolutionaries. They wanted political democracy and civil liberties and favored the gradual elimination of capitalism. They were also German nationalists, appalled by the prospect of civil war and revolutionary terror. Of crucial importance was the fact that the moderate Social Democrats quickly came to terms with the army and big business, which helped prevent total national collapse.

Yet the triumph of the Social Democrats brought violent chaos to Germany in 1918 to 1919. The new republic was attacked from both sides of the political spectrum. Radical Communists led by Karl Liebknecht and Rosa Luxemburg tried to seize control of the government in the Spartacist Uprising in Berlin in January 1919. The Social Democrats called in nationalist Free Corps militias, bands of demobilized soldiers who had kept their weapons, to crush the uprising. Liebknecht and Luxemburg were arrested and then brutally murdered by Free Corps soldiers. In Bavaria, a short-lived Bolshevik-style republic was violently overthrown on government orders by the Free Corps. Nationwide strikes by leftist workers and a short-lived, right-wing military takeover — the Kapp Putsch — were repressed by the central government.

By the summer of 1920 the situation in Germany had calmed down, but the new republican government faced deep discontent. Communists and radical socialists blamed the Social Democrats for the murders of Liebknecht and Luxemburg and the repression in Bavaria. Right-wing nationalists, including the new Nazi Party, despised the government from the start. They spread the myth that the German army had never actually lost the war — instead, the nation was "stabbed in the back" by socialists and pacifists at home. In

MAPPING THE PAST

MAP 25.4 Territorial Changes After World War I

World War I brought tremendous changes to eastern Europe. New nations and new boundaries were established, and a dangerous power vacuum was created by the relatively weak states established between Germany and Soviet Russia.

ANALYZING THE MAP What territory did Germany lose, and to whom? Why was Austria referred to as a head without a body in the 1920s? What new independent states were formed from the old Russian Empire?

CONNECTIONS How were the principles of national self-determination applied to the redrawing of Europe after the war, and why didn't this theory work in practice?

Germany, the end of the war brought only a fragile sense of political stability.

The Treaty of Versailles

In January 1919 over seventy delegates from twenty-seven nations met in Paris to hammer out a peace accord. The conference produced several treaties, including the **Treaty of Versailles**, which laid out the terms of the postwar settlement with Germany. The peace negotiations inspired great expectations. A young British diplomat later wrote that the victors "were journeying to Paris . . . to found a new order in Europe. We were preparing not Peace only, but Eternal Peace."[9]

This idealism was greatly strengthened by U.S. president Wilson's January 1918 peace proposal, the **Fourteen Points**. The plan called for open diplomacy, a reduction in armaments, freedom of commerce and trade, and the establishment of a **League of Nations**, an international body designed to provide a place for peaceful resolution of international problems. Perhaps most important, Wilson demanded that peace be based on the principle of **national self-determination**, meaning that peoples should be able to choose their own national governments through democratic majority-rule elections and live free from outside interference in territories with clearly defined, permanent borders. Despite the general optimism inspired by these ideas, the conference and the treaty itself quickly generated disagreement.

The "Big Three"—the United States, Great Britain, and France—controlled the conference. Germany, Austria-Hungary, and Russia were excluded, though their lands were placed on the negotiating table. Italy took part, but its role was quite limited. Representatives from the Middle East, Africa, and East Asia attended as well, but their concerns were largely ignored.

Almost immediately, the Big Three began to quarrel. Wilson, who was wildly cheered by European crowds as the champion of democratic international cooperation, was almost obsessed with creating the League of Nations. He insisted that this question come first, for he passionately believed that only a permanent international organization could avert future wars. Wilson had his way—the delegates agreed to create the League, though the details would be worked out later and the final structure was too weak to achieve its grand purpose. Prime Ministers Lloyd George of Great Britain and Georges Clemenceau of France were unenthusiastic about the League. They were primarily concerned with punishing Germany.

The question of what to do with Germany dominated discussions among the Big Three. Clemenceau wanted Germany to pay for its aggression. The war in the west had been fought largely on French soil, and like most French people, Clemenceau wanted revenge, economic retribution, and lasting security for France. This,

he believed, required the creation of a buffer state between France and Germany, the permanent demilitarization of Germany, and vast reparation payments. Lloyd George supported Clemenceau, but was less harsh. Wilson disagreed. Clemenceau's demands seemed vindictive, and they violated Wilson's sense of Christian morality and the principle of national self-determination. By April the conference was deadlocked, and Wilson packed his bags to go home.

In the end, Clemenceau, fearful of future German aggression, agreed to a compromise. Clemenceau gave up the French demand for a Rhineland buffer state in return for French military occupation of the region for fifteen years and a formal defensive alliance with the United States and Great Britain. Both Wilson and Lloyd George promised that their countries would come to France's aid in the event of a German attack. The Allies moved quickly to finish the settlement, believing that further adjustments would be possible within the dual framework of a strong Western alliance and the League of Nations.

The various agreements signed at Versailles redrew the map of Europe, and the war's losers paid the price. The new independent nations carved out of the Austro-Hungarian and Russian Empires included Poland, Czechoslovakia, Finland, the Baltic States, and Yugoslavia. The Ottoman Empire was also split apart, or "partitioned," its territories placed under the control of the victors.

The Treaty of Versailles, signed by the Allies and Germany, was key to the settlement. Germany's African and Asian colonies were given to France, Britain, and Japan as League of Nations mandates or administered territories, though Germany's losses within Europe were relatively minor, thanks to Wilson. Alsace-Lorraine was returned to France. Ethnic Polish territories seized by Prussia during the eighteenth-century partition of Poland (see Chapter 16) were returned to a new independent Polish state. Predominantly German Danzig was also placed within the Polish border but as a self-governing city under League of Nations protection. Germany had to limit its army to one hundred thousand men, agree to build no military fortifications in the Rhineland, and accept temporary French occupation of that region.

■ **Treaty of Versailles** The 1919 peace settlement that ended war between Germany and the Allied powers.

■ **Fourteen Points** Wilson's 1918 peace proposal calling for open diplomacy, a reduction in armaments, freedom of commerce and trade, the establishment of the League of Nations, and national self-determination.

■ **League of Nations** A permanent international organization, established during the 1919 Paris Peace Conference, designed to protect member states from aggression and avert future wars.

■ **national self-determination** The notion that peoples should be able to choose their own national governments through democratic majority-rule elections and live free from outside interference in nation-states with clearly defined borders.

More harshly, in Article 231, the famous **war guilt clause**, the Allies declared that Germany (with Austria) was entirely responsible for the war and thus had to pay reparations equal to all civilian damages caused by the fighting. This much-criticized clause expressed French and to some extent British demands for revenge. For the Germans, reparations were a crippling financial burden. Moreover, the clause was a cutting insult to German national pride. Many Germans believed wartime propaganda that had repeatedly claimed that Germany was an innocent victim, forced into war by a circle of barbaric enemies. When presented with these terms, the new German government protested vigorously but to no avail. On June 28, 1919, representatives of the German Social Democrats signed the treaty in Louis XIV's Hall of Mirrors at Versailles, where Bismarck's empire had been joyously proclaimed almost fifty years before (see Chapter 23).

The rapidly concluded Versailles treaties were far from perfect, but within the context of war-shattered Europe they were a beginning. Germany had been punished but not dismembered. A new world organization complemented a traditional defensive alliance of satisfied powers: Britain, France, and the United States. The remaining serious problems, the Allies hoped, could be worked out in the future. Allied leaders had seen speed as essential because they feared that the Bolshevik Revolution might spread. The best answer to Lenin's unending calls for worldwide upheaval, they believed, was peace and tranquillity.

Yet the great hopes of early 1919 had turned to ashes by the end of the year. The Western alliance had collapsed, and a grandiose plan for permanent peace had given way to a fragile truce. There were several reasons for this turn of events. First, the U.S. Senate and, to a lesser extent, the American people rejected Wilson's handiwork. Republican senators led by Henry Cabot Lodge believed that the treaty gave away Congress's constitutional right to declare war and demanded changes in the articles. In failing health, the self-righteous Wilson rejected all compromise. In doing so, he ensured that the Senate would never ratify the treaty and that the United States would never join the League of Nations. Moreover, the Senate refused to ratify treaties forming a defensive alliance with France and Great Britain. America in effect had turned its back on Europe. The new American gospel of isolationism represented a tragic renunciation of international responsibility. Using U.S. actions as an excuse, Great Britain too refused to ratify its defensive alliance with France. Bitterly betrayed by its allies, France stood alone.

A second cause for the failure of the peace was that the principle of national self-determination, which had engendered such enthusiasm, was good in theory but flawed in practice. In Europe, the borders of new states such as Poland, Czechoslovakia, and Yugoslavia cut through a jumble of ethnic and religious groups that often despised each other. The new central European nations would prove to be economically weak and politically unstable, the source of conflict in the years to come. In the colonies, desires for self-determination were simply ignored, leading to problems particularly in the Middle East.

The Peace Settlement in the Middle East

Although Allied leaders at Versailles focused mainly on European issues, they also imposed a political settlement on what had been the Ottoman Empire. Their decisions, made in Paris and at other international conferences, brought radical and controversial changes to the region. The Allies dismantled or partitioned the Ottoman Empire, Britain and France expanded their influence in the region, Jewish peoples were promised a "national homeland" in British-controlled Palestine, and Arab nationalists felt cheated and betrayed.

The British government had encouraged the wartime Arab revolt against the Ottoman Turks and had even made vague promises of an independent Arab kingdom, most clearly in the McMahon-Hussein correspondence (see page 839). However, when the fighting stopped, the British and the French chose instead to honor their own secret wartime agreements to divide and rule the Ottoman lands. Most important was the Sykes-Picot Agreement of 1916, named after the British and French diplomats who negotiated the deal.

In the secret accord, Britain and France agreed that former Ottoman territories would be administered by the European powers under what they called the **mandate system**. Under the terms of the mandates, individually granted to European powers by the League of Nations, former Ottoman territories (and former German colonies) would be placed under the "tutelage" of European authorities until they could "stand alone." France would receive a mandate to govern modern-day Lebanon and Syria and much of southern Turkey, and Britain would control Palestine, Transjordan, and Iraq. Though the official goal of the mandate system was to eventually grant these regions national independence, it quickly became clear that the Allies hardly intended to do so. Critics labeled the system colonialism under another name, and when Britain and France set about implementing their agreements

■ **war guilt clause** An article in the Treaty of Versailles that declared that Germany (with Austria) was solely responsible for the war and had to pay reparations equal to all civilian damages caused by the fighting.

■ **mandate system** The plan to allow Britain and France to administer former Ottoman territories, put into place after the end of the First World War.

■ **Balfour Declaration** A 1917 British statement that declared British support of a National Home for the Jewish People in Palestine.

The War in the Middle East   An Ottoman camel corps prepares for action in the Sinai Peninsula in 1915. The defeat of the Ottoman Empire in the First World War helped shape the modern Middle East as we know it today. (Library of Congress Prints and Photographs Division, Washington, D.C./LC-DIG-ppmsca-13709-00037)

after the armistice, Arab nationalists reacted with understandable surprise and resentment.

British plans for the former Ottoman lands that would become Palestine further angered Arab nationalists. The **Balfour Declaration** of November 1917, written by British foreign secretary Arthur Balfour, had announced that Britain favored a "National Home for the Jewish People" in Palestine, but without discriminating against the civil and religious rights of the non-Jewish communities already living in the region. Some members of the British cabinet believed the declaration would appeal to German, Austrian, and American Jews and thus help the British war effort. Others sincerely supported the Zionist vision of a Jewish homeland (see Chapter 23), which they hoped would also help Britain maintain control of the Suez Canal. Whatever the motives, the declaration enraged Arabs.

In 1914 Jews accounted for about 11 percent of the population in the three Ottoman districts that the British would lump together to form Palestine; the rest of the population was predominantly Arab. Both groups understood that Balfour's "National Home" implied the establishment of some kind of Jewish state that would violate majority rule. Moreover, a state founded on religious and ethnic exclusivity was out of keeping with Islamic and Ottoman tradition, which had historically been more tolerant of religious diversity and minorities than Christian Europe had been.

Though Arab leaders attended the Versailles Peace Conference, their efforts to secure autonomy in the Middle East came to nothing. Only the kingdom of Hejaz—today part of Saudi Arabia—was granted independence. In response, Arab nationalists came together in Damascus as the General Syrian Congress in 1919 and unsuccessfully called again for political independence. The congress proclaimed Syria an independent kingdom; a similar congress declared Iraqi independence.

The Western reaction was swift and decisive. A French army stationed in Lebanon attacked Syria, taking Damascus in July 1920. The Arab government fled, and the French took over. Meanwhile, the British bloodily put down an uprising in Iraq and established control there. Brushing aside Arab opposition, the British mandate in Palestine formally incorporated the Balfour Declaration and its commitment to a Jewish national home. Western imperialism, in the form of the mandate system authorized by the League of Nations, appeared to have replaced Ottoman rule in the Middle East. In the following decades, deadly anti-imperial riots and violent conflicts between Arabs and Jews would repeatedly undermine the region's stability. (See "Thinking Like a Historian: The Partition of the Ottoman Empire and the Mandate System," page 858.)

The Partition of the Ottoman Empire and the Mandate System

During and after the First World War, representatives of the Entente governments made various agreements to carve up Ottoman territories into spheres of interest and "mandates," managed much like colonies by the European powers. Such agreements were subject to competing claims and criticism, including wartime strategic needs, Zionist desires for an independent state in Palestine, and Arab aspirations for national independence. The outcome satisfied no one. What were the mandate system's strengths and weaknesses?

1 **Resolution of the General Syrian Congress at Damascus, July 2, 1919.** President Woodrow Wilson insisted at Versailles that the right of self-determination should be applied to the conquered Ottoman territories. In the selection below, a group of Arab nationalists from Syria offer their response to the King-Crane Commission, a group of Americans on a fact-finding mission to investigate the partition of the Ottoman Arab territories. The Arabs demand national independence and critique the League of Nations mandate system and the Balfour Declaration.

We the undersigned members of the General Syrian Congress . . . provided with credentials and authorizations by the inhabitants of our various districts, Moslems, Christians, and Jews, have agreed upon the following statement of the desires of the people of the country who have elected us to present them to the American Section of the International Commission. . . .

1. We ask absolutely complete political independence for Syria within these boundaries. [Request includes the present-day states of Syria, Lebanon, Israel, and Jordan; the congress rejected any French rule or interference in the area and requested "complete independence" for present-day Iraq.]

2. We ask that the Government of this Syrian country should be a democratic civil constitutional Monarchy on broad decentralization principles, safeguarding the rights of minorities, and that the King be the Emir Faisal, who carried on a glorious struggle in the cause of our liberation and merited our full confidence and entire reliance.

3. Considering the fact that the Arabs inhabiting the Syrian area are not naturally less gifted than other more advanced races and that they are by no means less developed than the Bulgarians, Serbians, Greeks, and Romanians at the beginning of their independence, we protest against Article 22 of the Covenant of the League of Nations, placing

us among the nations in their middle stage of development which stand in need of a mandatory power. . . .

7. We oppose the pretensions of the Zionists to create a Jewish commonwealth in the southern part of Syria, known as Palestine, and oppose Zionist migration to any part of our country; for we do not acknowledge their title but consider them a grave peril to our people from the national, economical, and political points of view. Our Jewish compatriots shall enjoy our common rights and assume the common responsibilities. . . .

The noble principles enunciated by President Wilson strengthen our confidence that our desires emanating from the depths of our hearts, shall be the decisive factor in determining our future; and that President Wilson and the free American people will be our supporters for the realization of our hopes, thereby proving their sincerity and noble sympathy with the aspiration of the weaker nations in general and our Arab people in particular.

2 **Article 22 of the Covenant of the League of Nations, ratified January 1920.** In one of its first acts, the League of Nations defined the terms of the mandate system, under which the victors in the First World War would govern territories disrupted by the war, primarily former lands of the Ottoman and German Empires.

To those colonies and territories which as a consequence of the late war have ceased to be under the sovereignty of the States which formerly governed them and which are inhabited by peoples not yet able to stand by themselves under the strenuous conditions of the modern world, there should be applied the principle that the well-being and development of such peoples form a sacred trust of civilisation and that securities for the performance of this trust should be embodied in this Covenant. . . . [T]he tutelage of such peoples

ANALYZING THE EVIDENCE

1. Compare and contrast the maps in Sources 3 and 4. What are the key differences? What historical events account for these differences?
2. In Source 1, why do the representatives at the Syrian Congress appeal to the "noble principles" associated with U.S. president Wilson? How did the mandate system deal with demands for national self-determination?
3. The sources above present contradictions that proved difficult if not impossible for contemporary negotiators to resolve. What were the sticking points? In what ways did the partition of the Ottoman Empire leave unresolved problems for future generations?

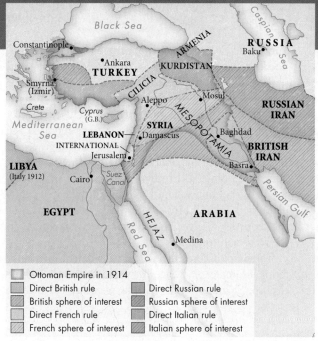

3 **Entente proposals for the partition of the Ottoman Empire, 1915–1917.** In secret treaties and agreements negotiated during the war, Britain, France, Russia, and Italy planned to divide up the territories of the Ottoman Empire.

4 **The partition of the Ottoman Empire, 1914–1923.** The division of the Ottoman Arab states between Britain and France and the creation of a separate Palestinian state under British mandate would set the stage for decades of conflict.

should be entrusted to advanced nations who by reason of their resources, their experience or their geographical position can best undertake this responsibility, and who are willing to accept it, and that this tutelage should be exercised by them as Mandatories on behalf of the League.

The character of the mandate must differ according to the stage of the development of the people, the geographical situation of the territory, its economic conditions and other similar circumstances. Certain communities formerly belonging to the Turkish Empire have reached a stage of development where their existence as independent nations can be provisionally recognized subject to the rendering of administrative advice and assistance by a Mandatory until such time as they are able to stand alone. The wishes of these communities must be a principal consideration in the selection of the Mandatory.

5 **The British mandate for Palestine, July 24, 1922.** The League of Nations granted Britain the mandate for Palestine, a disputed territory that included significant Christian, Jewish, and Islamic holy territories and sites.

Whereas His Britannic Majesty has accepted the Mandate in respect of Palestine and undertaken to exercise it on behalf of the League of Nations in conformity with the following provisions. . . .

Article 1. The Mandatory shall have full powers of legislation and of administration [in Palestine].

Article 2. The Mandatory shall be responsible for placing the country under such political, administrative, and economic conditions as will secure the establishment of the Jewish National Home . . . and the development of self-governing institutions, and also for safeguarding the civil and religious rights of all the inhabitants of Palestine, irrespective of race and religion. . . .

Article 4. An appropriate Jewish Agency shall be recognized as a public body for the purpose of advising and co-operating with the Administration of Palestine in such economic, social and other matters as may affect the establishment of the Jewish National Home and the interests of the Jewish population in Palestine. . . . The Zionist organization . . . shall be recognized as such agency. . . .

Article 6. The Administration of Palestine, while ensuring that the rights and position of other sections of the population are not prejudiced, shall facilitate Jewish immigration under suitable conditions and shall encourage, in co-operation with the Jewish Agency . . . close settlement by Jews on the land.

PUTTING IT ALL TOGETHER

Notions of national self-determination, Western superiority, and strategic diplomacy inspired the European powers who dissolved the Ottoman Empire. Few could predict the intractable conflicts that followed. Using the sources above, along with what you have learned in class and in Chapters 24 and 25, write a short essay that evaluates the motivations of these actors. Was the mandate system a fair way to resolve their conflicting needs and interests?

Sources: (1) "Resolution of the General Syrian Congress at Damascus, 2 July 1919," from the King-Crane Commission Report, in *Foreign Relations of the United States: Paris Peace Conference, 1919*, 12:780–781; (2) The Covenant of the League of Nations, Yale Law School, The Avalon Project: Documents in Law, History and Diplomacy, http://avalon.law.yale.edu/20th_century/leagcov.asp; (5) Charles D. Smith, *Palestine and the Arab-Israeli Conflict: A History with Documents*, 8th ed. (Boston: Bedford/St. Martin's, 2013), pp. 100–102.

The Allies sought to impose even harsher terms on the defeated Turks than on the "liberated" Arabs. A treaty forced on the Ottoman sultan dismembered the Turkish heartland. Great Britain and France occupied parts of modern-day Turkey, and Italy and Greece claimed shares. There was a sizable Greek minority in western Turkey, and Greek nationalists wanted to build a modern Greek empire modeled on long-dead Byzantium. In 1919 Greek armies carried by British ships landed on the Turkish coast at Smyrna (SMUHR-nuh; today's Izmir) and advanced unopposed into the interior, while French troops moved in from the south. Turkey seemed finished.

Turkey survived the postwar invasions. A Turkish National Movement emerged, led by Mustafa Kemal (1881–1938), a prominent general in the successful Turkish defeat of the British at the Battle of Gallipoli. The leaders of the movement overthrew the sultan and refused to acknowledge the Allied dismemberment of their country. Under Kemal's direction, a revived Turkish army gradually mounted a forceful resistance, and despite staggering losses, his troops repulsed the invaders. The Greeks and British sued for peace. In 1923, after long negotiations, the resulting Treaty of Lausanne (loh-ZAN) recognized the territorial integrity of Turkey and solemnly abolished the hated capitulations that the European powers had imposed over the centuries to give their citizens special privileges in the Ottoman Empire.

The peace accords included an agreement for a shattering example of what we would now call "ethnic cleansing," under which Greeks were forced to leave

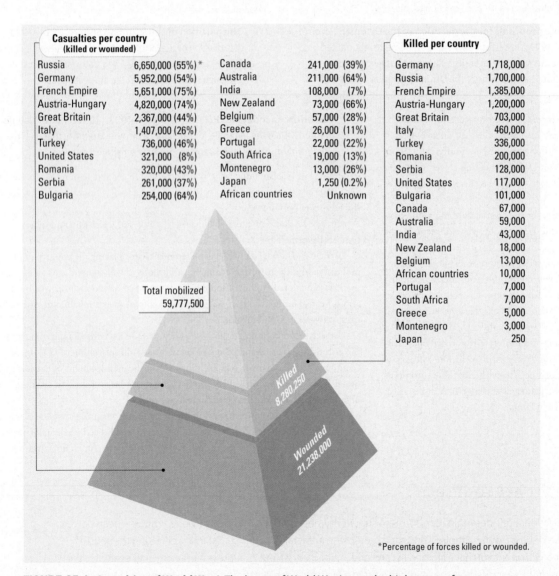

FIGURE 25.1 Casualties of World War I The losses of World War I were the highest ever for a war in Europe. These numbers are approximate because of problems with record keeping caused by the destructive nature of total war.

Turkish-majority lands for Greece, while Turks moved from Greece and former Balkan territories to the Turkish mainland. The result, driven by ideals of national self-determination and racial purity, was a humanitarian disaster. Ethnic Greeks constituted about 16 percent of the Turkish population, and now between 1.5 and 2 million people had to pick up and move west. At the same time, 500,000 to 600,000 ethnic Turks moved out of Greece and Bulgaria to the Anatolian peninsula (modern-day Turkey). Very few wanted to leave their homes, and though the authorities set up refugee camps, refugees faced harsh conditions, rampant looting, and physical abuse. In this case, race trumped religion: Muslim Greeks were forced west, and Christian Turks forced east, and the population exchange destroyed a vital, multicultural ethnic patchwork. The agreements at Lausanne became a model for future examples of ethnic cleansing, most notably the exchange of Germans and Slavs in central Europe after the Second World War, and the exchange of Hindus and Muslims that followed Indian independence in 1947.

Kemal, a nationalist without religious faith, believed that Turkey should modernize and secularize along Western lines. He established a republic, was elected president, and created a one-party system—partly inspired by the Bolshevik example—to transform his country. The most radical reforms pertained to religion and culture. For centuries, Islamic religious authorities had regulated most of the intellectual, political, and social activities of Ottoman citizens. Profoundly influenced by the example of western Europe, Kemal set out to limit the place of religion and religious leaders in daily affairs. He decreed a controversial separation of church and state, promulgated law codes inspired by European models, and established a secular public school system. Women received rights that they never had before. By the time of his death in 1938, Kemal had implemented much of his revolutionary program and had moved Turkey much closer to Europe, foretelling current efforts by Turkey to join the European Union as a full-fledged member.

The Human Costs of the War

World War I broke empires, inspired revolutions, and changed national borders on a world scale. It also had immense human costs, and ordinary people in the combatant nations struggled to deal with its legacy in

The Human Costs of War   A disabled German veteran works as a carpenter around 1919. The war killed millions of soldiers and left many more permanently disabled, making the sight of men missing limbs or disfigured in other ways a common one in the 1920s. (FPG/Hulton Archive/Getty Images)

the years that followed. The raw numbers are astonishing: estimates vary, but total deaths on the battlefield numbered about 8 million soldiers. Russia had the highest number of military casualties, followed by Germany. France had the highest proportionate number of losses; about one out of every ten adult males died in the war. The other belligerents paid a high price as well (Figure 25.1). Between 7 and 10 million civilians died because of the war and war-related hardships, and another 20 million people died in the worldwide influenza epidemic that followed the war in 1918.

The number of dead, the violence of their deaths, and the nature of trench warfare made proper burials difficult, if not impossible. Soldiers were typically interred where they fell, and by 1918 thousands of ad hoc military cemeteries were scattered across northern France and Flanders. When remains were gathered, the chaos and danger of the battlefield limited accurate identification. After the war, the bodies were moved to more formal cemeteries, but hundreds of thousands remained unidentified. British and German soldiers ultimately remained in foreign soil, in graveyards managed by national commissions. After some delay, the bodies of most of the French combatants were brought home to local cemeteries.

Millions of ordinary people grieved, turning to family, friends, neighbors, and the church for comfort. Towns and villages across Europe raised public memorials to honor the dead and held ceremonies on important anniversaries: on November 11, the day the war ended, and in Britain on July 1, to commemorate the Battle of the Somme. These were poignant and often tearful moments for participants. For the first time, many nations built a Tomb of the Unknown Soldier as a site for national mourning. Memorials were also built on the main battlefields of the war. All expressed the general need to recognize the great sorrow and suffering caused by so much death.

The victims of the First World War included millions of widows and orphans and huge numbers of emotionally scarred and disabled veterans. Countless soldiers suffered from what the British called "shell shock" — now termed post-traumatic stress disorder (PTSD). Contemporary physicians and policymakers poorly understood this complex mental health issue, and though some soldiers suffering from PTSD received medical treatment, others were accused of cowardice and shirking, and were denied veterans' benefits after the war. In addition, some 10 million soldiers came home physically disfigured or mutilated. Governments tried to take care of the disabled and the survivor families, but there was rarely enough money to adequately fund pensions and job-training programs. Artificial limbs were expensive, uncomfortable, and awkward, and some employers refused to hire disabled workers. Crippled veterans were often forced to beg on the streets, a common sight for the next decade.

The German case is illustrative. Nearly 10 percent of German civilians were direct victims of the war in one way or another, and the new German government struggled to take care of them. Veterans' groups organized to lobby for state support, and fully one-third of the federal budget of the Weimar Republic was tied up in war-related pensions and benefits. With the onset of the Great Depression in 1929, benefits were cut, leaving bitter veterans vulnerable to Nazi propagandists who paid homage to the sacrifices of the war while calling for the overthrow of the republican government. The human cost of the war thus had another steep price. Across Europe, newly formed radical right-wing parties, including the German Nazis and the Italian Fascists, successfully manipulated popular feelings of loss and resentment to undermine fragile parliamentary governments.

NOTES

1. Quoted in J. Remak, *The Origins of World War I* (New York: Holt, Rinehart & Winston, 1967), p. 84.
2. On the mood of 1914, see J. Joll, *The Origins of the First World War* (New York: Longman, 1992), pp. 199–233.
3. Quoted in G. L. Mosse, *Fallen Soldiers: Reshaping the Memory of the World Wars* (New York: Oxford University Press, 1990), p. 64.
4. Quoted in N. Malcolm, *Bosnia: A Short History* (New York: New York University Press, 1996), p. 153.
5. Quoted in S. Audoin-Rouzeau, *Men at War, 1914–1918: National Sentiment and Trench Journalism in France During the First World War* (Oxford Berg, 1992), p. 69.
6. V. G. Liulevicius, *War Land on the Eastern Front: Culture, National Identity, and German Occupation in World War I* (New York: Cambridge University Press, 2000), pp. 54–89; quotation on p. 71.
7. Quoted in F. P. Chambers, *The War Behind the War, 1914–1918* (London: Faber & Faber, 1939), p. 168.
8. J. Reed, *Ten Days That Shook the World* (New York: International Publishers, 1967), p. 126.
9. Quoted in H. Nicolson, *Peacemaking 1919* (New York: Grosset & Dunlap Universal Library, 1965), pp. 8, 31–32.
10. Quoted in C. Barnett, *The Swordbearers: Supreme Command in the First World War* (New York: Morrow, 1964), p. 40.

LOOKING BACK LOOKING AHEAD

When chief of the German general staff Count Helmuth von Moltke imagined the war of the future in a letter to his wife in 1905, his comments were surprisingly accurate. "It will become a war between peoples which will not be concluded with a single battle," the general wrote, "but which will be a long, weary struggle with a country that will not acknowledge defeat until the whole strength of its people is broken."[10] As von Moltke predicted, World War I broke peoples and nations. The trials of total war increased the power of the centralized state and brought down the Austro-Hungarian, Ottoman, and Russian Empires. The brutal violence shocked and horrified observers across the world; ordinary citizens were left to mourn their losses.

Despite high hopes for Wilson's Fourteen Points, the Treaty of Versailles hardly brought lasting peace. The war's disruptions encouraged radical political conflict in the 1920s and 1930s and the rise of totalitarian regimes across Europe, which led to the even more extreme violence of the Second World War. Indeed, some historians believe that the years from 1914 to 1945 might most accurately be labeled a modern Thirty Years' War, since the problems unleashed in August 1914 were only really resolved in the 1950s. This strong assertion contains a great deal of truth. For all of Europe, World War I was a revolutionary conflict of gigantic proportions with lasting traumatic effects.

Make Connections

Think about the larger developments and continuities within and across chapters.

1. While the war was being fought, peoples on all sides of the fighting often referred to the First World War as "the Great War." Why would they find this label appropriate?

2. How did the First World War draw on long-standing political rivalries and tensions among the European powers (Chapters 19, 23, and 24)?

3. To what extent was the First World War actually a "world" war?

25 REVIEW & EXPLORE

Identify Key Terms

Identify and explain the significance of each item below.

Triple Alliance (p. 829)

Triple Entente (p. 830)

Schlieffen Plan (p. 833)

total war (p. 833)

trench warfare (p. 835)

February Revolution (p. 846)

Petrograd Soviet (p. 847)

Bolsheviks (p. 848)

Treaty of Brest-Litovsk (p. 851)

War Communism (p. 851)

Treaty of Versailles (p. 855)

Fourteen Points (p. 855)

League of Nations (p. 855)

national self-determination (p. 855)

war guilt clause (p. 856)

mandate system (p. 856)

Balfour Declaration (p. 857)

Review the Main Ideas

Answer the focus questions from each section of the chapter.

◆ What caused the outbreak of the First World War? (p. 828)

◆ How did the First World War differ from previous wars? (p. 833)

◆ In what ways did the war transform life on the home front? (p. 841)

◆ Why did world war lead to revolution in Russia, and what was its outcome? (p. 846)

◆ In what ways was the Allied peace settlement flawed? (p. 852)

Suggested Reading and Media Resources

BOOKS

◆ Barthas, Louis. *Poilu: The World War I Notebooks of Corporal Louis Barthas, Barrelmaker, 1914–1918*. Trans. Edward M. Strauss. 2014. This French corporal's wartime diary offers a gritty yet humane description of daily life in the trenches.

◆ Clark, Christopher. *The Sleepwalkers: How Europe Went to War in 1914*. 2013. This narrative-driven, comprehensive view of the political-diplomatic crises that led to the First World War suggests that all Europe's Great Powers—not just Germany and Austria-Hungary—share responsibility for the war's outbreak.

◆ Davis, Belinda J. *Home Fires Burning: Food, Politics, and Everyday Life in Berlin in World War I*. 2000. A moving account of women struggling to feed their families on the home front and their protests against the imperial German state.

◆ Englund, Peter. *The Beauty and the Sorrow: An Intimate History of the First World War*. 2011. An everyday-life history of the war told through the

personal stories of twenty men and women, from more than a dozen different nations and from all walks of life.

◆ Fitzpatrick, Sheila. *The Russian Revolution, 1917–1932*. 1982. An important interpretation that considers the long-term effects of the revolution.

◆ Fromkin, David. *A Peace to End All Peace*. 2001. A brilliant reconsideration of the collapse of the Ottoman Empire and its division by the Allies.

◆ Grayzel, Susan R. *Women and the First World War*. 2002. A thorough overview of women's experience of war across Europe.

◆ Joll, James. *The Origins of the First World War*. 1992. A thorough review of the causes of the war that brings together military, diplomatic, economic, political, and cultural history.

◆ Larson, Erik. *Dead Wake: The Last Crossing of the Lusitania*. 2015. An accessible and detailed history of the doomed ocean liner, focusing on the people involved in the tragedy.

- Liulevicius, Vejas Gabriel. *War Land on the Eastern Front: Culture, National Identity, and German Occupation in World War I.* 2000. An important and pathbreaking work on the eastern front.

- Macmillan, Margaret. *Paris, 1919: Six Months That Changed the World.* 2001. A comprehensive, exciting account of all aspects of the peace conference.

- Mosse, George L. *Fallen Soldiers: Reshaping the Memory of the World Wars.* 1990. An innovative yet accessible account of how Europeans remembered the world wars.

- Neiberg, Michael S. *Fighting the Great War: A Global History.* 2006. A lively and up-to-date account.

- Rogan, Eugene. *The Fall of the Ottomans: The Great War in the Middle East.* 2015. A readable narrative on the key role played by the Ottoman Middle East in the conflict.

- Whalen, Robert Weldon. *Bitter Wounds: German Victims of the Great War.* 1984. An excellent treatment of the human costs of the war in Germany.

DOCUMENTARIES

- *The Battle of the Somme* (Geoffrey Malins, 1916). One of the very first wartime propaganda films, this famous documentary was originally released in August 1916. Though several scenes are clearly staged, the realistic battle sequences shocked contemporary audiences.

- *Paris 1919: Inside the Peace Talks That Changed the World* (BFS Entertainment and Multimedia, 2009). Through historical re-enactments, archival footage, and contemporary photos, this documentary takes viewers "behind the scenes" at the Versailles Conference to explore the controversial decisions made in Paris in 1919.

- *Russian Revolution in Color* (Shanachie Studio, 2005). Covers the Russian Revolution and civil war using colorized archival footage, historical re-enactments, and expert testimonies.

FEATURE FILMS

- *All Quiet on the Western Front* (Lewis Milestone, 1930). This graphic antiwar film about the frontline experiences and growing disillusionment of a young German volunteer is based on the famous novel of the same name by Erich Maria Remarque, first published in 1928.

- *A Farewell to Arms* (Frank Borzage, 1932). The tragic story of a romance between an American ambulance driver and a Red Cross nurse, set on the Italian front. Based on a novel by Ernest Hemingway.

- *J'Accuse* (Abel Gance, 1938). This French remake, based on a film first produced in 1919, tells the story of an angry veteran who travels to the former frontlines and calls forth the ghosts of the war dead to help him prevent a second world war.

- *Testament of Youth* (James Kent, 2014). A moving feature film based on the autobiography of Vera Brittain, the renowned British nurse and pacifist.

WEB SITES

- *The Great War and the Shaping of the 20th Century.* The companion to a PBS documentary, this site offers an array of material on various aspects of the First World War. **www.pbs.org/greatwar**

- *Imperial War Museums.* These famous museums and research center were founded in 1917 to preserve artifacts and record events from the then ongoing world war. Its world-class collections include materials from all conflicts involving Great Britain, the British Commonwealth, and former colonies, from the First World War to the present day. **www.iwm.org.uk**

- *1914–1918-Online: International Encyclopedia of the First World War.* This open access encyclopedia, with authors from over fifty countries, is an impressive and comprehensive collection of recent scholarly articles on all aspects of the war. **http://www.1914-1918-online.net/**

26

The Age of Anxiety

1880–1940

When Allied diplomats met in Paris in early 1919 with their optimistic plans for building a lasting peace, many people looked forward to happier times. After the terrible trauma of total war, they hoped that life would return to normal and would make sense in the familiar prewar terms of peace, progress, and prosperity. Their hopes were in vain. World War I and the Russian Revolution had mangled too many things beyond repair. Great numbers of people felt themselves increasingly adrift in an age of anxiety and continual change.

Late-nineteenth-century thinkers had already called attention to the pessimism, uncertainty, and irrationalism that seemed to accompany modern life. By 1900 radical developments in philosophy and the sciences had substantiated and popularized such ideas. The modernist movement had begun its sweep through literature, music, and the arts, as avant-garde innovators rejected old cultural forms and began to experiment with new ones. Radical innovations in the arts and sciences dominated Western culture in the 1920s and 1930s and remained influential after World War II. A growing consumer society, and the new media of radio and film, transformed the habits of everyday life and leisure.

Even as modern science, art, and culture challenged received wisdom of all kinds, international relations spiraled into crisis. Despite some progress in the mid-1920s, political stability remained short-lived, and the Great Depression that began in 1929 cast millions into poverty and shocked the status quo. Democratic liberalism was besieged by the rise of authoritarian and Fascist governments, and another world conflict seemed imminent. In the early 1920s the French poet and critic Paul Valéry described his widespread "impression of darkness," where "almost all the affairs of men remain in a terrible uncertainty. We think of what has disappeared, and we are almost destroyed by what has been destroyed; we do not know what will be born, and we fear the future, not without reason."[1] Valéry's words captured the gloom and foreboding that dominated the decades between the wars. ■

CHAPTER PREVIEW

Life in the Age of Anxiety
Dadaist George Grosz's disturbing *Inside and Outside* portrays the rampant inequality wrought by the economic crises of the 1920s. Wealthy and bestial elites celebrate a luxurious New Year's Eve "inside," while "outside" a veteran with disabilities begs in vain from uncaring passersby. (Art © Estate of George Grosz/Licensed by VAGA, New York, NY/ photo: akg-images)

Uncertainty in Modern Thought

FOCUS QUESTION *How did intellectual developments reflect the general crisis in Western thought?*

The decades surrounding the First World War—from the 1880s to the 1930s—brought intense cultural and intellectual experimentation. As people grappled with the costs of the war and the challenges of postwar recovery, philosophers and scientists questioned and even abandoned many of the cherished values and beliefs that had guided Western society since the eighteenth-century Enlightenment and the nineteenth-century triumph of industry and science. Radical intellectuals dismissed the possibility that rational thought could lead to greater human understanding or social progress. Though some thinkers embraced Christianity, others rejected Christian teachings. Modern thought thus dovetailed with the ongoing political and social crises of the 1920s and 1930s.

Historians find it relatively easy to set precise dates for political events, such as the outbreak of wars or the outcome of national elections. Exact dates for the rise and fall of intellectual and cultural developments are more difficult to define. The emergence of modern philosophy, for example, did not follow the clear-cut timelines of political history. Thus to understand the history of modern thought, we must investigate trends dating back to the last decades of the nineteenth century and follow them into the 1950s.

Modern Philosophy

Before 1914 most people still believed in Enlightenment ideals of progress, reason, and individual rights. At the turn of the century supporters of these philosophies had some cause for optimism. Women and workers were gradually gaining support in their struggles for political and social recognition, and the rising standard of living, the taming of the city, and the growth of state-supported social programs suggested that life was indeed improving. Such developments encouraged faith in the ability of a rational human mind to discover the laws of society and then wisely act on them.

Nevertheless, in the late nineteenth century a small group of serious thinkers mounted a determined attack on these optimistic beliefs. These critics rejected the general faith in progress and the rational human mind. The German philosopher Friedrich Nietzsche (NEE-chuh) (1844–1900) was particularly influential, though not until after his death. Never a systematic philosopher, he wrote more as a prophet in a provocative and poetic style. In the first of his *Untimely Meditations* (1873), he argued that ever since classical Athens, the West had overemphasized rationality and stifled the authentic passions and animal instincts that drive human activity and true creativity.

Nietzsche questioned the conventional values of Western society. He believed that reason, progress, and respectability were outworn social and psychological constructs that suffocated self-realization and excellence. Though he was the son of a Lutheran minister, Nietzsche famously rejected religion. In his 1887 book, *On the Genealogy of Morals*, he claimed that Christianity embodied a "slave morality" that glorified weakness, envy, and mediocrity. In one of his most famous lines, an apparent madman proclaims that "God is dead," metaphorically murdered by lackadaisical modern Christians who no longer really believed in him. (See "Evaluating the Evidence 26.1: Friedrich Nietzsche Pronounces the Death of God," page 870.)

Nietzsche painted a dark world, perhaps foreshadowing his own loss of sanity in 1889. He warned that Western society was entering a period of nihilism—the philosophical idea that human life is entirely without meaning, truth, or purpose. Nietzsche asserted that all moral systems were invented lies and that liberalism, democracy, and socialism were corrupt systems designed

Philosophy with a Hammer German philosopher Friedrich Nietzsche claimed that his "revaluation of all values" was like writing "philosophy with a hammer." His ideas posed a radical challenge to conventional Western thought and had enormous influence on later thinkers. (akg-images)

to promote the weak at the expense of the strong. The West was in decline; false values had triumphed; the death of God left people disoriented and depressed. According to Nietzsche, the only hope for the individual was to accept the meaninglessness of human existence and then make that very meaninglessness a source of self-defined personal integrity and hence liberation. In this way, at least a few superior individuals could free themselves from the humdrum thinking of the masses and become true heroes.

Little read during his active years, Nietzsche's works attracted growing attention in the early twentieth century. Artists and writers experimented with his ideas, which were fundamental to the rise of the philosophy of existentialism in the 1920s. Subsequent generations remade Nietzsche to suit their own needs, and his influence remains enormous to this day.

The growing dissatisfaction with established ideas before 1914 was apparent in other important thinkers as well. In the 1890s French philosophy professor Henri Bergson (1859–1941), for one, argued that immediate experience and intuition were as important as rational and scientific thinking for understanding reality. According to Bergson, a religious experience or mystical poem was often more accessible to human comprehension than a scientific law or a mathematical equation.

The First World War accelerated the revolt against established certainties in philosophy, but that revolt went in two very different directions. In English-speaking countries, the main development was the acceptance of logical positivism in university circles. In the continental countries, the primary development in philosophy was existentialism.

Logical positivism was truly revolutionary. Adherents of this worldview argued that what we know about human life must be based on rational facts and direct observation. They concluded that theology and most traditional philosophy were meaningless because even the most cherished ideas about God, eternal truth, and ethics were impossible to prove using logic. This outlook is often associated with the Austrian philosopher Ludwig Wittgenstein (VIHT-guhn-shtine) (1889–1951), who later immigrated to England, where he trained numerous disciples.

Chronology

1887	Nietzsche publishes *On the Genealogy of Morals*
1900	Freud publishes *The Interpretation of Dreams*
1913	Stravinsky's *The Rite of Spring* premieres in Paris
1919	Treaty of Versailles; Freudian psychology gains popularity; Keynes publishes *The Economic Consequences of the Peace*; Rutherford splits the atom; Bauhaus school founded
1920s	Existentialism, Dadaism, and Surrealism gain prominence
1922	Eliot publishes *The Waste Land*; Joyce publishes *Ulysses*; Woolf publishes *Jacob's Room*; Wittgenstein writes on logical positivism
1922	First radio broadcast by British Broadcasting Company (BBC)
1923	French and Belgian armies occupy the Ruhr; Corbusier publishes *Towards a New Architecture*
1924	Dawes Plan
1925	Berg's opera *Wozzeck* first performed; Kafka publishes *The Trial*
1926	Germany joins the League of Nations
1927	Heisenberg formulates the "uncertainty principle"
1928	Kellogg-Briand Pact
1929	Faulkner publishes *The Sound and the Fury*
1929–1939	Great Depression
1932	Franklin Roosevelt announces "New Deal for the forgotten man"
1933	The National Socialist Party takes power in Germany
1935	Release of Riefenstahl's documentary film *Triumph of the Will*
1936	Formation of Popular Front in France

In his pugnacious *Tractatus Logico-Philosophicus* (Essay on Logical Philosophy), published in 1922, Wittgenstein argued that philosophy is only the logical clarification of thoughts and that therefore it should concentrate on the study of language, which expresses thoughts. In his view, the great philosophical issues of the ages—God, freedom, morality, and so on—were quite literally senseless, a great waste of time, for neither scientific experiments nor mathematical logic could demonstrate their validity. Statements about

■ **logical positivism** A philosophy that sees meaning in only those beliefs that can be empirically proven, and that therefore rejects most of the concerns of traditional philosophy, from the existence of God to the meaning of happiness, as nonsense.

Friedrich Nietzsche Pronounces the Death of God

In this selection from philosopher Friedrich Nietzsche's The Gay Science *(1882), one of the best-known passages in his entire body of work, a "madman" pronounces the death of God and describes the anxiety and despair — and the opportunities — faced by people in a world without faith.*

The Madman. Haven't you heard of that madman, who on a bright morning day lit a lantern, ran into the market-place, and screamed incessantly: "I am looking for God! I am looking for God!" Since there were a lot of people standing around who did not believe in God, he only aroused great laughter. Is he lost? asked one person. Did he lose his way like a child? asked another. Or is he in hiding? Is he frightened of us? Has he gone on a journey? Or emigrated? And so they screamed and laughed. The madman leaped into the crowd and stared straight at them. "Where has God gone?" he cried. "I will tell you! *We have killed him.* You and I! All of us are his murderers! But how did we do this? How did we manage to drink up the sea? Who gave us the sponge to wipe away the entire horizon? What were we doing when we unchained this earth from its sun? Where is it going now? Where are we going? Away from all the suns? Aren't we ceaselessly falling? Backward, sideways, forward, in all directions? Is there an up or a down at all? Aren't we just roaming through an infinite nothing? Don't you feel the breath of this empty space? Hasn't it gotten colder? Isn't night and ever more night falling? Don't we have to light our lanterns in the morning? Do we hear anything yet of the noise of the gravediggers who are burying God? Do we smell anything yet of the rot of God's decomposition? Gods decompose too! God is dead! God will stay dead! And we have killed him! How do we console ourselves, the murderers of all murderers? The holiest and mightiest the world has ever known has bled to death against our knives — who will wipe the blood off? Where is the water to cleanse ourselves? What sort of rituals of atonement, what sort of sacred games, will we have to come up with now? Isn't the greatness of this deed too great for us? Don't we have to become gods ourselves simply to appear worthy of it? There has never been a greater deed, and whoever will be born after us will belong to a history greater than any history up to now!"

EVALUATE THE EVIDENCE

1. Does Nietzsche believe that the "death of God" is a positive experience? In what ways can people come to grips with this "great deed"?
2. How does the nihilism expressed in this passage foreshadow many of the main ideas in the philosophy of existentialism?

Source: *Nietzsche and the Death of God: Selected Writings*, trans. and ed. Peter Fritzsche (Boston: Bedford/St. Martin's, 2007), pp. 71–72. Used by permission of Bedford/St. Martin's.

such matters reflected only the personal preferences of a given individual. As Wittgenstein put it in the famous last sentence of this work, "Of what one cannot speak, of that one must keep silent." Logical positivism, which has remained dominant in England and the United States to this day, drastically reduced the scope of philosophical inquiry and offered little solace to ordinary people.

On the continent, others looked for answers in **existentialism**. This new philosophy loosely united highly diverse and even contradictory thinkers in a search for usable moral values in a world of anxiety and uncertainty. Modern existentialism had many nineteenth-century forerunners, including Nietzsche, the Danish religious philosopher Søren Kierkegaard (1813–1855), and the Russian novelist Fyodor Dostoyevsky (1821–1881). The philosophy gained recognition in Germany in the 1920s when philosophers Martin Heidegger (1889–1976) and Karl Jaspers (1883–1969) found a sympathetic audience among disillusioned postwar university students. These writers placed great emphasis on the loneliness and meaninglessness of human existence and the need to come to terms with the fear caused by this situation.

Most existential thinkers in the twentieth century were atheists. Often inspired by Nietzsche, they did not believe that a supreme being had established humanity's fundamental nature and given life its meaning. In the words of French existentialist Jean-Paul Sartre (ZHAWN-pawl SAHR-truh) (1905–1980), "existence precedes essence." By that, Sartre meant that there are no God-given, timeless truths outside or independent of individual existence. Only after they are born do people struggle to define their essence, entirely on their own. According to thinkers like Sartre and his lifelong intellectual partner Simone de Beauvoir (1908–1986), existence itself is absurd. Human beings are terribly alone, for there is no God to help them. They are left to confront the inevitable arrival of death and so are hounded by despair. The crisis of the existential thinker epitomized the modern intellectual crisis — the shattering of beliefs in God, reason, and progress.

At the same time, existentialists recognized that human beings must act in the world. Indeed, in the words of Sartre, "man is condemned to be free." Because life is meaningless, existentialists believe that individuals are forced to create their own meaning and define themselves through their actions. Such radical freedom is frightening, and Sartre concluded that most people try to escape it by structuring their lives around conventional social norms. According to Sartre, to escape is to live in "bad faith," to hide from the hard truths of existence. To live authentically, individuals must become "engaged" and choose their own actions in full awareness of their responsibility for their own behavior. Existentialism thus had a powerful ethical component. It placed great stress on individual responsibility and choice, on "being in the world" in the right way.

Existentialism had important precedents in the late nineteenth and early twentieth centuries, but the philosophy really came of age in France during and immediately after World War II. The terrible conditions of that war, discussed in the next chapter, reinforced the existential view of and approach to life. After World War II, French existentialists such as Sartre and Albert Camus (1913–1960) became enormously influential. They offered powerful but unsettling answers to the profound moral issues and the crises of the first half of the twentieth century.

The Revival of Christianity

Though philosophers such as Nietzsche, Wittgenstein, and Sartre all argued that religion had little to teach people in the modern age, the decades after the First World War witnessed a tenacious revival of Christian thought. Christianity—and religion in general—had been on the defensive in intellectual circles since the Enlightenment. In the years before 1914 some theologians, especially Protestant ones, had felt the need to interpret Christian doctrine and the Bible so that they did not seem to contradict science, evolution, and common sense. They saw Christ primarily as a great moral teacher and downplayed the mysterious, spiritual aspects of his divinity. Indeed, some modern theologians were embarrassed by the miraculous, unscientific aspects of Christianity and rejected them.

Especially after World War I, a number of thinkers and theologians began to revitalize the fundamental beliefs of Christianity. Sometimes called Christian existentialists because they shared the loneliness and despair of atheistic existentialists, they stressed human beings' sinful nature, their need for faith, and the mystery of God's forgiveness. The revival of Christian belief after World War I was fed by the rediscovery of the work of the nineteenth-century Danish theologian Søren Kierkegaard (KIHR-kuh-gahrd), whose ideas became extremely influential. Kierkegaard believed it

was impossible for ordinary individuals to prove the existence of God, but he rejected the notion that Christianity was an empty practice. In his classic *Sickness unto Death* (1849), Kierkegaard mastered his religious doubts by suggesting that people must take a "leap of faith" and accept the existence of an objectively unknowable but nonetheless awesome and majestic God.

In the 1920s the Swiss Protestant theologian Karl Barth (1886–1968) propounded similar ideas. In brilliant and influential writings, Barth argued that human beings were imperfect, sinful creatures whose reason and will are hopelessly flawed. Religious truth is therefore made known to human beings only through God's grace, not through reason. People have to accept God's word and the supernatural revelation of Jesus Christ with awe, trust, and obedience, not reason or logic.

Among Catholics, the leading existential Christian was Gabriel Marcel (1889–1973). Born into a cultivated French family, Marcel found in the Catholic Church an answer to what he called the postwar "broken world." Catholicism and religious belief provided the hope, humanity, honesty, and piety for which he hungered. Marcel and his countryman Jacques Maritain (1882–1973) denounced anti-Semitism and supported closer ties with non-Catholics.

After 1914 religion became much more meaningful to intellectuals than it had been before the war. Between about 1920 and 1950, in addition to Marcel and Maritain, poets T. S. Eliot and W. H. Auden, novelists Evelyn Waugh and Aldous Huxley, historian Arnold Toynbee, writer C. S. Lewis, psychoanalyst Karl Stern, and physicist Max Planck all either converted to a faith or became attracted to religion for the first time. Religion, often of a despairing, existential variety, was one meaningful answer to uncertainty and anxiety and the horrific costs of the First and Second World Wars. In the words of English novelist Graham Greene, a Roman Catholic convert, "One began to believe in heaven because one believed in hell."[2]

The New Physics

Ever since the Scientific Revolution of the seventeenth century, scientific advances and their implications had greatly influenced the beliefs of thinking people. By the late nineteenth century science was one of the main pillars supporting Western society's optimistic and rationalistic worldview. Progressive minds believed that science, unlike religion or philosophical speculation, was based on hard facts and controlled experiments. Unchanging natural laws seemed to determine physical processes and permit useful solutions to more and more problems. All this was comforting, especially

existentialism A philosophy that stresses the meaninglessness of existence and the importance of the individual in searching for moral values in an uncertain world.

Unlocking the Power of the Atom
Many of the fanciful visions of science fiction came true in the twentieth century, although not exactly as first imagined. This 1927 Swedish reprint of a drawing by American cartoonist Robert Fuller satirizes a pair of professors who have split the atom and unwittingly destroyed their building and neighborhood in the process. In the Second World War, professors indeed harnessed the atom in bombs and decimated faraway cities and foreign civilians. (© Mary Evans Picture Library/The Image Works)

En amerikansk tecknares bekymmer för framtiden.

Då professorn äntligen efter årslånga experiment lyckades sönderdela en atom.

to people no longer committed to traditional religious beliefs. And all this was challenged by the new physics.

An important first step came at the end of the nineteenth century with the discovery that atoms were not like hard, permanent little billiard balls. They were actually composed of many far-smaller, fast-moving particles, such as electrons and protons. Polish-born physicist Marie Curie (1867–1934) and her French husband, Pierre, discovered that radium constantly emits subatomic particles and thus does not have a constant atomic weight. Building on this and other work in radiation, German physicist Max Planck (1858–1947) showed in 1900 that subatomic energy is emitted in uneven little spurts, which Planck called

"quanta," and not in a steady stream, as previously believed. Planck's discovery called into question the old sharp distinction between matter and energy: the implication was that matter and energy might be different forms of the same thing. The view of atoms as the stable basic building blocks of nature, with a different kind of unbreakable atom for each of the ninety-two chemical elements, was badly shaken.

In 1905 the German-Jewish genius Albert Einstein (1879–1955) went further than the Curies and Planck in undermining Newtonian physics. His **theory of special relativity** postulated that time and space are relative to the viewpoint of the observer and that only the speed of light is constant for all frames of reference in the universe. In order to make his revolutionary and paradoxical idea somewhat comprehensible to the nonmathematical

■ **theory of special relativity** Albert Einstein's theory that time and space are relative to the observer and that only the speed of light remains constant.

layperson, Einstein used analogies involving moving trains. For example, if a woman in the middle of a moving car got up and walked forward to the door, she had gone, relative to the train, a half car length. But relative to an observer on the embankment, she had gone farther. To Einstein, this meant that time and distance were not natural universals but depended on the position and motion of the observer.

In addition, Einstein's theory stated that matter and energy are interchangeable and that even a particle of matter contains enormous levels of potential energy. These ideas unified an apparently infinite universe with the incredibly small, fast-moving subatomic world. In comparison, the closed framework of the Newtonian physics developed during the Scientific Revolution, exemplified by Newton's supposedly immutable laws of motion and mechanics, was quite limited (see Chapter 16).

The 1920s opened the "heroic age of physics," in the apt words of Ernest Rutherford (1871–1937), one of its leading pioneers. Breakthrough followed breakthrough. In 1919 Rutherford showed that the atom could be split. By 1944 seven subatomic particles had been identified, the most important of which was the neutron. Physicists realized that the neutron's capacity to shatter the nucleus of another atom could lead to chain reactions of shattered atoms that would release unbelievable force. This discovery was fundamental to the subsequent development of the nuclear bomb.

Although few nonscientists truly understood the revolution in physics, its implications, as presented by newspapers and popular science fiction writers, were disturbing to millions of men and women in the 1920s and 1930s. As unsettling as Einstein's ideas was a notion popularized by German physicist Werner Heisenberg (VER-nuhr HIGH-zuhn-buhrg) (1901–1976). In 1927 Heisenberg formulated the "uncertainty principle," which postulates that nature itself is ultimately unknowable and unpredictable. He suggested that the universe lacked any absolute objective reality. Everything was "relative," that is, dependent on the observer's frame of reference. Such ideas caught on among ordinary people, who found the unstable, relativistic world described by the new physicists strange and troubling. Instead of Newton's dependable, rational laws, there seemed to be only tendencies and probabilities in an extraordinarily complex and uncertain universe. Like modern philosophy, physics no longer provided comforting truths about natural laws or optimistic answers about humanity's place in an understandable world.

Freudian Psychology

With physics presenting an uncertain universe so unrelated to ordinary human experience, questions regarding the power and potential of the rational human mind assumed special significance. The findings and speculations of Sigmund Freud were particularly influential, yet also deeply disturbing.

Before Freud, poets and mystics had probed the unconscious and irrational aspects of human behavior. But most scientists assumed that the conscious mind processed sense experiences in a rational and logical

Freud's Couch As part of his "talking cure," Austrian neurologist Sigmund Freud invited neurotic patients to lie back on a couch and speak about their dreams and innermost thoughts. This photo shows Freud's famous couch in his office in Vienna. His theories about the unconscious and instinctual motivation of human behavior cast doubt on Enlightenment ideals of rationalism and progress. (© Peter Aprahamian/Corbis)

way. Human behavior in turn was the result of rational calculation—of "thinking." Beginning in the late 1880s Freud developed a very different view of the human psyche. Basing his insights on the analysis of dreams and of "hysteria," a sort of nervous breakdown, Freud concluded that human behavior was basically irrational, governed by the unconscious, a mental reservoir that contained vital instinctual drives and powerful memories. Though the unconscious profoundly influenced people's behavior, it was unknowable to the conscious mind, leaving people unaware of the source or meaning of their actions. Freud explained these ideas in his magisterial book *The Interpretation of Dreams*, first published in 1900.

Freud eventually described three structures of the self—the **id**, the **ego**, and the **superego**—that were basically at war with one another. The primitive, irrational id was entirely unconscious. The source of sexual, aggressive, and pleasure-seeking instincts, the id sought immediate fulfillment of all desires and was totally amoral. Keeping the id in check was the superego, the conscience or internalized voice of parental or social control. For Freud, the superego was also irrational. Overly strict and puritanical, it was constantly in conflict with the pleasure-seeking id. The third component was the ego, the rational self that was mostly conscious and worked to negotiate between the demands of the id and the superego.

For Freud, the healthy individual possessed a strong ego that effectively balanced the id and superego. Neurosis, or mental illness, resulted when the three structures were out of balance. Since the id's instinctual drives were extremely powerful, the danger for individuals and indeed whole societies was that unacknowledged drives might overwhelm the control mechanisms of the ego in a violent, distorted way. Freud's "talking cure"—in which neurotic patients lay back on a couch and shared their innermost thoughts with the psychoanalyst—was an attempt to resolve such unconscious tensions and restore the rational ego to its predominant role.

Yet Freud, like Nietzsche, believed that the mechanisms of rational thinking and traditional moral values could be too strong. In his book *Civilization and Its Discontents* (1930), Freud argued that civilization was

possible only when individuals renounced their irrational instincts in order to live peaceably in groups. Such renunciation made communal life possible, but it left basic instincts unfulfilled and so led to widespread unhappiness. Freud gloomily concluded that Western civilization was itself inescapably neurotic.

Freudian psychology and clinical psychiatry had become an international medical movement by 1910, but only after 1919 did they receive more public attention, especially in northern Europe. In the United States, Freud's ideas attained immense popularity after the Second World War. Many opponents and even some enthusiasts interpreted Freud as saying that the first requirement for mental health was an uninhibited sex life—popular understandings of Freud thus reflected and encouraged growing sexual experimentation, particularly among middle-class women. For more serious students, the psychology of Freud and his followers contributed to the weakening of the old easy optimism about the rational and progressive nature of the human mind.

Modernism in Architecture, Art, Literature, and Music

FOCUS QUESTION *How did modernism revolutionize Western culture?*

Like the scientists and intellectuals who were part of this increasingly unsettled modern culture, creative artists rejected old forms and old values. **Modernism** in architecture, art, literature, and music meant constant experimentation and a search for new kinds of expression. Even today the modernism of the first half of the twentieth century seems strikingly fresh and original. And though many people still find the varied modern visions of the arts strange and perhaps disturbing, these decades, so dismal in many respects, stand as one of Western society's great artistic eras.

Architecture and Design

Already in the late nineteenth century, architects inspired by modernism had begun to transform the physical framework of urban society. The United States, with its rapid urban growth and lack of rigid building traditions, pioneered the new architecture. In the 1890s the Chicago School of architects, led by Louis H. Sullivan (1856–1924), used inexpensive steel, reinforced concrete, and electric elevators to build skyscrapers and office buildings lacking almost any exterior ornamentation. In the first decade of the twentieth century, Sullivan's student Frank Lloyd Wright (1867–1959)

■ **id, ego, and superego** Freudian terms to describe the three parts of the self and the basis of human behavior, which Freud saw as basically irrational.

■ **modernism** A label given to the artistic and cultural movements of the late nineteenth and early twentieth centuries, which were typified by radical experimentation that challenged traditional forms of artistic expression.

■ **functionalism** The principle that buildings, like industrial products, should serve as well as possible the purpose for which they were made, without excessive ornamentation.

■ **Bauhaus** A German interdisciplinary school of fine and applied arts that brought together many leading modern architects, designers, and theatrical innovators.

built a series of radically modern houses featuring low lines, open interiors, and mass-produced building materials. Europeans were inspired by these and other American examples of functional construction, like the massive, unadorned grain elevators of the Midwest.

Promoters of modern architecture argued that buildings and living spaces in general should be ordered according to a new principle: **functionalism**. Buildings, like industrial products, should be "functional"—that is, they should serve, as well as possible, the purpose for which they were made. According to the Franco-Swiss architect Le Corbusier (luh cowr-booz-YAY) (1887–1965), one of the great champions of modernism, "a house is a machine for living in."[3]

Le Corbusier's polemical work *Towards a New Architecture*, published in 1923, laid out guidelines meant to revolutionize building design. Le Corbusier argued that architects should affirm and adopt the latest technologies. Rejecting fancy ornamentation, they should find beauty in the clean, straight lines of practical construction and efficient machinery. The resulting buildings, fashioned according to what was soon called the "International Style," were typically symmetrical rectangles made of concrete, glass, and steel.

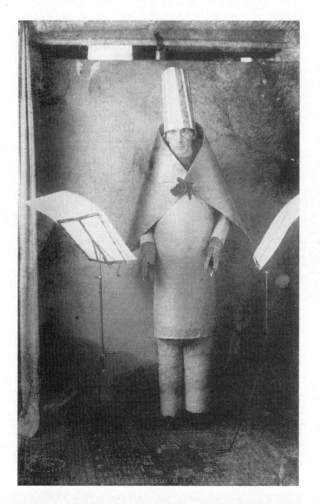

In Europe, architectural leadership centered in German-speaking countries until Hitler took power in 1933. In 1911 twenty-eight-year-old Walter Gropius (1883–1969) broke sharply with the past in his design of the Fagus shoe factory at Alfeld, Germany—a clean, light, elegant building of glass and iron. In 1919 Gropius merged the schools of fine and applied arts at Weimar into a single interdisciplinary school, the **Bauhaus**. The Bauhaus brought together many leading modern architects, designers, and theatrical innovators. Working as an effective, inspired team, they combined the study of fine art, including painting and sculpture, with the study of applied art in the crafts of printing, weaving, and furniture making. Throughout the 1920s the Bauhaus, with its stress on functionalism and quality design for everyday goods, attracted enthusiastic students from all over the world. (See "Living in the Past: Modern Design for Everyday Use," page 876.)

Another leading modern architect, Ludwig Mies van der Rohe (1886–1969), followed Gropius as director of the Bauhaus in 1930. Like many modernist intellectuals, after 1933 he emigrated to the United States to escape the repressive Nazi regime. His classic steel-frame and glass-wall Lake Shore Apartments in Chicago, built between 1948 and 1951, epitomized the spread and triumph of the modernist International Style in the great building boom that followed the Second World War.

New Artistic Movements

In the decades surrounding the First World War, the visual arts also experienced radical change and experimentation. For the last several centuries, artists had tried to produce accurate representations of reality. Now a new artistic avant-garde emerged to challenge that practice. From Impressionism and Expressionism to Dadaism and Surrealism, a sometimes-bewildering array of artistic movements followed one after another. Modern painting and sculpture became increasingly abstract as artists turned their backs on figurative representation and began to break down form into its constituent parts: lines, shapes, and colors.

Berlin, Munich, Moscow, Vienna, New York, and especially Paris became famous for their radical artistic undergrounds. Commercial art galleries and exhibition halls promoted the new work, and schools and institutions, such as the Bauhaus, emerged to train a

The Shock of the Avant-Garde   Dadaist Hugo Ball recites his nonsense poem "Karawane" at the notorious Cabaret Voltaire in Zurich, Switzerland, in 1916. Avant-garde artists such as Ball consciously used their work to overturn familiar artistic conventions and challenge the assumptions of the European middle classes. (Aplc/Getty Images)

LIVING IN THE PAST
Modern Design for Everyday Use

European design movements of the early twentieth century had a lasting impact on everyday lifestyles. Many ordinary elements of living, from apartment buildings to interior furnishings, were transformed by modernist experimentation. The Bauhaus (or House of Building), an institute founded in Germany by architect Walter Gropius in 1919, exemplified modern design at its most influential. It attracted an array of highly talented artists, designers, architects, and students, including the Russian painter Wassily Kandinsky, the Swiss artist Paul Klee, and the Hungarian-Jewish photographer and painter László Moholy-Nagy.

The instructors and students at the Bauhaus sought to revolutionize product design by unifying art, craft, and technology. They argued that everyday objects should reflect the highly rationalized, industrialized, and modern society in which—and for which—they were made. Bauhaus adherents believed that form should follow function and that, as director Ludwig Mies van der Rohe put it in a famous aphorism, "less is more." The results were streamlined, functional designs stripped of all ornamentation that were nonetheless works of great style and lasting beauty.

No everyday item was too insignificant to be treated as an object of high design. The industrial ethos of the Bauhaus was brought to bear on textiles, typography, dishware, and furniture. The famous steel tube and canvas "Wassily chair," created by architect and designer Marcel Breuer, exemplified Bauhaus concepts and remains an icon of modernism. Such goods were mass-produced and marketed at affordable prices, bringing high-concept design into the lives of ordinary Europeans. Bauhaus architects applied the same principles in designing buildings, from factories to working-class housing projects and private homes.

In 1933 Adolf Hitler and the Nazi Party, zealous opponents of modern art of all kinds, shut down the Bauhaus. Many of its prominent teachers and students fled persecution. Gropius, Breuer, Mies, and numerous others moved to the United States, where they helped spread Bauhaus ideas around the world after the end of the Second World War.

QUESTIONS FOR ANALYSIS

1. How do the Bauhaus designs shown here reflect the modern industrial society in which they were created?
2. Why did Bauhaus designers work in so many different fields?
3. Why are Bauhaus designs still influential today?

The Bauhaus School in Dessau, Germany, designed by Walter Gropius opened in 1926. Its glass, steel, and concrete construction is typical of functionalism in modern architecture. (imageBROKER/ SuperStock)

generation in modern techniques. Young artists flocked to these cultural centers to participate in the new movements, earn a living making art, and perhaps change the world with their revolutionary ideas.

One of the earliest modernist movements was Impressionism, which blossomed in Paris in the 1870s. French artists such as Claude Monet (1840–1926) and Edgar Degas (1834–1917) and the American Mary Cassatt (1844–1926), who settled in Paris in 1875, tried to portray their sensory "impressions" in their work. Impressionists looked to the world around them for subject matter, turning their backs on traditional themes such as battles, religious scenes, and wealthy elites. Monet's colorful and atmospheric paintings of farmland haystacks and Degas's many pastel drawings of ballerinas exemplify the way Impressionists moved toward

The angular, streamlined furnishings and patterns in the Bauhaus director's office (ca. 1923) exemplify the school's efforts to use modern materials and design to combine beautiful form and practical function, as do Marcel Breuer's famous "Wassily chair," made of bent tubular steel and canvas (1927), and Marianne Brandt's striking teapot (1924). (teapot: Designed by Marianne Brandt [1893–1983]/© Artists Rights Society (ARS), New York/ VG Bild-Kunst, Bonn/Private Collection/Photo © The Fine Art Society, London, UK/Bridgeman Images; chair: akg-images; office: © 2016 Artists Rights Society [ARS], New York/VG Bild-Kunst, Bonn/Digital Image © The Museum of Modern Art/Licensed by SCALA/Art Resource, NY)

abstraction. Capturing a fleeting moment of color and light, in often blurry and quickly painted images, was far more important than making a heavily detailed, precise rendering of an actual object.

In the next decades an astonishing array of new artistic movements emerged one after another. Postimpressionists and Expressionists, such as Vincent van Gogh (1853–1890), built on Impressionist motifs

of color and light but added a deep psychological element to their pictures, reflecting the attempt to search within the self and reveal (or "express") deep inner feelings on the canvas.

After 1900 avant-garde artists increasingly challenged the art world status quo. In Paris in 1907 painter Pablo Picasso (1881–1973), along with other artists, established Cubism—a highly analytical

The Futurist Manifesto

In the founding manifesto of the Futurist movement, published in 1909, the Italian poet Filippo Tommaso Marinetti called for works of art and literature that embraced the speed and confusion of modernity and the energy and beauty he saw in modern technology.

1. We intend to sing the love of danger, the habit of energy and fearlessness.

2. Courage, audacity, and revolt will be essential elements of our poetry.

3. Up to now literature has exalted a pensive immobility, ecstasy, and sleep. We intend to exalt aggressive action, a feverish insomnia, the racer's stride, the mortal leap, the punch and the slap.

4. We say that the world's magnificence has been enriched by a new beauty: the beauty of speed. A racing car whose hood is adorned with great pipes, like serpents of explosive breath—a roaring car that seems to ride on grapeshot—is more beautiful than the *Victory of Samothrace*.

5. We want to hymn the man at the wheel, who hurls the lance of his spirit across the Earth, along the circle of its orbit.

6. The poet must spend himself with ardor, splendor, and generosity, to swell the enthusiastic fervor of the primordial elements.

7. Except in struggle, there is no more beauty. No work without an aggressive character can be a masterpiece. Poetry must be conceived as a violent attack on unknown forces, to reduce and prostrate them before man.

8. We stand on the last promontory of the centuries! . . . Why should we look back, when what we want is to break down the mysterious doors of the Impossible? Time and Space died yesterday. We already live in the absolute, because we have created eternal, omnipresent speed.

9. We will glorify war—the world's only hygiene—militarism, patriotism, the destructive gesture of freedom-bringers, beautiful ideas worth dying for, and scorn for woman.

10. We will destroy the museums, libraries, academies of every kind, will fight moralism, feminism, every opportunistic or utilitarian cowardice.

11. We will sing of great crowds excited by work, by pleasure, and by riot; we will sing of the multicolored, polyphonic tides of revolution in the modern capitals; we will sing of the vibrant nightly fervor of arsenals and shipyards blazing with violent electric moons; greedy railway stations that devour smoke-plumed serpents; factories hung on clouds by the crooked lines of their smoke; bridges that stride the rivers like giant gymnasts, flashing in the sun with a glitter of knives; adventurous steamers that sniff the horizon; deep-chested locomotives whose wheels paw the tracks like the hooves of enormous steel horses bridled by tubing; and the sleek flight of planes whose propellers chatter in the wind like banners and seem to cheer like an enthusiastic crowd.

EVALUATE THE EVIDENCE

1. Why is Marinetti so fascinated by the products of modern industry, and why does he want to do away with the great institutions of Italian culture?
2. How did Futurism lay the foundation for future radical avant-garde cultural movements?

Source: *Marinetti: Selected Writing* by F. T. Marinetti, edited by R. W. Flint, translated by R. W. Flint and Arthur A. Coppotelli. Translation copyright © 1972 by Farrar, Straus & Giroux, Inc. Reprinted by permission of Farrar, Straus & Giroux, LLC.

approach to art concentrated on a complex geometry of zigzagging lines and sharply angled overlapping planes that exemplified the ongoing trend toward abstract, nonrepresentational art. In 1909 Italian Filippo Tommaso Marinetti (1876–1944) announced the founding of Futurism, a radical art and literary movement determined to transform the mentality of an anachronistic society. According to Marinetti, traditional culture could not deal with the advances of modern technology—automobiles, radios, telephones, phonographs, ocean liners, airplanes, the cinema, the newspaper—and the way these had changed human consciousness. Marinetti embraced the future and cast away the past, calling for radically new art forms that would express the modern condition. (See "Evaluating the Evidence 26.2: The Futurist Manifesto," above.)

The shock of World War I encouraged further radicalization. In 1916 a group of international artists and intellectuals in exile in Zurich, Switzerland, championed a new movement they called **Dadaism**, which attacked all the familiar standards of art and delighted in outrageous behavior. The war had shown once and for all that life was meaningless, the Dadaists argued, so art should be meaningless as well. Dadaists tried to shock their audiences with what they called "anti-art," works and

Salvador Dalí, *Metamorphosis of Narcissus*   Dalí was a leader of the Surrealist art movement, which emerged in the late 1920s. Surrealists were deeply influenced by the theories of Sigmund Freud and used strange and evocative symbols in their work to capture the inner workings of dreams and the unconscious. In this 1937 painting, Dalí plays with the Greek myth of Narcissus, who fell in love with his own reflection and drowned in a pool. What mysterious significance, if any, lies behind this surreal reordering of everyday reality? (© Salvador Dalí, Fundació Gala–Salvador Dalí, Artists Rights Society [ARS], New York 2016/photo: Granger, NYC—All rights reserved)

public performances that were insulting and entirely nonsensical. A well-known example is a reproduction of Leonardo da Vinci's *Mona Lisa* in which the masterpiece is ridiculed with the addition of a hand-drawn mustache and an obscene inscription. Like Futurists, Dadaists embraced the modern age and grappled with the horrors of modern war. "Art in its execution and direction is dependent on the time in which it lives, and artists are creatures of their epoch," wrote Richard Huelsenbeck (1892–1974), one of the movement's founders. "The highest art will be that which in its conscious content presents the thousand-fold problems of the day, the art which has been visibly shattered by the explosions of last week, which is forever trying to collect its limbs after yesterday's crash."[4] After the war, Dadaism became an international movement, spreading to Paris, New York, and particularly Berlin in the early 1920s.

During the mid-1920s some Dadaists were attracted to Surrealism. Surrealists such as Salvador Dalí (1904–1989) were deeply influenced by Freudian psychology and portrayed images of the unconscious in their art. They painted fantastic worlds of wild

dreams and uncomfortable symbols, where watches melted and giant metronomes beat time in precisely drawn but impossible alien landscapes.

Many modern artists sincerely believed that art had a radical mission. By calling attention to the bankruptcy of mainstream society, they believed, art had the power to change the world. The sometimes-nonsensical manifestos written by members of the Dadaist, Futurist, and Surrealist movements were meant to spread their ideas, challenge conventional assumptions of all kinds, and foment radical social change.

By the 1920s art and culture had become increasingly politicized. Many avant-garde artists sided with the far left; some became committed Communists. Such artists and art movements had a difficult time surviving the political crises of the 1930s. Between 1933 and 1945, when the National Socialist (Nazi) Party came to power in Germany and brought a

■ **Dadaism** An artistic movement of the 1920s and 1930s that attacked all accepted standards of art and behavior and delighted in outrageous conduct.

second world war to the European continent, hundreds of artists and intellectuals—often Jews and leftists—fled to the United States to escape the war and the repressive Nazi state. After World War II, New York greatly benefited from this transfusion of talent and replaced Paris and Berlin as the world capital of modern art.

Twentieth-Century Literature

In the decades that followed the First World War, Western literature was deeply influenced by the general intellectual climate of pessimism and alienation and the turn toward radical experimentation sweeping through the other arts. The great nineteenth-century novelists had typically written as all-knowing narrators, describing realistic characters and their relationships to an understandable, if sometimes harsh, society (see Chapter 22). Modernist writers now developed new techniques to express new realities. In the twentieth century many authors adopted the limited, often confused viewpoint of a single individual. Like Freud, they focused their attention on the complexity and irrationality of the human mind, where feelings, memories, and desires are forever scrambled. French novelist Marcel Proust (1871–1922), in his semi-autobiographical, multivolume *Remembrance of Things Past* (1913–1927), recalled bittersweet memories of childhood and youthful love and tried to discover their innermost meaning. To do so, Proust lived like a hermit in a soundproof Paris apartment for ten years, withdrawing from the present to dwell on the past.

Some novelists used the **stream-of-consciousness technique**, relying on internal monologues to explore the human psyche. In *Jacob's Room* (1922), the English author Virginia Woolf (1882–1941) created a novel made up of a series of such monologues in which she tried to capture the inner voice in prose. In this and other stories, Woolf portrayed characters whose ideas and emotions from different periods of their lives bubble up as randomly as from a patient on a psychoanalyst's couch. William Faulkner (1897–1962), one of America's greatest novelists, used the same technique in *The Sound and the Fury* (1929), with much of its intense drama confusedly seen through the eyes of a man who is mentally disabled.

The most famous and perhaps most experimental stream-of-consciousness novel is *Ulysses* (1922) by Irish novelist James Joyce (1882–1941). Into an account of a single day in the life of an ordinary man, Joyce weaves an extended ironic parallel between the aimless wanderings of his hero through the streets and pubs of Dublin and the adventures of Homer's hero Ulysses on his way home from Troy. *Ulysses* was surely one of the most dis-

turbing novels of its generation. Abandoning any sense of a conventional plot, breaking rules of grammar, and blending foreign words, puns, bits of knowledge, and scraps of memory together in bewildering confusion, *Ulysses* is intended to mirror modern life: a gigantic riddle impossible to unravel. Since Joyce included frank descriptions of the main character's sexual thoughts and encounters, the novel was considered obscene in Great Britain and the United States and was banned there until the early 1930s.

As creative writers turned their attention from society to the individual and from realism to psychological relativity, they rejected the idea of progress. Some described "anti-utopias," nightmare visions of things to come, as in the T. S. Eliot poem *The Waste Land* (1922), which depicts a world of growing desolation:

> April is the cruelest month, breeding
> Lilacs out of the dead land, mixing
> Memory and desire, stirring
> Dull roots with spring rain.
> . . .
> What are the roots that clutch, what branches grow
> Out of this stony rubbish? Son of man,
> You cannot say, or guess, for you know only
> A heap of broken images, where the sun beats,
> And the dead tree gives no shelter, the cricket no relief,
> And the dry stone no sound of water.[5]

With its biblical references, images of a ruined and wasted natural world, and general human incomprehension, Eliot (1888–1965) expressed the widespread despair that followed the First World War. The Czech writer Franz Kafka (1883–1924) likewise portrayed an incomprehensible, alienating world. Kafka's novels *The Trial* (1925) and *The Castle* (1926) are stories about helpless individuals crushed by inexplicably hostile forces, as is his famous novella *The Metamorphosis* (1915), in which the main character turns into a giant insect. The German-Jewish Kafka died young, at forty-one, and was spared the horror of seeing the world of his nightmares materialize in the Nazi state. In these and many other works, authors between the wars used new literary techniques and dark imagery to capture the anxiety of the age.

Modern Music

Developments in modern music paralleled those in painting and fiction. Composers and performers expressed the emotional intensity and shock of modernism in radically experimental forms. The ballet *The Rite of Spring* by Russian composer Igor Stravinsky (1882–1971), for example, practically caused a riot

■ **stream-of-consciousness technique** A literary technique, found in works by Virginia Woolf, James Joyce, and others, that uses interior monologue—a character's thoughts and feelings as they occur—to explore the human psyche.

Modern Dance   Dancers in Russian composer Igor Stravinsky's avant-garde ballet *The Rite of Spring* perform at the Paris premiere. The dissonant music, wild sets and costumes, and unpredictable dance movements shocked and insulted the audience, which rioted on the opening night in May 1913. (© Lebrecht/The Image Works)

when it was first performed in Paris in 1913. The combination of pulsating rhythms and dissonant sounds from the orchestra pit with earthy representations of lovemaking by the strangely dressed dancers on the stage shocked audiences accustomed to traditional ballet.

After the First World War, when irrationality and violence had seemed to pervade human experience, modernism flourished in opera and ballet. One of the most powerful examples was the opera *Wozzeck*, by Alban Berg (1885–1935), first performed in Berlin in 1925. Blending a half-sung, half-spoken kind of dialogue with harsh, atonal music, *Wozzeck* is a gruesome tale of a soldier driven by Kafka-like inner terrors and vague suspicions of infidelity to murder his mistress.

Some composers turned their backs on long-established musical conventions. Just as abstract painters arranged lines and color but did not draw identifiable objects, so modern composers arranged sounds without creating recognizable harmonies. Led by Viennese composer Arnold Schönberg (SHURN-buhrg) (1874–1951), they abandoned traditional harmony and tonality. The musical notes in a given piece were no longer united and organized by a key; instead they were independent and unrelated. Schönberg's twelve-tone music of the 1920s arranged all twelve notes of the scale in an abstract mathematical pattern, or "tone row." This pattern sounded like no pattern at all to the ordinary

listener and could be detected only by a highly trained eye studying the musical score. Accustomed to the harmonies of classical and romantic music, audiences generally resisted atonal music. Only after the Second World War did it begin to win acceptance.

An Emerging Consumer Society

FOCUS QUESTION *How did consumer society change everyday life?*

Fundamental innovations in the basic provision and consumption of goods and services accompanied the radical transformation of artistic and intellectual life. After the First World War, modern business forms of credit, retail, and advertising helped sell increasing numbers of mass-produced goods—the products of a highly industrialized factory system—to ever-larger numbers of people. With the arrival of cinema and radio, commercial entertainment increasingly dominated the leisure time of ordinary people. The consumer revolution had roots in the prosperous decades before World War I and would not be fully consolidated until the 1950s and 1960s. Yet in the interwar years the outlines of a modern consumer society emerged with startling clarity.

Mass Culture

The emerging consumer society of the 1920s is a good example of the way technological developments can lead to widespread social change. The arrival of a highly industrialized manufacturing system dedicated to mass-producing inexpensive goods, the establishment of efficient transportation systems that could bring these goods to national markets, and the rise of professional advertising experts to sell them were all part of a revolution in the way consumer goods were made, marketed, and used by ordinary people.

Contemporaries viewed the new mass culture as a distinctly modern aspect of everyday life. It seemed that consumer goods themselves were modernizing society by changing so many ingrained habits. Some people embraced the new ways; others worried that these changes threatened familiar values and precious traditions.

Critics had good reason to worry. Mass-produced goods had a profound impact on the lives of ordinary people. Housework and private life were increasingly organized around an array of modern appliances, from electric ovens, washing machines, and refrigerators to telephones and radios. The aggressive marketing of fashionable clothing and personal care products, such as shampoo, perfume, and makeup, encouraged a cult of youthful "sex appeal." Advertisements increasingly linked individual attractiveness to the use of brand-name products. The mass production and marketing of automobiles and the rise of tourist agencies opened roads to increased mobility and travel.

Commercialized mass entertainment likewise prospered and began to dominate the way people spent their leisure time. Movies and radio thrilled millions. Professional sporting events drew throngs of fans. Thriving print media brought readers an astounding variety of newspapers, inexpensive books, and glossy illustrated magazines. Flashy restaurants, theatrical revues, and nightclubs competed for evening customers.

Department stores epitomized the emergence of consumer society. Already well established across Europe and the United States by the 1890s, they had become veritable temples of commerce by the 1920s. The typical store sold an enticing variety of goods, including clothing, magazines, housewares, food, and spirits. Larger stores included travel bureaus, movie theaters, and refreshment stands. Aggressive advertising campaigns, youthful and attractive salespeople, and easy credit and return policies helped attract customers in droves.

The emergence of modern consumer culture both undermined and reinforced existing social differences. On one hand, consumerism helped democratize Western society. Since everyone with the means could pur-chase any good, mass culture helped break down old social barriers based on class, region, and religion. Yet it also reinforced social differences. Manufacturers soon realized they could profit by marketing goods to specific groups. Catholics, for example, could purchase their own popular literature and inexpensive devotional items; young people eagerly bought the latest fashions marketed directly to them. In addition, the expense of many items meant that only the wealthy could purchase them. Automobiles and, in the 1920s, even vacuum cleaners cost so much that ownership became a status symbol.

The changes in women's lives were particularly striking. The new household items transformed how women performed housework. Advice literature of all kinds encouraged housewives to rush out and buy the latest appliances so they could "modernize" the home. Consumer culture brought growing public visibility to women, especially the young. Girls and young women worked behind the counters and shopped in the aisles of department stores, and they went out on the street alone in ways unthinkable in the nineteenth century. Contemporaries spoke repeatedly about the arrival of the **"modern girl,"** a surprisingly independent female who could vote and held a job, spent her salary on the latest fashions, applied makeup and smoked cigarettes, and used her sex appeal to charm any number of young men. The modern girl had precedents in the assertive, athletic, and independent "new woman" of the 1890s, but she became a dominant global figure in the 1920s. "The woman of yesterday," wrote one German feminist in 1929, yearned for marriage and children and "honor[ed] the achievements of the 'good old days.'" The "woman of today," she continued, "refuses to be regarded as a physically weak being . . . and seeks to support herself through gainful employment. . . . Her task is to clear the way for equal rights for women in all areas of life."[6]

Despite such enthusiasm, the modern girl was in some ways a stereotype, a product of marketing campaigns dedicated to selling goods to the masses. Few young women could afford to live up to this image, even if they did have jobs. Yet the changes associated with the First World War (see Chapter 25) and the emergence of consumer society did loosen traditional limits on women's behavior.

The emerging consumer culture generated a chorus of complaint from cultural critics of all stripes. On the left, socialist writers worried that its appeal undermined working-class radicalism, because mass culture created passive consumers rather than active, class-conscious revolutionaries. On the right, conservatives complained that money spent on frivolous consumer goods sapped the livelihood of industrious artisans and undermined proud national traditions. Religious leaders protested that modern consumerism encouraged

■ **"modern girl"** Somewhat stereotypical image of the modern and independent working woman popular in the 1920s.

The Modern Girl: Image or Reality?   A young woman enjoys a dessert at the Romanesque Café in Berlin in 1924 (left). The independence of this "modern girl," wearing fashionable clothes with a revealing hemline and lacking an escort, transgressed familiar gender roles and shocked and fascinated contemporaries. Images of the modern girl appeared in movies, illustrated magazines, and advertisements, such as this German poster selling "this winter's perfume." Did the emerging consumer society of the 1920s open doors to liberating behavior for women, or did it set new standards that limited women's options? (photo: bpk, Berlin/Art Resource, NY; poster: Lordprice Collection/Alamy Stock Photo)

rampant individualism and that greedy materialism was replacing spirituality. Others bemoaned the supposedly loose morals of the modern girl and fretted over the decline of traditional family values.

Despite such criticism—which continued after World War II—consumer society was here to stay. Ordinary people enjoyed the pleasures of mass consumption, and individual identities were tied ever more closely to modern mass-produced goods. Yet the Great Depression of 1929 (see page 891) soon made actual participation in the new world of goods elusive. The promise of prosperity would only truly be realized during the economic boom that followed the Second World War.

The Appeal of Cinema

Nowhere was the influence of mass culture more evident than in the rapid growth of commercial entertainment, especially cinema and radio. (See "Thinking Like a Historian: The Radio Age," page 884.) Both became

major industries in the interwar years, and an eager public enthusiastically embraced them, spending their hard-earned money and their leisure hours watching movies or listening to radio broadcasts. These mass media overshadowed and began to replace the traditional amusements of people in cities, and then in small towns and villages, changing familiar ways of life.

Cinema first emerged in the United States around 1880, driven in part by the inventions of Thomas Edison. By 1910 American directors and business people had set up "movie factories," at first in the New York area and then in Los Angeles. Europeans were quick to follow. By 1914 small production companies had formed in Great Britain, France, Germany, and Italy, among others. World War I quickened the pace. National leaders realized that movies offered distraction to troops and citizens and served as an effective means of spreading propaganda. Audiences lined up to see *The Battle of the Somme*, a British film released in August 1916 that was frankly intended to encourage popular support for the war. For the audience, watching this early example of cinematic

The Radio Age

In the late 1920s and 1930s radio became a mass medium that reached millions of people around the world. How did the arrival of radio change the way Europeans and others experienced everyday life?

1 **John Reith, *Broadcast over Britain*, 1924.** In a spirited defense of public radio, published shortly after the BBC's first official broadcast, the corporation's founding director championed the potential of wireless broadcasting.

Broadcasting brings relaxation and interest to many homes where such things are at a premium. It does far more; it carries direct information on a hundred subjects to innumerable men and women who will after a short time be in a position to make up their own minds on many matters of vital moment, matters which formerly they had either to receive according to the dictated and partial versions and opinions of others, or to ignore altogether. . . .

As we conceive it, our responsibility is to carry into the greatest possible number of homes everything that is best in every department of human knowledge, endeavour and achievement, and to avoid the things which are, or may be hurtful. It is occasionally indicated to us that we are apparently setting out to give the public what we think they need—and not what they want, but few know what they want, and very few what they need. There is often no difference. . . .

I expect the day will come when, for those who wish it, in the home or office, the news of the world may be received in any quarter of the globe. . . .

Because we broadcast certain items with no permanent value, ethical or educational, it does not follow that we have failed in an ideal to transmit good things, and such as will tend to raise the general ethical or educational standard. There is no harm in trivial things; in themselves they may even be unquestionably beneficial for they may assist the more serious work by providing the measure of salt which seasons. . . .

The whole service which is conducted by wireless broadcasting may be taken as the expression of a new and better relationship between man and man. . . . The genius and the fool, the wealthy and the poor listen simultaneously, and to the same extent, and the satisfaction of the one may be as great as that of the other. . . . There need be no first and third class. . . .

Broadcasting may help to show that mankind is a unity and that the mighty heritage, material, moral, and spiritual, if meant for the good of any, is meant for the good of all, and this is conveyed in its operations.

2 **The Broadcaster, ca. 1925.** Radio transformed the way millions of listeners spent their leisure time and organized their households, and fan magazines like *The Broadcaster* helped broaden its appeal. As this cover illustration suggests, excited listeners would often install a radio set in a prominent location in the family living room.

(The Advertising Archives)

ANALYZING THE EVIDENCE

1. What, according to director John Reith in Source 1, are the main goals of the BBC?
2. What do Sources 2–5 reveal about radio's impact on everyday life? Does this evidence help explain the larger impact of modern consumer culture on Western society?
3. How would listening to radio change the experience of a "traditional" Christmas (see Source 3)? Who is the target audience for the holiday broadcast?
4. Consider the figures in Source 5. Do these numbers accurately represent the number of listeners in the radio audience? Can historians use them to estimate the popularity of radio in the 1920s and 1930s?

3 **Christmas Day radio programming in western Germany, 1928.** By the late 1920s the radio audience in the Münster-Cologne-Aachen region could enjoy a full day of Christmas Day programming.

Tuesday, 25 December

6:00   **Broadcast of the Christmas Mass from the [Protestant] Mother Church in Unterbarmen.** [Includes community and choir singing, a Christmas sermon, and organ music by J. S. Bach.]

9:00   **Ringing Church Bells from St. Gereon's Basilica, Cologne.**

9:05   **Catholic Morning Service.** [Includes sermon on the "Christmas Message," solo and choir performances of Christmas music.]

11:00   **University Professor Dr. J. Verweyen: On the Origins of the Christmas Holiday.** . . .

12:35   **Hanns Brauckmann, Christmas in the Holy Lands.** . . .

2:40   **Pastor Dr. Girkon Soest: Christmas in the Fine Arts.** . . .

3:30   **Children's Hour. "The Christ Child's Way Home."** . . .

4:40   **Broadcast of the Glockenspiel Concert from St. John's Cathedral in Hertogenbosch [Holland].** [Includes performances of church and family Christmas carols.]

5:40   **Christmas Songs.** . . . [Performance by a trio of vocalists includes "Oh Christmas Tree" and other carols.]

7:00   **"Holy Night."** A Christmas legend by Ludwig Thoma recited in Upper Bavarian dialect . . . with zither.

8:00   **Christmas Concert.** [Includes a variety of classical Christmas music] . . .

Intermission: An Hour for the Betrothed. [Includes wedding music by famous composers; it was customary for Germans to get engaged on Christmas Eve and Day.]

Until

1:00 A.M.   **Evening Music and Dance Music.** [Includes waltz, foxtrot, slowfox, tango, and one-step ballroom dance music.]

(akg-images)

4 **Listening to the radio in a Romanian village, ca. 1935.** Radio took some time to penetrate Europe's less wealthy, rural areas. Eventually, however, broadcasting's transformative effects reached the European hinterlands.

5 **Official listening numbers, Germany, 1923–1938.**

Number of Radios Registered in Germany, 1923–1938			
1923	467	1931	3,509,509
1924	1,580	1932	3,981,000
1925	548,749	1933	4,307,722
1926	1,022,299	1934	5,052,607
1927	1,376,564	1935	6,142,921
1928	2,009,842	1936	7,192,000
1929	2,635,567	1937	8,167,975
1930	3,066,682	1938	9,087,454

PUTTING IT ALL TOGETHER

According to BBC director John Reith, radio broadcasts embodied a "new and better relationship between man and man." Radio, for Reith, had the potential to level social differences, by bringing the "material, moral, and spiritual" heritage of Western society to broad masses of ordinary people. Using the sources above, along with what you have learned in class and in this chapter, write a short essay explaining whether or not you agree. Did radio fulfill its democratic promise?

Sources: (1) John Reith, *Broadcast over Britain* (London: Hodder and Stoughton, 1924), pp. 19, 34, 212–213, 217–218. Copyright © John Reith. Reproduced by permission of Hodder & Stoughton Ltd; (3) "Die Ründfunkwoche," *Die Sendung,* December 21, 1928, p. 12, translated by Joe Perry; (5) Kate Lacey, *Feminine Frequencies: Gender, German Radio, and the Public Sphere, 1923–1945* (Ann Arbor: University of Michigan Press, 1996), pp. 32, 247.

propaganda could be heart wrenching. "The tears in many people's eyes and the silence that prevailed when I saw the film showed that every heart was full of love and sympathy for our soldiers," wrote one viewer to the *London Times* that September.[7]

Cinema became a true mass medium in the 1920s, the golden age of silent film. The United States was again a world leader, but European nations also established important national studios. Germany's Universal Film Company (or UFA) was particularly renowned. In the massive Babelsberg Studios just outside Berlin, talented UFA directors produced classic Expressionist films such as *Nosferatu* (1922), a creepy vampire story, and *Metropolis* (1927), about a future society in the midst of a working-class revolt. Such films made use of cutting-edge production techniques, thrilling audiences with fast and slow motion, montage sequences, unsettling close-ups, and unusual dissolves.

Film making became big business on an international scale. Studios competed to place their movies on foreign screens, and European theater owners were sometimes forced to book whole blocks of American films to get the few pictures they really wanted. In response, European governments set quotas on the number of U.S. films they imported. By 1926 U.S. money was drawing German directors and stars to Hollywood and consolidating America's international domination. These practices put European producers at a disadvantage until "talkies" permitted a revival of national film industries in the 1930s, particularly in France.

Motion pictures would remain the central entertainment of the masses until after the Second World War and the rise of television. People flocked to the gigantic movie palaces built across Europe in the mid-1920s, splendid theaters that could seat thousands. There they viewed the latest features, which were reviewed by critics in newspapers and flashy illustrated magazines. Cinema audiences grew rapidly in the 1930s. In Great Britain in the late 1930s, one in every four adults went to the movies twice a week, and two in five went at least once a week. Other countries had similar figures.

As these numbers suggest, motion pictures could be powerful tools of indoctrination, especially in countries with dictatorial regimes. Lenin encouraged the development of Soviet film making, believing that the new medium was essential to the social and ideological transformation of the country. Beginning in the mid-1920s, a series of epic films, the most famous of which were directed by Sergei Eisenstein (1898–1948), brilliantly dramatized the Communist view of Russian history. In Nazi Germany, a young and immensely talented woman film maker, Leni Riefenstahl (REE-fuhn-shtahl) (1902–2003), directed a masterpiece of documentary propaganda, *Triumph of the Will*, based

on the 1934 Nazi Party rally at Nuremberg. Riefenstahl combined stunning aerial photography with mass processions of young Nazi fanatics and images of joyful crowds welcoming Adolf Hitler. Her film, released in 1935, was a brilliant yet chilling documentary of the rise of Nazism.

The Arrival of Radio

Like film, radio became a full-blown mass medium in the 1920s. Experimental radio sets were first available in the 1880s; the work of Italian inventor Guglielmo Marconi (1874–1937) around 1900 and the development of the vacuum tube in 1904 made possible primitive transmissions of speech and music. But the first major public broadcasts of news and special events occurred only in the early 1920s, in Great Britain and the United States.

Every major country quickly established national broadcasting networks. In the United States such networks were privately owned and were financed by advertising, but in Europe the typical pattern was direct control by the government. In Great Britain, Parliament set up an independent public corporation, the British Broadcasting Corporation (BBC), supported by licensing fees. Whatever the institutional framework, radio enjoyed a meteoric growth in popularity. By the late 1930s more than three out of every four households in both democratic Great Britain and dictatorial Germany had at least one radio. (See "Thinking Like a Historian: The Radio Age," page 884.)

Like the movies, radio was well suited for political propaganda and manipulation. Dictators such as Hitler and Italy's Benito Mussolini controlled the airwaves and could reach enormous national audiences with their dramatic speeches. In democratic countries, politicians such as American president Franklin Roosevelt and British prime minister Stanley Baldwin effectively used informal "fireside chats" to bolster their popularity.

The Search for Peace and Political Stability

FOCUS QUESTION *What obstacles to lasting peace did European leaders face?*

As established patterns of thought and culture were further challenged and mangled by the ferocious impact of World War I, so too was the political fabric stretched and torn. The Versailles settlement had established a shaky truce, not a solid peace. After the war, leaders faced a gigantic task as they sought to create a stable international order within the general context of intellectual crisis, halting economic growth, and political turmoil.

The pursuit of real and lasting peace proved difficult for many reasons. Germany hated the Treaty of Versailles. France was fearful and isolated. Britain was undependable, and the United States turned its back on European problems. Eastern Europe was in ferment, and Communist Russia had an unpredictable future. Moreover, the international economic situation was weak and greatly complicated by war debts and disrupted patterns of trade. Yet from 1925 to late 1929, it appeared that peace and stability were within reach. When the economic collapse of the 1930s mocked these hopes and brought the rise of brutal dictators, the disillusionment of liberals in the democracies intensified.

Germany and the Western Powers

Germany was the key to lasting stability. Yet to Germans of all political parties, the Treaty of Versailles represented a harsh dictated peace, to be revised or repudiated as soon as possible. Germany still had the potential to become the strongest country in Europe but remained a source of uncertainty. Moreover, with ominous implications, France and Great Britain did not see eye to eye on Germany.

Immediately after the war, the French wanted to stress the harsh elements in the Treaty of Versailles. Most of the war in the west had been fought on French soil, and the expected costs of reconstruction, as well as of repaying war debts to the United States, were staggering. Thus French politicians believed that massive reparations from Germany were vital for economic recovery. After having compromised with President Wilson only to be betrayed by America's failure to ratify the treaty, many French leaders saw strict implementation of all provisions of the Treaty of Versailles as France's last best hope. Large reparation payments could hold Germany down indefinitely, ensuring French security.

The British soon felt differently. Before the war Germany had been Great Britain's second-best market in the world; after the war a healthy, prosperous Germany appeared to be essential to the British economy. Many Brits agreed with the analysis of the English economist John Maynard Keynes (1883–1946), who eloquently denounced the Treaty of Versailles in his book *The Economic Consequences of the Peace* (1919). Ac-

cording to Keynes, astronomical reparations and harsh economic measures would impoverish Germany, encourage Bolshevism, and increase economic hardship in all countries. Only a complete revision of the treaty could save Germany—and Europe. Keynes's attack engendered much public discussion and became very influential. It created sympathy for Germany in the English-speaking world, which often paralyzed English and American leaders in their relations with Germany over the next two decades.

In addition, British politicians were suspicious of both France's army—the largest in Europe, and authorized at Versailles to occupy the German Rhineland until 1935—and France's expansive foreign policy. Since 1890 France had looked to Russia as a powerful ally against Germany. But with Russia hostile and Communist, and with Britain and the United States unwilling to make any firm commitments, France turned to the newly formed states of central Europe for diplomatic support. In 1921 France signed a mutual defense pact with Poland and associated itself closely with the so-called Little Entente, an alliance that joined Czechoslovakia, Romania, and Yugoslavia against defeated and bitter Hungary.

While French and British leaders drifted in different directions, the Allied commission created to determine German reparations completed its work. In April 1921 it announced that Germany had to pay the enormous sum of 132 billion gold marks ($33 billion) in annual installments of 2.5 billion gold marks. Facing possible occupation of more of its territory, the young German republic—generally known as the Weimar Republic—made its first payment in 1921. Then in 1922, wracked by rapid inflation and political assassinations and motivated by hostility and arrogance as well, German leaders announced their inability to pay more. They proposed a moratorium on reparations for three years, with the clear implication that thereafter the payments would be either drastically reduced or eliminated entirely.

The British were willing to accept a moratorium, but the French were not. Led by their tough-minded prime minister, Raymond Poincaré (1860–1934), they decided they had to either call Germany's bluff or see the entire peace settlement dissolve to France's great disadvantage. If the Germans refused to pay reparations, France would use occupation to paralyze Germany and force it to accept the Treaty of Versailles. So, despite strong British protests, in early January 1923 French and Belgian armies moved out of the Rhineland

French Occupation of the Ruhr, 1923–1925

Jugend Nr. 36

**Ihr Mütter der Welt,
starben dafür Eure Söhne?**

"Mothers of the World, Did Your Sons Die for This?"   In 1923 the French army occupied the industrial district of the Ruhr in Germany in an effort to force reparation payments. The occupying forces included colonial troops from West Africa, and Germans responded with a racist propaganda campaign that cast the West African colonial soldiers as uncivilized savages intent on ravaging German women. (Kharbine-Tarabor/ The Art Archive at Art Resource, NY)

and began to occupy the Ruhr district, the heartland of industrial Germany, creating the most serious international crisis of the 1920s.

Strengthened by a wave of German patriotism, the German government ordered the people of the Ruhr to stop working and offer passive resistance to the occupation. The coal mines and steel mills of the Ruhr fell silent, leaving 10 percent of Germany's population out of work. The French responded by sealing off the Ruhr and the Rhineland from the rest of Germany, letting in only enough food to prevent starvation. German opinion was

■ **Dawes Plan** War reparations agreement that reduced Germany's yearly payments, made payment dependent on economic prosperity, and granted large U.S. loans to promote recovery.

incensed when the French sent over forty thousand colonial troops from North and West Africa to control the territory. German propagandists labeled these troops the "black shame," warning that the African soldiers were savages, eager to brutalize civilians and assault German women. These racist attacks, though entirely unfounded, nonetheless intensified tensions.

By the summer of 1923 France and Germany were engaged in a great test of wills. French armies could not collect reparations from striking workers at gunpoint, but the occupation was paralyzing Germany and its economy. To support the workers and their employers, the German government began to print money to pay its bills, causing runaway inflation. Prices soared as German money rapidly lost all value. People went to the store with bags of banknotes; they returned home with handfuls of groceries. Catastrophic inflation cruelly mocked the old middle-class virtues of thrift, caution, and self-reliance as savings were wiped out. Many Germans felt betrayed. They hated and blamed the Western governments, their own government, big business, the Jews, the workers, and the Communists for their misfortune. Right-wing nationalists— including Adolf Hitler and the newly established National Socialist (Nazi) Party—eagerly capitalized on the widespread discontent.

In August 1923, as the mark lost value and unrest spread throughout Germany, Gustav Stresemann (GOOS-tahf SHTRAY-zuh-mahn) (1878–1929) assumed leadership of the government. Stresemann tried compromise. He called off passive resistance in the Ruhr and in October agreed in principle to pay reparations, but asked for a re-examination of Germany's ability to pay. Poincaré accepted. His hard line had become unpopular in France, and it was hated in Britain and the United States. (See "Individuals in Society: Gustav Stresemann," at right.) In addition, power in both Germany and France was passing to more moderate leaders who realized that continued confrontation was a destructive, no-win situation. Thus, after five long years of hostility and tension, culminating in a kind of undeclared war in the Ruhr in 1923, Germany and France both decided to try compromise. The British, and even the Americans, were willing to help. The first step was to reach an agreement on the reparations question.

Hope in Foreign Affairs

In 1924 an international committee of financial experts headed by American banker Charles G. Dawes met to re-examine reparations from a broad perspective. The resulting **Dawes Plan** (1924) was accepted by France, Germany, and Britain. Germany's yearly reparation payments were reduced and linked to the level of German economic output. Germany would also

Gustav Stresemann

German foreign minister Gustav Stresemann is a controversial historical figure. Hailed in the 1920s as a hero of peace, he was denounced as a traitor by radical German nationalists and Hitler's Nazis. After World War II, revisionist historians stressed Stresemann's persistent nationalism and cast doubt on his peaceful intentions. Weimar Germany's most renowned leader is a fascinating example of the restless quest for convincing historical interpretation.

Stresemann's origins were modest. His parents were Berlin innkeepers and beer retailers, and of their five children only Gustav attended high school. Attracted first to literature and history, Stresemann later turned to economics, earned a doctoral degree, and quickly reached the top as a manager and director of German trade associations. A highly intelligent extrovert with a knack for negotiation, Stresemann became a deputy in the German Reichstag (parliament) in 1907 as a business-oriented liberal and nationalist. When World War I erupted, he believed, like most Germans, that Germany had acted defensively and was not at fault. A strident nationalist, he urged German annexation of conquered foreign territories. Germany's collapse in defeat and revolution devastated Stresemann. He seemed a prime candidate to join the hateful extremism of the far right.

Yet although Stresemann opposed the Treaty of Versailles as unjust and unrealistic, he turned toward the center. He accepted the new Weimar Republic and played a growing role in the Reichstag as the leader of his own small probusiness party. His hour came when French and Belgian troops occupied the Ruhr. Named chancellor in August 1923, he called off passive resistance and began talks with the French. His government also quelled Communist uprisings; put down rebellions in Bavaria, including Hitler's attempted coup; and ended runaway inflation with the introduction of a new currency. Stresemann fought to preserve German unity, and he succeeded.

Voted out as chancellor in November 1923, Stresemann remained as foreign minister in every German government until his death in 1929. Proclaiming a policy of peace and agreeing to pay reparations, he achieved his greatest triumph in the Locarno agreements of 1925. But these agreements did not lead the French to make any further concessions that might have disarmed Germany's extremists. Stresemann made little additional progress in achieving international reconciliation and true sovereignty for Germany. His premature death in office was a serious blow to German pragmatism, encouraging the turn to a more aggressive and nationalist foreign policy.

Stresemann was no fuzzy pacifist. Historians debunking his legend are right in seeing an enduring nationalism in his defense of German interests. But Stresemann, like his French counterpart Aristide Briand, was a statesman of goodwill who

Foreign Minister Gustav Stresemann greets a crowd after accepting the 1926 Nobel Peace Prize in Oslo, Norway.
(ullstein bild/ullstein bild via Getty Images)

wanted peace through mutually advantageous compromise. A realist trained by business and politics in the art of the possible, Stresemann perceived that Germany had to be a satisfied and equal partner for peace to be secure. His unwillingness to guarantee Germany's eastern borders (see Map 25.4, page 854), which is often criticized as contributing to the coming of the Second World War, reflected his conviction that keeping some Germans under Polish and Czechoslovakian rule created a ticking time bomb in Europe. Stresemann was also convinced that war on Poland would almost certainly recreate the Allied coalition that had crushed Germany in 1918.* The mighty coalition that formed after Hitler's 1939 invasion of Poland proved this view prophetic.

QUESTIONS FOR ANALYSIS

1. What did Gustav Stresemann do to promote reconciliation in Europe? How did his policy toward France differ from that toward Poland and Czechoslovakia?
2. What is your interpretation of Stresemann? Does he arouse your sympathy or your suspicion and hostility? Why?

*Robert Grathwol, "Stresemann: Reflections on His Foreign Policy," *Journal of Modern History* 45 (March 1973): 52–70.

receive large loans from the United States to promote economic recovery. In short, Germany would get private loans from the United States in order to pay reparations to France and Britain, thus enabling those countries to repay the large war debts they owed the United States.

This circular flow of international payments was complicated and risky, but for a while it worked. With continual inflows of American capital, the German republic experienced a shaky economic recovery. Germany paid about $1.3 billion in reparations in 1927 and 1928, enabling France and Britain to repay the United States. In this way the Americans belatedly played a part in the general economic settlement that, though far from ideal, facilitated a worldwide recovery in the late 1920s.

A political settlement accompanied the economic accords. In 1925 the leaders of Europe signed a number of agreements at Locarno, Switzerland. Germany and France solemnly pledged to accept their common border, and both Britain and Italy agreed to fight either France or Germany if one invaded the other. Stresemann reluctantly agreed to settle boundary disputes with Poland and Czechoslovakia by peaceful means, although he did not agree on permanent borders to Germany's east. In response, France reaffirmed its pledge of military aid to those countries if Germany attacked them. The refusal to settle Germany's eastern borders angered the Poles, and though the "spirit of Locarno" lent some hope to those seeking international stability, political tensions deepened in central Europe.

Other developments suggested possibilities for international peace. In 1926 Germany joined the League of Nations, and in 1928 fifteen countries signed the Kellogg-Briand Pact, initiated by French prime minister Aristide Briand and U.S. secretary of state Frank B. Kellogg. The signing states agreed to "renounce [war] as an instrument of international policy" and to settle international disputes peacefully. The pact made no provisions for action in case war actually occurred and would not prevent the arrival of the Second World War in 1939. In the late 1920s, however, it fostered a cautious optimism and encouraged the hope that the United States would accept its responsibilities as a great world power by contributing to European stability.

Hope in Democratic Government

Domestic politics also offered reason to hope. During the occupation of the Ruhr and the great inflation, republican government in Germany had appeared on the verge of collapse. In 1923 Communists momentarily entered provincial governments, and in November an obscure politician named Adolf Hitler leaped onto a table in a beer hall in Munich and proclaimed a "national socialist revolution." But the young republican government easily crushed Hitler's plot to seize control, and he was sentenced to prison. In the late 1920s liberal democracy seemed to take root in Weimar Germany. Elections were held regularly, and republican democracy appeared to have growing support among a majority of Germans. A new currency was established, and the economy stabilized. The moderate businessmen who tended to dominate the various German coalition governments were convinced that economic prosperity demanded good relations with the Western powers, and they supported parliamentary government at home.

Sharp political divisions remained, however. Throughout the 1920s Hitler's Nazi Party attracted support from fanatical anti-Semites, ultranationalists, and disgruntled ex-servicemen. Many unrepentant nationalists and monarchists populated the right and the army. On the left, members of Germany's recently formed Communist Party were noisy and active. The Communists, directed from Moscow, reserved their greatest hatred and sharpest barbs for their cousins the Social Democrats, whom they accused of betraying the revolution. Though the working class was divided, a majority supported the nonrevolutionary Social Democrats.

The situation in France was similar to that in Germany. Communists and Socialists battled for workers' support. After 1924 the democratically elected government rested mainly in the hands of coalitions of moderates, with business interests well represented. France's great accomplishment was the rapid rebuilding of its war-torn northeastern region. The expense of this undertaking led, however, to a large deficit and substantial inflation. By early 1926 the franc had fallen to 10 percent of its prewar value, causing a severe crisis. Poincaré was recalled to office, while Briand remained minister for foreign affairs. Poincaré slashed spending and raised taxes, restoring confidence in the economy. The franc was stabilized at about one-fifth of its prewar value, and the economy remained fairly stable until 1930.

Britain, too, faced challenges after 1920. The great problem was unemployment. In June 1921 almost 2.2 million people—or 23 percent of the labor force—were out of work, and throughout the 1920s unemployment hovered around 12 percent, leading to a massive general strike in 1926. Yet the state provided unemployment benefits and supplemented the payments with subsidized housing, medical aid, and increased old-age pensions. These and other measures kept living standards from seriously declining, helped moderate class tensions, and pointed the way toward the welfare state Britain would establish after World War II.

Relative social harmony was accompanied by the rise of the Labour Party as a determined champion of the working class and of greater social equality. Committed to the kind of moderate revisionist socialism that had emerged before World War I (see Chapter 23), the Labour Party replaced the Liberal Party as the main opposition to the Conservatives. This shift reflected the decline of old liberal ideals of competitive capitalism, limited government control, and individual responsibility. In 1924 and from 1929 to 1931, the Labour Party under Ramsay MacDonald (1866–1937) governed the country with the support of the smaller Liberal Party. Yet Labour moved toward socialism gradually and democratically, so as not to antagonize the middle classes.

The British Conservatives showed the same compromising spirit on social issues. In 1922 Britain granted southern, Catholic, Ireland full autonomy after a bitter guerrilla war, thereby removing a key source of prewar friction. Despite conflicts such as the 1926 strike by hard-pressed coal miners, which led to an unsuccessful general strike, social unrest in Britain was limited in the 1920s and 1930s. Developments in both international relations and the domestic politics of the leading democracies across western Europe gave cause for optimism in the late 1920s.

The Great Depression, 1929–1939

FOCUS QUESTION *What were the causes and consequences of the Great Depression?*

This fragile optimism was short-lived. Beginning in 1929, a massive economic downturn struck the entire world with ever-greater intensity. Recovery was slow and uneven, and contemporaries labeled the economic crisis the **Great Depression**, to emphasize its severity and duration. Only with the Second World War did the depression disappear in much of the world.

The social and political consequences of the Great Depression were enormous. Mass unemployment and failing farms made insecurity and unemployment a reality for millions of people (Map 26.1). In Europe and the United States, governments instituted a variety of social welfare programs intended to manage the crisis. Yet the prolonged economic collapse shattered the fragile political stability of the mid-1920s and encouraged the growth of extremists on both ends of the political spectrum. Democratic government faltered, and authoritarian and Fascist parties gained power across Europe.

The Economic Crisis

Though economic activity was already declining moderately in many countries by early 1929, the crash of the stock market in the United States in October of that year initiated a worldwide crisis. The American economy had prospered in the late 1920s, but there were large inequalities in income and a serious imbalance between actual business investment and stock market speculation. Thus net investment—in factories, farms, equipment, and the like—actually fell from $3.5 billion in 1925 to $3.2 billion in 1929. In the same years, as money flooded into stocks, the value of shares traded on the exchanges soared from $27 billion to $87 billion. Such inflated prices should have raised serious concerns about economic solvency, but even experts failed to predict the looming collapse.

This stock market boom—or "bubble" in today's language—was built on borrowed money. Many wealthy investors, speculators, and people of modest means bought stocks by paying only a small fraction of the total purchase price and borrowing the remainder from their stockbrokers. Such buying "on margin" was extremely dangerous. When prices started falling in 1929, the hard-pressed margin buyers had to either put up more money, which was often impossible, or sell their shares to pay off their brokers. Thousands of people started selling all at once. The result was a financial panic. Countless investors and speculators were wiped out in a matter of days or weeks.

The consequences were swift and severe. Stripped of wealth and confidence, battered investors and their fellow citizens started buying fewer goods. Prices fell, production began to slow down, and unemployment began to rise. Soon the entire American economy was caught in a spiraling decline.

The financial panic triggered an international financial crisis. Throughout the 1920s American bankers and investors had lent large amounts of capital to many countries. Once the panic broke, U.S. bankers began recalling the loans they had made to foreign businesses. Gold reserves began to flow rapidly out of European countries, particularly Germany and Austria, toward the United States. It became very hard for European businesses to borrow money, and panicky Europeans began to withdraw their savings from banks. These banking problems eventually led to the crash of the largest bank in Austria in 1931 and then to general financial chaos. The recall of loans by American bankers also accelerated a collapse in world prices when businesses dumped industrial goods and agricultural commodities in a frantic attempt to get cash to pay their loans.

■ **Great Depression** A worldwide economic depression from 1929 through 1939, unique in its severity and duration and with slow and uneven recovery.

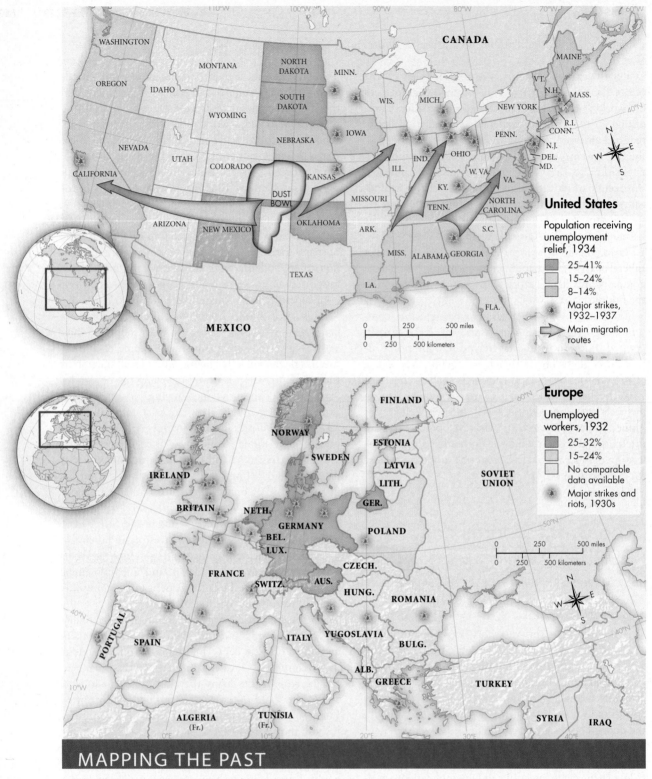

MAP 26.1 The Great Depression in the United States and Europe, 1929–1939

These maps show that unemployment was high almost everywhere, but that national and regional differences were also substantial.

ANALYZING THE MAP Which European countries had the highest rate of unemployment? How do the rates of people on unemployment relief in the United States compare to the percentage of unemployed workers in Europe? In the United States, what were the main channels of migration?

CONNECTIONS What tactics of reform and recovery did European nations use to combat the deprivations of the Great Depression?

The financial crisis led to a general crisis of production: between 1929 and 1933 world output of goods fell by an estimated 38 percent. As this happened, each country turned inward and tried to manage the crisis alone. In 1931, for example, Britain went off the gold standard, refusing to convert banknotes into gold, and reduced the value of its money. Britain's goal was to make its goods cheaper and therefore more salable in the world market. But more than twenty other nations, including the United States in 1934, also went off the gold standard, so few countries gained a real advantage from this step—though Britain was an exception. Similarly, country after country followed the example of the United States when in 1930 it raised protective tariffs to their highest levels ever and tried to seal off shrinking national markets for domestic producers. Such actions further limited international trade. Within this context of fragmented and destructive economic nationalism, a recovery did not begin until 1933 and it was a halting one at that.

Although opinions differ, two factors probably best explain the relentless slide to the bottom from 1929 to early 1933. First, the international economy lacked leadership able to maintain stability when the crisis came. Neither Britain nor the United States—the world's economic leaders at the time—successfully stabilized the international economic system in 1929. The American decisions to cut back on international lending and erect high tariffs, as we have seen, had damaging ripple effects.

The second factor was poor national economic policy in almost every country. Governments generally cut their budgets when they should have raised spending and accepted large deficits in order to stimulate their economies. After World War II, this "countercyclical policy," advocated by John Maynard Keynes, became a well-established weapon against downturn and depression. But in the 1930s orthodox economists who believed balanced budgets to be the key to economic growth generally regarded Keynes's prescription with horror.

British Unemployment, 1932

Insured workers
unemployed
■ More than 35%
▨ 25–35%
□ 15–24%
□ Less than 15%

Homelessness in London The Great Depression of the 1930s disrupted the lives of millions across the United States and Europe. The frustration and agony of unemployment are evident in this common scene of homeless Londoners wrapping themselves in newspaper against the cold. (© Mary Evans Picture Library/The Image Works)

George Orwell on Life on the Dole

Periodic surges in unemployment were an old story in capitalist economies, but the long-term joblessness of millions in the Great Depression was something new and unexpected. In Britain especially, where the depression followed a weak postwar recovery, large numbers suffered involuntary idleness for years at a time. Whole families lived "on the dole," the weekly welfare benefits paid by the government.

One of the most insightful accounts of unemployed workers was written by the British journalist and novelist George Orwell (1903–1950), who studied the conditions in northern England and wrote The Road to Wigan Pier *(1937), an excerpt of which follows. An independent socialist who distrusted rigid Marxism, Orwell believed that socialism could triumph in Britain if it came to mean commonsense "justice and liberty" for a broad sector of the working classes. Orwell's disillusionment with authoritarian socialism and Soviet-style communism pervades his other famous works,* Animal Farm *(1945) and* 1984 *(1949).*

When you see the unemployment figures quoted at two millions, it is fatally easy to take this as meaning that two million people are out of work and the rest of the population is comparatively comfortable. . . . [Adding in the destitute,] you might take the number of underfed people in England (for *everyone* on the dole or thereabouts is underfed) as being, at the very most, five millions.

This is an enormous under-estimate, because, in the first place, the only people shown on unemployment figures are those actually drawing the dole — that is, in general, heads of families. An unemployed man's dependants do not figure on the list unless they too are drawing a separate allowance. . . . In addition there are great numbers of people who are in work but who, from a financial point of view, might equally be unemployed, because they are not drawing anything that can be described as a living wage.

Allow for these and their dependants, throw in as before the old-age pensioners, the destitute and other nondescripts, and you get an *underfed* population of well over ten millions. . . . Take the figures for Wigan, which is typical enough of the industrial and mining districts. . . . The total population of Wigan is a little under 87,000; so that at any moment more than one person in three out of the whole population — not merely the registered workers — is either drawing or living on the dole. . . .

Nevertheless, in spite of the frightful extent of unemployment, it is a fact that poverty — extreme poverty — is less in evidence in the industrial North than it is in London. Everything is poorer and shabbier, there are fewer motor-cars and fewer well-dressed people; but also there are fewer people who are obviously destitute. . . . In the industrial towns the old communal way of life has not yet broken up, tradition is still strong and almost everyone has a family — potentially, therefore, a home. In a town of 50,000 or 100,000 inhabitants there is no casual and as it were unaccounted-for population; nobody sleeping in the streets, for instance. Moreover, there is just this to be said for the unemployment regulations, that they do not discourage people from marrying. A man and wife on twenty-three shillings a week are not far from the starvation line, but they can make a home of sorts; they are vastly better off than a single man on fifteen shillings. . . .

But there is no doubt about the deadening, debilitating effect of unemployment upon everybody, married or single, and upon men more than upon women. . . . Everyone who saw Greenwood's play *Love on the Dole* must remember that dreadful moment when the poor, good, stupid working man beats on the table and cries out, "O God, send me some work!" This was not dramatic exaggeration, it was a touch from life. That cry must have been uttered, in almost those words, in tens of thousands, perhaps hundreds of thousands of English homes, during the past fifteen years.

But, I think not again — or at least, not so often. . . . When people live on the dole for years at a time they grow used to it, and drawing the dole, though it remains unpleasant, ceases to be shameful. Thus the old, independent, workhouse-fearing tradition is undermined. . . .

So you have whole populations settling down, as it were, to a lifetime of the P.A.C. [Public Assistance Committees, which means-tested recipients and set benefit levels]. . . . Take, for instance, the fact that the working class think nothing of getting married on the dole. . . . Life is still fairly normal, more normal than one really has the right to expect. Families are impoverished, but the family-system has not broken up. The people are in effect living a reduced version of their former lives.

Instead of raging against their destiny they have made things tolerable by lowering their standards. But they don't necessarily lower their standards by cutting out luxuries and concentrating on necessities; more often it is the other way about — the more natural way, if you come to think of it. Hence the fact that in a decade of unparalleled depression, the consumption of all cheap luxuries has increased. The two things that have probably made the greatest difference of all are the movies and the mass-production of cheap smart clothes since the war. The youth who leaves school at fourteen and gets a blind-alley job is out of work at twenty, probably for life; but for two pounds ten on the hire-purchase system he can buy himself a suit which, for a little while and at a little distance, looks as though it had been tailored in Savile

Row. The girl can look like a fashion plate at an even lower price. . . . You can stand on the street corner, indulging in a private daydream of yourself as Clark Gable or Greta Garbo, which compensates you for a great deal. . . .

Trade since the war has had to adjust itself to meet the demands of underpaid, underfed people, with the result that a luxury is nowadays almost always cheaper than a necessity. One pair of plain solid shoes costs as much as two ultra-smart pairs. . . . And above all there is gambling, the cheapest of all luxuries. Even people on the verge of starvation can buy a few days' hope ("Something to live for," as they call it) by having a penny on a sweepstake. . . . Twenty million people are underfed but literally everyone in England has access to a radio. What we have lost in food we have gained in electricity. Whole sections of the working class who have been plundered of all they really need are being compensated, in part, by cheap luxuries which mitigate the surface of life.

Do you consider all this desirable? No, I don't. But it may be that the psychological adjustment which the working class are visibly making is the best they could make in the circumstances. They have neither turned revolutionary nor lost their self-respect; merely they have kept their tempers and settled down to make the best of things on a fish-and-chip standard. The alternative would be God knows what continued agonies of despair; or it might be attempted insurrections which, in a strongly governed country like England, could only lead to futile massacres and a régime of savage repression.

EVALUATE THE EVIDENCE

1. According to Orwell, "extreme poverty" was less visible in the northern industrial towns than in London. How did family relations contribute to social stability in the face of growing poverty?
2. What were the consequences of long-term unemployment for English workers? How did joblessness change attitudes and behaviors?
3. Judging from Orwell's description, did radical revolution seem likely in England in the Great Depression? Why?

Source: Excerpts from Chapter V in *The Road to Wigan Pier* by George Orwell. Copyright © George Orwell, 1937. Copyright © 1958 and renewed 1986 by the Estate of Sonia B. Orwell. Reprinted by permission of Houghton Mifflin Harcourt Publishing Company, from *The Complete Works of George Orwell*. All rights reserved.

Mass Unemployment

The lack of large-scale government spending contributed to the rise of mass unemployment. As the financial crisis led to production cuts, workers lost their jobs and had little money to buy goods. In Britain, where unemployment had averaged 12 percent in the 1920s, it averaged more than 18 percent between 1930 and 1935. Far worse was the case of Germany, where in 1932 one in every three workers was jobless. In the United States, unemployment had averaged only 5 percent in the 1920s. In 1933 it soared to about 30 percent: almost 13 million people were out of work (see Map 26.1).

Mass unemployment created great social problems. Poverty increased dramatically, although in most countries unemployed workers generally received some kind of meager unemployment benefits or public aid that prevented starvation. (See "Evaluating the Evidence 26.3: George Orwell on Life on the Dole," at left.) Millions of people lost their spirit, condemned to an apparently hopeless search for work. Homes and ways of life were disrupted in millions of personal tragedies. Young people postponed marriages, and birthrates fell sharply. There was an increase in suicide and mental illness. Poverty or the threat of poverty became a grinding reality. In 1932 the workers of Manchester, England, appealed to their city officials—a typical plea echoed throughout the Western world:

> We tell you that thousands of people . . . are in desperate straits. We tell you that men, women, and children are going hungry. . . . We tell you that great numbers are being rendered distraught through the stress and worry of trying to exist without work. . . . If you do not do this—if you do not provide useful work for the unemployed—what, we ask, is your alternative? Do not imagine that this colossal tragedy of unemployment is going on endlessly without some fateful catastrophe. Hungry men are angry men.[8]

Only strong government action could deal with mass unemployment, a social powder keg preparing to explode.

The New Deal in the United States

The Great Depression and the government response to it marked a major turning point in American history. President Herbert Hoover (U.S. pres. 1929–1933) and his administration initially reacted to the stock market crash and economic decline with dogged optimism but limited action. When the full force of the financial crisis struck Europe in the summer of 1931 and boomeranged back to the United States, people's worst fears became reality. Banks failed; unemployment soared. Between 1929 and 1932 industrial production fell by about 50 percent.

In these dire circumstances, Franklin Delano Roosevelt (U.S. pres. 1933–1945) won a landslide presidential victory in 1932 with grand but vague promises of a "New Deal for the forgotten man." Roosevelt's goal was to reform capitalism in order to save it. Though Roosevelt rejected socialism and government ownership of industry, he advocated forceful government intervention in the economy and instituted a broad range of government-supported social programs designed to stimulate the economy and provide jobs.

In the United States, innovative federal programs promoted agricultural recovery, a top priority. Almost half of the American population still lived in rural areas, and the depression hit farmers hard. Roosevelt took the United States off the gold standard and devalued the dollar in an effort to raise American prices and rescue farmers. The Agricultural Adjustment Act of 1933 also aimed at raising prices—and thus farm income—by limiting agricultural production. These measures worked for a while, and in 1936 farmers repaid Roosevelt with overwhelming support in his re-election campaign.

The most ambitious attempt to control and plan the economy was the National Recovery Administration (NRA). Intended to reduce competition among industries by setting minimum prices and wages, the NRA broke with the cherished American tradition of free competition. Though participation was voluntary, the NRA aroused conflicts among business people, consumers, and bureaucrats and never worked well. The program was abandoned when declared unconstitutional by the Supreme Court in 1935.

Roosevelt and his advisers then attacked the key problem of mass unemployment. The federal government accepted the responsibility of employing as many people as financially possible. New agencies like the Works Progress Administration (WPA), set up in 1935, were created to undertake a vast range of projects. One-fifth of the entire U.S. labor force worked for the WPA at some point in the 1930s, constructing public buildings, bridges, and highways. The WPA was enormously popular, and the opportunity of taking a government job helped check the threat of social revolution in the United States.

In 1935 the U.S. government also established a national social security system with old-age pensions and unemployment benefits. The National Labor Relations Act of 1935 gave union organizers the green light by guaranteeing rights of collective bargaining. Union membership more than doubled from 4 million in

1935 to 9 million in 1940. In general, between 1935 and 1938 government rulings and social reforms chipped away at the privileges of the wealthy and tried to help ordinary people.

Programs like the WPA were part of the New Deal's fundamental commitment to use the federal government to provide relief welfare for all Americans. This commitment marked a profound shift from the traditional stress on family support and community responsibility. Embraced by a large majority in the 1930s, this shift in attitudes proved to be one of the New Deal's most enduring legacies.

Despite undeniable accomplishments in social reform, the New Deal was only partly successful in responding to the Great Depression. At the height of the recovery in May 1937, 7 million workers were still unemployed—better than the high of about 13 million in 1933 but way beyond the numbers from the 1920s. The economic situation then worsened seriously in the recession of 1937 and 1938, and unemployment had risen to a staggering 10 million when war broke out in Europe in September 1939. The New Deal never pulled the United States out of the depression; it took the Second World War to do that.

The Scandinavian Response to the Depression

Of all the Western democracies, the Scandinavian countries under Social Democratic leadership responded most successfully to the challenge of the Great Depression. Having grown steadily in the late nineteenth century, the Social Democrats became the largest political party in Sweden and then in Norway after the First World War. In the 1920s they passed important social reform legislation that benefited both peasants and workers and developed a unique kind of socialism. Flexible and nonrevolutionary, Scandinavian socialism grew out of a strong tradition of cooperative community action. Even before 1900 Scandinavian agricultural cooperatives had shown how individual peasant families could join together for everyone's benefit. Labor leaders and capitalists were also inclined to cooperate with one another.

When the economic crisis struck in 1929, socialist governments in Scandinavia built on this pattern of cooperative social action. Sweden in particular pioneered in the use of large-scale deficits to finance public works and thereby maintain production and employment. In ways that paralleled some aspects of Roosevelt's New Deal, Scandinavian governments also increased such social welfare benefits as old-age pensions, unemployment insurance, subsidized housing, and maternity allowances. All this spending required a

Oslo Breakfast   Scandinavian Social Democrats championed cooperation and practical welfare measures, playing down strident rhetoric and theories of class conflict. The "Oslo Breakfast" portrayed in this pamphlet from the mid-1930s exemplified the Scandinavian approach. It provided every schoolchild in the Norwegian capital with a good breakfast free of charge. (Courtesy, Directorate for Health and Social Affairs, Oslo)

large bureaucracy and high taxes, first on the rich and then on practically everyone. Yet both private and co-operative enterprise thrived, as did democracy. Some observers saw Scandinavia's welfare socialism as an appealing middle way between sick capitalism and cruel communism or fascism.

Recovery and Reform in Britain and France

In Britain, MacDonald's Labour government and then, after 1931, the Conservative-dominated coalition government followed orthodox economic theory. The budget was balanced, spending was tightly controlled, and unemployed workers received barely enough welfare to live. Nevertheless, the economy recovered considerably after 1932. By 1937 total production was about 20 percent higher than in 1929. In fact, for Britain the years after 1932 were actually somewhat better than the 1920s had been, the opposite of the situation in the United States and France.

This good but by no means brilliant performance reflected the gradual reorientation of the British economy. After going off the gold standard in 1931 and establishing protective tariffs in 1932, Britain concentrated increasingly on the national, rather than the international, market. The old export industries of the Industrial Revolution, such as textiles and coal, continued to decline, but new industries, such as automobiles and electrical appliances, grew in response to British home demand. Moreover, low interest rates encouraged a housing boom. By the end of the decade, there were highly visible differences between the old, depressed industrial areas of the north and the new, growing areas of the south.

Because France was relatively less industrialized and thus more isolated from the world economy, the Great Depression came to it late. But once the depression hit France, it stayed and stayed. Decline was steady until 1935, and a short-lived recovery never brought production or employment back up to predepression levels. Economic stagnation both reflected and heightened an ongoing political crisis. There was no stability in government. As before 1914, the French parliament was made up of many political parties that could never cooperate for long. In 1933, for example, five coalition cabinets formed and fell in rapid succession.

The French, however, had lost the underlying unity that had made government instability bearable before

1914. Fascist organizations agitated against parliamentary democracy and turned to Mussolini's Italy and Hitler's Germany for inspiration. In February 1934 French Fascists rioted and threatened to take over the republic. At the same time, the Communist Party and many workers opposed to the existing system looked to Stalin's Russia for guidance. The vital center of moderate republicanism was weakened by attacks from both sides.

Frightened by the growing strength of the Fascists at home and abroad, the Communists, Socialists, and Radicals formed an alliance — the **Popular Front** — for the national elections of May 1936. Their clear victory reflected the trend toward polarization. The number of Communists in the parliament jumped dramatically from 10 to 72, while the Socialists, led by Léon Blum, became the strongest party in France, with 146 seats. The Radicals — who were actually quite moderate — slipped badly, and the conservatives lost ground to the far right.

In the next few months, Blum's Popular Front government made the first and only real attempt to deal with the social and economic problems of the 1930s in France. Inspired by Roosevelt's New Deal, it encouraged the union movement and launched a far-reaching program of social reform, complete with paid vacations and a forty-hour workweek. Supported by workers and the lower middle class, these measures were quickly sabotaged by rapid inflation and accusations of revolution from Fascists and frightened conservatives. Wealthy people sneaked their money out of the country, labor unrest grew, and France entered a severe financial crisis. Blum was forced to announce a "breathing spell" in social reform.

Political dissension in France was encouraged by the Spanish Civil War (1936–1939), during which authoritarian Fascist rebels overthrew the democratically elected republican government. French Communists demanded that the government support the Spanish republicans, while many French conservatives would gladly have joined Hitler and Mussolini in aiding the Spanish Fascists. Extremism grew, and France itself was within sight of civil war. Blum was forced to resign in June 1937, and the Popular Front quickly collapsed. An anxious and divided France drifted aimlessly once again, preoccupied by Hitler and German rearmament.

NOTES

1. P. Valéry, *Variety*, trans. M. Cowley (New York: Harcourt Brace, 1927), pp. 27–28.
2. G. Greene, *Another Mexico* (New York: Viking Press, 1939), p. 3.
3. C. E. Jeanneret-Gris (Le Corbusier), *Towards a New Architecture* (London: J. Rodker, 1931), p. 15.
4. R. Huelsenbeck, "Collective Dada Manifesto (1920)," in *The Dada Painters and Poets*, ed. Robert Motherwell and Jack D. Flam (Boston: G. K. Hall, 1981), pp. 242–246.
5. From *The Waste Land* by T. S. Eliot. Used by permission of Faber and Faber Ltd.
6. E. Herrmann, *This Is the New Woman* (1929), quoted in *The Weimar Republic Sourcebook*, ed. A. Kaes, M. Jay, and E. Dimendberg (Berkeley: University of California Press, 1994), pp. 206–208.
7. Quoted in R. Smither, ed., *The Battles of the Somme and Ancre* (London: Imperial War Museum, 1993), p. 67.
8. Quoted in S. B. Clough et al., eds., *Economic History of Europe: Twentieth Century* (New York: Harper & Row, 1968), pp. 243–245.
9. S. Freud, *Civilization and Its Discontents* (New York: W. W. Norton, 1961), p. 112.

■ **Popular Front** A short-lived New Deal–inspired alliance in France led by Léon Blum that encouraged the union movement and launched a far-reaching program of social reform.

LOOKING BACK LOOKING AHEAD

The decades before and especially after World War I brought intense intellectual and cultural innovation. The results were both richly productive and deeply troubling. From T. S. Eliot's poem *The Waste Land* to Einstein's theory of special relativity to the sleek glass and steel buildings of the Bauhaus, the intellectual products of the time stand among the highest achievements of Western arts and sciences. At the same time, mass culture, embodied in cinema, radio, and an emerging consumer society, transformed everyday life. Yet the modern vision was often bleak and cold. Modern art and consumer society alike challenged traditional values, contributing to feelings of disorientation and pessimism that had begun late in the nineteenth century and were exacerbated by the searing events of the war. The situation was worsened by ongoing political and economic turmoil. The Treaty of Versailles had failed to create a lasting peace or resolve the question of Germany's role in Europe. The Great Depression revealed the fragility of the world economic system and cast millions out of work. In the end, perhaps, the era's intellectual achievements and the overall sense of crisis were closely related.

Sigmund Freud captured the general mood of gloom and foreboding in 1930. "Men have gained control over the forces of nature to such an extent that . . . they would have no difficulty in exterminating one another to the last man," he wrote. "They know this, and hence comes a large part of their current unrest, their unhappiness and their mood of anxiety."[9] Freud's dark words reflected the extraordinary human costs of World War I and the horrific power of modern weaponry. They also expressed his despair over the growing popularity of repressive dictatorial regimes. During the interwar years, many European nations — including Italy, Germany, Spain, Poland, Portugal, Austria, and Hungary — would fall one by one to authoritarian or Fascist dictatorships, succumbing to the temptations of totalitarianism. Liberal democracy was severely weakened. European stability was threatened by the radical programs of Soviet Communists on the left and Fascists on the right, and Freud uncannily predicted the great conflict to come.

Make Connections

Think about the larger developments and continuities within and across chapters.

1. How did trends in politics, economics, culture, and the arts and sciences come together to create a general sense of crisis in the 1920s and 1930s?

2. To what extent did the problems of the 1920s and 1930s have roots in the First World War (Chapter 25)?

3. What made modern art and intellectual thought "modern"?

26 REVIEW & EXPLORE

Identify Key Terms

Identify and explain the significance of each item below.

logical positivism (p. 869)

existentialism (p. 870)

theory of special relativity (p. 872)

id, ego, and superego (p. 874)

modernism (p. 874)

functionalism (p. 875)

Bauhaus (p. 875)

Dadaism (p. 878)

stream-of-consciousness technique (p. 880)

"modern girl" (p. 882)

Dawes Plan (p. 888)

Great Depression (p. 891)

Popular Front (p. 898)

Review the Main Ideas

Answer the focus questions from each section of the chapter.

◆ How did intellectual developments reflect the general crisis in Western thought? (p. 868)

◆ How did modernism revolutionize Western culture? (p. 874)

◆ How did consumer society change everyday life? (p. 881)

◆ What obstacles to lasting peace did European leaders face? (p. 886)

◆ What were the causes and consequences of the Great Depression? (p. 891)

Suggested Reading and Media Resources

BOOKS

◆ Bowler, Peter J., and Iwan Rhys Morus. *Making Modern Science: A Historical Survey.* 2005. An accessible survey covering the main developments in scientific thinking from the seventeenth to the twentieth centuries.

◆ Burrow, J. W. *The Crisis of Reason: European Thought, 1848–1914.* 2002. A rewarding intellectual history.

◆ Durozoi, Gerard, and Vincent Bouvet. *Paris Between the Wars, 1919–1939: Art, Life, and Culture.* 2010. A cultural history of the Parisian avant-garde in a defining period and place for Western art.

◆ Eksteins, Modris. *Rites of Spring: The Great War and the Birth of the Modern Age.* 1989. A penetrating analysis of the links between World War I and modern culture and politics.

◆ Ezra, Elizabeth, ed. *European Cinema.* 2004. A concise history of European cinema from its origins to the present.

◆ Gay, Peter. *Modernism: The Lure of Heresy.* 2008. An encyclopedic compendium by a renowned cultural historian that covers modernism in arts and culture from the mid-nineteenth century to the 1960s.

◆ Jackson, Julian. *The Popular Front in France: Defending Democracy, 1934–38.* 1990. Explores the rise and fall of the political, social, and cultural aspects of the Popular Front.

◆ Mazower, Mark. *Dark Continent: Europe's Twentieth Century.* 2000. A sophisticated survey that pays close attention to the crises of the interwar era.

◆ Rothermund, Dietmar. *The Global Impact of the Great Depression, 1929–1939.* 1996. A compact account that examines the causes and consequences of the Great Depression and covers events in the United States, Europe, Asia, and Latin America.

◆ Slater, Don. *Consumer Culture and Modernity.* 1997. An informative introduction to scholarly interpretations of consumer society.

* Weinbaum, Alys Eve, et al., eds. *The Modern Girl Around the World: Consumption, Modernity, and Globalization*. 2008. A collection of essays on how the "modern girl" of the 1920s and 1930s challenged conventions in major cities across the globe.
* Weitz, Eric D. *Weimar Germany: Promise and Tragedy*. 2007. A thorough exploration of modern art, culture, and politics in interwar Germany.

DOCUMENTARIES

* *Picasso and Braque Go to the Movies* (Arne Glimcher, 2010). This film depicts the influence of early film making on modern art—especially Cubism.
* *Triumph of the Will* (Leni Riefenstahl, 1935). A chilling Nazi propaganda film that covers the 1934 Nuremberg rally and demonstrates the new political possibilities of the mass media.

FEATURE FILMS

* *The Artist* (Michel Hazanavicius, 2011). A romantic tale of two actors who must grapple with the end of the silent film era and the emergence of talking films. Winner of the 2012 Academy Award for Best Picture.
* *The Grapes of Wrath* (John Ford, 1940). Set in the United States during the 1930s, this famous film adaptation of John Steinbeck's novel shows the suffering of a family displaced by the Great Depression.
* *Metropolis* (Fritz Lang, 1927). Famous for its early use of special effects, this silent sci-fi classic from UFA studios in Berlin portrays a working-class revolution in a city of the future.

* *The Rules of the Game* (Jean Renoir, 1939). A favorite of cinema buffs, this dark comedy portrays the banality and corruption of the French aristocracy and subtly anticipates the brutality of the Second World War.
* *Un Chien Andalou* (Luis Buñuel, 1929). Written by Buñuel and his Surrealist collaborator Salvador Dalí, this short silent film is a Surrealist classic that seems to portray the Freudian, dreamlike fantasies of a young man. The sixteen-minute film is available free online at several Web sites.

WEB SITES

* *Internet Encyclopedia of Philosophy: Friedrich Nietzsche*. Provides a look at the life and theories of Friedrich Nietzsche. **www.iep.utm.edu/nietzsch**
* *Internet Encyclopedia of Philosophy: Sigmund Freud*. Examines the life and theories of Sigmund Freud. **www.iep.utm.edu/freud**
* *Modernism: Searching for Utopia*. The Victoria and Albert Museum of Art and Design offers an overview of modernist experimentation and links to primary and secondary sources, focused on modernism in material culture, the decorative arts, and architecture. **www.vam.ac.uk/content/articles/m/modernism/**

27

Dictatorships and the Second World War

1919–1945

The intense wave of artistic and cultural innovation in the 1920s and 1930s, which shook the foundations of Western thought, was paralleled by radical developments in the realm of politics. In the age of anxiety, Communist and Fascist states undertook determined assaults on democratic government and individual rights across Europe. On the eve of the Second World War, popularly elected governments survived only in Great Britain, France, Czechoslovakia, the Low Countries, Scandinavia, and Switzerland.

Totalitarian regimes in the Communist Soviet Union, Fascist Italy, and Nazi Germany practiced a ruthless and dynamic tyranny. Their attempts to revolutionize state and society went far beyond traditional forms of conservative authoritarianism. Communist and Fascist states ruled with unprecedented severity. They promised to greatly improve the lives of ordinary citizens and intervened radically in those lives in pursuit of utopian schemes of social engineering. Their drive for territorial expansion threatened neighboring nations. The human costs of these policies were appalling. Millions died as Stalin forced communism on the Soviet Union in the 1930s. Attempts to build a "racially pure" New Order in Europe by Hitler's Nazi Germany led to the deaths of tens of millions more in World War II and the Holocaust, a scale of destruction far beyond that of World War I.

Such brutalities may seem a thing of the distant past that "can't happen again." Yet horrible atrocities in Rwanda, Bosnia, and Sudan show that they continue to plague the world in our time. It remains vital that we understand Europe's era of overwhelming violence in order to guard against the possibility of its recurrence in the future. ■

CHAPTER PREVIEW

Life at Auschwitz

This rough painting by an anonymous inmate of the Auschwitz-Birkenau Nazi concentration camp is preserved on the ceiling of a camp barracks. Guarded by SS officers, prisoners labor on a drainage canal under the worst conditions, while two carry a dead worker off the field. (De Agostini/ Getty Images)

Authoritarian States

FOCUS QUESTION *How were Fascist and Communist totalitarian dictatorships similar and different?*

Both conservative and radical dictatorships took power in Europe in the 1920s and 1930s. Although these two types of dictatorship shared some characteristics, in essence they were quite different. Conservative authoritarian regimes, which had a long history in Europe, were limited in scope. Radical totalitarian dictatorships, based on the ideologies of communism and fascism, were a new and frightening development aimed at the radical reconstruction of society.

Conservative Authoritarianism and Radical Totalitarian Dictatorships

The traditional form of antidemocratic government in European history was conservative authoritarianism. Like Catherine the Great in Russia and Metternich in Austria, the leaders of such governments relied on obedient state bureaucracies in their efforts to control society. Though political opponents were often jailed or exiled, these older authoritarian governments were limited in both power and objectives. They had neither the ability nor the desire to control many aspects of their subjects' lives. As long as the people did not try to change the system, they were typically allowed considerable personal independence.

After the First World War, authoritarianism revived, especially in eastern Europe. What emerged, however, were new kinds of radical dictatorship that went much further than conservative authoritarianism, particularly in the Soviet Union, Germany, and Italy. In addition, both Communist and Fascist political parties became well established in all major European nations and mounted challenges to democratic rule.

Some scholars use the term **totalitarianism** to describe these radical dictatorships, which made unprecedented "total claims" on the beliefs and behavior of their citizens. The totalitarian model emphasizes the characteristics that Fascist and Communist dictatorships had in common. One-party totalitarian states used violent political repression and intense propaganda to gain

complete power. In addition, the state tried to dominate the economic, social, intellectual, and cultural aspects of people's lives.

Most historians agree that totalitarianism owed much to the experience of total war in 1914 to 1918 (see Chapter 25). World War I required state governments to limit individual liberties and intervene in the economy in order to achieve one supreme objective: victory. Totalitarian leaders were inspired by the example of the modern state at war. They showed a callous disregard for human life and greatly expanded the power of the state in pursuit of social control.

Communist and Fascist dictatorships shared other characteristics. Both rejected parliamentary government and liberal values. Classical liberals (see Chapter 21) sought to limit the power of the state and protect the rights of the individual. Totalitarians, on the other hand, believed that individualism undermined equality and unity, and rejected democracy in favor of one-party political systems.

A charismatic leader typically dominated the totalitarian state—Stalin in the Soviet Union, Mussolini in Italy, Hitler in Germany. All three created political parties of a new kind, dedicated to promoting idealized visions of collective harmony. They used force and terror to intimidate and destroy political opponents and pursued policies of imperial expansion to exploit other lands. They censored the mass media and instituted propaganda campaigns to advance their goals. Finally, and perhaps most important, totalitarian governments engaged in massive projects of state-controlled social engineering dedicated to replacing individualism with a unified "people" capable of exercising the collective will.

Communism and Fascism

Communism and fascism clearly shared a desire to revolutionize state and society. Yet some scholars—arguing that the differences between the two systems are more important than the similarities—have moved beyond the totalitarian model. What were the main differences between these two systems? To answer this question, it is important to consider the way ideology, or a guiding political philosophy, was linked to the use of state-sponsored repression and violence.

Following Marx, Soviet Communists strove to create an international brotherhood of workers. In the Communist utopia ruled by the revolutionary working class, economic exploitation would supposedly disappear and society would be based on radical social equality (see Chapter 21). Under Stalinism—the name given to the Communist system during Stalin's rule—the state aggressively intervened in all walks of life to pursue this social leveling. Using brute force to destroy the upper and middle classes, the Stalinist state

■ **totalitarianism** A radical dictatorship that exercises "total claims" over the beliefs and behavior of its citizens by taking control of the economic, social, intellectual, and cultural aspects of society.

■ **fascism** A movement characterized by extreme, often expansionist nationalism; anti-socialism; a dynamic and violent leader; and glorification of war and the military.

■ **eugenics** A pseudoscientific doctrine saying the selective breeding of human beings can improve the general characteristics of a national population, which helped inspire Nazi ideas about national unity and racial exclusion and ultimately contributed to the Holocaust.

nationalized private property, pushed rapid industrialization, and collectivized agriculture (see pages 906–915).

The Fascist vision of a new society was quite different. Leaders who embraced **fascism**, such as Mussolini and Hitler, claimed that they were striving to build a new community on a national — not an international — level. Extreme nationalists, and often racists, Fascists glorified war and the military. For them, the nation was the highest embodiment of the people, and the powerful leader was the materialization of the people's collective will.

Like Communists, Fascists promised to improve the lives of ordinary workers. Fascist governments intervened in the economy, but unlike Communist regimes they did not try to level class differences and nationalize private property. Instead, they presented a vision of a community bound together by nationalism. In the ideal Fascist state, all social strata and classes would work together to build a harmonious national community.

Communists and Fascists differed in another crucial respect: the question of race. Where Communists sought to build a new world around the destruction of class differences, Fascists typically sought to build a new national community grounded in racial homogeneity. Fascists embraced the doctrine of **eugenics**, a pseudoscience that maintained that the selective breeding of human beings could improve the general characteristics of a national population. Eugenics was popular throughout the Western world in the 1920s and 1930s and was viewed by many as a legitimate social policy. But Fascists, especially the German National Socialists, or Nazis, pushed these ideas to the extreme.

Adopting a radicalized view of eugenics, the Nazis maintained that the German nation had to be "purified" of groups of people deemed "unfit" by the regime. Following state policies intended to support what they called "racial hygiene," Nazi authorities attempted to control, segregate, or eliminate those of "lesser value," including Jews, Sinti and Roma (often called Gypsies, a term that can have pejorative connotations) and other ethnic minorities, homosexuals, and people suffering from chronic mental or physical disabilities. The pursuit of "racial hygiene"

Chronology

1921	New Economic Policy (NEP) in U.S.S.R.
1922	Mussolini gains power in Italy
1924	Mussolini seizes dictatorial powers
1924–1929	Buildup of Nazi Party in Germany
1927	Stalin comes to power in U.S.S.R.
1928	Stalin's first five-year plan
1929	Lateran Agreement; start of collectivization in Soviet Union
1929–1939	Great Depression
1931	Japan invades Manchuria
1932–1933	Famine in Ukraine
1933	Hitler appointed chancellor in Germany; Reichstag passes the Enabling Act, granting Hitler absolute dictatorial power
1935	Nuremberg Laws deprive Jews of citizenship rights
1936	Start of great purges under Stalin; Spanish Civil War begins
1937	Japanese army invades China
1938	Kristallnacht marks beginning of more aggressive anti-Jewish policy in Germany
1939	Germany occupies Czech lands and invades western Poland; Britain and France declare war on Germany, starting World War II; Soviet Union occupies eastern Poland
1940	Germany defeats and occupies France; Battle of Britain begins
1941	Germany invades U.S.S.R.; Japan attacks Pearl Harbor; United States enters war
1941–1945	The Holocaust
1942–1943	Battle of Stalingrad
1944	Allied invasion at Normandy
1945	Soviet and U.S. forces enter Germany; United States drops atomic bombs on Japan; World War II ends

ultimately led to the Holocaust, the attempt to purge Germany and Europe of all Jews and other undesirable groups by mass killing during World War II (see page 932). Though the Soviets readily persecuted specific ethnic groups they believed were disloyal to the Communist state, in general they justified these attacks using ideologies of class rather than race or biology.

Perhaps because both championed the overthrow of existing society, Communists and Fascists were sworn

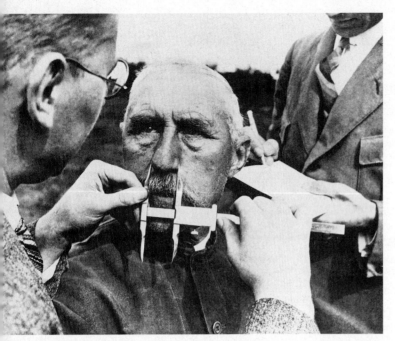

Eugenics in Nazi Germany Nazi "race scientists" believed they could use the eugenic methods of social engineering to build a powerful Aryan race. In this photograph, published in a popular magazine in 1933, a clinician measures a man's nose. Such pseudoscientific methods were used to determine an individual's supposed "racial value." (© Hulton-Deutsch Collection/Corbis)

Stalin's Soviet Union

FOCUS QUESTION *How did Stalin and the Communist Party build a totalitarian state in the Soviet Union?*

Lenin's harshest critics claim that he established the basic outlines of a modern totalitarian dictatorship after the Bolshevik Revolution and during the Russian civil war. If so, Joseph Stalin (1879–1953) certainly finished the job. A master of political infighting, Stalin cautiously consolidated his power and eliminated his enemies in the mid-1920s. Then in 1928, as undisputed leader of the ruling Communist Party, Stalin launched the first **five-year plan**—the "revolution from above," as he aptly termed it—the beginning of a radical attempt to transform Soviet society into a Communist state. The ultimate goal of this immensely ambitious effort was to generate new attitudes, new loyalties, and a new socialist humanity. The means were constant propaganda, enormous sacrifice by the people, harsh repression that included purges and executions, and rewards for those who followed the party line. Thus the Soviet Union in the 1930s became a dynamic totalitarian state.

From Lenin to Stalin

By spring 1921 Lenin and the Bolsheviks had won the civil war, but they ruled a shattered and devastated land. Many farms were in ruins, and food supplies were exhausted. In southern Russia, drought combined with the ravages of war to produce the worst famine in generations. Industrial production had broken down completely. In the face of economic disintegration, riots by peasants and workers, and an open rebellion by previously pro-Bolshevik sailors at Kronstadt, Lenin was tough but, as ever, flexible. He repressed the Kronstadt rebels, and in March 1921 he replaced War Communism with the **New Economic Policy (NEP)**, which re-established limited economic freedom in an attempt to rebuild agriculture and industry. During the civil war, the Bolsheviks had simply seized grain without payment. Now peasant producers were permitted to sell their surpluses in free markets, and private traders and small handicraft manufacturers were allowed to reappear. Heavy industry, railroads, and banks, however, remained wholly nationalized.

The NEP was a political and economic success. Politically, it was a necessary but temporary compromise with the Soviet Union's overwhelming peasant majority. Realizing that his government was not strong enough to take land from the peasants and turn them into state workers, Lenin made a deal with the only force capable of overturning his government. The

enemies. The result was a clash of ideologies, which was in large part responsible for the horrific destruction and loss of life in the middle of the twentieth century. Explaining the nature of totalitarian dictatorships thus remains a crucial project for historians, even as they look more closely at the ideological differences between communism and fascism.

One important set of questions explores the way dictatorial regimes generated popular consensus. Neither Hitler nor Stalin ever achieved the total control each sought. Nor did they rule alone; modern dictators need the help of large state bureaucracies and the cooperation of large numbers of ordinary people. Which was more important for generating popular support: terror and coercion or material rewards? Under what circumstances did people resist or perpetrate totalitarian tyranny? These questions lead us toward what Holocaust survivor Primo Levi called the "gray zone" of moral compromise, which defined everyday life in totalitarian societies. (See "Individuals in Society: Primo Levi," at right.)

■ **five-year plan** A plan launched by Stalin in 1928, and termed the "revolution from above," aimed at modernizing the Soviet Union and creating a new Communist society with new attitudes, new loyalties, and a new socialist humanity.

■ **New Economic Policy (NEP)** Lenin's 1921 policy to re-establish limited economic freedom in an attempt to rebuild agriculture and industry in the face of economic disintegration.

Primo Levi never stopped thinking, writing, and speaking about the Holocaust.
(© Gianni Giansanti/ Sygma/Corbis)

Most Jews deported to Auschwitz-Birkenau were murdered soon after arriving, but the Nazis used some prisoners as slave laborers, and a few of them survived. Primo Levi (1919–1987), one of these laborers, lived to become one of the most influential witnesses to the Holocaust.

Like much of Italy's small Jewish community, Levi's family belonged to the urban professional classes. Levi graduated from the University of Turin with highest honors in chemistry in 1941. Growing discrimination against Italian Jews led him to join the antifascist resistance two years later. Captured, he was deported to Auschwitz with 650 Italian Jews in February 1944. Stone-faced SS men picked 96 men, Levi among them, and 29 women from this group to work in labor camps; the rest were gassed upon arrival.

Levi and his fellow prisoners were kicked, punched, stripped, branded with tattoos, crammed into huts, and worked unmercifully. Hoping for some prisoner solidarity, Levi found only a desperate struggle of each against all and enormous status differences among prisoners. Many bewildered newcomers, beaten and demoralized by their bosses — the most privileged prisoners — collapsed and died. Others struggled to secure their own privileges, however small, because food rations and working conditions were so abominable that prisoners who were not bosses usually perished in two to three months.

Sensitive and noncombative, Levi found himself sinking into oblivion. But instead of joining the mass of the "drowned," he became one of the "saved" — a complicated surprise with moral implications that he would ponder all his life. As Levi explained in *Survival in Auschwitz* (1947), the usual road to salvation in the camps was some kind of collaboration with German power. Savage German criminals were released from prison to become brutal camp guards; non-Jewish political prisoners competed for jobs entitling them to better conditions; and, especially troubling for Levi, a few Jews plotted and struggled to gain the power of life and death over other Jewish prisoners.

Though not one of these Jewish bosses, Levi believed that he, like almost all survivors, had entered the "gray zone" of moral compromise. "Nobody can know for how long and under what trials his soul can resist before yielding or breaking," Levi wrote. "The harsher the oppression, the more widespread among the oppressed is the willingness, with all its infinite nuances and motivations, to collaborate."* The camps held no saints, he believed: the Nazi system degraded its victims, forcing them to commit sometimes-bestial acts against their fellow prisoners in order to survive.

For Levi, salvation came from his education. Interviewed by a German technocrat for work in the camp's synthetic rubber program, Levi was chosen for this relatively easy labor because he spoke fluent German, including scientific terminology. Work in the warm camp laboratory offered Levi opportunities to pilfer equipment he could then trade to other prisoners for food and necessities. Levi also gained critical support from three prisoners who refused to do wicked and hateful acts. And he counted luck as essential for his survival: in the camp infirmary with scarlet fever in February 1945 as advancing Russian armies prepared to liberate the camp, Levi was not evacuated by the Nazis and shot to death like most Jewish prisoners.

After the war, Levi was haunted by the nightmare that the Holocaust would be ignored or forgotten. Ashamed that so many people whom he considered better than himself had perished, and wanting the world to understand the genocide in all its complexity so that people would never again tolerate such atrocities, he turned to writing about his experiences. Primo Levi, while revealing Nazi guilt, tirelessly grappled with his vision of individual responsibility and moral ambiguity in a hell designed to make the victims collaborate and persecute each other.

QUESTIONS FOR ANALYSIS

1. Describe Levi's experience at Auschwitz. How did camp prisoners treat each other? Why?
2. What does Levi mean by the "gray zone"?
3. Will a vivid historical memory of the Holocaust help prevent future genocide?

*Primo Levi, *The Drowned and the Saved* (New York: Vintage, 1989), pp. 43, 60. See also Levi, *Survival in Auschwitz: The Nazi Assault on Humanity* (London: Collier Books, 1961). These powerful testimonies are highly recommended.

NEP brought rapid economic recovery, and by 1926 industrial output surpassed, and agricultural production almost equaled, prewar levels.

In 1924, as the economy recovered and the government partially relaxed its censorship and repression, Lenin died without a chosen successor, creating an intense struggle for power in the inner circles of the Communist Party. The principal contenders were Stalin and Trotsky. Joseph Dzhugashvili (joo-guhsh-VEEL-yih)—later known as Stalin (from the Russian for "steel")—was a good organizer but a poor speaker and writer, and he had no experience outside of Russia. Trotsky, a great and inspiring leader who had planned the 1917 Bolshevik takeover and then created the victorious Red Army, appeared to have all the advantages in the power struggle. Yet Stalin won because he was more effective at gaining the all-important support of the party. Having risen to general secretary of the party's Central Committee in 1922, he used his office to win friends and allies with jobs and promises.

Stalin also won because he was better able to relate Marxist teaching to Soviet realities in the 1920s. Stalin developed a theory of "socialism in one country" that was more appealing to the majority of party members than Trotsky's doctrine of "permanent revolution." Stalin argued that the Russian-dominated Soviet Union had the ability to build socialism on its own. Trotsky maintained that socialism in the Soviet Union could succeed only if a socialist revolution swept throughout Europe. To many Russian Communists, this view sold their country short and promised risky conflicts with capitalist countries. Stalin's willingness to revoke NEP reforms furthermore appealed to young party militants, who detested the NEP's reliance on capitalist free markets.

Stalin's ascendancy had a momentous impact on the policy of the new Soviet state toward non-Russians.

The Communists had inherited the vast multiethnic territories of the former Russian Empire. Lenin initially argued that these ethnic groups should have the right to self-determination even if they claimed independence from the Soviet state. In 1922, reflecting such ideas, the Union of Soviet Socialist Republics (or U.S.S.R.) was organized as a federation of four Soviet republics: the Russian Soviet Federative Socialist Republic, Ukraine, Belorussia, and a Transcaucasian republic. The last was later split into Armenia, Azerbaijan, and Georgia, and five Central Asian republics were established in the 1920s and 1930s (Map 27.1).

In contrast to Lenin, Stalin argued for more centralized Russian control of these ethnic regions. His view would dominate state policy until the breakup of the Soviet Union in the early 1990s. The Soviet republics were granted some cultural independence but no true political autonomy. Party leaders allowed the use of non-Russian languages in regional schools and government institutions, but the right to secede was a fiction, and real authority remained in Moscow, in the hands of the Russian Communist Party. The Stalinists thus established a far-flung Communist empire on the imperial holdings of the former tsars.

With cunning skill, Stalin achieved supreme power between 1922 and 1927. First he allied with Trotsky's personal enemies to crush his rival, and then he moved against all who might challenge his ascendancy, including former allies. Stalin's final triumph came at the party congress of December 1927, which condemned all "deviation from the general party line" that he had formulated. The dictator and his followers were ready to launch the revolution from above, radically changing the lives of millions of people.

Ethnic Minorities in the U.S.S.R. The Soviet Union inherited the vast and diverse territories of the former Russian Empire. In this propaganda poster, titled "The Great Stalin Is the Banner of Friendship Between the Peoples of the U.S.S.R.!" the Soviet dictator receives flowers from a diverse group of Soviet citizens, including ethnic Russians and East and Central Asians. This idealized testament to peaceful coexistence within the Soviet empire masked the tensions aroused by Russian domination. How does this poster represent the relationship between Stalin and the Soviet people? (rps—ullstein-bild/ Granger, NYC—All rights reserved)

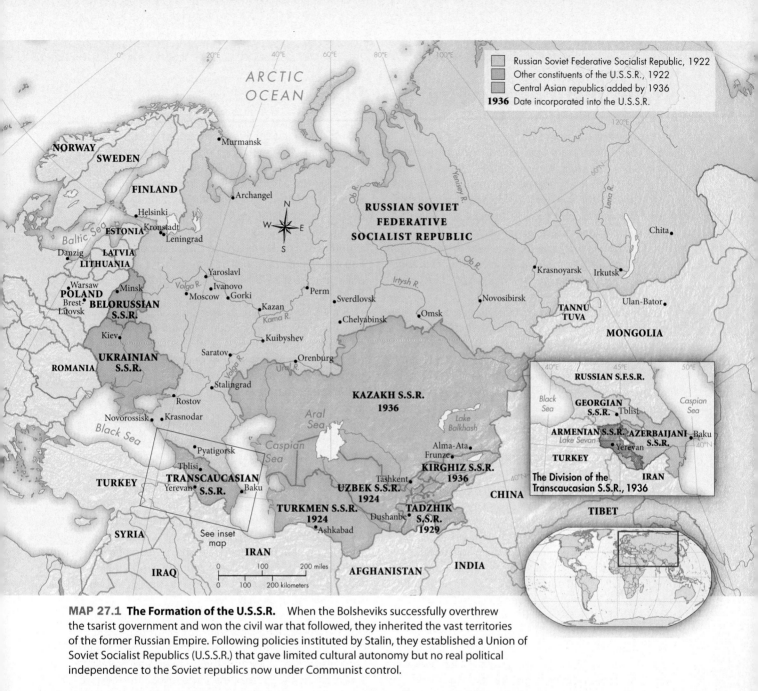

MAP 27.1 The Formation of the U.S.S.R. When the Bolsheviks successfully overthrew the tsarist government and won the civil war that followed, they inherited the vast territories of the former Russian Empire. Following policies instituted by Stalin, they established a Union of Soviet Socialist Republics (U.S.S.R.) that gave limited cultural autonomy but no real political independence to the Soviet republics now under Communist control.

The Five-Year Plans

The party congress of 1927, which ratified Stalin's consolidation of power, marked the end of the NEP. The following year marked the beginning of the era of socialist five-year plans. The first of these plans had staggering economic objectives. In just five years, total industrial output was to increase by 250 percent, with heavy industry, the preferred sector, growing even faster. Agricultural production was slated to increase by 150 percent, and one-fifth of the peasants in the Soviet Union were to give up their private plots and join collective farms.

Stalin unleashed his "second revolution" for a variety of interrelated reasons. There were, first of all, ideological considerations. Stalin and his militant supporters were deeply committed to socialism as they understood

it. They feared a gradual restoration of capitalism and wished to promote the working classes. Moreover, Communist leaders were eager to abolish the NEP's private traders, independent artisans, and property-owning peasants. Economic motivations were also important. A fragile economic recovery stalled in 1927 and 1928, and a new offensive seemed necessary to ensure industrial and agricultural growth. Such economic development would allow the U.S.S.R. to catch up with the West and so overcome traditional Russian "backwardness." (See "Evaluating the Evidence 27.1: Stalin Justifies the Five-Year Plan," page 910.)

The independent peasantry remained a major problem as well. For centuries the peasants had wanted to own the land, and finally they had it. Sooner or later, Stalinists reasoned, landowning peasants would embrace conservative capitalism and pose a threat to the regime.

Stalin Justifies the Five-Year Plan

On February 4, 1931, Joseph Stalin delivered the following address, titled "No Slowdown in Tempo!" to the First Conference of Soviet Industrial Managers. Published the following day in Pravda, *the newspaper of the Communist Party, and widely publicized at home and abroad, Stalin's speech reaffirmed the leader's commitment to the breakneck pace of industrialization and collectivization set forth in the first five-year plan. Arguing that more sacrifices were necessary, Stalin sought to rally the people and generate support for the party's program. His address captures the spirit of Soviet ideology in the early 1930s.*

Stalin's concluding idea, that Bolsheviks needed to master technology and industrial management, reflected another major development. The Soviet Union was training a new class of Communist engineers and technicians, who were beginning to replace foreign engineers and "bourgeois specialists," Russian engineers trained in tsarist times who were grudgingly tolerated in the first years after the revolution.

It is sometimes asked whether it is not possible to slow down the tempo somewhat, to put a check on the movement. No, comrades, it is not possible! The tempo must not be reduced! On the contrary, we must increase it as much as is within our powers and possibilities. This is dictated to us by our obligations to the workers and peasants of the U.S.S.R. This is dictated to us by our obligations to the working class of the whole world.

To slacken the tempo would mean falling behind. And those who fall behind get beaten. But we do not want to be beaten. No, we refuse to be beaten! One feature of the history of old Russia was the continual beatings she suffered because of her backwardness. She was beaten by the Mongol khans, . . . the Turkish beys, . . . and the Japanese barons. All beat her — because of her backwardness, cultural backwardness, political backwardness, industrial backwardness, agricultural backwardness. They beat her because to do so was profitable and could be done with impunity. . . . Such is the law of the exploiters — to beat the backward and the weak. It is the jungle law of capitalism. You are backward, you are weak — therefore you are wrong; hence you can be beaten and enslaved. You are mighty — therefore you are right; hence we must be wary of you. That is why we must no longer lag behind.

In the past we had no fatherland, nor could we have had one. But now that we have overthrown capitalism and power is in our hands, in the hands of the people, we have a fatherland, and we will uphold its independence. Do you want our socialist fatherland to be beaten and to lose its independence?

If you do not want this, you must put an end to its backwardness in the shortest possible time and develop a genuine Bolshevik tempo in building up its socialist economy. There is no other way. That is why Lenin said on the eve of the October Revolution: "Either perish, or overtake and outstrip the advanced capitalist countries."

We are fifty or a hundred years behind the advanced countries. We must make good this distance in ten years. Either we do it, or we shall go under. That is what our obligations to the workers and peasants of the U.S.S.R. dictate to us.

But we have yet other, more serious and more important, obligations. They are our obligations to the world proletariat. . . . We achieved victory not solely through the efforts of the working class of the U.S.S.R., but also thanks to the support of the working class of the world. Without this support we would have been torn to pieces long ago. . . .

Why does the international proletariat support us? How did we merit this support? By the fact that we were the first to hurl ourselves into the battle against capitalism, we were the first to establish working-class state power, we were the first to begin building socialism. By the fact that we are engaged on a cause which, if successful, will transform the whole world and free the entire working class. But what is needed for success? The elimination of our backwardness, the development of a high Bolshevik tempo of construction. We must march forward in such a way that the working class of the whole world, looking at us, may say:

There you have my advanced detachment, my shock brigade, my working-class state power, my fatherland; they are engaged on their cause, *our* cause, and they are working well; let us support them against the capitalists and promote the cause of the world revolution. Must we not justify the hopes of the world's working class, must we not fulfill our obligations to them? Yes, we must if we do not want to utterly disgrace ourselves.

Such are our obligations, internal and international.

As you see, they dictate to us a Bolshevik tempo of development.

I will not say that we have accomplished nothing in regard to management of production during these years. In fact, we have accomplished a good deal. . . . But we could have accomplished still more if we had tried during this period really to master production, the technique of production, the financial and economic side of it. In ten years at most we must make good the distance that separates us from the advanced capitalist countries. We have all the "objective" possibilities for this. The only thing lacking is the ability to make proper use of these possibilities.

And that depends on us. *Only* on us! . . . If you are a factory manager—interfere in all the affairs of the factory, look into everything, let nothing escape you, learn and learn again. Bolsheviks must master technique. It is time Bolsheviks themselves became experts. . . .

It is said that it is hard to master technique. That is not true! There are no fortresses that Bolsheviks cannot capture. We have solved a number of most difficult problems. We have overthrown capitalism. We have assumed power.

We have built up a huge socialist industry. We have transferred the middle peasants on the path of socialism. We have already accomplished what is most important from the point of view of construction. What remains to be done is not so much: to study technique, to master science. And when we have done that we shall develop a tempo of which we dare not even dream at present. And we shall do it if we really want to.

EVALUATE THE EVIDENCE

1. What reasons does Stalin give to justify an unrelenting "Bolshevik" tempo of industrial and social change? In the light of history, which reason seems most convincing? Why?

2. Imagine that the year is 1931 and you are a Soviet student reading Stalin's speech. Would Stalin's determination inspire you, frighten you, or leave you cold? Why?

3. Some historians argue that Soviet socialism was a kind of utopianism, where the economy, the society, and even human beings could be completely remade and perfected. What utopian elements do you see in Stalin's declaration?

Source: Joseph Stalin, "No Slowdown in Tempo!" *Pravda*, February 5, 1931, excerpted from "Reading No. 14" in *Soviet Economic Development: Operation Outstrip, 1921–1965*, by Anatole G. Mazour.

At the same time, the Communists—mainly urban dwellers—believed that the feared and despised "class enemy" in the villages could be squeezed to provide the enormous sums needed for all-out industrialization.

To resolve these issues, in 1929 Stalin ordered the **collectivization of agriculture**—the forced consolidation of individual peasant farms into large, state-controlled enterprises that served as agricultural factories. Peasants across the Soviet Union were compelled to move off their small plots onto large state-run farms, where their tools, livestock, and produce would be held in common and central planners could control all work.

The increasingly repressive measures instituted by the state first focused on the **kulaks**, the class of well-off peasants who had benefited the most from the NEP. The kulaks were small in number, but propagandists cast them as the great enemy of progress. Stalin called for their "liquidation" and seizure of their property. Stripped of land and livestock, many starved or were deported to forced-labor camps for "re-education."

Forced collectivization led to disaster. Large numbers of peasants opposed to the change slaughtered their animals and burned their crops rather than turn them over to state commissars. Between 1929 and 1933 the number of horses, cattle, sheep, and goats in the Soviet Union fell by at least half. Nor were the state-controlled collective farms more productive. The output of grain barely increased over the first five-year plan, and collectivized agriculture was unable to make any substantial financial contribution to Soviet industrial development in the first five-year plan.

Collectivization in the fertile farmlands of the Ukraine was more rapid and violent than in other Soviet territories. The drive against peasants snowballed into an assault on Ukrainians in general, who had sought independence from Soviet rule after the First World War. Stalin and his associates viewed this peasant resistance as an expression of unacceptable anti-Soviet nationalism. In 1932, as collectivization and deportations continued, party leaders set levels of grain deliveries for the Ukrainian collectives at excessively high levels and refused to relax those quotas or allow food relief when Ukrainian Communist leaders reported that starvation was occurring. The result was a terrible man-made famine in Ukraine in 1932 and 1933, which claimed 3 to 3.5 million lives. (See "Evaluating the Evidence 27.2: Famine and Recovery on a Soviet Collective Farm," page 912.)

Collectivization was a cruel but real victory for Stalinist ideologues. Though millions died, by the end of 1938 government representatives had moved 93

■ **collectivization of agriculture** The forcible consolidation of individual peasant farms into large state-controlled enterprises in the Soviet Union under Stalin.

■ **kulaks** The better-off peasants who were stripped of land and livestock under Stalin and were generally not permitted to join collective farms; many of them starved or were deported to forced-labor camps for "re-education."

Famine and Recovery on a Soviet Collective Farm

Fedor Belov describes daily life on a kolkhoz, or collective farm, in the Soviet Ukraine during the famine of the early 1930s and the recovery that followed. Belov, a former collective farm chairman, fled the Soviet Union for the West, where he published this critical account in 1955.

In these kolkhozes the great bulk of the land was held and worked communally, but each peasant household owned a house of some sort, a small plot of ground and perhaps some livestock. All the members of the kolkhoz were required to work on the kolkhoz a certain number of days each month; the rest of the time they were allowed to work on their own holdings. They derived their income partly from what they grew on their garden strips and partly from their work in the kolkhoz. . . .

By late 1932 more than 80 per cent of the peasant households in the raion [district] had been collectivized. . . . That year the peasants harvested a good crop and had hopes that the calculations would work out to their advantage and would help strengthen them economically. These hopes were in vain. The kolkhoz workers received only 200 grams of flour per labor day for the first half of the year; the remaining grain, including the seed fund, was taken by the government. The peasants were told that industrialization of the country, then in full swing, demanded grain and sacrifices from them.

That autumn the "red broom" [government agents who requisitioned grain] passed over the kolkhozes and the individual plots, sweeping the . . . "surpluses," [and] everything was collected. . . . As a result, famine, which was to become intense by the spring of 1933, already began to be felt in the fall of 1932.

The famine of 1932–1933 was the most terrible and destructive that the Ukrainian people have ever experienced. The peasants ate dogs, horses, rotten potatoes, the bark of trees, grass — anything they could find. Incidents of cannibalism were not uncommon. The people were like wild beasts, ready to devour one another. And no matter what they did, they went on dying, dying, dying. . . .

There was no one to gather the bumper crop of 1933, since the people who remained alive were too weak and exhausted. More than a hundred persons — office and factory workers from Leningrad — were sent to assist on the kolkhoz; two representatives of the Party arrived to help organize the harvesting. . . .

That summer (1933) the entire administration of the kolkhoz — the bookkeeper, the warehouseman, the manager of the flour mill, and even the chairman himself — were put on trial on charges of plundering the kolkhoz property and produce. All the accused were sentenced to terms of seven to ten years, and a new administration was elected. . . .

After 1934 a gradual improvement began in the economic life of the kolkhoz and its members. . . . In general, from the mid-1930s until 1941, the majority of kolkhoz members in the Ukraine lived relatively well.

EVALUATE THE EVIDENCE

1. How did party leaders respond to widespread starvation? Did government policy contribute to the intensity of the famine in 1932?
2. How did the organization of the collective farm express the basic ideas of communist ideology?

Source: *History of a Soviet Collective Farm* by Fedor Belov, Research Program on the USSR (Praeger, 1955). Reproduced with permission of PRAEGER in the format Republish in a book via Copyright Clearance Center.

percent of peasant households onto collective farms, neutralizing them as a political threat. Nonetheless, peasant resistance had forced the supposedly all-powerful state to make modest concessions. Peasants secured the right to limit a family's labor on the state-run farms and to cultivate tiny family plots, which provided them with much of their food. In 1938 these family plots produced 22 percent of all Soviet agricultural produce on only 4 percent of all cultivated land.

The rapid industrialization mandated by the five-year plans was more successful — indeed, quite spectacular. A huge State Planning Commission, the "Gosplan," was created to set production goals and control deliveries of raw and finished materials. This was a complex and difficult task, and production bottlenecks and slowdowns often resulted. In addition, Stalinist planning favored heavy industry over the production of consumer goods, which led to shortages of basic necessities. Despite such problems, Soviet industry produced about four times as much in 1937 as it had in 1928. No other major country had ever achieved such rapid industrial growth.

Steel was the idol of the Stalinist age. The Soviet state needed heavy machinery for rapid development, and an industrial labor force was created almost overnight as peasant men and women began working in the huge steel mills built across the country. Independent trade unions lost most of their power. The government could assign workers to any job anywhere in the U.S.S.R., and an internal passport system ensured that individuals could move only with permission. When factory managers needed more hands, they called on their counterparts on the collective farms, who sent them millions of "unneeded" peasants over the years. Rapid industrial growth led to urban development: more than 25 million people, mostly peasants, migrated to cities during the 1930s.

The new workers often lived in deplorable conditions in hastily built industrial cities such as Magnitogorsk (Magnetic Mountain City) in the Ural Mountains. Yet they also experienced some benefits of upward mobility. In a letter published in the Magnitogorsk newspaper, an ordinary electrician described the opportunities created by rapid industrialization:

> In old tsarist Russia, we weren't even considered people. We couldn't dream about education, or getting a job in a state enterprise. And now I'm a citizen of the U.S.S.R. Like all citizens I have the right to a job, to education, to leisure. . . . In 1931, I came to Magnitogorsk. From a common laborer I have turned into a skilled worker. . . . I live in a country where one feels like living and learning. And if the enemy should attack this country, I will sacrifice my life in order to destroy the enemy and save my country.[1]

We should read such words with care, since they appeared in a state-censored publication. Yet the enthusiasm was at least partly authentic. The great industrialization drive of 1928 to 1937 was an awe-inspiring achievement, purchased at enormous sacrifice on the part of ordinary Soviet citizens.

Life and Culture in Soviet Society

Daily life was difficult in Stalin's Soviet Union. The lack of housing was a particularly serious problem. Millions were moving into the cities, but the government built few new apartments. A relatively lucky family received one room for all its members and shared both a kitchen and a toilet with others living on the same floor.

There were constant shortages of goods as well. Because consumption was reduced to pay for investment, there was little improvement in the average standard of living in the years before World War II. The average nonfarm wage purchased only about half as many goods in 1932 as it had in 1928. After 1932 real wages rose slowly, but by 1937 workers could still buy only about 60 percent of what they had bought in 1928 and less than they could purchase in 1913. Collectivized peasants experienced greater hardships.

Life was by no means hopeless, however. Idealism and ideology had real appeal for many Communists and ordinary citizens, who saw themselves heroically building the world's first socialist society while capitalism crumbled in a worldwide depression and degenerated into fascism in the West. This optimistic belief in the future of the Soviet Union attracted many disillusioned Westerners to communism in the 1930s. On a more practical level, Soviet workers received important social benefits, such as old-age pensions, free medical services, free education, and day-care centers for children. Unemployment was almost unknown.

Communism also opened possibilities for personal advancement. Rapid industrialization required massive numbers of skilled workers, engineers, and plant managers. In the 1930s the Stalinist state broke with the egalitarian policies of the 1920s and offered tremendous incentives to those who could serve its needs. It paid the mass of unskilled workers and collective farmers very low wages, but provided high salaries and special privileges to its growing technical and managerial elite. This group joined with the political and artistic elites in a new upper class, whose members grew rich and powerful.

The radical transformation of Soviet society had a profound impact on women's lives. Marxists had traditionally believed that both capitalism and middle-class husbands exploited women, and the Russian Revolution of 1917 immediately proclaimed complete equality for women. In the 1920s divorce and abortion were made easily available, and women were urged to work outside the home. After Stalin came to power, he reversed this trend. The government revoked many laws supporting women's emancipation in order to strengthen the traditional family and build up the state's population.

At the same time, women saw lasting changes in education. The Soviets opened higher education to women, who could now enter the ranks of the better-paid specialists in industry and science. Medicine practically became a woman's profession. By 1950, 75 percent of all doctors in the Soviet Union were female.

Alongside such advances, however, Soviet society demanded great sacrifices from women. The vast majority of women had to work outside the home. Wages were so low that it was almost impossible for a family or couple to live only on the husband's earnings. Peasant women continued to work on farms, and millions of women toiled in factories and in heavy construction, building dams, roads, and steel mills in summer heat and winter frost. Men continued to dominate the very best jobs. Finally, rapid change and economic hardship led to many broken families, creating further physical and emotional strains for women. In any event, the massive mobilization of women was a striking characteristic of the Soviet state.

Culture was thoroughly politicized for propaganda and indoctrination purposes. Party activists lectured workers in factories and peasants on collective farms, while newspapers, films, and radio broadcasts endlessly revealed capitalist plots and recounted socialist achievements. Whereas the 1920s had seen considerable modernist experimentation in art and theater, in the 1930s intellectuals were ordered by Stalin to become

Day Shift at Magnitogorsk
Beginning in 1928, Stalin's government issued a series of ambitious five-year plans designed to rapidly industrialize the Soviet Union. The plans focused primarily on boosting heavy industry and included the building of a gigantic steel complex at Magnitogorsk in the Ural Mountains. Here steelworkers review production goals at the Magnitogorsk foundry. (© Sovfoto/UIG via Getty Images)

"engineers of human minds." Following the dictates of "Socialist Realism," they were instructed to exalt the lives of ordinary workers and glorify Russian nationalism. Russian history was rewritten so that early tsars such as Ivan the Terrible and Peter the Great became worthy forerunners of the greatest Russian leader of all—Stalin. Writers and artists who could effectively combine genuine creativity and political propaganda became the darlings of the regime.

Stalin seldom appeared in public, but his presence was everywhere—in portraits, statues, books, and quotations from his writings. Although the government persecuted those who practiced religion and turned churches into "museums of atheism," the state had both an earthly religion and a high priest—Marxism-Leninism and Joseph Stalin.

Stalinist Terror and the Great Purges

In the mid-1930s the great offensive to build socialism and a new society culminated in ruthless police terror and a massive purging of the Communist Party. First used by the Bolsheviks in the civil war to maintain their power, terror as state policy was revived in the collectivization drive against the peasants. Top members of the party and government publicly supported Stalin's initiatives, but there was some grumbling. At a small gathering in November 1932, even Stalin's wife complained bitterly about the misery of the people and the horrible

famine in Ukraine. Stalin showered her with insults, and she committed suicide that night. In late 1934 Stalin's number-two man, Sergei Kirov, was mysteriously killed. Stalin—who probably ordered Kirov's murder—blamed the assassination on "Fascist agents" within the party. He used the incident to launch a reign of terror that purged the Communist Party of supposed traitors and solidified his own control.

Murderous repression picked up steam over the next two years. It culminated in the "great purge" of 1936 to 1938, a series of spectacular public show trials in which false evidence, often gathered using torture, was used to incriminate party administrators and Red Army leaders. In August 1936 sixteen "Old Bolsheviks"—prominent leaders who had been in the party since the Russian Revolution—confessed to all manner of contrived plots against Stalin. All were executed. In 1937 the secret police arrested a mass of lesser party officials and newer members, using torture to extract confessions and precipitating more show trials. In addition to the party faithful, union officials, managers, intellectuals, army officers, and countless ordinary citizens were accused of counter-revolutionary activities. At least 6 million people were arrested, and probably 1 to 2 million of these were executed or never returned from prisons and forced-labor camps.

Stalin's mass purges remain baffling, for most historians believe that the victims posed no threat and were innocent of their supposed crimes. Some scholars have argued that the terror was a defining characteristic of the totalitarian state, which must always fight real or imaginary enemies. Certainly the highly publicized purges sent a warning: no one was secure; everyone had to serve the party and its leader with redoubled devotion.

The long-standing interpretation that puts most of the blame for the purges on Stalin has been confirmed by recent research in newly opened Soviet archives. Apparently fearful of active resistance, Stalin and his allies used the harshest measures against their political enemies, real or imagined. Moreover, many in the general population shared such fears. Bombarded with ideology and political slogans, numerous people responded energetically to Stalin's directives. Investigations and trials snowballed into mass hysteria, resulting in a modern witch-hunt that claimed millions of victims. In this view of the 1930s, a deluded Stalin found large numbers of willing collaborators for crime as well as for achievement.[2]

The purges seriously weakened the Soviet Union in economic, intellectual, and military terms. But they left Stalin in command of a vast new state apparatus, staffed by the 1.5 million new party members enlisted to replace the purge victims. Thus more than half of all Communist Party members in 1941 had joined since the purges, and they experienced rapid social advance. Often the children of workers, they had usually studied in the new technical schools, and they soon proved capable of managing the government and large-scale production. Despite their human costs, the great purges thus brought substantial practical rewards to this new generation of committed Communists. They would serve Stalin effectively until his death in 1953, and they would govern the Soviet Union until the early 1980s.

Mussolini and Fascism in Italy

FOCUS QUESTION *What kind of government did Mussolini establish in Italy?*

Mussolini's Fascist movement and his seizure of power in 1922 were important steps in the rise of dictatorships in Europe between the two world wars. Mussolini and his supporters were the first to call themselves "Fascists" — revolutionaries determined to create a new totalitarian state based on extreme nationalism and militarism.

The Seizure of Power

In the early twentieth century, Italy was a liberal constitutional monarchy that recognized the civil rights of Italians. On the eve of World War I, the parliament granted universal male suffrage, and Italy appeared to be moving toward democracy. But there were serious

problems. Much of the Italian population was still poor, and many peasants were more attached to their villages and local interests than to the national state. Moreover, the papacy, many devout Catholics, conservatives, and landowners remained strongly opposed to liberal institutions, and relations between church and state were often tense. Class differences were also extreme, leading to the development of a powerful revolutionary socialist movement.

World War I worsened the political situation. To win support for the war effort, the Italian government had promised territorial expansion as well as social and land reform, which it could not deliver. Instead, the Versailles treaty denied Italy any territorial gains, and soaring unemployment and inflation after the war created mass hardship. In response, the Italian Socialist Party followed the Bolshevik example, and radical workers and peasants began occupying factories and seizing land in 1920. These actions mobilized the property-owning classes. Moreover, after the war the pope lifted his ban on participation by Catholics in Italian politics, and a

Mussolini and Hitler   Italian dictator Benito Mussolini and Nazi leader Adolf Hitler, in front of the Shrine of Fallen Nazis, review a military parade passing by in their honor. In September 1937 Mussolini visited Hitler in Germany to cement the Rome-Berlin Axis alliance. (Istituto Nazionale Luce/ Alinari via Getty Images)

Fascist Youth on Parade Totalitarian governments in Italy and Nazi Germany established mass youth organizations to instill the values of national unity and train young soldiers for the state. These members of the Balilla, Italy's Fascist youth organization, raise their rifles in salute at a mass rally in 1939. (© Hulton-Deutsch Collection/Corbis)

strong Catholic party quickly emerged. Thus by 1921 revolutionary socialists, conservatives, Catholics, and property owners were all opposed—though for different reasons—to the liberal government.

Into these crosscurrents of unrest and fear stepped bullying, blustering Benito Mussolini (1883–1945). Mussolini began his political career before World War I as a Socialist Party leader and radical newspaper editor. In 1914 he had urged that Italy join the Allies, a stand for which he was expelled from the Socialist Party. Returning home after being wounded at the front in 1917, Mussolini began organizing bitter war veterans like himself into a band of Fascists—from the Italian word for "a union of forces."

At first Mussolini's program was a radical combination of nationalist and socialist demands. As such, it competed directly with the well-organized Socialist

Party and failed to get off the ground. When Mussolini saw that his violent verbal assaults on rival Socialists won him growing support from conservatives and the frightened middle classes, he shifted gears in 1920 and became a sworn enemy of socialism. Mussolini and his private militia of **Black Shirts** grew increasingly violent. Few people were killed, but Socialist Party newspapers, union halls, and local headquarters were destroyed, and the Black Shirts managed to push Socialists out of city governments in northern Italy.

Fascism soon became a mass movement, one which Mussolini claimed would help the little people against the established interests. In 1922, in the midst of chaos largely created by his Black Shirt militias, Mussolini stepped forward as the savior of order and property. Striking a conservative, anticommunist note in his speeches and gaining the support of army leaders, Mussolini demanded the resignation of the existing government. In October 1922 a band of armed Fascists marched on Rome to threaten the king and force him to appoint Mussolini prime minister of Italy. The

■ **Black Shirts** Mussolini's private militia that destroyed socialist newspapers, union halls, and Socialist Party headquarters, eventually pushing Socialists out of the city governments of northern Italy.

■ **Lateran Agreement** A 1929 agreement that recognized the Vatican as an independent state, with Mussolini agreeing to give the church heavy financial support in return for public support from the pope.

threat worked. Victor Emmanuel III (r. 1900–1946)—who himself had no love for the liberal regime—asked Mussolini to take over the government and form a new cabinet. Thus, after widespread violence and a threat of armed uprising, Mussolini seized power using the legal framework of the Italian constitution.

The Regime in Action

Mussolini became prime minister in 1922, but moved cautiously in his first two years in office to establish control of the government. At first, he promised a "return to order" and consolidated his support among Italian elites. Fooled by Mussolini's apparent moderation, the Italian parliament passed a new electoral law that gave two-thirds of the representatives in the parliament to the party that won the most votes. This change allowed the Fascist Party and its allies to win an overwhelming majority in April 1924. Shortly thereafter, a group of Fascist extremists kidnapped and murdered the leading Socialist politician Giacomo Matteotti (JAHK-oh-moh mat-tee-OH-tee). Alarmed, a group of prominent parliamentary leaders demanded that Mussolini's armed squads be dissolved and all violence be banned.

Mussolini may not have ordered Matteotti's murder, but he took advantage of the resulting political crisis. Declaring his desire to "make the nation Fascist," he imposed a series of repressive measures. The government ruled by decree, abolished freedom of the press, and organized fixed elections. Mussolini arrested his political opponents, disbanded all independent labor unions, and put dedicated Fascists in control of Italy's schools. Mussolini trumpeted his goal in a famous slogan: "Everything in the state, nothing outside the state, nothing against the state." By the end of 1926 Italy was a one-party dictatorship under Mussolini's unquestioned leadership.

Mussolini's Fascist Party drew support from broad sectors of the population, in large part because he was willing to compromise with the traditional elites that controlled the army, the economy, and the state. He left big business to regulate itself, and there was no land reform. Mussolini also drew increasing support from the Catholic Church. In the **Lateran Agreement** of 1929, he recognized the Vatican as an independent state, and he agreed to give the church significant financial support in return for the pope's support. Because he was forced to compromise with these conservative elites, Mussolini never established complete totalitarian control.

Mussolini's government nonetheless proceeded with attempts to bring fascism to Italy. The state engineered popular consent by staging massive rallies and sporting events, creating Fascist youth and women's movements, and providing new welfare benefits. Newspapers, radio, and film promoted a "cult of the Duce" (leader), portraying Mussolini as a powerful strongman who embodied the best qualities of the Italian people. Like other Fascist regimes, his government was vehemently opposed to liberal feminism and promoted traditional gender roles. Mussolini also gained support by manipulating popular pride in the grand history of the ancient Roman Empire—as one propagandist put it, "Fascism, in its entirety, is the resurrection of Roman-ness."[3]

Mussolini matched his aggressive rhetoric with military action: Italian armies invaded the African nation of Ethiopia in October 1935. After surprising setbacks at the hands of the poorly armed Ethiopian army, the Italians won in 1936, and Mussolini could proudly declare that Italy again had its empire. Though it shocked international opinion, the war resulted in close ties between Italy and Nazi Germany. After a visit to Berlin in the fall of 1937, the Italian dictator pledged support for Hitler and promised that Italy and Germany would "march together right to the end."[4]

Italy's Ethiopian Campaign, 1935–1936

→ Italian campaigns, 1935–1936

Deeply influenced by Hitler's example (see below), Mussolini's government passed a series of anti-Jewish racial laws in 1938. Though the laws were unpopular, Jews were forced out of public schools and dismissed from professional careers. Nevertheless, extreme anti-Semitic persecution did not occur in Italy until late in World War II, when Italy was under Nazi control. Though Mussolini's repressive tactics were never as ruthless as those in Nazi Germany, his government did much to turn Italy into a totalitarian police state.

Hitler and Nazism in Germany

FOCUS QUESTION *What policies did Nazi Germany pursue, and how did they lead to World War II?*

The most frightening dictatorship developed in Nazi Germany. National Socialism (or Nazism) shared some characteristics with Italian fascism, but Nazism was far more interventionist. Under Hitler, the Nazi dictatorship smashed or took over most independent organizations, established firm control over the German state and society, and violently persecuted the Jewish population and non-German peoples. Truly totalitarian in aspiration, Nazi Germany acted with a dynamism, based on racial aggression and territorial expansion, that led to history's most destructive war.

The Roots of National Socialism

National Socialism grew out of many complex developments, of which the most influential were nationalism and racism. These two ideas captured the mind of the young Adolf Hitler (1889–1945), and he dominated Nazism until the end of World War II.

The son of an Austrian customs official, Hitler spent his childhood in small towns in Austria. A mediocre student, Hitler dropped out of high school at age fourteen. He then moved to Vienna, where he was exposed to extreme Austro-German nationalists who believed Germans to be a superior people and the natural rulers of central Europe. They advocated the union of Austria with Germany and the violent expulsion of "inferior" peoples as the means of maintaining German domination of the Austro-Hungarian Empire.

In Vienna, Hitler developed an unshakable belief in the crudest distortions of Social Darwinism (see Chapter 24), the superiority of Germanic races, and the inevitability of racial conflict. Exposure to poor eastern European Jews contributed to his anti-Semitic prejudice. Jews, Hitler now claimed, directed an international conspiracy of finance capitalism and Marxist socialism against German culture, German unity, and the German people.

Hitler was not alone. Racist anti-Semitism became wildly popular on the far-right wing of European politics in the decades surrounding the First World War. Such irrational beliefs, rooted in centuries of Christian anti-Semitism, were given pseudoscientific legitimacy by nineteenth-century developments in biology and eugenics. These ideas came to define Hitler's worldview and would play an immense role in the ideology and actions of National Socialism.

Hitler greeted the outbreak of the First World War as a salvation. The struggle and discipline of war gave life meaning, and Hitler served bravely as a dispatch carrier on the western front. Germany's defeat shattered his world. Convinced that Jews and Marxists had "stabbed Germany in the back," he vowed to fight on.

In late 1919 Hitler joined a tiny extremist group in Munich called the German Workers' Party. In addition to denouncing Jews, Marxists, and democrats, the party promised a uniquely German National Socialism that would abolish the injustices of capitalism and create a mighty "people's community." By 1921 Hitler had gained control of this small but growing party, which had been renamed the National Socialist German Workers' Party, or Nazis for short. Hitler became a master of mass propaganda and political showmanship. In wild, histrionic speeches, he worked his audience into a frenzy with demagogic attacks on the Versailles treaty, Jews, war profiteers, and the Weimar Republic.

In late 1923 that republic seemed on the verge of collapse, and Hitler, inspired by Mussolini's recent victory, organized an armed uprising in Munich—the so-called Beer Hall Putsch. Despite the failure of the poorly planned coup and Hitler's arrest, National Socialism had been born.

Hitler's Road to Power

At his trial, Hitler gained enormous publicity by denouncing the Weimar Republic. He used his brief prison term to dictate his book *Mein Kampf* (My Struggle), where he laid out his basic ideas on "racial purification" and territorial expansion that would define National Socialism.

In *Mein Kampf*, Hitler claimed that Germans were a "master race" that needed to defend its "pure blood" from groups he labeled "racial degenerates," including Jews, Slavs, and others. The German race was destined to triumph and grow, and, according to Hitler, it needed *Lebensraum* (living space). This space could be found to Germany's east, which Hitler claimed was inhabited by the "subhuman" Slavs and Jews. The future dictator outlined a sweeping vision of war and conquest in which the German master race would colonize east and central Europe and ultimately replace the "subhumans" living there. He championed the idea of the leader-dictator, or *Führer* (FYOUR-uhr), whose unlimited power would embody the people's will and lead the German nation to victory. These ideas would ultimately propel the world into the Second World War.

In the years of relative prosperity and stability between 1924 and 1929, Hitler built up the Nazi Party. From the failed beer hall revolt, he had concluded that he had to come to power through electoral competition rather than armed rebellion. To appeal to middle-class voters, Hitler de-emphasized the anticapitalist elements of National Socialism and vowed to fight communism. The Nazis still remained a small splinter group in 1928, when they received only 2.6 percent of the vote in the general elections and only twelve seats in the Reichstag, the German parliament. There the Nazi deputies pursued the legal strategy of using democracy to destroy democracy.

The Great Depression of 1929 brought the ascent of National Socialism. Now Hitler promised German voters economic as well as political salvation. His appeals for "national rebirth" appealed to a broad spectrum of voters, including middle- and lower-class groups—small business owners, officeworkers, artisans, peasants, and skilled workers. Seized by panic as bankruptcies increased, unemployment soared, and the Communists made dramatic election gains, voters deserted conservative and moderate parties for the

■ **National Socialism** A movement and political party driven by extreme nationalism and racism, led by Adolf Hitler; its adherents ruled Germany from 1933 to 1945 and forced Europe into World War II.

■ **Enabling Act** An act pushed through the Reichstag by the Nazis that gave Hitler absolute dictatorial power for four years.

Nazis. In the election of 1930 the Nazis won 6.5 million votes and 107 seats, and in July 1932 they gained 14.5 million votes—38 percent of the total. They were now the largest party in the Reichstag.

The breakdown of democratic government helped the Nazis seize power. Chancellor Heinrich Brüning (BROU-nihng) tried to overcome the economic crisis by cutting back government spending and ruthlessly forcing down prices and wages. His conservative policies intensified Germany's economic collapse and convinced many voters that the country's republican leaders were stupid and corrupt, adding to Hitler's appeal.

Division on the left also contributed to Nazi success. Even though the two left-wing parties together outnumbered the Nazis in the Reichstag, the Communists refused to cooperate with the Social Democrats. Failing to resolve their differences, these parties could not mount an effective opposition to the Nazi takeover.

Finally, Hitler excelled in the dirty backroom politics of the decaying Weimar Republic. In 1932 Hitler cleverly gained the support of the conservative politicians in power, who thought they could use Hitler for their own advantage, to resolve the political crisis, but also to clamp down on leftists. They accepted Hitler's demand to be appointed chancellor in a coalition government, reasoning that he could be used and controlled. On January 30, 1933, Adolf Hitler, leader of the most popular political party in Germany, was appointed chancellor by President Hindenburg.

State and Society in Nazi Germany

Hitler moved rapidly and skillfully to establish an unshakable dictatorship that would pursue the Nazi program of racial segregation and spatial expansion. First, Hitler and the Nazi Party worked to consolidate their power. To maintain appearances, Hitler called for new elections. In February 1933, in the midst of an electoral campaign plagued by violence—much of it caused by Nazi toughs—the Reichstag building was partly destroyed by fire. Hitler blamed the Communists and convinced Hindenburg to sign emergency acts that abolished freedom of speech and assembly as well as most personal liberties.

The façade of democratic government was soon torn asunder. When the Nazis won only 44 percent of

Events Leading to World War II	
1919	Treaty of Versailles signed
1922	Mussolini gains power in Italy
1927	Stalin takes full control in the Soviet Union
1931	Japan invades Manchuria
January 1933	Hitler appointed chancellor of Germany
October 1933	Germany withdraws from the League of Nations
March 1935	Hitler announces German rearmament
October 1935	Mussolini invades Ethiopia
1936–1939	Civil war in Spain, culminating in establishment of Fascist regime under Franco
March 1936	German armies move unopposed into the Rhineland
October 1936	Rome-Berlin Axis created
1937	Japan invades China
March 1938	Germany annexes Austria
September 1938	Munich Conference: Britain and France agree to German seizure of the Sudetenland from Czechoslovakia
March 1939	Germany occupies the rest of Czechoslovakia; appeasement ends in Britain
August 1939	Nazi-Soviet pact signed
September 1, 1939	Germany invades Poland
September 3, 1939	Britain and France declare war on Germany

the vote in the elections, Hitler outlawed the Communist Party and arrested its parliamentary representatives. Then on March 23, 1933, the Nazis pushed through the Reichstag the **Enabling Act**, which gave Hitler dictatorial power for four years. The Nazis' deceitful stress on legality, coupled with divide-and-conquer techniques, disarmed the opposition until it was too late for effective resistance.

Germany became a one-party Nazi state. Elections were farces. The new regime took over the government bureaucracy intact, installing Nazis in top positions. At the same time, it created a series of overlapping Nazi Party organizations responsible solely to Hitler. As recent research has shown, the resulting system of dual government was riddled with rivalries, contradictions, and inefficiencies. The Nazi state was often disorganized and lacked the all-encompassing unity that its propagandists claimed. Yet this fractured system suited Hitler and his purposes. The lack of unity encouraged competition among state personnel, who worked to outdo each other to fulfill Hitler's vaguely expressed goals. The Führer thus played the established bureaucracy against his personal party government and maintained dictatorial control.

Once the Nazis were firmly in command, Hitler and the party turned their attention to constructing a National Socialist society defined by national unity and racial exclusion. First they eliminated political enemies. Communists, Social Democrats, and trade-union leaders were forced out of their jobs or arrested

Mothers in the Fatherland Nazi ideologues promoted strictly defined gender roles for men and women, and the Nazi state implemented a variety of social programs to encourage "racially correct" women to stay home and raise "Aryan" children. This colorful poster portrays the joy of motherhood and calls for donations to the Mother and Child division of the National Socialist People's Welfare office. A woman who had four children was awarded the bronze Cross of Honor for the German Mother (left). The medal came with a letter of appreciation signed by Hitler. (medal: Private Collection/Peter Newark Military Pictures/Bridgeman Images; poster: akg-images)

and taken to hastily built concentration camps. The Nazis outlawed strikes and abolished independent labor unions, which were replaced by the Nazi-controlled German Labor Front.

Hitler then purged the Nazi Party itself of its more extremist elements. The Nazi storm troopers (the SA), the quasi-military band of 3 million toughs in brown shirts who had fought Communists and beaten up Jews before the Nazis took power, now expected top positions in the army. Some SA radicals even talked of a "second revolution" that would create equality among all Germans by sweeping away capitalism. Now that he was in power, however, Hitler was eager to win the support of the traditional military and maintain social order. He decided that the leadership of the SA had to be eliminated. On the night of June 30, 1934, Hitler's elite personal guard—the SS—arrested and executed about one hundred SA leaders and other political enemies. Afterward, the SS grew rapidly. Under its methodical, ruthless leader Heinrich Himmler (1900–1945), the SS took over the political police and the concentration camp system.

The Nazis instituted a policy called "coordination," which forced existing institutions to conform to National Socialist ideology. Professionals—doctors and lawyers, teachers and engineers—saw their previously independent organizations swallowed up by Nazi associations. Charity and civic organizations were also put under Nazi control, and universities, publishers, and writers were quickly brought into line. Democratic, socialist, and Jewish literature was put on ever-growing blacklists. Passionate students and radicalized professors burned forbidden books in public squares. Modern art and architecture—which the Nazis considered "degenerate"—were prohibited. Life became violently anti-intellectual. By 1934 a brutal dictatorship characterized by frightening dynamism and obedience to Hitler was largely in place.

Acting on its vision of racial eugenics, the party began a many-faceted campaign against those deemed incapable of making positive biological contributions to the "master race." The Nazis persecuted a number of groups. Jews headed the list, but Slavic peoples, Sinti and Roma, homosexuals, and Jehovah's Witnesses were also considered social "deviants." Nazi bureaucrats furthermore invented two categories targeted for "racial hygiene": the "hereditarily ill" and "asocials." The "hereditarily ill" included people with chronic mental or physical disabilities, such as schizophrenics, manic depressives, epileptics, and people suffering from what Nazi physicians called "congenital feeblemindedness." The catchall category of "asocials" included common criminals, alcoholics, prostitutes, the "work shy" (or chronically unemployed), beggars and vagrants, and others on the margins of German society.

Nazi leaders used a variety of measures to convince Germans that "racial hygiene" was justified and necessary. In what some historians term the Nazi "racial state," barbarism and race hatred were institutionalized with the force of science and law.[5] New university academies, such as the German Society for Racial Research, wrote studies that measured and defined racial differences; prejudice was thus presented in the guise of enlightened medical science, a means for creating a strong national race. Schoolroom lessons, articles in the popular press, feature films, traveling exhibitions, and even children's board games touted the benefits of racist eugenic practice. (See "Thinking Like a Historian: Normalizing Eugenics and 'Racial Hygiene' in Nazi Germany," page 922.)

The results were monstrous, a barbaric violation of the ethical norms most of us take for granted. Thousands of innocent people faced social ostracism and then brutal repression, simply because the Nazis deemed them racial outsiders. Convinced by their own racial ideology, Nazi authorities denied outsiders welfare benefits and put them out of work, forced people with disabilities into special hospitals where they could be segregated from "healthy" Germans, and imprisoned homosexuals and "asocials" in concentration camps for "re-education." A series of sterilization laws exemplified the ethical breakdown. Nazi medical workers forcibly sterilized some four hundred thousand German citizens, mainly "asocials" or the "hereditarily ill," so their "degenerate blood" would not pollute the "Aryan race." The eugenics campaign reached a crescendo in 1938, when the authorities initiated a coldhearted euthanasia program—dubbed "mercy killing" by Nazi physicians and administrators—and systematically murdered about seventy thousand Germans with chronic disabilities (see page 932).

From the beginning, German Jews were a special target of Nazi racial persecution. Anti-Jewish propaganda was ever present in Nazi Germany. Ugly posters of stereotypical Jews; feature films and documentaries about the Jewish "menace"; signs in shop windows, banks, and parks forbidding Jewish entry—all and more were used to stigmatize German Jews. Such means were backed up with harsh legal oppression. Shortly after they took power, Nazi authorities issued the Professional Civil Service Restoration Act, which banned Jews from working in government jobs; by 1934 many Jewish lawyers, doctors, professors, civil servants, and musicians had been summarily dismissed from their jobs. In 1935 the infamous Nuremberg Laws classified as Jewish anyone having three or more Jewish grandparents, outlawed marriage and sexual relations between Jews and those defined as German, and deprived Jews of all rights of citizenship. Conversion to Christianity and abandonment of the Jewish faith made no difference. For the vast majority of German citizens not targeted by such laws, the creation of a demonized outsider group may well have contributed to feelings of national unity and support for the Hitler regime.

In late 1938 the assault on the Jews accelerated. During a well-organized wave of violence known as Kristallnacht (or the Night of Broken Glass pogrom), Nazi gangs smashed windows and looted over 7,000 Jewish-owned shops, destroyed many homes, burned down over 200 synagogues, and killed dozens of Jews. German Jews were then rounded up and made to pay for the damage. By 1939 some 300,000 of Germany's 500,000 Jews had emigrated, sacrificing almost all their property in order to escape persecution. Some Germans privately opposed these outrages, but most went along or looked the other way. Historians still debate the degree to which this lack of opposition expressed popular anti-Semitism. In any case, it revealed widespread support for Hitler's government.

Popular Support for National Socialism

Why did millions of ordinary Germans back a brutally repressive, racist regime? A combination of coercion and reward enlisted popular support for the racial state. Using the secret police and the growing concentration camp system in a reign of ruthless terror, the regime persecuted its political and "racial" enemies. Yet for the large majority of ordinary German citizens who were not Jews, Communists, or members of other targeted groups, Hitler's government brought new opportunities. The German "master race" clearly benefited from Nazi policies and programs.

Hitler had promised the masses economic recovery, and he delivered. The Nazi state launched a large public works program to help pull Germany out of the depression. Work began on superhighways, offices, gigantic sports stadiums, and public housing, which created jobs and instilled pride in national recovery. By 1938 unemployment had fallen to 2 percent, and there was a shortage of workers. Between 1932 and 1938 the standard of living for the average worker increased moderately. Business profits rose sharply.

The persecution of Jews brought substantial benefits to ordinary Germans as well. As Jews were forced out of their jobs and compelled to sell their homes and businesses, Germans stepped in to take their place in a process known as Aryanization (named after the "Aryan master race" prized by the Nazis for their supposedly pure German blood). For millions of so-called Aryans, a rising standard of living—at whatever ethical price—was tangible evidence that Nazi promises were more than show and propaganda.

Normalizing Eugenics and "Racial Hygiene" in Nazi Germany

The Nazi regime issued a number of laws and regulations that institutionalized racial eugenics, including the Civil Service Restoration Act (1933) and the Nuremberg Laws (1935). Notions of "racial hygiene" also penetrated the very fabric of everyday life in the Third Reich. What means did Nazi supporters use to teach Germans that racial engineering was legitimate and even desirable?

1 **Adolf Hitler, *Mein Kampf* (My Struggle).** The dictator of the Nazi state explained the importance of racial education in his infamous political manifesto, first published in 1925.

~ If, as the first task of the State in the service and for the welfare of its nationality we recognize the preservation, care, and development of the best racial elements, it is natural that this care must not only extend to the birth of every little national and racial comrade, but that it must educate the young sapling to become a valuable link in the chain of future reproduction.

2 **Joseph Goebbels, party rally speech.** Propaganda Minister Goebbels sums up his view of welfare benefits in a 1938 speech, delivered to functionaries working in the Nazi welfare agency.

~ Our starting point is not the individual, and we do not subscribe to the view that one should feed the hungry, give drink to the thirsty, or clothe the naked—those are not our objectives. Our objectives are entirely different. They can be put most crisply in the sentence: we must have a healthy people [*Volk*] in order to prevail in the world.

(akg-images)

3 **An anti-Semitic children's book.** In this scene from a notorious 1936 anti-Semitic children's book, blond-haired "Aryan" schoolchildren laugh and jeer as a Jewish schoolteacher and a group of Jewish students are forcibly ejected from a German grade school. The portrayal of the Jewish teacher and students draws on the most ugly racist stereotypes. Approximately one hundred thousand copies of the book were printed by a Nazi publisher, and it was used in many German schoolrooms.

ANALYZING THE EVIDENCE

1. In Source 1, why does Hitler emphasize the importance of education for the development of "the best racial elements"?
2. Review Goebbels's statement on the relationship between the individual and the "people" in Source 2. How do his ideas, and those expressed in Sources 5 and 6, challenge the rationale behind Christian charity and/or liberal-democratic ideals of individual human rights?
3. How do Sources 3–6 bring Nazi assumptions about "racial hygiene" to ordinary Germans?
4. The evidence presented here is "top down"—it was created by propagandists who supported the Nazis' racial ideas. Given these limitations, how can historians tackle the question of reception? Can we really know what ordinary people thought about these sources?

So würde es enden

Qualitativer Bevölkerungsabstieg bei zu schwacher Fortpflanzung der höherwertigen.

So wird es kommen
wenn Minderwertige 4 Kinder und höherwertige 2 Kinder haben.

(bpk, Berlin/Art Resource, NY)

4 **A lesson in racial biology.** In 1935 educator Jakob Graf wrote a series of exercises designed to teach young students to identify a person's "racial soul" by observing their habits and physical characteristics.

How We Can Learn to Recognize a Person's Race

ASSIGNMENTS

1. Summarize the spiritual characteristics of the individual races.
2. Collect from stories, essays, and poems examples of ethnological illustrations. Underline those terms which describe the type and mode of the expression of the soul.
3. What are the expressions, gestures, and movements which allow us to make conclusions as to the attitude of the racial soul?
4. Determine also the physical features which go hand in hand with the specific racial soul characteristics of the individual figures.
5. Try to discover the intrinsic nature of the racial soul through the characters in stories and poetical works in terms of their inner attitude. Apply this mode of observation to persons in your own environment.
6. Collect propaganda posters and caricatures for your race book and arrange them according to a racial scheme. . . .
7. Collect from illustrated magazines, newspapers, etc., pictures of great scholars, statesmen, artists, and others who distinguish themselves by their special accomplishments (for example, in economic life, politics, sport). Determine the preponderant race and admixture, according to physical characteristics. Repeat this exercise with the pictures of great men of all nations and times.

. . .

9. Observe people whose special racial features have drawn your attention, also with respect to their bearing when moving or when speaking. Observe their expressions and gestures.
10. Observe the Jew: In his way of walking, his bearing, gestures, and movements when talking.
11. What strikes you about the way a Jew talks and sings?
12. What are the occupations engaged in by the Jews of your acquaintance?
13. What are the occupations in which Jews are not to be found? Explain this phenomenon on the basis of the character of the Jew's soul.

5 **Envisioning "racial decline."** Visitors to the 1935 Wonders of Life eugenics exposition in Berlin could view this poster titled "The Qualitative Decline of the Population Due to Weak Reproduction Rates Among the Highly Valued." The poster graphs population rates, using the symbol of a chronically disabled "Lowly Valued" man that grows to tower over the "Highly Valued" figure. The text explains that "This Is How It Will End" after 120 years if each "Lowly Valued" family continues to have four children while each "Highly Valued" family has only two.

6 **A lesson in mathematics.** A great variety of Nazi propaganda materials—including feature films, traveling exhibits, and these 1936 math exercises—brought home the message that the chronically ill and handicapped were an expensive and ultimately unnecessary burden on German society.

Question 95: The construction of a lunatic asylum costs 6 million RM [Reich Marks]. How many houses at 15,000 RM each could have been built for that amount? . . .

Question 97: To keep a mentally ill person costs approx. 4 RM per day, a cripple 5.50 RM, a criminal 3.5 RM. Many civil servants receive only 4 RM per day, white-collar employees barely 3.5 RM, unskilled workers not even 2 RM per head for their families.

(a) Illustrate these figures with a diagram.

According to conservative estimates there are 300,000 mentally ill, epileptics, etc., in care.

(b) How much do these people cost to keep in total, at a cost of 4 RM per head?
(c) How many marriage loans at 1,000 RM each . . . could be granted from this money?

PUTTING IT ALL TOGETHER

Historians have often argued that victims of Nazi racial policy and the Holocaust—Jews, homosexuals, people with chronic mental illness, and others considered "less worthy"—were subjected to processes of dehumanization before they were persecuted or even murdered. Using the sources above, along with what you have learned in class and in this chapter, write a short essay that outlines this process. What are the most important eugenic ideas, and how are they "normalized"—made acceptable to ordinary people—in Nazi propaganda?

Sources. (1, 2) Michael Burleigh and Wolfgang Wippermann, *The Racial State: Germany 1933–1945* (New York: Cambridge University Press, 1991), pp. 202, 69; (4) George Mosse, ed., *Nazi Culture: A Documentary History* (New York: Schocken Books, 1981), pp. 80–81; (6) Burleigh and Wippermann, *The Racial State*, p. 154.

LIVING IN THE PAST
Nazi Propaganda and Consumer Goods

t is easy to forget that the Volkswagens that zip around America's streets today got their start in Hitler's Germany, introduced as part of a Nazi campaign to provide inexpensive but attractive consumer goods to the *Volk* (people). Marketed to Aryans, but not to Jews and other "racial enemies," the Volkswagen (or People's Car) and other People's Products, including the People's Radio, the People's Refrigerator, and even the People's Single-Family Home, symbolized a return to German prosperity. As the advertisements shown here suggest, the appeal of material abundance was a central plank in Nazi propaganda.

Despite Hitler's promise of a "new, happier age" that would "make the German people rich,"* many of these consumer goods remained out of reach of ordinary Germans. The Volkswagen was a case in point. The car was sold by subscription, and a purchaser made weekly deposits into a savings account. When the balance was paid off, the customer would receive a car. By 1939 some 340,000 Germans had opened such savings accounts. Yet because of problems with production, the car's relatively

"All Germany listens to the Führer on the People's Radio."
(radio: De Agostini/Getty Images; poster: © Mary Evans Picture Library/Alamy Stock Photo)

*Peter Fritzsche, *Life and Death in the Third Reich* (Cambridge, Mass.: Harvard University Press, 2008), p. 59.

Economic recovery was accompanied by a wave of social and cultural innovation intended to construct what Nazi propagandists called the *Volksgemeinschaft*—a "people's community" for racially pure Germans. The party set up mass organizations to spread Nazi ideology and enlist volunteers for the Nazi cause. Millions of Germans joined the Hitler Youth, the League of German Women, and the German Labor Front. Mass rallies, such as annual May Day celebrations and Nazi Party conventions in Nuremberg, brought together thousands of participants. Glowing reports on such events in the Nazi-controlled press brought the message home to millions more.

As the economy recovered, the government proudly touted a glittering array of inexpensive and enticing people's products. Items such as the Volkswagen (the "People's Car") were intended to link individuals' desire

for consumer goods to the collective ideology of the "people's community." (See "Living in the Past: Nazi Propaganda and Consumer Goods," above.) Though such programs faltered as the state increasingly focused on rearmament for the approaching war, they suggested to all that the regime was working hard to improve German living standards.

Women played a special role in the Nazi state. Promising to "liberate women from women's liberation," Nazi ideologues championed a return to traditional family values. They outlawed abortion, discouraged women from holding jobs or obtaining higher education, and glorified domesticity and motherhood. Women were cast as protectors of the hearth and home and were instructed to raise young boys and girls in accordance with Nazi ideals. In the later 1930s, facing labor shortages, high price, and the concentration on armament production in the late 1930s, not one People's Car was delivered to a private customer.

In contrast, the People's Radio was a unique success. The modest VE-301 radio was much less expensive than standard models, and between 1934 and 1942 the number of Germans who owned radios doubled. Many people could now sit at home and listen to broadcasts ranging from popular and classical music to speeches from regime leaders like Minister of Propaganda Joseph Goebbels, whose tirades were so inescapable that Germans nicknamed the VE-301 (shown at left) the "Goebbels snout."

QUESTIONS FOR ANALYSIS

1. What do these images suggest about everyday life in Nazi Germany? What do they reveal about the aspirations of the German people for a good life in the 1930s?
2. Consider why both the government and commercial manufacturers attached the prefix *Volk*, or "people," to products like the Volkswagen. What larger message did these two groups seek to convey through the use of this prefix?
3. How are these images similar to advertisements today? How are they different?

This 1938 advertisement for the Volkswagen, produced by the Nazi Strength Through Joy organization, highlights the pleasures of a family vacation. (Deutsches Historisches Museum, Berlin, Germany/© DHM/Bridgeman Images)

the Nazis had to reluctantly reverse course and encourage women to enter the labor force. Whatever the employment situation, the millions of women enrolled in Nazi mass organizations, which organized charity drives and other social programs, experienced a sense of freedom and community in these public activities.

Few historians today believe that Hitler and the Nazis brought about a real social revolution, as an earlier generation of scholars thought. Yet Hitler's rule promoted economic growth, and Nazi propagandists continually played up the supposed accomplishments of the regime. The vision of a "people's community," national pride in recovery, and feelings of belonging created by acts of racial exclusion led many Germans to support the regime. Hitler himself remained popular with broad sections of the population well into the war.

Not all Germans supported Hitler, however, and a number of groups actively resisted him after 1933. But opponents of the Nazis were never unified, which helps explain their lack of success. Furthermore, the regime harshly clamped down on dissidents: tens of thousands of political enemies were imprisoned, and thousands were executed. After Communists and socialists were smashed by the SS system, a second group of opponents arose in the Catholic and Protestant churches. Their efforts, however, were directed primarily at preserving religious life, not at overthrowing Hitler. In 1938 and again during the war, a few high-ranking army officers, who feared the consequences of Hitler's reckless aggression, plotted against him, but their plans were unsuccessful.

Aggression and Appeasement

The nazification of German society fulfilled only part of the Nazi agenda. While building the "people's community," the regime aggressively pursued policies meant to achieve territorial expansion for the supposedly superior German race. At first, Hitler carefully camouflaged his expansionist goals. Germany was still militarily weak, and the Nazi leader proclaimed his peaceful intentions. Germany's withdrawal from the League of Nations in October 1933 nonetheless indicated that Gustav Stresemann's policy of peaceful cooperation was dead (see Chapter 26). Then in March 1935 Hitler declared that Germany would no longer abide by the disarmament clauses of the Treaty of Versailles. He established a military draft and began to build up the German army. France and Great Britain protested strongly and warned against future aggressive actions.

Any hope of a united front against Hitler quickly collapsed. Britain adopted a policy of **appeasement**, granting Hitler what he demanded to avoid war. British appeasement, which practically dictated French policy, was motivated in large part by the pacifism of a population still horrified by the memory of the First World War. As in Germany, many powerful conservatives in Britain underestimated Hitler. They believed that Soviet communism was the real danger and that Hitler could be used to stop it. Such strong anticommunist feelings made an alliance between the Western powers and Stalin against Hitler highly unlikely.

When Hitler suddenly marched his armies into the demilitarized Rhineland in March 1936, brazenly violating the treaties of Versailles and Locarno (Map 27.2), Britain refused to act. France could do little without British support. Emboldened, Hitler moved ever more aggressively, enlisting powerful allies in international affairs.

MAP 27.2 The Growth of Nazi Germany, 1933–1939 Until March 1939 Hitler's conquests brought ethnic Germans into the Nazi state; then he turned on the Slavic and Jewish peoples he had always hated. He stripped Czechoslovakia of its independence and prepared to attack Poland in September 1939.

A Republican Militia in the Spanish Civil War   The enthusiasm of the republican forces of the demo-cratically elected government of Spain could not overcome the rebel Fascist armies of Francisco Franco during the Spanish Civil War (1936–1939). Once in power, Franco ruled over a repressive dictatorial state in Spain until his death in 1975. Women combatants like the *milicianas* pictured here, carrying rifles with their male comrades, made a significant contribution to the republican cause. (Universal History Archive/Getty Images)

Italy and Germany established the so-called Rome-Berlin Axis in 1936. Japan, also under the rule of a Fascist dicta-torship, joined the Axis alliance that same year.

At the same time, Germany and Italy intervened in the Spanish Civil War (1936–1939), where their military aid helped General Francisco Franco's revolutionary Fascist movement defeat the democratically elected republican government. Republican Spain's only official aid in the fight against Franco came from the Soviet Union, for public opinion in Britain and especially in France was hopelessly divided on whether to intervene.

In late 1937 Hitler moved forward with plans to seize Austria and Czechoslovakia as the first step in his long-contemplated drive for living space in the east. By threatening Austria with invasion, Hitler forced the Austrian chancellor to put local Nazis in control of the government in March 1938. The next day, in the An-schluss (annexation), German armies moved in unop-posed, and Austria became part of Greater Germany (see Map 27.2).

Simultaneously, Hitler demanded that territories in-habited mostly by ethnic Germans in western Czechoslo-vakia—the Sudetenland—be ceded to Nazi Germany. Though democratic Czechoslovakia was allied with France and the Soviet Union and prepared to defend it-self, appeasement triumphed again. In negotiations British prime minister Arthur Neville Chamberlain and the French agreed with Hitler that Germany should immediately take over the Sudetenland. Returning to

"Peace for Our Time"   British prime minister Neville Chamberlain speaks at the London airport after a meeting with Adolf Hitler in Munich in September 1938. In return for acceptance of the German annexation of the Czech Sudetenland, Hitler promised to halt foreign aggression, and Chamberlain famously announced that he had negotiated "peace for our time" with the Nazi leader. Less than a year later, Germany invaded Poland and Europe was at war. (Central Press/Getty Images)

▪ appeasement   The British policy toward Germany prior to World War II that aimed at granting Hitler's territorial demands, including western Czechoslovakia, in order to avoid war.

London from the Munich Conference in September 1938, Chamberlain told cheering crowds that he had secured "peace with honor . . . peace for our time." Sold out by the Western powers, Czechoslovakia gave in.

Chamberlain's peace was short-lived. In March 1939 Hitler's armies invaded and occupied the rest of Czechoslovakia. The effect on Western public opinion was electrifying. This time, there was no possible rationale of self-determination for Nazi aggression, since Hitler was seizing ethnic Czechs and Slovaks—not Germans—as captive peoples. When Hitler next used the question of German minorities in Danzig as a pretext to confront Poland, a suddenly militant Chamberlain declared that Britain and France would fight if Hitler attacked his eastern neighbor. Hitler did not take these warnings seriously.

In August 1939, in an about-face that stunned the world, sworn enemies Hitler and Stalin signed a non-aggression pact that paved the road to war. Each dictator promised to remain neutral if the other became involved in open hostilities. An attached secret protocol ruthlessly divided Poland, the Baltic nations, Finland, and a part of Romania into German and Soviet spheres of influence. Stalin agreed to the pact because he remained distrustful of Western intentions and because Hitler offered immediate territorial gain.

For Hitler, everything was now set. On September 1, 1939, German armies and warplanes smashed into Poland from three sides. Two days later, Britain and France, finally true to their word, declared war on Germany. The Second World War had begun.

German Bomber over Warsaw Germany opened its September 1939 attack on Poland by subjecting the Polish capital to repeated bombardment. By the end of the war, both sides had engaged in massive air campaigns against civilian targets, taking the lives of hundreds of thousands of civilians and leading finally to the use of the atomic bomb against Japan in 1945. (© INTERFOTO/Alamy Stock Photo)

The Second World War

FOCUS QUESTION *How did Germany and Japan conquer enormous empires during World War II, and how did the Allies defeat them?*

Nazi Germany's unlimited ambition unleashed an apocalyptic cataclysm. Hitler's armies quickly conquered much of western and eastern Europe, establishing a vast empire of expropriation, destruction, and death. At the same time, Japanese armies overran much of Southeast Asia and created their own racial empire. This reckless aggression brought together a coalition of unlikely but powerful allies determined to halt the advance of fascism: Britain, the United States, and the Soviet Union. After years of slaughter that decimated much of Europe and East Asia, this "Grand Alliance" decisively defeated the Axis powers.

German Victories in Europe

Using planes, tanks, and trucks in the first example of a blitzkrieg, or "lightning war," Hitler's armies crushed Poland in four weeks. While the Soviet Union quickly took its part of the booty—the eastern half of Poland and the independent Baltic states of Lithuania, Estonia, and Latvia—French and British armies prepared their defenses in the west.

In spring 1940 the Nazi lightning war struck again. After Germany occupied Denmark, Norway, and Holland, motorized columns broke into France through southern Belgium, split the Franco-British forces, and trapped the entire British army on the French beaches of Dunkirk. By heroic efforts, the British withdrew their troops—although equipment could not be saved. Soon after, France was taken by the Nazis. By July 1940 Hitler ruled practically all of continental Europe. Italy was a German ally. Romania, Hungary, and Bulgaria joined the Axis powers, and the Soviet Union, Spain, and Sweden were friendly neutrals. Only the Balkans and Britain, the nation led by the uncompromising Winston Churchill (1874–1965), remained unconquered.

To prepare for an amphibious invasion of Britain, Germany sought to gain control of the air. In the Battle of Britain, which began in July 1940, up to a thousand

Everyday Life in the London Blitz

In 1941 Hilde Marchant, a young English journalist, published an account of her experiences in the streets of London during the Battle of Britain the year before. Here she speaks of Mr. Smith, an air raid warden. Mr. Smith, she reported, was neither strong nor brave, but he nonetheless learned to effectively manage the destruction of the blitz.

~

But perhaps the greatest battle of all in those early days was a personal one. Smith had to adjust his warm, sentimental, domestic nature to the grim agonising sights of the night. He loves humanity, in all its virtue and vice, and it was a shock for him to see the pain and distortion of life around him. Yet he corseted his sentimentality with the months of training he had had and became the handyman of the blitz. . . .

Smith began to tell me about that first night, the night he fell in the road and broke his glasses. A bomb just a few yards from him had hit a block of buildings, and there were eleven people trapped on the ground floor.

"It was a noisy night, but every time we bent low we could hear the groans of the people underneath. I thought I'd be sick. I held a man's hand that was clear. It took us nine hours to get him out. An hour later we got a woman out. They were in a bad way. There was dirt and blood caked on the woman's face. We wiped it off. She must have been about thirty. They both died. We were all a bit quiet. It was the first we'd seen. We couldn't have got them out quicker—we'd torn our hands up dragging the stones away. But it was awful seeing them take the last gasps as they lifted them into the ambulance."

Smith was quiet, even retelling the story, and one of the [other wardens] said:

"It was the first, you see."

Then Smith told me about the next night—the night when he was really "blooded." Incendiaries had started a fire in one of the smaller streets and high explosives began to fall into the fire. Smith approached the houses from the back and got through to the kitchen of one of the houses.

"I fell over something. I picked it up and it was a leg. I stood there with it in my hand wondering what I should do with it. I knew it was a woman's leg. I put it down and went to look for the ambulance. They had got the fire out at the front. The ambulance men brought a stretcher and I showed them the leg. Then we looked farther in and there were pieces all over. All they said was they didn't need a stretcher."

As Smith sat thinking, his whole body seemed to pause. . . .

"You see, how we look at things now is like this. If they're alive you work like the devil to keep 'em alive and get 'em out. . . . If they're dead there's nothing we can do. Getting upset hampers your work."

So Smith learned not to over-indulge his sensitivity on seeing death, or torn limb and flesh. His job was with the spark of life that survived.

EVALUATE THE EVIDENCE

1. Does Marchant's story have a political message for the British people?
2. What does this passage reveal about the resilience of human beings in times of war?

Source: James M. Brophy et al., *Perspectives from the Past: Primary Sources in Western Civilizations*, 4th ed., vol. 2 (New York: W. W. Norton, 2009), pp. 766–767.

German planes a day attacked British airfields and key factories, dueling with British defenders high in the skies. Losses were heavy on both sides. In September 1940 Hitler angrily turned from military objectives to indiscriminate bombing of British cities in an attempt to break British morale. British aircraft factories increased production, and the heavily bombed people of London defiantly dug in. By October Britain was beating Germany three to one in the air war, and the Battle of Britain was over. (See "Evaluating the Evidence 27.3: Everyday Life in the London Blitz," above.) Stymied there, the Nazi war machine invaded and occupied Greece and the Balkans.

Hitler now allowed his lifetime obsession of creating a vast eastern European empire ruled by the master race to dictate policy. In June 1941 he broke his pact with Stalin and launched German armies into the Soviet Union along a vast front (Map 27.3). By October most of Ukraine had been conquered, Leningrad was practically surrounded, and Moscow was besieged. But the Soviets did not collapse, and when a severe winter struck German armies outfitted only in summer uniforms, the invaders retreated. Nevertheless, Hitler and his allies ruled over a vast European empire stretching from eastern Europe to the English Channel. Hitler, the Nazi leadership, and the loyal German army were positioned to greatly accelerate construction of their so-called New Order in Europe.

Europe Under Nazi Occupation

Hitler's New Order was based firmly on the guiding principle of National Socialism: racial imperialism.

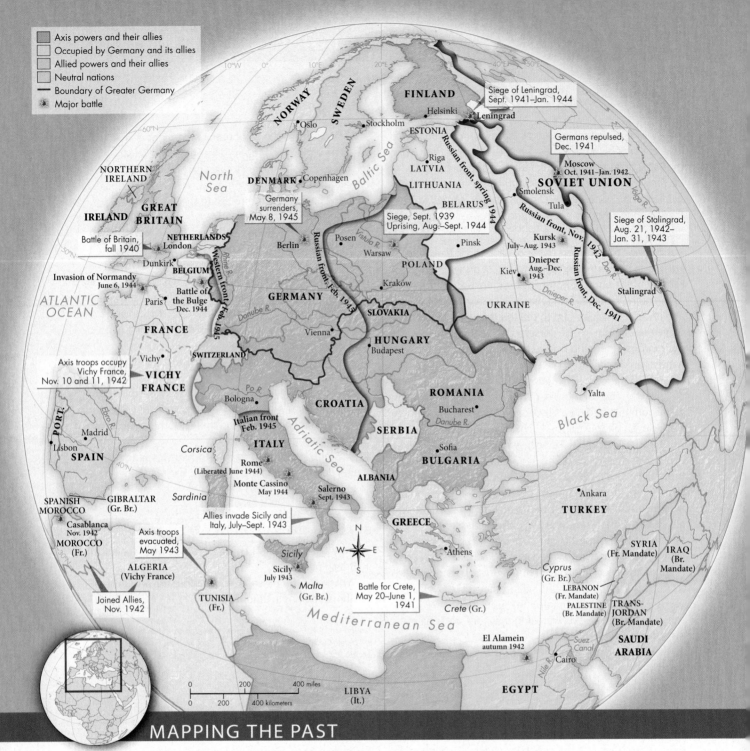

Legend:
- Axis powers and their allies
- Occupied by Germany and its allies
- Allied powers and their allies
- Neutral nations
- Boundary of Greater Germany
- Major battle

Siege of Leningrad, Sept. 1941–Jan. 1944

Germans repulsed, Dec. 1941

Moscow Oct. 1941–Jan. 1942

Siege of Stalingrad, Aug. 21, 1942– Jan. 31, 1943

Russian front, spring 1944

Russian front, Nov. 1942

Russian front, Dec. 1941

Russian front, Feb. 1945

Siege, Sept. 1939 Uprising, Aug.–Sept. 1944

Germany surrenders, May 8, 1945

Kursk July–Aug. 1943

Dnieper Aug.–Dec. 1943

Battle of Britain, fall 1940

Western front, Feb. 1945

Invasion of Normandy, June 6, 1944

Battle of the Bulge Dec. 1944

Axis troops occupy Vichy France, Nov. 10 and 11, 1942

Italian front Feb. 1945

Rome (Liberated June 1944)

Monte Cassino May 1944

Salerno Sept. 1943

Allies invade Sicily and Italy, July–Sept. 1943

Casablanca Nov. 1942

Axis troops evacuated, May 1943

Sicily July 1943

Battle for Crete, May 20–June 1, 1941

Joined Allies, Nov. 1942

El Alamein autumn 1942

MAPPING THE PAST

MAP 27.3 World War II in Europe and Africa, 1939–1945

This map shows the extent of Hitler's empire before the Battle of Stalingrad in late 1942 and the subsequent advances of the Allies until Germany surrendered on May 8, 1945. Compare this map with Map 27.2 on page 926 to trace the rise and fall of the Nazi empire over time.

ANALYZING THE MAP What was the first country conquered by Hitler (see Map 27.2)? Locate Germany's advance and retreat on the Russian front in December 1941, November 1942, spring 1944, and February 1945. How does this compare to the position of British and American forces on the battlefield at similar points in time?

CONNECTIONS What implications might the battle lines on February 1945 have had for the postwar settlement in Europe?

Occupied peoples were treated according to their place in the Nazi racial hierarchy. All were subject to harsh policies dedicated to ethnic cleansing and the plunder of resources for the Nazi war effort.

Within this **New Order**, the so-called Nordic peoples—the Dutch, Danes, and Norwegians—received preferential treatment, for the Germans believed them related to the Aryan master race. In Holland, Denmark, and Norway, the Nazis established puppet governments of various kinds. Though many people hated the conquerors, the Nazis found willing collaborators who ruled in accord with German needs. France was divided into two parts. The German army occupied the north, including Paris. The southeast remained nominally independent. There the aging First World War general Marshal Henri-Philippe Pétain formed a new French government—the Vichy (VIH-shee) regime—that adopted many aspects of National Socialist ideology and willingly placed French Jews in the hands of the Nazis.

In all conquered territories, the Nazis used a variety of techniques to enrich Germany and support the war effort. Occupied nations were forced to pay for the costs of the war and for the occupation itself, and the price was high. Nazi administrators stole goods and money from local Jews, set currency exchanges at favorable rates, and forced occupied peoples to accept worthless wartime scrip. Soldiers were encouraged not only to steal but also to purchase goods at cheap exchange rates and send them home. A flood of plunder thus reached Germany, helping maintain high living standards and preserving home-front morale well into the war. Nazi victory, furthermore, placed national Jewish populations across Europe under German control, allowing the mass murder of Europe's Jews.

In central and eastern Europe, the war and German rule were far more ruthless and deadly than in the west. From the start, the Nazi leadership had cast the war in the east as one of annihilation. The Nazis now set out to build a vast colonial empire where Jews would be exterminated and Poles, Ukrainians, and Russians would be enslaved and forced to die out. According to the plans, ethnic

Vichy France, 1940

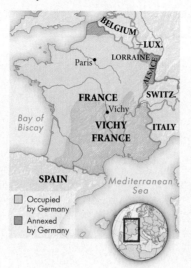

☐ Occupied by Germany
■ Annexed by Germany

Nazi Occupation of Poland and East-Central Europe, 1939–1942

— Boundary of Poland, 1938
■ Germany, 1938
☐ Annexed by Germany, 1939
☐ German civil administration, 1942
■ German military occupation, 1942
— Boundary of Greater Germany, 1942

German peasants would resettle the resulting abandoned lands, a "mass settlement space." In pursuit of such goals, large parts of western Poland were incorporated into Germany. Another part of Poland was placed under the rule of a merciless civilian administration.

With the support of military commanders, German policemen, and bureaucrats in the occupied territories, Nazi administrators and Himmler's elite SS corps now implemented a program of destruction and annihilation to create a "mass settlement space" for racially pure Germans. Across the east, the Nazi armies destroyed cities and factories, stole crops and farm animals, and subjected conquered peoples to forced starvation and mass murder. Nazi occupation in the east destroyed the lives of millions.[6]

In response to such atrocities, small but determined underground resistance groups fought back. They were hardly unified. Communists and socialists often disagreed with more centrist or nationalist groups on long-term goals and short-term tactics. In Yugoslavia, for example, Communist and royalist military resistance groups attacked the Germans, but also each other. The resistance nonetheless presented a real challenge to the Nazi New Order. Poland, under German occupation longer than any other nation, had the most determined and well-organized resistance. The Nazis had closed all Polish universities and outlawed national newspapers, but the Poles organized secret classes and maintained a thriving underground press. Underground members of the Polish Home Army, led by the government in exile in London, passed intelligence about German operations to the Allies and committed sabotage. The famous French resistance undertook similar actions, as did groups in Italy, Greece, Russia, and the Netherlands.

The German response was swift and deadly. The Nazi army and the SS tortured captured resistance members and executed hostages in

■ **New Order** Hitler's program based on racial imperialism, which gave preferential treatment to the "Nordic" peoples; the French, an "inferior" Latin people, occupied a middle position; and Slavs and Jews were treated harshly as "subhumans."

A "Transport" Arrives at Auschwitz Upon arrival at Auschwitz in May 1944, Jews from Subcarpathian Rus, a rural district on the border of Czechoslovakia and Ukraine, undergo a "selection" managed by Nazi officers and prisoners in striped uniforms. Camp guards will send the fittest people to the barracks, where they will probably soon die from forced labor under the most atrocious conditions. The aged, ill, very young, or otherwise infirm will be murdered immediately in the Auschwitz gas chambers. The tower over the main gate to the camp, which today opens onto a vast museum complex, is visible in the background. (Galerie Bildwelt/Getty Images)

reprisal for attacks. Responding to actions undertaken by resistance groups, the German army murdered the male populations of Lidice (Czechoslovakia) and Oradour (France) and leveled the entire towns, brutal examples of Nazi barbarism in pursuit of a racial New Order. Despite reprisals, Nazi occupiers were never able to eradicate popular resistance to their rule.

The Holocaust

The ultimate abomination of Nazi racism was the condemnation of all European Jews and other peoples considered racially inferior to extreme racial persecution and then annihilation in the **Holocaust**, a great spasm of racially inspired mass murder.

As already described, the Nazis began to use social, legal, and economic means to persecute Jews and other "undesirable" groups immediately after taking power. Between 1938 and 1940 persecution turned deadly in the Nazi euthanasia (mercy killing) campaign, an important step toward genocide. Just as Germany be-

gan the war, some 70,000 people with physical and mental disabilities were forced into special hospitals, barracks, and camps. Deemed by Nazi administrators to be "unworthy lives" who might "pollute" the German race, they were murdered in cold blood. The victims were mostly ethnic Germans, and the euthanasia campaign was stopped after church leaders and ordinary families spoke out. The staff involved took what they learned in implementing this program with them to the extermination camps the Nazis would soon build in the east (Map 27.4).

The German victory over Poland in 1939 brought some 3 million Jews under Nazi control. Jews in German-occupied territories were soon forced to move into urban districts termed "ghettos." In walled-off ghettos in cities large and small—two of the most important were in Warsaw and Lodz—hundreds of thousands of Polish Jews lived in crowded and unsanitary conditions, without real work or adequate sustenance. Over 500,000 people died under these conditions.

The racial violence reached new extremes when Germany invaded the Soviet Union in 1941. Three

MAP 27.4 **The Holocaust, 1941–1945** The leaders of Nazi Germany established an extensive network of ghettos and concentration and extermination camps to persecute their political opponents and those people deemed "racially undesirable" by the regime. The death camps, where the Nazi SS systematically murdered millions of European Jews, Soviet prisoners of war, and others, were located primarily in Nazi-occupied territories in eastern Europe, but the conditions in the concentration camps within Germany's borders were almost as brutal.

military death squads known as Special Task Forces (*Einsatzgruppen*) and other military units followed the advancing German armies. They moved systematically from town to town, shooting Jews and other target populations. The victims of these mobile killing units were often forced to dig their own graves in local woods or fields before they were shot. In this way the German armed forces murdered some 2 million civilians.

In late 1941 Hitler and the Nazi leadership, in some still-debated combination, ordered the SS to implement the mass murder of all Jews in Europe. What the Nazi leadership called the "final solution of the Jewish question" had begun. The Germans set up an industrialized killing machine that remains unparalleled, with an extensive network of concentration camps, factory

complexes, and railroad transport lines to imprison and murder Jews and other so-called undesirables, and to exploit their labor before they died. In the occupied east, the surviving residents of the ghettos were loaded onto trains and taken to camps such as Auschwitz-Birkenau, the best known of the Nazi killing centers, where over 1 million people—the vast majority of them Jews—were murdered in gas chambers. Some few were put to work as expendable laborers. The Jews of Germany and then of occupied western and central Europe were likewise rounded up, put on trains, and sent to the camps. Even after it was quite clear that Germany would lose the war, the killing continued.

■ **Holocaust** The systematic effort of the Nazi state to exterminate all European Jews and other groups deemed racially inferior during the Second World War.

Given the scope and organization of Nazi persecution, there was little opportunity for successful Jewish resistance, yet some Jews did evade or challenge the killing machine. Some brave Jews went underground or masqueraded as Christian to escape Nazi roundups; others fled to rural areas and joined bands of anti-Nazi partisans. Jews also organized secret resistance groups in ghettos and concentration camps. When news of pending deportation to the Treblinka killing center reached the Jews still living in the Warsaw Ghetto in January 1943, poorly armed underground resistance groups opened fire on German troops. The Ghetto Uprising, with sporadic fighting dominated by the vastly superior German forces, lasted until May, when the last Jews were taken to extermination camps and the ghetto was razed to the ground. In Auschwitz itself, in October 1944, a group of Jewish prisoners revolted and burned down one of the camp's crematoriums before all were captured and summarily executed.

The murderous attack on European Jews was the ultimate monstrosity of Nazi "racial hygiene" and racial imperialism. By 1945 the Nazis had killed about 6 million Jews and some 5 million other Europeans, including millions of ethnic Poles and Russian POWs. (See "Individuals in Society: Primo Levi," page 907.) Who was responsible for this terrible crime? Historians continue to debate this critical question. Some lay the guilt on Hitler and the Nazi leadership, arguing that ordinary Germans had little knowledge of the extermination camps or were forced to participate by Nazi terror and totalitarian control. Other scholars conclude that far more Germans knew about and were at best indifferent to the fate of "racial inferiors."

The question remains: what inspired those who actually worked in the killing machine—the "desk murderers" in Berlin who sent trains to the east, the soldiers who shot Jews in the Polish forests, the guards at Auschwitz? Some historians believe that widely shared anti-Semitism led "ordinary Germans" to become Hitler's "willing executioners." Others argue that heightened peer pressure, the desire to advance in the ranks, and the need to prove one's strength under the most brutalizing wartime violence turned average Germans into reluctant killers. The conditioning of racist Nazi propaganda clearly played a role. Whatever the motivation, numerous Germans were somehow prepared to join the SS ideologues and perpetrate ever-greater crimes, from mistreatment to arrest to mass murder.[7]

Japanese Empire and the War in the Pacific

The racist war of annihilation in Europe was matched by racially inspired warfare in East Asia. In response to political divisions and economic crisis, a Fascist government had taken control of Japan in the 1930s. As in Germany and Italy, the Japanese government was highly nationalistic and militaristic, and it was deeply committed to imperial expansion. According to Japanese race theory, the Asian races were far superior to Western ones. In speeches, schools, and newspapers, ultranationalists eagerly voiced the extreme anti-Western views that had risen in the 1920s and 1930s. They glorified the warrior virtues of honor and sacrifice and proclaimed that Japan would liberate East Asia from Western colonialists.

Japan soon acted on its racial-imperial ambitions. In 1931 Japanese armies invaded and occupied Manchuria, a vast territory bordering northeastern China. In 1937 Japan brutally invaded China itself. Seeking to cement ties with the Fascist regimes of Europe, in 1940 the Japanese entered into a formal alliance with Italy and Germany, and in summer 1941 Japanese armies occupied southern portions of the French colony of Indochina (now Vietnam and Cambodia).

The goal was to establish what the Japanese called the Greater East Asia Co-Prosperity Sphere. Under the slogan "Asia for Asians," Japanese propagandists maintained that this expansion would free Asians from hated Western imperialists. By promising to create a mutually advantageous union for long-term development, the Japanese tapped currents of nationalist sentiment, and most local populations were glad to see the Westerners go.

But the Co-Prosperity Sphere was a sham. Real power remained in the hands of the Japanese. They exhibited great cruelty toward civilian populations and prisoners of war, and exploited local peoples for Japan's wartime needs, arousing local populations against them. Nonetheless, the ability of the Japanese to defeat the Western colonial powers set a powerful example for national liberation groups in Asia, which would become important in the decolonization movement that followed World War II.

Japanese expansion from 1937 to 1941 evoked a sharp response from U.S. president Franklin Roosevelt, and Japan's leaders came to believe that war with the United States was inevitable. After much debate, they decided to launch a surprise attack on the U.S. fleet based at Pearl Harbor in the Hawaiian Islands. On December 7, 1941, the Japanese sank or crippled every American battleship, but by chance all the American aircraft carriers were at sea and escaped unharmed. Pearl Harbor brought the Americans into the war in a spirit of anger and revenge.

As the Americans mobilized for war, Japanese armies overran more European and American colonies in Southeast Asia. By May 1942 Japan controlled a vast empire (Map 27.5) and was threatening Australia. The Americans pushed back and engaged the Japanese in a series of hard-fought naval battles. In July 1943 the Americans and their Australian allies opened a successful island-hopping campaign that slowly forced Japan out of its conquered territories. The war in the Pacific

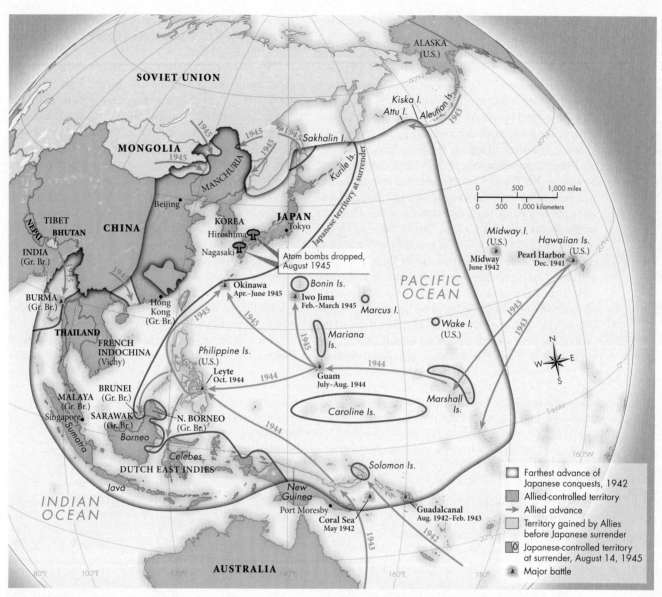

MAP 27.5 World War II in the Pacific   In 1942 Japanese forces overran an enormous amount of territory, which the Allies slowly recaptured in a long, bitter struggle. As this map shows, Japan still held a large Asian empire in August 1945, when the unprecedented devastation of atomic warfare suddenly forced it to surrender.

was extremely brutal—a "war without mercy," in the words of a leading American scholar—and soldiers on both sides committed atrocities. A product of spiraling violence, mutual hatred, and dehumanizing racial stereotypes, the fighting intensified as the United States moved toward Japan.[8]

The "Hinge of Fate"

While the Nazis and the Japanese built their savage empires, Great Britain, the United States, and the Soviet Union joined together in a military pact Churchill termed the Grand Alliance. This was a matter of circumstance more than of choice. It had taken the Japanese surprise attack to bring the isolationist United States

into the war. Moreover, the British and Americans were determined opponents of Soviet communism, and disagreements between the Soviets and the capitalist powers during the course of the war sowed mutual distrust. Stalin repeatedly urged Britain and the United States to open a second front in France to relieve pressure on Soviet forces, but Churchill and Roosevelt refused until the summer of 1944. Despite such tensions, the overriding goal of defeating the Axis powers brought together these reluctant allies.

In one area of agreement, the Grand Alliance concurred on a policy of "Europe first." Only after Hitler was defeated would the Allies mount an all-out attack on Japan, the lesser threat. The Allies also agreed to concentrate on immediate military needs, postponing tough political questions about the eventual peace settlement that might have divided them. To further encourage mutual trust, the Allies adopted the principle of the unconditional surrender of Germany and Japan. This policy cemented the Grand Alliance because it denied Hitler any hope of dividing his foes. It also meant that Soviet and Anglo-American armies would almost certainly be forced to invade and occupy all of Germany, and that Japan would fight to the bitter end.

The military resources of the Grand Alliance were awesome. The United States harnessed its vast industrial base to wage global war and in 1943 outproduced not only Germany, Italy, and Japan, but all of the rest of the world combined. Great Britain became an impregnable floating fortress, a gigantic frontline staging area for a decisive blow to the heart of Germany. After a determined push, the Soviet Union's military strength was so great that it might well have defeated Germany without Western help. Stalin drew heavily on the heroic resolve of the Soviet people, especially those in the central Russian heartland. Broad-based Russian nationalism, as opposed to narrow communist ideology,

became a powerful unifying force in what the Soviet people appropriately called the Great Patriotic War of the Fatherland.

The combined might of the Allies forced back the Nazi armies on all fronts (see Map 27.3). Through early 1942 heavy fighting between British and Axis forces had resulted in significant German advances in North Africa. At the Second Battle of El Alamein (el al-uh-MAYN) in October–November 1942, however, British forces decisively defeated combined German and Italian armies and halted Axis penetration of North Africa. Winston Churchill called the battle the "hinge of fate" that opened the door to Allied victory. Shortly thereafter, an Anglo-American force landed in Morocco and Algeria. These French possessions, which were under the control of Pétain's Vichy government, went over to the Allies. Fearful of an Allied invasion across the Mediterranean, German forces occupied Vichy France in November 1942, and the collaborationist French government effectively ceased to exist.

After driving the Axis powers out of North Africa, U.S. and British forces invaded Sicily in the

German Prisoners of War After the Battle of Stalingrad   Wrapped in coats and blankets to protect against the bitter Russian winter, these German prisoners of war were marched through the destroyed streets of Stalingrad in February 1943 after their defeat. The battle was a major turning point that marked the start of the destruction of Nazi Germany. Hundreds of thousands of soldiers on both sides lost their lives, and of the approximately 100,000 German prisoners taken by the Red Army only about 5,000 returned home after the war. (© Corbis)

summer of 1943 and mainland Italy that autumn. Mussolini was overthrown by a coup d'état, and the new Italian government publicly accepted unconditional surrender. In response, Nazi armies invaded and seized control of northern and central Italy, and German paratroopers rescued Mussolini in a daring raid and put him at the head of a puppet government. Facing stiff German resistance, the Allies battled their way slowly up the Italian peninsula. The Germans still held northern Italy, but they were clearly on the defensive.

The spring of 1943 brought crucial Allied victories at sea and in the air. In the first years of the war, German submarines had successfully attacked North Atlantic shipping, severely hampering the British war effort. New antisubmarine technologies favored the Allies. Soon massive convoys of hundreds of ships were streaming across the Atlantic, bringing much-needed troops and supplies from the United States to Britain.

The German air force had never really recovered from its defeat in the Battle of Britain. With almost unchallenged air superiority, the United States and Britain now mounted massive bombing raids on German cities to maim industrial production and break civilian morale. By the war's end, hardly a German city of any size remained untouched, and many—including Dresden, Hamburg, and Cologne—lay in ruins.

Great Britain and the United States had made critical advances in the western theater, but the worst German defeats came at the hands of the Red Army on the eastern front. Although the Germans had almost captured the major cities of Moscow and Leningrad in early winter 1941, they were forced back by determined Soviet counterattacks. The Germans mounted a second and initially successful invasion of the Soviet Union in the summer of 1942, but the campaign turned into a disaster. The downfall came at the Battle of Stalingrad, when in November 1942 the Soviets surrounded and systematically destroyed the entire German Sixth Army of 300,000 men. In January 1943 only 123,000 soldiers were left to surrender. Hitler, who had refused to allow a retreat, suffered a catastrophic defeat. For the first time, German public opinion turned decisively against the war. In summer 1943 the larger, better-equipped Soviet armies took the offensive and began to push the Germans back along the entire eastern front (see Map 27.3).

Allied Victory

The balance of power was now clearly in Allied hands, yet bitter fighting continued in Europe for almost two years. Germany, less fully mobilized for war in 1941 than Britain, stepped up its efforts. The German war industry, under the Nazi minister of armaments Albert Speer, put to work millions of prisoners of war and slave laborers from across occupied Europe. Between early 1942 and July 1944, German war production tripled despite heavy Anglo-American bombing.

German resistance against Hitler also failed to halt the fighting. An unsuccessful attempt by conservative army leaders to assassinate Hitler in July 1944 only brought increased repression by the fanatic Nazis who had taken over the government. Closely disciplined by the regime, frightened by the prospect of unconditional surrender, and terrorized by Nazi propaganda that portrayed the advancing Russian armies as rapacious Slavic beasts, the Germans fought on with suicidal resolve.

On June 6, 1944, American and British forces under General Dwight Eisenhower landed on the beaches of Normandy, France, in history's greatest naval invasion. In a hundred dramatic days, more than 2 million men and almost half a million vehicles broke through the German lines and pushed inland. Rejecting proposals to strike straight at Berlin in a massive attack, Eisenhower moved forward cautiously on a broad front. Not until March 1945 did American troops cross the Rhine and enter Germany. By spring of 1945 the Allies had finally forced the Germans out of the Italian peninsula. That April, Mussolini was captured in northern Italy by Communist partisans and executed, along with his mistress and other Fascist leaders.

The Soviets, who had been advancing steadily since July 1943, reached the outskirts of Warsaw by August 1944. Anticipating German defeat, the Polish underground Home Army ordered an uprising, so that the Poles might take the city on their own and establish independence from the Soviets. The Warsaw Uprising was a tragic miscalculation. Citing military pressure, the Red Army refused to enter the city. Stalin and Soviet leaders thus allowed the Germans to destroy the Polish insurgents, a cynical move that paved the way for the establishment of a postwar Communist regime. Only after the decimated Home Army surrendered did the Red Army continue its advance. Warsaw lay in ruins, and between 150,000 and 200,000 Poles—mostly civilians—had lost their lives.

Over the next six months, the Soviets moved southward into Romania, Hungary, and Yugoslavia. In January 1945 the Red Army crossed Poland into Germany, and on April 26 met American forces on the Elbe River. The Allies had overrun Europe and closed their vise on Nazi Germany. As Soviet forces fought their way into Berlin, Hitler committed suicide, and on May 8 the remaining German commanders capitulated.

The war in the Pacific also drew to a close. Despite repeated U.S. victories through the summer of 1945, Japanese troops had continued to fight with enormous courage and determination. American commanders believed the invasion and conquest of Japan itself might cost 1 million American casualties and claim 10 to 20 million Japanese lives. In fact, Japan was almost helpless, its industry and dense, fragile wooden cities

Nuclear Wasteland at Hiroshima   Only a handful of buildings remain standing in the ruins of Hiroshima in September 1945. Fearing the costs of a prolonged ground and naval campaign against the Japanese mainland, the United States dropped atomic bombs on Hiroshima and Nagasaki in August 1945. The bombings ended the war and opened the nuclear age. (AP Photo/AP Images)

largely destroyed by intense American bombing. Yet the Japanese seemed determined to fight on, ready to die for a hopeless cause.

After much discussion at the upper levels of the U.S. government, American planes dropped atomic bombs on Hiroshima and Nagasaki in Japan on August 6 and 9, 1945. The mass bombing of cities and civilians, one of the terrible new practices of World War II, now ended in the final nightmare—unprecedented human destruction in a single blinding flash. On August 14, 1945, the Japanese announced their surrender. The Second World War, which had claimed the lives of more than 50 million soldiers and civilians, was over.

NOTES

1. Quoted in S. Kotkin, *Magnetic Mountain: Stalinism as a Civilization* (Berkeley: University of California Press, 1997), pp. 221–222.
2. R. Thurston, *Life and Terror in Stalin's Russia, 1934–1941* (New Haven, Conn.: Yale University Press, 1996), esp. pp. 16–106; also M. Malia, *The Soviet Tragedy: A History of Socialism in Russia, 1917–1991* (New York: Free Press, 1995), pp. 227–270.
3. Quoted in C. Duggan, *A Concise History of Italy* (New York: Cambridge University Press, 1994), p. 227.
4. Quoted ibid, p. 234.
5. M. Burleigh and W. Wippermann, *The Racial State: Germany, 1933–1945* (New York: Cambridge University Press, 1991).
6. See, for example, the population statistics on the German occupation of Belarus in C. Gerlach, "German Economic Interests, Occupation Policy, and the Murder of the Jews in Belorussia, 1941–43," in *National Socialist Extermination Policies: Contemporary German Perspectives and Controversies*, U. Herbert, ed. (New York: Berghan Books, 2000), pp. 210–239. See also M. Allen, *The Business of Genocide: The SS, Slave Labor, and the Concentration Camps* (Chapel Hill: University of North Carolina Press, 2002), pp. 270–285.
7. D. Goldhagen, *Hitler's Willing Executioners: Ordinary Germans and the Holocaust* (New York: Vintage Books, 1997); for an alternate explanation, see C. Browning, *Ordinary Men: Reserve Police Battalion 101 and the Final Solution in Poland* (New York: Harper, 1992).
8. J. Dower, *War Without Mercy: Race and Power in the Pacific War* (New York: Pantheon, 1986).
9. E. Hobsbawm, *The Age of Extremes: A History of the World, 1914–1991* (New York: Vintage, 1996), p. 21.

LOOKING BACK LOOKING AHEAD

The first half of the twentieth century brought almost unimaginable violence and destruction, leading historian Eric Hobsbawm to label the era the "age of catastrophe."[9] Shaken by the rapid cultural change and economic collapse that followed the tragedy of World War I, many Europeans embraced the radical politics of communism and fascism. Some found appeal in visions of a classless society or a racially pure national community, and totalitarian dictators like Stalin and Hitler capitalized on these desires for social order, building dictatorial regimes that demanded total allegiance to an ideological vision. Even as these regimes rewarded supporters and promised ordinary people a new age, they violently repressed their enemies, real and imagined. The vision proved fatal: the great clash of ideologies that emerged in the 1920s and 1930s led to history's most deadly war, killing millions and devastating large swaths of Europe and East Asia.

Only the reluctant Grand Alliance of the liberal United States and Great Britain with the Communist Soviet Union was able to defeat the Axis powers. After 1945 fascism was finished, discredited by total defeat and the postwar revelation of the Holocaust. To make sure, the Allies would occupy the lands of their former enemies. Rebuilding a devastated Europe proved a challenging but in the end manageable task: once recovery took off, the postwar decades brought an economic boom that led to levels of prosperity unimaginable in the interwar years. Maintaining an alliance between the capitalist West and the Communist East was something else. Trust quickly broke down. Europe would be divided into two hostile camps, and Cold War tensions between East and West would dominate European and world politics for the next fifty years.

Make Connections

Think about the larger developments and continuities within and across chapters.

1. Historians continue to disagree on whether "totalitarianism" is an appropriate way to describe Communist and Fascist dictatorships in Europe. How would you define this term? Is it a useful label to describe state and society under Stalin, Mussolini, and Hitler? Why is the debate over totalitarianism still important today?

2. Why would ordinary people support dictatorships that trampled on familiar political freedoms and civil rights?

3. Summarize the key issues in the origins of World War II and the key turning points in the war itself. Was political ideology the main driving force behind these events or were other factors at play?

27 REVIEW & EXPLORE

Identify Key Terms

Identify and explain the significance of each item below.

totalitarianism (p. 904)

fascism (p. 905)

eugenics (p. 905)

five-year plan (p. 906)

New Economic Policy (NEP) (p. 906)

collectivization of agriculture (p. 911)

kulaks (p. 911)

Black Shirts (p. 916)

Lateran Agreement (p. 917)

National Socialism (p. 918)

Enabling Act (p. 919)

appeasement (p. 926)

New Order (p. 931)

Holocaust (p. 932)

Review the Main Ideas

Answer the focus questions from each section of the chapter.

◆ How were Fascist and Communist totalitarian dictatorships similar and different? (p. 904)

◆ How did Stalin and the Communist Party build a totalitarian state in the Soviet Union? (p. 906)

◆ What kind of government did Mussolini establish in Italy? (p. 915)

◆ What policies did Nazi Germany pursue, and how did they lead to World War II? (p. 917)

◆ How did Germany and Japan conquer enormous empires during World War II, and how did the Allies defeat them? (p. 928)

Suggested Reading and Media Resources

BOOKS

◆ Aly, Götz. *Hitler's Beneficiaries: Plunder, Racial War, and the Nazi Welfare State*. 2005. A controversial interpretation of popular support for the Hitler regime, focused on the material benefits of wartime plunder.

◆ Applebaum, Anne. *Gulag: A History*. 2004. An excellent study of Soviet police terror.

◆ Bergen, Doris L. *War and Genocide: A Concise History of the Holocaust*, 3d ed. 2016. A concise and accessible discussion of National Socialism and the murderous Nazi assault on European Jews and other groups.

◆ Bosworth, R. J. B. *Mussolini's Italy: Life Under the Fascist Dictatorship, 1915–1945*. 2007. An outstanding study of Italy under Mussolini.

◆ Browning, Christopher R. *Ordinary Men: Reserve Police Battalion 101 and the Final Solution in Poland*, 2d ed. 2001. A carefully researched, unnerving account of German atrocities in Poland during World War II.

◆ Geyer, Michael, and Sheila Fitzpatrick, eds. *Beyond Totalitarianism: Stalinism and Nazism Compared*. 2009. A collection of essays that compares the two dictatorships and challenges the usefulness of the totalitarian model.

◆ Kaplan, Marion A. *Between Dignity and Despair: Jewish Life in Nazi Germany*. 1998. A deeply moving book about the Jewish response to the Holocaust, with a compelling focus on women's history.

◆ Kotkin, Stephen. *Magnetic Mountain: Stalinism as a Civilization*. 1997. An extraordinary account of Stalinism and forced industrialization in the 1930s.

◆ Merridale, Catherine. *Ivan's War: Life and Death in the Red Army, 1939–1945*. 2007. An in-depth look at the lives of ordinary Soviet soldiers.

◆ Roberts, David D. *The Totalitarian Experiment in Twentieth-Century Europe: Understanding the Poverty of Great Politics*. 2006. Makes a case for the totalitarian model by comparing Stalinism, Nazism, and Italian fascism.

- Snyder, Timothy. *Bloodlands: Europe Between Hitler and Stalin*. 2010. A new synthesis that examines the murderous policies and practices of Nazi and Soviet authorities in east-central Europe before and during World War II.
- Weinberg, Gerhard L. *World at Arms: A Global History of World War II*, new ed. 2005. A masterful military history of World War II.

DOCUMENTARIES

- *A Film Unfinished* (Yael Hersonski, 2010). This documentary takes a critical look at the infamous Nazi propaganda film of the Warsaw Ghetto.
- *History of World War II* (BBC, 2005). With thirty hours of programming, this collection of ten BBC programs offers a wide range of analysis of World War II.
- *Night and Fog* (Alain Resnais, 1955). A justly famous, existentialism-influenced documentary about the Holocaust by a noted French film director.

FEATURE FILMS AND TELEVISION

- *Burnt by the Sun* (Nikita Mikhalkov, 1994). In a subtle, Oscar-winning film that ably expresses Russian attempts to come to grips with memories of Stalinism, Commander Sergei Kotov, an "Old Bolshevik," senior Red Army officer, and civil war hero, is unexpectedly trapped in his summer house by the great purges of the late 1930s.

- *The Conformist* (Bernardo Bertolucci, 1970). This art film explores the Fascist mentality through an investigation of a young man who joins the Fascist secret police and helps assassinate his former professor.
- *Hitler Youth Quex* (Hans Steinhoff, 1933). A Nazi propaganda film about a youth in the last years of the Weimar Republic who spurns the Communists and joins the Nazi Hitler Youth. The film can be streamed from the Internet and is easy to understand despite the lack of English subtitles.

WEB SITES

- *Eyewitness to History: World War II*. A remarkable collection of firsthand accounts from a variety of people, covering all theaters of the war. **www.eyewitnesstohistory.com/w2frm.htm**
- *Gulag: Many Days, Many Lives*. Explores the history of the Soviet Gulags through various exhibits, such as "Days and Lives," "Soviet Forced Labor Camps and the Struggle for Freedom," and "Tour a Gulag Camp." **gulaghistory.org/**
- *United States Holocaust Memorial Museum*. A vast collection of material on all aspects of the Holocaust and other acts of genocide. **www.ushmm.org**
- *Windows on War: Soviet Posters, 1943–1945*. A colorful collection of Soviet propaganda posters from the last years of the war. **http://windowsonwar.nottingham.ac.uk/**

28

Cold War Conflict and Consensus

1945–1965

The defeat of the Nazis and their allies in 1945 left Europe in ruins. In the immediate postwar years, as Europeans struggled to overcome the effects of rampant death and destruction, the victorious Allies worked to shape an effective peace accord. Disagreements between the Soviet Union and the Western allies emerged during this process and quickly led to an apparently endless Cold War between the two new superpowers—the United States and the Soviet Union. This conflict split much of Europe into a Soviet-aligned Communist bloc and a U.S.-aligned capitalist bloc and spurred military, economic, and technological competition.

Amid these tensions, battered western European countries fashioned a remarkable recovery, building strong democratic institutions and vibrant economies. In the Soviet Union and the "East Bloc" (the label applied to central and eastern European countries governed by Soviet-backed Communist regimes), Communist leaders repressed challenges to one-party rule but also offered limited reforms, leading to stability there as well. Yet the postwar period was by no means peaceful. Anti-Soviet uprisings in East Bloc countries led to military intervention and death and imprisonment for thousands. Colonial independence movements in the developing world sometimes erupted in violence, even after liberation was achieved. Cold War hostilities had an immense impact on the decolonization process, often to the detriment of formerly colonized peoples.

Cold War conflicts notwithstanding, the postwar decades witnessed the construction of a relatively stable social and political consensus in both Communist and capitalist Europe. At the same time, changing class structures, new migration patterns, and new roles for women and youths had a profound impact on European society, laying the groundwork for major transformations in the decades to come. ■

CHAPTER PREVIEW

Life in Eastern Europe
This relief sculpture, a revealing example of Socialist Realism from 1952, portrays (from left to right) a mail carrier, a builder, industrial workers, and peasants. It adorns the wall of the central post office in Banská Bystrica, a regional capital in present-day Slovakia (formerly part of Czechoslovakia). Citizens in the Soviet Union and its satellite countries of the East Bloc saw many such works of public art, which idealized the dignity of ordinary laborers and the advantages of communism. (© Georgios Makkas/Alamy Stock Photo)

Postwar Europe and the Origins of the Cold War

FOCUS QUESTION *Why was World War II followed so quickly by the Cold War?*

In 1945 the Allies faced the momentous challenges of rebuilding a shattered Europe, dealing with Nazi criminals, and creating a lasting peace. Reconstruction began and war crimes were punished, but the Allies found it difficult to cooperate in peacemaking. Motivated by different goals and hounded by misunderstandings, Great Britain and the United States found themselves at loggerheads with the Soviet Union (U.S.S.R.). Though a handful of countries maintained a neutral stance, by 1949 most of Europe was divided into East and West Blocs allied with the U.S.S.R. and the United States, respectively. For the next forty years, the competing superpowers engaged in the **Cold War**, a determined competition for political and military superiority around the world.

The Legacies of the Second World War

In the summer of 1945 Europe lay in ruins. Across the continent, the fighting had destroyed cities and landscapes and obliterated buildings, factories, farms, rail tracks, roads, and bridges. Many cities—including Leningrad, Warsaw, Vienna, Budapest, Rotterdam, and Coventry—were completely devastated. Postwar observers compared the remaining piles of rubble to moonscapes. Surviving cities such as Prague and Paris were left relatively unscathed, mostly by chance.

The human costs of the Second World War are almost incalculable (Map 28.1). The death toll far exceeded the mortality figures for World War I. At least 20 million Soviets, including soldiers and civilians, died in the war. Between 9 and 11 million noncombatants lost their lives in Nazi concentration camps, including approximately 6 million Jews and over 220,000 Sinti and Roma (sometimes called Gypsies). One out of every five Poles died in the war, including 3 million of Poland's 3.25 million Jews. German deaths numbered 5 million, 2 million of them civilians. France and Britain both lost fewer soldiers than in World War I, but about 350,000 French civilians were killed in the fighting. Over 400,000 U.S. soldiers died in the European and Pacific campaigns, and other nations across Europe and the globe also lost staggering numbers. In total, about 50 million human beings perished in the conflict.

The destruction of war also left tens of millions homeless—25 million in the U.S.S.R. and 20 million in Germany alone. The wartime policies of Hitler and Stalin had forced some 30 million people from their homes in the hardest-hit war zones of central and eastern Europe. The end of the war and the start of the peace

Displaced Persons in the Ruins of Berlin   The end of the war in 1945 stopped the fighting but not the suffering. For the next two years, millions of displaced persons wandered across Europe searching for sustenance, lost family members, and a place to call home. (Fred Rampage/Getty Images)

increased their numbers. Some 13 million ethnic Germans fled west before the advancing Soviet troops or were expelled from eastern Europe under the terms of Allied agreements. Forced laborers from Poland, France, the Balkans, and other nations, brought to Germany by the Nazis, now sought to go home. A woman in Berlin described the flow of refugees passing through the city in spring 1945:

> The streets were filled with small, tired caravans of people.... All the vehicles looked the same: pitiful handcarts piled high with sacks, crates, and trunks. Often I saw a woman or an older child in front, harnessed to a rope, pulling the cart forward, with the smaller children or a grandpa pushing from behind. There were people perched on top, too, usually very little children or elderly relatives. The old people look terrible amid all the junk, the men as well as the women—pale, dilapidated, apathetic. Half-dead sacks of bones.[1]

These **displaced persons** or DPs—their numbers increased by concentration camp survivors and freed prisoners of war, and hundreds of thousands of orphaned children—searched for food and shelter. From 1945 to 1947 the newly established United Nations Relief and Rehabilitation Administration (UNRRA) opened over 760 DP camps and spent $10 billion to house, feed, clothe, and repatriate the refugees.

For DPs, going home was not always the best option. Soviet citizens who had spent time in the West were seen as politically unreliable by political leaders in the U.S.S.R. Many DPs faced prison terms, exile to labor camps in the Siberian gulag, and even execution upon their return to Soviet territories. Jewish DPs faced unique problems. Their families and communities had been destroyed, and persistent anti-Semitism often made them unwelcome in their former homelands. Many stayed in special Jewish DP camps in Germany for years. After the creation of Israel in 1948 (see page 967), over 330,000 European Jews left for the new Jewish state. By 1952 about 100,000 Jews had also immigrated to the United States; smaller numbers moved to other western European countries, South America, and the British Commonwealth countries. When the last DP camp closed in 1957, the UNRRA had cared for and resettled many millions of refugees, Jews and non-Jews alike.

When the fighting stopped, Germany and Austria had been divided into four occupation zones, each governed by one of the Allies—the United States, the Soviet Union, Great Britain, and France. The Soviets collected substantial reparations from their zone in eastern Germany and from former German allies Hungary and Romania. In Soviet-occupied Germany, administrators seized factories and equipment, even tearing up railroad tracks and sending the rails to the U.S.S.R.

The authorities in each zone tried to punish those guilty of Nazi atrocities. Across Europe, almost 100,000 Germans and Austrians were convicted of war crimes. Many more were investigated or indicted. In Soviet-dominated central and eastern Europe—where the worst crimes had taken place—retribution was particularly intense. There and in other parts of Europe, collaborators, non-Germans who had assisted the German occupiers during the war, were also punished. In the days and months immediately after the war, spontaneous acts of retribution brought some collaborators to account. In both France and Italy, unofficial groups seeking revenge summarily executed some 25,000 persons. French women accused of "horizontal

Chronology

1945	Yalta Conference; end of World War II in Europe; Potsdam Conference; Nuremberg trials begin
1945–1960s	Decolonization of Asia and Africa
1945–1965	United States takes lead in Big Science
1947	Truman Doctrine; Marshall Plan
1948	Foundation of Israel
1948–1949	Berlin airlift
1949	Creation of East and West Germany; formation of NATO; establishment of COMECON
1950–1953	Korean War
1953	Death of Stalin
1954–1962	Algerian War of Independence
1955	Warsaw Pact founded
1955–1964	Khrushchev in power; de-Stalinization of Soviet Union
1956	Suez crisis
1957	Formation of Common Market; Pasternak publishes *Doctor Zhivago*
1961	Building of Berlin Wall
1962	Cuban missile crisis; Solzhenitsyn publishes *One Day in the Life of Ivan Denisovich*
1964	Brezhnev replaces Khrushchev as Soviet leader

■ **Cold War** The rivalry between the Soviet Union and the United States that divided much of Europe into a Soviet-aligned Communist bloc and a U.S.-aligned capitalist bloc between 1945 and 1989.

■ **displaced persons** Postwar refugees, including 13 million Germans, former Nazi prisoners and forced laborers, and orphaned children.

MAP 28.1 The Aftermath of World War II in Europe, ca. 1945–1950

By 1945 millions of people displaced by war and territorial changes were on the move. The Soviet Union and Poland took land from Germany, which the Allies partitioned into occupation zones. Those zones subsequently formed the basis of the East and West German states. Austria was detached from Germany and similarly divided, but the Soviets subsequently permitted Austria to reunify as a neutral state.

ANALYZING THE MAP Which groups fled west? Who went east? How would you characterize the general direction of most of these movements?

CONNECTIONS What does the widespread movement of people at the end of the war suggest about the war? What does it suggest about the ensuing political climate?

collaboration"—having sexual relations with German soldiers during the occupation—were publicly humiliated by angry mobs. Newly established postwar governments also formed official courts to sanction collaborators or send them to prison. A small number received the death sentence.

In Germany and Austria, occupation authorities set up "denazification" procedures meant to identify and punish former Nazi Party members responsible for the worst crimes and eradicate National Socialist ideology from social and political institutions. At the Nuremberg trials (1945–1946), an international military tribunal organized by the four Allied powers tried the highest-ranking Nazi military and civilian leaders who had survived the war, charging them with war crimes and crimes against humanity. After chilling testimony from victims of the regime, which revealed the full systematic horror of Nazi atrocities, twelve were sentenced to death and ten more to lengthy prison terms.

The Nuremberg trials marked the last time the four Allies worked closely together to punish former Nazis. As the Cold War developed and the Soviets and the Western Allies drew increasingly apart, each carried out separate denazification programs in their own zones of occupation. In the Western zones, military courts at first actively prosecuted leading Nazis. But the huge numbers implicated in Nazi crimes, German opposition to the proceedings, and the need for stability in the looming Cold War made thorough denazification impractical. Except for the worst offenders, the Western authorities had quietly shelved denazification by 1948. The process was similar in the Soviet zone. At first, punishment was swift and harsh. About 45,000 former party officials, upper-class industrialists, and large landowners identified as Nazis were sentenced to prison or death. As in the West, however, former Nazis who cooperated with the Soviet authorities could avoid prosecution. Thus many former Nazis found leading positions in government and industry in both the Soviet and Western zones.

The Peace Settlement and Cold War Origins

In the years immediately after the war, as ordinary people across Europe struggled to come to terms with the war and recover from the ruin, the victorious Allies—the U.S.S.R., the United States, and Great Britain—tried to shape a reasonable and lasting peace. Yet the Allies began to quarrel almost as soon as the unifying threat of Nazi Germany disappeared, and the interests of the Communist Soviet Union and the capitalist Britain and United States increasingly diverged. The hostility between the Eastern and Western superpowers was the sad but logical outgrowth of military developments, wartime agreements, and long-standing political and ideological differences that stretched back to the Russian Revolution.

Once the United States entered the war in late 1941, the Americans and the British had made military victory their highest priority. They did not try to take advantage of the Soviet Union's precarious position in 1942, because they feared that hard bargaining would encourage Stalin to consider making a separate peace with Hitler. Together, the Allies avoided discussion of postwar aims and the shape of the eventual peace settlement and focused instead on pursuing a policy of German unconditional surrender to solidify

the alliance. By late 1943 negotiations about the postwar settlement could no longer be postponed. The conference that the "Big Three"—Stalin, Roosevelt, and Churchill—held in the Iranian capital of Teheran in November 1943 proved crucial for determining the shape of the postwar world.

At Teheran, the Big Three jovially reaffirmed their determination to crush Germany, followed by tense discussions of Poland's postwar borders and a strategy to win the war. Stalin, concerned that the U.S.S.R. was bearing the brunt of the fighting, asked his allies to relieve his armies by opening a second front in German-occupied France. Churchill, fearing the military dangers of a direct attack, argued that American and British forces should follow up their Italian campaign with an indirect attack on Germany through the Balkans. Roosevelt, however, agreed with Stalin that an American-British assault through France would be better, though the date for the invasion was set later than the Soviet leader desired. This decision had momentous implications for the Cold War. While the delay in opening a second front fanned Stalin's distrust of the Allies, the agreement on a British-U.S. invasion of France also ensured that the American-British and Soviet armies would come together in defeated Germany along a north-south line, and that Soviet troops would play the predominant role in pushing the Germans out of eastern and central Europe. Thus the basic shape of postwar Europe was cast even as the fighting continued.

When the Big Three met again in February 1945 at Yalta, on the Black Sea in southern Russia, advancing Soviet armies had already occupied Poland, Bulgaria, Romania, Hungary, part of Yugoslavia, and much of Czechoslovakia, and were within a hundred miles of Berlin. The stalled American-British forces had yet to cross the Rhine into Germany. Moreover, the United States was far from defeating Japan. In short, the U.S.S.R.'s position on the ground was far stronger than that of the United States and Britain, which played to Stalin's advantage.

The Allies agreed at Yalta that each of the four victorious powers would occupy a separate zone of Germany and that the Germans would pay heavy reparations to the Soviet Union. At American insistence, Stalin agreed to declare war on Japan after Germany's defeat. As for Poland, the Big Three agreed that the U.S.S.R. would permanently incorporate the eastern Polish territories its army had occupied in 1939 and that Poland would be compensated with German lands to the west. They also agreed in an ambiguous compromise that the new governments in Soviet-occupied Europe would be freely elected but "friendly" to the Soviet Union.

The Yalta compromise over elections in these countries broke down almost immediately. Even before the conference, Communist parties were taking control in Bulgaria and Poland. Elsewhere, the Soviets formed coalition governments that included Social Democrats

The Big Three   In 1945 a triumphant Winston Churchill, an ailing Franklin Roosevelt, and a determined Stalin met at Yalta in southern Russia to plan for peace. Cooperation soon gave way to bitter hostility, and the decisions made by these leaders transformed the map of Europe. (Franklin D. Roosevelt Presidential Library and Museum of the National Archives and Records Administration/U.S. National Archives)

and other leftist parties but reserved key government posts for Moscow-trained Communists. At the Potsdam Conference of July 1945, the differences over elections in Soviet-occupied Europe surged to the fore. Roosevelt had died and had been succeeded by Harry Truman (U.S. pres. 1945–1953), who demanded immediate free elections throughout central and eastern Europe. Stalin refused point-blank. "A freely elected government in any of these East European countries would be anti-Soviet," he admitted simply, "and that we cannot allow."[2]

Here, then, were the keys to the much-debated origins of the Cold War. While fighting Germany, the Allies could maintain an alliance of necessity. As the war drew to a close, long-standing hostility between East and West re-emerged. Mutual distrust, security concerns, and antagonistic desires for economic, political, and territorial control began to destroy the former partnership.

Stalin, who had lived through two enormously destructive German invasions, was determined to establish a

- **Truman Doctrine** America's policy geared to containing communism to those countries already under Soviet control.

- **Marshall Plan** American plan for providing economic aid to western Europe to help it rebuild.

buffer zone of sympathetic states around the U.S.S.R. and at the same time expand the reach of communism and the Soviet state. Stalin believed that only Communists could be dependable allies, and that free elections would result in independent and possibly hostile governments on his western border. With Soviet armies in central and eastern Europe, there was no way short of war for the United States to control the region's political future, and war was out of the question. The United States, for its part, pushed to maintain democratic capitalism and open access to free markets in western Europe. The Americans quickly showed that they, too, were willing to use their vast political, economic, and military power to maintain predominance in their sphere of influence.

West Versus East

The Cold War took shape over the next five years, as both sides hardened their positions. After Japan's surrender in September 1945, Truman cut off aid to the ailing U.S.S.R. In October he declared that the United States would never recognize any government established by force against the will of its people. In March 1946 former British prime minister Churchill ominously informed an American audience that an "iron curtain" had fallen across the continent, dividing Europe into two antagonistic camps (Map 28.2).

The Soviet Union was indeed consolidating its hold on central and eastern Europe. In fact, the Soviets enjoyed some popular support in the region, though this varied from country to country. After all, the Red Army had thrown out the German invaders, and after the abuses of fascism the ideals of Communist equality retained some appeal. Yet the Communist parties in these areas quickly recognized that they lacked enough support to take power in free elections. In Romania, Bulgaria, Poland, and Hungary, Communist politicians, backed by Moscow, repressed their liberal opponents and engineered phony elections that established Communist-led regimes. They purged the last remaining noncommunists from the coalition governments set up after the war and by 1948 had established Soviet-style, one-party Communist dictatorships. The pattern was somewhat different in Czechoslovakia, where Communists enjoyed success in open elections and initially formed a coalition government with other parties. When the noncommunist ministers resigned in February 1948, the Communists took over the government and began Stalinizing the country. This seizure of power in Czechoslovakia greatly contributed to Western fears of limitless Communist expansion.

In western Europe, communism also enjoyed some support. In Italy, which boasted the largest Communist Party outside of the Soviet bloc, Communists won 19 percent of the vote in 1946; French Communists earned 28 percent of the vote the same year. These

MAP 28.2 Cold War Europe in the 1950s The Cold War divided Europe into two hostile military alliances that formed to the east and west of an "iron curtain."

large, well-organized parties criticized the growing role of the United States in western Europe and challenged their own governments with violent rhetoric and large strikes. At the same time, bitter civil wars in Greece and China pitted Communist revolutionaries against authoritarian leaders backed by the United States.

By early 1947 it appeared to many Americans that the U.S.S.R. was determined to export communism by subversion throughout Europe and around the world. The United States responded with the **Truman Doctrine**, aimed at "containing" communism to areas already under Communist governments, a policy first advocated by U.S. diplomat George Kennan in 1946. The United States, President Truman promised, would use diplomatic, economic, and even military means to resist the expansion of communism anywhere on the globe. In the first examples of containment policies in action, Truman asked Congress to provide military aid to anticommunist forces in the Greek Civil War (1944–1949) and counter the threat of Soviet expansion in Turkey. With American support, both countries remained in the Western bloc. The American determination to enforce containment hardened when the Soviets exploded their own atomic bomb in 1949, raising popular fears of a looming nuclear holocaust. At home

and abroad, the United States engaged in an anticommunist crusade. Emotional, moralistic denunciations of Stalin and Communist regimes became part of American public life. By the early 1950s the U.S. government was restructuring its military to meet the Soviet threat, pouring money into defense spending, and testing nuclear weapons that dwarfed the destructive power of atomic bombs.

Military aid and a defense buildup were only one aspect of Truman's policy of containment. In 1947 western Europe was still on the verge of economic collapse. Food was scarce, inflation was high, and black markets flourished. Recognizing that an economically and politically stable western Europe would be an effective block against the popular appeal of communism, U.S. secretary of state George C. Marshall offered Europe economic aid—the **Marshall Plan**— to help it rebuild. As Marshall wrote in a State Department bulletin, "Its purpose should be the revival of a working economy in the world so as to permit the emergence of political and social conditions in which free institutions can exist."[3]

The Marshall Plan was one of the most successful foreign aid programs in history. When it ended in 1951, the United States had given about $13 billion in aid (equivalent to over $200 billion in 2015 dollars) to fifteen western European nations, and Europe's economy was on the way to recovery. Marshall Plan funding was initially offered to East Bloc countries as well, but fearing Western interference in the Soviet sphere, they rejected the offer. In 1949 the Soviets established the **Council for Mutual Economic Assistance (COMECON)**, an economic organization of Communist states intended to rebuild the East Bloc independently of the West. Thus the generous aid of the Marshall Plan was limited to countries in the Western bloc, which further increased Cold War divisions.

In the late 1940s Berlin, the capital city of Germany, was on the frontline of the Cold War. Like the rest of Germany and Austria, Berlin had been divided into four zones of occupation. In June 1948 the Western allies replaced the currency in the western zones of Germany and Berlin, an early move in plans to establish a separate West German state sympathetic to U.S. interests. The currency reform violated the peace settlement and raised Stalin's fears of the American presence in Europe. In addition, growing ties among Britain, France, Belgium, and the Netherlands convinced Stalin that a Western bloc was forming against the Soviet Union. In response, the Soviet dictator used the one card he had to play—access to Berlin—to force the allies to the bargaining table. Stalin blocked all traffic through the Soviet zone of Germany to Berlin in an attempt to win concessions and perhaps reunify the city under Soviet control. Acting firmly, the Western allies coordinated around-the-clock flights of hundreds of planes over the Soviet roadblocks, supplying provisions to West Berliners and thwarting Soviet efforts to swallow up the western half of the city. After 324 days, the Berlin airlift succeeded, and the Soviets reopened the roads.

Success in breaking the Berlin blockade had several lasting results. First, it paved the way for the creation of two separate German states in 1949: the Federal Republic of Germany (West Germany), aligned with the United States, and the German Democratic Republic (East Germany), aligned with the U.S.S.R. Germany would remain divided for the next forty-one years, a radical solution to the "German problem" that satisfied people fearful of the nation's possible military resurgence.

The Berlin crisis also seemed to show that containment worked, and thus strengthened U.S. resolve to maintain a strong European and U.S. military presence in western Europe. In 1949 the United States formed **NATO** (the North Atlantic Treaty Organization), an anti-Soviet military alliance of Western governments. As one British diplomat put it, NATO was designed "to keep the Russians out, the Americans in, and the Germans down."[4] With U.S. backing, West Germany joined NATO in 1955 and was allowed to rebuild its military to help defend western Europe against possible Soviet attack. That same year, the Soviets countered by organizing the **Warsaw Pact**, a military alliance among the U.S.S.R. and its Communist satellites. In both political and military terms, most of Europe was divided into two hostile blocs.

The superpower confrontation that emerged from the ruins of World War II took shape in Europe, but it quickly spread around the globe. The Cold War turned hot in East Asia. When Soviet-backed Communist North Korea invaded South Korea in 1950, President Truman swiftly sent U.S. troops. In the end, the Korean War was indecisive: the fragile truce agreed to in 1953 left Korea divided between a Communist north and a capitalist south. The war nonetheless showed that though the superpowers might maintain a fragile peace in Europe, they were perfectly willing to engage in open conflict in non-Western territories.

By 1955 the Soviet-American confrontation had become an apparently permanent feature of world affairs. For the next thirty-five years, despite intermittent periods of relaxation, the superpowers would struggle to win political influence and territorial control and to achieve technological superiority. Cold War hostilities helped foster a nuclear arms race, a space race, and the computer revolution, all made possible by stunning advances in science and technology.

Big Science in the Nuclear Age

During the Second World War, theoretical science lost its innocence when it was joined with practical technology (applied science) on a massive scale. Many leading university scientists went to work on top-secret projects to help their governments fight the war. The development by British scientists of radar to detect enemy aircraft was a particularly important outcome of this new kind of sharply focused research. The air war also greatly stimulated the development of rocketry and jet aircraft. The most spectacular and deadly result of directed scientific research during the war was the atomic bomb, which showed the world both the awesome power and the heavy moral responsibilities of modern science and its high priests.

The impressive results of this directed research inspired a new model for science—Big Science. By combining theoretical work with sophisticated engineering in a large bureaucratic organization, Big Science could tackle extremely difficult problems, from new and improved weapons for the military to better products for consumers. Big Science was extremely

---

■ **Council for Mutual Economic Assistance (COMECON)** An economic organization of Communist states meant to help rebuild East Bloc countries under Soviet auspices.

■ **NATO** The North Atlantic Treaty Organization, an anti-Soviet military alliance of Western governments.

■ **Warsaw Pact** Soviet-backed military alliance of East Bloc Communist countries in Europe.

The Soviet View of the Arms Race
During the 1950s and 1960s the United States and the Soviet Union (with its east European satellite allies) engaged in an all-out nuclear arms race. The battle to stockpile massive numbers of atomic weapons involved rapid scientific advance, public displays of powerful weaponry, and accusatory propaganda campaigns. On the twentieth anniversary of victory in World War II, Communist authorities in Prague, the capital of Czechoslovakia, watched a parade of the latest Soviet ballistic missiles (above). The Soviet cartoon (right) depicting the United States masking its nuclear threat as the dove of peace reads, "Washington 'Dove'—Though cleverly disguised, it does not hide its cowardly insides." (missiles: Friedrich/Interfoto/akg-images; cartoon: Private Collection/Peter Newark Military Pictures/Bridgeman Images)

expensive, requiring large-scale financing from governments and large corporations.

After the war, scientists continued to contribute to advances in military technologies, and a large portion of all postwar scientific research supported the growing arms race. New weapons such as missiles, nuclear submarines, and spy satellites demanded breakthroughs no less remarkable than those responsible for radar and the first atomic bomb. After 1945 roughly one-quarter of all men and women trained in science and engineering in the West—and perhaps more in the Soviet Union—were employed full-time in the production of weapons to kill other humans. By the 1960s both sides had enough nuclear firepower to destroy each other and the rest of the world many times over.

Sophisticated science, lavish government spending, and military needs came together in the space race of the 1960s. In 1957 the Soviets used long-range rockets developed in their nuclear weapons program to launch Sputnik, the first man-made satellite to orbit the earth. In 1961 they sent the world's first cosmonaut circling the globe. Embarrassed by Soviet triumphs, the United States caught "Sputnikitis" and made an all-out commitment to catch up with the Soviets. The U.S. National Aeronautics and Space Administration (NASA), founded in 1958, won a symbolic victory by landing a manned spacecraft on the moon in 1969. Four more moon landings followed by 1972.

Advanced nuclear weapons and the space race were made possible by the concurrent revolution in computer technology. The search for better weaponry in World War II boosted the development of sophisticated data-processing machines, including the electronic Colossus computer used by the British to break German military codes. The massive mainframe ENIAC (Electronic Numerical Integrator and Computer), built for the U.S. Army at the University of Pennsylvania, went into operation in 1945. The invention of the transistor in 1947 further advanced computer design. From the mid-1950s on, this small, efficient electronic switching device increasingly replaced bulky vacuum tubes as the key computer components. By the 1960s sophisticated computers were indispensable tools for a variety of military, commercial, and scientific uses, foreshadowing the rise of personal computers in the decades to come.

Big Science had tangible benefits for ordinary people. During the postwar green revolution, directed agricultural research greatly increased the world's food supplies. Farming was industrialized and became more and more productive per acre, resulting in far fewer people being needed to grow food. The application of scientific advances to industrial processes made consumer goods less expensive and more available to larger numbers of people. The transistor, for example, was used in computers but also in portable radios, kitchen appliances, and many other consumer products. In sum, in the nuclear age, Big Science created new sources of material well-being and entertainment as well as destruction.

The Western Renaissance/ Recovery in Western Europe

FOCUS QUESTION *What were the sources of postwar recovery and stability in western Europe?*

In the late 1940s the outlook for Europe appeared bleak. Ruins still covered urban areas, economic conditions were the worst in generations, and Cold War confrontations divided the continent. Yet Europe recovered, with the nations of western Europe in the vanguard. In less than a generation, many western European countries constructed democratic political institutions and entered a period of unprecedented economic growth. As a consumer revolution brought improved living standards and a sense of prosperity to ever-larger numbers of people, politicians entered collective economic agreements and established the European Economic Community, the first steps toward broader European unity.

■ **economic miracle** Term contemporaries used to describe rapid economic growth, often based on the consumer sector, in post–World War II western Europe.

■ **Christian Democrats** Center-right political parties that rose to power in western Europe after the Second World War.

The Search for Political and Social Consensus

In the first years after the war, economic conditions in western Europe were terrible. Infrastructure of all kinds barely functioned, and runaway inflation and a thriving black market testified to severe shortages and hardships. In 1948, as Marshall Plan dollars poured in, the battered economies of western Europe began to improve. The outbreak of the Korean War in 1950 further stimulated economic activity, and Europe entered a period of rapid economic progress that lasted into the late 1960s. Never before had the European economy grown so fast. By the late 1950s contemporaries were talking about a widespread **economic miracle** that had brought robust growth to most western European countries.

There were many reasons for this stunning economic performance. American aid got the process off to a fast start. Moreover, economic growth became a basic objective of all western European governments, for leaders and voters alike were determined to avoid a return to the dangerous and demoralizing stagnation of the 1930s.

The postwar governments in western Europe thus embraced new political and economic policies that led to a remarkably lasting social consensus. They turned to liberal democracy and generally adopted Keynesian economics (see Chapter 26) in successful attempts to stimulate their economies. In addition, whether they leaned to the left or to the right, national leaders in the core European states applied an imaginative mixture of government planning and free-market capitalism to promote economic growth. They nationalized (or established government ownership of) significant sectors of the economy, used economic regulation to encourage growth, and established generous welfare provisions, paid for with high taxes, for all citizens. This consensual framework for good government lasted until the middle of the 1970s.

In politics, the Nazi occupation and the war had discredited old ideas and old leaders, and a new team of European politicians emerged to guide the postwar recovery. Across the West, newly formed Christian Democratic parties became important power brokers. Rooted in the Catholic parties of the prewar decades (see Chapters 23 and 27), the **Christian Democrats** offered voters tired of radical politics a center-right vision of reconciliation and recovery. Socialists and Communists, active in the resistance against Hitler, also increased their power and prestige, especially in France and Italy. They, too, provided fresh leadership as they pushed for social change and economic reform.

Across much of continental Europe, the centrist Christian Democrats defeated their left-wing competition. In Italy, the Christian Democrats were the leading party in the first postwar elections in 1946, and in early 1948 they won an absolute majority in the parliament in a landslide victory. In France, the Popular

Western European Recovery and the Promise of Prosperity

Christian Democrat Ludwig Erhard, minister for economic affairs (1949–1963) and then chancellor (1963–1966) of West Germany, was an outspoken proponent of liberal capitalism and free markets in the years of the "economic miracle." In this newspaper article from June 16, 1953, Erhard defends the use of consumer credit and the expansion of consumption, starting with the wealthy, as an engine of postwar economic growth.

~

I have often pointed out that the consumption of quality goods can only be expanded provided we tolerate their use being confined initially to a relatively small number of people in the higher income brackets. If this is not accepted, and if the enjoyment of such goods is regarded as indulgence and made the subject of social obloquy and hostility, then the economy will be forced to abandon production in this sector, and there will be a corresponding loss of potential national income (and jobs) and the growth of the country's productive capacity will be forcibly curtailed. One section of the press actually challenged me to say how an old-age pensioner was to set about getting his refrigerator. To this puerile question I replied that the first motor-cars in America were presumably not run by pensioners but by millionaires, and I do not consider this reply unduly flippant. Does not the history of the world in the last hundred years afford abundant proof of the fact that every single improvement in the standard of living can only be effected step by step, spreading progressively over a gradually mounting proportion of the population? . . .

Ever since 1948 I have been propounding an economic policy which puts the consumer at the very centre of all economic processes, by ensuring freedom of choice to him and restoring him to a position of dignity and power. . . .

Responding to a critique of shoppers purchasing goods on credit, Erhard continues:

~

At first sight, this argument seems reasonable enough, but in the balance-sheet of the economy as a whole the picture looks different. Consumer credit enables goods to be produced which could otherwise not find a market. . . . Now, consumer credit goes a step further and initiates an expansion of production (e.g. of refrigerators), and this expanded production creates new income which in its turn appears as additional purchasing power on the market. The volume of goods at the disposal of the economy has in other words been built up to a higher level, the national product and the national income have been extended. . . .

In this connection of course the question of magnitude is of vital importance. Consumer credit cannot carry, but can usefully supplement an upswing of the economy as a whole. . . . The use of consumer credit [is] one of the means capable of subserving a general policy aimed at expanded consumption. . . .

Consumer credit can be a means of increasing employment, creating additional returns, and thus enlarging the national product and the national income. The wider the choice of goods available to the consumer, the more active competition becomes, and the more prices will tend to come down, to the benefit of us all.

EVALUATE THE EVIDENCE

1. How, according to Erhard, does expanded consumption and the use of credit lead to economic growth?
2. Why would promises of looming prosperity — such as Erhard's — play an important role in Cold War rhetoric?

Source: Ludwig Erhard, *The Economics of Success*, trans. J. A. Arengo-Jones and D. J. S. Thomson (Princeton: D. Van Nostrand Co., 1963). Used by permission of Ludwig-Erhard-Stiftung e.V.

Republican Movement, a Christian Democratic party, provided some of the best postwar leaders after General Charles de Gaulle (duh GOHL) resigned from his position as head of the provisional government in January 1946. West Germans, too, elected a Christian Democratic government from 1949 until 1969.

As they provided effective leadership for their respective countries, Christian Democrats drew inspiration from a common Christian and European heritage. They firmly rejected authoritarianism and narrow nationalism and placed their faith in democracy and liberalism. The anticommunist rhetoric of these steadfast cold war-

riors was unrelenting. Rejecting the class politics of the left, they championed a return to traditional family values, a vision with great appeal after a war that left many broken families and destitute households; the Christian Democrats often received a majority of women's votes.

Following their U.S. allies, Christian Democrats advocated free-market economics and promised voters prosperity and ample supplies of consumer goods. (See "Evaluating the Evidence 28.1: Western European Recovery and the Promise of Prosperity," above.) At the same time, they established education subsidies, family and housing allowances, public transportation, and public health insurance throughout continental Europe. When necessary, Christian Democratic leaders accepted the need for limited government planning. In France, the government established modernization commissions for key industries, and state-controlled banks funneled money into industrial development. In West Germany, the Christian Democrats broke decisively with the straitjacketed Nazi economy and promoted a "social-market economy" based on a combination of free-market liberalism, some state intervention, and an extensive social benefits network.

Though Portugal, Spain, and Greece generally supported NATO and the United States in the Cold War, they proved exceptions to the rule of democratic transformation outside the Soviet bloc. In Portugal and Spain, nationalist authoritarian regimes had taken power in the 1930s. Portugal's authoritarian state was overthrown in a left-wing military coup only in 1974, while Spain's dictator Francisco Franco remained in power until his death in 1975. The authoritarian monarchy established in Greece when the civil war ended in 1949, bolstered by military support and kept in power in a series of army coups, was likewise replaced by a democratic government only in 1975.

By contrast, the Scandinavian countries and Great Britain took decisive turns to the left. Norway, Denmark, and especially Sweden earned a global reputation for long-term Social Democratic governance, generous state-sponsored welfare benefits, tolerant lifestyles, and independent attitudes toward Cold War conflicts. In Britain, the social-democratic Labour Party took power after the war and ambitiously established a "cradle-to-grave" welfare state. Although the Labour Party suffered defeats throughout much of the 1950s and early 1960s, its Conservative opponents maintained much of the welfare state when they came to power.

Many British industries were nationalized, including banks, iron and steel industries, and utilities and public transportation networks. The British government gave its citizens free medical services and hospital care, generous retirement pensions, and unemployment benefits, all subsidized by progressive taxation that pegged tax payments to income levels, with the wealthy paying significantly more than those below them. Even though wartime austerity and rationing programs were in place until the mid-1950s, Britain offered the most comprehensive state benefit programs outside Scandinavia. Economic growth and state-sponsored welfare measures meant that, by the early 1960s, western European living standards were higher than ever before.

Toward European Unity

Though there were important regional differences across much of western Europe, politicians and citizens supported policies that brought together limited state planning, strong economic growth, and democratic government, and this political and social consensus accompanied the first tentative steps on the long road toward a more unified Europe. Christian Democrats were committed to cultural and economic cooperation, and other groups shared their dedication. Many European intellectuals believed that only a new "European nation" could effectively rebuild the war-torn continent and reassert the continent's influence in world affairs.

A number of new financial arrangements and institutions encouraged slow but steady moves toward European integration, as did cooperation with the United States. The Bretton Woods agreement of 1944 had already linked Western currencies to the U.S. dollar and established the International Monetary Fund and the World Bank to facilitate free markets and world trade. To receive Marshall Plan aid, the European states were required by the Americans to cooperate with one another, leading to the creation of the Organization for European Economic Cooperation and the Council of Europe in 1948, both of which promoted commerce and cooperation among European countries.

European federalists hoped that the Council of Europe would evolve into a European parliament with sovereign rights, but this did not happen. Britain, with its still-vast empire and its close relationship with the United States, consistently opposed conceding sovereignty to the council. On the continent, many prominent nationalists and Communists agreed with the British view.

Frustrated in political consolidation, European federalists turned to economics as a way of working toward genuine unity. In 1950 two far-seeing French statesmen, the diplomat and political economist Jean Monnet and Foreign Minister Robert Schuman, called for a special international organization to control and integrate all European steel and coal production. Christian Democratic governments in West Germany, Italy, Belgium, the Netherlands, and Luxembourg accepted the French proposal and founded the European Coal and Steel Community in 1951 (the British refused to join). The founding states quickly attained their immediate economic goal—a single, transnational market for steel and coal without national tariffs or quotas. Close economic ties, advocates hoped, would eventually bind the six member nations so closely together that war among them would become unthinkable.

In 1957 the six countries of the Coal and Steel Community signed the Treaty of Rome, which created the European Economic Community, or **Common Market**. The first goal of the treaty was a gradual reduction of all tariffs among the six in order to create a single market almost as large as that of the United States. Other goals included the free movement of capital and labor and common economic policies and institutions. The Common Market encouraged trade among European states, promoted global exports, and helped build shared resources for the modernization of national industries.

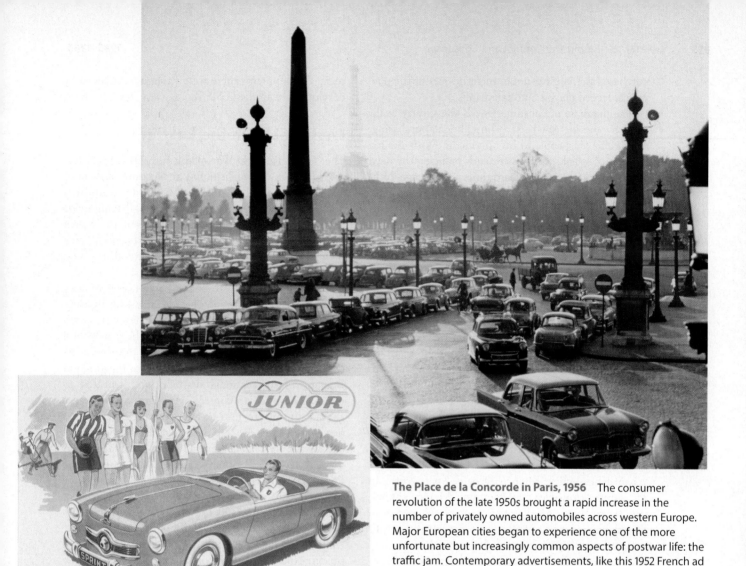

The Place de la Concorde in Paris, 1956 The consumer revolution of the late 1950s brought a rapid increase in the number of privately owned automobiles across western Europe. Major European cities began to experience one of the more unfortunate but increasingly common aspects of postwar life: the traffic jam. Contemporary advertisements, like this 1952 French ad for the Dyna Panhard Junior 130 Sprint, played up the youthful, sporty aspects of the new auto-mobility. (traffic: Peter Cornelius/akg-images; ad: akg-images)

European integration thus increased transnational cooperation even as it bolstered economic growth on the national level.

The development of the Common Market fired imaginations and encouraged the hopes of some for rapid progress toward political as well as economic union. In the 1960s, however, these hopes were frustrated by a resurgence of nationalism. France again took the lead. French president Charles de Gaulle, re-elected to office in 1958, was at heart a romantic nationalist. De Gaulle viewed the United States as the main threat to genuine French (and European) independence. He withdrew all French military forces from what he called an "American-controlled" NATO, developed France's own nuclear weapons, and vetoed the scheduled advent of majority rule within the Common Market. Thus the 1950s and 1960s established a lasting pattern: Europeans would establish ever-closer economic ties, but the Common Market remained a union of independent, sovereign states.

The Consumer Revolution

In the late 1950s western Europe's rapidly expanding economy led to a rising standard of living and remarkable growth in the number and availability of standardized consumer goods. Modern consumer society had precedents in the decades before the Second World War (see Chapter 26), but the years of the "economic miracle" saw the arrival of a veritable consumer revolution: as the percentage of income spent on necessities such as housing and food declined dramatically, near full employment and high wages meant that more Europeans could buy more things than ever before. Shaken by war and eager to rebuild their homes and families, western Europeans embraced the new products of consumer society. Like North Americans, they filled their houses and apartments with modern appliances such as washing machines, and they eagerly

■ **Common Market** The European Economic Community, created by six western and central European countries in the West Bloc in 1957 as part of a larger search for European unity.

purchased the latest entertainment devices of the day: radios, record players, and televisions.

The purchase of consumer goods was greatly facilitated by the increased use of installment purchasing, which allowed people to buy on credit. With the expansion of social security safeguards reducing the need to accumulate savings for hard times and old age, ordinary people were increasingly willing to take on debt, and new banks and credit unions offered loans for consumer purchases on easy terms. The consumer market became an increasingly important engine for general economic growth. For example, the European automobile industry expanded phenomenally after lagging far behind that of the United States since the 1920s. In 1948 there were only 5 million cars in western Europe; by 1965 there were 44 million. Car ownership was democratized and became possible for better-paid workers—the consumer revolution brought a vast array of new items into everyday activities, changing both lifestyles and attitudes.

Visions of consumer abundance became a powerful weapon in an era of Cold War competition. Politicians in both East and West claimed that their respective systems could best provide citizens with ample consumer goods. (See "Evaluating the Evidence 28.2: The Nixon-Khrushchev 'Kitchen Debate,'" page 960.) In the competition over consumption, Western capitalism clearly surpassed Eastern planned economies in the production and distribution of inexpensive products. Western leaders boasted about the abundance of goods on store shelves and promised new forms of social equality in which all citizens would have equal access to consumer items—rather than relying on class leveling mandated by the state, as in the despised East Bloc. The race to provide ordinary people with higher living standards would be a central aspect of the Cold War, as the Communist East Bloc struggled to catch up to Western standards of prosperity.

Developments in the Soviet Union and the East Bloc

FOCUS QUESTION *What was the pattern of postwar development in the Soviet bloc?*

While western Europe surged ahead economically and increased its independent political power as American influence gradually waned, East Bloc countries followed a different path. The Soviet Union first tightened its grip on peoples it had "liberated" during the Second World War and then refused to let go. Though limited reforms after Stalin's death in 1953 led to some economic improvement and limited gains in freedoms, postwar recovery in Communist central and eastern Europe proceeded along Soviet lines, and political and social developments there were strongly influenced by developments in the U.S.S.R.

Postwar Life in the East Bloc

The "Great Patriotic War of the Fatherland" had fostered Russian nationalism and a relaxation of dictatorial terror. It also had produced a rare but real unity between Soviet rulers and most citizens. Having made a heroic war effort, the vast majority of the Soviet people hoped in 1945 that a grateful party and government would grant greater freedom and democracy. Such hopes were soon disappointed.

Even before the war ended, Stalin was moving the U.S.S.R. back toward rigid dictatorship. By early 1946 Stalin was arguing that another war was inevitable as long as capitalism existed. Working to extend Communist influence across the globe, the Soviets established the Cominform, or Communist Information Bureau, an international organization dedicated to maintaining Russian control over Communist parties abroad, in western Europe and the East Bloc. Stalin's new superpower foe, the United States, served as an excuse for re-establishing a harsh dictatorship in the U.S.S.R. itself. Stalin reasserted the Communist Party's control of the government and his absolute mastery of the party. Rigid ideological indoctrination, attacks on religion, and the absence of civil liberties were soon facts of life for citizens of the Soviet empire. Millions of supposed political enemies were sent to prison, exile, or forced-labor camps.

As discussed earlier, in the satellite states of central and eastern Europe—including East Germany, Poland, Hungary, Czechoslovakia, Romania, Albania, and Bulgaria—national Communist parties remade state and society on the Soviet model. Though there were significant differences in these East Bloc countries, postwar developments followed a similar pattern. Popular Communist leaders who had led the resistance against Germany were ousted and replaced by politicians who supported Stalinist policies. With Soviet backing, national Communist parties absorbed their Social Democratic rivals and established one-party dictatorships subservient to the Communist Party in Moscow. State security services arrested, imprisoned, and sometimes executed dissenters. Show trials of supposedly disloyal Communist Party leaders took place across the East Bloc from the late 1940s into the 1950s, but were particularly prominent in Bulgaria, Czechoslovakia, Hungary, and Romania. They testified to the influence of Soviet advisers and the unrestrained power of the domestic secret police in the satellite states, as well as Stalin's urge to establish complete control—and his increasing paranoia.

Only Josip Broz Tito (TEE-toh) (1892–1980), the resistance leader and Communist chief of Yugoslavia, was able to proclaim political independence and successfully resist Soviet domination. Tito stood up to Stalin in

Rebellion in East Germany In June 1953 disgruntled construction workers in East Berlin walked off the job to protest low pay and high work quotas, setting off a nationwide rebellion against the Communist regime. The protesters could do little against the Soviet tanks and troops that put down the revolt. (Photo by Wolfgang Albrecht/ Deutsches Historisches Museum, Berlin, Germany/© DHM/Bridgeman Images)

1948, and because there was no Russian army in Yugoslavia, he got away with it. Though Communist led, Yugoslavia remained outside of the Soviet bloc. The country prospered as a multiethnic state until it began to break apart in 1991.

Within the East Bloc, the newly installed Communist governments moved quickly to restructure national economies along Soviet lines, introducing five-year plans to cope with the enormous task of economic reconstruction. Most industries and businesses were nationalized. These efforts transformed prewar patterns of everyday life, even as they laid the groundwork for industrial development later in the decade. (See "Living in the Past: A Model Socialist Steel Town," page 958.)

In their attempts to revive the economy, Communist planners gave top priority to heavy industry and the military. At the same time, East Bloc planners neglected consumer goods and housing, in part because they were generally suspicious of Western-style consumer culture. A glut of consumer goods, they believed, created waste, encouraged rampant individualism, and led to social inequality. Thus, for practical and ideological reasons, the provision of consumer goods lagged in the East Bloc, leading to complaints and widespread disillusionment with the constantly deferred promise of socialist prosperity.

Communist regimes also moved aggressively to collectivize agriculture, as the Soviets had done in the 1930s (see Chapter 27). By the early 1960s independent farmers had virtually disappeared in most of the East Bloc. Poland was the exception: there the Stalinist

regime tolerated the existence of private agriculture, hoping to maintain stability in the large and potentially rebellious country.

For many people in the East Bloc, everyday life was hard throughout the 1950s. Socialist planned economies often led to production problems and persistent shortages of basic household items. Party leaders encouraged workers to perform almost superhuman labor to "build socialism," often for low pay and under poor conditions. In East Germany, popular discontent with this situation led to open revolt in June 1953. A strike by Berlin construction workers protesting poor wages and increased work quotas led to nationwide demonstrations that were put down with Soviet troops and tanks. At least fifty-five protesters were killed and about five thousand were arrested during the uprising. When the revolt ended, the authorities rescinded the increased work quotas, but despite this apparent concession the protest strengthened the position of hardliner Stalinists within the East German government.

Communist censors purged culture and art of independent voices in aggressive campaigns that imposed rigid anti-Western ideological conformity. In the 1950s and 1960s the Communist states required artists and writers to conform to the dictates of **Socialist Realism**, which idealized the working classes and the Soviet Union. Party propagandists denounced artists who strayed from the party line, and forced many talented

■ **Socialist Realism** Artistic movement that followed the dictates of Communist ideals, enforced by state control in the Soviet Union and East Bloc countries in the 1950s and 1960s.

LIVING IN THE PAST
A Model Socialist Steel Town

Steel was king in the postwar Soviet bloc. On both sides of the iron curtain, economic recovery required the development of heavy industry, but socialist planners were especially eager to promote large-scale industrial production centered on coal, iron, and steel. Following Soviet examples, East Bloc countries built massive industrial works and model socialist cities to house the workers. Among these was Nowa Huta (NOH-vuh HOO-tuh; New Foundry), a steel town erected in the early 1950s on the outskirts of Kraków, Poland.

Nowa Huta was one of the grandest construction projects of the Stalinist era. By the mid-1960s Polish leaders bragged that the massive Lenin Steelworks produced more steel per day than any foundry in Europe. They were equally proud of the city that surrounded the mills, also built with Soviet assistance. The monumental Central Square, complete with an imposing statue of Lenin, was the center of the planned city. Streets radiated out into blocks of workers' apartment buildings designed by socialist architects. In theory, Nowa Huta brought together working and living space and included everything a working family might need: green space, department and grocery stores, recreation facilities, kindergartens and schools, cultural centers, and an extensive streetcar system. And indeed, Nowa Huta created real opportunities for Polish workers. Many moved from the farm to the city, where they enjoyed relatively good housing and good wages. By 1957

over one hundred thousand people lived in Nowa Huta, many of them employed at the steelworks.

According to propagandists, cities like Nowa Huta proved that the East could surpass the West in terms of industrial output while creating humane and equitable living spaces. At mass rallies and workplace meetings—attendance was mandatory—workers and their families listened to lengthy speeches about the honor of simple labor and the superiority of socialism. But the grand experiment revealed some of the

At the opening of the blast furnace at the Lenin Steelworks in Nowa Huta in July 1954, the vice-chairman of the Polish Council of Ministers awards the "Standard of Labor" to a production engineer. Such official ceremonies were common practice during the Communist years.
(Sovfoto/UIG via Getty Images)

The main square of Nowa Huta with the Lenin Steelworks foundry in the background.
(Sovfoto/UIG via Getty Images)

According to socialist planners, the newly built workers' apartments at Nowa Huta had everything a growing family could want, though the pleasant scene depicted in this photo stands in contrast to the difficult working conditions and the state repression of Catholicism that led to popular unrest. (Sovfoto/UIG via Getty Images)

weaknesses of the East Bloc economy. Under party oversight and strict workplace discipline, workers labored to meet demanding production quotas. Despite protests from the mostly Catholic workers, the Communist authorities sought to repress religious belief and refused to build a church until 1966. Pollution from the foundry fouled the air and damaged Kraków's historic architecture. And by the mid-1970s the steel produced by the "tiger nations" of East Asia was better and less expensive than that made at Nowa Huta; the foundry could no longer compete in global markets. The Communist Party clung to its vision of the workers' state, and continued government subsidies helped bankrupt the Polish state. Today, most of the steel plant is closed, but visitors can still explore an important example of socialist planning and ponder everyday life in a model industrial suburb.

QUESTIONS FOR ANALYSIS

1. How did planned cities like Nowa Huta reflect and promote socialist values?
2. Why would Polish leaders continue to support Nowa Huta when its products were no longer competitive?
3. Imagine yourself a worker in Nowa Huta. What would you find appealing about the living conditions? What would you find objectionable?

writers, composers, and film directors to produce works that conformed to the state's political goals. In short, the postwar East Bloc resembled the U.S.S.R. in the 1930s, although police terror was far less intense (see Chapter 27).

Reform and De-Stalinization

In 1953 the aging Stalin finally died, and the dictatorship that he had built began to change. Even as Stalin's heirs struggled for power, they realized that reforms were necessary because of the widespread fear and hatred created by Stalin's political terrorism. The power of the secret police was curbed, and many forced-labor camps were gradually closed. Change was also necessary to spur economic growth, which had sputtered in the postwar years. Moreover, Stalin's belligerent foreign policy had led directly to a strong Western alliance, which had taken steps to isolate the Soviet Union.

The Soviet leadership was badly split on the question of just how much change could be permitted while still preserving the system. Conservatives wanted to move slowly. Reformers, led by the remarkable Nikita Khrushchev (1894–1971), argued for major innovations. Khrushchev (kroush-CHAWF), who had joined the party as a coal miner in 1918 and risen to a high-level position in Ukraine in the 1930s, emerged as the new Soviet premier in 1955.

To strengthen his position and that of his fellow reformers, Khrushchev launched a surprising attack on Stalin and his crimes at a closed session of the Twentieth Party Congress in 1956. In his famous "secret speech," Khrushchev told Communist delegates startled by his open admission of errors that Stalin had "supported the glorification of his own person with all conceivable methods" to build a propagandistic "cult of personality." The delegates applauded when Khrushchev reported that Stalin had bungled the country's defense in World War II and unjustly imprisoned and tortured thousands of loyal Communists:

> [Stalin] discarded the Leninist method of convincing and educating . . . for that of administrative violence, mass repressions, and terror. . . . Mass arrests and deportations of many thousands of people, execution without trial and without normal investigation created conditions of insecurity, fear, and even desperation.[5]

The U.S.S.R. now entered a period of genuine liberalization — or **de-Stalinization**, as it was called in the West. Khrushchev's speech was read at Communist Party meetings held throughout the country, and it strengthened the reform movement. The party jealously maintained its monopoly on political power, but

■ **de-Stalinization** The liberalization of the post-Stalin Soviet Union led by reformer Nikita Khrushchev.

The Nixon-Khrushchev "Kitchen Debate"

During the Cold War, the United States and the Soviet Union waged political battles in Europe, wars of influence in the former colonies, and contests for national prestige in space and the nuclear arms race. But the two superpowers also sparred over which system — communism or capitalism — provided the best lifestyle for its citizens. In an effort to move beyond Cold War tensions, the Americans and Soviets set up public displays in each other's territory. The American National Exhibition in Moscow in 1959 included a model U.S. suburban home, complete with modern kitchen appliances, a television and stereo console, and a Cadillac sedan, all meant to demonstrate the superiority of capitalism.

During a visit to the exhibit, U.S. vice president Richard Nixon and Soviet premier Nikita Khrushchev engaged in an impromptu and sometimes ham-fisted argument over the merits of their respective political systems. As this exchange from the famous "kitchen debate" suggests, dishwashers were also on the frontline of the Cold War.

KHRUSHCHEV: We want to live in peace and friendship with Americans because we are the two most powerful countries and if we live in friendship then other countries will also live in friendship. But if there is a country that is too war-minded we could pull its ears a little and say: Don't you dare; fighting is not allowed now; this is a period of atomic armament; some foolish one could start a war and then even a wise one couldn't finish the war. Therefore, we are governed by this idea in our policy — internal and foreign. How long has America existed? Three hundred years?

NIXON: One hundred and fifty years.

KHRUSHCHEV: One hundred and fifty years? Well then we will say America has been in existence for 150 years and this is the level she has reached. We have existed not quite 42 years and in another seven years we will be on the same level as America. When we catch you up, in passing you by, we will wave to you. Then if you wish we can stop and say: Please follow up. Plainly speaking, if you want capitalism you can live that way. That is your own affair and doesn't concern us. We can still feel sorry for you but since you don't understand us — live as you do understand. . . . [Wrapping his arms about a Soviet workman.] Does this man look like a slave laborer? [Waving at others.] With men with such spirit how can we lose?

NIXON: [Pointing to American workmen.] With men like that we are strong. But these men, Soviet and American, work together well for peace, even as they have worked together in building this exhibition. This is the way it should be. Your remarks are in the tradition of what we have come to expect — sweeping and extemporaneous. Later on we will both have an opportunity to speak and consequently I will not comment on the various points that you raised, except to say this — this color television is one of the most advanced developments in communication that we have. I can only say that if this competition in which you plan to outstrip us is to do the best for both of our peoples and for peoples everywhere, there must be a free exchange of ideas. After all, you don't know everything.

KHRUSHCHEV: If I don't know everything you don't know anything about communism except fear of it.

NIXON: There are some instances where you may be ahead of us, for example in the development of the thrust of your rockets for the investigation of outer space; there may be some instances in which we are ahead of you — in color television, for instance.

KHRUSHCHEV: No, we are up with you on this, too. We have bested you in one technique and also in the other.

NIXON: You see, you never concede anything.

KHRUSHCHEV: I do not give up.

NIXON: Wait till you see the picture [on the TV set]. Let's have far more communication and exchange in this very area that we speak of. We should hear you more on our televisions. You should hear us more on yours.

KHRUSHCHEV: That's a good idea. Let's do it like this. You appear before our people. We will appear before your people. People will see and appreciate this. . . .

NIXON: [Halting Khrushchev at the model kitchen in the model house.] You had a very nice house in your exhibition in New York. My wife and I saw and enjoyed it very much. I want to show you this kitchen. It is like those of our houses in California.

KHRUSHCHEV: [After Nixon points to a built-in panel-controlled washing machine.] We have such things.

NIXON: This is the newest model. This is the kind which is built in thousands of units for direct installation in the houses. [He adds that Americans are interested in making life easier for their women.]

Khrushchev remarked that in the Soviet Union, they did not have "the capitalist attitude toward women."

NIXON: I think that this attitude toward women is universal. What we want to do is make easier the life of our housewives.

Nixon explained that the house could be built for $14,000 and that most veterans had bought houses for between $10,000 and $15,000.

NIXON: Let me give you an example you can appreciate. Our steelworkers, as you know, are on strike. But any steelworker could buy this house. They earn $3 an hour. This house costs about $100 a month to buy on a contract running 25 to 30 years.

KHRUSHCHEV: We have steelworkers and we have peasants who also can afford to spend $14,000 for a house. . . .

KHRUSHCHEV: Don't you have a machine that puts food into the mouth and pushes it down? Many things you've shown us are interesting but they are not needed in life. They have no useful purpose. They are merely gadgets. We have a saying, if you have bedbugs you have to catch one and pour boiling water into the ear.

NIXON: We have another saying. This is that the way to kill a fly is to make it drink whisky. But we have a better use for whisky. [Aside] I like to have this battle of wits with the Chairman. He knows his business. . . .

KHRUSHCHEV: The Americans have created their own image of the Soviet man and think he is as you want him to be. But he is not as you think. You think the Russian people will be dumbfounded to see these things, but the fact is that newly built Russian houses have all this equipment right now. Moreover, all you have to do to get a house is to be born in the Soviet Union. You are entitled to housing. I was born in the Soviet Union. So I have a right to a house. In America, if you don't have a dollar — you have the right to choose between sleeping in a house or on the pavement. Yet you say that we are slaves of communism. . . .

NIXON: We do not claim to astonish the Russian people. We hope to show our diversity and our right to choose. We do not wish to have decisions made at the top by government officials who say that all homes should be built in the same way. Would it not be better to compete in the relative merits of washing machines than in the strength of rockets? Is this the kind of competition you want?

KHRUSHCHEV: Yes that's the kind of competition we want. But your generals say: "Let's compete in rockets. We are strong and we can beat you." But in this respect we can also show you something.

NIXON: To me you are strong and we are strong. In some ways, you are stronger. In others, we are stronger. We are both strong not only from the standpoint of weapons but from the standpoint of will and spirit.

EVALUATE THE EVIDENCE

1. Why did Nixon and Khrushchev focus so heavily on the lives of workers in the United States and the Soviet Union?

2. What does the kitchen debate reveal about the role of consumer goods in the Cold War?

Source: Transcript of the "Kitchen Debate" at the opening of the American National Exhibition at Sokolniki Park in Moscow, July 24, 1959.

Khrushchev brought in new members. Calling for a relaxation of tensions with the West, the new premier announced a policy of "peaceful coexistence." In domestic policies, state planners shifted resources from heavy industry and the military toward consumer goods and agriculture, and relaxed Stalinist workplace controls. Leaders in other Communist countries grudgingly adopted similar reforms, and the East Bloc's generally low standard of living began to improve.

Khrushchev was proud of Soviet achievements and liked to boast that East Bloc living standards and access to consumer goods would soon surpass those of the West. (See "Evaluating the Evidence 28.2: The Nixon-Khrushchev 'Kitchen Debate,'" at left.) Soviet and East Bloc reforms did spark a limited consumer revolution. Consumers' options were more modest than those in the West, but people in Communist countries also purchased automobiles, televisions, and other consumer goods in increasing numbers in the 1960s.

De-Stalinization created great ferment among writers and intellectuals who sought freedom from the constraints of Socialist Realism, such as Russian author Boris Pasternak (1890–1960), who published his great novel *Doctor Zhivago* in 1957. Appearing in the West but not in the Soviet Union until 1988, *Doctor Zhivago* is both a literary masterpiece and a powerful challenge to communism. It tells the story of a poet who rejects the violence and brutality of the October Revolution of 1917 and the Stalinist years. Mainstream Communist critics denounced Pasternak, whose book was circulated in secret — but in an era of liberalization he was neither arrested nor shot. Other talented writers followed Pasternak's lead, and courageous editors let the sparks fly. Aleksandr Solzhenitsyn (sohl-zhuh-NEET-suhn) (1918–2008) created a sensation when his *One Day in the Life of Ivan Denisovich* was published in 1962. Solzhenitsyn's novel portrays in grim detail life in a Stalinist concentration camp — a life to which Solzhenitsyn himself had been unjustly condemned — and is a damning indictment of the Stalinist past.

Foreign Policy and Domestic Rebellion

Khrushchev also de-Stalinized Soviet foreign policy. "Peaceful coexistence" with capitalism was possible, he argued, and war was not inevitable. Khrushchev negotiated with Western diplomats, agreeing in 1955, for example, to independence for a neutral Austria after ten long years of Allied occupation. As a result, Cold War tensions relaxed considerably between 1955 and 1957. At the same time, Khrushchev began wooing the new nations of Asia and Africa — even those that were not Communist — with promises of support and economic aid.

The Kitchen Debate   Khrushchev and Nixon discuss the merits of the American way during the famous kitchen debate. Leonid Brezhnev, the future leader of the Soviet Union (from 1964 to 1982), stands on the far right, just behind Nixon. (AP Photo/ AP Images)

In the East Bloc states, Communist leaders responded in complex ways to de-Stalinization. In East Germany the regime stubbornly resisted reform, but in Poland and Hungary de-Stalinization stimulated rebelliousness. Poland took the lead in 1956, when extensive popular demonstrations brought a new government to power. The new First Secretary of the Polish Communist Party argued that there were "many roads to socialism." By promising to remain loyal to the Warsaw Pact, the Polish Communists managed to win greater autonomy from Soviet control. The new leadership maintained Communist control even as it tolerated a free peasantry and an independent Catholic Church.

Hungary experienced an ultimately tragic revolution the same year. Led by students and workers—the classic urban revolutionaries—the people of Budapest installed Imre Nagy (im-rey nadge), a liberal Communist reformer, as the new prime minister in October 1956. Encouraged by extensive popular protests and joined by other Communist reformers, Nagy proposed to democratize Hungary. Though never renouncing communism, he demanded open, multiparty elections, the relaxation of political repression, and other reforms. Bold moves in Hungary raised widespread hopes that Communist states could undergo substantial but peaceful change, driven from within.

At first, it seemed that the Soviets might negotiate, but the breathing space was short-lived. When Nagy announced that Hungary would leave the Warsaw Pact and asked the United Nations to protect the country's neutrality, the Soviets grew alarmed about the possibility that Hungary's independent course would affect other East Bloc countries. On November 4 Soviet troops moved in on the capital city of Budapest and crushed the revolution. Around 2,700 Hungarians died in the crackdown. Fighting was bitter until the end, for the Hungarians hoped that the United Nations would come to their aid. This did not occur—in part because the Western powers were involved in the Suez crisis (see page 968) and were, in general, reluctant to directly confront the Soviets in Europe with military force. When a new, more conservative Communist regime executed Nagy and other protest leaders and sent thousands more to prison, many people in the East Bloc concluded that their best hope was to strive for internal reform without openly challenging Soviet control.

The outcome of the Hungarian uprising weakened support for Soviet-style communism in western Europe—the brutal repression deeply discouraged those who still believed in the possibility of an equitable socialist society, and tens of thousands of Communist Party members in the West resigned in disgust. At the same time, Western politicians saw that the U.S.S.R. would use military force to defend its control of the East Bloc, and that only open war between East and West had the potential to overturn Communist rule there. This price was too high, and it seemed that Communist domination of the satellite states was there to stay.

The Limits of Reform

By late 1962 opposition to Khrushchev's reformist policies had gained momentum in party circles. Khrushchev's Communist colleagues began to see de-Stalinization as a dangerous threat to the authority of the party. Moreover, Khrushchev's policy toward the West was erratic and ultimately unsuccessful. In 1958, in a failed attempt to staunch the flow of hundreds of thousands of disgruntled East German residents who used the open border between East and West Berlin to move permanently to the West, Khrushchev tightened border controls and ordered the Western allies to evacuate the city within six months. In response, the allies reaffirmed their unity in West Berlin, and Khrushchev backed down. Then, with Khrushchev's backing, in 1961 the East German authorities built a wall between East and West Berlin, sealing off West Berlin, in clear violation of existing access agreements between the Great Powers. The recently elected U.S. president, John F. Kennedy (U.S. pres. 1961–1963), insisted publicly that the United States would never abandon Berlin. Privately hoping that the wall would lessen Cold War tensions by easing hostilities in Berlin, Kennedy did little to prevent its construction.

Emboldened by American acceptance of the Berlin Wall and seeing a chance to change the balance of military power decisively, Premier Khrushchev secretly ordered missiles with nuclear warheads installed in Fidel Castro's Communist Cuba in 1962. When U.S. intelligence discovered missile sites under construction, Kennedy countered with a naval blockade of Cuba. After a tense diplomatic crisis, Khrushchev agreed to remove the Soviet missiles in return for American pledges not to disturb Castro's regime. In a secret agreement, Kennedy also promised to remove U.S. nuclear missiles from Turkey.

Khrushchev's influence in the party, already slipping, declined rapidly after the Cuban missile crisis. In 1964 the reformist premier was displaced in a bloodless coup, and he spent the rest of his life under house arrest. Under his successor, Leonid Brezhnev (1906–1982), the U.S.S.R. began a period of limited re-Stalinization and economic stagnation. Almost immediately, Brezhnev (BREHZH-nehf) and his supporters started talking quietly of Stalin's "good points" and downplaying his crimes. This change informed Soviet citizens that further liberalization could not be expected at home. Soviet leaders, determined never to suffer Khrushchev's humiliation in the face of American nuclear superiority, launched a massive arms buildup. Yet Brezhnev and company proceeded cautiously in the mid-1960s and avoided direct confrontation with the United States.

Despite popular protests and changes in leadership, the U.S.S.R. and its satellite countries had achieved some stability by the late 1950s. Communist regimes addressed dissent and uprisings with an effective combination of military force, political repression, and limited economic reform. East and West traded propaganda threats, but both sides basically accepted the division of Europe into spheres of influence. Violent conflicts now took place in the developing world, where decolonization was opening new paths for Cold War confrontation.

The End of Empires

FOCUS QUESTION *What led to decolonization after World War II, and how did the Cold War influence the process?*

In the postwar era, in one of world history's great turning points, Europe's long-standing overseas expansion was dramatically reversed. The retreat from imperial control—a process Europeans called **decolonization**—remade the world map. In just two decades, over fifty new nations in Africa, Asia, and the Middle East joined the global community (Map 28.3). In some cases, decolonization proceeded relatively smoothly, with an orderly transition and little violence. In others, the European powers were determined to preserve colonial rule—long a source of profit and national pride—and colonized peoples won independence only after long and bloody struggles.

The Cold War had a profound impact on decolonization. Independence movements often had to choose sides in the struggle between the superpowers. After independence was won, both the United States and the Soviet Union struggled to exert influence in the former colonies, and economic growth and political stability remained elusive in much of Europe's former empire. Liberation from colonial domination was a proud achievement that brought fundamental gains in human freedom but left lasting problems for the former colonized and colonizers alike.

Decolonization and the Global Cold War

The most basic cause of imperial collapse was the rising demand of non-Western peoples for national self-determination, racial equality, and personal dignity. This demand spread from intellectuals to ordinary people in nearly every colonial territory after the First World War. By 1939 the colonial powers were already on the defensive; the Second World War prepared the way for the eventual triumph of independence movements.

European empires had been based on an enormous power differential between the rulers and the ruled, a difference that had greatly declined by 1945. Western Europe was economically devastated and militarily weak immediately after the war. Moreover, the Japanese had driven imperial rulers from large parts of East Asia during the war in the Pacific, shattering the myth of European superiority and invincibility. In Southeast Asia, European imperialists confronted strong anti-colonial nationalist movements that re-emerged with new enthusiasm after the defeat of the Japanese.

■ **decolonization** The postwar reversal of Europe's overseas expansion caused by the rising demand of the colonized peoples themselves, the declining power of European nations, and the freedoms promised by U.S. and Soviet ideals.

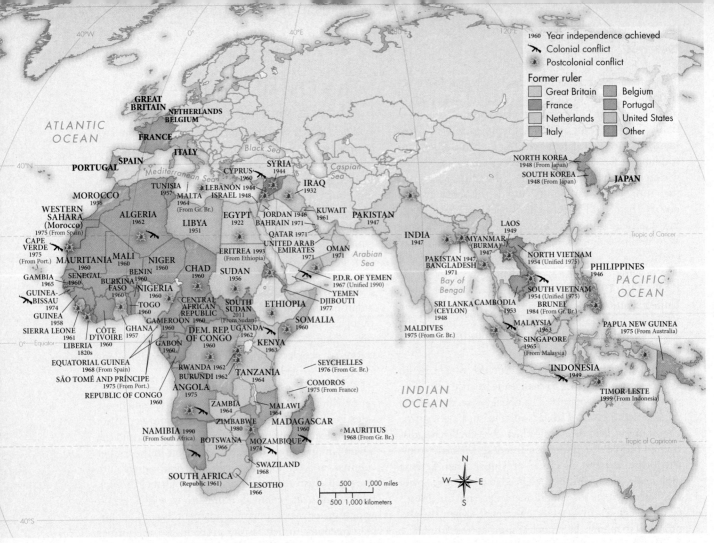

MAP 28.3 Decolonization in Africa and Asia, 1947 to the Present Divided primarily along religious lines into two states, British India led the way to political independence in 1947. Most African territories achieved statehood by the mid-1960s as European empires passed away, unlamented.

To some degree, the Great Powers regarded their empires very differently after 1945 than before 1914, or even before 1939. Empire had rested on self-confidence and self-righteousness; Europeans had believed their superiority to be not only technical and military but also spiritual, racial, and moral. The horrors of the First and Second World Wars undermined such complacent arrogance and gave opponents of imperialism much greater influence in Europe. Increasing pressure from the United States, which had long presented itself as an enemy of empire despite its own imperialist actions in the Philippines and the Americas, encouraged Europeans to let go of their former colonies. Indeed, Americans were eager to extend their own influence in Europe's former colonies. Economically weakened, and with their political power and moral authority in tatters, the imperial powers preferred to avoid bloody colonial wars and generally turned to rebuilding at home.

Furthermore, the imperial powers faced dedicated anticolonial resistance. Popular politicians, including China's Mao Zedong, India's Mohandas Gandhi,

Egypt's Gamal Abdel Nasser, and many others, provided determined leadership in the struggle against European imperialism. A new generation of intellectuals, such as Jomo Kenyatta of Kenya and Aimé Césaire and Frantz Fanon, both from Martinique, wrote trenchant critiques of imperial power, often rooted in Marxist ideas. (See "Evaluating the Evidence 28.3: Frantz Fanon on Violence, Decolonization, and Human Dignity," at right.) Anticolonial politicians and intellectuals alike helped inspire colonized peoples to resist and overturn imperial rule.

Around the globe, the Cold War had an inescapable impact on decolonization. Liberation from colonial rule had long been a central goal for proponents of Communist world revolution. The Soviets and, after 1949, the Communist Chinese advocated rebellion in the developing world and promised to help end colonial exploitation and bring freedom and equality in a socialist state. They supported Communist independence movements with economic and military aid, and the guerrilla insurgent armed with a Soviet-made AK-47 machine gun became the new symbol of Marxist revolution.

Frantz Fanon on Violence, Decolonization, and Human Dignity

Frantz Fanon shocked Western audiences with his assertion that only violence could restore political freedom and human dignity to colonized peoples, an argument forcefully expressed in his famous book The Wretched of the Earth *(1961). Born in the French colony of Martinique in 1925 and educated as a psychiatrist, Fanon held radical views that were profoundly influenced by his work as a doctor in Algeria during the colonial war (1954–1962) that ultimately led to independence from French rule.*

~

National liberation, national renaissance, the restoration of nationhood to the people, commonwealth: whatever may be the heading used or the new formulas introduced, decolonization is always a violent phenomenon. At whatever level we study it — relationships between individuals, new names for sports clubs, the human admixture at cocktail parties, in the police, on the directing boards of national or private banks — decolonization is quite simply the replacing of a certain "species" of men by another "species" of men. Without any period of transition, there is a total, complete, and absolute substitution. . . .

Decolonization is the meeting of two forces, opposed to each other by their very nature. . . . Their first encounter was marked by violence and their existence together — that is to say the exploitation of the native by the settler — was carried on by dint of a great array of bayonets and cannons. The settler and the native are old acquaintances. . . .

The naked truth of decolonization evokes for us the searing bullets and bloodstained knives which emanate from it. For if the last shall be first, this will only come to pass after a murderous and decisive struggle between the two protagonists. . . . [We] can only triumph if we use all means to turn the scale, including, of course, that of violence. . . .

In the colonial countries the peasants alone are revolutionary, for they have nothing to lose and everything to gain. The starving peasant, outside the class system, is the first among the exploited to discover that only violence pays. For him there is no compromise, no possible coming to terms; colonization and decolonization are only a question of relative strength. . . .

The mobilization of the masses, when it arises out of the war of liberation, introduces into each man's consciousness the ideas of a common cause, of a national destiny, and of a collective history. In the same way the second phase, that of the building-up of the nation, is helped on by the existence of this cement which has been mixed with blood and anger. . . .

At the level of individuals, violence is a cleansing force. It frees the native from his inferiority complex and from his despair and inaction; it makes him fearless and restores his self-respect. . . .

Violence alone, violence committed by the people, violence organized and educated by its leaders, makes it possible for the masses to understand social truths and gives the key to them. Without that struggle, without that knowledge of the practice of action, there's nothing but a fancy dress parade and the blare of the trumpets. There's nothing save a minimum of readaptation, a few reforms at the top, a flag waving: and down there at the bottom an undivided mass, still living in the middle ages, endlessly marking time.

EVALUATE THE EVIDENCE

1. Why, according to Fanon, is violence required for both the political and psychological success of the anti-imperial struggle?
2. How do advocates of nonviolent reform, such as Mohandas Gandhi or Martin Luther King, Jr., challenge Fanon's ideas about the positive potential of violent revolt? Who makes the better case?

Source: Excerpts from *The Wretched of the Earth* by Frantz Fanon, copyright © 1963 by *Présence Africaine*. Used by permission of Grove/Atlantic, Inc. Any third party use of this material, outside of this publication, is prohibited.

Western Europe and particularly the United States offered a competing vision of independence, based on free-market economics and, ostensibly, liberal democracy—though the United States was often willing to support authoritarian regimes that voiced staunch anticommunism. Like the U.S.S.R., the United States extended economic aid and weaponry to decolonizing nations. The Americans promoted cautious moves toward self-determination in the context of containment, attempting to limit the influence of communism in newly liberated states.

After they had won independence, the leaders of the new nations often found themselves trapped between the superpowers, compelled to voice support for one bloc or the other. Many new leaders followed a third way, adopting a policy of **nonalignment**, remaining neutral in the Cold War and playing both sides for what they could get.

■ **nonalignment** Policy of postcolonial governments to remain neutral in the Cold War and play both the United States and the Soviet Union for what they could get.

The Struggle for Power in Asia

The first major fight for independence that followed World War II, between the Netherlands and anticolonial insurgents in the Dutch East Indies (today's Indonesia), in many ways exemplified decolonization in the Cold War world. The Dutch had been involved in Indonesia since the early seventeenth century (see Chapter 14) and had extended their colonial power over the centuries. During World War II, however, the Japanese had overrun the archipelago, encouraging hopes among the locals for independence from Western control. Following the Japanese defeat in 1945, the Dutch returned, hoping to use Indonesia's raw materials, particularly rubber, to support economic recovery at home. But Dutch imperialists faced a determined group of rebels inspired by a powerful combination of nationalism, Marxism, and Islam. Four years of deadly guerrilla war followed, and in 1949 the Netherlands reluctantly accepted Indonesian independence. The new Indonesian president became an effective advocate of nonalignment. He had close ties to the Indonesian Communist Party but received foreign aid from the United States as well as the Soviet Union.

A similar combination of communism and anticolonialism inspired the independence movement in parts of French Indochina (now Vietnam, Cambodia, and Laos), though noncommunist nationalists were also involved. France desperately wished to maintain control over these prized colonies and tried its best to re-establish colonial rule after the Japanese occupation collapsed at the end of World War II. Despite substantial American aid, the French army fighting in Vietnam was defeated in 1954 by forces under the guerrilla leader Ho Chi Minh (hoh chee mihn) (1890–1969), who was supported by the U.S.S.R. and China. Vietnam was divided. As in Korea, a shaky truce established a Communist North and a pro-Western South Vietnam, which led to civil war and subsequent intervention by the United States. Cambodia and Laos also gained independence under noncommunist regimes, though Communist rebels remained active in both countries.

India, Britain's oldest, largest, and most lucrative imperial possession, played a key role in the decolonization process. Nationalist opposition to British rule coalesced after the First World War under the leadership of British-educated lawyer Mohandas (sometimes called "Mahatma," or "Great-Souled") Gandhi (1869–1948), one of the twentieth century's most significant and influential figures. In the 1920s and 1930s Gandhi (GAHN-dee) built a mass movement preaching nonviolent "noncooperation" with the British. In 1935 Gandhi wrested from the frustrated and unnerved British a new, liberal constitution that was practically a blueprint for independence. The Second World War interrupted progress toward Indian self-rule, but when the Labour Party came to power in Great Britain in 1945, it was ready to relinquish sovereignty. British socialists had long been critics of imperialism, and the heavy cost of governing India had become a large financial burden to the war-wracked country.

A Refugee Camp During the Partition of India A young Muslim man, facing an uncertain future, sits above a refugee camp established on the grounds of a medieval fortress in the northern Indian city of Delhi. In the camp, Muslim refugees wait to cross the border to the newly founded Pakistan. The chaos that accompanied the mass migration of Muslims and Hindus during the partition of India in the late summer and autumn of 1947 cost the lives of up to 1 million migrants and disrupted the livelihoods of millions more. (Margaret-Bourke White/The LIFE Picture Collection/Getty Images)

Britain withdrew peacefully, but conflict between India's Hindu and Muslim populations posed a lasting dilemma for South Asia. As independence neared, the Muslim minority grew increasingly anxious about their status in an India dominated by the Hindu majority. Muslim leaders called for partition—the division of India into separate Hindu and Muslim states—and the British agreed. When independence was made official on August 15, 1947, predominantly Muslim territories on India's eastern and western borders became Pakistan (the eastern section is today's Bangladesh). Seeking relief from ethnic conflict that erupted, some 10 million Muslim and Hindu refugees fled both ways across the new borders, a massive population exchange that left mayhem and death in its wake. In just a few summer weeks, up to 1 million people (estimates vary widely) lost their lives. Then in January 1948 a radical Hindu nationalist who opposed partition assassinated Gandhi, and Jawaharlal Nehru became Indian prime minister.

As the Cold War heated up in the early 1950s, Pakistan, an Islamic republic, developed close ties with the United States. Under the leadership of Nehru, India successfully maintained a policy of nonalignment. India became a liberal, if socialist-friendly, democratic state that dealt with both the United States and the U.S.S.R. Pakistan and India both joined the British Commonwealth, a voluntary and cooperative association of former British colonies that already included Canada, Australia, and New Zealand.

Where Indian nationalism drew on Western parliamentary liberalism, Chinese nationalism developed and triumphed in the framework of Marxist-Leninist ideology. After the withdrawal of the occupying Japanese army in 1945, China erupted again in open civil war. The authoritarian Guomindang (Kuomintang, National People's Party), led by Jiang Jieshi (traditionally called Chiang Kai-shek; 1887–1975), fought to repress the Chinese Communists, led by Mao Zedong (MA-OW zuh-DOUNG) and supported by a popular grassroots uprising. The Soviets gave Mao aid, and the Americans gave Jiang much more. Winning the support of the peasantry by promising to expropriate the holdings of the big landowners, the tougher, better-organized Communists forced the Guomindang to withdraw to the island of Taiwan in 1949. Mao and the Communists united China's 550 million inhabitants in a strong centralized state. Once in power, the "Red Chinese" began building a new society that adapted Marxism to Chinese conditions. The new government promoted land reform, extended education and health-care programs to the peasantry, and introduced Soviet-style five-year plans that boosted industrial production. It also brought Stalinist-style repression—mass arrests, forced-labor camps, and ceaseless propaganda campaigns—to the Chinese people.

Independence and Conflict in the Middle East

In some areas of the Middle East, the movement toward political independence went relatively smoothly. The French League of Nations mandates in Syria and Lebanon had collapsed during the Second World War, and Saudi Arabia and Transjordan had already achieved independence from Britain. But events in the British mandate of Palestine and in Egypt showed that decolonization in the Middle East could follow a dangerous and difficult path.

As part of the peace accords that followed the First World War, the British government had advocated a Jewish homeland alongside the Arab population (see Chapter 25). This tenuous compromise unraveled after World War II. Neither Jews nor Arabs were happy with British rule, and violence and terrorism mounted on both sides. In 1947 the frustrated British decided to leave Palestine, and the United Nations voted in a nonbinding resolution to divide the territory into two states—one Arab and one Jewish. The Jews accepted the plan and founded the state of Israel in 1948.

The Palestinians and the surrounding Arab nations viewed Jewish independence as a betrayal of their own interests, and they attacked the Jewish state as soon as it was proclaimed. The Israelis drove off the invaders and conquered more territory. Roughly nine hundred thousand Arab Palestinians fled or were expelled from their homes, creating a persistent refugee problem. Holocaust survivors from Europe streamed into Israel, as Theodor Herzl's Zionist dream came true (see Chapter 23). The next fifty years saw four more wars between the Israelis and the Arab states and innumerable clashes between Israelis and Palestinians.

The Arab defeat in 1948 triggered a powerful nationalist revolution in Egypt in 1952, led by the young army officer Gamal Abdel Nasser (1918–1970). The revolutionaries drove out the pro-Western king, and in 1954 Nasser became president of an Egyptian republic. A crafty politician, Nasser advocated nonalignment and expertly played the superpowers against each other, securing loans from the United States and purchasing Soviet arms.

In July 1956 Nasser abruptly nationalized the foreign-owned Suez Canal Company, the last symbol and substance of Western power in the Middle East.

Boundary of Israel after the first Arab-Israeli War, 1949

Cyprus
SYRIA
Mediterranean Sea
LEBANON
ISRAEL — Jerusalem
Dead Sea
EGYPT
JORDAN
SAUDI ARABIA

UN partition of Palestine, 1947
■ Jewish state
□ Arab state

Israel, 1948

Nasser Opens an Oil Refinery The charismatic Egyptian president inaugurates an oil refinery outside Cairo on July 25, 1956. The next day Nasser announced the nationalization of the Suez Canal, in order to fund the construction of the Aswan Dam after the United States and Britain had withdrawn their financial support. This set off the Suez crisis, a key event in the history of postwar decolonization.
(© Bettmann/Corbis)

The Suez Crisis, 1956

Infuriated, the British and the French, along with the Israelis, planned a secret military operation. The Israeli army invaded the Sinai Peninsula bordering the canal, and British and French bombers attacked Egyptian airfields. World opinion was outraged, and the United States feared that such a blatant show of imperialism would propel the Arab states into the Soviet bloc. The Americans joined with the Soviets to force the British, French, and Israelis to back down. Egyptian nationalism triumphed: Nasser got his canal, and Israel left the Sinai. The Suez crisis, a watershed in the history of European imperialism, showed that the European powers could no longer maintain their global empires and demonstrated the power and appeal of nonalignment.

Decolonization in Africa

In less than a decade, most of Africa won independence from European imperialism, a remarkable movement of world historical importance. In much of the continent south of the Sahara, decolonization proceeded relatively smoothly. Yet the new African states were quickly caught up in the struggles between the Cold War superpowers, and decolonization all too often left a lasting legacy of violence, economic decline, and political conflict (see Map 28.3).

Starting in 1957 most of Britain's African colonies achieved independence with little or no bloodshed and then entered a very loose association with Britain as members of the British Commonwealth. Ghana, Nigeria, Tanzania, and other countries gained independence in this way, but there were exceptions to this relatively smooth transfer of power. In Kenya, British forces brutally crushed the nationalist Mau Mau rebellion in the early 1950s, but nonetheless recognized Kenyan independence in 1963. In South Africa, the white-dominated government left the Commonwealth in 1961 and declared an independent republic in order to preserve apartheid—an exploitative system of racial segregation enforced by law.

The decolonization of the Belgian Congo was one of the great tragedies of the Cold War. Belgian leaders, profiting from the colony's wealth of natural resources and proud of their small nation's imperial status, maintained a system of apartheid there and dragged their feet in granting independence. These conditions sparked an anticolonial movement that grew increasingly aggressive in the late 1950s under the able leadership of the charismatic Patrice Lumumba. In January 1960 the Belgians gave in and hastily announced that the Congo would be independent six months later, a schedule that was irresponsibly fast. Lumumba was chosen prime minister in democratic elections, but when the Belgians pulled out on schedule, the new government was entirely unprepared. Chaos broke out when the Congolese army attacked Belgian military officers who remained in the country.

With substantial financial investments in the Congo, the United States and western Europe worried that the new nation might fall into Soviet hands. U.S. leaders cast Lumumba as a Soviet proxy, an oversimplification of his nonalignment policies, and American anxiety increased when Lumumba asked the U.S.S.R. for aid and protection. A cable from the CIA chief in the Congo revealed the way Cold War anxieties framed the situation:

> Embassy and station believe Congo experiencing classic Communist takeover government. . . . Whether or not Lumumba actually Commie or just playing Commie game to assist solidifying his power, anti-West forces rapidly increasing power [in] Congo and there may be little time left in which to take action to avoid another Cuba.[6]

In a troubling example of containment in action, the CIA helped implement a military coup against Lumumba, who was captured and then assassinated. The military set up a U.S.-backed dictatorship under the corrupt general Joseph Mobutu. Mobutu ruled until 1997 and became one of the world's wealthiest men, while the Congo remained one of the poorest, most violent, and most politically torn countries in the world.

French colonies in Africa followed several roads to independence. Like the British, the French offered most of their African colonies the choice of a total break or independence within a kind of French commonwealth. All but one of the new states chose the latter option, largely because they identified with French culture and wanted aid from their former colonizer. The French were eager to help—provided the former colonies accepted close economic ties on French terms. As in the past, the French and their Common Market partners, who helped foot the bill, saw themselves as continuing their civilizing mission in sub-Saharan Africa (see Chapter 24). More important, they saw in Africa raw materials for their factories, markets for their industrial goods, outlets for profitable investment, and good temporary jobs for their engineers and teachers.

Things were far more difficult in the French colony of Algeria, a large Muslim state on the Mediterranean Sea where some 1.2 million white European settlers, including some 800,000 French, had taken up permanent residency by the 1950s. Nicknamed pieds-noirs (literally "black feet"), many of these Europeans had raised families in Algeria for three or four generations, and they enforced a two-tiered system of citizenship, dominating politics and the economy. When Algerian rebels, inspired by Islamic fundamentalism and Communist ideals, established the National Liberation Front (FLN) and revolted against French colonialism in the early 1950s, the presence of the pieds-noirs complicated matters. Worried about their position in the col-

Decolonization in the Democratic Republic of the Congo   Flushed with victory, the democratically elected Congolese premier Patrice Lumumba waves as he leaves the National Senate on September 8, 1960. Lumumba had just received a 41–2 vote of confidence that confirmed his leadership position. Four months later he was assassinated in a military coup. (© Bettmann/Corbis)

ony, the pieds-noirs pressured the French government to help them. In response, France sent some 400,000 troops to crush the FLN and put down the revolt. (See "Thinking Like a Historian: Violence and the Algerian War," page 970.)

The resulting Algerian War—long, bloody, and marred by atrocities committed on both sides—lasted from 1954 to 1962. FLN radicals repeatedly attacked pied-noir civilians in savage terrorist attacks, while the French army engaged in systematic torture, mass arrests (often of innocent suspects), and the forced relocation and internment of millions of Muslim civilians suspected of supporting the insurgents. By 1958 French forces had successfully limited FLN military actions, but their disproportionate use of force effectively encouraged many Muslims to support or join the FLN. News reports about torture and abuse of civilians turned significant elements of French public opinion against the war, and international outrage further pressured French leaders to end the conflict. Efforts to open peace talks led to a revolt by the Algerian French and threats of a coup d'état by the French army. In 1958 the immensely popular General Charles de Gaulle was reinstated as French prime minister as part of the movement to keep Algeria French. His appointment at first calmed the army, the pieds-noirs, and the French public.

Violence and the Algerian War

In the course of the eight-year-long Algerian War, French soldiers and police, FLN insurgents, and OAS militiamen all used ferocious violence in pursuit of their military-political objectives. Though casualty numbers were small at the start, the Algerian War would ultimately claim the lives of hundreds of thousands of people. What sort of tactics did the combatants use, and how did they justify their actions?

1 An argument for revolutionary violence. While thinkers like Frantz Fanon called for anti-imperial violence in historical-psychological terms (see page 965), radicals like Brazilian urban guerrilla Carlos Marighella laid out the justification in chilling, practical terms. Similar ideas inspired the FLN.

It is necessary to turn political crisis into armed conflict by performing violent actions that will force those in power to transform the political situation of the country into a military situation. That will alienate the masses, who, from then on, will revolt against the army and the police and blame them for the state of things.

2 An argument for torture. French soldiers and police routinely tortured FLN members and other Algerians suspected of supporting the insurgents in order to gain information and intimidate the general population. Colonel Antoine Argoud, a commander of a French paratroop force sent to Algeria, argued for the necessity of torture.

Muslims will not talk as long... as long as we do not inflict acts of violence on them.... They will rally [to] our camp only if it [justice] responds to their respect and thirst for authority.... From our perspective, torture and capital executions are acts of war. Now, war is an act of violence aimed at compelling the enemy to execute our will, and violence is the means [by which to do it]....

Torture is an act of violence just like the bullet shot from a gun, the [cannon] shell, the flamethrower, the bomb, napalm, or gas. Where does torture really start, with a blow with the fist, the threat of reprisal, or electricity? Torture is different from other methods in that it is not anonymous. ... Torture brings the torturer and his victim face to face. The torturer at least has the merit of oper-

ating in the open. It is true that with torture the victim is disarmed, but so are the inhabitants of a city being bombed, aren't they? ...

It is my choice. I will carry out public executions, I'll shoot those absolutely guilty. Justice will therefore be just. It will conform to the first criterion of Christian justice. I'll expose their corpses to the public... not out of some sadist feeling, but to enhance the virtue of exemplary justice....

To the great astonishment of my men, I then decided to bring the corpses [of presumed insurgents killed in an air strike] back to M'sila to expose them to the population.... I ordered the driver to unload [the corpses] in M'sila on the main square [where they remained exposed for twenty-four hours]. When we left, the ambiance had completely changed. No more attacks, and the population, initially mute, opened up, and information began to pour out.

3 The Philippeville massacres, August 20, 1955. Faced by setbacks, the FLN decided to mount an open attack on the coastal region of Philippeville. A violent group, encouraged by FLN insurgents, massacred 123 European settlers. Enraged by the atrocities — the mob had brutally assaulted elderly men, women, and children — French army units, police, and settler vigilantes retaliated by killing at least 1,273 insurgents and Muslim-Arab residents; the FLN claimed that the actual number was 12,000. A French paratrooper described the scene.

[The bodies of French colonial settlers] literally strewed the town. The Arab children, wild with enthusiasm — to them it was a great holiday — rushed about yelling among the grown-ups. They finished off the dying. In one alley we found two of them kicking in an old woman's head. Yes, kicking it in! We had to kill them on the spot: they were crazed....

ANALYZING THE EVIDENCE

1. What are the main arguments made for the use of violence and terror in Sources 1 and 2, and in the Frantz Fanon selection (page 965)? Are any of these arguments legitimate?
2. Review the firsthand accounts by French soldiers who fought against FLN insurgents (Sources 2 and 3). What is their attitude toward Algerian Muslims?
3. Consider Sources 2–5. Did the use of violence and terror have unintended consequences?

[Catching up with a group of "rebels," mingled with civilians,] we opened fire into the thick of them, at random. Then as we moved on and found more bodies, our company commanders finally gave us the order to shoot down every Arab we met. You should have seen the result. . . . For two hours all we heard was automatic rifles spitting fire into the crowd. Apart from a dozen *fellagha* ["bandit," or FLN insurgent] stragglers, weapons in hand, whom we shot down, there were at least a hundred and fifty *boukaks* [another derogatory term for Muslims]. . . .

At midday, fresh orders: take prisoners. That complicated everything. It was easy when it was merely a matter of killing. . . . At six o'clock next morning all the l.m.g.s [light machine guns] and machine-guns were lined up in front of the crowd of prisoners, who immediately began to yell. But we opened fire; ten minutes later, it was practically over. There were so many of them they had to be buried with bulldozers.

(ullstein-bild/akg-images)

4 **A 1956 FLN terror bombing in Algiers.** The violence continued to escalate after the Philippeville massacres, and in 1956 the FLN formally embraced terrorism, expanding its attacks on the colonial state to include European civilians. This FLN bomb attack, intended to strike a French police patrol in a working-class district of Algiers, missed its target and hit customers in a coffeehouse instead. In the background, suspects are under arrest.

(Jacques Grevin/AFP/Getty Images)

5 **Pacification of the Algerian countryside.** Fighting took place in the capital of Algiers and other cities, but the Algerian War was largely fought in the countryside. In attempts to "pacify" the Algerian peasantry, French forces undertook numerous campaigns in rural areas like the one pictured here. Soldiers checked identity cards, searched for weapons, arrested villagers and moved them to internment centers, and at times tortured and summarily executed those they suspected of supporting the FLN.

PUTTING IT ALL TOGETHER

War inevitably involves the use of deadly, unrestrained violence, but historians agree that the Algerian War was particularly brutal. Using the sources above, along with what you have learned in class and in this chapter, write a short essay that explores the use of violence in the process of decolonization. Why was violence so central—and so savage—in the Algerian struggle for independence?

Sources: (1) Alejandro Colás and Richard Saull, eds., *The War on Terrorism and the American "Empire" After the Cold War* (New York: Routledge, 2007), p. 190; (2) Marnia Lazreg, *Torture and the Twilight of Empire: From Algiers to Baghdad* (Princeton, N.J.: Princeton University Press, 2008), pp. 89–92; (3) Alistair Horne, *A Savage War of Peace: Algeria 1954–1962* (New York: Viking, 1978), p. 121.

Yet to the dismay of the pieds-noirs and army hardliners, de Gaulle pragmatically moved toward Algerian self-determination. In 1961 furious pieds-noirs and army leaders formed the OAS (Secret Army Organization) and opened a terrorist revolt against Muslim Algerians and the French government. In April of that year the OAS mounted an all-out but short-lived putsch, taking over Algiers and threatening the government in Paris. Loyal army units defeated the rebellion, the leading generals were purged, and negotiations between the French government and FLN leaders continued. In April 1962, after more than a century of French rule, Algeria became independent under the FLN. Then in a massive postindependence exodus, over 1 million pieds-noirs fled to France and the Americas.

By the mid-1960s most African states had won independence, some through bloody insurrections. There were exceptions: Portugal, for one, waged war against independence movements in Angola and Mozambique until the 1970s. Even in liberated countries, the colonial legacy had long-term negative effects. South African blacks still longed for liberation from apartheid, and white rulers in Rhodesia continued a bloody civil war against African insurgents until 1979. Elsewhere African leaders may have expressed support for socialist or democratic principles in order to win aid from the superpowers. In practice, however, corrupt and authoritarian African leaders like Mobutu in the Congo often established lasting authoritarian dictatorships and enriched themselves at the expense of their populations.

Even after decolonization, western European countries managed to increase their economic and cultural ties with their former African colonies in the 1960s and 1970s. Above all, they used the lure of special trading privileges and provided heavy investment in French- and English-language education to enhance a powerful Western presence in the new African states. This situation led a variety of leaders and scholars to charge that western Europe (and the United States) had imposed a system of **neocolonialism** on the former colonies. According to this view, neocolonialism was a system designed to perpetuate Western economic domination and undermine the promise of political independence, thereby extending to Africa (and much of Asia) the kind of economic subordination that the United States had imposed on Latin America in the nineteenth century.

■ **neocolonialism** A postcolonial system that perpetuates Western economic exploitation in former colonial territories.

■ **guest worker programs** Government-run programs in western Europe designed to recruit labor for the booming postwar economy.

■ **postcolonial migration** The postwar movement of people from former colonies and the developing world into Europe.

Postwar Social Transformations

FOCUS QUESTION *How did changes in social relations contribute to European stability on both sides of the iron curtain?*

While Europe staged its astonishing political and economic recovery from the Nazi nightmare and colonized peoples won independence, the basic structures of Western society were also in transition. A changing class structure, new patterns of global migration, and new roles for women and youths had dramatic impacts on everyday life, albeit with different effects in the East Bloc and western Europe. Yet such large-scale changes had transformative effects on both sides of the iron curtain: social and cultural trends joined political and economic recovery to build stability in the postwar decades.

Changing Class Structures

The combination of rapid economic growth, growing prosperity and mass consumption, and the implementation of generous welfare policies went a long way toward creating a new society in Europe after the Second World War. Old class barriers relaxed, and class distinctions became fuzzier.

Changes in the structure of the middle class were particularly influential in this result. In the nineteenth and early twentieth centuries, the model for the middle class had been the independent, self-employed individual who owned a business or practiced a liberal profession such as law or medicine. Ownership of property—frequently inherited property—and strong family ties had often been the keys to wealth and standing within the middle class. After 1945 this pattern changed drastically in western Europe. A new breed of managers and experts—so-called white-collar workers—replaced property owners as the leaders of the middle class. The ability to serve the needs of a big organization largely replaced inherited property and family connections in determining an individual's social position in the middle and upper-middle classes. At the same time, the middle class grew massively and became harder to define.

There were several reasons for these developments. Rapid industrial and technological expansion and the consolidation of businesses created a powerful demand for technologists and managers in large corporations and government agencies. Moreover, the old propertied middle class lost control of many family-owned businesses. Numerous small businesses (including family farms) could no longer turn a profit, so their former owners regretfully joined the ranks of salaried employees.

Similar processes were at work in the Communist states of the East Bloc, where class leveling was an avowed goal of the authoritarian socialist state. The nationalization of industry, expropriation of property, and aggressive attempts to open employment opportunities to workers and equalize wage structures effectively reduced class differences. Communist Party members typically received better jobs and more pay than nonmembers, but by the 1960s the income differential between the top and bottom strata of East Bloc societies was far smaller than in the West.

In both East and West, managers and civil servants represented the model for a new middle class. Well paid and highly trained, often with backgrounds in engineering or accounting, these pragmatic experts were primarily concerned with efficiency and with practical solutions to concrete problems.

The structure of the lower classes also became more flexible and open. Continuing trends that began in the nineteenth century, large numbers of people left the countryside for the city. The population of one of the most traditional and least mobile groups in European society—farmers—drastically declined. Meanwhile, the number of industrial workers in western Europe also began to fall, as new jobs for white-collar and service employees grew rapidly. This change marked a significant transition in the world of labor. The welfare benefits extended by postwar governments also helped promote greater social equality because they raised lower-class living standards and were paid for in part by higher taxes on the wealthy. In general, European workers were better educated and more specialized than before, and the new workforce bore a greater resemblance to the growing middle class of salaried specialists than to traditional industrial workers.

Patterns of Postwar Migration

The 1850s to the 1930s had been an age of global migration, as countless Europeans moved around the continent and the world seeking economic opportunity or freedom from political or religious persecution (see Chapter 24). The 1950s and 1960s witnessed new waves of migration that had a significant impact on European society.

Some postwar migration took place within countries. Declining job prospects in Europe's rural areas encouraged many peasants and small farmers to seek better prospects in cities. In the poorer countries of Spain, Portugal, and Italy, millions moved to more developed regions of their own countries. The process was similar in the East Bloc, where the forced collectivization of agriculture and state subsidies for heavy industry opened opportunities in urban areas. And before the erection of the Berlin Wall in 1961, some 3.5 million East Germans moved to the Federal Republic of Germany, seeking higher pay and a better life.

Many other Europeans moved across national borders seeking work. The general pattern was from south to north. Workers from less developed countries like Italy, Spain, and socialist Yugoslavia moved to the industrialized north, particularly to West Germany, which—having lost 5 million people during the war—was in desperate need of able-bodied workers. In the 1950s and 1960s West Germany and other prosperous countries implemented **guest worker programs** designed to recruit much-needed labor for the booming economy. West Germany signed labor agreements with Italy, Greece, Spain, Portugal, Yugoslavia, Turkey, and the North African countries of Tunisia and Morocco. By the early 1970s there were 2.8 million foreign workers in Germany and another 2.3 million in France, where they made up 11 percent of the workforce.

Most guest workers were young, unskilled single men who labored for low wages in entry-level jobs and sent much of their pay to their families at home. (See "Individuals in Society: Armando Rodrigues," page 974.) According to government plans, these guest workers were supposed to return to their home countries after a specified period. Many built new lives, however, and, to the dismay of the authorities, chose to live permanently in their adoptive countries.

Europe was also changed by **postcolonial migration**, the movement of people from the former colonies and the developing world into prosperous Europe. In contrast to guest workers, who joined formal recruitment programs, postcolonial migrants could often claim citizenship rights from their former colonizers and moved spontaneously. Immigrants from the Caribbean, India, Africa, and Asia moved to Britain; people from North Africa, especially Algeria, and from sub-Saharan countries such as Cameroon and the Ivory Coast moved to France; Indonesians migrated to the Netherlands. Postcolonial immigrants also moved to eastern Europe, though in far fewer numbers.

These new migration patterns had dramatic results. Immigrant labor helped fuel economic recovery. Growing ethnic diversity changed the face of Europe and enriched the cultural life of the continent. The new residents were not always welcome, however. Adaptation to European lifestyles could be difficult, and immigrants often lived in separate communities where they spoke their own languages. They faced employment and housing discrimination, and the harsh anti-immigrant rhetoric and policies of xenophobic politicians. Even prominent European intellectuals worried aloud that Muslim migrants from North Africa and Turkey would never adopt European values and customs.

INDIVIDUALS IN SOCIETY

Armando Rodrigues

Popping flashbulbs greeted Portuguese worker Armando Rodrigues when he stepped off a train in Cologne in September 1964. Celebrated in the national media as West Germany's 1 millionth guest worker, Rodrigues was met by government and business leaders — including the Christian Democratic minister of labor — who presented him with a motorcycle and a bouquet of carnations.

In most respects, Rodrigues was hardly different from the many foreign workers recruited to work in West Germany and other northern European countries. Most foreign laborers were nobodies, written out of mainstream historical texts and treated as statistics. Yet given his moment of fame, Rodrigues is an apt symbol of a troubled labor program that helped turn Germany into a multiethnic society.

By the late 1950s the new Federal Republic desperately needed able-bodied men to fill the low-paying jobs created by rapid economic expansion. The West German government signed labor agreements with several Mediterranean countries to meet this demand. Rodrigues and hundreds of thousands of other young men signed up for the employment program and then submitted to an arduous application process. Rodrigues traveled from his village to the regional Federal Labor Office, where he filled out forms and took written and medical exams. Months later, after he had received an initial one-year contract from a German employer, Rodrigues and twelve hundred other Portuguese and Spanish men boarded a special train reserved for foreign workers and embarked for West Germany.

For labor migrants, life was hard in West Germany. In the first years of the guest worker program, most recruits were men between the ages of twenty and forty who were either single or willing to leave their families at home. They typically filled low-level jobs in construction, mines, and factories, and they lived apart from West Germans in special barracks close to their workplaces, with six to eight workers in a room.

West Germans gave Rodrigues and his fellow migrants a mixed reception. Though they were a welcome source of inexpensive labor, the men who emigrated from what West Germans called "the southern lands" faced discrimination and prejudice. "Order, cleanliness, and punctuality seem like the natural qualities of a respectable person to us," wrote one official in 1966. "In the south, one does not learn or know this, so it is difficult [for a person from the south] to adjust here."*

According to official plans, the so-called guest workers were supposed to return home after a specified period of time. Rodrigues, for one, went back to Portugal in the late

*Quoted in Rita Chin, *The Guest Worker Question in Postwar Germany* (New York: Cambridge University Press, 2007), p. 43.

Armando Rodrigues received a standing ovation and a motorcycle when he got off the train in Cologne in 1964. (Horst Ossinger/picture-allliance/dpa/AP Images)

1970s. Others did not. Resisting government pressure, millions of temporary "guests" raised families and became permanent West German residents, building substantial ethnic minorities in the Federal Republic. Because of strict naturalization laws, however, they could not become West German citizens.

Despite the hostility they faced, foreign workers established a lasting and powerful presence in West Germany, and they were a significant factor in the country's swift economic recovery. More than fifty years after Rodrigues arrived in Cologne, his motorcycle is on permanent display in the House of History Museum in Bonn. The exhibit is a remarkable testament to one man's history, to the contribution of migrant labor to West German economic growth, and to the ongoing struggle to come to terms with ethnic difference and integration in a democratic Germany.

QUESTIONS FOR ANALYSIS

1. How did Rodrigues's welcome at his 1964 reception differ from the general attitude toward guest workers in Germany at the time?
2. What were the long-term costs and benefits of West Germany's labor recruitment policies?

The tensions that surrounded changed migration patterns would pose significant challenges to social integration in the decades to come.

New Roles for Women

The postwar culmination of a one-hundred-year-long trend toward early marriage, early childbearing, and small family size in wealthy urban societies (see Chapter 22) had revolutionary implications for women. Above all, pregnancy and child care occupied a much smaller portion of a woman's life than in earlier times. The postwar baby boom did make for larger families and fairly rapid population growth of 1 to 1.5 percent per year in many European countries, but the long-term decline in birthrates resumed by the 1960s. By the early 1970s about half of Western women were having their last baby by the age of twenty-six or twenty-seven. When the youngest child trooped off to kindergarten, the average mother had more than forty years of life in front of her.

This was a momentous transition. Throughout history male-dominated society insisted on defining most women as mothers or potential mothers, and motherhood was very demanding. In the postwar years, however, motherhood no longer absorbed the energies of a lifetime, and more and more married women looked for new roles in the world of work outside the family. Three major forces helped women searching for jobs in the changing post–World War II workplace. First, the economic boom created strong demand for labor. Second, the economy continued its gradual shift away from the old male-dominated heavy industries, such as coal, steel, and shipbuilding, and toward the white-collar service industries in which some women already worked, such as government, education, trade, and health care. Third, young women shared fully in the postwar education revolution, positioning them to take advantage of the growing need for officeworkers and well-trained professionals. Thus more and more married women became full-time and part-time wage earners.

In the East Bloc, Communist leaders opened up numerous jobs to women, who accounted for almost half of all employed persons. Many women made their way into previously male professions, including factory work but also medicine and engineering. In western Europe and North America, the percentage of married women in the workforce rose from a range of roughly 20 to 25 percent in 1950 to anywhere from 30 to 60 percent in the 1970s.

All was not easy for women entering paid employment. Married women workers faced widespread and long-established discrimination in pay, advancement, and occupational choice in comparison to men. Moreover, many women could find only part-time work. As

the divorce rate rose in the 1960s, part-time work, with its low pay and scanty benefits, often meant poverty for many women with children. Finally, married working women in both the East and West still carried most of the child-rearing and housekeeping responsibilities, leaving them with an exhausting "double burden." Trying to live up to society's seemingly contradictory ideals was one reason that many women accepted part-time employment.

The injustices that married women encountered as wage earners contributed greatly to the movement for women's equality and emancipation that arose in the United States and western Europe in the 1960s. Sexism and discrimination in the workplace—and in the home—grew loathsome and evoked the sense of injustice that drives revolutions and reforms.

Youth Culture and the Generation Gap

The bulging cohort of so-called baby boomers born after World War II created a distinctive and very international youth culture, which brought remarkable changes to postwar youth roles and lifestyles. That subculture, found across western Europe and the United States, was rooted in fashions and musical tastes that set its members off from their elders and fueled anxious comments about a growing "generation gap."

Youth styles in the United States often provided inspiration for movements in Europe. Groups like the British Teddy boys, the West German *Halbstarken* (half-strongs), and the French *blousons noirs* (black jackets) modeled their rebellious clothing and cynical attitudes on the bad-boy characters played by U.S. film stars such as James Dean and Marlon Brando. American jazz and rock 'n' roll spread rapidly in western Europe, aided by the invention of the long-playing record album (or LP) and the 45 rpm "single" in the late 1940s, and the growth of the corporate music industry. American musicians such as Elvis Presley, Bill Haley and His Comets, and Gene Vincent thrilled European youths and worried parents, teachers, and politicians.

Youths played a key role in the consumer revolution. Marketing experts and manufacturers quickly recognized that the young people they now called "teenagers" had money to spend due to postwar prosperity. An array of advertisements and products consciously targeted the youth market. In France, for example, magazine advertising aimed at adolescents grew by 400 percent between 1959 and 1962. As the baby boomers entered their late teens, they eagerly purchased trendy clothing and the latest pop music hits, as well as record players, transistor radios, magazines, hair products, and makeup, all marketed for the "young generation."

British Rockers, July 1964   By the early 1960s, the postwar baby boom had brought remarkable changes to the lives of teenagers and young adults. New styles and behaviors, often based on American models, embraced youthful rebelliousness and challenged adult conventions. The British Rockers, a youth subculture centered on motorcycle clubs, epitomized the trend. (Terence Spencer/The LIFE Picture Collection/Getty Images)

The new youth culture became an inescapable part of Western society. One clear sign of this new presence was the rapid growth in the number of universities and college students. Before the 1960s, in North America and Europe, only a small elite received a university education. In 1950 only 3 to 4 percent of western European youths went on to higher education; numbers in the United States were only slightly higher. Then, as government subsidies made education more affordable to ordinary people, enrollments skyrocketed. By 1960 at least three times more European students attended some kind of university than they had before World War II, and the number continued to rise sharply until the 1970s.

The rapid expansion of higher education opened new opportunities for the middle and lower classes, but it also made for overcrowded classrooms. Many students felt that they were not getting the kind of education they needed for jobs in the modern world. At the same time, some reflective students feared that universities were doing nothing but turning out docile technocrats both to stock and to serve "the establishment." Thus it was no coincidence that students became leaders in a counterculture that attacked the ideals of the affluent society of the postwar world and shocked the West in the late 1960s.

NOTES

1. Anonymous, *A Woman in Berlin: Eight Weeks in the Conquered City: A Diary* (New York: Metropolitan Books, 2005), pp. 239–240.
2. Quoted in N. Graebner, *Cold War Diplomacy, 1945–1960* (Princeton, N.J.: Van Nostrand, 1962), p. 17.
3. From a speech delivered by G. Marshall at Harvard University on June 5, 1947, reprinted in *Department of State Bulletin* (June 15, 1947), pp. 1159–1160.
4. Quoted in T. Judt, *Postwar: A History of Europe Since 1945* (New York: Penguin, 2005), p. 150.
5. N. Khrushchev, "On the Cult of Personality and Its Consequences" (1956), quoted in J. M. Brophy et al., *Perspectives from the Past* (New York: W. W. Norton, 2009), pp. 804–805.
6. Quoted in M. Huband, *The Skull Beneath the Skin: Africa After the Cold War* (Boulder: Westview Press, 2001), p. 9.

LOOKING BACK LOOKING AHEAD

The unprecedented human and physical destruction of World War II left Europeans shaken, searching in the ruins for new livelihoods and a workable political order. A tension-filled peace settlement left the continent divided into two hostile political-military blocs, and the resulting Cold War, complete with the possibility of atomic annihilation, threatened to explode into open confrontation. Albert Einstein voiced a common anxiety when he said, "I do not know with what weapons World War III will be fought, but World War IV will be fought with sticks and stones."

Despite such fears, the division of Europe led to the emergence of a stable world system. In the West Bloc, economic growth, state provision of welfare benefits, and a strong alliance brought social and political consensus. In the East Bloc, a combination of political repression and partial reform likewise limited dissent and encouraged stability. During the height of the Cold War, Europe's former colonies won liberation in a process that was often flawed but that nonetheless resulted in political independence for millions of people. And large-scale transformations, including the rise of Big Science and rapid economic growth, opened new opportunities for women and immigrants and contributed to stability on both sides of the iron curtain.

By the early 1960s Europeans had entered a remarkable age of affluence that almost eliminated real poverty on most of the continent. Superpower confrontations had led not to European war but to peaceful coexistence. The following decades, however, would see substantial challenges to this postwar consensus. Youth revolts and a determined feminist movement, an oil crisis and a deep economic recession, and political dissent and revolution in the East Bloc would shake and remake the foundations of Western society.

Make Connections

Think about the larger developments and continuities within and across chapters.

1. How did the Cold War shape politics and everyday life in the United States and western Europe, the U.S.S.R. and the East Bloc, and the decolonizing world? Why was its influence so pervasive?

2. How were the postwar social transformations in class structures, patterns of migration, and the lives of women and youths related to the broad political and economic changes that followed World War II? How did they differ on either side of the iron curtain?

3. Compare and contrast the treaties and agreements that ended the First and Second World Wars (Chapter 25). Did the participants who shaped the peace accords face similar problems? Which set of agreements did a better job of resolving outstanding issues, and why?

28 REVIEW & EXPLORE

Identify Key Terms

Identify and explain the significance of each item below.

Cold War (p. 944)

displaced persons (p. 945)

Truman Doctrine (p. 949)

Marshall Plan (p. 949)

Council for Mutual Economic
   Assistance (COMECON) (p. 950)

NATO (p. 950)

Warsaw Pact (p. 950)

economic miracle (p. 952)

Christian Democrats (p. 952)

Common Market (p. 954)

Socialist Realism (p. 957)

de-Stalinization (p. 959)

decolonization (p. 963)

nonalignment (p. 965)

neocolonialism (p. 972)

guest worker programs (p. 973)

postcolonial migration (p. 973)

Review the Main Ideas

Answer the focus questions from each section of the chapter.

◆ Why was World War II followed so quickly by the Cold War? (p. 944)

◆ What were the sources of postwar recovery and stability in western Europe? (p. 952)

◆ What was the pattern of postwar development in the Soviet bloc? (p. 956)

◆ What led to decolonization after World War II, and how did the Cold War influence the process? (p. 963)

◆ How did changes in social relations contribute to European stability on both sides of the iron curtain? (p. 972)

Suggested Reading and Media Resources

BOOKS

◆ Abrams, Bradley F. *The Struggle for the Soul of the Nation: Czech Culture and the Rise of Communism.* 2004. This intellectual history of postwar Czechoslovak political culture argues that grassroots calls for radical change brought Communists to power and critiques claims that communism was simply imposed from above.

◆ Berstein, Serge. *The Republic of de Gaulle, 1958–1969.* 2006. An outstanding work on postwar France.

◆ Chamberlain, M. E. *Decolonization: The Fall of the European Empires,* 2d ed. 1999. A clear, accessible account.

◆ Chin, Rita. *The Guest Worker Question in Postwar Germany.* 2007. An engaging interpretation of postwar migration patterns in West Germany.

◆ de Grazia, Victoria. *Irresistible Empire: America's Advance Through Twentieth-Century Europe.* 2005. A lively, provocative account of the Americanization of Europe from 1900 to the 1950s.

◆ de Senarclens, Pierre. *From Yalta to the Iron Curtain: The Great Powers and the Origins of the Cold War.* 1995. A valuable work on the Cold War.

◆ Eksteins, Modris. *Walking Since Daybreak: A Story of Eastern Europe, World War II, and the Heart of Our Century.* 2000. A powerful, partly autobiographical account of the Baltic countries before, during, and after World War II.

◆ Hitchcock, William I. *The Struggle for Europe: The Turbulent History of a Divided Continent, 1945 to the Present.* 2004. A valuable general study with extensive bibliographies.

- Judt, Tony. *Postwar: A History of Europe Since 1945*. 2005. A masterful reconsideration, especially strong on smaller countries.
- Kertzer, David I., and Marzio Barbagli, eds. *Family Life in the Twentieth Century: The History of the European Family*, vol. 3. 2003. A distinguished collection of essays by experts.
- Lomax, Bill. *Hungary 1956*. 1976. A gripping and engaged book on the failed Hungarian revolution that explores the actions of ordinary people as well as prominent leaders.
- Westad, Odd Arne. *The Global Cold War: Third World Interventions and the Making of Our Times*. 2007. An up-to-date study of the Cold War's global impact.

DOCUMENTARIES

- *Cold War* (CNN, 1998). A twenty-four-part miniseries that examines the United States and the Soviet Union's relationship between World War II and the collapse of the Soviet Union.
- *In the Shadow of the Moon* (David Sington, 2007). Surviving crew members of NASA's Apollo missions tell their own stories.
- *Korean War Stories* (PBS, 2001). American war veterans recall their experiences of the Korean War.
- *Sputnik Mania* (David Hoffman, 2007). A documentary looking at the Soviet Union's launch of Sputnik and its worldwide effects.

FEATURE FILMS AND TELEVISION

- *The Battle of Algiers* (Gillo Pontecorvo, 1966). A justly famous and fairly accurate feature film about the "Battle of the Casbah" during the Algerian War, shot in black-and-white documentary style.
- *The Bicycle Thief* (Vittorio De Sica, 1948). This classic example of Italian Neorealist cinema explores the tribulations of ordinary Italian workers dealing with the hardships of the immediate postwar period.
- *Dr. Strangelove or: How I Learned to Stop Worrying and Love the Bomb* (Stanley Kubrick, 1964). A dark comedy produced during the Cold War that satirizes the fear of a nuclear holocaust.

WEB SITES

- *BBC: History: Cold War*. A great resource for overviews on the Korean War, Cuban missile crisis, weapons of the Cold War, and the fall of the Soviet Union. **www.bbc .co.uk/history/worldwars/coldwar/**
- *North Atlantic Treaty Organization*. NATO's homepage provides information about its origins and the nature of the organization today. **www.nato.int/cps/en/natolive /index.htm**
- *Nuremberg Trials*. Legal resources pertaining to the Nuremberg trials. **www.loc.gov/rr/frd/Military_Law /Nuremberg_trials.html**
- *Wilson Center: Cold War International History Project*. This Web site offers government documents from all sides of the Cold War. The project seeks to integrate materials and perspectives from the former East and West Blocs. **www.wilsoncenter.org/program/cold -war-international-history-project**

29

Challenging the Postwar Order

1960–1991

As Europe entered the 1960s, the political and social systems forged in the postwar era appeared sound. Centrist politicians in western Europe agreed that managed economic expansion, abundant jobs, and state-sponsored welfare benefits would continue to improve living standards and create social consensus. In the Soviet Union and the East Bloc, although conditions varied by country, modest economic growth and limited reforms amid continued political repression likewise contributed to a sense of stability. Cold War tensions diminished, and it seemed that a remarkable age of affluence would ease political differences and lead to social harmony.

By the late 1960s, however, this hard-won sense of stability had begun to disappear as popular protest movements in East and West arose to challenge dominant certainties. In the early 1970s the astonishing postwar economic advance ground to a halt, with serious consequences. In western Europe, a new generation of conservative political leaders advanced new policies to deal with economic decline and the growth of global competition. New political groups across the political spectrum, from feminists and environmentalists to national separatists and right-wing populists, added to the atmosphere of crisis and conflict.

In the East Bloc, leaders vacillated between central economic control and liberalization and left in place tight controls on social freedom, leading to stagnation and frustration. In the 1980s popular dissident movements emerged in Poland and other satellite states, and efforts to reform the Communist system in the Soviet Union from the top down snowballed out of control. In 1989, as revolutions swept away Communist rule throughout the entire Soviet bloc, the Cold War reached a dramatic conclusion. ■

CHAPTER PREVIEW

Reform and Protest in the 1960s
Why did the postwar consensus of the 1950s break down?

Crisis and Change in Western Europe
What were the consequences of economic decline in the 1970s?

The Decline of "Developed Socialism"
What led to the decline of Soviet power in the East Bloc?

The Revolutions of 1989
Why did revolution sweep through the East Bloc in 1989, and what were the immediate consequences?

Life in a Divided Europe
Watchtowers, armed guards, and minefields controlled the Communist eastern side of the Berlin Wall, a significant symbol of Cold War division in Europe. In the liberal West, to the contrary, ordinary folk turned what was an easily accessible blank wall into an ad hoc art gallery — whimsical graffiti art, like the examples pictured here, covered the western side of the wall. (Bernd Kammerer/picture-alliance/dpa/akg-images)

Reform and Protest in the 1960s

FOCUS QUESTION *Why did the postwar consensus of the 1950s break down?*

In the early 1960s politics and society in prosperous western Europe remained relatively stable. East Bloc governments, bolstered by modest economic growth and state-enforced political conformity, and committed to generous welfare benefits for their citizens, maintained control. As the 1960s progressed, politics in the West shifted noticeably to the left, and Social Democratic governments worked to normalize East-West relations. Amid this more liberalized society, a youthful counterculture emerged among the children of affluence to critique the status quo. In the East Bloc, Khrushchev's limited reforms also inspired rebellions. Thus activists around the world rose in protest against the perceived inequalities of both capitalism and communism, leading to dramatic events in 1968, exemplified in Paris and Prague.

Cold War Tensions Thaw

In western Europe, the first two decades of postwar reconstruction had been overseen for the most part by center-right Christian Democrats, who successfully maintained postwar stability around Cold War politics, free-market economics with limited state intervention, and welfare provisions (see Chapter 28). In the mid- to late 1960s, buoyed by the rapidly expanding economy, much of western Europe moved politically to the left. Socialists entered the Italian government in 1963. In Britain, the Labour Party returned to power in 1964, after thirteen years in opposition. In West Germany, the aging postwar chancellor Konrad Adenauer (1876–1967) retired in 1963, and in 1969 Willy Brandt (1913–1992) became the first Social Democratic West German chancellor; his party would govern Germany until 1982. There were important exceptions to this general trend. Though the tough-minded, independent French president Charles de Gaulle resigned in 1969, the centrist Gaullists remained in power in France until 1981. And in Spain, Portugal, and Greece, authoritarian regimes remained in power until the mid-1970s.

Despite these exceptions, the general leftward drift eased Cold War tensions. Though the Cold War continued to rage outside Europe and generally defined relations between the Soviet Union and the United States, western European leaders took major steps to normalize relations with the East Bloc. Willy Brandt took the lead. In December 1970 he flew to Poland for the signing of a historic treaty of reconciliation. In a dramatic moment rich in symbolism, Brandt laid a wreath at the tomb of the Polish unknown soldier and another at the monument commemorating the armed uprising of Warsaw's Jewish ghetto against occupying Nazi armies. Standing before the ghetto memorial, a somber Brandt fell to his knees as if in prayer. "I wanted," Brandt said later, "to ask pardon in the

A West German Leader Apologizes for the Holocaust In 1970 West German chancellor Willy Brandt knelt before the Jewish Heroes' Monument in Warsaw, Poland, to ask forgiveness for the German mass murder of European Jews and other groups during the Second World War. Brandt's action, captured in photo and film by the onlooking press, symbolized the chancellor's policy of Ostpolitik, the normalization of relations between the East and West Blocs. (bpk, Berlin/photographer: Hanns Hubmann, Inv. HU 17089-071/Art Resource, NY)

name of our people for a million-fold crime which was committed in the misused name of the Germans."[1]

Brandt's gesture at the Warsaw Ghetto memorial and the treaty with Poland were part of his broader, conciliatory foreign policy termed **Ostpolitik** (German for "Eastern policy"). Brandt aimed at nothing less than a comprehensive peace settlement for central Europe and the two postwar German states. Brandt believed that the building of the Berlin Wall in 1961 revealed the limitations of West Germany's official hard line toward the East Bloc. Accordingly, the chancellor negotiated new treaties with the Soviet Union and Czechoslovakia, as well as Poland, that formally accepted existing state boundaries—rejected by West Germany's government since 1945—in return for a mutual renunciation of force or the threat of force. Using the imaginative formula of "two German states within one German nation," he broke decisively with past policy and entered into direct relations with East Germany.

Brandt's Ostpolitik was part of a general relaxation of East-West tensions, termed **détente** (day-TAHNT), which began in the early 1970s. Though Cold War hostilities continued in the developing world, diplomatic relations between the United States and the Soviet Union grew less strained. The superpowers agreed to limit the testing and proliferation of nuclear weapons and in 1975 mounted a joint U.S.-U.S.S.R. space mission.

The move toward détente reached a high point when the United States, Canada, the Soviet Union, and all European nations (except isolationist Albania and tiny Andorra) met in Helsinki to sign the Final Act of the Conference on Security and Cooperation in Europe in 1975. Under what came to be called the Helsinki Accords, the thirty-five participating nations agreed that Europe's existing political frontiers could not be changed by force. They also accepted numerous provisions guaranteeing the civil rights and political freedoms of their citizens. The agreement helped diminish Cold War conflict. Although Communist regimes would continue to curtail domestic freedoms and violate human rights guarantees, the accords encouraged East Bloc dissidents, who could now demand that their governments respect international declarations on human rights. (See "Evaluating the Evidence 29.1: Human Rights Under the Helsinki Accords," page 984.)

Chronology

1961	Building of Berlin Wall suggests permanence of the East Bloc
1962–1965	Second Vatican Council
1963	Wolf publishes *Divided Heaven;* Friedan publishes *The Feminine Mystique*
1964	Civil Rights Act in the United States
1964–1973	Peak of U.S. involvement in Vietnam War
1966	Formation of National Organization for Women (NOW)
1968	Soviet invasion of Czechoslovakia; "May Events" protests in France
1971	Founding of Greenpeace
1973	OPEC oil embargo
1975	Helsinki Accords
1979	Margaret Thatcher becomes British prime minister; founding of West German Green Party; Soviet invasion of Afghanistan
1985	Mikhail Gorbachev named Soviet premier
1987	United States and Soviet Union sign arms reduction treaty
1989	Soviet withdrawal from Afghanistan
1989–1991	Fall of communism in eastern Europe
December 1991	Dissolution of the Soviet Union

Newly empowered Social Democrats in western Europe also engaged in reform at home. Building on the welfare systems established in the 1950s, politicians increased state spending on public services even further. These Social Democrats did not advocate "socialism" as practiced in the Soviet bloc, where strict economic planning, the nationalization of key economic sectors, and one-party dictatorships ensured rigid state control. To the contrary, they maintained a firm commitment to capitalist free markets and democracy. At the same time, they viewed welfare provisions as a way to ameliorate the inevitable inequalities of a competitive market economy. As a result, western European democracies spent more and more state funds on health care, education, old-age insurance, and public housing, all paid for with very high taxes.

By the early 1970s state spending on such programs hovered around 40 percent of the gross domestic product

■ **Ostpolitik** German for Chancellor Willy Brandt's new "Eastern policy"; West Germany's attempt in the 1970s to ease diplomatic tensions with East Germany, exemplifying the policies of détente.

■ **détente** The progressive relaxation of Cold War tensions that emerged in the early 1970s.

Human Rights Under the Helsinki Accords

At the conclusion of the two-year-long Conference on Security and Cooperation in Europe (1973–1975), the representatives of thirty-five West and East Bloc states solemnly pledged to "respect each other's sovereign equality" and to "refrain from any intervention, direct or indirect . . . in the internal or external affairs . . . of another participating state." East Bloc leaders, pleased that the West had at last officially accepted the frontiers and territorial integrity of the Communist satellite states established after World War II, agreed to recognize a lengthy list of "civil, political, economic, social, cultural and other rights and freedoms."

~

Principle VII on Human Rights and Freedoms, from the Final Act of the Conference on Security and Cooperation in Europe (August 1, 1975).

VII. Respect for human rights and fundamental freedoms, including the freedom of thought, conscience, religion or belief

The participating States will respect human rights and fundamental freedoms, including the freedom of thought, conscience, religion or belief, for all without distinction as to race, sex, language or religion.

They will promote and encourage the effective exercise of civil, political, economic, social, cultural and other rights and freedoms all of which derive from the inherent dignity of the human person and are essential for his free and full development.

Within this framework the participating States will recognize and respect the freedom of the individual to profess and practice, alone or in community with others, religion or belief acting in accordance with the dictates of his own conscience.

The participating States on whose territory national minorities exist will respect the right of persons belonging to such minorities to equality before the law, will afford them the full opportunity for the actual enjoyment of human rights and fundamental freedoms and will, in this manner, protect their legitimate interests in this sphere.

The participating States recognize the universal significance of human rights and fundamental freedoms, respect for which is an essential factor for the peace, justice and well-being necessary to ensure the development of friendly relations and co-operation among themselves as among all States.

They will constantly respect these rights and freedoms in their mutual relations and will endeavor jointly and separately, including in co-operation with the United Nations, to promote universal and effective respect for them.

They confirm the right of the individual to know and act upon his rights and duties in this field.

In the field of human rights and fundamental freedoms, the participating States will act in conformity with the purposes and principles of the Charter of the United Nations and with the Universal Declaration of Human Rights. They will also fulfill their obligations as set forth in the international declarations and agreements in this field, including *inter alia* the International Covenants on Human Rights, by which they may be bound.

EVALUATE THE EVIDENCE

1. How do the Helsinki Accords express the guiding principles of liberal democracy?
2. Why would Communist representatives publicly agree to recognize a list of rights that clearly challenged many of the repressive aspects of one-party rule in the East Bloc?

Source: "The Final Act of the Conference on Security and Cooperation in Europe, Aug. 1, 1975, 14 I.L.M. 1292 (Helsinki Declaration)," University of Minnesota Civil Rights Library, http://www1.umn.edu/humanrts/osce/basics/finact75.htm.

---

in France, West Germany, and Great Britain, and even more in Scandinavia and the Netherlands. Center-right Christian Democrats generally supported increased spending on entitlements—as long as the economy prospered. The economic slowdown of the mid-1970s, however, undermined support for the welfare state consensus (see page 992).

The Affluent Society

The political shift to the left in the 1960s was accompanied by rapid social change across western Europe. A decade of economic growth and high wages meant that an expanding middle class could increasingly enjoy the benefits of the consumer revolution that began in the 1950s (see Chapter 28). Yet this so-called age of affluence had clear limits. The living standards of workers and immigrants did not rise as fast as those of the educated middle classes, and the expanding economy did not always reach underdeveloped regions, such as southern Italy. The 1960s nonetheless brought general prosperity to millions, and the construction of a full-blown consumer society had a profound impact on daily life.

Many Europeans now had more money to spend on leisure time and recreational pursuits, and one of the most noticeable leisure-time developments was the blossoming of mass travel and tourism. With month-long paid vacations required by law in most western European countries and with widespread automobile ownership, travel to beaches and ski resorts came within the reach of the middle class and much of the working class. By the late 1960s packaged tours with cheap group airfares and bargain hotel accommodations had made even distant lands easily accessible.

Consumerism also changed life at home. Household appliances that were still luxuries in the 1950s were now commonplace; televisions overtook radio as a popular form of domestic entertainment while vacuum cleaners, refrigerators, and washing machines transformed women's housework. Studies later showed that these new "laborsaving devices" caused women to spend even more time cleaning and cooking to new exacting standards, but at the time electric appliances were considered indispensable to what contemporaries called a "modern lifestyle." The establishment of U.S.-style self-service supermarkets across western Europe changed the way food was produced, purchased, and prepared, and threatened to force independent bakers, butchers, and neighborhood grocers out of business. (See "Living in the Past: The Supermarket Revolution," page 986.)

Intellectuals and cultural critics greeted the age of affluence with a chorus of criticism. Some worried that rampant consumerism created a bland conformity that wiped out regional and national traditions. The great majority of ordinary people, they argued, now ate the same foods, wore the same clothes, and watched the same programs on television, sapping creativity and individualism. Others complained bitterly that these changes threatened to Americanize Europe. Neither group could do much to stop the spread of consumer culture.

Worries about the Americanization of Europe were overstated. European nations preserved distinctive national cultures even during the consumer revolution, but social change nonetheless occurred. The moral authority of religious doctrine lost ground before the growing materialism of consumer society. In predominantly Protestant lands—Great Britain, Scandinavia, and parts of West Germany—church membership and regular attendance both declined significantly. Even in traditionally Catholic countries, such as Italy, Ireland, and France, outward signs of popular belief seemed to falter. At the **Second Vatican Council**, convened from 1962 to 1965, Catholic leaders agreed on a number of reforms meant to democratize and renew the church and broaden its appeal. They called for new openness in Catholic theology and declared that masses would henceforth be said in local languages rather than in Latin, which few could understand.

Braniff Airways Hostesses, ca. 1968 Sporting the latest "mod" styles, hostesses for Braniff International Airways wear uniforms made by world-renowned Italian fashion designer Emilio Pucci. The 1960s counterculture helped popularize the use of kaleidoscopic fluorescent colors and wild shapes in fashion, the fine arts, and advertising. (© Bettmann/Corbis)

These resolutions, however, did little to halt the slide toward secularization.

Family ties also weakened in the age of affluence. The number of adults living alone grew remarkably, men and women married later, the nuclear family became smaller and more mobile, and divorce rates rose rapidly. By the 1970s the baby boom of the postwar decades was over, and population growth leveled out across Europe and even began to decline in prosperous northwestern Europe.

The Counterculture Movement

The dramatic emergence of a youthful counterculture, which came of age in the mid-1960s, accompanied growing economic prosperity. The "sixties generation" angrily criticized the comforts of the affluent society and challenged the social and political status quo.

What accounts for the emergence of the counterculture? Simple demographics played an important role. Young soldiers returning home after World War II in

■ **Second Vatican Council** A meeting of Catholic leaders convened from 1962 to 1965 that initiated a number of reforms, including the replacement of Latin with local languages in church services, designed to democratize the church and renew its appeal.

LIVING IN THE PAST
The Supermarket Revolution

In February 1961 Supermarket Italiani opened its first supermarket in Florence, Italy, home of Renaissance art and culture. The opening was an apparent triumph: police were needed to control the fifteen thousand customers who mobbed the store. Owned by a U.S.-based multinational corporation, Supermarket Italiani proudly advertised "self-service"—in English—the slogan expressing a new cachet for all things American. Yet all was not well. Small grocers greeted the supermarket with strikes. Demonstrators called for boycotts. Angry letters to local newspapers complained that Italian traditions were in decay.

No wonder. The supermarket brought dramatic changes to everyday life. For centuries Florentines—like most Europeans—had bought fresh food from local butchers, bakers, and produce dealers. In tiny neighborhood stores, a shopkeeper greeted customers and, while gossiping about neighborhood events, took an order, calculated the price, and weighed and wrapped the goods.

Shopping in an American-style supermarket changed all that. Consumers entered a well-lit, much larger store and filled their carts from long aisles stocked with pre-packaged, pre-priced goods. Frozen meat and canned vegetables meant that once-seasonal items were now available year-round. Competing brands introduced many versions of the same product, and advertising campaigns and cut-rate pricing enticed customers.

The new approach to shopping unleashed a host of changes. New farming methods, distribution networks, and packaging and advertising industries emerged. Huge international chains arose, such as Aldi, which started as a small chain in postwar Germany and now owns over eight thousand stores around the world. At home, meal plans, recipes, budgets, and shopping styles were altered. Supermarkets also transformed city space. Large stores on busy roads meant more traffic, and automobiles and parking lots threatened

For decades before the supermarket revolution of the 1950s, Europeans shopped in small stores featuring specialty selections, such as this pre–World War II butcher shop in Berlin, Germany. Customers asked for items displayed behind the counter and were typically served by the shopkeeper or members of his family or by part-time employees. (akg-images)

1945 eagerly established families, and the next two decades brought a dramatic increase in the number of births per year in Europe and North America. The children born during the postwar baby boom grew up in an era of political liberalism and unprecedented material abundance. They remembered the horrors of totalitarian government that caused World War II and watched as colonial peoples forged new paths to freedom during the decades of decolonization. The counterculture challenged the growing conformity that seemed to be an inherent part of consumer society and the unequal distribution of wealth that arose from market economics. In short, when the baby boomers came of age in the 1960s, they had the education to see problems like inequality and the lack of social justice, as well as the freedom from want to act on their concerns.

Counterculture movements in both Europe and the United States drew much inspiration from the

the existence of neighborhood stores. Though they never entirely displaced small grocers or dominated the food retail sector, as in the United States, by the 1980s supermarkets were part of daily life in Europe, vivid evidence of how the consumer revolution transformed the way Europeans shopped for, ate, and thought about food.

QUESTIONS FOR ANALYSIS

1. Why did Italians greet the arrival of supermarket shopping with both protest and enthusiasm?
2. In what ways does the supermarket exemplify the consumer revolution that swept through Europe in the late 1950s and the 1960s? What were its implications for family life?

At Sainsbury's Self-service shopping is EASY and QUICK

1—As you go in you are given a special wire basket for your purchases.

2—The prices and weight of all goods are clearly marked. You just take what you want.

3—Are you a fast shopper or a slow? You can be either when you shop at Sainsbury's!

4—Dairy produce, cooked meats, pies, sausages, bacon, poultry, rabbits and cheese—all hygienically packed.

5—Meat is served from Sainsbury's special refrigerated counters. Or you can serve yourself from the cabinets.

6—Pay as you go out. The assistant puts what you have bought into your own basket and gives you a receipt.

"Self-service shopping is easy and quick," claims this 1950s advertisement for the Sainsbury's supermarket chain in Great Britain, championing the pleasures of the modern grocery store. (Private Collection/© The Advertising Archives/Bridgeman Images)

In the new supermarkets, customers enjoyed self-service from a vastly expanded array of mass-produced goods, colorfully packaged and displayed on open shelves in long, impersonal aisles. Shoppers in this British supermarket in the 1960s carried their selections in baskets or carts to checkout counters at the front of the store. (© Mary Evans Picture Library/The Image Works)

American civil rights movement. In the late 1950s and early 1960s African Americans effectively challenged institutionalized inequality using the courts, public demonstrations, sit-ins, and boycotts, and thereby threw off a deeply entrenched system of segregation and repression. The landmark Civil Rights Act of 1964, which prohibited discrimination in public services and on the job, and the Voting Rights Act of 1965, which guaranteed all African Americans the

right to vote, were the crowning achievements of the long struggle against racism.

If dedicated African Americans and their white supporters could successfully reform entrenched power structures, student leaders reasoned, so could they. In 1964 and 1965, at the University of California–Berkeley, students consciously adapted the tactics of the civil rights movement, including demonstrations and sit-ins, to challenge limits on free speech and academic freedom at the university. Their efforts were contagious. Soon students across the United States and western Europe, where rigid rules controlled student activities at overcrowded universities, were engaged in active protests. The youth movement had come of age, and it mounted a determined challenge to the Western consensus.

Dreaming of economic justice and freer, more tolerant societies, student activists in western Europe and the United States embraced new forms of Marxism, creating a multidimensional and heterogeneous movement that came to be known as the **New Left**. In general, adherents of the various strands of the New Left felt that Marxism in the Soviet Union had been perverted to serve the needs of a repressive totalitarian state but that Western capitalism, with its cold disregard for social equality, was little better. What was needed was a more humanitarian style of socialism that could avoid the worst excesses of both capitalism and Soviet-style communism. New Left critics further attacked what they saw as the conformity of consumer society. The "culture industry," which controlled mass culture, fulfilled only false needs and so contributed to the dehumanization they saw at the core of Western society.

Such rarefied ideas fascinated student intellectuals, but much counterculture activity revolved around a lifestyle rebellion that seemed to have broad appeal. Politics and daily life merged, a process captured in the popular 1960s slogan "the personal is political." Nowhere was this more obvious than in the so-called sexual revolution. The 1960s brought frank discussion about sexuality, a new willingness to engage in premarital sex, and a growing acceptance of homosexuality. Sexual experimentation was facilitated by the development of the birth control pill, which helped eliminate the risk of unwanted pregnancy for millions of women after it went on the market in most western European countries in the 1960s. Much of the new openness about sex crossed generational lines, but for the young the idea of sexual emancipation was closely linked to radical politics. Sexual openness and "free love," the sixties generation claimed, moved people beyond traditional norms and might also shape a more humane society.

The revolutionary aspects of the sexual revolution are easily exaggerated. According to a poll of West German college students taken in 1968, the overwhelming majority wished to establish permanent families on traditional middle-class models. Yet the sexual behavior of young people did change in the 1960s and 1970s. More young people engaged in premarital sex, and they did so at an earlier age than ever before. A 1973 study reported that only 4.5 percent of West German youths born in 1945 and 1946 had experienced sexual relations before their seventeenth birthday, but

that 32 percent of those born in 1953 and 1954 had done so.[2] Such trends were found in other Western countries and continued in the following decades.

Along with sexual freedom, drug use and rock music inspired lifestyle rebellion. Taking drugs challenged conventional morals; users could "turn on, tune in, and drop out," in the infamous words of the American cult figure Timothy Leary. The popular music of the 1960s championed these alternative lifestyles. Rock bands like the Beatles, the Rolling Stones, and many others sang songs about drugs and casual sex. Counterculture "scenes" developed in cities such as San Francisco, Paris, and West Berlin. Carnaby Street, the center of "swinging London" in the 1960s, was world famous for its clothing boutiques and record stores, revealing the inescapable connections between generational revolt and consumer culture.

The United States and Vietnam

The growth of the counterculture movement was closely linked to the escalation of the Vietnam War. Although many student radicals at the time argued that imperialism was the main cause, American involvement in Vietnam was more clearly a product of the Cold War policy of containment (see Chapter 28). After Vietnam won independence from France in 1954, U.S. president Dwight D. Eisenhower (U.S. pres. 1953–1961) refused to sign the Geneva Accords that temporarily divided the country into a Communist north and an anticommunist south. When the South Vietnamese government declined to hold free elections that would unify the two zones, Eisenhower provided the south with military aid to combat guerrilla insurgents in South Vietnam who were supported by the Communist north. President John F. Kennedy (U.S. pres. 1961–1963) later increased the number of American "military advisers" to 16,000, and in 1964 President Lyndon B. Johnson (U.S. pres. 1963–1969) greatly expanded America's role in the Vietnam conflict, providing South Vietnam with massive military aid and eventually some 500,000 American troops. Though the United States bombed North Vietnam with ever-greater intensity, it did not invade the north or set up a naval blockade.

In the end, the American strategy of limited warfare backfired. The undeclared war in Vietnam, fought nightly on American television, eventually divided the nation. Initial support was strong. The politicians, the media, and the population as a whole saw the war as part of a legitimate defense against the spread of Communist totalitarianism. But an antiwar movement quickly emerged on college campuses, where the prospect of being drafted to fight savage battles in Asian jungles made male stomachs churn. In October 1965 student protesters joined forces with old-line socialists, New Left intellectuals, and pacifists in antiwar

■ **New Left** A 1960s counterculture movement that embraced updated forms of Marxism to challenge both Western capitalism and Soviet-style communism.

demonstrations in fifty American cities. The protests spread to western Europe. By 1967 a growing number of U.S. and European critics denounced the American presence in Vietnam as a criminal intrusion into a complex and distant civil war.

Criticism reached a crescendo after the Vietcong staged the Tet Offensive in January 1968, the Communists' first comprehensive attack on major South Vietnamese cities. The offensive was a military failure. The Vietcong, an army of Communist insurgents and guerrilla fighters located in South Vietnam, suffered heavy losses, but the Tet Offensive signaled that the war was not close to ending, as Washington had claimed. The American people grew increasingly weary of the war and pressured their leaders to stop the fighting. Within months of Tet, President Johnson announced that he would not stand for re-election and called for negotiations with North Vietnam.

President Richard M. Nixon (U.S. pres. 1969–1974) sought to gradually disengage America from Vietnam once he took office. Nixon intensified the bombing campaign against the north, opened peace talks, and pursued a policy of "Vietnamization" designed to give the South Vietnamese responsibility for the war and reduce the U.S. presence. He suspended the draft and cut American forces in Vietnam from 550,000 to 24,000 in four years. In 1973 Nixon finally reached a peace agreement with North Vietnam and the Vietcong that allowed the remaining American forces to complete their withdrawal and gave the United States the right to resume bombing if the accords were broken. Fighting declined markedly in South Vietnam, where the South Vietnamese army appeared to hold its own against the Vietcong.

Although the storm of criticism in the United States passed with the peace settlement, America's disillusionment with the war had far-reaching repercussions. In early 1974, when North Vietnam launched a general invasion against South Vietnamese armies, the U.S. Congress refused to permit any American military response. In 1974 the South Vietnamese were forced to accept a unified country under a Communist dictatorship, ending a conflict that had begun with the anticolonial struggle against the French at the end of World War II.

Student Revolts and 1968

While the Vietnam War had raged, American escalation had engendered worldwide opposition. New Left activists believed that the United States was fighting an immoral and imperialistic war against a small and heroic people, and the counterculture became increasingly radical. In western European and North American cities, students and sympathetic followers organized massive antiwar demonstrations and then extended their protests to support colonial independence movements, demand an end to the nuclear arms race, and call for world peace and liberation from social conventions of all kinds.

Political activism erupted in 1968 in a series of protests and riots that circled the globe. African Americans rioted across the United States after the assassination of civil rights leader Martin Luther King, Jr., and antiwar demonstrators battled police at the Democratic National Convention in Chicago. Young protesters marched for political reform in Mexico City, where police responded by shooting and killing several hundred. Students in Tokyo rioted against the war and for university reforms. Protesters clashed with police in the West and East Blocs as well. Berlin and London

Student Rebellion in Paris These rock-throwing students in the Latin Quarter of Paris, pictured on the cover of one of France's major newsmagazines, are trying to force education reforms and even topple de Gaulle's government. In May 1968, in a famous example of the protest movements that swept the world in the late 1960s, Parisian rioters clashed repeatedly with France's tough riot police in bloody street fighting. De Gaulle remained in power, but a reform of French education did follow. (Mai 68/Photo © Collection Gregoire/Bridgeman Images)

N° 882 - 13-19 mai 1968   2 Francs

Dix ans de gaullisme: débat Mitterrand-Giscard

L'EXPRESS

étudiants: L'INSURRECTION

LE QUARTIER LATIN, LUNDI DERNIER.

witnessed massive, sometimes-violent demonstrations, students in Warsaw protested government censorship, and youths in Prague were in the forefront of the attempt to radically reform communism from within (see page 991).

One of the most famous and perhaps most far-reaching of these revolts occurred in France in May 1968, when massive student protests coincided with a general strike that brought the French economy to a standstill. The "May Events" began when a group of students dismayed by conservative university policies and inspired by New Left ideals occupied buildings at the University of Paris. Violent clashes with police followed. When police tried to clear the area around the university on the night of May 10, a pitched street battle took place. At the end of the night, 460 arrests had been made by police, 367 people were wounded, and about 200 cars had been burned by protesters. The slogans that appeared as graffiti scrawled on walls in Paris captured the New Left spirit: "Power to the Imagination"; "Be Realistic, Demand the Impossible"; "Forget Everything You've Been Taught. Start by Dreaming."

The "May Events" might have been a typically short-lived student protest against overcrowded universities, U.S. involvement in Vietnam, and the abuses of capitalism, but the demonstrations triggered a national revolt. By May 18 some 10 million workers were out on strike, and protesters occupied factories across France. For a brief moment, it seemed as if counterculture dreams of a revolution from below would come to pass. The French Fifth Republic was on the verge of collapse, and a shaken President de Gaulle surrounded Paris with troops.

In the end, however, the New Left goals of the radical students contradicted the bread-and-butter demands of the striking workers. When the government promised workplace reforms, including immediate pay raises, the strikers returned to work. President de Gaulle dissolved the French parliament and called for new elections. His conservative party won almost 75 percent of the seats, showing that the majority of the French people supported neither general strikes nor student-led revolutions. The universities shut down for the summer, administrators enacted educational reforms, and the protests had dissipated by the time the fall semester began. The May Events marked the high point of counterculture activism in Europe; in the early 1970s the movement declined.

As the political enthusiasm of the counterculture waned, committed activists disagreed about the best way to continue to fight for social change. Some followed what West German student leader Rudi Dutschke called "the long march through the institutions" and began to work for change from within the system. They ran for office and joined the emerging feminist, antinuclear, and environmental groups that would gain increasing prominence in the following decades (see pages 997–1000).

Others followed a more radical path. Across Europe, but particularly in Italy and West Germany, fringe New Left groups tried to bring radical change by turning to violence and terrorism. Like the American Weather Underground, the Italian Red Brigades and the West German Red Army Faction robbed banks, bombed public buildings, and kidnapped and killed business leaders and conservative politicians. After spasms of violence in the late 1970s—in Italy, for example, the Red Brigades murdered former prime minister Aldo Moro in 1978—security forces succeeded in incarcerating most of the terrorist leaders, and the movement fizzled out.

Counterculture protests generated a great deal of excitement and trained a generation of activists. In the end, however, the protests of the sixties generation resulted in short-term and mostly limited political change. Lifestyle rebellions involving sex, drugs, and rock music certainly expanded the boundaries of acceptable personal behavior, but they hardly overturned the existing system.

The 1960s in the East Bloc

The building of the Berlin Wall in 1961 suggested that communism was there to stay, and NATO's refusal to intervene showed that the United States and western Europe basically accepted the premise. In the West, the wall became a potent symbol of the repressive nature of communism in the East Bloc, where halting experiments with economic and cultural liberalization brought only limited reform.

East Bloc economies clearly lagged behind those of the West, exposing the weaknesses of central planning. To address these problems, in the 1960s Communist governments implemented cautious forms of decentralization and limited market policies. The results were mixed. Hungary's so-called New Economic Mechanism, which broke up state monopolies, allowed some private retail stores, and encouraged private agriculture, was perhaps most successful. East Germany's New Economic System, inaugurated in 1963, also brought moderate success, though it was reversed when the government returned to centralization in the late 1960s. In other East Bloc countries, however, economic growth flagged.

Recognizing that the overwhelming emphasis on heavy industry was generating popular discontent, Communist planning commissions began to redirect resources to the consumer sector. Again, the results varied. By 1970, for example, ownership of televisions in the more developed nations of East Germany, Czechoslovakia, and Hungary approached that of the affluent nations of western Europe, and other consumer goods were also more available. In Poland, by contrast, the economy stagnated in the 1960s. In the more conservative Albania and Romania, where leaders held fast to Stalinist practices, provision of consumer goods faltered. In general, ordinary people in the East Bloc grew increasingly tired of the shortages of basic consumer goods that seemed an endemic problem in Communist society.

In the 1960s Communist regimes cautiously granted cultural freedoms. In the Soviet Union, the cultural thaw allowed dissidents like Aleksandr Solzhenitsyn to publish critical works of fiction (see Chapter 28), and this relative tolerance spread to other East Bloc countries as well. In East Germany, for example, during the Bitterfeld Movement — named after a conference of writers, officials, and workers held at Bitterfeld, an industrial city south of Berlin — the regime encouraged intellectuals to take a more critical view of life in the East Bloc, as long as they did not directly oppose communism. Author Christa Wolf's novel *Divided Heaven* (1963) is a classic example of the genre. Though the protagonist's boyfriend emigrates to West Germany in search of better work conditions and she sees very real problems in her small-town factory, she remains committed to building socialism.

Cultural openness only went so far, however. The most outspoken dissidents were harassed and often forced to emigrate to the West; other critics contributed to the rise of an underground *samizdat* (SAH-meez-daht) literature that emerged in the Soviet Union and the East Bloc. The label *samizdat*, a Russian term meaning "self-published," referred to books, periodicals, newspapers, and pamphlets published secretly and passed hand to hand by dissident readers because the works directly criticized communism and thus went far beyond the limits of criticism accepted by the state. Samizdat literature emerged in Russia, Poland,

and other countries in the mid-1950s and blossomed in the 1960s. These unofficial networks of communication kept critical thought alive and built contacts among dissidents, creating the foundation for the reform movements of the 1970s and 1980s.

The citizens of East Bloc countries sought political liberty as well, and the limits on reform were sharply revealed in Czechoslovakia during the 1968 "Prague Spring" (named for the country's capital city). In January 1968 reform elements in the Czechoslovak Communist Party gained a majority and voted out the long-time Stalinist leader in favor of Alexander Dubček (1921–1992), whose new regime launched dramatic reforms. Educated in Moscow, Dubček (DOOB-chehk) was a dedicated Communist, but he and his allies believed that they could reconcile genuine socialism with personal freedom and party democracy. They called for relaxed state censorship and replaced rigid bureaucratic planning with local decision making by trade unions, workers' councils, and consumers. The reform program — labeled "Socialism with a Human Face" — proved enormously popular.

Remembering that the Hungarian revolution had revealed the difficulty of reforming communism from within (see Chapter 28), Dubček constantly proclaimed his loyalty to the Soviet Union and the Warsaw Pact. But the determination of the Czechoslovak reformers to build a more liberal and democratic socialism nevertheless threatened hard-line Communists, particularly in Poland and East Germany, where leaders knew full well that they lacked popular support. Moreover, Soviet leaders feared that a liberalized Czechoslovakia would eventually be

The East German Trabi
This small East German passenger car, pictured here in a 1980s advertisement, was one of the best-known symbols of everyday life in East Germany. Produced between 1963 and 1990, the cars were notorious for their poor engineering. The growing number of Trabis on East German streets nonetheless testified to the increased availability of consumer goods in the East Bloc in the 1960s and 1970s. (akg-images)

drawn to neutrality or even to NATO. Thus the East Bloc leadership launched a concerted campaign of intimidation against the reformers. Finally, in August 1968, five hundred thousand Soviet and East Bloc troops occupied Czechoslovakia. The Czechoslovaks made no attempt to resist militarily, and the arrested leaders surrendered to Soviet demands. The reform program was abandoned, and the Czechoslovak experiment in humanizing communism from within came to an end.

Shortly after the invasion of Czechoslovakia, Soviet premier Leonid Brezhnev (1906–1982) announced that the Soviets would now follow the so-called **Brezhnev Doctrine**, under which the Soviet Union and its allies had the right to intervene militarily in any East Bloc country whenever they thought doing so was necessary to preserve Communist rule. The 1968 invasion of Czechoslovakia was the crucial event of the Brezhnev era: it demonstrated the determination of the Communist elite to maintain the status quo throughout the Soviet bloc, which would last for another twenty years. At the same time, the Soviet crackdown encouraged dissidents to change their focus from "reforming" Communist regimes from within to building a civil society that might bring internal freedoms independent of the regimes (see pages 1005–1007).

Crisis and Change in Western Europe

FOCUS QUESTION *What were the consequences of economic decline in the 1970s?*

The great postwar economic boom came to a close in the early 1970s, opening a long period of economic stagnation, widespread unemployment, and social dislocation. As a result, politics in western Europe drifted to the right, and leaders cut taxes and state spending and sold off (or privatized) state-owned companies. A number of new political groups entered national politics, including feminists and environmentalists on the left and neo-nationalists on the right. By the end of the 1980s the postwar consensus based on prosperity, full employment, modest regulation, and generous welfare provisions had been deeply shaken. Led by a new generation of conservative politicians, the West had restructured its economy and entered the information age.

Economic Crisis and Hardship

Starting in the early 1970s the West entered into a long period of economic decline. One of the early causes of

The Invasion of Czechoslovakia   Armed with Czechoslovakian flags, courageous Czechs in downtown Prague try to stop a Soviet tank and repel the invasion and occupation of their country by the Soviet Union and its eastern European allies. Realizing that military resistance would be suicidal, the Czechs capitulated to Soviet control. (AP Photo/Libor Hajsky/CTK/AP Images)

the downturn was the collapse of the international monetary system, which since 1945 had been based on the American dollar, valued in gold at $35 an ounce. In the postwar decades the United States spent billions of dollars on foreign aid and foreign wars, weakening the value of American currency. In 1971 President Nixon attempted to reverse this trend by abruptly stopping the exchange of U.S. currency for gold. The value of the dollar fell sharply, and inflation accelerated worldwide. Countries abandoned fixed rates of currency exchange, and great uncertainty replaced postwar predictability in international trade and finance.

Even more damaging to the global economy was the dramatic reversal in the price and availability of energy. The great postwar boom had been fueled in large part by cheap oil from the Middle East. The fate of the developed world was thus increasingly linked to this turbulent region, where strains began to show in the late 1960s. In 1967, in the Six-Day War, Israel quickly defeated Egypt, Jordan, and Syria and occupied more of the former territories of Palestine, angering Arab leaders and exacerbating anti-Western feeling in the Arab states. Economics fed tension between Arab states and the West. Over the years **OPEC**, the Organization of Petroleum Exporting Countries, had watched the price of crude oil decline consistently compared with the rising price of Western manufactured goods. OPEC decided to reverse that trend by presenting a united front against Western oil companies.

The stage was thus already set for a revolution in energy prices when Egypt and Syria launched a surprise attack on Israel in October 1973, setting off the fourth Arab-Israeli war. With the help of U.S. weapons, Israel again achieved a quick victory. In response, the Arab members of OPEC declared an embargo on oil shipments to the United States and other industrialized nations that supported Israel in the war, and they simultaneously raised oil prices. Within a year, crude oil prices quadrupled. Western nations realized that the rapid price increase was economically destructive, but together they did nothing. Thus governments, industry, and individuals dealt piecemeal with the so-called oil shock—a "shock" that turned out to be an earthquake.

Coming on the heels of the upheaval in the international monetary system, the revolution in energy prices plunged the world into its worst economic decline since the 1930s. Energy-intensive industries that had driven the economy up in the 1950s and 1960s now dragged it down. Unemployment rose, productivity and living standards declined, and inflation soared. Economists coined a new term—**stagflation**—to describe the combination of low growth and high inflation that drove the worldwide recession. By 1976 a modest recovery was in progress, but in 1979 a fundamentalist Islamic revolution overthrew the shah of Iran. When oil production in that country collapsed, the price of crude oil doubled again, and the world economy succumbed to its second oil shock. Unemployment and inflation rose dramatically before another uneven recovery began in 1982.

Anxious observers, recalling the disastrous consequences of the Great Depression, worried that the European Common Market would disintegrate in the face of severe economic dislocation and that economic nationalism would halt steps toward European unity. Yet the Common Market continued to attract new members. In 1973 Britain finally joined, as did Denmark and Ireland. After replacing authoritarian regimes with democratic governments in the 1970s, Greece joined in 1981, and Portugal and Spain entered in 1986. The nations of the Common Market cooperated more closely in international undertakings, and the movement toward western European unity stayed alive.

The developing world was hit hard by slow growth, and the global economic downturn widened the gap between rich and poor countries. Governments across South America, sub-Saharan Africa, and South Asia borrowed heavily from the United States and western Europe in attempts to restructure their economies, setting the stage for a serious international debt crisis. At the same time, the East Asian countries of Japan and then Singapore, South Korea, and Taiwan started exporting high-tech consumer goods to the West. Competition from these East Asian "tiger economies," whose labor costs were comparatively low, shifted manufacturing jobs away from the highly industrialized countries of northern Europe and North America.

Even though the world economy slowly began to recover in the 1980s, western Europe could no longer create enough jobs to replace those that were lost. By the end of the 1970s, the foundations of economic growth in the industrialized West had begun shifting to high-tech information industries, such as computing and biotechnology, and to services, including medicine, banking, and finance. Scholars spoke of the shift as the arrival of "the information age" or **postindustrial society**. Technological advances streamlined the production of many goods, making many industrial jobs superfluous. In western Europe, heavy industry, such as steel, mining, automobile manufacture, and shipbuilding, lost ground. Factory closings led to the

- **Brezhnev Doctrine** Doctrine created by Leonid Brezhnev that held that the Soviet Union had the right to intervene in any East Bloc country when necessary to preserve Communist rule.
- **OPEC** The Organization of Petroleum Exporting Countries.
- **stagflation** Term coined in the early 1980s to describe the combination of low growth and high inflation that led to a worldwide recession.
- **postindustrial society** A society that relies on high-tech and service-oriented jobs for economic growth rather than heavy industry and manufacturing jobs.

emergence of "rust belts"—formerly prosperous indus-trialized areas that were now ghost lands, with vacant lots, idle machinery, and empty inner cities. The highly industrialized Ruhr district in northwest West Germany and the once-extensive factory regions around Birming-ham (Great Britain) and Detroit, Michigan, were classic examples. By 1985 the unemployment rate in western Europe had risen to its highest level since the Great De-pression. Nineteen million people were jobless.

The crisis struck countless ordinary people, and there were heartbreaking human tragedies—bankruptcies, homelessness, and mental breakdowns. The punk rock songs of the late 1970s captured the mood of hostility and cynicism among young people. Yet on the whole, the welfare system fashioned in the postwar era pre-vented mass suffering and degradation. The responsive, socially concerned national state undoubtedly contrib-uted to the preservation of political stability and democ-racy in the face of economic difficulties that might have brought revolution and dictatorship in earlier times.

With the commitment of governments to sup-porting social needs, government spending in most European countries continued to rise sharply during the 1970s and early 1980s. In 1982 western European governments spent an average of more than 50 percent of all national income on social programs, as compared to only 37 percent fifteen years earlier. Across western Europe, people were willing to see their governments increase spending, but they resisted higher taxes. This imbalance contributed to the rapid growth of budget deficits, national debts, and inflation. While this in-creased spending was generally popular, a powerful re-action against government's ever-increasing role had set in by the late 1970s that would transform gover-nance in the 1980s.

The New Conservatism

The transition to a postindustrial society was led to a great extent by a new generation of conservative politi-cal leaders, who believed they had viable solutions for restructuring the relations between the state and the economy. During the thirty years following World War II, both Social Democrats and the more conserva-tive Christian Democrats had usually agreed that eco-nomic growth and social stability were best achieved through full employment and high wages, some gov-ernment regulation, and generous welfare provisions.

In the late 1970s, however, with a weakened economy and increased global competition, this consensus be-gan to unravel. Whether politics turned to the right, as in Great Britain, the United States, and West Germany, or to the left, as in France and Spain, leaders moved to cut government spending and regulation in attempts to improve economic performance.

The new conservatives of the 1980s followed a phi-losophy that came to be known as **neoliberalism** be-cause of its roots in the free market, laissez-faire policies favored by eighteenth-century liberal economists such as Adam Smith (see Chapter 21). Neoliberal theorists like U.S. economist Milton Friedman argued that gov-ernments should cut support for social services, in-cluding housing, education, and health insurance; limit business subsidies; and retreat from regulation of all kinds. (Neoliberalism should be distinguished from modern American liberalism, which supports welfare programs and some state regulation of the economy.) Neoliberals also called for **privatization**—the sale of state-managed industries to private owners. Placing government-owned industries such as transportation and communication networks and heavy industry in private hands, they argued, would both reduce govern-ment spending and lead to greater workplace effi-ciency. The main goal was to increase private profits, which neoliberals believed were the real engine of eco-nomic growth.

The effects of neoliberal policies are best illustrated by events in Great Britain. The broad shift toward greater conservatism, coupled with growing voter dis-satisfaction with high taxes and runaway state budgets, helped elect Margaret Thatcher (1925–2013) prime minister in 1979. A member of the Conservative Party and a convinced neoliberal, Thatcher was determined to scale back the role of government, and in the 1980s—the "Thatcher years"—she pushed through a series of controversial free-market policies that trans-formed Britain. Thatcher's government cut spending on health care, education, and public housing; reduced taxes; and privatized or sold off government-run enter-prises. In one of her most popular actions, Thatcher encouraged low- and moderate-income renters in state-owned housing projects to buy their apartments at rock-bottom prices. This initiative, part of Thatcher's broader privatization campaign, created a whole new class of property owners, thereby eroding the electoral base of Britain's socialist Labour Party. (See "Individuals in Society: Margaret Thatcher," page 996.)

Though Thatcher never eliminated all social pro-grams, her policies helped replace the interventionist ethos of the welfare state with a greater reliance on pri-vate enterprise and the free market. This transition in-volved significant human costs. In the first three years of her government, heavy industries such as steel, coal mining, and textiles shut down, and unemployment

■ **neoliberalism** Philosophy of 1980s conservatives who argued for privatization of state-run industries and decreased government spending on social services.

■ **privatization** The sale of state-managed industries such as transportation and communication networks to private owners; a key aspect of broader neoliberal economic reforms meant to control government spending, increase private profits, and foster economic growth, which were implemented in western Europe in response to the economic crisis of the 1970s.

The Social Consequences of Thatcherism
As police watch in the background, picketers outside the largest coal mine in Britain hold up a poster reading "Save the Pits" during the miners' strike of 1984 to 1985. Prime Minister Margaret Thatcher broke the strike, weakening the power of Britain's trade unions and easing the turn to free-market economic reforms. Thatcher's neoliberal policies revived economic growth but cut state subsidies for welfare benefits and heavy industries, leading to lower living standards for many working-class Britons and, as this image attests, to popular protest. (Peter Skingely/Bride Lane Library/Popperfoto/Getty Images)

rates in Britain doubled to over 12 percent. The gap between rich and poor widened, and increasing poverty led to discontent and crime. Strikes and working-class protests sometimes led to violent riots. Street violence often had racial overtones: immigrants from former British colonies in Africa, India, and the Caribbean, dismayed with poor jobs and racial discrimination, clashed repeatedly with police. Thatcher successfully rallied support by leading a British victory over Argentina in the brief Falklands War (1982), but over time her position weakened. By 1990 Thatcher's popularity had fallen to record lows, and she was replaced by Conservative Party leader John Major.

In the United States, two-term president Ronald Reagan (U.S. pres. 1981–1989) followed a similar path, though his success in cutting government was more limited. Reagan's campaign slogan — "government is not the solution to our problem, government is the problem" — summed up a movement in line with Thatcher's ideas, which was labeled the conservative movement in the United States. With widespread popular support and the agreement of most congressional Democrats as well as Republicans, Reagan pushed through major across-the-board cuts in income taxes in 1981. But Reagan and Congress failed to limit government spending, which increased as a percentage of national income in the course of his presidency. A massive military buildup was partly responsible, but spending on social programs — despite Reagan's pledges to rein them in — also grew rapidly. The harsh recession of the early 1980s required the government to spend more on unemployment benefits, welfare benefits, and medical treatment for the poor. Moreover, Reagan's antiwelfare rhetoric mobilized the liberal opposition and eventually turned many moderates against him. The budget deficit soared, and U.S. government debt tripled in a decade.

West Germany also turned to the right. After more than a decade in power, the Social Democrats foundered, and in 1982 Christian Democrat Helmut Kohl (b. 1930) became the new chancellor. Like Thatcher, Kohl cut taxes and government spending. His policies led to increasing unemployment in heavy industry but also to solid economic growth. By the mid-1980s West Germany was one of the most prosperous countries in the world. In foreign policy, Kohl drew close to President Reagan. The chancellor agreed to deploy U.S. cruise missiles and nuclear-armed Pershing missiles on West German territory, a decision that contributed to renewed superpower tensions. In power for sixteen years, Kohl and the Christian Democrats governed during the opening of the Berlin Wall in 1989, the reunification of East and West Germany in 1990, and the end of the Cold War.

The most striking temporary exception to the general drift to the right in European politics was François Mitterrand (1916–1996) of France. After his election as president in 1981, Mitterrand and his Socialist Party led France on a lurch to the left. This marked a significant change in French politics, which had been dominated by center-right parties for some twenty-five years. Working at first in a coalition that included the French Communist Party, Mitterrand launched a vast

Margaret Thatcher, the first woman elected to lead a major European state, was one of the late twentieth century's most significant political leaders. The controversial "Iron Lady" attacked socialism, promoted capitalism, and changed the face of modern Britain.

Raised in a lower-middle-class family in a small city in southeastern England, Thatcher entered Oxford in 1943 to study chemistry. She soon discovered a passion for politics and was elected president of student conservatives. Four years after her graduation, she ran for Parliament in 1950 in a solidly Labour district to gain experience. Articulate and attractive, she won the attention of Denis Thatcher, a wealthy businessman who drove her to campaign appearances in his Jaguar. Married a year later, the new Mrs. Thatcher abandoned chemistry, went to law school, gave birth to twins, and became a tax attorney. In 1959 she returned to politics and won a seat in that year's Conservative triumph.

For the next fifteen years Thatcher served in Parliament and held various ministerial posts when the Conservatives governed. In 1974, as the economy soured and the Conservatives lost two close elections, a rebellious Thatcher adroitly ran for the leadership of her party and won. Five years later, as the Labour government faced rampant inflation and crippling strikes, Thatcher promised to reduce union power, lower taxes, and promote free markets. Attracting swing votes from skilled workers, the Conservatives gained a majority, and she became prime minister.

A self-described "conviction politician," Thatcher rejected postwar Keynesian efforts to manage the economy, arguing that governments created inflation by printing too much money. Thus her government reduced the supply of money and credit and refused to retreat when interest rates and unemployment soared. Her popularity plummeted. But Thatcher remained in office, in part through an aggressive foreign policy. In 1982 the generals ruling Argentina suddenly seized the nearby Falkland Islands, home to 1,800 British citizens. A staunch nationalist, Thatcher detached a naval armada that recaptured the islands without a hitch. Britain admired Thatcher's determination and patriotism, and she was re-elected in 1983.

Margaret Thatcher as prime minister.
(Dave Caulkin/AP Photo/AP Images)

Thatcher's second term was the high point of her influence. Her commitment to privatization transformed British industry. More than fifty state-owned companies, ranging from the state telephone monopoly to the nationalized steel trust, were sold to private investors. Small investors were offered shares at bargain prices to promote "people's capitalism." Thatcher curbed the power of British labor unions, most spectacularly in 1984, when the once-mighty coal miners rejected more mine closings and doggedly struck for a year; the "Iron Lady" stood firm and beat them. This outcome had a profound psychological impact on the public, who blamed her for growing unemployment. Thatcher was also accused of mishandling a series of protest hunger strikes undertaken by the Irish Republican Army—in 1981 ten IRA members starved themselves to death in British prisons—but she refused to compromise with those she labeled criminals. As a result, the revolt in Northern Ireland entered one of its bloodiest phases.

Despite these problems, Thatcher was elected to a third term in 1987. Afterward, she became increasingly stubborn, overconfident, and uncaring. Working with her ideological soul mate, U.S. president Ronald Reagan, she opposed greater political and economic unity within the European Community. This, coupled with rising inflation, stubborn unemployment, and an unpopular effort to assert financial control over city governments, proved her undoing. In 1990, as in 1974, party stalwarts suddenly revolted and elected a new Conservative leader. The transformational changes of the Thatcher years nonetheless endured, consolidated by her Conservative successor, John Major, and largely accepted by the new Labour prime minister, the moderate Tony Blair, who served in office from 1997 to 2007.

QUESTIONS FOR ANALYSIS

1. "Thatcherism" has become a shorthand label for the neoliberal ideologies that gained popularity in the 1970s and 1980s. How did the policies promoted by Thatcher's government embody neoliberal ideas?
2. Would you say that Thatcher was a successful British leader? Why or why not?

program of nationalization and public investment designed to spend the country out of economic stagnation. By 1983 this attempt had clearly failed, and Mitterrand's Socialist government made a dramatic about-face. The Socialists were compelled to reprivatize industries they had just nationalized. They imposed a wide variety of austerity measures and maintained those policies for the rest of the decade.

Despite persistent economic crises and high social costs, by 1990 the developed nations of western Europe and North America were far more productive than they had been in the early 1970s. Western Europe was at the center of the emerging global economy, and its citizens were far richer than those in Soviet bloc countries (see page 1001). Even so, the collapse of the postwar consensus and the remaking of Europe in the transitional decades of the 1970s and 1980s helped generate new forms of protest and dissent across the political spectrum.

Challenges and Victories for Women

The 1970s marked the arrival of a diverse and widespread feminist movement devoted to securing genuine gender equality and promoting the general interests of women. Three basic reasons accounted for this dramatic development. First, ongoing changes in underlying patterns of motherhood and paid work created novel conditions and new demands (see Chapter 28).

Second, a vanguard of feminist intellectuals articulated a powerful critique of gender relations, which stimulated many women to rethink their assumptions and challenge the status quo. Third, taking a lesson from the civil rights movement in the United States and protests against the Vietnam War, dissatisfied women recognized that they had to band together if they were to influence politics and secure fundamental reforms.

Feminists could draw on a long heritage of protest, stretching back to the French Revolution and the women's movements of the late nineteenth century (see Chapters 19 and 22). They were also inspired by recent writings, such as the foundational book *The Second Sex* (1949) by the French writer and philosopher Simone de Beauvoir (1908–1986). Beauvoir, who worked closely with the existentialist philosopher Jean-Paul Sartre, analyzed the position of women within the framework of existential thought. Drawing on history, philosophy, psychology, biology, and literature, Beauvoir argued that women had almost always been trapped by particularly inflexible and limiting conditions. Only through courageous action and self-assertive creativity could a woman become a completely free person and escape the role of the inferior "other" that men had constructed for her gender. (See "Evaluating the Evidence 29.2: Simone de Beauvoir's Feminist Critique of Marriage," page 998.)

The Second Sex inspired a generation of women intellectuals, and by the late 1960s and the 1970s "second-wave feminism" had spread through North America and

Feminist Protest in London, 1982
In a protest organized by the grassroots Women's Fightback Network, women march for equal pay and employment opportunity.
(Roberto Koch/Contrasto/Redux)

Simone de Beauvoir's Feminist Critique of Marriage

Having grown up in Paris in a middle-class family and become a teacher, novelist, and intellectual, Simone de Beauvoir turned increasingly to feminist concerns after World War II. Her most influential work was The Second Sex *(1949), a massive declaration of independence for contemporary women.*

As an existentialist, Beauvoir believed that all individuals must accept responsibility for their lives and strive to overcome the tragic dilemmas they face (see Chapter 26). Studying the experience of women since antiquity, Beauvoir argued that men had generally used education and social conditioning to create a dependent "other," a negative nonman who was not permitted to grow and strive for freedom. Marriage — on men's terms — was part of this unjust and undesirable process. Beauvoir's conclusion that some couples could establish free and equal unions was based in part on her own experience with philosopher Jean-Paul Sartre, her encouraging companion and longtime lover.

All human existence is transcendence and immanence at the same time; to go beyond itself, it must maintain itself; to thrust itself toward the future, it must integrate the past into itself; and while relating to others, it must confirm itself in itself. These two moments are implied in every living movement: for *man*, marriage provides the perfect synthesis of them; in his work and political life, he finds change and progress, he experiences his dispersion through time and the universe; and when he tires of this wandering, he establishes a home, he settles down, he anchors himself in the world; in the evening he restores himself in the house, where his wife cares for the furniture and children and safeguards the past she keeps in store. But the wife has no other task save the one of maintaining and caring for life in its pure and identical generality; she perpetuates the immutable species, she ensures the even rhythm of the days and the permanence of the home she guards with locked doors; she is given no direct grasp on the future, nor on the universe; she goes beyond herself toward the group only through her husband as mouthpiece.

Marriage today still retains this traditional form. . . . The male's vocation is action; he needs to produce, fight, create, progress, go beyond himself toward the totality of the universe and the infinity of the future; but traditional marriage does not invite woman to transcend herself with him; it confines her in immanence. She has no choice but to build a stable life where the present, prolonging the past, escapes the threats of tomorrow, that is, precisely to create a happiness. . . .

It is through housework that the wife comes to make her "nest" her own; this is why, even if she has "help," she insists on doing things herself; at least by watching over, controlling, and criticizing, she endeavors to make her servants' results her own. By administrating her home, she achieves her social justification; her job is also to oversee the food, clothing, and care of the familial society in general. Thus she too realizes herself as an activity. But, as we will see, it is an activity that brings her no escape from her immanence and allows her no individual affirmation of herself. . . .

Few tasks are more similar to the torment of Sisyphus than those of the housewife; day after day, one must wash dishes, dust furniture, mend clothes that will be dirty, dusty, and torn again. The housewife wears herself out running on the spot; she does nothing; she only perpetuates the present; she never gains the sense that she is conquering a positive Good, but struggles indefinitely against Evil. . . .

Washing, ironing, sweeping, routing out tufts of dust in the dark places behind the wardrobe, this is holding away death but also refusing life: for in one movement time is created and destroyed; the housewife only grasps the negative aspect of it. . . .

So the wife's work within the home does not grant her autonomy; it is not directly useful to the group, it does not open onto the future, it does not produce anything. It becomes meaningful and dignified only if it is integrated into existences that go beyond themselves, toward the society in production or action: far from enfranchising the matron, it makes her dependent on her husband and children; she justifies her existence through them: she is no more than an inessential mediation in their lives. . . .

The drama of marriage is not that it does not guarantee the wife the promised happiness — there is no guarantee of happiness — it is that it mutilates her; it dooms her to repetition and routine. The first twenty years of a woman's life are extraordinarily rich; she experiences menstruation, sexuality, marriage, and motherhood; she discovers the world and her destiny. She is mistress of a home at twenty, linked from then on to one man, a child in her arms, now her life is finished forever. Real activity, real work, are the privilege of man: her only occupations are sometimes exhausting but never fulfill her. . . .

Marriage must combine two autonomous existences, not be a withdrawal, an annexation, an escape, a remedy. . . . The couple should not consider itself a community, a closed cell: instead, the individual as individual has to be integrated into a society in which he can thrive without assistance; he will then be able to create links in pure generosity with another individual equally adapted to the group, links founded on the recognition of two freedoms.

This balanced couple is not a utopia; such couples exist sometimes even within marriage, more often outside of it; some are united by a great sexual love that leaves them free in their friendships and occupations; others are linked by a friendship that does not hamper their sexual freedom; more rarely there are still others who are both lovers and friends but without seeking in each other their exclusive reason for living. Many nuances are possible in the relations of a man and a woman: in companionship, pleasure, confidence, tenderness, complicity, and love, they can be for each other the most fruitful source of joy, richness, and strength offered to a human being.

EVALUATE THE EVIDENCE

1. How did Beauvoir's analysis of marriage and marriage partners express the main ideas of existential philosophy?
2. To what extent does a married woman benefit from a "traditional" marriage, according to Beauvoir? Why?
3. What was Beauvoir's solution to the situation she described? Was her solution desirable? Realistic?
4. What have you learned about the history of women that supports or challenges Beauvoir's analysis? Include developments since World War II and your own reflections.

Source: Excerpt from THE SECOND SEX by Simone de Beauvoir and translated by Constance Borde and Sheila Malovany-Chevallier, translation copyright © 2009 by Constance Borde and Sheila Malovany-Chevallier. Used by permission of Alfred A. Knopf, an imprint of the Knopf Doubleday Publishing Group, a division of Penguin Random House LLC. All rights reserved. Any third-party use of this material, outside of this publication, is prohibited. Interested parties must apply directly to Penguin Random House LLC for permission.

Europe. In the United States, writer and organizer Betty Friedan's (1921–2006) pathbreaking study, *The Feminine Mystique* (1963) pointed the way. Friedan called attention to the stifling aspects of women's domestic life, devoted to the service of husbands and children. Housewives lived in a "gilded cage," she concluded, because they were usually not allowed to hold professional jobs or become mature adults and genuine human beings. In 1966 Friedan helped found the National Organization for Women (NOW) to press for women's rights. NOW flourished, growing from seven hundred members in 1967 to forty thousand in 1974.

Many other women's organizations rose in Europe and North America. The diverse groups drew inspiration from Marx, Freud, or political liberalism, but in general feminists attacked patriarchy (the domination of society by men) and sexism (the inequalities faced by women simply because they were female). Throughout the 1970s a proliferation of publications, conferences, and institutions devoted to women's issues reinforced the emerging international movement. Advocates of women's rights pushed for new statutes governing the workplace: laws against discrimination, acts requiring equal pay for equal work, and measures such as maternal leave and affordable day care designed to help women combine careers and family responsibilities.

The movement also addressed gender and family questions, including the right to divorce (in some Catholic countries), legalized abortion, the needs of single mothers, and protection from rape and physical violence. In almost every country, the effort to decriminalize abortion served as a catalyst in mobilizing an effective, self-conscious women's movement—and, as in the United States, in creating opposition to it.

In countries that had long placed women in a subordinate position, the legal changes were little less than revolutionary. In Italy, for example, new laws abolished restrictions on divorce and abortion that had been strengthened by Mussolini and defended energetically by the Catholic Church in the postwar era. By 1988 divorce and abortion were common in Italy, which had the lowest birthrate in Europe. While the women's movement of the 1970s won new rights for women, subsequently it became more diffuse, a victim of both its successes and the resurgence of an antifeminist opposition.

The Rise of the Environmental Movement

Like feminism, environmentalism had roots in the 1960s counterculture. Early environmentalists drew inspiration from writers like U.S. biologist Rachel Carson, whose book *Silent Spring*, published in 1962, was quickly translated into twelve European languages.

Carson's chilling title referred to a future spring, when people in developed society would wake up and hear no birds singing, because they had all been killed by the rampant use of pesticides. The book had a striking impact on the growth of environmental movements in Europe and North America.

By the 1970s the destructive environmental costs of industrial development in western Europe and the East Bloc were everywhere apparent. The mighty Rhine River, which flows from Switzerland, past France, and through Germany and the Netherlands, was an industrial sewer. The forests of southwestern Germany were dying from acid rain, a result of smokestack emissions. The pristine coast of Brittany, in northwest France, was fouled by oil spills from massive tanker ships. Rapid industrialization in the East Bloc, undertaken with little regard for environmental impact, severely polluted waterways, contaminated farmlands and forests, and degraded air quality. Nuclear power plants across Europe were generating toxic waste that would last for centuries; serious accidents at nuclear plants—at Three Mile Island in Pennsylvania (1979) and at Chernobyl in Soviet Ukraine (1986)—revealed nuclear

power's potential to create human and environmental disaster (Map 29.1). These were just some examples of the environmental threats that inspired a growing environmental movement to challenge government and industry to clean up their acts.

Environmentalists had two main agendas. First, they worked to lessen the ill effects of unbridled industrial development on the natural environment. Second, they argued that local environmental problems often increased human poverty, inequality, and violence around the globe, and they sought ways to ameliorate the impact of environmental decline on human well-being. Environmental groups pursued their goals in various ways. Some used the mass media to reach potential supporters; some worked closely with politicians and public officials to change government policies. Others took a more activist stance. In Denmark in March 1969, in a dramatic example, student protesters at the University of Copenhagen took over a scientific conference on natural history. They locked the conference hall doors, sprayed the professors in attendance with polluted lake water, and held up an oil-doused duck, shouting, "Come and save it . . . you talk about pollution, why don't you do anything about it!"[3] (See "Thinking Like a Historian: The New Environmentalism," page 1002.)

Environmental protesters also built new institutions, particularly in North America and western Europe. In 1971 Canadian activists established Greenpeace, a nongovernmental organization dedicated to environmental conservation and protection. Greenpeace quickly grew into an international organization, with strong support in Europe and the United States. In West Germany in 1979 environmentalists founded the Green Party, a political party to fight for environmental causes. The West German Greens met with astounding success when they elected members to parliament in 1983, the first time in sixty years that a new political party had been seated in Germany. Their success was a model for like-minded activists in Europe and North America, and Green Party members were later elected to parliaments in Belgium, Italy, and Sweden. In the East Bloc, government planners increasingly recognized and tried to ameliorate environmental problems in the 1980s, but official censorship meant that groups like the Greens would not emerge there until after the end of Communist rule.

MAP 29.1 Pollution in Europe, ca. 1990 Despite attempts to remedy the negative consequences of the human impact on the environment, pollution remains a significant challenge for Europeans in the twenty-first century.

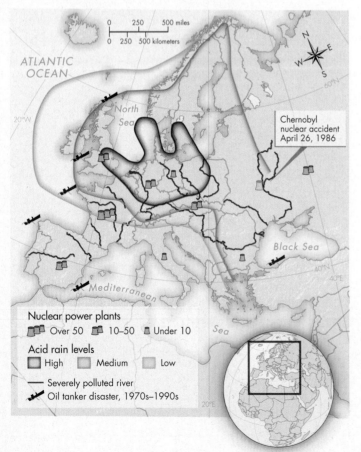

Separatism and Right-Wing Extremism

The 1970s also saw the rise of determined separatist movements across Europe. In Ireland, Spain, Belgium, and Switzerland—and in Yugoslavia and

Czechoslovakia in the East Bloc—regional ethnic groups struggled for special rights, political autonomy, and even national independence. This separatism was most violent in Spain and Northern Ireland, where well-established insurgent groups used terrorist attacks to win government concessions. In the ethnic Basque region of northern Spain, the ETA (short, in the Basque language, for Basque Homeland and Freedom) tried to use bombings and assassinations to force the government to grant independence. After the death in 1975 of Fascist dictator Francisco Franco, who had ruled Spain for almost forty years, a new constitution granted the Basque region special autonomy, but it was not enough. The ETA stepped up its terrorist campaigns, killing over four hundred people in the 1980s.

The Provisional Irish Republican Army (IRA), a paramilitary organization in Northern Ireland, used similar tactics. Though Ireland had won autonomy in 1922, Great Britain retained control of six primarily Protestant counties in the north of the island (see Chapter 26). In the late 1960s violence re-emerged as the IRA, hoping to unite these counties with Ireland, attacked British security forces, which it saw as an occupying army. On Bloody Sunday in January 1972, British soldiers shot and killed thirteen demonstrators, who had been protesting anti-Catholic discrimination in the town of Derry, and the violence escalated. For the next thirty years the IRA attacked soldiers and civilians in Northern Ireland and in Britain itself. Over two thousand British soldiers, civilians, and IRA members were killed during "the Troubles" before negotiations between the IRA and the British government opened in the late 1990s; a settlement was finally reached in 1998.

Mainstream European politicians also faced challenges from newly assertive political forces on the far right. Right-wing political parties such as the National Front in France, the Northern League in Italy, the Austrian Freedom Party, and the National Democratic Party in West Germany were founded or gained popularity in the 1970s and 1980s. Populist leaders like Jean-Marie Le Pen, the founder of the French National Front, opposed European integration and called for a return to traditional national customs, often at the expense of the non-European immigrants who were a growing proportion of western Europe's working-class population (see Chapter 28). New right-wing politicians promoted themselves as the champions of ordinary (white) workers, complaining that immigrants swelled welfare rolls and stole jobs from native-born Europeans. Though their programs at times veered close to open racism, in the 1980s they began to win seats in national parliaments.

The Decline of "Developed Socialism"

FOCUS QUESTION *What led to the decline of Soviet power in the East Bloc?*

In the postwar decades the Communist states of the East Bloc had achieved a shaky social consensus based on a rising standard of living, an extensive welfare system, and political repression. When the Marxist utopia still had not arrived in the 1970s, Communist leaders told citizens that an egalitarian society would be realized sometime in the future; until then, they would have to accept the system as it was. In the long run, leaders promised, "developed socialism" would prove better than capitalism. Such claims were an attempt to paper over serious tensions in socialist society. Everyday life could be difficult. Limits on personal and political freedoms encouraged the growth of determined reform movements, and a revival of Cold War tensions accompanied the turn to the right in the United States and western Europe in the 1980s.

When Mikhail Gorbachev burst on the scene in 1985, the new Soviet leader opened an era of reform that was as sweeping as it was unexpected. Although many believed that Gorbachev would soon fall from power, his reforms rapidly transformed Soviet culture and politics and drastically reduced Cold War tensions. But communism, which Gorbachev wanted so desperately to revitalize, continued to stagnate and decline.

State and Society in the East Bloc

By the 1970s many of the professed goals of communism had been achieved. Communist leaders in central and eastern Europe and the Soviet Union adopted the term **developed socialism** (sometimes called "real existing socialism") to describe the accomplishments of their societies. Agriculture had been thoroughly collectivized, and though Poland was an exception, 80 to 90 percent of Soviet and East Bloc farmers worked on huge collective farms. Industry and business had been nationalized, and only a small portion of the economy remained in private hands in most East Bloc countries. The state had also done much to level class differences. Though some people—particularly party members—clearly had greater access to opportunities and resources, the gap between rich and poor was far smaller than in the West. An extensive system of government-supported welfare benefits included free medical care, guaranteed

---

■ **developed socialism** A term used by Communist leaders to describe the socialist accomplishments of their societies, such as nationalized industry, collective agriculture, and extensive social welfare programs.

The New Environmentalism

The environmentalism of the late 1960s and 1970s readily drew on earlier nineteenth-century concerns with the effects of an emerging industrial-urban society on human health and the natural landscape. Yet as the negative impact of industrial development became ever more apparent, arguments that stewardship of the environment should be a fundamental concern of humankind grew increasingly angry — and more widespread. How did a new generation of activists respond to the environmental degradation of the late twentieth century?

1 Rachel Carson, *Silent Spring*, 1962. Rachel Carson's highly readable polemic specifically targeted the U.S. pesticide industry, though the pathbreaking marine biologist and conservationist made larger claims about the great chains of being that enmeshed humans in their natural environment.

For each of us, as for the robin in Michigan or the salmon in the Miramichi, this is a problem of ecology, of interrelationships, of interdependence. We poison the caddis flies in a stream and the salmon runs dwindle and die. We poison the gnats in a lake and the poison travels from link to link of the food chain and soon the birds of the lake margins become its victims. We spray our elms and the following springs are silent of robin song, not because we sprayed the robins directly but because the poison traveled, step by step, through the now familiar elm leaf–earthworm–robin cycle. These are matters of record, observable, part of the visible world around us. They reflect the web of life — or death — that scientists know as ecology. . . .

We stand now where two roads diverge. But unlike the roads in Robert Frost's familiar poem, they are not equally fair. The road we have long been traveling is deceptively easy, a smooth superhighway on which we progress with great speed, but at its end lies disaster. The other fork of the road — the one less traveled by — offers our last, our only chance to reach a destination that assures the preservation of the earth.

The choice, is, after all, ours to make.

2 Arne Naess, "The Deep Ecology Platform," 1984. Norwegian philosopher Arne Naess was a founder of the Deep Ecology wilderness movement. His vision of "biospheric egalitarianism" rejected notions that humans stood above or outside of nature and called on activists to take a radical stand in defense of the natural world.

1. The well-being and flourishing of human and nonhuman life on Earth have value in themselves (synonyms: inherent worth, intrinsic value, inherent value). These values are independent of the usefulness of the nonhuman world for human purposes.

2. Richness and diversity of life forms contribute to the realization of these values and are also values in themselves.

3. Humans have no right to reduce this richness and diversity except to satisfy vital needs.

4. Present human interference with the nonhuman world is excessive, and the situation is rapidly worsening.

5. The flourishing of human life and cultures is compatible with a substantial decrease of the human population. The flourishing of nonhuman life requires such a decrease.

6. Policies must therefore be changed. The changes in policies affect basic economic, technological, and ideological structures. The resulting state of affairs will be deeply different from the present.

7. The ideological change is mainly that of appreciating life quality (dwelling in situations of inherent worth) rather than adhering to an increasingly higher standard of living. There will be a profound awareness of the difference between big and great.

8. Those who subscribe to the foregoing points have an obligation directly or indirectly to participate in the attempt to implement the necessary changes.

ANALYZING THE EVIDENCE

and contrast the arguments made in Sources 1, 2, and 3. What do they share? What significant differences?

5, how do environmental activists use visual presentation and symbolism political beliefs? In Source 5, how do the more traditionally dressed members react to the Green Party members in their midst?

s in these sources express continuities with the ideas of the 1960s r was the environmentalism of the 1970s and 1980s something new?

3 Rudolf Bahro, "Some Preconditions for Resolving the Ecology Crisis," 1979.

Rudolf Bahro, a founding member of the West German Green Party who compared the earth's environment to the doomed ocean liner *Titanic*, called for radical intervention in the structures of corporate capitalism to prevent the looming disaster.

⟣ The ecology crisis is insoluble unless we work at the same time at overcoming the confrontation of military blocs. It is insoluble without a resolute policy of détente and disarmament, one that renounces all demands for subverting other countries. . . .

The ecology crisis is insoluble without a world order on the North-South axis. And we must realize that our entire standard of living [in the North] is largely based on the exploitation and suppression of the rest of humanity. . . .

The ecology crisis is insoluble without a decisive breakthrough towards social justice in our own country and without a swift equalization of social differences throughout Western Europe. . . . The ecology crisis is insoluble without progress in human emancipation here and now, even while capitalism still exists. It is insoluble without countless individuals managing to rise above their immediate and compensatory interests. . . .

If all this is brought to a common denominator, the conclusion is as follows: The ecology crisis is insoluble under capitalism. We have to get rid of the capitalist manner of regulating the economy and above all of the capitalist driving mechanism, for a start at least bringing it under control. In other words, there is no solution to the ecology crisis without the combination of all anticapitalist and socialist tendencies for a peaceful democratic revolution against the dominant economic structure.

(Keystone/Getty Images)

4 "Please Save Me from Lead Pollution," 1978.

A nine-year-old schoolgirl stands in front of the British prime minister's residence to protest the proposed extension of the M25 highway through her local playing fields, warning that children will be hurt by lead poisoning if the project goes through.

(bpk, Berlin/photographer: Peter Strack/Art Resource, NY)

5 Green Party representatives enter the West German parliament, 1983.

Members of the West German "Greens" won enough votes to send several representatives to the Bundestag (parliament) for the first time in 1983, a significant victory for the environmental movements that emerged in the 1970s.

PUTTING IT ALL TOGETHER

The environmental activists of the 1970s and 1980s were a diverse group with diverse opinions about the ways to address environmental issues. Using the sources above, along with what you have learned in class and in Chapters 28 and 29, write a short essay that explores the impact of environmentalism on political debate in the late twentieth century. How did environmental activists combine ethical, economic, and scientific critiques?

Sources: (1) Rachel Carson, *Silent Spring* (New York: Houghton Mifflin, 2002), pp. 189, 277; (2) Bill Devall and George Sessions, *Deep Ecology* (Salt Lake City: G. M. Smith, 1985), p. 70; (4) Rudolf Bahro, *Socialism and Survival* (London: Merlin Books, 1982), pp. 41–43.

employment, inexpensive public transportation, and large subsidies for rent and food.

Everyday life under developed socialism was defined by an uneasy mixture of outward conformity and private disengagement—or apathy. The Communist Party dominated public life. Party-led mass organizations for youth, women, workers, and sports groups staged huge rallies, colorful festivals, and new holidays that exposed citizens to the values of the socialist state. East Bloc citizens might grudgingly participate in party-sponsored public events, but at home, and in private, they often grumbled about and sidestepped the Communist authorities.

East Bloc living standards were well above those in the developing world, but below those in the West. Centralized economic planning continued to lead to shortages, and people complained about the poor quality and lack of choice of the most basic goods. Under these conditions, informal networks of family and friends helped people find hard-to-get goods and offered support beyond party organizations. Though the secret police persecuted those who openly challenged the system and generated mountains of files on ordinary people, they generally left alone those who demonstrated the required conformity.

Women in particular experienced the contradictions of the socialist system. Official state policy guaranteed equal rights for women and encouraged them to join the workforce in positions formerly reserved for men, and an extensive system of state-supported child care freed women to accept these employment opportunities and eased the work of parenting. Yet women rarely made it into the upper ranks of business or politics, and they faced the same double burden as those in the West (see Chapter 28). In addition, government control of the public sphere meant that the independent groups dedicated to feminist reform that emerged in the West in the 1970s developed more slowly in the East Bloc and the Soviet Union. Women could complain to the Communist authorities about unequal or sexist conditions at work or at home, but until the 1980s they could not build private, nongovernmental organizations to lobby for change.

Though everyday life was fairly comfortable in the East Bloc, a number of deeply rooted structural problems undermined popular support for Soviet-style communism. These fundamental problems would contribute to the re-emergence of civic dissent and ultimately to the revolutions of 1989. East Bloc countries—like those in the West—were hard hit by the energy crisis and stagflation of the 1970s. For a time, access to inexpensive oil from the Soviet Union, which had huge resources, helped prop up faltering economies, but this cushion began to fall apart in the 1980s. For a number of reasons, East Bloc leaders refused to make the economic reforms that might have made developed socialism more effective.

First, a move toward Western-style postindustrial society would have required fundamental changes to the Communist system. As in the West, it would have

Crossing the Border Between East and West Berlin   It was relatively easy for Westerners to get into East Germany to visit friends and relatives, but the Communist state tightly controlled the border. Most East Germans were never allowed to visit the West. In this 1964 photo, a group of West Berliners cross the border to return home after a trip to East Berlin. The glass and steel building in the background—the East German border-crossing station—was nicknamed the "Palace of Tears" by local residents. Here departing West Germans and their East German relatives who could not leave East Germany said many tearful farewells. The limits on travel to the West were one of the most hated aspects of daily life in the East Bloc. (© AND-Bildarchiv/ullstein bild/The Image Works)

hurt the already-tenuous living standard of industrial workers. But Communist East Bloc states were publicly committed to supporting the working classes, including coal miners, shipbuilders, and factory and construction workers. To pursue the neoliberal reforms undertaken in the West would have undermined popular support for the government among these basic constituencies, which was already tenuous at best.

Second, East Bloc regimes refused to cut spending on the welfare state because that was, after all, one of the proudest achievements of socialism. Third, the state continued to provide subsidies to heavy industries such as steel and mining. High-tech industries failed to take off in Communist Europe, in part because the West maintained embargoes on technology exports. The industrial goods produced in the East Bloc became increasingly uncompetitive in the new global system. To stave off total collapse, governments borrowed massive amounts of hard currency from Western banks and governments, helping to convince ordinary people that communism was bankrupt, and setting up a cycle of indebtedness that helped bring down the entire system in 1989.

Economic decline was not the only reason people increasingly questioned one-party Communist rule. The best career and educational opportunities were reserved for party members or handed out as political favors, leaving many talented people underemployed and resentful. Tight controls on travel continually called attention to the burdens of daily life in a repressive society. The one-party state had repeatedly quashed popular reform movements, retreated from economic liberalization, and jailed or exiled dissidents, even those who wished to reform communism from within. Though many East Bloc citizens still found the promise of Marxist egalitarian socialism appealing, they increasingly doubted the legitimacy of Soviet-style communism: the dream of distributing goods "from each according to his means, to each according to his needs" (as Marx had once put it) hardly made up for the great structural weaknesses of developed socialism.

Dissent in Czechoslovakia and Poland

Stagnation in the East Bloc encouraged small numbers of dedicated people to try to change society from below. Developments in Czechoslovakia and Poland were the most striking and significant, and determined protest movements re-emerged in both countries in the mid-1970s. Remembering a history of violent repression and Soviet invasion, dissenters carefully avoided direct challenges to government leaders. Nor did they try to reform the Communist Party from within, as Dubček and his followers had attempted in Prague in 1968. Instead, they worked to build a civil society from below—to create a realm of freedom beyond formal

politics, where civil liberties and human rights could be exercised independent of the Communist system.

In Czechoslovakia in 1977 a small group of citizens, including future Czechoslovak president Václav Havel (VAH-slahf HAH-vuhl) (1936–2011), signed a manifesto that came to be known as Charter 77. The group criticized the government for ignoring the human rights provision of the Helsinki Accords and called on Communist leaders to respect civil and political liberties. They also criticized censorship and argued for improved environmental policies. (See "Evaluating the Evidence 29.3: Dissent in the Czechoslovak Socialist Republic," page 1006.) Despite immediate state repression, the group challenged passive acceptance of Communist authority and voiced public dissatisfaction with developed socialism.

In Poland, an unruly satellite from the beginning, the Communists had failed to dominate society to the extent seen elsewhere in the East Bloc. Most agricultural land remained in private hands, and the Catholic Church thrived. The Communists also failed to manage the economy effectively. The 1960s brought stagnation, and in 1970 Poland's working class rose again in angry protest. A new Communist leader came to power, and he wagered that massive inflows of Western capital and technology, especially from rich and now-friendly West Germany, could produce a Polish economic miracle. Instead, bureaucratic incompetence and the first oil shock in 1973 sent the economy into a nosedive. Workers, intellectuals, and the church became increasingly restive. Then the real Polish miracle occurred: Cardinal Karol Wojtyla (KAH-rohl voy-TIH-wah), archbishop of Kraków, was elected pope in 1978 as John Paul II. In June 1979 he returned to Poland from Rome, preaching love of Christ and country and the "inalienable rights of man." The pope drew enormous crowds and electrified the Polish nation.

In August 1980 strikes broke out across Poland; at the gigantic Lenin Shipyards in Gdansk (formerly known as Danzig) sixteen thousand workers laid down their tools and occupied the plant. As other workers joined "in solidarity," the strikers advanced the ideals of civil society, including the right to form trade unions free from state control, freedom of speech, release of political prisoners, and economic reforms. After the strikers occupied the shipyard for eighteen days, the government gave in and accepted the workers' demands in the Gdansk Agreement. In a state in which the Communist Party claimed to rule on behalf of the proletariat, a working-class revolt had won an unprecedented, even revolutionary, victory.

Led by feisty Lenin Shipyards electrician and devout Catholic Lech Wałęsa (lehk vah-WEHN-suh) (b. 1943), the workers proceeded to organize a free and democratic trade union called **Solidarity**. As had been

> ■ **Solidarity** Independent Polish trade union that worked for workers' rights and political reform throughout the 1980s.

Dissent in the Czechoslovak Socialist Republic

First published in West Germany in January 1977, the Manifesto of the Czechoslovak dissident group Charter 77 called on the Communist regime to recognize the human rights codified in the country's 1960 constitution, the 1975 Helsinki Accords (see "Evaluating the Evidence 29.1: Human Rights Under the Helsinki Accords," page 984), and other international agreements on civil and political rights. The 243 courageous individuals who signed the Charter faced harsh state retaliation and their opposition had little immediate impact, but their ideas expressed a deep desire for civil rights and helped lay the intellectual foundations for the revolutions of 1989.

The human rights and freedoms underwritten by these covenants [on international civil and political rights, including the Helsinki Accords, signed by the Czechoslovak government] constitute features of civilized life for which many progressive movements have striven throughout history and whose codification could greatly assist humane developments in our society.

We accordingly welcome the Czechoslovak Socialist Republic's accession to those agreements.

Their publication, however, serves as a powerful reminder of the extent to which basic human rights in our country exist, regrettably, on paper alone.

The right to freedom of expression, for example, guaranteed by Article 19 of the first-mentioned covenant, is in our case purely illusory. Tens of thousands of our citizens are prevented from working in their own fields for the sole reason that they hold views differing from official ones, and are discriminated against and harassed in all kinds of ways by the authorities and public organizations. Deprived as they are of any means to defend themselves, they become victims of a virtual apartheid. . . .

Freedom of religious confession, emphatically guaranteed by Article 18 of the first covenant, is continually curtailed by arbitrary official action. . . .

This state of affairs likewise prevents workers and others from exercising the unrestricted right to establish trade unions and other organizations to protect their economic and social interests. . . .

Further civic rights, including the explicit prohibition of "arbitrary interference with privacy, family, home or correspondence" (Article 17 of the first covenant), are seriously vitiated by the various forms of interference in the private life of citizens exercised by the Ministry of the Interior, for example by bugging telephones and houses, opening mail, following personal movements, searching homes, setting up networks of neighborhood informers (often recruited by illicit threats or promises) and in other ways. . . .

Clause 2, Article 12 of the first covenant, guaranteeing every citizen the right to leave the country, is consistently violated, or under the pretense of "defense of national security" is subjected to various unjustifiable conditions (Clause 3). . . .

Responsibility for the maintenance of rights in our country naturally devolves in the first place on the political and state authorities. Yet not only on them: everyone bears his share of responsibility for the conditions that prevail and accordingly also for the observance of legally enshrined agreements, binding upon all individuals as well as upon governments.

It is this sense of co-responsibility, our belief in the importance of its conscious public acceptance and the general need to give it new and more effective expression that led us to the idea of creating Charter 77, whose inception we today publicly announce. . . .

We believe that Charter 77 will help to enable all citizens of Czechoslovakia to work and live as free human beings.

EVALUATE THE EVIDENCE

1. Why does the Charter call on ordinary citizens to take responsibility for observing the "legally enshrined agreements" on human rights?
2. How did the 1975 Helsinki Accords provide a legal basis for dissidents to challenge the Czechoslovak one-party state?

Source: "Appendix D: Manifesto of Charter 77 — Czechoslovakia," in *Czechoslovakia (Former): A Country Study*, Library of Congress, https://archive.org/details/czechoslovakiaco00gawd.

---

the case in Czechoslovakia, Solidarity worked cautiously to shape an active civil society. Joined by intellectuals and supported by the Catholic Church, it became a national union with a full-time staff of 40,000 and 9.5 million members. Cultural and intellectual freedom blossomed in Poland, and Solidarity enjoyed tremendous public support. But Solidarity's leaders pursued a self-limiting revolution, meant only to defend the concessions won in the Gdansk Agreement. Solidarity thus practiced moderation, refusing to challenge directly the Communist monopoly on political power. At the same time, the ever-present threat of calling a nationwide strike gave them real leverage in ongoing negotiations with the Communist bosses.

Lech Wałęsa and Solidarity
An inspiration for fellow workers at the Lenin Shipyards in the dramatic and successful strike against the Communist leaders in August 1980, Wałęsa played a key role in Solidarity before and after it was outlawed. Here he speaks at a protest rally in the port city of Gdansk during the strike. Members of the crowd hold flags with the Polish national eagle and the red and white Solidarity banner. Wałęsa personified the enduring opposition to Communist rule in eastern Europe. (Camera Press/Redux)

Solidarity's combination of strength and moderation postponed a showdown, as the Soviet Union played a waiting game of threats and pressure. After a confrontation in March 1981, Wałęsa settled for minor government concessions, and Solidarity dropped plans for a massive general strike. Criticism of Wałęsa's moderate leadership gradually grew, and Solidarity lost its cohesiveness. The worsening economic crisis also encouraged radical actions among disgruntled Solidarity members, and the Polish Communist leadership shrewdly denounced the union for promoting economic collapse and provoking a possible Soviet invasion. In December 1981 Wojciech Jaruzelski (VOY-chehk yahr-oo-ZEHL-skee), the general who headed Poland's Communist government, suddenly proclaimed martial law and arrested Solidarity's leaders.

Outlawed and driven underground, Solidarity survived in part because of the government's unwillingness (and probably its inability) to impose full-scale terror. Moreover, millions of Poles decided to continue acting as if they were free—the hallmark of civil society—even though they were not. Cultural and intellectual life remained extremely vigorous as the Polish economy continued to deteriorate. Thus popular support for outlawed Solidarity remained strong under martial law in the 1980s, preparing the way for the union's political rebirth toward the end of the decade.

The rise and survival of Solidarity showed that ordinary Poles would stubbornly struggle for greater political and religious liberty, cultural freedom, trade-union rights, patriotic nationalism, and a more humane socialism. Not least, Solidarity's challenge encouraged fresh thinking in the Soviet Union, ever the key to lasting change in the East Bloc.

From Détente Back to Cold War

The Soviets and the leaders of the Soviet satellite states faced challenges from abroad as optimistic hopes for détente in international relations gradually faded in the late 1970s. Brezhnev's Soviet Union ignored the human rights provisions of the Helsinki agreement, and East-West political competition remained very much alive outside Europe. Many Americans became convinced that the Soviet Union was taking advantage of détente, steadily building up its military might and pushing for political gains and revolutions in Africa, Asia, and Latin America. The Soviet invasion of Afghanistan in December 1979, designed to save an increasingly unpopular Marxist regime, alarmed the West. Many Americans feared that the oil-rich states of the Persian Gulf would be next, and once again they looked to the NATO alliance and military might to thwart Communist expansion.

The Soviet War in Afghanistan, 1979–1989

President Jimmy Carter (U.S. pres. 1977–1981) tried to lead NATO beyond verbal condemnation of the Soviet Union and urged economic sanctions against it, but only Great Britain among the European allies supported the American initiative. The alliance showed the same lack of concerted action when the Solidarity movement rose in Poland. Some observers concluded that NATO had lost the will to act decisively in dealing with the Soviet bloc.

The Atlantic alliance endured, however, and the U.S. military buildup launched by Carter in his last years in office was greatly accelerated by President Reagan, who was swept into office in 1980 by a wave of patriotism and economic discontent. The new American leadership acted as if the military balance had tipped in favor of the Soviet Union, which Reagan anathematized as the "evil empire." Increasing defense spending enormously, the Reagan administration deployed short-range nuclear missiles in western Europe and built up the navy to preserve American power in the post-Vietnam age. The broad shift toward greater conservatism in the 1980s gave Reagan invaluable allies in western Europe. Margaret Thatcher worked well with Reagan and was a forceful advocate for a revital-

Mikhail Gorbachev Soviet president Mikhail Gorbachev (center, with red tie) walks with a crowd of delegates to the twenty-eighth and last congress of the Soviet Communist Party in July 1990. Gorbachev took office in 1985 with the goal of reforming communism from within. His plans spiraled out of control. By 1991 the Soviet Union and the East Bloc had disintegrated into independent, noncommunist states. (© Pascal Le Segretain/Sygma/Corbis)

ized Atlantic alliance, and under Helmut Kohl West Germany likewise worked with the United States to coordinate military and political policy toward the Soviet bloc.

Gorbachev's Reforms in the Soviet Union

Cold War tensions aside, the Soviet Union's Communist elite seemed safe from any challenge from below in the early 1980s. A well-established system of administrative controls stretched downward from the central ministries and state committees to provincial cities and from there to factories, neighborhoods, and villages. At each level of this massive state bureaucracy, the overlapping hierarchy of the 17.5-million-member Communist Party maintained tight state control. Organized opposition was impossible, and average people left politics to the bosses.

Although the massive state and party bureaucracy safeguarded the elite, it promoted widespread apathy and stagnation. When the ailing Brezhnev finally died in 1982, his successor, the long-time chief of the secret police, Yuri Andropov (1914–1984), tried to invigorate the system. Relatively little came of his efforts, but they combined with a sharply worsening economic situation to set the stage for the emergence in 1985 of Mikhail Gorbachev (b. 1931), the most vigorous Soviet leader in a generation.

A lawyer and experienced Communist Party official, Gorbachev was smart, charming, and tough. He believed in communism, but realized that the Soviet Union was failing to keep up with the West and was losing its superpower status. Thus Gorbachev tried to revitalize the Soviet system with fundamental reforms. An idealist who wanted to improve conditions for ordinary citizens, Gorbachev understood that the enormous expense of the Cold War arms race had had a disastrous impact on living conditions in the Soviet Union; improvement at home, he realized, required better relations with the West.

In his first year in office, Gorbachev attacked corruption and incompetence in the bureaucracy and consolidated his power. He condemned alcoholism and drunkenness, which were deadly scourges of Soviet society, and worked out an ambitious reform program designed to transform and restructure the economy in order to provide for the real needs of the Soviet population. To accomplish this economic restructuring, or **perestroika** (pehr-uh-STROY-kuh), Gorbachev and his supporters permitted an easing of government price controls on some goods, more independence for state enterprises, and the creation of profit-seeking private cooperatives to provide personal services. These timid reforms initially produced a few improvements, but shortages grew as the economy

■ **perestroika** Economic restructuring and reform implemented by Premier Mikhail Gorbachev in the Soviet Union in 1985.

■ **glasnost** Soviet premier Mikhail Gorbachev's popular campaign for openness in government and the media.

stalled at an intermediate point between central planning and free-market mechanisms. By late 1988 widespread consumer dissatisfaction posed a serious threat to Gorbachev's leadership and the entire reform program.

Gorbachev's bold and far-reaching campaign for greater freedom of expression was much more successful. Very popular in a country where censorship, dull uniformity, and outright lies had long characterized public discourse, the newfound openness, or **glasnost** (GLAZ-nohst), of the government and the media marked an astonishing break with the past. Long-banned émigré writers sold millions of copies of their works in new editions, while denunciations of Stalin and his terror became standard fare in plays and movies. In another example of glasnost in action, after several days of hesitation the usually secretive Soviet government issued daily reports on the 1986 nuclear plant accident at Chernobyl, one of the worst environmental disasters in history. Indeed the initial openness in government pronouncements quickly went much further than Gorbachev intended and led to something approaching free speech, a veritable cultural revolution.

Democratization was another element of reform. Beginning as an attack on corruption in the Communist Party, it led to the first free elections in the Soviet Union since 1917. Gorbachev and the party remained in control, but a minority of critical independents was elected in April 1989 to a revitalized Congress of People's Deputies. Millions of Soviets then watched the new congress for hours on television as Gorbachev and his ministers saw their proposals debated and even rejected. Thus millions of Soviet citizens took practical lessons in open discussion, critical thinking, and representative government. An active civil society was emerging—a new political culture at odds with the Communist Party's monopoly of power and control.

Democratization also ignited demands for greater political and cultural autonomy and even national independence among non-Russian minorities living in the fifteen Soviet republics. The Soviet population numbered about 145 million ethnic Russians and 140.6 million non-Russians, including 55 million Muslims in the Central Asian republics and over 44 million Ukrainians. Once Gorbachev opened the doors to greater public expression, tensions flared between central Soviet control and national separatist movements. Independence groups were particularly active in the Baltic Soviet socialist republics of Lithuania, Latvia, and Estonia; in western Ukraine; and in the Transcaucasian republics of Armenia, Azerbaijan, and Georgia.

Finally, Gorbachev brought reforms to the field of foreign affairs. He withdrew Soviet troops from Afghanistan in February 1989 and sought to reduce East-West tensions. Of enormous importance, the Soviet leader sought to halt the arms race with the United States and convinced President Reagan of his sincerity. In a Washington summit in December 1987, the two leaders agreed to eliminate all land-based intermediate-range missiles in Europe, setting the stage for more arms reductions. Gorbachev pledged to respect the political choices of the peoples of East Bloc countries, repudiating the Brezhnev Doctrine and giving encouragement to reform movements in Poland, Czechoslovakia, and Hungary. By early 1989 it seemed that if Gorbachev held to his word, the tragic Soviet occupation of eastern Europe might wither away, taking the long Cold War with it once and for all.

The Revolutions of 1989

FOCUS QUESTION *Why did revolution sweep through the East Bloc in 1989, and what were the immediate consequences?*

In 1989 Gorbachev's plan to reform communism from within snowballed out of control. A series of largely peaceful revolutions swept across eastern Europe, overturning existing Communist regimes (Map 29.2). The revolutions of 1989 had momentous consequences. First, the peoples of the East Bloc gained political freedom after about forty years of dictatorial Communist rule. Second, West Germany absorbed its East German rival, and a reunified Germany emerged as the most influential country in Europe. Third, as Gorbachev's reforms boomeranged, a complicated anticommunist revolution swept through the Soviet Union, and the multinational empire broke into a large Russia and fourteen other independent states. The Cold War came to an end, and the United States suddenly stood as the world's only superpower.

The Collapse of Communism in the East Bloc

The collapse of Communist rule in the Soviet satellite states surprised many Western commentators, who had expected Cold War divisions to persist for many years. Yet while the revolutions of 1989 appeared to erupt quite suddenly, long-standing, structural weaknesses in the Communist system had in some ways made revolt inevitable. East Bloc economies never really recovered from the economic catastrophe of the 1970s. State spending on outdated industries and extensive welfare systems led to massive indebtedness to Western banks and undermined economic growth,

MAPPING THE PAST

MAP 29.2 Democratic Movements in Eastern Europe, 1989

Countries that had been satellites in the orbit of the Soviet Union began to set themselves free in 1989.

ANALYZING THE MAP Why did the means by which communism was overthrown in the East Bloc vary from country to country? What accounts for the rapid spread of these democratic movements?

CONNECTIONS How did Gorbachev's reforms in the Soviet Union contribute to the spread of democratic movements in eastern Europe, and how did his actions hasten the end of the Cold War?

while limits on personal and political freedoms fueled a growing sense of injustice (see page 1004).

In this general climate of economic stagnation and popular anger, Solidarity and the Polish people led the way to revolution. In 1988 widespread strikes, raging inflation, and the outlawed Solidarity's refusal to cooperate with the military government had brought Poland to the brink of economic collapse. Poland's frustrated Communist leaders offered to negotiate with Solidarity if the outlawed union's leaders could get the strikers back to work and resolve the political stalemate and the economic crisis. The subsequent

agreement in April 1989 legalized Solidarity and declared that a large minority of representatives to the Polish parliament would be chosen by free elections that June. Still guaranteed a parliamentary majority and expecting to win many of the contested seats, the Communists believed that their rule was guaranteed for four years and that Solidarity would keep the workers in line.

Lacking access to the state-run media, Solidarity succeeded nonetheless in mobilizing the country and winning all but one of the contested seats in an overwhelming victory. Moreover, many angry voters crossed off the names of unopposed party candidates, so that the Communist Party failed to win the majority its leaders had anticipated. Solidarity members jubilantly entered the Polish parliament, and a dangerous stalemate quickly developed. But Lech Wałęsa, a gifted politician who always repudiated violence, adroitly obtained a majority by securing the allegiance of two minor procommunist parties that had been part of the coalition government after World War II. In August 1989 Tadeusz Mazowiecki (Ta-DAY-ush MAH-zoe-vee-ETS-key) (1927–2013), the editor of one of Solidarity's weekly newspapers, was sworn in as Poland's new noncommunist prime minister.

In its first year and a half, the new Solidarity government cautiously introduced revolutionary political changes. It eliminated the hated secret police, the Communist ministers in the government, and finally Communist Party leader Jaruzelski himself, but it did so step-by-step in order to avoid confrontation with the army or the Soviet Union. In economics, however, the Solidarity government was radical from the beginning. It applied economic shock therapy, an intense dose of neoliberal policy designed to make a clean break with state planning and move quickly to market mechanisms and private property (see Chapter 30). Thus the government abolished controls on many prices on January 1, 1990, and reformed the monetary system with a big bang.

Hungary followed Poland. Hungary's moderate Communist Party leader János Kádár (KAH-dahr) had permitted liberalization of the rigid planned economy after the 1956 uprising in exchange for political loyalty and continued Communist control. In May 1988, in an effort to retain power by granting modest political concessions, the party replaced the ill and aging Kádár with a reform-minded Communist. But liberal opposition groups rejected piecemeal progress, and in the summer of 1989 the Hungarian Communist Party agreed to hold free elections the following March. Welcoming Western investment and moving rapidly toward multiparty democracy, Hungary's Communists now enjoyed considerable popular support, and they believed, quite mistakenly, that they could defeat the opposition in the upcoming elections.

In an effort to strengthen their support at home, the Hungarians opened their border to East Germans and tore down the barbed wire curtain separating Hungary from Austria. Tens of thousands of dissatisfied East German "vacationers" then poured into Hungary, crossed into Austria as refugees, and continued on to immediate resettlement in thriving West Germany.

The flight of East Germans fed the rapid growth of a homegrown, spontaneous protest movement in East Germany. Workers joined intellectuals, environmentalists, and Protestant ministers in huge candlelight demonstrations, arguing that a democratic but still so-

The Collapse of Communism

1977	Charter 77 reform movement founded in Czechoslovakia
1980	Polish Solidarity movement formed
1981	Solidarity outlawed by Communist leaders
1982	Soviet premier Leonid Brezhnev dies
1985	Mikhail Gorbachev becomes Soviet premier and institutes perestroika and glasnost reforms
1988	Polish workers strike throughout country
1989	
April	Solidarity legalized in Poland
August	Noncommunist prime minister elected in Poland
November	Berlin Wall opened
November–December	Velvet Revolution ends communism in Czechoslovakia
December	Communist dictator of Romania executed
1990	
February	Communist Party defeated in Soviet elections
March	Free elections in Hungary
May	Boris Yeltsin elected leader of Russian Soviet Republic
October	Reunification of Germany
November	Paris Accord: arms reductions across Europe
1991	
August	Communist hardliners kidnap Gorbachev and try to overthrow Soviet government
December	Soviet Union dissolved

cialist East Germany was both possible and desirable. These "stayers" failed to convince the "leavers," however, who continued to depart en masse. In a desperate attempt to stabilize the situation, the East German government opened the Berlin Wall in November 1989, and people danced for joy atop that grim symbol of the prison state. A new, reformist government took power and scheduled free elections.

In Czechoslovakia, Communist rule began to dissolve peacefully in November to December 1989. This so-called **Velvet Revolution** grew out of popular demonstrations led by students and joined by intellectuals and a dissident playwright-turned-moral-revolutionary

■ **Velvet Revolution** The term given to the relatively peaceful overthrow of communism in Czechoslovakia; the label came to signify the collapse of the East Bloc in general in 1989 to 1990.

named Václav Havel (1936–2011). When the protesters took control of the streets, the Communist government resigned, leading to a power-sharing arrangement
termed the "Government of National Understanding."
As 1989 ended, the Czechoslovakian assembly elected
Havel president.

In Romania, popular revolution turned violent and
bloody. There the dictator Nicolae Ceauşescu (chow-
SHESS-koo) (1918–1989) had long combined tight
party control with stubborn independence from Moscow. Faced with mass protests in December 1989,
Ceauşescu ordered his ruthless security forces to quell
unrest, sparking an armed uprising. Perhaps 750
people were killed in the fighting; the numbers were
often exaggerated. After the dictator and his wife were
captured and executed by a military court, Ceauşescu's
forces were defeated. A coalition government emerged,
although the legacy of Ceauşescu's long and oppressive
rule left a troubled country.

German Unification and
the End of the Cold War

The dissolution of communism in East Germany that
began in 1989 reopened the "German question" and
raised the threat of renewed Cold War conflict over
Germany. Taking power in October 1989, East
German reform Communists, enthusiastically supported by leading intellectuals and former dissidents,
wanted to preserve socialism by making it genuinely
democratic and responsive to the needs of the people.
They argued for a "third way" that would go beyond
the failed Stalinism they had experienced and the ruthless capitalism they saw in the West. These reformers
supported closer ties with West Ger-
many but feared unification, hoping
to preserve a distinct East German
identity with a socialist system.

Over the next year, however, East
Germany was absorbed into an enlarged West Germany, much as a faltering company is swallowed by a
stronger rival and ceases to exist.
Three factors were particularly important in this outcome. First, in the
first week after the Berlin Wall was
opened, almost 9 million East
Germans—roughly half of the total
population—poured across the border into West Germany. Almost all
returned to their homes in the east,
but the joy of warm welcomes from
long-lost friends and relatives and the
exhilaration of crossing a long-closed
border aroused long-dormant hopes
of unity among ordinary citizens.

Second, West German chancellor Helmut Kohl and
his closest advisers skillfully exploited the historic opportunity handed them. Sure of support from the
United States, whose leadership he had steadfastly followed, in November 1989 Kohl presented a ten-point
plan for step-by-step unification in cooperation with
both East Germany and the international community.
Kohl then promised the struggling citizens of East
Germany an immediate economic bonanza—a generous though limited exchange of East German marks
in savings accounts and pensions into much more
valuable West German marks. This offer helped popularize the conservative-liberal Alliance for Germany,
a well-financed political party established in East
Germany with the support of Kohl's West German Christian Democrats. In March 1990 the Alliance won almost 50 percent of the votes in an East
German parliamentary election, outdistancing the
Party of Democratic Socialism (the renamed East
German Communist Party) (16 percent) and the revived Social Democratic Party (22 percent). The Alliance for Germany quickly negotiated an economic and
political union on favorable terms with Kohl. The
rapid pace of reunification quickly overwhelmed those
who argued for the preservation of an independent socialist society in East Germany.

Third, in the summer of 1990 the crucial international aspect of German unification was successfully
resolved. Unification would once again make Germany
the strongest state in central Europe and would directly affect the security of the Soviet Union. But Gorbachev swallowed hard—Western cartoonists showed
Stalin turning over in his grave—and negotiated the
best deal he could. In a historic agreement signed by
Gorbachev and Kohl in July 1990,
Kohl solemnly affirmed Germany's
peaceful intentions and pledged
never to develop nuclear, biological,
or chemical weapons. The Germans
sweetened the deal by promising
enormous loans to the hard-pressed
Soviet Union. In October 1990 East
Germany merged into West Germany,
forming a single nation under the West
German laws and constitution.

The peaceful reunification of Germany accelerated the pace of agreements to liquidate the Cold War. In
November 1990 delegates from
twenty-two European countries
joined those from the United States
and the Soviet Union in Paris and
agreed to a scaling down of all their
armed forces. The delegates also solemnly affirmed that all existing borders in Europe, including those of

The Reunification of Germany, 1990

DENMARK
Hamburg
NETH.
Berlin
GERMANY
Cologne, Bonn, Leipzig, Dresden
LUX.
Frankfurt
FRANCE
CZECH.
Munich
AUSTRIA
— Former boundary between East and West Germany

The Opening of the Berlin Wall
The sudden and unanticipated opening of the Berlin Wall on November 10, 1989, dramatized the spectacular fall of communism throughout east-central Europe. West Berliners welcomed the East Germans who piled into their "Trabi" automobiles to cross the border. Millions of East German citizens traveled into West Berlin and the Federal Republic of Germany in the first few days after the surprise relaxation of inter-German travel controls. (© DPA/Courtesy Everett Collection)

unified Germany and the emerging Baltic States, were legal and valid. The Paris Accord was for all practical purposes a general peace treaty bringing an end to both World War II and the Cold War.

Peace in Europe encouraged the United States and the Soviet Union to scrap a significant portion of their nuclear weapons in a series of agreements. In September 1991 a confident President George H. W. Bush canceled the around-the-clock alert status for American bombers outfitted with atomic bombs, and a floundering Gorbachev quickly followed suit with his own forces. For the first time in four decades, Soviet and American nuclear weapons were not standing ready for mutual destruction.

The Disintegration of the Soviet Union

As 1990 began, the tough work of dismantling some forty-five years of Communist rule had begun in all but two East Bloc states—tiny Albania and the vast Soviet Union. The great question now became whether the Soviet Union would follow its former satellites.

In February 1990, as competing Russian politicians noisily presented their programs and nationalists in the non-Russian republics demanded autonomy or independence from the Soviet Union, the Communist Party suffered a stunning defeat in local elections throughout the country. As in East Bloc countries, democrats and anticommunists won clear majorities in the leading cities of the Russian Soviet Federative Socialist Republic (SFSR), by far the largest republic in the Soviet Union. Moreover, in Lithuania the people elected an uncompromising nationalist as president, and the newly chosen parliament declared Lithuania an independent state.

Gorbachev responded by placing an economic embargo on Lithuania, but he refused to use the army to crush the separatist government. The result was a tense political stalemate that undermined popular support for Gorbachev. Separating himself further from Communist hardliners, Gorbachev asked Soviet citizens to ratify a new constitution that formally abolished the Communist Party's monopoly of political power and expanded the power of the Congress of People's Deputies. While retaining his post as party secretary, Gorbachev then convinced a majority of deputies to elect him president of the Soviet Union.

Despite his victory, Gorbachev's power continued to erode, and his unwillingness to risk a universal suffrage election for the presidency strengthened his great rival, Boris Yeltsin (1931–2007). A radical reform

Revolution in Romania
A man holding a Romanian flag with the Communist symbol torn from its center stands on a balcony overlooking the tanks, soldiers, and citizens filling Palace Square in Bucharest, the capital city, during the revolution of 1989. Deadly violence accompanied the overthrow of communism in Romania. Elsewhere the collapse of the East Bloc was relatively peaceful. (© Peter Turnley/Corbis)

Communist, Yeltsin embraced the democratic movement, and in May 1990 he was elected parliamentary leader of the Russian Soviet Republic. He boldly announced that Russia would put its interests first and declare its independence from the Soviet Union, broadening the base of the anticommunist movement by joining the patriotism of ordinary Russians with the democratic aspirations of big-city intellectuals. Gorbachev tried to save the Soviet Union with a new treaty that would link the member republics in a looser, freely accepted confederation, but six of the fifteen Soviet republics rejected his plan.

Opposed by democrats and nationalists, Gorbachev was also challenged by the Communist old guard. In August 1991 a gang of hardliners kidnapped him and his family in the Caucasus and tried to seize the Soviet government. The attempted coup collapsed in the face of massive popular resistance that rallied around Yeltsin. As the spellbound world watched on television, Yeltsin defiantly denounced the rebels from atop a stalled tank in central Moscow and declared the "rebirth of Russia." The army supported Yeltsin, and Gorbachev was rescued and returned to power as head of the Soviet Union.

The leaders of the coup had wanted to preserve Communist power, state ownership, and the multina-

tional Soviet Union; they succeeded in destroying all three. An anticommunist revolution swept Russia as Yeltsin and his supporters outlawed the Communist Party and confiscated its property. Locked in a personal and political duel with Gorbachev, Yeltsin and his democratic allies declared Russia independent, withdrew from the Soviet Union, and changed the country's name from the Russian Soviet Republic to the Russian Federation. All the other Soviet republics also withdrew. Gorbachev resigned on December 25, 1991, and the next day the Supreme Soviet dissolved itself, marking the end of the Soviet Union. The independent republics of the old Soviet Union then established a loose confederation, the Commonwealth of Independent States, which played only a minor role in the 1990s.

NOTES

1. Quoted in Kessing's Research Report, *Germany and East Europe Since 1945: From the Potsdam Agreement to Chancellor Brandt's "Ostpolitik"* (New York: Charles Scribner's Sons, 1973), pp. 284–285.
2. M. Mitterauer, *The History of Youth* (Oxford: Basil Blackwell, 1992), p. 40.
3. See R. Guha, *Environmentalism: A Global History* (New York: Longman, 2000), p. 79.

LOOKING BACK LOOKING AHEAD

The unexpected collapse of Communist Europe capped three decades of turbulent change. In the 1960s the counterculture challenged the status quo and steered western Europe to the left as reformists attempted (but failed) to liberalize East Bloc communism. In the 1970s a global recession had devastating effects in the West and East Blocs alike. In the 1980s conservative Western leaders pushed neoliberal plans to revive growth and meet growing global competition. In the East Bloc, structural problems and spontaneous revolt brought down communism, dissolved the Soviet Union, and ended the Cold War.

With the world economy on the road to recovery and new free-market systems in place across the former East Bloc, all of Europe would now have the opportunity to enter the information age. After forty years of Cold War division, the continent regained an underlying unity as faith in democratic government and market economics became the common European creed. In 1991 hopes for peaceful democratic progress were almost universal. According to philosopher Francis Fukuyama, the world had reached "the end of history" — the end of the Cold War, he argued, would lead to peaceful development based on growing tolerance, free-market economics, and liberal democracy.

The post–Cold War years saw the realization of some of these hopes, but the new era brought its own problems and tragedies. New ethnic and nationalist tensions flared, leading to a disastrous civil war in the former Yugoslavia. The struggle to rebuild the shattered societies of the former East Bloc countries was far more difficult than the people living in them had hoped. Poor economic growth continued to complicate attempts to deal with the wide-open global economy. New conflicts with Islamic nations in the Middle East involved some European nations in war. The European Union expanded, but political disagreements, environmental issues, increased anxiety about non-Western immigrants, and a host of other problems undermined moves toward true European unity. History was far from over — the realities of a post–Cold War world continued to produce difficult challenges as Europe entered the twenty-first century.

Make Connections

Think about the larger developments and continuities within and across chapters.

1. How did the revolts that shook western European countries and the East Bloc develop out of issues left unresolved in the 1950s era of postwar reconstruction (Chapter 28)?

2. Both East and West Blocs faced similar economic problems in the 1970s, yet communism collapsed in the East and capitalism recovered. How do you account for the difference? Were economic problems the main basis for popular opposition to communism?

3. What were some of the basic ideas behind the neoliberal economic policies that emerged in the West in the 1970s and 1980s? Why are they still popular today?

29 REVIEW & EXPLORE

Identify Key Terms

Identify and explain the significance of each item below.

Ostpolitik (p. 983)

détente (p. 983)

Second Vatican Council (p. 985)

New Left (p. 988)

Brezhnev Doctrine (p. 992)

OPEC (p. 993)

stagflation (p. 993)

postindustrial society (p. 993)

neoliberalism (p. 994)

privatization (p. 994)

developed socialism (p. 1001)

Solidarity (p. 1005)

perestroika (p. 1008)

glasnost (p. 1009)

Velvet Revolution (p. 1011)

Review the Main Ideas

Answer the focus questions from each section of the chapter.

◆ Why did the postwar consensus of the 1950s break down? (p. 982)

◆ What were the consequences of economic decline in the 1970s? (p. 992)

◆ What led to the decline of Soviet power in the East Bloc? (p. 1001)

◆ Why did revolution sweep through the East Bloc in 1989, and what were the immediate consequences? (p. 1009)

Suggested Reading and Media Resources

BOOKS

◆ Ash, Timothy Garton. *The Magic Lantern: The Revolution of '89 Witnessed in Warsaw, Budapest, Berlin, and Prague*. 1993. An exciting firsthand narrative of the collapse of the East Bloc in 1989 and 1990.

◆ Cohen, Stephen F. *Soviet Fates and Lost Alternatives: From Stalinism to the New Cold War*. 2011. An up-to-date book by an acclaimed historian that challenges conventional interpretations of the rise and fall and aftermath of the Soviet Union.

◆ Guha, Ramachandra. *Environmentalism: A Global History*. 2000. A powerful and readable overview of environmentalism that puts Europe in world context.

◆ Kurlansky, Mark. *1968: The Year That Rocked the World*. 2003. Popular history at its best; a gripping account of the 1960s generation and 1968 across the globe.

◆ McLeod, Hugh. *The Religious Crisis of the 1960s*. 2007. A comparative study of Western religion in decline.

◆ Okey, Robin. *The Demise of Communist East Europe: 1989 in Context*. 2004. A measured overview of the collapse of the East Bloc that avoids accusatory Cold War rhetoric.

◆ Pittaway, Mark. *Eastern Europe, 1939–2000*. 2004. A survey of east-central Europe from the start of World War II to the end of communism, with a welcome emphasis on social history.

◆ Port, Andrew I. *Conflict and Stability in the German Democratic Republic*. 2007. A penetrating analysis of popular support for communism in this major East Bloc country.

◆ Reitan, Earl A. *Tory Radicalism: Margaret Thatcher, John Major, and the Transformation of Modern Britain, 1979–1997*. 1997. Clear, concise, and very useful.

◆ Ross, Kristin. *May '68 and Its Afterlives*. 2004. An important book on the way contested memories continue to shape our understanding of France's May Events.

* Smith, Bonnie G. *Global Feminisms Since 1945.* 2000. A broad overview of feminism after World War II that puts European and American movements in global context.
* Williams, Kieran. *The Prague Spring and Its Aftermath: Czechoslovak Politics, 1968–1970.* 1997. Explores the events of the Prague Spring and the political changes that followed the revolt.
* Zubok, Vladislav M. *A Failed Empire: The Soviet Union in the Cold War from Stalin to Gorbachev.* 2008. An in-depth account of Soviet leaders and elites during the Cold War.

DOCUMENTARIES

* *The Beatles Anthology* (EMI Records, 1995). This series about the British rock band the Beatles includes clips of many of their songs as well as a detailed look at the lives of the artists.
* *My Perestroika* (Robin Hessman, 2010). Documents the story of five individuals who were born in the Soviet Union and came of age during its collapse.
* *Vietnam's Unseen War: Pictures from the Other Side* (National Geographic, 2001). A look at the Vietnam War through the lenses of Vietnamese photographers.

FEATURE FILMS

* *Apocalypse Now* (Francis Ford Coppola, 1979). In this famous film, loosely based on Joseph Conrad's *Heart of Darkness*, a special operations captain undertakes a secret mission into the jungle of Cambodia that reveals the cruelty and absurdity of the war in Vietnam.
* *The Iron Lady* (Phyllida Lloyd, 2011). A film about the life of Great Britain's first female prime minister, Margaret Thatcher, who is renowned for her neoliberal policies in the 1980s.

* *The Lives of Others* (Florian Henckel von Donnersmarck, 2006). An East German secret agent spies on a prominent writer and his lover and becomes obsessed with their lives.
* *Man of Marble* (Andrzej Wajda, 1977). By a noted Polish director, this film tells the story of the first decade of Communist rule in Poland through the experiences of a young bricklayer and a documentary film maker who seeks to make a film about the bricklayer's life and times.
* *Omagh* (Pete Travis, 2004). A dramatic film about the tragic 1998 bombing in Omagh by the Irish Republican Army.

WEB SITES

* *BBC News Special Report: The Thatcher Years in Statistics.* An interactive Web site that allows users to compare and contrast various sets of economic and social statistics in Britain during the Thatcher years. **news.bbc.co .uk/2/hi/in_depth/4447082.stm**
* *Making the History of 1989.* Primary sources, scholarly interviews, and case studies on the fall of communism in eastern Europe. **chnm.gmu.edu/1989/**
* *MSU Billings Library Research Guide: Europe in the 1960s.* A library research guide, hosted by Montana State University, that includes a wide variety of links to online primary and secondary sources on all aspects of Europe's experience of the 1960s. **http://libguides .msubillings.edu/c.php?g=242173&p=1610604**

30

Life in an Age of Globalization

1990 TO THE PRESENT

On November 9, 2009, the twentieth anniversary of the opening of the Berlin Wall, jubilant crowds filled the streets around the Brandenburg Gate at the former border between East and West Berlin. World leaders and tens of thousands of onlookers applauded as former Polish president Lech Wałęsa pushed over a line of one thousand eight-foot-tall foam dominos, symbolizing the collapse of communism.

The crowd had reason to celebrate. The revolutions of 1989 had opened a new chapter in European and world history. Capitalism spread across the former Eastern bloc and Soviet Union (now the Russian Federation and fourteen other republics), along with the potential for political reform. Some of these hopes were realized, but the new era also brought problems and tragedies. The process of remaking formerly Communist societies was more difficult than expected. At the same time, across the West and around the world, globalization, the digital revolution, and the ongoing flow of immigrants into western Europe had impacts both positive and negative.

As Europeans faced serious tensions and complex changes in the twenty-first century, they also came together to form a strong new European Union that would prove a formidable economic competitor to the United States. Ties between western Europe and the United States began to loosen, but Europe and North America—as well as the rest of the world—confronted common challenges. Finding solutions to problems in the Middle East and addressing challenges regarding economic growth, energy needs, the environment, and human rights would require not only innovation but also creative cooperation. ■

CHAPTER PREVIEW

Life in a Globalizing World
This French-American collaboration, titled *The Standing March*, was exhibited on the façade of the National Assembly building in Paris during the United Nations–sponsored climate conference in December 2015, when world leaders gathered to negotiate an international deal to control climate change. Using cutting-edge technology, the creators projected a video of faces from around the world to remind the negotiators about the impact of global warming on ordinary people. (*The Standing March* is the collaborative work by the French artist known as JR and the U.S. filmmaker Darren Aronofsky/photo: Eric Feferberg/AFP/Getty Images)

Reshaping the Soviet Union and the Former East Bloc

FOCUS QUESTION *How did life change in Russia and the former East Bloc countries after 1989?*

Establishing stable democratic governments in the former East Bloc countries and the diverse territories of the Soviet Union, now divided into fifteen republics with Russia at its core, was not easy. While Russia initially moved toward economic reform and political openness, by 2010 it had returned to its authoritarian traditions. Stability proved elusive in many of the former Soviet Socialist Republics, and conflict undermined Russia's relations with some of these new nation-states.

The transformation of the Communist East Bloc was also difficult. After a period of tense reform, some countries, such as Poland, the Czech Republic, and Hungary, established relatively prosperous democracies and joined NATO and then the European Union. Others, such as Romania and Bulgaria, lagged behind. In multiethnic Yugoslavia, the collapse of communism and the onset of a disastrous civil war broke the country apart. All these changes produced mixed results for ordinary folk.

Economic Shock Therapy in Russia

Politics and economics were closely intertwined in Russia after the dissolution of the Soviet Union (see Chapter 29). President Boris Yeltsin (pres. 1991–1999), his democratic supporters, and his economic ministers

wanted to create conditions that would prevent a return to communism and right the faltering economy. Following the example of Poland (see Chapter 29), and agreeing with neoliberal Western advisers who argued that a quick turn to free markets would speed economic growth, Russian reformers opted in January 1992 for liberalization at breakneck speed.

To implement the plan, the Russians abolished price controls on most consumer goods, with the exception of bread, vodka, oil, and public transportation. The government launched a rapid privatization program, selling formerly state-owned industries and agricultural concerns to private investors. As a result, thousands of factories and mines were turned over to new private companies. In an attempt to share the wealth privatization was expected to generate, each citizen received a voucher worth 10,000 rubles (about $22) to buy stock in these private companies. Ownership of these formerly public assets, however, usually remained in the hands of the old bosses—the managers and government officials from the Communist era—undermining the reformers' goal of worker participation.

President Yeltsin and his economic advisers believed that shock therapy would revive production and bring widespread prosperity. The results were quite different. Prices increased 250 percent on the very first day and kept on soaring, increasing by a factor of twenty-six in the course of 1992. At the same time, production fell a staggering 20 percent. Nor did the situation stabilize quickly. After 1995 inflation still raged, though at slower rates, and output continued to fall. According to most estimates, Russia produced from one-third to one-half less in 1996 than it had in 1991. The Russian economy crashed again in 1998 in the wake of Asia's financial crisis.

Rapid economic liberalization worked poorly in Russia for several reasons. Soviet industry had been highly monopolized and strongly tilted toward military goods. Production of many items had been concentrated in one or two gigantic factories or in interconnected combines. With privatization, these powerful state monopolies became powerful private monopolies that cut production and raised prices in order to maximize profits. Moreover, Yeltsin's government handed out enormous subsidies to corporate managers and bureaucrats, ostensibly to reinforce faltering firms and avoid bankruptcies, but also to buy political allegiance. New corporate leaders included criminals who intimidated would-be rivals in attempts to prevent the formation of competing businesses.

Rich and Poor in Postcommunist Russia   A woman sells knitted scarves in front of a department store window in Moscow in September 2005. The collapse of the Soviet Union and the use of shock therapy to reform the Russian economy created new poverty as well as new wealth. (Sovfoto/UIG via Getty Images)

Runaway inflation and poorly executed privatization brought a profound social revolution to Russia. The new capitalist elite—the so-called Oligarchs—acquired great wealth and power, while large numbers of people fell into abject poverty and the majority struggled to make ends meet. Managers, former Communist officials, and financiers who came out of the privatization process with large shares of the old state monopolies stood at the top. The Oligarchs, Yeltsin's main supporters, maintained control with corrupt business practices and rampant cronyism. The new elite held more wealth than ever before.

At the other extreme, the vast majority of people saw their savings become practically worthless. Pensions lost much of their value, living standards drastically declined, and many people sold their personal goods to survive. Under these conditions, effective representative government failed to develop, and many Russians came to equate democracy with the corruption, poverty, and national decline they experienced throughout the 1990s. Yeltsin became increasingly unpopular; only the backing of the Oligarchs kept him in power.

Russian Revival Under Vladimir Putin

This widespread disillusionment set the stage for the rise of Vladimir Putin (POO-tihn) (b. 1952), who was elected president as Yeltsin's chosen successor in 2000 and re-elected in a landslide in March 2004. A colonel in the secret police during the Communist era, Putin maintained relatively liberal economic policies but re-established semi-authoritarian political rule. Critics labeled Putin's system an "imitation democracy," and indeed a façade of democratic institutions masked authoritarian rule from above in postcommunist Russia.[1] Putin's government maintained control with rigged elections, weak parliamentary rule, the intimidation of political opponents, and the distribution of state-owned public assets to win support of the new elite. Yet Putin's argument that the transition to free markets required strong political rule to control corruption and prevent a collapse into complete chaos resonated with ordinary Russians worried about the disintegration of the Communist state. The president enjoyed strong popular support, at least in the first years of his rule.

Putin's government combined authoritarian politics with economic reform. The regime clamped down on the excesses of the Oligarchs, lowered corporate and business taxes, and re-established some government control over key industries. Such reforms—aided greatly by high world prices for oil and natural gas, Russia's most important exports—led to a decade of economic expansion, encouraging the growth of a new middle class. In 2008, however, the global financial crisis and a rapid drop in the price of oil caused a downturn, and the Russian stock market collapsed. The government initiated a $200 billion rescue plan, and the economy stabilized and returned to modest growth in 2010.

During his first two terms as president, Putin's domestic and foreign policies proved immensely popular with a majority of Russians. His housing, education, and health-care reforms significantly improved living

Vladimir Putin on Vacation in 2009 After two terms as Russian president (2000–2008), Putin served as prime minister for four years before returning to the presidency in 2012. Putin's high approval ratings were due in part to his carefully crafted image of strength and manliness. (Alexsey Druginyn/AFP/Getty Images)

standards. Putin repeatedly evoked the glories of Russian history, expressed pride in the accomplishments of the Soviet Union, and downplayed the abuses of the Stalinist system; he thus capitalized on popular feelings of Russian patriotism. In addition, the Russian president centralized power in the Kremlin, increased military spending, and expanded the secret police. Putin's carefully crafted manly image and his forceful international diplomacy soothed the country's injured pride and symbolized its national revival.

In foreign relations, the president generally championed assertive anti-Western policies in an attempt to bolster Russia's status as a great Eurasian power and world player. (See "Evaluating the Evidence 30.1: President Putin on Global Security," at right). Putin forcefully opposed the expansion of NATO into the former East Bloc and regularly challenged U.S. and NATO foreign policy goals. In the Syrian civil war that broke out in 2011, for example, Russian backing of Syrian president Bashar al-Assad flew in the face of U.S. attempts to depose him. Putin's support in summer 2015 for a deal to limit Iran's nuclear capabilities marked a

rare moment of Russian cooperation with the United States, the EU, and the United Nations.

Putin's Russia has taken an aggressive and at times interventionist stance toward the Commonwealth of Independent States, a loose confederation of most of the former Soviet republics (Map 30.1). The annexation of the Crimea in 2014 and support for insurrectionist pro-Russian rebels in eastern Ukraine are only the latest examples.

Putin's government moved decisively to limit political opposition at home. The 2003 arrest and imprisonment for tax evasion and fraud of the corrupt oil billionaire Mikhail Khodorkovsky, an Oligarch who had openly supported opposition parties, showed early on that Putin and his United Russia Party would use state powers to stifle dissent. Though the Russian constitution guarantees freedom of the press, the government cracked down on the independent media. Using a variety of tactics, officials and pro-government businessmen influenced news reports and intimidated critical journalists. The suspicious murder in 2006 of journalist Anna Politkovskaya, a prominent critic of the government's human rights abuses and its war in Chechnya, reinforced Western worries that the country was returning to Soviet-style press censorship.

Putin stepped down when his term limits expired in 2008. His handpicked successor, Dmitry Medvedev (mehd-VEHD-yehf) (b. 1965), easily won election that year and then appointed Putin prime minister, leading observers to believe that the former president was still the dominant figure. This suspicion was confirmed when Putin won the presidential election of March 2012 with over 60 percent of the vote. International observers agreed that the election itself was democratic, but reported irregularities during the vote-counting process. Some fifteen thousand protesters marched through downtown Moscow to protest election fraud and the authoritarian aspects of Putin's rule, and demonstrations accompanied the president's inauguration that May.

Tensions between political centralization and openness continue to define Russia's difficult road away from communism. On one hand, Putin's return to the presidency seemed to reinforce Russia's system of authoritarian central control. On the other, the fact that mass assemblies and marches against the president took place with relatively little repression attests to some degree of political openness and new limits on Russian state power in the twenty-first century.

Coping with Change in the Former East Bloc

Developments in the former East Bloc paralleled those in Russia in important ways. The former satellites worked to replace state planning and socialism with market mechanisms and private property. Western-style electoral politics also took hold.

President Putin on Global Security

In this wide-ranging speech, delivered to representatives of over forty nations at the Munich Conference on Security Policy in 2007, Russian president Vladimir Putin explained his views on achieving global security. He attacked the militarization of outer space, the expansion of NATO into former East Bloc countries, and unlimited nuclear proliferation — all key elements of Russian foreign policy after communism — but reserved his sternest comments for U.S. actions in what he called a "unipolar world."

What is a unipolar world? However one might embellish this term, at the end of the day it . . . is [a] world in which there is one master, one sovereign. And at the end of the day this is pernicious not only for all those within this system, but also for the sovereign itself because it destroys itself from within. . . .

I consider that the unipolar model is not only unacceptable but also impossible in today's world. . . . The model itself is flawed because at its basis there is and can be no moral foundations for modern civilization. . . .

Today we are witnessing an almost uncontained hyper use of force — military force — in international relations, force that is plunging the world into an abyss of permanent conflicts. As a result we do not have sufficient strength to find a comprehensive solution to any one of these conflicts. Finding a political settlement also becomes impossible.

We are seeing a greater and greater disdain for the basic principles of international law. And independent legal norms are, as a matter of fact, coming increasingly closer to one state's legal system. One state and, of course, first and foremost the United States, has overstepped its national borders in every way. This is visible in the economic, political, cultural and educational policies it imposes on other nations. Well, who likes this? Who is happy about this? . . .

But do we have the means to counter these threats [of authoritarian regimes and the proliferation of weapons of mass destruction]? Certainly we do. It is sufficient to look at recent history. Did not our country have a peaceful transition to democracy? Indeed, we witnessed a peaceful transformation of the Soviet regime — a peaceful transformation! And what a regime! With what a number of weapons, including nuclear weapons! Why should we start bombing and shooting now at every available opportunity? Is it the case when without the threat of mutual destruction we do not have enough political culture, respect for democratic values and for the law? . . .

The use of force can only be considered legitimate if the decision is sanctioned by the UN. And we do not need to substitute NATO or the EU for the UN. When the UN will truly unite the forces of the international community and can really react to events in various countries, when we will leave behind this disdain for international law, then the situation will be able to change. Otherwise the situation will simply result in a dead end, and the number of serious mistakes will be multiplied. . . .

The stones and concrete blocks of the Berlin Wall have long been distributed as souvenirs. But we should not forget that the fall of the Berlin Wall was possible thanks to a historic choice — one that was also made by our people, the people of Russia — a choice in favour of democracy, freedom, openness and a sincere partnership with all the members of the big European family.

And now they are trying to impose new dividing lines and walls on us — these walls may be virtual but they are nevertheless dividing, ones that cut through our continent. And is it possible that we will once again require many years and decades, as well as several generations of politicians, to dissemble and dismantle these new walls?

EVALUATE THE EVIDENCE

1. Putin's speech often seems overly general or vague. Exactly which U.S. actions draw his concern, and why would he worry about them?
2. How do Putin's words reflect the diminished stature of Russia in global affairs after the end of the Cold War? Why does he claim that "new walls" are being built between Russia and the West?

Source: Global Research, http://www.globalresearch.ca/the
-universal-indivisible-character-of-global-security/4741.

New leaders across the former East Bloc faced similar economic problems: how to restructure Communist economic systems and move state-owned businesses and property into private hands. Under Soviet-style communism, central planners determined production and distribution goals and often set wage and price controls; now former East Bloc countries would adopt market-based economic systems. In addition, industries, businesses, and farms, considered the "people's property" and managed by the state in the name of the entire population, would now be privatized.

The methods of restructuring and privatization varied from country to country. Poland's new leaders turned to "shock therapy," the most rapid and comprehensive form of economic transformation, advocated by neoliberal Western institutions, including the International Monetary Fund and the World Bank. Starting in 1990, the Poles liberalized prices and trade policies,

Boundary of the
Soviet Union, 1991

BELARUS Member of the
CIS, 1991

ARCTIC
OCEAN

N
W   E
S

20°E   40°E   60°E   80°E   100°E

**Conflicts in
the Caucasus**

RUSSIAN FEDERATION

ABKHAZIA

Declared independence
1991; ongoing war with
Russia

CHECHNYA
• Grozny

*Black
Sea*

Breakaway republic
established 2008

SOUTH
OSSETIA

DAGESTAN

42°N

GEORGIA
• Tblisi

AJARIA

☐ Ongoing
conflict

TURKEY

42°E   44°E   46°E

ARMENIA

AZER.

NORWAY   SWEDEN

FINLAND

*Baltic
Sea*   • Tallinn

ESTONIA   • St. Petersburg

(RUS.
FED.)   • Riga
LATVIA
LITHUANIA
⊛ Vilnius

**RUSSIAN
FEDERATION**

POLAND   • Minsk

BELARUS

Volga R.   ⊛ Moscow

Ob R.

Kama R.

Irtysh R.

60°N

UKRAINE   • Chernobyl
• Kiev

MONGOLIA

MOLDOVA

ROMANIA ⊛   • Chisinau

Volga R.

Ural R.

⊛ Astana
(since 1998)

CRIMEA

Black Sea

See inset
map

GEORGIA
• Tblisi

*Caspian
Sea*

KAZAKHSTAN

*Lake
Balkhash*

Almaty
(to 1997) ⊛

CHINA

TURKEY

ARMENIA
Yerevan ⊛   • Baku

*Aral
Sea*

UZBEKISTAN

Bishkek •

KYRGYZSTAN

Tashkent •

AZERBAIJAN

0   100   200 miles

0   100   200 kilometers

CYPRUS

SYRIA

LEBANON

IRAQ

TURKMENISTAN
⊛ Ashgabat

IRAN

Dushanbe •   **TAJIKISTAN**

AFGHANISTAN

MAP 30.1 Russia and the Successor States, 1991–2015   After the failure of an attempt in August 1991 to depose Gorbachev, an anticommunist revolution swept the Soviet Union. The republics that formed the Soviet Union each declared their sovereignty and independence, with Russia, under President Boris Yeltsin, being the largest. Eleven of the fourteen republics then joined with Russia to form a loose confederation called the Commonwealth of Independent States, but the integrated economy of the Soviet Union dissolved into separate national economies, each with its own goals and policies. Conflict continued to simmer over these goals and policies, as evidenced by the ongoing civil war in Chechnya, the struggle between Russia and Georgia over South Ossetia, the Russian annexation of the Crimea, and the Ukrainian separatist movement.

raised taxes, cut spending to reduce budget deficits, and quickly sold state-owned industries to private investors. As they would in Russia a few years later, these radical moves at first brought high inflation and a rapid decline in living standards, which generated public protests and strikes. But because the plan had the West's approval, Poland received Western financial support that eased the pain of transition. By the end of the decade, the country had one of the strongest economies in the former East Bloc.

Other countries followed alternate paths. Czechoslovakia took a more gradual approach. As in Russia, the Czechoslovak state issued vouchers to its citizens, which they could use to bid for shares in privatized

companies. In Slovenia, one of the countries carved out of the former Yugoslavia, privatization included the transfer of up to 60 percent of company ownership to employees. In Estonia, reformers experimented with employee ownership, vouchers, and worker cooperatives. Compared to Poland's approach, privatization in all three countries was slower, continued more practices from the Communist past, and caused less social disruption.

Economic growth in the former Communist countries was varied, but most observers agreed that Poland, the Czech Republic, and Hungary were the most successful. Each met the critical challenge of economic reconstruction more successfully than did Russia, and

1024

each could claim to be the economic leader in the former East Bloc, depending on the criteria selected. The reasons for these successes included considerable experience with limited market reforms before 1989, flexibility and lack of dogmatism in government policy, and an enthusiastic embrace of capitalism by a new entrepreneurial class. In its first five years of reform, Poland created twice as many new businesses as did Russia in a comparable period, despite having only a quarter of Russia's population.

Poland, the Czech Republic, and Hungary also did far better than Russia in creating new civic institutions, legal systems, and independent media outlets that reinforced political freedom and national revival. Lech Wałęsa in Poland and Václav Havel in Czechoslovakia were elected presidents of their countries and proved as remarkable in power as in opposition (see Chapter 29). After Czechoslovakia's Velvet Revolution in 1989, the Czechoslovak parliament accepted a "velvet divorce" in 1993, when Slovakian nationalists wanted to break off and form their own state, creating the separate Czech and Slovak Republics. Above all, and in sharp contrast to Russia, the popular goal of adopting the liberal democratic values of western Europe reinforced political moderation and compromise. In 1999 Poland, Hungary, and the Czech Republic were accepted into NATO, and in 2004 they and Slovakia gained admission to the European Union (EU) (see page 1029).

Romania and Bulgaria lagged behind in the postcommunist transition. Western traditions were weaker there, and both countries were poorer than their more successful neighbors. Romania and Bulgaria did make progress after 2000, however, and joined NATO in 2004 and the EU in 2007.

The social consequences of rebuilding the former East Bloc were similar to those in Russia, though people were generally spared the widespread shortages and misery that characterized Russia in the 1990s. Ordinary citizens and the elderly were once again the big losers, while the young and former Communist Party members were the big winners. Inequalities between richer and poorer regions also increased. Capital cities such as Warsaw, Prague, and Budapest concentrated wealth, power, and opportunity as never before, while provincial centers stagnated and old industrial areas declined. Crime, corruption, and gangsterism increased in both the streets and the executive suites.

Though few former East Bloc residents wanted to return to communism, some expressed longings for the stability of the old system. They missed the guaranteed jobs and generous social benefits provided by the Communist state, and they found the individualism and competitiveness of capitalism cold and difficult. One Russian woman living on a pension of $448 a month in 2003 summed up the dilemma: "What we want is for our life to be as easy as it was in the Soviet Union, with the guarantee of a good, stable future and low prices—and at the same time this freedom that did not exist before."[2]

The question of whether or how to punish former Communist leaders who had committed political crimes or abused human rights emerged as a pressing issue in the former East Bloc. Germany tried major offenders and opened the records of the East German secret police (the Stasi) to the public, and by 1996 more than a million former residents had asked to see their files.[3] Other countries designed various means to deal with former Communist elites who might have committed crimes, with right-wing leaders generally taking a more punitive stand. The search for fair solutions proceeded slowly and with much controversy, a reminder of the troubling legacies of communism and the Cold War.

Tragedy in Yugoslavia

The great postcommunist tragedy occurred in Yugoslavia, which under Josip Broz Tito had been a federation of republics under centralized Communist rule (see Chapter 28). After Tito's death in 1980, power passed increasingly to the sister republics, which encouraged a revival of centuries-old regional and ethnic conflicts that were exacerbated by charges of ethnically inspired massacres during World War II and a dramatic economic decline in the mid-1980s.

The revolutions of 1989 accelerated the breakup of Yugoslavia. Serbian president Slobodan Milošević (1941–2006), a former Communist bureaucrat, wished to strengthen the federation's centralized government under Serbian control. In 1989 Milošević (mee-LOH-sheh-veech) severely limited self-rule in the Serbian province of Kosovo, where ethnic Albanians constituted the overwhelming majority, but which held a medieval battleground that he claimed was sacred to Serbian identity. In 1990 Milošević supported calls to grab land from other republics and unite all Serbs, regardless of where they lived, in a "greater Serbia" (which included Kosovo). Milošević's moves strengthened the cause of national separatism in the federation, and in June 1991 relatively wealthy Slovenia and Croatia declared their independence. Milošević ordered the Yugoslavian federal army to invade both areas to assert Serbian control. The Serbs were quickly repulsed in Slovenia, but managed to take about 30 percent of Croatia.

In 1992 the civil war spread to Bosnia-Herzegovina, which had also declared its independence. Serbs—about 30 percent of that region's population—refused to live under the more numerous Bosnian Muslims, or Bosniaks (Map 30.2). Yugoslavia had once been a tolerant and largely successful multiethnic state with different groups living side by side and often intermarrying. The new goal of the armed factions in the Bosnian civil war was

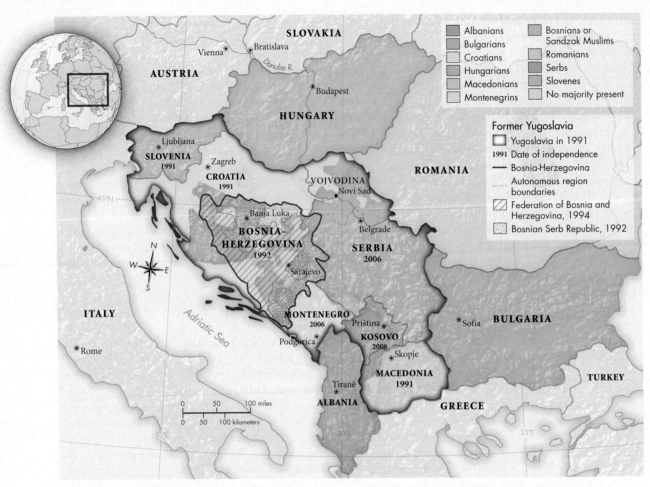

MAP 30.2 The Breakup of Yugoslavia, 1991–2006 Yugoslavia had the most ethnically diverse population in eastern Europe. The republic of Croatia had substantial Serbian and Muslim minorities. Bosnia-Herzegovina had large Muslim, Serbian, and Croatian populations, none of which had a majority. In June 1991 Serbia's brutal effort to seize territory and unite all Serbs in a single state brought a tragic civil war.

ethnic cleansing: the attempt to establish ethnically homogeneous territories by intimidation, forced deportation, and killing. The Yugoslavian army and irregular militias attempted to "cleanse" the territory of its non-Serb residents, unleashing ruthless brutality, with murder, rape, destruction, and the herding of refugees into concentration camps. Before the fighting in Bosnia ended, some three hundred thousand people were dead, and millions had been forced to flee their homes.

While appalling scenes of horror not seen in Europe since the Holocaust shocked the world, the Western nations had difficulty formulating an effective, unified response. The turning point came in July 1995 when Bosnian Serbs overran Srebrenica—a Muslim city previously declared a United Nations safe area. Serb forces killed about eight thousand of the city's Bosniak civilians, primarily men and boys. Public outrage prompted NATO to bomb Bosnian Serb military targets intensively, and the Croatian army drove all the Serbs from Croatia. In November 1995 President Bill Clinton helped the warring sides hammer out a complicated accord that gave Bosnian Serbs about 49 percent of Bosnia and gave Bosniaks and

the Roman Catholic Bosnian Croats the rest. Troops from NATO countries patrolled Bosnia to keep the peace; by 2013 only one thousand remained, suggesting that the situation had significantly improved.

The Kosovo Albanians, who hoped to establish self-rule, gained nothing from the Bosnian agreement. Frustrated Kosovar militants formed the Kosovo Liberation Army (KLA) and began to fight for independence. Serbian repression of the Kosovars increased, and in 1998 Serbian forces attacked both KLA guerrillas and unarmed villagers, displacing 250,000 people.

When Milošević refused to withdraw Serbian militias from Kosovo and accept self-government (but not independence) for Kosovo, NATO began bombing Serbia in March 1999. Serbian paramilitary forces responded by driving about 865,000 Albanian Kosovars into exile. NATO redoubled its destructive bombing campaign, which eventually forced Milošević to withdraw and allowed the Kosovars to regain their homeland. A United Nations and NATO peacekeeping force occupied Kosovo, ending ten years of Yugoslavian civil wars. Although U.S.-led NATO intervention finally

Srebrenica Refugees   More than 2,300 Bosnian Muslims packed into NATO trucks to flee the Serbian encirclement of Srebrenica in the spring of 1995. That July, the Serbian army massacred approximately 8,000 civilians in the city, and outraged public opinion in western Europe and North America finally led to decisive intervention against Serbia. In early 2016 twelve of the Serbian military leaders believed responsible were still on trial for crimes against humanity at the United Nations International Criminal Tribunal; eighty had been sentenced by the international court. (Michel Euler/AP Photo/AP Images)

brought an end to the conflict, the failure to take a stronger stand in the early years led to widespread and unnecessary suffering in the former Yugoslavia.

The war-weary and impoverished Serbs eventually voted the still-defiant Milošević out of office, and in July 2001 a new pro-Western Serbian government turned him over to a war crimes tribunal in the Netherlands to stand trial for crimes against humanity. After blustering his way through the initial stages of his trial, Milošević died in 2006 before the proceedings were complete. In 2008, after eight years of administration by the United Nations and NATO peacekeeping forces, the Republic of Kosovo declared its independence from Serbia. The United States and most states of the European Union recognized the declaration. Serbia and Russia did not, and the long-term status of this troubled emerging state remained uncertain.

Instability in the Former Soviet Republics

The collapse of the Soviet Union led to the establishment of the Russian Federation and fourteen other newly independent republics and brought major changes to east-central Europe and south-central Asia (see Map 30.1). In many ways, the transformation of this vast and diverse region paralleled the experience of the former East Bloc countries and Russia itself (see above). Though most of the fourteen new republics, which included almost one-half of the former Soviet Union's total population, adopted some sort of liberal market capitalism, political reforms varied broadly. In the Baltic republics, where Gorbachev's perestroika had quickly encouraged powerful separatist movements, reformers established working democratic government. While Ukrainians

struggled to construct a working democratic system, elsewhere—in Belarus, Kazakhstan and the other Central Asian republics, and the new republics in the Caucasus—systems of "imitation democracy" and outright authoritarian rule took hold.

Though Putin encouraged the former Soviet republics to join the Commonwealth of Independent States, a loose confederation dominated by Russia that supposedly represented regional common interests, stability and agreement proved elusive. Popular protests and revolts challenged local politicians and Russian interests alike. In Georgia, the so-called Rose Revolution (November 2003) brought a pro-Western, pro-NATO leader to power. In Ukraine, the Orange Revolution (November 2004–January 2005) challenged the results of a national election and expressed popular nationalist desires for more distance from Russia. Similar **Color Revolutions** in Belarus, Kyrgyzstan, and Moldova exemplified the unpredictable path toward democratization in the new republics that bordered the powerful Russian Federation.

Putin took an aggressive and at times interventionist stance toward anti-Russian revolt in the Commonwealth of Independent States and the Russian borderlands. Conflict has been particularly intense in the oil-rich Caucasus, where an unstable combination of nationalist separatism and ethnic and religious tensions challenges Russian dominance. Since the breakup of the Soviet Union, Russian troops have repeatedly invaded Chechnya (CHEHCH-nyuh), a tiny Muslim republic with

■ **ethnic cleansing** The attempt to establish ethnically homogeneous territories by intimidation, forced deportation, and killing.

■ **Color Revolutions** A series of popular revolts and insurrections that challenged regional politicians and Russian interests in the former Soviet republics during the first decade of the twenty-first century.

1 million inhabitants on Russia's southern border that declared its independence in 1991. Despite ultimate Russian victory in the Chechen wars, the cost of the conflict was high. Thousands lost their lives, and both sides committed serious human rights abuses. Moscow declared an end to military operations in April 2009, but Chechen insurgents, inspired by nationalism and Islamic radicalism, continued to fight. Russia also intervened in the independent state of Georgia, which won independence when the Soviet Union collapsed in 1991. Russian troops also invaded Georgia in 2008 to support a separatist movement in South Ossetia (ah-SEE-shuh), which eventually established a breakaway independent republic recognized only by Russia and a handful of small states.

Revolution broke out again in Ukraine in February 2014, and when popular protests brought down the pro-Russian government, Putin's response was rapid and radically interventionist. In late February Russian troops marched into Crimea, a strategically valuable peninsula in the Black Sea where pro-Russian sentiment ran high. The territory, with a major naval base in the city of Sevastopol and large reserves of oil and natural gas, was incorporated into the Russian Federation. Then, in response to the anti-Russian policies of the new Ukrainian government, in April 2014 a group of armed rebels took over the regional capital Donetsk and other cities in eastern Ukraine and declared the establishment of the separatist, pro-Russian Donetsk and Luhansk "People's Republics" (see Map 30.1).

A full-scale military assault by Ukrainian government troops failed to push back or defeat the separatist forces. According to Ukrainian and U.S. sources, only direct Russian intervention, including substantial supplies of weaponry and troops, prevented the defeat of the insurrection. In response, the United States and the European Union placed economic sanctions on Russia, and since February 2015 a shaky ceasefire has dampened hostilities in eastern Ukraine. Yet the outcome of the conflict remains uncertain, a telling example of the way great power interests continue to create instability in the former Soviet republics.

The New Global System

FOCUS QUESTION *How did globalization affect European life and society?*

Contemporary observers often assert that the world has entered a new era of **globalization**. Such assertions do not mean that there were never international connections before. Europe has long had close—sometimes productive, sometimes destructive—ties to other parts of the world. Yet new global relationships and increasing interdependence did emerge in the last decades of the twentieth century.

First, the growth of multinational corporations restructured national economies on a global scale. Second, an array of international governing bodies, such as the European Union, the United Nations, the World Trade Organization, and a number of nongovernmental organizations (or NGOs) increasingly set policies that challenged the autonomy of traditional nation-states. Finally, the expansion and ready availability of highly efficient computer and media technologies led to ever-faster exchanges of information and entertainment around the world. Taken together, these global transformations had a remarkable impact, both positive and negative, on many aspects of Western society.

The Global Economy

Though large business interests had long profited from international trade and investment, multinational corporations grew and flourished in a world economy increasingly organized around policies of free-market neoliberalism, which relaxed barriers to international trade (see Chapter 29). Multinational corporations built global systems of production and distribution that generated unprecedented wealth and generally escaped the control of regulators and politicians acting on the national level.

Conglomerates such as Siemens and Vivendi exemplified this business model. Siemens, with international headquarters in Berlin and Munich and offices around the globe, is one of the world's largest engineering companies, with vast holdings in energy, construction, health care, financial services, and industrial production. Vivendi, an extensive media and telecommunications company headquartered in Paris, controls a vast international network of producers and products, including music and film, publishing, television broadcasting, pay-TV, Internet services, and video games.

The development of sophisticated personal computer technologies and the Internet at the end of the twentieth century, coupled with the deregulation of national and international financial systems, further encouraged the growth of international trade. The ability to rapidly exchange information and capital meant that economic activity was no longer centered on national banks or stock exchanges, but rather flowed quickly across international borders. Large cities like London, Moscow, New York, and Hong Kong became global centers of banking, trade, and financial services. The influence of financial and insurance companies, communications conglomerates, and energy and legal firms headquartered in these global cities extended far beyond the borders of the traditional nation-state.

At the same time, the close connections between national economies also made the entire world vulnerable to economic panics and downturns. In 1997 a banking crisis in Thailand spread to Indonesia, South Korea,

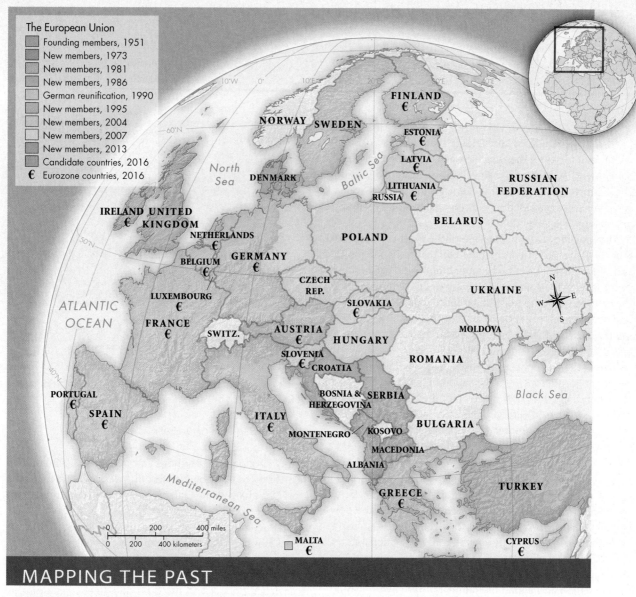

The European Union
- Founding members, 1951
- New members, 1973
- New members, 1981
- New members, 1986
- German reunification, 1990
- New members, 1995
- New members, 2004
- New members, 2007
- New members, 2013
- Candidate countries, 2016
- € Eurozone countries, 2016

MAPPING THE PAST

MAP 30.3 The European Union, 2016

No longer divided by ideological competition and the Cold War, much of today's Europe has banded together in a European Union that facilitates the open movement of people, jobs, and currency across national borders.

ANALYZING THE MAP Trace the expansion of membership from its initial founding as the European Economic Union to today. How would you characterize the most recent members? Whose membership is still pending?

CONNECTIONS Which countries are and are not part of the Eurozone, and what does this suggest about how successful the European Union has been in adopting the euro?

---

and Japan and then echoed around the world. The resulting slump in oil and gas prices hit Russia especially hard, leading to high inflation, bank failures, and the collapse of the Russian stock market. The crisis then spread to Latin America, plunging most countries there into a severe economic downturn. A decade later, a global recession triggered by a crisis in the U.S. housing market and financial system created the worst worldwide economic crisis since the Great Depression of the 1930s (see page 1049).

The New European Union

Global economic pressures encouraged the expansion and consolidation of the European Common Market, which in 1993 proudly rechristened itself the **European Union (EU)** (Map 30.3). The EU added the free

- **globalization** The emergence of a freer, more technologically connected global economy, accompanied by a worldwide exchange of cultural, political, and religious ideas.

- **European Union (EU)** The economic, cultural, and political alliance of twenty-eight European nations.

LIVING IN THE PAST
The Euro

On January 1, 2002, the residents of many European Union countries exchanged their familiar national currencies for the euro, the newly approved coins and banknotes that signaled the arrival of the EU monetary union. The German deutschmark, the French franc, the Italian lira, and many others passed into history, collectibles, perhaps, but no longer legal tender.

The move to the euro was one of the most controversial aspects of the Maastricht Treaty of 1991 that reshaped the EU and laid out a timetable for this monetary union. While some countries signed up, Britain, Denmark, and Sweden accepted the main terms of the treaty but refused to join the currency union (or Eurozone, the group of countries that use the new money). Citizens there rejected the euro, fearing its economic impact and its effects on national autonomy.

To join the Eurozone, a country had to maintain stringent economic conditions—low inflation, tight budgets, and small deficits. In 2016 only nineteen of the EU's twenty-eight member states used euros as their national currency. Though Latvia and Slovakia adopted the euro, other former East Bloc nations, such as Poland and Hungary (which joined the EU in 2004 and 2007), were excluded from the Eurozone and so remained something of second-class members.

The euro raised basic questions about a common European identity. What images could be portrayed on the new coins and bills that would do justice to both membership in a larger European community and the variety of national states that made up what was in fact a very diverse continent? The solution was ingenious. The front of the coins would show the denomination and a map of Europe, but the reverse would

A colorfully dressed anti-euro protester stands outside the British Houses of Parliament in June 2003. (Scott Barbour/Getty Images)

portray national images chosen by individual EU members. Thus the two-euro coin minted in Ireland features a traditional Celtic harp, while that made in Lithuania portrays a Teutonic knight on horseback. Banknotes, by contrast, would feature generic architectural images on both sides that looked real but were not, in order to prevent any national prejudice. Thus the arches on the five-euro note resemble a Roman viaduct; the bridge on the ten-euro note resembles a Renaissance bridge; and the glass and steel façade on the

The president of Cyprus withdraws the country's first euros on January 1, 2008, after the country formally adopted the euro as its official currency. (Petros Karadjias/AP Images)

A selection of euro bills (above). The reverse side of the Lithuanian (top) and the Greek (below) euro coins. (bills: © RTimages/ Shutterstock; Lithuanian euro coin: © Jjustas/Shutterstock; Greek euro coin: © MattiaATH/Shutterstock)

five-hundred-euro note resembles a modern urban office building. All are imaginary structures that look "European" but do not actually exist.

QUESTIONS FOR ANALYSIS

1. Why did the leaders of the European Union push for a common currency?
2. How do the images portrayed on euro coins and banknotes reflect the dilemmas of establishing a workable European identity?

movement of capital and services and eventually individuals across national borders to the existing free trade in goods. In addition, member states sought to create a monetary union in which all EU countries would share a single currency. Membership in the monetary union required states to meet strict financial criteria defined in the 1991 **Maastricht Treaty**, which also set legal standards and anticipated the development of common policies on defense and foreign affairs.

Western European elites and opinion makers generally supported the economic integration embodied in the Maastricht Treaty. They felt that membership requirements, which imposed financial discipline on national governments, would combat Europe's ongoing economic problems and viewed the establishment of a single European currency as an irreversible historic step toward basic political unity. This unity would allow Europe as a whole to regain its place in world politics and to deal with the United States as an equal.

Support for the Maastricht Treaty was hardly universal. Ordinary people, leftist political parties, and right-wing nationalists expressed considerable opposition to the new rules. Many people resented the EU's ever-growing bureaucracy in Brussels, which imposed common standards on everything from cheese production to day care, supposedly undermining national customs and local traditions. Moreover, increased unity meant yielding still more power to distant "Eurocrats" and political insiders, which limited national sovereignty and democratic control.

Above all, many citizens feared that the European Union would operate at their expense. Joining the monetary union required national governments to meet stringent fiscal standards, impose budget cuts, and contribute to the EU operating budget. The resulting reductions in health care and social benefits hit ordinary citizens and did little to reduce high unemployment. When put to the public for a vote, ratification of the Maastricht Treaty was usually very close. In France, for example, the treaty passed with just 50.1 percent of the vote. Even after the treaty was ratified, battles over budgets, benefits, and high unemployment continued throughout the EU in the 1990s.

Then in 2002, brand-new euros finally replaced the national currencies of all Eurozone countries. (See "Living in the Past: The Euro," at left.) The establishment of the European monetary union built confidence in member nations and increased their willingness to accept new members. On May 1, 2004, the European Union began admitting its former East Bloc neighbors. By 2016, with the recent admission of Croatia, the EU was home to about 500 million citizens in twenty-eight countries. It included most of the

■ **Maastricht Treaty** The basis for the formation of the European Union, which set financial and cultural standards for potential member states and defined criteria for membership in the monetary union.

former East Bloc and, with the Baltic nations, three republics of the former Soviet Union.

This rapid expansion underscored the need to reform the EU's unwieldy governing structure. In June 2004 a special commission presented a new EU constitution that created a president, a foreign minister, and a voting system weighted to reflect the populations of the different states. The proposed constitution moved toward a more centralized federal system, though each state retained veto power over taxation, social policy, foreign affairs, and other sensitive areas. After many contentious referendum campaigns across the continent, the constitution failed to win the unanimous support required to take effect. Ultimately, nationalist fears about losing sovereignty and cultural identity outweighed the perceived benefits of a more unified Europe. Fears that an unwieldy European Union would grow to include Ukraine, Georgia, and Muslim Turkey—countries with cultures and histories that were very different from those of western Europe—were particularly telling.

Though the constitution did not go into effect, the long postwar march toward greater European unity did not stop. In 2007 the rejected constitution was replaced with the Treaty of Lisbon. The new treaty kept many sections of the constitution, but further streamlined the EU bureaucracy and reformed its political structure. When the Treaty of Lisbon went into effect on December 1, 2009, after ratification by all EU states, it capped a remarkable fifty-year effort to unify what had been a deeply divided and war-torn continent.

Yet profound questions about the meaning of European unity and identity remained. Would the European Union expand as promised to include the postcommunist nations of the former Soviet Union, and if so, how could Muslim Turkey's long-standing application be ignored? Could a union of twenty-eight diverse countries have any real cohesion and common identity? Would the EU remain closely linked with the United States in NATO, or would it develop an independent defense policy? Could member states agree on an economic policy to master the stubborn recession that emerged in 2008 and the Greek debt crisis of 2015 and keep the nineteen-state Eurozone intact (see page 1050)? Would they be able to manage the refugee crisis that emerged in 2015? The EU struggled to shape institutions and policies to address these complicated issues.

Supranational Organizations

Beyond the European Union, the trend toward globalization empowered a variety of other supranational organizations that had tremendous reach. National governments still played the leading role in defining and implementing policy, but they increasingly had to take the policies of institutions such as the United Nations and the World Trade Organization into consideration.

The United Nations (UN), established in 1945 after World War II, remains an important player on the world stage. Representatives from all independent countries meet in the UN General Assembly in New York City to try to forge international agreements. UN agencies deal with issues such as world hunger and poverty, and the International Court of Justice in The Hague, Netherlands, hears cases that violate international law. The UN also sends troops in attempts to preserve peace between warring parties—as in Yugoslavia in the 1990s. While the smaller UN Security Council has broad powers, including the ability to impose sanctions to punish uncooperative states and even to endorse military action, its five permanent members—the United States, Russia, France, Great Britain, and China—can each veto resolutions introduced in that body. The predominance of the United States and western European powers on the Security Council has led some critics to accuse the UN of implementing Western neocolonial policies (see Chapter 28). Others argue that UN policies should never take precedence over national needs, and UN resolutions are at times ignored or downplayed.

A trio of nonprofit international financial institutions have also gained power in a globalizing world. Like the United Nations, the World Bank and the International Monetary Fund (IMF) were established in the years following World War II. Initially founded to help rebuild war-torn Europe, these organizations now provide loans to the developing world. Their funding comes primarily from donations from the United States and western Europe, and they typically extend loans on the condition that recipient countries adopt neoliberal economic reforms, including budget reduction, deregulation, and privatization. In the 1990s the World Bank and the IMF played especially active roles in shaping economic and social policy in the former East Bloc.

The third economic supranational, the **World Trade Organization (WTO)**, is one of the most powerful supranational financial institutions. It sets trade and tariff agreements for over 150 member countries, thus helping manage a large percentage of the world's import-export policies. Like the IMF and the World Bank, the WTO generally promotes neoliberal policies.

The rise of these institutions, which typically represent the shared interests of national governments, was paralleled by the emergence of a variety of **nongovernmental organizations (NGOs)**. Some NGOs act as lobbyists on specific issues; others conduct international programs and activities. Exemplary NGOs include Doctors Without Borders, a charitable organization of physicians headquartered in France; Greenpeace, an international environmental group; and Oxfam, a British-based group dedicated to alleviating famine, disease, and poverty in the developing world. Though financed by donations from governments and private citizens, NGOs' annual budgets can total hundreds of millions of dollars and their work can be quite extensive.

The Human Side of Globalization

Globalization transformed the lives of millions of people, as the technological changes associated with postindustrial society (see Chapter 29) remade workplaces and lifestyles around the world. Low labor costs in the industrializing world—including the former East Bloc, Latin America, and East Asia—encouraged corporations to outsource labor-intensive manufacturing jobs to these regions. Widespread adoption of neoliberal free-trade policies and low labor costs in developing countries made it less expensive to manufacture steel, automotive parts, computer components, and all manner of consumer goods in developing countries and then import them for sale in the West. In the 1990s China, with its low wages and rapidly growing industrial infrastructure, emerged as an economic powerhouse that supplied goods across the world—even as the West's industrial heartlands continued to decline. Under these conditions, a car made by Volkswagen could still be sold as a product of high-quality German engineering despite being assembled in Chattanooga, Tennessee, using steel imported from South Korea and computer chips made in Taiwan.

The outsourcing of manufacturing jobs dramatically changed the nature of work in western Europe and North America. In France in 1973, for example, some 40 percent of the employed population worked in industry—in mining, construction, manufacturing, and utilities. About 49 percent worked in services, including retail, hotels and restaurants, transportation, communications, financial and business services, and social and personal services. In 2004 only 24 percent of the French worked in industry, and a whopping 72 percent worked in services. The numbers varied country by country, yet across Europe the trend was clear: by 2005 only about one in three workers was still employed in the once-booming manufacturing sector.[4]

The deindustrialization of Europe established a multitiered society with winners and losers. At the top was a small, affluent group of experts, executives, and professionals—about one-quarter of the total population—who managed the new global enterprises. In the second, larger tier, the middle class struggled with stagnating incomes and a declining standard of living as once-well-paid industrial workers faced stubborn unemployment and cuts in both welfare and workplace benefits. Many were forced to take low-paying jobs in the retail service sector.

In the bottom tier—in some areas as much as a quarter of the population—a poorly paid underclass

Antiglobalization Activism   French protesters carry the figure of Ronald McDonald through the streets to protest the trial of José Bové, a prominent leader in campaigns against the human and environmental costs associated with globalization. Bové was accused of demolishing a McDonald's franchise in a small town in southern France. With its worldwide fast-food restaurants that pay little attention to local traditions, McDonald's has often been the target of antiglobalization protests. (Witt/Haley/Sipa)

performed the unskilled jobs of a postindustrial economy or were chronically unemployed. In western Europe and North America, inclusion in this lowest segment of society was often linked to race, ethnicity, and a lack of educational opportunity. Recently arrived immigrants had trouble finding jobs and often lived in unpleasant, hastily built housing, teetering on the edge of poverty. In London, unemployment rates among youths and particularly young black men soared above those of their white compatriots. Frustration over these conditions, coupled with anger at a police shooting, boiled over in immigrant neighborhoods across the city in August 2011, when angry youths rioted in the streets, burning buildings and looting stores.

Geographic contrasts further revealed the unequal aspects of globalization. Regions in Europe that had successfully shifted to a postindustrial economy, such as northern Italy and southern Germany and Austria, enjoyed prosperity. Lagging behind were regions historically dependent on heavy industry, such as the former East Bloc countries and the factory districts north

---

■ **World Trade Organization (WTO)** A powerful supranational financial institution that sets trade and tariff agreements for over 150 member countries and so helps manage a large percentage of the world's import-export policies. Like the IMF and the World Bank, the WTO promotes neoliberal policies around the world.

■ **nongovernmental organizations (NGOs)** Independent organizations with specific agendas, such as humanitarian aid or environmental protection, that conduct international programs and activities.

of London, or underdeveloped areas, such as rural sections of southern Italy, Spain, and Greece. In addition, a global north-south divide increasingly separated Europe and North America—both still affluent despite their economic problems—from the industrializing nations of Africa and Latin America. Though India, China, and other East Asian nations experienced solid growth, other industrializing nations struggled to overcome decades of underdevelopment.

The human costs of globalization resulted in new forms of global protest. Critics accused global corporations and financial groups of doing little to address problems caused by their activities, such as social inequality, pollution, and unfair labor practices. The Slow Food movement that began in Italy, for example, criticized American-style fast-food chains that proliferated in Europe and the world in the 1990s. Cooking with local products and traditional methods, followers argued, was healthier and kept jobs and profits in local neighborhoods. The fast-food giant McDonald's was often targeted as an example of the ills of corporate globalization. José Bové, a French farmer and antiglobalization activist, made world headlines by driving his truck through the windows of a McDonald's in a small French village to protest the use of hormone-fed beef and genetically modified foods as well as the reach of corporate capital.

The general tone of the antiglobalization movement was captured at the 1999 meeting of the WTO in Seattle, Washington. Tens of thousands of protesters from around the world, including environmentalists, consumer and antipoverty activists, and labor rights groups, marched in the streets and disrupted the meeting. Comparable demonstrations took place at later meetings of the WTO, the World Bank, and other supranational groups.

Similar feelings inspired the Occupy movement, which began in the United States in 2011 and quickly spread to over eighty countries. Under the slogan "We are the 99 percent," thousands of people camped out in (or "occupied") public places to protest the rapidly growing social inequality that divided a tiny wealthy elite (the "1 percent") from the vast majority of ordinary people. Though the diverse groups in the Occupy movement failed to mount a sustained and successful challenge to the public officials and business leaders who profited from globalization, their calls for greater social equality and democracy showed that the struggle for reform continued.

Life in the Digital Age

The growing sophistication of information technologies—a hallmark of the globalizing age—has had a profound and rapidly evolving effect on patterns of communications, commerce, and politics. As tiny digital microchips replaced bulky transistors and the Internet grew in scope and popularity, more and more people organized their everyday lives around the use of ever-smaller and more powerful high-tech devices.

Leisure-time pursuits were a case in point. The arrival of cable television, followed swiftly by DVDs and then online video streaming, enabled individuals to watch full-length movies or popular television shows on their personal computers or smartphones at any time and greatly diversified the options for home entertainment. Europe's once-powerful public broadcasting systems, such as the BBC, were forced to compete with a variety of private enterprises, including Netflix, a U.S. online video provider that entered the European media market in 2014. Music downloads and streaming audio files replaced compact discs, which themselves had replaced vinyl records and cassettes; digital cameras eliminated the need for expensive film; e-book readers, including Kindles and iPads, offered a handheld portable library; smartphone apps provided an apparently endless variety of conveniences and distractions.

Digitalization transformed familiar forms of communication in a few short decades. Many of these changes centered on the Internet, which began its rapid expansion around the globe in the late 1980s. In the first decade of the twenty-first century, the evolution of the cell phone into the smartphone, with its multimedia telecommunications features and more functions and power than the desktop computers of the previous decade, hastened the change. The growing popularity of Internet-based communication tools such as e-mail, text messaging, Facebook, Twitter, and other social media changed the way friends, families, and businesses kept in touch. Letter writing with pen and paper became a quaint relic of the past. Skype, first introduced in 2003, offered personal computer and smartphone users video telecommunications around the world. The old-fashioned "landline," connected to a stationary telephone, seemed ready to join the vinyl LP and the handwritten letter in the junk bin of history.

Entire industries were dramatically changed by the emergence of the Internet. With faster speeds and better online security came online shopping. People increasingly relied on the Internet to purchase goods from clothes to computers to groceries. Online file sharing of books and popular music transformed the publishing and music industries, while massive online retailers such as Amazon and eBay, which sell millions of goods across the globe without physical storefronts, transformed familiar retail systems.

The rapid growth of the Internet and social media raised complex questions related to personal privacy and politics. Governments and businesses used online tracking systems to amass an extraordinary amount of information on individuals and then monitor their political activities or target them with advertising. Privacy advocates worked with government regulators to shape laws that might preserve key elements of online privacy, and in general, rules were more stringent in Europe than in the United States.

The vast amount of information circulating on the Internet could also lead to the exposure of government and business secrets. The numerous materials posted online by the nonprofit organization WikiLeaks, dedicated to the publication of secret information and news leaks, documented numerous examples of government and corporate misconduct. The classified U.S. National Security Agency information leaked in 2013 by former CIA contractor Edward Snowden embarrassed U.S. diplomats and fueled further debates about Internet surveillance, national security, and privacy protection. (See "Individuals in Society: Edward Snowden," page 1036.) In addition, individuals could use smartphones and social media sites to organize protest campaigns. Facebook and Twitter, for example, helped mobilize demonstrators in Egypt during the Arab Spring (see page 1048) and allowed members of the Occupy movement to share news and shape strategy. A number of authoritarian states from North Korea to Iran to Cuba, recognizing the disruptive powers of the Internet, strictly limited online access.

Life in the Digital Age   Conference attendees examine a cutting-edge smartphone on display at the Mobile World Congress in Barcelona in 2014. The annual conference, which explores the impact of mobile information technologies on individuals and businesses, is the world's largest mobile trade fair and a telling example of the way digitalization has transformed everyday life. (Albert Llop/Anadolu Agency/Getty Images)

Ethnic Diversity in Contemporary Europe

FOCUS QUESTION *What are the main causes and effects of growing ethnic diversity in contemporary Europe?*

As the twenty-first century opened and ongoing globalization transformed European society and politics, Europeans witnessed the remaking of their ethnic communities. First, Europe experienced a remarkable decline in birthrates that seemed to predict a shrinking and aging population in the future. Second, the peaceful, wealthy European Union attracted rapidly growing numbers of refugees and immigrants from the former Soviet Union and East Bloc, North Africa, and the Middle East. The unexpected arrival of so many newcomers raised perplexing questions about ethnic diversity and the costs and benefits of multiculturalism.

The Prospect of Population Decline

In 2016 population rates were still growing rapidly in many poor countries but not in the world's industrialized nations. In 2000 families in developed countries had only 1.6 children on average; only in the United States did families have, almost exactly, the 2.1

children necessary to maintain a stable population. In Europe, where birthrates had been falling since the 1950s, national fertility rates ranged from 1.2 to 1.8 children per woman of childbearing age. By 2013 Italy and Ireland, once known for large Catholic families, had each achieved one of Europe's lowest birthrates—a mere 1.3 babies per woman. None of the twenty-eight countries in the EU had birthrates above 2.0; the average fertility rate was about 1.55 children per woman.[5]

If the current baby bust continues, the long-term consequences could be dramatic, though hardly predictable. At the least, Europe's population would decline and age. Projections for Germany are illustrative. Total German population, barring much greater immigration, would gradually decline from about 81 million in 2015 to just under 72 million around 2050. The number of people of working age would fall, and due to longer life spans, nearly a third of the population would be over sixty. Social security taxes paid by the shrinking labor force would need to soar to meet the skyrocketing costs of pensions and health care for seniors—a recipe for generational conflict. As the premier of Bavaria, Germany's biggest state, has warned, the prospect of demographic decline is a "ticking time bomb under our social welfare system and entire economy."[6]

Why, in times of peace, did Europeans fail to reproduce? Studies showed that European women and men in their twenties, thirties, and early forties still wanted two or even three children—like their parents. But

Edward Snowden

Edward Snowden — traitor or hero? When the former CIA operative leaked a trove of classified documents about American surveillance programs to the world press, he was praised by some, vilified by others, and ultimately indicted on espionage charges by the U.S. government.

Snowden perhaps seems an unlikely candidate for masterminding the biggest intelligence leak in history. Born in 1983, the gun-owning, political conservative never finished high school and took computer classes at a community college. In 2006 he got a job in information technology with the CIA. From 2009 to 2013 he worked as a contractor for the National Security Agency.

As a systems analyst with a high-level security clearance, Snowden had access to highly classified NSA materials. Over the years, he grew increasingly outraged by the extent of secret government surveillance. In contravention of NSA regulations, he began to copy files on a personal thumb drive and ultimately collected tens of thousands of top-secret documents from NSA archives.

In January 2013 a journalist working for the liberal British newspaper the *Guardian* and an American documentary film maker received e-mails from an anonymous source asking for an exchange of encrypted (highly encoded) information. "I am a senior member of the intelligence community," read the anonymous e-mail. "This won't be a waste of your time."* Enticed, they agreed to meet the source in a Hong Kong hotel. There Snowden disclosed his identity and handed over a selection of documents. Recognizing a scoop, the *Guardian* revealed the secret surveillance programs. Other media outlets pounced on the story, and Snowden's revelations became a global sensation.

The explosive news reports described extensive U.S. spy programs that shocked people around the world. The leaks revealed that the NSA had collected phone records from virtually every person in the United States and had misled the U.S. Congress about the extent of the surveillance. The agency had accessed the Internet servers of major telecommunications providers and could thus collect information about e-mail messages, Internet searches, and individual friends and contacts from Facebook and Google. The documents described programs that monitored the telephone calls of notable politicians in friendly nations. Chancellor Angela Merkel of Germany, a close ally of the United States, was infuriated to find out that the NSA had tapped her cell phone; so were the presidents of Mexico and Brazil, among others.

The response took many forms. Foreign leaders were dismayed by the extensive leaks from a major allied security service and by the pervasiveness of U.S. surveillance programs. Conservative pundits and U.S. officials condemned Snowden, arguing that the leaked materials revealed secret antiterrorism operations and could even endanger the lives of agents in the field. As President Barack Obama put it, "If any

Former NSA contractor and antisurveillance whistleblower Edward Snowden receives the 2015 Bjornson Prize from the Norwegian Academy of Literature and Freedom of Expression. (© SVEIN OVE EKORNESVAAG/epa/Corbis)

individual who objects to government policy can take it in their own hands to publicly disclose classified information, then we will not be able to keep our people safe, or conduct foreign policy."†

Proponents of civil liberties, defenders of the right to online privacy, and critics of U.S. foreign policy nonetheless welcomed Snowden's revelations. "It is time for President Obama to offer clemency to Edward Snowden, the courageous U.S. citizen who revealed the Orwellian reach of the National Security Agency's sweeping surveillance of Americans," wrote a liberal commentator in the *Washington Post*. "His actions may have broken the law, but his act . . . did the nation a great service."‡

Fearing for his freedom, Snowden went underground in Hong Kong. Several weeks later, he surfaced in Russia, where he received an offer of temporary asylum. Snowden now lives somewhere around Moscow, where he continues to comment on electronic surveillance and privacy rights.

QUESTIONS FOR ANALYSIS

1. Why did the arrival of the digital age lead to heated debates about the individual's right to privacy?
2. Where would you draw the line between the need for online privacy and the government's need to collect personal information in order to protect society from terrorist attacks? Where does Snowden fit in?

* Luke Harding, "How Edward Snowden Went from Loyal NSA Contractor to Whistleblower," *Guardian*, February 1, 2014, http://www.theguardian.com /world/2014/feb/01/edward-snowden-intelligence-leak-nsa-contractor-extract.
† Josh Gerstein, "Obama Hits Snowden over NSA Leaks," *Politico*, January 17, 2014, http://www.politico.com/story/2014/01/barack-obama-edward-snowden-nsa -leaks-102316.
‡ Katrina vanden Heuval, "Justice for Edward Snowden," *Washington Post*, October 28, 2014.

unlike their parents, young couples did not realize their ideal family size. Many women postponed the birth of their first child into their thirties in order to finish their education and establish careers. Then, finding that balancing a child and a career was more difficult than anticipated, new mothers tended to postpone and eventually forgo having a second child. The better educated and the more economically successful a woman was, the more likely she was to have just one child or no children at all. In addition, the uneven, uninspiring European economic conditions since the mid-1970s played a role. High unemployment fell heavily on young people, especially after the recession of 2008, convincing youths to delay settling down and having children.

In 2013 some population experts concluded that European birthrates had stablized, though women continued to postpone having children. Moreover, the frightening implications of dramatic population decline emerged as a major public issue. Opinion leaders, politicians, and the media started to advocate for larger families and propose policies to provide more support for families with children. Europeans may yet respond with enough vigor to reverse their population decline and avoid societal crisis.

Changing Immigration Flows

As European demographic vitality waned in the 1990s, a surge of migrants from the former Soviet Bloc, Africa, and most recently the Middle East headed for western Europe. Some migrants entered the European Union legally, with proper documentation, but increasing numbers were smuggled in past beefed-up border patrols. Large-scale immigration, both documented and undocumented, emerged as a critical and controversial issue.

Historically a source rather than a destination of immigrants, western Europe saw rising numbers of immigrants in postcolonial population movements beginning in the 1950s, augmented by the influx of manual laborers in its boom years from about 1960 until about 1973 (see Chapter 28). A new and different surge of migration into western Europe began in the 1990s. The collapse of communism in the East Bloc and savage civil wars in Yugoslavia drove hundreds of thousands of refugees westward. Equally brutal conflicts in Somalia and Rwanda, the U.S.-led invasions of Afghanistan and Iraq, and then the turmoil in North Africa and the Middle East unleashed by the "Arab Spring," brought hundreds of thousands more. In 2013 immigration to the EU from nonmember countries topped 1.7 million people.

Undocumented or irregular immigration into the European Union also exploded. The number of irregular migrants is difficult to quantify, but in 2014 approximately 260,000 non-European nationals were turned back at Europe's borders, while almost 550,000 irregular migrants already lived in the EU. That same year, about 275,000 migrants entered Europe irregularly, an increase of almost 140 percent from 2013.[7]

Why was Europe such an attractive destination for non-European migrants, regular and irregular? First, even with all the economic problems of western Europe, economic opportunity undoubtedly was a major attraction for immigrants. Germans, for example, earned on average three and a half times more than neighboring Poles, who in turn earned much more than people farther east and in North Africa. In 1998 most European Union states abolished all border controls; entrance into one country allowed for unimpeded travel almost anywhere (though Ireland and the United Kingdom opted out of this agreement). This meant that irregular migrants could enter across the relatively lax borders of Greece and south-central Europe, and then move north across the continent in search of refuge and jobs.

Second, EU immigration policy offered migrants the possibility of acquiring asylum status, if they could demonstrate that they faced severe persecution, based on race, nationality, religion, political belief, or membership in a specific social group in their home countries. Many migrants turned to Europe as they fled civil wars in Syria and Iraq, violence in Libya, and poverty and harsh social and political repression in parts of Africa. The rules for attaining asylum status varied by nation, though Germany and Sweden offered relatively liberal policies, housing for applicants, and high benefit payments (still only about $425 per month, per adult). The regulations were nonetheless restrictive: though numerous migrants applied for asylum, after an average fifteen-month wait many were rejected, classified as illegal job seekers, and expelled.

Irregular immigration was aided by powerful criminal gangs that smuggled people for profit. In the 1990s these gangs contributed to the large number of young female illegal immigrants from eastern Europe, especially Russia and Ukraine. Often lured by criminals promising jobs as maids or waitresses, these women were often trafficked into the most prosperous parts of Europe and forced into prostitution.

More recently, immigration flows have shifted to reflect the dislocation that emerged in North Africa and the Middle East in the wake of the failed "Arab Spring" and the war against the Islamic State (see page 1049). Smugglers with a callous disregard for the well-being of their charges can demand thousands of euros to bring undocumented migrants from North Africa and the Middle East across the Mediterranean into Spain and Italy; the safer and less expensive route across Turkey and Greece and the north into more prosperous European countries is particularly well traveled (Map 30.4).

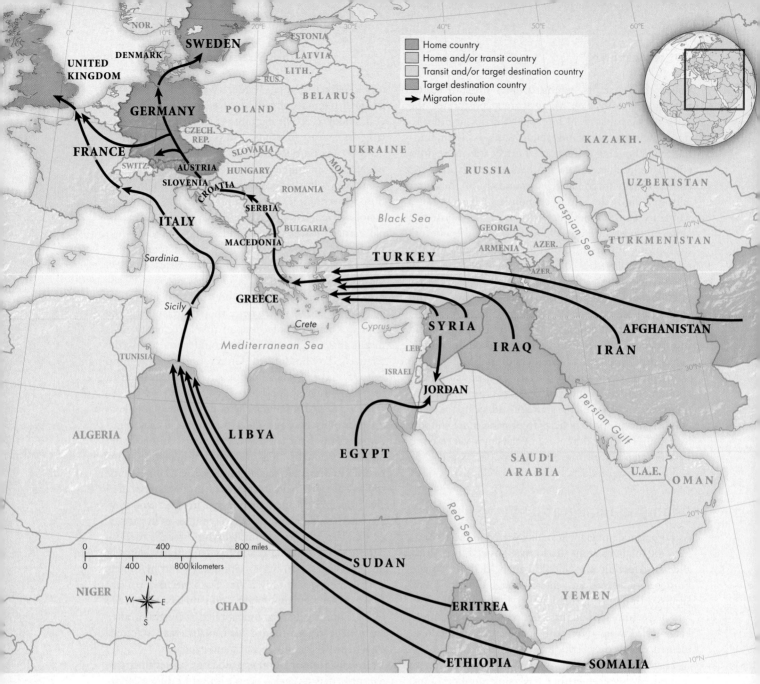

MAP 30.4 Major Migration Routes into Contemporary Europe In the wake of wars and the collapse of the Arab Spring, in-migration from northern Africa and the Middle East into Europe reached crisis proportions. Aided by smugglers, thousands of migrants traveled two main routes: through Libya and across the Mediterranean Sea into southern Italy, and across Turkey to close-by Greek islands and then north through the Balkans. Countries with relatively lenient refugee regulations, such as Sweden and Germany, were favorite destinations. Under the so-called Schengen Agreement, the EU's open-border policy made travel through Europe fairly easy. As the number of migrants increased in fall 2015 and spring 2016, however, European politicians began to close national borders, and many migrants were stranded in quickly built refugee camps.

In the summer of 2015 the migration issue reached crisis proportions. Tens of thousands of migrants, most displaced by war in Syria and Iraq, entered Hungary through Serbia and struggled to travel into more hospitable Austria, Germany, and northern Europe. Others continued to enter the EU through the relatively accessible Greek islands. As Germany promised homes for eight hundred thousand migrants and encouraged other EU nations to take their share, thousands of migrants choked train and bus stations on the Hungarian-Austrian border. Others languished in quickly established refugee camps built in northern Greece and the Hungarian countryside, and Hungary's anti-immigrant government quickly built a 108-mile razor-wire fence along the border with Serbia to squelch further movement.

Europe's Refugee Crisis
A volunteer helps Middle Eastern refugees ashore at the Greek island of Lesbos on November 29, 2015. Exhausted and emotional, they traveled by boat from Turkey. Under Europe's system of open internal borders, the island's thinly patrolled, easily accessible coastline, within sight of the Turkish coast, offered a tempting entry into the European Union for migrants ultimately seeking residence in Germany or Sweden. In fall and early winter of 2015–2016, about five thousand refugees reached Europe each day along the so-called Balkan migrant route. Their unprecedented numbers stoked anti-immigrant tensions across Europe and called into question the internal open-border system. (Oage Elif Kizil/Anadolu Agency/Getty Images)

The discovery of seventy-one dead migrants locked in an abandoned truck on an Austrian highway—and the deaths of thousands more who in the last several years attempted to cross the Mediterranen in rudimentary rubber rafts and leaky boats—underscored the venality of the smugglers and the human costs of uncontrolled immigration. As this text was being written, European leaders were still struggling to contain the humanitarian crisis caused by the largest movement of peoples across Europe since the end of World War II, with little end in sight.

Toward a Multicultural Continent

By 2015 immigration to Europe had profoundly changed the ethnic makeup of the continent, though the effects were unevenly distributed. One way to measure the effect of these new immigrants is to consider the rapid rise of their numbers. Since the 1960s the foreign population of western European nations has grown by two to ten times. In the Netherlands in 1960, only 1 percent of the population was foreign-born. In 2006 the foreign born made up 10 percent. Over the same years the proportion of immigrants grew from 1.2 percent to 12.3 percent in Germany and from 4.7 percent to almost 11 percent in France.[8] In 2005 immigrants constituted about 10 percent of most western European nations (though a far smaller share of the former East Bloc nations). For centuries the number of foreigners living in Europe had been relatively small. Now, permanently displaced ethnic groups, or **diasporas**, brought ethnic diversity to the continent.

The new immigrants were divided into two main groups. A small percentage were highly trained specialists who could find work in the upper ranks of education, business, and high-tech industries. Engineers from English-speaking India, for example, could find positions in international computer companies. Most immigrants, however, did not have access to high-quality education or language training, which limited their employment opportunities and made integration more difficult. They often lived in separate city districts marked by poor housing and crowded conditions, which set them apart from more established residents. Districts of London were home to tens of thousands of immigrants from the former colonies, and in Paris North Africans dominated some working-class *banlieues* (suburbs).

A variety of new cultural forms, ranging from sports and cuisine to music, the fine arts, and film, brought together native and foreign traditions and transformed European lifestyles. Food was a case in point. Recipes and cooks from former colonies in North Africa enlivened French cooking, while the döner kebab—the Turkish version of a gyro sandwich—became Germany's "native" fast food. Indian restaurants proliferated across Britain, and controversy raged when the British foreign minister announced in 2001 that chicken tikka masala—a spicy Indian stew—was Great Britain's new national dish.[9]

The **multiculturalism** and ethnic diversity associated with globalization have inspired numerous works in literature, film, and the fine arts. From rap to reggae to rai,

---

■ **diasporas** Enclaves of ethnic groups settled outside of their homelands

■ **multiculturalism** The mixing of ethnic styles in daily life and in cultural works such as film, music, art, and literature.

The Changing Face of London's Arsenal Football Club Growing ethnic diversity is transforming many aspects of everyday life in contemporary Europe, including the ethnic makeup of European football (soccer) teams. In 1950 the Arsenal Football Club of northern London was composed entirely of white ethnic Britons (right). Today, its diverse roster includes players from around the globe (above). (1950 team: Bob Thomas/Getty Images; 2015 team: Michael Regan/The FA via Getty Images)

multiculturalism has also had a profound effect on popular music, a medium with a huge audience. Rai, which originated in the Bedouin culture of North Africa, exemplified the new pop music forms that emerged from cultural mixing. In the 1920s rai traveled with Algerian immigrants to France. In its current form, it blends Arab and North African folk music, U.S. rap, and French and Spanish pop styles. Lyrics range from sentimental love stories to blunt and sometimes critical descriptions of daily life in immigrant communities.

The growth of immigration and ethnic diversity created rich social and cultural interactions but also generated controversy and conflict in western Europe. In most EU nations, immigrants can become full citizens if they meet certain legal qualifications; adopting the culture of the host country is not a requirement. This legal process has raised questions about who, exactly, could or should be European, and about the way these new citizens might change European society. The idea that cultural and ethnic diversity could be a force for vitality and creativity has run counter to deep-seated beliefs about national homogeneity. Some commentators have accused the newcomers of taking jobs from unemployed native

Europeans and undermining national unity. Government welfare programs intended to support struggling immigrants have been criticized by some as a misuse of money, especially in times of economic downturn.

Europe and Its Muslim Population

General concerns with migration often fused with fears of Muslim migrants and Muslim residents who have grown up in Europe. Islam is now the largest minority religion in Europe. The EU's 15 to 20 million Muslims outnumber Catholics in Europe's mainly Protestant north, and they outnumber Protestants in Europe's Catholic south. Major cities have substantial Muslim minorities. Muslim residents make up about 25 percent of the population in Marseilles and Rotterdam, 15 percent in Brussels, and about 10 percent in Paris, Copenhagen, and London.[10]

Worries increased after the September 11, 2001, al-Qaeda attack on New York's World Trade Center (see page 1046) and the subsequent war in Iraq. Terrorist attacks in Europe organized by Islamist extremists heightened anxieties. On a morning in March 2004, radical Moroccan Muslims living in Spain exploded bombs planted on trains bound for Madrid, killing 191 commuters and wounding 1,800 more. A year later, an attack on the London transit system carried out by British citizens of Pakistani descent killed over 50 people. Since then, a number of attacks have kept Islamist terrorism in the public eye—including the murderous January 2015 assault on the staff of the satiric French magazine *Charlie Hebdo*, which had published cartoons critical of the Prophet Muhammad, and the even more deadly attacks in Paris in November 2015, when extremists motivated by the ideologies of the Islamic State killed 130 people.

The vast majority of Europe's Muslims clearly supported democracy and rejected violent extremism, but these spectacular attacks and other assaults by Islamist militants nonetheless sharpened the debate on immigration. Security was not the only focus of concern. Critics across the political spectrum warned that Europe's rapidly growing Muslim population posed a dire threat to the West's liberal tradition, which embraced freedom of thought, representative government, toleration, separation of church and state, and, more recently, equal rights for women and gays. Islamist extremists and radical clerics living in Europe, critics proclaimed, rejected these fundamental Western values and preached the supremacy of Islamic laws for Europe's Muslims.

Secular Europeans at times had a hard time understanding the depths of Muslim spirituality. French attempts to enforce a ban on wearing the hijab (the headscarf worn by many faithful Muslim women) in public schools expressed the tension between Western secularism and Islamic religiosity on a most personal level and evoked outrage and protests in the Muslim community. As busy mosques came to outnumber dying churches in European cities, nationalist politicians exploited widespread doubts that immigrant populations from Muslim countries would ever assimilate into Western culture. A Danish-Muslim imam (spiritual leader) captured the dilemma: "The Danish shelves for faith and spirituality are empty," he reported. "They fill them instead with fear of the 'strong foreigner.'"[11] Time was on the side of Euro-Islam, critics warned. Europe's Muslim population, estimated at 20 million in 2010, appeared likely to grow to 30 million by 2025 and to increase rapidly thereafter—even though that total would only be 4 percent of Europe's then-projected 750 million people.

By the 1990s in France, some 70 percent of the population believed that there were "too many Arabs," and 30 percent supported right-wing politician Jean-Marie Le Pen's calls to rid France of its immigrants altogether.[12] In the last decade, Le Pen's National Front and other anti-immigration, far-right political parties, such as the Danish People's Party and Austria's Freedom Party, have made impressive gains in national elections. Their success has been aided by bigotry and popular misconceptions. According to one 2013 poll, about 50 percent of respondents in Spain, Germany, France, Switzerland, Britain, and Sweden believe that "Islam is not compatible with the West." Other polls show that Europeans routinely overestimate the number of Muslims in Europe. In France, for example, the public believes that 31 percent of the population is Muslim, when the actual number is about 8 percent; the British believe that 21 percent of the population is Muslim, when the actual number is only 5 percent.[13]

Terrorist Attacks in Paris, November 2015   At a makeshift memorial made of flowers, candles, and messages left by mourners and passersby, onlookers observe a moment of silence for the victims of the November 13, 2015, terrorist attacks in central Paris. Islamic State jihadists claimed responsibility for the series of coordinated assaults, which killed 130 people and wounded hundreds more at a concert hall (Le Bataclan), restaurants, and the national stadium. (Jacques Demarthon/AFP/ Getty Images)

William Pfaff, Will the French Riots Change Anything?

In late November 2005 young Muslim males rioted for several nights in the suburbs of Paris and other French cities. Receiving saturation coverage from the media, their explosion of car burning and arson ignited controversy and debate throughout France and across Europe. Similar outbreaks occurred in 2007 and 2009. What caused the riots, and why did they persist? Anti-immigrant conservatives interpret the outbursts as an example of the inevitable conflict between Christians and Muslims. More liberal observers have blamed dismal living conditions and failures of assimilation.

One penetrating commentary, written after the unrest in 2005 and aimed at an American audience, came from William Pfaff, a noted author and political columnist with many years of European experience. As you read Pfaff's analysis, note in particular the portrait he draws of daily life in France's immigrant ghettos and the role of religion in French Muslim society.

~

The rioting in France's ghetto suburbs is a phenomenon of futility — but a revelation nonetheless. It has no ideology and no purpose other than to make a statement of distress and anger. It is beyond politics. It broke out spontaneously and spread in the same way, communicated by televised example, ratified by the huge attention it won from the press and television and the politicians, none of whom had any idea what to do.

It has been an immensely pathetic spectacle, whose primary meaning has been that it happened. It has been the most important popular social phenomenon in France since the student uprisings of 1968. But those uprisings . . . had consequences for power. The new riots have nothing to do with power.

They started with the accidental electrocutions of two boys hiding from the police, who they thought were after them. The police say there was no pursuit and they had no interest in the boys. However, under the policies of the minister of interior — the presidential candidate Nicolas Sarkozy — there had been a general police crackdown in these ugly suburban clusters of deteriorating high-rise apartments built years ago to house immigrant workers. They were meant to be machines for living. The police attention meant random identity checks, police suspicion, and harassment of young men hanging about — maybe dealing in drugs, maybe simply doing nothing because there is nothing for them to do. (In the past, they at least had to do national military service, which was a strong integrative force, but now France has a professional army.)

Their grandfathers came to France, mostly from North Africa, to do the hard labor in France's industrial reconstruction after the Second World War. Their fathers saw the work gradually dry up as Europe's economies slowed, following the first oil shock in the early 1970s. After that came unemployment. The unemployment rate in the zones where there has been the most violence is nearly 40 percent and among young people it is higher. Many of the young men in these places have never been offered a job. When they applied, their names often excluded them.

Their grandfathers were hard-working men. Their fathers saw their manhood undermined by unemployment. These young men are doomed to be boys. They often take their frustration out on their sisters and girlfriends, who are more likely to have done well in school and found jobs — and frequently a new life — outside the ghetto. . . .

The Muslim mothers and wives of the French ghetto are often confined in the home. Drugs are big business in the American ghetto; they are not that big in France. The crimes of the French ghetto are robbery and shoplifting, stealing mobile phones, stealing cars for joyrides, burning them afterward to eliminate fingerprints, or burning cars just for the hell of it, as well as robbing middle-class students in the city and making trouble on suburban trains, looking for excitement.

Religion is important . . . in the French ghetto, it provides the carapace that protects against the France that excludes Muslims. To the European Muslim, it seems that all of the powerful in the world are in collusion to exclude Muslims — or are at war with them. The war in Iraq, on television, is the constant backdrop to Muslim life in Europe. There are itinerant imams who can put the young ghetto Muslim on the road to danger and adventure in Afghanistan, Pakistan, Iraq — or elsewhere. There are plenty more who preach a still deeper ghettoization: a retreat inside Islamic fundamentalism, totally shutting out a diabolized secular world.

One would think there would be a revolutionary potential in these ghettos, vulnerability to a mobilizing ideology. This seems not to be so. We may be living in a religious age, but it is not one of political ideology. In any case, it is difficult to imagine how the marginalized, thirteen- to twenty-three-year-old children of the Muslim immigration could change France other than by what they are doing, which is to demonstrate that the French model of assimilating immigrants as citizens, and not as members of religious or ethnic groups, has failed for them. It has failed because it has not seriously been tried.

The ghettoization of immigrant youth in France is the consequence of negligence. It has been as bad as the ghettoization through political correctness of Muslims in Britain and the Netherlands, where many people who thought of themselves as enlightened said that assimilation efforts were acts of cultural aggression. The immigrant in France is told that he or she is a citizen just like everyone else, with all the rights and privileges of citizenship—including the right to be unemployed.

Nicolas Sarkozy's zero tolerance of crime and of the petty mafias in the ghetto contributed to touching off these riots, but until recently he was the only French politician to say there has to be affirmative action to get an immigrant elite out of the ghettos and into important roles in French life, where they can pull their communities after them. Some affirmative action has been attempted in recruiting candidates for the elite *grandes écoles* [state schools] that train the French administrative and political class, where the cultural hurdles are immense for candidates. Virtually no children of the Muslim immigration are prominent in mainstream electoral politics; the political parties have yet to make a serious effort to include them. The present government has one junior minister of Algerian origin. I am not aware of any Muslims of immigrant origin in French diplomacy or the top ranks of police and military.*

President Jacques Chirac has announced a civilian national service agency to give training and employment to 50,000 young people from the troubled zones by 2007. The age of apprenticeship has been lowered to fourteen, with a corresponding drop in the age of compulsory academic schooling and new measures to support apprenticeships. There will be more money for schools, local associations, and housing construction and renovation. This is change. Whether it is enough, and in time, is another matter.

EVALUATE THE EVIDENCE

1. Describe the situation of young Muslims in France. What elements of their situation strike you most forcefully? How might these contribute to ongoing outbreaks of civic unrest?

2. France has maintained that, since all citizens are equal, they should all be treated the same way. Why has this policy failed for French Muslims? What alternatives would you suggest? Why?

Source: William Pfaff, "The French Riots: Will They Change Anything?" *The New York Review of Books*, vol. 52, no. 20, December 15, 2005, pp. 88–89. Copyright © 2005 by William Pfaff.

*In 2013 William Pfaff added the following comment: "This no longer is true. All recent French government cabinets have included appointments of immigrant origin or descent."

In Germany, tens of thousands of people have joined the anti-immigrant movement called Pegida (Patriotic Europeans Against the Islamization of the West), and in the first six months of 2015 the German authorities recorded over two hundred attacks against migrant housing or against the migrants themselves. Immigration and the supposed "Islamization" of Europe, along with fundamentalist terrorism, have become highly charged political issues, and conservative and far-right pundits and politicians across Europe offer a variety of diagnoses and solutions to these perceived problems. (See "Thinking Like a Historian: The Conservative Reaction to Immigration and Islamist Terrorism," page 1044.)

Admitting that Islamist extremism could pose a serious challenge, some observers focused instead on the issue of integration. Whereas the first generation of Muslim migrants—predominantly Turks in Germany, Algerians in France, Pakistanis in Britain, and Moroccans in the Netherlands—had found jobs as unskilled workers in Europe's great postwar boom, they and their children had been hard hit after 1973 by the general economic downturn and the decline of manufacturing. Immigrants also suffered from a lack of educational opportunities. Provided with modest welfare benefits and housed minimally in dilapidated housing projects, many second- and third-generation Muslim immigrants were outcasts in their adopted countries. To these observers, economics, inadequate job training, and discrimination had more influence on immigrant attitudes about their host communities than did religion and extremist teachings.

This argument was strengthened by widespread rioting by Muslim youths in France in 2005 and again in 2007 and 2009. Almost always French by birth, language, and education, marauding groups labeled "Arabs" in press reports torched hundreds of automobiles night after night in Paris suburbs and other large cities. (See "Evaluating the Evidence 30.2: William Pfaff, Will the French Riots Change Anything?" at left.) The rioters complained bitterly of high unemployment, systematic discrimination, and exclusion, and studies sparked by the rioting showed that religious ideology had almost no influence on their thinking.

A minority used such arguments to challenge anti-immigrant, anti-Muslim discrimination and its racist overtones. They argued that Europe badly needed newcomers—preferably talented newcomers—to limit the impending population decline and provide valuable technical skills. Some asserted that Europe should recognize that Islam has for centuries been a European religion and a vital part of European life. This recognition might open the way to political and cultural acceptance of European Muslims and head off the resentment that can drive a tiny minority to separatism and acts of terror.

The Conservative Reaction to Immigration and Islamist Terrorism

The impact of immigration on European values and society, the connections between immigration and Islamist terrorism, and the best means to stop terrorist attacks are among the most critical and controversial issues in contemporary Europe. In these selections, conservative politicians offer their diagnoses and prescriptions. What are the main problems, according to these leaders? What solutions do they propose?

1 Immigration and the German welfare state. Former Social Democratic senator and German central bank board member Thilo Sarrazin's bestselling book *Germany Does Itself In* (2010), a radical critique of the Muslim presence in Germany, generated heated controversy. Sarrazin explained his views in an interview with the newspaper *Kurier*.

KURIER: What does [Germany's national debt crisis] have to do with immigration?

SARRAZIN: At this time in Berlin there is massive influx of Roma and Bulgarian Turks. In 2014 they will all have permanent residence rights and a claim on the German benefits system. It won't work, financing the growing burdens of demographic aging as well as further uncontrolled immigration on the German welfare state by raising taxes on the so-called rich. . . .

KURIER: And you would very much like to stop it. How?

SARRAZIN: First: change the benefits system—immigrants receive no benefits for at least ten years. Second: change the permanent residency law—only those able and willing to make a long-term, highly skilled contribution to Germany receive residency rights. Third: social and family benefits in Germany should be dependent on adequate knowledge of the language and efforts at integration. Fourth: we must clearly say to the Muslim immigrants who are already here: at some point you become German, even if you obviously continue to cook Turkish food and go to the mosque, and if you don't want to do that, it's best you return home. Opinion polls show that more than 60 percent of Turks in Germany speak no German at all or cannot speak it well, and a third would leave Germany immediately if there were no German welfare benefits.

2 Popular opposition to the "islamization" of Europe. The programs offered by conservative politicians evoked substantial popular support, seen in demonstrations across Europe, such as this January 2015 anti-immigrant/anti-Islam rally in Dresden, Germany. Organized by the grassroots group Pegida (a German acronym for Patriotic Europeans Against Islamization of the West), thousands protested the supposedly pro-Islam stance of the German federal government. The poster in the foreground, with a fake photo of Chancellor Angela Merkel in a Muslim headscarf, mocks the chancellor's commitment to accept large numbers of refugees from the Middle East. The text, which reads "Ms. Merkel, here are

(Jens Meyer/AP Photo)

the people," suggests that "real" Germans should recognize and oppose Islamic extremism and the potential "islamization" of Europe. Pro-immigration groups organized counter demonstrations calling for tolerance and diversity.

ANALYZING THE EVIDENCE

1. Why and how do the conservative politicians evoke Western values and ideals in their critiques of Islamist extremism?
2. Why would conservative critics of Islamic fundamentalism, as represented in the sources here, be more likely to challenge the immigration policies of the European Union than more left-wing politicians would?
3. Examine the statistics in Source 3. What conclusions can you draw about popular concerns with Islamist extremism in contemporary Europe?

3 **Islamist extremism in Europe: some statistics on popular attitudes.** This Pew Research Center poll taken in spring 2015 suggested that popular concerns about Islamist extremism varied significantly across national borders and that gender, age, and ideology were statistically significant factors in such concerns.

Percentage responding they are very concerned about Islamic extremism in their country:

	Total %	By age (percent)			By gender (percent)		By ideology (percent)		
		18–29	30–49	50+	Male	Female	Left	Moderate	Right
Germany	46	22	39	56	42	50	33	48	55
UK	52	33	49	64	51	52	37	53	56
Spain	61	47	55	70	54	67	52	65	61
France	67	54	63	74	62	71	52	68	73
Italy	53	49	48	58	46	59	48	61	52
Poland	22	18	18	27	21	23	30	21	22
Russia	23	16	18	32	24	23	—	—	—

4 **The Dutch government turns away from multiculturalism.** The 2010 Dutch elections brought to power a conservative government that announced plans to restrict immigration, ban face-covering garments for Muslim women, and ensure that immigrants "integrate" into Dutch society. The new interior minister, P. H. Donner, mounted a trenchant critique of multiculturalism.

The government distances itself explicitly from the relativism contained in the concept of a multicultural society and envisions a society which may change, also through the influence of immigrants who settle here, but is not interchangeable with any other society. The fundamental elements which determine Dutch society are rooted in its history and constitute reference points which many Dutchmen share and which cannot be discarded.

5 **The British crackdown on Islamic extremism.** In July 2015 British prime minister David Cameron announced that his Conservative Party government would seek new policies to combat Islamist extremism. The key problem, he argued, was a "radical ideology" that was violent and subversive of Western liberal values but also an exciting temptation for youths facing identity crises and failures of integration.

We should expose their extremism for what it is—a belief system that glorifies violence and subjugates its people—not least Muslim people. We should contrast their bigotry, aggression and theocracy with our values. . . . We are all British. We respect democracy and the rule of law. We believe in freedom of speech, freedom of the press, freedom of worship, equal rights regardless of race, sex, sexuality or faith. . . . Whether you are Muslim, Hindu, Jewish, Christian or Sikh . . . we can all feel part of this country—and we must now all come together and stand up for our values with confidence and pride. . . .

We must . . . deglamorize the extremist cause, especially ISIL [the Islamic State]. . . . This isn't a pioneering movement—it is vicious, brutal, and a fundamentally abhorrent existence. And here's my message to any young person here in Britain thinking of going out there. . . . You are cannon fodder for them. . . . If you are a boy, they will brainwash you, strap bombs to your body and blow you up. If you are a girl, they will enslave and abuse you. That is the sick and brutal reality of ISIL. . . .

We need our internet companies to go further in helping us identify potential terrorists online. . . . It's now time for [Internet companies] to protect their users from the scourge of radicalization. . . .

Government has a key role to play in this. It's why we ban hate preachers from our country. . . . We need to put out of action the key extremist influencers who are careful to operate just inside the law, but who clearly detest British society and everything we stand for. . . . So as part of our Extremism Bill, we are going to introduce new narrowly targeted powers to enable us to deal with these facilitators and cult leaders, and stop them peddling their hatred. . . . This is not about clamping down on free speech. It's just about applying our shared values uniformly.

PUTTING IT ALL TOGETHER

Using the sources above, along with what you have learned in class and in Chapters 29 and 30, write a short essay that summarizes the conservative viewpoint on Islamist extremism. Are the conservative critics able to reconcile Western democratic traditions of freedom and tolerance with the perceived need to limit immigration, clamp down on fundamentalism, and prevent terrorist attacks?

Sources: (1) Andreas Schwarz, "Thilo Sarrazin legt nach," *Kurier*, December 5, 2011, http://kurier.at/politik/thilo-sarrazin-legt-nach/731.594, translated by Joe Perry; (3) Spring 2015 Global Attitudes survey, Q23, Pew Research Center, http://www.pewglobal.org/2015/07/16/extremism-concerns-growing-in-west-and-predominantly-muslim-countries/extremism-concerns-08. Used by permission of the Pew Research Center; (4) Quoted in Geert Wilders, *Marked for Death: Islam's War Against the West and Me* (Washington, D.C.: Regnery, 2011), p. 206; (5) "David Cameron Extremism Speech," *Independent*, July 20, 2015, www.independent.co.uk. Used by permission of The Independent.

Confronting Long-Term Challenges

FOCUS QUESTION *What challenges will Europeans face in the coming decades?*

Russian irredentism, uncontrolled immigration, and radical Islamic terrorism posed major problems for Europeans in the second decade of the twenty-first century. Yet with goodwill, one could believe that these might be temporary crises, resolvable with determined government action. At the same time, European societies faced a number of interconnected challenges that seemed to pose longer-term challenges. The growing distance in international affairs between the United States and Europe revealed differences in social values and political goals, though both struggled to deal with turmoil in the Muslim world. A persistent economic recession had a devastating impact on the lives of millions and called into question the unity of the Eurozone. Climate change and environmental degradation exposed the dangers of industrial development and the heavy dependence on fossil fuels for energy. At the same time, the relative wealth of European societies in the global context provoked serious thinking about European identity and Europe's humanitarian mission in the community of nations.

Growing Strains in U.S.-European Relations

In the fifty years after World War II, the United States and western Europe generally maintained close diplomatic relations. Though they were never in total agreement, they usually worked together to promote international consensus under U.S. guidance, as represented by the NATO alliance. For example, a U.S.-led coalition that included thousands of troops from France and the United Kingdom and smaller contributions from other NATO allies attacked Iraqi forces in Kuwait in the 1990–1991 Persian Gulf War, freeing the small nation from attempted annexation by Iraqi dictator Saddam Hussein. Over time, however, the growing power of the European Union and the new unilateral thrust of Washington's foreign policy created strains in traditional transatlantic relations.

The growing gap between the United States and Europe had several causes. For one, the European Union was now the world's largest trading block, challenging the predominance of the United States. Prosperous European businesses invested heavily in the United States, reversing a decades-long economic relationship in which investment dollars had flowed the other way. For another, under Presidents George W. Bush (U.S. pres. 2001–2009) and Barack Obama (U.S. pres. 2009–), the United States

often ignored international opinion in pursuit of its own interests. Citing the economic impact, Washington refused to ratify the Kyoto Protocol of 1997, which was intended to limit global warming and which had been agreed to by nearly two hundred countries. Nor did the United States join the International Criminal Court, a global tribunal meant to prosecute individuals accused of crimes against humanity, which nearly 140 states agreed to join. These positions troubled EU leaders, as did unflagging U.S. support for Israel in the ongoing Palestinian-Israeli crisis.

A values gap between the United States and Europe contributed to cooler relations. Ever more secular Europeans had a hard time understanding the religiosity of many Americans. Relatively lax gun control laws and use of capital punishment in the United States were viewed with dismay in Europe, where most countries had outlawed private handgun ownership and abolished the death penalty. Despite President Obama's health-care reforms—which evoked controversy among Americans—U.S. reluctance to establish a single-payer, state-funded program surprised Europeans, who saw their own such programs as highly advantageous.

Hardball geopolitical issues relating to NATO further widened the gap. The dissolution of the Communist Warsaw Pact left NATO without its Cold War adversaries. Yet NATO continued to expand, primarily in the territories in the former East Bloc—the defensive belt the Soviet Union had established after World War II. NATO's expansion angered Russia's leaders, particularly when President Bush moved to deploy missile defense systems in Poland and the Czech Republic in 2008. Even within the alliance there were tensions. By 2009, with twenty-eight member states, it was difficult to shape unanimous support for NATO actions. France, for example, did not support NATO's engagement in Bosnia in 1995 because the alliance failed to get UN approval for the action, and in 2011 Germany and Poland refused to back NATO air strikes against the Libyan regime. As the EU expanded, some argued that Europe should determine its own military and defense policy without U.S. or NATO guidance.

American-led wars in Afghanistan and Iraq, undertaken in response to the September 11 terrorist attacks against the United States, further strained U.S.-European relations. On the morning of September 11, 2001, passenger planes hijacked by terrorists destroyed the World Trade Center towers in New York City and crashed into the Pentagon. Perpetrated by the radical Islamist group al-Qaeda, the attacks took the lives of more than three thousand people from many countries and put the personal safety of ordinary citizens at the top of the West's agenda.

Immediately after the September 11 attacks, the peoples and governments of Europe and the world joined Americans in heartfelt solidarity. Over time, however, tensions between Europe and the United States re-emerged and deepened markedly, particularly after President Bush declared a unilateral U.S. **war on terror**—a determined effort to fight terrorism in all its forms, around the world. The main acts in Bush's war on terror were a U.S.-led war in Afghanistan, which started in 2001, and another in Iraq, which lasted from 2003 to 2011. Both succeeded in quickly bringing down dictatorial regimes. At the same time, they fomented anti-Western sentiment in the Muslim world and failed to stop regional violence driven by ethnic and religious differences.

The U.S. invasion of Iraq and subsequent events caused some European leaders, notably in France and Germany, to question the rationale for and indeed the very effectiveness of a "war" on terror. Military victory, even over rogue states, would hardly end terrorism, since terrorist groups easily moved across national borders. Terrorism, they concluded, was better fought through police and intelligence measures. Europeans certainly shared U.S. worries about stability in the Middle East, and they faced their own problems with Islamist terrorism, especially after the Madrid and London train bombings of 2004 and 2005, and the attacks in Paris in 2015. But European leaders worried that the tactics used in the Iraq War, exemplified by Washington's readiness to use its military without international agreements or UN backing, violated international law.

American conduct of the war on terror also raised serious human rights concerns. The revelation of the harsh interrogation techniques used on prisoners held by American forces and abuse of prisoners in Iraq shocked many Europeans. U.S. willingness to engage in "extraordinary rendition"—secretly moving terrorism suspects to countries that allow coercive interrogation techniques—caused further concern.

The election of Barack Obama, America's first African American president, in 2008, and his re-election in 2012, brought improvement to U.S.-European foreign relations. Upon election, Obama announced that he would halt deployment of missiles in central Europe and reduce nuclear arms, easing tensions with Russia. He took U.S. troops out of Iraq in 2011 and Afghanistan in 2014, and quietly shelved the language of the "war on terror." Despite these changes, many Europeans continued to find U.S. willingness to undertake unilateral military action disturbing—American drone attacks on suspected terrorists along the Afghanistan-Pakistan border were particularly unpopular.[14] In the long run, though ties with the United States remained firm, European states increasingly responded independently to global affairs.

Turmoil in the Muslim World

Over the past decade, civil wars, terrorist sectarian attacks, civilian dislocation and misery, and a loss of social, political, and economic stability have shaken much of the Muslim world in North Africa and the Middle East. In many ways, these problems were the results of recent historical events. Yet the turmoil in North Africa and the Middle East, along with Islamic challenges to Western interests and policies, had a much deeper history, which included the legacies of European colonialism and the mandate system established after World War I, Cold War power plays, and the Palestinian-Israeli conflict.

Radical political Islam, a mixture of traditional religious beliefs and innovative social and political reform ideas, was at first a reaction against the foreign control and secularization represented by the mandate system established in the Middle East after World War I (see Chapter 25). Groups like the **Muslim Brotherhood**, founded in Egypt in 1928, called for national liberation from European control and a return to shari'a law (based on Muslim legal codes), and demanded land reform, extensive social welfare programs, and economic independence. The appeal of such ideas crossed class lines and national borders. By the 1960s the Brotherhood had established chapters across the Middle East and North Africa, and a variety of other groups and leaders advocated similar ideas about the need for Islamic revival and national autonomy. The broad spectrum of Islamist ideas is difficult to summarize, but adherents tended to fall into two main groups: a moderate or centrist group that worked peacefully to reform society within existing institutions, and a much smaller, more militant minority willing to use violence to achieve its goals.

Decolonization and the Cold War sharpened anti-Western and particularly anti-U.S. sentiments among radical Islamists. As the western European powers loosened their ties to the Middle East, the Americans stepped in. Applying containment policy to limit the spread of communism, and eager to preserve steady supplies of oil, the United States supported secular, authoritarian regimes friendly to U.S. interests in Egypt, Saudi Arabia, Iran, and elsewhere. Such regimes often played on U.S. concerns about communism or the threat of radical Islam to bolster American support.

U.S. policies in the Middle East at times produced "blowback," or unforeseen and unintended consequences. One example was the Iranian revolution of

---

■ **war on terror** American policy under President George W. Bush to fight global terrorism in all its forms.

■ **Muslim Brotherhood** Islamic social and political reform group founded in Egypt in 1928 that called for national liberation from European control and a return to shari'a law (based on Muslim legal codes), and demanded land reform, extensive social welfare programs, and economic independence.

1979, when Islamist radicals antagonized by Western intervention, state corruption, and secularization overthrew the U.S.-supported shah and established an Islamic republic. The successful revolution encouraged militant Islamists elsewhere. So did the example of the mujahideen, the Muslim guerrilla fighters in Afghanistan who successfully fought off the Soviet army from 1979 to 1989 (see Chapter 29). U.S. military aid and arms, funneled to the mujahideen during the war, also generated blowback. Many of the U.S.-armed mujahideen would go on to support the Taliban, a militant Islamist faction that came to rule Afghanistan in 1996. The Taliban established a strict Islamist state based on shari'a law that denied women's right to education and banned Western movies and music. The Taliban also provided a safe haven for the Saudi-born millionaire Osama bin Laden and the al-Qaeda terrorist network.

As a result of these policies, the United States, along with western Europe, became the main target for Islamist militants. During the 1990s bin Laden and al-Qaeda mounted several terrorist attacks on U.S. installations, leading up to the horrific September 11 assault. After that attack, President Bush declared with some justification that the terrorists "hate our freedoms: our freedom of religion, our freedom of speech, our freedom to vote."[15] In public calls for jihad (or struggle) against the United States and the West, however, bin Laden gave a more pragmatic list of grievances, including U.S. support for Israel in the Israeli-Palestinian crisis, the sanctions on Iraq that followed the Persian Gulf War, and the presence of U.S. military bases in Saudi Arabia—seen as an insult to the Muslim holy sites in Mecca and Medina.[16]

The Bush administration hoped that the invasions of Afghanistan—a direct response to the September 11 attacks—and Iraq would end the terrorist attacks and bring peace and democracy to the Middle East, but both brought chaos instead. The military campaign in Afghanistan quickly achieved one of its goals, bringing down the Taliban, and the United States installed a friendly government. But U.S. troops failed to find bin Laden or disable al-Qaeda, and Taliban insurgents mounted a determined and lasting guerrilla war.

With heavy fighting still under way in Afghanistan in late 2001, the Bush administration turned its attention to Saddam Hussein's Iraq, arguing that it was necessary to expand the war on terror to other hostile regimes in the Middle East. U.S. leaders effectively played on American fears of renewed terrorism and

charged that Saddam Hussein was still developing weapons of mass destruction in flagrant disregard of his 1991 promise to end all such programs. Some Americans shared the widespread doubts held by Europeans about the legality—and wisdom—of an American attack on Iraq, especially after UN inspectors found no weapons of mass destruction in the country. Though they failed to win UN approval, in March 2003 the United States and Britain, with token support from a handful of other European states, invaded Iraq.

The U.S.-led invasion quickly overwhelmed the Iraqi army, and Saddam's dictatorship collapsed in April, but America's subsequent efforts to establish a stable pro-American Iraq proved difficult. Poor postwar planning and management by administration officials was one factor, but there were others. Iraq, a creation of Western imperialism after the First World War (see Chapter 25), was a fragile state with three distinct groups: non-Arab Kurds, Arab Sunni Muslims, and Arab Shi'ite Muslims. By 2006 deadly sectarian conflicts among these groups and against the United States and its Iraqi supporters had taken hold. Casualties in Iraq began to decline after President Bush sent additional troops to the country in 2007, and when President Obama took office in 2009 his administration moved forward with agreements to withdraw all U.S. forces in 2011. The shaky Iraqi government continued to struggle with ethnic divisions and terrorist violence, however.

Areas that are predominantly
☐ Sunni (ca. 36%)
☐ Shi'ite (ca. 60%)
☐ Mixed
– Kurdish

Iraq, ca. 2010

Although U.S. commandos finally killed Osama bin Laden in Pakistan in May 2011, the apparently unwinnable guerrilla war in Afghanistan became increasingly unpopular in the United States and among NATO allies in Europe. Though the conflict continued, President Obama withdrew U.S. combat troops from the country in 2014.

In early 2011 an unexpected chain of events that came to be called the **Arab Spring** further destabilized the Middle East and North Africa. In a provincial town in Tunisia, a poor fruit vendor set himself on fire to protest official harassment. His death eighteen days later unleashed a series of spontaneous mass protests that brought violence, chaos, and regime change; six weeks later, Tunisia's authoritarian president fled the country, opening the way for reform. Massive popular demonstrations calling for more open democractic government and social tolerance broke out across the Middle East. In Egypt, demonstrators forced the resignation of President Hosni Mubarak, a U.S.-friendly leader who had ruled for thirty years. An armed uprising in Libya, supported by NATO air strikes, brought down the dictatorial government of Muammar Gaddafi that October. A civil war broke out in Syria in July 2011, but dragged on into 2016 as Bashar al-Assad, with Russian support, hurled his army at the rebels and Western powers disagreed about what to do. Protests arose in other countries in the region as well, evoking a mixed response of repression and piecemeal reform.

As the popular movements inspired by the Arab Spring faltered, the emergence of the **Islamic State** (sometimes called ISIS or ISIL) suggested that events in the Middle East had spiraled out of control. The Islamic State, an extremist Islamist militia dedicated to the establishment of a new caliphate to unify Muslims around the world, grew out of al-Qaeda and the various other insurgent groups fighting in Iraq and the Syrian civil war. By summer 2015 Islamic State soldiers had taken control of substantial parts of central Syria and Iraq—including Mosul, Ramadi, and Fallujah, cities central to U.S. combat missions in the Iraq war. Over 4 million Syrians and Iraqis lost their homes during the fighting, and hundreds of thousands streamed north in attempts to find asylum in Europe (see page 1037).

In the territories under their control, Islamic State militants set up a terroristic government based on an extremist reading of shari'a law. Islamic State terror tactics included the violent persecution of sectarian religious groups; use of sexual assault and rape as tools of conquest; mass executions and beheadings of military, political, or sectarian enemies; and the "cultural cleansing" (destruction and looting) of ancient cultural monuments and shrines that failed to meet its stringent religious ideals, most recently in the classical city of Palmyra in Syria. All these actions were well documented in widespread Internet propaganda campaigns; videos recorded by militants, intended to demonstrate their power and entice recruits, were regularly posted on the Internet.

In summer 2016, as this was being written, the outcome of the turmoil in the Middle East was difficult to predict. The Arab Spring seemed, for the most part, a dismal failure. The young activists who sought greater political and social liberties from authoritarian regimes quickly lost control of the changes they unleashed. Multiple players now vied for power: military leaders and old elites, local chieftains representing ethnic or sectarian interests, and moderate and radical Islamists. In Egypt, the first open elections in decades brought to power representatives of the moderate wing of the Muslim Brotherhood; a year later, military leaders overthrew this elected government. In Libya, Yemen, and especially Syria, persistent civil wars undermined the search for stability. The hold of the Islamic State was likewise difficult to

shake. In Iraq, air strikes by a U.S.-NATO coalition and assaults by Iraqi ground troops only slowly repulsed the extremists.

In the period leading up to 2016, Western policymakers grappled in vain for clear and effective ways to help defeat the Islamic State and bring order to the region. Their efforts were especially freighted, since the turmoil in the Muslim world was at the center of many of Europe's problems. These included the immigration emergency of 2015–2016, the persistent extremist Islamist terrorist attacks, the destabilization of Europe's energy supplies, and the disastrous human rights crisis faced by millions of Middle East residents.

The Global Recession and the Viability of the Eurozone

While chaos and change roiled the Muslim world, economic crisis sapped growth and political unity in Europe and North America. In 2008 the United States entered a deep recession, caused by the burst of the housing boom, bank failures, and an overheated financial securities market. The U.S. government spent massive sums to recharge the economy. Banks, insurance agencies, auto companies, and financial services conglomerates received billions of dollars in federal aid. By 2016 the economy had improved and much of the housing market had recovered, though some critics claimed that income inequality was higher than ever.

The 2008 recession swept across Europe, where a housing bubble, high national deficits, and a weak bond market made the crisis particularly acute. One of the first countries affected, and one of the hardest hit, was Iceland, where the currency and banking system collapsed outright. Other countries followed—Ireland and Latvia made deep and painful cuts in government spending to balance national budgets. By 2010 Britain was deeply in debt, and Spain, Portugal, and especially Greece were close to bankruptcy.

This sudden "euro crisis" put the very existence of the Eurozone in question. The common currency grouped together countries with vastly divergent economies. Germany and France, the zone's two strongest economies, felt pressure to provide financial support to ensure the stability of far weaker countries, including Greece and Portugal. They did so with strings attached: recipients of EU support were required to reduce deficits through austerity measures. Even so, the transfer of monies within the Eurozone angered the citizens of wealthier countries, who felt they were being asked to

■ **Arab Spring** A series of popular revolts in several countries in the Middle East and North Africa that sought an end to authoritarian, often Western-supported regimes.

■ **Islamic State** A radical Islamist militia in control of substantial parts of central Syria and Iraq, where it applies an extremist version of shari'a law.

Anti-Austerity Protests in Greece   With protest marches and a rally in front of the Greek parliament, thousands of anti-austerity voters celebrated the results of the July 2015 Greek referendum in the streets of Athens. The popular vote soundly rejected a bailout deal proposed by the IMF, the European Common Bank, and the European Union, which would have required the Greek government to implement harsh austerity measures. Just days after the vote, Greek leaders backed down and accepted the plan anyway. (© Bjorn Kietzmann/Demotix/Corbis)

subsidize countries in financial difficulties of their own making. Such feelings were particularly powerful in Germany, forcing Chancellor Angela Merkel (r. 2005–), the nation's first woman chancellor, to move cautiously in providing financial stimulus to troubled Eurozone economies.

The difficulty dealing with the stubborn Greek debt crisis prompted debates about the viability of a single currency for nations with vastly different economies as well as widespread speculation that the Eurozone might fall apart. In 2010 and 2012 Greece received substantial bailouts from the IMF, the European Common Bank, and the European Union (the so-called Troika). In return for loans and some debt relief, Greek leaders were required to implement a painful austerity plan—which meant raising taxes, privatizing state-owned businesses, reforming labor markets, and drastically reducing government spending on employee wages, pensions, and other popular social benefits. Greek unemployment hit a record 25 percent in 2012, and more than half of young adults lacked jobs. Rampant joblessness meant declining tax revenues and the Greek economy continued to weaken. As the government cut popular social programs, demonstrators took to the streets to protest declining living standards and the lack of work; in Athens, protests large and small were almost a daily occurrence.

The 2015 Greek elections brought the left-wing Syriza Party and the charismatic prime minister Alexis Tsipras to power. In the Thessaloniki Programme, Tsipras and his party promised voters a tough stand against the Troika's fiscal demands and an end to austerity. (See "Evaluating the Evidence 30.3: The Thessaloniki Programme," page 1052.) Yet Troika negotiators, led by Germany, maintained an uncompromising line: if Tsipras and Syriza failed to meet Greek debt payments, they would be forced into a "Grexit" (a Greek exit from the Eurozone). After a dramatic series of events, which included a resounding "no" vote in a Greek referendum on the deal proposed by the Troika, Tsipras backtracked and accepted further austerity measures in return for yet another bailout loan. Among other conditions, Greek leaders promised to sell off about 50 billion euros' worth of government-owned property, including airports, power plants and energy assets, roads and railroads, and the national post office.

Even as the Greek crisis shook European unity, in June 2016 Great Britain voted to leave the EU all together. The campaign for the "Brexit" (British exit from the EU) was intense. The narrow victory of those wanting "out" showed that many Brits did not want "Eurocrats" in Brussels intruding on national policy and did not appreciate the EU's relatively open immigration policies. Prime Minister David Cameron (r. 2010–2016) resigned immediately. Though Britain had two years to negotiate the terms of the exit, global financial markets fell, far-right populist parties on the continent rejoiced, and EU supporters expressed deep concern about the future of the union.

Dependence on Fossil Fuels

One of the most significant long-term challenges facing Europe and the world in the early twenty-first century was the need for adequate energy resources. Maintaining standards of living in industrialized countries and modernizing the developing world required extremely high levels of energy use, and supplies were heavily dependent on fossil fuels: oil, coal, and natural gas. In 2011 Europe and Russia combined had about 12 percent of the world's population but annually consumed about 34 percent of the world's natural gas production, 22 percent of oil production, and 13 percent of coal output. Scientists warned that such high levels of usage were unsustainable over the long run and predicted that fossil fuel supplies will eventually run out, especially as the countries of the developing world—including giants such as India and China—increased their own rates of consumption.[17]

Struggles to control and profit from these shrinking resources often resulted in tense geopolitical conflicts. The need to preserve access to oil, for example, has led to a transformation in military power in the post–Cold War world. Between 1945 and 1990 the largest areas of military buildup were along the iron curtain in Europe and in East Asia, as U.S. forces formed a bulwark against the spread of communism. Today military power is increasingly concentrated in oil-producing areas such as the Middle East, which holds about 65 percent of the world's oil reserves. One scholar labeled conflicts in the Persian Gulf and Central Asia "resource wars" because they are fought, in large part, to preserve the West's access to the region's energy supplies.[18]

The global struggle for ample energy has placed Russia, which in 2011 became the world's number-one oil producer (surpassing Saudi Arabia) and the number-two natural gas producer, in a powerful but strained position. The Russian invasions of Chechnya and Georgia, and intervention in Ukraine, were attempts to maintain political influence in these territories, but also to preserve Russian control of the region's rich energy resources.

Beyond military action, Russian leaders readily use their control over energy to assert political influence. The Russian corporation Gazprom, one of the world's largest producers of natural gas, sells Europe about 30 percent of its natural gas, and the EU treads softly with Russia to maintain this supply. Russia is willing to play hardball: it has engaged in over fifty politically motivated disruptions of natural gas supply in the former Soviet republics, including one in January 2009 when Russia shut off supplies to Ukraine for three weeks, resulting in closed factories and no heat for hundreds of thousands of people. "Yesterday tanks, to-

day oil," a Polish politician remarked about Russia's willingness to use energy to exert influence in central Europe.[19]

Climate Change and Environmental Degradation

Even setting aside the question of the supply of fossil fuels, their use has led to serious environmental problems. Burning oil and coal releases massive amounts of carbon dioxide (CO_2) into the atmosphere, the leading cause of **climate change**, or global warming. While the future effects of climate change are difficult to predict, the vast majority of climatologists agree that global warming is proceeding far more quickly than previously predicted and that some climatic disruption is now unavoidable. Rising average temperatures already play havoc with familiar weather patterns, melting glaciers and polar ice packs, and drying up freshwater resources. Moreover, in the next fifty years rising sea levels may well flood low-lying coastal areas around the world.

Since the 1990s the EU has spearheaded efforts to control energy consumption and contain climate change. EU leaders have imposed tight restrictions on CO_2 emissions, and Germany, the Netherlands, and Denmark have become world leaders in harnessing alternative energy sources such as solar and wind power. Some countries, hoping to combat the future effects of global warming, have also taken pre-emptive measures. The Dutch government, for example, has spent billions of dollars constructing new dikes, levees, and floodgates. These efforts provided models for U.S. urban planners after floodwaters churned up by Hurricane Sandy swamped low-lying swaths of New York City in October 2012.

Environmental degradation encompasses a number of problems beyond climate change. Overfishing and toxic waste threaten the world's oceans and freshwater lakes, which once seemed to be inexhaustible sources of food and drinking water. The disaster that resulted when an offshore oil rig exploded in the Gulf of Mexico in April 2010, spewing millions of gallons of oil into the gulf waters, underscored the close connections between energy consumption and water pollution. Deforestation, land degradation, soil erosion, and over-fertilization; species extinction related to habitat loss; the

Primary Oil and Gas Pipelines to Europe, ca. 2005

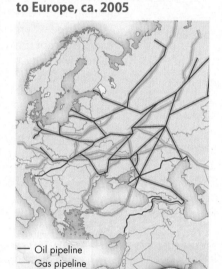

— Oil pipeline
— Gas pipeline
■ Supplied by Russia

■ **climate change** Changes in long-standing weather patterns caused primarily by carbon dioxide emissions from the burning of fossil fuels.

The Thessaloniki Programme

Under the leadership of soon-to-be Greek prime minister Alexis Tsipras, the left-wing Syriza Party unanimously adopted the Thessaloniki Programme in September 2014. The reformist manifesto called for a "European Debt Conference" to write down Greece's public debt and end the austerity policies enforced by bailout deals with the EU, and announced a series of measures to grow the Greek economy. In elections in January 2015, Syriza took power from the center-right government led by Prime Minister Antonis Samaras. Though Tsipras boldly announced that the terms of the Programme were "non-negotiable," in July 2015 his government accepted a new EU bailout and a new round of strict austerity requirements.

We demand immediate parliamentary elections and a strong negotiation mandate with the goal to:

Write-off the greater part of public debt's nominal value so that it becomes sustainable in the context of a "European Debt Conference." It happened for Germany in 1953. It can also happen for the South of Europe and Greece.

Include a "growth clause" in the repayment of the remaining part so that it is growth-financed and not budget-financed.

Include a significant grace period ("moratorium") in debt servicing to save funds for growth.

Exclude public investment from the restrictions of the Stability and Growth Pact.

A "European New Deal" of public investment financed by the European Investment Bank.

Quantitative easing by the European Central Bank with direct purchases of sovereign bonds.

Finally, we declare once again that the issue of the Nazi Occupation forced loan from the Bank of Greece is open for us. Our partners know it. It will become the country's official position from our first days in power.

On the basis of this plan, we will fight and secure a socially viable solution to Greece's debt problem so that our country is able to pay off the remaining debt from the creation of new wealth and not from primary surpluses, which deprive society of income.

With that plan, we will lead with security the country to recovery and productive reconstruction by:

Immediately increasing public investment by at least €4 billion.

Gradually reversing all the Memorandum injustices.

Gradually restoring salaries and pensions so as to increase consumption and demand.

Providing small and medium-sized enterprises with incentives for employment, and subsidizing the energy cost of industry in exchange for an employment and environmental clause.

Investing in knowledge, research, and new technology in order to have young scientists, who have been massively emigrating over the last years, back home.

Rebuilding the welfare state, restoring the rule of law and creating a meritocratic state.

We are ready to negotiate and we are working towards building the broadest possible alliances in Europe.

The present Samaras government is once again ready to accept the decisions of the creditors. The only alliance which it cares to build is with the German government.

This is our difference and this is, at the end, the dilemma:

European negotiation by a SYRIZA government, or acceptance of the creditors' terms on Greece by the Samaras government.

EVALUATE THE EVIDENCE

1. How did the Thessaloniki Programme challenge the economic policies promoted by international organizations like the European Union and the International Monetary Fund?
2. Why did Tsipras and the Syriza Party drop these demands? How do you think the Greek public responded to that action?

Source: "Syriza: The Thessaloniki Programme," Syriza, http://www.syriza.gr /article/SYRIZA---THE-THESSALONIKI-PROGRAMME.html#.VfXCt87WFJk.

accumulation of toxins in the air, land, and water; the disposal of poisonous nuclear waste—all will continue to pose serious problems in the twenty-first century.

Though North American and European governments, NGOs, and citizens have taken a number of steps to limit environmental degradation and regulate energy use, the overall effort to control energy consumption has been an especially difficult endeavor, underscoring the interconnectedness of the contemporary world. Rapidly industrializing countries such as India and China—the latter surpassed the United States in 2008 as the largest emitter of CO_2—have had a difficult time balancing environmental concerns and the energy use necessary for economic growth. Because of growing demand for electricity, for example, China currently accounts for about 47 percent of the world's coal consumption, causing hazardous air pollution in Chinese cities and contributing to climate change.[20]

Can international agreements and good intentions make a difference? In December 2015 representatives of almost two hundred nations met at the annual United Nations Climate Change Conference in Paris, France. They extended the Kyoto Protocol on climate change, set ambitious goals for the reduction of CO_2 emissions by 2020, and promised to help developing countries manage the effects of climate change. Such changes would require substantial modifications in the planet's consumption of energy derived from fossil fuels, however, and the ultimate success of ambitious plans to limit the human impact on the environment remains uncertain.

Promoting Human Rights

Though regional differences persisted in the twenty-eight EU member states, Europeans entering the twenty-first century enjoyed some of the highest living standards in the world, the sweet fruit of more than fifty years of peace, security, and overall economic growth. The recent agonies of barbarism and war in the former Yugoslavia as well as the memories of the horrors of World War II and the Holocaust cast in bold relief the ever-present reality of collective violence. (See "The Past Living Now: Remembering the Holocaust," page 1054.) For some Europeans, the realization that they had so much and so many others had so little kindled a desire to help. As a result, European intellectuals and opinion makers began to envision a new historic mission for Europe: the promotion of domestic peace and human rights in lands plagued by instability, violence, and oppression.

European leaders and humanitarians believed that more global agreements and new international institutions were needed to set moral standards and to regu-late countries, leaders, armies, corporations, and individuals. In practice, this meant more curbs on the sovereign rights of the world's states, just as the states of the European Union had imposed increasingly strict standards of behavior on themselves in order to secure the rights and welfare of EU citizens. As one EU official concluded, the European Union has a "historical responsibility" to make morality "a basis of policy" because "human rights are more important than states' rights."[21]

In practical terms, this mission raised questions. Europe's evolving human rights policies would require military intervention to stop civil wars and to prevent tyrannical governments from slaughtering their own people. Thus the EU joined the United States to intervene militarily to stop the killing and protect minority rights in Bosnia, Croatia, and Kosovo. The EU states vigorously supported UN initiatives to verify compliance with anti–germ warfare conventions, outlaw the use of land mines, and establish a new international court to prosecute war criminals.

Europeans also broadened definitions of individual rights. Having abolished the death penalty in the EU, they condemned its continued use in China, the United States, and other countries. At home, Europe expanded personal rights. The pacesetting Netherlands gave pensions and workers' rights to prostitutes and provided assisted suicide (euthanasia) for the terminally ill. The Dutch recognized same-sex marriage in 2001. By the time France followed suit in 2013, nine western European countries had legalized same-sex marriage and twelve others recognized alternative forms of civic union. (The United States Supreme Court guaranteed the right to same-sex marriage in

Demonstrating for Peace
Holding torches, some 3,500 people form the peace sign in Heroes Square in central Budapest, the capital of Hungary, in 2006. The rally marked the third anniversary of the U.S.-led invasion of Iraq. Millions long for peace, but history and current events suggest that bloody conflicts will continue. Yet Europeans have cause for cautious optimism: despite episodes of intense violence and suffering, since 1945 wars have been localized; cataclysmic catastrophes like World Wars I and II have been averted; and Europe has become a world leader in the push for human rights. (© Peter Kollanyi/epa/Corbis)

THE PAST LIVING NOW

Remembering the Holocaust

Berlin's Memorial to the Murdered Jews of Europe, a somber monument of 2,711 concrete slabs on a vast, uneven plain, stands just footsteps away from the Brandenburg Gate at the city's center. Opened in 2005, the memorial commemorates the almost 6 million Jews murdered by the Nazis during World War II. Its blank walls and forbidding passageways symbolize the brutality of crimes against humanity that stretch the limits of understanding, but may also remind viewers of the difficulty of remembering those monstrous events, which played out in such vastly different ways across Europe.

In the first postwar decades, Europeans paid little attention to Nazi genocide. Though Allied leaders promised liberation from Nazi barbarism, they seldom mentioned Jews; the Allies aimed to push back the Germans, not stop genocide. After the war Europeans rebuilt cities, homes, and families and remembered their personal losses; the Jews, now gone, were too easy to forget. There was another reason: German occupiers were responsible for deporting and murdering Jews, but they were not alone. Across occupied Europe, non-German collaborators were partners in genocide. They kept quiet.

In the 1960s the silence started to crack — first in Germany, the land of the perpetrators. The 1961 trial in Jerusalem of Nazi official Adolf Eichmann for crimes against humanity raised awareness, as did trials of concentration camp guards from 1963 to 1965. The youth generation of the 1960s challenged their parents' silence about the past, and the 1979 German broadcast of the U.S.-made television miniseries *Holocaust*, watched by some 20 million viewers, put Nazi crimes at the center of German public consciousness.

Visitors explore the Memorial to the Murdered Jews of Europe in Berlin. (Markus Schreiber/AP Photo/AP Images)

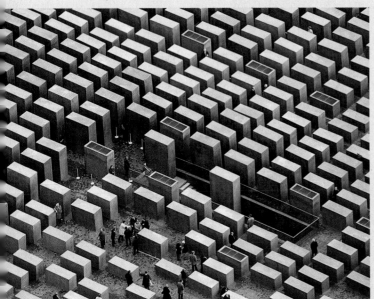

In countries occupied by the Germans during World War II, remembering the Holocaust posed troublesome questions about complicity and collaboration. France was a key example. During the war, French officials of the Nazi-friendly Vichy regime had voluntarily introduced anti-Semitic legislation and arrested and deported Jews, with relatively little pressure from the Germans. Such actions were hardly mentioned until the mid-1990s, when, after several trials of high-ranking Vichy officials, the French president belatedly acknowledged the country's role in mass murder. Later, in 2005, the Shoah Memorial, dedicated to remembering the Holocaust with a museum and resource center, opened in Paris.

In the East Bloc, Communist leaders readily publicized Nazi crimes, but failed to explain that Jews were the primary target of Nazi genocide. Because Marxist ideology championed the working classes, Communist interpretations of Nazi barbarism focused on workers, not Jews. At the Auschwitz Museum in Communist Poland, for example, those murdered in the camp were labeled "workers" and listed by nationality, not ethnicity or religion, thus masking the fact that over 90 percent of the camp's 1.5 million victims were Jewish.* After communism collapsed, Poles dealt more openly with the facts; the museum at Auschwitz now clearly recognizes Jewish victims. But this new openness raised tough questions — historians have recently called attention to Polish anti-Semitism and the Poles' own varied reactions to Nazi-led genocide. The new Museum of the History of Polish Jews, opened in 2013, shows a new acknowledgment of Poland's troubled past.

Over the past twenty-five years, Europeans have grappled with Holocaust memories from a variety of perspectives, and debates over appropriate forms of commemoration continue. New museums and monuments reveal a growing willingness to confront the difficult legacies of the Holocaust and offer hope that remembering the past might help avert crimes against humanity in the future.

QUESTIONS FOR ANALYSIS

1. Why would memories of the Holocaust vary from country to country and change over time? What accounts for the growing commemoration of the Holocaust?
2. Find the Web sites for the museums and monuments discussed above, and compare and contrast the ways they present the Holocaust. What are the stated goals of these institutions? Can you see national differences in the ways they depict the past?

*Tony Judt, *Postwar: A History of Europe Since 1945* (New York: Penguin Books, 2005), p. 811. Judt's epilogue provides a concise overview of Europeans' attempts to adequately commemorate the Holocaust.

June 2015.) The countries of the former East Bloc, where people were generally less supportive of gay rights, lagged behind in this regard.

Europeans extended their broad-based concept of human rights to the world's poorer countries. Such efforts often included sharp criticism of globalization and unrestrained neoliberal capitalism. For example, Europe's moderate Social Democrats joined human rights campaigners in 2001 to secure drastic price cuts from international pharmaceutical corporations selling drugs to combat Africa's AIDS crisis. Advocating greater social equality and state-funded health care, European socialists embraced morality as a basis for the global expansion of human rights.

The record was not always perfect. Critics accused the European Union (and the United States) of selectively promoting human rights in their differential responses to the Arab Spring—the West was willing to act in some cases, as in Libya, but dragged its feet in others, as in Egypt and Syria. The conflicted response to the immigration emergency of 2015 underscored the difficulties of shaping unified human rights policies that would satisfy competing political and national interests. Attempts to extend rights to women, indigenous peoples, and immigrants remained controversial. Even so, the general trend suggested that Europe's leaders and peoples alike took very seriously the ideals articulated in the 1948 UN Universal Declaration of Human Rights.

NOTES

1. P. Anderson, "Managed Democracy," *London Review of Books*, August 27, 2015, pp. 19–27.
2. Quoted in T. Judt, *Postwar: A History of Europe Since 1945* (New York: Penguin, 2005), p. 691.
3. Ibid., pp. 698–699.
4. *Quarterly Labor Force Statistics*, vol. 2004/4 (Paris: OECD Publications, 2004), p. 64.
5. "Fertility Statistics," Eurostat: Statistics Explained, accessed August 7, 2015, http://ec.europa.eu/eurostat/statistics-explained/index.php/Fertility_statistics.
6. Quoted in *The Economist*, January 6, 2001, p. 6.
7. European Commission, *European Migration Network Annual Report on Immigration and Asylum 2014*, p. 9; European Commission, Migration and Home Affairs, "Irregular Migration and Return," accessed August 7, 2015, http://ec.europa.eu/dgs/home-affairs/what-we-do/policies/irregular-migration-return-policy/index_en.htm.
8. Mark Mazower, *Dark Continent: Europe's Twentieth Century* (New York: Vintage, 2000), p. 415; *United Nations International Migration Report 2006* (UN Department of Economic and Social Affairs), http://www.un.org/esa/populationpublications/2006_MigrationRep/report.htm.
9. L. Collingham, *Curry: A Tale of Cooks and Conquerors* (London: Oxford University Press, 2006), pp. 2, 9.
10. J. Klausen, *The Islamic Challenge: Politics and Religion in Western Europe* (New York: Oxford University Press, 2006), p. 16; Malise Ruthven, "The Big Muslim Problem!" *New York Review*, December 17, 2009, p. 62.
11. Quoted in Klausen, *The Islamic Challenge*, p. 16.
12. J. Gross, D. McMurray, and T. Swedenborg, "Rai, Rap, and Ramadan Nights: Franco-Maghribi Cultural Identities," in *Political Islam: Essays from Middle East Report*, ed. Joel Beinin and Joe Stork (London: I. B. Tauris, 1997), p. 258.
13. "Islam in Europe," *Wall Street Journal*, January 7, 2015, http://www.economist.com/blogs/graphicdetail/2015/01/daily-chart-2.
14. "Global Opinion of Obama Slips, International Policies Faulted," *Pew Research Global Attitudes Research Project*, June 13, 2012, http://www.pewglobal.org/2012/06/13/global-opinion-of-obama-slips-international-policies-faulted/.
15. Quoted in "Text: President Bush Addresses the Nation," *Washington Post Online*, September 20, 2001, http://www.washingtonpost.com/wp-srv/nation/specials/attacked/transcripts/bushaddress_092001.html.
16. See M. H. Hunt, ed., *The World Transformed, 1945 to the Present: A Documentary Reader* (Boston: Bedford/St. Martin's), pp. 410–411.
17. Statistics in *BP Statistical Review of World Energy June 2012*, http://www.bp.com/en_no/norway/media/press-releases-and-news/2012/bp-statistical-review-of-world-energy-2012.html.
18. M. T. Klare, *Resource Wars: The New Landscape of Global Conflict* (New York: Henry Holt, 2001), pp. 25–40.
19. A. E. Kramer, "Eastern Europe Fears New Era of Russian Sway," *New York Times*, October 13, 2009, p. A1.
20. Edward Wong, "Beijing Takes Steps to Fight Pollution as Problem Worsens," *New York Times*, January 31, 2013, p. A4.
21. Quoted in *International Herald Tribune*, June 15, 2001, p. 6.

LOOKING BACK LOOKING AHEAD

The twenty-first century opened with changes and new challenges for the Western world. The collapse of the East Bloc brought more-representative government to central and eastern Europe, but left millions struggling to adapt to a different way of life in market economies. High-tech information systems that quickened the pace of communications and the global reach of new supranational institutions made the world a smaller place, yet globalization left some struggling to maintain their livelihoods. New contacts between peoples, made possible by increased migration, revitalized European society, but the massive influx of refugees in 2015–2016 raised concerns about cultural tolerance and the EU's open internal borders policy.

One thing is sure: despite the success of European democracy and liberalism, and despite the high living standards enjoyed by most Europeans, the challenges won't go away. The search for solutions to environmental degradation and conflicts between ethnic and religious groups, and the promotion of human rights across the globe, will clearly occupy European and world leaders for some time to come.

However these issues play out, the study of the past puts the present and the future in perspective. Others before us have trodden the paths of uncertainty and crisis, and the historian's ability to analyze and explain the choices they made helps us understand our current situation and helps save us from exaggerated self-pity in the face of our own predicaments. Perhaps our Western heritage may rightly inspire us with measured pride and self-confidence. We stand, momentarily, at the head of the long procession of Western civilization. Sometimes the procession has wandered, or backtracked, or done terrible things. But it has also carried the efforts and sacrifices of generations of toiling, struggling ancestors. Through no effort of our own, we are the beneficiaries of those sacrifices and achievements. Now that it is our turn to carry the torch onward, we may remember these ties with our forebears.

To change the metaphor, we in the West are like card players who have been dealt many good cards. Some of them are obvious, such as our technical and scientific heritage, our environmental resources, and our commitment to human rights and individual freedoms. Others are not so obvious, sometimes half-forgotten or even hidden up the sleeve. Think, for example, of the almost-miraculous victory of peaceful revolution in the East Bloc in 1989 — an expression of what Czech playwright-turned-president Václav Havel called "the power of the powerless." Here we again see the regenerative strength of the Western ideals of individual rights and democratic government. We hold a good hand.

Our study of history, of mighty struggles and fearsome challenges, of shining achievements and tragic failures, gives a sense of the essence of life itself: the process of change over time. Again and again we have seen how peoples and societies evolve, influenced by ideas, human passions, and material conditions. This process of change will continue as the future becomes the present and then the past. Students of history are better prepared to make sense of this unfolding process because they have closely observed it. They understand that change is rooted in existing historical forces, and they have tools to explore the intricate web of activity that propels life forward. Students of history are prepared for the new and unexpected in human development, for they have already seen great breakthroughs and revolutions. They have an understanding of how things really happen.

Make Connections

Think about the larger developments and continuities within and across chapters.

1. Did people's lives really change dramatically during the wave of globalization that emerged in the late twentieth century? How have they stayed the same?

2. The globalization of today's world seems inseparable from advances in digital technology. How are the two connected? Were there other times in the history of Western society during which technological developments drove social, political, or cultural change?

3. How are the challenges that confront Europeans in the twenty-first century rooted in events and trends that came before?

30 REVIEW & EXPLORE

Identify Key Terms

Identify and explain the significance of each item below.

ethnic cleansing (p. 1026)

Color Revolutions (p. 1027)

globalization (p. 1028)

European Union (EU) (p. 1029)

Maastricht Treaty (p. 1031)

World Trade Organization (WTO) (p. 1032)

nongovernmental organizations
(NGOs) (p. 1032)

diasporas (p. 1039)

multiculturalism (p. 1039)

war on terror (p. 1047)

Muslim Brotherhood (p. 1047)

Arab Spring (p. 1048)

Islamic State (p. 1049)

climate change (p. 1051)

Review the Main Ideas

Answer the focus questions from each section of the chapter.

* How did life change in Russia and the former East Bloc countries after 1989? (p. 1020)

* How did globalization affect European life and society? (p. 1028)

* What are the main causes and effects of growing ethnic diversity in contemporary Europe?
(p. 1035)

* What challenges will Europeans face in the coming decades? (p. 1046)

Suggested Reading and Media Resources

BOOKS

* Berend, Ivan T. *Europe Since 1980*. 2010. A useful introduction to contemporary European history, including the crash of 2008 and its consequences.

* Caldwell, Christopher. *Reflections on the Revolution in Europe: Immigration, Islam, and the West*. 2009. A controversial and thought-provoking book that emphasizes the problems associated with growing numbers of Muslim immigrants in Europe.

* Gillingham, John. *European Integration, 1950–2003: Superstate or New Market Economy?* 2003. A brilliant interpretive history.

* Jordan, Andrew. *Environmental Policy in the European Union: Actors, Institutions and Processes*. 2005. A critical look at the European Union's response to major environmental problems.

* Klausen, Jytte. *The Islamic Challenge: Politics and Religion in Western Europe*. 2006. Reviews the goals of Europe's Islamic leaders and takes a positive view of future Muslim integration in western Europe.

* Laqueur, Walter. *Putinism: Russia and Its Future with the West*. 2015. A critical look at Russia's leader and Russian-U.S. relations after the Cold War, by a renowned historian.

* Noueihed, Lin, and Alex Warren. *The Battle for the Arab Spring: Revolution, Counter-Revolution, and the Making of a New Era*. 2012. Explores the causes and results of the popular revolutions in the Middle East and North Africa.

* Pinder, John, and Simon Usherwood. *The European Union: A Very Short Introduction*, 3d ed. 2013. A readable overview of the history, institutions, and policies of the European Union.

* Ramet, Sabrina P. *Balkan Babel: The Disintegration of Yugoslavia from the Death of Tito to the Fall of Milošević*. 2002. A thorough history of the collapse of Yugoslavia.

* Ryan, Johnny. *A History of the Internet and the Digital Future*. 2011. An accessible review of the way electronic communications are changing commercial, political, and cultural life.

+ Soros, George. *Financial Turmoil in Europe and the United States: Essays.* 2012. A collection of accessible articles on the 2008 global recession that offers explanations and prescriptions for overcoming the crisis in the United States and Europe.

+ Stiglitz, Joseph E. *Making Globalization Work.* 2006. An excellent overview of the successes and failures of globalization, by a distinguished economist.

+ Tarrow, Sidney. *The New Transnational Activism.* 2005. A sympathetic account of the transnational activism opposed to corporate globalization.

DOCUMENTARIES

+ *Citizenfour* (Laura Poitras, 2014). A documentary about Edward Snowden and the NSA leaks scandal.

+ *Debtocracy* (Aris Chatzistefanou and Katerina Kitidi, 2011). Explores the causes of the Greek debt crisis and critiques the government austerity plans intended to resolve it.

+ *Global Warming: The Signs and the Science* (PBS, 2005). Documents the evidence and effects of global warming; includes interviews with scientists on particular ways people can cope with or change this environmental problem.

+ *Once Brothers* (ESPN, 2010). A dramatized documentary about Drazen Petrovic and Vlade Divac, friends who played together on the Yugoslavian National Basketball team, but ended up on separate sides of the civil war.

FEATURE FILMS AND TELEVISION

+ *The Class* (Laurent Cantet, 2008). A teacher attempts to connect with his culturally diverse students in a working-class neighborhood in Paris.

+ *Good Bye Lenin!* (Wolfgang Becker, 2003). This comedy drama depicts Ostalgie through the story of a young man's efforts to re-create East Germany for his mother, who has recently awoken from a coma after the reunification of Germany.

+ *Leviathan* (Andrey Zvyagintsev, 2014). This moving film explores the challenges faced by ordinary people in postcommunist Russia.

WEB SITES

+ *European Union.* The European Union sponsors this Web site that explains "How the EU Works" and gives access to documents pertaining to the EU, among other resources. **europa.eu/**

+ *The History Place: Genocide in the 20th Century: Bosnia-Herzegovina.* An overview of the ethnic cleansing in Bosnia in the 1990s. **www.historyplace.com /worldhistory/genocide/bosnia.htm**

+ *Riots in France.* An online forum set up by the Social Science Research Council for scholars to discuss the 2005 riots in France. **riotsfrance.ssrc.org/**

+ *World Trade Organization.* The homepage of the World Trade Organization, which includes official documents pertaining to the WTO. **www.wto.org/**

Afrikaners Descendants of the Dutch settlers in the Cape Colony in southern Africa. (p. 805)

appeasement The British policy toward Germany prior to World War II that aimed at granting Hitler's territorial demands, including western Czechoslovakia, in order to avoid war. (p. 926)

Arab Spring A series of popular revolts in several countries in the Middle East and North Africa that sought an end to authoritarian, often Western-supported regimes. (p. 1048)

Atlantic slave trade The forced migration of Africans across the Atlantic for slave labor on plantations and in other industries; the trade reached its peak in the eighteenth century and ultimately involved more than 12 million Africans. (p. 562)

Aztec Empire A large and complex Native American civilization in modern Mexico and Central America that possessed advanced mathematical, astronomical, and engineering technology. (p. 440)

Balfour Declaration A 1917 British statement that declared British support of a National Home for the Jewish People in Palestine. (p. 857)

Battle of Peterloo The army's violent suppression of a protest that took place at Saint Peter's Fields in Manchester in reaction to the revision of the Corn Laws. (p. 704)

Bauhaus A German interdisciplinary school of fine and applied arts that brought together many leading modern architects, designers, and theatrical innovators. (p. 875)

Berlin Conference A meeting of European leaders held in 1884 and 1885 in order to lay down some basic rules for imperialist competition in sub-Saharan Africa. (p. 806)

"Black Legend" The notion that the Spanish were particularly ruthless and cruel in their conquest and domination of the Americas, an idea often propagated by Spain's rivals. (p. 458)

Black Shirts Mussolini's private militia that destroyed socialist newspapers, union halls, and Socialist Party headquarters, eventually pushing Socialists out of the city governments of northern Italy. (p. 916)

blood sports Events such as bullbaiting and cockfighting that involved inflicting violence and bloodshed on animals and that were popular with the eighteenth-century European masses. (p. 586)

Bloody Sunday A massacre of peaceful protesters at the Winter Palace in St. Petersburg in 1905, triggering a revolution that overturned absolute tsarist rule and made Russia into a conservative constitutional monarchy. (p. 770)

Bolsheviks Lenin's radical, revolutionary arm of the Russian party of Marxist socialism, which successfully installed a dictatorial socialist regime in Russia. (p. 848)

bourgeoisie The middle-class minority who owned the means of production and, according to Marx, exploited the working-class proletariat. (p. 697)

boyars The highest-ranking members of the Russian nobility. (p. 485)

Brezhnev Doctrine Doctrine created by Leonid Brezhnev that held that the Soviet Union had the right to intervene in any East Bloc country when necessary to preserve Communist rule. (p. 992)

cameralism View that monarchy was the best form of government, that all elements of society should serve the monarch, and that, in turn, the state should use its resources and authority to increase the public good. (p. 533)

caravel A small, maneuverable, three-mast sailing ship developed by the Portuguese in the fifteenth century that gave the Portuguese a distinct advantage in exploration and trade. (p. 433)

carnival The few days of revelry in Catholic countries that preceded Lent and that included drinking, masquerading, dancing, and rowdy spectacles that upset the established order. (p. 588)

Cartesian dualism Descartes's view that all of reality could ultimately be reduced to mind and matter. (p. 515)

charivari Degrading public rituals used by village communities to police personal behavior and maintain moral standards. (p. 578)

Christian Democrats Center-right political parties that rose to power in western Europe after the Second World War. (p. 952)

class-consciousness Awareness of belonging to a distinct social and economic class whose interests might conflict with those of other classes. (p. 676)

climate change Changes in long-standing weather patterns caused primarily by carbon dioxide emissions from the burning of fossil fuels. (p. 1051)

Cold War The rivalry between the Soviet Union and the United States that divided much of Europe into a Soviet-aligned Communist bloc and a U.S.-aligned capitalist bloc between 1945 and 1989. (p. 944)

collectivization of agriculture The forcible consolidation of individual peasant farms into large state-controlled enterprises in the Soviet Union under Stalin. (p. 911)

Color Revolutions A series of popular revolts and insurrections that challenged regional politicians and Russian interests in the former Soviet republics during the first decade of the twenty-first century. (p. 1027)

Columbian exchange The exchange of animals, plants, and diseases between the Old and the New Worlds. (p. 449)

Combination Acts British laws passed in 1799 that outlawed unions and strikes, favoring capitalist business people over skilled artisans. Bitterly resented and widely disregarded by many craft guilds, the acts were repealed by Parliament in 1824. (p. 677)

Common Market The European Economic Community, created by six western and central European countries in the West Bloc in 1957 as part of a larger search for European unity. (p. 954)

community controls A pattern of cooperation and common action in a traditional village that sought to uphold the economic, social, and moral stability of the closely knit community. (p. 578)

companionate marriage Marriage based on romantic love and middle-class family values that became increasingly dominant in the second half of the nineteenth century. (p. 736)

Congress of Vienna A meeting of the Quadruple Alliance (Russia, Prussia, Austria, and Great Britain), restoration France, and smaller European states to fashion a general peace settlement that began after the defeat of Napoleon's France in 1814. (p. 685)

conquistador Spanish for "conqueror"; Spanish soldier-explorers, such as Hernán Cortés and Francisco Pizarro, who sought to conquer the New World for the Spanish crown. (p. 433)

constitutionalism A form of government in which power is limited by law and balanced between the authority and power of the government, on the one hand, and the rights and liberties of the subjects or citizens on the other hand; could include constitutional monarchies or republics. (p. 492)

consumer revolution The wide-ranging growth in consumption and new attitudes toward consumer goods that emerged in the cities of northwestern Europe in the second half of the eighteenth century. (p. 589)

Continental System A blockade imposed by Napoleon to halt all trade between continental Europe and Britain, thereby weakening the British economy and military. (p. 637)

Copernican hypothesis The idea that the sun, not the earth, was the center of the universe. (p. 509)

Corn Laws British laws governing the import and export of grain, which were revised in 1815 to prohibit the importation of foreign grain unless the price at home rose to improbable levels, thus benefiting the aristocracy but making food prices high for working people. (p. 704)

Cossacks Free groups and outlaw armies originally comprising runaway peasants living on the borders of Russian territory from the fourteenth century onward. By the end of the sixteenth century they had formed an alliance with the Russian state. (p. 485)

cottage industry A stage of industrial development in which rural workers used hand tools in their homes to manufacture goods on a large scale for sale in a market. (p. 551)

Council for Mutual Economic Assistance (COMECON) An economic organization of Communist states meant to help rebuild East Bloc countries under Soviet auspices. (p. 950)

Crimean War A conflict fought between 1853 and 1856 over Russian desires to expand into Ottoman territory; Russia was defeated by France, Britain, and the Ottomans, underscoring the need for reform in the Russian Empire. (p. 766)

Crystal Palace The location of the Great Exhibition in 1851 in London; an architectural masterpiece made entirely of glass and iron. (p. 657)

Dadaism An artistic movement of the 1920s and 1930s that attacked all accepted standards of art and behavior and delighted in outrageous conduct. (p. 878)

Dawes Plan War reparations agreement that reduced Germany's yearly payments, made payment dependent on economic prosperity, and granted large U.S. loans to promote recovery. (p. 888)

debt peonage A form of serfdom that allowed a planter or rancher to keep his workers or slaves in perpetual debt bondage by periodically advancing food, shelter, and a little money. (p. 562)

decolonization The postwar reversal of Europe's overseas expansion caused by the rising demand of the colonized peoples themselves, the declining power of European nations, and the freedoms promised by U.S. and Soviet ideals. (p. 963)

deism Belief in a distant, noninterventionist deity; common among Enlightenment thinkers. (p. 520)

de-Stalinization The liberalization of the post-Stalin Soviet Union led by reformer Nikita Khrushchev. (p. 959)

détente The progressive relaxation of Cold War tensions that emerged in the early 1970s. (p. 983)

developed socialism A term used by Communist leaders to describe the socialist accomplishments of their societies, such as nationalized industry, collective agriculture, and extensive social welfare programs. (p. 1001)

diasporas Enclaves of ethnic groups settled outside of their homelands. (p. 1039)

displaced persons Postwar refugees, including 13 million Germans, former Nazi prisoners and forced laborers, and orphaned children. (p. 945)

Dreyfus affair A divisive case in which Alfred Dreyfus, a Jewish captain in the French army, was falsely accused and convicted of treason. The Catholic Church sided with the anti-Semites against Dreyfus; after Dreyfus was declared innocent, the French government severed all ties between the state and the church. (p. 776)

Duma The Russian parliament that opened in 1906, elected indirectly by universal male suffrage but controlled after 1907 by the tsar and the conservative classes. (p. 770)

economic liberalism A belief in free trade and competition based on Adam Smith's argument that the invisible hand of free competition would benefit all individuals, rich and poor. (p. 557)

economic miracle Term contemporaries used to describe rapid economic growth, often based on the consumer sector, in post–World War II western Europe. (p. 952)

empiricism A theory of inductive reasoning that calls for acquiring evidence through observation and experimentation rather than deductive reason and speculation. (p. 514)

Enabling Act An act pushed through the Reichstag by the Nazis that gave Hitler absolute dictatorial power for four years. (p. 919)

enclosure The movement to fence in fields in order to farm more effectively, at the expense of poor peasants who relied on common fields for farming and pasture. (p. 545)

encomienda system A system whereby the Spanish crown granted the conquerors the right to forcibly employ groups of Indians in exchange for providing food, shelter, and Christian teaching. (p. 446)

enlightened absolutism Term coined by historians to describe the rule of eighteenth-century monarchs who, without renouncing their own absolute authority, adopted Enlightenment ideals of rationalism, progress, and tolerance. (p. 532)

Enlightenment The influential intellectual and cultural movement of the late seventeenth and eighteenth centuries that introduced a new worldview based on the use of reason, the scientific method, and progress. (p. 517)

estates The three legal categories, or orders, of France's inhabitants: the clergy, the nobility, and everyone else. (p. 620)

Estates General A legislative body in prerevolutionary France made up of representatives of each of the three classes, or estates. It was called into session in 1789 for the first time since 1614. (p. 620)

ethnic cleansing The attempt to establish ethnically homogeneous territories by intimidation, forced deportation, and killing. (p. 1026)

eugenics A pseudoscientific doctrine that maintains that the selective breeding of human beings can improve the general characteristics of a national population, which helped inspire Nazi ideas about national unity and racial exclusion and ultimately contributed to the Holocaust. (p. 905)

European Union (EU) The economic, cultural, and political alliance of twenty-eight European nations. (p. 1029)

evolution The idea, applied by thinkers in many fields, that stresses gradual change and continuous adjustment. (p. 748)

existentialism A philosophy that stresses the meaninglessness of existence and the importance of the individual in searching for moral values in an uncertain world. (p. 870)

Factory Acts English laws passed from 1802 to 1833 that limited the workday of child laborers and set minimum hygiene and safety requirements. (p. 666)

fascism A movement characterized by extreme, often expansionist nationalism; anti-socialism; a dynamic and violent leader; and glorification of war and the military. (p. 905)

February Revolution Unplanned uprisings accompanied by violent street demonstrations begun in March 1917 (old calendar February) in Petrograd, Russia, that led to the abdication of the tsar and the establishment of a provisional government. (p. 846)

five-year plan A plan launched by Stalin in 1928, and termed the "revolution from above," aimed at modernizing the Soviet Union and creating a new Communist society with new attitudes, new loyalties, and a new socialist humanity. (p. 906)

Fourteen Points Wilson's 1918 peace proposal calling for open diplomacy, a reduction in armaments, freedom of commerce and trade, the establishment of the League of Nations, and national self-determination. (p. 855)

Fronde A series of violent uprisings during the early reign of Louis XIV triggered by growing royal control and increased taxation. (p. 474)

functionalism The principle that buildings, like industrial products, should serve as well as possible the purpose for which they were made, without excessive ornamentation. (p. 875)

German Social Democratic Party (SPD) A German working-class political party founded in the 1870s, the SPD championed Marxism but in practice turned away from Marxist revolution and worked instead in the German parliament for social and workplace reforms. (p. 774)

germ theory The idea that disease was caused by the spread of living organisms that could be controlled. (p. 723)

Girondists A moderate group that fought for control of the French National Convention in 1793. (p. 629)

glasnost Soviet premier Mikhail Gorbachev's popular campaign for openness in government and the media. (p. 1009)

globalization The emergence of a freer, more technologically connected global economy, accompanied by a worldwide exchange of cultural, political, and religious ideas. (p. 1028)

global mass migration The mass movement of people from Europe in the nineteenth century; one reason that the West's impact on the world was so powerful and many-sided. (p. 799)

Grand Empire The empire over which Napoleon and his allies ruled, encompassing virtually all of Europe except Great Britain and Russia. (p. 637)

Great Depression A worldwide economic depression from 1929 through 1939, unique in its severity and duration and with slow and uneven recovery. (p. 891)

Greater Germany A liberal plan for German national unification that included the German-speaking parts of the Austrian Empire, put forth at the national parliament in 1848 but rejected by Austrian rulers. (p. 714)

Great Famine The result of four years of potato crop failure in the late 1840s in Ireland, a country that had grown dependent on potatoes as a dietary staple. (p. 707)

Great Fear The fear of noble reprisals against peasant uprisings that seized the French countryside and led to further revolt. (p. 623)

Great Rebellion The 1857 and 1858 insurrection by Muslim and Hindu mercenaries in the British army that spread throughout northern and central India before finally being crushed. (p. 819)

guest worker programs Government-run programs in western Europe designed to recruit labor for the booming postwar economy. (p. 973)

guild system The organization of artisanal production into trade-based associations, or guilds, each of which received a monopoly over its trade and the right to train apprentices and hire workers. (p. 556)

gunboat diplomacy The use or threat of military force to coerce a government into economic or political agreements. (p. 798)

Haskalah The Jewish Enlightenment of the second half of the eighteenth century, led by the Prussian philosopher Moses Mendelssohn. (p. 538)

Holocaust The systematic effort of the Nazi state to exterminate all European Jews and other groups deemed racially inferior during the Second World War. (p. 932)

Holy Alliance An alliance formed by the conservative rulers of Austria, Prussia, and Russia in September 1815 that became a symbol of the repression of liberal and revolutionary movements all over Europe. (p. 688)

Homestead Act An American law enacted during the Civil War that gave western land to settlers, reinforcing the concept of free labor in a market economy. (p. 766)

hundred days of reform A series of Western-style reforms launched in 1898 by the Chinese government in an attempt to meet the foreign challenge. (p. 822)

id, ego, and superego Freudian terms to describe the three parts of the self and the basis of human behavior, which Freud saw as basically irrational. (p. 874)

illegitimacy explosion The sharp increase in out-of-wedlock births that occurred in Europe between 1750 and 1850, caused by low wages and the breakdown of community controls. (p. 579)

Inca Empire The vast and sophisticated Peruvian empire centered at the capital city of Cuzco that was at its peak from 1438 until 1532. (p. 441)

Industrial Revolution A term first coined in 1799 to describe the burst of major inventions and economic expansion that began in Britain in the late eighteenth century. (p. 651)

industrious revolution The shift that occurred as families in northwestern Europe focused on earning wages instead of producing goods for household consumption; this reduced their economic self-sufficiency but increased their ability to purchase consumer goods. (p. 553)

iron law of wages Theory proposed by English economist David Ricardo suggesting that the pressure of population growth prevents wages from rising above the subsistence level. (p. 657)

Islamic State A radical Islamist militia in control of substantial parts of central Syria and Iraq, where it applies an extremist version of shari'a law. (p. 1049)

Jacobin Club A political club in revolutionary France whose members were well-educated radical republicans. (p. 628)

janissary corps The core of the sultan's army, composed of slave conscripts from non-Muslim parts of the empire; after 1683 it became a volunteer force. (p. 489)

Jansenism A sect of Catholicism originating with Cornelius Jansen that emphasized the heavy weight of original sin and accepted the doctrine of predestination; it was outlawed as heresy by the pope. (p. 600)

Junkers The nobility of Brandenburg and Prussia, they were reluctant allies of Frederick William in his consolidation of the Prussian state. (p. 482)

just price The idea that prices should be fair, protecting both consumers and producers, and that they should be imposed by government decree if necessary. (p. 588)

Karlsbad Decrees Issued in 1819, these repressive regulations were designed to uphold Metternich's conservatism, requiring the German states to root out subversive ideas and squelch any liberal organizations. (p. 689)

kulaks The better-off peasants who were stripped of land and livestock under Stalin and were generally not permitted to join collective farms; many of them starved or were deported to forced-labor camps for "re-education." (p. 911)

Kulturkampf Bismarck's attack on the Catholic Church within Germany from 1870 to 1878, resulting from Pius IX's declaration of papal infallibility. (p. 774)

labor aristocracy The highly skilled workers, such as factory foremen and construction bosses, who made up about 15 percent of the working classes from about 1850 to 1914. (p. 731)

laissez faire A doctrine of economic liberalism that calls for unrestricted private enterprise and no government interference in the economy. (p. 691)

Lateran Agreement A 1929 agreement that recognized the Vatican as an independent state, with Mussolini agreeing to give the church heavy financial support in return for public support from the pope. (p. 917)

law of inertia A law formulated by Galileo that states that motion, not rest, is the natural state of an object, and that an object continues in motion forever unless stopped by some external force. (p. 510)

law of universal gravitation Newton's law that all objects are attracted to one another and that the force of attraction is proportional to the objects' quantity of matter and inversely proportional to the square of the distance between them. (p. 510)

League of Nations A permanent international organization, established during the 1919 Paris Peace Conference, designed to protect member states from aggression and avert future wars. (p. 855)

liberalism The principal ideas of this movement were equality and liberty; liberals demanded representative government and equality before the law as well as individual freedoms such as freedom of the press, freedom of speech, freedom of assembly, freedom of worship, and freedom from arbitrary arrest. (p. 691)

logical positivism A philosophy that sees meaning in only those beliefs that can be empirically proven, and that therefore rejects most of the concerns of traditional philosophy, from the existence of God to the meaning of happiness, as nonsense. (p. 869)

Luddites Group of handicraft workers who attacked factories in northern England in 1811 and later, smashing the new machines that they believed were putting them out of work. (p. 673)

Maastricht Treaty The basis for the formation of the European Union, which set financial and cultural standards for potential member states and defined criteria for membership in the monetary union. (p. 1031)

mandate system The plan to allow Britain and France to administer former Ottoman territories, put into place after the end of the First World War. (p. 856)

Marshall Plan American plan for providing economic aid to western Europe to help it rebuild. (p. 949)

Marxism An influential political program based on the socialist ideas of German radical Karl Marx, which called for a working-class revolution to overthrow capitalist society and establish a Communist state. (p. 696)

Meiji Restoration The restoration of the Japanese emperor to power in 1867, leading to the subsequent modernization of Japan. (p. 820)

mercantilism A system of economic regulations aimed at increasing the power of the state based on the belief that a nation's international power was based on its wealth, specifically its supply of gold and silver. (p. 478)

Methodists Members of a Protestant revival movement started by John Wesley, so called because they were so methodical in their devotion. (p. 599)

millet system A system used by the Ottomans whereby subjects were divided into religious communities, with each millet (nation) enjoying autonomous self-government under its religious leaders. (p. 489)

Mines Act of 1842 English law prohibiting underground work for all women and girls as well as for boys under ten. (p. 669)

"modern girl" Somewhat stereotypical image of the modern and independent working woman popular in the 1920s. (p. 882)

modernism A label given to the artistic and cultural movements of the late nineteenth and early twentieth centuries, which were typified by radical experimentation that challenged traditional forms of artistic expression. (p. 874)

Mountain, the Led by Robespierre, the French National Convention's radical faction, which seized legislative power in 1793. (p. 629)

multiculturalism The mixing of ethnic styles in daily life and in cultural works such as film, music, art, and literature. (p. 1039)

Muslim Brotherhood Islamic social and political reform group founded in Egypt in 1928 that called for national liberation from European control and a return to shari'a law (based on Muslim legal codes), and demanded land reform, extensive social welfare programs, and economic independence. (p. 1047)

Napoleonic Code French civil code promulgated in 1804 that reasserted the 1789 principles of the equality of all male citizens before the law and the absolute security of wealth and private property, as well as restricting rights accorded to women by previous revolutionary laws. (p. 636)

National Assembly The first French revolutionary legislature, made up primarily of representatives of the third estate and a few from the nobility and clergy, in session from 1789 to 1791. (p. 621)

nationalism The idea that each people had its own genius and specific identity that manifested itself especially in a common language and history, and often led to the desire for an independent political state. (p. 692)

national self-determination The notion that peoples should be able to choose their own national governments through democratic majority-rule elections and live free from outside interference in nation-states with clearly defined borders. (p. 855)

National Socialism A movement and political party driven by extreme nationalism and racism, led by Adolf Hitler; its adherents ruled Germany from 1933 to 1945 and forced Europe into World War II. (p. 918)

nativism Policies and beliefs, often influenced by nationalism, scientific racism, and mass migration, that give preferential treatment to established inhabitants over immigrants. (p. 804)

NATO The North Atlantic Treaty Organization, an anti-Soviet military alliance of Western governments. (p. 950)

natural philosophy An early modern term for the study of the nature of the universe, its purpose, and how it functioned; it encompassed what we would call "science" today. (p. 507)

Navigation Acts A series of English laws that controlled the import of goods to Britain and British colonies. (p. 559)

neocolonialism A postcolonial system that perpetuates Western economic exploitation in former colonial territories. (p. 972)

neo-Europes Settler colonies with established populations of Europeans, such as North America, Australia, New Zealand, and Latin America, where Europe found outlets for population growth and its most profitable investment opportunities in the nineteenth century. (p. 796)

neoliberalism Philosophy of 1980s conservatives who argued for privatization of state-run industries and decreased government spending on social services. (p. 994)

New Economic Policy (NEP) Lenin's 1921 policy to re-establish limited economic freedom in an attempt to rebuild agriculture and industry in the face of economic disintegration. (p. 906)

New Imperialism The late-nineteenth-century drive by European countries to create vast political empires abroad. (p. 804)

New Left A 1960s counterculture movement that embraced updated forms of Marxism to challenge both Western capitalism and Soviet-style communism. (p. 988)

New Order Hitler's program based on racial imperialism, which gave preferential treatment to the "Nordic" peoples; the French, an "inferior" Latin people, occupied a middle position; and Slavs and Jews were treated harshly as "subhumans." (p. 931)

nonalignment Policy of postcolonial governments to remain neutral in the Cold War and play both the United States and the Soviet Union for what they could get. (p. 965)

nongovernmental organizations (NGOs) Independent organizations with specific agendas, such as humanitarian aid or environmental protection, that conduct international programs and activities. (p. 1032)

OPEC The Organization of Petroleum Exporting Countries. (p. 993)

Opium Wars Two mid-nineteenth-century conflicts between China and Great Britain over the British trade in opium, which were designed to "open" China to European free trade. In defeat, China gave European traders and missionaries increased protection and concessions. (p. 797)

Orientalism A term coined by literary scholar Edward Said to describe the way Westerners misunderstood and described colonial subjects and cultures. (p. 813)

Ostpolitik German for Chancellor Willy Brandt's new "Eastern policy"; West Germany's attempt in the 1970s to ease diplomatic tensions with East Germany, exemplifying the policies of détente. (p. 983)

Peace of Utrecht A series of treaties, from 1713 to 1715, that ended the War of the Spanish Succession, ended French expansion in Europe, and marked the rise of the British Empire. (p. 479)

Peace of Westphalia The name of a series of treaties that concluded the Thirty Years' War in 1648 and marked the end of large-scale religious violence in Europe. (p. 468)

People's Budget A bill proposed after the Liberal Party came to power in Britain in 1906, it was designed to increase spending on social welfare services, but was initially vetoed in the House of Lords. (p. 776)

perestroika Economic restructuring and reform implemented by Premier Mikhail Gorbachev in the Soviet Union in 1985. (p. 1008)

Petrograd Soviet A huge, fluctuating mass meeting of two to three thousand workers, soldiers, and socialist intellectuals modeled on the revolutionary soviets of 1905. (p. 847)

philosophes A group of French intellectuals who proclaimed that they were bringing the light of knowledge to their fellow humans in the Age of Enlightenment. (p. 519)

Pietism A Protestant revival movement in early-eighteenth-century Germany and Scandinavia that emphasized a warm and emotional religion, the priesthood of all believers, and the power of Christian rebirth in everyday affairs. (p. 598)

Popular Front A short-lived New Deal–inspired alliance in France led by Léon Blum that encouraged the union movement and launched a far-reaching program of social reform. (p. 898)

postcolonial migration The postwar movement of people from former colonies and the developing world into Europe. (p. 973)

postindustrial society A society that relies on high-tech and service-oriented jobs for economic growth rather than heavy industry and manufacturing jobs. (p. 993)

privatization The sale of state-managed industries such as transportation and communication networks to private owners; a key aspect of broader neoliberal economic reforms meant to control government spending, increase private profits, and foster economic growth, which were implemented in western Europe in response to the economic crisis of the 1970s. (p. 994)

proletarianization The transformation of large numbers of small peasant farmers into landless rural wage earners. (p. 548)

proletariat The industrial working class who, according to Marx, were unfairly exploited by the profit-seeking bourgeoisie. (p. 697)

Protectorate The English military dictatorship (1653–1658) established by Oliver Cromwell following the execution of Charles I. (p. 494)

Ptolemy's *Geography* A second-century-C.E. work that synthesized the classical knowledge of geography and introduced the concepts of longitude and latitude. Reintroduced to Europeans about 1410 by Arab scholars, its ideas allowed cartographers to create more accurate maps. (p. 433)

public sphere An idealized intellectual space that emerged in Europe during the Enlightenment, where the public came together to discuss important issues relating to society, economics, and politics. (p. 529)

Puritans Members of a sixteenth- and seventeenth-century reform movement within the Church of England that advocated purifying it of Roman Catholic elements, like bishops, elaborate ceremonials, and wedding rings. (p. 492)

putting-out system The eighteenth-century system of rural industry in which a merchant loaned raw materials to cottage workers, who processed them and returned the finished products to the merchant. (p. 551)

rationalism A secular, critical way of thinking in which nothing was to be accepted on faith, and everything was to be submitted to reason. (p. 518)

Realism A literary movement that, in contrast to Romanticism, stressed the depiction of life as it actually was. (p. 749)

Red Shirts The guerrilla army of Giuseppe Garibaldi, who invaded Sicily in 1860 in an attempt to liberate it, winning the hearts of the Sicilian peasantry. (p. 760)

Reform Bill of 1832 A major British political reform that increased the number of male voters by about 50 percent and gave political representation to new industrial areas. (p. 705)

Reichstag The popularly elected lower house of government of the new German Empire after 1871. (p. 774)

Reign of Terror The period from 1793 to 1794 during which Robespierre's Committee of Public Safety tried and executed thousands suspected of treason and a new revolutionary culture was imposed. (p. 631)

republicanism A form of government in which there is no monarch and power rests in the hands of the people as exercised through elected representatives. (p. 492)

revisionism An effort by moderate socialists to update Marxist doctrines to reflect the realities of the late nineteenth century. (p. 788)

Rocket The name given to George Stephenson's effective locomotive that was first tested in 1829 on the Liverpool and Manchester Railway at 35 miles per hour. (p. 656)

rococo A popular style in Europe in the eighteenth century, known for its soft pastels, ornate interiors, sentimental portraits, and starry-eyed lovers protected by hovering cupids. (p. 528)

Romanticism An artistic movement at its height from about 1790 to the 1840s that was in part a revolt against classicism and the Enlightenment, characterized by a belief in emotional exuberance, unrestrained imagination, and spontaneity in both art and personal life. (p. 697)

salon Regular social gathering held by talented and rich Parisians in their homes, where philosophes and their followers met to discuss literature, science, and philosophy. (p. 528)

sans-culottes The laboring poor of Paris, so called because the men wore trousers instead of the knee breeches of the aristocracy and middle class; the word came to refer to the militant radicals of the city. (p. 629)

Schlieffen Plan Failed German plan calling for a lightning attack through neutral Belgium and a quick defeat of France before turning on Russia. (p. 833)

Second Industrial Revolution The burst of industrial creativity and technological innovation that promoted strong economic growth in the last third of the nineteenth century. (p. 745)

second revolution From 1792 to 1795, the second phase of the French Revolution, during which the fall of the French monarchy introduced a rapid radicalization of politics. (p. 629)

Second Vatican Council A meeting of Catholic leaders convened from 1962 to 1965 that initiated a number of reforms, including the replacement of Latin with local languages in church services, designed to democratize the church and renew its appeal. (p. 985)

sensationalism The idea that all human ideas and thoughts are produced as a result of sensory impressions. (p. 519)

separate spheres A gender division of labor with the wife at home as mother and homemaker and the husband as wage earner. (pp. 666, 739)

Social Darwinism A body of thought drawn from the ideas of Charles Darwin that applied the theory of biological evolution to human affairs and saw the human race as driven by an unending economic struggle that would determine the survival of the fittest. (p. 748)

socialism A backlash against the emergence of individualism and the fragmentation of industrial society, and a move toward cooperation and a sense of community; the key ideas were economic planning, greater social equality, and state regulation of property. (p. 693)

Socialist Realism Artistic movement that followed the dictates of Communist ideals, enforced by state control in the Soviet Union and East Bloc countries in the 1950s and 1960s. (p. 957)

Solidarity Independent Polish trade union that worked for workers' rights and political reform throughout the 1980s. (p. 1005)

spinning jenny A simple, inexpensive, hand-powered spinning machine created by James Hargreaves in 1765. (p. 652)

stadholder The executive officer in each of the United Provinces of the Netherlands, a position often held by the princes of Orange. (p. 497)

stagflation Term coined in the early 1980s to describe the combination of low growth and high inflation that led to a worldwide recession. (p. 993)

steam engines A breakthrough invention by Thomas Savery in 1698 and Thomas Newcomen in 1705 that burned coal to produce steam, which was then used to operate a pump;

the early models were superseded by James Watt's more efficient steam engine, patented in 1769. (p. 655)

stream-of-consciousness technique A literary technique, found in works by Virginia Woolf, James Joyce, and others, that uses interior monologue—a character's thoughts and feelings as they occur—to explore the human psyche. (p. 880)

suffrage movement A militant movement for women's right to vote led by middle-class British women around 1900. (p. 743)

sultan The ruler of the Ottoman Empire; he owned all the agricultural land of the empire and was served by an army and bureaucracy composed of highly trained slaves. (p. 489)

sweated industries Poorly paid handicraft production, often carried out by married women paid by the piece and working at home. (p. 734)

Tanzimat A set of reforms designed to remake the Ottoman Empire on a western European model. (p. 772)

tariff protection A government's way of supporting and aiding its own economy by laying high taxes on imported goods from other countries, as when the French responded to cheaper British goods flooding their country by imposing high tariffs on some imported products. (p. 663)

Test Act Legislation, passed by the English Parliament in 1673, to secure the position of the Anglican Church by stripping Puritans, Catholics, and other dissenters of the right to vote, preach, assemble, hold public office, and teach at or attend the universities. (p. 496)

theory of special relativity Albert Einstein's theory that time and space are relative to the observer and that only the speed of light remains constant. (p. 872)

Thermidorian reaction A reaction to the violence of the Reign of Terror in 1794, resulting in the execution of Robespierre and the loosening of economic controls. (p. 634)

thermodynamics A branch of physics built on Newton's laws of mechanics that investigated the relationship between heat and mechanical energy. (p. 745)

totalitarianism A radical dictatorship that exercises "total claims" over the beliefs and behavior of its citizens by taking control of the economic, social, intellectual, and cultural aspects of society. (p. 904)

total war A war in which distinctions between the soldiers on the battlefield and civilians at home are blurred, and where the government plans and controls economic and social life in order to supply the armies at the front with supplies and weapons. (p. 833)

Treaty of Brest-Litovsk Peace treaty signed in March 1918 between the Central Powers and Russia that ended Russian participation in World War I and ceded Russian territories containing a third of the Russian Empire's population to the Central Powers. (p. 851)

Treaty of Paris The treaty that ended the Seven Years' War in Europe and the colonies in 1763, and ratified British victory on all colonial fronts. (p. 560)

Treaty of Tordesillas The 1494 agreement giving Spain everything to the west of an imaginary line drawn down the Atlantic and giving Portugal everything to the east. (p. 437)

Treaty of Versailles The 1919 peace settlement that ended war between Germany and the Allied powers. (p. 855)

trench warfare A type of fighting used in World War I behind rows of trenches, mines, and barbed wire; the cost in lives was staggering and the gains in territory minimal. (p. 835)

Triple Alliance The alliance of Austria, Germany, and Italy. Italy left the alliance when war broke out in 1914 on the grounds that Austria had launched a war of aggression. (p. 829)

Triple Entente The alliance of Great Britain, France, and Russia prior to and during the First World War. (p. 830)

Truman Doctrine America's policy geared to containing communism to those countries already under Soviet control. (p. 949)

utilitarianism The idea of Jeremy Bentham that social policies should promote the "greatest good for the greatest number." (p. 722)

Velvet Revolution The term given to the relatively peaceful overthrow of communism in Czechoslovakia; the label came to signify the collapse of the East Bloc in general in 1989 to 1990. (p. 1011)

viceroyalties The name for the four administrative units of Spanish possessions in the Americas: New Spain, Peru, New Granada, and La Plata. (p. 445)

War Communism The application of centralized state control during the Russian civil war, in which the Bolsheviks seized grain from peasants, introduced rationing, nationalized all banks and industry, and required everyone to work. (p. 851)

war guilt clause An article in the Treaty of Versailles that declared that Germany (with Austria) was solely responsible for the war and had to pay reparations equal to all civilian damages caused by the fighting. (p. 856)

war on terror American policy under President George W. Bush to fight global terrorism in all its forms. (p. 1047)

Warsaw Pact Soviet-backed military alliance of East Bloc Communist countries in Europe. (p. 950)

water frame A spinning machine created by Richard Arkwright that had a capacity of several hundred spindles and used waterpower; it therefore required a larger and more specialized mill—a factory. (p. 653)

wet-nursing A widespread and flourishing business in the eighteenth century in which women were paid to breast-feed other women's babies. (p. 581)

white man's burden The idea that Europeans could and should civilize more primitive nonwhite peoples and that imperialism would eventually provide nonwhites with modern achievements and higher standards of living. (p. 812)

World Trade Organization (WTO) A powerful supranational financial institution that sets trade and tariff agreements for over 150 member countries and so helps manage a large percentage of the world's import-export policies. Like the IMF and the World Bank, the WTO promotes neoliberal policies around the world. (p. 1032)

Young Turks Fervent patriots who seized power in a 1908 coup in the Ottoman Empire, forcing the conservative sultan to implement reforms. (p. 773)

Zionism A movement dedicated to building a Jewish national homeland in Palestine, started by Theodor Herzl. (p. 783)

Ellis, Sarah Stickney, *Women of England, The: Their Social Duties and Domestic Habits,* 676(d)
Ellis Island, 802(b)
Emancipation
    of Jews, 782–783
    of slaves, 618
Embargo, on OPEC oil, 993
Emigration. *See also* Immigrants and immigration; Migrants and migration
    from Asia, 802–804, 804(i)
    from Europe, 800–801, 800(f), 801(f)
    family and friendship ties in, 801
    from Ireland, 666, 707
    of Jews, 921, 945
    use of term, 799
Emile or On Education (Rousseau), 584
Emperors. *See* Empire(s)Holy Roman Empire; specific emperors
Empire(s). *See also* Colonies and colonization; Imperialism; New imperialism; specific empires
    in Africa, 806–808, 807(m), 809(b)
    in Asia and Pacific region, 569–571
    Austrian, 778
    Aztec, 440–441, 443(d), 506
    Communist, 908
    decolonization and, 963–972
    after First World War, 855
    in France, 610, 636–640, 756(i), 757
    German, 774–775
    Inca, 441, 444, 448(i), 451(b)(i)
    Japanese, 934–935
    multinational, 829
    natural history and, 511–512
    Nazi, 929
    New Imperialism and, 804–805
    Ottoman, 430–431, 489–490, 490(m), 492, 766, 772–773
    Persian, 430
    Portuguese, 435
    Russian, 485–487, 766–772
    seaborne trade, 431, 452(m)
    technology and, 810(i)
    women and, 814–815(d), 815(d)(i)
Empiricism, 514, 515, 516
Employment. *See also* Labor; Unemployment; Workers
    of women, 734, 843–844, 843(i)
Enabling Act (Germany, 1933), 919
Enclosure, 545, 546–548, 547(d), 551
Encomienda system, 446, 448, 449
Encyclopedia (Diderot and d'Alembert), 520–521, 526(i), 527(d), 528, 533
Energy
    electricity as, 745
    environment and, 1051, 1052
    matter and, 872–873
    new physics and, 872–873
    prices of, 993
    resource uses and, 1051
Energy crisis, 993
    in East Bloc, 1004
Engels, Friedrich, 673, 696, 696(i), 697
Engine. *See also* Steam power
    internal combustion engine, 745
Engineers and engineering, urban, 725(b)
England (Britain). *See also* Britain; British East India Company; Decolonization; First World War; London; Parliament (England); Second World War
    absolutism and, 494
    Act of Union with Scotland and Ireland, 521

Africa and, 806, 808
    agriculture in, 546–547
    American Revolution and, 615–616
    Asia and, 569, 810
    Bill of Rights in, 496, 617
    birthrate in, 741(f)
    British Empire and, 819–820
    Catholic Church in, 496
    China trade and, 797
    cinema in, 883–886
    cities in, 721
    civil war in, 493–494, 494(i)
    coal industry in, 651, 653, 655, 668–669
    coffeehouse in, 530–531(b), 530(b)(i)
    colonies of, 444–445, 565–566, 808, 809(b)
    common law in, 495
    in Common Market, 993
    constitutional monarchy in, 464, 468, 492, 496–497
    cottage industry in, 551, 552(m), 650(m), 651–652
    Crystal Palace exhibit in, 656, 657, 660(i), 718, 719(i)
    death rate decline in, 723(f)
    decolonization and, 968
    domestic servants in, 734
    at Dunkirk, 928
    economy after First World War and, 887
    Egypt and, 799, 811
    electricity in, 746–747(d), 746(d)(i)
    emigrants from, 800
    enclosure in, 545, 546–548, 547(d)
    EU membership vote in, 1050
    exploration by, 439
    exports of manufactured goods by, 562, 562(f)
    farming in, 546–547
    before First World War, 829–830, 832
    First World War and, 828, 829, 833, 835, 844
    after First World War, 855, 856–860, 887, 890–891
    France and, 559–560, 887
    general strike in (1926), 890
    government of, 492
    Great Depression in, 893, 895, 897
    immigrants to, 973
    imperialism by, 810
    imports and, 562, 795
    income in, 727–728, 794(f)
    India and, 569–570, 570(i)
    industrialization in, 648, 650–660, 654(b), 657(m), 658–659(b), 661(f), 721
    industrial labor from, 665
    Industrial Revolution in, 794
    infant mortality in, 581
    Ireland and, 493, 495, 496, 776–777, 844, 1001
    Islamic extremism and, 1055(d)
    Jews in, 495
    labor in, 678, 692, 787
    Labour Party in, 788, 891, 954
    laws in, 496, 498
    liberalism in, 623, 691
    literacy in, 585
    London blitz and, 929, 929(d)
    mandates of, 856–860
    manufacturing in, 562, 651
    Napoleon and, 636–637
    nationalism in, 830
    navy of, 471, 559, 651
    neoliberalism in, 994
    Ottoman Empire and, 772

peasants in, 544
    politics in, 776
    population in, 549(f), 657
    postwar occupation by, 945
    Protestantism in, 496
    Puritans in, 492, 494–495
    radio networks in, 886
    railroads in, 656, 658–659(b), 658(b)(i), 659(b)(i)
    Realism in, 751
    recession in, 1049
    reform in, 704–706
    reparations after First World War and, 890
    Restoration in, 495–496
    Rockers in, 976(i)
    Romantic poets in, 698(d), 699
    rural textile production in, 551
    Scotland and, 496
    Second World War and, 928, 935–937
    after Second World War, 954
    Seven Years' War and, 532, 560, 614–615
    slave trade and, 543(i), 563
    smallpox in, 605
    socialists in, 788
    social welfare in, 776
    and South Africa, 805–806
    taxation in, 651
    tea party in India, 815(b)(i)
    Thirty Years' War and, 468, 492
    trade and, 543(i)
    travel restrictions and, 1037
    unemployment in, 548, 893(m)
    welfare state in, 954
    wives in, 742
    women's fashion in, 732–733(b), 732(b)(i), 733(b)(i)
    women's voting rights in, 776
    wool trade and, 431, 650
    youth styles in, 975
English East India Company. *See* British East India Company
ENIAC (Electronic Numerical Integrator and Computer), 952
Enlightened absolutism, 532–536, 538, 569
Enlightenment, 517–532
    18th-century revolutions and, 517
    American, 567, 569
    Atlantic, 567, 569
    in Austria, 534–536, 538
    children and, 521, 528, 583
    China and, 525
    coffeehouses in, 529, 530–531(b), 530(b)(i), 531(b)(i)
    colonial, 567, 569
    culture in, 524–525, 528–529, 532, 586
    defined, 517
    in Dutch Republic, 518
    early, 518–519
    English, 524, 525, 528
    French, 519–520
    German, 524
    impact on society, 504
    industrialization and, 650, 655
    international, 521, 524
    Islam and, 525
    Italian, 524
    Jews in, 537(b), 538
    major figures of, 519
    philosophes in, 518, 519–521, 520(i), 526, 528
    Prussian, 532–533
    race and, 525–526, 565, 782
    religious tolerance and, 522–523(d)

"Oslo Breakfast," as welfare, 897(i)
Ostpolitik policy, 982(i), 983
Othello (Shakespeare), 460
Ottoman Empire. *See also* Ottoman Turks; Turkey
   Armenian deportation from, 839, 840(i)
   Austria and, 482, 483(m)
   Balkan wars and, 832
   Egypt and, 428, 798
   in 1566, 490(m)
   First World War and, 831, 831(m), 833, 839
   after First World War, 855, 856–861
   government of, 489
   as Great Power (1815), 686(m)
   Hungary and, 482, 492
   Jews in, 857
   military in, 489, 492
   modernization of, 766, 772–773
   nationalism in, 778
   partition of, 858–859(d), 859(d)(m)
   reform in, 772–773
   religion in, 430
   religious toleration in, 484, 489
   Romanticism and nationalism in, 701
   Russia and, 766, 770
   trade and, 430–431
   Transylvania and, 482, 483(m), 492
Ottoman Turks. *See also* Ottoman Empire; Turks
   Constantinople and, 430
Outsourcing, 1033
Overfertilization, 1051
Overfishing, 1051
Overseas expansion. *See* Expansion; Exploration
Owen, Robert, 666, 675(d), 678, 693, 787
Owen, Wilfred, "Dulce et Decorum Est," 838(d)
Oxen, plowing with, 546
Oxfam, 1032–1033
Ozymandias (Shelley), 698(d)

Pacific Ocean region
   First World War and, 840
   Magellan in, 438–439
   Second World War in, 934–935, 935(m)
   trade and empire in, 569–571
   United States and, 766
Pacifism, in First World War, 841
Paine, Thomas, 586, 616
Painting. *See also* Art(s)
   baroque, 499–500(i), 500
   castas, 569(i)
   modern, 875
   Realism in, 749(i)
   Romantic, 699(i), 701–702, 701(i)
Pakistan
   creation of, 967
   U.S. drone attacks and, 1047
Palaces
   of absolute monarchs, 476–477(b), 476(b)(i), 477(b)(i)
   of Electricity (Paris), 746(d)(i)
Pale of Settlement, 538, 538(m), 801
Palermo, 471
Palestine. *See also* Israel
   Balfour Declaration and, 857
   British and, 856, 967
   First World War and, 839–840
   Israel and, 967, 967(m), 1047
   Jews in, 783
   U.S. support for Israel and, 1046
Palm d'Aelders, Etta, 627(d)
Palmyra, Syria, 1049
Panama Canal, 795

Panics
   financial, 891
   worldwide, 1028–1029
Pankhurst, Emily, 743(i)
Papa, Mama, and Baby (Droz), 741
Papacy. *See also* Catholic Church; Protestant Reformation; specific popes
   Italy and, 758, 915
Papal States, 760
Paper, in China, 506
Paracelsus, 516
Pareja, Juan de, 453(b), 453(b)(i)
Paris. *See also* France; French Revolution; Paris, Treaty of; Parlement of Paris
   apartment living in, 729(i)
   autobiography of boyhood in, 583(d)
   Bastille in, 611(i), 622
   clothing in, 591, 592
   coffeehouse in, 530(b)
   guilds in, 556, 557
   immigrants in, 1039
   lifestyle in, 590–591(d)
   modernization of, 725–726, 726(m)
   newspaper publishing in, 710(b), 711(b)(i)
   republicanism in (1848), 709
   revolution of 1830 in, 706–707(i), 708
   revolutions of 1848 and, 709–712
   scientific academy in, 517
   in Second Empire, 756(i)
   Second World War and, 931, 944
   student protests in, 989(i)
   terrorist attacks in, 1041(i)
   Universal Exhibition in (1900), 746(d)(i)
   University of, 990
   urban planning in, 725–726, 726(m)
Paris, Treaty of
   of 1763, 560, 570, 615
   of 1783, 617
   in 1815, 687
Paris Accord (1990), 1013
Paris Commune (1871), 764, 775
Parish churches, 597
Paris peace conference (1919). *See* Versailles, Treaty of
Parlement of Paris, 474, 620
Parlements (France), 619
Parliament. *See also* Parliament (England)
   in Germany, 762–763, 918
   in Prussia, 762
Parliament (England). *See also* House of Commons (England); House of Lords (England)
   American Revolution and, 616
   Charles I and, 492, 493, 494
   constitutional monarchy and, 492, 496
   Cromwell and, 494
   liberalism and, 616, 776
   restoration of, 495
   sovereignty in, 496, 519
   voting for, 496
Parliamentary government
   communism, fascism, and, 904
   in England, 492
Partisans, Belgian, 833
Partitions. *See also* East Germany; West Germany
   of Africa, 807(m)
   of India, 966(i), 967
   of Ottoman Empire, 855, 858–859(d), 859(d)(m)
   of Poland, 534, 535(m), 855
Party of Democratic Socialism (Germany), 1012
Passive citizenship, 626(d)
Pasternak, Boris, 961

Pasteur, Louis, and pasteurization, 723, 725, 745
Patriarchy
   in 17th century, 466
   feminism and, 999
Patriotism. *See also* Nationalism
   in First World War, 842(b)
   in Germany, 888
   images of, 780(i)
   Russian, 851
   workers and, 787
Patronage, in French court, 476
Peace
   Chamberlain on (1938), 927–928, 927(i)
   after Cold War, 1013
   demonstration for (2006), 1053(i)
   after First World War, 852–853, 855–861
   Russia in First World War and, 851
   after Second World War, 942
   UN troops for, 1032
   between world wars, 886–891
"Peace, Land, and Bread for the Russian People" (Lenin), 850(d)
Peaceful coexistence policy, 961
Peace of Augsburg, 468
Peace of Utrecht, 479, 480(m), 560
Peace of Westphalia, 468, 469(m)
Pearl Harbor, Japanese attack on, 934
Peasants. *See also* Agriculture; Land; Serfs and serfdom
   in 17th century, 466–467, 466(i)
   in Austria, 536
   in England, 544
   in France, 544
   in French Revolution, 623
   in Italy, 915
   labor of, 466(i), 467
   marriage by, 576
   open-field system and, 544
   in Prussia, 481
   in Russia, 485, 486, 486(i), 533–534, 766–767, 768–769(b), 768(b)(i), 769(b)(i), 770
   as serfs, 467
   social order and, 466–467
   Soviet, 906, 909–912, 913
Peel, Robert (factory owner), 667(d), 706
Pegida (Patriotic Europeans Against the Islamization of the West, Germany), 1043
Penal system, reform of, 524
Pendulum clock, 507
Peninsulares, 691
Penn, William, 496
Pennsylvania, 445
Pensions
   in England, 890
   in Germany, 775
   in Soviet Union, 913
Peonage, debt, 562
People's Budget (England), 776
People's Charter (England, 1838), 705
People's Republic of China. *See* China
"People's Will" (Russia), 770
Perestroika, 1008
Periodic law and table, 745
Permanent revolution, Trotsky on, 908
Perry, Matthew, 798, 820
Persecution, by Nazis, 920
Persia. *See* Iran; Persian Empire
Persian Empire
   religion in, 430
   trade and, 430
Persian Gulf region
   energy resources in, 1051
   Soviet Union and, 1007

Timeline · A History of Western Society: A Brief Overview

	Government	Society and Economy
3000 B.C.E.	Emergence of first cities in Mesopotamia, ca. 3800 Unification of Egypt; Archaic Period, ca. 3100–2600 Old Kingdom of Egypt, ca. 2660–2180 Dominance of Akkadian empire in Mesopotamia, ca. 2331–2200 Middle Kingdom in Egypt, ca. 2080–1640	Neolithic peoples rely on settled agriculture, while others pursue nomadic life, ca. 7000–3000 Expansion of Mesopotamian trade and culture into the modern Middle East and Turkey, ca. 2600
2000 B.C.E.	Babylonian empire, ca. 2000–1595 Code of Hammurabi, ca. 1755 Hyksos invade Egypt, ca. 1640–1570 Hittite Empire, ca. 1600–1200 New Kingdom in Egypt, ca. 1570–1075	First wave of Indo-European migrants, by ca. 2000 Extended commerce in Egypt, by ca. 2000 Horses introduced into Asia and North Africa, by ca. 2500
1500 B.C.E.	Third Intermediate Period in Egypt, ca. 1070–712 Unified Hebrew kingdom under Saul, David, and Solomon, ca. 1025–925	Use of iron increases in western Asia, by ca. 1300–1100 Second wave of Indo-European migrants, by ca. 1200 "Dark Age" in Greece, ca. 1100–800
1000 B.C.E.	Hebrew kingdom divided into Israel and Judah, 925 Assyrian Empire, ca. 900–612 Phoenicians found Carthage, 813 Kingdom of Kush conquers and reunifies Egypt, ca. 800–700 Roman monarchy, ca. 753–509 Medes conquers Persia, 710 Babylon wins independence from Assyria, 626 Dracon issues law code at Athens, 621 Solon's reforms at Athens, ca. 594 Cyrus the Great conquers Medes, founds Persian Empire, 550 Persians complete conquest of ancient Near East, 521–464 Reforms of Cleisthenes in Athens, 508	Phoenician seafaring and trading in the Mediterranean, ca. 900–550 First Olympic games, 776 Concentration of landed wealth in Greece, ca. 750–600 Greek overseas expansion, ca. 750–550 Beginning of coinage in western Asia, ca. 640
500 B.C.E.	Persian wars, 499–479 Struggle of the Orders in Rome, ca. 494–287 Growth of the Athenian Empire, 478–431 Peloponnesian War, 431–404 Rome captures Veii, 396 Gauls sack Rome, 387 Roman expansion in Italy, 390–290 Philip II of Macedonia conquers Greece, 338 Conquests of Alexander the Great, 334–324 Punic Wars, 264–146 Reforms of the Gracchi, 133–121	Growth of Hellenistic trade and cities, ca. 330–100 Beginning of Roman silver coinage, 269 Growth of slavery, decline of small farmers in Rome, ca. 250–100 Agrarian reforms of the Gracchi, 133–121

Religion and Philosophy	Science and Technology	Arts and Letters
Growth of anthropomorphic religion in Mesopotamia, ca. 3000–2000 Emergence of Egyptian polytheism and belief in personal immortality, ca. 2660 Spread of Mesopotamian and Egyptian religious ideas as far north as modern Turkey and as far south as central Africa, ca. 2600	Development of wheeled transport in Mesopotamia, by ca. 3000 Use of widespread irrigation in Mesopotamia and Egypt, ca. 3000 Construction of Stonehenge monument in England, ca. 2500 Construction of first pyramid in Egypt, ca. 2600	Cuneiform and hieroglyphic writing, ca. 3200
Emergence of Hebrew monotheism, ca. 1700 Mixture of Hittite and Near Eastern religious beliefs, ca. 1595	Construction of first ziggurats in Mesopotamia, ca. 2100 Widespread use of bronze in ancient Near East, ca. 1900 Babylonian mathematical advances, ca. 1800	*Epic of Gilgamesh*, ca. 1900
Exodus of the Hebrews from Egypt into Palestine, ca. 1300–1200	Hittites introduce iron technology, ca. 1400	Phoenicians develop alphabet, ca. 1400 Naturalistic art in Egypt under Akhenaten, 1367–1350 Egyptian *Book of the Dead*, ca. 1300
Era of the prophets in Israel, ca. 1100–500 Beginning of the Hebrew Bible, ca. 950–800 Intermixture of Etruscan and Roman religious cults, ca. 753–509 Growing popularity of local Greek religious cults, ca. 700 B.C.E.–337 C.E. Introduction of Zoroastrianism, ca. 600 Babylonian Captivity of the Hebrews, 587–538	Babylonian astronomical advances, ca. 750–400 Construction of Parthenon in Athens begins, 447	Homer, traditional author of *Iliad* and *Odyssey*, ca. 800 Hesiod, author of *Theogony* and *Works and Days*, ca. 800 Aeschylus, first significant Athenian tragedian, ca. 525–456
Pre-Socratic philosophers, ca. 500–400 Socrates executed, 399 Plato, student of Socrates, 427–347 Diogenes, leading proponent of cynicism, ca. 412–323 Aristotle, student of Plato, 384–322 Epicurus, founder of Epicurean philosophy, 340–270 Zeno, founder of Stoic philosophy, 335–262 Emergence of Mithraism, ca. 300 Greek cults brought to Rome, ca. 200 Spread of Hellenistic mystery religions, ca. 200–100	Hippocrates, formal founder of medicine, ca. 430 Building of the Via Appia begins, 312 Aristarchos of Samos, advances in astronomy, ca. 310–230 Euclid codifies geometry, ca. 300 Herophilus, discoveries in medicine, ca. 300–250 Archimedes, works on physics and hydrologics, ca. 287–212	Sophocles, tragedian whose plays explore moral and political problems, ca. 496–406 Herodotus, "father of history," ca. 485–425 Euripides, most personal of the Athenian tragedians, ca. 480–406 Thucydides, historian of Peloponnesian War, ca. 460–440 Aristophanes, greatest Athenian comic playwright, ca. 445–386

	Government	Society and Economy
100 B.C.E.	Dictatorship of Sulla, 88–79 B.C.E. Civil war in Rome, 88–31 B.C.E. Dictatorship of Caesar, 45–44 B.C.E. Principate of Augustus, 31 B.C.E.–14 C.E. "Five Good Emperors" of Rome, 96–180 C.E. "Barracks Emperors'" civil war, 235–284 C.E.	Reform of the Roman calendar, 46 B.C.E. "Golden age" of Roman prosperity and vast increase in trade, 96–180 C.E. Growth of serfdom in Roman Empire, ca. 200–500 C.E. Economic contraction in Roman Empire, ca. 235–284 C.E.
300 C.E.	Constantine removes capital of Roman Empire to Constantinople, ca. 315 Visigoths defeat Roman army at Adrianople, 378 Bishop Ambrose asserts church's independence from the state, 380 Odoacer deposes last Roman emperor in the West, 476 Clovis issues Salic law of the Franks, ca. 490	Barbarian migrations throughout western and northern Europe, ca. 378–600
500	Law code of Justinian, 529 Spread of Islam across Arabia, the Mediterranean region, Spain, North Africa, and Asia as far as India, ca. 630–733	Gallo-Roman aristocracy intermarries with Germanic chieftains, ca. 500–700 Decline of towns and trade in the West; agrarian economy predominates, ca. 500–1800
700	Charles Martel defeats Muslims at Tours, 732 Pippin III anointed king of the Franks, 754 Charlemagne secures Frankish crown, r. 768–814	Height of Muslim commercial activity with western Europe, ca. 700–1300
800	Imperial coronation of Charlemagne, Christmas 800 Treaty of Verdun divides Carolingian kingdom, 843 Viking, Magyar, and Muslim invasions, ca. 850–1000 Establishment of Kievan Rus, ca. 900	Invasions and unstable conditions lead to increase of serfdom in western Europe, ca. 800–900 Height of Byzantine commerce and industry, ca. 800–1000
1000	Seljuk Turks conquer Muslim Baghdad, 1055 Norman conquest of England, 1066 Penance of Henry IV at Canossa, 1077	Decline of Byzantine free peasantry, ca. 1025–1100 Growth of towns and trade in the West, ca. 1050–1300 *Domesday Book* in England, 1086
1100	Henry I of England, r. 1100–1135 Louis VI of France, r. 1108–1137 Frederick I of Germany, r. 1152–1190 Henry II of England, r. 1154–1189	Henry I of England establishes the Exchequer, 1130 Beginnings of the Hanseatic League, 1159

Religion and Philosophy	Science and Technology	Arts and Letters
Mithraism spreads to Rome, 27 B.C.E.–270 C.E. Life of Jesus, ca. 3 B.C.E.–29 C.E.	Engineering advances in Rome, ca. 100 B.C.E.–180 C.E.	Flowering of Latin literature: Virgil, 70–19 B.C.E.; Livy, ca. 59 B.C.E.–17 C.E.; Ovid, 43 B.C.E.–17 C.E.
Constantine legalizes Christianity, 312 Theodosius declares Christianity the official state religion, 380 Donatist heretical movement at its height, ca. 400 St. Augustine, *Confessions*, ca. 390; *The City of God*, ca. 425 Clovis adopts Roman Christianity, 496	Construction of Arch of Constantine, ca. 315	St. Jerome publishes Latin *Vulgate*, late 4th c. Byzantines preserve Greco-Roman culture, ca. 400–1000
Rule of St. Benedict, 529 Life of the Prophet Muhammad, ca. 571–632 Pope Gregory the Great publishes *Dialogues, Pastoral Care, Moralia*, 590–604 Monasteries established in Anglo-Saxon England, ca. 600–700 Publication of the Qur'an, 651 Synod of Whitby, 664	Using watermills, Benedictine monks exploit energy of fast-flowing rivers and streams, by 600 Heavy plow and improved harness facilitate use of multiple-ox teams; harrow widely used in northern Europe, by 600 Byzantines successfully use "Greek fire" in naval combat against Arab fleets attacking Constantinople, 673, 717	Boethius, *The Consolation of Philosophy*, ca. 520 Justinian constructs church of Santa Sophia, 532–537
Bede, *Ecclesiastical History of the English Nation*, ca. 700 Missionary work of St. Boniface in Germany, ca. 710–750 Iconoclastic controversy in Byzantine Empire, 726–843 Pippin III donates Papal States to the papacy, 756		Lindisfarne Gospel Book, ca. 700 *Beowulf*, ca. 700 Carolingian Renaissance, ca. 780–850
Foundation of abbey of Cluny, 909 Byzantine conversion of Russia, late 10th c.	Stirrup and nailed horseshoes become widespread in combat, 900–1000 Paper (invented in China, ca. 150) enters Europe through Muslim Spain, ca. 900–1000	Byzantines develop Cyrillic script, late 10th c.
Schism between Roman and Greek Orthodox churches, 1054 Lateran Council restricts election of pope to College of Cardinals, 1059 Pope Gregory VII, 1073–1085 Theologian Peter Abelard, 1079–1142 First Crusade, 1095–1099 Founding of Cistercian order, 1098	Arab conquests bring new irrigation methods, cotton cultivation, and manufacture to Spain, Sicily, southern Italy, by 1000 Avicenna, Arab scientist, d. 1037	Muslim musicians introduce lute, rebec (stringed instruments, ancestors of violin), ca. 1000 Romanesque style in architecture and art, ca. 1000–1200 *Song of Roland*, ca. 1095
Universities begin, ca. 1100–1300 Concordat of Worms ends investiture controversy, 1122 Height of Cistercian monasticism, 1125–1175	Europeans, copying Muslim and Byzantine models, construct castles with rounded towers and crenellated walls, by 1100	Troubadour poetry, especially of Chrétien de Troyes, circulates widely, ca. 1100–1200 *Rubaiyat of Umar Khayyam*, ca. 1120 Dedication of abbey church of Saint-Denis launches Gothic style, 1144

	Government	Society and Economy
1100 (CONT.)	Thomas Becket, archbishop of Canterbury, murdered 1170 Philip Augustus of France, r. 1180–1223	
1200	Spanish victory over Muslims at Las Navas de Tolosa, 1212 Frederick II of Germany and Sicily, r. 1212–1250 Magna Carta, charter of English political and civil liberties, 1215 Louis IX of France, r. 1226–1270 Mongols end Abbasid caliphate, 1258 Edward I of England, r. 1272–1307 Philip IV (the Fair) of France, r. 1285–1314	European revival, growth of towns; agricultural expansion leads to population growth, ca. 1200–1300 Crusaders capture Constantinople (Fourth Crusade) and spur Venetian economy, 1204
1300	Philip IV orders arrest of Pope Boniface at Anagni, 1303 Hundred Years' War between England and France, 1337–1453 Political disorder in Germany, ca. 1350–1450 Merchant oligarchies or despots rule Italian city-states, ca. 1350–1550	"Little ice age," European economic depression, ca. 1300–1450 Black Death appears ca. 1347; returns intermittently until ca. 1720 Height of the Hanseatic League, 1350–1450 Peasant and working-class revolts: Flanders, 1328; France, 1358; Florence, 1378; England, 1381
1400	Joan of Arc rallies French monarchy, 1429–1431 Medici domination of Florence begins, 1434 Princes in Germany consolidate power, ca. 1450–1500 Ottoman Turks under Mahomet II capture Constantinople, May 1453 Wars of the Roses in England, 1455–1471 Establishment of the Inquisition in Spain, 1478 Ferdinand and Isabella complete reconquista in Spain, 1492 French invasion of Italy, 1494	Population decline, peasants' revolts, high labor costs contribute to decline of serfdom in western Europe, ca. 1400–1650 Flow of Balkan slaves into eastern Mediterranean, of African slaves into Iberia and Italy, ca. 1400–1500 Christopher Columbus reaches the Americas, 1492 Portuguese gain control of East Indian spice trade, 1498–1511
1500	Charles V, Holy Roman emperor, 1519–1556 Habsburg-Valois Wars, 1521–1559 Philip II of Spain, r. 1556–1598 Revolt of the Netherlands, 1566–1598 St. Bartholomew's Day massacre in France, 1572 English defeat of the Spanish Armada, 1588 Henry IV of France issues Edict of Nantes, 1598	Consolidation of serfdom in eastern Europe, ca. 1500–1650 Balboa discovers the Pacific, 1513 Magellan's crew circumnavigates the earth, 1519–1522 Spain and Portugal gain control of regions of Central and South America, ca. 1520–1550 Peasants' Revolt in Germany, 1524–1525 "Time of Troubles" in Russia, 1598–1613

Religion and Philosophy	Science and Technology	Arts and Letters
Aristotle's works translated into Latin, ca. 1140–1260 Third Crusade, 1189–1192 Pope Innocent III, height of the medieval papacy, 1198–1216	Underground pipes with running water and indoor latrines installed in some monasteries, such as Clairvaux and Canterbury Cathedral Priory, by 1100; elsewhere rare until 1800 Windmill invented, ca. 1180	
Founding of the Franciscan order, 1210 Fourth Lateran Council accepts seven sacraments, 1215 Founding of Dominican order, 1216 Thomas Aquinas, height of scholasticism, 1225–1274	*Notebooks* of architect Villard de Honnecourt, a major source for Gothic engineering, ca. 1250 Development of double-entry bookkeeping in Florence and Genoa, ca. 1250–1340 Venetians purchase secrets of glass manufacture from Syria, 1277 Mechanical clock invented, ca. 1290	*Parzifal, Roman de la rose, King Arthur and the Round Table* celebrate virtues of knighthood and chivalry, ca. 1200–1300 Height of Gothic style, ca. 1225–1300
Pope Boniface VIII declares all Christians subject to the pope in *Unam Sanctam*, 1302 Babylonian Captivity of the papacy, 1309–1376 Theologian John Wyclif, ca. 1330–1384 Great Schism in the papacy, 1378–1417	Edward III of England uses cannon in siege of Calais, 1346 Clocks in general use throughout Europe, by 1400	Paintings of Giotto mark emergence of Renaissance movement in the arts, ca. 1305–1337 Dante, *Divine Comedy*, ca. 1310 Petrarch develops ideas of humanism, ca. 1350 Boccaccio, *The Decameron*, ca. 1350 Jan van Eyck, Flemish painter, 1366–1441 Brunelleschi, Florentine architect, 1377–1446 Chaucer, *Canterbury Tales*, ca. 1387–1400
Council of Constance ends the schism in the papacy, 1414–1418 Pragmatic Sanction of Bourges affirms special rights of French crown over French church, 1438 Expulsion of Jews from Spain, 1492	Water-powered blast furnaces operative in Sweden, Austria, the Rhine Valley, Liège, ca. 1400 Leonardo Fibonacci's *Liber Abaci* popularizes use of Hindu-Arabic numerals, important in rise of Western science, 1402 Paris and largest Italian cities pave streets, making street cleaning possible, ca. 1450 European printing and movable type, ca. 1450	Height of Renaissance movement: Masaccio, 1401–1428; Botticelli, 1444–1510; Leonardo da Vinci, 1452–1519; Albrecht Dürer, 1471–1528; Michelangelo, 1475–1564; Raphael, 1483–1520
Machiavelli, *The Prince*, 1513 More, *Utopia*, 1516 Luther, *Ninety-five Theses*, 1517 Henry VIII of England breaks with Rome, 1532–1534 Merici establishes Ursuline order for education of women, 1535 Loyola establishes Society of Jesus, 1540 Calvin establishes theocracy in Geneva, 1541 Council of Trent shapes essential character of Catholicism until the 1960s, 1545–1563 Peace of Augsburg, official recognition of Lutheranism, 1555	Scientific revolution in western Europe, ca. 1540–1690: Copernicus, *On the Revolutions of the Heavenly Bodies*, 1543; Galileo, 1564–1642; Kepler, 1571–1630; Harvey, 1578–1657	Erasmus, *The Praise of Folly*, 1509 Castiglione, *The Courtier*, 1528 Baroque movement in arts, ca. 1550–1725: Rubens, 1577–1640; Velasquez, 1599–1660 Shakespeare, West's most enduring and influential playwright, 1564–1616 Montaigne, *Essays*, 1598

	Government	Society and Economy
1600	Thirty Years' War begins, 1618 Richelieu dominates French government, 1624–1643 Frederick William, Elector of Brandenburg, r. 1640–1688 English Civil War, 1642–1649 Louis XIV, r. 1643–1715 Peace of Westphalia ends the Thirty Years' War, 1648 The Fronde in France, 1648–1660	Chartering of British East India Company, 1600 English Poor Law, 1601 Chartering of Dutch East India Company, 1602 Height of Dutch commercial activity, ca. 1630–1665
1650	Anglo-Dutch wars, 1652–1674 Protectorate in England, 1653–1658 Leopold I, Habsburg emperor, r. 1658–1705 English monarchy restored, 1660 Ottoman siege of Vienna, 1683 Glorious Revolution in England, 1688–1689 Peter the Great of Russia, r. 1689–1725	Height of mercantilism in Europe, ca. 1650–1750 Agricultural revolution in Europe, ca. 1650–1850 Principle of peasants' hereditary subjugation to their lords affirmed in Prussia, 1653 Colbert's economic reforms in France, ca. 1663–1683 Cossack revolt in Russia, 1670–1671
1700	War of the Spanish Succession, 1701–1713 Peace of Utrecht redraws political boundaries of Europe, 1713 Frederick William I of Prussia, r. 1713–1740 Louis XV of France, r. 1715–1774 Maria Theresa of Austria, r. 1740–1780 Frederick the Great of Prussia, r. 1740–1786	Foundation of St. Petersburg, 1701 Last appearance of bubonic plague in western Europe, ca. 1720 Growth of European population, ca. 1720–1789 Enclosure movement in England, ca. 1730–1830
1750	Seven Years' War, 1756–1763 Catherine the Great of Russia, r. 1762–1796 Partition of Poland, 1772–1795 Louis XVI of France, r. 1774–1792 American Revolution, 1775–1783 French Revolution, 1789–1799 Slave insurrection in Saint-Domingue, 1791	Growth of illegitimate births in Europe, ca. 1750–1850 Industrial Revolution in western Europe, ca. 1780–1850 Serfdom abolished in France, 1789
1800	Napoleonic era, 1799–1815 Haitian republic declares independence, 1804 Congress of Vienna re-establishes political power after defeat of Napoleon, 1814–1815 Greece wins independence from Ottoman Empire, 1830 French conquest of Algeria, 1830 Revolution in France, 1830 Great Britain: Reform Bill of 1832; Poor Law reform, 1834; Chartists, repeal of Corn Laws, 1838–1848 Revolutions in Europe, 1848	British takeover of India complete, 1805 British slave trade abolished, 1807 German Zollverein founded, 1834 European capitalists begin large-scale foreign investment, 1840s Great Famine in Ireland, 1845–1851 First public health law in Britain, 1848

Religion and Philosophy	Science and Technology	Arts and Letters
Huguenot revolt in France, 1625	Further development of scientific method: Bacon, *The Advancement of Learning*, 1605; Descartes, *Discourse on Method*, 1637	Cervantes, *Don Quixote*, 1605, 1615 Flourishing of French theater: Molière, 1622–1673; Racine, 1639–1699 Golden age of Dutch culture, ca. 1625–1675: Rembrandt van Rijn, 1606–1669; Vermeer, 1632–1675
Social contract theory: Hobbes, *Leviathan*, 1651; Locke, *Second Treatise on Civil Government*, 1690 Patriarch Nikon's reforms split Russian Orthodox Church, 1652 Test Act in England excludes Roman Catholics from public office, 1673 Revocation of Edict of Nantes, 1685 James II tries to restore Catholicism as state religion, 1685–1688	Tull (1674–1741) encourages innovation in English agriculture Newton, *Principia Mathematica*, 1687	Construction of baroque palaces and remodeling of capital cities, central and eastern Europe, ca. 1650–1725 Bach, great late baroque German composer, 1685–1750 Enlightenment begins, ca. 1690: Fontenelle, *Conversations on the Plurality of Worlds*, 1686; Voltaire, French philosopher and writer whose work epitomizes Enlightenment, 1694–1778 Pierre Bayle, *Historical and Critical Dictionary*, 1697
Wesley, founder of Methodism, 1703–1791 Montesquieu, *The Spirit of Laws*, 1748	Newcomen develops steam engine, 1705 Charles Townsend introduces four-year crop rotation, 1730	
Hume, *The Natural History of Religion*, 1755 Rousseau, *The Social Contract* and *Emile*, 1762 Fourier, French utopian socialist, 1772–1837 Papacy dissolves Jesuits, 1773 Smith, *The Wealth of Nations*, 1776 Church reforms of Joseph II in Austria, 1780s Kant, *What Is Enlightenment?*, 1784 Reorganization of church in France, 1790s Wollstonecraft, *A Vindication of the Rights of Woman*, 1792 Malthus, *Essay on the Principle of Population*, 1798	Hargreaves's spinning jenny, ca. 1765 Arkwright's water frame, ca. 1765 Watt's steam engine promotes industrial breakthroughs, 1780s Jenner's smallpox vaccine, 1796	*Encyclopedia*, edited by Diderot and d'Alembert, published 1751–1765 Classical style in music, ca. 1770–1830: Mozart, 1756–1791; Beethoven, 1770–1827 Wordsworth, English romantic poet, 1770–1850 Romanticism in art and literature, ca. 1790–1850
Napoleon signs Concordat with Pope Pius VII regulating Catholic Church in France, 1801 Spencer, Social Darwinist, 1820–1903 Comte, *System of Positive Philosophy*, 1830–1842 Height of French utopian socialism, 1830s–1840s List, *National System of Political Economy*, 1841 Nietzsche, radical and highly influential German philosopher, 1844–1900 Marx, *Communist Manifesto*, 1848	First railroad, Great Britain, 1825 Faraday studies electromagnetism, 1830–1840s	Staël, *On Germany*, 1810 Balzac, *The Human Comedy*, 1829–1841 Delacroix, *Liberty Leading the People*, 1830 Hugo, *The Hunchback of Notre Dame*, 1831

	Government	Society and Economy
1850	Second Empire in France, 1852–1870 Crimean War, 1853–1856 Britain crushes Great Rebellion in India, 1857–1858 Unification of Italy, 1859–1870 U.S. Civil War, 1861–1865 Bismarck leads Germany, 1862–1890 Unification of Germany, 1864–1871 Britain's Second Reform Bill, 1867 Third Republic in France, 1870–1940	Crédit Mobilier founded in France, 1852 Japan opened to European influence, 1853 Russian serfs emancipated, 1861 First Socialist International, 1864–1871
1875	Congress of Berlin, 1878 European "scramble for Africa," 1880–1900 Britain's Third Reform Bill, 1884 Dreyfus affair in France, 1894–1899 Spanish-American War, 1898 South African War, 1899–1902	Full property rights for women in Great Britain, 1882 Second Industrial Revolution; birthrate steadily declines in Europe, ca. 1880–1913 Social welfare legislation, Germany, 1883–1889 Second Socialist International, 1889–1914 Witte directs modernization of Russian economy, 1892–1899
1900	Russo-Japanese War, 1904–1905 Revolution in Russia, 1905 Balkan wars, 1912–1913	Women's suffrage movement, England, ca. 1900–1914 Social welfare legislation, France, 1904, 1910; Great Britain, 1906–1914 Agrarian reforms in Russia, 1907–1912
1914	World War I, 1914–1918 Armenian genocide, 1915 Easter Rebellion, 1916 U.S. declares war on Germany, 1917 Bolshevik Revolution, 1917–1918 Treaty of Versailles, World War I peace settlement, 1919	Planned economics in Europe, 1914 Auxiliary Service Law in Germany, 1916 Bread riots in Russia, March 1917
1920	Mussolini seizes power in Italy, 1922 Stalin comes to power in U.S.S.R., 1927 Hitler gains power in Germany, 1933 Rome-Berlin Axis, 1936 Nazi-Soviet Non-Aggression Pact, 1939 World War II, 1939–1945	New Economic Policy in U.S.S.R., 1921 Dawes Plan for reparations and recovery, 1924 Great Depression, 1929–1939 Rapid industrialization in U.S.S.R., 1930s Start of Roosevelt's New Deal in U.S., 1933
1940	United Nations founded, 1945 Decolonization of Asia and Africa, 1945–1960s Cold War begins, 1947 Founding of Israel, 1948 Communist government in China, 1949 Korean War, 1950–1953 De-Stalinization of Soviet Union under Khrushchev, 1953–1964	Holocaust, 1941–1945 Marshall Plan enacted, 1947 European economic progress, ca. 1950–1970 European Coal and Steel Community founded, 1952 European Economic Community founded, 1957

Religion and Philosophy	Science and Technology	Arts and Letters
Decline in church attendance among working classes, ca. 1850–1914 Mill, *On Liberty*, 1859 Pope Pius IX, *Syllabus of Errors*, denounces modern thoughts, 1864 Marx, *Das Capital*, 1867 Doctrine of papal infallibility, 1870	Modernization of Paris, ca. 1850–1870 Great Exhibition in London, 1851 Freud, founder of psychoanalysis, 1856–1939 Darwin, *On the Origin of Species*, 1859 Pasteur develops germ theory of disease, 1860s Suez Canal opened, 1869 Mendeleev develops periodic table, 1869	Realism in art and literature, ca. 1850–1870 Flaubert, *Madame Bovary*, 1857 Tolstoy, *War and Peace*, 1869 Impressionism in art, ca. 1870–1900 Eliot (Mary Ann Evans), *Middlemarch*, 1872
Growth of public education in France, ca. 1880–1900 Growth of mission schools in Africa, 1890–1914	Emergence of modern immunology, ca. 1875–1900 Electrical industry: lighting and streetcars, ca. 1880–1900 Trans-Siberian Railroad, 1890s Marie Curie, discovery of radium, 1898	Zola, *Germinal*, 1885 Kipling, "The White Man's Burden," 1899
Separation of church and state in France, 1901–1905 Hobson, *Imperialism*, 1902 Schweitzer, *Quest of the Historical Jesus*, 1906	Planck develops quantum theory, ca. 1900 First airplane flight, 1903 Einstein develops theory of special relativity, 1905–1910	Modernism in art and literature, ca. 1900–1929 Conrad, *Heart of Darkness*, 1902 Cubism in art, ca. 1905–1930 Proust, *Remembrance of Things Past*, 1913–1927
Keynes, *Economic Consequences of the Peace*, 1919	Submarine warfare introduced, 1915 Ernest Rutherford splits atom, 1919	Spengler, *The Decline of the West*, 1918
Emergence of modern existentialism, 1920s Revival of Christianity, 1920s–1930s Wittgenstein, *Essay on Logical Philosophy*, 1922 Heisenberg's principle of uncertainty, 1927	"Heroic age of physics," 1920s First major public radio broadcasts in Great Britain and U.S., 1920 First talking movies, 1930 Radar system in England, 1939	Gropius, Bauhaus, 1920s Dadaism and surrealism, 1920s Woolf, *Jacob's Room*, 1922 Joyce, *Ulysses*, 1922 Eliot, *The Waste Land*, 1922 Remarque, *All Quiet on the Western Front*, 1929 Picasso, *Guernica*, 1937
De Beauvoir, *The Second Sex*, 1949 Communists fail to break Catholic Church in Poland, 1950s	U.S. drops atomic bombs on Japan, 1945 Big Science in U.S., ca. 1945–1965 Watson and Crick discover structure of DNA molecule, 1953 Russian satellite in orbit, 1957	Cultural purge in Soviet Union, 1946–1952 Van der Rohe, Lake Shore Apartments, 1948–1951 Orwell, *1984*, 1949 Pasternak, *Doctor Zhivago*, 1956 "Beat" movement in U.S., late 1950s

	Government	Society and Economy
1960	Building of Berlin Wall, 1961	Civil rights movement in U.S., 1960s
	U.S. involvement in Vietnam War, 1964–1973	Stagflation, 1970s
	Student rebellion in France, 1968	Feminist movement, 1970s
	Soviet tanks end Prague Spring, 1968	Collapse of postwar monetary system, 1971
	Détente between U.S. and U.S.S.R., 1970s	OPEC oil price increases, 1973, 1979
	Soviet occupation of Afghanistan, 1979–1989	
1980	U.S. military buildup, 1980s	Growth of debt in the West, 1980s
	Solidarity in Poland, 1980	Economic crisis in Poland, 1988
	Unification of Germany, 1989	Maastricht Treaty proposes monetary union, 1990
	Revolutions in eastern Germany, 1989–1990	European Community becomes European Union, 1993
	Persian Gulf War, 1990–1991	Migration to western Europe increases, 1990s
	Dissolution of Soviet Union, 1991	Former Soviet bloc nations adopt capitalist economies, 1990s
	Civil war in Yugoslavia, 1991–2001	
	Separatist war breaks out in Chechnya, 1991	
2000	Vladimir Putin elected president of Russian Federation, 2000	Same-sex marriage legalized in the Netherlands, 2001
	Terrorist attacks on U.S., Sept. 11, 2001	Euro enters circulation, 2002
	War in Afghanistan begins, 2001	Voters reject new European Union constitution, 2005
	Iraq War, 2003–2011	Immigrant riots in France, 2005, 2009
	Angela Merkel elected chancellor of Germany, 2005	Worldwide financial crisis begins, 2008
	Growing popularity of anti-immigrant, far-right political parties across Europe, 2010s	European financial crisis intensifies, 2010
	NATO intervenes in Libyan civil war, 2011	Anti-austerity protests across Europe begin, 2010
	Al-Qaeda leader Osama bin Laden killed, 2011	Arab Spring uprisings in the Middle East and North Africa, 2011
	Vladimir Putin re-elected, 2012	France legalizes same-sex marriage, 2013
	Ex-NSA contractor Edward Snowden leaks classified U.S. government information, 2013	Occupy Movement begins in the United States, spreads to Europe, 2011
	Russia annexes Crimea (southern Ukraine) and supports pro-Russian Ukrainian rebels, 2014	Greek debt crisis, 2015
	Growth of Islamic State, 2014–2015	Massive influx of refugees from the Middle East, 2015–2016
	Terrorist attacks in Paris organized by Islamic State kill 130 people, 2015	Refugee crisis undermines European unity, 2016
	Terrorist attacks in Brussels organized by Islamic State kill 32 people, 2016	

Religion and Philosophy	Science and Technology	Arts and Letters
Second Vatican Council announces sweeping Catholic reforms, 1962–1965 Pope John II, 1978–2005	European Council for Nuclear Research founded, 1960 Space race, 1960s Russian cosmonaut first to orbit globe, 1961 American astronaut first person on moon, 1969	The Beatles, 1960s Solzhenitsyn, *One Day in the Life of Ivan Denisovich*, 1962 Carson, *Silent Spring*, 1962 Friedan, *The Feminine Mystique*, 1963 Servan-Schreiber, *The American Challenge*, 1967
Revival of religion in Soviet Union, 1985– Growth of Islam in Europe, 1990s Fukuyama proclaims "end of history," 1991	Reduced spending on Big Science, 1980s Computer revolution continues, 1980s–1990s U.S. Genome Project begins, 1990 First World Wide Web server and browser, 1991 Pentium processor invented, 1993 First genetically cloned sheep, 1996	Consolidation and popularization of postmodernism in fine arts and literature, 1980s Solzhenitsyn returns to Russia, 1994; dies 2008 Author Salman Rushdie exiled from Iran, 1989 Gehry, Guggenheim Museum, Bilbao, 1997
Number of Europeans who claim to be religious continues to decline, 2000– UN announces first World Philosophy Day to "honor philosophical reflection" across the globe, 2002 Ramadan, *Western Muslims and the Future of Islam*, 2004 Pontificate of Benedict XVI, 2005–2013 Jorge Mario Bergoglio elected as Pope Francis, 2013 Noted Slovenian philosopher Slavoj Žižek critiques contemporary Western notions of freedom, 2014	Google emerges as popular Internet search engine, 2000s Growing concern about global warming, 2000s First hybrid car, 2003 Facebook founded, 2004 YouTube founded, 2005 iPhone introduced to consumers, 2007 Copenhagen summit on climate change, 2009 Paris summit on climate change, 2015	Middle East conflict leads to looting and destruction of archaeological sites and museums, 2000– Growing importance of artists and art centers outside of Europe: in Latin America, Africa, and Asia, 2000– Digital methods of production and display grow increasingly popular in works of art, 2000– Movies and books exploring clash between immigrants and host cultures popular: *Bend It Like Beckham*, 2002; *The Namesake*, 2003; *White Teeth*, 2003; *The Class*, 2008; *Brooklyn*, 2015

About the Authors

John P. McKay (Ph.D., University of California, Berkeley) is professor emeritus at the University of Illinois. He has written or edited numerous works, including the Herbert Baxter Adams Prize–winning book *Pioneers for Profit: Foreign Entrepreneurship and Russian Industrialization, 1885–1913*.

Bennett D. Hill (Ph.D., Princeton University), late of Georgetown University, published *Church and State in the Middle Ages* and numerous articles and reviews, and he was one of the contributing editors to *The Encyclopedia of World History*. He taught for many years at the University of Illinois and was a Benedictine monk of St. Anselm's Abbey in Washington, D.C.

John Buckler (Ph.D., Harvard University), late of the University of Illinois, published numerous works, including *Theban Hegemony, 371–362 B.C.*; *Philip II and the Sacred War*; and *Aegean Greece in the Fourth Century B.C.* With Hans Beck, he published *Central Greece and the Politics of Power in the Fourth Century*.

Clare Haru Crowston (Ph.D., Cornell University) teaches at the University of Illinois, where she is currently professor of history and department chair. She is the author of *Credit, Fashion, Sex: Economies of Regard in Old Regime France* and *Fabricating Women: The Seamstresses of Old Regime France, 1675–1791*, which won the Berkshire and Hagley Prizes. She edited two special issues of the *Journal of Women's History*, has published numerous journal articles and reviews, and is one of the editors of the *Journal of Social History* and past president of the Society for French Historical Studies.

Merry E. Wiesner-Hanks (Ph.D., University of Wisconsin–Madison) taught first at Augustana College in Illinois, and since 1985 at the University of Wisconsin–Milwaukee, where she is currently UWM Distinguished Professor in the department of history. She is the senior editor of the *Sixteenth Century Journal*, one of the editors of the *Journal of Global History*, and the author or editor of more than twenty books, including *A Concise History of the World* (2015). She is the former Chief Reader for Advanced Placement World History.

Joe Perry (Ph.D., University of Illinois at Urbana-Champaign) is associate professor of modern German and European history at Georgia State University. He has published numerous articles and is author of *Christmas in Germany: A Cultural History*. His current research interests focus on issues of consumption, gender, and popular culture in West Germany and Western Europe after World War II.